Studies in American Tort Law

Third Edition

Studies in American Tort Law

Third Edition

Vincent R. Johnson

ASSOCIATE DEAN AND PROFESSOR OF LAW
ST. MARY'S UNIVERSITY

and

Alan Gunn

JOHN N. MATTHEWS PROFESSOR OF LAW
UNIVERSITY OF NOTRE DAME

CAROLINA ACADEMIC PRESS
Durham, North Carolina

ISBN 978-1-59460-034-0

LCCN 2004111964

CAROLINA ACADEMIC PRESS
700 Kent Street
Durham, NC 27701
Telephone (919) 489-7486
Fax (919) 493-5668
www.cap-press.com

Printed in the United States of America

To my parents,
Harry Paul Johnson and Anna Ruth Gozlick Johnson
for providing a world of support

———————

To the memory of my mother,
Helen Whitnall Gunn

Summary of Contents

Contents

Table of Cases

Principal cases, and the pages on which they begin, are italicized.

Books and Articles Cited

Abraham, Kenneth S., *What Is a Tort Claim? An Interpretation of Contemporary Tort Reform*, 51 Md. L. Rev. 172, 190–191 (1992), 191

Abraham, Kenneth, *Individual Action and Collective Responsibility: The Dilemma of Mass Tort Reform*, 73 Va. L. Rev. 845 (1987), 404

Abraham, Kenneth S., *Collective Justice in Tort Law*, 78 Va. L. Rev. 1481 (1993), 404

Adams, Arlin M., & Charles J. Emmerich, *A Heritage of Religious Liberty*, 137 U. Pa. L. Rev. 1559, 1671 n. 361 (1989), 604

Ahrend, George M. & Randall T. Thomsen, *Tort Claims and Judgments as Debts for "Wilful and Malicious Injury" Nondischargeable Under Section 523(a)(6) of the Bankruptcy Code*, 100 Comm. L.J. 498, 499 (1995), 31

American Law Institute, Restatement of Torts (various editions), 5–6

Anderson, David A., *Is Libel Law Worth Reforming?*, 140 U. Pa. L. Rev. 487, 488–90 (1991), 1028, 1030

Antolini, Denise E., *Modernizing Public Nuisance: Solving the Paradox of the Special Injury Rule*, 28 Ecology L.Q. 755 (2001), 914

Arnold, Roy W., Note, *The Persistence of Caveat Emptor: Publisher Immunity from Liability for Inaccurate Factual Information*, 53 U. Pitt. L. Rev. 777 (1992), 962

Austin, Regina, *Employer Abuse, Worker Resistance, and the Tort of Intentional Infliction of Severe Emotional Distress*, 41 Stan. L. Rev. 1, 55 (1988), 78

Baldus, David, John C. MacQueen, M.D., and George Woodworth, *Improving Judicial Oversight of Jury Damages Assessments: A Proposal for the Comparative Additur/Remittitur Review of Awards for Nonpecuniary Harms and Punitive Damages*, 80 Iowa. L. Rev. 1109, 1119 n. 17 (1995), 185

Bloomquist, Harry L., III, *Geophysical Trespass? The Guessing Game Created by the Awkward Combination of Outmoded Law and Soaring Technology*, 48 Baylor L. Rev. 21 (1996), 882

Boston, Gerald W., *Strict Liability for Abnormally Dangerous Activity: The Negligence Barrier*, 36 San Diego L. Rev. 597 (1999), 695

Brennwald, Stephen F., *Proving Causation in "Loss of a Chance" Cases: A Proportional Approach*, 34 Cath. U. L. Rev. 747, 779 n. 254 (1985), 384

Breslo, James A., *Comment: Taking the Punitive Damage Windfall Away from the Plaintiff: An Analysis*, 86 Nw. U. L. Rev. 1130 (1992), 231

Brokaw, Katherine, *Genetic Screening in the Workplace and Employers' Liability*, 23 Colum. J. L. & Soc. Prob. 317, 341–45 (1990), 502

Brown, William M., *Deja Vu All Over Again: The Exodus from Contraceptive Research and How to Reverse It*, 40 Brandeis L.J. 1, 40–41 (2001), 218

Burnham, Scott J., *What Attorneys Should Know About the Fair Debt Collection Practices Act, Or, The 2 Do's and the 200 Don'ts of Debt Collection*, 59 Mont. L. Rev. 179 (1998), 95

Calabresi, Guido, & Douglas Melamed, *Property Rules, Liability Rules, and Inalienability: One View of the Cathedral*, 85 Harv. L. Rev. 1089 (1972), 922

Calabresi, Guido & Jon T. Hirschoff, *Toward a Test for Strict Liability in Torts*, 81 Yale L.J. 1055 (1972), 742

Calvert, Robert W., *"...In the Interest of Justice,"* 4 St. Mary's L. J. 291 (1972), 611

Cantu, Charles E., *Negligent Infliction of Emotional Distress: Expanding the Rule Evolved Since Dillon*, 17 Tex. Tech. L. Rev. 1557, 1565 (1986), 612

Cantu, Charles E., *A New Look at an Old Conundrum: The Determinative Test for the Hybrid Sales/Service Transaction Under Section 402A of the Restatement (Second) of Torts*, 45 Ark. L. Rev. 913 (1993), 710

Carpenter, Charles E., *Intentional Invasion of Interest of Personality*, 13 Or. L. Rev. 227, 237 & n. 57 (1934), 57

Cavico, Frank J., and Nancy M. Cavico, *The Nursing Profession in the 1990s: Negligence and Malpractice Liability*, 43 Clev. St. L. Rev. 557, 574 (1995), 285

Chamallas, Martha, *The Architecture of Bias: Deep Structures in Tort Law*, 146 U. Pa. L. Rev. 463 (1998), 93, 203, 292

Coase, Ronald, *The Problem of Social Cost*, 3 J. L. & Econ. 1 (1960), 902, 903, 905, 906

Cobb, William D., Jr., *Tactical Considerations in Defending Assigned Legal Malpractice Claims*, 34 St. Mary's L.J. 941 (2003), 282

Cox, Barbara J., *Alternative Families: Obtaining Traditional Family Benefits Through Litigation, Legislation and Collective Bargaining*, 15 Wis. Women's L.J. 93, 133–37 (2000), 597

Danforth, Mary Taylor, *Cells, Sales, and Royalties: The Patient's Right to a Portion of the Profits*, 6 Yale L. & Pol'y Rev. 179 (1988), 133

Davis, Theodore H., and Catherine B. Bowman, *No-Fault Compensation for Unavoidable Injuries: Evaluating the National Childhood Vaccine Injury Compensation Program*, 16 U. Dayton L. Rev. 277, 311–12 (1991), 26

Dillon, Thomas P., Note, *Source Compensation for Tissues and Cells Used in Biotechnical Research: Why a Source Shouldn't Share in the Profits*, 64 Notre Dame L. Rev. 628 (1989), 133

Dobbs, Dan B., The Law of Torts (2000), 6

Easterbrook, Frank H., & Daniel R. Fischel, *Optimal Damages in Securities Cases*, 52 U. Chi. L. Rev. 611 (1985), 954

Ellman, Ira Mark, and Stephen D. Sugarman, *Spousal Emotional Abuse as a Tort?*, 55 Md. L. Rev. 1268, 1343 (1996), 84

Emerson, Thomas, *The Right of Privacy and Freedom of the Press*, 14 Harv. C.R.-C.L. L. Rev. 329, 333 (1979), 1055

Epstein, Richard A., *Was* New York Times v. Sullivan *Wrong?*, 53 U. Chi. L. Rev. 782 (1986), 986, 991

Esbeck, Carl H., *Tort Claims Against Churches and Ecclesiastical Officers: the First Amendment Considerations*, 89 W. Va. L. Rev. 1 (1986), 604

Eschweiler, Thomas G., Comment, *Educational Malpractice in Sex Education*, 49 S.M.U. L. Rev. 101 (1995), 286

Esquibel, Amanda K., *The Case of the Conflicted Mediator: An Argument for Liability and Against Immunity*, 31 Rutgers L.J. 131 (1999), 859

Ezra, David B., Note, *Smoker Battery: An Antidote to Second-Hand Smoke*, 63 S. Cal. L. Rev. 1061–112 (1990), 69

Farnbauch, David L., Note, *Pre-Impact Pain and Suffering Damages in Aviation Accidents*, 20 Val. U. L. Rev. 219 (1986), 199

Feinman, Jay M., *Attorney Liability to Nonclients*, 31 Tort & Ins. L.J. 735, 736 (1996), 281

Finley, Lucinda M., *A Break in the Silence: Including Women's Issues in a Torts Course*, 1 Yale J. L. & Fem. 41, 48–51 (1989), 203

Finley, Lucinda M., *Female Trouble: The Implications of Tort Reform for Women*, 64 Tenn. L. Rev. 847 (1997), 235

Fischer, David A., *Causation in Fact in Omission Cases*, 1992 Utah L. Rev. 1335, 366

Fischer, David A., *Fraudulently Induced Consent to Intentional Torts*, 46 U. Cinn. L. Rev. 71 (1977), 147

Fischer, David A., *Tort Recovery for Loss of a Chance*, 36 Wake Forest L. Rev. 605 (2001), 383

Flynn, Michael, *Physician Business (Mal)Practice*, 20 Hamline L. Rev. 333 (1996), 292

Gautier, Virginia Smith, *Comment, Hedonic Damages: A Variation in Paths, the Questionable Expert and a Recommendation for Clarity in Mississippi*, 65 Miss. L.J. 735, 746 (1996), 186

Gifford, Donald G., *Public Nuisance as a Mass Products Liability Tort*, 71 U. Cinn. L. Rev. 743, 747 (2003), 911

Glesner, B.A., *Landlords as Cops: Tort, Nuisance & Forfeiture Standards Imposing Liability on Landlords for Crime on the Premises*, 42 Case W. Res. L. Rev. 679, 790 (1992), 483

Goodenough, Oliver R., *Go Fish: Evaluating the Restatement's Formulation of the Law of Publicity*, 47 S.C. L. Rev. 709 (1996), 1060

Green, Michael D., *The Unanticipated Ripples of Comparative Negligence: Superseding Cause in Products Liability and Beyond*, 53 S.C. L. Rev. 1103 (2002), 463

Gregory, Charles O., *Breach of Criminal Licensing Statutes in Civil Litigation*, 36 Cornell L.Q. 622 (1951), 312

Handler, Milton, *False and Misleading Advertising*, 39 Yale L.J. 22, 706

Harrison, Jeffrey L., *Reconceptualizing the Expert Witness: Social Costs, Current Controls, and Proposed Responses*, 18 Yale J. on Reg. 253 (2001), 291

Hemphill, James A., Note, *Libel-Proof Plaintiffs and the Question of Injury*, 71 Tex. L. Rev. 401 (1992), 1003

Henderson, James A., Jr. & Aaron D. Twerski, *Closing the American Products Liability Frontier: The Rejection of Liability Without Defect*, 66 N.Y.U. L. Rev. 1263 (1991), 762

Henderson, James A., Jr., *Extending the Boundaries of Strict Products Liability: Implications of the Theory of the Second Best*, 128 U. Pa. L. Rev. 1036 (1980), 709

Henderson, James A., Jr., *Judicial Review of Manufacturers' Conscious Design Choices: The Limits of Adjudication*, 73 Colum. L. Rev. 1531 (1973), 727

Henderson, James A., Jr., & Aaron D. Twerski, *Achieving Consensus on Defective Product Design*, 83 Cornell L. Rev. 867, 869 (1998), 727, 728

Hollister, Gail D., *Using Comparative Fault to Replace the All-or-Nothing Lottery Imposed in Intentional Torts Suits in Which Both Plaintiff and Defendant Are at Fault*, 46 Vand. L. Rev. 121, 124–25 (1993), 801

Jensen, Erik M., Note, *The Standard of Proof of Causation in Legal Malpractice Cases*, 63 Cornell L. Rev. 666 (1978), 386

Johnson, Vincent R., *"Absolute and Perfect" Candor to Clients*, 34 St. Mary's L.J. 737 (2003), 298, 935

Johnson, Vincent R., *Ethical Campaigning for the Judiciary*, 29 Tex. Tech. L. Rev. 811, 816–837 (1998), 995

Johnson, Vincent R., *Ethical Limitations on Creative Financing of Mass Tort Litigation*, 54 Brook. L. Rev. 539 (1988), 405

Johnson, Vincent R., *Liberating Progress and the Free Market From the Specter of Tort Liability*, 83 Nw. U. L. Rev. 1027, 1048–54 (1989), 324

Johnson, Vincent R., *Solicitation of Law Firm Clients by Departing Partners and Associates: Tort, Fiduciary, and Disciplinary Liability*, 50 U. Pitt. L. Rev. 1, 111–14 (1988), 286

Johnson, Vincent R., *Tort Law in America at the Beginning of the 21st Century*, 1 Renmin Univ. of China L. Rev. 237 (2000), 22

Johnson, Vincent R., *Transferred Intent in American Tort Law*, 87 Marquette L. Rev. (2004), 52

Jones, William K., *Strict Liability for Hazardous Enterprise*, 92 Colum. L. Rev. 1705, 1707–13 (1992), 691

Jorgenson, Linda, Rebecca Randles, and Larry Strasburger, *The Furor Over Psychotherapist-Patient Sexual Contact: New Solutions to an Old Problem*, 32 Wm. & Mary L. Rev. 645, 689 (1991), 291

Jung, David J., and David I. Levine, *Whence Knowledge Intent? Whither Knowledge Intent?*, 20 U.C. Davis L. Rev. 551, 554–55 (1987), 15

Kearney, Mary Kate, *Breaking the Silence: Tort Liability for Failing to Protect Children from Abuse*, 42 Buff. L. Rev. 405 (1994), 518

Keating, Patrick J., Kevin R. Sutherland, Gerald V. Cleary III, and Timothy J. Walsh, *Recent Developments in Aviation and Space Law*, 38 Tort Trial & Ins. Prac. L.J. 205 (2003), 404

Keeton, W. Page, et al, *Prosser and Keeton on Torts* (1984), 6

Keeton, W. Page, *Product Liability and the Meaning of Defect* (1973) 5 St. Mary's L.J. 30, 33, 723

Keeton, W. Page, *Fraud—Concealment and Non-Disclosure*, 15 Tex. L. Rev. 1, 930 (1936).

Kelley, Patrick J., *Who Decides? Community Safety Conventions at the Heart of Tort Liability*, 38 Clev. St. L. Rev. 315, 390 (1990), 10

King, Joseph H., Jr., *Defining the Internal Context for Communications Containing Allegedly Defamatory Headline Language*, 71 U. Cinn. L. Rev. 863 (2003), 967

King, Joseph H., Jr., *"Reduction of Likelihood" Reformulation and Other Retrofitting of the Loss-of-a-Chance Doctrine*, 28 U. Memphis L. Rev. 491 (1998), 383

King, Joseph H., Jr., *Causation, Valuation, and Chance in Personal Injury Torts Involving Preexisting Conditions and Future Consequences*, 90 Yale L.J. 1353, 1354 (1981), 379

Kinney, Judith M., *Note: Tort Law—Expansion of Hospital Liability Under the Doctrine of Corporate Negligence*, 65 Temple L. Rev. 787 (1992), 291

Krause, Harry D., *On the Dangers of Allowing Marital Fault to Re-Emerge in the Guise of Torts*, 73 Notre Dame L. Rev. 1355 (1998), 837

Leibson, David J., *Recovery of Damages for Emotional Distress Caused by Physical Injury to Another*, 15 J. Fam. L. 163, 198 (1977), 590

Levmore, Saul & Jeffrey O'Connell, *A Reply to Landes: A Faulty Study of No-Fault's Effect on Fault*, 48 Mo. L. Rev. 649 (1983), 40

Levy, Steven Mark, *Liability of the Art Expert for Professional Malpractice*, 1991 Wis. L. Rev. 595, 650–51, 275

Llewellyn, *On Warranty of Quality and Society*, 36 Col. L. Rev. 699, 704, 706

Logan, David A., *Libel Law in the Trenches: Reflections on Current Data on Libel Litigation*, 87 Va. L. Rev. 503, 511 (2001), 1030

Logan, David A., *Masked Media: Judges, Juries, and the Law of Surreptitious Newsgathering*, 83 Iowa L. Rev. 161 (1997), 1016

Love, Jean C., *Discriminatory Speech and the Tort of Intentional Infliction of Emotional Distress*, 47 Wash. & Lee L. Rev. 123 (1990), 71, 92

Maguigan, Holly, *Battered Women and Self-Defense: Myths and Misconceptions in Current Reform Proposals*, 140 U. Pa. L. Rev. 379 (1991), 153

McClurg, Andrew Jay, *Handguns as Products Unreasonably Dangerous Per Se*, 13 U. Ark. Little Rock L.J. 599 (1991), 761

McNamara, John W., Note, *Murder and the Tort of Intentional Infliction of Emotional Distress*, 1986 Duke L.J. 572, 572–85, 98

Miller, Ted R., *Willingness to Pay Comes of Age: Will the Tort System Survive?*, 83 Nw. U. L. Rev. 876 (1989), 206

Montgomery, John E. and David A. Owen, "*Reflections on the Theory and Administration of Strict Tort Liability for Defective Products*," 27 S.C. L. Rev. 803, 826 (1976), 760

Moretti, Barbara, *Note, Outing: Justifiable or Unwarranted Invasion of Privacy? The Private Facts Tort as a Remedy for Disclosure of Sexual Orientation*, 11 Cardozo Arts & Ent. L. Rev. 857, 864 (1993), 1038

Noah, Barbara A., *The Managed Care Dilemma: Can Theories of Tort Liability Adapt to the Realities of Cost Containment?*, 48 Mercer L. Rev. 1219, 1230–32 (1997), 291

Nolte, Steffen, *The Spoliation Tort: An Approach to Underlying Principles*, 26 St. Mary's L.J. 351, 391 (1995), 362

Note, *An Economic Analysis of the Plaintiff's Windfall From Punitive Damages Litigation*, 105 Harv. L. Rev. 1900 (1992), 231

Note, *Government Tort Liability*, 111 Harv. L. Rev. 2009 (1998), 848

Note, *Plaintiff's Conduct as a Defense to Claims Against Cigarette Manufacturers*, 99 Harv. L. Rev. 809 (1986), 754

O'Connell, Jeffrey, "*Taming the Automobile*," 58 Nw. U. L. Rev. 299, 348 (1963), 716

Orloff, Neil and Jery Stedinger, *A Framework for Evaluating the Preponderance-of-the-Evidence Standard*, 131 U. Pa. L. Rev. 1159 (1983), 384

Ormsten, Franklin D., Norman B. Arnoff, and Gregg R. Evangelist, *Securities Broker Malpractice and Its Avoidance*, 25 Seton Hall L. Rev. 190, 190 (1994), 275

Pearson, Richard N., *Liability to Bystanders for Negligently Inflicted Emotional Harm—A Comment on the Nature of Arbitrary Rules*, 34 U. Fla. L. Rev. 477, 511 (1982), 610

Peck, Cornelius J., *Comments on Judicial Creativity*, 69 Iowa L. Rev. 1, 13 (1983), 868

Peck, Cornelius J., *The Role of the Courts and Legislatures in the Reform of Tort Law*, 48 Minn. L. Rev. 265, 268–70 (1963), 868

Pedrick, Willard H., *Intentional Infliction: Should Section 46 Be Revised?*, 13 Pepperdine L. Rev. 1 (1985), 78

Piacun, Joseph S., *The Abolition of Strict Liability in Louisiana: A Return to a Fairer Standard or an Impossible Burden for Plaintiffs?*, 43 Loyola L. Rev. 215, 237–38 (1997), 693

Pomeroy, Jeremy, *Reason, Religion, and Avoidable Consequences: When Faith and the Duty to Mitigate Collide*, 67 N.Y.U. L. Rev. 1111, 1145–1147 (1992), 265

Poplar, David E., *Tolling the Statute of Limitations for Battered Women After Giovine v. Giovine: Creating Equitable Exceptions for Victims of Domestic Abuse*, 101 Dick. L. Rev. 161, 170, 175 (1996), 87

Probert, Walter, *A Case Study in Interpretation in Torts: Garratt v. Dailey*, 19 Toledo L. Rev. 73, 85 n.65 (1987), 28

Prosser, William L., *Injurious Falsehood: The Basis of Liability*, 59 Colum. L. Rev. 425, 969

Prosser, William L., *Palsgraf Revisited*, 52 Mich. L. Rev. 1, 15 (1953), 237

Prosser, William L., *Privacy*, 48 Cal. L. Rev. 383 (1960), 1033

Prosser, William L., *Private Action for Public Nuisance*, 52 Va. L. Rev. 997, 1005

Prosser, William L., *Strict Liability to the Consumer*, 69 Yale L.J. 1099, 712

Prosser, William L., *Transferred Intent*, 45 Tex. L. Rev. 650 (1967), 52, 421, 882

Pryor, Ellen S., *The Stories We Tell: Intentional Harm and the Quest for Insurance Funding*, 75 Texas L. Rev. 1721 (1997), 32

Rabin, Robert L., *Tort Recovery for Negligently Inflicted Economic Loss: A Reassessment*, 37 Stan. L. Rev. 1513, 1526 (1985), 610

Raisty, Laura M., *Bystander Distress and Loss of Consortium: An Examination of the Relationship Requirements in Light of Romer v. Evans*, 65 Fordham L. Rev. 2647, 2648 (1997), 593

Razin, Cathrael, Comment, *"Nowhere To Go and Chose To Stay": Using the Tort of False Imprisonment to Redress Involuntary Confinement of Elderly in Nursing Homes and Hospitals*, 137 U. Pa. L. Rev. 903 (1989), 106

Reamey, Gerald S., *When Special Needs Meet Probable Cause: Denying the Devil Benefit of Law*, 19 Hastings Const. L.Q. 295 (1992), 108

Reesman, David A., Note, *Parental Liability and the Extension of Social Host Liability to Minors*, 16 Dayton L. Rev. 827 (1991), 54

Remmers, Donald H., *Recent Legislative Trends in Defamation by Radio*, 64 Harv. L. Rev. 727 (1951), 984

Reynolds, Osborne M., Jr., *Tortious Battery: Is "I Didn't Mean Any Harm" Relevant?*, 37 Okla. L. Rev. 717 (1984), 59

Robbennolt, Jennifer K., *Determining Punitive Damages: Empirical Insights and Implications for Reform*, 50 Buffalo L. Rev. 103, 161–65 (2002), 219

Robertson, David W., *The Common Sense of Cause in Fact*, 75 Texas L. Rev. 1765 (1997), 376

Rosen, Richard A., *On Self-Defense, Imminence, and Women Who Kill Their Batterers*, 71 N.C. L. Rev. 371 (1993), 153

Rosenberg, David, *Class Actions for Mass Torts: Doing Justice by Collective Means*, 62 Ind. L.J. 561 (1987), 404

Rosenberg, David, *The Causal Connection in Mass Exposure Cases: A "Public Law" Vision of the Tort System*, 97 Harv. L. Rev. 851 (1984), 404

Ruder, Lisa, Comment, *Caps on Noneconomic Damages and the Female Plaintiff*, 44 Case W. Res. L. Rev. 197 (1993), 234

Rustad, Michael, *In Defense of Punitive Damages in Products Liability: Testing Tort Anecdotes with Empirical Data*, 78 Iowa L. Rev. 1, 7 n.23 & n. 29 (1992), 218

Saine, Christian D., *Preserving the Collateral Source Rule: Modern Theories of Tort Law and a Proposal for Practical Application*, 47 Case Western Res. L. Rev. 1075, 1119 (1997), 191

Sanzo, Michael, *Vaccines and the Law*, 19 Pepperdine L. Rev. 29, 45 (1991), 26

Schlanger, Margo, *Injured Women Before Common Law Courts, 1860–1930*, 21 Harv. Women's L.J. 79 (1998), 300

Schuerman, Sue Ellen, *Establishing a Tort Duty for Police Failure to Respond to Domestic Violence*, 34 Ariz. L. Rev. 355, 369 (1992), 524

Schulman, "*The Standard of Care Required of Children*," 37 Yale L.J. 618, 619 (1928), 267

Schwab, Stewart J., & Theodore Eisenberg, *Explaining Constitutional Tort Litigation: The Influence of the Attorney Fees Statute and the Government as Defendant*, 73 Cornell L. Rev. 719 (1988), 448

Schwartz, Gary T., *The Myth of the Ford Pinto Case*, 43 Rutgers L. Rev. 1013, 1038 (1991), 728

Scott, David A., *An Employer's Guide to Defending Workplace Defamation Claims*, 37 So. Tex. L. Rev. 84, 854 (1996), 1026

Scott, L. Wayne, *Liability of Parents for the Conduct of Their Child Under Section 33.01 of the Texas Family Code: Defining the Requisite Standards of "Culpability,"* 20 St. Mary's L.J. 69 (1988), 54

Seavey, Warren A., *Principles of Torts*, 56 Harv. L. Rev. 72, 90–93 (1942), 432

Sharp, Rodney M., Comment, *Intentional Infliction of Emotional Distress: Recovery of Damages for Victims of Parental Kidnapping*, 1984 S. Ill. U. L.J. 145, 80

Sims, Andrew B., *Tort Liability for Physical Injuries Allegedly Resulting from Media Speech: A Comprehensive First Amendment Approach*, 34 Ariz. L. Rev. 231 (1992), 418

Spitz, Stephen A., *From Res Ipsa Loquitur to Diethylstilbestrol: The Unidentified Tortfeasor in California*, 65 Ind. L.J. 591 (1990), 343, 405

Squires-Lee, Debra, *Note, In Defense of Floyd: Appropriately Valuing Companion Animals in Tort*, 70 N.Y.U. L. Rev. 1059 (1995), 125

Sugarman, Stephen D., *Assumption of Risk*, 31 Valparaiso L. Rev. 833 (1997), 774, 787

Swerdlow, Janet, *Negligent Referral: A Potential Theory of Employer Liability*, 64 S. Cal. L. Rev. 1645, 1671 (1991), 493

Symposium, *Blackmail*, 141 U. Pa. L. Rev. 1565 (1993), 1045

Symposium, *Punitive Damages*, 87 Georgetown L.J. 285 (1998), 218

Temkin, Barry R., *Can Negligent Referral to Another Attorney Constitute Legal Malpractice?*, 17 Touro L. Rev. 639 (2001), 285

Tobias, Carl, *Interspousal Tort Immunity in America*, 23 Ga. L. Rev. 359 (1989), 837

Traynor, Roger J., *The Ways and Meanings of Defective Products and Strict Liability*, *supra*, 32 Tenn. L. Rev. 363, 366, 722

Trebilcock, Michael and Don Dewees, *The Efficacy of the Tort System and Its Alternatives: A Review of Empirical Evidence*, 30 Osgoode Hall L.J. 57, 66–67 (1992), 40

Tribe, Laurence H., *Trial by Mathematics: Precision and Ritual in the Legal Process*, 84 Harv. L. Rev. 1329, 1340–41 (1971), 404

Tullier, Kelly Mahon, *Governmental Liability for Negligent Failure to Detain Drunk Drivers*, 77 Cornell L. Rev. 873, 874 (1992), 625

Twerski, A. D., A. S. Weinstein, W. A. Donaher & H. R. Piehler, *The Use and Abuse of Warnings in Products Liability Design—Defect Litigation Comes of Age*, 61 Cornell L. Rev. 495 (1976), 732

Uchendu, Vincent, *Attorney's Commingling, Misappropriation, and Conversion of Client's Funds: Sanctions*, 31 How. L.J. 331 (1988), 126

Wade, John, *On the Nature of Strict Tort Liability for Products*, 44 Miss. L.J. 825 (1973), 722, 723, 740

Walker, L. Mark, and Dale E. Cottingham, *An Abridged Primer on the Law of Public Nuisance*, 30 Tulsa L.J. 355, 355 (1994), 910

Warren, Charles D., & Louis D. Brandeis, *The Right to Privacy*, 4 Harv. L. Rev. 193, 196 (1890), 1033

Weiler, Paul C., Howard H. Hyatt, Joseph P. Newhouse, William G. Johnson, Troyen A. Brennan & Lucian L. Leape, *A Measure of Malpractice: Medical Injury, Malpractice Litigation, and Patient Compensation* (1993), 293

Weinstein, Jack B., *Preliminary Reflections on Law's Reaction to Disaster*, 11 Colum. J. Envtl. L. 1 (1986), 404

Werdegar, Matthew Mickle, *Enjoining the Constitution: The Use of Public Nuisance Abatement Injunctions Against Urban Street Gangs*, 51 Stan. L. Rev. 409, 409 (1999), 910

Wilhoit, Bart S., Comment, *Spoliation of Evidence: The Viability of Four Emerging Torts*, 46 U.C.L.A. L. Rev. 631 (1998), 360

Winfield, Percy H., *The Foundation of Liability in Tort*, 27 Colum. L. Rev. 1, 4–5 (1927), 4

Wriggins, Jennifer, *Domestic Violence Torts*, 75 So. Cal. L. Rev. 121 (2001), 70, 861

Wriggins, Jennifer, *Interspousal Tort Immunity and Insurance "Family Member Exclusions": Shared Assumptions, Relational and Liberal Feminist Challenges*, 17 Wis. Women's L.J. 251 (2002), 837

Ziles, Zigurd L., *Vosburg v. Putney: A Centennial Story*, 1992 Wis. L. Rev. 877–996, 12

Zimmerman, Diane L., *Requiem for a Heavyweight: A Farewell to Warren and Brandeis's Privacy Tort*, 68 Cornell L. Rev. 291 (1983), 1038

Third Edition Preface and Acknowledgments

The third edition of Studies in American Tort Law attempts to capture the immense range of activity that continues to take place in this field of law. Seventeen new principal cases address emerging issues, such as constitutional limitations on punitive damages and on the right of publicity, intentional interference with intangible property (including domain names), and tort remedies for victims of domestic violence. The text seeks to demonstrate how states are grappling with critical doctrinal matters, such as defining the boundary between products-liability law and public-nuisance law (*e.g.*, in cases involving handguns and tobacco), or are applying established principles to new contexts (*e.g.*, Internet information brokers, mass marketers of products, and non-traditional families).

The notes in the third edition cite more than a hundred new cases and reflect, frequently by way of statutory excerpts, both the fruits of continuing "tort reform" campaigns and the contemporary preference for crafting statutory solutions to virtually every significant legal issue. State legislatures, for example, have recently passed a myriad of new laws limiting the liability of professionals and purveyors of goods; modifying joint and several liability; restoring or creating immunities for teachers, volunteers, mediators, and others; lengthening statutes of limitations for sexual abuse; and altering, in dozens of ways, the rules for determining damages.

Careful attention has been paid to the emerging Restatement, Third, of Torts, which has been cited and discussed throughout the volume. Every effort has been made to reflect, in their rich complexity, the rules, preferences, and policy determinations that today shape American tort law. The casebook continues to offer an economic analysis of tort rules in areas where that is particularly useful, as well as perspectives reminding students about the special ethical obligations of attorneys.

Since the second edition of Studies in American Tort Law was published in 1999, its companion volume, Mastering Torts (2d ed. 1999), has appeared in two Chinese editions published by China Renmin University Press in Beijing, under the title American Tort Law. One edition is a full Chinese translation; the other is published in English with Chinese keywords. Both editions were translated by Professor Zhao Xiuwen of Renmin University.

We thank the faculty members at other schools who have offered useful suggestions and kind words about earlier editions of this book, especially Jennifer Wriggins of University of Maine School of Law, Sheila Foster of Fordham University School of Law, Sally F. Goldfarb of Rutgers School of Law-Camden, Robert F. Blomquist of Valparaiso University School of Law, and Wang Liming of Renmin University of China.

At St. Mary's University School of Law, work on the third edition was ably assisted by several upper-level students, including Teresa Ahnberg, Brian T. Bagley, Kellie Billings, Leila Ben Debba, Benjamin J. Carbajal, Jacqueline Dieterle, Carlos Garcia, Suzanne Jost, Kathleen Kilanowski, Armistead M. Long, Michael Norris, Daniel Austin Ortiz, Joseph Pena, Jeannemarie Wilson, Patricia Zarate, and, particularly, Claire G. Hargrove.

Vincent R. Johnson
San Antonio, Texas
November 15, 2004

First Edition Preface

Tort law is a prime battleground in the ongoing debate over social policy. This book attempts to illuminate that debate through the use of cases and materials that clearly reflect not only the current rules on injury compensation, but also the policy choices underlying those rules.

Lawyers must know what the law is now, and how to apply it to the facts of a client's case. But they must also understand public policy, if they are to effectively participate in the important (and inevitable) legal processes through which existing rules are continually challenged, reaffirmed, discarded, and replaced.

As an instructional text, Studies in American Tort Law (SATL) does not speak from an ideological perspective. In that sense, the book is intended to be both "balanced" and "mainstream." Within a clear doctrinal framework (which is undoubtedly influenced by the work of the late William Prosser), a range of views is presented, reflecting dominant themes and issues in tort law, such as fault, proportionality, deterrence, internalization of costs, and distribution of losses. These views are then linked, juxtaposed, and explored with the purpose of assisting students in the task of assessing the merits and limitations of these positions. In the end, however, the evaluation of the public policies which have shaped the current tangle of rules on liability for personal injury and property damage is left to the reader. This book attempts to promote a better understanding of the values advanced and the interests sacrificed by the adoption or application of particular rules in given contexts.

In terms of organization, SATL moves from simple concepts and elementary rules to ones that are more complex or elusive. The book has a strong doctrinal framework and strives for clarity, to the extent that clarity is possible, on the assumption that if simple points are dealt with efficiently, time can then be profitably spent on difficult or uncertain questions.

In selecting or writing material for the book, students and professors have been foremost in mind. At each juncture, the test has been whether the selection is both readable and teachable. The goal has been to include material that is vivid, provocative, and worthy of the reader's time.

A few features of SATL deserve mention. First, although cases are used as the principal vehicle for teaching torts, a special effort has been made to integrate statutory law into the text. In particular, careful attention has been paid to the give-and-take process through which judge-made law and legislation influence one another. Second, the significance of liability insurance is highlighted, for students must come to appreciate the critical role that insurance (or the lack of it) plays in the resolution of real cases. Third, "ethics notes" have been included throughout the book for the purpose of sensitizing students to the difficult ethical questions that practicing lawyers face each day. These notes demonstrate, in part, that lawyers are subject to higher standards than persons in other callings. Fourth, the materials in SATL explore a number of issues associated with the law and feminism movement. These issues raise questions of social justice that should be of concern to all lawyers.

SATL introduces students to—but is careful not to overwhelm them with—law and economics. At appropriate junctures in SATL, economic issues are explored, as in connection with the negligence balancing test and the materials discussing computation of damages, liability for nuisance, and strict liability. The goal is not to view all of tort law through an economic lens, but to employ economic analysis when it is particularly useful. This approach allows professors from the law-and-economics "school" to use the materials in the text as a starting point for classroom discussions; those faculty members who eschew economic analysis can allow the economic commentary to stand on its own, without need for in-class elaboration.

By emphasizing doctrinal clarity and the role of public policy, SATL seeks to afford professors maximum flexibility in teaching the law of torts. At the same time, it endeavors to ensure that all students develop a firm foundation in both what the law is and what it can be. We hope that SATL will prove to be a book that can be productively taught by professors and readily grasped by students.

Vincent R. Johnson
San Antonio, Texas

Alan Gunn
Notre Dame, Indiana

June 18, 1994

First Edition Acknowledgments

This book has been long in the making—so long, in fact, that it is almost embarrassing to recount the tale. The book began in the summer of 1985, when, after three years of teaching, and with a long career ahead of me, I decided that I wanted to use in my classes a set of materials which I truly enjoyed, and which my students could enjoy and benefit from, too. The first rough draft of SATL was made available to my classes at St. Mary's University in installments during the 1985-86 academic year. Those students were infinitely patient for allowing the manuscript to be parceled out piece-meal as it became available throughout the year, and I owe each of those persons a debt of gratitude for allowing the project to get started.

During the ensuing years, successive drafts appeared, with the work progressing in fits and starts. The manuscript grew and was continually refined, but the task was interrupted by all manner of diversions: the writing of law review articles; the founding of an international law program in Innsbruck, Austria; a year at the Supreme Court of the United States as the Judicial Fellow; a visitorship at Vermont Law School; and the renovation of a home in a San Antonio historic district.

By spring of 1991, it became clear that I should bring the project to completion; the draft then ran about 1000 pages, but still needed substantial work. With the help of Dean David T. Link of Notre Dame Law School, I began what I regard as an extraordinarily effective collaboration with a professor I had never met before, Alan Gunn. Alan brought to the text perspectives on tort law that complemented my own, as well as the experience and discipline of a seasoned author. His work on all parts of the manuscript has added immeasurably to the quality of the book. Alan is principally responsible for the law-and-economics gloss on the text.

There are both advantages and disadvantages to a project covering a long span of time. In this case, the advantages have included the opportunity to test and hone the materials over a span of years. If the cases are tightly edited (as I hope they are), that is due in part to the fact that they have been re-edited, at least annually, over the course of many seasons. In addition, the fact that the text of SATL has been taught at least nine times (in various versions) at St. Mary's, Vermont, and Notre Dame has allowed it to benefit from the comments and insights of many students.

In fairness, the disadvantages of an extended project should not be understated. Aside from the annoyance of having an unfinished task hanging over one's head, there are more practical problems. In this case, the word processing software with which the project began became obsolete, secretaries changed, and the "blue book" revised the rules on parallel state citations, all of which necessitated seemingly endless tinkering with the manuscript format.

For almost a decade, I have been assisted by a legion of highly qualified research assistants, many of whom are now successful attorneys in private practice or public service. The pleasure of working with these young lawyers would have made the endeavor worthwhile, even if the book had never been brought to completion. The project began with the help of Mike Bassett and Chris Warren, but soon included the assistance of Kay Reamey, Laura Johnson Urbis, Lee Parsons, Mark Brewster, Bill McMurrey, Sara Murray, Pat Barsalou, Michael Warren, Jamie Bagnall, Cassandra Johnson, and Kathleen Lucas. I particularly enjoyed working with John Palmer, Susan Bowen, John Carroll, Philip Lionberger, Joseph Gay, Curt Cukjati, Jared Woodfill, Cory Hawryluk, and Daniel Chalker, as well as with Scott Crutchfield and Allen Nye, Rob Dickinson, Brett Kraemer, John Love, and "Four" Price. In the latter stages of the project, I needed research assistants with an eye for detail, and was ably served by David Wiley, Laura Gabrysch, Tracy Caldwell, Frank Alvarez, Phillip Hall, David Rivela, Greg Geerdes, Kristina Weber, Chris Hebner, and Shawn Paschall.

Secretarial support for this book was provided by Cecilia Aguilar, Hortense Cannon, Claudia Apolinar, Aurelia Vincent, Maria Sanchez, Kathleen Worthington, and Rachel Butera at St. Mary's University, and Laura Gillan at Vermont Law School. Becky Ortiz, who cheerfully assists me on a range of projects, did excellent work locating photographs for this book. At the Law Book Company of Texas, Mrs. Katie Lee has played a valuable role in the distribution of successive drafts of SATL since the very beginning of the work.

I am indebted to Dean Barbara Bader Aldave for her support of this project, and, more importantly, for her continuing encouragement of faculty scholarship at St. Mary's University. Several of my friends on the faculty have assisted me indirectly by cultivating a climate at the law school conducive to scholarship, particularly Michael Ariens, Victoria Mather, Mark Cochran, Jeff Pokorak, Marsha Huie, David Dittfurth, Doug Haddock, Jon Dubin, Laura Burney, Faye Bracey, and Beto Juarez. My colleagues in the torts field Charles Cantu, Paul Ferguson, and John Teeter have graciously shared their insights with me over the course of many years. Since 1982, my good friend Geary Reamey, now our Associate Dean, has acted as a valuable sounding board for all manner of ideas, including many of which are part of this book.

Alan acknowledges his gratitude to Marlou Hall for secretarial support and to Dave Link and the Notre Dame Law School for financial support.

Several of the photographs in SATL were provided either by the individuals pictured or by law schools with which they were associated. Additional credit is given to: the New York State Court of Appeals for the portraits of William S. Andrews and Charles D. Breitel; the Supreme Court Historical Society for the photograph of Sandra Day O'Connor (copyright held by the National Geographic Society); and the Curator's Office at Supreme Court of the United States for the photograph of Benjamin N. Cardozo. The photograph of Judge Learned Hand was obtained through the kind assistance of Steven Smith of the Harvard Law Art Collection.

The excerpts from the Restatement of Torts (1934-39), the Restatement (Second) of Agency (1957), and the Restatement (Second) of Torts (1965, vols. I and II; 1977, vol. III; and 1979, vol. IV) are reprinted with the permission of the American Law Institute, which holds the copyrights on those works.

Since before this project began, I have had the friendship and counsel of my dear wife Jill Torbert, an attorney whose intelligence, independence, and integrity brings honor to the practice of law.

Vincent R. Johnson
June 18, 1994

About the Editing

With minor exceptions, the material quoted in the text appears in its original form. However, some changes have been made, usually for the purpose of standardizing the appearance of quoted sources.

In general, the deletion of footnotes has not been noted. Otherwise, the omission of text is shown by ellipses. If only supporting authority (and no text) has been deleted, the word "citation" or "citations" appears in brackets. The use of italics and caps in the names of cases, books, articles, and judges, and for Latin terms, has sometimes been changed. In many instances, the words "section" and "sections," or related abbreviations, have been converted to section symbols. Quotation marks normally have been deleted from block paragraphs.

Studies in American Tort Law

Chapter 1

An Overview of Modern Tort Liability: Intentional Injury, Failure to Exercise Care, and Strict Liability

Personal Injury and Property Damage. Tort law is a dynamic field not easily described. Its rules are nowhere set down in a single comprehensive code, and indeed they continually evolve in response to the felt needs of society.

In general, tort law is a vehicle of legal redress for victims of physical injury or damage to tangible property. It also, on occasion, provides compensation or other relief for such diverse forms of harm as mental distress, impairment of reputation, and non-tangible economic injuries.

The disputes which fall within the bounds of tort law are as broad as the range of human activities. Litigants include individuals and corporations, governmental bodies and non-profit institutions, professionals and volunteers. Indeed, every person whose conduct or inaction precipitates a result which another perceives as harmful is a potential tort defendant.

Tort law encompasses many distinct causes of action—including, for example, claims for defamation, invasion of privacy, negligence, and false imprisonment, to mention but a few. Some torts (such as trespass to land) are ancient in origin, while others (such as strict products liability) have emerged only recently; a number of actions (for example, deceit) are well-defined and consistently recognized, though others (for example, wrongful birth and wrongful life) are only loosely understood or are the subject of little consensus.

New Rights and Remedies. New torts are constantly being elevated to legal status as ideas change concerning the duties persons owe to one another. In fact, that process has been underway since not long after William defeated Harold at the Battle of Hastings in 1066. Thus, early in the twentieth century, an English writer reflecting on his country's contribution to Anglo-American tort jurisprudence aptly remarked:

> [I]t has never been of much use to contend that *merely* because an action is new it cannot be brought....If the judges thought that a new remedy was necessary, they invented it, unless the invention of it would have shocked public opinion, in which event they left...[the task] to Parliament....
>
> ....Torts of a specific character have increased steadily in number throughout our legal history, and the courts can even now, if they think fit, enlarge the list....

> [At times, the willingness of English courts to recognize new remedies was
> so great that it] was more difficult for jurists to state this branch of the law sci-
> entifically than for judges to make the law itself. Writers on the law were like
> map-makers whose rulers conquer territory so rapidly that the bounds of their
> realms cannot be traced.

Percy H. Winfield, *The Foundation of Liability in Tort*, 27 Colum. L. Rev. 1, 4–5 (1927).
This is not to suggest that judges are indiscriminate in recognizing new rights. As one
court recently explained:

> This Court treads cautiously when deciding whether to recognize a new tort.
> [Citations.] While the law must adjust to meet society's changing needs, we
> must balance that adjustment against boundless claims in an already crowded
> judicial system.

Trevio v. Ortega, 969 S.W.2d 950, 951–52 (Tex. 1998).

Common Law and Statutory Law. In large measure, tort law is a "common law" subject, meaning that its principles often have been articulated not by legislatures, but by
courts. Indeed, for centuries—beginning long before legislative lawmaking was popu-
larized by the leaders of the Progressive era and the New Deal—judges have defined
standards of civil liability as part of the process of deciding the disputes that come before them. It is well recognized that when A sues B, alleging that a wrong has been committed, the court may decide that the complaint states a cause of action in tort entitling
A to relief *either* because B's conduct violates a command of the legislature *or* because
B's conduct transgresses the common (non-statutory) law of the jurisdiction. When a
court rests its decision on the latter ground, it must necessarily state, either expressly or
implicitly, what the common law is. Non-statutory common-law principles articulated
by courts impose legal obligations which are binding upon all members of the community, notwithstanding the absence of legislation. Where applicable, common-law rules
govern not only the instant dispute, but similar future cases as well.

Earlier generations might have described the judge's role in common-law adjudication as that of merely "finding" the law through a disciplined process of legal analysis
and reasoning. Today, however, most members of the legal profession candidly acknowledge that the process involves considerable discretion. At times, judges are in fact
engaged in a process of making law, rather than in the scientific discovery of preor-
dained principles. Contrary, perhaps, to contemporary public opinion, such law-making
by courts is not a new encroachment by activist judges upon established prerogatives of
the legislature. Rather, common-law adjudication antedates the ascendancy of statute; it
is a time-honored process the origins of which can be traced back for the better part of
a millennium.

Nevertheless, today's tort law is significantly shaped by legislative intervention into
what was once almost exclusively the domain of the judiciary. Statutes are an increasingly present feature of the legal landscape. When they speak to an issue, whether directly or indirectly, they cannot be ignored. Tort lawyers must be as familiar with books
of statutes as with volumes containing court opinions. Note, however, that many judges
are wary of legislative intrusions into the field of torts, and they have sometimes reacted
by holding statutes invalid.

> In a little over a decade, over *sixty* state court decisions have used provisions
> in *state* constitutions to nullify attempts by state legislatures to reform Amer-
> ica's tort law.... Never before have *state* constitutional provisions been used on
> so grand a scale to overturn state legislative policy decisions.

Victor E. Schwartz, Mark A. Behrens, and Mark D. Taylor, Who Should Make America's Tort Law: Courts or Legislatures?, at 2-15 (Wash. Legal Found. 1997) ("scholars have hailed this development as one of the most important...occurrences in the development of tort law in the past fifty years") (emphasis in original).

Primarily State Law. For the most part, tort law is a creature of the state, rather than the national, government. Under America's federal system, each state has broad leeway to define the conditions under which a person will be subject to tort liability for causing harm to another. This state power is restricted only by the relatively limited demands of the federal constitution (*e.g.,* with respect to free speech or due process) and by federal legislation of such a nature as to preempt contrary state enactments. Because reasonable persons may differ on issues of individual responsibility and social accountability for personal injury or property damage, the principles of tort law governing a particular issue may vary from one jurisdiction to the next.

Re-forming Tort Law. Not only do state lawmakers (courts and legislatures) sometimes diverge on questions of accident compensation, but attitudes shift with the passage of time. Rules once thought to strike a sound balance between competing interests may come to be regarded as out of step with changed circumstances. Not surprisingly, the standards of tort law are regularly subject to re-examination. Interest groups urge legislatures to "re-form" the law governing accidents, and each court case involving a common law issue presents a potential occasion for the judiciary to decide whether to follow an existing rule. To be sure, there is a strong presumption—embodied in the doctrine of "*stare decisis*"—that courts should stand by their earlier decisions. But, not infrequently, a point is reached where the reasoning underlying an old rule is insufficiently persuasive to justify its continued application. In such instances, the only intelligent course is for the rule to be abandoned in favor of a new, sounder standard— whether through judicial decision or legislative action.

The Restatement of Torts and the Prosser Hornbook. It is not surprising that over the years there have been efforts to articulate in simple but comprehensive terms the mass of tort law that has emerged from the courts. In this regard, one authority has achieved preeminence: the Restatement of Torts by the American Law Institute. Respected for its clarity, as well as its wisdom in identifying the "best" view in areas where there are competing positions, the Restatement of Torts has been widely influential. The "blackletter" provisions of the Restatement of Torts, and the reasoning advanced by the Restatement commentary in support of those rules, have been cited in judicial decisions more than 65,000 times.

Founded early in the twentieth century, the American Law Institute is an organization of highly respected judges, professors, and practitioners. A principal focus of the ALI's work has been to "restate" the principles governing torts, contracts, agency, and other fields of law. The first Restatement of Torts was completed in four volumes in 1939. That work was replaced by the second Restatement, another four-volume treatise, the various books of which were published between 1965 and 1979. Portions of the second Restatement remain in effect, but work on the third Restatement of Torts is now underway.

The section on harm caused by defective products (now called the Restatement, Third, of Torts: Products Liability) was finalized in 1998, and the section on comparative principles (called the Restatement, Third, of Torts: Apportionment of Liability) was completed in 2000. Three tentative drafts of key material relating to central concepts in tort law (called the Restatement, Third, of Torts: Liability for Physical Harm (Basic

William L. Prosser

Principles)) have also been completed. Other topics will be addressed by the ALI in the near future.

At this juncture, it is envisioned that some portions of the second Restatement will continue to be authoritative. Thus, on some matters, the third Restatement supersedes the second Restatement, and on other matters it does not. Until the work on the third Restatement is finished and a table of continuingly authoritative provisions from the second Restatement is published, one must exercise care in citing Restatement provisions. Of course, the Restatement is merely a guide—albeit a very persuasive guide— for students, scholars, practitioners, and courts. However, it is not the law anywhere until its provisions, one by one, are adopted by judicial decision. Courts are free to endorse the Restatement or reject it. States that follow the Restatement on one subject may embrace divergent positions on others.

There is one other important work of torts scholarship that should be noted, at least for historical purposes: namely, the hornbook on tort law by the late William L. Prosser. Dean Prosser's hornbook on the law of torts was first published in 1941, and before his death in the early 1970s the book, in various editions, achieved legendary status among law students, professors, judges, and the bar. It was cited in thousands of decisions and was probably the single most influential law book written in America during the twentieth century. The Prosser hornbook was last published under the editorship of other scholars (W. Page Keeton, Dan B. Dobbs, Robert E. Keeton, and David G. Owen), with the title "Prosser and Keeton on Torts" (5th ed. 1984). The fifth edition continues to be cited by courts and scholars, but a more current source of guidance is the new hornbook by Professor Dan B. Dobbs, The Law of Torts (2000).

Tort Law and Public Policy. The substantive content of tort law cannot be explained by reference to a single objective or goal. Rather, the contours of the field have been shaped by the pursuit of a variety of ends, each of which has commanded some degree of support as being a socially desirable objective. It is useful to identify these sometimes-congruent, sometimes-conflicting public policies. A clear understanding of them does much to explain the content of particular rules. It also makes possible the evaluation of tort standards by clarifying the interests advanced or sacrificed through adherence to a given position.

To be sure, there is no comprehensive list of relevant public policy considerations. Yet some arguments have been invoked with such regularity that their historical significance cannot be ignored. What follows is a brief, introductory sketch of several important public-policy arguments.

It has often been urged that:

Liability should be based on "fault." The fault principle has been strongly influential for more than a century, and it accounts for much of the law of negligence, and other tort rules as well. In part, it is intended to allow individuals a maximum sphere of action free of the risk of tort liability. According to the fault principle, only if the defendant's conduct is blameworthy should liability be imposed. In general, the term "fault" is used in torts to encompass situations where harm is the product of intentionally tortious conduct or failure to exercise care.

Liability should be proportional to fault. The proportionality principle seeks to limit or refine application of the fault principle. In part, it holds that liability should not be levied on an individual tortfeasor, even if fault is shown, if doing so would expose the defendant to a burden that is disproportionately heavy or perhaps unlimited. In addition, the principle of proportionality holds that where the tortious conduct of two or more persons contributes to the production of harm, liability for the loss should be allocated among the actors in accordance with the degree to which their conduct has precipitated the damage.

Liability should be used to deter accidents. The deterrence principle recognizes that tort law is concerned not only with fairly allocating past losses, but also with minimizing the costs of future accidents. According to this principle, tort rules should discourage persons from engaging in those forms of conduct which pose an excessive risk of personal injury or property damage. In some cases, this means nothing more than that liability should be imposed on those who deliberately inflict injury or cause harm by ignoring foreseeable risks. In other situations, such as those where a risk of harm is foreseeable to more than one person, the policy of deterrence may favor placing the threat of liability on the party best situated to avoid the loss, or, as some might say, the cheapest cost avoider, or taking fault on the part of all such persons into account in determining damages, so that all relevant actors have an incentive to avoid causing losses.

The costs of accidents should be spread broadly. The idea underlying the "spreading" rationale is that the financial burden of accidents may be diminished by spreading losses broadly so that no person is forced to bear a large share of the damages. For example, some argue that when a defective product unforeseeably causes injury to a consumer, it is best to place the loss on the manufacturer, even in the absence of fault, for unlike the unfortunate consumer, the manufacturer can distribute the loss to a large segment of the public by incrementally adjusting the price of its products. Losses can be spread not only through increases in the costs of goods and services, but through other devices such as taxation and insurance. Though controversial, the spreading principle revolutionized the law of products liability and has catalyzed other changes in tort doctrine.

The costs of accidents should be shifted to those best able to bear them. Although this principle is not concerned with identifying which persons are in a good position to spread liability, the "shifting" rationale is closely related to the spreading principle insofar as it seeks to use the process of loss allocation to minimize the economic burden of accidents. According to this view, a loss will be less severely felt if it is placed on one with substantial resources than on one with limited wealth, and therefore losses should be shifted to those financially able to bear them. Proponents of this view argue, for example, that it is undesirable to force an accident victim with only $100 in assets to bear the full amount of a $100 loss, for doing so means than the accident will have a devastating financial impact. In contrast, shifting that same loss to a defendant with a million dollars in assets may be desirable, for then the loss will not really be felt by either the plaintiff or the defendant. To be sure, the law has never held that a poor person should always be able to recover from a rich one, or that a wealthy person is precluded from seeking damages from one financially less well to do. Indeed, in many quarters, there is great reluctance to applying one law to the rich and another to the poor. Yet, the shifting rationale—sometimes pejoratively referred to as the search for the "deep pocket"—has not been without influence. However, its impact on tort doctrine has been less overt than the impact of many other policy considerations.

Those who benefit from dangerous activities should bear resulting losses. Certain activities—*e.g.,* owning a dog that may bite or using explosives—entail a serious risk of harm to third persons even if care is exercised by the actor. According to this principle, fairness requires that those who enjoy the benefits of such conduct should bear resulting losses, even in the absence of fault. In a related vein, it is sometimes said that an activity "must pay its own way." What this means is that there is good reason for the law to force the promoters of activities to "internalize" the costs that their endeavors inflict on third persons. Only when those costs are taken into account, it is argued, are promoters likely to make decisions that are not only personally beneficial, but socially responsible.

Tort law should foster predictability in human affairs. The idea here is that persons should not be forced to act at their peril, uncertain as to what the law requires of them or what they may expect of others. Depending on how this principle is interpreted, it can be used to support a variety of views, including those holding that tort rules should provide clear notice of the type of conduct that is expected in particular circumstances; that standards should not be unnecessarily subjective, if an objective standard is feasible; that tort rules prospectively enacted by the legislature are preferable to those retroactively created by the judiciary; or even that bright-line rules are preferable to flexible norms which require a jury to second-guess the propriety of an actor's conduct after it has occurred.

Tort law should facilitate economic growth and the pursuit of progress. A century ago, this principle held great sway, and many rules were crafted to limit the tort liability of commercial enterprises. The theory was that a greater benefit for the community would be produced by freeing the engines of industrialization and economic expansion from the spectre of tort liability than by requiring such concerns to compensate those injured by their products or activities. In recent years, there has been growing recognition that the pursuit of progress is not an unqualified good, and increased support for holding businesses accountable for the losses they cause. Nevertheless, there is continuing concern that tort liability not be so readily imposed that industrial creativity is stifled, that entrepreneurship is chilled, that professionals are unwilling to render important services, or that American businesses become globally uncompetitive.

Tort law should be administratively convenient and efficient, and should avoid intractable inquiries. Only a limited amount of resources can be devoted to the administration of justice in any society. This principle holds that tort rules should be shaped so that the dollars spent on accident compensation are efficiently employed. Thus, legal standards should not be so complex or uncertain that their application entails an undue expenditure of judicial resources or imposes unnecessarily high litigation costs on parties. So, too, convenience and efficiency discourage the pursuit of what might be called intractable inquiries, matters where the facts are such that even after expenditure of considerable time and money, there is a substantial risk that an erroneous result will be reached.

Tort law should promote individual responsibility and discourage the waste of resources. According to this view, tort law should encourage individuals to employ available resources to protect their own interests, rather than depend upon others to save them from harm. Many would argue that this policy has been on the wane in recent years, as changes in tort doctrine have made it easier for accident victims to lay responsibility for their losses at the doorstep of others. Yet, the continued vitality of the anti-waste or self-protection principle can be seen in various areas of the law, including those defenses based on the plaintiff's conduct which limit the plaintiff's ability to recover damages even when the defendant is shown to have engaged in tortious conduct. There is a continuing struggle to define how much one must do for oneself, and how much one can expect from others.

Courts should accord due deference to co-equal branches of government. Although courts have traditionally created and updated the common law, there are occasions when the judiciary should eschew action in favor of other branches of government. Thus, it is often urged that certain questions are best left to the legislature because of its ability to gather facts through the legislative hearing process, to craft comprehensive solutions to broad-ranging questions, or to represent the will of the public on highly controversial issues. Presumably, the policy favoring deference to co-equal branches of government has less force where legislative or executive action is likely to be distorted by the lobbying of special interest groups, the under-representation of victims in the decision-making process, or lack of adequate funding.

Accident victims should be fully compensated. There is a strong public interest in insuring that accident victims obtain the financial resources needed to overcome the injuries they have sustained. Proponents of this view argue that tort rules should be crafted and applied with an eye toward this goal, even if that means diminished respect for the fault or proportionality principles or other tort policies. A corollary to the compensation principle is the argument that a system that awards compensation on a regular, predictable, and consistent basis is preferable to one in which doctrinal and administrative vicissitudes render the availability of compensation a matter of chance.

These various perspectives on public policy are sometimes antagonistic. Adherence to the fault principle may mean that an actor will not be held liable for an unforeseeable injury, but also that the victim of that accident will not be compensated. Yet, it is often possible for a decision on issues of accident compensation to advance more than one tort goal. For example, a court may hold that a driver who causes an auto accident by exceeding the prescribed speed limit is liable to an injured pedestrian for all resulting damages. In that case, it may be said that the decision bases liability on fault (because the conduct was unreasonable and the harm was foreseeable), deters future accidents by this driver or others (by showing that violators will be held liable), fully compensates the victim (by imposing liability for resulting damages), embraces a predictable standard (namely the posted speed limit), and defers to the legislature's judgment as to the maximum reasonable speed on the road (by holding that violation of the speed limit constitutes actionable negligence).

Much of tort law can be understood in terms of the congruence and competition between the policies identified above.

An Alternative to "Policy Analysis." Until the middle of the twentieth century, very few judges explicitly justified their decisions by invoking policy arguments. Instead, the common law of torts was seen as redressing wrongs caused by those who violated accepted standards of conduct in the community. The defendant who had behaved acceptably was not liable (save in a handful of cases involving "strict liability"); the defendant whose misbehavior caused harm to the plaintiff had to make amends. The rules of tort law grew from decisions reached in particular cases, with novel situations being dealt with largely by analogy. Today, many legal scholars view most of the history of the common law as the product of unenlightened and slovenly reasoning; some go so far as to say that reasoning by analogy is not "reasoning" at all. Today, the idea that judges are making and implementing policy decisions in their rulings is often taken for granted.

The "modern" view of torts, in which the rules are seen as implementing policies, is central to this book because it is widespread, not because it is necessarily right. Much can be said for the older view. For one thing, the body of tort law that emerged over the course of several hundred years of decisions that were largely indifferent (at least explicitly) to policy concerns was quite satisfactory: much of it survives today. Furthermore, as some of the opinions reproduced in this book will show, judges are not necessarily very good at making decisions about public policy: they receive no training in disciplines relevant to policymaking (such as economics and statistics); they are not selected for their offices on the basis of their past success as policymakers; and they have no facilities for conducting even the most basic empirical research on the factual questions relevant to policy issues. Nor does our system of government explicitly charge judges with responsibility for policy-making; that function is assigned to legislatures and administrative agencies. As one scholar has put it:

> If courts in tort cases decide whether the defendant wronged the plaintiff by referring to the accepted community safety conventions at the time of the injury, they are not telling us after the fact how we should act, based on their view of appropriate social policy.... Judges in tort cases... are called on to adjudicate and redress claims of wrong. When they go further, and tell us how the defendant ought to have acted and how we ought to act in the future, based on their views of social policy, they go beyond what we expect of them.

Patrick J. Kelley, *Who Decides? Community Safety Conventions at the Heart of Tort Liability*, 38 Clev. St. L. Rev. 315, 390 (1990).

The judicial opinions that make up most of this book were written by judges with a variety of approaches to the law. Some rest explicitly on policy grounds; some apply existing rules more or less just because they are there; some seem to rest on policy considerations that have not been spelled out; some rely on convention; some apply (explicitly or otherwise) accepted community standards. Whatever else it may be, the common law is diverse.

Three Categories of Liability. In modern tort law, there are three overarching categories of tort liability: actions for intentionally inflicted injury (including a diverse array of intentional torts); actions based on failure to exercise care (including claims under the doctrines of negligence and recklessness); and actions in which liability is imposed without regard to the actor's state of mind or exercise of care (strict liability). A given course of injurious conduct may give rise to claims falling within one or more of these categories. Outside of these three categories there is no tort liability.

A. Intentionally Inflicted Injury

Vosburg v. Putney
Supreme Court of Wisconsin
50 N.W. 403 (Wis. 1891)

LYON, J.

[This]…action was brought to recover damages for an assault and battery, alleged to have been committed by the defendant upon the plaintiff on February 20, 1889,…[when] plaintiff was a little more than 14 years of age, and the defendant a little less than 12 years of age. The injury complained of was caused by a kick inflicted by defendant upon the leg of the plaintiff, a little below the knee. The transaction occurred in a school-room…, during school hours, both parties being pupils in the school. A former trial…resulted in a verdict and judgment for the plaintiff for $2,800. The defendant appealed…to this court, and the same was reversed for error, and a new trial awarded. [Citation.] The case has been again tried…and the trial resulted in a verdict for plaintiff for $2,500.…

….

[The evidence showed that the defendant reached across an aisle with his foot and touched the shin of the plaintiff's right leg. The plaintiff did not feel the kick, either because it was so slight or because it produced a loss of sensation. However, moments later the plaintiff experienced severe pain. Despite various treatments and a subsequent operation, plaintiff lost the use of his limb. Several weeks before the kicking incident, plaintiff had injured the same leg above the knee in a coasting accident. At least one medical expert opined at trial that the limb was in a diseased condition when the kick was given and that the kick had aggravated the condition. There was medical agreement that the kick was the exciting cause of the destruction of the bone in plaintiff's leg. At the second trial, in response to the question "Did the defendant, in touching the plaintiff with his foot, intend to do any harm?," the jury answered "No."]

The jury having found that the defendant, in touching the plaintiff with his foot, did not intend to do him any harm, counsel for defendant maintain that the plaintiff has no cause of action.…If the intended act is unlawful, the intention to commit it must necessarily be unlawful. Hence,…if the kicking of the plaintiff by the defendant was an unlawful act, the intention of the defendant to kick him was also unlawful. Had the parties been upon the play-grounds of the school, engaged in the usual boyish sports, the defendant being free from malice, wantonness, or negligence, and intending no harm to plaintiff in what he did, we should hesitate to hold the act of the defendant unlawful, or that he could be held liable in this action. Some consideration is due to the implied license of the play-grounds. But it appears that the injury was inflicted in the school, after it had been called to order by the teacher, and after the regular exercises of the school had commenced. Under these circumstances, no implied license to do the act complained of existed, and such act was a violation of the order and decorum of the school, and necessarily unlawful. Hence we are of the opinion that, under the evidence and verdict, the action may be sustained.

. . . .

[Because the court found that there had been an error in the admission of expert testimony, the judgment was reversed and the case was remanded for a new trial.]

Notes

1. The simple classroom incident described above spawned four years of costly litigation, involving prominent lawyers and physicians, local, state, and national politicians, and three appearances before the Supreme Court of Wisconsin. In the end, the high court affirmed a judgment for the plaintiff in the amount of $1200, but—interestingly—the victor never bothered to collect the award. The Wisconsin Supreme Court's three opinions have influenced the teaching of the law of evidence, damages, and torts, and the one quoted above has been used as the lead opinion in several torts casebooks. The full story of the *Vosburg* litigation and its numerous participants is recounted in Zigurd L. Ziles, *Vosburg v. Putney: A Centennial Story*, 1992 Wis. L. Rev. 877–996.

2. Why sue a child? See the notes beginning at p. 53, *infra*.

Garratt v. Dailey

Supreme Court of Washington
279 P.2d 1091 (Wash. 1955)

HILL, Justice.

The liability of an infant for an alleged battery is presented to this court for the first time. Brian Dailey (age five years, nine months) was visiting with Naomi Garratt, an adult and a sister of the plaintiff, Ruth Garratt, likewise an adult, in the back yard of the plaintiff's home, on July 16, 1951. It is plaintiff's contention that she came out into the back yard to talk with Naomi and that, as she started to sit down in a wood and canvas lawn chair, Brian deliberately pulled it out from under her. The only one of the three persons present so testifying was Naomi Garratt. (Ruth Garratt, the plaintiff, did not testify as to how or why she fell.) The trial court, unwilling to accept this testimony, adopted instead Brian Dailey's version of what happened, and made the following findings:

> III...that while Naomi Garratt and Brian Dailey were in the back yard the plaintiff, Ruth Garratt, came out of her house into the back yard. Some time subsequent thereto defendant, Brian Dailey, picked up a lightly built wood and canvas lawn chair which was then and there located in the back yard of the above described premises, moved it sideways a few feet and seated himself therein, at which time he discovered the plaintiff, Ruth Garratt, about to sit down at the place where the lawn chair had formerly been, at which time he hurriedly got up from the chair and attempted to move it toward Ruth Garratt to aid her in sitting down in the chair; that due to the defendant's small size and lack of dexterity he was unable to get the lawn chair under the plaintiff in time to prevent her from falling to the ground....

> IV. That the preponderance of the evidence in this case establishes that when the defendant, Brian Dailey, moved the chair in question...*he did not have any intent to injure the plaintiff, or any intent to bring about any unauthorized or offensive contact with her person or any...purpose, intent or design to perform a prank or to effect an assault and battery upon the person of the plaintiff.*

(Italics ours, for a purpose hereinafter indicated.)

It is conceded that Ruth Garratt's fall resulted in a fractured hip and other painful and serious injuries. To obviate the necessity of a retrial in the event this court determines that she was entitled to a judgment against Brian Dailey, the amount of her damage was found to be $11,000. Plaintiff appeals from a judgment dismissing the action and asks for the entry of a judgment in that amount or a new trial.

The authorities generally, but with certain notable exceptions…, state that when a minor has committed a tort with force he is liable to be proceeded against as any other person would be. [Citations.]

In our analysis of the applicable law, we start with the basic premise that Brian, whether five or fifty-five, must have committed some wrongful act before he could be liable for appellant's injuries.

….

It is urged that Brian's action in moving the chair constituted a battery. A definition (not all-inclusive but sufficient for our purpose) of a battery is the intentional infliction of a harmful bodily contact upon another. The rule that determines liability for battery is given in 1 Restatement, Torts, 29, §13, as:

> An act which, directly or indirectly, is the legal cause of a harmful contact with another's person makes the actor liable to the other, if
>
> (a) the act is done with the intention of bringing about a harmful or offensive contact or an apprehension thereof to the other or a third person, and
>
> (b) the contact is not consented to by the other or the other's consent thereto is procured by fraud or duress, and
>
> (c) the contact is not otherwise privileged.

Rule (Battery defined)

assumption of risk
consent

We have in this case no question of consent or privilege. We therefore proceed to an immediate consideration of intent and its place in the law of battery. In the comment on clause (a), the Restatement says:

> *Character of actor's intention.* In order that an act may be done with the intention of bringing about a harmful or offensive contact or an apprehension thereof to a particular person, either the other or a third person, the act must be done for the purpose of causing the contact or apprehension or with knowledge on the part of the actor that such contact or apprehension is substantially certain to be produced.…

We have here the conceded volitional act of Brian, i.e., the moving of a chair. Had the plaintiff proved to the satisfaction of the trial court that Brian moved the chair while she was in the act of sitting down, Brian's action would patently have been for the purpose or with the intent of causing the plaintiff's bodily contact with the ground, and she would be entitled to a judgment against him for the resulting damages. [Citations.]

The plaintiff based her case on that theory, and the trial court held that she failed in her proof and accepted Brian's version of the facts rather than that given by the eyewitness who testified for the plaintiff.…

….

Analysis

A battery would be established if, in addition to plaintiff's fall, it was proved that, when Brian moved the chair, he knew with substantial certainty that the plaintiff would attempt to sit down where the chair had been. If Brian had any of the intents which the trial court found, in the italicized portions of the findings of fact quoted above, that he did not have, he would of course have had the knowledge to which we have referred. The mere absence of any intent to injure the plaintiff or to play a prank on her or to embarrass her, or to commit an assault and battery on her would not absolve him from liability if in fact he had such knowledge....

While a finding that Brian had no such knowledge can be inferred from the findings made, we believe that before the plaintiff's action in such a case should be dismissed there should be no question but that the trial court had passed upon that issue; hence, the case should be remanded for clarification of the findings to specifically cover the question of Brian's knowledge, because intent could be inferred therefrom. If the court finds that he had such knowledge the necessary intent will be established and the plaintiff will be entitled to recover, even though there was no purpose to injure or embarrass the plaintiff....

....The only circumstance where Brian's age is of any consequence is in determining what he knew, and there his experience, capacity, and understanding are of course material.

....

Costs on this appeal will abide the ultimate decision of the superior court....

Remanded for clarification.

[Following the remand, which resulted in a judgment for plaintiff in the amount of $11,000, there was a second appeal, 304 P.2d 681 (Wash. 1956).]

ROSELLINI, Justice.

....

....[O]n remand, the judge who heard the case stated that...[i]n order to determine whether the defendant knew that the plaintiff would sit in the place where the chair had been, it was necessary for him to consider carefully the time sequence, as he had not done before; and this resulted in his finding that the arthritic woman had begun the slow process of being seated when the defendant quickly removed the chair and seated himself upon it, and that he knew, with substantial certainty, at that time that she would attempt to sit in the place where the chair had been. Such a conclusion, he stated, was the only reasonable one possible....[T]he record...is sufficient to charge the defendant with intent to commit a battery.

The judgment is affirmed.

Note

1. *Intent and Culpability.* According to Professors David Jung and David Levine:

> "Knowledge intent" is the Restatement's creation. Until the Reporter for the first Restatement, Professor Francis Bohlen, drawing on the criminal law and the scholarly literature, introduced the concept, it did not appear at all under that name in the torts cases. Yet, once introduced, the definition gained prominence, and it is the most frequently cited definition of intent.

> ....

> For Professor Bohlen and the drafters of the first Restatement...[a]cting with knowledge that harm was certain to follow was the same as acting for the

purpose of causing that harm because both reflected culpable states of mind. "One who embarks upon a particular course of action with knowledge that it involves as a necessary result an invasion of another's legally protected interest is as culpable as though the act were done for the very purpose of invading the interest." Both actors were culpable because both made a subjective choice to act in a way that invaded the plaintiff's interests....

David J. Jung and David I. Levine, *Whence Knowledge Intent? Whither Knowledge Intent?*, 20 U.C. Davis L. Rev. 551, 554–55 (1987).

B. Actions Based on Lack of Care

Negligence is the breach of a duty to exercise reasonable care on behalf of another. Put differently, conduct which foreseeably subjects another to an unreasonable risk of harm is negligent.

Doe v. Roe
Court of Appeal of California
267 Cal. Rptr. 564 (Ct. App. 1990)

SMITH, Acting Presiding Justice.

....

Defendant Richard Roe[1] appeals from a judgment after a court trial finding him liable to plaintiff Jane Doe for $150,000 in damages based on negligent transmittal of the virus herpes simplex II (hereafter herpes) sometime in early 1985. Defendant does not contest the court's finding that he transmitted the disease to plaintiff or the amount of damages assessed. Rather he argues that he had no duty to... [protect plaintiff from the disease] as a matter of law because the risk of asymptomatic transmission was unforeseeable in 1985.

....

Defendant and plaintiff became acquainted in early 1985....Soon after he asked her out, the subject of venereal disease came up. Plaintiff told defendant that she and her boyfriend were "clean," and that she would not want to put herself in a position where she could possibly contract a sexual disease. Defendant replied, "I don't blame you, I wouldn't want one either," but did not tell her he had previously contracted herpes.

In fact, defendant had suffered three prior outbreaks of herpes....Each time the lesions healed by themselves.

Defendant and plaintiff began dating....Over a four-month period, they had sex once or twice a week. Defendant never disclosed the existence of his herpes condition, nor did he ever wear a condom during sexual relations. Up to that time, he made no attempt to educate himself about the disease, nor did he tell plaintiff about it because he didn't think he could give it to anybody.

---

1. By stipulation of the parties and order of this court the parties have been designated by fictitious names to protect their privacy.

....[P]laintiff contracted genital herpes from defendant. Unlike defendant, who experienced only mild manifestations of the illness, plaintiff suffered greatly. She came down with 102-degree fever, swollen lymph glands, a sore throat and painful lesions on her genitalia which lasted three weeks. Since the onset of disease, she suffers outbreaks on the average of twice a month, each of which lasts about 10 days. She has undergone humiliation, severe physical discomfort and emotional distress....

....

....The [trial] court found...that defendant was negligent in either not disclosing that he was infected with herpes or taking precautions such as the use of a condom, to prevent its transmission. The court found the total damages to plaintiff to be $200,000, but it reduced that figure by 25 percent due to contributory negligence on her part[2]....

....

Defendant contends...that as a matter of law he was relieved of a duty to plaintiff to disclose his condition or take measures to prevent its spread because he believed that he could not transmit the disease unless he had an active manifestation of the infection. Defendant cites several medical articles and pamphlets...in an attempt to show that as of 1985 the existence of asymptomatic shedding (transmission without lesions) was not well known.... Since the risk of harm was unforeseeable, defendant argues, there can be no duty of care....

In determining whether a duty should be imposed, the courts are guided by the basic principle expressed in Civil Code section 1714 that everyone is responsible for injury occasioned to another by his own want of ordinary care or skill. [Citation.] Departures from this rule are warranted only by balancing a number of policy considerations, including the foreseeability of the harm suffered, the degree of certainty the plaintiff suffered injury, the closeness of the connection between defendant's conduct and the injury suffered, the moral blame attached to the defendant's conduct and the consequences to the community of imposing a duty to exercise care.... With the exception of foreseeability, defendant does not dispute that *all* of them substantially weigh in favor of the imposition of a duty of care on his part to warn...or at least take precautions....

Since the court's judgment implied a finding that defendant exposed plaintiff to a foreseeable risk, we must view the record in the light most favorable to the judgment to determine whether a reasonable trier of fact could have found the risk of harm foreseeable. [Citation.] "Ordinarily foreseeability is a question of fact....It may be decided as a question of law only if 'under the undisputed facts there is no room for a reasonable difference of opinion.'...." [Citation.] "'The degree of foreseeability necessary to warrant the finding of a duty will...vary from case to case. For example, in cases where the burden of preventing future harm is great, a high degree of foreseeability may be required. [Citation.] On the other hand, in cases *where there are strong policy reasons for preventing the harm, or the harm can be prevented by simple means, a lesser degree of foreseeability may be required.'*...." [Citation.] In the present case, it is beyond question that our state's policy of preventing the spread of venereal disease is great and that the burden of warning a prospective sex partner is small. Thus, only a slight degree of foreseeability was needed to warrant the imposition of a duty of due care in the present case.

Policy Reason [margin annotation]

---

2. The court cited evidence that midway through the relationship plaintiff discovered that defendant's female roommate (who plaintiff suspected might have a venereal disease) was romantically interested in defendant. The court held that once she obtained this knowledge, plaintiff should have either ended the relationship or required that precautions be taken during intercourse.

The evidence shows defendant knew he had herpes and that it could be transmitted by sexual contact. Although he had several outbreaks of the virus prior to 1985, defendant did absolutely nothing to find out about its contagiousness or what steps could be taken to prevent his giving it to a prospective partner. Defendant also testified that his lesions would appear at times without warning. Knowing that he had this infectious condition and that plaintiff was concerned about contracting venereal disease, defendant entered into a sexual liaison with plaintiff and continued to have intercourse with her on a regular basis for four months without revealing to her this material fact, electing to gamble with her health rather than inform her of his condition or educate himself about the disease. Under these facts, the record supports the court's implied finding that the risk of harm was foreseeable and that defendant unreasonably failed to exercise due care to guard against this risk....

Holding

Our conclusion is not altered by the fact that defendant did not have an active outbreak of the disease during the relationship. There is no evidence in the record to support defendant's repeated assertion that he "relied on his doctors," in failing to disclose the condition or take precautionary measures during sex. No one, much less a physician, told plaintiff that he could not transmit herpes as long as he did not have lesions; defendant simply made up his mind that such was the case. Dr. Norman, whom defendant consulted in 1987, testified that, as of 1985 he believed that asymptomatic transmission was *improbable*, not impossible; moreover, defendant did not hear this as a medical opinion until after he was served with the lawsuit. On the other hand, there was evidence at trial that the phenomenon of asymptomatic transmission was not only known in the medical community but reported in lay literature long before defendant commenced his affair with plaintiff.

Kozup v. Georgetown University (D.D.C. 1987) 663 F. Supp. 1048 (*affd. in pertinent part* (D.C. Cir. 1988) 851 F.2d 437), relied on by defendant as controlling, is inapposite. In that case, a blood bank was held not liable for negligently transmitting AIDS to a blood donor recipient because as of October 1982, it was not known that AIDS could be transmitted by blood. [Citation.] Here, defendant admittedly had *actual knowledge* that herpes was sexually transmissible....Finally, plaintiff testified that if such a disclosure had been made to her, she would never have consented to sexual relations. We therefore find substantial evidence to support the trial court's finding that there was a duty of care and that defendant's breach of that duty proximately resulted in plaintiff's injuries.

....

The judgment is affirmed.

Notes

1. *Negligence.* According to the third Restatement:

> A person acts with negligence if the person does not exercise reasonable care under all the circumstances. Primary factors to consider in ascertaining whether the person's conduct lacks reasonable care are the foreseeable likelihood that it will result in harm, the foreseeable severity of the harm that may ensue, and the burden that would be borne by the person and others if the person takes precautions that eliminate or reduce the possibility of harm.

Restatement, Third, of Torts: Liability for Physical Harm (Basic Principles) §3 (Tent. Draft No. 1, 2001).

2. *Recklessness.* Recklessness is a more-blameworthy variety of tortious conduct than negligence, and according to many authorities the difference between the two is a mat-

ter of degree. Both depend upon failure to exercise care. Negligence is the failure to use that degree of care which an ordinary, reasonable, prudent person would use under similar circumstances; recklessness involves something more, and it has been defined at least two ways. Objectively, recklessness consists of an extreme lack of care; subjectively, it is defined as carelessness accompanied by conscious indifference to a known risk of serious harm. Some authorities employ the objective definition; others the subjective definition; and still others both definitions, either interchangeably, alternatively, or in special combination. For example, according to the Third Restatement:

A person acts with recklessness in engaging in conduct if:

(a) the person knows of the risk of harm created by the conduct or knows facts that make that risk obvious to anyone in the person's situation, and

(b) the precaution that would eliminate or reduce that risk involves burdens that are so slight relative to the magnitude of the risk as to render the person's failure to adopt the precaution a demonstration of the person's indifference to the risk.

Restatement, Third, of Torts: Liability for Physical Harm (Basic Principles) §2 (Tent. Draft No. 1, 2001).

A gym teacher who forces a student to play dodge ball despite knowing that a doctor has sent a note indicating that the student should not participate in any sport involving side-to-side movement may be found to have acted recklessly. *See* Brugger v. Joseph Academy, Inc., 760 N.E.2d 135 (Ill. App. Ct. 2001).

The manner in which recklessness is defined may determine whether it can be proved under the facts in a particular case. For example, it may be easier to establish that the defendant knew of an unreasonable danger and disregarded it, than to show that the defendant's conduct fell so far below what was required as to amount to an extreme departure from acceptable conduct.

Recklessness is sometimes viewed as more blameworthy than negligence, but less blameworthy than intentionally harmful conduct. Whether it is more akin to intentional wrongdoing than to negligence, or vice versa, depends upon the matter at issue. Recklessness serves just as well as intent in satisfying the scienter requirement in an action for deceit (*see* Chapter 21); in proving "actual malice" in a defamation action by a public official or public figure (*see* Chapter 22); and as a predicate for imposition of punitive damages (*see* Chapter 4). Conduct that is merely negligent fulfills none of those purposes. In contrast, recklessness generally stands with negligence, rather than intent, when it comes to defenses based on misconduct by the plaintiff. As discussed below, many states hold that a plaintiff's carelessness (contributory negligence) or venturesomeness (assumption of the risk) will reduce or bar a plaintiff's recovery in an action based on negligence or recklessness, but not in an action based on intentional wrongdoing.

It is important to be attentive to terminology. Some authorities use the terms "wilful," "wanton," and "reckless" interchangeably. *See* Restatement, Second, of Torts §282 Comment e (Special Note). Others say that "'[w]ilful misconduct' sometimes refers to conduct involving an intent to cause harm; but 'wanton misconduct' is commonly understood to mean recklessness." Restatement, Third, of Torts: Liability for Physical Harm (Basic Principles) §2 cmt. a (Tent. Draft No. 1, 2001).

Note that the "word 'negligent' is often used [imprecisely] to include all conduct [including recklessness and mere negligence] which, although not intended to invade any legally protected interest, has the element of social fault." Restatement, Second, of Torts §282 Comment e (Special Note) (brackets added).

3. *Contributory Negligence, Comparative Negligence, and Comparative Fault.* At common law, there were two major defenses, either of which totally defeated a claim based on negligence: contributory negligence and assumption of the risk. Contributory negligence existed wherever the plaintiff's failure to exercise care for personal safety or self-protection contributed to the plaintiff's injury or loss. This defense could be raised at common law only in a negligence action, but where it was proved, it had dramatic effect. In general, any contributory negligence on the part of the plaintiff, however small, absolved the defendant from all liability for negligence, however great. *See* Restatement, Second, of Torts §467. (Under a related rule, "contributory recklessness" fully defeated an action based on recklessness. *See* Restatement, Second, of Torts §482(2).)

In recent years, the harsh common law rule on contributory negligence has been modified by two developments, the first of which means that such conduct is no longer always a total bar to recovery, and the second of which holds that contributory negligence can be raised as a defense not only in negligence cases, but in certain other actions as well.

The first development, the replacement of contributory negligence by comparative negligence, represents a doctrinal change in the law of more than 45 jurisdictions, which in many states took place during the 1960s or 1970s. In general, there are two basic schemes for comparative negligence, "pure" and "modified." In states adopting pure comparative negligence, a contributorily negligent plaintiff is not barred from recovery, but damages are reduced in proportion to the plaintiff's fault. Thus, a plaintiff 65% responsible for an accident can recover compensation for 35% of any damages sustained. In states adopting a modified system of comparative negligence, there is typically a 50% threshold. If the plaintiff's contributory negligence exceeds (some jurisdictions say "equals or exceeds") 50% of the total negligence in the case, there can be no recovery. If the plaintiff's contributory negligence is below that threshold, the plaintiff can recover from a negligent defendant, but damages will be proportionally reduced. Thus, typically, in a state with a modified comparative negligence system, a plaintiff 65% responsible for an accident can recover nothing, but a plaintiff 49% responsible can recover 51% of any losses suffered. *See, e.g.,* State v. Tidwell, 735 S.W.2d 629 (Tex. Ct. App. 1987) (where game wardens stopped their vehicle to allow an intoxicated hunter in their custody to attempt to catch a rattlesnake, the hunter's recovery from the State for snake-bite injuries was reduced by 40%).

As the terminology in the foregoing paragraph suggests, courts and others sometimes continue to refer to the plaintiff's failure to exercise care as "contributory negligence," even though in most jurisdictions the common law rule of contributory negligence has been supplanted by a comparative approach. In such instances, the better practice may be to refer to the plaintiff's failure to exercise care as "comparative negligence," but old habits die hard and not everyone conforms to that usage.

The second stage in modification of the traditional rules on plaintiff negligence was the adoption of comparative fault (an approach that is sometimes termed "comparative causation," "comparative responsibility," or "proportionate responsibility"). Under the doctrine of comparative fault, which replaced comparative negligence in many jurisdictions beginning in the 1970s or 1980s, contributory negligence may be invoked to offset liability for recklessness or strict liability, as well as liability for negligence, on either a pure or a modified basis. Other forms of fault on the part of the plaintiff, such as recklessness, are treated similarly under most comparative fault systems. Under comparative fault, many states hold that negligence or recklessness by the plaintiff cannot be compared with intentionally tortious conduct. However, there is a small, but growing, number of states to the contrary. Without adopting comparative fault, some—but not all—comparative negligence states permit negligence by the plaintiff to be raised as a defense to recklessness.

Today, some jurisdictions still follow the common law rule on contributory negligence, others have comparative negligence, and yet others adhere to comparative fault. *See* Chapter 16.

4. *Assumption of the Risk.* The second major defense to negligence at common law—assumption of the risk—existed when a person (a) subjectively appreciated a danger, (b) voluntarily chose to confront it, and (c) manifested a willingness to relieve the defendant of any obligation to exercise care or had no expectation that care would be exercised. *See* Restatement, Second, of Torts §§496A–G. This defense, which totally barred recovery, could be raised at common law not only in suits based on negligence, but also in actions predicated on recklessness or strict liability. And consent, a doctrine jurisprudentially related to assumption of the risk, likewise precluded actions based on intentional wrongdoing.

Today, in jurisdictions subscribing to comparative negligence or comparative fault, assumption of the risk, like contributory negligence, is often treated as a limited or partial defense in actions based on recklessness, negligence, or strict liability, although in certain situations it survives as a complete defense. *See* Chapter 16. Consent is still a total bar to recovery for an intentionally perpetrated tort. *See* Chapter 3.

Students tend to overestimate the applicability of assumption of the risk, thinking that the defense is established anytime one suffers injury after confronting a known danger. That is not the case—at least with respect to dangers that are not inherently part of an activity. As to those kinds of dangers, the courts have been diligent in requiring convincing proof of each of the defense's three elements. Not only must the plaintiff have been subjectively aware of the danger, but the decision to confront the danger must have been voluntary, rather than coerced. In addition, the facts must show that the plaintiff agreed to run the risks in such a way as to absolve the defendant of any need to exercise care on the plaintiff's behalf. Those demanding requirements will not often be met.

Cohen v. Petty

Court of Appeals of the District of Columbia
65 F.2d 820 (D.C. Cir. 1933)

GRONER, Associate Justice.

Facts

Plaintiff's declaration alleged that on December 14, 1930, she was riding as a guest in defendant's automobile; that defendant failed to exercise reasonable care in its operation, and drove it at a reckless and excessive rate of speed so that he lost control of the car and propelled it off the road against an embankment on the side of the road, as the result of which plaintiff received permanent injuries. The trial judge gave binding instructions, and the plaintiff appeals.

There were four eyewitnesses to the accident, namely, plaintiff and her sister on the one side, and defendant and his wife on the other. All four were occupants of the car. Defendant was driving the car, and his wife was sitting beside him. Plaintiff and her sister were in the rear seat....They had known one another for a number of years, and plaintiff and her sister frequently drove out in the country with defendant and his wife....After passing the Country Club..., the automobile suddenly swerved out of the road, hit the abutment of a culvert, and ran into the bank, throwing plaintiff and her sister through the roof of the car onto the ground.

Facts

....Plaintiff testified that just before the accident, perhaps a minute, she heard the defendant, who, as we have said, was driving the car, exclaim to his wife, "I feel sick," and a moment later heard his wife exclaim in a frightened voice to her husband, "Oh, John, what is the matter?" Immediately thereafter the car left the road and the crash occurred....Plaintiff, when she heard defendant's wife exclaim, "What is the matter?" instead of looking at the driver of the car, says she continued to look down the road, and as a result she did not see and does not know what subsequently occurred, except that there was a collision with the embankment.

Defendant's evidence as to what occurred just before the car left the road is positive and wholly uncontradicted. His wife, who was sitting beside him, states that they were driving along the road at a moderate rate of speed when all of a sudden defendant said, "Oh, Tree, I feel sick"—defendant's wife's name is Theresa, and he calls her Tree. His wife looked over, and defendant had fainted. "His head had fallen back and his hand had left the wheel, and I immediately took hold of the wheel with both hands, and then I do not remember anything else until I waked up on the road in a strange automobile." The witness further testified that her husband's eyes were closed when she looked, and that his fainting and the collision occurred in quick sequence to his previous statement, "Oh, Tree, I feel so sick." The defendant himself testified that he had fainted just before the crash, that he had never fainted before, and that so far as he knew he was in good health, that on the day in question he had breakfast late, and had no luncheon, but that he was not feeling badly until the moment before the illness and the fainting occurred. He explained the incident as follows: "I was going along, just casually along, and I said 'My, Tree, I feel awfully sick,' and with that I went back like that [indicating]. I just remember my hands getting away from the wheel. I did not have time to think of any danger or anything else. I just fainted out and passed out."

Facts

....

The sole question is whether, under the circumstances we have narrated, the trial court was justified in taking the case from the jury. We think its action was in all respects correct.

Issue

It is undoubtedly the law that one who is suddenly stricken by an illness, which he had no reason to anticipate, while driving an automobile, which renders it impossible for him to control the car, is not chargeable with negligence. [Citations.]

Rule

In the present case the positive evidence is all to the effect that defendant did not know and had no reason to think he would be subject to an attack such as overcame him. Hence negligence cannot be predicated in this case upon defendant's recklessness in driving an automobile when he knew or should have known of the possibility of an accident from such an event as occurred.

Holding

As the plaintiff wholly failed to show any actionable negligence prior to the time the car left the road, or causing or contributing to that occurrence, and as the defendant's positive and uncontradicted evidence shows that the loss of control was due to defendant's sudden illness, it follows the action of the lower court was right....

Affirmed.

D wins!

Notes

1. *Contingent Fees.* Many injured persons could not afford to hire an attorney if they had to pay money up front. To address that reality, the American legal system embraces the type of contingent fee system than many other countries have rejected.

A cornerstone of the American tort system is the contingent fee contract. This arrangement for financing legal services enables anyone who is seriously injured and has a plausibly meritorious claim to obtain a lawyer—often a very good lawyer—even if that person has no money to pay for representation.

A contingent fee contract gives a lawyer a financial interest in the client's case that is dependent upon its success. If the lawyer wins the case and recovers money for the client, the lawyer gets to keep a percentage of the recovery—often something on the order of 30 to 35%, depending on the terms of the contract. In contrast, if the case is unsuccessful and the client recovers nothing, the lawyer receives no payment for the services rendered. Thus, if the client wins, the lawyer wins; if the client loses, the lawyer loses. Needless to say, a lawyer whose fee is contingent on success has an incentive to work hard, for if the client does not prevail, the lawyer is denied compensation for the work performed.

The contingent fee arrangement provides not only a device for financing legal services, but a mechanism for screening the merits of potential claims. A lawyer ordinarily will be unwilling to accept a contingent fee for working on a case that lacks merit. Only suits that have a reasonable basis in law and in fact are likely to be undertaken on such terms. Consequently, contingent fees help to ensure both that meritorious cases reach the courts and that legally or factually frivolous claims do not.

Although it is possible, and sometimes desirable, for a lawyer and client to agree to a different form of fee arrangement, virtually all plaintiffs in American tort litigation are represented on a contingent fee basis. In contrast, the defendants in tort actions typically pay their lawyers by the hour for the services they perform. Hourly billing, like contingent fees, creates an incentive for thoroughness in the preparation of a case. The more hours worked, the greater the fee earned by the lawyer. So long as the defendant (or the defendant's insurance company) is willing to pay the bill, there is little reason for a lawyer to forgo steps which reasonably should be undertaken for the purpose of mounting a robust defense.

Consequently, as presently structured, the financing of attorneys fees in the American tort system tends to ensure that the claims decided in litigation are throughly investigated, well prepared, and vigorously asserted. That, of course, is appropriate in the American adversarial system of justice, which depends for its success on the clash of competing interests as a vehicle for learning the truth about the facts and fairly resolving claims.

Vincent R. Johnson, *Tort Law in America at the Beginning of the 21st Century*, 1 Renmin Univ. of China L. Rev. 237 (2000).

2. *The "American Rule" on Attorneys Fees.* Under the "American rule" on attorneys fees, each side bears its own costs of legal representation. However, plans are frequently put forth to discard the American approach in favor of the "English rule," the "loser pays" principle. Under that approach, the loser in litigation must pay the winner's at-

torneys fees. Needless to say, if many persons cannot afford to pay the fees of their own lawyer, except on a contingent basis, those same persons, when unsuccessful in litigation, can hardly afford to pay the fees charged by their opponent's attorney. Rather than risk incurring liability for the fees of one's opponent, many persons would simply forgo bringing claims, at least in the large range of cases in which the issue of liability is less than clear. Loser-pays proposals continue to be a common element in tort-reform legislation.

3. *Statutory Attorneys Fees*. At both the state and federal level, many statutes dealing with particular types of actions—including a few relating to the field of torts, which are discussed below in the text—permit the prevailing party to recover, in addition to money damages, reimbursement for their attorneys fees.

C. Strict Liability Conduct

Hossenlopp v. Cannon
Supreme Court of South Carolina
329 S.E.2d 438 (S.C. 1985)

LITTLEJOHN, Chief Justice

....Eric John Hossenlopp, a four-year old child, brings this action to recover for injuries sustained when the dog of defendants-appellants, William J. Cannon, Jr. and Yong H. Cannon, attacked him causing personal injuries of nineteen puncture wounds requiring sutures, surgery and hospitalization. It is a tort action alleging negligence on the part of the owners.... Based on depositions and affidavits, the trial judge granted summary judgment in favor of the child as to liability, leaving the assessment of damages for trial by jury in the usual fashion....

The showing made to the trial judge revealed that young Hossenlopp and another young boy were...at the home of a babysitter. They were playing outside the babysitter's residence watching her own dogs which were fenced in. The Cannons' dog charged toward them; to avoid the attack, both boys tried to climb over the fence. The plaintiff herein failed in his efforts and was attacked by the dog which dragged him by the ankle and leg causing the injuries which inspired this action.

Under Rule 44 of the Circuit Court, it is appropriate to grant summary judgment on all issues or on specified issues if there is no genuine issue of fact to be determined. The conventional dog-bite law in this state heretofore set forth in several cases is as follows:

> ....It is the rule in this State that domestic animals are not presumed to be dangerous to persons, and before recovery of damages may be had against the owner, the injured party must prove that the particular animal was of a dangerous, or vicious nature, and that his dangerous propensity was either known, or should have been known to the owner. The negligence that imposes liability upon the owner is the keeping of a dangerous animal with knowledge of its dangerous tendencies, or in the failure to restrain it from injuring persons....

[Citations.]

....

Issue

The sole contention of the Cannons is that there is a contested issue as to their knowledge of the fact that their dog had, on previous occasions, harmed others or had dangerous propensities....

The deposition of William J. Cannon, Jr. admits that he was aware of the fact that on a previous occasion this dog attacked a six-year old boy leaving what he described as "...a little small scratch mark right here on the inside of his arm. I immediately took the child into my bathroom, I took a Q-tip, some alcohol and I attempted to clean it.... There was not enough blood to even pink the Q-tip." Mr. Cannon averred that he was unable to keep the dog in the fence because she was able to climb the fence even after he put an extension on it. When he wanted to truly restrain the dog, he kept her on a chain. We think that his own admission is sufficient to establish guilty knowledge.

We are of the opinion, under our established rule of law, that the trial judge correctly granted a summary judgment on the liability issue. In addition, this Court under Rule 4, §8 may affirm the trial court on any ground appearing in the record. In 1978 in the case of McQuaig v. Brown,...[242 S.E.2d 688], the court alerted the bench and bar to the fact that the dog-bite law in this state was antiquated....

The dog-bite law is of common law origin. It may be changed by common law mandate. The time has come when our rule must give way to the more commonly accepted rule of law indicated in other states by both case law and by statute.

Holding

Strict Liability

When a child, as in this case, has been injured by the dog of another, the burden of damages, medical expenses, hospital, etc. must be paid by either the owner of the dog or the parents of the child. It is common knowledge that dogs have a tendency to bite. The owners know this and should be made to respond in damages when the dogs they keep do injuries to others regardless of whether the injury is a result of the first bite, the second or other bite. In this state, we have a paradoxical situation in that §15-75-30 Code of Laws of South Carolina (1976) gives to an injured party the right to collect damages from parents where an unmarried minor child under the age of seventeen years does damages to the property of another; but if that same parents' dog does damage to the property of another, money may not be collected unless it be shown that he had bitten before or was known to be of a mischievous nature. In tort cases, the culpable party should be responsible for not only the second delict but the first.

CA Law

California has dealt with this matter by way of statute. Out of that statute has come a jury instruction found in *California Jury Instructions—Civil* (1950 Supp.). We approve. It reads as follows:

> The law of California provides that the owner of any dog which bites a person while such person is on or in a public place or is lawfully on or in a private place, including the property of the owner of such dog, is liable for such damages as may be suffered by the person bitten regardless of whether or not the dog previously had been vicious, regardless of the owner's knowledge or lack of knowledge of any such viciousness, and regardless of whether or not the owner has been negligent in respect to the dog, provided, however, that if a person knowingly and voluntarily invites attack upon himself [herself], or if, when on the property of the dog owner, a person voluntarily, knowingly, and without reasonable necessity, exposes himself [herself] to the danger, the owner of the dog is not liable for the consequences....

Holding (CA) law

We think the California rule is sound. It is short of the rule of strict liability for dogs. We sustain the trial court on this additional ground. All cases heretofore decided by this Court inconsistent with the view herein expressed are hereby overruled....Affirmed.

HARWELL, Justice:

I concur in the result.... However,...I believe our traditional dog-bite law, requiring a dog-owner to know or have reason to know of the dog's dangerous propensity before being held liable, is sound. This rule should remain the law in South Carolina until the General Assembly sees fit to liberalize it.

GREGORY, Justice:

I concur in the result.... However, I dissent insofar as the majority adopts the California rule. Such a holding as an additional sustaining ground is clearly gratuitous. This case is not the proper vehicle for such a far-reaching change in the law.

Notes

1. In some states, the arguments voiced by the dissenters in *Hossenlopp* have been found persuasive. *See* Borns v. Voss, 70 P.3d 262 (Wyo. 2003) (declining to adopt strict liability for dog bites because "it would be better for the matter to be addressed by the legislature").

However, statutes have frequently reached the same result as the decision in *Hossenlopp* by abolishing the traditional common-law fault requirement and imposing strict liability for all harm caused to human beings and livestock by dogs. *See* Restatement, Third, of Torts: Liability for Physical Harm (Basic Principles) §23 Cmt. d (Tent. Draft No. 1, 2001) ("[i]n about half of all jurisdictions, statutes exist that impose strict liability"). In Indiana, a dog-bite statute renders dog owners strictly liable if their dogs bite a postal delivery worker or other public servant without provocation, but otherwise a plaintiff must prove negligence. *See* Cook v. Whitsell-Sherman, 796 N.E.2d 271 (Ind. 2003). Why would a legislature draw that distinction?

2. *Defining Strict Liability and Absolute Liability*. Although the majority in *Hossenlopp* states that the decision stopped "short of strict liability," most authorities use that term to refer to a rule of law which (like the rule in *Hossenlopp*) dispenses with one or both of the two chief elements of any fault-based approach to compensation, namely foreseeability of injury and blameworthy conduct.

In cases based on strict liability, the defendant may assert the defenses of assumption of the risk and comparative fault (if the latter has been adopted) for the purpose of precluding or limiting recovery by the plaintiff. However, in some strict-liability cases, such defenses may not be raised. In those instances, which are rare, the tort rule is sometimes said to impose "absolute liability." Clearly, the decision in *Hossenlopp* did not go that far. *See* Seim v. Garavalia, 306 N.W.2d 806 (Minn. 1981), *infra* at 324 (holding that a dog bite statute imposed not merely strict, but absolute, liability).

3. Strict liability has frequently been applied to cases involving harm caused by defective products, abnormally dangerous activities, or dangerous animals, and employers are held strictly liable for torts committed by employees within the scope of their employment. *See* Chapters 14 & 15. The policy basis for the doctrine varies somewhat from field to field. In some instances, strict liability is used to ensure maximum deterrence by increasing the likelihood that an actor will be held liable. In other cases, the doctrine is an instrument for simplifying or making more dependable the compensation process. In yet other situations, strict liability serves as a vehicle for allocating losses to those persons best able to bear or spread the losses. Finally, in some cases, strict liability tends to ensure that those who benefit from hazardous activities bear the

costs arising therefrom. Of course, any given application of strict liability may be intended to further more than one of these objectives.

4. *Strict Liability by Statute.* Just as courts sometimes dispense with proof of fault in accident cases, some legislative schemes provide for no-fault compensation. For example, in 1986 Congress enacted the National Childhood Vaccine Injury Act to provide swift and certain compensation to victims of vaccine-related injuries, while at the same time protecting vaccine manufacturers from potentially crushing tort liability. *See* 42 U.S.C. §§300aa-1 to 33 (Westlaw 2003). Under the Act, a fatal injury results in an automatic payment of $250,000, and persons who are injured receive compensation for virtually all past and future economic losses, plus no more than $250,000 for actual and projected pain and suffering and emotional distress. Theoretically, victims may reject an award under the Act and sue in tort, but the doctrinal limitations imposed by the Act on tort actions make that an undesirable course. *See* Theodore H. Davis and Catherine B. Bowman, *No-Fault Compensation for Unavoidable Injuries: Evaluating the National Childhood Vaccine Injury Compensation Program*, 16 U. Dayton L. Rev. 277, 311–12 (1991) (terming the program a "remarkable success"). The Act applies only to seven compulsory childhood vaccines and does not include vaccines used primarily by adults or noncompulsory vaccines administered to children. *See* Michael Sanzo, *Vaccines and the Law*, 19 Pepperdine L. Rev. 29, 45 (1991). The Act does not include tort actions by victims' relatives to obtain compensation for their own related injuries. *See* Schafer v. American Cyanamid Co., 20 F.3d 1 (1st Cir. 1994) (loss of consortium action permitted).

5. *Consequences of Classification.* Important legal consequences flow from classification of the defendant's conduct as intentional, reckless, negligent, or strict liability. Those consequences concern, among other matters:

(a) *Scope of Liability.* Typically, the law is willing to extend liability to a larger class of persons and to award greater compensatory damages in cases involving high culpability, such as intentional or reckless conduct, than in cases predicated upon mere negligence or strict liability. *See generally* Restatement, Third, of Torts: Liability for Physical Harm (Basic Principles) §33(b) (Tent. Draft No. 3, 2003). In part, the reason here is that where conduct is highly blameworthy there is a reduced risk of imposing liability disproportionate to fault.

Consider suits for harm done by misrepresentation. An action based on intentional misrepresentation of a material fact (deceit) may normally be commenced by a person who expectedly relies upon the false communication, regardless of whether its content reaches that person directly or indirectly. *See* Restatement, Second, of Torts §531. However, in many jurisdictions, a similar suit may not be maintained by one who foreseeably relies on a negligently made misstatement, unless the evidence establishes that there have been direct dealings or the equivalent between the plaintiff and the defendant. *See* Credit Alliance Corp. v. Arthur Andersen & Co., 483 N.E.2d 110 (N.Y. 1985), *infra* at 955. So, too, many courts hold that proof of an intentional misrepresentation in a business transaction entitles the victim to compensation for not only out-of-pocket losses and expected consequential damages, but, to the extent that they can be proved, damages sufficient to give the plaintiff the benefit of the contract which had been entered into with the defendant. *See* Restatement, Second, of Torts §549. However, benefit-of-the-bargain damages cannot normally be recovered in an action for negligent misrepresentation, and compensation is limited to out-of-pocket losses and consequential damages. *See* Restatement, Second, of Torts §552B. *See generally* Chapter 21 discussing misrepresentation.

(b) *Punitive or Exemplary Damages.* In some cases, punitive or exemplary damages are awarded to punish or make an example of the defendant. Punitive damages are intended to deter and are available only in the most egregious cases, where the conduct of the defendant not only deviates from accepted standards of behavior, but is highly culpable. Accordingly, cases based on ordinary negligence will not support punitive damages. *See, e.g.*, Miles v. Kohli & Kalher Assoc., Ltd., 917 F.2d 235, 252 (6th Cir. 1990). However, on appropriate facts, reckless or intentional conduct may justify such an award. *See, e.g.*, Micari v. Mann, 481 N.Y.S.2d 967 (Sup. Ct. 1984) (standard was satisfied where a respected acting teacher exploited his position of trust by inducing his students to engage in various sexual acts). In an action based on strict liability, punitive damages are available only where the evidence establishes a high degree of blameworthiness on the part of the defendant. *See, e.g.*, Glasscock v. Armstrong Cork Co., 946 F.2d 1085 (5th Cir. 1991).

Some states permit an award of punitive damages where the defendant has acted with "gross negligence" or "gross neglect." *See* Buzzard v. Farmers Ins. Co., 824 P.2d 1105, 1115 (Okla. 1991); Wisker v. Hart, 766 P.2d 168, 172 (Kan 1988); Tex. Civ. Prac. & Rem. Code §41.003 (Westlaw 2003). As defined in Texas, "gross negligence" is roughly equivalent to the level of wrongdoing which other jurisdictions refer to as recklessness. *See* Tex. Civ. Prac. & Rem. Code §41.001(11) (Westlaw 2003) ("'Gross negligence' means an act or omission: (A) which when viewed objectively from the standpoint of the actor at the time of its occurrence involves an extreme degree of risk, considering the probability and magnitude of the potential harm to others; *and* (B) of which the actor has actual, subjective awareness of the risk involved, but nevertheless proceeds with conscious indifference to the rights, safety, or welfare of others"; emphasis added). Punitive damages are discussed in detail in Chapter 4.

(c) *Defenses.* As indicated earlier in this chapter, defenses based on the plaintiff's own failure to exercise care may be invoked to reduce or preclude liability in actions based on recklessness, negligence, or, if comparative fault has been adopted, strict liability. However, except in a small minority of states, negligence on the part of the plaintiff is not a defense in suits predicated on intentional conduct.

(d) *Respondeat Superior. Respondeat superior* — meaning "let the master answer" or "look to the one higher up" — is a legal doctrine under which one person, who is without fault, is vicariously held liable for the tortious actions of another. An important application of this principle is to the field of employment. In traditional work settings, an employer will be held liable for the torts of an employee occurring within the "scope of employment." The issue of whether harmful conduct is within that scope frequently turns upon such facts as the time and place of the tort and whether the employee's conduct was actuated, at least in part, by a desire to serve the business purposes of the employer. *See generally* Chapter 14, discussing *respondeat superior* as a form of strict liability.

An employer is less readily held liable for an employee's intentional wrongdoing than for negligent conduct. *See* Medlin v. Bass, 398 S.E.2d 460, 464 (N.C. 1990) (noting that "[i]ntentional tortious acts are rarely considered to be within the scope of an employee's employment" and rejecting a *respondeat superior* claim based on sexual assault). Predictably, vicarious liability for recklessness falls between those two extremes. *Cf.* Price v. Viking Penguin, Inc., 881 F.2d 1426 (8th Cir. 1989) (recognizing that in a defamation action reckless disregard for the truth can be imputed on a *respondeat superior* theory). Of course, an employee's strict liability conduct may be imputed to an employer, if the acts occur within the scope of the employment. *Cf.* Richard v. A. Waldman and Sons, Inc., 232 A.2d 307 (Conn. 1967), *infra* at 951.

The imputation of vicarious liability to an employer does not absolve the employee from liability. The employee ordinarily remains subject to suit by the victim, and if the employer is forced to pay a judgment based on the agent's tort, the employer may normally seek reimbursement from the agent.

(e) *Insurance.* The nature of the defendant's tortious conduct may determine whether resulting losses will be compensated by the defendant's insurance. "Intentional injuries, generally, are not covered. Otherwise a liability policy could be used as a license to wreak havoc at will." Appleman Insurance Law and Practice (Berdal ed.) §4501.09 (2003 Supp.).

The operative question is ordinarily whether the damage falls within the terms of a policy provision excluding coverage for harm "expected or intended from the standpoint of the insured." The facts surrounding many intentional torts are such that it is possible to conclude that injury or damage was "intended" by the insured, as that term is used in insurance contracts. *See* Allstate Ins. Co. v. Mugavero, 589 N.E.2d 365, 370 (N.Y. 1992) (holding that injuries to children as a result of alleged sodomy and sexual abuse were "intentionally caused" within the meaning of an insurance coverage exclusion because the alleged harm "was inherent in the nature of the alleged acts"). However, not all intentional torts may be so characterized—which is not surprising in view of cases such as Vosburg v. Putney, 50 N.W. 403 (Wis. 1891), *supra* at 11, showing that intent to do harm is not a prerequisite to intentional tort liability.

Interpretations of standard insurance contract language differ from state to state, and it is difficult to generalize about the meaning of provisions denying coverage for intentional harm. The most that can be said is that insurance coverage will be denied for some, but not all, intentional torts. *Cf.* Tal v. Franklin Mut. Ins. Co., 410 A.2d 1194 (N.J. Super. Ct. 1980) (recovery under policy was not barred where a jury found liability based on both negligence and intentional conduct); Walter Probert, *A Case Study in Interpretation in Torts: Garratt v. Dailey,* 19 Toledo L. Rev. 73, 85 n.65 (1987) (noting that in *Garratt, supra* at 12, "Even though Brian was held [liable] for an intentional tort, the insurance company involved paid the claim").

Many decisions interpreting the intentional-harm exclusion in insurance contracts hold that for coverage to be denied, subjective intent to cause harm must be proven. *See* State Auto Mut. Ins. Co. v. McIntyre, 652 F. Supp. 1177 (D.C. Ala. 1987); *see also* Sherwood v. Sepulvado, 362 So. 2d 1161 (La. Ct. App. 1978) (although shove was intended, back injury was not). However, courts may differ as to what inferences may be drawn from similar facts. *Compare* Loveridge v. Chartier, 468 N.W.2d 146, 153 (Wis. 1991) (intent to harm could not be inferred as a matter of law from fact that an adult violated a criminal law by having consensual sex with a 16- or 17-year-old girl who contracted herpes from him), *with* Linebaugh v. Berdish, 376 N.W.2d 400 (1985) (for purposes of intentional-harm exclusion, adult who had consensual sex with a minor intended to injure her as a matter of law). The reluctance of some courts to find that harm was "intended from the standpoint of the insured" probably reflects their "desire to aid the innocent victim" inasmuch as "application of the exclusionary clause may limit…[the victim's] recovery to a tortfeasor whose pocket is less deep than the insurer's." Kersh v. Heffner, 542 So. 2d 1118, 1120 (La. Ct. App. 1989).

The term "expected injury," as used in an insurance policy provision denying coverage for harm "expected or intended from the standpoint of the insured," "[o]bviously,… cannot be equated with the [merely] foreseeable injury." Appleman Insurance Law and Practice (Berdal ed.) §4501.09 (2003 Supp.). Otherwise few persons would find purchasing insurance worthwhile. Consequently, harm foreseeably resulting from the defendant's negligent, reckless, or strict-liability conduct may be compensable under the defendant's liability insurance, subject of course to the many limitations of the law of insurance.

(f) *Immunities.* At common law, a wide array of immunities barred litigation of certain categories of tort actions. For example, sovereign immunity precluded suits against the government; spousal immunity forbade claims between spouses; parental immunity prevented suits by children against parents; and charitable immunity foreclosed actions against charities. For varying reasons, these kinds of litigation were viewed as detrimental to the common good.

Beginning around 1940, there was a marked trend toward abrogating immunities in whole or in part, on the theory that, except in extraordinary circumstances, persons should be held accountable for the harm they tortiously cause. In jurisdictions retaining some diminished form of these no-liability rules, the line separating what is permissible from what is forbidden has frequently been drawn with reference to the various forms of tort liability. For example, some states bar claims between spouses based on negligence, but allow suits for intentional wrongdoing. *See* Lusby v. Lusby, 390 A.2d 77 (Md. 1978). And, under the Federal Tort Claims Act, it is possible to sue the federal government for injuries resulting from negligence (28 U.S.C. §1346(b) (Westlaw 2003)), but not for claims arising out of such intentional torts as battery, assault, false imprisonment, and deceit (28 U.S.C. §2680 (Westlaw 2003)). As these examples suggest, it is difficult to generalize about the legal contours of partial immunities. In some instances, the law is willing to entertain only those torts involving a high degree of blameworthiness; in other areas, the contrary is true.

In recent years, some persons have argued that the widespread abrogation of common law immunities has left important endeavors vulnerable to ruin via tort litigation. To address that risk, some immunities have been legislatively restored or newly created to protect non-profit organizations and individuals who assist their efforts. See the notes in Chapter 18. In these areas, too, the scope of immunity may be defined with reference to the nature of the defendant's tortious conduct. *See* Conn. Gen. Stat. Ann. §52-557m (Westlaw 2003) (providing that uncompensated directors, officers, and trustees of certain nonprofit organizations are immune from liability, except where damage or injury is caused by "reckless, wilful, or wanton misconduct"); N.Y. Not-for-Profit Corp. Law §720-a (Westlaw 2003) (immunizing uncompensated directors, officers, and trustees of certain not-for-profit corporations from liability, except where the conduct constitutes "gross negligence or was intended to cause the resulting harm").

(g) *Workers' Compensation.* Under workers' compensation laws, persons injured in on-the-job accidents are compensated pursuant to special statutory schemes, rather than via the traditional tort system. A covered employee whose injury arises "out of and in the course of employment" is entitled to an insurance award without proof that the injury resulted from tortious conduct of the employer. The amount of the award is computed according to schedules, which typically take into account the nature of the injury and the resulting degree of disability. The size of the payout is generally much less than what might be recovered in tort litigation.

To encourage employers to participate in workers' compensation systems by paying insurance premiums, statutes immunize participating employers from suit in tort based upon work-related accidents. The immunity bars actions based on negligence, but does not preclude a claim predicated on intentional wrongdoing. *See* Sitzman v. Schumaker,

718 P.2d 657, 659 (Mont. 1986) (actions by an employee and his wife were not barred where the employer allegedly struck the employee in the head with a pipe during an argument, for otherwise, by participating in the workers' compensation system, the employer "would have bought the right to hit his employees"); Kissinger v. Mannor, 285 N.W.2d 214, 217 (Mich. Ct. App. 1979) (an action for intentional infliction of severe mental distress was not barred where plaintiff's foreman disclosed to 40 co-workers that plaintiff had "crapped [in] his pants"); Caudle v. Betts, 512 So. 2d 389 (La. 1987) (an action for battery was not barred where the defendant's C.E.O. intentionally shocked the plaintiff with an auto condensor as a practical joke); *but see* Estate of New v. Dairy Mart Conv. Stores, 2001 W.L. 792931 (Ohio. App.) (holding that a convenience store chain was not liable under intentional-tort exception to workers' compensation immunity for the murder and abduction of an employee; although there had allegedly been an "epidemic of violent crimes" in the employer's other stores, only one documented crime in the area was an armed robbery, and therefore the employer could not have known with substantial certainty that the decedent would be the victim of a future crime).

Actions based on recklessness and other forms of tortious behavior falling short of intentional injury are also typically precluded by workers' compensation immunity.

(h) *Statutes of Limitations.* A statute of limitations bars commencement of a suit after expiration of a certain period of time. *See generally* Chapter 19. The length of the period is determined by the nature of the claim or the type of damage alleged. Consequently, a suit framed as an action based on one variety of tortious conduct may be subject to a different period of limitations than might apply if the suit were framed differently. The provisions applicable in New York under its Civil Practice Law and Rules, N.Y. C.P.L.R. §215(3) (Westlaw 2003), provide a useful illustration. A personal-injury claim litigated as an intentional battery will be subject to a one-year period of limitations under the terms of C.P.L.R. §215, which provides in relevant part:

> The following actions shall be commenced within one year:
>
> ....
>
> (3) an action to recover damages for assault, battery, false imprisonment, malicious prosecution, libel, slander, false words causing special damages, or a violation of the right of privacy....

A suit for negligence, rather than for battery, would fall within the broad provisions of N.Y. C.P.L.R. §214 (Westlaw 2003), which require the following actions to be commenced within three years:

> 3. an action to recover a chattel or damages for the taking and detaining of a chattel;
>
> 4. an action to recover damages for injury to property except as provided in §214-c [dealing with toxic torts];
>
> 5. an action to recover damages for a personal injury except as provided in §§214-b [dealing with "Agent Orange" cases], 214-c [toxic torts] and 215 [certain intentional torts];
>
> 6. an action to recover damages for malpractice, other than medical, dental or podiatric malpractice, regardless of whether the underlying theory is based on contract or tort....

So too, while an action for negligent misrepresentation resulting in property damage might fall within the three-year rule imposed by §214 quoted above, an action for fraud—which normally requires a showing of intentional or reckless misrepresentation—would be subject to a longer period of limitations under N.Y. C.P.L.R. §213(8) (Westlaw 2003). That section provides that actions based upon fraud must be commenced within six years of "the time the plaintiff...discovered the fraud, or could with reasonable diligence have discovered it."

(i) *Discharge in Bankruptcy.* Like other debts, tort liability generally may be discharged through bankruptcy proceedings. *See* Burnam v. Patterson, 2003 WL 202433 (Tex. App.) (discharge in bankruptcy barred continuation of negligence lawsuit). However, there are at least two important exceptions.

First, it is not possible to discharge a debt "for willful and malicious injury by the debtor to another entity or to the property of another entity." *See* 11 U.S.C.A. §523 (a)(6) (Westlaw 2003). Ordinary negligence will never fall within this non-dischargeable category, but many intentional torts will. *See generally* George M. Ahrend & Randall T. Thomsen, *Tort Claims and Judgments as Debts for "Wilful and Malicious Injury" Nondischargeable Under Section 523(a)(6) of the Bankruptcy Code,* 100 Comm. L.J. 498, 499 (1995) (courts differ in their interpretation of the section and litigation has "dramatically increased as creditors have creatively tried to avoid discharge of debts owed to them").

Second, bankruptcy will not discharge a debt for "money, property, [or] services... obtained by...actual fraud." *See* 11 U.S.C.A. §523 (a)(2)(A) (Westlaw 2003). Tort actions for fraud are discussed in Chapter 21 and normally require proof of an intentionally or recklessly false misstatement. *See* Cohen v. De La Cruz, 523 U.S. 213 (1998) (holding that the discharge exception for actual fraud prevented the discharge of all liability arising from the debtor's fraud, including treble damages, attorney fees, and costs).

D. An Introduction to Insurance

Although courts seldom mention insurance in explaining their decisions in tort cases, the importance of insurance to the tort system should not be underestimated. An award of damages means little or nothing to a plaintiff who cannot collect the judgment. Unless the defendant is wealthy, the existence of liability insurance which will cover a judgment for the plaintiff may determine whether it is worthwhile for the plaintiff to sue. When the defendant does have liability insurance that will cover the plaintiff's claim, the insurance company is usually solely responsible for defending the action and for deciding whether to settle. Furthermore, two of the major policy concerns which shape the law of torts—deterrence and risk-spreading—implicate insurance. With respect to deterrence, the availability and cost of liability insurance will sometimes determine whether one undertakes an activity that may cause harm, and liability insurers often insist that their insureds take particular kinds of precautions. As for risk-spreading, the availability of first-party insurance (insurance that covers the insured's own loss) provides a method by which those who may suffer losses can spread their risks. This means that a court's decision to impose a particular kind of liability to promote "risk-spreading" should, in principle, be based not simply upon a belief that risk-spreading is good, but upon a showing that first-party insurance does not already provide adequate risk-spreading.

1.   Liability Insurance

Liability insurance pays amounts which the insureds (the owner of the policy and others specified in the policy) become liable to pay to accident victims. No liability-insurance policy covers all potential claims. Automobile liability insurance, which in some states is mandatory for car owners, covers claims against the owner or driver for damages arising out of automobile accidents. Homeowners' insurance often covers homeowners and their family members for liability arising from causes not involving the use of an automobile. (Liability coverage under most homeowners' policies is not limited to accidents sustained in the insured's home.) Many businesses carry liability insurance covering claims arising out of their business activities.

Almost all liability insurance excludes coverage for harms inflicted intentionally by the insured, so in many, if not most, intentional-tort cases, the insurance company need not defend the claim or pay damages if they are awarded. This puts some pressure on plaintiffs—as well as defendants—to characterize claims as arising out of negligence or strict liability, rather than as intentional torts, such as battery. For a heroic but unsuccessful attempt at this, see Saba v. Darling, 575 A.2d 1240 (Md. 1990), in which someone who had been punched by a drunkard sued, not for battery, but for the drunkard's "negligence" in becoming intoxicated. *See also* Farmers Alliance Mut. Ins. Co. v. Salazar, 77 F.3d 1291 (10th Cir. 1996) (homeowners' policy did not provide coverage for claims against mother for negligent supervision of her son, who was involved in a drive-by-shooting murder, because the "occurrence" that gave rise to the injury was an intentional act, not an accident). Attempting to plead and prove negligence in a case involving the intentional infliction of harm has been called "underlitigating." For an analysis of the phenomenon, see Ellen S. Pryor, *The Stories We Tell: Intentional Harm and the Quest for Insurance Funding*, 75 Texas L. Rev. 1721 (1997).

Liability insurance is always limited in amount; it is therefore desirable for a seriously injured victim to hold as many persons as possible liable for the injury. A million-dollar judgment against someone whose liability insurance covers damages only up to $50,000 may be worth only $50,000.

Insurance companies are businesses, not charities. They must earn more from premiums and from investing those premiums than they pay out in claims. This means that insureds must, in the aggregate, pay more for insurance than they would pay in damages if they were not insured. Why, then, does anyone buy insurance? One answer is that some kinds of liability insurance are compulsory—automobile liability insurance in some states, for example. Another answer is that many insureds are "risk averse"—they would rather pay a relatively small sum each year than take a chance (even a very small chance) of having to pay a much larger amount as damages. Finally, most liability insurance covers not only damages assessed against the insured but also the costs of the defense, and the defense is usually handled by the insurance company. Some insureds therefore buy liability insurance as a way of hiring an insurance company to handle claims.

Cases in which the plaintiff sues for more than the amount of the defendant's liability insurance can create serious conflict-of-interest problems. Suppose, for example, that an insured who has coverage for $100,000 of liability is sued for $300,000. Suppose further that there is a 50–50 chance that the plaintiff will win the suit. If the plaintiff offers to settle the suit for the policy limit of $100,000, the insured would want to accept the offer: the settlement is within the policy limits, so the insurer would pay the entire amount and the insured would pay nothing. For the insurer, however, taking the case to trial looks attractive: settlement means that the company will have to pay $100,000; going to trial means that the company will pay the cost of the trial but will face only a 50-percent chance of having to pay $100,000 in damages (with the insured liable for the rest if the plaintiff wins). The language of most policies gives the right to decide whether to settle to the insurer, but the courts, noting the conflict between the interests of the insurer and the insured, have created a cause of action for "bad-faith" conduct in settling.

Crisci v. Security Insurance Co. of New Haven

Supreme Court of California
426 P.2d 173 (Cal. 1967)

PETERS, Justice.

In an action against The Security Insurance Company of New Haven, Connecticut, the trial court awarded Rosina Crisci $91,000 (plus interest) because she suffered a judgment in a personal injury action after Security, her insurer, refused to settle the claim. Mrs. Crisci was also awarded $25,000 for mental suffering. Security has appealed.

June DiMare and her husband were tenants in an apartment building owned by Rosina Crisci. Mrs. DiMare was descending the apartment's outside wooden staircase when a tread gave way. She fell through the resulting opening up to her waist and was left hanging 15 feet above the ground. Mrs. DiMare suffered physical injuries and developed a very severe psychosis. In a suit brought against Mrs. Crisci the DiMares alleged that the step broke because Mrs. Crisci was negligent in inspecting and maintaining the stairs. They contended that Mrs. DiMare's mental condition was caused by the accident, and they asked for $400,000 as compensation for physical and mental injuries and medical expenses.

Mrs. Crisci had $10,000 of insurance coverage under a general liability policy issued by Security. The policy obligated Security to defend the suit against Mrs. Crisci and authorized the company to make any settlement it deemed expedient. Security hired an experienced lawyer, Mr. Healy, to handle the case. Both he and defendant's claims manager believed that unless evidence was discovered showing that Mrs. DiMare had a prior mental illness, a jury would probably find that the accident precipitated Mrs. DiMare's psychosis. And both men believed that if the jury felt that the fall triggered the psychosis, a verdict of not less than $100,000 would be returned. An extensive search turned up no evidence that Mrs. DiMare had any prior mental abnormality. As a teenager Mrs. DiMare had been in a Washington mental hospital, but only to have an abortion. Both Mrs. DiMare and Mrs. Crisci found psychiatrists who would testify that the accident caused Mrs. DiMare's illness, and the insurance company knew of this testimony. Among those who felt the psychosis was not related to the accident were the doctors at the state mental hospital where Mrs. DiMare had been committed following the accident. All the psychiatrists agreed, however, that a psychosis could be triggered by a sudden fear of falling to one's death.

.... [B]y the time the DiMares' attorney reduced his settlement demands to $10,000, Security had doctors prepared to support its position and was only willing to pay $3,000 for Mrs. DiMare's physical injuries. Security was unwilling to pay one cent for the possibility of a plaintiff's verdict on the mental illness issue. This conclusion was based on the assumption that the jury would believe all of the defendant's psychiatric evidence and none of the plaintiff's. Security also rejected a $9,000 settlement demand at a time when Mrs. Crisci offered to pay $2,500 of the settlement.

A jury awarded Mrs. DiMare $100,000 and her husband $1,000. After an appeal... the insurance company paid $10,000 of this amount, the amount of its policy. The DiMares then sought to collect the balance from Mrs. Crisci. A settlement was arranged by which the DiMares received $22,000, a 40 percent interest in Mrs. Crisci's claim to a particular piece of property, and an assignment of Mrs. Crisci's cause of action against Security. Mrs. Crisci, an immigrant widow of 70, became indigent. She worked as a babysitter, and her grandchildren paid her rent. The change in her financial condition was accompanied by a decline in physical health, hysteria, and suicide attempts. Mrs. Crisci then brought this action.

The liability of an insurer in excess of its policy limits for failure to accept a settlement offer within those limits was considered by this court in Comunale v. Traders & General Ins. Co., 50 Cal.2d 654, 328 P.2d 198. It was there reasoned that in every contract, including policies of insurance, there is an implied covenant of good faith and fair dealing that neither party will do anything which will injure the right of the other to receive the benefits of the agreement; that it is common knowledge that one of the usual methods by which an insured receives protection under a liability insurance policy is by settlement of claims without litigation; that the implied obligation of good faith and fair dealing requires the insurer to settle in an appropriate case although the express terms of the policy do not impose the duty; that in determining whether to settle the insurer must give the interests of the insured at least as much consideration as it gives to its own interests; and that when "there is great risk of a recovery beyond the policy limits so that the most reasonable manner of disposing of the claim is a settlement which can be made within those limits, a consideration in good faith of the insured's interest requires the insurer to settle the claim." (50 Cal.2d at p. 659.)

In determining whether an insurer has given consideration to the interests of the insured, the test is whether a prudent insurer without policy limits would have accepted the settlement offer. [Citations.]

Several cases, in considering the liability of the insurer, contain language to the effect that bad faith is the equivalent of dishonesty, fraud, and concealment. [Citations.] Obviously a showing that the insurer has been guilty of actual dishonesty, fraud, or concealment is relevant to the determination whether it has given consideration to the insured's interest in considering a settlement offer within the policy limits. The language used in the cases, however, should not be understood as meaning that in the absence of evidence establishing actual dishonesty, fraud, or concealment no recovery may be had for a judgment in excess of the policy limits....Liability is imposed not for a bad faith breach of the contract but for failure to meet the duty to accept reasonable settlements, a duty included within the implied covenant of good faith and fair dealing....

Amicus curiae argues that, whenever an insurer receives an offer to settle within the policy limits and rejects it, the insurer should be liable in every case for the amount of any final judgment whether or not within the policy limits....

The proposed rule is a simple one to apply and avoids the burdens of a determination whether a settlement offer within the policy limits was reasonable. The proposed rule would also eliminate the danger that an insurer, faced with a settlement offer at or near the policy limits, will reject it and gamble with the insured's money to further its own interests. Moreover, it is not entirely clear that the proposed rule would place a burden on insurers substantially greater than that which is present under existing law. The size of the judgment recovered in the personal injury action when it exceeds the policy limits, although not conclusive, furnishes an inference that the value of the claim is the equivalent of the amount of the judgment and that acceptance of an offer within those limits was the most reasonable method of dealing with the claim.

Finally, and most importantly, there is more than a small amount of elementary justice in a rule that would require that, in this situation where the insurer's and insured's interests necessarily conflict, the insurer, which may reap the benefits of its determination not to settle, should also suffer the detriments of its decision. On the basis of these and other considerations, a number of commentators have urged that the insurer should be liable for any resulting judgment where it refuses to settle within the policy limits. [Citations.]

We need not, however, here determine whether there might be some countervailing considerations precluding adoption of the proposed rule because, under Comunale v. Traders & General Ins. Co., *supra*, and the cases following it, the evidence is clearly sufficient to support the determination that Security breached its duty to consider the interests of Mrs. Crisci in proposed settlements. Both Security's attorney and its claims manager agreed that if Mrs. DiMare won an award for her psychosis, that award would be at least $100,000. Security attempts to justify its rejection of a settlement by contending that it believed Mrs. DiMare had no chance of winning on the mental suffering issue. That belief in the circumstances present could be found to be unreasonable. Security was putting blind faith in the power of its psychiatrists to convince the jury when it knew that the accident could have caused the psychosis, that its agents had told it that without evidence of prior mental defects a jury was likely to believe the fall precipitated the psychosis, and that Mrs. DiMare had reputable psychiatrists on her side. Further, the company had been told by a psychiatrist that in a group of 24 psychiatrists, 12 could be found to support each side.

The trial court found that defendant "knew that there was a considerable risk of substantial recovery beyond said policy limits" and that "the defendant did not give as much consideration to the financial interests of its said insured as it gave to its own interests." That is all that was required. The award of $91,000 must therefore be affirmed.

We must next determine the propriety of the award to Mrs. Crisci of $25,000 for her mental suffering. In Comunale v. Traders & General Ins. Co., *supra*, 50 Cal.2d 654, 663, it was held that an action of the type involved here sounds in both contract and tort and that "where a case sounds both in contract and tort the plaintiff will ordinarily have freedom of election between an action of tort and one of contract. Eads v. Marks, 39 Cal.2d 807, 811, 249 P.2d 257....

. . . .

The general rule of damages in tort is that the injured party may recover for all detriment caused whether it could have been anticipated or not. (Civ. Code, §3333; *see* Hunt Bros. Co. v. San Lorenzo etc. Co., 150 Cal. 51, 56, 87 P. 1093, 7 L.R.A. N.S. 913.) In accordance with the general rule, it is settled in this state that mental suffering constitutes an aggravation of damages when it naturally ensues from the act complained of....

We are satisfied that a plaintiff who as a result of a defendant's tortious conduct loses his property and suffers mental distress may recover not only for the pecuniary loss but also for his mental distress.... The principal reason for limiting recovery of damages for mental distress is that to permit recovery of such damages would open the door to fictitious claims, to recovery for mere bad manners, and to litigation in the field of trivialities. (Prosser, Torts (3d ed. 1964) §11, p. 43.) Obviously, where, as here, the claim is actionable and has resulted in substantial damages apart from those due to mental distress, the danger of fictitious claims is reduced, and we are not here concerned with mere bad manners or trivialities but tortious conduct resulting in substantial invasions of clearly protected interests.

Recovery of damages for mental suffering in the instant case does not mean that in every case of breach of contract the injured party may recover such damages. Here the breach also constitutes a tort. Moreover, plaintiff did not seek by the contract involved here to obtain a commercial advantage but to protect herself against the risks of accidental losses, including the mental distress which might follow from the losses. Among the considerations in purchasing liability insurance, as insurers are well aware, is the peace of mind and security it will provide in the event of an accidental loss, and recovery of damages for mental suffering has been permitted for breach of contracts which directly concern the comfort, happiness or personal esteem of one of the parties. [Citation.]

. . . .

The judgment is affirmed.

TRAYNOR, C.J., McCOMB, J., TOBRINER, J., MOSK, J., and BURKE, J., concurred.

Notes

1. *Settlement.* The vast majority of tort cases are resolved through settlement rather than litigation; the percentage is often put at 95% or higher. Settlement may come at any stage: before suit is filed; after filing, but before the trial; during trial; or even after a verdict has been returned. Whether a case settles prior to judgment is to some extent a function of whether the parties agree, at least generally, on what the result will be if the case is tried to a final judgment. If the law or the facts are so uncertain that the parties significantly differ in their predictions of the outcome, there is a good chance that the case will not settle—at least if the amount in controversy is worth fighting over.

Sometimes the terms of a settlement are confidential and related court records are sealed. However, secrecy can contribute to dangerous products remaining in the market. *See* Charles Noteboom, *Courts Get Wise to Harmful Secret Settlements*, Tex. Law. Oct. 11, 2002. In some states, court records are presumptively open and can be sealed only for compelling reasons. For example:

TEXAS RULES OF CIVIL PROCEDURE
Rule 76(a) (Westlaw 2003)

1. …No court order or opinion issued in the adjudication of a case may be sealed. Other court records, as defined in this rule, are presumed to be open to the general public and may be sealed only upon a showing of all of the following:

(a) a specific, serious and substantial interest which clearly outweighs:

(1) this presumption of openness;

(2) any probable adverse effect that sealing will have upon the general public health or safety;

(b) no less restrictive means than sealing records will adequately and effectively protect the specific interest asserted....

2. *Ethics in Law Practice: Settlement Offers.* A "lawyer who receives from opposing counsel an offer of settlement in a civil controversy...must promptly inform the client of its substance unless the client has previously indicated that the proposal will be acceptable or unacceptable or has authorized the lawyer to accept or to reject the offer." Model Rules of Professional Conduct Rule 1.4 Cmt. 2 (2003).

3. *Settlement Incentives.* "Tort reform" efforts often try to discourage litigation and encourage settlement. For example, new legislation in Texas will dramatically change the incentives relevant to the settlement process in tort cases in that state. *See* Tex. Civ. Prac. & Rem. Code §42.001 *et seq.* (Westlaw 2003).

Under the new law, if a settlement offer is made and rejected and the judgment ultimately rendered is "significantly less favorable" (which essentially means 20% less favorable) to the rejecting party than was the settlement offer, the offering party may recover litigation costs from the rejecting party.

"'Litigation costs' means money actually spent and obligations actually incurred that are directly related to the case in which a settlement offer is made...[including]:...court costs;...reasonable fees for not more than two testifying expert witnesses; and...reasonable attorney's fees." The recoverable amount is limited to those litigation costs incurred by the offering party after the date the rejecting party declined the settlement offer. More important, litigation costs may not be greater than the sum of 50% of the economic damages plus 100% of non-economic and exemplary damages awarded to the claimant (with certain other adjustments). This means that recovery of litigation costs is available only the extent that the plaintiff wins something and not where the defense prevails on summary judgment or take-nothing judgment. Thus, if the defendant is the rejecting party, the plaintiff may rely on these provisions to enhance the plaintiff's recovery; if the plaintiff is the rejecting party, the defendant can take away part of the plaintiff's recovery.

"The settlement procedures...apply only to claims for monetary relief," and only after a declaration has been filed with the court. The new rules expressly do not apply to "a class action;...a shareholder's derivative action;...an action by or against a governmental unit;...an action brought under the Family Code;...an action to collect workers' compensation benefits...; or an action filed in a justice of the peace court," so presumably they will affect a wide range of tort cases that do not fall within those exceptions. The Texas legislature has directed the state Supreme Court to promulgate rules governing the new process.

4. *No Strict Liability for Failure to Settle within Policy Limits.* No court has yet held insurers strictly liable for failure to accept a settlement offer within policy limits whenever a judgment exceeding those limits is awarded. That is somewhat surprising, for a strict liability approach has considerable appeal. In theory, under ideal conditions, a strict-liability rule gives an insurance company the same incentive as a "reasonableness" rule with regard to whether to accept settlements. *See* Chapter 14. And, as the *Crisci* court points out, a strict-liability rule should be easier to apply in practice than a standard requiring case-by-case inquiries into the insurer's reasonableness in rejecting settlement offers.

5. *Duty to Defend and Duty to Pay.* The standard liability insurance policy imposes two duties on an insurer: a duty to defend and a duty to pay. These duties are separate, so the duty to defend a suit seeking covered damages may exist even if, on the facts as eventually established, the insurer has no duty to pay. This would be the case, for instance, if *A* ran over *B* and *B* sued *A*, alleging battery and negligence. Because the suit

alleges negligence (which is typically a covered claim) the insurer would have a duty to defend it. This is true even though the insurer will have no duty to pay if the factfinder determines that A ran B down on purpose (because intentional harm is normally excluded from coverage).

The duties to defend and to pay arise at different points in time. The duty to defend attaches when the insured is sued, even though the facts are yet to be determined. The duty to pay does not arise until the litigation has terminated through adjudication or settlement.

6. *Reservation of Rights.* An insurance company unsure of whether the policy covers the loss in question will often proceed with a defense under a "reservation of rights" so that, if the insured loses the case, the company can assert that the policy does not cover the award.

7. *Ethics in Law Practice: Coverage Disputes.* A source of conflict between insured and insurer is uncertainty about whether the policy covers the loss in question. Suppose, for instance, that the lawyer retained by the company to defend the insured learns, in the course of the representation, that the insured may have run down the plaintiff deliberately. The policy does not require the company to defend or pay claims for intentional injuries. The plaintiff offers to settle with the insurance company for a sum well within the policy limits. The insured would like to have the settlement accepted; the company would, if it knew the facts, disclaim coverage. The lawyer, who represents the insured but is hired and paid by the insurance company, must respect the confidences of the client (the insured) and so cannot inform the company of the facts giving rise to the dispute without the insured's consent. *See* Model Rules of Professional Conduct Rule 1.6 (2003) (stating the general rule on confidentiality of client information). However, if the facts showed that the policy *clearly* did not cover the injury, the lawyer could not help the insured persist in a course of conduct that would lead to the company's settling the case, as doing that would help the insured perpetrate a fraud against the company. *See* Model Rules of Professional Conduct Rule 1.2(d) (2003) ("A lawyer shall not counsel a client to engage, or assist a client, in conduct that the lawyer knows is criminal or fraudulent").

A complex body of law has emerged to address these and other difficult ethical questions in insurance defense practice. *See* Charles W. Wolfram, Modern Legal Ethics 428–33 (1986). Because the rules differ from state to state, it is difficult to generalize about an attorney's obligations and essential to consult the law of the jurisdiction. At some point the conflict may be so severe as to require the attorney to withdraw from the case. *See, e.g.*, Employers Casualty Co. v. Tilley, 496 S.W.2d 552 (Tex. 1973).

San Diego Navy Federal Credit Union v. Cumis, 208 Cal. Rptr. 494 (Ct. App. 1984), held that an insurance company which proposes to defend an action against the insured despite the existence of a coverage dispute must pay for independent counsel for the insured. *Accord* Public Serv. Mut. Ins. Co. v. Goldfarb, 425 N.E.2d 810, 815 (N.Y. 1981). The problem in this kind of case is that a lawyer retained by the insurance company might have an incentive to conduct the trial in such a way as to bring out facts that would help the company disclaim coverage later on. Cal. Civ. Code §2860 (Westlaw 2003) now spells out in some detail the insurer's rights to insist that the insured's counsel have specified minimum qualifications.

8. *Automobile Liability Insurance and Deterrence.* Many drivers, particularly young drivers, have assets insufficient to pay large judgments, and so the prospect of a large judgment does not create much of a deterrent effect. In theory, a system of compulsory liability insurance could enhance automobile safety. Persons without insurance could not drive, and insurance companies would charge the most dangerous kinds of drivers

(those with convictions for drunken driving, for example) premiums so large that many of them would give up driving.

In practice, things have not worked out so tidily. For one thing, drivers in most states can meet compulsory-insurance requirements by buying policies that provide coverage much lower than that needed to satisfy even routine judgments for death or serious injuries. Furthermore, "assigned-risk" pools provide insurance at relatively low cost even to very dangerous drivers. Finally, considerations other than safety play an important role in insurance rate regulation. To take but one example, some states prohibit insurance companies from charging young male drivers higher premiums than young female drivers, even though it is well established that young male drivers are, statistically, much worse risks than young female drivers. By insisting that men and women pay the same premiums, these states make insurance more expensive for women and cheaper for men, thus discouraging women from driving and encouraging men to do so. This may well contribute to equality of the sexes in some sense, at the cost of making the roads more dangerous.

2. First-Party Insurance

Common examples of first-party insurance include life insurance, medical insurance, fire insurance, and collision and comprehensive coverage for automobiles. This kind of insurance creates a form of loss-spreading. All of those who buy the insurance pay for the losses that occur; without insurance like this, the losses would fall upon fewer people. The existence of insurance does not, of course, make losses go away, it just shifts the financial burdens of the losses from the few people who would bear them if there were no insurance to all policy holders. Indeed, because some people whose losses will be covered by insurance will act more carelessly than if they did not have insurance,[d] the institution of insurance probably causes the total amount of losses to increase.

First-party insurance does not play the same direct role in the tort process as liability insurance. Its existence does have some effect on the law of torts, however. For example, in New York, damages caused by a fire started by the defendant's negligence are quite limited; one reason is the courts' belief that most property owners will have fire insurance, and that holding a defendant whose negligence has burned down 50 houses liable to all 50 owners would unduly concentrate the loss on the defendant. *See* Ryan v. New York Central R. Co., 35 N.Y. 210 (1866), a decision which has not generally been accepted in other jurisdictions. *See also* Weinberg v. Dinger, 524 A.2d 366 (N.J. 1987) (holding that water companies are no longer immune from negligence liability for fail-

---

d. Some people deny this at first, but it is almost certainly true. Consider, for example, how knowledge that the theft insurance on a new $20,000 car had lapsed would affect the owner's willingness to leave the car parked at a mall while attending a movie. Or imagine the owner of a $200,000 house: would that person not seriously consider installing a sprinkler system if unable to get fire insurance? Even if some people's behavior would be the same with or without insurance, losses will increase because of insurance even if only a few insureds act more carelessly than if they did not have coverage.

The tendency of insurance to make insureds somewhat more willing to engage in risky behavior is called "moral hazard" in the insurance business. Some features of first-party insurance exist largely to limit the effects of moral hazard. For example, a "deductible" in an automobile-insurance policy may require the owner to pay for part of any damage sustained; this encourages owners to take precautions (as well as to refrain from submitting a claim for every little scratch).

ure to provide water to fire hydrants, except with respect to subrogation claims asserted by fire-insurance companies).

"No-Fault" Automobile Insurance. One form of first-party insurance—"no-fault" automobile insurance—has in many states displaced a portion of the tort system. Under most no-fault plans, automobile owners give up the right to sue others for certain kinds of harms (typically property damage, up to a specified dollar limit, and in many states minor personal injuries as well). In exchange, the victim's own insurance company pays for the damage. An important idea behind no-fault insurance was to reduce the role of lawyers and claims adjusters and so to allow a larger portion of the money paid as insurance premiums to go to accident victims. This would reduce the cost of insurance considerably. Studies have shown that, in cases which go through the tort system, victims end up with about half of the money spent by the insurance companies and defendants: the rest goes toward resolving disputes. Furthermore, no-fault benefits are usually paid promptly; litigation of a tort case may not be over until years after the accident. Another advantage of no-fault, with respect to "compensation," is that no-fault systems cover all victims, not just those who can convince a factfinder that someone else was at fault.

No-fault was originally proposed as a complete substitute for the tort system for auto-accident cases, but political forces have squelched that. (In New Zealand, by contrast, a no-fault system run by the government has replaced almost all of the law of torts.) A few of today's no-fault systems provide benefits (subject to stringent limits) to an accident victim without affecting the victim's right to sue whoever caused the accident. Most no-fault laws limit tort actions to cases in which the victim's medical expenses exceed an amount specified by statute, or to cases in which the victim suffers disfiguring injuries.

A controversial 1982 study concluded that displacement of the tort system, even in part, by no-fault insurance increases fatal accident rates, and that the higher the threshold for tort claims, the higher the rate of fatal accidents. *See* Elisabeth M. Landes, *Insurance, Liability, and Accidents: A Theoretical and Empirical Investigation of No-Fault Accidents*, 25 J.L. & Econ. 49 (1982). To put the matter starkly, the argument is that hundreds of people have been killed because the states in which they lived adopted no-fault insurance. At first glance, this conclusion seems implausible, as no-fault systems do not displace tort liability for fatal accidents. It may well be, however, that drivers who know that they cannot be sued for "fender-benders," and that minor damage to their own cars will be covered under a no-fault system, will tend to drive more carelessly. And the more careless (some) drivers become, the more fatal accidents a state will have. The Landes study is criticized in Jeffrey O'Connell & Saul Levmore, *A Reply to Landes: A Faulty Study of No-Fault's Effect on Fault*, 48 Mo. L. Rev. 649 (1983). The dispute here is about the extent to which displacing the tort system with no-fault increases accidents; it is almost inevitable that the change will have *some* effect on safety. In Quebec and Australia, which have adopted no-fault systems much more extensive than those in the United States, the introduction of no-fault has been followed by substantial increases in fatal accidents. These increases may, however, have resulted in part from flaws in the no-fault systems rather than from the displacement of tort law by first-party insurance. For example, insurance rates under Quebec's system do not distinguish between high-risk drivers and others. *See* Don Dewees & Michael Trebilcock, *The Efficacy of the Tort System and Its Alternatives: A Review of Empirical Evidence*, 30 Osgoode Hall L.J. 57, 66–67 (1992).

Chapter 2

Basic Intentional Torts

A. The Concept of Intent

Focus on Consequences. Intent is a state of mind about consequences or results, and exactly what must be intended varies with the tort in issue. For example, false imprisonment requires intent to confine; trespass to land, intent to be present at the place in question; and conversion, intent to exercise dominion and control over personal property.

Purpose and Knowledge. As indicated in Garratt v. Dailey, 279 P.2d 1091 (Wash. 1955), *supra* at 12, there are two varieties of intent. The first—purpose—depends upon the defendant's subjective wishes and exists whenever the defendant acts with the purpose of causing the consequence which the law forbids. The other variety of intent—knowledge—is present if the defendant, regardless of subjective purposes, knows with substantial certainty that the act in question will cause the prohibited result. While substantial certainty does not mean absolute certainty, it means certainty for all practical purposes.

See generally Restatement, Third, of Torts: Liability for Physical Harm (Basic Principles) §1 (Tent. Draft No. 1, 2001) (discussing purpose and knowledge).

As the following cases indicate, many questions can be raised about intent. Must the alleged tortfeasor intend to injure or harm the plaintiff? How does a mistake about the surrounding facts affect a finding of intent? Can liability be based on intent produced by insanity or some other mental deficiency? Should a defendant who intends to cause one kind of harm escape liability if a different kind of harm results?

1. Intent to Injure

Lambertson v. United States

United States Court of Appeals for the Second Circuit
528 F.2d 441 (2d Cir. 1976)

VAN GRAAFEILAND, Circuit Judge.

....

Appellant, an employee of Armour & Co., sustained serious injuries to his mouth as a result of the actions of one William Boslet, a meat inspector for the United States Department of Agriculture....

Facts

On August 30, 1972, a truck shipment of beef arrived at the receiving dock of Armour's Syracuse plant. Plaintiff was one of the employees assigned to unload this truck. While he was so engaged, he was suddenly and without warning jumped by Boslet who, screaming "boo," pulled plaintiff's wool stocking hat over his eyes and, climbing on his back, began to ride him piggyback. As a result of this action, plaintiff fell forward and struck his face on some meat hooks located on the receiving dock[2] suffering severe injuries to his mouth and teeth.

It is apparently agreed by all witnesses that the mishap was the result of one-sided horseplay and with no intention on Boslet's part to injure plaintiff. Indeed, immediately after the incident Boslet apologized to plaintiff, telling him that he was only playing around and meant no harm.

Seeking redress for his injuries, plaintiff commenced the instant action against the United States pursuant to the Federal Tort Claims Act, 28 U.S.C. §1346(b).

Fed. Tort Claims Act

Traditionally, the sovereign has always been immune from suit. To alleviate the harshness of this rule, Congress enacted the Federal Tort Claims Act which permits civil actions against the United States for personal injury and property damage caused by the "negligent or wrongful act or omission of any employee of the Government while acting within the scope of his office or employment." 28 U.S.C. §1346(b). 28 U.S.C. §2680, however, lists several claims expressly excepted from the purview of the Act, among which are any claims arising out of an assault or battery.[3] Since the United States has not consented to be sued for these torts, federal courts are without jurisdiction to entertain a suit based on them....

... [T]he parties agree that the sole basis for Judge Port's dismissal was his conclusion that Boslet's actions constituted a battery. Appellant contests this conclusion and steadfastly maintains that his complaint sounds in negligence.

....

intent to make contact NOT intent to injure Rule

It is hornbook law in New York, as in most other jurisdictions, that the intent which is an essential element of the action for battery is the intent to make contact, not to do injury. [Citations.] As the court stated in Masters [v. Becker, 254 N.Y.S.2d 633, 635 (App. Div. 1964)]:

> A plaintiff in an action to recover damages for an assault founded on bodily contact must prove only that there was bodily contact; that such contact was offensive; and that the defendant intended to make the contact. The plaintiff is not required to prove that defendant intended physically to injure him. Certainly he is not required to prove an intention to cause the specific injuries resulting from the contact.

Analysis

Harper and James put it that "it is a battery for a man...to play a joke upon another which involves a harmful or offensive contact." Prosser says that a "defendant may be liable where he has intended only a joke." *Accord* Restatement (Second) of Torts §13,

---

2. These meat hooks were no more than six inches away from plaintiff's head when Boslet jumped on his back.

3. Section 2680 reads in pertinent part as follows:

The provisions of this chapter and section 1346(b) of this title shall not apply to

....

(h) Any claim arising out of assault, battery, false imprisonment, false arrest, malicious prosecution, abuse of process, libel, slander, misrepresentation, deceit, or interference with contract rights.

comment c (1965). Since there is not the remotest suggestion that Boslet's leap onto plaintiff's back, his piggy back ride and his use of plaintiff's hat as a blindfold might have been accidental, there was no error in the District Court's determination that it was a battery.

To say that plaintiff's claim was not one "arising out of" a battery would be to blink at the exclusionary provisions of §2680....

We would find it much more pleasant to reach a decision based on what we wish Congress had said, rather than what it did say. However, to permit plaintiff to recover by "dressing up the substance" of battery in the "garments" of negligence would be to "judicially admit at the back door that which has been legislatively turned away at the front door." [Citation.]

Affirmed.

[The concurring opinion of Judge Oakes has been omitted.]

Notes

1. *Degrees of Probability.* To some extent, the difference between knowledge, reck-lessness, and negligence is a matter of degree. According to the Restatement:

> If the actor knows that the consequences are certain, or substantially certain, to result from his act, and still goes ahead, he is treated by the law as if he had in fact desired to produce the result. As the probability that the consequences will follow decreases, and becomes less than substantial certainty, the actor's con-duct loses the character of intent, and becomes mere recklessness....As the probability decreases still further, and amounts only to a risk that the result will follow, it becomes ordinary negligence....

Restatement, Second, of Torts §8A cmt. b.

2. *Motive.* An individual's motivation is not dispositive of whether a particular result was intended. For example, in Ruple v. Brooks, 352 N.W.2d 652, 655 (S.D. 1984), the victim of a series of obscene telephone calls sued the caller for intentional infliction of severe mental distress, a tort which, as its name suggests, requires proof of intent to cause emotional anguish. The defendant admitted making two of the vulgar calls and had previously pled guilty to criminal charges of using "a telephone to call another per-son with intent to...harass...." In affirming a judgment for the plaintiff, the court wrote:

> Defendant claims that the directed verdict on the issue of liability at the close of plaintiff's case foreclosed him from presenting evidence of his motivations for making the obscene telephone calls. He alleges that his motives were anger and frustration over the difficulties his wife encountered in working with plaintiff, and that such motives would show a lack of intent to cause emotional distress. We find this argument to be unconvincing. No matter what defendant's specific motivation may have been, such motivation does not negate the fact that the act was done intentionally. In fact, defendant's admitted anger when making the telephone calls greatly strengthens a finding of intent to cause emotional harm. While defendant's motivation may be relevant on the question of mitigation of damages, [citations], it is not conclusive as to intent; one may have any number of motives for doing a particular act and yet still do the act intentionally....

3. *"Intentional Acts."* The *Ruple* court's suggestion that the defendant was liable be-cause his "act was done intentionally" is extremely misleading. The law almost never

holds someone liable simply for performing an "intentional act" which caused harm. For example, suppose that the defendant intentionally fires a rifle at a target. Unknown to the defendant, the plaintiff is sleeping in tall grass near the target and is hit by the bullet. Is the defendant, having intentionally done an act that caused harm to the plaintiff, liable for the intentional tort of battery? Certainly not: the defendant did not intend to inflict any contact—let alone a harmful or offensive one—on the plaintiff or anyone else. (If the defendant's shooting was careless under the circumstances, the plaintiff may have a negligence claim.) Similarly, someone who intentionally drives at ten miles an hour over the speed limit and who, as a result, accidentally crashes into another car, may be liable for *negligence*, but has certainly not committed an intentional tort. Intention has to do with results, not just with "acts." A competent lawyer should never argue that a defendant committed an intentional tort on the sole ground that the defendant "acted intentionally."

What should the court in *Ruple* have said instead of "the act was done intentionally"?

See Hennessey v. Pyne, 694 A.2d 691, 696 (R.I. 1997) (rejecting argument that defendant was liable for battery because he "intentionally hit the golf ball" which in turn struck the plaintiff).

2. Intent and Mistake

Ranson v. Kitner

Appellate Court of Illinois
31 Ill. App. 241 (1888)

CONGER, J.

This was an action brought by appellee against appellants to recover the value of a dog killed by appellants, and a judgment [was] rendered for $50.

The defense was that appellants were hunting for wolves, that appellee's dog had a striking resemblance to a wolf, that they in good faith believed it to be one, and killed it as such.

Many points were made, and a lengthy argument failed to show that error in the trial below was committed, but we are inclined to think that no material error occurred to the prejudice of appellants.

The jury held them liable for the value of the dog, and we do not see how they could have done otherwise under the evidence. Appellants are clearly liable for the damages caused by their mistake, notwithstanding they were acting in good faith.

We see no reason for interfering with the conclusion reached by the jury, and the judgment will be affirmed.

Notes

1. *Mistake and Intent.* In addition to the principal case, *see* La Bruno v. Lawrence, 166 A.2d 822 (N.J. Super. Ct. 1960) (mistake as to a boundary line was no defense to an action for intentional trespass to land); Seigel v. Long, 53 So. 753 (Ala. 1910) (mistake as to the plaintiff's identity did not preclude a finding of battery where the defendant pushed the plaintiff's hat from behind). *Cf.* York Industrial Center, Inc. v. Michigan Mutual Liability Co., 155 S.E.2d 501 (N.C. 1967) (insurer held liable for amounts paid by the insured as the result of a trespass action involving a bona fide mistake as to the

ownership of property). These cases do not mean, however, that mistake is never relevant to the question whether the defendant intended to interfere with the person or property of another. Consider again the example (page 44, above) of the defendant who shoots at a target and hits the plaintiff, sleeping nearby. This is not an intentional tort, even though the case might be described as one in which the defendant made a "mistake" about whether anyone was in a position to be shot. How is this case to be distinguished from Ranson v. Kitner?

2. *Mistake and Privilege.* While a mistake as to the surrounding facts will not necessarily preclude a finding of tortious intent, the existence of a mistake may bear upon whether the defendant can assert a privilege (*e.g.*, self-defense, defense of property, recapture of chattels, etc.) that will defeat the plaintiff's action, notwithstanding proof of intent. *See generally* Chapter 3.

3. *Induced Mistake.* Conduct based upon a mistake induced by the plaintiff does not ordinarily give rise to liability. *See, e.g.*, Tousley v. Board of Education, 40 N.W. 509 (Minn. 1888) (plaintiff was not allowed to recover for the conversion of wood where his words and conduct had caused the defendant to believe that the wood belonged to a third person).

4. *Volitional-Act Requirement.* There is no tort liability for an involuntary act. *See* Henrickson v. Sebanc, 336 P.2d 201 (Cal. Ct. App. 1959) (the touching of a boy's face was not an actionable battery where it was caused by the boy's abrupt movement and was not intentional).

If a third person takes hold of the defendant's hand and strikes plaintiff with it, the only voluntary act is that of the third person, and thus the third person, not the defendant, will be liable for battery. *Cf.* Reynolds v. Pierson, 64 N.E. 484 (Ind. Ct. App. 1902) (A jerked B's arm, causing C, who was leaning on B, to fall).

3. Intent and Insanity

McGuire v. Almy
Supreme Judicial Court of Massachusetts
8 N.E.2d 760 (Mass. 1937)

QUA, Justice.

This is an action of tort for assault and battery. [At trial, the jury returned a verdict for plaintiff in the amount of $1,500.] The only question of law reported is whether the judge should have directed a verdict for the defendant.

The following facts are established by the plaintiff's own evidence: In August, 1930, the plaintiff was employed to take care of the defendant. The plaintiff was a registered nurse.... The defendant was an insane person. Before the plaintiff was hired she learned that the defendant was a "mental case and was in good physical condition,".... During the period of "fourteen months or so" while the plaintiff cared for the defendant, the defendant "had a few odd spells," when she showed some hostility to the plaintiff and said that "she would like to try and do something to her."....

On April 19, 1932, the defendant, while locked in her room, had a violent attack. The plaintiff heard a crashing of furniture and then knew that the defendant was ugly, violent and dangerous. The defendant told the plaintiff and a Miss Maroney, "the maid,"...that if they came into the defendant's room, she would kill them. The plaintiff and Miss Maroney looked into the defendant's room, "saw what the defendant had done," and "thought it best to take the broken stuff away before she did any harm to herself with it." They sent for a Mr. Emerton, the defendant's brother-in-law. When he arrived the defendant was in the middle of her room about ten feet from the door, holding upraised the leg of a low-boy as if she were going to strike. The plaintiff stepped into the room and walked toward the defendant, while Mr. Emerton and Miss Maroney remained in the doorway. As the plaintiff approached the defendant and tried to take hold of the defendant's hand which held the leg, the defendant struck the plaintiff's head with it, causing...[injuries].

Facts

The extent to which an insane person is liable for torts has not been fully defined in this Commonwealth....

Turning to authorities elsewhere, we find that courts in this country almost invariably say in the broadest terms that an insane person is liable for his torts....Thus it is said that a rule imposing liability tends to make more watchful those persons who have charge of the defendant and who may be supposed to have some interest in preserving his property; that as an insane person must pay for his support, if he is financially able, so he ought also to pay for the damage which he does; that an insane person with abundant wealth ought not to continue in unimpaired enjoyment of the comfort which it brings while his victim bears the burden unaided; and there is also a suggestion that courts are loath to introduce into the great body of civil litigation the difficulties in determining mental capacity which it has been found impossible to avoid in the criminal field.

The rule established in these cases has been criticized severely by certain eminent text writers both in this country and in England, principally on the ground that it is an archaic survival of the rigid and formal medieval conception of liability for acts done, without regard to fault, as opposed to what is said to be the general modern theory that liability in tort should rest upon fault. Notwithstanding these criticisms, we think, that as a practical matter, there is strong force in the reasons underlying these decisions.... Fault is by no means at the present day a universal prerequisite to liability, and the theory that it should be such has been obliged very recently to yield at several points to what have been thought to be paramount considerations of public good....

Rule ...[W]here an insane person by his act does intentional damage to the person or property of another he is liable for that damage in the same circumstances in which a normal person would be liable. This means that in so far as a particular intent would be necessary in order to render a normal person liable, the insane person, in order to be liable, must have been capable of entertaining that same intent and must have entertained it in fact. But the law will not inquire further into his peculiar mental condition with a view to excusing him if it should appear that delusion or other consequence of his affliction has caused him to entertain that intent or that a normal person would not have entertained it.

....

Coming now to the application of the rule to the facts of this case, it is apparent that the jury could find that the defendant was capable of entertaining and that she did entertain an intent to strike and to injure the plaintiff and that she acted upon that intent....

D's argument (creative) The defendant further argues that she is not liable because the plaintiff, by undertaking to care for the defendant with knowledge of the defendant's condition and by walking into the room in spite of the defendant's threat under the circumstances shown, consented to the injury, or, as the defendant puts it, assumed the risk, both contractually and voluntarily....[W]e think that the defendant was not entitled to a directed verdict on this ground. Although the plaintiff knew when she was employed that the defendant was a mental case, and despite some show of hostility and some violent and unruly conduct, there was no evidence of any previous attack or even of any serious threat against anyone. The plaintiff had taken care of the defendant for "fourteen months or so." We think that the danger of actual physical injury was not, as matter of law, plain and obvious up to the time when the plaintiff entered the room on the occasion of the assault. But by that time an emergency had been created. The defendant was breaking up the furniture, and it could have been found that the plaintiff reasonably feared that the defendant would do harm to herself. Something had to be done about it. The plaintiff had assumed the duty of caring for the defendant. We think that a reasonable attempt on her part to perform that duty under the peculiar circumstances brought about by the defendant's own act did not necessarily indicate a voluntary consent to be injured. Consent does not always follow from the intentional incurring of risk. "The degree of danger, the stress of circumstances, the expectation or hope that others will fully perform the duties resting on them, may all have to be considered." [Citations.]

Judgment for the plaintiff on the verdict.

Notes

1. *McGuire* is the leading case on whether an insane person can be held liable for an intentional tort, and its holding is consistent with the great weight of authority. *See* Restatement, Second, of Torts §895 ("One who has deficient mental capacity is not immune from tort liability solely for that reason"); Polmatier v. Russ, 537 A.2d 468 (Conn. 1988) (holding that the defendant, who acted under an insane delusion, was liable in tort for wrongful death, even though the defendant had been found not guilty of murder by reason of insanity).

In Williams v. Kearbey, 775 P.2d 670, 672 (Kan. Ct. App. 1989), an insane 14-year-old was held liable for injuries he inflicted during a shooting spree at a junior high school. The *Williams* court quoted the well-known opinion in Seals v. Snow, 254 P. 348 (Kan. 1927):

> "Undoubtedly, there is some appearance of hardship, even of injustice, in compelling one to respond for that which, for want of the control of reason, he was unable to avoid; that it is imposing upon a person already visited with the inexpressible calamity of mental obscurity an obligation to observe the same care and precaution respecting the rights of others that the law demands of one in the full possession of his faculties. But the question of liability in these cases…is a question of policy; and it is to be disposed of as would be the question whether the incompetent person should be supported at the expense of the public, or of his neighbors, or at the expense of his own estate. If his mental disorder makes him dependent, and at the same time prompts him to commit injuries, there seems to be no greater reason for imposing upon the neighbors or the public one set of these consequences, rather than the other; no more propriety or justice in making others bear the losses resulting from his unreasoning fury, when it is spent upon them or their property, than there would be in calling upon them to pay the expense of his confinement in an asylum, when his own estate is ample for the purpose." 123 Kan. at 90–91, 254 P. 348 (quoting 1 Cooley on Torts 172 [3d ed. 1906]).

Although the above language is somewhat dated, the reasoning is still well grounded in sound public policy. Someone must bear the loss and, as between the tortfeasor, the injured party, and the general public, sound public policy favors placing the loss on the person who caused it, whether sane or not.

A similar result was reached in Goff v. Taylor, 708 S.W.2d 113, 115 (Ky. Ct. App. 1986), another shooting case, in which the defendant argued unsuccessfully that liability should turn upon whether the actor could distinguish right from wrong and was able to conform his conduct to the law. The court wrote:

> That the subjective standard would afford fairer treatment of a defendant afflicted with a mental disability cannot be disputed. The question the commentators [favoring that standard] do not attempt to reach is the fairness to the victim of the wrongful conduct. Is a victim any less entitled to compensation for his loss because of the mental deficiencies of his tortfeasor? We believe that the answer is no....

2. *Avoiding Intractable Inquiries.* The rule that insanity and lesser degrees of mental incompetency create no immunity from tort liability is accounted for, in part, by the reluctance of courts to embark upon intractable inquiries into the workings of the mind. Among the factors contributing to that reluctance, the Restatement has noted:

> [T]he unsatisfactory character of the evidence of mental deficiency in many cases, together with the ease with which it can be feigned, the difficulty of estimating its existence, nature and extent; and some fear of introducing into the law of torts the confusion that has surrounded the defense of insanity in the criminal law.

Restatement, Second, of Torts §895J cmt. a.

3. *Mental Deficiencies That Preclude Intent.* Although a mental deficiency does not, by itself, confer an immunity from liability in tort, the condition may bear upon the matter of whether the defendant acted with the necessary intent. For example, a mental condition may deprive the defendant of the intent to deceive that is essential to an action for deceit or the wrongful purpose that is required in an action for malicious prosecution. Or suppose that an insane delusion causes a defendant to think that if he throws a knife at the plaintiff the knife will disintegrate in the air before striking the victim. The defendant throws the knife and the plaintiff is hurt. The defendant has not intentionally injured the plaintiff. In this case, the defendant is not using insanity as a *defense* to an intentional tort; he is using it to show that he lacked the intent necessary for that tort.

4. *Related Legislation.* In some jurisdictions, the common-law rule holding insane persons liable for their intentional torts has been echoed in legislation. *See, e.g.,* Cal. Civ. Code §41 (Westlaw 2003) ("A person of unsound mind, of whatever degree, is civilly liable for a wrong done by the person, but is not liable in exemplary damages unless at the time of the act the person was capable of knowing that the act was wrongful").

5. *Minority Rule.* In Anicet v. Gant, 580 So. 2d 273 (Fla. Dist. Ct. App. 1991), the court described the issues as "straight from a difficult exam question in Torts I." In a rare departure from the majority rule, the court held that an insane resident confined in a hospital ward designed "for the lowest functioning and most dangerous patients" was not liable for injuries sustained by an attendant who was struck by a heavy ashtray thrown by the resident. The court recognized that imposing liability on an insane person is normally justified on the grounds that "as between an innocent injured person and an incompetent injuring one, the latter should bear the loss," and that "imposition of liability...encourage[s] the utmost restriction of the insane person so that he may cause no unnecessary damage to the innocent." However, the court found those rationales inapplicable to the case before it. Expressly refusing to decide the case under the doctrine of assumption of the risk, the court wrote:

[Plaintiff] was not an innocent member of the public unable to anticipate or safeguard himself against the intrusions of a lunatic. In all meaningful respects, his position was directly to the contrary: he was employed to encounter, and knowingly did encounter, just the dangers which injured him. Importantly, any economic loss caused by damage from one of those dangers is invariably borne, as it was in this case, by workers' compensation coverage....

. . . .

[In addition, the defendant,]...his relatives, and society did as much as they could do...[to prevent harm] by confining him in the most restrictive area of a restricted institution that could be found. Hence, it would serve no salutary purpose to impose the extra financial burden of a tort recovery.

As to the "fairness" issue, it is likewise clear that the imposition of liability would in fact counter our notions of what would be just to [a defendant] who has no control over his actions and is thus innocent of any wrongdoing in the most basic sense of that term....

. . . .

In sum, we revert to the basic rule that where there is no fault, there should be no liability....

The *Anicet* court distinguished McGuire v. Almy on the ground that there the defendant was being cared for at home, making "encouragement of further restriction" possible.

6. *Insanity and Insurance.* What bearing, if any, does insanity have on insurance? Courts differ as to whether policy provisions denying coverage for intentionally caused harm preclude coverage of injuries resulting from severe mental disability. *Compare* Shelter Mutual Ins. Co. v. Williams, 804 P.2d 1374 (Kan. 1991) (homeowner's policy did not cover injuries caused by a mentally ill teenager who went on a shooting spree at a junior high school), *with* Western States Ins. Co. v. Kelley-Williamson Co., 569 N.E.2d 1289 (Ill. Ct. App. 1991) (homeowner's policy covered damages caused by an insane insured who attempted to commit suicide by ramming his truck into a gas station).

7. *Intoxication.* Courts have been unwilling to allow persons charged with intentional wrongdoing to raise a defense based on intoxication. If the defendant was able to form a tortious intent, it is irrelevant that the intent would not have existed but for the intoxication. *Cf.* Saba v. Darling, 575 A.2d 1240 (Md. 1990) (the defendant committed a battery, for he was "not so intoxicated that he could not perform intentional acts" and he "was able to form a conscious intent to punch" the plaintiff).

4. Transferred Intent

Keel v. Hainline

Supreme Court of Oklahoma
331 P.2d 397 (Okla. 1958)

WILLIAMS, Justice.

In this action [for assault and battery], Patricia Ann Burge, a minor, hereinafter referred to as plaintiff, obtained a judgment against...[six minors], for damages for personal injury. Defendant Keel alone appeals.

As his first proposition of error defendant asserts that...there was no evidence that the injury was willfully or intentionally inflicted or that the injury was the proximate result of wrongful and unlawful activity on the part of Keel and the other defendants.

The evidence reveals that on February 1, 1956, some thirty five to forty students... went to a class room for instruction in music. The class met at the hour of 10:30 a.m., but, for some unknown reason, their instructor did not make an appearance until some thirty or forty minutes later. During the absence of the instructor, several of the male students indulged in what they termed "horse play." This activity consisted of throwing wooden blackboard erasers, chalk, cardboard drum covers, and, in one instance, a "coke" bottle, at each other. It appears that two or three of the defendants went to the north end of the class room and the remaining defendants went to the south end of the room. From vantage points behind the blackboard on the north end and the piano on the south end, they threw the erasers and chalk back and forth at one another. This activity was carried on for a period of some 30 minutes, and terminated only when an eraser, thrown by defendant Jennings, struck plaintiff in the eye, shattering her eye glasses, and resulting in the loss of the use of such eye. Plaintiff was sitting in her chair near the center of the room engaged in studying her lessons at the time she was struck by the eraser, and had not been participating in the so called "horse play" in any manner. None of the defendants intended to strike or injure plaintiff. They were, however, throwing at each other, with the intention of striking each other, although in sport and apparently without intent to cause injury.

The case of Peterson v. Haffner, 59 Ind. 130, 26 Am. Rep. 81, involved a situation in which the defendant, between 13 and 14 years of age, was playing in the street with some boys, and in sport threw a piece of mortar at another boy, and the mortar hit a third boy in the eye, putting it out. In the opinion affirming the judgment for the plaintiff, the court held that it was clear that an assault and battery had been committed. In the body of the opinion it is stated:

> He did not intend to inflict the injury, but he intended to do the wrongful act from which the injury resulted and he is answerable for that result....

The case of Singer v. Marx, 144 Cal. App.2d 637, 301 P.2d 440, 442, involved a situation in which a 9 year old boy threw a rock which struck and injured an 8 year old girl.... [The court stated:]

> While throwing rocks at trees or into the street ordinarily is an innocent and lawful pastime, that same act when directed at another person is wrongful. The evidence at bar...warrants an inference that Tim threw at Barbara and inadvertently struck Denise. In such circumstances the doctrine of 'transferred intent' renders him liable to Denise.

Defendant strenuously argues that the class had not been called to order by the teacher and that the defendants were merely playing until the teacher arrived, and therefore could not be said to have been engaged in any wrongful or unlawful acts. We do not agree. We do not believe and are not willing to hold that the willful and deliberate throwing of wooden blackboard erasers at other persons in a class room containing 35 to 40 students is an innocent and lawful pastime, even though done in sport and without intent to injure. Such conduct is wrongful, and we so hold....

> ....

[The court then held that Keel aided and abetted the wrongful activity, though his participation was limited to retrieving erasers and handing them to others for further throwing.]

....As is well stated at 52 Am. Jur. 454, Torts, §114:

> One who commands, directs, advises, encourages, procures, instigates, pro-
> motes, controls, aids, or abets a wrongful act by another has been regarded as
> being as responsible as the one who commits the act so as to impose liability
> upon the former to the same extent as if he had performed the act himself.

Judgment affirmed.

Notes

1. *Writs at Early Common Law.* Following the Norman conquest, justice in England
was administered by many local courts. Gradually, the King began to permit some cases
to come before his Council, usually for a fee. The formal document commencing this
litigation was called a "writ." Bearing the royal seal, the writ directed the King's judges to
hear the matter. Because the exercise of royal jurisdiction interfered with and impaired
the income of local courts, it was strongly resisted. Writs were available to cover only a
limited, though ever-expanding, number of situations. *See generally* Charles A. Keig-
win, *Cases in Common Law Pleading* 1–10, 15–16 (2d ed. 1934).

Two writs of a distinctly tortious nature emerged: "trespass" and "trespass on the
case" (the latter sometimes called simply "case"). In general, the writ of trespass lay for
injuries directly inflicted (e.g., where a person was struck by a rock thrown by defendant or a dog was given poison); whereas case would lie for harm caused indirectly
(e.g., where a person was injured by tripping over an object left in the road or a dog ate
poison which had been left for it to find). The intricate complexities attending the development of these writs and their influence on the law of torts has been chronicled
elsewhere and need not be repeated here. *See generally* W. Page Keeton, Dan B. Dobbs,
Robert E. Keeton, and David G. Owen, *Prosser and Keeton on Torts* §6 (5th ed. 1984).
Two features of today's law can be linked to the writ of trespass: nominal damages and
transferred intent.

2. *Nominal Damages.* First, because the writ of trespass was quasi-criminal in nature
and would issue in cases of serious and forcible breaches of the King's peace, for which
a fine would be imposed under penalty of imprisonment, it did not require proof of actual damages. Case, in contrast, necessitated a showing of actual loss on the part of the
plaintiff. Even today, those torts descended from the writ of trespass—battery, assault,
false imprisonment, trespass to land, and trespass to chattels—still do not require
proof of actual damages.[a] In cases involving no actual harm, the plaintiff will receive
judgment for a nominal sum, typically one dollar. In virtually all other areas of tort law,
the plaintiff must prove that the defendant caused actual harm.

3. *Transferred Intent.* The history of the writ of trespass is thought by some to determine the scope of the doctrine of transferred intent. In the simplest of terms, that
doctrine holds that if the defendant intended to cause any one of the five trespassory
torts, then the defendant "intended" to cause any invasion within that range of actions that befalls either the intended victim or a third party. Thus, if the defendant
shoots to frighten *A* (which is an assault), but actually strikes *A*, there is an intentional battery. The same is true if the bullet fired to frighten *A* misses *A* and strikes *B*.
This is true even if *B*'s presence was wholly unexpected. Indeed, under the doctrine,

---

a. Except for trespass to chattels, in some circumstances. *See* Glidden v. Syzbiak, 63 A.2d 233
(N.H. 1949).

if the bullet fired to scare *A* passes through *A* and also strikes *B*, whose presence was unknown, there are *two* intentional batteries. As Prosser said, the "intention follows the bullet." William L. Prosser, *Transferred Intent*, 45 Texas L. Rev. 650, 661–62 (1967).

The concept of transferred intent originally took root in a world of all-or-nothing compensation before the theory of negligence liability was well established and long before the advent of comparative fault principles. Does the doctrine of transferred intent still make sense?

To answer this question it is useful to distinguish unexpected injuries to intended victims from unexpected injuries to third parties. Treating unintended injury to an intended victim as an intentional tort is hardly shocking. The defendant intended to invade the interests of the plaintiff, and in that sense the resulting harm was not accidental, even if unexpected. To call that type of invasion an intentional tort appeals to common sense. It also alleviates some of the difficulties of proving exactly what the defendant intended.

In contrast, in cases involving unexpected harm to third parties (particularly third parties not known to be present), the defendant never intended to harm the plaintiff, and it is purely fictional to treat the case as if the defendant did. Why should the law do this? Could not the unexpected victim simply sue for negligence or recklessness? Is an intentional-tort suit preferable to those actions? Recall the consequences of classification (relating to insurance, bankruptcy, *respondeat superior*, and the like) discussed in Chapter 1. *See generally* Vincent R. Johnson, *Transferred Intent in American Tort Law*, 87 Marquette L. Rev. 903 (2004) (arguing that transferred intent should not be applied in the third-party context, because actions based on lack of care (negligence and recklessness) provide a better route to recovery).

Virtually all of the modern transferred-intent cases have involved assault and battery, though there are those who say it can also apply with respect to false imprisonment, trespass to land, and trespass to chattels. In the second Restatement, the sections defining assault and battery are crafted so that either tort will lie if there is intent to commit an assault or a battery involving the same person or a different person. *See* Restatement, Second, of Torts §§ 13 and cmt. b, 16, 18, 20 and 21 (1965). And the section on false imprisonment is drafted so that liability is imposed if there was intent to confine either the plaintiff or a third person. *Id.* at §35(1). *See also* Restatement, Third, of Torts: Liability for Physical Harm (Basic Principles) §1 cmt. b (Tent. Draft No. 1, 2001); *id.* at §33 cmt. c (Tent. Draft No. 3, 2003).

4. The doctrine of transferred intent has no counterpart in the law of negligence. *Cf.* Palsgraf v. Long Island R.R. Co., 162 N.E. 99 (N.Y. 1928), *infra* at 238 (there is no liability in negligence unless a danger to plaintiff was reasonably to be anticipated, regardless of whether a risk was posed to others). To that extent, the doctrine illustrates a general tendency of the law to extend liability more readily if the defendant's conduct rises to the level of intentional wrongdoing.

5. *Children and Intent.* The general rule at common law is that children are liable for their torts, whether they are committed intentionally, negligently, or as a matter of strict liability. However, the immaturity of the child is taken into account in determining whether, in the first instance, a tort has been committed. For example, with battery, a child may be of such tender years, and so unaware of surrounding circumstances, as to be incapable of forming the required intent to make a harmful or offensive contact. If so, there is no tort even if the child pokes someone in the eye: only an unavoidable accident.

A few states treat a child below a certain age as incapable of forming a tortious intent. *See, e.g.,* De Luca v. Bowden, 329 N.E.2d 109 (Ohio 1975) (children under the age of seven cannot be held liable for intentional torts); *cf.* Hatch v. O'Neill, 202 S.E.2d 44 (Ga. 1973) (minor under the age of criminal responsibility is immune from suit in tort). Other states have declined to do so. *See* Bailey v. C.S., 12 S.W.3d 159 (Tex. App. 2000) (holding that minority, standing alone, was insufficient to prove that a four-year-old child lacked intent to commit a battery when he struck his babysitter in the throat when she delayed playing a game with him).

See also Chapter 5, discussing the negligence liability of minors.

6. *Why Sue a Minor Child?* There are several reasons to sue a minor child. To begin with, a tort judgment against a minor may be satisfied out of personal holdings of the child, if any, or periodically renewed at statutorily prescribed intervals until such time as the child obtains sufficient assets to cover the judgment. However, upon reaching the age of legal majority, the child may discharge the debt through bankruptcy proceedings, unless the underlying conduct was "wilful and malicious" within the meaning of the Bankruptcy Code. *See* 11 U.S.C.A. §523(a)(6) (Westlaw 2003).

Of much greater practical importance today is the possibility that a judgment against a minor may be covered by liability insurance. The parent's homeowner's policy may include children living at home within the definition of an "insured." *See* John A. Appleman, Insurance Law and Practice (Berdal ed.), §4501.04 (2003 Supp.). However, liability-insurance policies generally exclude coverage for harm "expected or intended from the standpoint of the insured." *Id.* at §4501.09.

In some cases, it may be best, for the purpose of reaching insurance proceeds, for the plaintiff to style the action as one for accidental wrongdoing (negligence), rather than intentional battery, if the facts support that characterization. Not all cases afford the plaintiff that kind of flexibility. *See, e.g.,* Clark v. Allstate Ins. Co., 529 P.2d 1195 (Ariz. Ct. App. 1975) (an insured high school student admitted that he intended to strike the victim in the face; the liability-insurance policy did not apply even though the defendant claimed that he did not mean to injure the victim).

7. *Common-Law Parental Liability for the Torts of Minor Children.* In the absence of statute, a parent is not liable for the torts of a minor child by the mere fact of parentage. *See* Ross v. Souter, 464 P.2d 911 (N.M. 1970); Littenberg v. McNamara, 136 N.Y.S.2d 178 (Sup. Ct. 1954).

However, vicarious liability—meaning liability for the wrongs of another—may arise in some cases. For example, if a child is an employee of the parent, the parent will be liable for torts committed in the course of the employment because employers are liable for their employees' torts. *See* Schmidt v. Adams, 18 Mo. App. 432 (1885); Trahan v. Smith, 239 S.W. 345 (Tex. Civ. App. 1922). Similarly, liability under agency law principles may sometimes extend to non-business settings. *See* Butler v. Moore, 188 S.E.2d 142, 144 (Ga. Ct. App. 1972) (child acted as the agent of the parent in making home repairs); De Anda v. Blake, 562 S.W.2d 497, 499 (Tex. Civ. App. 1978) (minor operated a car at the insistence of her mother for her mother's benefit). So, too, vicarious liability may be imposed if a parent subsequently ratifies a child's independent tortious conduct. *See* Hower v. Ulrich, 27 A. 37 (Pa. 1893) (father accepted corn after learning that his children had stolen it).

Liability of a personal (rather than vicarious) nature—that is, liability for one's own wrongdoing—will be found if a parent directs a child to commit a tortious act or knowingly assists in tortious conduct. *See* Harrington v. Hall, 63 A. 875, 876 (Del.

1906) (parent instructed child to shoot a foxhound); Langford v. Shu, 128 S.E.2d 210 (N.C. 1962) (parent approved of and participated in a practical joke that her children played on a neighbor, who jumped with fright and was injured when a furry object sprang out of a box said to contain a snake-eating mongoose). And a parent may be liable for failure to control a child with specifically known dangerous tendencies (*see* Snow v. Nelson, 450 So. 2d 269 (Fla. Dist. Ct. App. 1984), *approved*, 475 So. 2d 225 (Fla. 1985)). This matter is explored further in Chapter 9.

8. *Parental-Liability Statutes.* Frequently prompted by rising tides of juvenile vandalism, states have enacted laws which, to some extent, modify the common law and make parents vicariously liable for some harms inflicted by their minor children. *See* L. Wayne Scott, *Liability of Parents for the Conduct of Their Child Under Section 33.01 of the Texas Family Code: Defining the Requisite Standards of "Culpability,"* 20 St. Mary's L.J. 69 (1988) (containing an appendix summarizing provisions from all 50 States); David A. Reesman, Note, *Parental Liability and the Extension of Social Host Liability to Minors,* 16 Dayton L. Rev. 827 (1991) (similar appendix).

Parental-liability statutes vary widely in their coverage. Among the most important differences are those concerning the type of conduct which may serve as the basis of liability and limits, if any, on maximum dollar recovery. While many statutes limit a parent's exposure to a relatively small amount (perhaps $7500 or less), some allow much higher recoveries. *See* Fla. Stat. Ann. §741.24 (Westlaw 2004) (recovery for malicious or willful destruction or theft of property "shall be limited to the actual damages in addition to taxable court costs"). Indeed, the Hawaii statute appears to completely reverse the common law rule of no vicarious liability by providing that "The father and mother of unmarried minor children shall jointly and severally be liable in damages for tortious acts committed by their children...." Haw. Rev. Stat. Ann. §577-3 (Westlaw 2003); *see also* La. Civ. Code Ann. art. 2318 (Westlaw 2003) (similar).

Contrast the following civil-liability provisions from Oregon and Texas:

OR. REV. STAT. §30.765
(Westlaw 2001)

(1) In addition to any other remedy provided by law, the parent or parents of an unemancipated minor child shall be liable for actual damages to person or property caused by any tort intentionally or recklessly committed by such child. However, a parent who is not entitled to legal custody of the minor child at the time of the intentional or reckless tort shall not be liable for such damages.

(2) The legal obligation of the parent or parents of an unemancipated minor child to pay damages under this section shall be limited to not more than $7,500, payable to the same claimant, for one or more acts.

TEX. FAM. CODE §§41.001–.002
(Westlaw 2003)

§41.001 Liability

A parent or other person who has the duty of control and reasonable discipline of a child is liable for any property damage proximately caused by...the wilful and malicious conduct of a child who is at least 10 years of age but under 18 years of age.

§41.002 Limits of Recovery

Recovery for damage caused by wilful and malicious conduct is limited to actual damages, not to exceed $25,000 per occurrence, plus court costs and reasonable attorneys' fees.

The legislative compromises that attend the enactment of parental-liability laws may lead to anomalous results. For example, under the Texas statute, if a teenager fires a gun across the street toward a neighbor's house, intentionally blowing a hole through the front door, there will be parental liability for the property damage. If the bullet kills or wounds someone standing by the door, the parent will not be liable for death or personal injury.

Many parental liability tort statutes impose a "living with" or "residing with" requirement; others refer to "custody and control" or use similar language; and still others have no control, custody, or residence restrictions at all. *See* Canida v. Canida, 751 So. 2d 647, 649 n. 1 (Fla. Ct. App. 1999) (holding that strict construction necessitated the conclusion that a non-custodial father's overnight visitation privilege with his son every other weekend did not constitute "living with" the father for purposes of imposing liability).

Some, but not all, losses under parental-liability statutes will be covered by the parent's liability insurance policy.

In addition to statutes creating civil liability, a new wave of laws in at least 17 states imposes criminal penalties on parents who fail to control their minor children. *See* Lisa Stansky, *The Sins of the Children*, Student Law., at 37–38 (Nov. 1997).

Brudney v. Ematrudo

United States District Court for the District of Connecticut
414 F. Supp. 1187 (D. Conn. 1976)

ZAMPANO, District Judge.

The plaintiff, Karen Brudney, a former student at Yale University, commenced this action against Peter Ematrudo, a member of the New Haven Police Department, to recover damages...for assault and battery....

....

After a careful review of the evidence, the Court accepts neither of the parties' complete version of the facts and finds as follows. On May 11, 1972, at approximately 11:00 A.M., a peaceful anti-war demonstration held in front of the Yale-in-China building in New Haven turned into a serious physical encounter between students and police. Scuffles and fights occurred. The defendant, observing that detective Giannotti had been knocked to the ground and was under attack by several students, left his post on the steps of the building and rushed to assist his fellow officer. After issuing a verbal warning that went unheeded, he lashed out with his blackjack in order to subdue a male demonstrator (probably Cruz) who was assaulting Giannotti. As the blackjack descended and hit the head of the demonstrator, it accidentally glanced the head of the plaintiff, causing a mild injury. Because the blackjack struck its intended target, the defendant did not realize the weapon also touched the plaintiff's body as it came down in and among a pushing, shoving, fighting group of persons. The plaintiff, on the other hand, feeling an unexpected, sharp and sudden force against her head, reasonably assumed she was the object of the defendant's blackjack.

....There is not a scintilla of credible evidence to support an inference that the action of any other person caused the injury to the plaintiff. But, contrary to the plaintiff's allegation, the Court concludes she was not the victim of an unprovoked act of police brutality....

. . . .

. . . . The defendant resorted to the use of force to aid another policeman under assault only after his verbal warning was ignored. His use of a blackjack was necessary, reasonable, limited and relatively controlled under the circumstances. Due to the crush of the crowd and the plaintiff's close proximity to the demonstrators who were attacking the officer, the blackjack accidentally grazed the plaintiff's head. Immediately after the release of the fallen officer by the protestors, the defendant ceased using the blackjack and retreated to call for assistance from uniformed police. It seems evident, therefore, that the defendant's application of force was restricted to a good faith effort to extricate a fellow police officer from great potential harm and to restore order and discipline within the crowd. Finally, the minor nature of the injury inflicted negates any suggestion by the plaintiff and her witnesses that the defendant acted maliciously or sadistically.

. . . .

. . . [T]he Court is impelled to the conclusion that the defendant did not commit an actionable assault and battery against the plaintiff. It is evident that the defendant acted within reasonable limits in determining the type and amount of force required in order to rescue officer Giannotti during the altercation with the demonstrators. [Citation.] It is unfortunate that the plaintiff received an injury through no fault on her part, yet the record fails to convince the Court that she proved her claims by a preponderance of the evidence.

Accordingly, judgment may enter for the defendant.

Notes

1. Is *Brudney* inconsistent with *Keel*? Did the plaintiff's attorney forget to argue the doctrine of transferred intent, or is the doctrine inapplicable?

2. Is *Brudney* consistent with Smith v. Moran, 193 N.E.2d 466, 469 (Ill. App. Ct. 1963)? There, the defendant entered a tavern and fired twice at a waitress who she believed was "improperly keeping company" with defendant's husband. The bullets struck not only the intended victim but also a second waitress. In an action by the latter for assault and battery, the court held there was nothing to prevent the defendant from pleading and proving facts showing that the action was "accidental, excusable, justified, or provoked." "If any or all of them," the court wrote, "would have established that the acts of the defendant were lawful acts lawfully done[,] they were material."

3. In *Keel*, the court took pains to point out that the deliberate throwing of the erasers, in a classroom containing 35 to 40 students, not all of whom participated in the battle, was not an innocent pastime. Rather, the court found, the conduct constituted a "wrongful act." Would *Keel* have turned out differently if all of the persons in the room had been consensual participants in the horseplay? Would the act have still been wrongful? Or, what if A and B were the only participants in the eraser battle, both had consented to the risks, and an eraser somehow struck C, whose presence could not possibly have been anticipated?

B. Battery and Assault

Two Distinct Actions. The torts of assault and battery are conceptually distinct. Battery is the intentional infliction of unconsented bodily contact that is harmful or offensive, whereas assault is the intentional creation of apprehension of imminent battery.

A tort victim unaware of an offer of physical contact prior to its infliction suffers a battery without an assault. And if the victim is cognizant of an imminent threat, but the perpetrator desists before the blow is struck, there is an assault without a battery. Thus, either tort may exist independently of the other, although the two actions frequently co-exist, as where, during a dispute, the defendant grabs the plaintiff by the throat and physically prepares to strike. *See* Carrell v. Richie, 697 S.W.2d 43, 46 (Tex. Ct. App. 1985). *See generally* Restatement, Second, of Torts §§13–34.

Policy Basis. The existence of the tort of assault, even when no battery follows, shows that the law sometimes redresses purely emotional injury, not just physical harm. In an action for assault, the loss of mental tranquility is treated as a significant injury.

The actions for assault and battery serve deterrence functions. Assault penalizes intentional conduct that is likely to result in a breach of the peace, whether because once a threat of contact is made the actor is apt to carry through, or because the endangered victim may resort to force in self-defense. Battery deters the purposeful infliction of unnecessary harm. Moreover, even in cases of mere technical battery, unaccompanied by intent to harm—as in Vosburg v. Putney, 50 N.W. 403 (Wis. 1891), *supra* at 11—the action for battery deters conduct which "violates the rule of society…that a person must keep his hands to himself." Osborne M. Reynolds, Jr., *Tortious Battery: Is "I Didn't Mean Any Harm" Relevant?*, 37 Okla. L. Rev. 717, 731 (1984).

Historical Development. The torts of assault and battery are ancient in origin. *See generally* Charles E. Carpenter, *Intentional Invasion of Interest of Personality*, 13 Or. L. Rev. 227, 237 & n. 57 (1934). This is not surprising, for "[o]ne of the first functions of orderly government is the maintenance of peace and order in the community." Fowler V. Harper, Fleming James, Jr., and Oscar S. Gray, The Law of Torts §3.1 (2d ed. 1986). The earliest known case of assault dates back to the mid-fourteenth century, where, in I de S et ux. v. W de S, YB Lib. Assis, Edw. III, f. 99, pl. 60 (1348), "the court upheld a jury's award of half a mark to a tavern keeper's wife who successfully dodged the hatchet cast at her by an irate, turned-away customer." Stuart M. Speiser, Charles F. Krause, and Alfred W. Gans, The American Law of Torts §26.16 (1990).

Requirement of Intent. Some authorities opine that battery requires a showing of intent to cause contact and that assault requires proof of intent to cause apprehension of contact. However, other authorities, including the Restatement, indicate that either tort will lie if the defendant "acts intending to cause…contact with the person of the other or a third person, or an imminent apprehension of such a contact." Given the availability of the doctrine of transferred intent to an intended victim, it makes no practical difference which approach a court takes.

Terminology. Criminal law has frequently used the terms "assault" and "battery" interchangeably (often in the same breath) to denote the unconsented infliction of bodily harm. Perhaps for that reason, civil courts have not always employed these terms correctly. For example, O'Brien v. Cunard S.S. Co., 28 N.E. 266 (Mass. 1891), *infra*, at 138 (incorrectly referring to injection of a smallpox vaccine as assault, rather than battery). One jurisdiction has abandoned efforts to distinguish the two torts. *See* Charles E. Cantu, *Assault and Battery*, Texas Torts and Remedies (1987) (indicating that the state Penal Code, which has combined assault and battery into the criminal offense of assault, is controlling in civil suits). Thus, in Texas, the tort of assault covers contact, as well as apprehension of contact.

Noble v. Louisville Transfer Co.

Court of Appeals of Kentucky
255 S.W.2d 493 (Ky. Ct. App. 1952)

MILLIKEN, Justice.

....

Marcella Noble and her five year old daughter, Sherry, arrived at Union Station, Louisville, about 1:45 a.m.... The mother hired the defendant's taxicab to take them to their home.... Mrs. Noble, a young woman, was pregnant at the time and her little daughter, Sherry, was nauseated. Sherry vomited in the defendant's taxicab on their way home, and this became the *casus belli* of this litigation.

Mrs. Noble avers that the driver of the cab, appellee, James Wood, Sr., ordered her to clean up the vomit, and that she went into her dark house to get a rag for that purpose while Wood detained Sherry just outside the cab. The street was dark, slumbering neighbors were near, Wood was a big man (6 feet 1½ inches, 210 pounds), Sherry was sick, and Mrs. Noble "was not feeling very well...."

According to Mrs. Noble she cleaned up the floor of the cab because she was afraid of Wood, who still held Sherry. According to Wood when Sherry got out of the cab "the little tot started to heave again and she vomited against my leg where I was standing by the side of the door and I reached down and touched this little baby on her shoulder, and I said: 'Why, honey, you are not through vomiting yet, are you?'" Wood said Mrs. Noble attempted to clean the cab with kleenex, and that she went into the house to get cash for her fare. Mrs. Noble construed Wood's holding of Sherry to be a detention of the child. On the other hand, Wood, when asked, "When did you have her (Sherry) in your arms—when she was vomiting over there?" answered: "I never had her in my arms. I got more sense than that.... I touched her with my little finger to keep her from falling over."

....

[Suits were filed on behalf of Sherry and Mrs. Noble alleging battery and false imprisonment of the daughter and assault of both women. On appeal, the court found the false imprisonment and assault claims to be without merit.]

.... When Wood placed his hand on Sherry his manifest intention was to help the sick child and not to harm her. There was neither the harmful or offensive physical contact with Sherry nor the manifest intention to harm her which are required to constitute a battery. Restatement of the Law of Torts, Sections 13 through 20.

We concur with the view of the trial judge that there was not sufficient evidence of any conduct on the part of Wood to constitute an offense. We conclude that the evidence given at the trial, with all inferences that the jury could justifiably draw from it, is insufficient to support a verdict for the plaintiffs, so that such a verdict, if returned, would have to be set aside. As a consequence, the court was correct in directing verdicts for the defendants. [Citations.]

Notes

1. *Harmfulness.* To be actionable as battery, contact must be harmful or offensive. "Harmful" is a term of art denoting any unconsented alteration of a structure or function of the body, even if the change does not affect the plaintiff's health.

2. *Offensiveness and Presumed Consent.* Contact is offensive if it would offend a reasonable person's sense of personal dignity. Those contacts which are ordinarily and necessarily incident to the conduct of everyday affairs do not meet this requirement. A tap on the shoulder to obtain information will not give rise to liability. *See* Coward v. Baddeley, 4 H. & N. 478, 157 Eng. Rep. 927 (1859). Nor will the rendering of assistance to an intoxicated person, *see* Hoffman v. Eppers, 41 Wis. 251 (1866), or the casual jostling of another to clear a passage through congested quarters, *see* Cole v. Turner, 6 Mod. Rep. 149, 90 Eng. Rep. 958 (1709).

To some extent, the question is one of what should reasonably be expected, for by engaging in particular forms of conduct, one knowingly runs certain risks. Some bodily contact may be inevitable where a patron frequents a crowded bar, but an action for battery will still lie where one patron gives another a hard elbow to the stomach. Similarly, if the defendant excitedly grasps the plaintiff's shoulder, it may make a difference whether the two are spectators at a football game or users of a public library. The issue is whether the "conduct is unwarranted by the social usages prevalent at the time and place." Restatement, Second, of Torts §19 cmt. a.

In Brzoska v. Olson, 668 A.2d 1355, 1363–64 (Del. 1995), 38 former patients of a dentist who died of AIDS sued for battery based on the contact that occurred during dental treatment. The court wrote:

> [W]ithout actual exposure to HIV, the risk of its transmission is so minute that any fear of contracting AIDS is per se unreasonable. We therefore hold, as a matter of law, that the incidental touching of a patient by an HIV-infected dentist while performing ordinary, consented-to dental procedures is insufficient to sustain a battery claim in the absence of a channel for HIV infection. In other words, such contact is "offensive" only if it results in actual exposure to the HIV virus....

See note 3 *infra* at p. 579.

3. *Intent to Harm or Offend.* An occasional case holds that intent to harm or offend is a prerequisite to liability for battery. But the great weight of authority seems to be to the contrary: consider, for example, Vosburg v. Putney, 50 N.W. 403 (Wis. 1891), p. 11, *supra*, and Lambertson v. United States, 528 F.2d 441 (2d Cir. 1976), p. 41, *supra*. Even acts done with the best of motives can give rise to liability for battery, as when a well-meaning bystander insists on administering first aid over the victim's objections.

If intent to harm or offend is not needed for battery, does it follow that any intentional touching that leads to harm will suffice? Some writers have said so. For instance, Osborn M. Reynolds, *Tortious Battery: Is "I Didn't Mean Any Harm" Relevant?*, 37 Okla. L. Rev. 717, 718 (1984), says, "[t]here must simply be intent...to cause contact, followed by contact that in fact *is* either harmful or reasonably offensive." This seems to be an overstatement: no one considers a friendly tap on the shoulder to get someone's attention or a gentle social hug a battery, even if the recipient suffers serious harm as a result because of some peculiar susceptibility to injury, unknown to the person doing the tapping or hugging.

One answer to the problem may be to say, as the Restatement does, that "the intent required...[for] an intentional tort is the intent to bring about harm" (Restatement, Third, of Torts: Liability for Physical Harm (Basic Principles) §1 cmt. b (Tent. Draft No. 1, 2001), while defining "harm" broadly. The tortfeasor in *Lambertson*, for example, did not intend to hurt the plaintiff, but he did intend to touch the plaintiff in a way that

most people would find unacceptable. Similarly, the physician who performs an operation without consent or the bystander who attempts first aid over the victim's objections
has tried to "harm" the plaintiff by seriously meddling with the plaintiff's person without consent: this can be seen as a harm to the plaintiff's right of bodily integrity even if
the outcome is entirely benign. As to the unauthorized-operation case, see Restatement,
Second, of Torts, § 15, Comment a and Illus. 1; Karl J. Pizzalotto, M.D., Ltd. v. Wilson,
437 So. 2d 859 (La. 1983) (surgeon's removal of the plaintiff's apparently non-func-
tional reproductive organs without her consent was a battery, regardless of the reasonableness of the surgery).

Those who prefer to say that intent to harm is not required may reach the result of
no liability in the friendly-tap and social-hug cases by saying that consent to such
conduct is implied from the custom in the community. Contact is a battery only if it
is unconsented.

4. *Plaintiff's Protestations.* Normally, consent to contact cannot be implied in the
face of another's express assertions to the contrary. *See* Restatement, Second, of Torts
§892 cmt. c; Childers v. A.S., 909 S.W.2d 282, 293 (Tex. Ct. App. 1995) (evidence that,
during "sexual games" between children, the plaintiff told the defendant "to stop" precluded summary judgment for the defendant child).

Can a sensitive person render generally permitted contacts tortious merely by manifesting an objection and refusing to consent? Perhaps. *See* Cohen v. Smith, 648 N.E.2d
329 (Ill. Ct. App. 1995) (patient stated a cause of action against a male nurse and a
hospital for battery and intentional infliction of emotional distress by alleging that she
informed them of her religious beliefs against being seen unclothed by a man and that
the male nurse was nonetheless present during her cesarean delivery and touched the
patient's naked body). Certainly, to the extent that the defendant has no good reason
for the action and seeks only to annoy the plaintiff, it is likely that liability will attach.
Tort law has traditionally disfavored those who seek to exploit the known sensitivities
of others.

5. *Good Intentions and Important Goals.* If the evidence establishes an intentional,
unconsented touching that is harmful or offensive, it is irrelevant to the issue of liability
that defendant sought merely to advance the plaintiff's interests or acted in furtherance
of some other important goal. The "Good Samaritan" who insists, over objection, on
setting the plaintiff's fracture will be subject to a claim for damages. *See* Clayton v. New
Dreamland Roller Skating Rink, 82 A.2d 458 (N.J. Super. Ct. 1951). And a corporation
that deliberately exposes a worker to vented radioactive steam cannot defeat a battery
action by arguing that such steps were necessary to keep a power plant operational. *See*
Field v. Philadelphia Elec. Co., 565 A.2d 1170, 1178 (Pa. Super. Ct. 1989). *See also* Mink
v. University of Chicago, 460 F. Supp. 713 (N.D. Ill. 1978) (women who had unknowingly been given the drug DES as part of a medical experiment to determine the drug's
effectiveness as a miscarriage preventative stated a claim for battery).

6. *Damages for Battery and Unanticipated Consequences.* In an action for battery,
the plaintiff may obtain an award for compensatory damages for losses actually suffered, including physical and mental harm. If no losses are established, nominal damages (traditionally one dollar) may be awarded to vindicate the plaintiff's technical
right. In cases involving highly culpable conduct, punitive damages may be awarded.

If the elements of battery are shown, it is irrelevant that the resulting injuries are
more extensive than might reasonably have been anticipated. "[A]s a matter of sound
social policy it is clearly better that the risk of such unintended and unforeseeable con-

sequences should fall on the intentional wrongdoer than on the victim." Fowler V. Harper, Fleming James, Jr., & Oscar S. Gray, The Law of Torts §3.3 (2d ed. 1986). *See* White v. University of Idaho, 768 P.2d 827 (Idaho Ct. App. 1989) (a touch on the back "in a movement later described as one a pianist would make in striking and lifting the fingers from a keyboard" required removal of a rib); Saba v. Darling, 575 A.2d 1240 (Md. 1990) (unintended broken jaw). This is commonly called the "eggshell skull" principle, though there is really no such thing as an "eggshell skull." *See* note p. 436 *infra*.

7. *Affirmative Act.* An action for battery cannot be predicated upon mere inaction; there must be some affirmative action on the part of the defendant. In Vernon Village Inc. v. Gottier, 755 F. Supp. 1142 (D. Ct. 1990), the court rejected a claim for battery based on the alleged presence of excessive contaminants in drinking water because the defendant had merely failed to test a water supply or notify affected individuals of contamination.

Picard v. Barry Pontiac-Buick, Inc.

Supreme Court of Rhode Island
654 A.2d 690 (R.I. 1995)

LEDERBERG, Justice.

[After having difficulties with a garage over whether her brakes needed to be repaired, plaintiff contacted a television news reporter, who was described as a "troubleshooter." Thereafter, the plaintiff took a picture of the defendant, "presumably as evidence for the troubleshooter reporter." The photograph clearly showed the defendant fully facing the camera, standing upright while pointing his index finger at the plaintiff.]

. . . .

The defendant testified that as he was looking at the car, plaintiff had come up behind him and aimed the camera toward him. He then pointed at plaintiff and said, "who gave you permission to take my picture?," then walked around the car to plaintiff, placed his index finger on the camera and again asked, "who gave you permission to take my picture?" The defendant denied grabbing plaintiff, touching her body, threatening her or making any threatening gestures, scuffling with her or reaching for the photograph. He also testified that he did not intend to cause plaintiff any bodily harm. *Facts*

. . . .

[In a subsequent action for assault and battery, the jury awarded compensatory and punitive damages.]

. . . . The defendant appealed the judgment. . . .

. . . .

The plaintiff testified that she was frightened by defendant's actions. A review of the attendant circumstances attests that such a reaction was reasonable. The defendant admitted approaching plaintiff, and the photograph taken that day clearly showed defendant pointing his finger at plaintiff as defendant approached her. Because plaintiff's apprehension of imminent bodily harm was reasonable at that point, plaintiff has established a prima facie case of assault.

. . . .

. . . [D]efendant contended that a battery did not occur because defendant did not intend to touch or injure plaintiff. Rather, defendant argued, the evidence showed that he intended to touch plaintiff's camera, not plaintiff's person, and therefore the contact *D's argument* was insufficient to prove battery. With this contention we must disagree. Even if this court were to accept defendant's characterization of the incident, a battery had nonetheless occurred. The defendant failed to prove that his actions...were accidental or involuntary. Therefore, defendant's offensive contact with an object attached to or identified with plaintiff's body was sufficient to constitute a battery. As noted in the comments to the Restatement (Second) Torts §18, cmt. c at 31 (1965):

Rule {

> "Unpermitted and intentional contacts with anything so connected with the body as to be customarily regarded as part of the other's person and therefore as partaking of its inviolability is actionable as an offensive contact with his person. *There are some things such as clothing or a cane or, indeed, anything directly grasped by the hand which are so intimately connected with one's body as to be universally regarded as part of the person.*" (Emphasis added.)

Holding The defendant's contact with the camera clutched in plaintiff's hand was thus sufficient to constitute a battery....

....

[The court found that the award of compensatory damages was grossly excessive and that the facts would not support an award of punitive damages.]

....

....We remand the case to the Superior Court for a new trial on...[damages].

Notes

1. *See also* Fisher v. Carrousel Motor Hotel, Inc., 424 S.W.2d 627 (Tex. 1967) (plate grabbed from hand); S.H. Kress & Co. v. Brashier, 50 S.W.2d 922 (Tex. Civ. App. 1932) (book grabbed from hand).

2. *Personal Effects.* At some point the connection between the plaintiff's body and the item which is struck becomes so slight that an action for battery will not lie. According to the Second Restatement, the line of distinction is difficult to draw and depends upon the emotional reaction of a reasonable person. "The ordinary man might well regard a horse upon which he is riding as part of his personality but, a passenger in a public omnibus or other conveyance would clearly not be entitled so to regard the vehicle merely because he is seated in it." *See* Restatement, Second, of Torts §18 Cmt. c.

3. *Ethics in Law Practice: Assault and Battery.* An attorney who commits an assault or battery is subject not merely to tort liability and criminal prosecution, but to professional discipline in the form of reprimand, suspension, or removal from practice. *See* Matter of Hickox, 57 P.3d 403 (Colo. 2002) (six-month suspension based, in part, on evidence of domestic violence); Matter of Runyon, 491 N.E.2d 189 (Ind. 1986) (attorney disbarred based, in part, on evidence that he struck his ex-wife with a club and held her at gunpoint).

Moore v. El Paso Chamber of Commerce

Court of Civil Appeals of Texas
220 S.W.2d 327 (Tex. Civ. App. 1949)

SUTTON, Justice.

[To promote its annual rodeo and Livestock Show, the El Paso Chamber of Commerce encouraged residents to go "Western" for a week by wearing some sort of distinguishing regalia. People on the street who were not attired in western wear were roped and lifted into wagons and conveyed to "corrals" where many of them were invited or caused to occupy a "hot seat," a chair wired with hot wires, wherein they were lightly "shocked." Persons subjected to the horseplay were released when they purchased rodeo tickets or handkerchiefs which, when worn about the neck, satisfied the attire requirement.]

   ....

...[D]uring the rodeo week, plaintiff and her mother had been down town shopping....They were approached by three young ropers, who, plaintiff said, had their eyes on her, and [were] about forty feet away. One of them said: "let's get that girl," or "let's get that one," or something to that effect. Plaintiff was a young woman just past seventeen and married for some two months. The young woman said to her mother "Let's duck in here," and ran into the drug store. One of the young men with his rope followed her. She said she was frightened and not interested in the play and sought to escape from the drug store into the lobby of the Hilton where she thought she would be safe from the apprehension. To do so she had to pass through a door connecting the drug store and the lobby. The door had a glass panel. She ran against the door and pushed her left hand through the glass and received very severe cuts....

Plaintiff...charged the Chamber of Commerce, acting through its agents, servants and representatives, with the responsibility and liability for the injuries received....She charged...that the defendant, its agents, servants and employees negligently, carelessly, recklessly and wilfully, in violation of the laws of the State, assaulted plaintiff by chasing her for the purpose of roping her and imprisoning her without her consent....

[Following the submission of special issues, the jury returned findings that Claude Weaver, the young man who chased the plaintiff in the drug store was acting at the direction of one "Shorty"; that Shorty was within the actual or implied scope of his authority from the Chamber of Commerce; that Weaver caused Plaintiff to push the glass and was negligent; that Plaintiff was negligent in failing to properly care for her own safety; and that Plaintiff had been damaged in the sum of $6,163.00. The trial court granted judgment for the Defendant.]

   ....

Apparently the trial court considered contributory negligence a defense in this case and that the findings of the jury on the issues of contributory negligence defeated her right to recover on the verdict otherwise favorable to her. In our opinion this is not a negligence case. All that young Weaver did he willed or purposed to do, save to become responsible for the serious injury inflicted as a consequence of what he did that led to it. He intended to do exactly what he did do, except the infliction of the injury. What he did then was an intentional and not a negligent wrong....[C]ontributory negligence is no defense to an intentional wrong....We conclude, therefore, the findings of contributory negligence do not defeat the right of recovery.

Trial Ct.'s Decision

   ....

....[P]laintiff had the legal right to make a lawful use of the streets of the city without hindrance, interference and molestation, and that right was violated by young Weaver in his pursuit or chase of her in an effort to restrain her and compel her submission to the "horse-play" of the day and in doing so he caused her "to push the glass in the door between the Hilton Hotel Drug Store and the lobby in the Hilton Hotel and to be injured thereby."....

   ....

It is clear to us the Chamber of Commerce must be liable for the acts of Claude Weaver. The corrals were set up and maintained by the Chamber of Commerce through its Livestock Committee in the interest of and as a part of the rodeo and Livestock Show. It is true the Chamber of Commerce employed no one in the sense people were engaged for hire to do the things that were done in the operation of the corrals but "one good fellow after another would just go ahead and take a hand at it." Their services to that extent were voluntary and gratuitous, but nevertheless all they did was for and in the interest of the Chamber of Commerce in furthering its projects. What Claude Weaver did was the chief activity of the corrals—the matter of going out and bringing in the people. The Chamber of Commerce had a representative in charge all the time and Weaver worked there, using the rope and bringing in people along with the others for more than a day and a half. The Chamber of Commerce may not permit him to openly engage in those activities peculiarly their own until an unfortunate accident and injury happens and then say he was not acting for them but that he was a mere volunteer and acting for himself....

"The relation of agency does not depend upon an express appointment and acceptance thereof, but it may be, and frequently is, implied from the words and conduct of the parties and circumstances of the particular case. It may be implied from a single transaction....It is often difficult to determine upon general principles whether any agency exists; rather it must be determined from the facts and circumstances of the particular case, and if it appears from such facts and circumstances that there was at least an implied intention to create the relation, it will by implication be held to exist." [Citations.]

....

It is difficult to find, we think, stronger facts than the facts of the instant case from which agency may be implied and held to exist.

....The judgment of the trial court will be accordingly reversed and judgment here rendered for the plaintiff for her damages and costs.

Notes

1. *Indirect Force.* Indirect contact may give rise to battery. The defendant who throws water on or sets a dog upon the plaintiff, or drives a truck fast, knowing that the plaintiff will be thrown from its bed, commits a battery. *See* Restatement, Second, of Torts §18 cmt. c. *See also* Field v. Philadelphia Elec. Co., 565 A.2d 1170 (Pa. Super. Ct. 1989) (release of radioactive steam); Lambrecht v. Schreyer, 152 N.W. 645 (Minn. 1915) (defendant whipped a horse which the plaintiff was driving, causing the horse and surrey to collide with a stump).

2. *Knowledge of Contact.* The plaintiff's lack of awareness of the contact at the time it occurs—for example, because plaintiff is asleep or under anesthetic—will not defeat an action for battery. *See* Restatement, Second, of Torts §18 cmt. d.

Western Union Telegraph Co. v. Hill

Court of Appeals of Alabama
150 So. 709 (Ala. Ct. App. 1933)

SAMFORD, Judge.

The action in this case is based upon an alleged assault on the person of plaintiff's wife by one Sapp, an agent of defendant in charge of its office in Huntsville, Ala. The assault complained of consisted of an attempt on the part of Sapp to put his hand on the person of plaintiff's wife coupled with a request that she come behind the counter in defendant's office, and that, if she would come and allow Sapp to love and pet her, he "would fix her clock."

.... Was there such an assault as will justify an action for damages?

....

While every battery includes an assault, an assault does not necessarily require a battery to complete it. What it does take to constitute an assault is an unlawful attempt to commit a battery, incomplete by reason of some intervening cause; or, to state it differently, to constitute an actionable assault there must be an intentional, unlawful, offer to touch the person of another in a rude or angry manner under such circumstances as to create in the mind of the party alleging the assault a well-founded fear of an imminent battery, coupled with the apparent present ability to effectuate the attempt, if not prevented....

Rule

....

What are the facts here?.... Defendant was under contract with plaintiff to keep in repair and regulated an electric clock in plaintiff's place of business. When the clock needed attention, that fact was to be reported to Sapp, and he in turn would report to a special man, whose duty it was to do the fixing. At 8:13 o'clock p.m. plaintiff's wife reported to Sapp over the phone that the clock needed attention, and, no one coming to attend the clock, plaintiff's wife went to the office of defendant about 8:30 p.m. There she found Sapp in charge and behind a desk or counter, separating the public from the part of the room in which defendant's operator worked. The counter is four feet and two inches high, and so wide that, Sapp standing on the floor, leaning against the counter and stretching his arm and hand to the full length, the end of his fingers reaches just to the outer edge of the counter. The photographs in evidence show that the counter was as high as Sapp's armpits. Sapp had had two or three drinks and was "still slightly feeling the effects of whisky; I felt all right; I felt good and amiable." When plaintiff's wife came into the office, Sapp came from towards the rear of the room and asked what he could do for her. She replied: "I asked him if he understood over the phone that my clock was out of order and when he was going to fix it. He stood there and looked at me a few minutes and said: 'If you will come back here and let me love and pet you, I will fix your clock.' This he repeated and reached for me with his hand, he extended his hand toward me, he did not put it on me; I jumped back. I was in his reach as I stood there. He reached for me right along here (indicating her left shoulder and arm)." The foregoing is the evidence offered by plaintiff tending to prove an assault.

Facts

no battery

Per contra, aside from the positive denial by Sapp of any effort to touch Mrs. Hill, the physical surroundings as evidenced by the photographs of the locus tend to rebut any evidence going to prove that Sapp could have touched plaintiff's wife across that counter even if he had reached his hand in her direction unless she was leaning against the counter or Sapp should have stood upon something so as to elevate him and allow him to reach beyond the counter. However, there is testimony tending to prove that, notwithstanding the width of the counter and the height of Sapp, Sapp could have reached from six to eighteen inches beyond the desk in an effort to place his hand on Mrs. Hill. The evidence as a whole presents a question for the jury. This was the view taken by the trial judge, and in the several rulings bearing on this question there is no error.

The next question is, Was the act of Sapp towards Mrs. Hill, plaintiff's wife, such as to render this defendant liable under the doctrine of *respondeat superior*? It is admitted that at the time of the alleged assault Sapp was the manager of defendant's office... [and] that he was in and about his master's business incident to that office....

The defendant is a public service corporation, maintaining open offices for the transaction of its business with the public.... People entering these offices are entitled to courteous treatment, and if, while transacting the business of the corporation with the agent, an assault is made growing out of, or being related to the business there in hand, the corporation would be liable. [Citation.] But the assault in this case, if committed, was clearly from a motive or purpose solely and alone to satisfy the sensuous desires of Sapp, and not in furtherance of the business of defendant. In such case the liability rests with the agent and not the master.... [W]hile Sapp was the agent of defendant, in the proposal and technical assault made by him on plaintiff's wife he stepped aside wholly from his master's business to pursue a matter entirely personal. Where this is so, the doctrine of *respondeat superior* does not apply....

The rulings of the trial court with reference to this question were erroneous....

Reversed and remanded.

Notes

1. *Present Apparent Ability.* The tort of assault protects the plaintiff's "interest in freedom from apprehension of... contacts" and is actionable only if the defendant's actions "actually have put the plaintiff in apprehension of an immediate contact." Thus, there is no assault if the defendant's attempt to inflict harmful or offensive contact is unknown to the plaintiff before the battery is accomplished or the effort is abandoned. *See* Restatement, Second, of Torts §22. Nor is there an assault if the plaintiff believes— even mistakenly—that the defendant lacks the ability to commit a battery.

> Thus, if the actor, believing a revolver to be loaded, points it at another and threatens to shoot him, the actor is not liable... if the other believes that the revolver is unloaded. This is true though the other is mistaken in his belief, the revolver is in fact loaded, and the actor is only prevented from carrying out his purpose by a bystander snatching the revolver from him.

Restatement, Second, of Torts §24 Comment a. Of course, once the plaintiff has been placed in apprehension, the defendant is subject to liability, even though the defendant's acts are thereafter terminated or frustrated. Restatement, Second, of Torts §23. In a similar vein, liability for assault does not depend upon the defendant's actual ability or intention to carry out the threat:

> The actor may know that he is incapable of carrying out the threat of harm of which he intends to put the other in apprehension. It is only necessary that the other believe that the actor have the ability and that the actor intend to bring about such belief on the part of the other.

Restatement, Second, of Torts §33 cmt. a.

2. *Apprehension of Contact.* Apprehension is not equivalent to fear. According to the Restatement:

> It is not necessary that the other believe that the act done by the actor will be effective in inflicting the intended contact upon him. It is enough that he believes that the act is capable of immediately inflicting the contact upon him

unless something further occurs. Therefore, the mere fact that he can easily prevent the threatened contact by self-defensive measures which he feels amply capable of taking does not prevent the actor's attempt to inflict the contact upon him from being an actionable assault....

Restatement, Second, of Torts §24 cmt. b.

Whether the plaintiff was placed in apprehension will normally be an issue for the fact finder to resolve. *See* Lesser v. Neosho County Comm. Coll., 741 F. Supp. 854, 866 (D. Kan. 1990) (where a student-athlete doubted assurances from other students that the coach would not strike him in the genitals during a "cup check," the issue of reasonable apprehension was a jury question sufficient to preclude summary judgment).

3. *Reasonableness of Reaction.* There is some dispute as to whether the plaintiff's apprehension of contact must be reasonable or merely genuine. According to the Restatement, if the defendant succeeds in intentionally placing the plaintiff in apprehension of imminent contact, it is irrelevant that the defendant's acts would not have placed a person of ordinary courage in such apprehension. Restatement, Second, of Torts §27. In that situation, the actor has intentionally invaded the legally protected interests of the plaintiff, and "the mere fact that the actor succeeds in accomplishing his purpose by conduct which ordinarily would not accomplish it, is no basis for an immunity...." *Id.* at cmt. a. *See also* Newell v. Whitcher, 53 Vt. 589 (1880) (in an action by a blind girl, the trial court properly refused an instruction denying recovery unless the defendant's conduct would have injured a person of ordinary nerve and courage).

However, many cases appear to reach a different conclusion. For example, in Bouton v. Allstate Ins. Co., 491 So. 2d 56 (La. Ct. App. 1986), the court held that a homeowner was not assaulted by trick-or-treaters, one of whom wore military fatigues and another of whom flashed a camera in the homeowner's face, for a "reasonable person expects to see an endless array of ghouls, beasts, and characters" on Halloween. Should the result be the same if the trick-or-treaters know of the plaintiff's extreme sensitivity?

4. *Imminent versus Future Threats.* A threat of future harm will not support an action for assault:

> The apprehension created must be one of imminent contact, as distinguished from any contact in the future. "Imminent" does not mean immediate, in the sense of instantaneous contact, as where the other sees the actor's fist about to strike his nose. It means rather that there will be no significant delay. It is not necessary that one shall be within striking distance of the other, or that a weapon pointed at the other shall be in a condition for instant discharge. It is enough that one is so close to striking distance that he can reach the other almost at once, or that he can make the weapon ready for discharge in a very short interval of time.

Restatement, Second, of Torts §29 cmt. b.

In S & F Corporation v. Daley, 376 N.E.2d 699 (Ill. App. Ct. 1978), Buchta and Gomez, customers at a bar called the "Candy Store," were told by a waitress to pay for drinks they had not ordered for women they did not know. According to the court:

> When the customers objected to paying for these "drinks" the waitress pointed to two men at the bar and said "They're not going to like it." She told the customers to pay or else, and made a motion to the two men at the bar, approximately 15 feet away. Buchta and Gomez then paid the waitress $20 each... [and] left the premises....

In finding that an assault had been committed, the court wrote:

> The threat to Buchta was an immediate one, and not merely a threat to act in the future....The necessity of a "present ability" to inflict a battery upon the victim [citation] is satisfied by the immediate presence of these bouncers, especially when coupled with the waitress' gestures toward them.

What if the bouncers had been outside in the parking lot, or in another room, or 50 feet away, or not scheduled to come on duty for a half hour?

5. *Conditional Threats.* Whether a conditional threat to commit a battery constitutes an assault depends upon whether the condition is one which the defendant is privileged to enforce through physical contact or a threat to inflict the same. Thus, an action for assault may lie where the defendant screams "Get right out of my house or I will shoot you dead," but not where the defendant heatedly states "I will give you one minute to leave my house. If you don't, I will put you out." The difference is that there is a privilege to use physical force, but not deadly force, to eject an unwanted guest, and one may threaten only that degree of force that it would be permissible to use. *See* Restatement, Second, of Torts §30 and Illus. 1 & 2.

6. *Verbal Nuances and Words Alone.* Words accompanying conduct provide a basis for determining whether the plaintiff was placed in apprehension of imminent contact. Such language may reveal, for example, that despite appearances to the contrary, the defendant had no intention of striking the plaintiff, as where the defendant raises a whip, exclaiming, "If you were not an old man, I would knock you down." State v. Crow, 23 N.C. 375 (1841); *cf.* Restatement, Second, of Torts §31 cmt. b and illus. 2 ("If it were not assize time, I would not take such language from you").

So too, words may clarify the significance of ambiguous conduct. Whether an actor causes an assault by reaching into his coat pocket during a quarrel may depend upon whether he simultaneously states, "'I will blow out your brains,' or 'Wait a minute; I need a handkerchief.'" Restatement, Second, of Torts §31 illus. 3.

However, words unaccompanied by some form of threatening gesture are generally said to be insufficient to support an action for assault. *See* Bollaert v. Witter, 792 P.2d 465 (Or. Ct. App. 1990) (no assault where the defendant stated, without an overt act, "I'm a Vietnam Vet...let's duke it out....I wouldn't be surprised if my wife...took a gun and shot you").

> Apparently the origin of this rule [that words alone are not enough] lay in nothing more than the fact that in the early days the King's courts had their hands full when they intervened at the first threatening gesture, or in other words, when the fight was about to start; and taking cognizance of all the belligerent language which the foul mouths of merrie England could dispense was simply beyond their capacity.

W. Page Keeton, Dan B. Dobbs, Robert E. Keeton, and David G. Owen, Prosser and Keeton on Torts §10, at 45 (5th ed. 1984). Constraints based on limited judicial resources still obtain. However, the Restatement opines:

> [T]here may be...situations in which...words themselves, without any accompanying gesture, are sufficient under the circumstances to arouse a reasonable apprehension of imminent bodily contact....An entirely motionless highwayman, standing with a gun in his hand and crying "Stand and deliver!" creates quite as much apprehension as one who draws the gun; and any rule which insists upon such a gesture as essential to liability is obviously quite artificial and unreasonable.

Restatement, Second, of Torts §31 cmts. a and d.

In Castiglione v. Galpin, 325 So. 2d 725 (La. Ct. App. 1976), the plaintiffs went to the defendant's residence to turn off the water because the bill had not been paid. The court held that there was an assault when the defendant, after stating, "I'll get a gun and shoot you if you dare to close that water," retrieved his gun and either placed it on his lap or pointed it at the plaintiffs. Would the case have turned out differently, if the gun was on the defendant's lap when the plaintiffs arrived and remained there at all times? What if the gun was in the house and the defendant never moved to retrieve it after making his threat?

7. *Sexual Advances.* Because words unaccompanied by a threatening gesture are normally insufficient to constitute an assault, no action will lie where one person does nothing more than *verbally* solicit another to engage in sexual relations. *See, e.g.*, Davis v. Richardson, 89 S.W. 318 (Ark. 1905); Reed v. Maley, 74 S.W. 1079 (Ky. 1905). Thus, generations of law students were taught that "there is no harm in asking." The cases cited for this proposition are old, and offensive conduct toward women has become widespread in some circles. Do not rule out the possibility that verbal advances, especially if repeated, vulgar, or otherwise particularly objectionable, may be or become actionable on some theory in some jurisdictions.

An unwanted, *physical* sexual advance is a battery, and the threat of such an advance can be an assault. In McDonald v. Ford, 223 So. 2d 553 (Fla. Dist. Ct. App. 1969), plaintiff and defendant spent an evening together, then returned to defendant's home. While plaintiff was putting records on the stereo, defendant came up behind her, laughingly embraced her, and, though she resisted, "kissed her hard." A violent struggle ensued, during which plaintiff struck her head on an unknown object. The court held that, although the initial stages of the struggle did not constitute an assault and battery, the latter stages did, when plaintiff tried to free herself and get away.

8. *Damages for Assault.* In an action for assault, the plaintiff can recover compensatory damages for mental disturbance, including fright, humiliation, and the like, as well as damages for resulting physical illness. In the absence of proof of harm, the jury can award nominal damages to vindicate the plaintiff's legal right to be safe from apprehension of battery. Punitive damages may be recovered for an assault involving egregious facts.

9. *Battery by Smoke?* Can contact with smoke be a battery? *See* Leichtman v. WLW Jacor Comm., Inc., 634 N.E.2d 697 (Ohio Ct. App. 1994) (antismoking advocate sufficiently alleged that a radio talk show host committed "battery" by intentionally blowing cigar smoke in the advocate's face when the advocate was in the studio to discuss the harmful effects of smoking and breathing secondary smoke); Annot, *Secondary Smoke as Battery*, 46 A.L.R. 5th 813 (1997); David B. Ezra, Note, *Smoker Battery: An Antidote to Second-Hand Smoke*, 63 S. Cal. L. Rev. 1061–112 (1990).

10. *Battery, Assault, and Domestic Violence.* Do actions for assault and battery offer effective avenues of relief for victims of domestic violence? Perhaps not.

> People who commit domestic violence generally are, in theory, liable under intentional tort theories, in addition to whatever liability they may face under criminal law. But despite the frequency with which people are injured by "domestic violence torts," very few tort suits are brought to seek recovery for the harms domestic violence causes. This underenforcement is caused by several factors. First, standard liability insurance policies generally do not cover domestic violence torts. Second, many defendants have limited or no assets.

Third, statutes of limitations are typically shorter for intentional torts than for negligence. A consequence of the dearth of lawsuits is that one of the key aims of the tort system—deterrence—is failing. These harms are not compensated through the tort system; the losses simply remain where they fall. Second, other commonly recognized policy aims of the tort system (such as loss spreading) fail in the case of domestic violence torts. Third, because the injuries fall outside the tort system, they are less visible or even invisible to the public and the behavior of the perpetrator is not condemned through the tort system.

Jennifer Wriggins, *Domestic Violence Torts*, 75 So. Cal. L. Rev. 121, 122–23 (2001). Professor Wriggins argues that a more effective approach to civil liability for domestic violence torts can be achieved through insurance reform.

C. Intentional or Reckless Infliction of Severe Emotional Distress

1. In General

Historical Development. Although threats of future harm or words alone generally cannot sustain an action for assault, they may support a claim for intentional or reckless infliction of severe mental distress (sometimes called the "tort of outrage"). Most jurisdictions now recognize this action, and its elements are well established. In contrast to the relatively ancient lineage of assault, battery, and other torts descended from the writ of trespass, the tort of outrage is a recent judicial development. As recently as 1934, the first Restatement explained the tort of assault as an historical anomaly, boldly stating that:

> The interest in mental and emotional tranquility and, therefore, in freedom from mental and emotional disturbance[,] is not, *as a thing in itself*, regarded as of sufficient importance to require others to refrain from conduct intended or recognizably likely to cause such a disturbance.

(Emphasis added.) However, even at that date, courts permitted recovery of mental-distress damages in at least two situations. First, in cases of tortiously inflicted physical injury, damages for emotional pain and suffering could be recovered in addition to compensation for physical harm. Second, certain other traditional torts not involving physical harm (such as assault, libel, slander, malicious prosecution, and false imprisonment) permitted an award of damages for mental anguish, as well as compensation for more-tangible losses. Consequently, the doctrinal question posed during the middle years of the twentieth century was not whether emotional distress damages could ever be recovered, but whether a claim for mental anguish was actionable absent proof of physical injury or some other tort. According to one source:

> The rule denying recovery for intentionally inflicted emotional distress in the absence of physical injury or conduct constituting a traditionally recognized tort began, in the 1930's, to come under increasing attack by commentators who pointed out the hypocrisy of allowing recovery for mental anguish in cases involving trivial and perhaps adventitious physical impact but denying recovery for perhaps even more serious mental anguish in cases lacking that element.

Annot. 38 A.L.R.4th 998 (1985). Eventually, the courts relented and recognized an independent cause of action. Recounting the history of this development, one court has written:

> Traditionally, at common law an action for mental distress alone could not be brought.... This reluctance to fashion a direct remedy reflected a policy consideration that because these damages were difficult to assess and prove[,] a flood of fictitious and trivial claims might result if an independent tort were recognized. [Citation.]
>
> This narrow approach was gradually eroded as courts reflected society's increasing valuation of an individual's interest in privacy and emotional well-being. This culminated in 1948 when the American Law Institute recognized as an independent cause of action outrageous conduct causing severe emotional distress....
>
> ....
>
> The tort of intentional infliction of mental distress as described by section 46 of the Restatement has gained sufficient acceptance to be characterized as the general rule....

Sheltra v. Smith, 392 A.2d 431, 432 (Vt. 1978). Over the years, the doctrinal contours of the tort of outrage have shifted. Professor Jean C. Love writes:

> In 1948 the American Law Institute adopted the following proposition as section 46: "One who, without a privilege to do so, intentionally causes severe emotional distress to another is liable (a) for such emotional distress and (b) for bodily harm resulting from it."
>
> Ten years later, Professor [William] Prosser, as the Reporter for the Restatement (Second) of Torts, announced that there were over one hundred cases dealing with the question of liability for intentional infliction of emotional distress. Professor Prosser redrafted section 46 "to keep the courts from running wild on this thing" and added numerous comments designed to "spell out some boundaries, qualifications and limitations" to the new tort. As a result, section 46 of the Restatement (Second) of Torts imposes liability for damages on a defendant who "by extreme and outrageous conduct intentionally or recklessly causes severe emotional distress to another...."

Jean C. Love, *Discriminatory Speech and the Tort of Intentional Infliction of Emotional Distress*, 47 Wash. & Lee L. Rev. 123, 126–27 (1990).

The Problem of Genuineness. In an attempt to assure that the plaintiff had in fact suffered mental distress, some jurisdictions initially required proof that the alleged suffering resulted in physical harm to the plaintiff, such as a miscarriage, a heart attack, or a less-serious physical illness. Eventually, courts questioned the soundness of that approach, and today most permit recovery even though the mental distress is unaccompanied by physical illness or other tangible consequences. In a typical opinion, the Supreme Judicial Court of Massachusetts wrote:

> There has been a concern that...there can be no objective measurement of the extent or the existence of emotional distress. [Citation.] There is a fear that "[i]t is easy to assert a claim of mental anguish and very hard to disprove it." [Citations.]
>
> While we are not unconcerned with these problems, we believe that "the problems presented are not...insuperable" and that "administrative difficul-

ties do not justify the denial of relief for serious invasions of mental and emotional tranquility...." [Citation.] "That some claims may be spurious should not compel those who administer justice to shut their eyes to serious wrongs and let them go without being brought to account. It is the function of courts and juries to determine whether claims are valid or false. This responsibility should not be shunned merely because the task may be difficult to perform." [Citation.]

Furthermore, the distinction between the difficulty which juries may encounter in determining liability and assessing damages where no physical injury occurs and their performance of that same task where there has been resulting physical harm may be greatly overstated. "The jury is ordinarily in a better position...to determine whether outrageous conduct results in mental distress than whether that distress in turn results in physical injury. From their own experience jurors are aware of the extent and character of the disagreeable emotions that may result from the defendant's conduct, but a difficult medical question is presented when it must be determined if emotional distress resulted in physical injury....Greater proof that mental suffering occurred is found in the defendant's conduct designed to bring it about than in physical injury that may or may not have resulted therefrom."....

Agis v. Howard Johnson Co., 355 N.E.2d 315, 317–18 (Mass. 1976).

Relationship to Negligent Infliction of Emotional Distress. In recent years, some courts have recognized an independent tort action for *negligent* infliction of severe mental distress. That tort differs from the tort of outrage in several respects, the most important of which is that it may be predicated on conduct that is merely unreasonable, rather than extreme and outrageous. Consequently, the negligence-based action raises heightened concerns about the genuineness of the alleged emotional loss and the risk of imposing liability disproportionate to fault—concerns which are less weighty in cases involving highly egregious conduct. Some courts have imposed special requirements on the negligence action to address those concerns; other courts have not. Negligent infliction of emotional distress will be examined in detail in Chapter 11.

Four Avenues for Recovery. Ignoring many details and variations among states, compensation for mental distress is potentially recoverable in at least four different ways: (1) as a "parasitic" claim incidental to a tort involving physical injury; (2) as one element of recovery in an action for certain non-physical-injury torts other than the "tort of outrage" or negligent infliction (*e.g.*, libel, slander, malicious prosecution, assault, false imprisonment, and others); (3) in an independent action for intentional or reckless infliction of severe emotional distress; or (4) in an independent action for negligent infliction of severe emotional distress.

Harris v. Jones
Court of Appeals of Maryland
380 A.2d 611 (Md. 1977)

MURPHY, Chief Judge.

In Jones v. Harris, 35 Md. App. 556, 371 A.2d 1104 (1977), a case of first impression in Maryland, the Court of Special Appeals...recognized intentional infliction of emotional distress as a new and independent tort in this jurisdiction....We granted certiorari to review the decision of the Court of Special Appeals and to decide whether, if intentional infliction of emotional distress is a viable tort in Maryland, the court erred in reversing judgments entered on jury verdicts for the plaintiff....

The plaintiff, William R. Harris, a 26-year-old, 8-year employee of General Motors Corporation (GM), sued GM and one of its supervisory employees, H. Robert Jones.... The declaration alleged that Jones, aware that Harris suffered from a speech impediment which caused him to stutter, and also aware of Harris' sensitivity to his disability, and his insecurity because of it, nevertheless "maliciously and cruelly ridiculed... [him]." It was also alleged in the declaration that Jones' actions occurred within the course of his employment with GM and that GM ratified Jones' conduct.

(P's) the claim

The evidence at trial showed that Harris stuttered throughout his entire life. While he had little trouble with one syllable words, he had great difficulty with longer words or sentences....

....Harris worked under Jones' supervision at a GM automobile assembly plant. Over a five-month period, between March and August of 1975, Jones approached Harris over 30 times at work and verbally and physically mimicked his stuttering disability. In addition, two or three times a week during this period, Jones approached Harris and told him, in a "smart manner," not to get nervous. As a result of Jones' conduct, Harris was "shaken up" and "felt like going into a hole and hide."

On June 2, 1975, Harris asked Jones for a transfer to another department; Jones refused, called Harris a "troublemaker" and chastised him for repeatedly seeking the assistance of his committeeman, a representative who handles employee grievances. On this occasion, Jones, "shaking his head up and down" to imitate Harris, mimicked his pronunciation of the word "committeeman," which Harris pronounced "mmitteeman."....

Facts

Harris had been under the care of a physician for a nervous condition for six years prior to the commencement of Jones' harassment. He admitted that many things made him nervous, including "bosses." Harris testified that Jones' conduct heightened his nervousness and his speech impediment worsened. He saw his physician on one occasion during the five-month period that Jones was mistreating him; the physician prescribed pills for his nerves.

Harris admitted that other employees at work mimicked his stuttering....He said that a bad day at work caused him to become more nervous than usual. He admitted that he had problems with supervisors other than Jones, that he had been suspended or relieved from work 10 or 12 times, and that after one such dispute, he followed a supervisor home on his motorcycle, for which he was later disciplined.

Harris' wife testified that her husband was "in a shell" at the time they were married, approximately seven years prior to the trial. She said that it took her about a year to get him to associate with family and friends and that while he still had a difficult time talking, he thereafter became "calmer."....

....The jury awarded Harris $3,500 compensatory damages and $15,000 punitive damages against both Jones and GM.

Jury award

In concluding that the intentional infliction of emotional distress, standing alone, may constitute a valid tort action, the Court of Special Appeals relied upon [the] Restatement (Second) of Torts..., which provides, in pertinent part:

§46. Outrageous Conduct Causing Severe Emotional Distress

(1) One who by extreme and outrageous conduct intentionally or recklessly causes severe emotional distress to another is subject to liability for

Restate

such emotional distress, and if bodily harm to the other results from it, for such bodily harm.

. . . .

Illustrative of the cases which hold that a cause of action will lie for intentional infliction of emotional distress, unaccompanied by physical injury, is Womack v. Eldridge, 215 Va. 338, 210 S.E.2d 145 (1974). There, the defendant was engaged in the business of investigating cases for attorneys. She deceitfully obtained the plaintiff's photograph for the purpose of permitting a criminal defense lawyer to show it to the victims in several child molesting cases in an effort to have them identify the plaintiff as the perpetrator of the offenses, even though he was in no way involved in the crimes. While the victims did not identify the plaintiff, he was nevertheless questioned by the police, called repeatedly as a witness and required to explain the circumstances under which the defendant had obtained his photograph. As a result, plaintiff suffered shock, mental depression, nervousness and great anxiety as to what people would think of him and he feared that he would be accused of molesting the boys. The court, in concluding that a cause of action had been made out, . . . identified four elements which must coalesce to impose liability for intentional infliction of emotional distress:

Precedent

(1) The conduct must be intentional or reckless;

(2) The conduct must be extreme and outrageous;

(3) There must be a causal connection between the wrongful conduct and the emotional distress;

(4) The emotional distress must be severe.

Factors (Rule)

. . . . We agree that the independent tort of intentional infliction of emotional distress should be sanctioned in Maryland, and that by closely adhering to the four elements outlined in *Womack*, two problems which are inherent in recognizing a tort of this character can be minimized: (1) distinguishing the true from the false claim, and (2) distinguishing the trifling annoyance from the serious wrong. [Citations.]

. . . . Section 46 of the Restatement, comment d, states that "Liability has been found only where the conduct has been so outrageous in character, and so extreme in degree, as to go beyond all possible bounds of decency, and to be regarded as atrocious, and utterly intolerable in a civilized community." The comment goes on to state that liability does not extend, however:

Restatement Definition

to mere insults, indignities, threats, annoyances, petty oppressions, or other trivialities. The rough edges of our society are still in need of a good deal of filing down, and in the meantime plaintiffs must necessarily be expected and required to be hardened to a certain amount of rough language, and to occasional acts that are definitely inconsiderate and unkind. . . .

Comment f states that the extreme and outrageous character of the conduct "may arise from the actor's knowledge that the other is peculiarly susceptible to emotional distress, by reason of some physical or mental condition or peculiarity." The comment continues:

The conduct may become heartless, flagrant, and outrageous when the actor proceeds in the face of such knowledge, where it would not be so if he did not know. It must be emphasized . . . that major outrage is essential to the tort. . . .

In his now classic article, *Mental and Emotional Disturbance in the Law of Torts*, 49 Harv. L. Rev. 1033 (1936), Professor Calvert Magruder warned against imposing liability for conduct which is not outrageous and extreme; he observed at 1035 that "Against a large part of the frictions and irritations and clashing of temperaments incident to participation in a community life, a certain toughening of the mental hide is a better protection than the law could ever be," and at 1053, he said:

"....No pressing social need requires that every abusive outburst be converted into a tort; upon the contrary, it would be unfortunate if the law closed all the safety valves through which irascible tempers might legally blow off steam."

In determining whether conduct is extreme and outrageous, it should not be considered in a sterile setting, detached from the surroundings in which it occurred. [Citation.] The personality of the individual to whom the misconduct is directed is also a factor. "There is a difference between violent and vile profanity addressed to a lady, and the same language to a Butte miner and a United States marine." [Citation.]

...[C]ases decided by other courts reflect an application of these principles. For example, in Pakos v. Clark,...[453 P.2d 682 (Or. 1969)], the court held that the conduct of a police officer who told the plaintiff that he was crazy as a bedbug and would be put back in an asylum and his children taken from him, and the conduct of another official who puffed up his cheeks and bulged his eyes 7 or 8 times at the plaintiff, was not extreme and outrageous conduct. In Paris v. Division of State Compensation Ins. Funds, 517 P.2d 1353 (Colo. App. 1973), a supervisor delivered a letter of reprimand to the plaintiff, a paraplegic, which contained the statement: "You must realize that your job was created for you because of your handicap." The court there affirmed the trial court's ruling that this conduct was not so outrageous as to support an action for the intentional infliction of emotional distress....

It is for the court to determine, in the first instance, whether the defendant's conduct may reasonably be regarded as extreme and outrageous; where reasonable men may differ, it is for the jury to determine whether, in the particular case, the conduct has been sufficiently extreme and outrageous to result in liability.... *Issue*

In cases where the defendant is in a peculiar position to harass the plaintiff, and cause emotional distress, his conduct will be carefully scrutinized by the courts. [Citation.] Thus, in Alcorn [v. Anbro Engineering, Inc., 468 P.2d 216 (Cal. 1970),]...the court referred to comment e of the Restatement, *supra*, §46, i.e., that the extreme and outrageous character of the defendant's conduct may arise from his abuse of a position, or relation with another person, which gives him actual or apparent authority over him, or power to affect his interests. In that case, the Supreme Court of California said that a plaintiff's status as an employee should entitle him to a greater degree of protection from insult and outrage than if he were a mere stranger....

The Court of Special Appeals found that Jones' conduct was intended to inflict emotional distress and was extreme and outrageous. As to the other elements of the tort, it concluded that the evidence was legally insufficient to establish either that a causal connection existed between Jones' conduct and Harris' emotional distress, or that Harris' emotional distress was severe. *Holding*

While it is crystal clear that Jones' conduct was intentional, we need not decide whether it was extreme or outrageous, or causally related to the emotional distress which Harris allegedly suffered. The fourth element of the tort—that the emotional distress must be severe—was not established by legally sufficient evidence justifying submission of the case to the jury. That element of the tort requires the plaintiff to

show that he suffered a severely disabling emotional response to the defendant's conduct. The severity of the emotional distress is not only relevant to the amount of recovery, but is a necessary element to any recovery. [Citation.] Comment j of §46 of the Restatement, *supra*, elaborates on this requirement:

> Emotional distress passes under various names, such as mental suffering,
> mental anguish, mental or nervous shock, or the like. It includes all highly un-
> pleasant mental reactions, such as fright, horror, grief, shame, humiliation,
> embarrassment, anger, chagrin, disappointment, worry, and nausea. It is only
> where it is extreme that the liability arises.... The intensity and the duration of
> the distress are factors to be considered in determining its severity. Severe dis-
> tress must be proved; but in many cases the extreme and outrageous character
> of the defendant's conduct is in itself important evidence that the distress has
> existed....

> ...[T]here is no liability where the plaintiff has suffered exaggerated and
> unreasonable emotional distress, unless it results from a peculiar susceptibility
> to such distress of which the actor has knowledge.

> It is for the court to determine whether on the evidence severe emotional
> distress can be found; it is for the jury to determine whether, on the evidence,
> it has in fact existed.

> ....

Thus, in Johnson v. Woman's Hospital, 527 S.W.2d 133 (1975), the Court of Appeals
of Tennessee found that severe emotional distress was established by evidence showing
nervous shock sustained by a mother whose newly born deceased infant was displayed
to her in a jar of formaldehyde. *See also* Reeves v. Melton, 518 P.2d 57 (Okl. Ct. App.
1973). In Swanson v. Swanson, 121 Ill. App.2d 182, 257 N.E.2d 194 (1970), the court
held that severe emotional distress was not shown by evidence of plaintiff's nervous
shock resulting from the deliberate refusal of his brother to inform him of their
mother's death, or to publish her obituary.

...[W]e find no evidence, legally sufficient for submission to the jury, that the distress was "severe".... The evidence that Jones' reprehensible conduct humiliated Harris
and caused him emotional distress, which was manifested by an aggravation of Harris'
pre-existing nervous condition and a worsening of his speech impediment, was vague
and weak at best. It was unaccompanied by any evidentiary particulars other than that
Harris, during the period of Jones' harassment, saw his physician on one occasion for
his nerves, for which pills were prescribed—the same treatment which Harris had been
receiving from his physician for six years prior to Jones' mistreatment. The intensity
and duration of Harris' emotional distress is nowhere reflected in the evidence. All that
was shown was that Harris was "shaken up" by Jones' misconduct and was so humiliated
that he felt "like going into a hole and hide." While Harris' nervous condition may have
been exacerbated somewhat by Jones' conduct, his family problems antedated his encounter with Jones and were not shown to be attributable to Jones' actions. Just how, or
to what degree, Harris' speech impediment worsened is not revealed by the evidence.
Granting the cruel and insensitive nature of Jones' conduct toward Harris, and considering the position of authority which Jones held over Harris, we conclude that the humiliation suffered was not, as a matter of law, so intense as to constitute the "severe"
emotional distress required to recover for the tort of intentional infliction of emotional
distress.

Judgment affirmed; costs to be paid by appellant.

Notes

1. *Unendurable-Distress Requirement.* The Maryland court is not alone in demanding convincing proof of mental distress. The plaintiff in Russo v. White, 400 S.E.2d 160 (Va. 1991), alleged that over a period of about two months she had received 340 "hang-up" calls from the defendant. The calls were particularly threatening because of their frequency, because the plaintiff was a single parent of a young child, and because the plaintiff had little basis for judging the defendant's proclivity for violence. The majority held that even if the defendant's conduct rose to the level of outrageousness, liability should be denied. Opining that independent actions for infliction of mental distress are "'not favored' in the law," *id.* at 162, the court set a high standard of proof, quoting comment j to section 46 of the Restatement, Second, of Torts, which provides that "liability arises only when the emotional distress is extreme, and *only where the distress is so severe that no reasonable person could be expected to endure it.*" *Id.* at 163. Applying that standard to the facts of the case, the court wrote:

> The plaintiff has alleged that she was nervous, could not sleep, experienced stress and "its physical symptoms," withdrew from activities, and was unable to concentrate at work. There is no claim, for example, that she had any objective physical injury caused by the stress, that she sought medical attention, that she was confined at home or in a hospital, or that she lost income. Consequently, we conclude that the alleged effect on the plaintiff's sensitivities is not the type of extreme emotional distress that is so severe that no reasonable person could be expected to endure it.

See also Williams v. First Tenn. Nat. Corp., 97 S.W.3d 798 (Tex. App. 2003) (a former employee failed to prove that he suffered unendurable distress as a result of termination because although he "was emotionally reeling" at the time he was fired, "lost his appetite," and became "cranky," "within a few weeks, he was able to 'bounce back'"); Villasenor v. Villasenor, 911 S.W.2d 411 (Tex. App. 1995) (former husband who felt "hurt" and "angry" because of his former wife's manipulation of their children failed to prove unendurable distress; there was no evidence of physical consequences, interrupted work or social interests, need for professional help, or pecuniary losses).

2. *Egregious-Conduct Requirement.* Like the requirement that distress be severe, the requirement of "extreme and outrageous conduct" has often been read as imposing an exceptionally demanding standard. In Hamilton v. Ford Motor Credit Co., 502 A.2d 1057 (Md. Ct. Spec. App. 1986), the evidence showed that a debt collector had engaged in a "wide array of objectionable and harassing conduct," including persistent telephone calls and a variety of threats. In holding that the conduct failed to qualify as extreme and outrageous, the court wrote:

> To satisfy that element, conduct must completely violate human dignity. "[E]xtreme and outrageous conduct exists only if 'the average member of the community must regard the defendant's conduct…as being a complete denial of the plaintiff's dignity as a person.'" [Citations.] The conduct must strike to the very core of one's being, threatening to shatter the frame upon which one's emotional fabric is hung. *Id.* at 1063–64.

3. *Compensation versus Deterrence.* Why should proof of severe harm be required in an action based on the tort of outrage, but not in an action for battery or assault? The difference is difficult to justify, unless there is reason to deter battery or assault unaccompanied by actual harm, but no similar reason to deter extreme and outrageous con-

duct unaccompanied by severe mental distress. Put differently, the mental distress action, by requiring proof of harm in all cases, seems to be animated more by the goal of compensation than by deterrence.

In *Intentional Infliction: Should Section 46 Be Revised?*, 13 Pepperdine L. Rev. 1 (1985), Professor Willard H. Pedrick argued that because deterrence of anti-social conduct is a major objective of the law, a plaintiff should not be required to prove "severe mental distress" in an action based on extreme and outrageous conduct.

> The intentional infliction of mental suffering by extreme and outrageous conduct on the part of the defendant needs to be recognized for what it is — a dignitary hurt appropriately classified with the old common law actions for assault, battery, false imprisonment and invasion of privacy. Section 46 enlarges the circle of protection for the individual's right to personal security from intentionally or recklessly inflicted nervous shock. This is surely good morals. It is, in addition, good social engineering. Is it not desirable that those individuals and those institutions whose employees may indulge in overreaching and harassing tactics be restrained by the law — without regard to whether their victims are persons of ordinary sensibility or of hardy, resilient nature?

Id. at 12–18. A similar argument addressed to workplace harassment was made in Regina Austin, *Employer Abuse, Worker Resistance, and the Tort of Intentional Infliction of Severe Emotional Distress*, 41 Stan. L. Rev. 1, 55 (1988):

> The severe harm requirement of section 46 insulates outrageous supervisory conduct from attack and penalizes those workers who, because of their own personal or social resources, have the strength to withstand abuse.... The emphasis must be on the conduct of the employer, not on the suffering and misery of the aggrieved workers. If their mental states are pertinent at all, anger, antipathy, and sullen contempt should suffice.

4. ***The Role of Motive.*** The defendant's motivation may play a role in the assessment of whether liability will be imposed for intentional or reckless infliction of severe mental distress. For example, in Burgess v. Perdue, 721 P.2d 239 (Kan. 1986), a doctor failed to relay the plaintiff's statement that she refused permission for an autopsy on her son's brain, and thereafter the procedure was performed. When a second doctor, the plaintiff's son's regular physician, learned what had happened, she contacted the plaintiff and told her that the State hospital had "her son's brain in a jar" and asked what should be done with it. In denying liability for the resulting mental distress, the court said:

> While the statements made to the mother were probably shocking, they were not outrageous.... The doctor called the mother because she knew the mother had not wanted the brain autopsied. The doctor was concerned that any impropriety be resolved. She did not intend to harass or intimidate or otherwise abuse the mother. No malice was involved.
>
> While the wording the doctor used in informing the mother of the problem was probably not the most tactful, the doctor's conduct was not outrageous....

A similar result was reached, on different grounds, in Ruth v. Fletcher, 377 S.E.2d 412 (Va. 1989). There, Ted alleged that Patty intentionally convinced him that she was pregnant with his child, fostered the development of a bond of love and affection between Ted and the child, caused Ted to pay monthly child support in return for visitation rights, and then, when it suited her purposes, cut off Ted's visitation rights and proved that he was not the child's father, causing Ted severe emotional distress. In reversing a judgment for the plaintiff, the court focused on testimony relating to the defendant's motivation:

> Ted was asked whether he thought Patty had told him he was the father of the child in order deliberately to hurt him. He replied, "I don't think so, not deliberately to hurt me." He also said that when she called to advise him of the adoption, she was crying. As she talked to him, she asked him why he was not yelling and screaming. He replied, "Because I can hear in your voice, Patty, this is the hardest thing you have ever done." According to Ted, she answered "You are right. You are absolutely right."
>
> ....
>
> We fail to discern from this record any proof that Patty's conduct was "intentional or reckless." There is no proof that she set out to convince Ted that the child was his, and, to cause him to develop a loving relationship with the child so that in the end, she could hurt Ted by taking the child away from him forever. Such proof was required to satisfy the "intentional or reckless" prong of the...test....

Arguably, the plaintiff intended to cause Ted's suffering because she "knew" that her revelation of nonpaternity would cause severe mental distress. A better justification for the *Ruth* court's holding might be that, without proof of a scheme to deceive, the defendant's conduct was not shown to have been extreme and outrageous.

5. *Outrageousness Established.* Conduct has been found to be extreme and outrageous where:

> An automobile club wrongfully denied a life insurance claim after altering an autopsy report falsely to reflect that plaintiff's wife, who never consumed alcohol during their 46-year marriage, was drunk when she died in a one-car accident, Tidelands Automobile Club v. Walters, 699 S.W.2d 939 (Tex. Ct. App. 1985);

> An obstetrician delegated responsibility for a complex premature delivery to an inexperienced resident, resulting in decapitation of the child, Lucchesi v. Frederic N. Stimmell, M.D., Ltd., 716 P.2d 1013 (Ariz. 1986);

> A woman recovering from a miscarriage was falsely informed that an arrest warrant had been issued for her husband, Neufeldt v. L.R. Foy Constr. Co., 693 P.2d 1194 (Kan. 1985);

> A neighbor harassed an elderly couple by making frequent telephone calls, sending them 1,400 pieces of nuisance mail, operating a strobe light and a lawn mower at night, hanging obscene signs near their property line, placing sharp objects on their driveway, and setting fire to their woods, Welty v. Heggy, 429 N.W.2d 546 (Wis. 1988);

> An attorney failed to fully advise a client of her rights, unilaterally increased the amount of his contingent fee, and arranged for a stop-payment order on an insurance company check endorsed to the client, Cummings v. Pinder, 574 A.2d 843 (Del. 1990).

6. *Outrageousness Wanting.* Extreme and outrageous conduct has been found wanting where:

> A business client "raised hell" with the widow of a concrete contractor, called her at home to complain on approximately 60 occasions, and threatened to terminate

the contracts if the construction site was closed on the day of her husband's funeral, Tiller v. McLure, 2003 W.L. 21026572 (Tex.);

An employee made false reports to the police about an employer's alleged scalping of professional football tickets and called the police to report that the employer was preventing her from leaving his office, Langeslag v. KYMN, Inc., 664 N.W.2d 860 (Minn. 2003);

Feuding neighbors retaliated by painting religious slogans on their roof facing the plaintiffs' property, Lybrand v. Trask, 31 P.3d 801 (Alaska 2001);

A newspaper published a picture of the plaintiff's deceased wife in her coffin, Cox Texas Newspapers v. Wooten, 59 S.W.3d 717 (Tex. App. 2001) (stating that pictures of dead bodies are frequently taken in a variety of situations);

An employer, in a severe and curt manner, questioned an employee about possible theft, Randall's Food Markets, Inc. v. Johnson, 891 S.W.2d 640 (Tex. 1995);

A patient, without disclosure, was given an HIV-positive roommate, Bain v. Wells, 936 S.W.2d 618 (Tenn. 1997);

The plaintiff was allegedly defrauded into disclosing his life story, which was then made into the movie "Saturday Night Fever," Robinson v. Paramount Pictures Corp., 504 N.Y.S.2d 472 (App. Div. 1986);

A known non-smoker was forced to work in one part of an 1,100-square-foot room in which smoking by two co-workers was permitted, Bernard v. Cameron and Colby Co. Inc., 491 N.E.2d 604 (Mass. 1986);

A nuclear power plant was alleged to have been slow in detecting problems with contradictory dosimeter readings and in reporting the aberrational readings to the Nuclear Regulatory Commission, Caputo v. Boston Edison Co., 924 F.2d 11 (1st Cir. 1991);

A newspaper published the name and address of the sole witness to a murder while the criminals were still at large, Hood v. Naeter Brothers Publishing Co., 562 S.W.2d 770 (Mo. 1978);

Employees were fired in front of co-workers in alleged retaliation for reporting sexual harassment, followed by defendant's immediate action to repossess its car phones from the employees, Southwestern Bell Mobile Systems, Inc. v. Franco, 971 S.W.2d 52 (Tex. 1998).

7. *Interference with Child Custody.* Interference with the plaintiff's right to child custody can give rise to an action for intentional or reckless infliction of severe mental distress. *See* Kajtazi v. Kajtazi, 488 F. Supp. 15 (E.D. N.Y. 1978); Wasserman v. Wasserman, 671 F.2d 832 (4th Cir. 1982); Rodney M. Sharp, Comment, *Intentional Infliction of Emotional Distress: Recovery of Damages for Victims of Parental Kidnapping*, 1984 S. Ill. U. L.J. 145. *But see* Towne v. Cole, 478 N.E.2d 895 (Ill. App. Ct. 1985) (holding that no action could be maintained by a grandmother against her son and his wife based on their refusal to allow her to see her only granddaughter).

Even if the plaintiff cannot show that the defendant's interference with custody constituted "extreme and outrageous conduct" which caused the plaintiff "severe mental distress," an action may be available under the terms of Restatement, Second, of Torts §700:

One who, with knowledge that the parent does not consent, abducts or otherwise compels or induces a minor child to leave a parent legally entitled to its custody or not to return to the parent after it has been left him, is subject to liability to the parent.

The tort of intentional interference with custodial rights has been recognized by a large number of jurisdictions. *See* Larson v. Dunn, 460 N.W.2d 39, 44 n.3 (Minn. 1990) (declining to endorse the action, but cataloguing prior decisions).

In Fenslage v. Dawkins, 629 F.2d 1107 (5th Cir. 1980), the court relied upon §700 of the Restatement to uphold an award against the plaintiff's ex-husband and others for fleeing with her two children to Canada. The court expressly rejected the argument that damages for mental anguish were not recoverable under §700.

8. *Workplace Distress.* In GTE Southwest, Inc. v. Bruce, 998 S.W.2d 605 (Tex. 1999), the court opined that an action for intentional infliction of emotional distress will not lie for ordinary employment disputes, which include at "a minimum such things as criticism, lack of recognition, and low evaluations" and that in the workplace "extreme conduct exists only in the most unusual of circumstances." The court, nevertheless, found that demanding standard satisfied where a supervisor's acts of harassment, intimidation, and humiliation, and daily obscene and vulgar behavior, continued over a two-year period. The employer was held liable for the supervisor's actions because they were closely connected to the supervisor's authorized duties.

See also Jarrard v. UPS, Inc., 529 S.E.2d 144 (Ga. Ct. App. 2000) (single brutal employment evaluation was not "outrageous").

2. Abusive Language

As noted in Harris v. Jones, the Restatement opines that "liability clearly does not extend to mere insults, indignities, threats, annoyances, petty oppressions, or other trivialities....There must still be freedom to express an unflattering opinion...." Restatement, Second, of Torts §46 cmt. d. While most courts would probably agree, abusive language may at some point go beyond the "mere[ly] insult[ing]" and warrant liability. This is especially likely if the abusive language is coupled with harmful action.

Slocum v. Food Fair Stores of Florida, Inc.

Supreme Court of Florida
100 So. 2d 396 (Fla. 1958)

DREW Justice.

This appeal is from an order dismissing a complaint for failure to state a cause of action. Simply stated, the plaintiff sought money damages for mental suffering or emotional distress, and an ensuing heart attack and aggravation of pre-existing heart disease, allegedly caused by insulting language of the defendant's employee directed toward her while she was a customer in its store. Specifically, in reply to her inquiry as to the price of an item he was marking, he replied: "If you want to know the price, you'll have to find out the best way you can...you stink to me." She asserts, in the alternative, that the language was used in a malicious or grossly reckless manner, "or with intent to inflict great mental and emotional disturbance to said plaintiff."

...[T]he central problem in this case,...[is] whether...the use of insulting language under the circumstances described, constituted an actionable invasion of a legally protected right....

. . . .

words alone

...[I]t is uniformly agreed that the determination of whether words or conduct are actionable in character is to be made on an objective rather than subjective standard, from common acceptation. The unwarranted intrusion must be calculated to cause "severe emotional distress" to a person of ordinary sensibilities, in the absence of special knowledge or notice. There is no inclination to include all instances of mere vulgarities, obviously intended as meaningless abusive expressions....

old rule

A broader rule has been developed in a particular class of cases, usually treated as a distinct and separate area of liability originally applied to common carriers. Rest. Torts, per. ed., §48. The courts have from an early date granted relief for offense reasonably suffered by a patron from insult by a servant or employee of a carrier, hotel, theater, and most recently, a telegraph office. The existence of a special relationship, arising either from contract or from the inherent nature of a non-competitive public utility, supports a right and correlative duty of courtesy beyond that legally required in general mercantile or personal relationships. [Citations.]

D wins here!

...[T]here is no impelling reason to extend the rule of the latter cases....

Affirmed.

Notes

1. *Carriers, Innkeepers, and Utilities.* As *Slocum* shows, one exception to the rule on "mere insults" involves common carriers, innkeepers, and utilities. During the formative days of tort law, such entities often enjoyed monopoly status, *de jure* (by reason of law) or *de facto* (as a matter of fact). Accordingly, the law held them to a higher standard of care than was required of other entities. For example, in Lipman v. Atlantic Coast Line R. Co., 93 S.E. 714 (S.C. 1917), the court ruled that a cause of action was stated where, with intent to cause mental distress, a train conductor allegedly addressed a passenger "in a rude and angry manner, in the presence of other passengers, [and told him] that he [the passenger] was a lunatic and his place was in a lunatic asylum, and that he [the conductor] would be glad to give him two black eyes if he were off duty." (Brackets added.) Citing authority, the *Lipman* court said:

> Passengers do not contract merely for transportation, but have the right to be treated by the servants and agents of the carrier with kindness, respect, courtesy, and due consideration, and to be protected against insult, indignity, and abuse from such servants and agents, and it is generally held that the use by an employee of abusive or insulting language, or rude and discourteous conduct on the part of such employee, toward a passenger, gives to the passenger a right of action against the carrier for damages....

This exception to the "mere insult" rule is described in section 48 of the Restatement, Second, of Torts:

> A common carrier or other public utility is subject to liability to patrons utilizing its facilities for gross insults which reasonably offend them, inflicted by the utility's servants while otherwise acting within the scope of their employment.

The Reporter's Notes recognize that the rule has been applied to innkeepers. Not all potential plaintiffs are entitled to the benefits of the rule, for, as comment b states, "[t]he rule...applies only to insults to patrons who are utilizing the facilities of the carrier or other public utility, for the purpose for which they are offered to the public." Moreover, not every indignity will qualify as a "gross insult[]," within the meaning of section 48. Comment c explains:

> Even at the hands of public servants the public must be expected and required to be hardened to a certain amount of rudeness or minor insolence.... Even profanity may not be grossly insulting, where it obviously amounts to nothing more than mere emphasis or a habit of speech, or where it is so customary in the particular community that it may be said to be generally tolerated.... No passenger on a railroad can mulct the carrier in damages merely because he is told to "Hurry up! We haven't got all night!"
>
> The obvious condition of the plaintiff must, however, be taken into account in determining whether the conduct is grossly insulting; and language addressed to a pregnant or a sick woman may be actionable where the same words would not be if they were addressed to a United States Marine....

"Common carriers" are businesses which transport persons, goods, or messages for compensation. In California, the term has been broadly construed. *See* McIntyre v. Smoke Tree Ranch Stables, 23 Cal. Rptr. 339 (1962) (guided tour mule ride); Squaw Valley Ski Corp. v. Superior Ct., 3 Cal. Rptr. 2d 897 (1992) (chair lift); Neubauer v. Disneyland, Inc., 875 F. Supp. 672 (C.D. Cal. 1995) ("Pirates of the Carribean" amusement ride).

2. *Known Sensitivity.* A second exception to the rule that abusive language is generally not actionable exists where the defendant exploits a known sensitivity of the plaintiff. Comment f to section 46 of the Restatement provides:

> The extreme and outrageous character of the conduct may arise from the actor's knowledge that the other is peculiarly susceptible to emotional distress, by reason of some physical or mental condition or peculiarity. The conduct may become heartless, flagrant, and outrageous when the actor proceeds in the face of such knowledge, where it would not be so if he did not know. It must be emphasized again, however, that major outrage is essential to the tort; and the mere fact that the actor knows that the other will regard the conduct as insulting, or will have his feelings hurt, is not enough.

For example, in LaBrier v. Anheuser Ford, Inc., 612 S.W.2d 790 (Mo. Ct. App. 1981), the evidence showed that the defendant's employees knew that the plaintiff was easily distraught and had previously suffered severe emotional problems. Notwithstanding that knowledge, they appeared at her residence in the presence of two neighbors and, in a loud and threatening voice, attempted to humiliate and harass the plaintiff, asking the whereabouts of her husband (a salesman for defendant) and his demonstrator automobile, and threatening to have the husband arrested by issuing an "all-points bulletin." The court held that the facts stated a claim upon which relief could be granted and that, in determining whether the defendant's conduct was extreme and outrageous and whether mental distress was intentionally or recklessly inflicted, the jury could take into account the employees' knowledge of the plaintiff's past emotional problems.

Other cases include: Archer v. Farmer Bros., 70 P.3d 495 (Colo. Ct. App. 2002) (liability imposed where, five days after an employee suffered a heart attack, two supervisors barged into the house where he was staying and fired the employee while he lay partially clothed in bed); Mellaly v. Eastman Kodak Co., 597 A.2d 846 (Conn. Super. Ct. 1991) (an allegation of outrageousness was sufficient to go to the jury where an employer used an employee's history of alcoholism to badger him); Zalnis v. Thoroughbred Datsun Car Co., 645 P.2d 292, 294 (Colo. Ct. App. 1982) (liability imposed for bullying customer; defendant knew she had watched her husband kill himself and was mentally unstable); *but see* Kentucky Fried Chicken Natl. Mgt. Co. v. Weathersby, 607 A.2d 8 (Md. 1992) (employee who had a nervous breakdown in response to being demoted was denied recovery because her employer did not know that her psychological makeup was other than that of any competent and industrious employee).

3. *Ethics in Practice: Rudeness to Clients and Others.* In Mobley Law Firm PA v. Lisle Law Firm PA, 120 S.W.3d 537 (Ark. 2003), a lawyer who neglected a client's case responded to the client's anxiety about the apparent lack of progress by stating "I don't have a speedometer up my ass." The court found that statement "shocking" and relied on it as a reason for holding that the attorney was fired for cause and was not entitled to his full contractual fee. As a result, the attorney lost several thousand dollars, not to mention the permanent embarrassment of being the subject of a published opinion based on the statement.

In Comuso v. National Railroad Passenger Corp., 2000 W.L. 502707 (E.D. Pa.), an attorney who, among other things, threatened to kill the defendant and uttered various profanities at the defendant in the courtroom was disqualified from further participation in the matter, assessed fees and costs, and reported to disciplinary authorities.

4. *Statutory Relief for Insults.* Even if insulting language is insufficient to support an action under the tort of outrage, relief may be available pursuant to statute. In a few jurisdictions, statutes create a civil remedy for insulting words tending to provoke a breach of the peace. For example:

Va. Code Ann. §8.01-45
(Westlaw 2004)

> All words shall be actionable which from their usual construction and common acceptance are construed as insults and tend to violence and breach of the peace.

See also Miss. Code Ann. §95-1-1 (Westlaw 2004) (similar); W. Va. Code §55-7-2 (Westlaw 2004) (similar). An action under such a law resembles an action for defamation, and is therefore subject to the constitutional limitations which have been imposed in recent years on suits for defamatory libel or slander. *See* Potomac Valve & Fitting, Inc. v. Crawford Fitting Co., 829 F.2d 1280 (4th Cir. 1987). Defamation is discussed in Chapter 22.

3. Domestic Violence and Harassment

If spouse abuse does not amount to battery or assault, should it be actionable under the tort of outrage? Does it matter whether such a *fault-based* claim is asserted incidental to a *no-fault* divorce? *See* Ira Mark Ellman and Stephen D. Sugarman, *Spousal Emotional Abuse as a Tort?*, 55 Md. L. Rev. 1268, 1343 (1996). Ellman and Sugarman "conclude that it is probably a mistake for the courts to make tort law available for claims between divorcing spouses, apart from cases in which the abusive conduct is criminal. This would bar most, if not all, claims for... [intentional infliction of emotional distress] or invasion of privacy, while allowing claims for physical violence and the like."

Feltmeier v. Feltmeier

Supreme Court of Illinois
798 N.E.2d 75 (Ill. 2003)

Justice RARICK delivered the opinion of the court:

Plaintiff, Lynn Feltmeier, and defendant, Robert Feltmeier, were married on October 11, 1986, and divorced on December 16, 1997. The judgment for dissolution of marriage incorporated the terms of a December 10, 1997, marital settlement agreement. On August 25, 1999, Lynn sued Robert for the intentional infliction of emotional distress. According to the allegations contained in the complaint, Robert engaged in a pattern of domestic abuse, both physical and mental in nature, which began shortly after the marriage and did not cease even after its dissolution.

.... [The circuit court denied the defendant's motions to dismiss and certified three questions of law for appellate review.]

.... The [intermediate] appellate court concluded that Lynn, as plaintiff, could "maintain an action at law to recover monetary damages...." ....

....

The first matter... is whether Lynn's complaint states a cause of action for intentional infliction of emotional distress....

According to the... complaint, since the parties' marriage in October 1986, and continuing for over a year after the December 1997 dissolution of their marriage:... [Robert entered into a continuous and outrageous course of conduct toward Lynn]..., including... on repeated occasions: battering Lynn by striking, kicking, shoving, pulling hair and bending and twisting her limbs and toes; preventing Lynn from leaving the house to escape the abuse; yelling insulting and demeaning epithets at Lynn; engaging in verbal abuse which included threats and constant criticism of Lynn in such a way as to demean, humiliate, and degrade her; throwing items at Lynn with the intent to cause her harm; attempting to isolate Lynn from her family and friends; getting very upset if Lynn would show the marks and bruises resulting from Robert's abuse to others; and, since the divorce, engaging in stalking behavior.

The complaint further alleged, as examples of conduct within the categories set forth above, dozens of episodes of abusive behavior, including specific details and time frames for the various physical and emotional attacks.

....

...Robert first contends that the allegations of Lynn's complaint do not sufficiently set forth conduct which was extreme and outrageous when considered "[i]n the context of the subjective and fluctuating nature of the marital relationship."...Robert cites several cases from other jurisdictions that have addressed the policy ramifications of allowing a spouse to maintain an action for intentional infliction of emotional distress based upon acts occurring during the marriage. In Pickering v. Pickering, 434 N.W.2d 758, 761 (S.D.1989), the Supreme Court of South Dakota held that the tort of intentional infliction of emotional distress should be unavailable as a matter of public policy when predicated on conduct which leads to the dissolution of a marriage. However, unlike the case at bar, the conduct serving as the basis for the tort in *Pickering* was the wife's extramarital affair, and the court noted that South Dakota law already provided a remedy for this type of claim in the form of an action against the paramour for alienation of affections. [Citation.] Next, Robert cites Hakkila v. Hakkila,...812 P.2d 1320, 1327 (N.M. Ct. App.1991)], in which the Court of Appeals of New Mexico found that a husband's insults and occasional violent outbursts over the course of the parties' 10-year marriage were insufficiently outrageous to establish liability for intentional infliction of emotional distress....

Finally, Robert cites a Texas case, Villasenor v. Villasenor, 911 S.W.2d 411, 415 n. 2 (Tex. App.1995), wherein the court, in *dicta,* noted that because the marital relationship "'is highly subjective and constituted by mutual understandings and interchanges which are constantly in flux [,]'...[f]or purposes of determining outrageous conduct, the insults, indignities, threats, annoyances, petty oppressions, or other trivialities associated with marriage and divorce must be considered upon the individual facts of each case." However, Illinois case law makes clear that under no circumstances would "'mere insults, indignities, threats, annoyances, petty oppressions, or other trivialities'" qualify as outrageous conduct....Thus, while we agree that special caution is required in dealing with actions for intentional infliction of emotional distress arising from conduct occurring within the marital setting, our examination of both the law...and the most commonly raised policy concerns leads us to conclude that no valid reason exists to restrict such actions or to require a heightened threshold for outrageousness in this context.

One policy concern that has been advanced is the need to recognize the "mutual concessions implicit in marriage," and the desire to preserve marital harmony. *See* Henriksen v. Cameron, 622 A.2d 1135, 1138–39 (Me.1993). However, in this case, brought after the parties were divorced, "there is clearly no marital harmony remaining to be preserved." [Citation.] Moreover, we agree with the Supreme Judicial Court of Maine that "behavior that is 'utterly intolerable in a civilized society' and is intended to cause severe emotional distress is not behavior that should be protected in order to promote marital harmony and peace." [Citation.]

Indeed, the Illinois legislature, in creating the Illinois Domestic Violence Act of 1986 (Act) (750 ILCS 60/101 *et seq.* (West 2002)), has recognized that domestic violence is "a serious crime against the individual and society" and that "the legal system has ineffectively dealt with family violence in the past, allowing abusers to escape effective prosecution or financial liability." [Citation.] However,...while the Act created the crime of domestic battery and "provides a number of remedies in an effort to protect abused spouses and family members, it did not create a civil cause of action to remedy the damages done." [Citation.] Thus, it would seem that the public policy of this state would be furthered by recognition of the action at issue.

A second policy concern is the threat of excessive and frivolous litigation if the tort is extended to acts occurring in the marital setting. Admittedly, the likelihood of vindictive litigation is of particular concern following a dissolution of marriage, because "the events leading to most divorces involve some level of emotional distress." [Citation.] However, we believe that the showing required of a plaintiff in order to recover damages for intentional infliction of emotional distress provides a built-in safeguard against excessive and frivolous litigation....

Another policy consideration...is that a tort action for compensation would be redundant. However, as earlier noted, while our legislature has recognized the inadequacy of our legal system in allowing abusers to escape financial liability for domestic violence, the laws of this state provide no compensatory relief for injuries sustained. An action for dissolution of marriage also provides no compensatory relief for domestic abuse. [Citation.] In Illinois, as in most other states, courts are not allowed to consider marital misconduct in the distribution of property when dissolving a marriage. *See* 750 ILCS 5/503(d) (West 2002).

After examining case law from courts around the country, we find the majority have recognized that public policy considerations should not bar actions for intentional infliction of emotional distress between spouses or former spouses based on conduct occurring during the marriage. *See Henriksen,* 622 A.2d at 1140 (and cases cited therein)....

....

...Illinois cases in which the tort of intentional infliction of emotional distress has been sufficiently alleged have very frequently involved a defendant who stood in a position of power or authority relative to the plaintiff. [Citation.] While these past cases have generally involved abuses of power by employers, creditors, or financial institutions, we see no reason to exclude the defendant at issue here, a spouse/former spouse, from the many types of individuals who may be positioned to exercise power over a plaintiff. *See* [citation]; D. Poplar, *Tolling the Statute of Limitations for Battered Women After Giovine v. Giovine: Creating Equitable Exceptions for Victims of Domestic Abuse,* 101 Dick. L. Rev. 161, 170, 175 (1996) (many battered women remain in an abusive relationship because they are economically dependent upon their spouses, they fear for the well-being of their children, or fear that leaving will only encourage their spouses to commit more severe violence; indeed, constant physical and mental abuse causes a battered woman to develop a belief in the strength and omnipotence of her abuser).

....

The issue of whether domestic abuse can be sufficiently outrageous to sustain a cause of action for intentional infliction of emotional distress is apparently one of first impression in Illinois. Other jurisdictions, however, have found similar allegations of recurring cycles of physical and verbal abuse, wherein the conduct went far beyond the "trials of everyday life between two cohabiting people," to be sufficiently outrageous to fall within the parameters of section 46 of the Restatement (Second) of Torts. Curtis v. Firth,... [850 P.2d 749, 757 (Idaho 1993)], *see also* Toles v. Toles, 45 S.W.3d 252, 262 (Tex. App. 2001) (when abusive conduct such as being assaulted, intimidated, and threatened becomes a regular pattern of behavior, it should not be accepted in a civilized society).

In the instant case,...when the...allegations of the complaint are viewed in their entirety, they show a type of domestic abuse that is extreme enough to be actionable....

Therefore, where we find that a reasonable trier of fact could easily conclude that Robert's conduct was so outrageous as to be regarded as intolerable in a civilized community, we reject his contention that the complaint fails to sufficiently allege this element.

It is equally clear...that Robert either intended to inflict, or knew that his conduct was likely to inflict, severe emotional distress upon Lynn. However, Robert does contest the adequacy of the complaint as to the third necessary element, that his conduct in fact caused severe emotional distress. He argues that Lynn's complaint "contains no factual allegations from which the level of severity of the emotional distress could be inferred." We must disagree.

Lynn's complaint specifically alleges that, "[a]s a direct and proximate result of the entirety of [Robert's] course of conduct, [she] has sustained severe emotional distress including, but not limited to[,] loss of self-esteem and difficulty in forming other relationships, and a form of Post Traumatic Stress Disorder sustained by battered and abused women as a result of being repeatedly physically and verbally abused and harassed over a long period of time." The complaint also alleges that Lynn has suffered depression and a "fear of being with other men," and that her enjoyment of life has been substantially curtailed. Finally, it is alleged that Lynn has incurred, and will continue to incur, medical and psychological expenses in an effort to become cured or relieved from the effects of her mental distress.

.... We, of course, express no opinion on the substantive merits of Lynn's complaint. We simply hold that, taking the allegations of the complaint as true,... the complaint is sufficient to survive a motion to dismiss.

The second certified question we examine is whether Lynn's claim for intentional infliction of emotional distress based on conduct prior to August 25, 1997, is barred by the applicable statute of limitations. Robert contends that each separate act of abuse triggered a new statute of limitations so that "all claims by Lynn based upon incidents occurring prior to August 25, 1997," or more than two years before the date on which Lynn filed her complaint, would be time-barred. Lynn responds that Robert's actions constitute a "continuing tort" for purposes of the statute of limitations and that her complaint, filed within two years of the occurrence of the last such tortious act, is therefore timely....

.... We agree that the applicable statute of limitations for intentional infliction of emotional distress is two years, because the tort is a form of personal injury. [Citation]. The ultimate question, however, is when the statute of limitations began to run in the instant case.

Generally, a limitations period begins to run when facts exist that authorize one party to maintain an action against another. [Citation.] However, under the "continuing tort" or "continuing violation" rule, "where a tort involves a continuing or repeated injury, the limitations period does not begin to run until the date of the last injury or the date the tortious acts cease." [Citations.]

... [W]e believe it important to note what does *not* constitute a continuing tort. A continuing violation or tort is occasioned by continuing unlawful acts and conduct, not by continual ill effects from an initial violation. [Citations.] Thus, where there is a single overt act from which subsequent damages may flow, the statute begins to run on the date the defendant invaded the plaintiff's interest and inflicted injury, and this is so despite the continuing nature of the injury. [Citations.] For example, in Bank of Ravenswood [v. City of Chicago, 717 N.E.2d 478 (Ill. App. Ct. 1999)], the appellate court rejected the plaintiffs' contention that the defendant city's construction of a subway tunnel under the plaintiffs' property constituted a continuing trespass violation. The plaintiffs' cause of action arose at the time its interest was invaded, *i.e.*, during the period of the subway's construction, and the fact that the subway was present below ground would be a continual effect from the initial violation, but not a continual violation. [Citations.]

....

...Robert...maintains that "each of the alleged acts of abuse inflicted by Robert upon Lynn over a 12 year period are separate and distinct incidents which give rise to separate and distinct causes of action, rather than one single, continuous, unbroken, violation or wrong which continued over the entire period of 12 years." We must disagree. While it is true that the conduct set forth in Lynn's complaint could be considered separate acts constituting separate offenses of, *inter alia,* assault, defamation and battery, Lynn has alleged, and we have found, that Robert's conduct *as a whole* states a cause of action for intentional infliction of emotional distress....

...[W]e find the case of Pavlik v. Kornhaber,...[761 N.E.2d 175 (Ill. App. Ct. 2001)], to be instructive. In *Pavlik,* the court first found that plaintiff's complaint stated a cause of action for intentional infliction of emotional distress, where the defendant's persistent notes, sexually explicit comments, insistence on meetings to discuss his desire for sexual contact and lewd behavior in their employer-employee relationship were such that a reasonable person would perceive them to be sufficiently offensive and sinister to rise to the level of extreme and outrageous behavior. [Citation.] The court in *Pavlik* then found that the trial court had erred in dismissing the plaintiff's claim as untimely. While the defendant argued that his sexual advances took place outside the two-year statute of limitations for personal injury, the plaintiff had alleged an ongoing campaign of offensive and outrageous sexual pursuit that established a continuing series of tortious behavior, by the same actor, and of a similar nature, such that the limitations period did not commence until the last act occurred or the conduct abated. [Citation.]

We find the following passage, wherein the *Pavlik* court explains its reasons for applying the continuing tort rule to the plaintiff's action for intentional infliction of emotional distress, to be particularly cogent:

> "Illinois courts have said that in many contexts, including employment, repetition of the behavior may be a critical factor in raising offensive acts to actionably outrageous ones. [Citation.] It may be the pattern, course and accumulation of acts that make the conduct sufficiently extreme to be actionable, whereas one instance of such behavior might not be. [Citation.] It would be logically inconsistent to say that each act must be independently actionable while at the same time asserting that often it is the cumulative nature of the acts that give rise to the intentional infliction of emotional distress. Likewise, we cannot say that cumulative continuous acts may be required to constitute the tort but that prescription runs from the date of the first act. [Citations.] Because it is impossible to pinpoint the specific moment when enough conduct has occurred to become actionable, the termination of the conduct provides the most sensible place to begin the running of the prescriptive period." [Citation.]

....

The purpose behind a statute of limitations is to prevent stale claims, not to preclude claims before they are ripe for adjudication....

Therefore,...the continuing tort rule should be extended to apply in cases of intentional infliction of emotional distress.

...[E]mbracing the concept of a continuing tort in the area of intentional infliction of emotional distress "does not throw open the doors to permit filing these actions at any time." [Citation.] As with any continuing tort, the statute of limitations is only held in abeyance until the date of the last injury suffered or when the tortious acts cease. Thus, we find that the two-year statute of limitations for this action began to run in August 1999, because Lynn's complaint includes allegations of tortious behavior by Robert occurring as late as that month. Applying the continuing tort rule to the instant case, Lynn's complaint, filed August 25, 1999, was clearly timely and her claims based on conduct prior to August 25, 1997, are not barred by the applicable statute of limitations.

Robert contends that even if the acts of alleged abuse are considered to be a continuing tort, the discovery rule should apply to determine when the statute of limitations began to run. Contrary to Robert's contention, the discovery rule is inapplicable here. The discovery rule, like the continuing tort rule, is an equitable exception to the statute of limitations. However, under the discovery rule, a cause of action accrues, and the limitations period begins to run, when the party seeking relief knows or reasonably should know of an injury and that it was wrongfully caused. [Citation.]

By contrast, in the case of a continuing tort, such as the one at bar, a plaintiff's cause of action accrues, and the statute of limitations begins to run, at the time the last injurious act occurs or the conduct is abated. [Citation.] Thus,...a continuing tort does not involve tolling the statute of limitations because of delayed or continuing injuries, but instead involves viewing the defendant's conduct as a continuous whole for prescriptive purposes. [Citation.] We therefore have no need to consider application of the discovery rule here, because we have found that Lynn's complaint was filed within two years of the accrual of her action for the continuing tort of intentional infliction of emotional distress....

The third certified question is whether Lynn's claim against Robert for intentional infliction of emotional distress has been released by the language of their marital settlement agreement. Robert argues that two provisions within the agreement operate to release him from liability.[b]...[W]e believe, as did the appellate court, that "the question can be simply answered in the negative in light of our holding on the continuing-tort theory."....

The marital settlement agreement was executed by the parties on December 11, 1997. We have found that Lynn's cause of action did not accrue until the date of the last tortious act, in August 1999. It is clear that a contractual release cannot be construed to include claims not within the contemplation of the parties, and it will not be extended to cover claims that may arise in the future. *See* [citations]; *see also* Farm Credit Bank of St. Louis v. Whitlock,...581 N.E.2d 664 (Ill. 1991) (a general release is inapplicable to an unknown claim). Indeed, "a release covering all claims that might later arise between the parties 'would constitute a consent to the foregoing of legal protection for the future and would plainly be against public policy.'" [Citations.] Thus, we agree with the appel-

---

b. Paragraph 8(a) of the agreement provided in part:

"To the fullest extent by law permitted to do so, and except as herein otherwise provided, each of the parties does hereby forever relinquish, release, waive, and forever quitclaim and grant to the other,...all rights of dower, inheritance, descent, distribution, community interest, marital property, and all other right, title, claim, tort claims, interest, and estate as husband and wife, widow or widower, or otherwise, by reason of the marital relations existing between the parties hereto, under any present or future law, or which he or she otherwise has or might have or be entitled to claim in, to, or against the property and assets of the other..., and each party further covenants and agrees...that neither of them will at any time hereafter sue the other...for the purpose of enforcing any of the rights specified in and relinquished under this paragraph 8(a), and further agrees that in the event any suit shall be commenced, this release, when pleaded, shall be and constitute a complete defense to any claim or suit so instituted by either party hereto...."

Paragraph 8(d) provided in part:

"Save and except as herein otherwise provided, and to the fullest extent that they may lawfully do so, all the rights, claims, and demands of every kind, nature[,] and description[ ] which each party has, or may hereafter have, or claim to have against the other[ ] shall be and the same hereby are forever discharged, extinguished, released, and ended, and all matters and charges whatsoever, and any and all manner of actions or causes of actions,...judgments, claims, and demands whatsoever, in law or in equity, which each party ever had [or] now has[ ] or which he or she...hereafter can, shall, or may have against the other (as the case may be) for or by reason of any cause, matter[,] or thing whatsoever, from the beginning of the world to the effective date hereof, shall be and the same are[ ] extinguished...."—Eds. (*quoting* 777 N.E.2d 1044–45 (Ill. App. Ct.).

late court's conclusion that "[a] release with very general boilerplate language, such as the two provisions at issue, cannot be construed to release future causes of action between the parties." [Citation.]

....

....The appellate court's judgment is...affirmed.

Notes

1. *Spouse Abuse*. *See also* Christians v. Christians, 637 N.W.2d 377 (S.D. 2001) (permitting an outrage action based on a husband's conduct after the filing of a divorce, which included accusing his wife of child abuse, having the child repeatedly examined by law enforcement authorities, and causing his wife to lose her job); McCulloh v. Drake, 24 P.3d 1162 (Wyo. 2001) (holding that "extreme and outrageous conduct by one spouse which results in severe emotional distress to the other spouse should not be ignored by virtue of the marriage of the victim to the aggressor and...that such behavior can create an independent cause of action"); Twyman v. Twyman, 855 S.W.2d 619, 620 n.1 (Tex. 1993) (permitting outrage action incidental to divorce where husband subjected wife to sadomasochistic bondage activities, knowing that she feared such activities because she had been raped at knife-point before their marriage).

At least one state has opted to recognize a separate tort for "battered woman's syndrome." *See* Giovine v. Giovine, 663 A.2d 109 (N.J. Super. 1995). *See also* James C. Stuchell, *Tradition, Distortion, and Creation: Three Approaches to "Battered Woman's Syndrome,"* 8 Regent U.L. Rev. 83 (1997).

The law's abhorrence for domestic violence may be evident from the fact that, in some states, such actions enjoy a longer statute of limitations.

Mich. Stat. Ann. §600.5805
(Westlaw 2004)

....

(2) The period of limitations is 2 years for an action charging assault, battery, or false imprisonment.

(3) The period of limitations is 5 years for an action charging assault or battery brought by a person who has been assaulted or battered by his or her spouse or former spouse, an individual with whom he or she has had a child in common, or a person with whom he or she resides or formerly resided....

(4) The period of limitations is 5 years for an action charging assault and battery brought by a person who has been assaulted or battered by an individual with whom he or she has or has had a dating relationship....

2. *Racial and Ethnic Harassment*. In Contreras v. Crown Zellerbach Corp., 565 P.2d 1173 (Wash. 1977), a case involving the use of ethnic epithets, the court held that the plaintiff's membership in a particular ethnic group could be taken into account in determining whether the defendant's conduct was extreme and outrageous. Nevertheless, it may be difficult to succeed on an outrage claim predicated mainly on racial or ethnic slurs. *See* Walker v. Thompson, 214 F.3d 615 (5th Cir. 2000) (racist remarks did not amount to intentional infliction of emotional distress); Thomas v. Clayton Williams Energy, Inc., 2 S.W.3d 734 (Tex. App. 1999) (supervisor's alleged frequent use of racial epithets was not actionable); McCray v. DPC Industries, Inc., 875 F.

Supp. 384 (E.D. Tex. 1995) (conduct of co-workers who made racial slurs and jokes was not "outrageous"); Bouie v. Autozone, Inc., 959 F.2d 875 (10th Cir. 1992) (recovery denied based on racial slurs by a supervisor; "[n]either party cites a single state or federal case where recovery under the tort of intentional or reckless infliction of emotional distress has been allowed for racial slurs which are repeated by a third party to a plaintiff").

It may make a great deal of difference whether racial or ethnic abuse occurs on one occasion or on many. *Compare* Colon v. Wal-Mart Stores, Inc., 703 N.Y.S. 2d 863 (Sup. Ct. 1999) (stating that "an isolated ethnic epithet will not support a cause of action for intentional infliction of emotional distress"), *with* Weathers v. Marshalls of MA, Inc., 2002 WL 1770927 (E.D. La.) (finding that a complaint passed muster where it alleged that an assistant manager, along with other white store employees, berated plaintiff with constant racial epithets and made derogatory remarks based on race).

Should the question whether the words are extreme and outrageous be judged under an objective standard or a subjective standard? That is, should the issue be whether an ordinary member of the community would regard the conduct as extreme and outrageous, or whether a person in the plaintiff's position would have regarded the language as extreme and outrageous? The articulation of the standard may make a difference in result. *See* Jean C. Love, *Discriminatory Speech and the Tort of Intentional Infliction of Emotional Distress*, 47 Wash. & Lee L. Rev. 123, 147–53 (1990) ("there are reported cases of racial, ethnic, and religious epithets in which the victim's claim has been dismissed, even though members of the minority community to which the plaintiff belongs surely would have exclaimed, 'Outrageous'!").

3. *Sexual Harassment.* In some instances, evidence of sexual harassment may be sufficient to form the basis of an action for intentional or reckless infliction of severe emotional distress. *See* Maidy v. Guerzon, 2001 W.L. 830579 (D. Md.) (refusing to dismiss an action against a mental hospital intern who allegedly had a romantic relationship with a patient, but expressing doubt that the patient could prove severe emotional distress); Kerans v. Porter Paint Co., 575 N.E.2d 428 (Ohio 1991) (summary judgment for employer denied in a case involving five incidents of sexual molestation).

However, in other cases, courts have reached a contrary conclusion. *See* Bailey v. Fed. Home Loan Bank of Topeka, 1998 W.L. 982900 (D. Kan.) (conduct was not outrageous where a supervisor referred to the female workers as "gals," occasionally stared inappropriately at female workers, and took female workers to a restaurant called "Hooters"); Lahr v. Fulbright & Jaworski, L.L.P., 1996 W.L. 673438 (N.D. Tex.) (even if conduct can be said to constitute sexual harassment, the standard for intentional infliction of emotional distress is higher); Prunty v. Arkansas Freightways, Inc., 16 F.3d 649, 654 (5th Cir. 1994) (only in the most unusual case will a sexual harassment violation constitute intentional infliction of emotional distress).

In Dillard Dept. Stores v. Gonzalez, 72 S.W.3d 398 (Tex. App. 2002), the court held that the evidence was insufficient to support a finding that the actions of male employee's former supervisor constituted intentional infliction of emotional distress where the supervisor hugged the employee, called him pet names, made off-color remarks implying homosexuality, and leaned against the employee. The court noted "We find nothing in the law of intentional infliction of emotional distress mandating a lower standard for homosexual, rather than heterosexual, boorishness."

Is it extreme and outrageous to make false allegations of sexual harassment? Henderson v. Wellman, 43 S.W.3d 591 (Tex. App. 2001), said that false allegations and other conduct failed to rise to the required level of egregiousness.

An employer who fosters a corporate culture that allows a manager to sexually harass employees is subject to liability. *See* Manning v. Metropolitan Life Ins., 127 F.3d 686 (8th Cir. 1997) (whether employer's alleged acts of tolerating various forms of sexual harassment by a supervisor and coworker constituted the tort of outrage, under Arkansas law, was a question for the jury); Hoffman-La Roche, Inc. v. Zeltwanger, 69 S.W.3d 634 (Tex. App. 2002) (upholding an award based on fostering a corporate culture that allowed managers to sexually harass employees).

Does failure to investigate and respond promptly to an employee's complaint of sexual harassment itself constitute outrageous conduct? Probably not. *See* Martin v. Baer, 928 F.2d 1067 (11th Cir. 1991) (holding that failure to investigate rumors of sexual harassment was at most a negligent omission which fell well below the required level of outrageous conduct); Ammon v. Baron Automotive Group, 270 F. Supp. 2d 11293 (D. Kan. 2003) (alleged lack of response to sexually abusive comments of its employees, if proven, was not extreme and outrageous); Farris v. Bd. of County Comm'r, 924 F. Supp. 1041, 1051 (D. Kan. 1996) (stating that failure to investigate alleged harassment was not extreme and outrageous conduct even though employee had filed two EEOC charges and a complaint with the defendant employer); *but see* Ford v. Revlon, Inc., 734 P.2d 580 (Ariz. 1987).

Today, claims of sexual harassment in the workplace are often litigated under Title VII of the Civil Rights Act of 1964, which creates a federal statutory action for sex-based discrimination.

See generally Martha Chamallas, *The Architecture of Bias: Deep Structures in Tort Law*, 146 U. Pa. L. Rev. 463, 515 (1998):

> Tort law has never provided a solid basis for recovering for sexual harassment. This significant gap in the law is largely a product of the nonprivileged status of emotional harm. Although some harassment takes the form of physical contact amounting to battery or assault, the far more common type of harassment consists of claims of hostile working or educational environments, and involves verbal conduct and patterns of abuse that do not fall neatly into the traditional intentional tort categories. It is telling that no legal category captures the full dimensions of sexual harassment as an injury. Tort law treats it primarily as a dignitary harm under the rubric of emotional distress.

4. *Stalking.* On appropriate facts, stalking might support an action for the tort of outrage. However, in some states there are also statutorily defined civil actions for stalking that permit recovery of emotional distress damages on terms that may be more favorable to the victim. *See* Veile v. Martinson, 258 F.3d 1180 (10th Cir. 2001) (affirming a judgment in a statutory action where a funeral home owner was stalked by a competitor).

5. *Debt Collection.* A creditor may take reasonable steps to collect a debt, even though the effort is likely to cause the debtor severe mental distress. Indeed, the Restatement specifically recognizes that a creditor's calling a debtor a "deadbeat" and "demand[ing] payment in a rude and insolent manner," may not be so extreme and outrageous as to warrant liability. Restatement, Second, of Torts §46 illus. 8.

In some cases, however, unwarrantedly oppressive debt collection practices have supported successful actions under the tort of outrage. *See, e.g.*, Turman v. Central Billing Bureau, 568 P.2d 1382 (Or. 1977) (blind woman was subjected to repeated telephone calls during which the defendant used profane and abusive language, calling her a "scum" and a "deadbeat").

Nevertheless, as a remedy for debt collection abuses, the tort of outrage has been largely superseded by the terms of the federal Fair Debt Collection Practices Act, 15 U.S.C. §§1692A–1692K (Westlaw 2003) (FDCPA). The Act provides for administrative enforcement of its provisions and also permits persons injured by an intentional violation of its terms to maintain a civil cause of action against an offending debt collector for actual damages (including emotional distress), costs and attorney fees, and, in the case of an individual plaintiff, additional damages not exceeding $1000. *Id.* at 1692k. By proceeding under the civil remedy provisions of the FDCPA, rather than under the tort of outrage, a plaintiff can avoid the necessity of proving "extreme and outrageous conduct" or intolerably "severe mental distress." In cases falling outside of the statute, it is still possible to sue for outrage. *See* Meads v. Citicorp Credit Services, Inc., 686 F. Supp. 330 (S.D. Ga. 1988).

The FDCPA restricts communications by debt collectors with debtors and third persons, and compels certain written disclosures. *Id.* at 1692c and 1692e. A number of provisions in the Act directly address the types of conduct which traditionally gave rise to tort actions. Section 1692c provides in part:

> ...[A] debt collector may not communicate with a consumer in connection with the collection of any debt—

> (1) at any unusual time or place or a time or place known or which should be known to be inconvenient to the consumer. In the absence of knowledge of circumstances to the contrary, a debt collector shall assume that the convenient time for communicating with a consumer is after 8 o'clock antemeridian [sic] and before 9 o'clock postmeridian, local time at the consumer's location;

> ....

> (3) at the consumer's place of employment if the debt collector knows or has reason to know that the consumer's employer prohibits the consumer from receiving such communication.

In addition, section 1692d provides:

> A debt collector may not engage in any conduct the natural consequence of which is to harass, oppress, or abuse any person in connection with the collection of a debt. Without limiting the general application of the foregoing, the following conduct is a violation of this section:

> (1) The use or threat of use of violence or other criminal means to harm the physical person, reputation, or property of any person.

> (2) The use of obscene or profane language or language the natural consequence of which is to abuse the hearer or reader.

> (3) The publication of a list of consumers who allegedly refuse to pay debts, except to a consumer reporting agency or to persons...[who lawfully may receive reports from such agencies].

> (4) The advertisement for sale of any debt to coerce payment of the debt.

(5) Causing a telephone to ring or engaging any person in telephone conversation repeatedly or continuously with intent to annoy, abuse, or harass any person at the called number.

(6) Except as provided in section 1692b of this title [which imposes limitations on collection of information about the location of a consumer], the placement of telephone calls without meaningful disclosure of the caller's identity.

The Federal Debt Collection Practices Act is a good example of the law's tendency to replace common-law developments with statutory "solutions." Some states have also enacted debt-collection laws. *See* Hamilton v. Ford Motor Credit Co., 502 A.2d 1057 (Md. Ct. Spec. App. 1986) (holding that an action was stated under the Maryland statute even though the facts failed to establish a claim for intentional or reckless infliction of severe mental distress).

6. *Ethics in Law Practice: Collections Work.* The requirements of the Fair Debt Collection Practices Act apply to any attorney or law firm that "regularly" collects debts on behalf of third parties, as many attorneys and law firms do. *See* Heintz v. Jenkins, 514 U.S. 291 (1995); *see also* Nielsen v. Dickerson, 307 F.3d 623 (7th Cir. 2002) (attorney liable for misleading nature of debt collection letters sent on creditor's behalf); Bartlett v. Heibl, 128 F.3d 497 (7th Cir. 1997) (liability imposed on an attorney whose letter was not clear enough about debtor's right to dispute the debt within 30 days); Clomon v. Jackson, 988 F.2d 1314 (2d Cir. 1993) (liability imposed on an attorney who allowed his name and signature to be used by a collection agency). This means that lawyers who "engage[] in collection activities more than a handful of times per year must comply with the FDCPA." R. Hobbs, *Attorneys Must Now Comply with Fair Debt Collection Law*, X. Pa. J.L. Rptr., Nov. 21, 1987, at 3, *quoted with approval in* Crossley v. Lieberman, 868 F.2d 566 (3d Cir. 1989) (affirming award against attorney). Although the Act does not govern collections from corporate debtors, it applies to debts incurred by natural persons for personal, family, or household purposes. *See* Scott J. Burnham, *What Attorneys Should Know About the Fair Debt Collection Practices Act, Or, The 2 Do's and the 200 Don'ts of Debt Collection*, 59 Mont. L. Rev. 179 (1998).

In mandating fair treatment of third persons, the FDCPA is consistent with state rules of attorney ethics patterned on the American Bar Association's Model Rules of Professional Conduct (2003). Rule 4.4 provides:

> In representing a client, a lawyer shall not use means that have no substantial purpose other than to embarrass, delay, or burden a third person, or use methods of obtaining evidence that violate the legal rights of such a person.

Amplifying this provision, the comment to Rule 4.4 says that "Responsibility to a client requires a lawyer to subordinate the interests of others to those of the client, but that responsibility does not imply that a lawyer may disregard the rights of third persons."

Section 1692c(a)(2) of the FDCPA prohibits a debt collector from communicating with a debtor who is represented by an attorney, unless the attorney fails to respond to the collector within a reasonable period of time, or unless the attorney permits direct communications with the debtor. A similar obligation is imposed on attorneys by most state ethics codes. *See* Model Rules of Professional Conduct Rule 4.2 (2003). Consequently, an attorney who engages in impermissible communication with a represented debtor may be subject both to an action for damages under the FDCPA and to professional discipline, such as reprimand, suspension or disbarment.

4. Bystanders and Third Persons

Taylor v. Vallelunga

District Court of Appeal of California
339 P.2d 910 (Cal. Dist. Ct. App. 1959)

O'DONNELL, JUSTICE pro tem.

Facts

....In the first count, plaintiff Clifford Gerlach alleges that on December 25, 1956, defendants struck and beat him causing him bodily injury for which he seeks damages. In the second count, plaintiff and appellant Gail E. Taylor incorporates by reference the charging allegations of the first count and proceeds to allege that she is the daughter of plaintiff Clifford Gerlach, that she was present at and witnessed the beating inflicted upon her father by defendants, and that as a result thereof, she suffered severe fright and emotional distress. She seeks damages for the distress so suffered....A general demurrer to the second count of the complaint was interposed by defendants....

Rule

...[Section 46 of the Restatement provides]: "One who, without a privilege to do so, intentionally causes severe emotional distress to another is liable (a) for such emotional distress, and (b) for bodily harm resulting from it." In explanation of the meaning of the term "intentionally" as it is employed in said section 46, the Reporter says in subdivision (a) of that section: "An intention to cause severe emotional distress exists when the act is done for the purpose of causing the distress or with knowledge on the part of the actor that severe emotional distress is substantially certain to be produced by his conduct. See Illustration 3." Illustration 3 referred to reads as follows: "A is sitting on her front porch watching her husband B, who is standing on the sidewalk. C, who hates B and is friendly to A, *whose presence is known to him*, stabs B, killing him. C is liable to A for the mental anguish, grief and horror he causes." (Emphasis added.)

Holding

The failure of the second count of the complaint in the case at bar to meet the requirements of section 46 of the Restatement of Torts is at once apparent. There is no allegation that defendants knew that appellant was present and witnessed the beating that was administered to her father; nor is there any allegation that the beating was administered for the purpose of causing her to suffer emotional distress, or, in the alternative, that defendants knew that severe emotional distress was substantially certain to be produced by their conduct.

....

Judgment affirmed.

Notes

1. *Actions Based on Recklessness.* As suggested by the principal case, section 46 of the Restatement initially encompassed only intentional conduct. It now extends liability to cases where extreme and outrageous conduct intentionally *or recklessly* inflicts mental distress. Under the expanded coverage of section 46, would *Taylor* be decided differently?

2. *Bystanders and the Requirement of Bodily Harm.* In an attempt to place reasonable limitations on liability to third parties, section 46(2) of the Restatement, Second, of Torts provides:

(2) Where [extreme and outrageous] conduct is directed at a third person, the actor is subject to liability if he intentionally or recklessly causes severe emotional distress

> (a) to a member of such person's immediate family who is present at the time, whether or not such distress results in bodily harm, or

> (b) to any other person who is present at the time, if such distress results in bodily harm.

Rule

A caveat to the section "expresses no opinion as to whether there may be other circumstances" giving rise to liability.

In Bettis v. Islamic Republic of Iran, 315 F.3d 325 (D.C. Cir. 2003), the court held that the nieces and nephews of a victim who was kidnaped and tortured by a state-sponsored terrorist group could not recover on a tort of outrage claim because they were not direct victims entitled to recover emotional distress damages because of conduct directed at them and they were not members of the victim's immediate family.

See Courtney v. Courtney, 413 S.E.2d 418 (W. Va. 1991) (a child who witnesses his father's verbal abuse and physical assault of his mother has a cause of action for intentional infliction of emotional distress, even if there is no physical injury to the child).

3. *Requirement of Presence.* Marlene F. v. Psychiatric Med. Clinic, 770 P.2d 278 (Cal. 1989), involved a mother and child who were patients of a therapist. Outside of the presence of the mother, the therapist sexually molested the child. The court held that the mother could sue for the tort of *negligent* infliction of severe emotional distress (discussed in Chapter 11). In a separate concurrence, Justice Arguelles argued that the facts were sufficient to make out an action for *intentional* infliction of emotional distress. He noted that a caveat to section 46(2) of the Restatement, Second, of Torts leaves "open the possibility of situations in which presence... [by a bystander] may not be required," then added:

> Courts have been slow to accept this invitation to determine whether the presence requirement should be dispensed with in certain situations. The prevailing rule appears still to be that absent family members may not recover for the distress caused by outrageous conduct aimed at another member of the family, but there is authority for the contrary point of view as well....I would suggest that the fact a parent is not present when a child is molested by one occupying a position of trust should not stand as a bar to a cause of action for the intentional infliction of emotional distress, because no purpose is served by the presence requirement in such a case, whatever validity it might have in other situations.

> ....

> In Nancy P. v. D'Amato (1988), 401 Mass. 516, 517 N.E.2d 824, the Supreme Judicial Court of Massachusetts touched on this question in considering a claim for intentional infliction of emotional distress made by a mother whose daughter was molested by a neighbor. Although recovery was denied, primarily because there was insufficient evidence of severe emotional distress..., the court considered the import of Restatement, Second, of Torts section 46(2) and the caveat thereto and noted that "[a] custodial parent of a young child sexually abused by a trusted adult neighbor might present a particularly appealing case for not imposing a presence requirement." (Nancy P. 517 N.E.2d at p. 838.)....

Other cases support the view that in an action by a third person neither presence, nor knowledge of presence, is essential if other factors, such as the nature of the defendant's conduct, or the relationship between the victim and the plaintiff, establish a high probability or substantial certainty that the plaintiff would suffer mental distress. *See, e.g.,* Papieves v. Lawrence, 263 A.2d 118 (Pa. 1970) (parents permitted to recover where 14-year-old son was struck by a motor vehicle driven by the defendant, and the defendant, without attempting to obtain medical assistance, removed the body from the scene of the accident, stored it in his garage, and a few days later buried it in a field); Cahalin v. Rebert, 10 Pa. D. & C.3d 142, 150 (Pa. Dist. Ct. 1979) (custodial parent who was not present when his former spouse kidnaped their daughter stated an action for intentional infliction of emotional distress).

Even if the facts show that the defendant was aware of the presence of a bystander, recovery may be denied on the ground that the defendant's conduct was not extreme and outrageous. *See* Star v. Rabello, 625 P.2d 90 (Nev. 1981) (although the plaintiff witnessed an assault on her father, and her presence was known to the defendant, the assault was insufficient to support an action).

4. *Murder.* In John W. McNamara, Note, *Murder and the Tort of Intentional Infliction of Emotional Distress*, 1986 Duke L.J. 572, 572–85, a student author argued that the presence requirement is insupportable in cases involving the murder of an immediate family member.

5. *Punitive Damages.* Although the large majority of courts hold that the tort of outrage will support an award of punitive damages, a few courts have reached a contrary result. *See* Knierim v. Izzo, 174 N.E.2d 157 (Ill. 1961) (denying punitive damages on the ground that the outrageous conduct of the defendant forms the basis of the action and thus an award of compensatory damages is sufficiently punitive); Hall v. May Stores Co., 637 P.2d 126 (Or. 1981) (an award of punitive damages was precluded by the free expression provision of the Oregon constitution).

6. *Constitutional Restrictions.* Conduct that would otherwise be tortious may be protected under the free-speech or free-exercise-of-religion clauses of the First Amendment. For example, Paul v. Watchtower Bible and Tract Society of N.Y., Inc., 819 F.2d 875 (9th Cir. 1987), held that the free-exercise clause barred an action for intentional infliction of emotional distress by a former Jehovah's Witness who was "shunned" pursuant to church doctrine. But Guinn v. Church of Christ of Collinsville, Okl., 775 P.2d 766 (Okla. 1989), allowed an action for invasion of privacy and intentional infliction of severe mental distress to a plaintiff whose sexual activities were publicly disclosed to church members by the elders of her church. The plaintiff had wanted to withdraw from the church.

The plaintiffs in Nally v. Grace Community Church of the Valley, 763 P.2d 948 (Cal. 1988), were the parents of a 24-year-old man who committed suicide. They sued their son's church for negligent failure to prevent the suicide and for intentional infliction of emotional distress. The parents' claim was based in part on a tape-recorded statement the church's pastor had made—long after the suicide—in which he expressed his belief that committing suicide did not bar someone from heaven. (The parents were Catholics; their son had become a Protestant while in college.) The trial court thought that admitting this evidence would raise serious First Amendment problems, as this part of the plaintiff's claim was essentially that the defendant church's doctrine caused, or at least contributed to, severe emotional distress. The California Supreme Court found it unnecessary to reach the First Amendment issues because the recording was inadmissable on purely secular grounds and because the admissible evidence was insufficient to support the plaintiff's claims.

Hustler Magazine v. Falwell, 485 U.S. 46 (1988), invoked freedom of speech to invalidate an intentional infliction of mental distress case on Constitutional grounds. The defendant had published a parody describing a fictitious incestuous affair between the plaintiff, a minister, and his mother during a rendezvous in an outhouse. Based on precedent holding that the First Amendment prohibits states from imposing liability for a statement of pure opinion, the lower courts had rejected the plaintiff's defamation claim on the ground that no reasonable person could interpret the parody as a statement of fact. The Supreme Court upheld that decision, and held also that the plaintiff could not recover for intentional infliction of severe mental distress, even though the parody may have been extreme and outrageous, and the plaintiff's mental distress both severe and real.

In Tran v. Fiorenza, 934 S.W.2d 740 (Tex. Ct. App. 1996), the court held that excommunication is an ecclesiastical matter and therefore claims for defamation and intentional infliction of emotional harm were not subject to judicial review.

However, in Esposito-Hilder v. SFX Broadcasting, Inc., 665 N.Y.S.2d 697 (App. Div. 1997), a radio station business manager alleged that on-air personalities at a competing station had engaged in a routine known as the "Ugliest Bride" contest, in which they made derogatory and disparaging comments about the manager's appearance after her bridal photograph appeared in a local newspaper and invited the audience to do the same, disclosing the manager's full name and place of employment. The court held that the allegations stated a claim for intentional infliction of emotional distress, even though the statements were opinion protected by the First Amendment, and thus could not form the basis for a defamation action.

7. *Criminal Conversation and Alienation of Affections.* Koestler v. Pollard, 471 N.W.2d 7 (Wis. 1991), illustrates a statutory barrier to an action for outrage. At common law, a spouse could bring an action for "criminal conversation" against a third party who engaged in adultery with the spouse's marriage partner. However, these claims were legislatively abolished in Wisconsin, as in many other states. Koestler sued for intentional infliction of severe mental distress, alleging that Pollard had intentionally concealed from him the fact that Pollard was the biological father of a child born to Koestler's wife and revealed that fact only after Koestler developed a bond of affection with the child. The court held that the plaintiff's claim was legislatively barred because it was, in substance, a claim for criminal conversation. Compare Figueiredo-Torres v. Nickel, 584 A.2d 69 (Md. 1991), in which the complaint alleged that the defendant, a psychologist, had inflicted mental distress upon the plaintiff by seducing his wife while treating the couple for marital problems. The court held that the claim was not barred by the abolition of actions for criminal conversation and alienation of affections.

At common law, an action for alienation of affections would lie if wrongful conduct of a third party, perhaps involving conferral of gifts or other benefits, caused one spouse to lose the affection or consortium of the other spouse. The action is still recognized in a few states. *See* Gorman v. McMahon, 792 So. 2d 307 (Miss. Ct. App. 2001).

D. False Imprisonment

One of the earliest torts known to the common law, the action for false imprisonment protects the plaintiff's interest in freedom of movement. Sometimes called "false arrest," the action is available to a plaintiff who suffers an unconsented, intentional con-finement within fixed boundaries as a result of the defendant's unlawful use of force, threat of force, or assertion of legal authority. The plaintiff must be aware of the con-finement or must suffer harm as a result of it. *See generally* Restatement, Second, of Torts §§35–45A.

Rule

1. Unconsented Intentional Confinement within Boundaries

Bird v. Jones
Queen's Bench
7 A. & E. 742, 115 Eng. Rep. 668 (1845)

[In an action for false imprisonment, plaintiff had a verdict, and thereafter defen-dant obtained a rule nisi[c] for a new trial.]

COLERIDGE, J.

....

A part of a public highway was enclosed, and appropriated for spectators of a boat race paying a price for their seats. The plaintiff was desirous of entering this part, and was opposed by the defendant, but after a struggle, during which no momentary detention of his person took place, he succeeded in climbing over the enclosure. Two policemen were then stationed by the defendant to prevent, and they did prevent him from passing onwards in the direction in which he declared his wish to go; but he was allowed to remain unmolested where he was, and was at liberty to go, and was told that he was so, in the only other direction by which he could pass. This he refused for some time, and during that time, remained where he had thus placed himself....

... [A]lthough thus obstructed, the plaintiff was at liberty to move his person and go in any other direction, at his free will and pleasure....

I am of opinion that there was no imprisonment. To call it so appears to me to con-found partial obstruction and disturbance with total obstruction and detention. A prison may have its boundary large or narrow, visible or tangible...; it may itself be movable or fixed, but a boundary it must have; and that boundary the party imprisoned must be pre-vented from passing; he must be prevented from leaving that place, within the ambit of which the party imprisoning would confine him, except by prison-breach. Some confusion seems to me to arise from confounding imprisonment of the body with mere loss of free-dom; it is one part of the definition of freedom to be able to go wheresoever one pleases; but imprisonment is something more than the mere loss of this power; it includes the no-tion of restraint within some limits defined by a will or power exterior to our own....

If, in the course of a night, both ends of a street were walled up, and there was no egress from the house but into the street, I should have no difficulty in saying that the inhabitants were thereby imprisoned; but, if only one end were walled up, and an armed force stationed outside to prevent any scaling of the wall or passage that way, I

---

c. A "rule nisi" is a device in English law for securing review of a verdict. It is a court order ob-tained by the losing party stating that it shall have a new trial unless the prevailing party shows good cause why the verdict should stand. If good cause is not shown, the rule is made "absolute" by strik-ing the conditional language ("unless..."), in which case there will be a new trial. If good cause is established, the rule is "discharged" and the verdict stands.—Eds.

should feel equally clear that there was no imprisonment. If there were, the street would obviously be the prison; and yet, as obviously, none would be confined to it.

[Rule absolute.]

[The concurring opinions of WILLIAMS, J. and PATTERSON, J. are omitted.]

LORD DENMAN, C.J. [dissenting]:

....A Company unlawfully obstructed a public way for their own profit, extorting money from passengers, and hiring policemen to effect this purpose. The plaintiff, wishing to exercise his right of way, is stopped by force, and ordered to move in a direction which he wished not to take....

...I consider these acts as amounting to imprisonment. That word I understand to mean any restraint of the person by force....

I had no idea that any person in these times supposed any particular boundary to be necessary to constitute imprisonment, or that the restraint of a man's person from doing what he desires ceases to be an imprisonment because he may find some means of escape.

It is said that the party here was at liberty to go in another direction....But this liberty to do something else does not appear to me to affect the question of imprisonment. As long as I am prevented from doing what I have a right to do, of what importance is it that I am permitted to do something else?

    ....

Notes

1. *Partial Interference with Freedom of Movement.* In addition to *Bird*, see Randall's Food Markets, Inc. v. Johnson, 891 S.W.2d 640, 645–46 (Tex. 1995) (employer's request that employee stay away from a particular area of the business premises during work hours did not constitute "false imprisonment").

2. *Intent Requirement.* False imprisonment is an intentional tort; confinement resulting from negligence or even recklessness is not redressable by this action. However, someone injured by negligence which leads to confinement may have a negligence claim, subject to defenses like contributory negligence, which are not available in cases of intentional torts.

The intent required to support an action for false imprisonment is intent to confine, not just an intent to do something wrong. For a creative (if not plainly erroneous) effort to find the necessary intent, see Oviatt v. Pearce, 954 F.2d 1470 (9th Cir. 1992). A jail's lack of internal procedures for keeping track of whether inmates attended scheduled court appearances led to the plaintiff's detention for 114 days without arraignment, in violation of a law requiring trial or release within 60 days. The defendant's decision to maintain the procedures, which were known to be defective, was held to be "tantamount to an intent to confine."

The defendant in Green v. Donroe, 440 A.2d 973 (Conn. 1982), shot himself, then called the police. Embarrassed to admit that he had inflicted his own wound, he described a fictitious person who he said had tried to rob him. The plaintiff, who resembled the description, was picked up. When the defendant refused to identify the plaintiff, plaintiff was released from custody, after being detained for about ten minutes. In an action by plaintiff for false imprisonment, the court wrote:

"A person is not liable for false imprisonment unless his act is done for the purpose of imposing a confinement, or with knowledge that such confinement will, to a substantial certainty, result from it." [Citations.] The facts found by the trial court...negate any intention on the part of the defendant to bring about the detention of the plaintiff, or, indeed, of anybody. [Citation.] His contrivance of the bogus robbery was found to have been motivated solely by his embarrassment over shooting himself. The trial court was not compelled to infer from the description he gave to the police that he intended or expected any arrest to result....

...."It is not enough that the actor realizes or should realize that his actions involve a risk of causing a confinement, so long as the likelihood that it will do so falls short of a substantial certainty."....

The *Green* court noted that an action for negligence is available for an unintended imprisonment which causes harm. However, the complaint contained no allegations of negligence or damage, and a party "may not allege one cause of action and recover upon another."

3. *Transferred Intent.* The Restatement says that the rule of transferred intent applies to false imprisonment actions. Restatement, Second, of Torts §43. However, there are few, if any, recent cases.

4. *Reasonable Means of Escape.* Confinement is not complete, and there is no false imprisonment, if the plaintiff knows of a reasonable means of escape. *See* Restatement, Second, of Torts §36 and cmt. a. An avenue of escape that poses a risk of substantial harm to the person or property of the plaintiff or others, or which would otherwise offend a reasonable sense of decency or personal dignity, is not "reasonable." False imprisonment cannot be maintained by one who fails to take advantage of a means of escape which would entail only "slight inconvenience" or a mere "technical invasion" of another's property interests. *Id.*

The plaintiff in Davis & Alcott Co. v. Boozer, 110 So. 28 (Ala. 1926), took ill at work and was denied permission by her supervisor to go home. The court held that, although the door through which the plaintiff had entered the plant had been locked, there was no false imprisonment because another door to which workers had access was unlocked, as it normally was during the day. Would the case have turned out differently if the second door had regularly been locked and plaintiff had simply failed to discover that it was open on that occasion?

5. *Modes of Confinement.* Confinement may be caused by:

Imposition of physical barriers (e.g., locking a door, taking the plaintiff's crutches, or removing a ladder);

Use of force (e.g., grabbing the plaintiff's person or garments);

Threatening the immediate application of force to the plaintiff's person, to members of plaintiff's family, or to plaintiff's property (e.g., threatening to shoot plaintiff's child or keep plaintiff's valise); or

Assertion of legal authority (e.g., purporting to place the plaintiff under arrest, or falsely informing an accident victim that the law requires the victim to complete a report before leaving the scene).

See Restatement, Second, of Torts §§38, 39, 40, 40A, and 41; Whittaker v. Sanford, 85 A. 399 (Me. 1912) (refusal to provide a boat to go ashore after an ocean voyage).

6. *Being Forced to Follow.* According to Restatement, Second, of Torts §36 cmt. c:

If the actor by force or threats of force, or by exerting legal authority, compels another to accompany him from place to place, he has effectively confined the other as though he had locked him in a room.

7. *Retention of Property.* False imprisonment may result from the defendant's exercise of control over the plaintiff's property if the plaintiff elects to remain with the property. For example, in Fischer v. Famous-Barr Co., 646 S.W.2d 819 (Mo. Ct. App. 1982), the defendant's employee seized the plaintiff's package and told her that she would "have to come back up on the fourth floor" to have a security device, which had set off an alarm, removed from clothing plaintiff had purchased. *See also* Restatement, Second, of Torts §40A Illus. 2 (retention of a customer's purse to keep her from leaving the store is actionable).

Some decisions appear to embrace a contrary rule, taking the view that "not every inducement to remain can rise to the level of false imprisonment." Marcano v. Northwestern Chrysler-Plymouth Sales, Inc., 550 F. Supp. 595, 603 (N.D. Ill. 1982) (quoting Prosser) (plaintiff remained with a repossessed automobile for hours before leaving defendant's premises without interference; no false imprisonment); *see also* Warren v. Parrish, 436 S.W.2d 670 (Mo. 1969) (defendant sequestered plaintiffs' automobile for three hours to coerce payment of a disputed debt; plaintiffs "were at liberty...to invoke the assistance of the police department in obtaining the return of their auto, to call upon friends to return them to their residence [40 miles away], to seek public transportation, or to do anything which they might have chosen except drive their auto home"; no false imprisonment).

8. *Consent.* Consent will bar an action for false imprisonment if the defendant's actions are within the scope of the consent. *See* Morgan v. Greenwaldt, 786 So. 2d 1037 (Miss. 2001) (plaintiff's voluntary signing of a consent-to-treatment form precluded her suit against the those treating her for psychiatric problems); Lolley v. Charter Woods Hospital, Inc., 572 So. 2d 1223 (Ala. 1990) (plaintiff had allowed her husband to sign the consent form); Childers v. A.S., 909 S.W.2d 282, 293 (Tex. Ct. App. 1995) (testimony of minor child that her friend never stopped her from leaving precluded, as matter of law, false imprisonment cause of action).

The plaintiff in Noguchi v. Nakamura, 638 P.2d 1383 (Haw. Ct. App. 1982), was injured when she fell from the open door of her boyfriend's car when he suddenly drove off. A claim of false imprisonment was not barred by the plaintiff's having voluntarily entered the car. The court wrote:

> ...[Plaintiff] had refused to go anywhere on the day in question with the appellee but to the store and back. She was back; she was in front of her parents' house, and she had the car door open when appellee suddenly started off. The jury could well have found...that her consent...was limited to going to the store and back; that she had previously expressly told him she would not go out with him that evening, so that the limited consent had expired; and that her having the door open in the stopped car...reindicated her lack of consent to any further movement.

2. Unlawful Force, Threat of Force, or Assertion of Legal Authority

Morales v. Lee

Court of Appeals of Texas
668 S.W.2d 867 (Tex. Ct. App. 1984)

CADENA, Chief Justice.

Defendant, Dr. Cesar Morales, appeals from a judgment following trial to a jury, granting actual damages and exemplary damages to the plaintiff, Linda Lee, for alleged false imprisonment....

Plaintiff was a part-time employee in Dr. Morales' office.... The incident of which plaintiff complained occurred in Dr. Morales' medical office on... the day on which she was fired.

At 6:00 p.m.... Linda Lee was called into Dr. Morales' private office, in the presence of a co-worker, Mrs. Lydia Martinez, and the doctor's son, Guillermo. Five dollars was missing: he asked her if she took the money. She replied "no." By her testimony, the doctor then "got mad...just went crazy.... He got all mad and he had a chart in his hand and he slammed the chart down on the desk...he was screaming and hollering and he was cussing at me and he was threatening me. He told me 'don't leave.' He said, 'If you leave, I'll call the police and the police will be here in a minute.'" Later she testified: "I was scared of him, I thought he was going to hit me." When asked whether she was subsequently allowed to leave the office, she answered "yes...after he decided to let me go, he said, 'get the hell out of here. I don't want to see you any more.'" The plaintiff then left the doctor's private office, but waited outside in the waiting room to get her paycheck before going home. A co-worker testified that she was shaking and crying, and couldn't talk after the incident. Linda Lee testified that she couldn't sleep at night, that she had nightmares, couldn't eat, and would throw up afterwards. She stated that she consulted a doctor for these problems, and that she was out of work for five or six months afterwards because she was upset, confused, and unable to work. Linda's mother testified that her daughter had been in excellent health prior to this incident, but afterwards was depressed, unable to sleep at night, unable to eat, and lost twenty pounds.

We agree that there is no evidence supporting a finding of false imprisonment.

False imprisonment consists of a willful detention of another without his consent without legal justification. [Citations.]

....

.... Threats of future action, such as to call the police and have the plaintiff arrested, are not ordinarily sufficient in themselves to effect an unlawful imprisonment. W. Prosser, Torts, §11. The Texas cases allowing false imprisonment to be found where there were threats to call police, were such that the offense of false imprisonment could be established from other events occurring at the same time, such as extended interrogation and intimidation. [Citations.]

The judgment of the trial court is reversed and judgment is here rendered that plaintiff take nothing.

TIJERINA, Justice, dissenting.

"....*A wrongful detention may be effected by acts alone or by words alone*, or by both operating together, if the effect thereof is to operate on the will of the individual so as to prevent his free motion." [Citations.]

The majority is correct in saying that a threat to call the police, standing alone, is not sufficient to conclude that the complainant was unlawfully detained. But, the jury, as the fact finder, heard, observed and weighed all the other factors such as the age, sex, relative size of the parties, demeanor of the witnesses, employer-employee relationship, and susceptibility of the complainant to intimidation.... It is settled that the imprisonment need not be for more than an appreciable length of time and that it is not necessary that any damage result from it other than the confinement itself, since the tort is complete with even a brief restraint of the plaintiff's freedom. Prosser, Torts §11 at 43 (4th ed. 1971). Thus, in the instant case, the jury could have found or reasonably inferred that the angry outburst of hollering and threats by appellant was calculated to operate upon the mind of appellee and inspire fear of injury to her person.... We should not substitute our judgment for that of the jury. [Citations.]

I... would affirm....

Notes

1. *Future Harm*. A threat is a future threat if it proposes the use of force at an "appreciably later" time. Restatement, Second, of Torts §40 cmt. b.

Compare Morales with Marcus v. Liebman, 375 N.E.2d 486, 489 (Ill. App. Ct. 1978). The plaintiff, suffering mental difficulties, had voluntarily entered one hospital. She later requested her release within five days by signing a form. The defendant doctor threatened to have the plaintiff involuntarily committed to a second hospital unless she signed another paper revoking her earlier request for discharge; she signed this paper. The court found a present threat establishing a cause of action for false imprisonment:

> The defendant could have initiated commitment procedures immediately. The fact that these procedures could not have been concluded immediately does not change the threat to one in the future. At the time the alleged threat was made plaintiff was already confined. It was certainly reasonable for the plaintiff to believe that before her release commitment procedures could have been concluded.

2. *Moral Pressure and Economic Coercion*. Moral pressure and economic coercion are normally insufficient predicates for false imprisonment.

In Faniel v. Chesapeake & Potomac Telephone Co., 404 A.2d 147 (D.C. 1979), plaintiff alleged that she was falsely imprisoned in a car when she accompanied her superiors and a security officer to her home to recover an unauthorized company telephone which she had admitted using. Plaintiff testified that she was told that "a trip to her home would be necessary to recover the equipment," that she "just assumed that [she] had to go," and that she feared discipline if she did not cooperate. The court rejected the claim:

> ... [I]t is not enough for plaintiff to feel "mentally restrained" by the actions of the defendant. [Citations.] The evidence must establish a restraint against the plaintiff's will, as where she yields to force, to the threat of force or to the assertion of authority. [Citation.] Although plaintiff may submit to a confine-

ment without resistance, if the submission is voluntary, as where an accused voluntarily accompanies his accusers to vindicate himself, then no false imprisonment occurs. [Citation.]

Submission to the mere verbal direction of another, unaccompanied by force or threats of any character does not constitute false imprisonment. [Citation.] Similarly, fear of losing one's job, although a powerful incentive, does not render involuntary the behavior induced. [Citation.]

Other cases involving employees have reached similar results. *See, e.g.,* Johnson v. United Parcel Services, Inc., 722 F. Supp. 1282 (D. Md. 1989), *aff'd without op.* 927 F.2d 596 (4th Cir. 1991) (plaintiff submitted to three to four hours of questioning about employee theft and drug dealing allegations and took a polygraph test "out of fear that he would lose his job if he refused"; no false imprisonment).

3. *Confinement of the Elderly.* An action for false imprisonment can be used to redress involuntary confinement of senior citizens in nursing homes or hospitals. *See* Cathrael Razin, Comment, *"Nowhere To Go and Chose To Stay": Using the Tort of False Imprisonment to Redress Involuntary Confinement of Elderly in Nursing Homes and Hospitals,* 137 U. Pa. L. Rev. 903 (1989). The leading case is Big Town Nursing Home, Inc. v. Newman, 461 S.W.2d 195 (Tex. Civ. App. 1970), a suit involving a 67-year-old retired printer who was taken to the defendant nursing home by a nephew who signed the admission papers and paid in advance for one month's care. The court said:

On September 22, 1968, plaintiff decided he wanted to leave and tried to telephone for a taxi. Defendant's employees advised plaintiff he could not use the phone, or have any visitors unless the manager knew them, and locked plaintiff's grip and clothes up.... Plaintiff tried to escape from the nursing home five or six times but was caught and brought back each time against his will.... There was never any court proceeding to confine plaintiff....

The court found ample evidence to support a finding of false imprisonment and an award of compensatory and punitive damages.

4. *Criminal Liability.* False imprisonment may be a crime as well as a tort. *Cf.* Massey v. State, 624 S.W.2d 576 (Tex. Crim. App. 1981) (evidence insufficient to convict a nursing home administrator of false imprisonment by intimidation).

Enright v. Groves
Court of Appeals of Colorado
560 P.2d 851 (Colo. Ct. App. 1977)

SMITH, Judge.

Defendants Groves and City of Ft. Collins appeal from judgments entered against them upon jury verdicts awarding plaintiff $500 actual damages and $1,000 exemplary damages on her claim of false imprisonment, $1,500 actual damages and $3,000 exemplary damages on her claim of intentional infliction of mental distress, also referred to as outrageous conduct, and $500 actual damages and $1,000 exemplary damages on her claim of battery....

The evidence at trial disclosed that on August 25, 1974, Officer Groves, while on duty as a uniformed police officer of the City of Fort Collins, observed a dog running loose in violation of the city's "dog leash" ordinance. He observed the animal approaching what was later identified as the residence of Mrs. Enright, the plaintiff. As Groves approached the house, he encountered Mrs. Enright's eleven-year old son, and asked him if the dog belonged to him. The boy replied that it was his dog, and told Groves that his mother was sitting in the car parked at the curb by the house. Groves then ordered the boy to put the dog inside the house, and turned and started walking toward the Enright vehicle.

Groves testified that he was met by Mrs. Enright with whom he was not acquainted. She asked if she could help him. Groves responded by demanding her driver's license. She replied by giving him her name and address. He again demanded her driver's license, which she declined to produce. Groves thereupon advised her that she could either produce her driver's license or go to jail. Mrs. Enright responded by asking, "Isn't this ridiculous?" Groves thereupon grabbed one of her arms, stating, "Let's go!"

One eyewitness testified that Mrs. Enright cried out that Groves was hurting her. Her son who was just a few feet away at the time of the incident testified that his mother also screamed and tried to explain that her arm dislocated easily. Groves refused to release her arm, and Mrs. Enright struck him in the stomach with her free hand. Groves then seized both arms and threw her to the ground. With her lying on her stomach, he brought one of her arms behind her in order to handcuff her. She continued to scream in pain and asked him to stop hurting her. Groves pulled her up and propelled her to his patrol car where, for the first time, he advised her that she was under arrest.

She was taken to the police station where a complaint was signed charging her with violation of the "dog leash" ordinance and bail was set. Mrs. Enright was released only after a friend posted bail. She was later convicted of the ordinance violation.

. . . .

Appellants contend that Groves had probable cause to arrest Mrs. Enright, and that she was in fact arrested for and convicted of violation of the dog-at-large ordinance. They assert, therefore, that her claim for false imprisonment or false arrest cannot lie, and that Groves' use of force in arresting Mrs. Enright was permissible. We disagree.

False arrest arises when one is taken into custody by a person who claims but does not have proper legal authority. W. Prosser, Torts §11 (4th ed.). Accordingly, a claim for false arrest will not lie if an officer has a valid warrant or probable cause to believe that an offense has been committed and that the person who was arrested committed it. Conviction of the crime for which one is specifically arrested is a complete defense to a subsequent claim of false arrest. [Citation.]

Here, however, the evidence is clear that Groves arrested Mrs. Enright, not for violation of the dog leash ordinance, but rather for refusing to produce her driver's license. This basis for the arrest is exemplified by the fact that he specifically advised her that she would either produce the license or go to jail. We find no statute or case law in this jurisdiction which requires a citizen to show her driver's license upon demand, unless, for example, she is a driver of an automobile and such demand is made in that connection. [Citations.]

. . . .

We conclude that Groves' demand for Mrs. Enright's driver's license was not a lawful order and that refusal to comply therewith was not therefore an offense in and of itself. Groves was not therefore entitled to use force in arresting Mrs. Enright. Thus Groves' defense based upon an arrest for and conviction of a specific offense must, as a matter of law, fail.

. . . .

Judgment affirmed.

Notes

1. *Probable Cause and Reasonable Suspicion.* Probable cause for an arrest exists when the apparent state of facts would induce a reasonably intelligent and prudent person to believe that a crime has been, or is being, committed. As noted in *Enright*, an officer who makes an arrest based on probable cause normally has an absolute defense to a claim of false imprisonment. Recent Supreme Court precedent allows something less than probable cause—"reasonable suspicion"—as a basis for investigative detention. *See* Gerald S. Reamey, *When Special Needs Meet Probable Cause: Denying the Devil Benefit of Law*, 19 Hastings Const. L.Q. 295 (1992). If that standard has been satisfied, an action for false arrest will be barred. *See* Fulk v. Roberts, 517 N.E.2d 1098 (Ill. App. Ct. 1987) (conservation officers had specific and articulable basis for conducting investigatory stop on first day of hunting season).

An arrest made with probable cause or reasonable suspicion may be actionable for other reasons, such as the use of excessive force or unreasonable delay in bringing the arrestee before a magistrate. *Cf.* Thompson v. Olson, 798 F.2d 552, 555 (1st Cir. 1986).

An action involving an arrest by a law enforcement officer may be barred by the doctrines of official immunity (if the suit is against the officer) or sovereign immunity (if the suit is against the government). *See* Chapter 18.

2. *Bond Forfeiture.* Forfeiture of a criminal bond typically justifies the preceding arrest. The theory is that "there is, in a compromise or settlement, such an admission of probable cause that a plaintiff cannot afterwards retract it and try the question waived by settlement; or that the accused, having consented to a termination which leaves open the question of guilt and possible conviction, cannot take advantage of it." Neff v. Engle, 501 N.E.2d 675, 676 (Ohio Ct. App. 1986).

3. *Assertion of Legal Authority by Laypersons.* The defendant in a false arrest action need not be a law enforcement officer or entity. *See* Whitman v. Atchison, Topeka & Santa Fe Ry. Co., 116 P. 234 (Kan. 1911) (liability imposed because defendant's conductor told an accident victim that the law required him to furnish a statement before leaving the scene).

Under limited circumstances, a layperson may legally make an arrest. The rules vary from state to state.

4. *Relevance of Guilt.* Some authorities hold that "regardless of the unreasonableness of a party's arrest, if he actually committed the crime…, he cannot maintain an action for false arrest…." Taco Bell, Inc. v. Saleme, 701 S.W.2d 78 (Tex. Ct. App. 1985). *See* Fowler V. Harper, Fleming James, Jr., and Oscar S. Gray, The Law of Torts §3.18, at 372–73 (2d ed. 1986).

5. *Shoplifters.* A false imprisonment action by a suspected shoplifter may be barred by the privilege a merchant has to detain, for purposes of investigation, one reasonably suspected of theft. *See* Chapter 3.

6. *Knowledge of Confinement or Damage.* Liability for false imprisonment requires that the plaintiff know of the confinement or be harmed by it. *See* Parvi v. City of Kingston, 362 N.E.2d 960 (N.Y. 1977) (although the plaintiff's recollection was wiped

out as a result of the alcohol he had consumed and the injuries he sustained, the plaintiff's awareness of the confinement was established by the testimony of arresting officers who said that plaintiff had asked to be let out of the car).

Absent proof of actual damages, nominal damages may be recovered to vindicate the plaintiff's right to freedom of movement. Punitive damages may be awarded in a case involving egregious conduct. *See* Haryanto v. Saeed, 860 S.W.2d 913 (Tex. Ct. App. 1993) (affirming an award of $2 million in punitive damages, on top of $1 million in compensatory damages, where an aide to a Saudi prince took a hotel employee hostage and threatened to kill him).

In Dayton Hudson Corp. v. Altus, 715 S.W.2d 670 (Tex. Ct. App. 1986), a customer was arrested for shoplifting and jailed for nine to eleven hours in a dirty, noisy cell, with filthy prisoners, including apparent drug users. She later stopped teaching Sunday school because her children were teased about the event. In the customer's suit for false imprisonment against the store owner, the court held that evidence of jail conditions, as well as length of confinement and resulting public embarrassment, could be taken into account in determining actual and exemplary damages.

7. *Liability for Instigating an Arrest.* Can a person be held liable for false imprisonment merely because the person provided information to the police that led to the arrest of an innocent individual? Generally not. This result makes sense from a public policy standpoint, for society wants to encourage citizens to assist law enforcement efforts. According to many courts, the line is drawn between intentionally providing false information to the police (which may give rise to liability) and merely providing inaccurate information (which does not give rise to liability). *See, e.g.,* Wal-Mart Stores, Inc. v. Rodriguez, 92 S.W.3d 502 (Tex. 2002) (no liability for false imprisonment based on submitting a "hot check complaint form" to the district attorney's office). Although some decisions speak in terms of whether the informant has "caused" the arrest, it is probably better to analyze such cases in terms of privilege. That is, there is a privilege to disclose potentially useful information to law enforcement officers; there is no privilege to supply information that is known to be false.

8. *Negligent Identification.* Similar issues arise in cases where a plaintiff sues not for false imprisonment, but on some other ground, such as negligence. In Davis v. Equibank, 603 A.2d 637, 638 (Pa. Super. Ct. 1992), a bank teller, reviewing a police display of photographs, misidentified the plaintiff as the perpetrator of a robbery. Thereafter, the plaintiff was held in police custody for 17 days until the teller testified at a preliminary hearing that she believed the robber was taller than the plaintiff. In a negligence action against the teller and bank, the court held that, despite the seriousness of the plaintiff's loss of freedom, sound public policy precluded recognition of a cause of action for "negligent identification." The court wrote:

> [T]o allow recovery where an individual's provision of incorrect or mistaken information results in the arrest of another would have a substantial chilling effect upon the willingness of citizens to come forward with information relevant to criminal investigations.... [I]t is difficult enough under the present status of the law to conduct investigations and gather information without the natural dissuasion that potential liability would create.

The weight of authority is consistent with *Davis,* so long as the misidentification is made in good faith. *See* Smith v. Sneed, 938 S.W.2d 181 (Tex. Ct. App. 1997); Turner v. Mellon, 257 P.2d 15 (Cal. 1953); Manis v. Miller, 327 So. 2d 117 (Fla. Dist. Ct. App. 1976); Shires v. Cobb & Mayfair Market, 534 P.2d 188 (Or. 1975).

9. *Malicious Prosecution Distinguished.* A private person who initiates or procures the institution of criminal proceedings against someone not guilty of the offense commits the tort of malicious prosecution if (a) the actor lacks probable cause and acts primarily for a purpose other than bringing the offender to justice, and (b) the proceedings have terminated in favor of the accused. *See* Restatement, Second, of Torts §653. According to one source, "[t]he distinction between false imprisonment and malicious prosecution in the area of arrest depends on whether or not the arrest was made pursuant to a warrant." Burt v. Ferrese, 871 F.2d 14 (3d Cir. 1989) ("[t]he tort of false arrest and detention is available when a person has been confined without legal process; if a person has been arrested pursuant to a warrant, his remedy is to sue for malicious prosecution, as the 'essence of [this tort] is the perversion of proper legal procedures'"). *See* Restatement, Second, of Torts §35 cmt. a, §37 cmt. b, §41, and §654 cmt. e; *see also id.* at §653, cmt. g (no tort action for malicious prosecution against one who furnishes information to a public prosecutor in good faith).

3. Defenses

Peterson v. Sorlien

Supreme Court of Minnesota
299 N.W.2d 123 (Minn. 1980)

SHERAN, Chief Justice.

This action by plaintiff Susan Jungclaus Peterson for false imprisonment and intentional infliction of emotional distress arises from an effort by her parents, in conjunction with other individuals named as defendants, to prompt her disaffiliation from an organization known as The Way Ministry.

.... The jury returned a verdict exonerating Mr. and Mrs. Jungclaus and the other remaining defendants of the charge of false imprisonment; however, the jury found defendants Veronica Morgel and Kathy Mills liable for intentional infliction of emotional distress, assessing against each of them $1 compensatory damages and $4,000 and $6,000 respectively as punitive damages.

....

.... [T]his case marks the emergence of a new cultural phenomenon: youth-oriented religious or pseudo-religious groups which utilize the techniques of what has been termed "coercive persuasion" or "mind control" to cultivate an uncritical and devoted following...

At the time of the events in question, Susan Jungclaus Peterson was 21 years old.... In 1973, she graduated with honors from high school, ranking second in her class. She matriculated that fall at Moorhead State College. A dean's list student during her first year, her academic performance declined and her interests narrowed after she joined the local chapter of...The Way....

....

.... As her sophomore year began, Susan committed herself significantly, selling the car her father had given her and working part-time as a waitress to finance her contributions to The Way. Susan spent the following summer in South Dakota, living in conditions described as appalling and overcrowded, while recruiting, raising money and conducting training sessions for The Way.

As her junior year in college drew to a close, the Jungclauses grew increasingly alarmed by the personality changes they witnessed in their daughter; overly tired, unusually pale, distraught and irritable, she exhibited an increasing alienation from family, diminished interest in education and decline in academic performance. The Jungclauses, versed in the literature of youth cults and based on conversations with former members of The Way, concluded that through a calculated process of manipulation and exploitation Susan had been reduced to a condition of psychological bondage.

On May 24, 1976, defendant Norman Jungclaus, father of plaintiff, arrived at Moorhead to pick up Susan following the end of the third college quarter. Instead of returning to their family home, defendant drove with Susan to Minneapolis to the home of Veronica Morgel. Entering the home of Mrs. Morgel, Susan was greeted by Kathy Mills and several young people who wished to discuss Susan's involvement in the ministry. Each of these present had been in some way touched by the cult phenomenon. Kathy Mills, the leader of the group, had treated a number of former cult members, including Veronica Morgel's son....

The avowed purpose of deprogramming is to break the hold of the cult over the individual through reason and confrontation. Initially, Susan was unwilling to discuss her involvement; she lay curled in a fetal position, in the downstairs bedroom where she first stayed, plugging her ears and crying while her father pleaded with her to listen to what was being said. This behavior persisted for two days during which she intermittently engaged in conversation, at one point screaming hysterically and flailing at her father. But by Wednesday Susan's demeanor had changed completely; she was friendly and vivacious and that night slept in an upstairs bedroom. Susan spent all day Thursday reading and conversing with her father and on Saturday night went roller-skating. On Sunday she played softball at a nearby park, afterwards enjoying a picnic lunch. The next week Susan spent in Columbus, Ohio, flying there with a former cult member who had shared with her the experiences of the previous week. While in Columbus, she spoke every day by telephone to her fiancé who, playing tapes and songs from the ministry's headquarters in Minneapolis, begged that she return to the fold. Susan expressed the desire to extricate her fiancé from the dominion of the cult.

Susan returned to Minneapolis on June 9. Unable to arrange a controlled meeting so that Susan could see her fiancé outside the presence of other members of the ministry, her parents asked that she sign an agreement releasing them from liability for their past weeks' actions. Refusing to do so, Susan stepped outside the Morgel residence with the puppy she had purchased in Ohio, motioned to a passing police car and shortly thereafter was reunited with her fiancé in the Minneapolis headquarters of The Way. Following her return to the ministry, she was directed to counsel and initiated the present action.

....Plaintiff seeks a judgment notwithstanding the verdict on the issue of false imprisonment, alleging that defendants unlawfully interfered with her personal liberty by words or acts which induced a reasonable apprehension that force would be used against her if she did not otherwise comply. [Citation.] The jury, instructed that an informed and reasoned consent is a defense to an allegation of false imprisonment and that a nonconsensual detention could be deemed consensual if one's behavior so indicated, exonerated defendants with respect to the false imprisonment claim.

The period in question... [covered] 16 days. The record clearly demonstrates that Susan willingly remained in the company of defendants for at least 13 of those days.

During that time she took many excursions into the public sphere, playing softball and picnicking in a city park, roller-skating at a public rink, flying aboard public aircraft and shopping and swimming while relaxing in Ohio. Had Susan desired, manifold opportunities existed for her to alert the authorities of her allegedly unlawful detention; in Minneapolis, two police officers observed at close range the softball game in which she engaged; en route to Ohio, she passed through the security areas of the Twin Cities and Columbus airports in the presence of security guards and uniformed police; in Columbus she transacted business at a bank, went for walks in solitude and was interviewed by an F.B.I. agent who sought assurances of her safety. At no time during the 13-day period did she complain of her treatment or suggest that defendants were holding her against her will. If one is aware of a reasonable means of escape that does not present a danger of bodily or material harm, a restriction is not total and complete and does not constitute unlawful imprisonment. Damages may not be assessed for any period of detention to which one freely consents. [Citations.]

....The central issue for the jury, then, was whether Susan voluntarily participated in the activities of the first three days. The jury concluded that her behavior constituted a waiver.

    ....

...[T]he behavior Susan manifested during the initial three days at issue must be considered in light of her actions in the remainder of the period. Because, it is argued, the cult conditioning process induces dramatic and non-consensual change giving rise to a new temporary identity on the part of the individuals whose consent is under examination, Susan's volitional capacity prior to treatment may well have been impaired. Following her readjustment, the evidence suggests that Susan was a different person, "like her old self." As such, the question of Susan's consent becomes a function of time. We therefore deem Susan's subsequent affirmation of defendants' actions dispositive.

    ....

....Although carried out under colorably religious auspices, the method of cult indoctrination, viewed in a light most favorable to the prevailing party, is predicated on a strategy of coercive persuasion that undermines the capacity for informed consent. While we acknowledge that other social institutions may utilize a degree of coercion in promoting their objectives, none do so to the same extent or intend the same consequences. Society, therefore, has a compelling interest favoring intervention. The facts in this case support the conclusion that plaintiff only regained her volitional capacity to consent after engaging in the first three days of the deprogramming process. As such, we hold that when parents, or their agents, acting under the conviction that the judgmental capacity of their adult child is impaired, seek to extricate that child from what they reasonably believe to be a religious or pseudo-religious cult, and the child at some juncture assents to the actions in question, limitations upon the child's mobility do not constitute meaningful deprivations of personal liberty sufficient to support a judgment for false imprisonment. But owing to the threat that deprogramming poses to public order, we do not endorse self-help as a preferred alternative....[2]

    ....

---

2. ...[S]ome courts have permitted the creation of temporary guardianships to allow the removal of cult members to therapeutic settings. If the individuals desire, at the end of the conservatorship they may return to the cult....

[The court further held that plaintiff's other arguments, relating in part to her intentional infliction of mental distress claim, did not warrant reversal.]

WAHL, Justice (dissenting in part, concurring in part).

I must respectfully dissent. In every generation, parents have viewed their children's religious and political beliefs with alarm and dismay if those beliefs were different from their own. Under the First Amendment, however, adults in our society enjoy freedoms of association and belief. In my view, it is unwise to tamper with those freedoms and with longstanding principles of tort law out of sympathy for parents seeking to help their "misguided" offspring, however well-intentioned and loving their acts may be....

.... Any imprisonment "which is not legally justifiable" is false imprisonment, [Citation]; therefore, the fact that the tortfeasor acted in good faith is no defense to a charge of false imprisonment....

The unrebutted evidence shows that defendant Norman Jungclaus, the father of the 21-year-old plaintiff in this case, took his adult daughter, kicking and screaming, to a small bedroom in the basement of the Morgel home on Monday, May 23. Norman Jungclaus admitted that she did not go with him willingly.... Defendant Perkins testified that plaintiff screamed and cried and pleaded with several people to let her go, but her pleas were ignored. This situation continued until 3 a.m. Tuesday. At one point that morning, plaintiff flew at her father, and he held her arms around her from the back, in his words, "for maybe a half an hour, until she calmed down again."....

....

The majority opinion finds, in plaintiff's behavior during the remainder of the 16 day period of "deprogramming," a reasonable basis for acquitting defendant Jungclaus of the false imprisonment charge for the initial three days, during which time he admittedly held plaintiff against her will. Under this theory, plaintiff's "acquiescence" in the later stages of deprogramming operates as consent which "relates back" to the events of the earlier three days, and constitutes a "waiver" of her claims for those days. Cases cited by the majority do not lend support to this proposition....

....

Certainly, parents who disapprove of or disagree with the religious beliefs of their adult offspring are free to exercise their own First Amendment rights in an attempt, by speech and persuasion without physical restraints, to change their adult children's minds. But parents who engage in tortious conduct in their "deprogramming" attempts do so at the risk that the deprogramming will be unsuccessful and the adult children will pursue tort remedies against their parents. To allow parents' "conviction that the judgmental capacity of their [adult] child is impaired [by her religious indoctrination]" to excuse their tortious conduct sets a dangerous precedent.

Here, the evidence clearly supported a verdict against Norman Jungclaus on the false imprisonment claim.... The trial court's holding in this regard should be reversed.

....

OTIS, Justice (dissenting in part).

I join in the views expressed by Justice Wahl, and particularly take issue with a rule which authorizes what is euphemistically described as "limitations upon the adult child's mobility" whenever a parent, or indeed a stranger acting for a parent, subjectively decides, without the benefit of a professional opinion or judicial intervention, that the adult child's "judgmental capacity" is impaired and that she should be "extricated" from what is deemed to be a religious or pseudo-religious cult.

. . . .

We furnish no guidelines or criteria for what constitutes "impaired judgmental capacity" other than the fact that the adult child has embraced an unorthodox doctrine with a zeal which has given the intervenor cause for alarm, a concern which may be well-founded, ill-founded or unfounded.

. . . .

At age 21, a daughter is no longer a child....Susan Peterson was not only an adult in 1976 but she was a bright, well-educated adult. For whatever reason, she was experiencing a period of restlessness and insecurity which is by no means uncommon in students of that age. But to hold that for seeking companionship and identity in a group whose proselyting tactics may well be suspect, she must endure without a remedy the degrading and humiliating treatment she received at the hands of her parents, is, in my opinion, totally at odds with the basic rights of young people to think unorthodox thoughts, join unorthodox groups, and proclaim unorthodox views. I would reverse the denial of recovery as to that cause of action.

Notes

1. One finds in the majority opinion threads of at least four different arguments:

(1) that plaintiff waived her right to sue for false imprisonment during the initial three-day confinement by failing to object or commence suit during the subsequent 13-day period;

(2) that during the three-day period plaintiff lacked the capacity either to consent or not consent, and therefore the confinement was not unconsented;

(3) that the confinement was not a "meaningful deprivation of liberty": *de minimis non curat lex*;

(4) that the parents had a privilege to engage in otherwise tortious conduct, perhaps on the ground that one may inflict lesser harm to prevent greater harm from occurring.

Which of these rationales is the most persuasive? The defenses of consent and private necessity will be examined in Chapter 3.

2. *Actions by Minor Children.* Some jurisdictions give parents great latitude in exercising control over their minor children. Courts may also be reluctant to impose liability on persons who assist parents in their efforts to discipline or control an unemancipated minor child. *See* R.D.J. v. Vaughan Clinic, P.C., 572 So. 2d 1225 (Ala. 1990) (holding that the trial court did not err in finding that none of the defendants "unlawfully detained" R.D.J. in treating her, because each defendant admitted her and provided treatment in reliance upon her mother's consent).

3. *Tort Liability of Religious "Cults."* A religious organization which engages in indoctrination through brainwashing, or other forms of coercive conduct, may be subject to tort liability. *See* Eilers v. Coy, 582 F. Supp. 1093 (D. Minn. 1984) (false imprisonment proved); Lewis v. Holy Spirit Ass'n for Unification, 589 F. Supp. 10, 12 (D. Mass. 1983) (an outrage action was "conceivable," but adequate facts were not alleged).

However, courts are reluctant to review the indoctrination practices, initiation procedures, or conditions of membership in religious organizations, in part because of the free-exercise-of-religion and free-association guarantees of the First Amendment. In Murphy v. I.S.K. Con. of New England, Inc., 571 N.E.2d 340 (Mass. 1991), an action by a mother and her minor daughter against practitioners of Krishna Consciousness, the court overturned a verdict for the plaintiffs because evidence admitted by the trial court had permitted the jury to punish the defendants for their beliefs, rather than their practices.

E. Trespass to Land

The tort of trespass to land ("trespass *quare clausum fregit*" or "trespass q.c.f.") protects a possessor's interest in exclusive possession of real property. A person who intentionally and without consent or privilege enters on, under, or above the land of another commits a trespass. Taking an unauthorized shortcut across the plaintiff's lot, tunneling under it, stringing utility lines above it, or building a structure on it may be trespasses.

Indirect invasions, like throwing trash onto property without personally crossing the boundary, are also actionable. If A deliberately pushes B onto C's land, A commits a trespass. Because B had no intent to enter, B will not be held liable unless B fails to leave the property with reasonable dispatch. In addition, one who enters property with the permission of the possessor commits a trespass by failing to leave once the consent has expired.

If the defendant's entry causes no harm, nominal damages will be awarded to vindicate the plaintiff's legal right to exclusive possession of the land. It is no defense to liability that the defendant was mistaken about the ownership of the property: all that is required is the intent to be present (or transferred intent); intent to be present *on someone else's land* is not necessary.

Although, strictly speaking, trespass q.c.f. is an intentional tort, some authorities speak of negligent or reckless trespasses. When they do, they are using the term "trespass" in a generic sense to refer to unprivileged physical presence on another's land. Negligent or reckless invasion of another's land is actionable if harm results.

Trespass to land is best considered in tandem with the tort of nuisance, an action which protects a possessor from non-trespassory interference with the use or enjoyment of land (such as the discomforts that result from bright lights, noise, and odors). Trespass q.c.f. and nuisance are considered in detail in Chapter 20.

F. Trespass to Chattels and Conversion

Two Tort Actions. The intentional exercise of dominion or control over another's personal property may give rise to an action for conversion or for trespass to chattels. (The latter tort is also known as trespass *de bonis asportatis*, or trespass d.b.a., and although the Latin means "for goods taken away," a "taking" is not essential to the tort). In general, conversion will lie in cases of major interference with the plaintiff's rights; trespass to chattels applies to relatively minor interference.

The distinction between conversion and trespass to chattels can be important because of the way in which damages are calculated. Conversion uses an unusual measure of damages, as explained in this excerpt from Pearson v. Dodd, 410 F.2d 701 (D.C. Cir. 1969):

> Conversion is the substantive tort theory which underlay the ancient common law form of action for trover. A plaintiff in trover alleged that he had lost a chattel which he rightfully possessed, and that the defendant had found it and converted it to his own use. With time, the allegations of losing and finding became fictional, leaving the question of whether the defendant had "converted" the property the only operative one.
>
> The most distinctive feature of conversion is its measure of damages, which is the value of the goods converted. The theory is that the "converting" defendant has in some way treated the goods as if they were his own, so that the plaintiff can properly ask the court to decree a forced sale of the property from the rightful possessor to the converter.
>
> Because of this stringent measure of damages, it has long been recognized that not every wrongful interference with the personal property of another is a conversion. Where the intermeddling falls short of the complete or very substantial deprivation of possessory rights in the property, the tort committed is not conversion, but the lesser wrong of trespass to chattels.
>
> The Second Restatement of Torts has marked the distinction by defining conversion as: "[A]n intentional exercise of dominion or control over a chattel which so seriously interferes with the right of another to control it that the actor may justly be required to pay the other the full value of the chattel."
>
> Less serious interferences fall under the Restatement's definition of trespass [d.b.a.]....

The difference is more than a semantic one. The measure of damages in trespass is not the whole value of the property interfered with, but rather the actual diminution in its value caused by the interference.

Kinds and Degrees of Interference. A person may interfere with a chattel by taking possession of it, using it, moving it from one place to another, transferring possession to a third person, withholding possession, or destroying or otherwise altering the chattel. Section 222A(2) of the Restatement, Second, of Torts provides that:

> In determining the seriousness of the interference and the justice of requiring the actor to pay the full value, the following factors are important:
>
> (a) the extent and duration of the actor's exercise of dominion and control;
>
> (b) the actor's intent to assert a right in fact inconsistent with the other's right of control;
>
> (c) the actor's good faith;
>
> (d) the extent and duration of the resulting interference with the other's right of control;
>
> (e) the harm done to the chattel;
>
> (f) the inconvenience and expense caused to the other.

"No one factor is always predominant in determining the seriousness of the interference...," nor is the proffered list "intended to be exclusive." *Id.* at cmt. d.

Intent Required. Conversion and trespass to chattels are intentional torts; the intent necessary is intent to affect the chattel. Good motives are no defense, and, while a mistake of fact or law will not preclude a finding of intent, mistake may bear upon whether the actor can establish a privilege *See id.* at §§217 and 244; privileges, such as public and private necessity, are discussed in Chapter 3.

Unintentional harmful interference with personal property may be actionable under the principles of negligence, recklessness, or strict liability.

CompuServe Inc. v. Cyber Promotions, Inc.

United States District Court for the Southern District of Ohio
962 F. Supp. 1015 (S.D. Ohio 1997)

GRAHAM, District Judge.

....

Plaintiff CompuServe Incorporated ("CompuServe") is one of the major national commercial online computer services.... CompuServe... provides its subscribers with a link to the much larger resources of the Internet. This allows its subscribers to send and receive electronic messages, known as "e-mail," by the Internet. Defendants Cyber Promotions, Inc. and its president Sanford Wallace are in the business of sending unsolicited e-mail advertisements on behalf of themselves and their clients to hundreds of thousands of Internet users, many of whom are CompuServe subscribers. CompuServe has notified defendants that they are prohibited from using its computer equipment to process and store the unsolicited e-mail and has requested that they terminate the practice. Instead, defendants have sent an increasing volume of e-mail solicitations....

....

In an effort to shield its equipment from defendants' bulk e-mail, CompuServe has implemented software programs designed to screen out the messages and block their receipt. In response, defendants have modified their equipment and the messages they send in such a fashion as to circumvent CompuServe's screening software....

....

The Restatement §217(b) states that a trespass to chattel may be committed by intentionally using or intermeddling with the chattel in possession of another. Restatement §217, Comment e defines physical "intermeddling" as follows:

> ... intentionally bringing about a physical contact with the chattel....

Electronic signals generated and sent by computer have been held to be sufficiently physically tangible to support a trespass cause of action. Thrifty-Tel, Inc., v. Bezenek,... [54 Cal. Rptr.2d 468 (Cal. Ct. App. 1996)]; State v. McGraw, 480 N.E.2d 552, 554 (Ind.1985) (...recognizing in dicta that a hacker's unauthorized access to a computer was more in the nature of trespass than criminal conversion); and State v. Riley,... [846 P.2d 1365 (Wash. 1993)] (computer hacking as the criminal offense of "computer trespass" under Washington law). It is undisputed that plaintiff has a possessory interest in its computer systems. Further, defendants' contact with plaintiff's computers is clearly intentional. Although electronic messages may travel through the Internet over various routes, the messages are affirmatively directed to their destination.

Defendants, citing Restatement (Second) of Torts §221, which defines "dispossession," assert that not every interference with the personal property of another is actionable and that physical dispossession or substantial interference with the chattel is required. Defendants then argue that they did not, in this case, physically dispossess plaintiff of its equipment or substantially interfere with it. However, the Restatement (Second) of Torts §218 defines the circumstances under which a trespass to chattels may be actionable:

> One who commits a trespass to a chattel is subject to liability to the possessor of the chattel if, but only if,
>
> (a) he dispossesses the other of the chattel, or
>
> (b) the chattel is impaired as to its condition, quality, or value, or
>
> (c) the possessor is deprived of the use of the chattel for a substantial time, or
>
> (d) bodily harm is caused to the possessor, or harm is caused to some person or thing in which the possessor has a legally protected interest.

Therefore, an interference resulting in physical dispossession is just one circumstance under which a defendant can be found liable. Defendants suggest that "[u]nless an alleged trespasser actually takes physical custody of the property or physically damages it, courts will not find the 'substantial interference' required to maintain a trespass to chattel claim." (Defendant's Memorandum at 13). To support this rather broad proposition, defendants cite only two cases which make any reference to the Restatement. In Glidden v. Szybiak,...[63 A.2d 233 (N.H. 1949)], the court simply indicated that an action for trespass to chattels could not be maintained in the absence of some form of damage. The court held that where plaintiff did not contend that defendant's pulling on her pet dog's ears caused any injury, an action in tort could not be maintained. *Id.* 63 A.2d at 235. In contrast, plaintiff in the present action has alleged that it has suffered several types if injury as a result of defendants' conduct. In Koepnick v. Sears Roebuck & Co.,...[762 P.2d 609 (Ariz. 1988)] the court held that a two-minute search of an individual's truck did not amount to a "dispossession" of the truck as defined in Restatement §221 or a deprivation of the use of the truck for a substantial time. It is clear from a reading of Restatement §218 that an interference or intermeddling that does not fit the §221 definition of "dispossession" can nonetheless result in defendants' liability for trespass. The *Koepnick* court did not discuss any of the other grounds for liability under Restatement §218.

....In the present case, any value CompuServe realizes from its computer equipment is wholly derived from the extent to which that equipment can serve its subscriber base. Michael Mangino, a software developer for CompuServe..., states by affidavit that handling the enormous volume of mass mailings that CompuServe receives places a tremendous burden on its equipment. [Citation.] Defendants' more recent practice of evading CompuServe's filters by disguising the origin of their messages commandeers even more computer resources because CompuServe's computers are forced to store undeliverable e-mail messages and labor in vain to return the messages to an address that does not exist. [Citation.] To the extent that defendants' multitudinous electronic mailings demand the disk space and drain the processing power of plaintiff's computer equipment, those resources are not available to serve CompuServe subscribers. Therefore, the value of that equipment to CompuServe is diminished even though it is not physically damaged by defendants' conduct.

Next, plaintiff asserts that it has suffered injury aside from the physical impact of defendants' messages on its equipment. Restatement §218(d) also indicates that recovery may be had for a trespass that causes harm to something in which the possessor has a legally protected interest. Plaintiff asserts that defendants' messages are largely unwanted by its subscribers, who pay incrementally to access their e-mail, read it, and discard it. . . . These inconveniences decrease the utility of CompuServe's e-mail service and are the foremost subject in recent complaints from CompuServe subscribers. . . . Defendants contend that CompuServe subscribers are provided with a simple procedure to remove themselves from the mailing list. However, the removal procedure must be performed by the e-mail recipient at his expense, and some CompuServe subscribers complain that the procedure is inadequate. . . .

Many subscribers have terminated their accounts specifically because of the unwanted receipt of bulk e-mail messages. [Citation.] Defendants' intrusions into CompuServe's computer systems, insofar as they harm plaintiff's business reputation and goodwill with its customers, are actionable under Restatement §218(d).

. . . . [D]efendants' persistent affirmative efforts to evade plaintiff's security measures have circumvented any protection those self-help measures might have provided. . . . However, . . . the implementation of technological means of self-help, to the extent that reasonable measures are effective, is particularly appropriate in this type of situation and should be exhausted before legal action is proper.

. . . .

[The court held that the free speech guarantees of the First Amendment did not provide a defense for the defendant's conduct because the plaintiff is a private company.]

Defendants' intentional use of plaintiff's proprietary computer equipment . . . after repeated demands that defendants cease . . . is an actionable trespass to plaintiff's chattel. . . .

. . . .

Normally, a preliminary injunction is not appropriate where an ultimate award of monetary damages will suffice. [Citation.] However, money damages are only adequate if they can be reasonably computed and collected. Plaintiff has demonstrated that defendants' intrusions into their computer systems harm plaintiff's business reputation and goodwill. This is the sort of injury that warrants the issuance of a preliminary injunction because the actual loss is impossible to compute. [Citations.]

. . . . It is so ORDERED.

Notes

1. *See* Intel Corp. v. Hamidi, 71 P.3d 296 (Cal. 2003) (holding that trespass to chattels does not encompass electronic communications that neither damage the recipient computer system nor impair its functioning; temporary use of some portion of computer processors or storage is not cognizable injury, nor is loss of productivity caused by employee's reading or trying to block unwanted messages).

2. *Dispossession.* Section 218 of the Second Restatement now makes clear that damage will be inferred from any "dispossession." A plaintiff "may recover at least nominal damages for the loss of possession, even though it is of brief duration and he is not deprived of the use of the chattel for any substantial length of time." Restatement, Second, of Torts §218 cmt. d. However:

> [A]n intermeddling with a chattel is not a dispossession unless the actor intends to exercise a dominion and control over it inconsistent with a possession in any person other than himself. Thus, a trivial removal of a chattel from one

position to another with no intention to exercise further control over it or deprive the possessor of its use is not a dispossession.

Id. at §221 cmt. b.

3. In Johnson v. Weedman, 5 Ill. 495 (1843), the defendant, a bailee, rode the plaintiff's horse fifteen miles, contrary to the terms of the bailment. In an action for conversion, in which the defendant was represented by Abraham Lincoln, the court held that there was no conversion and that the plaintiff was entitled only to nominal damages, as the unauthorized ride caused no injury to the horse.

Zaslow v. Kroenert

Supreme Court of California, in Bank
176 P.2d 1 (Cal. 1946)

EDMONDS, Justice.

[Plaintiff Zaslow and Defendant Kroenert owned a house as tenants in common, which contained furniture belonging to the former. During a property dispute, Defendant and one Chapman entered the house and changed the locks. They removed and placed in storage plaintiff's furniture, after informing him that they would do so if he failed to remove it. At some time thereafter, plaintiff was informed of the furniture's location, but, rather than retrieve it, sued for conversion and recovered a judgment for $3,500. Defendant appeals.]....

.... "Conversion is any act of dominion wrongfully exerted over another's personal property in denial of or inconsistent with his rights therein." [Citations.] The liability of one in possession of real property for the conversion of personal property which he finds upon it, depends in most cases, upon a determination of whether the conduct of the defendant indicates an assumption of control or ownership over the goods.... [U]nder some circumstances, refusal of one in possession of real property to permit, upon demand, the owner of chattels which were left there to remove his goods, constitutes conversion. [Citations.] And if the possessor of the real estate appropriates the chattels to his own use in obvious defiance of the owner's rights, he is liable to the owner for the conversion of them. [Citations.]

However, every failure to deliver is not such a serious interference with the owner's dominion that the defendant should be required to pay the full value of the goods. [Citation.] And the act of taking possession of a building and locking it does not, of itself, constitute a conversion of the personal property therein.... Thus, in Poor v. Oakman,... [104 Mass. 309], a person rightfully took possession of a building and put a new lock on the door. He knew that the owner of some furniture then in the building had a key to the old lock. It was held that, in the absence of any evidence tending to prove a claim to the furniture, or any act which hindered the owner from removing it, as the contest was for the possession of the building, the possessor of the real estate was not liable for conversion of the furniture.... And ordinarily the courts have declared that one rightfully in possession of real property who removes, to a warehouse or other place, chattels found on it belonging to another, does not assert ownership or control over them to the extent of making him liable for conversion. [Citation.]

...[T]he court found only that Mrs. Kroenert and Chapman "took and carried away all the personal property and effects" of Zaslow, such taking being without his consent, express or implied. Admittedly, what Chapman did in this regard was to place the goods in storage: there is no evidence tending to prove that either he or Mrs. Kroenert other-wise exerted any dominion over Zaslow's personal property in denial of or inconsistent with his rights. If, upon demand for the return of the chattels, they had prevented the removal of the goods, such acts would have constituted evidence of a conversion. But here...no demand was made for the return of the personal property. While there is no evidence showing any conduct amounting to conversion, there is proof that Chapman, as the agent of Mrs. Kroenert, acted as custodian of the goods, recognizing Zaslow's complete title and right to them. The defendants did not use the goods. About a month and one-half after Mrs. Kroenert, by Chapman, took possession of the realty, she stated in a letter either received by or shown to Zaslow, that he could secure possession of his personal property by applying at the attorney's office. Zaslow neither said nor did any-thing in response thereto.

Where the conduct complained of does not amount to a substantial interference with possession or the right thereto..., the owner has a cause of action for trespass or case, and may recover only the actual damages suffered by reason of the impairment of the property or the loss of its use. [Citation.] As Zaslow was a cotenant and had the right of possession of the realty, which included the right to keep his personal property thereon, Chapman's act of placing the goods in storage, although not con-stituting the assertion of ownership and a substantial interference with possession to the extent of a conversion, amounted to an intermeddling. Therefore, Zaslow is enti-tled to actual damages in an amount sufficient to compensate him for any impair-ment of the property or loss of its use. But as the evidence shows $3,500 as the high-est value placed upon the goods and it is undisputed that they were not damaged while in storage for about four months, the amount awarded by the judgment has no support in the evidence

.... [T]he judgment is reversed with directions to the trial court to redetermine the amount of damages....

Notes

1. *See also* Russell v. American Real Estate Corp., 89 S.W.3d 204 (Tex. App. 2002) (in a case where a tenant's belongings were removed from a house, the defendant commit-ted trespass to personal property with respect to items that were promptly returned upon request, and conversion with respect to items that were damaged or lost).

2. *Demand for Return.* The mere retention of goods which the defendant obtained legitimately does not constitute conversion unless the plaintiff demands their return, and the demand is refused (*see* Kansas City Diesel Power Co., Inc. v. Kirloskar, Inc., 647 S.W.2d 841, 845 (Mo. Ct. App. 1983)), or unless there is some other independent act of conversion (see Frost v. Eggeman, 638 P.2d 141, 144 (Wyo. 1981)).

In Moorehouse v. Chase Manhattan Bank, 76 S.W.3d 608 (Tex. App. 2002), the plaintiff, who wished to cash a check, was paid five dollars less than the face value of the check because the bank charged a fee for services to non-customers. The court held that the check was not converted, even though the plaintiff personally objected and re-quested a receipt for the fee, because she did not demand return of the check, nor did the bank refuse to return it.

Proof of a refused demand is not required if the demand would have been useless. Thus, there is no need to demand return from a thief. *See* State v. Seventh Regiment Fund, Inc., 774 N.E.2d 702 (N.Y. 2002).

3. *Qualified Refusal.* A person does not become a converter merely by making a qualified refusal to surrender a chattel under circumstances making immediate surrender unreasonable, as in the case of goods not readily accessible or a demand made after business has closed. *See* Restatement, Second, of Torts §238 and Comments b and c. In most cases, refusal to return goods before checking on the claimant's right to them is permissible. *See id.* at §§239 and 240.

4. *Bona Fide Purchasers.* A person who obtains property through theft or fraud is liable for conversion. So is one who later acquires the goods with notice of their illegitimate origin. *See* Morrow Shoe Mfg. Co. v. New England Shoe Co., 57 F. 685 (7th Cir. 1893) (auctioneer had notice of fraud).

Whether a subsequent good faith purchaser of improperly acquired goods is liable for conversion depends upon the manner in which the goods were first procured. A thief has no title to stolen property and can pass no rights to a subsequent party. Hence, a subsequent bona fide purchaser who pays full value is a converter. *See* Lovinger v. Hix Green Buick Co., 140 S.E.2d 83 (Ga. Ct. App. 1964); Restatement, Second, of Torts §229 cmt. d.

A defrauder, in contrast, has "voidable" title to goods acquired by fraud. Although the victim of the fraud may equitably rescind the transaction and sue the defrauder for conversion, a bona fide purchase cuts off any equitable rights and precludes suit by the fraud victim against the good faith purchaser (but not against the person who committed the fraud). *See* Guckeen Farmers Elevator Co. v. South Soo Grain Co., 109 N.W.2d 728 (Neb. 1961); Restatement, Second, of Torts §229 cmt. d.

These rules produce the anomalous result that some bona fide purchasers are liable for conversion and others are not. This disparity reflects the law's efforts to strike a workable balance between the need for consumers to have confidence in commercial transactions and the need of possessors for property protection. The differing treatment of bona fide purchasers can be justified on the ground that there is greater reason to protect possessors from losses by theft, to which they have never consented, than from losses by fraud, where consent was given and there was some opportunity to scrutinize the facts.

Special rules apply to certain commercial dealings. For example, Uniform Commercial Code §2-403(2) (Westlaw 2002) provides that "[a]ny entrusting of possession of goods to a merchant who deals in goods of that kind gives him power to transfer all rights of the entruster to a buyer in the ordinary course of business."

5. *Bailees.* Detailed rules have evolved to protect bailees—persons temporarily holding goods belonging to others. The rules seek to avoid the inconvenience and delay of requiring bailees to inquire into the title of the items delivered to them. In general, at common law:

(a) A bailee without notice that a chattel is lost or stolen is not liable for conversion merely by reason of receiving it. *See* Williams v. Roberts, 1 S.E.2d 587 (Ga. Ct. App. 1939).

(b) A bailee who, without notice of other claims, redelivers a chattel to its bailor is not liable for conversion, even though the bailor is not the rightful possessor. *See* Thomas v. D.C. Andrews & Co., 54 F.2d 250 (2d Cir. 1931).

(c) A bailee who redelivers a chattel to one entitled to immediate possession is not liable to the actual bailor for conversion. *See* Texas Diamond Int'l v. Tiffany & Co., 47 S.W.3d 589, 592 (Tex. App. 2001); Restatement, Second, of Torts §234 cmt. d.

On the other hand:

> (d) A bailee with knowledge or reason to know that the bailor has no right to deliver the chattel becomes liable for conversion by receiving the goods. *See* Restatement, Second, of Torts §230.

> (e) A bailee with notice of multiple claims to a chattel is under an absolute duty to redeliver the chattel to its true owner. *See* Edwards v. Max Thieme Chevrolet Co., 191 So. 569 (La. Ct. App. 1939). (The bailee's difficulty may be avoided by a relatively simple procedure whereby, pursuant to statute, the bailee deposits the goods in court and asks the court to resolve the dispute. *See* Cass v. Higenbotam, 3 N.E. 189, 192 (N.Y. 1885).)

Russell-Vaughn Ford, Inc. v. Rouse

Supreme Court of Alabama
206 So. 2d 371 (Ala. 1968)

SIMPSON, Justice.

[Appellee Rouse went to Russell-Vaughn Ford, Inc., to discuss trading his Falcon in on a new Ford. One of the salesmen asked Mr. Rouse for the keys to his Falcon. The keys were given to him and Mr. Rouse looked at new cars for a time and then proceeded with the negotiations. The salesman offered to trade a new Ford for the Falcon, plus $2,400; plaintiff declined to trade on this basis.]

....Mr. Rouse asked for the return of the keys to the Falcon....[B]oth salesmen... said that they did not know where the keys were. Mr. Rouse then asked several people who appeared to be employees of Russell-Vaughn for the keys....Several mechanics and salesmen were, according to plaintiff's testimony, sitting around on cars looking at him and laughing at him.

After a period of time the plaintiff called the police....Shortly after the arrival of the policeman..., the salesman Parker threw the keys to Mr. Rouse with the statement that he was a cry baby and that "they just wanted to see him cry a while."

....

....The jury returned a general verdict in favor of the plaintiff in the amount of $5,000....

....Initially it is argued that the facts of this case do not make out a case of conversion. It is argued that the conversion if at all, is a conversion of the keys to the automobile, not of the automobile itself....We are not persuaded that the law of Alabama supports this proposition....

> ...[C]onversion may consist, not only in an appropriation of the property to one's own use, but in its destruction, *or in exercising dominion over it in exclusion or defiance of plaintiff's right....*

....A remarkable admission...was elicited by the plaintiff in examining one of the witnesses for the defense. It seems that according to [a] salesman for Russell-Vaughn Ford, Inc. it is a rather usual practice in the automobile business to "lose keys" to cars belonging to potential customers....

Further, appellants argue that there was no conversion since the plaintiff could have called his wife, at home, who had another set of keys and thereby gained the ability to move his automobile. We find nothing in our cases which would require the plaintiff to exhaust all possible means of gaining possession of a chattel which is withheld from him by the defendant, after demanding its return....

....In Compton v. Sims,...[96 So. 185 (Ala. 1923)] this court sustained a finding that there had been a conversion of cotton where the defendant refused to deliver to the plaintiff "warehouse tickets" which would have enabled him to gain possession of the cotton. The court spoke of the warehouse tickets as a symbol of the cotton and found that the retention of them amounted to a conversion of the cotton. So here, we think that the withholding from the plaintiff after demand of the keys to his automobile, without which he could not move it, amounted to a conversion of the automobile.

....[The amount of the verdict was not excessive because an award of punitive damages was justified by the evidence.]

....

Affirmed.

Notes

1. *Damages for Conversion.* The rules governing damages in conversion cases are complex. *See generally* Restatement, Second, Torts §911 and 927. In general:

a. *Time and Place.* In the usual case, the plaintiff is entitled to recover the market value of the chattel—what a willing buyer would pay a willing seller when neither is compelled to buy or to sell—at the time and place of the conversion. Successive converters may therefore be liable for different amounts. Where one person commits serial acts of conversion (*e.g.*, by stealing the chattel, refusing a demand to return it, and then destroying it), each conversion may give rise to a different amount of damages, and the plaintiff may elect to recover damages based on any one of the conversions, although damages for conversion may be recovered only once.

b. *Unmarketable and Irreplaceable Items.* Some items, such as a personal manuscript, an artificial eye, or a dog trained to obey only one master, are unmarketable, in the sense that they have little value to persons other than the owner. In these cases, damages are limited to replacement value, less an amount for depreciation.

If a chattel cannot be replaced, as in the case of a family portrait, the owner may recover an amount for its special value to the owner, as evidenced by its original cost and its condition at the time of the loss.

Traditionally, sentimental value has been disregarded in calculating damages. *See* MacGregor v. Watts, 5 N.Y.S.2d 525 (App. Div. 1938). However, some courts have endorsed a less restrictive rule. The defendant in Mieske v. Bartell Drug Co., 593 P.2d 1308 (Wash. 1979), negligently lost thirty-two rolls of movie film which contained pictures, taken over several decades, of plaintiff and his family. The court affirmed an award of $7500, noting that "the [only] type of sentiment which is not compensable is that which relates to 'indulging in feeling to an unwarranted extent' or 'being affectedly or mawkishly emotional.'" The jury instruction, which allowed an award for the "actual or intrinsic value" of the film to the plaintiffs, but denied recovery of "unusual sentimental value," was deemed correct.

c. *Commodities.* In the case of commodities which fluctuate in value, such as stocks, bonds, other securities, and fungible goods such as grain, cotton, and oil, most courts agree that the plaintiff may recover the highest value of the commodity between the date of the conversion and a reasonable time for replacement. This rule prevents defendants from appropriating the speculative possibilities of increases in market values, while encouraging plaintiffs to mitigate damages by securing replacements.

   d. *Mental Distress*. Damages for mental distress may be awarded if the defendant should have foreseen that psychic suffering would follow from the tort. In Fredeen v. Stride, 525 P.2d 166 (Or. 1974), a veterinarian advised the plaintiff, who could not afford expensive surgery for her injured dog, to have the dog put to sleep. Although plaintiff reluctantly agreed, the doctor failed to carry out the agreement and gave the dog to a third person. The plaintiff learned what had happened several months later. The court upheld an award of mental distress damages in a conversion action.

   e. *Punitive Damages*. Punitive damages may be awarded in cases involving particularly outrageous conduct.

2. *Damages for Loss of a Pet*. Most states limit recovery for the tortious death of a pet to the animal's market value, which is usually so low that it is not worthwhile for the owner to sue. Some writers have argued that damages should include an amount in compensation of the lost relationship between the owner and pet. *See* Debra Squires-Lee, *Note, In Defense of Floyd: Appropriately Valuing Companion Animals in Tort*, 70 N.Y.U. L. Rev. 1059 (1995). There is some evidence that the law may be beginning to change. *See* Cherie Song, *Pet Deaths Trigger Pain, Suffering Suits*, Nat'l L.J., Jul. 14, 2003, at 4 (stating that some companion-animal emotional distress claims survive motions to dismiss). Indeed, a few states have recently enacted statutes providing for civil liability for non-economic damages relating to the death or injury of a pet. For example:

TENN. CODE ANN. §44-17-403
(Westlaw 2004)

   (a) If a person's pet is killed or sustains injuries which result in death caused by the unlawful and intentional, or negligent, act of another or the animal of another, the trier of fact may find the individual causing the death or the owner of the animal causing the death liable for up to four thousand dollars ($4,000) in non-economic damages....

   (b) As used in this section, "pet" means any domesticated dog or cat normally maintained in or near the household of its owner.

   (c) Limits for non-economic damages set out in subsection (a) shall not apply to causes of action for intentional infliction of emotional distress or any other civil action other than the direct and sole loss of a pet.

   (d) Non-economic damages awarded pursuant to this section shall be limited to compensation for the loss of the reasonably expected society, companionship, love and affection of the pet.

   (e) This section shall not...be construed to authorize any award of non-economic damages in an action for professional negligence against a licensed veterinarian....

ILL. COMP. STAT. 70/16.3
(Westlaw 2004)

   Any person who has a right of ownership in an animal that is subjected to an act of aggravated cruelty...or torture...in violation of this Act or in an animal that is injured or killed as a result of actions taken by a person who acts in bad faith...under...this Act may bring a civil action to recover the damages sustained by that owner. Damages may include, but are not limited to, the monetary value of the animal, veterinary expenses incurred on behalf of the animal, any other expenses incurred by the owner in rectifying the effects of the cruelty, pain, and suffering of the animal, and emotional distress suffered by the owner. In addition..., the owner is also entitled to punitive or exemplary damages of not less than $500 but not more than $25,000 for each act of abuse or neglect....In addition, the court must award reasonable attorney's fees and costs....

The remedies provided in this Section are in addition to any other remedies allowed by law.

In an action under this Section, the court may enter any injunctive orders reasonably necessary to protect animals from any further acts of abuse, neglect, or harassment by a defendant....

3. *Ethics in Law Practice: Treatment of Client Property.* Lawyers often hold money or property for clients. For example, a client may advance funds to pay expenses of litigation (filing fees, expert witness costs, etc.) as they are incurred, or the lawyer may receive from a third person the proceeds of an executed court judgment or an amount paid in settlement of a claim. An attorney who appropriates client funds or property for personal use is subject not merely to a tort action (such as an action for conversion or fraud), but to professional discipline such as suspension from practice or disbarment. *See* Vincent Uchendu, *Attorney's Commingling, Misappropriation, and Conversion of Client's Funds: Sanctions,* 31 How. L.J. 331 (1988).

In an effort to avoid appearances of impropriety and to reduce the likelihood of harm to clients, the legal profession has adopted stringent rules for handling client funds and property. Rule 1.15 of the American Bar Association's Model Rules of Professional Conduct (2003) provides in part:

(a) A lawyer shall hold property of clients or third persons that is in a lawyer's possession in connection with a representation separate from the lawyer's own property. Funds shall be kept in a separate account....Other property shall be identified as such and appropriately safeguarded. Complete records of such account funds and other property shall be kept...[for a period of years].

....

(d) Upon receiving funds or other property in which a client or third person has an interest, a lawyer shall promptly notify the client or third person... [and] promptly deliver to the client or third person any funds or other property that the client or third person is entitled to receive and...render a full accounting regarding such property....

Similar duties are owed to prospective clients. *See* In Re Spencer, 58 P.3d 228 (Or. 2002) (attorney suspended for 60 days for allowing documents entrusted by would-be client to be destroyed).

Commingling—the failure to segregate clients' property from the lawyer's—is a serious breach of ethical standards, even if the infraction is unintentional. Commingling not only creates an appearance of impropriety and subjects the client's property to jeopardy, it is often the first step toward conversion.

4. *Replevin.* Someone whose property has been converted may wish to recover the chattel itself rather than receive the proceeds of the forced judicial sale which is the usual result of a conversion action. One alternative is to sue for replevin. An action for replevin allows the plaintiff to recover possession of the chattel *in specie*, and to recover incidental damages.

A number of replevin actions have arisen from the recent worldwide explosion in art theft. *See* Solomon R. Guggenheim Foundation v. Lubell, 569 N.E.2d 426 (N.Y. 1991) (Marc Chagall gouache); Mucha v. King, 792 F.2d 602 (7th Cir. 1986) (Art Nouveau poster by Alphonse Mucha, a famous Czech artist); O'Keeffe v. Snyder, 416 A.2d 862 (N.J. 1980) (paintings by Georgia O'Keeffe). When artwork has been missing for many years and has passed through various hands, issues of when the plaintiff's cause of action first accrues and whether transfers subsequent to the initial conversion are subject to a new period of limitations may arise.

In *O'Keeffe*, the court held that the plaintiff's cause of action accrues according to a "discovery rule":

> O'Keeffe's cause of action accrued when she first knew, or reasonably should have known through the exercise of due diligence, of the cause of action, including the identity of the possessor of the paintings.
>
> ....
>
> ...[U]nder the discovery rule, if an artist diligently seeks the recovery of a lost or stolen painting, but cannot find it or discover the identity of the possessor, the statute of limitations will not begin to run. The rule permits an artist who uses reasonable efforts to report, investigate, and recover a painting to preserve the rights of title and possession.

416 A.2d at 870–72. The court rejected the plaintiff's argument that each transfer of a chattel subsequent to the initial conversion was a separate act of conversion sufficient to start the statute of limitations running anew. Finding that the plaintiff's proposed rule would "tend to undermine the purpose of the statute in quieting titles and protecting against stale claims," the court said that the "majority and better view is to permit tacking, the accumulation of consecutive periods of possession by parties in privity with each other." *Id.* at 875. Under this view, the statute of limitations runs only once in cases of continuous dispossession, regardless of the number of acts of conversion. "The important point is not that there has been a substitution of possessors, but that there has been a continuous dispossession of the former owner." *Id.* at 874–75. *Accord* Restatement, Second, of Torts §899 cmt. c.

Kremen v. Cohen

United States Court of Appeals for the Ninth Circuit
337 F.3d 1024 (9th Cir. 2003)

KOZINSKI, Circuit Judge.

....

"Sex on the Internet?," they all said. "*That*'ll never make any money." But computer-geek-turned-entrepreneur Gary Kremen knew an opportunity when he saw it. The year was 1994; domain names were free for the asking.... With a quick e-mail to the domain name registrar Network Solutions, Kremen became the proud owner of sex.com. He registered the name to his business, Online Classifieds, and listed himself as the contact.

Con man Stephen Cohen, meanwhile, was doing time for impersonating a bankruptcy lawyer. He, too, saw the potential of the domain name.... Once out of prison, he sent Network Solutions what purported to be a letter he had received from Online Classifieds. It claimed the company had been "forced to dismiss Mr. Kremen," but "never got around to changing our administrative contact with the internet registration [sic] and now our Board of directors has decided to *abandon* the domain name sex.com." Why was this unusual letter being sent via Cohen rather than to Network Solutions directly? It explained:

> Because we do not have a direct connection to the internet, we request that you notify the internet registration on our behalf, to delete our domain name sex.com. Further, we have no objections to your use of the domain name sex.com and this letter shall serve as our authorization to the internet registration to transfer sex.com to your corporation.

Despite the letter's transparent claim that a company called "*Online* Classifieds" had no Internet connection, Network Solutions made no effort to contact Kremen. Instead, it accepted the letter at face value and transferred the domain name to Cohen. When Kremen contacted Network Solutions some time later, he was told it was too late to undo the transfer. Cohen went on to turn sex.com into a lucrative online porn empire.

.... [Kremen obtained a judgment against Cohen but was unable to collect it because Cohen "skipped the country, and his money is stashed in some offshore bank account."]

...Kremen seeks to hold someone else responsible for his losses. That someone is Network Solutions, the exclusive domain name registrar at the time of Cohen's antics. Kremen...argues that Network Solutions was a "bailee" of his domain name and seeks to hold it liable for "conversion by bailee."

....

Kremen...had an intangible property right in his domain name, and a jury could find that Network Solutions "wrongful[ly] dispos[ed] of" that right to his detriment by handing the domain name over to Cohen. [Citation.] The district court nevertheless rejected Kremen's conversion claim. It held that domain names, although a form of property, are intangibles not subject to conversion. This rationale derives from a distinction tort law once drew between tangible and intangible property: Conversion was originally a remedy for the wrongful taking of another's lost goods, so it applied only to tangible property. [Citation.] Virtually every jurisdiction, however, has discarded this rigid limitation to some degree. [Citation.] Many courts ignore or expressly reject it. [Citations, including Astroworks, Inc. v. Astroexhibit, Inc., 257 F. Supp. 2d 609, 618 (S.D.N.Y.2003) (holding that the plaintiff could maintain a claim for conversion of his website).] Others reject it for some intangibles but not others. The *Restatement*, for example, recommends the following test:

> (1) Where there is conversion of a document in which intangible rights are merged, the damages include the value of such rights.

> (2) One who effectively prevents the exercise of intangible rights of the kind customarily *merged in a document* is subject to a liability similar to that for conversion, even though the document is not itself converted.

Restatement (Second) of Torts § 242 (1965) (emphasis added). An intangible is "merged" in a document when, "by the appropriate rule of law, the right to the immediate possession of a chattel and the power to acquire such possession is *represented by* [the] document," or when "an intangible obligation [is] *represented by* [the] document, which is regarded as equivalent to the obligation.".... [6] The district court applied this test and found no evidence that Kremen's domain name was merged in a document.

The court assumed that California follows the Restatement on this issue. Our review, however, revealed that "there do not appear to be any California cases squarely addressing whether the 'merged with' requirement is a part of California law."....

We conclude that California does not follow the *Restatement's* strict merger requirement....

....

...[I]n Palm Springs-La Quinta Development Co. v. Kieberk Corp., 46 Cal. App.2d 234, 115 P.2d 548 (1941), the court of appeal allowed a conversion claim for intangible information in a customer list when some of the index cards on which the information was recorded were destroyed. The court allowed damages not just for the value of the cards, but for the value of the intangible information lost. [Citation.] Section 242(1) of the Restatement, however, allows recovery for intangibles only if they are merged in the converted document. Customer information is not merged in a document in any meaningful sense. A Rolodex is not like a stock certificate that actually *represents* a property interest; it is only a means of recording information.

....

California courts ignored the Restatement again in A & M Records, Inc. v. Heilman, 75 Cal. App.3d 554, 142 Cal. Rptr. 390 (1977), which applied the tort to a defendant who sold bootlegged copies of musical recordings. The court held broadly that "such misappropriation and sale of the intangible property of another without authority from the owner is conversion." [Citation.] It gave no hint that its holding depended on whether the owner's intellectual property rights were merged in some document. One might imagine physical things with which the intangible was associated—for example, the medium on which the song was recorded. But an intangible intellectual property right in a song is not merged in a phonograph record in the sense that the record *represents* the composer's intellectual property right. The record is not like a certificate of ownership; it is only a medium for one instantiation of the artistic work.

....

In short, California does not follow the Restatement's strict requirement that some document must actually represent the owner's intangible property right. On the contrary, courts routinely apply the tort to intangibles without inquiring whether they are merged in a document and, while it's often possible to dream up *some* document the intangible is connected to in some fashion, it's seldom one that represents the owner's property interest.... [Endorsement of a] strict merger rule...is against the weight of authority. That rule cannot be squared with a jurisprudence that recognizes conversion of music recordings, radio shows, customer lists, regulatory filings, confidential information and even domain names.

Were it necessary to settle the issue once and for all, we would toe the line...and hold that conversion is "a remedy for the conversion of every species of personal property." [Citation.] But we need not do so to resolve this case. Assuming *arguendo* that

---

6. The *Restatement* does note that conversion "has been applied by some courts in cases where the converted document is not in itself a symbol of the rights in question, but is merely essential to their protection and enforcement, as in the case of account books and receipts." *Id.* cmt. b.

California retains some vestigial merger requirement, it is clearly minimal, and at most requires only *some* connection to a document or tangible object—not representation of the owner's intangible interest in the strict *Restatement* sense.

Kremen's domain name falls easily within this class of property. He argues that the relevant document is the Domain Name System, or "DNS"—the distributed electronic database that associates domain names like sex.com with particular computers connected to the Internet. We agree that the DNS is a document (or perhaps more accurately a collection of documents). That it is stored in electronic form rather than on ink and paper is immaterial. *See, e.g., Thrifty-Tel,* 46 Cal. App.4th at 1565, 54 Cal. Rptr. 2d 468 (recognizing conversion of information recorded on floppy disk); *A & M Records,* 75 Cal. App.3d at 570, 142 Cal. Rptr. 390 (same for audio record); *Lone Ranger Television,* 740 F.2d at 725 (same for magnetic tape). It would be a curious jurisprudence that turned on the existence of a *paper* document rather than an electronic one. Torching a company's file room would then be conversion while hacking into its mainframe and deleting its data would not. That is not the law, at least not in California.

   ....

Network Solutions also argues that the DNS is not a document because it is refreshed every twelve hours when updated domain name information is broadcast across the Internet.... A document doesn't cease being a document merely because it is often updated.... Whether a document is updated by inserting and deleting particular records or by replacing an old file with an entirely new one is a technical detail with no legal significance.

Kremen's domain name is protected by California conversion law, even on the grudging reading we have given it. Exposing Network Solutions to liability when it gives away a registrant's domain name on the basis of a forged letter is no different from holding a corporation liable when it gives away someone's shares under the same circumstances. [Citation.] We have not "creat[ed] new tort duties" in reaching this result. [Citation.] We have only applied settled principles of conversion law to what the parties and the district court all agree is a species of property.

The district court...was reluctant to apply the tort of conversion because of its strict liability nature. This concern rings somewhat hollow...because the district court effectively exempted Network Solutions from liability to Kremen altogether, whether or not it was negligent. Network Solutions made no effort to contact Kremen before giving away his domain name, despite receiving a facially suspect letter from a third party. A jury would be justified in finding it was unreasonably careless.

...[T]here is nothing unfair about holding a company responsible for giving away someone else's property even if it was not at fault.... The question becomes whether Network Solutions should be open to liability for its decision to hand over Kremen's domain name. Negligent or not, it was Network Solutions that gave away Kremen's property. Kremen never did anything. It would not be unfair to hold Network Solutions responsible and force *it* to try to recoup its losses by chasing down Cohen. This, at any rate, is the logic of the common law, and we do not lightly discard it.

The district court was worried that "the threat of litigation threatens to stifle the registration system by requiring further regulations by [Network Solutions] and potential increases in fees." [Citation.] Given that Network Solutions's "regulations" evidently allowed it to hand over a registrant's domain name on the basis of a facially suspect letter without even contacting him, "further regulations" don't seem like such a bad idea. And the prospect of higher fees presents no issue here that it doesn't in any other context. A bank could lower its ATM fees if it didn't have to pay security guards, but we doubt most depositors would think that was a good idea.

The district court thought there were "methods better suited to regulate the vagaries of domain names" and left it "to the legislature to fashion an appropriate statutory scheme." *Id.* The legislature, of course, is always free (within constitutional bounds) to refashion the system that courts come up with. But that doesn't mean we should throw up our hands and let private relations degenerate into a free-for-all in the meantime. We apply the common law until the legislature tells us otherwise. And the common law does not stand idle while people give away the property of others.

The evidence supported a claim for conversion, and the district court should not have rejected it.

    ....

Kremen's complaint finally alleges a separate claim for "conversion by bailee." The district court granted summary judgment, holding that Network Solutions was not a bailee of Kremen's property.

We need not decide the issue because Kremen's "conversion by bailee" claim does not state a cause of action independent of his conversion claim. As we read California law, "conversion by bailee" is not a distinct tort, but merely the tort of conversion committed by one who is a bailee. [Citations.] Kremen's complaint does not allege any claim of bailee liability other than conversion... [Citation.] To prove "conversion by bailee," Kremen must establish all the elements of conversion but, having done so, he gains nothing by also showing that Network Solutions is a bailee.

....The judgment of the district court is reversed on this count, and the case is remanded for further proceedings.

Notes

1. ***Absence of a Property Right.*** Even if a case clearly involves a document, the plaintiff ordinarily must have a property interest in the document in question to be able to state a claim for conversion. In Wieder v. Chemical Bank, 608 N.Y.S.2d 195 (App. Div. 1994), a former employee sued based on alleged removal of "writing samples" he had prepared during his three-year employment with the defendant. The action failed because "it is axiomatic that materials or products developed by an employee in the course of his or her employment, absent any agreement to the contrary, belong to his or her employer." *See also* Mauriceville National Bank v. Zernial, 892 S.W.2d 858 (Tex. 1995) (a bank was not liable in conversion to payees of checks which went unpaid when the bank exercised its right to setoff deposits against overdue payments, because the funds were not held in trust for the plaintiffs); Parker v. Kowalsky & Hirschhorn, P.A., 722 A.2d 441 (Md. Ct. Spec. App. 1999) (attorney did not have a possessory interest in fees at the time that client files were removed by a lawyer leaving the firm, and thus the attorney failed to state a cause of action for conversion against the law firm that hired the departing lawyer).

However, consider FMC Corp. v. Capital Cities/ABC Inc., 915 F.2d 300 (7th Cir. 1990). During an evening news program, the defendant displayed documents (or copies thereof) relating to the plaintiff's pricing policies and contract with the Defense Department. The documents were missing from the plaintiff's files. It was undisputed that the defendant was not directly responsible for the loss of the plaintiff's documents and that whatever it possessed had been provided by a third-party. In a suit for conversion, the court held that if an inspection revealed that the defendant had the original documents, it had to return them to the plaintiff "for it is axiomatic that property known to belong to another must be returned." More interestingly, the court held that the defendant could be liable for conversion if the documents it had were mere photocopies of the originals.

> ...."[T]he receipt of copies of documents, rather than the documents themselves, should not ordinarily give rise to a claim for conversion."....In cases where the alleged converter has only a copy of the owner's property and the owner still possesses the property itself, the owner is in no way being deprived of the use of his property....

> But this case is different. Here, the owner, FMC [the plaintiff], does not have a copy of the documents known to be in the possession of the alleged converter, ABC [the defendant]....

> ....Where, as here, the owner does not have the originals and the alleged converter has the originals or the only known copies of the originals, the retention of such property—to the exclusion of the owner—constitutes conversion.

> In such a case the copies become the functional equivalents of the originals. Because ABC has refused to return copies of the documents that FMC has a right to use, ABC's retention of the documents amounts to the exercise of unlawful dominion over them. Hence, ABC is chargeable with conversion.

Does this make sense?

2. *Merger in a Document.* Notwithstanding the principal case and the authorities cited therein, some courts still retain the "merger in a document" requirement for conversion of information. *See* Hurst v. Dezer/Reyes Corp., 82 F.3d 232, 236 (8th Cir. 1996) (holding that, even under New York's "expanded definition of the tort," the business concept and appearance of a diner could not be "converted" since the claimed property rights were not rights customarily merged in a document); Berger v. Hanlon, 129 F.3d 505 (9th Cir. 1997) (the media's capture of the plaintiffs' images and voices could not support a conversion claim).

3. *Conversion of Human Tissue.* Moore v. Regents of the Univ. of Cal., 793 P.2d 479 (Cal. 1990), addressed the question whether the plaintiff stated a cause of action against his physician and other defendants for using rare cells removed from his body in potentially lucrative medical research without his permission. The court held that the complaint stated a cause of action for breach of the physician's fiduciary disclosure obligations, which generally require a doctor to inform a patient of all information material to the patient's decision on a course of treatment. (*See* Chapter 5.) In rejecting the plaintiff's conversion claim, the court found that "To establish a conversion, [a] plaintiff must establish an actual interference with his ownership or right of possession...." It noted that Moore clearly did not expect to retain possession of his cells following their removal and that statutory law drastically limited any continuing interest of a patient in excised cells. Justice Panelli said:

> ....While we do not purport to hold that excised cells can never be property for any purpose whatsoever, the novelty of Moore's claim demands express consideration of the policies to be served by extending liability....

>   ....

> To be sure, the threat of liability for conversion might help to enforce patients' rights indirectly....Unfortunately, to extend the conversion theory would utterly sacrifice the...goal of protecting innocent parties....[I]t would

impose liability on all those into whose hands the cells come, whether or not the particular defendant participated in, or knew of, the inadequate disclosures that violated the patient's right to make an informed decision. In contrast to the conversion theory, the fiduciary-duty and informed-consent theories protect the patient directly, without punishing innocent parties or creating disincentives to the conduct of socially beneficial research.

    ....

The extension of conversion law into this area will hinder research by restricting access to the necessary raw materials. Thousands of human cell lines already exist in tissue repositories....At present, human cell lines are routinely copied and distributed to other researchers for experimental purposes, usually free of charge. This exchange of scientific materials, which still is relatively free and efficient, will surely be compromised if each cell sample becomes the potential subject matter of a lawsuit. [Citation.]

    ....

...[T]he theory of liability that Moore urges us to endorse threatens to destroy the economic incentive to conduct important medical research. If the use of cells in research is a conversion, then with every cell sample a researcher purchases a ticket in a litigation lottery....

Id. at 487–97. *See generally* Thomas P. Dillon, Note, *Source Compensation for Tissues and Cells Used in Biotechnical Research: Why a Source Shouldn't Share in the Profits*, 64 Notre Dame L. Rev. 628 (1989); Mary Taylor Danforth, *Cells, Sales, and Royalties: The Patient's Right to a Portion of the Profits*, 6 Yale L. & Pol'y Rev. 179 (1988).

Chapter 3

Defenses and Privileges

A. Consent

Total Bar to Liability. The plaintiff's consent to an otherwise-tortious act negates the wrongful element of the defendant's conduct and prevents the existence of a tort. This idea is captured in the well-known Latin maxim *volenti non fit injuria*: to one who is willing, no wrong is done. In the context of intentional torts, it is said that "[a]ll intended wrongs...have in common the element that they are inflicted without the consent of the victim." Fricke v. Owens-Corning Fiberglass Corp., 571 So. 2d 130, 132 (La. 1990).

Burden of Pleading and Proving. Consent is normally treated not as a defense or privilege for the defendant to plead and prove, but as an issue relevant to the plaintiff's prima facie case. The burden of proving lack of consent is upon the plaintiff for each of the basic intentional torts, except for trespass to land. *See* W. Page Keeton, Dan B. Dobbs, Robert E. Keeton, & David G. Owen, Prosser and Keeton on Torts 112 & n. 2 (5th ed. 1984).

Three Kinds of Consent. There are at least three kinds of consent, any one of which bars an action for an intentional tort: actual consent, apparent consent, and implied consent. Actual consent (sometimes called "consent in fact") exists if the plaintiff is in fact willing that the conduct (but not necessarily the consequences thereof) occur. Apparent consent is found whenever the plaintiff's conduct reasonably leads another to believe that the plaintiff has consented, even though the plaintiff did not actually consent. And implied consent is a legal fiction which the courts indulge in the absence of consent (either actual or apparent) to justify desirable conduct which would otherwise be tortious. Not all courts use these terms precisely.

Relation to Assumption of Risk. The *volenti* principle applies to tort actions not based on intentional conduct. In those cases, the principle is embodied in the doctrine of assumption of the risk, which will be examined in Chapter 16.

1. Consent in Fact

Davies v. Butler

Supreme Court of Nevada
602 P.2d 605 (Nev. 1979)

MOWBRAY, Chief Justice.

....

In their wrongful death action, the Davies claimed that...the respondents, the Sun-

135

downers, a voluntary unincorporated association, and nine of its individual members…caused to be administered to their son excessive and unreasonably dangerous amounts of alcohol, and that they subjected him to physical and mental abuse which resulted in his death.…

The club…is a social "drinking club" which sponsors various activities in conjunction with extra-curricular events at the University of Nevada, Reno.

….On Thursday morning, October 9, 1975, Davies and four others were informed of their selection as initiates. From that time until Saturday night, initiates were directed to participate in morning, afternoon and evening activities, all of which were focused on their ability to consume alcoholic beverages. By Saturday evening, one of Davies' fellow initiates described himself as physically and mentally "exhausted."

On Saturday evening,…[at] midnight,…the initiates were taken outside to a parking lot and lined against a wall. There the "final ceremony" commenced. The five initiates, including Davies, were given and admonished to drink large quantities of alcohol, including 190 proof "Everclear", within a 20 to 30 minute period. After they had consumed the liquor, the initiates were instructed to climb into the open bed of a pickup truck.…[T]hey made two brief stops, then drove some 40 to 50 miles from Reno to a point near Pyramid Lake. There it was discovered that Davies had ceased breathing.…Davies eventually was taken to the nearest hospital, where he was pronounced dead.…

> Facts

….

Testimony of witnesses regarding the treatment and condition of Davies during the "final ceremony" varied. Davies' sister and two of her friends, who observed the event from a car parked across the street, testified that they saw Davies struck in the stomach and on the head by either respondent Sallee or respondent Johnson. Two of these witnesses testified that they heard the decedent shout out "Stop" in protest.

Three other observers…testified that they saw Davies fall to the ground, where he was kicked and screamed at, and that they then saw him picked up and held against the wall, while a bottle was forced into his mouth. Two of these witnesses testified that Davies definitely appeared unable to stand on his own.

The respondents, however, generally denied that Davies or any other initiate had been struck or kicked, though they admitted that the initiates had been shoved or held up, and verbally hazed, while bottles of liquor were held to their mouths.…

The jury, by a six to three vote, returned a general verdict in favor of all defendants.…Appellants contend that reversal and a new trial are mandated by prejudicial errors in the instructions to the jury.…

….

> Jury Instruction

The trial court instructed the jury, over appellants' objection, that "[a] person may expressly or by voluntarily participating in an activity consent to an act which would otherwise be a battery." In the context of this case, the giving of this instruction was reversible error.

> Jury found for the D!

….The jury may well have deduced from this instruction that one who voluntarily participates in an activity in legal contemplation assumes the risk of all negligent or intentional conduct by others.…

…[I]n the context of this case, the instruction was so incomplete as to be misleading. "To be effective, consent must be (a) by one who has the capacity to consent…and

Rule

(b) to the particular conduct, or to substantially the same conduct." 4 Restatement (Second), Torts §892A, at 364 (1979). As this court has held, consent is not effective as a defense to battery "where the beating is excessively disproportionate to the consent, given or implied, or where the party injured is exposed to loss of life or great bodily harm." [Citation.] Furthermore, capacity to consent requires the mental ability to appreciate the "nature, extent and probable consequences of the conduct consented to." Restatement, Torts, *supra*, comment b, at 365. As noted by Prosser, Law of Torts, §18, at 102 (4th ed. 1971), [i]f the plaintiff is known to be incapable of giving consent because of... intoxication...his failure to object, or even his active manifestation of consent will not protect the defendant."

Analysis

In McCue v. Klein,...[60 Tex. 168 (1883)], the widow of a man who had died as a result of drinking a toxic quantity of alcohol sued those who had furnished him the alcohol and induced him to drink it, on a wager. The court held, 60 Tex. at 169,

> [T]he maxim of *volenti non fit injuria* presupposes that the party is capable of giving consent to his own injury. If he is divested of the power of refusal by mental faculties, the damage cannot be excused on the ground of consent given. A consent given by a person in such condition is no consent at all,—more especially when his state of mind is well known to the party doing the injury...And so if one whose mental faculties are suspended by intoxication is induced to swallow spiritous liquors to such excess as to endanger his life, the persons taking advantage of his condition of helplessness and mental darkness and imposing the draught upon him must answer to him if such injury should fall short of the destruction of life, and to his family if death should be the result.

We conclude that "in view of all the circumstances the instruction may have misled the jury, and it should not have been given." [Citation.]

Holding

....

...[W]e must reverse the order of the district court denying appellants' motion for a new trial and remand the case to the lower court for that purpose.

[The dissenting opinion of BATJER, J., is omitted.]

Notes

1. *Fraternity Hazing.* Most jurisdictions have outlawed hazing, usually by classifying the conduct as a criminal misdemeanor unless the acts would otherwise constitute a felony. *See, e.g.,* Conn. Gen. Stat. Ann. §53-23a (Westlaw 2003) (defining hazing as "any action which recklessly or intentionally endangers the health or safety of a person for the purpose of initiation, admission into or affiliation with, or as a condition for continued membership in, a student organization"); Idaho Code §18-917 (Westlaw 2002) (specifying examples of prohibited activities, such as compelled ingestion of any substance, sleep deprivation, and transportation and abandonment of a pledge).

Hazing may give rise to tort liability. *See* Ballou v. Sigma Nu Gen. Frat., 352 S.E.2d 488 (S.C. Ct. App. 1986) (national fraternity held liable for actual and punitive damages under a theory of apparent agency for the death of a pledge following a "hell night" initiation); Haben v. Anderson, 597 N.E.2d 655 (Ill. Ct. App. 1992) (cause of action stated against members of a university club that had a *de facto* drinking requirement for membership).

2. *Manifestation of Consent.* Consent in fact may be manifested by words, by affirmative action, or by silence or inaction under circumstances showing that the silence or

inaction gives consent. Actual consent bars an action even if it is not communicated to the defendant. *See* Restatement, Second, of Torts §892, Comment b. If, for example, the owner of a swimming pool tells a neighbor that anyone in the neighborhood can use the pool, another neighbor who uses the pool without knowing of this invitation has not committed a trespass; *id.*, illus. 1.

3. *Capacity to Consent.* Consent is ineffective if youth or mental deficiency precludes a person from appreciating the nature, extent, and probable consequences of the conduct allegedly consented to. *See* Restatement, Second, of Torts §892A, Comment b.

4. *Scope of Consent.* An action will be barred only if the invasion is within the scope of the plaintiff's consent. In Vitale v. Henchey, 24 S.W.3d 651 (Ky. 2000), a patient consented to surgery being performed by two doctors, but was operated on by a third. The court held that a suit for battery against the third doctor was not barred because that surgery was not within the scope of the consent. In addition, the fact that the first two doctors consented to the operation's being performed by the third was irrelevant because consent must be given by one with capacity to consent. The first two doctors had no capacity to consent to surgery on the plaintiff.

2. Apparent Consent

O'Brien v. Cunard S.S. Co.

Supreme Judicial Court of Massachusetts
28 N.E. 266 (Mass. 1891)

KNOWLTON, J.

This case presents two questions: *First*, whether there was any evidence to warrant the jury in finding that the defendant, by any of its servants or agents, committed an assault on the plaintiff; *secondly*, whether there was evidence on which the jury could have found that the defendant was guilty of negligence towards the plaintiff. To sustain the first count...the plaintiff relied on the fact that the surgeon who was employed by the defendant vaccinated her on ship-board, while she was on her passage from Queenstown to Boston....In determining whether the act was lawful or unlawful, the surgeon's conduct must be considered in connection with the surrounding circumstances. If the plaintiff's behavior was such as to indicate consent on her part, he was justified in his act, whatever her unexpressed feelings may have been. In determining whether she consented, he could be guided only by her overt acts and the manifestations of her feelings. [Citations.] It is undisputed that at Boston there are strict quarantine regulations in regard to the examination of emigrants, to see that they are protected from small-pox by vaccination, and that only those persons who hold a certificate from the medical officer of the steam-ship, stating that they are so protected, are permitted to land without detention in quarantine, or vaccination by the port physician. It appears that the defendant is accustomed to have its surgeons vaccinate all emigrants who desire it, and who are not protected by previous vaccination, and give them a certificate which is accepted at quarantine as evidence of their protection. Notices of the regulations at quarantine, and of the willingness of the ship's medical officer to vaccinate such as needed vaccination, were posted about the ship in various languages, and on the day when the operation was performed the surgeon had a right to presume that she and the other women who were vaccinated understood the importance and purpose of vaccination for those who bore no marks to show that they were protected. By the plaintiff's testimony, which, in this particular, is undisputed, it appears that about 200 women passengers were assembled below, and she understood from conversation with them that they were to be vaccinated; that she stood about 15 feet from the surgeon, and saw them form in a line, and pass in turn before him; that he "examined their arms, and, passing some of them by, proceeded to vaccinate those that had no mark;" that she did not hear him say anything to any of them; that upon being passed by they each received a card, and went on deck; that when her turn came she showed him her arm; he looked at it, and said there was no mark, and that she should be vaccinated; that she told him she had been vaccinated before, and it left no mark; "that he then said nothing; that he should vaccinate her again;" that she held up her arm to be vaccinated; that no one touched her; that she did not tell him she did not want to be vaccinated; and that she took the ticket which he gave her, certifying that he had vaccinated her, and used it at quarantine. She was one of a large number of women who were vaccinated on that occasion, without, so far as appears, a word of objection from any of them. They all indicated by their conduct that they desired to avail themselves of the provisions made for their benefit. There was nothing in the conduct of the plaintiff to indicate to the surgeon that she did not wish to obtain a card which would save her from detention at quarantine, and to be vaccinated, if necessary, for that purpose. Viewing his conduct in the light of the surrounding circumstances, it was lawful; and there was no evidence tending to show that it was not. The ruling of the court on this part of the case was correct....

[The court found the negligence claim to be without merit.]....Exceptions overruled.

Notes

1. To similar effect is Lesser v. Neosho County Comm. Coll., 741 F. Supp. 854, 865 (D. Kan. 1990) (a student-athlete's claim of battery, based on the military-style haircut he received as a member of a baseball team, was barred by consent).

2. *Consent Manifested by Participation.* In Smith v. Calvary Christian Church, 614 N.W.2d 590 (Mich. 2000), claims for the tort of outrage and invasion of privacy were alleged after a church publicly shamed one of its errant members. The member had expressly consented in writing to accept church discipline, but then had formally resigned his membership. The court held that the tort actions were barred because the plaintiff, after resignation, "by active engagement and participation in the church" manifested his consent to the church's practices.

3. Implied Consent

In the absence of actual or apparent consent, special circumstances such as a medical emergency may make it desirable for a person to engage in conduct that would otherwise be tortious. In such instances, the law holds that consent is implied because the interests to be furthered by the invasion (*e.g.,* preservation of life or limb) are more important than those which will be sacrificed (*e.g.,* personal bodily integrity and freedom from unconsented contact). In such instances, there is really no consent at all, actual or apparent, only a legal fiction called implied consent, which completely bars liability.

In Kozup v. Georgetown Univ., 851 F.2d 437 (D.C. Cir. 1988), an infant contracted AIDS as a result of a blood transfusion. The court recognized the medical emergency rule, but held that the trial court erred in granting summary judgment, for there was a material issue of fact as to whether an emergency in fact existed at the time the transfusion was administered. On remand, the jury was instructed on the issue of emergency as it related to a battery claim. Georgetown prevailed, and on appeal the judgment was affirmed, 906 F.2d 783 (D.C. Cir. 1990).

The following case illustrates the rule relating to medical emergencies, although it rejects the rubric of "implied consent." (The *Miller* court seems to reserve that phrase for actual or apparent consent inferred from conduct.)

Miller v. HCA, Inc.
Supreme Court of Texas
118 S.W.3d 758 (Tex. 2003)

Justice ENOCH delivered the opinion of the Court.

The narrow question we must decide is whether Texas law recognizes a claim by parents for either battery or negligence because their premature infant, born alive but in distress at only twenty-three weeks of gestation, was provided resuscitative medical treatment by physicians at a hospital without parental consent. The court of appeals, with one justice dissenting, held that neither claim could be maintained....

....First, there is no dispute in the evidence that the Millers' premature infant could not be fully evaluated for medical treatment until birth. As a result, any decisions concerning treatment for the Millers' child would not be fully informed decisions until birth. Second, the evidence further established that once the infant was born, the physician attending the birth was faced with emergent circumstances—*i.e.*, the child might survive with treatment but would likely die if treatment was not provided before either parental consent or a court order overriding the withholding of such consent could be obtained.

....

...[A]pproximately four months before her due date, Karla Miller was admitted to Woman's Hospital of Texas (the "Hospital") in premature labor. An ultrasound revealed that Karla's fetus weighed about 629 grams or 1 1/4 pounds....

....The physicians...informed the Millers that if the infant was born alive, it would most probably suffer severe impairments, including cerebral palsy, brain hemorrhaging, blindness, lung disease, pulmonary infections, and mental retardation....

After their discussion, Drs. Jacobs and Kelley asked the Millers to decide whether physicians should treat the infant upon birth....At approximately noon that day, the Millers informed Drs. Jacob and Kelley that they wanted no heroic measures performed on the infant and they wanted nature to take its course. Mark testified that he understood heroic measures to mean performing resuscitation, chest massage, and using life support machines. Dr. Kelley recorded the Millers' request in Karla's medical notes, and Dr. Jacobs informed the medical staff at the Hospital that no neonatologist would be needed at delivery. Mark then left the Hospital to make funeral arrangements for the infant.

....An afternoon of meetings involving Hospital administrators and physicians followed. Between approximately 4:00 p.m. and 4:30 p.m. that day, Anna Summerfield, the director of the Hospital's neonatal intensive care unit, and several physicians, including Dr. Jacobs, met with Mark upon his return to the Hospital....Mark testified that Ms. Summerfield announced at the meeting that the Hospital had a policy requiring resuscitation of any baby who was born weighing over 500 grams....

Moreover, the physicians at the meeting testified that they and Hospital administrators agreed only that a neonatologist would be present to evaluate the Millers' infant at birth and decide whether to resuscitate based on the infant's condition at that time. As Dr. Jacobs testified:

> [W]hat we finally decided that everyone wanted to do was to not make the call prior to the time we actually saw the baby. Deliver the baby, because you see there was this [question] is the baby really 23 weeks, or is the baby further along, how big is the baby, what are we dealing with. We decided to let the neonatologist make the call by looking directly at the baby at birth.

> ....

Although Dr. Eduardo Otero, the neonatologist present in the delivery room when Sidney was born, did not attend that meeting, he confirmed that he needed to actually see Sidney before deciding what treatment, if any, would be appropriate....

Mark testified that, after the meeting, Hospital administrators asked him to sign a consent form allowing resuscitation according to the Hospital's plan, but he refused. Mark further testified that when he asked how he could prevent resuscitation, Hospital administrators told him that he could do so by removing Karla from the Hospital, which was not a viable option given her condition....

...[T]hat night, Karla delivered a premature female infant weighing 615 grams, which the Millers named Sidney....[Sidney] was born alive.

Dr. Otero noted that Sidney had a heart beat....He immediately "bagged" and "intubated" Sidney to oxygenate her blood; he then placed her on ventilation....Neither Karla nor Mark objected at the time to the treatment provided.

Sidney initially responded well to the treatment....But at some point during the first few days after birth, Sidney suffered a brain hemorrhage—a complication not uncommon in infants born so prematurely.

There was conflicting testimony about whether Sidney's hemorrhage occurred because of the treatment provided or in spite of it....At the time of trial, Sidney was seven years old and could not walk, talk, feed herself, or sit up on her own. The evidence demonstrated that Sidney was legally blind, suffered from severe mental retardation, cerebral palsy, seizures, and spastic quadriparesis in her limbs. She could not be toilet-trained and required a shunt in her brain to drain fluids that accumulate there and needed care twenty-four hours a day....

The Millers sued...[HCA] and the Hospital, a subsidiary of HCA. They did not sue any physicians...[T]he Millers asserted battery and negligence claims....

....The Millers...alleged that the Hospital's acts and/or omissions were performed with HCA's full knowledge and consent. Although the Millers did not sue Dr. Otero, they alleged that he and other Hospital personnel were the Hospital's apparent or ostensible agents.

....The trial court granted HCA's motion for a separate trial from the Hospital and then, at the Millers' request, tried the Millers' claims against HCA first.

....The jury found that the Hospital, without the consent of Karla or Mark Miller, performed resuscitative treatment on Sidney....The jury concluded that HCA and the Hospital were grossly negligent and that the Hospital acted with malice. The jury also determined that Dr. Otero acted as the Hospital's agent in resuscitating Sidney and that HCA was responsible for the Hospital's conduct under alter ego and single business enterprise theories. The trial court rendered judgment…on the jury's verdict of $29,400,000 in actual damages for medical expenses, $17,503,066 in prejudgment interest, and $13,500,000 in exemplary damages.

....

Generally speaking, the custody, care, and nurture of an infant resides in the first instance with the parents. As the United States Supreme Court has acknowledged, parents are presumed to be the appropriate decision-makers for their infants.…

The Texas Legislature has likewise recognized that parents are presumed to be appropriate decision-makers, giving parents the right to consent to their infant's medical care and surgical treatment. A logical corollary of that right,…is that parents have the right not to consent to certain medical care for their infant, *i.e.,* parents have the right to refuse certain medical care.

Of course, this broad grant of parental decision-making authority is not without limits. The State's role as *parens patriae* permits it to intercede in parental decision-making under certain circumstances. As the United States Supreme Court has noted:

> ….In the exercise of this authority, the state not only punishes parents whose conduct has amounted to abuse or neglect of their children but may also supervene parental decisions before they become operative to ensure that the choices made are not so detrimental to a child's interests as to amount to neglect and abuse.

But the Supreme Court has also pointed out:

> [A]s long as parents choose from professionally accepted treatment options the choice is rarely reviewed in court and even less frequently supervened.…

The Texas Legislature has acknowledged the limitations on parental decision-making. For example, the Legislature has provided in the Family Code that the rights and duties of parents are subject to modification by court order. And Texas courts have recognized their authority to enter orders, under appropriate circumstances, appointing a temporary managing conservator who may consent to medical treatment refused by a child's parents.

With respect to consent, the requirement that permission be obtained before providing medical treatment is based on the patient's right to receive information adequate for him or her to exercise an informed decision to accept or refuse the treatment. Thus, the general rule in Texas is that a physician who provides treatment without consent commits a battery. But there are exceptions. For example, in Gravis v. Physicians & Surgeons Hospital [427 S.W.2d 310, 311 (Tex.1968)], this Court acknowledged that "consent will be implied where the patient is unconscious or otherwise unable to give express consent and an immediate operation is necessary to preserve life or health."

In Moss v. Rishworth [222 S.W. 225, 226-27 (Tex. Comm'n App.1920, *judgm't approved*)], the court held that a physician commits a "legal wrong" by operating on a minor without parental consent when there is "an absolute necessity for a prompt operation, but not emergent in the sense that death would likely result immediately upon the failure to perform it." But the court in *Moss* expressly noted that "it [was] not contended [there] that any real danger would have resulted to the child had time been taken to consult the parent with reference to the operation." *Moss* therefore implicitly acknowledges that a physician does not commit a legal wrong by operating on a minor without consent when the operation is performed under emergent circumstances—*i.e.,* when death is likely to result immediately upon the failure to perform it.

Moss guides us here. We hold that a physician, who is confronted with emergent circumstances and provides life-sustaining treatment to a minor child, is not liable for not first obtaining consent from the parents. The Millers cite to Texas Family Code section 32.001, Texas Health & Safety Code section 773.008, and Texas Revised Civil Statutes article 4590i, section 6.07(a)(2), as illustrating that implied consent does not arise from an emergency context when a healthcare provider has actual notice of lack of consent. Because these statutes apply when a parent is not present to consent, the Millers suggest that this must mean that emergency services cannot be provided when the parents refuse consent. But that is not so.

Providing treatment to a child under emergent circumstances does not imply consent to treatment despite actual notice of refusal to consent. Rather, it is an exception to the general rule that a physician commits a battery by providing medical treatment without consent. As such, the exception is narrowly circumscribed and arises only in emergent circumstances when there is no time to consult the parents or seek court intervention if the parents withhold consent before death is likely to result to the child. Though in situations of this character, the physician should attempt to secure parental consent if possible, the physician will not be liable under a battery or negligence theory solely for proceeding with the treatment absent consent.

We recognize that the Restatement (Second) of Torts § 892D provides that an individual is not liable for providing emergency treatment without consent if that individual has no reason to believe that the other, if he or she had the opportunity to consent, would decline. But that requirement is inapplicable here because, as we have discussed, the emergent circumstances exception does not imply consent.

Further, the emergent circumstances exception acknowledges that the harm from failing to treat outweighs any harm threatened by the proposed treatment, because the harm from failing to provide life-sustaining treatment under emergent circumstances is death. And as we acknowledged in Nelson v. Krusen [678 S.W.2d 918, 925 (Tex.1984)], albeit in the different context of a wrongful life claim, it is impossible for the courts to calculate the relative benefits of an impaired life versus no life at all.

.... The jury found that the Hospital, through Dr. Otero, treated Sidney without the Millers' consent. The parties do not challenge that finding. Thus, we only address whether the Hospital was required to seek court intervention to overturn the lack of parental consent—which it undisputedly did not do—before Dr. Otero could treat Sidney without committing a battery.

The Millers...contend that, as a matter of law, no emergency existed that would excuse the Hospital's treatment of Sidney without their consent or a court order overriding their refusal to consent. The Millers point out that before Sidney's birth, Drs. Jacobs and Kelley discussed with them the possibility that Sidney might suffer from the numerous physical and mental infirmities that did, in fact, afflict her. And some eleven hours before Sidney's birth, the Millers indicated that they did not want any heroic measures performed on Sidney. The Millers note that these factors prompted the dissenting justice in the court of appeals to conclude that "[a]nytime a group of doctors and a hospital administration ha[ve] the luxury of multiple meetings to change the original doctors' medical opinions, without taking a more obvious course of action, there is no medical emergency."

We agree that a physician cannot create emergent circumstances from his or her own delay or inaction and escape liability for proceeding without consent. But the Millers' reasoning fails to recognize that, in this case, the evidence established that Sidney could only be properly evaluated when she was born. Any decision the Millers made before

Sidney's birth concerning her treatment at or after her birth would necessarily be based on speculation. Therefore, we reject the Millers' argument that a decision could adequately be made pre-birth that denying all post-birth resuscitative treatment would be in Sidney's best interest. Such a decision could not control whether the circumstances facing Dr. Otero were emergent because it would not have been a fully informed one according to the evidence in this case.

... [T]he...time for evaluating Sidney was when she was born. The evidence further reflected that Sidney was born alive but in distress. At that time, Dr. Otero had to make a split-second decision on whether to provide life-sustaining treatment. While the Millers were both present in the delivery room, there was simply no time to obtain their consent to treatment or to institute legal proceedings to challenge their withholding of consent, had the Millers done so, without jeopardizing Sidney's life. Thus, although HCA never requested a jury instruction, nor challenged the absence of a jury instruction, on whether Dr. Otero treated Sidney under emergent circumstances, the evidence conclusively established that Dr. Otero was faced with emergent circumstances when he treated Sidney. Those circumstances resulted from not being able to evaluate Sidney until she was born, not because of any delay or inaction by HCA, the Hospital, or Dr. Otero....

We acknowledge that certain physicians in this case initially asked the Millers to decide whether Sidney should be resuscitated some eleven hours before her birth. And certain physicians and Hospital administrators asked the Millers to consent to the subsequent plan developed to have a neonatologist present at Sidney's delivery to evaluate and possibly treat her. We agree that, whenever possible, obtaining consent in writing to evaluate a premature infant at birth and to render any warranted medical treatment is the best course of action. And physicians and hospitals should always strive to do so. But if such consent is not forthcoming, or is affirmatively denied, we decline to impose liability on a physician solely for providing life-sustaining treatment under emergent circumstances to a new-born infant without that consent.

Holding

....

.... [T]he Millers' only negligence claim was that HCA and the Hospital had policies, or lacked policies, and took actions that allowed Sidney to be treated without their consent. Thus, their negligence claim is based on the lack of consent before treatment, just like their battery claim.

If the phrase refers to Dr. Otero resuscitating Sidney against the Millers' wishes, it was not HCA's or the Hospital's policies, or lack thereof, that permitted Dr. Otero to treat Sidney without consent. Rather, it was the emergent circumstances that caused that to happen. Because Dr. Otero treated Sidney under emergent circumstances, he did not commit a battery. And because Dr. Otero did not commit a battery, HCA is not liable derivatively. Nor was the Hospital negligent for allowing Dr. Otero to treat Sidney under the circumstances without the Millers' consent.

....

.... We affirm the court of appeals' judgment.

Justice O'NEILL and Justice SMITH did not participate in the decision.

Note

1. *Implied Consent in Medical Emergencies.* In Barnett v. Bachrach, 34 A.2d 626, 628 (D.C. 1943), the court observed:

... [I]n case of emergency a surgeon may lawfully perform, and it is his duty to perform, such operation as good surgery demands even when it means extending the operation further than was originally contemplated, and...for doing so he is neither to be held [liable] in damages, or denied recovery of his fee.

} Rule

.... The law does not insist that a surgeon shall perform every operation according to plans and specifications, approved in advance by the patient, and carefully tucked away in his office-safe for courtroom purposes.

4. Consent Given Because of a Mistake

DeMay v. Roberts

Supreme Court of Michigan
9 N.W. 146 (Mich. 1881)

MARSTON, C.J.

The declaration in this case...sets forth that the plaintiff was at a time and place named a poor married woman, and being confined in child-bed and a stranger, employed in a professional capacity defendant De May who was a physician; that defendant visited the plaintiff as such, and against her desire and intending to deceive her wrongfully, etc., introduced and caused to be present at the house and lying-in room of the plaintiff and while she was in the pains of parturition the defendant Scattergood, who intruded upon the privacy of the plaintiff, indecently, wrongfully and unlawfully laid hands upon and assaulted her, the said Scattergood, which was well known to defendant De May, being a young unmarried man, a stranger to the plaintiff and utterly ignorant of the practice of medicine, while the plaintiff believed that he was an assistant physician, a competent and proper person to be present and to aid her in her extremity.

....

The evidence on the part of the plaintiff tended to prove the allegations of the declaration. On the part of the defendants evidence was given tending to prove that Scattergood very reluctantly accompanied Dr. De May at the urgent request of the latter; that the night was a dark and stormy one, the roads over which they had to travel in getting to the house of the plaintiff were so bad that a horse could not be rode or driven over them; that the doctor was sick and very much fatigued from overwork, and therefore asked the defendant Scattergood to accompany and assist him in carrying a lantern, umbrella and certain articles deemed necessary upon such occasions; that upon arriving at the house of the plaintiff the doctor knocked, and when the door was opened by the husband of the plaintiff, De May said to him, "that I had fetched a friend along to help carry my things;" he, plaintiff's husband, said all right, and seemed to be perfectly satisfied. They were bid to enter, treated kindly and no objection whatever made to the presence of defendant Scattergood. That while there Scattergood, at Dr. De May's request, took hold of plaintiff's hand and held her during a paroxysm of pain, and that both of the defendants in all respects throughout acted in a proper and becoming manner actuated by a sense of duty and kindness.

.... The plaintiff when examined as a witness was asked, what idea she entertained in reference to Scattergood's character and right to be in the house...and answered that she thought he was a student or a physician. To this there could be no good legal objection. It was not only important to know the character in which Scattergood went there, but to learn what knowledge the plaintiff had upon that subject. It was not claimed that the plaintiff or her husband, who were strangers in that vicinity, had ever met Scattergood before this time or had any knowledge or information concerning him beyond what they obtained on that evening, and it was claimed by the defendant that both the plaintiff and her husband must have known, from certain ambiguous expressions used, that he was not a physician.

We are of [the] opinion that the plaintiff and her husband had a right to presume that a practicing physician would not, upon an occasion of that character, take with him and introduce into the house, a young man in no way, either by education or otherwise, connected with the medical profession; and that something more clear and certain as to his non-professional character would be required to put the plaintiff and her husband upon their guard, or remove such presumption, than the remark made by De May that he had brought a friend along to help carry his things....

    ....

....To the plaintiff the occasion was a most sacred one and no one had a right to intrude unless invited or because of some real and pressing necessity which it is not pretended existed in this case. The plaintiff had a legal right to the privacy of her apartment at such a time, and the law secures to her this right by requiring others to observe it, and to abstain from its violation. The fact that at the time, she consented to the presence of Scattergood supposing him to be a physician, does not preclude her from maintaining an action and recovering substantial damages upon afterwards ascertaining his true character. In obtaining admission at such a time and under such circumstances without fully disclosing his true character, both parties were guilty of deceit, and the wrong thus done entitles the injured party to recover the damages afterwards sustained, from shame and mortification upon discovering the true character of the defendants.

    ....

It follows therefore that the judgment must be affirmed with costs.

Notes

1. *Consent Given Because of a Mistake: The Traditional Dichotomy and Recent Scholarship.* Consent intentionally procured by fraud is invalid, making the tort in question actionable. Some authorities limit this rule to situations in which the misrepresentation relates to the "essence" of the transaction, holding that consent is vitiated only by a deception bearing upon (1) the nature of the invasion, (2) the degree of harm reasonably to be expected, or (3) the existence of facts (perhaps relating to the relationship of the parties or the necessity of medical procedures) which make the interference harmful or offensive. This form of misrepresentation is called "fraud in the essence" or "fraud in the *factum*." In contrast, "fraud in the inducement" is a misrepresentation that relates merely to a person's collateral reasons for agreement (as opposed to the nature of the invasion or the harm, if any, to be anticipated). Fraud in the inducement is insufficient to destroy consent.

Although superficially appealing, the *factum*-versus-inducement dichotomy breaks down in application and has little predictive value. It is often difficult or impossible to differentiate between essential and collateral matters. For example, the Restatement, Second, of Torts sets forth two illustrations. The first says that a person who unknowingly accepts counterfeit money in exchange for submitting to intimate familiarities has no action for battery; the second, based on the same facts, allows a battery action to a person who unwittingly takes counterfeit money in exchange for agreeing to a blood transfusion. The distinction between these two situations—if it exists at all—is surely too elusive to provide useful guidance to the courts or the public. The drafters of the Restatement's illustration may have assumed, without making their premises clear, that selling sexual services is more objectionable than selling blood. Consider whether the alleged mistake in *DeMay* would be termed fraud in the essence or fraud in the inducement.

Recent scholarship rejects the traditional *factum*-inducement dichotomy and argues that any mistake sufficiently material to play a role in the plaintiff's decision-making process will invalidate consent. This approach is sound, for if the defendant has knowingly precluded the plaintiff from making an honest assessment of the facts, why not bar the defendant from the benefits flowing from the deception?

Under both the traditional and modern views, consent will be invalidated only if the defendant knows that the plaintiff has labored under a misconception. Other factual misunderstandings—for example, those negligently caused by the defendant or arising from circumstances independent of the defendant's conduct—will not bar the defendant from raising consent as a defense to a tort action. However, a plaintiff who has given consent because of a mistake may have some legal remedy even if the mistake bars an action for an intentional tort. In some instances, the remedies of contract rescission or restitution for unjust enrichment may be invoked by a plaintiff whose mistake was "unilateral" (that is, unknown to the defendant). *See* Restatement, Third, of Restitution and Unjust Enrichment §5, 11, 12, & 13 (Tent. Draft No. 1, 2001). Moreover, the tort of deceit, and the parallel actions for negligent misrepresentation and certain types of innocent misrepresentation, may provide redress. *See* Chapter 21.

On the traditional view, see Restatement, Second, of Torts §892B. Among the authorities rejecting the *factum*-inducement dichotomy are: David A. Fischer, *Fraudulently Induced Consent to Intentional Torts*, 46 U. Cinn. L. Rev. 71 (1977); Stuart M. Speiser, Charles F. Krause & Alfred W. Gans, The American Law of Torts, §5:7, p. 800 (1983). *See also* Fowler V. Harper, Fleming James, Jr., & Oscar S. Gray, Law of Torts §3.10, p. 303 (2d ed. 1986) ("Case law is thin…as to the proposed distinction [between collateral and non-collateral matters]"). For an interesting discussion of whether fraud vitiates consent, see Desnick v. ABC, 44 F.3d 1345, 1351-53 (7th Cir. 1995) (Posner, C.J.).

2. Consider Micari v. Mann, 481 N.Y.S.2d 967 (Sup. Ct. 1984). A distinguished acting teacher in his mid-sixties induced female students in their early twenties to engage in various sexual acts with him and with each other in his presence. The defendant used or threatened no physical force; he told the students that "this sexual activity was intended to release their inhibitions and thus improve their acting skills." Should the consent of the students bar actions for assault and battery? The jury was instructed that consent would be a complete defense "unless i) the defendant falsely represented to the plaintiffs that their performance of such acts was related to their training as actresses, and ii) plaintiffs relied upon such misrepresentation." The jury found the defendant liable for compensatory damages, and the court ordered a new trial unless the defendant paid punitive damages as well.

3. *Mutual Mistake.* A mutual[a] mistake does not invalidate consent. In Fricke v. Owens-Corning Fiberglass Corp., 571 So. 2d 130, 131-33 (La. 1990), the plant foreman, Fricke, discovered an employee, Davillier, unconscious at the bottom of an 18-

---

a. In an odd departure from ordinary English usage, lawyers use the term "mutual" to mean "common"; a "mutual" mistake is one that has been made by both of the parties.

foot-deep mustard tank. The foreman immediately notified the 76-year-old plant superintendent, Baumer. "Baumer started to descend a rope ladder inside the tank to
rescue Davillier, but Fricke persuaded the older man to let him go instead." As a result of mustard-gas poisoning, Fricke collapsed at the bottom of the tank and suffered brain damage, and Davillier died. In an action arising from the injuries to
Fricke, the court held that the supervisor, Baumer, had not committed an intentional
tort by acquiescing in Fricke's descent into the tank. (Under the workers' compensation laws, those injured by on-the-job negligence have no remedy except workers'
compensation; intentional tort claims are not limited in this way.) The court found
that "It is uncontroverted that neither Fricke nor Baumer knew that the mustard
tank contained lethal or gravely damaging vapors; and that neither knew what had
felled Davillier at the bottom." The court noted, however, "Of course, if Fricke in
consenting to contact with the offensive vapors had been induced to do so by a substantial mistake as to the nature of the vapor or the extent of harm to be expected
from it and the mistake had been known to Baumer or induced by Baumer's misrepresentation, Fricke's consent would not have been effective for the unexpected invasion or harm."

4. *Consent and Duress.* Consent is not effective if it is given under duress, such as the
use or threat of force against one's person or property, or against the person or property
of family members. *See* Restatement, Second, of Torts §892B, Comment j. *See also* Trot-
ter v. Okawa, 445 S.E.2d 121 (Va. 1994) (mentally ill patient's consent to sexual intercourse was vitiated by duress).

Courts have been reluctant to accept arguments that consent is vitiated by economic
duress. For example, in Quinn v. Limited Express, Inc., 715 F. Supp. 127 (W.D. Pa.
1989), the court held that an employee's consent negated any cause of action for assault
and battery arising from her employer's use of a polygraph examination as a part of an
investigation of missing funds. The court wrote:

> Our conclusion that plaintiff impliedly consented to the polygraph exami-
> nation is supported by the absence of duress. Plaintiff testified that neither the
> examiner nor any representative from the company told her she had to take the
> polygraph test. Likewise, neither the examiner nor any company representative
> told her she had to sign the consent forms. In addition, plaintiff's feeling of
> compulsion was at best an assumption on her part. Plaintiff was never told she
> would be fired if she did not submit to the exam. We recognize that plaintiff
> "felt that if I did not submit to it that I would either be terminated or looked
> upon with disfavor and suspicion by my superiors." The plaintiff's perceptions
> of economic duress, however, are insufficient to negate plaintiff's conduct
> which manifested her implied consent.

(Citations to the case record omitted.)

5. *Consent to a Criminal Act.* There is a split of authority as to whether consent to a
criminal act bars tort liability. The everyday case is that of two people who agree to
"step outside and settle their differences": conduct which typically violates laws about
assault (in the criminal sense) and disturbing the peace. Some courts say that the consent does not bar a tort action, on the theory that no person has the right to consent to
what the law forbids. According to these authorities, when two persons engage in criminal conduct, there are really three parties, the third being the state, and neither of the
individual actors has the right to speak for the state or waive its interests. Under this
view, respect for the law demands that consent to a criminal act be held invalid.

The other position—which has been embraced by the Restatement as the better view—holds that "consent is effective to bar recovery in a tort action although the conduct consented to is a crime." Restatement, Second, of Torts §829C(1). According to this view, the state's interests can be adequately advanced through criminal prosecutions (in which consent of the participants would not be a defense); protecting the interests of the state does not require giving one collaborator in criminal conduct a civil claim against the other. *See generally* the famous case of Hart v. Geysel, 294 P. 570 (Wash. 1930) (affirming the dismissal of a wrongful death action arising from the decedent's participation in an illegal prize fight).

6. *Deterrence of Criminal Acts.* Which rule better deters a breach of the peace: one which announces, "if you win the fight, you can still be held liable for damages" (the view holding consent to a criminal act invalid), or one which proclaims, "if you lose the fight, you may not seek a re-match in the courts" (the view holding consent to a criminal act valid)?

"As a practical matter it may reasonably be doubted that in either case the parties are at all influenced by any thought of tort liability before they engage in criminal acts." Restatement, Second, of Torts §829C(1), Comment b. While the Restatement may be right about the thoughts of many—even most—of those who fight in the street or commit other crimes, is it possible that *no one* contemplating a fight has ever been influenced by the possibility of having to pay damages to the other party? Deterrence of undesirable behavior is worthwhile even if it cannot eliminate that behavior entirely. It seems doubtful, however, that more than a handful of potential participants in fights know whether their state follows the majority or minority rule about consent to criminal conduct. The choice between these rules is therefore likely to have very little effect on deterrence.

7. *Parties Not* **In Pari Delicto.** Consent to a criminal act will bar liability only if the parties were *in pari delicto*.[b] For example, the Restatement, Second, of Torts §892C(2), provides that "If conduct is made criminal in order to protect a certain class of persons irrespective of their consent, the consent of members of that class to the conduct is not effective to bar a tort action." In Hudson v. Craft, 204 P.2d 1 (Cal. 1949), an 18-year-old participant in an illegal boxing match sued the promoter of the match for injuries he sustained. The court found that the boxing law, which required licensing and safety precautions, was intended to protect persons engaging in the activity from physical harm; the law was not intended to protect boxing promoters. Consequently, the plaintiff participant and the defendant promoter were not *in pari delicto*, and a suit against the promoter could be maintained, even though the plaintiff might have been criminally liable and would have been barred from suing another participant.

Statutes intended to protect a particular class of persons include those which forbid the sale of intoxicating liquor to a person who is already intoxicated and those which forbid sexual intercourse with a child under sixteen, regardless of consent. *See* Restatement, Second, of Torts §892C, illus. 7 & 8; Wilson v. Tobiassen, 777 P.2d 1379 (Or. Ct. App. 1989) (in an action holding scouting organizations liable for damages arising from a leader's sexual abuse of a troop member, the court extended to civil cases the statutory incapacity of a person under 18 to consent to a sexual act).

---

b. Parties stand "*in pari delicto*" when they are equally at fault. "The *in pari delicto* doctrine is based upon the premise that there is no recourse between wrongdoers." Patten v. Raddatz, 895 P.2d 633 (Mont. 1995) (tort action arising from long-term relationship involving drug use and prostitution was barred).

B. Defense of Self and Others

Silas v. Bowen

United States District Court for the District of South Carolina
277 F. Supp. 314 (D. S.C. 1967)

DONALD RUSSELL, District Judge.

[At defendant's parking lot, plaintiff engaged a mechanic to repair his car. The mechanic, though present at the lot, was not employed by the defendant. After receiving the car a week later, taking it for a drive, and discovering that the repairs were defective, plaintiff returned to the lot and heatedly demanded that the defendant immediately rectify the problem.]

. . . .

Facts

The testimony of the defendant and his two corroborating witnesses, one of whom, it is true, is his wife, seems [to be the] more credible. According to them, the plaintiff was drinking when he arrived at the parking lot; he was quite belligerent, was cursing, refused to depart when told to leave, approached the defendant in a threatening manner and grabbed him. When the difference in the size and age of the plaintiff and defendant is considered, the situation of the defendant was such as to strike fear and terror in the latter. The plaintiff was a young man, a professional athlete, robust, standing some six feet six inches, in perfect physical condition, weighing 225 to 230 pounds. The defendant, on the other hand, was of middle age, weighing about 135 pounds and standing five feet six inches. Facing a threat from the plaintiff, unable to induce him and his companions to leave his premises, already assaulted by the plaintiff, the defendant, under the emergency thus created and with reasonable cause to fear serious bodily harm from an individual so much more overpowering than he, fired his shotgun, not, I am convinced, with the intent of striking the plaintiff, but for the purpose of frightening him into desisting from his attack and into leaving his premises. Unfortunately, the shot, though directed downward towards the ground, struck the plaintiff in the foot. . . .

. . . .

The commission of an assault and battery by the defendant on the plaintiff is conceded and defendant seeks exoneration on his affirmative plea of self-defense. . . .

. . . . While entry of the defendant's premises by the plaintiff was lawful, the defendant had a plain right to order the plaintiff and his companions to depart; and, when the plaintiff refused to withdraw voluntarily after such demand, to use reasonable force to eject them. [Citation.]

Rule

. . . . While this right to use reasonable force does not ordinarily encompass the use of a deadly weapon, such use will be authorized, by way of self-defense, if the conduct of the trespasser under all the circumstances is such as to produce in the mind of a person of reasonable prudence and courage an apprehension of an assault by such trespasser involving serious bodily harm. [Citations.]

. . . .

. . . . In determining whether there was reasonable cause and justification for the use of a deadly weapon in such a situation, all the circumstances must be considered. Accordingly, it is generally stated that a defendant, in his own place of business, where he has a right to be, as the defendant was in this case, is not required to retreat in the face of a threatened assault in order to be able to plead self-defense. [Citation.] Again, while it is well-settled that mere words, however "abusive, insulting, vexatious or threatening," will not in themselves justify the use of a deadly weapon, such words if "accompanied by an actual offer of physical violence" reasonably warranting fear of serious bodily harm, may be an integral part of a plea of self-defense against liability for an assault and battery. [Citations.] Moreover, in determining whether there was reasonable cause for the apprehension of serious bodily harm, the difference in age, size, and relative physical strength of the parties to the controversy is a proper matter for consideration. [Citations.] As the Court said in State v. Floyd (1859), 51 N.C. (6 Jones) 392, "One cannot be expected to encounter a lion as he would a lamb."

....Of course, the defendant, in order to support his plea of self-defense must not have been at fault in provoking the difficulty [citation], but, by demanding that the plaintiff and his companions leave his parking lot, the defendant acted within his legal rights and can in no way be regarded as provoking the difficulty in this case....

Holding

This plea of self-defense, if sustained, is a bar to recovery in this action. One, who has acted in justifiable self-defense "can neither be punished criminally, nor held responsible for damages in a civil action." [Citations.]

D wins!

In my opinion, the defendant has made out his plea of self-defense under the facts and applicable law, as I have found and concluded. He acted in reasonable apprehension of serious bodily harm and to repel what he reasonably feared would be a serious and dangerous assault by a person of overpowering size.

Let judgment be entered for defendant, and

It is so ordered.

Notes

1. *Unlawful Provocation.* The privilege of self-defense is not available to an aggressor: one who unlawfully provokes an attack. *See, e.g.,* Tripoli v. Gurry, 218 So. 2d 563 (La. 1969); Webb v. Snow, 132 P.2d 114, 120 (Utah 1942). Thus, if A strikes B without justification, and B, using reasonable force, returns the blow in self-defense, A is liable for any harm inflicted on B in the course of an effort to "defend" against B's response.

The status of aggressor may shift as a confrontation escalates. For example, if B, the victim of the initial unlawful attack, responds by using *excessive* force, B is liable for those injuries caused by the unreasonableness of the force. *See* Ogden v. Claycomb, 52 Ill. 365, 366 (1869); Livesay v. Ambassador Operating Co., 92 S.W.2d 961, 963 (Mo. Ct. App. 1936). Moreover, it would be absurd for the law to conclude that A's only recourse in the face of excessive force is to bring an action for damages. Rather, A, despite being the initial instigator, gains a limited right of self-defense. *See* Fraguglia v. Sala, 62 P.2d 783 (Cal. Ct. App. 1936). Though A will be responsible for the harm resulting from the initial attack on B, A will not be held liable for those damages proximately caused to B by a reasonable response to B's use of excessive force. Each party may therefore be liable to the other for portions of the resulting damage.

2. *Abandonment.* An aggressor may regain a right of self-defense by communicating to the plaintiff an intent to cease the attack. *See* Jelly v. Dabney, 581 P.2d 622, 624 (Wyo. 1978); Penn v. Henderson, 146 P.2d 760, 766 (Or. 1944). This may be difficult to do persuasively, especially if the attacker retains control of a weapon. *Cf.* Dan B. Dobbs, The Law of Torts 161 (2000) ("the original attacker is privileged to defend against the

excess force, once the original attacker has attempted to withdraw from his aggressive posture and no longer poses a threat").

3. Because factual nuances unique to each case color the assessment of whether force used in defense of self or defense of others is reasonable in amount, similar confrontations have given rise to divergent legal results. For example, in both McCullough v. McAnelly, 248 So. 2d 7 (La. Ct. App. 1971), and Lopez v. Surchia, 246 P.2d 111 (Cal. Ct. App. 1952), a father fired one or more shots in an attempt to aid his son, who was being attacked on the family's front lawn. The attacker, in each instance, suffered death or serious bodily injury. In *McCullough*, the force used was held to be reasonable; in *Lopez* the privilege was denied on the ground that the response was excessive. A lawyer presenting a claim of self-defense or defense of others must carefully develop for the factfinder the circumstances of the particular case.

4. *Mistake about Need for Self-Defense.* The defendant in Courvoisier v. Raymond, 47 P. 284 (Colo. 1896), was asleep in his bed when the building in which he lived was attacked by a mob, for reasons which do not appear in the opinion. The defendant got up, took his revolver, and attempted unsuccessfully to scare the mob away by firing into the air. Raymond, a police officer, emerged from the crowd and approached Courvoisier, who, perhaps believing that Raymond was one of the rioters, shot him. The trial court charged the jury that if it found from the evidence that Raymond was not assaulting Courvoisier, it should find Courvoisier liable for Raymond's injuries. This was held to be error: If Courvoisier reasonably, though mistakenly, believed that Raymond was attacking him, Courvoisier had a privilege to use force in self defense.

The *Courvoisier* court gave no reason why the burden of a mistake in such a case should fall upon the plaintiff, rather than upon the defendant who made the mistake, however reasonable it may have been. If the plaintiff creates the appearance of danger, the rule makes some sense—the Restatement gives the example of a plaintiff who, as a joke, pretends to attack the defendant. But if the plaintiff is not at all at fault, as may have been the case in *Courvoisier*, it is hard to see why one who decides to use force should not bear the risk that an innocent person may be harmed. Nevertheless, the Restatement presents the *Courvoisier* rule as settled law, with no indication that a minority view even exists; Restatement, Second, of Torts §63 Comment h. Compare the rule concerning mistake about whether the plaintiff has consented to contact, pp. 146–48, *supra*.

5. *Retaliation.* The privilege is one of defense, not retaliation. It does not allow a victim to "get even," but merely sanctions reasonable efforts to avoid the infliction of harm. The "law does not countenance an eye for an eye or a tooth for a tooth." Fowler V. Harper, Fleming James, Jr., & Oscar S. Gray, The Law of Torts §3.11, p. 309 (2d ed. 1986).

6. *Mere Words.* Mere words, unaccompanied by a hostile act, do not justify self defense. *See* Penn v. Henderson, 146 P.2d 760, 765 (Or. 1944). However, abusive language is relevant to whether one reasonably believes there is an attack. *See* Pattershall v. Jenness, 485 A.2d 980, 985 (Me. 1984).

7. *Duty to Retreat.* There is no duty to retreat rather than use *non-deadly* force. However, a duty to retreat rather than to defend oneself may arise if the situation calls for *deadly* force (force likely to cause death or serious bodily injury).

Many older cases (now of questionable validity) held that a person had no duty to flee rather than fight, even if that meant inflicting grievous harm on another. Other decisions accorded preservation of human life priority over notions of personal honor, and held that one under attack had a duty to retreat, rather than use deadly force, if it was possible to retreat with complete safety.

Even in jurisdictions recognizing the "duty to retreat," the duty generally does not apply to one attacked at home, or perhaps at work, unless that place was also the home or workplace of the assailant. The thought is that one's home is one's "castle." *See generally* Restatement, Second, of Torts §65 & Comments g—i (recognizing a duty to retreat and a "castle" exception).

In recent years, courts have struggled to reconcile the tort rules on self-defense with the parallel defense in criminal law, which is often defined by legislation. *See* Duplechain v. Turner, 444 So. 2d 1322 (La. Ct. App. 1984) (applying criminal standards on justifiable homicide in a civil action); *see also* Tex. Penal Code Ann. §9.32(a)(2) (Westlaw 2003) (a "person is justified in using deadly force against another... if a reasonable person in the actor's situation would not have retreated").

8. *Battered-Woman Syndrome.* Traditionally, self-defense may be invoked only if harm appears to be imminent. Despite that limitation, there have been efforts in criminal law to extend the defense to cases involving prolonged abuse of a spouse or significant other in which renewed harm is likely, though not imminent; cases in which, for example, wives who have been subjected to repeated beatings kill their husbands while they are sleeping. *See* Richard A. Rosen, *On Self-Defense, Imminence, and Women Who Kill Their Batterers*, 71 N.C. L. Rev. 371 (1993) (noting "continuing reports of jury nullifications... and executive clemencies in such cases" and arguing that since "[i]t is no longer considered moral or legal for a man to beat his wife or girlfriend or to forcibly rape her... [,] [p]erhaps society no longer considers it a moral imperative that a woman delay taking defensive action until a man who has already threatened to kill her begins to demonstrate again that he meant what he said"); Holly Maguigan, *Battered Women and Self-Defense: Myths and Misconceptions in Current Reform Proposals*, 140 U. Pa. L. Rev. 379 (1991). As yet, no reported tort case has ruled on the issue.

Drabek v. Sabley

Supreme Court of Wisconsin
142 N.W.2d 798 (Wis. 1966)

Action for damages for false imprisonment and assault and battery.

The jury found no false imprisonment and no assault and battery... [T]he court entered judgment dismissing the complaint. Plaintiff has appealed.

Plaintiff Thomas Drabek, 10 years old, lived with his parents on highway 67.... Tom and four other boys were across the highway from the Drabek home, throwing snowballs at passing cars. Defendant, Dr. Nanito Sabley, drove by, and his car was hit by a snowball, apparently thrown by one of the other boys. Dr. Sabley stopped his car and the boys ran. Dr. Sabley pursued Tom for about 100 yards, caught him, and, holding him by the arm, took him to the car and directed him to enter it. Dr. Sabley asked and was told Tom's name, but did not ask where he lived. Dr. Sabley, who had been driving north, turned his car around and drove into the village. He located a police officer, and turned Tom over to him. Tom told the officer the names of the other boys involved, and the officer took Tom to his home. Tom was with the defendant some 15 to 20 minutes.

Facts

....

FAIRCHILD, Justice.

Interpreting the evidence, where in conflict, most favorably to the verdict, defendant effectively restrained Tom's physical liberty, and took him into the village for the pur-

Thomas E. Fairchild

pose of having him tell the police officer the names of the other boys. Defendant held Tom by the arm both on the way to the car before driving into the village, and, at times, while they were in the village.

Thus there was false imprisonment unless the restraint was legally justified. Except for possible justification, the offensive holding of the arm was also a battery, albeit nominal.

   ....

Defendant claims justification in that he witnessed acts that were dangerous to defendant and others and took reasonable steps to prevent further dangerous activities.

It is recognized that one may be privileged to interfere with the liberty of another, within limits, for the purpose of defending one's self, defending a third person, or preventing the commission of a crime. Dr. Sabley did not act in self defense, since he was no longer in danger. It is true that the boys momentarily terminated their offensive activity when he stopped his car, but it was reasonable to expect them to renew it. We perceive that throwing snowballs at moving cars creates a danger, as much because of the likelihood of startling the driver as of damage to the cars. Although it is a close question whether the threat to the safety of others was sufficiently immediate, after the boys had run away, it seems to us that Dr. Sabley, though not an officer, was privileged to take reasonable steps to prevent the resumption of the activity.

Analysis

We conclude that Dr. Sabley's actions presented a jury question of reasonableness up to the time he put the boy in his car and drove away. Up to that time he had obtained the boy's name, and admonished him, according to the defendant's testimony, against carrying on the activity. The jury was entitled to believe that in holding the boy he used only such force as was reasonable for the purpose. Dr. Sabley may well have been justified in marching Tom across the road to his home and notifying his parents. We conclude, however, that it was unreasonable, as a matter of law, for Dr. Sabley to put 10-year-old Tom in his car a few yards from his home and drive him into the village for the purposes he did and under the circumstances of this case.

....

Accordingly we conclude that the jury finding, in effect, that Dr. Sabley's conduct was reasonable exonerates him up to the time he put Tom in the car, but not afterward. The restraint of Tom's liberty continued, and after that point there was false imprisonment. Dr. Sabley admitted holding Tom while they looked for the officer, and this was a battery, though nominal.

Holding

It follows that there must be a determination of compensatory damages, though the record will not support a very substantial award, for the period of false imprisonment after the point just mentioned, and for the battery, consisting of the holding of the arm for a time after reaching the village. We think the first jury's findings that there was no false imprisonment and no assault and battery, imply a finding that there was no malice, and hence no punitory damages are recoverable....

Judgment reversed, cause remanded for further proceedings.

[The dissenting opinion of BEILFUSS, J., is omitted.]

Notes

1. *See also* Young v. Warren, 383 S.E.2d 381 (N.C. Ct. App. 1989). There, after breaking into his girlfriend's house, the plaintiff was ordered out by her father at gunpoint, then shot in the back. The facts failed to show that the father acted in "defense of family" for "at the time of the shooting...the plaintiff stood outside the house with his back to the defendant" and defendant's "daughter and children were inside the house, removed from any likely harm from plaintiff."

2. *Range of Response.* In a given situation, more than one response may be reasonable, in which case the defender will not be faulted for not having selected the very best course of action. As the court wrote in Wilson v. Dimitri, 138 So. 2d 618 (La. Ct. App. 1962):

> It was sufficient that he reasonably believed the danger to his brother's life to be imminent....[I]mmunity from liability is not judicially withdrawn because some other reasonable man may have perceived the idea of disabling the assailant instead of shooting him. Detached reflection, or a pause for consideration, cannot be demanded under such trying circumstances which by their very nature require a split second decision. To reason otherwise would be to establish a premise totally unrelated to normal human conduct under the stress of a spontaneous overflow of powerful emotions.

3. *Mistaken Intervention.* Some (generally older) decisions discourage defense of others by holding that an intervenor steps into the shoes of the one being assisted; if that person has no right of self-defense, the intervenor's conduct is not privileged, regardless of what the intervenor believes. *See, e.g.,* Webb v. Snow, 132 P.2d 114, 120 (Utah 1942). Other jurisdictions encourage (or at least do not penalize) reasonable intervention efforts by holding that a reasonable mistake as to another's right of self-defense does not destroy the privilege to defend the other. *See, e.g.,* Duplechain v. Turner, 444 So. 2d 1322 (La. Ct. App. 1984) (privilege barred recovery for the death of an off-

duty officer who was shot and killed after being mistaken as the aggressor in a barroom fight). Compare the rule for self-defense, p. 152, *supra*.

C. Privileges Relating to Property

1. Defense of Property

Katko v. Briney

Supreme Court of Iowa
183 N.W.2d 657 (Iowa 1971)

MOORE, Chief Justice.

Issue

The primary issue presented here is whether an owner may protect personal property in an unoccupied boarded-up farm house against trespassers and thieves by a spring gun capable of inflicting death or serious injury.

We are not here concerned with a man's right to protect his home and members of his family. Defendants' home was several miles from the scene of the incident....Plaintiff's action is for damages resulting from serious injury caused by a shot from a 20-gauge spring shotgun set by defendants in a bedroom of an old farm house which had been uninhabited for several years. Plaintiff and his companion, Marvin McDonough, had broken and entered the house to find and steal old bottles and dated fruit jars which they considered antiques.

....The jury returned a verdict for plaintiff and against defendants for $20,000 actual and $10,000 punitive damages.

....

....Most of the facts are not disputed. In 1957 defendant Bertha L. Briney inherited her parents' farm land....Included was an 80-acre tract in southwest Mahaska County where her grandparents and parents had lived. No one occupied the house thereafter. Her husband, Edward, attempted to care for the land. He kept no farm machinery thereon. The outbuildings became dilapidated.

For about 10 years, 1957 to 1967, there occurred a series of trespassing and housebreaking events with loss of some household items, the breaking of windows and "messing up of the property in general." The latest occurred June 8, 1967, prior to the event on July 16, 1967 herein involved.

Facts

Defendants through the years boarded up the windows and doors in an attempt to stop the intrusions. They had posted "no trespass" signs on the land several years before 1967. The nearest one was 35 feet from the house. On June 11, 1967 defendants set "a shotgun trap" in the north bedroom. After Mr. Briney cleaned and oiled his 20-gauge shotgun, the power of which he was well aware, defendants took it to the old house where they secured it to an iron bed with the barrel pointed at the bedroom door. It was rigged with wire from the doorknob to the gun's trigger so it would fire when the door was opened. Briney first pointed the gun so an intruder would be hit in the stomach but at Mrs. Briney's suggestion it was lowered to hit the legs. He admitted he did so "because I was mad and tired of being tormented" but "he did not intend to injure anyone." He gave no explanation of why he used a loaded shell and set it to hit a person already in the house. Tin was nailed over the bedroom window. The spring gun could not be seen from the outside. No warning of its presence was posted.

….Prior to July 16, 1967 plaintiff and McDonough had been to the premises….On the latter date about 9:30 p.m. they made a second trip to the Briney property. They entered the old house by removing a board from a porch window which was without glass….As…[plaintiff] started to open the north bedroom door the shotgun went off striking him in the right leg above the ankle bone. Much of his leg, including part of the tibia, was blown away. Only by McDonough's assistance was plaintiff able to get out of the house and after crawling some distance was put in his vehicle and rushed to a doctor and then to a hospital. He remained in the hospital 40 days.

….

….Plaintiff testified he knew he had no right to break and enter the house with intent to steal….He further testified he had entered a plea of guilty to larceny in the nighttime of property of less than $20 value from a private building….

….The main thrust of defendants' defense…is that "the law permits use of a spring gun in a dwelling or warehouse for the purpose of preventing the unlawful entry of a burglar or thief." They repeated this contention in their exceptions to the trial court's instructions….

….In instruction 2 the court referred to the early case history of the use of spring guns and stated under the law their use was prohibited except to prevent the commission of felonies of violence and where human life is in danger. The instruction included a statement breaking and entering is not a felony of violence.

Instruction 5 stated: "You are hereby instructed that one may use reasonable force in the protection of his property, but such right is subject to the qualification that one may not use such means of force as will take human life or inflict great bodily injury. Such is the rule even though the injured party is a trespasser and is in violation of the law himself."

Instruction 6 stated: "An owner of premises is prohibited from willfully or intentionally injuring a trespasser by means of force that either takes life or inflicts great bodily injury; and therefore a person owning a premise is prohibited from setting out 'spring guns' and like dangerous devices which will likely take life or inflict great bodily injury, for the purpose of harming trespassers…."

….

Prosser on Torts, Third Edition, pages 116-118, states:

"…[because] the law has always placed a higher value upon human safety than upon mere rights in property, it is the accepted rule that there is no privilege to use any force calculated to cause death or serious bodily injury to repel the threat to land or chattels, unless there is also such a threat to the defendant's personal safety as to justify a self-defense….[S]pring guns and other man-killing devices are not justifiable against a mere trespasser, or even a petty thief…."

Restatement of Torts, section 85, page 180, states: "…A possessor of land cannot do indirectly and by a mechanical device that which, were he present, he could not do immediately and in person. Therefore, he cannot gain a privilege to install, for the purpose of protecting his land from intrusions harmless to the lives and limbs of the occupiers or users of it, a mechanical device whose only purpose is to inflict death or serious harm upon such as may intrude, by giving notice of his intention to inflict, by mechanical means and indirectly, harm which he could not, even after request, inflict directly were he present."

....

In Phelps v. Hamlett, 207 S.W. 425 (Tex. Civ. App. 1918), defendant rigged a bomb inside his outdoor theater so that if anyone came through the door the bomb would explode. The court reversed plaintiff's recovery because of an incorrect instruction but at page 426 said: "While the law authorizes an owner to protect his property by such reasonable means as he may find to be necessary, yet considerations of humanity preclude him from setting out, even on his own property, traps and devices dangerous to the life and limb of those whose appearance and presence may be reasonably anticipated, even though they may be trespassers."

In United Zinc & Chemical Co. v. Britt, 258 U.S. 268, 275, 42 S. Ct. 299, 66 L. Ed. 615, 617, the court states: "The liability for spring guns and mantraps arises from the fact that the defendant has…expected the trespasser and prepared an injury that is no more justified than if he had held the gun and fired it."

In addition to civil liability many jurisdictions hold a land owner criminally liable for serious injuries or homicide caused by spring guns or other set devices.…

[handwritten: Holding: Gun is unreasonable!]

Study and careful consideration of defendant's contentions on appeal reveal no reversible error.

Affirmed.

All Justices concur except LARSON, J., who dissents.

[The dissenting opinion of Justice Larson has been omitted.]

Notes

1. *Mistake of Fact.* With respect to defense of property, a mistake about the degree of force necessary does not destroy the privilege. However, a mistake in concluding that the intruder is not acting in the exercise of a superior privilege (such as to conduct a lawful search and seizure) does destroy the privilege, unless the mistake has been induced by the intruder (such as where police officers carrying out a warrant fail to knock and announce their warrant). *See* Dan B. Dobbs, The Law of Torts 173 (2000).

2. *Conduct Threatening Persons as Well as Property.* Cases involving harm to property may also pose a risk of harm to persons, in which case the defendant's use of deadly force may be permissible. The defendant in Bennett v. Dunn, 507 So. 2d 451 (Ala. 1987), was aroused from his sleep by an intruder who was attempting to steal his truck. According to the court, when the intruder failed to respond to barking dogs or the defendant's shouts and warning shots, the defendant did not act unreasonably in shooting the intruder. "[H]is actions taken to protect his family, himself, and his home were fully justified."

But some courts are less willing to conclude that a risk to property also involves a risk to persons. *See* Goldfuss v. Davidson, 679 N.E.2d 1099 (Ohio 1997) (evidence did not warrant a jury instruction on self-defense in an action by a trespasser's estate claiming that a homeowner negligently shot and killed the trespasser, who was attempting to break into the homeowner's barn located at least 100 feet away from house).

3. *Defense against Animals.* *See also* Harrington v. Hall, 63 A. 875, 876 (Del. 1906). There, in an action for the killing of a foxhound, the court instructed the jury:

> A person may not maliciously injure or kill a dog for a mere trespass upon his premises, and the posting of notices against trespassing by dogs will not thereafter excuse or justify an unlawful killing of a dog found upon the premises. The remedy against such trespassing is, in a proper case, against the owner of the dog.
>
> ....[But] if the dog was upon the land of the defendant in the act of destroying his turkeys, the defendant was justified in killing him....

2. Recapture of Chattels

Efforts to recover personal property taken by fraud, force, or other tortious conduct may fall within the privilege to recapture chattels. A person suffering that kind of loss may use reasonable, non-deadly force to retake the goods, if the dispossession is discovered promptly and there is "fresh pursuit" of the wrongdoer. Any unreasonable delay in either discovery or pursuit destroys the privilege. And, to discourage persons from taking the law into their own hands over mere property interests, one exercising the privilege is liable for any mistake as to the facts which create the privilege—unless that mistake is knowingly induced by the plaintiff. *See generally* Restatement, Second, of Torts §§101–11. If the dispossessor resists the recapture efforts by using force against the person asserting the privilege, the privilege becomes one of self-defense, subject to the usual rules on that subject.

In the famous case of Hodgeden v. Hubbard, 18 Vt. 504 (1846), plaintiff purchased a stove by making fraudulent representations as to his ability to pay and signing a promissory note. On the same day, soon after the sale, defendants discovered the fraud, chased the plaintiff, and took the stove from him during a scuffle in which, after the plaintiff drew a knife, the defendants allegedly "used violence and applied force to his person with great rudeness and outrage." In reversing a $1 judgment for the plaintiff, the court ruled that the plaintiff had no right to resist the defendants' efforts to regain the property, and "it was the right of the defendants to hold him by force, and, if they made use of no unnecessary violence, they were justified" in their actions.

Contrast *Hodgeden* with a case in which a buyer under a conditional sales contract merely defaults on payments. In that case, absent additional facts, there has been no dispossession by fraud, force, or other tortious conduct, and the seller has no right to retake the goods by force. In Roberts v. Speck, 14 P.2d 33 (Wash. 1932), a couple failed to make payments on their new car and the wife refused to get out of the vehicle when the seller came to reclaim it. Both the car and the wife were forcibly towed away. In a suit by the wife for damages resulting from wrongful arrest, the court reversed a judgment for the seller and granted a new trial, quoting an earlier decision:

> Because a party to a contract violates his contract, and refuses to do what he agreed to do, is no reason why the other party to the contract should compel the performance of the contract by force. The adoption of such a rule would lead to a breach of the peace, and it is never the policy of the law to encourage a breach of the peace. The right to an enforcement of this part of the contract must, in the absence of a consent on the part of the mortgagor, be enforced by due process of law, the same as any other contract.

3. Detention for Investigation

Bonkowski v. Arlan's Department Store

Court of Appeals of Michigan
162 N.W.2d 347 (Mich. Ct. App. 1968)

NEAL E. FITZGERALD, Judge.

....

The plaintiff, Mrs. Marion Bonkowski, accompanied by her husband, had left the defendant's Saginaw, Michigan store about 10:00 p.m. on the night of December 18, 1962 after making several purchases, when Earl Reinhardt, a private policeman on duty that night in the defendant's store, called to her to stop as she was walking to her car about 30 feet away in the adjacent parking lot. Reinhardt motioned to the plaintiff to return toward the store, and when she had done so, Reinhardt said that someone in the store had told him the plaintiff had put three pieces of costume jewelry into her purse without having paid for them. Mrs. Bonkowski denied she had taken anything unlawfully, but Reinhardt told her he wanted to see the contents of her purse. On a cement step in front of the store, plaintiff emptied the contents of her purse into her husband's hands. The plaintiff produced sales slips for the items she had purchased, and Reinhardt, satisfied that she had not committed larceny, returned to the store.

Plaintiff brought this action against Earl Reinhardt and Arlan's Department Store, seeking damages on several counts. She complains that as a result of defendant's tortious acts she has suffered numerous psychosomatic symptoms, including headaches, nervousness, and depression....On the counts of false arrest and slander the case went to the jury, who returned a verdict of $43,750. The defendant's motions for judgment notwithstanding the verdict, remittitur, and new trial were denied by the trial court.

....

We conclude the plaintiff established a case entitling her to go to the jury on a charge of false arrest....

....

To the common-law tort of false arrest, privilege is a common-law defense, and we recognize as applicable here a privilege similar to that recognized by the American Law Institute in the Restatement of Torts, 2d. In section 120A, the Institute recognizes a privilege in favor of a merchant to detain for reasonable investigation a person whom he reasonably believes to have taken a chattel unlawfully. We adopt the concept embodied in section 120A, and we state the rule for this action as follows: if defendant Arlan's agent, Earl Reinhardt, reasonably believed the plaintiff had unlawfully taken goods held for sale in defendant's store, then he enjoyed a privilege to detain her for a reasonable investigation of the facts.

The...[Restatement] comment states the strong reason behind recognizing such a privilege:

> The privilege stated in this section is necessary for the protection of a shop-keeper against the dilemma in which he would otherwise find himself when he reasonably believes that a shoplifter has taken goods from his counter. If there

were no such privilege, he must either permit the suspected person to walk out of the premises and disappear, or must arrest him, at the risk of liability for false arrest if the theft could not be proved.

1 Restatement of Torts, 2d, page 202.

That the problem of shoplifting, faced by merchants, has reached serious dimensions is common knowledge, and we find compelling reason to recognize such a privilege, similar to that recognized in other jurisdictions. [Citations.]

....

The privilege we recognize here goes beyond that set forth in the Restatement, for..."the Institute expresses no opinion as to whether there may be circumstances under which this privilege may extend to the detention of one who has left the premises but is in their immediate vicinity." 1 Restatement of Torts, 2d, page 202.

....We think the privilege should be so extended here because we think it entirely reasonable to apply it to the circumstances of the case at bar, for the reason that a merchant may not be able to form the reasonable belief justifying a detention for a reasonable investigation before a suspected person has left the premises....

On remand on the cause for false arrest, therefore, it will be the duty of the jury to determine in accordance with the rule we have set down, whether or not the defendant's agent, Earl Reinhardt, reasonably believed the plaintiff had unlawfully taken any goods held for sale at the defendant's store. If the jury finds the defendant's agent did so reasonably believe, then it must further determine whether the investigation that followed was reasonable under all the circumstances. If the jury finds the defendant does not come within this privilege, then from the facts as discussed above, it could find a false arrest.

....

[The court then held that the evidence was insufficient to state a slander cause of action.]

Reversed and remanded for new trial in accordance with this opinion. The award of costs to await final determination of this cause.

[On a subsequent appeal, 174 N.W.2d 765, the Michigan Supreme Court held that proof of intention to take the plaintiff into custody was absent and that in any event the false arrest claim had been abandoned on appeal. The court ordered a new trial on the issue of slander only.]

Notes

1. *Recapture of Chattels Contrasted.* Comment e to the Restatement section quoted in *Bonkowski* provides:

> The privilege stated in this Section differs from the privilege to use reasonable force for the recapture of chattels, in that it protects the actor who has made a reasonable mistake as to the wrongful taking.

Although *Bonkowski* holds that the investigation privilege may apply outside of the defendant's premises, it seems clear that at some point the distance from the premises will be so great that the applicable privilege, if any, will be recapture of chattels rather than temporary detention for purposes of investigation.

2. *Historical Development.* The recognition of a privilege to detain for investigation was due in part to changes in merchandising practices. As explained in Alvarado v. City of Dodge City, 708 P.2d 174, 180-81 (Kan. 1985):

> [T]he merchant of days past, who owned a small shop and kept all of his goods stacked on shelves behind him or in a counter between him and his customers, may have been adequately protected by the common-law rule [on recapture of chattels], because there could be no doubt in his mind when someone was stealing from him. That situation changed, however, when modern methods of marketing goods came into existence. In modern department stores or super-markets, where nearly all of the goods are on open shelves within reach of the customer, and where the shopper is expected to pick up and examine the goods before purchasing them, it is difficult for a merchant to be sure, even under ap-parently obvious circumstances, that a particular customer is pilfering from the shelves. Under these circumstances, the common-law rule did not work. Annot., 47 A.L.R.3d 998.

In the late 1950's, the need for a change in the law became clear....

3. *Reasonableness of Detention.* [T]he commentary to Section 120A of the Restate-ment, Second, of Torts observes:

> f. The privilege is one of detention...for only the time necessary for a rea-sonable investigation. Investigation does not mean discovery of all of the facts, but only such inquiry as may reasonably be made under the circumstances, promptly and without undue detention. What is a reasonable time will depend upon all of the circumstances, including the nature of the misconduct sus-pected, the amount involved, the explanation or denial offered by the other, his willingness to cooperate, and the time required to consult readily available sources of information. Normally, such a reasonable time will be short. Fifteen minutes may be too long where all that is necessary is to ask a clerk whether the other has paid. If the detention is continued beyond the time reasonably neces-sary for investigation, the actor is liable for the excessive detention.

> g. The privilege is one of detention for investigation only and it does not ex-tend to the coercion of payment, which is imprisonment for debt. Nor does it extend to the extortion of a confession of theft; and the actor is liable if he de-tains the other for that purpose....

> h. Reasonable force may be used to detain the suspected person; but, as in the case of recapture of chattels..., the use of force intended or likely to cause serious bodily harm is never privileged for the sole purpose of detention to in-vestigate, and it becomes privileged only where the resistance of the other makes it necessary for the actor to use such force in self-defense. In the ordi-nary case, the use of any force at all will not be privileged until the other has been requested to remain; and it is only where there is no time for such a re-quest, or it would obviously be futile, that force is justified.

See also Dillard Dept. Stores, Inc. v. Silva, 106 S.W.3d 789 (Tex. App. 2003) (holding, under the state's investigation-privilege statute, that a one-hour detention was not too long, but that there was sufficient evidence to support a jury finding that the store acted in an unreasonable manner, and was therefore liable for false imprisonment, because the patron testified that the store's agent placed him on the ground and handcuffed him, emptied the patron's shopping bag onto the floor, and escorted him upstairs in handcuffs when people were around).

4. *Resisting Detention.* A shoplifter owes a duty to submit peaceably to lawful arrest or detention, and may be liable to a store employee who is injured while endeavoring to capture the shoplifter. *See* Smitherman v. McCafferty, 622 So. 2d 322 (Ala. 1993).

5. *Nonmerchants.* Although the common-law privilege to detain for purposes of investigation is frequently asserted by merchants, the privilege may be invoked by others. *See, e.g.,* Thornhill v. Wilson, 504 So. 2d 1205, 1208 (Miss. 1987) (detention of plaintiff for 15 minutes by police officers investigating frantic telephone calls regarding gunfire was not unreasonable).

6. *Shoplifting Statutes.* In a number of jurisdictions, the common law privilege to detain a suspected shoplifter has been recognized in, or expanded by, statute. Concerning such legislation, the court in Alvarado v. City of Dodge City, 708 P.2d 174, 181 (Kan. 1985), wrote:

> [M]any state legislatures…[have enacted] statutes specifically giving a merchant a qualified privilege to detain suspected shoplifters. The various state statutes vary somewhat in form but they all are consistent in providing that merchants or their employees or agents may detain in good faith and upon probable cause or reasonable grounds any person who it is believed was removing goods for sale from the store without paying for them, provided that such detention is for a reasonable time and is conducted in a reasonable manner.…The fact that under the statute the merchant can act upon probable cause or reasonable grounds leaves room for honest mistake. Under these statutes, the question of whether the merchant or his employee had reasonable grounds or probable cause for detention of the suspected shoplifter is the issue most frequently arising in false arrest cases involving suspected shoplifters.…

See also Jury v. Giant of Md., Inc., 491 S.E.2d 718 (Va. 1997) (holding that, in connection with detention of a suspected shoplifter, a merchant has statutory immunity from civil liability based on a wide range of torts, but not in circumstances in which the tort is committed in a willful, wanton, or otherwise unreasonable or excessive manner).

Some statutes have extended the privilege to detain to persons other than merchants. *See, e.g.,* Cal. Penal Code §490.5(f)(1) (Westlaw 2003) (persons employed by library facilities); Fla. Stat. Ann. §812.015(3)(a) (Westlaw 2003) (law enforcement officer, merchant, farmer, or transit agency employee or agent); Tex. Civ. Prac. & Rem. Code Ann. §124.001 (Westlaw 2003) (any "person who reasonably believes that another has stolen or is attempting to steal property").

7. *Civil Fines for Shoplifting.* A shoplifter is subject to criminal prosecution. In addition, in virtually all states, store owners can impose civil shoplifting fines ranging, for example, from $40 to three times "actual damages," and often including the value of the item and the wages of employees who process the case. There are many statutory variations. *See, e.g.,* Tex. Civ. Prac. & Rem. Code Ann. §134.005 (Westlaw 2003) (in addition to court costs and attorney's fees, the plaintiff may recover actual damages plus a $1000 maximum penalty from the person who commits the theft, or up to $5000 in actual damages from a parent or other person who had a duty to control the offender). Typically, the retailer passes the shoplifter's name to a lawyer or collection agency; if the fine is not paid, the person is sued civilly. Some major retailers recover over a million dollars in fines annually. In most states, a store's right to collect a civil fine does not preclude it from also initiating a criminal action. However, the criminal process tends to be slow and rarely permits a store to recover money.

D. Public Necessity and Private Necessity

Surocco v. Geary
Supreme Court of California
3 Cal. 69 (Cal. 1853)

MURRAY, Chief Justice, delivered the opinion of the Court.

....

This was an action...to recover damages for blowing up and destroying the plaintiffs' house and property, during the fire of the 24th of December, 1849.

Geary, at that time Alcalde of San Francisco, justified, on the ground that he had the authority, by virtue of his office, to destroy said building, and also that it had been blown up by him to stop the progress of the conflagration then raging.

It was in proof, that the fire passed over and burned beyond the building of the plaintiffs, and that at the time said building was destroyed, they were engaged in removing their property, and could, had they not been prevented, have succeeded in removing more, if not all of their goods.

The cause was tried by the court sitting as a jury, and a verdict rendered for the plaintiffs, from which the defendant prosecutes this appeal....

The only question for our consideration is, whether the person who tears down or destroys the house of another, in good faith, and under apparent necessity, during the time of a conflagration, for the purpose of saving the buildings adjacent, and stopping its progress, can be held personally liable in an action by the owner of the property destroyed.

This point has been so well settled in the courts of New York and New Jersey, that a reference to those authorities is all that is necessary to determine the present case.

The right to destroy property, to prevent the spread of a conflagration, has been traced to the highest law of necessity, and the natural rights of man, independent of society or civil government. "It is referred by moralists and jurists to the same great principle which justifies the exclusive appropriation of a plank in a shipwreck, though the life of another be sacrificed; with the throwing overboard goods in a tempest, for the safety of a vessel; with the trespassing upon the lands of another, to escape death by an enemy..."

....

....At...times, the individual rights of property give way to the higher laws of impending necessity.

A house on fire, or those in its immediate vicinity, which serve to communicate the flames, becomes a nuisance, which it is lawful to abate, and the private rights of the individual yield to the considerations of general convenience, and the interests of society. Were it otherwise, one stubborn person might involve a whole city in ruin, by refusing to allow the destruction of a building which would cut off the flames and check the progress of the fire, and that, too, when it was perfectly evident that his building must be consumed.

....

The counsel for the respondent has asked, who is to judge of the necessity of the destruction of property?

This must, in some instances, be a difficult matter to determine. The necessity of blowing up a house may not exist, or be as apparent to the owner, whose judgment is clouded by interest, and the hope of saving his property, as to others. In all such cases the conduct of the individual must be regulated by his own judgment as to the exigencies of the case. If a building should be torn down without apparent or actual necessity, the parties concerned would undoubtedly be liable in an action of trespass. But in every case the necessity must be clearly shown. It is true, many cases of hardship may grow out of this rule, and property may often in such cases be destroyed, without necessity, by irresponsible persons, but this difficulty would not be obviated by making the parties responsible in every case, whether the necessity existed or not.

Rule

....

In the absence of any legislation on the subject, we are compelled to fall back upon the rules of the common law.

The evidence in this case clearly establishes the fact, that the blowing up of the house was necessary, as it would have been consumed had it been left standing. The plaintiffs cannot recover for the value of the goods which they might have saved; they were as much subject to the necessities of the occasion as the house in which they were situate; and if in such cases a party was held liable, it would too frequently happen, that the delay caused by the removal of the goods would render the destruction of the house useless.

Holding

....

Judgment reversed.

Notes

1. *Imminent Peril*. In City of Rapid City v. Boland, 271 N.W.2d 60 (S.D. 1978), plaintiff's building was leveled during government clean-up efforts following a massive flood. The clean-up was intended to prevent the spread of disease. The court held that compensation for the building need not be paid if, at the time of the destruction, there was an imminent and impending peril to the public and it appeared to be necessary to destroy the property to prevent the spread of the peril. In remanding the case, the court quoted an 1848 decision:

> To fall within the privilege, there must be "[a] necessity, extreme, imperative, or overwhelming, [to] constitute such a justification, but mere expediency, or public good, or utility, will not answer."

See also Allen v. Camp, 70 So. 290 (Ala. 1915) (although it is permissible to kill a dog to fend off an attack, one who fails to do so cannot decapitate the animal days later to determine whether it was rabid).

2. *Private Citizens*. The privilege of public necessity is not confined to official representatives of the public and may be exercised by private citizens. *See* Restatement, Second, of Torts §262 Comment b.

3. *Privilege No Greater than the Necessity*. An actor seeking to avert a public disaster cannot cause greater harm than appears to be necessary. Thus, a firefighter needing to reach a conflagration cannot forcibly take the plaintiff's car, if the plaintiff is willing to drive the firefighter to the scene. Restatement, Second, of Torts §262 illus. 3.

Wegner v. Milwaukee Mutual Insurance Co.

Supreme Court of Minnesota
479 N.W.2d 38 (Minn. 1991)

TOMLJANOVICH, Justice.

Facts

[The Minneapolis police department severely damaged a house owned by Harriet Wegner while attempting to apprehend an armed suspect who had fled into the house. In an attempt to expel the suspect, a "SWAT" team fired at least 25 rounds of chemical munitions and three "flash-bang" concussion grenades into the dwelling. Eventually the suspect was apprehended.]

.... Wegner sought compensation from the City of Minneapolis on trespass and constitutional "taking" theories. The district court granted the City's motion for summary judgment on the "taking" issue. The court of appeals affirmed, reasoning that although there was a "taking" within the meaning of the Minnesota Constitution, the "taking" was noncompensable under the doctrine of public necessity. We reverse.

....

Article I, section 13, of the Minnesota Constitution provides "Private property shall not be taken, destroyed or damaged for public use without just compensation, first paid or secured." ....

....

Holding

We hold that where an innocent third party's property is damaged by the police in the course of apprehending a suspect, that property is damaged within the meaning of the constitution.

....

We briefly address the application of the doctrine of public necessity to these facts. The Restatement (Second) of Torts §196 describes the doctrine as follows:

Rule

> One is privileged to enter land in the possession of another if it is, or if the actor reasonably believes it to be, necessary for the purpose of averting an imminent public disaster.[6]

See McDonald v. City of Red Wing, 13 Minn. 38 (Gil. 25) (1868) (city excused from paying compensation under the doctrine of "public safety" where city officers destroyed building to prevent the spread of fire). Prosser, apparently somewhat troubled by the potential harsh outcomes of this doctrine, states:

---

6. Prosser explains:
   Where the danger affects the entire community, or so many people that the public interest is involved, that interest serves as a complete justification to the defendant who acts to avert the peril to all. Thus, one who dynamites a house to stop the spread of a conflagration that threatens a town, or shoots a mad dog in the street, or burns clothing infected with smallpox germs, or in time of war, destroys property which should not be allowed to fall into the hands of the enemy, is not liable to the owner, so long as the emergency is great enough, and he has acted reasonably under the circumstances. This notion does not require the "champion of the public" to pay for the general salvation out of his own pocket. The number of persons who must be endangered in order to create a public necessity has not been determined by the courts.
   Prosser and Keeton, The Law of Torts, §24 (5th ed. 1984).

It would seem that the moral obligation upon the group affected to make compensation in such a case should be recognized by the law, but recovery usually has been denied.

Prosser and Keeton, The Law of Torts, §24 (5th ed. 1984); *see also* Restatement (Second) of Torts §196 comment h. Here, the police were attempting to apprehend a dangerous felon who had fired shots at pursuing officers. The capture of this individual most certainly was beneficial to the whole community. In such circumstances, an individual in Wegner's position should not be forced to bear the entire cost of a benefit conferred on the community as a whole.

. . . .

We are not inclined to allow the city to defend its actions on the grounds of public necessity under the facts of this case. *But see* Steele [v. City of Houston, 603 S.W.2d 786, 792 (Tex. 1980)].c We believe the better rule, in situations where an innocent third party's property is taken, damaged or destroyed by the police in the course of apprehending a suspect, is for the municipality to compensate the innocent party for the resulting damages. The policy considerations in this case center around the basic notions of fairness and justice. At its most basic level, the issue is whether it is fair to allocate the entire risk of loss to an innocent homeowner for the good of the public. We do not believe the imposition of such a burden on the innocent citizens of this state would square with the underlying principles of our system of justice. Therefore, the City must reimburse Wegner for the losses sustained.

As a final note, we hold that the individual police officers, who were acting in the public interest, cannot be held personally liable. Instead, the citizens of the City should all bear the cost of the benefit conferred.

The judgments of the courts below are reversed and the cause remanded for trial on the issue of damages.

Affirmed in part, reversed in part and remanded.

Notes

1. The rule in *Wegner* does not require compensation of property losses sustained by persons involved in criminal activity. *See* McGovern v. City of Minneapolis, 480 N.W.2d 121, 127 (Minn. Ct. App. 1992).

2. *Tort v. "Taking."* Federal and state constitutions require just compensation if the government takes private property for public use. Courts are divided on whether property damage caused by the police should be treated as a tort or a "taking." *Compare* Wallace v. City of Atlantic City, 608 A.2d 480 (N.J. Super. Ct. 1992) (in an action for damages caused during the execution of a search warrant, a landlord could not recover in tort, but could sue for a "taking"), *with* Customer Co. v. City of Sacramento, 41 Cal. Rptr. 2d 658, 670-73 (Cal. 1995) (in an action for damage to a convenience store caused by efforts to apprehend a suspect, the plaintiff could not recover under the theory of inverse condemnation, but could sue under provisions of the Tort Claims Act); Sullivant

---

c. In *Steele*, the police set fire to the plaintiff's house in an effort to recapture escaped convicts who were hiding there. In remanding the case for a new trial on the issue of compensation, the court noted that the city could defend its actions by proof of a "great public necessity," but that evidence of "[m]ere convenience" would not justify uncompensated destruction. — Eds.

v. City of Okla. City, 940 P.2d 220 (Okla. 1997) (potential tort, but no taking). The complexities of "takings" law are beyond the scope of a course in torts, but *Wegner* makes clear that the doctrine of public necessity and its underlying policies may have application to such actions.

3. *Public Necessity and Immunity.* Persons acting on behalf of the government may be protected not only by the public-necessity privilege, but by governmental or official immunity. *See, e.g.,* Kelly v. Storey County Sheriff, 611 N.W.2d 475 (Iowa 2000) (holding, in an action by the owner of a residence to recover damages caused by a forcible entry to execute an arrest warrant, that the county, the sheriff, and sheriff's department employees were entitled to immunity because the officers had exercised "due care" within the terms of a state statute conferring immunity).

Vincent v. Lake Erie Transp. Co.

Supreme Court of Minnesota
124 N.W. 221 (Minn. 1910)

O'BRIEN, J.

The steamship Reynolds, owned by the defendant, was for the purpose of discharging her cargo on November 27, 1905, moored to plaintiff's dock in Duluth. While the unloading of the boat was taking place a storm from the northeast developed, which at about 10 o'clock p.m., when the unloading was completed, had so grown in violence that the wind was then moving at 50 miles per hour and continued to increase during the night. There is some evidence that one, and perhaps two, boats were able to enter the harbor that night, but it is plain that navigation was practically suspended....After the discharge of the cargo the Reynolds signaled for a tug to tow her from the dock, but none could be obtained because of the severity of the storm. If the lines holding the ship to the dock had been cast off, she would doubtless have drifted away; but, instead, the lines were kept fast, and as soon as one parted or chafed it was replaced, sometimes with a larger one. The vessel lay upon the outside of the dock, her bow to the east, the wind and waves striking her starboard quarter with such force that she was constantly being lifted and thrown against the dock, resulting in its damage, as found by the jury, to the amount of $500.

....One witness testified upon the trial that the vessel could have been warped into a slip, and that, if the attempt to bring the ship into the slip had failed, the worst that could have happened would be that the vessel would have been blown ashore upon a soft and muddy bank. The witness was not present in Duluth at the time of the storm, and, while he may have been right in his conclusions, those in charge of the dock and the vessel at the time of the storm were not required to use the highest human intelligence, nor were they required to resort to every possible experiment which could be suggested for the preservation of their property. Nothing more was demanded of them than ordinary prudence and care, and the record in this case fully sustains the contention of the appellant that, in holding the vessel fast to the dock, those in charge of her exercised good judgment and prudent seamanship.

....

The appellant contends by ample assignments of error that, because its conduct during the storm was rendered necessary by prudence and good seamanship under conditions over which it had no control, it cannot be held liable for any injury resulting to the property of others, and claims that the jury should have been so instructed....

The situation was one in which the ordinary rules regulating property rights were suspended by forces beyond human control, and if, without the direct intervention of some act by the one sought to be held liable, the property of another was injured, such injury must be attributed to the act of God, and not to the wrongful act of the person sought to be charged. If during the storm the Reynolds had entered the harbor, and while there had become disabled and been thrown against the plaintiffs' dock, the plaintiffs could not have recovered. Again, if while attempting to hold fast to the dock the lines had parted, without any negligence, and the vessel carried against some other boat or dock in the harbor, there would be no liability upon her owner. But here those in charge of the vessel deliberately and by their direct efforts held her in such a position that the damage to the dock resulted, and, having thus preserved the ship at the expense of the dock, it seems to us that her owners are responsible to the dock owners to the extent of the injury inflicted.

In Depue v. Flateau, 100 Minn. 299, 111 N.W. 1, 8 L.R.A. (N.S.) 485, this court held that where the plaintiff, while lawfully in the defendants' house, became so ill that he was incapable of traveling with safety, the defendants were responsible to him in damages for compelling him to leave the premises. If, however, the owner of the premises had furnished the traveler with proper accommodations and medical attendance, would he have been able to defeat an action brought against him for their reasonable worth?

....

Theologians hold that a starving man may, without moral guilt, take what is necessary to sustain life; but it could hardly be said that the obligation would not be upon such person to pay the value of the property so taken when he became able to do so....

Let us imagine in this case that for the better mooring of the vessel those in charge of her had appropriated a valuable cable lying upon the dock. No matter how justifiable such appropriation might have been, it would not be claimed that, because of the overwhelming necessity of the situation, the owner of the cable could not recover its value.

This is not a case where life or property was menaced by any object or thing belonging to the plaintiff, the destruction of which became necessary to prevent the threatened disaster. Nor is it a case where, because of the act of God, or unavoidable accident, the infliction of the injury was beyond the control of the defendant, but is one where the defendant prudently and advisedly availed itself of the plaintiff's property for the purpose of preserving its own more valuable property, and the plaintiffs are entitled to compensation for the injury done.

Order affirmed.

LEWIS, J.

I dissent....

In my judgment, if the boat was lawfully in position at the time the storm broke, and the master could not, in the exercise of due care, have left that position without subjecting his vessel to the hazards of the storm, then the damage to the dock, caused by the pounding of the boat, was the result of an inevitable accident. If the master was in the exercise of due care, he was not at fault. The reasoning of the opinion admits that if the ropes, or cables, first attached to the dock had not parted, or if, in the first instance, the master had used the stronger cables, there would be no liability. If the master could not, in the exercise of reasonable care, have anticipated the severity of the storm and sought a place of safety before it became impossible, why should he be required to anticipate the severity of the storm, and, in the first instance, use the stronger cables?

I am of the opinion that one who constructs a dock to the navigable line of waters, and enters into contractual relations with the owner of a vessel to moor at the same, takes the risk of damage to his dock by a boat caught there by a storm, which event could not have been avoided in the exercise of due care, and further, that the legal status of the parties in such a case is not changed by renewal of cables to keep the boat from being cast adrift at the mercy of the tempest.

Notes

1. *Avoiding Greater Harm.* The idea behind private necessity is that one may inflict some harm in order to avoid greater harm. "Thus one whose chattel of small value is threatened with serious harm or even with complete destruction may not be privileged to destroy a far more valuable chattel of another in order to protect it." Restatement, Second, of Torts §263, Comment d.

2. *Compensation in Cases of Private Necessity.* The privilege of private necessity is incomplete in the sense that one who acts to protect personal interests, or the interests of a third person, is liable to another whose interests are invaded by the act. However, the privilege is complete, and no compensation is owed, if the person whose interest is being protected is the owner of the property in question. For example, a defendant who uses the plaintiff's scarf as a tourniquet to stop the plaintiff's bleeding following an accident is not liable for the value of the scarf. Restatement, Second, of Torts §263, Comment e and illus. 1. Cases like this are, one suspects, rare, as it would be an ungrateful plaintiff indeed who would even bring such a case. It is not unheard of, however, for those saved even from death to sue their rescuers. Carter v. Buscher, 973 F.2d 1328 (7th Cir. 1992), was a wrongful-death action by the widow of a man killed by police officers. The officers killed the plaintiff's husband when he fired at them while they were trying to arrest him for conspiracy to have the plaintiff murdered. The plaintiff did not deny that her husband was plotting to kill her; she argued, however, that the police could have arrested him without violence if they had planned the arrest more carefully. She lost.

Ploof v. Putnam

Supreme Court of Vermont
71 A. 188 (Vt. 1908)

MUNSON, J.

It is alleged as the ground of recovery that on the 13th day of November, 1904, the defendant was the owner of a certain island in Lake Champlain, and of a certain dock attached thereto,...that the plaintiff was then possessed of and sailing upon said lake a certain loaded sloop, on which were the plaintiff and his wife and two minor children; that there then arose a sudden and violent tempest, whereby the sloop and the property and persons therein were placed in great danger of destruction; that, to save these from destruction or injury, the plaintiff was compelled to, and did, moor the sloop to defendant's dock; that the defendant, by his servant, unmoored the sloop, whereupon it was driven upon the shore by the tempest, without the plaintiff's fault; and that the sloop and its contents were thereby destroyed, and the plaintiff and his wife and children cast into the lake and upon the shore, receiving injuries. This claim is set forth in two counts—one in trespass, charging that the defendant by his servant with force and arms willfully and designedly unmoored the sloop; the other in case, alleging that it was the duty of the defendant by his servant to permit the plaintiff to moor his sloop to the dock, and to permit it to remain so moored during the continuance of the tempest, but that the defendant by his servant, in disregard of this duty, negligently, carelessly, and wrongfully unmoored the sloop. Both counts are demurred to generally.

There are many cases in the books which hold that necessity…will justify entries upon land and interferences with personal property that would otherwise have been trespasses.…A traveler on a highway who finds it obstructed from a sudden and temporary cause may pass upon the adjoining land without becoming a trespasser because of the necessity. [Citations.] An entry upon land to save goods which are in danger of being lost or destroyed by water or fire is not a trespass.…

This doctrine of necessity applies with special force to the preservation of human life. One assaulted and in peril of his life may run through the close of another to escape from his assailant. 37 Hen. VII, pl. 26. One may sacrifice the personal property of another to save his life or the lives of his fellows. In Mouse's Case, 12 Co. 63, the defendant was sued for taking and carrying away the plaintiff's casket and its contents. It appeared that the ferryman of Gravesend took 47 passengers into his barge to pass to London, among whom were the plaintiff and defendant; and the barge being upon the water a great tempest happened, and a strong wind, so that the barge and all the passengers were in danger of being lost if certain ponderous things were not cast out, and the defendant thereupon cast out the plaintiff's casket. It was resolved that in case of necessity, to save the lives of the passengers, it was lawful for the defendant, being a passenger, to cast the plaintiff's casket out of the barge.…

Rule

It is clear that an entry upon the land of another may be justified by necessity, and that the declaration before us discloses a necessity for mooring the sloop. But the defendant questions the sufficiency of the counts because they do not negative the existence of natural objects to which the plaintiff could have moored with equal safety. The allegations are, in substance, that the stress of a sudden and violent tempest compelled the plaintiff to moor to defendant's dock to save his sloop and the people in it. The averment of necessity is complete, for it covers not only the necessity of mooring, but the necessity of mooring to the dock; and the details of the situation which created this necessity, whatever the legal requirements regarding them, are matters of proof, and need not be alleged.…

….

Judgment affirmed and cause remanded.

Notes

1. A similar case is Rossi v. Del Duca, 181 N.E.2d 591 (Mass. 1962). There, an eight-year-old girl, frightened and chased by a dog, sought to make her escape by crossing private property. On that land, she was unexpectedly attacked by the landowner's two Great Danes. In an action against the property owner, the court held that the doctrine of private necessity saved the girl from liability for technical trespass and permitted her to recover for her injuries under a dog-bite statute that would have denied compensation if she was trespassing.

2. *Overcoming Resistance to Privileged Entry*. Assuming that Rossi's entry was privileged, would Rossi have been liable for harm to the dogs or for property damage reasonably inflicted in an attempt to escape or resist the attack? According to the Restatement, Second, of Torts:

The important difference between the status of one who is a trespasser on land and one who is on the land pursuant to an incomplete privilege is that the latter is entitled to be on the land and therefore the possessor of the land is under a duty to permit him to come and remain there and hence is not privileged to resist his entry. Consequently, where the possessor of the land resists such a privileged entry, the actor's use of reasonable force to overcome such resistance to his entry or remaining on the land so long as the necessity continues is *completely* privileged. Therefore he is not liable for harm so occasioned.

(§197 Comment k; emphasis added.)

3. *Emergencies of the Actor's Own Making.* Even if the plaintiff in *Rossi* had provoked the incident by taunting the first dog, the result might have been the same, for the doctrine of private necessity is available even in an emergency of the actor's own making. Note, however, that a restriction may apply:

> [I]f the entry is [only] for the purpose of protecting the actor's land or chattels, such an entry would be reasonable only where the property sought to be saved is of considerably greater value than the amount of probable harm to the possessor's land or chattels likely to be done by saving the actor's property.

Restatement, Second, of Torts §197 Comment d (brackets added).

4. *Reasonableness and Necessity.* The privilege of private necessity must be exercised at a reasonable time and in a reasonable manner. *See* Restatement, Second, of Torts §197 cmts. a & c. Courts sometimes seize upon lack of reasonableness as a basis for concluding that the privilege does not apply. In Benamon v. Soo Line R.R. Co., 689 N.E.2d 366 (Ill. App. Ct. 1997), a 15-year-old boy fleeing from a gang ran up a railway incline where his foot got caught between steel grates and was severed by a passing train. The court held that the boy was a trespasser, rather than a person present on the property pursuant to a privilege of private necessity, and that therefore the railroad was not required to exercise care on his behalf. The court wrote:

> [W]e must conclude as a matter of law that, given the existence of less dangerous options, and given the known risks associated with the railroad tracks, that William's presence on or near those tracks was not reasonable and thus his presence on those tracks was not a private necessity....

E. Unlawful Conduct

Barker v. Kallash
Court of Appeals of New York
468 N.E.2d 39 (N.Y. 1984)

WACHTLER, Judge.

The question on this appeal is whether the 15-year-old plaintiff, who was injured while constructing a "pipe bomb," can maintain a tort action against the 9-year-old defendant who allegedly sold the firecrackers from which the plaintiff's companions extracted the gunpowder used to construct the bomb. The trial court granted summary judgment dismissing the cause of action against the defendant and his parents for alleged negligent supervision. The Appellate Division affirmed....

The facts are in dispute; however, for the purposes of this appeal, dealing with a motion for summary judgment, we must accept the plaintiff's version of the events, as the lower courts have done.

...[T]he plaintiff, George Barker, and two companions, Ayman and Anas Kallash, made a "pipe bomb" in the backyard of the Barker home in Brooklyn. At the time the plaintiff was nearly 15 years old and the Kallash brothers were 14 and 15, respectively. The bomb was made by filling a metal pipe, three or four inches long and one inch wide, with gunpowder.

The plaintiff concededly obtained the pipe from his father's home workshop where he also found the caps to seal it and a power drill he used to make a hole for the fuse. Although his father also used gunpowder to reload shotgun shells at home, the plaintiff contends that the gunpowder used in the bomb was supplied by the Kallash brothers who extracted it from firecrackers. He testified, at an examination before trial, that they had told him that the day before the incident they had purchased firecrackers from the defendant Daniel Melucci, Jr., who was not quite nine years old at the time. Indeed, the plaintiff testified that he had told the Kallash brothers where the firecrackers could be purchased. The injury occurred after the pipe had been capped at one end and the plaintiff, and one of the Kallash brothers, had poured the gunpowder into it. As the plaintiff was screwing the second cap on to the pipe it exploded, severely injuring his hands.

Plaintiff, through his father, brought an action against the Kallash brothers for their part in constructing the bomb, against Daniel Melucci, Jr., for allegedly selling the firecrackers to the Kallashes, and against Robert Judge, another infant, who allegedly sold the firecrackers to Melucci. In each instance the plaintiff also sued the infants' parents for negligent supervision.

....

At the outset a distinction must be drawn between lawful activities regulated by statute and activities which are entirely prohibited by law. In the first instance, it is familiar law that a violation of a statute governing the manner in which activities should be conducted, would merely constitute negligence or contributory negligence [citations]. Such cases would today be resolved under the rule of comparative negligence [citation]. However, when the plaintiff has engaged in activities prohibited, as opposed to merely regulated, by law, the courts will not entertain the suit if the plaintiff's conduct constituted a serious violation of the law and the injuries for which he seeks recovery were the direct result of that violation. In this latter instance recovery is denied, not because the plaintiff contributed to his injury, but because the public policy of this State generally denies judicial relief to those injured in the course of committing a serious criminal act (Reno v. D'Javid, 42 N.Y.2d 1040, 399 N.Y.S.2d 210, 369 N.E.2d 766). In the *Reno* case a woman who submitted to an illegal abortion could not recover for alleged negligence on the part of the physician performing the operation [citation]. The rule is based on "the paramount public policy imperative that the law, whatever its content at a given time or for however limited a period, be obeyed" [citation]. It extends the basic principle that one may not profit from his own wrong (Riggs v. Palmer, 115 N.Y. 506, 22 N.E. 188; Carr v. Hoy, 2 N.Y.2d 185, 158 N.Y.S.2d 572, 139 N.E.2d 531) to tort actions seeking compensation for injuries resulting from the plaintiff's own criminal activities of a serious nature.

The rule denying compensation to the serious offender would not apply in every instance where the plaintiff's injury occurs while he is engaged in illegal activity (*see* Restatement, Torts 2d, §889, Comment b). Thus if the plaintiff in the example cited above had been injured in an automobile accident as a result of another's negligence, she would not be denied access to the courts merely because she was on the way to have the illegal operation performed (*see, e.g.*, Restatement, Torts 2d, §889, Comment b, Illustration 3). A complaint should not be dismissed merely because the plaintiff's injuries were occasioned by a criminal act (*cf.* Humphrey v. State of New York, 60 N.Y.S.2d 742, 744, 469 N.Y.S.2d 661, 457 N.E.2d 767, *supra*; Scurti v. City of New York, 40 N.Y.2d 433, 387 N.Y.S.2d 55, 354 N.E.2d 794). However, when the plaintiff's injury is a direct result of his knowing and intentional participation in a criminal act he cannot seek compensation for the loss, if the criminal act is judged to be so serious an offense as to warrant denial of recovery (Reno v. D'Javid, *supra*). Thus a burglar who breaks his leg while descending the cellar stairs, due to the failure of the owner to replace a missing step cannot recover compensation from his victims....

The plaintiff urges that this rule should not apply to his case for a number of reasons....

First, he contends that his acts were not so egregious and that the case in essence involves nothing more than "a claim arising out of injuries suffered by one of several youngsters playing with fireworks shortly before the Fourth of July."....In the case before us the plaintiff's conduct may not fairly be characterized as a minor dereliction. By his own admission his injuries did not result from the mere use of firecrackers, but from his efforts to incorporate the gunpowder extracted from the firecrackers into a pipe bomb. Constructing a bomb is a far more dangerous activity not only to the maker, but to the public at large, and is treated as a far more serious offense under the law....

Secondly, the plaintiff claims dispensation from the general rule because of his age, not quite 15 at the time of the incident. He notes that at that age he could not be convicted of a criminal offense [citation] and urges that he should be granted a similar exemption from the rule precluding tort recovery for injuries resulting from an otherwise serious criminal act. Although the plaintiff may not be held criminally responsible for his conduct, the fact remains that constructing a bomb is prohibited by law [citation]. Notably even the criminal law does not grant a youth complete immunity from responsibility for illegal acts [citation]. There is nothing in this record which would justify such an exemption in this civil action.

The plaintiff was not a toddler. And building a bomb is not such an inherently innocuous activity that it can reasonably be presumed to be a legally permissible act by an average 15 year old. In fact, despite extensive pretrial proceedings below the plaintiff never claimed that he was ignorant of the fact that his conduct was wrongful or that he was unaware of the potential danger it posed to himself and other members of the public....

Finally the plaintiff urges that the rule precluding such recovery was abrogated when the Legislature adopted CPLR 1411 which provides that the "culpable conduct" of a plaintiff "shall not bar recovery, but the amount of damages otherwise recoverable shall be diminished in the proportion which the culpable conduct attributable to the claimant or decedent bears to the culpable conduct which caused the damages." The plaintiff contends that the term "culpable conduct" includes illegal conduct, thus permitting a plaintiff who was injured while violating the law to recover from those who may have contributed to his injury. Since this statute went into effect on September 1, 1975 (L. 1975, ch. 69), prior to the injury sustained by the plaintiff in this case, he urges that it permits him to recover a proportionate share of his loss.

CPLR 1411 abolished the contributory negligence rule which had previously denied a plaintiff any recovery for a cognizable tort if it was shown that the plaintiff had in any way contributed to his own injury.... The history of these statutes shows that by referring to "culpable" conduct, rather than negligence, the Legislature intended to include tortious conduct generally, breaches of warranty and the like which had previously served to defeat otherwise cognizable causes of action for damages, or bar contribution among defendants [citations].

The lower courts properly held that CPLR 1411 has no application to the rule precluding a plaintiff from recovering for injuries sustained as a direct result of his own illegal conduct of a serious nature involving risk of physical harm. That rule is not based on the theory that a plaintiff, with an otherwise cognizable cause of action, cannot recover for an injury to which he has contributed (McKay v. Syracuse R.T. Ry. Co., 208 N.Y. 359, 101 N.E. 885). It rests, instead, upon the public policy consideration that the courts should not lend assistance to one who seeks compensation under the law for injuries resulting from his own acts when they involve a substantial violation of the law [citations]. It simply means that proof of such an injury would not demonstrate any cause of action cognizable at law. The policy which applies to this case, has always existed independently from the rule of contributory negligence and its successor, comparative negligence....

The policy on which this rule rests has not diminished with time. Nor is there any indication in the history of the statute that the Legislature intended, by eliminating outmoded impediments to otherwise lawful recoveries, to create a new cause of action for those who suffer injuries as a direct result of voluntary participation in acts which the Legislature itself has defined as a serious offense involving risk of physical harm to the public....

Accordingly, the order of the Appellate Division should be affirmed.

SIMONS, Judge (dissenting).

. . . .

This case is factually and legally distinguishable from ... [Reno v. D'Javid, 42 N.Y.2d 1040, 399 N.Y.S.2d 210, 369 N.E.2d 766]. *Reno* dealt with an adult plaintiff and undisputed criminal liability for participating in an abortion. This plaintiff was 14 at the time of the accident, an age at which the majority concedes he cannot be held criminally responsible [citations]. Notwithstanding this, the majority insists that because of the seriousness of his conduct, his claim is barred. A plaintiff should not be foreclosed from seeking civil relief, however, because of the illegal character of his act as distinguished from an actual finding of criminal liability. Particularly is this so when the plaintiff is an infant plaintiff or one lacking capacity for other reasons, those whom the criminal law treats differently from competent adults....

Moreover, the *Reno* decision was based upon Riggs v. Palmer, 115 N.Y. 506, 22 N.E. 188, *supra* and that decision is inconsistent with the policies underlying present tort law. In *Riggs*, a legatee who murdered a testator was not allowed to inherit under the testator's will even though he was the named beneficiary. In denying the inheritance, this court relied upon the fundamental principle of public policy that one may not profit from his own wrong [citation]. As our later decisions demonstrate, however, the application of the principle has been restricted to preventing unjust enrichment in cases of competing claims to real or personal property [citations]. No New York tort case other than *Reno* has been brought to our attention in which *Riggs* was relied upon or even cited. A few other states have applied the *Riggs* principle in torts but those decisions have been described as contrary to the compensatory theory of torts and as "a barbarous relic of the worst there was in puritanism" (2 Harper and James, Torts, §17.6, pp. 995-997; *see, also*, Prosser, Torts [4th ed.], pp. 421, 422).

A plaintiff's unlawful conduct has never been applied consistently in New York to foreclose plaintiff's recovery. Thus, in Corbett v. Scott, 243 N.Y. 66, 152 N.E. 467, *supra*, a 16-year-old infant plaintiff was not denied recovery for his injuries when he had an accident while driving a motorcycle in violation of two statutes. In Connolly v. Knickerbocker Ice Co., 114 N.Y. 104, 21 N.E. 101, *supra*, an infant plaintiff riding unlawfully on the platform of a trolley was not denied recovery for the injuries he sustained when the trolley was involved in an accident. In Platz v. City of Cohoes, 89 N.Y. 219, *supra*, a plaintiff injured while violating the laws prohibiting driving a carriage on Sunday was permitted to recover (*see, also*, Carroll v. Staten Is. R.R. Co., 58 N.Y. 126). Similarly, plaintiff's criminal conduct has not been used to foreclose access to the courts for reckless or drunken drivers (*see* Humphrey v. State of New York, 60 N.Y.2d 742, 744, 469 N.Y.S.2d 661, 457 N.E.2d 767) or those guilty of criminal trespass when injured by a landowner's fault (*see* Scurti v. City of New York, 40 N.Y.2d 433, 387 N.Y.S.2d 55, 354 N.E.2d 794). The majority maintains liability will be foreclosed if the conduct is "serious"—the concurring opinion would apply the rule only if the conduct was "egregious"—and the injury the direct result of plaintiff's unlawful conduct.... A plaintiff's right to maintain an action, however, should not rest on a Judge's subjective view of whether the conduct is serious or egregious: Judges will differ in making such an evaluation. Indeed the Judges of this court disagreed on the "seriousness" of the plaintiff's conduct in *Reno*, as they do here....

There is another problem in applying the *Riggs* principle to questions of tort liability. It runs counter to the rule of comparative fault and the policy interests underlying that rule because *Riggs* produces an "all or nothing" result which precludes the wrongdoer from seeking judicial relief....

....

New York adopted comparative fault by a statute passed in 1975 (L. 1975, ch. 69). It provides that the culpable conduct attributable to the claimant shall not bar his recovery, only diminish it in the proportion which it bears to the culpable conduct of the defendant. The statute makes no exceptions for intentional acts or even criminal ones but applies alike to all culpable conduct, not just negligence [citations]. Thus, the statute provides the vehicle for evaluating plaintiff's conduct, whether it caused his damages and if so in what degree. It prevents a plaintiff from profiting from his own wrong because he can recover only the amount of his damages attributable to defendant's culpable conduct. In doing so, it provides a workable rule of law which reconciles the *Riggs* principle with the competing principle that a party injured by the fault of another is entitled to compensation.

....

Accordingly, I dissent and would vote to reverse the order granting summary judgment.

COOKE, C.J., and JONES and KAYE, JJ., concur with WACHTLER, J.

JASEN, J., concurs in a separate opinion [which has been omitted].

SIMONS, J., dissents and votes to reverse in another opinion in which MEYER, J., concurs.

Order affirmed, with costs.

Notes

1. *Claims Based on Illegal Acts.* Many other cases have denied aid to those whose claims are based upon their own illegal acts. *See* Amato v. United States, 549 F. Supp.

863, 867 (D. N.J. 1982), *aff'd without op.*, 729 F.2d 1445 (3d Cir. 1984) (suspect shot during robbery could not sue police for failing to arrest him prior to the robbery); Cole v. Taylor, 301 N.W.2d 766, 768 (Iowa 1981) (plaintiff barred from suing psychiatrist for negligently failing to prevent her from committing a murder); Adkinson v. Rossi Arms Co., 659 P.2d 1236 (Alaska 1983) (perpetrator of manslaughter had no claim against the manufacturer and seller of the shotgun for direct personal losses alleged to have resulted from the shooting); Lord v. Fogcutter Bar, 813 P.2d 660 (Alaska 1991) (drunken customer had no claim for damages against the bar that served him liquor in violation of a dramshop law); Burcina v. City of Ketchikan, 902 P.2d 817 (Alaska 1995) (patient who set fire to a mental health center and was convicted of arson did not have a cause of action against his psychiatrist or the facility at which he received treatment); Preston v. State, 543 N.Y.S.2d 823 (App. Div. 1989) (claimant convicted of assault barred from suing the State for alleged medical malpractice in not confining him prior to the incident); La Page v. Smith, 563 N.Y.S.2d 174 (App. Div. 1990) (estate barred from recovery for death of intoxicated driver during high-speed race); Vandenburg v. Brosnan, 514 N.Y.S.2d 784 (App. Div. 1987), *aff'd*, 524 N.Y.S.2d 672 (N.Y. 1988) (passenger who procured beer for minor driver had no cause of action against the seller); Saks v. Sawtelle, Goode, Davidson & Troilo, 880 S.W.2d 466 (Tex. Ct. App. 1994) (public policy barred a legal malpractice action for damages suffered by clients who were convicted of knowingly committing bank fraud after they had allegedly received negligent advice relating to a loan transaction); Lee v. Nationwide Mut. Ins. Co., 497 S.E.2d 328 (Va. 1998) (minor injured in an accident involving a stolen vehicle was barred from recovery against the driver).

But see Goldfuss v. Davidson, 679 N.E.2d 1099, 1104 (Ohio 1997) (holding, in an action based on the allegedly negligent shooting of a trespasser, that public policy does not preclude recovery for injuries sustained during the commission of a felony).

2. Some cases have reached opposite results on similar facts. *Compare* Zysk v. Zysk, 404 S.E.2d 721 (Va. 1990) (plaintiff barred from recovering damages for herpes contracted during participation in the crime of fornication with the defendant), *with* Long v. Adams, 333 S.E.2d 852, 855 (Ga. 1985) (contrary holding). Also, compare *Barker* with Craft v. Mid Island Dept. Stores, 492 N.Y.S.2d 780 (App. Div. 1985) (conduct of a minor in pouring pools of gasoline and lighting them with matches not such a serious violation of the law, or so criminal in nature, as to preclude recovery from marketers of allegedly flammable sweatshirt; "none of the defendants point to any penal statute applicable to the use of gasoline").

3. *Legislation Relating to Criminal Acts.* In some states, the common law rule relating to unlawful conduct has been modified by statute. Consider the following laws:

ALASKA STATUTES §09.65.210
(Westlaw 2002)

Damages resulting from commission of a felony
or while under the influence of alcohol or drugs

A person who suffers personal injury or death...may not recover damages for the personal injury or death if the injury or death occurred while the person was

(1) engaged in the commission of a felony, the person has been convicted of the felony, including conviction based on a guilty plea or plea of nolo contendere, and the party defending against the claim proves by clear and con-

vincing evidence that the felony substantially contributed to the personal injury or death;

(2) engaged in conduct that would constitute the commission of an unclassified felony, a class A felony, or a class B felony for which the person was not convicted and the party defending against the claim proves by clear and convincing evidence

(A) the felonious conduct; and

(B) that the felonious conduct substantially contributed to the personal injury or death;

. . . .

(4) operating a vehicle, aircraft, or watercraft while under the influence of intoxicating liquor or any controlled substance in violation of AS 28.35.030, was convicted, including conviction based on a guilty plea or plea of nolo contendere, and the party defending against the claim proves by clear and convincing evidence that the conduct substantially contributed to the personal injury or death; or

(5) engaged in conduct that would constitute a violation of AS 28.35.030 for which the person was not convicted if the party defending against the claim proves by clear and convincing evidence

(A) the violation of AS 28.35.030; and

(B) that the conduct substantially contributed to the personal injury or death.

CAL. CIV. CODE § 3333.3
(Westlaw 2003)

In any action for damages based on negligence, a person may not recover any damages if the plaintiff's injuries were in any way proximately caused by the plaintiff's commission of any felony, or immediate flight therefrom, and the plaintiff has been duly convicted of that felony.

OHIO ST. REV. CODE §2307.60
(Westlaw 2003)

Claim Barred Due to Conviction for Felony, or Misdemeanor Offense of Violence

. . . .

(B). . . . (2) Recovery on a claim for relief in a tort action is barred to any person. . . if the person has been convicted of or has pleaded guilty to a felony, or to a misdemeanor that is an offense of violence, arising out of criminal conduct that was a proximate cause of the injury or loss for which relief is claimed in the action.

(3) Division (B) of this section does not apply to civil claims based upon alleged intentionally tortious conduct, alleged violations of the United States Constitution, or alleged violations of statutes of the United States pertaining to civil rights.

4. *General Justification.* Because the common law continually adapts itself to new and changing circumstances, a defendant's conduct may be privileged under what might be called a doctrine of general justification even though it falls within none of the

traditional categories of defenses and privileges. The rough contours of this concept—which is essentially an inquiry into whether the defendant's conduct was acceptable under the circumstances—were outlined in Sindle v. N.Y.C. Transit Auth., 307 N.E.2d 245 (N.Y. 1973). There, a school bus driver was charged with false imprisonment. He asserted that he was privileged to drive the children to the police station when some of them continued to engage in repeated acts of vandalism despite requests to desist. The court agreed: "[A] school bus driver, entrusted with the care of his student-passengers and the custody of public property, has the duty to take reasonable measures for the safety and protection of both." The court held, in determining the existence of the privilege, that it was appropriate to take into account the need for the defendant to protect persons and property, the defendant's duty to aid in apprehending wrongdoers, the manner and place of the occurrence, and the feasibility of other alternative courses of action.

5. *Discipline of Children.* In Rodriguez v. Johnson, 504 N.Y.S.2d 379 (Civ. Ct. of City of N.Y. 1986), a school bus matron who struck a child was held liable for battery even though the slap did not constitute the use of excessive force. The evidence showed that the children on the bus were "noisy and troublesome" and that the plaintiff "was talking loudly and moving about in his seat." The court wrote:

> Physical violence should never be invoked, least of all against children who are so seriously harmed by it. Studies have consistently shown that not only do children themselves suffer when they are physically violated, but they often respond by being physically abusive to those weaker than themselves....

> ....

> ....Any person who physically assaults a child for any reason other than self-defense or defense of others is liable to that child for monetary damages.

Should the *Rodriguez* rule bar parents from using physical force to discipline their child? Section 147 of the Restatement, Second, of Torts provides in part:

> A parent is privileged to apply such reasonable force or to impose such reasonable confinement upon his child as he reasonably believes to be necessary for its proper control, training, or education.

In determining whether force or confinement is reasonable, the following factors are relevant: the age, sex, and physical and mental condition of the child; the nature of the offense and the child's apparent motive; the influence of the child's example upon other children of the same family; whether the force or confinement is reasonably necessary and appropriate to compel obedience to a proper command; whether it is disproportionate to the offense, unnecessarily degrading, or likely to cause serious or permanent harm.

Chapter 4

Damages

A. In General

1. Introduction

Anderson v. Sears, Roebuck & Co.

United States District Court for the Eastern District of Louisiana
377 F. Supp. 136 (E.D. La. 1974)

CASSIBRY, District Judge:

On April 23,1970 the Britains' home was completely consumed by a fire which was ignited by a defective Sears' heater. Both Mildred Britain and her infant daughter, Helen Britain, were severely burned and Helen Britain suffered multiple permanent injuries....

....

[At trial, a verdict was returned in favor of Helen Britain in the amount of $2 million]....The sole issue presently before the court is whether the damages awarded to Helen Britain were excessive.

....Defendants ground their argument of excessiveness merely on the size of the verdict. The reasonableness of quantum, however, is not to be decided in a vacuum but rather is to be considered in light of the evidence as to the injuries and actual damages sustained and the future effects thereof....

The legal standard on which to gauge a jury verdict for remittitur purposes is the "maximum recovery rule." [Citations.] This rule directs the trial judge to determine whether the verdict of the jury exceeds the maximum amount which the jury could reasonably find and if it does, the trial judge may then reduce the verdict to the highest amount that the jury could properly have awarded. Functionally, the maximum recovery rule both preserves the constitutionally protected role of the jury as finder of facts and prevents the predilections of the judge from infecting the jury's determination. Thus, the court's task is to ascertain, by scrutinizing all of the evidence as to each element of damages, what amount would be the maximum the jury could have reasonably awarded. In this case there are five cardinal elements of damages: past physical and mental pain; future physical and mental pain; future medical expenses; loss of earning capacity; and permanent disability and disfigurement.

Past Physical and Mental Pain

The infant child Helen Britain, was almost burned to death in the tragic fire that swept her home. She was burned over forty per cent of her entire body; third degree burns cover eighty per cent of her scalp and second and third degree burns of the trunk and of her extremities account for the remainder. Helen Britain's immediate post-trauma treatment required hospitalization for twenty-eight days, during which time the child developed pneumonia, required numerous transfusions, suffered fever, vomiting, diarrhea, and infection, and underwent skin graft surgery, under general anesthesia, to her scalp, which was only partially successful. Keloid scarring caused webbing and ankylosis of the child's extremities and severely limited her motion. The child's fingers became adhered together; scarring bent the arm at the elbow in a burdensome, fixed position; and thick scarring on the thighs and on the side of and behind the knees impaired walking.

This child had to undergo subsequent hospitalizations for further major operations and treatment. The second major operation under general anesthesia was undertaken to graft new skin from the back and stomach to the remaining bare areas of the scalp. The third operation under general anesthesia was an attempt to relieve the deformity of her left hand caused by the webbing scars which bound down the fingers of that hand. A fourth operation under general anesthesia was performed to reduce scars which had grown back on the left hand again webbing the fingers. I cannot envisage the breadth and intensity of the pain experienced by Helen Britain throughout this ordeal.

The undisputed testimony reveals that one of the most tragic aspects of this case is that the horrible mental and emotional trauma caused to this child occurred at an age which medical experts maintain is crucial to a child's entire psyche and personality formation. Helen Britain's persistent emotional and mental disturbance is evidenced by bed wetting, nightmares, refusing to sleep alone, withdrawal, and speech impediments. Dr. Cyril Phillips, a psychiatrist, and Dr. Diamond both indicated that the child manifested to them, even at this early age, emotional illness and retarded mental growth.

The evidence reflects that an award of six hundred thousand dollars for this element of damages alone would not be unreasonable.

Future Physical and Mental Pain

There is clear evidence that the stretching, pulling, and breaking down of scars inherent in growth will continue to cause severe pain and a crippling limitation of motion in varying degrees to all of Helen Britain's upper and lower extremities. Very little can be done to improve the condition of the scalp which will never be able to breathe, sweat or grow hair. There will be risks, trauma and pain, both physical and mental, with each of the recommended twenty-seven future operations which will extend over most of the child's adult life, if she is in fact fortunate enough to be able to risk undergoing these recommended surgeries. Furthermore, Helen Britain must vigilantly guard against irritation, infection and further injury to the damaged and abnormal skin, scars and grafts because any injury, however slight, can generate cancer in these adynamic areas.

The inherent stresses and tensions of each new phase of life will severely tax this little girl's debilitated and delicate mental and emotional capacity. Throughout her future life expectancy of seventy-five years, it is reasonable to expect, that she will be deprived of a normal social life and that she will never find a husband and raise a family. On top of this, Helen Britain will always be subjected to rejection, stares and tactless inquiries from children and adults.

The court concludes that an award of seven hundred fifty thousand dollars for this element of damages alone would not be excessive.

Future Medical Expenses

A large award for future medical expenses is justified. The uncontradicted testimony was that Helen Britain would need the guidance, treatment and counseling of a team of doctors, including plastic surgeons, psychiatrists and sociologists, throughout her lifetime. Add to this the cost of twenty-seven recommended operations and the cost of private tutoring necessitated by the child's mental and emotional needs and the jury could justifiably award a figure of two hundred and fifty thousand dollars to cover these future expenses.

Loss of Earning Capacity

The evidence of Helen Britain's disabilities both physical, mental and emotional was such that this court holds that the jury could properly find that these disabilities would prevent her from earning a living for the rest of her life. Not only do the physical impairments to her extremities disable her but her emotional limitations require avoiding stress and the combined effect is the permanent incapacity to maintain serious employment.

The jury was provided with actuarial figures which accurately calculated both the deduction of interest to be earned and the addition of an inflationary buffer, on any award made for future loss of earning capacity. In view of these incontrovertible projections at trial, it was within the province of the jury to award as much as $330,000.00 for the loss of earning capacity.

Permanent Disability and Disfigurement

The award for this element of damage must evaluate in monetary terms the compensation due this plaintiff for the permanent physical, mental and emotional disabilities and disfigurements proved by the evidence adduced at trial. A narration treating Miss Britain's permanent disabilities and disfigurements would be lengthy and redundant; therefore, I resort to listing.

1. The complete permanent loss of 80% of the scalp caused by the destruction of sweat glands, hair follicles and tissue—all of which effects a grotesque disfigurement and freakish appearance.

2. The permanent loss of the normal use of the legs.

3. The permanent impairment of the left fingers and hand caused by recurring webbing and resulting in limited motion.

4. The permanent impairment of the right hand caused by scars and webbing of the fingers.

5. The permanent injury to the left elbow and left arm with ankylosis and resulting in a crippling deformity.

6. The permanent destruction of 40% of the normal skin. As a result of this a large portion of the body is covered by "pigskin." Pigskin resembles the dry, cracked skin of an aged person and is highly susceptible to irritation from such ordinary things as temperature changes and washing.

7. Permanent scars over the majority of the body where skin donor sites were removed.

8. The permanent impairment of speech.

9. The loss of three years of formative and impressionable childhood.

10. Permanently reduced and impaired emotional capacity.

11. The permanent impairment of normal social, recreational and educational life.

12. The permanent imprint of her mother's hand on her stomach.

Considering each of the foregoing items, the court concludes that the jury had the prerogative of awarding up to one million, one hundred thousand dollars for this element of damages.

By totaling the estimated maximum recovery for each element of damages, the jury's actual award is placed in proper perspective. According to my calculations the maximum jury award supported by the evidence in this case could have been two million, nine hundred eighty thousand dollars. Obviously, the jury's two million dollar verdict is well within the periphery established by the maximum award test.

. . . .

[Two defendants] . . . argue that the introduction of photographs of the plaintiff was inflammatory. Since a part of plaintiff's claim for damages is for disfigurement and the humiliation and embarrassment resulting therefrom, I hold that these photographs were properly admitted to show the condition of the plaintiff as she appeared to others, at the time they were taken. [Citations.]

The defendants suggest that the presence of the child in the courtroom and in the corridors of the courthouse in some way inflamed or prejudiced the jury. This allegation is unfounded; the defendants have not pointed out any wrongful conduct on the part of Helen Britain, her parents, or counsel for plaintiffs. Helen Britain was well behaved and quiet the entire time she was in the courtroom. Accordingly I hold that there was not any bias, prejudice, or any other improper influence which motivated the jury in making its award.

The defendants' motions for a remittitur are denied.

Notes

1. *Controlling Excessive and Inadequate Damages: Remittitur and Additur.* A court has discretion to order a new trial if it finds the jury's verdict not to be supported by the weight of the evidence. When a court finds an award of damages to be excessive, a common practice is to order a new trial (on the issue of damages only) unless the plaintiff agrees to accept a smaller sum fixed by the court in place of the jury's award. This procedure is called "remittitur." The cost in money and time of a trial is so great that plaintiffs usually decide to take the lower sum, but they need not do so, and there are cases in which plaintiffs have gone through two or even three trials rather than accept a court's figure.

A similar technique—"additur"—allows a court to award the plaintiff a new trial on damages unless the defendant agrees to pay a larger amount than the jury awarded; as with remittitur, this can be done only if the award is against the weight of the evidence. For an example of additur, see Micari v. Mann, 481 N.Y.S.2d 967 (Sup. Ct. 1984) (holding that a small award of punitive damages in a case involving sexual abuse by an acting teacher was inadequate). Additur is not permitted in some states, and in such instances the sole remedy for an award that is manifestly too small is a new trial. *See* Guckian v. Fowler, 453 S.W.2d 323 (Tex. App. 1970); *see also* Bozeman v. Busby, 639 So.

2d 501 (Ala. 1994) (holding that a state statute that authorized a trial court to increase the amount of punitive damages awarded by a jury violated the state constitutional right to a jury trial).

A 1935 Supreme Court decision holds that Federal courts cannot use additur because the practice violates the Seventh Amendment's right to a jury trial; Dimick v. Schiedt, 293 U.S. 474 (1935). Remittitur is, however, practiced in Federal courts.

"In the absence of consent to an additur/remittitur order by the affected party, trial and appellate courts lack the authority to increase or decrease jury damage assessments." David Baldus, John C. MacQueen, M.D., and George Woodworth, *Improving Judicial Oversight of Jury Damages Assessments: A Proposal for the Comparative Additur/Remittitur Review of Awards for Nonpecuniary Harms and Punitive Damages*, 80 Iowa. L. Rev. 1109, 1119 n. 17 (1995).

Judges are not to set aside damages awards merely because they would have reached a judgment different from that of the jury. It is sometimes said that the standard for review is whether the jury's determination is "shocking to the judicial conscience or so grossly inadequate as to constitute a miscarriage of justice," or "indicates caprice or mistake or a clear abuse of its factfinding discretion or the clear influence of partiality, corruption, passion, prejudice, or a misconception of law." Tann v. Service Distrib., Inc., 56 F.R.D. 593 (E.D. Pa. 1972), *aff'd*, 481 F.2d 1399 (3d Cir. 1973). One kind of case in which judges tend to find damages excessive is that in which the jury awards a larger amount than the plaintiff's own witnesses' testimony supports.

Some states impose a lower standard for appellate review of mental distress damages. *See* Goady v. Utopia Home Care Agency, 759 N.Y.S.2d 183 (App. Div. 2003) (holding that a jury award of $200,000 for past pain and suffering, and $100,000 for future pain and suffering, to an infant upon whom a hot iron fell, deviated materially from what would be reasonable compensation, and a new trial on damages would be granted absent a stipulation reducing those damages to $125,000 and $25,000, respectively); Saenz v. Fidelity & Guar. Ins. Underwriters, 925 S.W.2d 607 (Tex. 1996) (requiring "evidence that the amount found is fair and reasonable").

In some states, the standards for remittitur and additur are set out by statute. *See,* *e.g.*, Fla. Stat. Ann. §768.74 (Westlaw 2003).

2. *"Hedonic" Damages.* Notably absent from the *Anderson* court's list of elements of tort damages is an award for the plaintiff's loss of ability to engage in enjoyable activities. Suppose, for example, that a minor injury to a plaintiff's arm causes permanent stiffness, which prevents the plaintiff from playing golf, which had been her favorite recreational activity. Traditionally, no award could be made for this loss; the plaintiff would be entitled to recover for pain and suffering, for medical expenses, for lost wages, if any, but not for this kind of loss. In recent years, some courts have approved awards of "hedonic" damages, to compensate for loss of some of life's pleasures.

The plaintiff in McDougald v. Garber, 536 N.E.2d 372 (N.Y. 1989), became permanently comatose as a result of brain injuries inflicted by the defendant's negligence. The jury's award included $3.5 million for the plaintiff's loss of enjoyment of life. The New York Court of Appeals refused to allow any recovery for loss of enjoyment of life as a category separate from pain and suffering. It also held that, if the plaintiff's neurological functions were so impaired that she could feel nothing, she was not entitled to an award for pain and suffering. The court felt that damages of this sort could not be compensatory and were, therefore, "punitive," and so improper. The *McDougald* opinion recognized, however, that the frustration of being unable to engage in one's favorite activities can be a component of a pain-and-suffering award if the plaintiff is conscious enough to suffer that kind of frustration. "A significant number of jurisdictions recognize the compensability of hedonic damages, but reject any contention that the loss of life's pleasures is a separate category of damages." Virginia Smith Gautier, *Comment, Hedonic Damages: A Variation in Paths, the Questionable Expert and a Recommendation for Clarity in Mississippi*, 65 Miss. L.J. 735, 746 (1996).

It may be difficult to introduce expert testimony on the issue of hedonic damages. *See* Ayers v. Robinson, 887 F. Supp. 1049 (N.D. Ill. 1995) (testimony, based on a "willingness-to-pay" model of valuing human life, was not admissible under the federal rules as "scientific knowledge" that would assist the trier of fact, and was also misleading and not admissible because of its low probative value).

3. *Per Diem Arguments.* To calculate damages for physical and mental pain and suffering, a majority of jurisdictions permit lawyers to make *per diem* arguments. Under this approach, counsel reduces the discomfort to small units of time, such as minutes, hours, or days; sets a value on each unit (*e.g.*, a penny a minute; a dollar an hour; ten dollars a day); and then argues that the jury should arrive at a total award by multiplying the unit value by the number of units of time that the discomfort may be expected to continue. Because a modest per unit figure may give rise to a very large long-term amount (*e.g.*, 10 cents per minute equals roughly $52,560 per year), some courts refuse to allow *per diem* arguments on the ground that they are inherently misleading.

4. *Pain and Suffering Awards in Similar Cases.* In Jutzi-Johnson v. U.S., 263 F.3d 753 (7th Cir. 2001), a case involving a jail suicide, Judge Richard Posner wrote:

> Most courts...treat the determination of how much damages for pain and suffering to award as a standardless, unguided exercise of discretion by the trier of fact, reviewable for abuse of discretion pursuant to no standard to guide the reviewing court either. To minimize the arbitrary variance in awards bound to result from such a throw-up-the-hands approach, the trier of fact should, as is done routinely in England, [citation], be informed of the amounts of pain and suffering damages awarded in similar cases. [Citations.] And when the trier of fact is a judge, he should be required as part of his Rule 52(a) obligation to set forth in his opinion the damages awards that he considered comparable. We make such comparisons routinely in reviewing pain and suffering awards, *see, e.g.*, Tullis v. Townley Engineering & Mfg. Co., 243 F.3d 1058, 1066 (7th Cir. 2001); Riemer v. Illinois Dept. of Transportation, 148 F.3d 800, 808 (7th Cir. 1998); DeBiasio v. Illinois Central R.R., 52 F.3d 678, 689 (7th Cir.1995), as do other courts. *See, e.g.*, Smith v. Kmart Corp., 177 F.3d 19, 31–32 (1st Cir. 1999); Mathie v. Fries, 121 F.3d 808, 813–14 (2d Cir.1997); Williams v. Chevron U.S.A., Inc., 875 F.2d 501, 506 (5th Cir.1989). It would be a wise practice to follow at the trial level as well.
>
> ....
>
> ...[B]oth parties have cited what they deem comparable cases. Only their notions of comparability are stunted. The plaintiff cites three cases in which damages for pain and suffering ranging from $600,000 to $1 million were awarded, but in each one the pain and suffering continued for hours, not minutes. The defendant confined its search for comparable cases to other prison suicide cases, implying that prisoners experience pain and suffering differently from other persons, so that it makes more sense to compare Johnson's pain and suffering to that of a prisoner who suffered a toothache than to that of a free

person who was strangled, and concluding absurdly that any award for pain and suffering in this case that exceeded $5,000 would be excessive. The parties should have looked at awards in other cases involving asphyxiation, for example cases of drowning, which are numerous. [Citations.] Had they done so, they would have come up with an award in the range of $15,000 to $150,000.

5. *"Day-in-the-Life" Videos.* An effective visual aid for dramatizing to the jury the hardships that an accident has imposed on the plaintiff is the "day-in-the-life" video. Such productions, which show a plaintiff's struggle with daily activities, such as dressing, bathing, eating, and therapy, are expensive and thus normally made only in cases involving serious injuries. Because a "day-in-the-life" video is prepared for admission into evidence, the defendant's attorney may have a right to be present during the filming, and the use of background music and other mechanisms for heightening drama will likely be precluded. Another type of video production used in personal injury cases is the "video settlement documentary." It differs from a "day-in-the-life" video in that it is intended for viewing not by a jury, but by the opposing attorney and client. The content of a video settlement documentary is not constrained by rules of evidence. It may include footage showing the demonstrative evidence (*e.g.*, models of the accident site) and the expert witnesses the plaintiff will seek to present at trial. The purpose is to persuade the defendant to settle the case on generous terms.

6. *Damages for "Loss of Consortium."* "Consortium" is a spouse's "legal right…to the company, affection, and service of the other" spouse; Webster's Ninth New Collegiate Dictionary (1987).

The common law of England allowed a husband whose wife was injured an action against the tortfeasor for "loss of consortium." A wife whose husband was injured had no comparable action. Today, in every state, the action is allowed either spouse. *See* Romero v. Byers, 872 P.2d 840, 843 (N.M. 1994). Damages in actions for loss of consortium include medical expenses paid by the plaintiff for the injured spouse, the costs of hiring someone to do the work an injured spouse can no longer do, and, in cases involving serious injuries, compensation for the loss of the companionship (sexual and other) and affection of the plaintiff's spouse.

In principle, one spouse's action for loss of consortium is an action distinct from the other spouse's action for his or her own injuries. However, in nearly all jurisdictions, the action for loss of consortium must be tried together with the principal action. *Cf.* Desjarlais v. USAA Ins. Co., 824 A.2d 1272 (R.I. 2003) (wife and children's claims were barred due to failure to join). Damages may also be subject to the same per-person insurance policy limits. *See* Ferrell v. Fireman's Fund Ins. Co., 696 So. 2d 569 (La. 1997) (holding that loss of consortium is a derivative claim and not a separate bodily injury, and therefore the per-person, rather than per-accident, limit applies). Furthermore, defenses—such as contributory negligence—that would affect recovery in the principal action will in most states have the same effect in an action for loss of consortium. Thus, if *D* negligently injures *H*, and if *H* was negligent as well, *H*'s negligence will eliminate or reduce not only his own award but also any award sought by *H*'s wife, *W*, for loss of consortium.

Of course, a jury is free to conclude, despite the testimony of the parties, that there was no loss of consortium with respect to household services and the like. In Dunn v. Bank-Tec South, 2003 W.L. 22438710 (Tex. App.), a jury found that a bank customer's injuries to his arm, which were caused when a mobile teller unit at a drive-in banking facility closed on it, were less than permanent, serious, and disabling, and that the customer's wife was not entitled to damages for loss of consortium. The appellate court concluded that the jury's determination was not manifestly unjust. The wife's testimony about her husband's inability as a result of the injury to do yard work, about the reduction in the amount of time he spent helping her around the house, and about his increased isolation and decreased physical affection, were inherently subjective in nature, and the wife was not a disinterested witness.

In fact, persons other than the spouse of the victim may suffer when someone is injured: unmarried cohabitants, the victim's parents, and the victim's children or grandchildren come to mind.

Many jurisdictions allow the parents of an injured child to recover for financial losses (principally medical expenses). In some states, legislation or case law allows a parent to recover for the loss of a child's companionship as well. *See, e.g.*, Gallimore v. Children's Hosp. Med. Ctr., 617 N.E.2d 1052 (Ohio 1993) (permitting recovery for loss of filial consortium, including loss of the child's services, companionship, comfort, love, and solace). *But see* Roberts v. Williamson, 111 S.W.3d 113, 117 (Tex. 2003) (rejecting claim for filial consortium and quoting precedent stating that "Although parents customarily *enjoy* the consortium of their children, in the ordinary course of events a parent does not *depend* on a child's companionship, love, support, guidance, and nurture in the same way and to the same degree that a husband depends on his wife, a wife depends on her husband, or a minor or disabled adult child depends on his or her parent").

At least one state has held that a grandparent standing in the place of a parent as caregiver and provider of affection may sue for loss of consortium. *See* Fernandez v. Walgreen Hastings Co., 968 P.2d 774 (N.M. 1998).

A few jurisdictions give the children of injured parents an action. *See Gallimore, supra* (including loss of parent's services, society, companionship, affection, comfort, guidance, and counsel). However, most states decline to do so. *See* Harrington v. Brooks Drugs, Inc., 808 A.2d 532, 534 (N.H. 2002) (quoting the second Restatement as indicating that "the overwhelming weight of authority…is against recognition of a cause of action for loss of parental consortium").

Some courts have permitted an award for loss of consortium in the case of siblings. *See, e.g.,* Sheahan v. Northeast Illinois Reg'l Commuter R.R. Corp., 496 N.E.2d 1179 (Ill. Ct. App. 1986).

Lozoya v. Sanchez, 66 P.3d 948 (N.M. 2003), was the first (unreversed) case in the nation to recognize the right of an unmarried cohabitant standing in an "intimate familial relationship" to the injured party to sue for loss of consortium.

Those close to an accident victim may sometimes recover for their own emotional distress, at least in cases in which they actually see the accident happen. *See* Chapter 11.

Considerable variation exists among jurisdictions as to who can maintain an action for loss of consortium, the measure of damages, procedural requirements, and the extent to which defenses in the principal case apply in the loss-of-consortium action.

7. *Medical Monitoring.* Some courts allow an award of damages for medical monitoring. "In the context of a toxic exposure action, a claim for medical monitoring seeks to recover the cost of future periodic medical examinations intended to facilitate early detection and treatment of disease caused by a plaintiff's exposure to toxic substances." Potter v. Firestone Tire and Rubber Co., 863 P.2d 795, 821 (Cal. 1993); Bower v. Westinghouse Elec. Corp., 522 S.E.2d 424, 429 (W. Va.1999) (holding that a cause of action

exists for the recovery of medical monitoring costs and that such recovery is permitted in at least six other states).

2. The Collateral-Source Rule

Helfend v. Southern California Rapid Transit District
Supreme Court of California, In Bank
465 P.2d 61 (Cal. 1970)

TOBRINER, Acting Chief Justice.

....

Plaintiff [who was injured in a bus-auto collision] filed a tort action against the Southern California Rapid Transit District, a public entity, and Mitchell, an employee of the transit district....Defendant requested permission to show that about 80 percent of the plaintiff's hospital bill had been paid by plaintiff's Blue Cross insurance carrier and that some of his other medical expenses may have been paid by other insurance.... The court ruled that defendants should not be permitted to show that plaintiff had received medical coverage from any collateral source.

....

The Supreme Court of California has long adhered to the doctrine that if an injured party receives some compensation for his injuries from a source wholly independent of the tortfeasor, such payment should not be deducted from the damages which the plaintiff would otherwise collect from the tortfeasor....

Although the collateral source rule remains generally accepted in the United States, nevertheless many other jurisdictions have restricted or repealed it. In this country most commentators have criticized the rule and called for its early demise....

....

The collateral source rule as applied here embodies the venerable concept that a person who has invested years of insurance premiums to assure his medical care should receive the benefits of his thrift. The tortfeasor should not garner the benefits of his victim's providence.

The collateral source rule expresses a policy judgment in favor of encouraging citizens to purchase and maintain insurance for personal injuries and for other eventualities. Courts consider insurance a form of investment, the benefits of which become payable without respect to any other possible source of funds. If we were to permit a tortfeasor to mitigate damages with payments from plaintiff's insurance, plaintiff would be in a position inferior to that of having bought no insurance, because his payment of premiums would have earned no benefit. Defendant should not be able to avoid payment of full compensation for the injury inflicted merely because the victim has had the foresight to provide himself with insurance.

Some commentators object that the above approach to the collateral source rule provides plaintiff with a "double recovery," rewards him for the injury, and defeats the principle that damages should compensate the victim but not punish the tortfeasor. We agree with Professor Fleming's observation, however, that "double recovery is justified only in the face of some exceptional, supervening reason, as in the case of accident or life insurance, where it is felt unjust that the tortfeasor should take advantage of the thrift and prescience of the victim in having paid the premiums." (Fleming, Introduction to the Law of Torts (1967) p. 131.)....

Furthermore, insurance policies increasingly provide for either subrogation or refund of benefits upon a tort recovery, and such refund is indeed called for in the present case. [Citation.] Hence, the plaintiff receives no double recovery; the collateral source rule simply serves as a means of by-passing the antiquated doctrine of nonassignment of tortious actions and permits a proper transfer of risk from the plaintiff's insurer to the tortfeasor by way of the victim's tort recovery. The double shift from the tortfeasor to the victim and then from the victim to his insurance carrier can normally occur with little cost in that the insurance carrier is often intimately involved in the initial litigation and quite automatically receives its part of the tort settlement or verdict.

Even in cases in which the contract or the law precludes subrogation or refund of benefits, or in situations in which the collateral source waives such subrogation or refund, the rule performs entirely necessary functions in the computation of damages. For example, the cost of medical care often provides both attorneys and juries in tort cases with an important measure for assessing the plaintiff's general damages. [Citation.] To permit the defendant to tell the jury that the plaintiff has been recompensed by a collateral source for his medical costs might irretrievably upset the complex, delicate, and somewhat indefinable calculations which result in the normal jury verdict. [Citation.]

We also note that generally the jury is not informed that plaintiff's attorney will receive a large portion of the plaintiff's recovery in contingent fees or that personal injury damages are not taxable to the plaintiff and are normally deductible by the defendant. Hence, the plaintiff rarely actually receives full compensation for his injuries as computed by the jury. The collateral source rule partially serves to compensate for the attorney's share and does not actually render "double recovery" for the plaintiff. Indeed, many jurisdictions that have abolished or limited the collateral source rule have also established a means for assessing the plaintiff's costs for counsel directly against the defendant rather than imposing the contingent fee system. In sum, the plaintiff's recovery for his medical expenses from both the tortfeasor and his medical insurance program will not usually give him "double recovery," but partially provides a somewhat closer approximation to full compensation for his injuries.[20]

If we consider the collateral source rule as applied here in the context of the entire American approach to the law of torts and damages, we find that the rule presently performs a number of legitimate and even indispensable functions. Without a thorough revolution in the American approach to torts and the consequent damages, the rule at least with respect to medical insurance benefits has become so integrated within our present system that its precipitous judicial nullification would work hardship. In this case the collateral source rule lies between two systems for the compensation of accident victims: the traditional tort recovery based on fault and the increasingly prevalent coverage based on non-fault insurance. Neither system possesses such universality of coverage or completeness of compensation that we can easily dispense with the collateral

---

20. Of course, only in cases in which the tort victim has received payments or services from a collateral source will he be able to mitigate attorney's fees by means of the collateral source rule. Thus the rule provides at best only an incomplete and haphazard solution to providing all tort victims with full compensation. Depriving some tort victims of the salutary protections of the collateral source rule will, short of a thorough reform of our tort system, only decrease the available compensation for injuries. [Citation.]

source rule's approach to meshing the two systems. [Citations.] The reforms which many academicians propose cannot easily be achieved through piecemeal common law development; the proposed changes, if desirable, would be more effectively accomplished through legislative reform....

....We therefore reaffirm our adherence to the collateral source rule in tort cases in which the plaintiff has been compensated by an independent collateral source—such as insurance, pension, continued wages, or disability payments—for which he had actually or constructively [citation] paid or in cases in which the collateral source would be recompensed from the tort recovery through subrogation, refund of benefits, or some other arrangement. Hence, we conclude that in a case in which a tort victim has received partial compensation from medical insurance coverage entirely independent of the tortfeasor the trial court properly followed the collateral source rule....

....

Defendants would have this court create a special form of sovereign immunity as a novel exception to the collateral source rule for tortfeasors who are public entities or public employees....We see no justification for such special treatment....The public entity or its insurance carrier is in at least as advantageous a position to spread the risk of loss as is the plaintiff's medical insurance carrier. To deprive Blue Cross of repayment for its expenditures on plaintiff's behalf merely because he was injured by a public entity rather than a private individual would constitute an unwarranted and arbitrary discrimination.

....

The judgment is affirmed.

McCOMB, PETERS, MOSK, BURKE and SULLIVAN, JJ., concur.

Notes

1. The collateral-source rule does not apply to amounts paid to the plaintiff by the tortfeasor, or by one acting on that person's behalf (*e.g.*, by an insurance company), or by one who erroneously believes that he or she is subject to liability. *See* Restatement, Second, Torts §920A. Thus, if a tortfeasor initially pays for part of plaintiff's medical expenses and then ceases such payments, the sums paid would fall outside of the rule and their value would not be recoverable in a subsequent tort action.

2. *Abrogation of the Collateral-Source Rule.* The rule has been criticized by some commentators and limited by certain courts, and its existence in a given context cannot be taken for granted. According to one writer:

> For years the traditional rule held out against its critics, but then it began to crumble. In the 1970s several jurisdictions abolished it by statute in medical malpractice cases; in the 1980s a larger number abolished it (again by statute) in all tort claims. In these jurisdictions, past and prospective insurance benefits paid or payable to the plaintiff are offset against the plaintiff's recovery.

Kenneth S. Abraham, *What Is a Tort Claim? An Interpretation of Contemporary Tort Reform*, 51 Md. L. Rev. 172, 190–191 (1992). At least, "25 jurisdictions have now enacted some form of legislation governing the collateral source rule." *Id.* at 191 n. 51. However, "[t]he collateral source rule debate is hardly over. Many states have not changed the traditional rule and some that have changed it have had the statute overturned by state supreme courts." Christian D. Saine, *Preserving the Collateral Source Rule: Modern Theo-*

ries of Tort Law and a Proposal for Practical Application, 47 Case Western Res. L. Rev. 1075, 1119 (1997). *See, e.g.*, Sorrell v. Thevenir, 633 N.E.2d 504 (Ohio 1994) (declaring a legislative reform of the collateral-source rule unconstitutional).

3. The Avoidable-Consequences Rule

Zimmerman v. Ausland
Supreme Court of Oregon, En Banc
513 P.2d 1167 (Or. 1973)

TONGUE, Justice.

This is an action for damages for personal injuries sustained in an automobile accident. Defendant admitted liability. The issue of damages was submitted to a jury, which returned a verdict of $7,500 in favor of plaintiff. Defendant appeals. We affirm.

Defendant contends that the trial court erred in submitting to the jury the issue whether plaintiff sustained a permanent injury, as alleged in her complaint, and in instructing the jury on plaintiff's life expectancy, after taking judicial notice of the Standard Mortality Tables.

In support of that contention defendant says that…there was no evidence from which the jury could properly find that plaintiff's injuries were permanent; that in this case the evidence established that plaintiff's condition, involving an injury to her knee, "is curable by routine surgery"; that all injured persons have a duty to mitigate damages by submitting to surgery "where the risk is small and a favorable result reasonably probable"; and that this "precludes any instruction on permanency."

    . . . .

Plaintiff testified…that as of the time of trial she still suffered swelling and pain in the knee after walking, as in shopping, and that as a substitute teacher she was no longer able to participate in physical education activities involving "physical games" or to play volleyball and tennis, as in the past.

Her doctor testified that plaintiff suffered from a torn semi-lunar cartilage in her knee; that "the probable future of this knee" was "one of gradual deterioration"; that her injury was "permanent"; and that it was "very probable" that she would "require a surgical procedure" to remove the torn cartilage. He also testified that after such an operation "the…[recovery] is fairly good" and that "the outlook for good recovery would be very optimistic."

In addition, plaintiff's doctor testified on cross-examination by defendant's attorney that he had not prescribed any "treatment" for plaintiff; that surgery is "not always" required in cases like this;…"it's pretty much a matter of how much it is bothering a patient."

Defendant's doctor, although disagreeing with the diagnosis that plaintiff suffered from a torn semi-lunar cartilage, testified that if she did have such an injury, as is "a very frequent injury seen in athletes," the torn cartilage should be "surgically exorcised," *i.e.*, "removed in total," and that after such an operation "the patient should recover completely" and be able "to return to all normal and usual activities."

    . . . .

This court has previously recognized the almost universal rule that admissibility of evidence of mortality tables in a personal injury case is dependent upon evidence that the injury is permanent.... [T]he same is true of the submission to a jury of allegations of permanent injury and of instructions to the jury on that subject.

It is equally well established that the plaintiff in a personal injury case cannot claim damages for what would otherwise be a permanent injury if the permanency of the injury could have been avoided by submitting to treatment by a physician, including possible surgery, when a reasonable person would do so under the same circumstances. [Citations.]

In considering whether plaintiff is required to mitigate her damages by submitting to surgery we must bear in mind that while plaintiff has the burden of proof that her injury is a permanent injury, defendant has the burden of proving that plaintiff unreasonably failed to mitigate her damages by submission to surgery. [Citation.]

Ordinarily, of course, the questions whether an injury is permanent and whether a reasonable person under the same circumstances would submit to surgery are questions of fact for the jury, assuming that substantial evidence is offered....

....

...[I]f under the circumstances, a reasonable person might well decline to undergo a surgical operation, a failure to do so imposes no disability against recovering full damages. [Citation.]

The factors to be considered for this purpose ordinarily include the risk involved (i.e., the hazardous nature of the operation), the probability of success, and the expenditure of money or effort required. [Citation.] Some courts also consider the pain involved as a factor, but no such question is presented for decision in this case. [Citation.]

....

...[I]t has been held that there must be evidence relating to the extent of the risk involved in a particular type of surgical operation before a jury may properly consider the contention that a plaintiff acted unreasonably in declining to submit to a surgical operation. [Citations.] The same must be true, *a fortiori*, when, as in this case, defendant contends that a court should hold as a matter of law that plaintiff unreasonably failed or refused to submit to a surgical operation. No such evidence was offered in this case.

Neither is there any evidence that plaintiff had been advised by any doctor that she should submit to a surgical operation on her knee and that she then failed or refused to do so. Indeed, both plaintiff's and defendant's doctors agreed that surgery was not indicated at the time of their examination....

....

In numerous cases involving the question whether a plaintiff, to minimize damages, should have submitted to surgery or other treatment for the correction of conditions consequent upon a fractured or dislocated bone, it has been held, usually upon conflicting evidence as to the seriousness and effect of the treatment, that the jury should be permitted to decide whether the refusal of treatment was justified....

Also, as stated by McCormick, [citation], "[t]he courts...are cautious about insisting that due care requires submission to an operation."

....

We hold [that the evidence was not] so clear and conclusive as to make it proper for the court to decide... [the questions at issue here] as a matter of law....

After examining the record in this case we also hold that testimony was offered by plaintiff from which, if believed by the jury, it could properly find that plaintiff has suffered a permanent injury....The verdict of the jury was supported by substantial evidence and the judgment of the trial court is affirmed.

Notes

1. *Avoidable Consequences as Comparative Fault.* In many states, unreasonable failure to mitigate damages is now treated as just one form of comparative fault. *See* Section 1 of the Uniform Comparative Fault Act, quoted in Chapter 16 at pp. 803–04.

2. *Religious Objections to Medical Treatment.* Suppose that the plaintiff suffers injuries that would be minor if the plaintiff received prompt medical care, but which become serious when the plaintiff refuses, for religious reasons, to undergo treatment. Is this just one more case of the "eggshell skull" rule, which provides that you must take the plaintiff the way he or she is; you can't complain that you deserve a different plaintiff (see Chapter 7)? Or can the defendant insist that the jury be allowed to determine whether the plaintiff's failure to receive treatment was "reasonable"? Many courts skirt the issue by instructing the jury that the plaintiff must take "reasonable" steps to mitigate damages and that they may consider the plaintiff's beliefs as "a factor" in determining whether failure to obtain treatment was reasonable. *See* Williams v. Bright, 658 N.Y.S.2d 910 (App. Div. 1997), *infra* at 262; Lange v. Hoyt, 159 A. 575 (Conn. 1932).

3. *Failure to Lose Weight.* Tanberg v. Ackerman Inv. Co., 473 N.W.2d 193 (Iowa 1991), was an action brought by a motel guest who fell in a whirlpool bathtub and injured his back. The court held that the guest's failure to follow medical advice to attempt to lose weight to decrease back pain, and thereby mitigate damages, could be considered fault under the state's modified comparative fault statute. Because the jury found the plaintiff 70% at fault, recovery was denied. *Tanberg* was overruled on other grounds by Greenwood v. Mitchell, 621 N.W.2d 200 (Iowa 2001), which held that the defendant's burden of proof as to causation in a failure-to-mitigate case is the same as the plaintiff's burden of proof on causation in proving fault on the part of the defendant.

4. Pre-Judgment Interest

Suppose that an injured plaintiff would be entitled to an award of $100,000 if the trial were held immediately after the injury. In fact, of course, the trial will not occur for years. If the plaintiff receives a judgment for $100,000 five years after the injury, should the defendant have to pay five years' interest on the $100,000? The traditional answer was no, but the unfairness of this outcome in an era of high interest rates (attributable mostly to inflation) has led a number of states to adopt legislation authorizing pre-judgment interest, and some courts have reached the same result by judicial decision.

A complicating factor is that some damages may not accrue until a date later than that of the injury. For instance, suppose that a jury awards the plaintiff $10,000 in lost wages for each of the five years the plaintiff has been out of work between the accident and the trial. In principle, the plaintiff should get approximately five years' worth of interest on the first year's wages, four years' worth on the second year's wages, and so on. The Texas Supreme Court took this into account (very roughly) by allowing pre-judgment interest on compensatory (but not punitive) damages for a period beginning six months after the date of the injury; Cavnar v. Quality Control Parking, Inc., 696 S.W.2d 549 (Tex. 1985). The Texas Legislature later enacted the following statute.

TEXAS FINANCE CODE §§304.102 *et seq.*
(Westlaw 2004)

§304.102.

A judgment in a wrongful death, personal injury, or property damage case must include prejudgment interest.

§304.103.

The prejudgment interest rate is equal to the postjudgment interest rate applicable at the time of judgment and is computed as simple interest.

§304.104.

... [P]rejudgment interest accrues on the amount of a judgment during the period beginning on the 180th day after the date the defendant receives written notice of a claim or on the date the suit is filed, whichever is earlier, and ending on the day preceding the date judgment is rendered.

§304.1045.

Prejudgment interest may not be assessed or recovered on an award of future damages.

§304.105.

(a) If judgment for a claimant is less than the amount of a settlement offer of the defendant, prejudgment interest does not accrue on the amount of the judgment during the period that the offer may be accepted.

(b) If judgment for a claimant is more than the amount of a settlement offer of the defendant, prejudgment interest does not accrue on the amount of the settlement offer during the period that the offer may be accepted.

§304.106.

To prevent the accrual of prejudgment interest under this subchapter, a settlement offer must be in writing and delivered to the claimant or the claimant's attorney or representative.

§304.107.

If a settlement offer does not provide for cash payment at the time of settlement, the amount of the settlement offer for the purpose of computing prejudgment interest is the cost or fair market value of the settlement offer at the time it is made.

B. Survival and Wrongful-Death Actions

Under the common law, the death of either party to most kinds of tort actions ended the action. Therefore, if *A* negligently injured *B*, *B*'s claim against *A* would vanish if either *A* or *B* died. (This rule did not apply to contract claims, or to some claims involving rights in personal property, such as claims for conversion.) Furthermore, the common law gave no right of recovery to the survivors of someone whom the defendant had negligently or intentionally killed, so that if *A's* misconduct caused the death of *B*, *B's* penniless survivors had no claim against *A* for either their pecuniary losses or for the loss of *B's* companionship. Today, these rules have been changed by statute in every state.

Statutes which prevent a lawsuit from coming to an end when one of the parties dies are called "survival statutes"—they provide (sometimes with exceptions for particular kinds of cases, such as defamation) that an action survives the death of either party. Another kind of statute—the "wrongful-death statute"—creates a cause of action for the benefit of those left behind when the defendant has tortiously killed someone. In some states, a single statute both provides for the survival of actions when a party dies and creates a right of recovery for wrongful death.

Here are selected portions of New York's survival statute. The term "personal representative" means the person authorized to administer the decedent's estate; that is, the administrator or executor.

New York Estates, Powers & Trusts Law §§11-3.1–11-3.3
(Westlaw 2003)

§11-3.1 Actions

Any action, other than an action for injury to person or property, may be maintained by and against a personal representative in all cases and in such manner as such action might have been maintained by or against his decedent.

§11-3.2 Action for injury to person or property survives despite death of person in whose favor or against whom cause of action existed

(a) Action against personal representative for injury to person or property.

(1) No cause of action for injury to person or property is lost because of the death of the person liable for the injury. For any injury, the action may be brought or continued against the personal representative of the decedent, but punitive damages shall not be awarded nor penalties adjudged in any such action brought to recover damages for personal injury....

(2)....

(b) Action by personal representative for injury to person or property.

No cause of action for injury to person or property is lost because of the death of the person in whose favor the cause of action existed. For any injury an action may be brought or continued by the personal representative of the decedent....No cause of action for damages caused by an injury to a third person is lost because of the death of the third person.

§11-3.3 Limitations upon recovery where injury causes death

(a) Where an injury causes the death of a person the damages recoverable for such injury are limited to those accruing before death and shall not include damages for or by reason of death, except that the reasonable funeral expenses of the decedent, paid by the estate or for the payment of which the estate is responsible, shall be recoverable in such action. The damages recovered become part of the estate of the deceased.

(b) Nothing contained herein shall affect the cause of action existing in favor of the next of kin under 5-4.1 [New York's wrongful-death statute, reproduced below—eds.], subject to the following:

(1) Such cause of action and the cause of action, under this section, in favor of the estate to recover damages may be prosecuted to judgment in a single action; a separate verdict, report or decision shall be rendered as to each cause of action.

(2) Where an action to recover damages for personal injury has been brought, and the injured person dies, as a result of the injury, before verdict, report or decision, his personal representative may enlarge the complaint in such action to include the cause of action for wrongful death under 5-4.1.

(3) Where an action to recover damages under this section and a separate action for wrongful death under 5-4.1 are pending against the same defendant, they may be consolidated on the motion of either party.

———————

Here is an edited version of New York's wrongful-death statute. The term "distributee" means someone allowed by statute to share in the property of a decedent who leaves no will.

New York Estates, Powers & Trusts Law §§5-4.1–5-4.5
(Westlaw 2003)

§5-4.1 Action by personal representative for wrongful act, neglect or default causing death of decedent

1. The personal representative...of a decedent who is survived by distributees may maintain an action to recover damages for a wrongful act, neglect or default which caused the decedent's death against a person who would have been liable to the decedent by reason of such wrongful conduct if death had not ensued. Such an action must be commenced within two years after the decedent's death. When the distributees do not participate in the administration of the decedent's estate under a will appointing an executor who refuses to bring such action, the distributees are entitled to have an administrator appointed to prosecute the action for their benefit....

§5-4.2 Trial and burden of proof of contributory negligence

On the trial of an action accruing before September first, nineteen hundred seventy-five to recover damages for causing death, the contributory negligence of the decedent shall be a defense, to be pleaded and proved by the defendant.

§5-4.3 Amount of recovery

(a) The damages awarded to the plaintiff may be such sum as the jury or, where issues of fact are tried without a jury, the court or referee deems to be fair and just compensation for the pecuniary injuries resulting from the decedent's death to the persons for whose benefit the action is brought. In every such action, in addition to any other lawful element of recoverable damages, the reasonable expenses of medical aid, nursing and attention incident to the injury causing death and the reasonable funeral expenses of the decedent paid by the distributees, or for the payment of which any distributee is responsible, shall also be proper elements of damage....

(b) Where the death of the decedent occurs on or after September first, nineteen hundred eighty-two, in addition to damages and expenses recoverable under paragraph (a) above, punitive damages may be awarded if such damages would have been recoverable had the decedent survived.

(c)(i) In any action in which the wrongful conduct is medical malpractice or dental malpractice, evidence shall be admissible to establish the federal, state and local personal income taxes which the decedent would have been obligated by law to pay....

§5-4.4 Distribution of damages recovered

(a) The damages, as prescribed by 5-4.3, whether recovered in an action or by settlement without an action, are exclusively for the benefit of the decedent's distributees and, when collected, shall be distributed to the persons entitled thereto under 4-1.1 and 5-4.5, subject to the following:

(1) Such damages shall be distributed by the personal representative to the persons entitled thereto in proportion to the pecuniary injuries suffered by them such proportions to be determined after a hearing, on application of the personal representative or any distributee....

....

(c) In the event that an action is brought, as authorized in this part, and there is no recovery or settlement, the reasonable expenses of such unsuccessful action, excluding counsel fees, shall be payable out of the assets of the decedent's estate.

§5-4.5 Non-marital children

For the purposes of this part, a non-marital child is the distributee of his father and paternal kindred and the father and paternal kindred of a non-marital child are that child's distributees to the extent permitted by 4-1.2.

Notes

1. To illustrate who can recover damages in wrongful-death and survivorship actions under the New York statutes reproduced above, suppose that *A*, a widow, dies as a result of *B's* tortious conduct. *A* leaves an adult child, *C*, and no other close relatives. *A's* will leaves half of her estate to *C* and the other half to her friend *D*. Suppose that litigation establishes that *A's* pre-death pain and suffering and medical expenses justify an award of $100,000 and that damages under the New York wrongful-death statute are $200,000. (Both figures are net of attorneys' fees.) Who gets how much?

The $100,000 awarded in the survivorship action will in this case be divided equally between *C* and *D*, because this action is brought on behalf of *A's* estate, and *C* and *D* are entitled by *A's* will to equal shares in that estate. Under the wrongful-death statute, the award of $200,000 goes to *C*. *C* is the only person who would have taken *A's* property under New York law if A had died without a will, and so *C* is the only "distributee." If *A* had been survived by more than one child, or by a child and a spouse, the calculation would have been more complex; *see* N.Y. EPTL §5-4.4 (Westlaw 2003), above. The principle underlying these rules is that the survival statute preserves *A's* right to recover damages from *B*, so these damages become part of *A's* estate. The wrongful-death claim is a claim by *C* for an injury—loss of support—suffered by *C*, so the terms of *A's* will are irrelevant in deciding who gets the wrongful-death award.

2. *"Pre-Impact Damages" in Survival Actions.* If the decedent survives the accident for several weeks and suffers greatly during that period, damages in the survival action will include a large award for the decedent's pain and suffering. But what if the decedent died immediately, as is common in cases involving plane crashes? Many courts allow juries to award substantial sums for the decedent's pre-impact terror, even though that terror may have lasted for only a few seconds, as when a plane crashes on takeoff or

landing (the most common kinds of aviation accidents). For example, in Beynon v. Montgomery Cablevision L.P., 718 A.2d 1161 (Md. 1998), a car skidded 71 feet prior to impact. Noting that seven other jurisdictions have allowed pre-impact fright damages, and four have disallowed them, the court affirmed a substantial award ($1 million for pre-impact fright, reduced to the statutory limit of $350,000). *But see* Ghotra v. Bandila Shipping, Inc., 113 F.3d 1050, 1061 (9th Cir. 1997) (ruling in a federal maritime action that "ten seconds of insensible consciousness does not meet the 'appreciable period of time' threshold for recovery of predeath pain and suffering damages").

The principal objection to awarding pre-impact damages is that they are speculative. In some aviation cases, testimony of passengers who survived the crash has been used to demonstrate the unpleasantness of experiencing the last seconds of the flight. *See generally* David L. Farnbauch, Note, *Pre-Impact Pain and Suffering Damages in Aviation Accidents*, 20 Val. U. L. Rev. 219 (1986).

3. *Elder-Abuse Laws*. In Arizona, the general survival statute (Ariz. Rev. Stat. §14-3110 (Westlaw 2003)) precludes an award of damages for the pain and suffering of a decedent prior to death. In Matter of Denton v. Superior Ct., 945 P.2d 1283, 1287–88 (Ariz. 1997), the court held that such damages were recoverable under the terms of the state's elder abuse statute, which was deemed to override the older, less specific survival-action law. "[T]he most likely forms of damages recoverable in these cases are for pain and suffering," and if the rule were otherwise with respect to survival "the tortfeasor would have a great incentive to delay litigation until the victim dies."

Gonzalez v. New York City Housing Authority

Court of Appeals of New York
572 N.E.2d 598 (N.Y. 1991)

KAYE, Judge.

Plaintiffs—the two grown grandchildren of a woman murdered in an apartment leased from defendant, New York City Housing Authority—were awarded damages for their grandmother's wrongful death, and for her conscious pain and suffering. Contesting neither liability nor the dollar amount of the award, defendant challenges the availability of wrongful death damages on the ground that plaintiffs have not established that they suffered any "pecuniary injuries" (EPTL 5-4.3[a]), and it challenges any award for conscious pain and suffering as lacking evidentiary basis. We conclude that damages for both wrongful death and conscious pain and suffering were properly allowed, and therefore affirm....

   ....

Then 76 years old, decedent was murdered in March 1984 in her apartment in the Isaac Homes Housing Project at First Avenue and 92nd Street, New York City. She was discovered with her hands tied behind her back, a gag wrapped around her jaw and mouth, and her right foot tied to the leg of a bureau. An autopsy revealed fractures of her neck and eight ribs, bleeding where teeth had been knocked out, and bruises on the back of her head and hand. The cause of death was described in the autopsy report as "Asphyxia by gagging. Contusions of scalp, fractures of ribs and cervical spine." Her assailant was subsequently convicted of the murder, and of raping and robbing two other women in the building.

Decedent was survived by her daughter-in-law and two grandchildren: plaintiffs Marta Gonzalez, 21 years old at the time of the murder, and her brother Antonio Freire, then 19. Decedent had raised them both, because their father (her son) had died in

Judith S. Kaye

1965 and their mother (her daughter-in-law) was mentally ill; as the Appellate Division observed, decedent had for many years been a "mother" to her grandchildren. At the time of the murder, however, both plaintiffs were financially independent and they no longer lived with her. The granddaughter lived separately with her husband, and the grandson had a construction job and an apartment a few blocks away.

Although decedent had retired from her job as a house-keeper several years before the crime, she remained active. She prepared dinner every night for her daughter-in-law, who was unable to cook for herself. Marta Gonzalez went to her mother's house every day, and frequently had her meals with them. She testified that her grandmother had more patience with her mother than she did, and would help her cope with her mother's condition. Antonio Freire testified that he visited his grandmother every other day, and that she frequently prepared his meals as well.

The decedent also helped her granddaughter in other ways. The month before the crime, when her granddaughter was having marital problems, decedent permitted her to live with her for a week until she could return home. At the time of the murder, Marta Gonzalez was pregnant, and together she and her grandmother planned that the grandmother would care for the child while she returned to school.

After trial, a jury awarded plaintiffs $1,250,000 for wrongful death and $1,000,000 for conscious pain and suffering, which the trial court reduced to $100,000 and $350,000. Defendant appealed to the Appellate Division solely on the damages issues. That court unanimously affirmed the plaintiffs' award, as do we.

. . . .

Under the common law of England, it was not possible to maintain a damages action for wrongful death. This was the law in New York and other American jurisdictions as well [citations]. "The result was that it was cheaper for the defendant to kill…than to injure [the plaintiff], and that the most grievous of all injuries left the bereaved family of the victim, who frequently were destitute, without a remedy." (Prosser and Keeton, Torts §127, at 945 [5th ed].)

That inequity was ameliorated in England in 1846 by passage of the Fatal Accidents Act [usually referred to as "Lord Campbell's Act"—Eds.], creating a remedy for wrongful death. New York was the first state to follow suit, and in 1847 adopted a statutory cause of action for wrongful death, now embodied in EPTL 5-4.1 [citation]. The statute authorizes the personal representative of a decedent survived by distributees to maintain an action for wrongful death. Since the statute is in derogation of common law, it must of course be strictly construed [citations].

The measure of damages obtainable in a wrongful death action "may be such sum as the jury or, where issues of fact are tried without a jury, the court or referee deems to be fair and just compensation for the pecuniary injuries resulting from the decedent's death to the persons for whose benefit the action is brought." (EPTL 5-4.3 [a].) In 1862, 15 years after enactment of the statute, we held that the statutory word "*pecuniary* was used in distinction to those injuries to the affections and sentiments which arise from the death of relatives, and which, though most painful and grievous to be borne, cannot be measured or recompensed by money. It excludes, also, those losses which result from the deprivation of the society and companionship of relatives, which are equally incapable of being defined by any recognized measure of value." [Citation.]

While other states now permit recovery for loss of society (Sea-Land Servs. v. Gaudet, 414 U.S. 573, 587, n.21 [listing jurisdictions]), New York since its first wrongful death statute has steadfastly restricted recovery to "pecuniary injuries," or injuries measurable by money, and denied recovery for grief, loss of society, affection, conjugal fellowship and consortium [citation]. Thus, the essence of the cause of action for wrongful death in this State is that the plaintiff's reasonable expectancy of future assistance or support by the decedent was frustrated by the decedent's death [citation]. Loss of support, voluntary assistance and possible inheritance, as well as medical and funeral expenses incidental to death, are injuries for which damages may be recovered [citation].

The "pecuniary injuries" caused by a wage earner's death may be calculated, in part, from factors relevant to the decedent's earning potential, such as present and future earnings, potential for advancement and probability of means to support heirs, as well as factors pertaining to the decedent's age, character and condition, and the circumstances of the distributees [citations omitted]. In the case of a decedent who was not a wage earner, "pecuniary injuries" may be calculated, in part, from the increased expenditures required to continue the services she provided, as well as the compensable losses of a personal nature, such as loss of guidance [citation].

Applying these principles to the facts before us, we first conclude that plaintiffs' status as adult financially independent grandchildren does not, of itself, preclude their recovery.

While defendant asks us to restrict recovery for loss of guidance to a decedent's children, the statute defines the class entitled to recover in a wrongful death action as distributees (*see*, EPTL 5-4.1[1]; 5-4.4[a]). There is no question that decedent's grandchildren were her distributees, and thus that they are members of the class the Legislature intended should be permitted to maintain this action [citations].

Nor is recovery barred solely because plaintiffs were self-supporting adults at the time of their grandmother's death. The argument that an adult distributee cannot state a claim for pecuniary injuries based on the loss of a parent's guidance was long ago rejected by this court. In Tilley v. Hudson Riv. R.R. Co., 29 N.Y. 252, a wrongful death action brought on behalf of the decedent's five surviving children, the oldest child was 23 and married at the time of her mother's death, and the next oldest 21. We held that the Trial Judge properly declined to limit damages to the minority of the children, finding in the wrongful death statute no "peremptory injunction to confine the damages absolutely to the minority of the children" [citations]. Defendant points to Bumpurs v. New York City Hous. Auth., 139 A.D.2d 438, as support for its contention that adults cannot claim pecuniary injuries from loss of a parent's guidance. There, adult children were denied recovery for loss of their mother's "companionship, comfort and assistance" on the ground that such injuries were not pecuniary in nature...; the court went on to note that the adult claimants could not state a claim for loss of their mother's nurture. However, the *Bumpurs* decision was properly distinguished by the Appellate Division in the present case: unlike the decedent here, the decedent in *Bumpurs* had provided no services to her adult children [citations].

Plaintiffs' status being no bar to recovery, the question then becomes whether the damages they have shown fall within the statutory confines of "pecuniary injuries."

Defendant urges that the only service decedent rendered to plaintiffs was the preparation of occasional meals outside their residences, which was not a compensable injury both because it was occasional and gratuitous and the plaintiffs therefore had no reason to rely on it, and because the service was not performed in their own households and plaintiffs therefore would not need to replace it.

As the record establishes, however, decedent contributed far more than "occasional meals," and her grandchildren relied upon her contributions. Decedent provided shelter for her granddaughter during a marital crisis, and helped both grandchildren cope with their mother's condition. The child care plan was more than occasional. Even the meals she furnished cannot accurately be called occasional—Marta Gonzalez testified that she ate dinner with her mother and grandmother every other day, while Antonio Freire testified that he visited his grandmother every other day and she frequently prepared his meals.

Nor is it significant that the decedent prepared meals in her daughter-in-law's home rather than in plaintiffs' homes. Wherever provided, the decedent's services would have to be replaced by plaintiffs. The same is equally true of her counseling, the shelter she provided for her granddaughter, and the meals she regularly prepared for both grandchildren.

Based upon this record, therefore, we conclude that plaintiffs presented evidence of "pecuniary injuries" they suffered by reason of their grandmother's wrongful death.

       . . . .

Defendant's remaining argument is addressed to the award of damages for decedent's conscious pain and suffering. Defendant contends that there was no showing that it was more likely than not that she suffered any pain before she died, because two of the causes of death noted by the medical examiner—contusion of the scalp and fracture of the cervical spine—were equally consistent with a simultaneous loss of consciousness and death.

We agree with the Appellate Division that there was sufficient circumstantial evidence to support the conclusion that decedent was conscious when most of the injuries were inflicted. As the Appellate Division noted, if she had been unconscious at the outset of the assault there would have been no reason for the murderer to have bound and gagged her elaborately and injured her as he did. Defendant's speculation that those other injuries might have been caused by a fall, or that they might have caused immediate unconsciousness, finds no support in the medical testimony or anywhere else in the record.

....

WACHTLER, C.J., and SIMONS, ALEXANDER, TITONE, HANCOCK and BELLA-COSA, JJ., concur.

Order affirmed, with costs.

Notes

1. *Compensation for the Death of Family Caretakers.* Courts have approved widely disparate awards in cases involving the deaths of women primarily devoted to the care of their families, rather than employed outside the home. Why? *See* Lucinda M. Finley, *A Break in the Silence: Including Women's Issues in a Torts Course*, 1 Yale J. L. & Fem. 41, 48–51 (1989).

See also Martha Chamallas, *The Architecture of Bias: Deep Structures in Tort Law*, 146 U. Pa. L. Rev. 463 (1998) ("Most empirical studies indicate that women of all races and minority men continue to receive significantly lower damage awards than white men in personal injury and wrongful death suits").

2. *Wrongful-Death Damages Measured by Pecuniary Loss.* The *Gonzalez* court, quoting Prosser, notes that it was cheaper under the common law for a defendant to kill someone than merely to inflict an injury. If, as in New York, the statute limits wrongful-death damages to "pecuniary" losses, that may still be the case, especially when the victim is a young child. The calculation of "pecuniary" loss generally proceeds by determining the amount of support the decedent would have provided the plaintiffs but for the death; as a result, the defendant who kills a surgeon or a partner in a law firm is likely to face much more liability than the defendant who kills a low-income worker or an unemployed person.

Some courts also allow a recovery for the loss of the inheritance the plaintiffs would have received had the decedent lived longer and saved more. *See* Yowell v. Piper Aircraft Corp., 703 S.W.2d 630 (Tex. 1986).

3. *Wrongful-Death Damages for Loss of Companionship and Society.* Most states now permit recovery in a wrongful-death action for the value of lost companionship, society, advice, and guidance. In some states, the issue is addressed by statute. Here is one example:

MASSACHUSETTS ANNOTATED LAWS
Chapter 229 §2 (Westlaw 2003)

A person who...by his negligence causes the death of a person, or...by willful, wanton or reckless act causes the death of a person under such circumstances that the deceased could have recovered damages for personal injuries if his death had not resulted...shall be liable in damages in the amount of:

(1) the fair monetary value of the decedent to [the decedent's survivors], including but not limited to compensation for the loss of the reasonably expected net income, services, protection, care, assistance, society, companionship, comfort, guidance, counsel, and advice of the decedent to the persons entitled to the damages recovered;

(2) the reasonable funeral and burial expenses of the decedent;

(3) punitive damages in an amount of not less than five thousand dollars in such case as the decedent's death was caused by the malicious, willful, wanton or reckless conduct of the defendant or by the gross negligence of the defendant....

Some courts have interpreted statutes providing for recovery of "actual damages" as allowing recovery for "loss of the decedent's society" and for mental anguish; *e.g.*

Sanchez v. Schindler, 651 S.W.2d 249 (Tex. 1983) (death of minor child); *see also* Moore v. Lillebo, 722 S.W.2d 683 (Tex. 1986) (death of adult son).

And some states allow "recovery for the survivor's loss of companionship, society, advice and guidance...on the theory that such elements have a pecuniary value." Dan B. Dobbs, The Law of Torts 812 (2000).

But see Kulish v. West Side Unlimited Corp., 545 N.W.2d 860 (Iowa 1996) (denying parents' loss-of-consortium claim based on death of adult son).

4. *Wrongful-Death Damages for Grief.* According to Professor Dobbs:

> Loss of companionship, society and the like—consortium rights—are usually viewed as something distinct from anguish or grief, so to allow consortium recovery is not necessarily to allow recovery for grief or anguish of survivors. However, by the 1990s many states were permitting recovery for emotional harm or anguish in wrongful death actions. Some of the statutes now provide for it directly, usually in addition to the claims for lost companionship, society, guidance and the like. Elsewhere, some courts have expanded liability to include mental anguish recovery under statutes that do not specifically authorize it.

Dan B. Dobbs, The Law of Torts 812 (2000).

Damages, Deterrence, and Compensation

Two goals commonly assigned to the tort system are deterrence of dangerous activities and compensation of victims. The calculation of damages for wrongful death provides an opportunity to examine the extent to which these goals are inconsistent with each other, for the measure of damages which is desirable for deterrence differs from the measure appropriate for a compensation system.

As an example of the way in which deterrence and compensation support different measures of recovery, consider cases in which defendants tortiously cause the deaths of young children. If the only goal of tort law were compensation, the appropriate measure of damages in these cases might well be zero. The loss is devastating to the parents, but it is not a financial loss. It is, in fact, quite the opposite, as raising children is expensive in dollar-and-cents terms. Furthermore, this kind of loss cannot in any sense be "made up for" by awarding the parents money. Discussions of compensation often proceed by assuming that a large enough award of money can make the victim as well off as before the injury. When the loss in question is largely financial, as when the plaintiff's house or car is destroyed, this can make some sense. When the loss is the loss of a child, an award of cash will not help. It may even hurt, as when parents enriched by a tort recovery are reminded of their loss every time they spend their riches.

From a deterrence perspective, the death of a child becomes an example of a case in which damages should be very high. One should not lightly undertake an activity which has more than a remote chance of killing anyone—especially a child. Someone who might, in the absence of any serious risk of liability, undertake a fairly dangerous activity in the hope that it will work out for the best may be deterred by the prospect of having to pay a large sum if things go wrong.

A possible objection to using damages to deter accidental death is that people will take precautions anyway, out of simple morality. This is, of course, true; but less so for some people than for others. Consider, for instance, a suburban homeowner installing a swimming pool. Swimming pools are very dangerous to children, whose ingenuity in getting through latched gates far exceeds their caution around water. It is very plausible to think that some homeowners (not all, but encouraging care can be useful even if it doesn't *always* work) take extra care to keep their pools fenced and their gates locked because they know, or suspect, that they will be held liable if a drowning takes place. And the homeowner's insurance agent may insist on precautions that the homeowner is too careless or ignorant to come up with. Furthermore, if homeowners' liability insurers charge extra for policies on homes with pools, some homeowners may decide that a pool is not worth the extra expense. Charging the owners of pools large sums when drownings do occur creates a desirable incentive to take precautions, even if not all owners will respond sensibly to those incentives.

How can the appropriate amount of damages for purposes of deterrence be calculated? One way is by looking at the amount people are willing to spend to protect themselves against small risks of dying. For instance, economists have estimated the amounts that people are willing to spend for safety precautions like smoke detectors, automobile airbags, and other safety devices which can be purchased. In addition, economists have investigated the amount of higher pay received by those engaged in dangerous occupations, like firefighting, police work, and logging, as compared with the pay of those in comparable but safer work. The difference may be a measure of the value people place on safety in their own lives. If studies like this show that, on the average, people are willing to spend $2.00 (but not more) to guard against a one-in-a-million chance of premature death, potential defendants could be encouraged to take the appropriate level of safety precautions by being held liable for $2,000,000 whenever their activities actually do cause an accidental death.

Economists tend to summarize the results of studies like those described above by coming up with a figure for "the value of a life." If, for instance, people will typically spend $2.00 to eliminate a one-in-a-million chance of death, an economist might say that the "value of a life" is $2,000,000. This is a misleading way of putting it, as hardly anyone would agree to die immediately for a $2,000,000 payment. Furthermore, few people—including economists—would say that it is permissible to murder someone if the payoff is more than $2,000,000. The "value of a life" notion is best understood as a shorthand way of expressing the value of taking precautions against small risks of death. Current estimates of the "value of a life" are $7.5 million or more. Note that this figure is much higher than the recovery in most wrongful-death cases, especially in cases in which the decedent had a low income or left no dependents. Indeed, in the extreme case of a decedent with no family and no close friends, the appropriate amount of "compensation" is very close to zero, yet no one would argue that no precautions should be taken to save the life of such a person.

While this discussion has focused on damages for wrongful death, similar considerations apply in other areas of torts. Generally speaking, if deterrence is the main goal, the law would want much higher damages than if it were concerned only with compensation. Consider damages for "pain and suffering." Suppose that a woman has had a car door accidentally slammed on her hand, breaking a couple of her fingers. Unless she is a concert pianist or a surgeon, or otherwise makes a living with her hands, an award of her medical expenses is probably all the "compensation" she should receive. (Although the experience was and may still be painful, giving her money will not make the pain go away, so that "loss" is, like the loss of a child, inherently incapable of being compensated.) So "compensation" for this kind of injury might be only a few hundred dollars. From the point of view of deterrence, however, a much higher award might be appropriate—few persons would let someone slam a car door on their hands for twice the medical bills that would be incurred.

Another example of the tension between deterrence and compensation is the collateral-source rule (pp. 189–92). Someone whose lost wages or medical bills have been picked up by insurance needs no "compensation" to be made whole for those losses. But it may be almost as important to deter prospective defendants from injuring the insured as from injuring the uninsured. Therefore, the collateral-source rule makes excellent sense, from the point of view of deterrence, even though it may overcompensate some plaintiffs. (Note that if the *only* concern were with deterrence, it would not matter whether the victim even got the money; deterrence requires that the careless defendant be made to pay, but not that the payment go to the victim.)

Although "deterrence" considerations support much higher damages awards than "compensation" would justify, a system aimed at deterrence would typically allow recovery in many fewer cases than a system seeking compensation. For example, someone who falls ill from natural causes, or who is struck by lightning through no one's fault, needs "compensation" as badly as someone whose injuries have been occasioned by the negligence of another. Yet deterrence can operate only in those cases in which someone could have prevented the harm at reasonable cost. Therefore, the tort system cannot effectively pursue both deterrence and compensation at the same time. Compensation-oriented systems like workers' compensation and Social Security disability insurance typically allow many persons to recover fairly small amounts. Deterrence-oriented systems would award much more to fewer victims.

For a discussion of "valuing lives" more extensive than can be presented here, *see* Ted R. Miller, *Willingness to Pay Comes of Age: Will the Tort System Survive?*, 83 Nw. U. L. Rev. 876 (1989).

Problem: The Ford Pinto. In the early 1970s, Ford became concerned that the Pinto, an inexpensive compact car, was unsafe. Ford prepared a cost-benefit analysis, which showed that the cost of making certain proposed changes in the Pinto's design would outweigh the benefits. In measuring the "benefits" of saving a life, Ford used the figure of $200,000 for each life saved. Ford obtained this figure from the National Highway Traffic Safety Administration, which had based its calculations on the expected lifetime earnings of those who would die. Was this a sensible figure to use?

C. Damages for Loss of Earning Capacity

As discussed above, one element of tort damages for a disabled plaintiff is loss of earning capacity. Calculating an award for this kind of loss presents several serious problems. One complication involves discounting future earnings to their present value. An award to a young plaintiff who might have worked for another 50 years will include, among other things, compensation for the earnings the plaintiff would have received in year 50. To give the plaintiff the full amount of the year-50 salary today would seriously overcompensate the victim. To see why, suppose that plaintiff's salary for year 50 would have been $50,000. A plaintiff who received $50,000 today could invest the money and let it grow for 50 years. At an interest rate of 4 percent a year, compounded semi-annually, $50,000 will grow to $362,232. Therefore, an award of $50,000 today compensates for a loss of $362,232 fifty years from now, not for a loss of $50,000.

By discounting future wages to present value, current awards can be made to correspond to some larger amount that would have been received in the future. The "present value" of an amount to be received in the future is the amount which, if invested today at a specified rate of interest, would grow to equal the future amount during the number of years in question. "Present value" calculations therefore depend upon the interest rate chosen and the time period in question — the higher the rate and the longer the time, the lower the present value of any particular future amount. The present value of $50,000 to be received in 50 years is $6902 at an interest rate of 4% a year, compounded semiannually. At an interest rate of 6%, compounded semiannually, the present value of $50,000 to be received in 50 years is only $2602. Note that a difference of only two percentage points changes the present value in this example by more than a factor of two.

Compulsory Periodic Payments. In Galayda v. Lake Hosp. Sys., Inc., 644 N.E.2d 298, 301 (Ohio 1994), a statute that required a trial court, upon the motion of a party, to order that any future damages award in excess of $200,000 be paid in a series of periodic payments was held to be an impermissible abridgement of the right under the state constitution to trial by jury. The court reasoned that under the "common law of Ohio, future damages must be reduced to present value, and a defendant is entitled to a jury instruction to that effect." The statute did "not merely mandate the *manner* in which a judgment shall be paid; rather, it require[d] the trial court to further reduce the jury's award of damages already once reduced to present value," with the result that a successful plaintiff would receive "less than the jury awarded."

1. Inflation

The following opinion illustrates some of the difficulties of reducing lost future wages to a present damage award.

O'Shea v. Riverway Towing Co.

United States Court of Appeals for the Seventh Circuit
677 F.2d 1194 (7th Cir. 1982)

POSNER, Circuit Judge.

This is a tort case under the federal admiralty jurisdiction. We are called upon to decide...in particular the question...whether, and if so how, to account for inflation in computing lost future wages.

[Margaret O'Shea, the plaintiff, was disabled in an accident caused by the defendant's negligence.]

. . . .

The more substantial issues in this appeal relate to the computation of lost wages. Mrs. O'Shea's job as a cook paid her $40 a day, and since the custom was to work 30 days consecutively and then have the next 30 days off, this comes to $7200 a year although...she never had earned that much in a single year. She testified that when the accident occurred she had been about to get another cook's job on a Mississippi towboat that would have paid her $60 a day ($10,800 a year). She also testified that she had been intending to work as a boat's cook until she was 70 — longer if she was able. An economist who testified on Mrs. O'Shea's behalf used the foregoing testimony as the basis for estimating the wages that she lost because of the accident. He first subtracted federal income tax from yearly wage estimates based on alternative assumptions about her wage rate (that it would be either $40 or $60 a day); assumed that this wage would have grown by between six and eight percent a year; assumed that she would have worked either to age 65 or to age 70; and then discounted the resulting lost-wage estimates to present value, using a discount rate of 8.5 percent a year. These calculations, being based on alternative assumptions concerning starting wage rate, annual wage increases, and length of employment, yielded a range of values rather than a single value. The bottom of the range was $50,000. This is the present value, computed at an 8.5 percent discount rate, of Mrs. O'Shea's lost future wages on the assumption that her starting wage was $40 a day and that it would have grown by six percent a year until she retired at the age of 65. The top of the range was $114,000, which is the present value (again discounted at 8.5 percent) of her lost future wages assuming she would have worked till she was 70 at a wage that would have started at $60 a day and increased by eight percent a year. The judge awarded a figure—$86,033—near the midpoint of this range. He did not explain in his written opinion how he had arrived at this figure, but in a preceding oral opinion he stated that he was "not certain that she would work until age 70 at this type of work," although "she certainly was entitled to" do so and "could have earned something"; and that he had not "felt bound by [the economist's] figure of eight per cent increase in wages" and had "not found the wages based on necessarily a 60 dollar a day job." If this can be taken to mean that he thought Mrs. O'Shea would probably have worked till she was 70, starting at $40 a day but moving up from there at six rather than eight percent a year, the economist's estimate of the present value of her lost future wages would be $75,000.

     . . . .

[The court held that, given the parties' litigating stances, the trial court had not erred by assuming that the plaintiff was totally disabled.]

Riverway argues next that it was wrong for the judge to award damages on the basis of a wage not validated, as it were, by at least a year's employment at that wage. Mrs. O'Shea had never worked full time, had never in fact earned more than $3600 in a full year, and in that year preceding the accident had earned only $900. But previous wages do not put a cap on an award of lost future wages. If a man who had never worked in his life graduated from law school, began working at a law firm at an annual salary of $35,000, and was killed the second day on the job, his lack of a past wage history would be irrelevant to computing his lost future wages. The present case is similar if less dramatic. Mrs. O'Shea did not work at all until 1974, when her husband died. She then lived on her inheritance and worked at a variety of part-time jobs till January 1979, when she started working as a cook on the towboat. According to her testimony, which the trial judge believed, she was then working full time. It is immaterial that this was her first full-time job and that the accident occurred before she had held it for a full year. Her job history was typical of women who return to the labor force after their children are grown or, as in Mrs. O'Shea's case, after their husband dies, and these women are, like any tort victims, entitled to damages based on what they would have earned in the future rather than on what they may or may not have earned in the past.

If we are correct so far, Mrs. O'Shea was entitled to have her lost wages determined on the assumption that she would have earned at least $7200 in the first year after the accident and that the accident caused her to lose that entire amount by disabling her from any gainful employment. And since Riverway neither challenges the district judge's (apparent) finding that Mrs. O'Shea would have worked till she was 70 nor contends that the lost wages for each year until then should be discounted by the probability that she would in fact have been alive and working as a boat's cook throughout the damage period, we may also assume that her wages would have been at least $7200 a year for the 12 years between the date of the accident and her seventieth birthday....

We come at last to the most important issue in the case, which is the proper treatment of inflation in calculating lost future wages. Mrs. O'Shea's economist based the six to eight percent range which he used to estimate future increases in the wages of a boat's cook on the general pattern of wage increases in service occupations over the past 25 years. During the second half of this period the rate of inflation has been substantial and has accounted for much of the increase in nominal wages in this period; and to use that increase to project future wage increases is therefore to assume that inflation will continue, and continue to push up wages. Riverway argues that it is improper as a matter of law to take inflation into account in projecting lost future wages. Yet Riverway itself wants to take inflation into account—one-sidedly, to reduce the amount of the damages computed. For Riverway does not object to the economist's choice of an 8.5 percent discount rate for reducing Mrs. O'Shea's lost future wages to present value, although the rate includes an allowance—a very large allowance—for inflation. To explain, the object of discounting lost future wages to present value is to give the plaintiff an amount of money which, invested safely, will grow to a sum equal to those wages. So if we thought that but for the accident Mrs. O'Shea would have earned $7200 in 1990, and we were computing in 1980 (when this case was tried) her damages based on those lost earnings, we would need to determine the sum of money that, invested safely for a period of 10 years, would grow to $7200. Suppose that in 1980 the rate of interest on ultra-safe (*i.e.*, federal government) bonds or notes maturing in 10 years was 12 percent. Then we would consult a table of present values to see what sum of money invested at 12 percent for 10 years would at the end of that time have grown to $7200. The answer is $2318. But a moment's reflection will show that to give Mrs. O'Shea $2318 to compensate her for lost wages in 1990 would grossly undercompensate her. People demand 12 percent to lend money risklessly for 10 years because they expect their principal to have much less purchasing power when they get it back at the end of the time. In other words, when long-term interest rates are high, they are high in order to compensate lenders for the fact that they will be repaid in cheaper dollars. In periods when no inflation is anticipated, the risk-free interest rate is between one and three percent. [Citation.] Additional percentage points above that level reflect inflation anticipated over the life of the loan. But if there is inflation it will affect wages as well as prices. Therefore to give Mrs. O'Shea $2318 today because that is the present value of $7200 10 years hence, computed at a discount rate—12 percent—that consists mainly of an allowance for anticipated inflation, is in fact to give her less than she would have been earning then if she was earning $7200 on the date of the accident, even if the only wage increases she would have received would have been those necessary to keep pace with inflation.

There are (at least) two ways to deal with inflation in computing the present value of lost future wages. One is to take it out of both the wages and the discount rate—to say to Mrs. O'Shea, "we are going to calculate your probable wage in 1990 on the assumption, unrealistic as it is, that there will be zero inflation between now and then; and, to be consistent, we are going to discount the amount thus calculated by the interest rate that would be charged under the same assumption of zero inflation." Thus, if we thought Mrs. O'Shea's real (*i.e.*, inflation-free) wage rate would not rise in the future, we would fix her lost earnings in 1990 as $7200 and, to be consistent, we would discount that to present (1980) value using an estimate of the real interest rate. At two percent, this procedure would yield a present value of $5906. Of course, she would not invest this money at a mere two percent. She would invest it at the much higher prevailing interest rate. But that would not give her a windfall; it would just enable her to replace her lost 1990 earnings with an amount equal to what she would in fact have earned in that year if inflation continues, as most people expect it to do. (If people did not expect continued inflation, long-term interest rates would be much lower; those rates impound investors' inflationary expectations.) An alternative approach, which yields the same result, is to use a (higher) discount rate based on the current risk-free 10-year interest rate, but apply that rate to an estimate of lost future wages that includes expected inflation. Contrary to Riverway's argument, this projection would not require gazing into a crystal ball. The expected rate of inflation can, as just suggested, be read off from the current long-term interest rate. If that rate is 12 percent, and if as suggested earlier the real or inflation-free interest rate is only one to three percent, this implies that the market is anticipating 9–11 percent inflation over the next 10 years, for a long-term interest rate is simply the sum of the real interest rate and the anticipated rate of inflation during the term.

Either approach to dealing with inflation is acceptable (they are, in fact, equivalent) and we by no means rule out others; but it is illogical and indefensible to build inflation into the discount rate yet ignore it in calculating the lost future wages that are to be discounted. That results in systematic undercompensation, just as building inflation into the estimate of future lost earnings and then discounting using the real rate of interest would systematically overcompensate. The former error is committed, we respectfully suggest, by those circuits…that refuse to allow inflation to be used in projecting lost future earnings but then use a discount rate that has built into it a large allowance for inflation. [Citation]. We align ourselves instead with those circuits (a majority, [citation]),…that require that inflation be treated consistently in choosing a discount rate and in estimating the future lost wages to be discounted to present value using that rate.…

Applying our analysis to the present case, we cannot pronounce the approach taken by the plaintiff's economist unreasonable. He chose a discount rate—8.5 percent—well above the real rate of interest, and therefore containing an allowance for inflation. Consistency required him to inflate Mrs. O'Shea's starting wage as a boat's cook in calculating her lost future wages, and he did so at a rate of six to eight percent a year. If this rate had been intended as a forecast of purely inflationary wage changes, his approach would be open to question, especially at the upper end of his range. For if the estimated rate of inflation were eight percent, the use of a discount rate of 8.5 percent would imply that the real rate of interest was only .5 percent, which is lower than most economists believe it to be for any substantial period of time. But wages do not rise just because of inflation. Mrs. O'Shea could expect her real wages as a boat's cook to rise as she became more experienced and as average real wage rates throughout the economy rose, as they usually do over a decade or more. It would not be outlandish to assume that even if there were no inflation, Mrs. O'Shea's wages would have risen by three percent a year.

If we subtract that from the economist's six to eight percent range, the inflation allowance built into his estimated future wage increases is only three to five percent; and when we subtract these figures from 8.5 percent we see that his implicit estimate of the real rate of interest was very high (3.5–5.5 percent). This means he was conservative, because the higher the discount rate used the lower the damages calculated.

If conservative in one sense, the economist was most liberal in another. He made no allowance for the fact that Mrs. O'Shea, whose health history quite apart from the accident is not outstanding, might very well not have survived—let alone survived and been working as a boat's cook or in an equivalent job—until the age of 70. The damage award is a sum certain, but the lost future wages to which that award is equated by means of the discount rate are mere probabilities. If the probability of her being employed as a boat's cook full time in 1990 was only 75 percent, for example, then her estimated wages in that year should have been multiplied by .75 to determine the value of the expectation that she lost as a result of the accident; and so with each of the other future years. *Cf.* Conte v. Flota Mercante del Estado, 277 F.2d 664, 670 (2d Cir. 1960). The economist did not do this, and by failing to do this he overstated the loss due to the accident.

But Riverway does not make an issue of this aspect of the economist's analysis....

Although we are not entirely satisfied with the economic analysis on which the judge, in the absence of any other evidence of the present value of Mrs. O'Shea's lost future wages, must have relied heavily, we recognize that the exactness which economic analysis rigorously pursued appears to offer is, at least in the litigation setting, somewhat delusive. Therefore, we will not reverse an award of damages for lost wages because of questionable assumptions unless it yields an unreasonable result....We cannot say the result here was unreasonable....

....

So we cannot say that the figure arrived at by the judge, $86,033, was unreasonably high. But we are distressed that he made no attempt to explain how he had arrived at that figure, since it was not one contained in the economist's testimony though it must in some way have been derived from that testimony. Unlike many other damage items in a personal injury case, notably pain and suffering, the calculation of damages for lost earnings can and should be an analytical rather than an intuitive undertaking. Therefore, compliance with Rule 52(a) of the Federal Rules of Civil Procedure requires that in a bench trial the district judge set out the steps by which he arrived at his award for lost future earnings, in order to assist the appellate court in reviewing the award....[F]or the future we ask the district judges in this circuit to indicate the steps by which they arrive at damage awards for lost future earnings.

Judgment affirmed.

Notes

1. *A Possible Shortcut.* Beaulieu v. Elliott, 434 P.2d 665 (Alaska 1967), held that the plaintiff should recover the total amount of estimated lost future wages without increasing those wages for inflation or for anticipated "real" increases or discounting the future wages to present value. It reasoned that the necessary increases and decreases would at least roughly offset each other. Pennsylvania adopted the Alaska rule in Kaczkowski v. Bolubasz, 421 A.2d 1027 (Pa. 1980). In evaluating this shortcut, consider the time a lawyer would have to spend preparing an expert witness to testify about the kind of information the *O'Shea* court held relevant. Consider also the challenge the lawyer would face in presenting expert testimony on present-value calculations to a financially unsophisticated jury.

2. *Loss of Earning Capacity.* Note that O'Shea's damages were for the loss of her "earning capacity," which is not necessarily the same thing as her lost future earnings. Therefore, if O'Shea had still been a homemaker at the time she was injured, her damages would, in theory, have been based on the income she could have earned if she had worked, not the (zero) income she was actually earning. As a practical matter, an actual work history helps a lot in determining the amount a plaintiff would have been capable

of earning but for an injury. Recall, however, that Helen Britain, who was a child at the time of her injuries, received a substantial award for loss of earning capacity (p. 183).

2. Taxation of Awards

Another problem in calculating damage awards for loss of earning capacity is how to treat income taxes. An award of compensatory damages in a case involving physical personal injuries is not taxable to the recipient; Internal Revenue Code of 1986, §104(a)(2) (Westlaw 2003). (Punitive damages are income to the plaintiff who gets them, as are some compensatory damages in cases involving non-physical injuries, such as harm to reputation or emotional distress.) The wages the plaintiff would have earned would have been taxable, however, and the interest or dividends the plaintiff earns by investing a lump-sum award will be taxable. If the case is settled, taxation of the earnings on the plaintiff's investment income can be avoided by arranging a "structured settlement." If, instead of paying the plaintiff a lump sum, the defendant (or, typically, the defendant's insurer) makes a series of payments, the full amount of the payments will be excludable from the plaintiff's income. So, instead of taking a lump sum payment of $100,000 and investing that amount to earn a $10,000 annual return (taxable), the plaintiff might agree to take $10,000 a year for 50 years, all tax-free. If there were no income tax, and if the appropriate interest rate is 10 percent, $100,000 now is worth more than $10,000 a year for 50 years. But the absence of any tax on payments under a structured settlement of $10,000 a year for 50 years could make that option more attractive to the plaintiff.

In re Air Crash Disaster Near Chicago on May 25, 1979
United States Court of Appeals for the Seventh Circuit
803 F.2d 304 (7th Cir. 1986)

ESCHBACH, Senior Circuit Judge.

Defendant McDonnell Douglas Corp. ("MDC") appeals from a judgment of $3,000,000 for plaintiff Lora Lux in this wrongful death action governed by Arizona law. The primary issues presented in this appeal are:...(2) whether evidence of the decedent's income tax liability should have been admitted; and (3) whether the jury should have been instructed that its award would not be subject to taxation....

....

The facts, as set forth in the district court's opinion, are as follows:

On May 25, 1979, Walter Lux was killed while piloting American Airlines Flight #191, which crashed shortly after takeoff at Chicago's O'Hare International Airport....

On the date of the accident, Walter Lux was 52 years old; [his wife] Lora Lux was 49 years old, and their only son, Michael, was 22 years old....Walter Lux' income from American Airlines as a captain pilot was $78,954 in 1978. In addition to his annual income, Walter Lux enjoyed various fringe benefits from his employment with American Airlines. These benefits included life insurance, medical and dental insurance, and pension benefits. At trial, plaintiff claimed a total of $1,589,930 in economic loss, of which approximately $1,000,000 represented lost income....

....

The district court excluded evidence of the income taxes Walter Lux would have paid on his earnings. MDC argues that this evidence was relevant to the measure of damages under Arizona's wrongful death statute and, therefore, should have been admitted under the Federal Rules of Evidence. We agree.

....Whether the measure of the plaintiff's pecuniary damages for lost support in wrongful death actions is the decedent's gross income or the surviving parties' net pecuniary loss (*i.e.*, the decedent's income less personal consumption expenses and taxes) has not been decided by any Arizona court.

....

....Whereas the purpose of pecuniary damages in a personal injury suit is to replace a plaintiff's lost earnings, the purpose of pecuniary damages in a wrongful death action is to replace the survivors' lost support. For this reason, the survivors' pecuniary damages in wrongful death actions are reduced by the amount that the decedent would have spent on personal consumption expenses. It would seem that, since a plaintiff in a wrongful death case is entitled to the amount that the decedent would have contributed to the plaintiff's support, the plaintiff's pecuniary damages similarly should be reduced by the amount that the decedent would have paid in income taxes....

Divining in the absence of any relevant authority how a state's highest court would rule ordinarily would be as exact as foretelling the future from the flight of birds; however, in this case we have been spared such an exercise. The Arizona Supreme Court has repeatedly reaffirmed that, in the absence of a controlling statute or precedent, it will follow the Restatement of the Law whenever it is applicable. [Citations.] We thus may turn to the Restatement (Second) of Torts to ascertain Arizona law on the admissibility of evidence of the decedent's income taxes in wrongful death actions.

The Restatement's position on the admissibility of evidence of income taxes in wrongful death suits is clear. In its comment to the section entitled "Effect of Taxation" on tort awards, the Restatement provides that

> When the injured party dies and action is brought under a wrongful death statute, the problem before the court [as to the admissibility of evidence of income taxes] is not the same [as it is in personal injury cases]. In the majority of states, the recovery of the statutory beneficiaries is measured by the contributions that the deceased would have made to them if he had lived.... This amount obviously could not be equivalent to his gross earnings, as he could not have given them funds that he spent on himself or paid in taxes or used for other purposes; and an appropriate percentage of his expected earnings, taking into consideration these various types of expenditures, is proper.

Restatement (Second) of Torts §914A comment b. The Restatement thus would allow evidence of the decedent's income taxes to reduce the survivors' pecuniary damages whenever a state's wrongful death statute measures damages by the amount that the decedent would have contributed to the survivors.

....We, therefore, hold that evidence of the decedent's income taxes is relevant to the plaintiff's pecuniary damages under Arizona's wrongful death statute, and, hence, should have been admitted under the Federal Rules of Evidence....

....

The district court also declined to instruct the jury that its award would not be taxed. MDC argues that such an instruction[7] was required in this case. We agree.

The Supreme Court has held, as a matter of generally applicable federal common law, that the jury should be instructed that damages for lost future wages are not subject to federal income taxation. *See* Gulf Offshore Co. v. Mobil Oil Corp., 453 U.S. 473, 484–88 (1981) (*Liepelt* "articulated a federal common-law rule"); Norfolk & Western Railway Co. v. Liepelt, 444 U.S. 490 (1980) (FELA defendant entitled to nontaxability instruction). The rationale for the federal rule is that, although most jurors are acutely aware of the effect of income taxes, few jurors appreciate that the amount of damages received on account of personal injuries is not taxable income. [Citations.] Thus, the jury, mistakenly believing that its award will be taxed, may inflate the amount of the plaintiff's damages so that the award, less the taxes that it presumes the plaintiff must pay, equals the amount to which the jury believes that the plaintiff is entitled. [Citation.] In contrast to the federal rule, however, Arizona law clearly states that the jury should not be instructed that its award will not be taxed. [Citations.] We therefore must decide whether to apply federal or state law as to the nontaxability instruction.

      . . . .

. . . [T]o determine whether state or federal law should be applied in this case, we must examine the grounds for refusing the instruction that have been expressed by the Arizona courts. The Arizona Supreme Court . . . has asserted three reasons: the instruction would complicate the trial; it is unnecessary if the jury is instructed on the proper measure of damages; and it would invite a flood of cautionary instructions. *See Mitchell*, 80 Ariz. at 403–05, 298 P.2d at 1037–38 . . . . Since Arizona has not articulated a substantive interest for not giving the instruction, federal law should apply.

We therefore hold that in this diversity case governed by Arizona law the jury should be instructed its award will not be subject to federal income taxation. To do otherwise would deny effect to the substantive federal interest for giving the instruction, *viz.*, preventing the jury from inflating its award.

      . . . .

For the reasons stated above, the judgment below is reversed and remanded for further proceedings consistent with this opinion.

Notes

1. ***Minority Rule Permits Full Recovery of Income.*** Contrary to the principal case, some states allow recovery of the decedent's income in a wrongful death action, without any reduction for amounts that would have been spent on personal consumption by the decedent. *See* Wehner v. Weinstein, 444 S.E.2d 27, 38 (W. Va. 1994) (declining, in the absence of any clear legislative language, to construe the phrase "reasonably expected loss of . . . income of the decedent" to mean "net income").

2. Some state statutes expressly address the issue of whether damages should be reduced because of tax considerations and what the jury should be told about taxation. For example:

---

7. The instruction proposed by MDC provided: "Any damages you award to the plaintiff will be exempt from any income taxes. Therefore, in fixing the amount of your award, you should not be concerned about or consider the effect of taxes imposed on the award."

Tex. Civ. Prac. & Rem. Code §18.091
(Westlaw 2004)

(a) Notwithstanding any other law, if any claimant seeks recovery for loss of earnings, loss of earning capacity, loss of contributions of a pecuniary value, or loss of inheritance, evidence to prove the loss must be presented in the form of a net loss after reduction for income tax payments or unpaid tax liability pursuant to any federal income tax law.

(b) If any claimant seeks recovery for loss of earnings, loss of earning capacity, loss of contributions of a pecuniary value, or loss of inheritance, the court shall instruct the jury as to whether any recovery for compensatory damages sought by the claimant is subject to federal or state income taxes.

D. Punitive Damages

As noted in Chapter 1, punitive damages are imposed in cases involving egregious conduct to punish or make an example of the defendant.

Type of Wrongdoing Required. Some states limit punitive damages awards to intentional acts of malice. For example, in Wisconsin, the punitive damages statute requires proof that "the defendant acted maliciously toward the plaintiff or in an intentional disregard of the rights of the plaintiff." Wis. Stat. Ann. §895.85 (Westlaw 2003).

Other states frame the standard differently and may require only wilful indifference, wanton or reckless conduct or gross negligence.

It may be difficult to demonstrate the type of egregious conduct that is a prerequisite to recovery of punitive damages. *See* Doe v. Issacs, 579 S.E.2d 174 (Va. 2003) (holding, in a state requiring "wilful recklessness" and not merely "gross negligence," that a motorist's behavior in rear-ending a vehicle and leaving the scene of an injury accident was not so willful or wanton as to show a conscious disregard for the rights of others, and therefore punitive damages could not be awarded).

In some states, a narrow definition of the predicate for punitive damages may produce unexpected results. In Komornik v. Sparks, 629 A.2d 721, 723–24 (Md. 1993), a driver whose blood alcohol was almost twice the level of *prima facie* intoxication caused an accident by depressing the clutch, rather than the brake, as he approached cars stopped at a traffic light. The court held that three prior instances of drunk driving did not warrant an award of punitive damages because what was needed was evidence of "evil motive, intent to injure, ill will, or fraud." The defendant's state of mind, the court found, was to the contrary of what was required, because his "intent was to avoid injury to those stopped ahead of him."

Factors Relevant to Liability for Punitive Damages. In Gyrc v. Dayton-Hudson Corp., 297 N.W.2d 727 (Minn. 1980), a four-year-old girl was severely burned when her pajamas burst into flames as she reached across an electric stove. The material used to make the pajamas complied with the Flammable Fabrics Act of 1953, a Federal statute requiring that fabrics sold in interstate commerce meet specified standards for flammability. Furthermore, the plaintiff's own expert witness testified that no mills produced flame-retardant flannelette in commercial quantities when the pajamas in question were manufactured. Nevertheless, the court upheld a punitive-damages award against the manufacturer, based on its failure to use "flame-retardant processes which could [have been] applied to the fabric without adversely affecting its qualities enough to make it unsalable." It said that in determining whether the defendant acted in wilful or reckless disregard of the plaintiff's rights, the jury may consider:

1. The existence and magnitude of the product danger to the public;

2. The cost or feasibility of reducing the danger to an acceptable level;

3. The manufacturer's awareness of the danger, the magnitude of the danger, and the availability of a feasible remedy;

4. The nature and duration of, and the reasons for, the manufacturer's failure to act appropriately to discover or reduce the danger;

5. The extent to which the manufacturer purposefully created the danger;

6. The extent to which the defendants are subject to federal safety regulation;

7. The probability that compensatory damages might be awarded against defendants in other cases; and, finally,

8. The amount of time which has passed since the actions sought to be deterred.

The defendant contended that the $750,000 compensatory damage award and the resulting loss of sales and damage to reputation was an adequate deterrent. It also argued that since it no longer manufactured cotton flannelette and since the Flammable Fabrics Act subsequently imposed more stringent standards for children's sleepwear, no additional deterrent was needed. In response, the court stated:

> This argument ignores the fact that Riegel [the defendant] was shown to have acted in reckless disregard of the public for purely economic reasons in the past. A punitive damages award serves to deter Riegel from acting in a similar manner with respect to other products manufactured by it in the future. Furthermore, since the potential of compensatory damages awards and loss of sales and reputation did not serve to deter Riegel in the past, Riegel cannot now argue that these considerations act as an adequate deterrent.

Clear and Convincing Evidence. "A growing majority of states requires clear and convincing evidence before punitive damages can be considered.... Twenty-four states have adopted a clear and convincing standard by statute. Six states and the District of Columbia have adopted the standard by judicial decision." Rodriguez v. Suzuki Motor Corp., 936 S.W.2d 104 (Mo. 1996). In Colorado, a punitive damages award requires proof beyond a reasonable doubt. *See* Colo. Rev. Stat. Ann. §13-25-127(2) (Westlaw 2003).

Compensatory Damages Predicate? There is a split of authority as to whether an award of compensatory damages is a necessary predicate for punitive damages. Most states so hold, but others allow punitive damages to be tacked onto an award of nominal damages. At least one state goes even further. *See* Hawkins v. Hawkins, 400 S.E.2d 472 (N.C. Ct. App. 1991) (upholding an award of punitive damages in a sexual abuse case where the jury, which found that a father had assaulted and battered his daughter, awarded punitive, but neither compensatory nor nominal damages). Consider the Texas statute:

Tex. Civ. Prac. & Rem. Code § 41.004
(Westlaw 2004)

(a) Except as provided by Subsection (b), exemplary damages may be awarded only if damages other than nominal damages are awarded.

(b) Exemplary damages may not be awarded to a claimant who elects to have his recovery multiplied under another statute.

See also Jensen v. Walsh, 623 N.W.2d 247 (Minn. 2001) (holding that a statute allowing punitive damages in cases involving "deliberate disregard of the rights *or* safety of others" reflected a legislative intent to safeguard rights other than those relating to a person's safety, and that therefore punitive damages are available in cases not involving personal injury).

Factors Relevant to Amount of Punitive Damages. Some states offer juries little guidance with respect to setting the amount of punitive damages, other than to say that the purpose of punitive damages is to punish or make an example of the defendant. However, more detailed guidance is feasible, as suggested by a model law.

MODEL PUNITIVE DAMAGES ACT §7
(Westlaw 2002)

§7. Amount of Punitive Damages.

(a) If a defendant is found liable for punitive damages, a fair and reasonable amount of damages may be awarded....The court shall instruct the jury in determining what constitutes a fair and reasonable amount of punitive damages to consider any evidence that has been admitted regarding the following factors:

(1) the nature of defendant's wrongful conduct and its effect on the claimant and others;

(2) the amount of compensatory damages;

(3) any fines, penalties, damages, or restitution paid or to be paid by the defendant arising from the wrongful conduct;

(4) the defendant's present and future financial condition and the effect of an award on each condition;

(5) any profit or gain, obtained by the defendant through the wrongful conduct, in excess of that likely to be divested by this and any other actions against the defendant for compensatory damages or restitution;

(6) any adverse effect of the award on innocent persons;

(7) any remedial measures taken or not taken by the defendant since the wrongful conduct;

(8) compliance or noncompliance with any applicable standard promulgated by a governmental or other generally recognized agency or organization whose function it is to establish standards; and

(9) any other aggravating or mitigating factors relevant to the amount of the award.

(b) If an award of punitive damages is authorized or governed by another statute of this State, any requirement as to amount or method of calculation established by that statute governs the award....

This particular provision of the model act was crafted before the Supreme Court's decision in State Farm v. Campbell, set forth below in the text.

A few states provide that the amount of punitive damages is to be determined by judges, not juries, either in all cases (*see* Kan. Stat. Ann §60-3702 (Westlaw 2003)) or at least in some suits (*see* Conn. Gen. Stat. Ann. §52-240b (Westlaw 2003) (products liability)).

Major Obstacles to Recovery of Punitive Damages. In Nebraska, a constitutional provision precludes an award of punitive damages. *See* Distinctive Printing & Packaging Co. v. Cox, 443 N.W.2d 566, 574 (Neb. 1989).

In Washington state, a similar rule applies as a result of an early judicial decision. *See* Spokane Truck & Dray Co. v. Hoefer, 25 P. 1072 (Wash. 1891) (barring punitive damages).

In New Hampshire, punitive damages are not available, unless expressly provided for by statute. *See* N.H. Rev. Stat. Ann. §507:16 (Westlaw 2002). In Connecticut, punitive damages may not exceed litigation expenses less taxable costs. *See* Triangle Sheet Metal Works, Inc. v. Silver, 222 A.2d 220 (Conn. 1966).

The Federal Tort Claims Act does not permit the federal government to be held liable for punitive damages. *See* 28 U.S.C. §1346(b), 2671, 2674 (Westlaw 2003).

Montana law requires that an "award of punitive damages must be unanimous as to liability and amount." Mont. Code Ann. §27-1-221(6) (Westlaw 2003).

"The FDA defense provides immunity from punitive liability to any manufacturer or seller of pharmaceuticals that markets its product in conformity with FDA regulations and who does not knowingly withhold or misrepresent information." Michael Rustad, *In Defense of Punitive Damages in Products Liability: Testing Tort Anecdotes with Empirical Data*, 78 Iowa L. Rev. 1, 7 n.23 & n. 29 (1992) (indicating that Arizona, New Jersey, Ohio, Oregon, and Utah have enacted the FDA defense). *See also* William M. Brown, *Deja Vu All Over Again: The Exodus from Contraceptive Research and How to Reverse It*, 40 Brandeis L.J. 1, 40–41 (2001) (discussing "FDA defense").

Do states that don't allow punitive damages have higher accident rates than those that do? Interestingly, and counterintuitively, the answer seems to be "no." *See* Symposium, *Punitive Damages*, 87 Georgetown L.J. 285 (1998).

Perspective. Large punitive damages awards attract media attention—perhaps too much attention.

> Empirical studies of punitive damages in actual cases have found that juries award punitive damages relatively infrequently. Studies conducted by researchers at the RAND Corporation found that punitive damages are only awarded in 1–8% of civil cases. Other studies have found punitive damages to be awarded at similar rates....
>
> ....
>
> ....Not only are punitive damages awarded infrequently, but they are typically not awarded in headline-grabbing amounts....Median awards tend to be relatively low; several studies have found that the median award is approximately $50,000....
>
> ....
>
> Mechanisms such as remittitur, appellate review, and settlement all contribute to the post-trial reduction of punitive awards, and judicial review of damage awards has become increasingly important. Studies that have examined post-trial reductions in punitive damage awards have found that awards were commonly reduced post-trial and that plaintiffs rarely received the amount awarded by the jury.
>
> ....

Recent decisions increasing the role of appellate judges in reviewing punitive damage awards may add fuel to this trend.

See Jennifer K. Robbennolt, *Determining Punitive Damages: Empirical Insights and Implications for Reform*, 50 Buffalo L. Rev. 103, 161–65 (2002).

State Farm Mutual Automobile Insurance Co. v. Campbell

Supreme Court of the United States
123 S. Ct. 1513 (2003)

Justice KENNEDY delivered the opinion of the Court.

.... The question is whether... an award of $145 million in punitive damages, where full compensatory damages are $1 million, is excessive and in violation of the Due Process Clause of the Fourteenth Amendment to the Constitution of the United States.

....

In 1981, Curtis Campbell (Campbell) was driving with his wife.... He decided to pass six vans traveling ahead of them on a two-lane highway. Todd Ospital was driving a small car.... To avoid a head-on collision with Campbell,... Ospital swerved onto the shoulder, lost control of his automobile, and collided with a vehicle driven by Robert G. Slusher. Ospital was killed, and Slusher was rendered permanently disabled....

... "[A] consensus was reached early on by the investigators and witnesses that Mr. Campbell's unsafe pass had indeed caused the crash." [Citation.] Campbell's insurance company,... (State Farm), nonetheless decided to contest liability and declined offers by Slusher and Ospital's estate (Ospital) to settle the claims for the policy limit of $50,000 ($25,000 per claimant). State Farm also ignored the advice of one of its own investigators and took the case to trial, assuring the Campbells that "their assets were safe, that they had no liability for the accident, that [State Farm] would represent their interests, and that they did not need to procure separate counsel." [Citation.] To the contrary, a jury determined that Campbell was 100 percent at fault, and a judgment was returned for $185,849, far more than the amount offered in settlement.

At first State Farm refused to cover the $135,849 in excess liability. Its counsel made this clear to the Campbells: "'You may want to put for sale signs on your property to get things moving.'".... Campbell obtained his own counsel to appeal the verdict. During the pendency of the appeal, in late 1984, Slusher, Ospital, and the Campbells reached an agreement whereby Slusher and Ospital agreed not to seek satisfaction of their claims against the Campbells. In exchange the Campbells agreed to pursue a bad faith action against State Farm.... Slusher and Ospital would receive 90 percent of any verdict against State Farm.

In 1989, the Utah Supreme Court denied Campbell's appeal in the wrongful death and tort actions. [Citation.] State Farm then paid the entire judgment, including the amounts in excess of the policy limits. The Campbells nonetheless filed a complaint against State Farm alleging bad faith, fraud, and intentional infliction of emotional distress.... State Farm moved *in limine* to exclude evidence of alleged conduct that occurred in unrelated cases outside of Utah, but the trial court denied the motion. At State Farm's request the trial court bifurcated the trial into two phases conducted before different juries. In the first phase the jury determined that State Farm's decision not to settle was unreasonable because there was a substantial likelihood of an excess verdict.

Before the second phase of the action against State Farm we decided BMW of North America, Inc. v. Gore, 517 U.S. 559...(1996), and refused to sustain a $2 million punitive damages award which accompanied a verdict of only $4,000 in compensatory damages. Based on that decision, State Farm again moved for the exclusion of evidence of dissimilar out-of-state conduct. [Citation.] The trial court denied State Farm's motion. [Citation.]

The second phase addressed State Farm's liability for fraud and intentional infliction of emotional distress, as well as compensatory and punitive damages. The Utah Supreme Court aptly characterized this phase of the trial:

> "State Farm argued during phase II that its decision to take the case to trial was an 'honest mistake' that did not warrant punitive damages. In contrast, the Campbells introduced evidence that State Farm's decision to take the case to trial was a result of a national scheme to meet corporate fiscal goals by capping payouts on claims company wide. This scheme was referred to as State Farm's 'Performance, Planning and Review,' or PP & R, policy. To prove the existence of this scheme, the trial court allowed the Campbells to introduce extensive expert testimony regarding fraudulent practices by State Farm in its nation-wide operations...." [Citation.]

Evidence pertaining to the PP & R policy concerned State Farm's business practices for over 20 years in numerous States. Most of these practices bore no relation to third-party automobile insurance claims, the type of claim underlying the Campbells' complaint against the company. The jury awarded the Campbells $2.6 million in compensatory damages and $145 million in punitive damages, which the trial court reduced to $1 million and $25 million respectively. Both parties appealed.

The Utah Supreme Court sought to apply the three guideposts we identified in *Gore*, [citation], and it reinstated the $145 million punitive damages award....We granted certiorari. [Citation.]

    ....

....Compensatory damages "are intended to redress the concrete loss that the plaintiff has suffered by reason of the defendant's wrongful conduct." [Citation.] By contrast, punitive damages serve a broader function; they are aimed at deterrence and retribution. [Citation.]

While States possess discretion over the imposition of punitive damages, it is well established that there are procedural and substantive constitutional limitations on these awards. [Citations.] The Due Process Clause of the Fourteenth Amendment prohibits the imposition of grossly excessive or arbitrary punishments on a tortfeasor. [Citation.] The reason is that "[e]lementary notions of fairness enshrined in our constitutional jurisprudence dictate that a person receive fair notice not only of the conduct that will subject him to punishment, but also of the severity of the penalty that a State may impose."....

Although these awards serve the same purposes as criminal penalties, defendants subjected to punitive damages in civil cases have not been accorded the protections applicable in a criminal proceeding....Jury instructions typically leave the jury with wide discretion in choosing amounts, and the presentation of evidence of a defendant's net worth creates the potential that juries will use their verdicts to express biases against big businesses, particularly those without strong local presences....

...[I]n *Gore, supra*, we instructed courts reviewing punitive damages to consider three guideposts: (1) the degree of reprehensibility of the defendant's misconduct; (2)

the disparity between the actual or potential harm suffered by the plaintiff and the punitive damages award; and (3) the difference between the punitive damages awarded by the jury and the civil penalties authorized or imposed in comparable cases. [Citation.] We reiterated the importance of these three guideposts in *Cooper Industries* and mandated appellate courts to conduct *de novo* review of a trial court's application of them to the jury's award....

....

Under the principles outlined in BMW of North America, Inc. v. Gore, this case is neither close nor difficult. It was error to reinstate the jury's $145 million punitive damages award. We address each guidepost of *Gore* in some detail.

....

"[T]he most important indicium of the reasonableness of a punitive damages award is the degree of reprehensibility of the defendant's conduct." [Citation.] We have instructed courts to determine the reprehensibility of a defendant by considering whether: the harm caused was physical as opposed to economic; the tortious conduct evinced an indifference to or a reckless disregard of the health or safety of others; the target of the conduct had financial vulnerability; the conduct involved repeated actions or was an isolated incident; and the harm was the result of intentional malice, trickery, or deceit, or mere accident. [Citation.] The existence of any one of these factors weighing in favor of a plaintiff may not be sufficient to sustain a punitive damages award; and the absence of all of them renders any award suspect. It should be presumed a plaintiff has been made whole for his injuries by compensatory damages, so punitive damages should only be awarded if the defendant's culpability, after having paid compensatory damages, is so reprehensible as to warrant the imposition of further sanctions to achieve punishment or deterrence. [Citation.]

...State Farm's handling of the claims against the Campbells merits no praise. The trial court found that State Farm's employees altered the company's records to make Campbell appear less culpable. State Farm disregarded the overwhelming likelihood of liability and the near-certain probability that, by taking the case to trial, a judgment in excess of the policy limits would be awarded. State Farm amplified the harm by at first assuring the Campbells their assets would be safe from any verdict and by later telling them, postjudgment, to put a for-sale sign on their house. While we do not suggest there was error in awarding punitive damages based upon State Farm's conduct toward the Campbells, a more modest punishment for this reprehensible conduct could have satisfied the State's legitimate objectives, and the Utah courts should have gone no further.

This case, instead, was used as a platform to expose, and punish, the perceived deficiencies of State Farm's operations throughout the country....

A State cannot punish a defendant for conduct that may have been lawful where it occurred. [Citations.] Nor, as a general rule, does a State have a legitimate concern in imposing punitive damages to punish a defendant for unlawful acts committed outside of the State's jurisdiction....

Here, the Campbells do not dispute that much of the out-of-state conduct was lawful where it occurred....Lawful out-of-state conduct may be probative when it demonstrates the deliberateness and culpability of the defendant's action in the State where it is tortious, but that conduct must have a nexus to the specific harm suffered by the plaintiff. A jury must be instructed, furthermore, that it may not use evidence of out-of-state conduct to punish a defendant for action that was lawful in the jurisdiction where it occurred. [Citation.] A basic principle of federalism is that each State may make its own reasoned judgment about what conduct is permitted or proscribed within its borders, and each State alone can determine what measure of punishment, if any, to impose on a defendant who acts within its jurisdiction. [Citation.]

For a more fundamental reason, however, the Utah courts erred in relying upon this and other evidence: The courts awarded punitive damages to punish and deter conduct that bore no relation to the Campbells' harm. A defendant's dissimilar acts, independent from the acts upon which liability was premised, may not serve as the basis for punitive damages. A defendant should be punished for the conduct that harmed the plaintiff, not for being an unsavory individual or business. Due process does not permit courts, in the calculation of punitive damages, to adjudicate the merits of other parties' hypothetical claims against a defendant under the guise of the reprehensibility analysis, but we have no doubt the Utah Supreme Court did that here. [Citation.] Punishment on these bases creates the possibility of multiple punitive damages awards for the same conduct; for in the usual case nonparties are not bound by the judgment some other plaintiff obtains. [Citation.]

... [T]he Utah Supreme Court's decision cannot be justified on the grounds that State Farm was a recidivist. Although "[o]ur holdings that a recidivist may be punished more severely than a first offender recognize that repeated misconduct is more reprehensible than an individual instance of malfeasance," [citation], in the context of civil actions courts must ensure the conduct in question replicates the prior transgressions. [Citations.]

The Campbells have identified scant evidence of repeated misconduct of the sort that injured them. Nor does our review of the Utah courts' decisions convince us that State Farm was only punished for its actions toward the Campbells. Although evidence of other acts need not be identical to have relevance in the calculation of punitive damages, the Utah court erred here because evidence pertaining to claims that had nothing to do with a third-party lawsuit was introduced at length.... The Campbells attempt to justify the courts' reliance upon this unrelated testimony on the theory that each dollar of profit made by underpaying a third-party claimant is the same as a dollar made by underpaying a first-party one.... [T]his argument is unconvincing. The reprehensibility guidepost does not permit courts to expand the scope of the case so that a defendant may be punished for any malfeasance, which in this case extended for a 20-year period. In this case, because the Campbells have shown no conduct by State Farm similar to that which harmed them, the conduct that harmed them is the only conduct relevant to the reprehensibility analysis.

....

Turning to the second *Gore* guidepost, we have been reluctant to identify concrete constitutional limits on the ratio between harm, or potential harm, to the plaintiff and the punitive damages award. *Gore, supra,* at 582... ("[W]e have consistently rejected the notion that the constitutional line is marked by a simple mathematical formula..."); [citation]. We decline again to impose a bright-line ratio which a punitive damages award cannot exceed. Our jurisprudence and the principles it has now established demonstrate, however, that, in practice, few awards exceeding a single-digit ratio between punitive and compensatory damages, to a significant degree, will satisfy due process.... While these ratios are not binding, they are instructive. They demonstrate what should be obvious: Single-digit multipliers are more likely to comport with due process, while still achieving the State's goals of deterrence and retribution, than awards with ratios in range of 500 to 1, *id.,* at 582,... or, in this case, of 145 to 1.

Nonetheless, because there are no rigid benchmarks that a punitive damages award may not surpass, ratios greater than those we have previously upheld may comport with due process where "a particularly egregious act has resulted in only a small amount of economic damages." [Citations.] The converse is also true, however. When compensatory damages are substantial, then a lesser ratio, perhaps only equal to compensatory damages, can reach the outermost limit of the due process guarantee. The precise award in any case, of course, must be based upon the facts and circumstances of the defendant's conduct and the harm to the plaintiff.

In sum, courts must ensure that the measure of punishment is both reasonable and proportionate to the amount of harm to the plaintiff and to the general damages recovered. In the context of this case, we have no doubt that there is a presumption against an award that has a 145-to-1 ratio. The compensatory award in this case was substantial; the Campbells were awarded $1 million for a year and a half of emotional distress. This was complete compensation. The harm arose from a transaction in the economic realm, not from some physical assault or trauma; there were no physical injuries; and State Farm paid the excess verdict before the complaint was filed, so the Campbells suffered only minor economic injuries for the 18-month period in which State Farm refused to resolve the claim against them. The compensatory damages for the injury suffered here, moreover, likely were based on a component which was duplicated in the punitive award. Much of the distress was caused by the outrage and humiliation the Campbells suffered at the actions of their insurer; and it is a major role of punitive damages to condemn such conduct. Compensatory damages, however, already contain this punitive element. *See* Restatement (Second) of Torts §908, Comment *c*, p. 466 (1977) ("In many cases in which compensatory damages include an amount for emotional distress, such as humiliation or indignation aroused by the defendant's act, there is no clear line of demarcation between punishment and compensation and a verdict for a specified amount frequently includes elements of both").

The Utah Supreme Court sought to justify the massive award by pointing to... the fact that State Farm's policies have affected numerous Utah consumers; the fact that State Farm will only be punished in one out of every 50,000 cases as a matter of statistical probability; and State Farm's enormous wealth....

... [T]he argument that State Farm will be punished in only the rare case, coupled with reference to its assets (which, of course, are what other insured parties in Utah and other States must rely upon for payment of claims) had little to do with the actual harm sustained by the Campbells. The wealth of a defendant cannot justify an otherwise unconstitutional punitive damages award. *Gore*, 517 U.S., at 585... ("The fact that BMW is a large corporation rather than an impecunious individual does not diminish its entitlement to fair notice of the demands that the several States impose on the conduct of its business")....

....

The third guidepost in *Gore* is the disparity between the punitive damages award and the "civil penalties authorized or imposed in comparable cases.".... The existence of a criminal penalty does have bearing on the seriousness with which a State views the wrongful action. When used to determine the dollar amount of the award, however, the criminal penalty has less utility. Great care must be taken to avoid use of the civil process to assess criminal penalties that can be imposed only after the heightened protections of a criminal trial have been observed, including, of course, its higher standards of proof. Punitive damages are not a substitute for the criminal process, and the remote possibility of a criminal sanction does not automatically sustain a punitive damages award.

Here, we need not dwell long on this guidepost. The most relevant civil sanction under Utah state law for the wrong done to the Campbells appears to be a $10,000 fine for an act of fraud, [citation], an amount dwarfed by the $145 million punitive damages award. The Supreme Court of Utah speculated about the loss of State Farm's business license, the disgorgement of profits, and possible imprisonment, but here again its references were to the broad fraudulent scheme drawn from evidence of out-of-state and dissimilar conduct. This analysis was insufficient to justify the award.

....

An application of the *Gore* guideposts to the facts of this case, especially in light of the substantial compensatory damages awarded (a portion of which contained a punitive element), likely would justify a punitive damages award at or near the amount of compensatory damages. The punitive award of $145 million, therefore, was neither reasonable nor proportionate to the wrong committed, and it was an irrational and arbitrary deprivation of the property of the defendant. The proper calculation of punitive damages under the principles we have discussed should be resolved, in the first instance, by the Utah courts.

The judgment of the Utah Supreme Court is reversed, and the case is remanded for proceedings not inconsistent with this opinion.

Justice SCALIA, dissenting.

I adhere to the view expressed in my dissenting opinion in BMW of North America, Inc. v. Gore, 517 U.S. 559, 598–99...(1996), that the Due Process Clause provides no substantive protections against "excessive" or "'unreasonable'" awards of punitive damages....

Justice THOMAS, dissenting.

I would affirm the judgment below because "I continue to believe that the Constitution does not constrain the size of punitive damages awards.".…

Justice GINSBURG, dissenting.

Not long ago, this Court was hesitant to impose a federal check on state-court judgments awarding punitive damages. In Browning-Ferris Industries of Vt., Inc. v. Kelco Disposal, Inc., 492 U.S. 257...(1989), the Court held that neither the Excessive Fines Clause of the Eighth Amendment nor federal common law circumscribed awards of punitive damages in civil cases between private parties. [Citation.] Two years later, in Pacific Mut. Life Ins. Co. v. Haslip, 499 U.S. 1...(1991), the Court observed that "unlimited jury [or judicial] discretion...in the fixing of punitive damages may invite extreme results that jar one's constitutional sensibilities," [citation]; the Due Process Clause, the Court suggested, would attend to those sensibilities and guard against unreasonable awards, [citation]. Nevertheless, the Court upheld a punitive damages award in *Haslip* "more than 4 times the amount of compensatory damages,...more than 200 times [the plaintiff's] out-of-pocket expenses," and "much in excess of the fine that could be imposed." [Citation.] And in TXO Production Corp. v. Alliance Resources Corp., 509 U.S. 443...(1993), the Court affirmed a state-court award "526 times greater than the actual damages awarded by the jury." [Citations.]

It was not until 1996, in BMW of North America, Inc. v. Gore, 517 U.S. 559... (1996), that the Court, for the first time, invalidated a state-court punitive damages assessment as unreasonably large. [Citation.] If our activity in this domain is now "well-established," [citation], it takes place on ground not long held.

In *Gore*, I stated why I resisted the Court's foray into punitive damages "territory traditionally within the States' domain." [Citation.] I adhere to those views....

....

Ample evidence allowed the jury to find that State Farm's treatment of the Campbells typified its "Performance, Planning and Review" (PP & R) program; implemented by top management in 1979, the program had "the explicit objective of using the claims-adjustment process as a profit center." [Citation.] "[T]he Campbells presented considerable evidence,"...documenting "that the PP & R program...has functioned, and continues to function, as an unlawful scheme...to deny benefits owed consumers by paying out less than fair value in order to meet preset, arbitrary payout targets designed to enhance corporate profits." [Citation.] That policy, the trial court observed, was encompassing in scope; it "applied equally to the handling of both third-party and first-party claims." [Citation.]

Evidence the jury could credit demonstrated that the PP & R program regularly and adversely affected Utah residents. Ray Summers, "the adjuster who handled the Campbell case and who was a State Farm employee in Utah for almost twenty years," described several methods used by State Farm to deny claimants fair benefits, for example, "falsifying or withholding of evidence in claim files." [Citation.] A common tactic, Summers recounted, was to "unjustly attac[k] the character, reputation and credibility of a claimant and mak[e] notations to that effect in the claim file to create prejudice in the event the claim ever came before a jury." [Citation.] State Farm manager Bob Noxon, Summers testified, resorted to a tactic of this order in the Campbell case when he "instruct[ed] Summers to write in the file that Todd Ospital (who was killed in the accident) was speeding because he was on his way to see a pregnant girlfriend." [Citation.] In truth, "[t]here was no pregnant girlfriend."....

The trial court also noted the testimony of two Utah State Farm employees, Felix Jensen and Samantha Bird, both of whom recalled "intolerable" and "recurrent" pressure to reduce payouts below fair value....At times, Bird said, she "was forced to commit dishonest acts and to knowingly underpay claims."....Utah managers superior to Bird, the evidence indicated, were improperly influenced by the PP & R program to encourage insurance underpayments. For example, several documents evaluating the performance of managers..."contained explicit preset average payout goals." [Citation.]

....

The trial court further determined that the jury could find State Farm's policy "deliberately crafted" to prey on consumers who would be unlikely to defend themselves....

The Campbells themselves could be placed within the "weakest of the herd" category. The couple appeared economically vulnerable and emotionally fragile. [Citation.] At the time of State Farm's wrongful conduct, "Mr. Campbell had residuary effects from a stroke and Parkinson's disease." [Citation.]

To further insulate itself from liability, trial evidence indicated, State Farm made "systematic" efforts to destroy internal company documents that might reveal its scheme....

....

State Farm's "policies and practices," the trial evidence thus bore out, were "responsible for the injuries suffered by the Campbells," and the means used to implement those policies could be found "callous, clandestine, fraudulent, and dishonest."....

. . . .

When the Court first ventured to override state-court punitive damages awards, it did so moderately. . . . Today's decision exhibits no such respect and restraint. No longer content to accord state-court judgments "a strong presumption of validity," *TXO*, 509 U.S., at 457 . . . the Court announces that "few awards exceeding a single-digit ratio between punitive and compensatory damages, to a significant degree, will satisfy due process." [Citation.] Moreover, the Court adds, when compensatory damages are substantial, doubling those damages "can reach the outermost limit of the due process guarantee." [Citation.] In a legislative scheme or a state high court's design to cap punitive damages, the handiwork in setting single-digit and 1-to-1 benchmarks could hardly be questioned; in a judicial decree imposed on the States by this Court under the banner of substantive due process, the numerical controls today's decision installs seem to me boldly out of order.

. . . . I would leave the judgment of the Utah Supreme Court undisturbed.

Notes

1. *Other Supreme Court Precedent.* In Honda Motor Co., Ltd. v. Oberg, 512 U.S. 415 (1994), the court ruled that an amendment to the Oregon Constitution, prohibiting judicial review of the amount of punitive damages awarded by a jury "unless the court can affirmatively say there is no evidence to support the verdict," violated due process.

In BMW of North America, Inc. v. Gore, 517 U.S. 559 (1996), the court overturned a $2 million punitive damage award to a car purchaser who had not been told about the predelivery damage and repair of the vehicle he purchased. The jury had awarded $4000 compensatory damages.

2. *Evidence of Defendant's Financial Condition.* It is generally held that the defendant's wealth or poverty is relevant to the issue of punitive damages. The reason is that an amount which may be sufficient to punish or deter a poor person may not be sufficient to achieve similar result with one who is rich. Many decisions throughout the country addressed this issue. However, all of that precedent is now subject to re-examination in light of the Supreme Court's statement in *Campbell* that "The wealth of a defendant cannot justify an otherwise unconstitutional punitive damages award."

3. *Bifurcated and Trifurcated Trials.* The introduction of evidence as to the defendant's wealth may prejudice the jury's assessment of the liability issue. Accordingly, many states hold that the better course is to divide the trial into separate stages dealing with compensatory damages liability, first, and punitive damages liability, second. This is called a bifurcated trial. *See, e.g.,* Cal. Civ. Code §3295(d) (Westlaw 2003); N.J. Stat. Ann. §2A:15-5.13 (Westlaw 2003); Tex. Civ. Prac. & Rem. Code §41.009 (Westlaw 2003). *But see* Life Ins. Co. of Ga. v. Johnson, 701 So. 2d 524 (Ala. 1997) (bifurcation of trials on merits and punitive damages is not necessary to assure due process).

Courts may even employ a three-part process (a trifurcated trial) that addresses: first, whether the defendant should be liable for compensatory damages and, if so, in what amount; second, whether punitive damages should be imposed; and third, the amount of punitive damages.

4. *Multiple Suits and Punitive Damages.* When a product injures several consumers, or an airplane crash kills many victims, there is a risk that the defendant may be exposed to multiple awards of punitive damages in separate actions. However, the ruling in *Campbell*—restricting consideration of extra-jurisdictional evidence, barring con-

sideration of hypothetical claims, and stating that the "precise award in any case...must be based upon the facts and circumstances of the defendant's conduct and the harm to the plaintiff"—would seem to go far toward reducing any risk of excessive punishment.

Georgia passed a tort reform act that allows only one recovery of punitive damages in products liability actions. *See* Ga. Code Ann. §51-12-5.1(e)(1) (Westlaw 2002). That provision has been held constitutional. *See* Mack Trucks, Inc. v. Conkle, 436 S.E.2d 635, 639 (Ga. 1993).

In attempting to grapple with the evidentiary questions relating to punitive damages in the mass tort context, one court wrote:

> ...[E]vidence about the profitability of a defendant's misconduct and about any settlement amounts for punitive damages or prior punitive damages awards that the defendant has actually paid for the same course of conduct is admissible when the defendant offers it in mitigation of punitive damages. Such evidence is relevant because it better informs the fact finder about the parties' situation and the amount of punitive damages necessary to fairly punish a party and to deter the conduct in question....
>
> Evidence that is not relevant, or is unduly prejudicial, and thus, not admissible to mitigate punitive damages, includes actual damage amounts paid by settlements or by judgments; the number of pending claims filed against a defendant for the same conduct; the number of anticipated claims for the same conduct; insurance coverage; unpaid punitive damages awards for the same course of conduct; and evidence of punitive damages that may be levied in the future. [Citations.]
>
> ....
>
> ...[O]nly prior paid awards and settlements for punitive damages should be considered by the fact finder. To hold otherwise risks unfair prejudice and jury confusion....[M]any punitive damage awards are reduced after trial, reversed on appeal, or settled at a discount. [Citations.]

Owens-Corning Fiberglas Corp. v. Malone, 972 S.W.2d 35, 40–42 (Tex. 1998).

5. *Punitive Damages Caps.* Some states have enacted limits on the amount of punitive damages. *See, e.g.*: Alaska Stat. §09.17.020(f)–(h) (Westlaw 2003) (greater of three times compensatory damages or $500,000, except when action is motivated by financial gain, in which case punitive damages are limited to the greater of four times compensatory damages, four times aggregate amount of financial gain, or $7,000,000; different rules apply to unlawful employment practices); Colo. Rev. Stat. Ann. §13-21-102 (Westlaw 2003) (award may not exceed actual damages or, if there are aggravating circumstances, three times actual damages); Conn. Gen. Stat. Ann. §52-240b (Westlaw 2003) (twice the compensatory award in a products liability action); Kan. Stat. Ann. §60-3701(1)(e)–(f) (Westlaw 2002) (no more than $5 million or the gross income of the defendant, whichever is less).

Suppose that a 85 year old patient in a nursing home is seriously injured as a result of conscious neglect by the staff. Would an award of punitive damages be capped under the following statute?

Tex. Civ. Prac. & Rem. Code §41.008
(Westlaw 2004)

§41.008. Limitation on Amount of Recovery

....

(b) Exemplary damages awarded against a defendant may not exceed an amount equal to the greater of:

(1) (A) two times the amount of economic damages; plus

(B) an amount equal to any noneconomic damages found by the jury, not to exceed $750,000; or

(2) $200,000.

(c) This section does not apply to a cause of action against a defendant from whom a plaintiff seeks recovery of exemplary damages based on conduct described as a felony in the following sections of the Penal Code if, except for Sections 49.07 and 49.08, the conduct was committed knowingly or intentionally:

(1) Section 19.02 (murder);

(2) Section 19.03 (capital murder);

(3) Section 20.04 (aggravated kidnapping);

(4) Section 22.02 (aggravated assault);

(5) Section 22.011 (sexual assault);

(6) Section 22.021 (aggravated sexual assault);

(7) Section 22.04 (injury to a child, elderly individual, or disabled individual, but not if the conduct occurred while providing health care as defined by Section 74.001);

(8) Section 32.21 (forgery);

(9) Section 32.43 (commercial bribery);

(10) Section 32.45 (misapplication of fiduciary property or property of financial institution);

(11) Section 32.46 (securing execution of document by deception);

(12) Section 32.47 (fraudulent destruction, removal, or concealment of writing);

(13) Chapter 31 (theft) the punishment level for which is a felony of the third degree or higher;

(14) Section 49.07 (intoxication assault); or

(15) Section 49.08 (intoxication manslaughter).

. . .

(f) This section does not apply to a cause of action for damages arising from the manufacture of methamphetamine....

6. *Insuring against Liability for Punitive Damages.* There is a split of authority as to whether an insurance contract term purporting to cover punitive damages is against public policy. In Price v. Hartford Accident and Indemnity Co., 502 P.2d 522 (Ariz. 1972), the court upheld the coverage. Turning aside arguments that the law should not allow irresponsible drivers to escape punishment and that permitting insurance would foist the burden of a punitive award onto the public at large, the court concluded that the insurance company was obliged to honor the clear language of the policy. Presumably, the company had been adequately compensated for taking the risk, and in any event the defendant and other drivers would be adequately deterred from misconduct

by fear of criminal liability, increased insurance premiums, and the risk that a punitive damage award would exceed insurance coverage limits.

Unlike *Price*, some courts hold that insuring punitive damage awards would frustrate public policy. *See, e.g.*, Johnson & Johnson v. Aetna Cas. & Surety Co., 667 A.2d 1087 (N.J. 1995) (declining to draw a distinction based on whether the insured's liability is direct or vicarious); Peterson v. Superior Court of Ventura Co., 642 P.2d 1305 (Cal. 1982); Hartford Accident and Indemnity Co. v. Village of Hempstead, 397 N.E.2d 737 (N.Y. 1979). However, others are in accord with *Price*. *See* Weschester Fire Ins. Co. v. Admiral Ins. Co., 2003 W.L. 21475423 (Tex. App.) (holding in the absence of clear authority from the state legislature or supreme court that insurance coverage for punitive damages did not violate Texas public policy).

Whether punitive damages are insurable can have important consequences. *See* John Council, *Insuring Punitive Damages Doesn't Violate Public Policy*, Tex. Law., July 21, 2003 (suggesting that eliminating insurance for punitive damages could be troubling "for doctors who do high-risk surgeries or work where mistakes often lead to accusations of gross negligence. Doctors who deliver babies might quit their practices if they can't get insurance for such damages").

7. ***Insurance Contract Exclusions.*** According to James J. Restivo, Jr., *Insuring Punitive Damages*, Nat'l L.J., July 24, 1995, at C1:

> In the late 1970s, the Insurance Services Office, the insurance industry's common trade and services organization, designed a standard-form punitive damages exclusion for comprehensive general liability policies. The standard exclusion would have excluded all coverage for any "punitive or exemplary damages or any fines or penalties, in whatever form assessed."
>
> The industry, however, never adopted this standard-form exclusion because of the increasing frequency of punitive damages, the intense competition among insurers at the time and the fear that they would lose policyholders if they added this exclusion. Since the [Universal Underwriters Ins. Co. v.] Lazenby decision [383 S.W.2d 1 (Tenn.)] in 1964, insurers have been on notice that without an explicit exclusion, there would be coverage for punitive damages in many states....

8. ***Vicarious Liability for Punitive Damages.*** Punitive damages may be imposed on an employer under a respondeat superior theory without violating due process. In Pacific Mutual Life Ins. Co. v. Haslip, 499 U.S. 1 (1991), the court wrote:

> Imposing exemplary damages on the corporation when its agent commits intentional fraud creates a strong incentive for vigilance by those in a position "to guard substantially against the evil to be prevented." [Citation.] If an insurer were liable for such damages only upon proof that it was at fault independently, it would have an incentive to minimize oversight of its agents. Imposing liability without independent fault deters fraud more than a less stringent rule. It therefore rationally advances the State's goal.

If a plaintiff seeks to hold a corporation liable for punitive damages based on the conduct of an employee or agent, it may be necessary to show that the employee or agent acted with malice. *See* Schropp v. Crown Eurocars, Inc., 654 So. 2d 1158 (Fla. 1995) (the jury's exoneration of the only employee with managerial responsibility from liability for maliciousness precluded an assessment of punitive damages against the employer).

Some states have addressed the issue of vicarious liability by statute. For example:

ALASKA STAT. §09.17.020(k)
(Westlaw 2003)

In a civil action in which an employer is determined to be vicariously liable for the act or omission of an employee, punitive damages may not be awarded against the employer under principles of vicarious liability unless

(1) the employer or the employer's managerial agent

(A) authorized the act or omission and the manner in which the act was performed or omission occurred; or

(B) ratified or approved the act or omission after the act or omission occurred; or

(2) the employee

(A) was unfit to perform the act or avoid the omission and the employer or the employer's managerial agent acted recklessly in employing or retaining the employee; or

(B) was employed in a managerial capacity and was acting within the scope of employment.

In this subsection, "managerial agent" means a management level employee with the stature and authority to exercise control, discretion, and independent judgment over a certain area of the employer's business and with some power to set policy for the employer.

9. *Punitive Damages Paid to the State.* While punitive damages are awarded because of the conduct of defendants, the awards also affect the behavior of plaintiffs. Traditionally, the full amount of a punitive damages award has been paid to the prevailing party. If a punitive award is larger than is necessary to compensate the plaintiff for the costs of litigation and losses not covered by compensatory damages, there is a threat that potential plaintiffs will be tempted to engage in risk-seeking behavior and excessive litigation, and that a disproportionate amount of legal talent will be misallocated to the representation of persons with punitive damages claims.

In an effort to address these problems—and to ease unrelated budgetary pressures—several states have enacted laws requiring some portion of each punitive damages award to be paid to the state, either to the general fund or to a special fund dealing, for example, with rehabilitation, medical assistance, or compensation of criminal injuries. Depending on the jurisdiction, the state's share of punitive damages may be a fixed percentage (sometimes up to 75% or more) or an amount determined by the discretion of the judge. *See, e.g.,* Ga. Code Ann. §51-12-5.1(e)(2) (Westlaw 2002) (in products liability actions, forfeiture of 75% less a proportionate part of the costs of litigation); 735 Ill. Comp. Stat. Ann. 5/2-1207 (Westlaw 2003) (discretionary amount); Iowa Code Ann. §668A.1(2)(b) (Westlaw 2002) (forfeiture of at least 75%, unless the defendant's conduct was directed specifically at the claimant); Mo. Rev. Stat. §537.675 (Westlaw 2003) (allowing state to receive 50%); Or. Rev. Stat. §18.540 (Westlaw 2001) (forfeiture of 60%); Utah Code Ann. §78-18-1(3) (Westlaw 2002) (giving state one-half of award in excess of $20,000, "after payment of attorneys' fees and costs").

In Pennsylvania, if punitive damages are awarded in a case involving violation of the Fine Arts Protection Act (which encompasses certain types of physical defacement, mutilation, alteration or destruction of a work of fine art), "the court shall, in its discretion, select an organization or organizations engaged in charitable or educational activities involving the fine arts in Pennsylvania to receive such damages." Pa. Cons. Stat. §2105(3) (Westlaw 2003).

Statutes forfeiting punitive damages to the state have been attacked as unconstitutional "takings" of private property or denials of equal protection—with mixed results. *Compare* Mack Trucks, Inc. v. Conkle, 436 S.E.2d 635 (Ga. 1993) (rejecting "takings" and equal protection challenges), *with* Kirk v. Denver Publishing Co., 818 P.2d 262, 273 (Colo. 1991) (finding state statute unconstitutional). In general, the legislation has produced less money for state programs than might be expected, because most large punitive damages awards do not survive on appeal. In addition, plaintiffs and defendants can, and presumably do, conspire to deprive a state of its anticipated share, and split that amount between themselves, by settling cases in which punitive damages awards are likely. To the extent that this happens, punitive damages are still paid by defendants, albeit in a reduced amount, even if they are not awarded. *See generally, Note, An Economic Analysis of the Plaintiff's Windfall From Punitive Damages Litigation*, 105 Harv. L. Rev. 1900 (1992); James A. Breslo, *Comment: Taking the Punitive Damage Windfall Away from the Plaintiff: An Analysis*, 86 Nw. U. L. Rev. 1130 (1992). *See generally* Life Ins. Co. of Ga. v. Johnson, 701 So. 2d 524 (Ala. 1997) (overruling earlier decision and holding that, as a matter of common law, sharing punitive awards with state treasury is not necessary in order to prevent windfalls).

10. *Ethics in Law Practice: Contingent Fees and Conflicts of Interest.* A client is entitled to the full benefit of an attorney's independent professional judgment, unclouded by improper personal interests of the attorney. One interest that most attorneys have relates to getting paid for the work they do. On the plaintiff's side of the bar, tort litigation is usually handled on a contingent fee basis. If the client does not recover, the lawyer does not get paid. The contingency of the lawyer's fee creates a powerful incentive for the lawyer to work hard to win. One might think, therefore, that such a contractual arrangement does not create a conflict of interest; that the arrangement is a win-win situation. But the ethical analysis is not so simple.

An attorney employed under a contingent fee contract may be induced to pursue risky litigation strategies in search of a large contingent fee, although a conservative course would be more consonant with the interests of the client. The attorney may also be tempted to settle a case quickly and with little expense in order to maintain a high volume of business, even though the specific client would be better served by more vigorous litigation. Despite these risks, ethics rules permit contingent fee contracts in all but a few areas (criminal representation and, in some jurisdictions, certain domestic relations matters). The dangers contingent fees pose to fair representation are generally thought to be outweighed by the fact that such agreements help to ensure that persons with colorable claims have access to the justice system, regardless of ability to pay.

Allocating a portion of a punitive damages award to the state may risk creating a conflict of interest between attorney and client, depending on how the arrangement is structured. If the attorney is permitted to receive a contingent fee out of the entire punitive damages award, and not simply the portion of the award eventually received by the client (*cf.* Life Ins. Co. of Ga. v. Johnson, 684 So. 2d 685, 699 (Ala. 1996), *overruled on remand*, 701 So. 2d 524 (Ala. 1997)), the interests of the lawyer and the client begin to differ. The attorney has a stronger incentive than the client to pursue punitive damages. One disadvantage for the client is that if a case goes to trial (for the purpose of securing a punitive award), the contingent fee contract may entitle the lawyer to a greater percentage as a fee (say, 40%, rather than 30%).

Aside from questions of forfeiture and diverging interests, it is worth remembering that, for tax reasons, a plaintiff may be better off if money received from a defendant is characterized as compensation, rather than punitive damages. The client has to pay federal income tax on receipt of punitive damages, but not on compensatory damages for personal physical injuries.

E. Statutory Limits on Damage Recoveries and Related "Reform" Legislation

Caps on Damages. Every few years there is a new perceived "crisis" created by large verdicts, followed by a new wave of tort reform ostensibly intended to control the costs of liability insurance. In particular, limits on recoveries for "non-economic" damages (such as damages for pain and suffering) have been very common. *See, e.g.,* Alaska Stat. 09.17.010 (Westlaw 2002) (limiting non-economic damages to the greater of $400,000 or the injured person's life expectancy in years multiplied by $8,000, unless the plaintiff "suffers severe physical impairment or severe disfigurement," in which case non-economic damages are limited to the greater of one million dollars or the injured person's life expectancy multiplied by $25,000). A few statutes, particularly in the medical malpractice field, also limit total recoveries.

Plaintiffs have argued, with some, but far from universal, success, that statutory damage limits violate the state or federal constitutions. In general, damage caps which purport to limit both economic damages (*e.g.,* medical expenses) and non-economic damages (*e.g.,* pain and suffering) have tended to be held unconstitutional, often on the ground that they irrationally discriminate between victims on the basis of the severity of the injury and tend to have the greatest adverse effect on those most seriously injured. In contrast, caps applicable only to non-economic damages have tended to survive constitutional scrutiny. The course in torts is no place to examine in detail the many constitutional arguments that can be made against this kind of legislation: arguments based on denial of "due process of law" or "equal protection of the laws" have been common, and some plaintiffs have persuaded courts that damage caps violate state constitutional rights of access to the courts and of trial by jury.

Illustrative of these decisions is Best v. Taylor Machine Works, 689 N.E.2d 1057 (Ill. 1997). The Illinois statute held unconstitutional in *Best* limited "noneconomic" damages, such as damages for pain and suffering and loss of consortium, to $500,000 in cases involving death, personal physical injury, or property damage. The legislation imposing this limit had described awards of noneconomic damages as "highly erratic," and had claimed (on questionable evidence) that health-care costs had decreased in the 20 states that had imposed limits on that kind of damage awards. The court held that the limit violated a state constitutional provision prohibiting any "special or local law when a general law is or can be made applicable." Because noneconomic damages were capped at $500,000 for all plaintiffs, no matter how serious their injuries, the legislation was held to discriminate between plaintiffs with slight injuries and those with serious injuries. Furthermore, the act was said to be irrational in limiting noneconomic damages in cases involving death, bodily injury, or property damage, while not limiting them in other cases, such as defamation. In addition, the court held that, because assessing damages is normally the province of the factfinder, with excessive awards reduced by the judge, using remittitur, the legislation violated the principle of separation of powers. The *Best* opinion cites ten state supreme court decisions upholding legislative limits on various kinds of damages and seven decisions invalidating caps.

Many damage-capping statutes apply only in limited contexts, such as medical malpractice actions. However, statutes limiting liability for damages may be found in a variety of other contexts. *See, e.g.,* Weinberg v. D-M Restaurant Corp., 426 N.E.2d 459 (N.Y. 1981) (applying a State statute drastically limiting a hotel or restaurant's liability for loss of a gratuitously checked coat or parcel).

Immunizing Tort Reform Legislation from Constitutional Attack. In 2003, the Texas legislature passed a law capping non-economic damages in medical malpractice cases. Then, in an effort to immunize the caps from constitutional review, the legislature sent to the voters a constitutional amendment which, on the election ballot, asked them to vote for or against "The constitutional amendment concerning civil lawsuits against doctors and health care providers, and other actions, authorizing the legislature to determine limitations on non-economic damages."

The amendment, known as Proposition 12, was a rare example of direct citizen involvement in tort reform. Aggressive public relations campaigns were waged relating to the proposal, with proponents rallying voters to "Save Your Doctor," and opponents urging voters to "Save the Courts." The amendment to the Texas constitution passed with less than 51% of the vote in favor of the proposal. It reads:

TEXAS CONSTITUTION
§ 66 (2003)

(a) In this section "economic damages" means compensatory damages for any pecuniary loss or damage. The term does not include any loss or damage, however characterized, for past, present, and future physical pain and suffering, mental anguish and suffering, loss of consortium, loss of companionship and society, disfigurement, or physical impairment.

(b) Notwithstanding any other provision of this constitution, the legislature by statute may determine the limit of liability for all damages and losses, however characterized, other than economic damages, of a provider of medical or health care with respect to treatment, lack of treatment, or other claimed departure from an accepted standard of medical or health care or safety, however characterized, that is or is claimed to be a cause of, or that contributes or is claimed to contribute to, disease, injury, or death of a person....

(c) Notwithstanding any other provision of this constitution, after January 1, 2005, the legislature by statute may determine the limit of liability for all damages and losses, however characterized, other than economic damages, in a claim or cause of action not covered by Subsection (b) of this section. This subsection applies...[to] any claim or cause of action based or sounding in tort, contract, or any other theory or any combination of theories of liability.

....

(e) A legislative exercise of authority under Subsection (c) of this section requires a three-fifths vote of all the members elected to each house and must include language citing this section.

Does § 66(c) effect a fundamental restructuring of judicial review in Texas? Is it likely that voters reading the one sentence description of the amendment on Texas election ballots were adequately apprised of the scope of the amendment? Does this amendment merely mean that persons attacking damages caps passed by the state legislature in the future must base Equal Protection and Due Process challenges on the federal rather than Texas constitution? Is that a serious disadvantage? In the 1980s, the Texas Supreme Court relied upon the Texas Constitution's guarantee of "open courts" as a basis for striking down various tort reform legislation. There is no "open courts" clause in the federal Constitution.

Efforts to Evade a Cap on Damages. A single set of events may give rise to several causes of action, only some of which may be subject to caps on damages. Logically, an attorney should consider whether it is possible to litigate the case in a way that produces a result that escapes limitations on damages. However, such planning may encounter serious obstacles. *See* Sasaki v. Class, 92 F.3d 232 (4th Cir. 1996) (in a sexual-harassment case involving a federal claim that was subject to a cap on non-economic damages and state law claims for assault and battery, the attorney committed reversible error by mentioning the federal cap and arguing that there was no cap on the state-law claims).

Caps on Attorneys' Fees. Like certain other states, California has restricted the amount a lawyer can earn on a contingent-fee basis in a medical malpractice case. An attorney can recover 40 percent of the first $50,000, 33⅓ percent of the next $50,000, 25 percent of the next $100,000 and 10 percent of any amount over $200,000. This legislation has survived constitutional attack; Roa v. Lodi Medical Group, Inc., 695 P.2d 164 (Cal. 1985). Many states have laws outside of the medical field limiting the size of the contingent fee a lawyer can charge for representing a client in a personal injury action. *See, e.g.,* Tex. Prob. Code Ann. §233 (Westlaw 2003) (fee for representing an estate ordinarily cannot exceed 33 1/3%).

Tort Reform and Public Opinion. In some parts of the country, the battle over "tort reform" is waged quite visibly. In Texas, for example, groups affiliated with Citizens Against Lawsuit Abuse, which is aligned with the insurance industry, erected billboards along major highways crying "Lawsuit Abuse . . . We All Pay, We All Lose." In some cities, it was almost impossible for a potential juror to reach the courthouse without reading these signs. The plaintiffs' bar has sometimes responded with its own billboards, ranging from the mildly amusing ("Prisons are for Common Criminals . . . Punitive Damages are for Corporate Criminals") to the more extreme ("Is 'Citizens Against Lawsuit Abuse' Racist?")

Tort Reform against Disfavored Classes. In the 1996 general election, California voters passed a referendum (Proposition 213) which by a 3–1 margin prohibited uninsured motorists and drunk drivers from collecting noneconomic damages arising from auto accidents, including pain and suffering, and prohibited fleeing felons from recovering any damages at all. *See* Cal. Civ. Code §§ 3333.3–3333.4 (Westlaw 2003). *See* Quackenbush v. Superior Ct., 70 Cal. Rptr.2d 271 (Cal. Ct. App. 1998) (rejecting constitutional challenges).

Gender Bias in Tort Reform? Do certain types of tort reform have a disparate impact on women? *See* Lisa Ruder, Comment, *Caps on Noneconomic Damages and the Female Plaintiff,* 44 Case W. Res. L. Rev. 197 (1993) (arguing that with caps on noneconomic damages "female plaintiffs may be the plaintiffs who suffer the most" because "[e]motional injuries are likely to be brought by and associated with women"); Pamela Anagnos Lipakis, *Tort Reform Could Leave Women Shortchanged,* Nat'l L. J., July 24, 1995, at

C2 (arguing that caps on recovery for non-economic loss (such as loss of fertility) and on punitive damages deny women equal access to the civil justice system and "intensify existing wage inequalities in the [job] market"); Lucinda M. Finley, *Female Trouble: The Implications of Tort Reform for Women*, 64 Tenn. L. Rev. 847 (1997) (analyzing Congressional proposals and their possible adverse impact on women's health).

Chapter 5

Negligence: Basic Principles

Unreasonable Conduct. Negligence is the largest and perhaps most important of the various categories of tort liability. Its flexible principles may be applied to virtually all types of conduct that give rise to accidental harm.

Unlike intentional tort liability, negligence is not directly concerned with the defendant's state of mind. Rather it is concerned with the character of the defendant's conduct; the defendant's state of mind matters only because conduct is judged in the light of what the defendant knew, or reasonably should have known. Conduct that poses an *unreasonable* risk of harm to others is negligent. One's conduct need not be free of all risks of harm, only free of those risks which under the circumstances are unreasonable.

A. The Concept of Duty

Prosser's Four Elements. Dean William Prosser was of the view that there are four elements to a negligence cause of action: duty, breach, causation, and damage. Many courts have adopted this formulation, but the cases bear witness to the fact that Prosser's categories are less clear in application than in theory. Not surprisingly, a number of authorities have articulated a somewhat different approach. Those sources collapse the duty and breach elements into a more general inquiry which asks simply whether the defendant's conduct was "negligent," then separately address the issue of causation of damages.

Even from a Prosserian perspective, the concept of duty is an elusive one. As Prosser himself recognized in a frequently quoted passage:

> There is a duty if the court says there is a duty; the law, like the constitution, is what we make it. Duty is only a word with which we state our conclusion that there is or is not to be liability; it necessarily begs the essential question.... The word serves a useful purpose in directing attention to the obligation to be imposed upon the defendant, rather than the causal sequence of events; beyond that it serves none.

William L. Prosser, *Palsgraf Revisited*, 52 Mich. L. Rev. 1, 15 (1953).

From Limited Duty to General Duty. The modern law of negligence is of recent origin, having developed, for the most part, during the past 125 years. During the 19th century, a person was obliged to exercise care on behalf of others only in a relatively limited range of situations. Over the years, however, the ambit of potential liability has expanded. Thus, as a practical matter, it is useful to assume today that one owes a duty of reasonable care to those who may be harmed by one's actions if harm is foreseeable,

Benjamin N. Cardozo

unless the conduct falls within one of a few important limited-duty categories. The chief limited-duty rules—relating to such matters as failure to rescue, premises liability, negligent infliction of emotional distress, and alcohol-related injuries—will be discussed in Chapters 9–12.

As to the general duty rule and its linkage to the concept of foreseeability, a useful perspective is presented by the majority opinion in Palsgraf v. Long Island R.R. Co., 162 N.E. 99 (N.Y. 1928). *Palsgraf* is recognized as the most famous (though not necessarily the most important) tort case of all time. It was decided by a group of highly esteemed jurists, who were described by Professor Irving Younger as "the greatest court that ever sat." Both the majority and the dissent in *Palsgraf* have been cited scores of times by courts throughout the country.

Palsgraf v. Long Island Railroad Co.

Court of Appeals of New York
162 N.E. 99 (N.Y. 1928)

CARDOZO, C.J.

Plaintiff was standing on a platform of defendant's railroad after buying a ticket to go to Rockaway Beach. A train stopped at the station, bound for another place. Two men ran forward to catch it. One of the men reached the platform of the car without mishap, though the train was already moving. The other man, carrying a package, jumped aboard the car, but seemed unsteady as if about to fall. A guard on the car, who had held the door open, reached forward to help him in, and another guard on the platform pushed him from behind. In this act, the package was dislodged, and fell upon the rails. It was a package of small size, about fifteen inches long, and was covered by a newspaper. In fact it contained fireworks, but there was nothing in its appearance to give notice of its contents. The fireworks when they fell exploded. The shock of the explosion threw down some scales at the other end of the platform many feet away. The scales struck the plaintiff, causing injuries for which she sues.

Facts

The conduct of the defendant's guard, if a wrong in its relation to the holder of the package, was not a wrong in its relation to the plaintiff, standing far away. Relatively to her it was not negligence at all. Nothing in the situation gave notice that the falling package had in it the potency of peril to persons thus removed. Negligence is not actionable unless it involves the invasion of a legally protected interest, the violation of a right. "Proof of negligence in the air, so to speak, will not do." Pollock, Torts (11th Ed.) p. 455....If no hazard was apparent to the eye of ordinary vigilance, an act innocent and harmless, at least to outward seeming, with reference to her, did not take to itself the quality of a tort because it happened to be a wrong, though apparently not one involving the risk of bodily insecurity, with reference to someone else. "In every instance, before negligence can be predicated on a given act, back of the act must be sought and found a duty to the individual complaining, the observance of which would have averted or avoided the injury." [Citations.] "The ideas of negligence and duty are strictly correlative." [Citation.] The plaintiff sues in her own right for a wrong personal to her, and not as the vicarious beneficiary of a breach of duty to another.

A different conclusion will involve us, and swiftly too, in a maze of contradictions.... In this case, the rights that are said to have been violated, the interests said to have been invaded, are not even of the same order. The man was not injured in his person nor even put in danger. The purpose of the act, as well as its effect, was to make his person safe. If there was a wrong to him at all, which may very well be doubted[,] it was a wrong to a property interest only, the safety of his package. Out of this wrong to property, which threatened injury to nothing else, there has passed, we are told, to the plaintiff by derivation or succession a right of action for the invasion of an interest of another order, the right to bodily security. The diversity of interests emphasizes the futility of the effort to build the plaintiff's right upon the basis of a wrong to someone else....

....What the plaintiff must show is "a wrong" to herself; *i.e.*, a violation of her own right, and not merely a wrong to some one else, nor conduct "wrongful" because unsocial, but not "a wrong" to any one....The risk reasonably to be perceived defines the duty to be obeyed and risk imports relation; it is risk to another or to others within the range of apprehension. [Citations.] This does not mean, of course, that one who launches a destructive force is always relieved of liability, if the force, though known to be destructive, pursues an unexpected path. "It was not necessary that the defendant should have had notice of the particular method in which an accident would occur, if the possibility of an accident was clear to the ordinarily prudent eye." [Citations.] Some acts, such as shooting are so imminently dangerous to anyone who may come within reach of the missile however unexpectedly, as to impose a duty of prevision not far from that of an insurer....The range of reasonable apprehension is at times a question for the court, and at times, if varying inferences are possible, a question for the jury. Here, by concession, there was nothing in the situation to suggest to the most cautious mind that the parcel wrapped in newspaper would spread wreckage through the station. If the guard had thrown it down knowingly and willfully, he would not have threatened the plaintiff's safety, so far as appearances could warn him. His conduct would not have involved, even then, an unreasonable probability of invasion of her bodily security. Liability can be no greater where the act is inadvertent.

William S. Andrews

Negligence, like risk, is thus a term of relation. Negligence in the abstract, apart from things related, is surely not a tort, if indeed it is understandable at all....

The law of causation, remote or proximate, is thus foreign to the case before us. The question of liability is always anterior to the question of the measure of the consequences that go with liability. If there is no tort to be redressed, there is no occasion to consider what damage might be recovered if there were a finding of a tort....

The judgment of the Appellate Division and that of the Trial Term should be reversed, and the complaint dismissed, with costs in all courts.

ANDREWS, J. (dissenting).

    ....

....The result we shall reach depends upon our theory as to the nature of negligence. Is it a relative concept—the breach of some duty owing to a particular person or to particular persons? Or, where there is an act which unreasonably threatens the safety of others, is the doer liable for all its proximate consequences, even where they result in injury to one who would generally be thought to be outside the radius of danger? This is not a mere dispute as to words. We might not believe that to the average mind the dropping of the bundle would seem to involve the probability of harm to the plaintiff standing many feet away whatever might be the case as to the owner or to one so near as to be likely to be struck by its fall. If, however, we adopt the second hypothesis, we have to inquire only as to the relation between cause and effect. We deal in terms of proximate cause, not of negligence.

    ....

But we are told that "there is no negligence unless there is in the particular case a legal duty to take care, and this duty must be one which is owed to the plaintiff himself and not merely to others." Salmond, Torts (6th Ed.) 24. This I think too narrow a conception. Where there is the unreasonable act, and some right that may be affected[,] there is negligence whether damage does or does not result. That is immaterial. Should we drive down Broadway at a reckless speed, we are negligent whether we strike an approaching car or miss it by an inch. The act itself is wrongful. It is a wrong not only to those who happen to be within the radius of danger, but to all who might have been there—a wrong to the public at large. Such is the language of the street....

Due care is a duty imposed on each one of us to protect society from unnecessary danger, not to protect A, B, or C alone.

It may well be that there is no such thing as negligence in the abstract. "Proof of negligence in the air, so to speak, will not do." In an empty world negligence would not exist. It does involve a relationship between man and his fellows, but not merely a relationship between man and those whom he might reasonably expect his act would injure; rather, a relationship between him and those whom he does in fact injure....

....

The proposition is this: Every one owes to the world at large the duty of refraining from those acts that may unreasonably threaten the safety of others. Such an act occurs. Not only is he wronged to whom harm might reasonably be expected to result, but he also who is in fact injured, even if he be outside what would generally be thought the danger zone. There needs be duty due to the one complaining, but this is not a duty to a particular individual because as to him harm might be expected. Harm to some one being the natural result of the act, not only that one alone, but all those in fact injured may complain. We have never, I think, held otherwise....Unreasonable risk being taken, its consequences are not confined to those who might probably be hurt.

....

....An overturned lantern may burn all Chicago. We may follow the fire from the shed to the last building. We rightly say the fire started by the lantern caused its destruction.

A cause, but not the proximate cause. What we do mean by the word "proximate" is that, because of convenience, of public policy, of a rough sense of justice, the law arbitrarily declines to trace a series of events beyond a certain point. This is not logic. It is practical politics....

Take the illustration given in an unpublished manuscript by a distinguished and helpful writer on the law of torts. A chauffeur negligently collides with another car which is filled with dynamite, although he could not know it. An explosion follows. A, walking on the sidewalk nearby, is killed. B, sitting in a window of a building opposite, is cut by flying glass. C, likewise sitting in a window a block away, is similarly injured. And a further illustration: A nursemaid, ten blocks away, startled by the noise, involuntarily drops a baby from her arms to the walk. We are told that C may not recover while A may. As to B it is a question for court or jury. We will agree that the baby might not. Because, we are again told, the chauffeur had no reason to believe his conduct involved any risk of injuring either C or the baby. As to them he was not negligent.

But the chauffeur, being negligent in risking the collision, his belief that the scope of the harm he might do would be limited is immaterial. His act unreasonably jeopardized the safety of any one who might be affected by it. C's injury and that of the baby were directly traceable to the collision. Without that, the injury would not have happened. C had the right to sit in his office, secure from such dangers. The baby was entitled to use the sidewalk with reasonable safety.

The true theory is, it seems to me, that the injury to C, if in truth he is to be denied recovery, and the injury to the baby, is that their several injuries were not the proximate result of the negligence. And here not what the chauffeur had reason to believe would be the result of his conduct, but what the prudent would foresee, may have a bearing — may have some bearing, for the problem of proximate cause is not to be solved by any one consideration. It is all a question of expediency. There are no fixed rules to govern our judgment. There are simply matters of which we may take account....There is in truth little to guide us other than common sense.

There are some hints that may help us. The proximate cause, involved as it may be with many other causes, must be, at the least, something without which the event would not happen. The court must ask itself whether there was a natural and continuous sequence between cause and effect. Was the one a substantial factor in producing the other? Was there a direct connection between them, without too many intervening causes? Is the effect of cause on result not too attenuated? Is the cause likely, in the usual judgment of mankind, to produce the result? Or, by the exercise of prudent foresight, could the result be foreseen? Is the result too remote from the cause, and here we consider remoteness in time and space....Clearly we must so consider, for the greater the distance either in time or space, the more surely do other causes intervene to affect the result. When a lantern is overturned, the firing of a shed is a fairly direct consequence. Many things contribute to the spread of the conflagration — the force of the wind, the direction and width of streets, the character of intervening structures, other factors. We draw an uncertain and wavering line, but draw it we must as best we can.

Once again, it is all a question of fair judgment, always keeping in mind the fact that we endeavor to make a rule in each case that will be practical and in keeping with the general understanding of mankind.

....

....We trace the consequences, not indefinitely, but to a certain point. And to aid us in fixing that point we ask what might ordinarily be expected to follow the fire or the explosion.

This last suggestion is the factor which must determine the case before us. The act upon which defendant's liability rests is knocking an apparently harmless package onto the platform. The act was negligent. For its proximate consequences the defendant is liable. If its contents were broken, to the owner; if it fell upon and crushed a passenger's foot, then to him; if it exploded and injured one in the immediate vicinity, to him also as to A in the illustration....

Under these circumstances I cannot say as a matter of law that the plaintiff's injuries were not the proximate result of the negligence....

The judgment appealed from should be affirmed, with costs.

POUND, LEHMAN and KELLOGG, JJ., concur with CARDOZO, C.J.

ANDREWS, J., dissents in opinion in which CRANE and O'BRIEN, JJ., concur.

Judgment reversed, etc.

Note

1. **Palsgraf** *Today.* The debate underlying the differing approaches of Judges Cardozo and Andrews to the issue of negligence continues today. Courts and scholars still

dispute, often in passionate terms, whether one owes a duty of care to the world in general (as Judge Andrews contended) or only to those foreseeably endangered (as Chief Judge Cardozo said). These questions were recently a focal point of discussions surrounding the new third Restatement. After vigorous debate, the American Law Institute voted to endorse a position that sides with Judge Andrews in dealing with the issue as one of causation, rather than duty, but which endorses Chief Judge Cardozo's result. Illustration 9 to § 29 of the third Restatement describes a fact situation identical to that of *Palsgraf* and concludes that, as a matter of law, the harm to the victim was not within the scope of the defendant's liability for negligence. The illustration goes on to observe:

> Generally, application of the risk standard should avoid much of the need for consideration of unforeseeable plaintiffs.... In cases in which the plaintiff was, because of time or geography, nevertheless truly beyond being subject to harm of the type risked by the tortious conduct, but the plaintiff somehow suffers such harm, the defendant is not liable to that plaintiff for the harm.

Restatement, Third, of Torts: Liability for Physical Harm (Basic Principles) (Tent. Draft No. 3, 2003) § 29, Illus. 9

There is support in recent cases for Chief Judge Cardozo's "duty" approach. In Holder v. Mellon Mortgage Co., 5 S.W.3d 654 (Tex. 1999), a woman was stopped by a police officer for an alleged traffic violation in the middle of the night. The officer took the woman's insurance and identification cards and told her to follow his squad car. The woman followed the officer for several blocks to a parking garage owned by Mellon Mortgage Company. Once inside the garage, the officer sexually assaulted the woman in his squad car. The woman then sued Mellon for negligence, arguing that the company had provided inadequate security at the garage. After a detailed review of the opinions in *Palsgraf*, Justice Greg Abbott wrote:

> Certainly, Mellon expected that its employees would use the garage, often at times when it would be relatively vacant and thus more dangerous. It is not unreasonable to conclude that Mellon could foresee that an employee or some other person who frequents the garage could be the victim of a violent crime in the garage. To protect these garage users, Mellon provided armed security patrols weekdays from 5:45 a.m. to 11:30 p.m., in addition to random patrols by off-duty police officers during business hours. Holder [the injured woman], however, was not a member of this class nor any other that Mellon could have reasonably foreseen would be the victim of a criminal act in its garage.

> Unlike any foreseeable victim, Holder was pulled over in her car at 3:30 a.m. by a third party over whom Mellon had no control, and she was led from several blocks away to the actual crime scene. Not only did Mellon have no control over the criminal, Potter [the police officer], it had no knowledge of him nor any reason to know that he would pick the garage as the scene of his reprehensible crime. Moreover, Mellon had no knowledge of Holder nor any reason to believe that she, or a person similarly situated, could be subject to a crime on Mellon's property. It simply was not foreseeable, beyond a remote philosophic sense, that this tragic event would occur to Holder on Mellon's property. With relation to Mellon's allegedly wrongful act of not securing its garage at three in the morning, Holder was not so situated that injury to her might reasonably have been foreseen. She was, in short, beyond Mellon's reasonable apprehension.

....Holder's summary judgment evidence provides little more than "proof of negligence in the air." [Citation.] She provides no evidence of a foreseeable risk in relation to her.

....

Accordingly, Mellon owed no legal duty to Holder. To the extent that Mellon's conduct may have created a risk of harm, it did not breach a duty to Holder because she was not so situated with relation to the wrongful act such that her injury might have been foreseen.

See also Waters v. New York City Hous. Auth., 505 N.E.2d 922 (N.Y. 1987) (owner of an occupied building who had not kept the security system in good repair could not be held liable in tort to a crime victim solely because the building was used as a place to complete a crime that began on a public street; neither the victim nor the crime were connected with the owner's building and the victim was not within zone of foreseeable harm); Bain v. Gillespie, 357 N.W.2d 47, 49 (Iowa App 1984) ("The law's standard is one of reasonable foresight, not prophetic vision"; so injury to novelty store owners' business interests was not a reasonably foreseeable result of a college basketball referee's call during a game which eliminated the local team from the conference championship, and the referee owed no duty to the store owners).

B. The Negligence Balancing Test

In light of the fact that, as *Palsgraf* suggests, foreseeability of harm is a critical consideration in the negligence calculus, the question arises as to how foreseeable harm must be before liability will attach. The following cases explore this question and suggest that the answer lies in a balancing test.

Nussbaum v. Lacopo
Court of Appeals of New York
265 N.E.2d 762 (N.Y. 1970)

BURKE, Judge.

Plaintiff's home is situate on land abutting the thirteenth hole of the defendant country club. Between plaintiff's patio and the thirteenth fairway are approximately *20 to 30 feet of rough*, and located in that golfer's no man's land is a natural barrier of *45- to 60-foot-high trees*. Although plaintiff's real property line runs parallel to the thirteenth fairway, the direct and proper line of flight from the tee to the green was at a substantial angle...far to the right of the plaintiff's property line....

On June 30, 1963, defendant Lacopo, a trespasser on the golf course, struck a ball from the thirteenth tee. At that time the rough was dense and the trees were in full foliage. The shot, a high, bad one, "hooked" and crossed over into the area of plaintiff's patio and there allegedly hit the plaintiff. Lacopo did not see plaintiff and did not shout the traditional golfer's warning: "Fore!"

....

Plaintiff, in his complaint,...argued that defendant failed to give a timely warning. That duty, which extends to other players [citations], did not extend to plaintiff. The duty is imposed to prevent accidents, and the relationship between the failure to warn and plaintiff's injuries is tenuous at best. It rests on the improbable assumption that plaintiff would have responded to it, even though no ball had ever struck his house. Living so close to a golf course, plaintiff would necessarily hear numerous warning shouts each day. As the warning would ordinarily be directed to other golfers, plaintiff could be expected to ignore them. We will not permit the submission of this case to the jury on the remote possibility that plaintiff could have recognized and acted upon any warning given by the golfer at this time.

...[A] warning is only required in favor of those who are "in such a position" that danger to them is reasonably anticipated.

The admission that this was a "bad shot" is not sufficient to warrant submission to a jury. Plaintiff made no effort to show that defendant failed to use due care in striking the ball. Pursuant to our rules of practice [citation], plaintiff took an examination before trial of defendant. Not a single question was directed at the manner in which defendant swung. Moreover, two witnesses, who observed the shot, were available to plaintiff. Thus plaintiff could have shown, for example, that defendant aimed so inaccurately as to unreasonably increase the risk of harm.... [W]e will not permit an inference of negligence to be drawn merely from the fact that this shot "hooked" sharply. *Holding*

...[E]ven the best professional golfers cannot avoid an occasional "hook" or "slice."....

One last comment on the lack of foreseeability is necessary.... The mere fact that a person may have been careless in the performance of an act does not necessarily result in actionable negligence. It is only required that the care be commensurate with the risk and danger. The plaintiff failed to show that the act of this player as to him had possibilities of danger so many and apparent as to entitle him to be protected against the doing of it. His burden of proof required that the act testified to, which he asserts constituted negligence, was not merely possible, but probable. Here, only an extraordinarily misdirected shot attaining great height could possibly drop on plaintiff's property because of the height and density of the protective barrier. Against this kind of unlikely misfortune, the law does not confer protection. Looking back from the alleged injury to the event, we consider it highly exceptional that a player's conduct would have brought about harm. *Holding*

.... Lack of due care is not demonstrated when the undisputed physical evidence proves that it could not have been reasonably anticipated that the harm complained of would result from the natural and probable consequences of the act claimed to be negligent. *Rule*

...[T]he dismissal of the complaint as against both defendants at the close of the plaintiff's case is well founded.

Accordingly, the order of the Appellate Division should be affirmed.

[The dissenting opinion of Judge BERGAN, in which Judges BREITEL and GIBSON concurred, has been omitted.]

Note

1. The analysis in negligence cases is typically fact-intensive, and a slight change in the facts can dictate a different result. *Compare Nussbaum with* Hennessey v. Pyne, 694 A.2d 691 (R.I. 1997) (issues of fact relating to whether a golfer should have foreseen harm to a resident of adjacent condominium precluded summary judgment).

Gulf Refining Co. v. Williams

Supreme Court of Mississippi
185 So. 234 (Miss. 1938)

GRIFFITH, Justice.

Appellants are the distributors of petroleum products....Shortly before the injury here complained of, appellants...sold and delivered to a planter in that vicinity a drum of gasoline for use in farm tractors. Appellee was the planter's employee and was engaged in operating a tractor. The drum of gasoline had been taken to the field, but no attempt had been made to use it, until, for the first time since its delivery, appellee undertook to remove the bunghole cap from the drum in order to replenish the fuel in the tractor, whereupon there was a sudden outburst of fire, caused, as the jury was justified in concluding..., by a spark which was produced by the condition of unrepair in the threads of the bung cap, as will be later mentioned.

Appellee was severely burned by the sudden fire, and recovered judgment....

The chief argument of appellants is that the proof shows that an explosion or fire in drawing gasoline from a drum when, or on account of, taking off the bung cap is an unusual, extraordinary, and improbable occurrence, so much so that some of the witnesses say that no such happening had ever before been heard of by them; and that, therefore, appellant cannot be held liable as for a failure to anticipate the danger of any such improbable occurrence....

The general language of the courts in stating the rule of the law of negligence in regard to the liability of the actor as to harmful results which are foreseeable is that he will be liable for all such harm as a reasonably prudent person would or should have anticipated as the natural and probable consequences of his act....

This general language has lead to the occasional misunderstanding as to what may be termed the degree of probability which is meant by these expressions, as used in the law of negligence; and it is sometimes supposed and argued that unless such a foreseeable consequence is one which is more likely to happen than not to happen there can be no liability. But these references to probability are in a different sense as compared with what is meant in the procedural law when there is under inquiry whether a certain event happened, or probably happened, in the past.

　　....

When the inquiry is upon an issue whether a certain alleged fact existed or happened in the past, it is not sufficient to prove only or no more than a possibility, however substantial the possibility may be, so long as it is only a possibility. There the proof must establish the fact as a probability, using that word in its ordinary and common acceptation....But when the inquiry is one of foreseeability, is as regards a thing that may happen in the future, and to which the law of negligence holds a party to anticipation as a measure of duty, that inquiry is not whether the thing is to be foreseen or anticipated as one which will probably happen,...but whether it is likely to happen, even though the likelihood may not be sufficient to amount to a comparative probability.

It is true, as already mentioned, that remote possibilities are not within the rules of negligence as respects foreseeability. As said in Illinois Central Railroad Co. v. Bloodworth, [145 So. 333 (Miss. 1933)], these rules do not demand "that a person should prevision or anticipate an unusual, improbable, or extraordinary occurrence, though such happening is within the range of possibilities...." On the other hand, in order to bring the rule of liability into operation, it is not necessary that the chances that a damage will result shall be greater than the chances that no damage will occur. The test as respects foreseeability is not the balance of probabilities, but the existence…of some real likelihood of some damage and the likelihood is of such appreciable weight and moment as to induce, or which reasonably should induce, action to avoid it on the part of a person of a reasonably prudent mind. [Citations.]

Rule

The vendor of an inherently dangerous commodity, such as gasoline, is under duty to use cautious care to distribute the same in reasonably safe containers, the degree of care thereinabout to be commensurate with the danger, and the obligation of this duty is not dependent upon contractual relations, but extends to all who may lawfully use, or be in the vicinity of, the container.…

Holding

The drum, or gasoline container, involved herein was of standard material, construction and manufacture, and of the kind in general use; and had it been in reasonably good repair there would, of course, be no liability. But the proof is that the drum had been in use nine years; that the threads in the bung plug or bung cap were broken, bent and jagged; that this condition had been brought about by repeated hammering on the bung cap during the course of its use—a condition which had attracted the attention of one of appellants' employees before the container was sent out on this occasion. There is no adequate proof to show that appellee had equal knowledge or appreciation of the significance of this fact, or any knowledge which was sufficient to put the use at his risk as by the so-called assumption thereof, as contended for by appellants—leaving aside whether, if the facts were otherwise, there would be assumption of risk, rather than contributory negligence. [Citation.] The proof is sufficient to show that a person of ordinary prudence, and mindful of the duty of cautious care with which appellants were charged, should have known of the condition aforesaid and should reasonably have anticipated, as a likelihood of weight and moment, that a sudden fire or explosion would be caused by the stated condition of unrepair; and hence appellants are liable for the injury to appellee which resulted.

Holding

. . . .

Affirmed.

United States v. Carroll Towing Co.

United States Court of Appeals for the Second Circuit
159 F.2d 169 (2d Cir. 1947)

[After the defendant's servants negligently shifted its mooring lines, libellant's barge broke adrift, collided with another vessel, and sank. The trial court, pursuant to a comparative negligence rule in admiralty, reduced the amount of damages recoverable by the libellant, finding that it was negligent in not having a custodian on board who could have called for help and possibly have avoided the sinking once the damage from the collision became apparent. As to the propriety of this reduction in damages:]

L. HAND, Circuit Judge.

. . . .

It appears from the foregoing review that there is no general rule to determine when the absence of a bargee or other attendant will make the owner of the barge liable for injuries to other vessels if she breaks away from her moorings. However, in any cases where he would be so liable for injuries to others, obviously he must reduce his dam-

Learned Hand

ages proportionately, if the injury is to his own barge. It becomes apparent why there can be no such general rule, when we consider the grounds for such a liability. Since there are occasions when every vessel will break from her moorings, and since, if she does, she becomes a menace to those about her, the owner's duty, as in other similar situations, to provide against resulting injuries is a function of three variables: (1) The probability that she will break away; (2) the gravity of the resulting injury, if she does; (3) the burden of adequate precautions. Possibly it serves to bring this notion into relief to state it in algebraic terms: if the probability be called P; the injury, L; and the Burden, B; liability depends upon whether B is less than L multiplied by P: i.e., whether $B < PL.$ Applied to the situation at bar, the likelihood that a barge will break from her fasts and the damage she will do, vary with the place and time; for example, if a storm threatens, the danger is greater; so it is, if she is in a crowded harbor where moored barges are constantly being shifted about. On the other hand, the barge must not be the bargee's prison, even though he lives aboard; he must go ashore at times. We need not say whether, even in such crowded waters as New York Harbor a bargee must be aboard at night at all; it may be that the custom is otherwise.... We leave that question open; but *Holding* we hold that it is not in all cases a sufficient answer to a bargee's absence without excuse, during working hours, that he has properly made fast his barge to a pier, when he leaves her. In the case at bar the bargee left at five o'clock in the afternoon of January 3rd, and the flotilla broke away at about two o'clock in the afternoon of the following day, twenty-one hours afterwards. The bargee had been away all the time, and we hold that his fabricated story was affirmative evidence that he had no excuse for his absence. At the *locus in quo*—especially during the short January days and in the full tide of war activity—barges were being constantly "drilled" in and out. Certainly it was not beyond reasonable expectation that, with the inevitable haste and bustle, the work might not be

done with adequate care. In such circumstances we hold ... that it was a fair requirement that the Conners Company should have a bargee aboard (unless he had some excuse for his absence), during the working hours of daylight.

Holding (handwritten)

....

[The judgment was affirmed insofar as concerns the reduction in damages.]

Notes

1. *Negligence as a Question of Fact.* Whether a defendant (or plaintiff) was negligent
is a question of fact. This means, in practical terms, that if it is unclear whether someone acted negligently the jury (or the trial judge, in a non-jury trial) decides the matter.
Because appellate courts do not ordinarily decide questions of fact, a litigant who has
lost at trial on the negligence issue cannot hope to win on appeal by arguing that the
factfinder's decision was wrong.

Although neither the trial judge (in a case tried to a jury) nor an appellate court can
overrule a factfinder's determination about negligence, it may be so clear from the
record that the factfinder's decision was wrong that a judge will rule that the party was,
or was not, negligent "as a matter of law." The standard for making this kind of decision
is whether reasonable persons can differ about whether someone was negligent. If they
cannot—if, for instance, any reasonable factfinder would have to conclude from the evidence that the defendant was negligent—a finding of fact going the other way will be
reversed.

To illustrate, consider Delao v. Carlson, 589 S.W.2d 525 (Texas Civ. App. 1979), a
wrongful-death action against the driver of a car that had struck and killed the plaintiffs' son at night. Plaintiffs argued that the defendant had acted negligently by having
his headlights on low beam at the time of the accident; reasonable care, they urged, required the use of high beams. The trial judge, acting as finder of fact in a non-jury proceeding, ruled that the defendant was not negligent. Holding that the question whether
a reasonable driver would have used high beams at the time was one for the factfinder,
the Court of Civil Appeals affirmed: not because it agreed on the merits with the
factfinder's decision, but because questions of fact are for the factfinder, not for appellate courts. If by contrast, the defendant had been driving at night with no headlights,
and if the factfinder had found this behavior not negligent, the appellate court would
surely have reversed. Absent special circumstances, such as the lights failing suddenly
and unexpectedly, reasonable factfinders cannot find it reasonable to drive at night
without headlights.

Because the question of negligence is for the factfinder if reasonable people can differ, it is a rare case in which a client can be assured in advance that a proposed course of
conduct will not someday be found negligent if something goes wrong. Suppose, for instance, that the operator of a fast-food store asks a lawyer whether certain proposed
measures to protect customers against crime will insulate the store from liability if a
customer is injured or killed during a robbery. The lawyer considers the proposed measures and concludes that they are "reasonable." Should the lawyer advise the client that
implementation of these measures will insure that the client will not be liable? Certainly
not. Although the lawyer considers those measures reasonable, a factfinder may disagree. Only if the lawyer can conclude that no reasonable person could find the proposed precautions inadequate—a standard very hard to satisfy—can the requested assurance be given.

See generally Restatement, Third, of Torts: Liability for Physical Harm (Basic Principles) §8 (Tent. Draft No. 1, 2001) (discussing the roles of judge and jury).

2. *Other Formulations of the Test.* The B < LP balancing test articulated by Judge Hand in *Carroll Towing* has been frequently quoted and widely influential. Nonetheless it is only one of many ways in which the negligence test may be articulated. *See* Restatement, Second, Torts §291. Indeed, the negligence inquiry was defined in somewhat different terms by Judge Hand in Conway v. O'Brien, 111 F.2d 611, 612 (2d Cir. 1940):

> The degree of care demanded of a person by an occasion is the resultant of three factors: the likelihood that his conduct will injure others, taken with the seriousness of the injury if it happens, and balanced against the interest which he must sacrifice to avoid the risk.

There, he candidly recognized:

> All these [factors] are practically not susceptible of any quantitative estimate, and the second two are not so even theoretically. For this reason a solution always involves some preference, or choice between incommensurables, and it is consigned to a jury because their decision is thought most likely to accord with commonly accepted standards, real or fancied.

See also U.S. Fid. & Guar. Co. v. Jadranska Slobodna Plovidba, 683 F.2d 1022, 1026 (7th Cir. 1982) (observing that B, P, and L have never been precisely quantified in any lawsuit).

Negligence as an Economic Concept

The question whether someone has taken enough safety precautions can be thought of as raising issues of economics. Resources are scarce, and so it would be wasteful either to devote too many of those resources to accident prevention or to devote too little to accident prevention. To take a simple example, injuries from automobile accidents could be reduced considerably if all drivers were prevented from exceeding fifteen miles an hour (perhaps by mandating that cars be designed so that they could not exceed that speed). Outlawing cars entirely would probably save thousands of lives each year. Yet these proposals are fantastic; the benefits people get—directly and indirectly—from driving are so great that few would be willing to give them up, even to save lives.

Judge Learned Hand's "formula" in the *Carroll Towing* opinion has been widely used by economic analysts of the legal system as a starting point for defining "negligence" in economic terms. Judge Hand himself seems to have intended the formula only as a guide to the considerations which, in particular cases, should be taken into account in determining negligence. Even looked at in that way, the formula invites re-expression in economic terms. It suggests, for example, that if the chance of an accident is high, it makes more sense to devote resources to safety than if the chance of an accident is low, other things being equal. (For instance, a city planning to add one traffic light would be better advised to put it at an intersection where accidents have been common than at one at which accidents are rare.) And the formula teaches that, other things being equal, resources spent to prevent accidents that threaten serious injury are better spent than if they had gone to reduce minor scrapes; this is why the law insists that drivers keep to the right on two-way streets, while not bothering to make pedestrians on sidewalks stay in lanes. Being bumped by a pedestrian is likely to produce a much smaller "L" than being hit by a car. Furthermore, and perhaps less obviously, the formula indicates that some measures to reduce the costs of accidents are not worth taking, because the benefits of added safety would amount to less than the costs. Whenever a car is started there is an increased risk that someone will be injured, even if the car is driven very carefully (for instance, a pedestrian may faint and fall in front of the car). But it is not negligent to drive; the costs of not driving exceed the very small benefit in safety. These are economic arguments.

Strictly speaking, the Learned Hand formula must be expressed in marginal terms to give an economically accurate guide to how much in the way of safety precautions is enough. Suppose, for example, that one knows that spending an additional $1000 on safety would reduce losses from accidents by $1500. At first glance, it might seem that the actor should spend the $1000, and if the only choice is between spending $1000 and spending nothing, that is indeed the right answer. But suppose that spending $900 would reduce losses by $1300, and that each additional dollar spent on safety would reduce losses by only fifty cents. In that case, one should not spend more than $900; each additional dollar saves less than a dollar in losses. Would it be even better to spend *less* than $900? It depends. Ideally, one should decide how much to spend by asking whether an additional dollar will produce more than an additional dollar in safety benefits. As long as the answer is "yes," it is wise to spend the additional dollar.

Marginal analysis is not a technique that one could reasonably expect juries to employ. Indeed, even without introducing the marginal-analysis wrinkle, the Learned Hand formula would probably confuse more jurors than it would help: the formula is not used in jury instructions. Nevertheless, the law does in some ways come fairly close to using marginal analysis. Suppose, for example, that the plaintiff, who has been struck by a car that was being driven at 50 miles an hour on a residential street, argues that the defendant was negligent simply because the defendant was driving; he should, according to the plaintiff, have taken a train or bus. That is, the plaintiff seeks to argue that the overall benefit of the defendant's driving (at 50 miles an hour) was less than the risk of harm created by driving at that speed. This would be a highly unconventional way of arguing for negligence, and it is not the approach lawyers take. Instead, the plaintiff will argue that reasonable care under the circumstances required the defendant to drive more slowly—perhaps 35 miles an hour—and that the plaintiff would not have been hurt if the defendant had done that. This kind of argument comes close to using marginal analysis: the starting point for evaluating the defendant's conduct is what the defendant actually did, and the plaintiff's proposed "reasonable" conduct is something fairly close to that.

In an article that has greatly clarified the place of negligence in the law of torts, Mark Grady has shown that approaching negligence questions by using the Learned Hand formula works much better in some kinds of cases than in others; Mark F. Grady, *Why Are People Negligent? Technology, Nondurable Precautions, and the Medical Malpractice Explosion*, 82 Nw. U.L. Rev. 293 (1988); *see also* Mark F. Grady, *Better Medicine Causes More Lawsuits, and New Administrative Courts Will Not Solve the Problem*, 86 Nw. U.L. Rev. 1068 (1992). In some cases—*Carroll Towing*, for example—someone actually made a decision that would affect safety. Whether that decision was "reasonable" determines whether the actor was negligent, and the Learned Hand formula can help to determine reasonableness. But in many negligence cases, the lapse in question consists not of a bad decision but rather of a momentary, inadvertent error, as when a normally careful driver fails to see a stop sign, or when a doctor accidentally overlooks a symptom. In cases like these, the Learned Hand formula does not help us determine whether the actor has been negligent. "Negligence" is in one sense obvious, as the actor has plainly made a mistake. As Grady points out, "negligence law does not forgive inadvertence, even reasonable amounts of it"; 82 Nw. U.L. Rev. at 295. Yet, according to the Learned Hand formula, the actor has not been "negligent" at all—no complex activity can be made error-free, and it is not "unreasonable" to drive, or to perform medical procedures, even if the actor knows that mistakes will occur.[a]

With respect to negligence of the "inadvertent lapse" variety, it may be more accurate to describe the law as imposing a sort of strict liability than to insist that liability is assigned according to "fault." Consider how the law of traffic accidents would differ in practice from the way it works now if, instead of saying that negligent drivers are liable for the harms they cause, the law said that drivers are strictly liable for abnormally dangerous driving (such as running stop signs, entering the wrong lane, failing to avoid pedestrians, and so on). One case in which it *would* make a difference is Cohen v. Petty, 65 F.2d 820 (D.C. Cir. 1933), *supra* at p. 20. Would holding the defendant in that case liable be any more unjust than holding someone with an excellent driving record liable for accidentally failing to notice a pedestrian stepping onto the road?

One reason for examining Grady's distinction between the two very different kinds of conduct the law treats as "negligent" is that the distinction explains why a central prediction of the law-and-economics school fails to correspond to everyday observation. According to traditional law-and-economics analysis, negligence should be rare in a world in which those who are negligent must pay for their mistakes. If cost-justified (according to the Learned Hand formula) precautions are not taken and harm ensues, the actor will pay for the harm, which by definition makes it cheaper to take the precautions. Therefore, the argument goes, only those who are irrational will fail to take cost-justified precautions, and those people will soon be bankrupted by the tort system. In fact, everyday observation shows that negligence is rampant. The explanation may be that much of the "negligence" which one can observe on the highway, in the hospital, or in the opinions in this casebook, is negligence of the "inadvertent lapse" variety, which occurs not because people have made bad cost-benefit calculations, but because of inherent human limitations.[b] This kind of negligence is not described by the Learned Hand formula, and is therefore beyond the scope of much traditional law-and-economics analysis. *See* Mark F. Grady, *Why Are People Negligent*, 82 Nw. U.L. Rev. at 294.

Chicago, B & Q. R.R. Co. v. Krayenbuhl

Supreme Court of Nebraska
91 N.W. 880 (Neb. 1902)

ALBERT, C.

This action was brought on behalf of Leo Krayenbuhl,...by his next friend, against the Chicago, Burlington & Quincy Railroad Company to recover for personal injuries received by the plaintiff while playing on a turntable belonging to the defendant.

---

a. If the actor knows that mistakes are very likely, engaging in the activity may be unreasonable, as when someone subject to seizures decides to drive a car.

b. This is not to say that "Learned Hand negligence" is never seen on the highway. Someone who decides to drive at 80 in a 35 mile zone has probably made a conscious but unreasonable decision about how much to take in the way of safety precautions. This is a different kind of negligence from that of someone who overlooked a "school-crossing" sign and failed to slow down, but would have if the sign had been seen.

. . . .

[Leo was four years old. The turntable was located between two branches of the defendant's line, 1600 feet from a passenger depot and 70 feet from common footpath used by the general public and members of Leo's family. There was evidence that defendant's employees frequently disregarded the company's rules that the turntable was to be locked when not in use and that one of the staples on the turntable was so loose that it could be unfastened without difficulty. On the day of the accident, the turntable was found unlocked and unguarded, and when set in motion by Leo's playmates, severed his foot at the ankle when it was caught between the rails. A verdict at trial was rendered in the child's favor.] . . . . [W]here the owner of a dangerous premises knows, or has good reason to believe, that children so young as to be ignorant of the danger will resort to such premises[,] he is bound to take such precautions to keep them from such premises, or to protect them from injuries likely to result from the dangerous condition of the premises, while there, as a man of ordinary care and prudence, under like circumstances, would take. At first sight, it would seem that the principle, thus stated, is too broad, and that its application would impose unreasonable burdens on owners, and intolerable restrictions on the use and enjoyment of property. But it must be kept in mind that it requires nothing of the owner that a man of ordinary care and prudence would not do of his own volition, under like circumstances. Such a man would not willingly take up unreasonable burdens, nor vex himself with intolerable restrictions.

It is true, as said in Loomis v. Terry, 17 Wend. 496, 31 Am. Dec. 306, "the business of life must go forward"; the means by which it is carried forward cannot be rendered absolutely safe. Ordinarily, it can be best carried forward by the unrestricted use of private property by the owner; therefore the law favors such use to the fullest extent consistent with the main purpose for which, from a social standpoint, such business is carried forward, namely, the public good. Hence, in order to determine the extent to which such use may be enjoyed, its bearing on such main purpose must be taken into account, and a balance struck between its advantages and disadvantages. If, on the whole, such use defeats, rather than promotes, the main purpose, it should not be permitted; on the other hand, if the restrictions proposed would so operate, they should not be imposed. The business of life is better carried forward by the use of dangerous machinery; hence the public good demands its use, although occasionally such use results in the loss of life or limb. It does so because the danger is insignificant, when weighed against the benefits resulting from the use of such machinery, and for the same reason demands its reasonable, most effective, and unrestricted use, up to the point where the benefits resulting from such use no longer outweigh the danger to be anticipated from it. At that point the public good demands restrictions. For example, a turntable is a dangerous contrivance, which facilitates railroading; the general benefits resulting from its use outweigh the occasional injuries inflicted by it; hence the public good demands its use. We may conceive of means by which it might be rendered absolutely safe, but such means would so interfere with its beneficial use that the danger to be anticipated would not justify their adoption; therefore the public good demands its use without them. But the danger incident to its use may be lessened by the use of a lock which would prevent children, attracted to it, from moving it; the interference with the proper use of the turntable occasioned by the use of such lock is so slight that it is outweighed by the danger to be anticipated from an omission to use it; therefore the public good, we think, demands the use of the lock. . . .

Hence, in all cases of this kind in the determination of the question of negligence, regard must be had to the character and location of the premises, the purpose for which they are used, the probability of injury therefrom, the precautions necessary to prevent such injury, and the relations such precautions bear to the beneficial use of the premises. The nature of the precautions would depend on the particular facts in each case. In some cases a warning to the children or the parents might be sufficient; in others, more active measures might be required. But in every case they should be such as a man of ordinary care and prudence would observe under like circumstances....

[The judgment was reversed on other grounds and remanded for further proceedings.]

Notes

1. *Utility of the Defendant's Conduct.* How heavily the burden of taking precautions will weigh in the negligence calculus is often inextricably bound to an assessment of the goals the defendant seeks to advance. Stopping a car suddenly in traffic to avoid hitting a squirrel may be negligent, while an identical action taken to avoid hitting a child would not be. The Restatement says that the risk of harm from the act must be balanced against the "utility" of the actor's conduct. "Utility," in turn, depends upon the "social value" of the interest the actor is trying to advance, the chance that the action will in fact advance that interest, and other "factors"; Restatement, Second, of Torts §§291–293.

The Restatement's reference to the "social value" of the defendant's action must not be taken too broadly. A doctor driving to work in the morning must drive just as carefully as a slumlord on the way to evict some widows and orphans, even though some would view the doctor's career as having more "social value" than the slumlord's. On the other hand, though, the driving of a doctor racing to the scene of a medical emergency would be evaluated quite differently than driving in other contexts.

See also Wassell v. Adams, 865 F.2d 849, 853 (7th Cir. 1989) ("[t]he loss of business from telling the truth [to prospective motel customers about crime in the area] is not a social loss; it is a social gain").

2. *Alternatives.* Section 292(c) of the Restatement points out that whether a particular course of conduct is negligent may depend upon whether alternatives are available. In Adams v. Bullock, 125 N.E. 93 (N.Y. 1919), a young boy was shocked and burned when a long wire he was swinging struck an uninsulated power line above the defendant's trolley tracks. In concluding that the verdict for the plaintiff could not stand, Judge Cardozo wrote for the New York Court of Appeals:

> There is...a distinction not to be ignored between electric light and trolley wires. The distinction is that the former may be insulated. Chance of harm, though remote, may betoken negligence, if needless. Facility of protection may impose a duty to protect. With trolley wires, the case is different. Insulation is impossible. Guards here and there are of little value. To avert the possibility of this accident and others like it at one point or another on the route, the defendant must have abandoned the overhead system, and put the wires underground. Neither its power nor its duty to make the change is shown.

3. *Advances in Technology.* Because circumstances change and technology advances, conduct which at one point may be considered reasonable may at another time be found unreasonable. In Davison v. Snohomish County, 270 P. 422 (Wash. 1928), plaintiffs sustained personal injuries and property damages when the car in which they were riding broke through allegedly insufficient guard rails on an elevated stretch of road. In reversing the jury's judgment in their favor, the court wrote:

[M]unicipalities cannot be required to protect long stretches of roadway with railings or guards capable of preventing an automobile, moving at a rapid rate, from leaving the road.... "[To so hold]...would be to put a burden upon the public that it could not bear...."

Yet, forty years later the same court, in Bartlett v. Northern Pac. Ry. Co., 447 P.2d 735 (Wash. 1968), allowed a similar case to go to the jury. Noting that its earlier decision could no longer be regarded as authoritative on engineering issues and financial matters, the court held that the parties should have the opportunity to present evidence as to the "practicality (costwise and otherwise)" of installing guard rails to stop slow-moving vehicles.

C. The Reasonable-Person Standard

In General. The negligence formula, under which unreasonableness is determined by balancing the gravity and probability of harm against the burden of avoidance and the utility of the defendant's conduct, serves many purposes. It directs the attention of counsel to those factors which should be taken into account in evaluating a case or presenting an argument to the jury. It also guides trial and appellate court rulings on the evidence. *See, e.g.,* U.S. Fid. & Guar. Co. v. Jadranska Slobodna Plovidba, 683 F.2d 1022 (7th Cir. 1982).

Nevertheless, the law has frequently elected to articulate the same inquiry in more anthropomorphic terms, asking simply whether the defendant acted as a reasonable, prudent person would have acted under the same or similar circumstances. For example, in Medlar v. Mohan, 409 S.E.2d 123 (Va. 1991), a negligence action arising from a collision at a very wet intersection, the court wrote that "the test is whether the driver used that degree of care which an ordinarily prudent person would have exercised, 'having regard to the duty of the driver to exercise increased caution in the face of the known and obvious dangerous condition of the highway.'"

For purposes of jury instruction, the reasonable-person standard has a clear advantage over the negligence formula. In contrast to the abstract, almost cold and mathematical, nature of the latter, the reasonable-person standard invites lay jurors to address the matter of reasonableness in more-familiar, human terms. To be sure, the issue is the same, regardless of which test is used. In either instance, the task is to determine whether the defendant's conduct posed an unacceptable risk of harm to the plaintiff. Presumably, the answer should be the same regardless of the test employed.

Four Ways of Establishing What a Reasonable Person Would Do. What a reasonable person would do in a given situation is frequently less than obvious. According to the Restatement, Second, of Torts §285, the conduct of a reasonable person may be established in any of four distinct ways.

(a) *Factfinder Determination.* First, and perhaps most frequently, the finder of fact, guided by applicable rules of law or appropriate instructions, and directing its attention to the circumstances of a single case, may determine on an *ad hoc* basis whether a particular defendant acted reasonably. Thus, the court or jury, within limits, defines the conduct of the reasonable prudent person. It is of course important for the factfinder to know what circumstances may be taken into account. For example, is the fact that defendant is faced with an emergency, or is blind, aged, well-educated, or experienced relevant to the determination? These and similar questions are considered below at pp. 257–300.

There are two chief difficulties with this facts-of-the-case approach to determining what is acceptable conduct. One is that by reason of being an after-the-fact determination, a prospective defendant is offered no advance warning of precisely what is expected. The other is that because such decisions are fact-specific and have no precedential force, juries can, and frequently do, arrive at inconsistent results in relatively similar cases. On the other hand, the flexibility of the case-by-case approach allows the decisionmaker to take into account numerous factual variables that might be ignored by a more-rigid rule of law.

(b) *Judge-Made Standards.* The second way the standard of conduct of a reasonable person may be established is by judicial decision. *See* pp. 300–04, below. Thus, when faced with a problem of a recurring nature, a court may state, as a matter of law, what conduct is required of a person confronted with those circumstances. The jury will be instructed that if it determines that the defendant failed to take the required steps, it must find that the defendant acted unreasonably and breached its duty of care to the plaintiff. The advance articulation of such a rule gives individuals clear notice of what conduct is expected and leads to consistency of results in similar cases. But as Justice Benjamin N. Cardozo wrote in Pokora v. Wabash Ry. Co., 292 U.S. 98 (1934), "Extraordinary situations may not wisely or fairly be subjected to tests or regulations that are fitting for the commonplace." Thus, the use of this approach may be undesirable where the factors legitimately bearing upon the question of reasonableness are too numerous or variable to adequately be taken into account by a hard-and-fast rule.

(c) *Legislatively Determined Standards.* Sometimes the standard of conduct is defined by a legislative body through an appropriate enactment. *See* pp. 300–05, below. Thus, where duly constituted representatives of the public expressly or implicitly declare that failure to take certain actions will give rise to civil liability, courts recognize such expressions as defining the applicable level of care. This approach not only lends itself to fair notice and uniformity of results, but allows the judiciary to express appropriate deference for the determinations of co-equal branches of government.

(d) *Judicially Declared Standards Based on Legislation.* Finally, even if a legislative enactment does not expressly or implicitly establish a standard of care, a court, in the exercise of its inherent nomothetic powers, may define the standard of care with reference to that legislative enactment if the court finds that the legislation calls for appropriate behavior. *See* pp. 305–27, below. Such a decision is in many respects similar to the second method of setting the standard of care, discussed above, since, in essence, the court is not required to adopt the standard, but is exercising its law-giving prerogative to do so. However, it differs from the second approach in that, among other things, it allows the court to draw upon the legislative history and vote underlying the enactment to support the reasonableness of its decision. Some courts have held that any legislative establishment of a safety standard determines the standard to be applied in tort cases, even though the legislation is not expressly addressed to torts.

Good Intentions Are Not Enough. An early case applying the reasonable person standard was Vaughan v. Menlove, 3 Bing. (N.C.) 467, 132 Eng. Rep. 490 (1837). There, the defendant constructed a hay rick in a location immediately adjacent to his neighbor's cottages. He was repeatedly warned by others that it might catch fire by spontaneous combustion, and thereby endanger the nearby buildings. Defendant replied that he would "chance it," and, predictably, the worst came to pass. In rejecting his argument that he should not be held liable for the destruction of the cottages if he had acted in good faith, "bona fide to the best of his judgment," Chief Justice Tindal wrote that to hold that liability for negligence was co-extensive with the judgment of each person would result in a standard "as variable as the length of the foot of each individual." "It is not enough that the defendant did the best he knew how." In other words, the reasonable person standard is intended to ensure some degree of predictability in the conduct of human affairs. (On the facts in *Vaughan*, it is hard to see how the defendant could reasonably have been held to have acted even in good faith—similar conduct today would almost surely lead to an award of punitive, as well as compensatory, damages.)

1. Considerations the Jury May Take into Account

a. *Emergencies*

Young v. Clark

Supreme Court of Colorado
814 P.2d 364 (Colo. 1991)

Justice VOLLACK delivered the Opinion of the Court.

....

.... The plaintiff, John Young (Young), and the defendant, Holly Clark (Clark), were both traveling eastbound in the center lane on Colorado Highway 36. Construction on the highway caused all traffic to slow.... One unidentified driver, who was four to five cars ahead of Young, pulled out of the center lane into the right-hand lane and then swerved abruptly back into the center-lane traffic, forcing all drivers behind him to apply their brakes. At that time, Clark had looked over her shoulder while attempting to change lanes. Her passenger, Susan Baldwin, yelled to Clark upon seeing that all traffic ahead had stopped. Clark applied her brakes and swerved to the left, but was unable to avoid colliding with the rear of Young's car.

Young filed suit against Clark....

The jury found that the Youngs' injuries were not caused by any negligence on Clark's part.... We granted certiorari to determine whether the trial court's submission of a "sudden emergency" instruction was improper....

....

The sudden emergency doctrine was developed by the courts to recognize that a person confronted with sudden or unexpected circumstances calling for immediate action is not expected to exercise the judgment of one acting under normal conditions. [Citation.]

> [T]he basis of the special rule is merely that the actor is left no time for adequate thought, or is reasonably so disturbed or excited that the actor cannot weigh alternative courses of action, and must make a speedy decision, based very largely upon impulse or guess. Under such conditions, the actor cannot reasonably be held to the same accuracy of judgment or conduct as one who has had full opportunity to reflect, even though it later appears that the actor made the wrong decision....

Id. The doctrine does not, however, impose a lesser standard of care on a person caught in an emergency situation; the individual is still expected to respond to the situation as a reasonably prudent person under the circumstances. The emergency is merely a circumstance to be considered in determining whether the actor's conduct was reasonable. [Citations.] Thus, a person may be found negligent if his actions are deemed unreasonable, despite the emergency....

....

...[T]he trial court submitted to the jury Colorado's pattern "sudden emergency" instruction, CJ-Civ.2d 9:10, which states: "A person who, through no fault of his or her own, is placed in a sudden emergency, is not chargeable with negligence if the person exercises that degree of care which a reasonably careful person would have exercised under the same or similar circumstances."....

....

The Youngs contend that it was improper to give the instruction because the rear-end collision was caused by Clark's lack of attention and failure to maintain a safe distance from Young's car. While it is true that the sudden emergency instruction is not available where a defendant, or a plaintiff, is obviously guilty of negligence, the question of whether an emergency arose because of some negligence by Clark was not so clear. No evidence was presented to show that Clark was following too closely to Young's car or that she was driving too fast under the circumstances....The factual dispute as to whether Clark was at fault for causing the accident was therefore appropriately submitted to the finder of fact....

....In our view, the sudden and unexpected reentry of the unknown driver into the flow of traffic provided sufficient evidence to support giving the sudden emergency instruction. *See* Restatement, Second, of Torts §296(1) comment a (1977) (the sudden emergency doctrine applies "where the sudden emergency is created in any way other than by the actor's own tortious conduct, as where it is created by the unexpected operation of a natural force *or by the innocent or wrongful act of a third person*") (emphasis added). We therefore conclude that the trial court did not act improperly in instructing the jury on the sudden emergency doctrine under the circumstances of this case.

....

The Youngs further urge this court to follow the lead of those jurisdictions that have abolished, or curtailed the use of, the sudden emergency doctrine. [Citations.] These courts generally have denounced the usefulness of the sudden emergency instruction..., reasoning that "[e]ven the wording of a well-drawn instruction intimates that ordinary rules of negligence do not apply to the circumstances constituting the claimed 'sudden emergency.'" Knapp [v. Stanford, 392 So. 2d 196, 198 (Miss. 1980)]. *See also* Simonson [v. White, 713 P.2d 983, 989 (Mont. 1986)]....

Such reasoning, in our view, is based on unfounded assumptions about how jurors perceive an instruction explaining the relatively simplistic sudden emergency doctrine. The pattern instruction used by Colorado courts, CJI-Civ. 2d 9:10, is a clear statement of the doctrine and obligates the finder of fact to do nothing more than apply the objective "reasonable person" standard to an actor in the specific context of an emergency situation. It thus does not operate to excuse fault but merely serves as an explanatory instruction, offered for purposes of clarification for the jury's benefit.

The Youngs also maintain that the sudden emergency doctrine should be abolished because its original purpose, to overcome the harsh effect of the former contributory negligence defense whereby a plaintiff's negligence acted as a complete bar to recovery, is no longer served with the enactment of comparative negligence in this state....

....Under...[Colorado's comparative-negligence statute], a plaintiff's contributory negligence shall not bar recovery if such negligence was not as great as the defendant's negligence, "but any damages allowed shall be diminished in proportion to the amount of negligence attributable to" the plaintiff....Significantly, the doctrine explains to the jury the standard of conduct expected of defendants *and* plaintiffs who act under the stress of an emergency situation. Finding no friction between the comparative negligence scheme of allocating fault and the sudden emergency doctrine, we conclude that abolishing the doctrine on this ground is unwarranted. [Citations.]

....

....We affirm the court of appeals judgment.

[The dissenting opinion of Justice LOHR, in which Justice ERICKSON joined, has been omitted.]

Notes

1. ***Emergency as a Relevant Factor.*** Most courts hold that evidence of an emergency does not require the application of a different standard. Instead, the emergency condition is a factor in determining the reasonable character of the defendant's choice of action.

See Helms v. Church's Fried Chicken, Inc., 344 S.E.2d 349 (N.C. Ct. App. 1986) (in an action by customers of a fast-food restaurant who were injured by a robber after an employee of the restaurant told another customer to call the police, the court reversed a grant of summary judgment to the defendant, noting that "[s]udden emergency" is not a legal defense but only one factor to consider in making the reasonable-person determination, with the question of due care being ordinarily for the jury).

2. ***Errors of Judgment.*** If reasonable minds can differ as to the preferred course of action in an emergency, a defendant who makes a reasonable choice will not be held liable for having failed to select what an expert or jury might later decide was the best course. *See* De Gregorio v. Malloy, 52 A.2d 195, 197–198 (Pa. 1947) (a police officer riding on the outside of a truck during an emergency was not contributorily negligent).

In upholding a judgment n.o.v. for the defendant-appellee in Murphy v. Neely, 179 A. 439 (Pa. 1935), a case arising out of the crash of a two-seater plane as it was flying about 250 feet above a prospective landing field, the court wrote:

> Appellee was bringing the ship around in a gentle bank to continue his examination of the field, when, three-quarters of the way around, in the turning movement, the nose dropped suddenly, and the ship fell almost vertically to the ground, injuring appellant. It was estimated that it was some five seconds from the time the fall began until the ship struck the ground. As the ship was falling, appellee cut the ignition switch in order to reduce the fire hazard when it crashed.
>
> ....
>
> The action of appellee in cutting off the ignition when confronted with an emergency not shown to have been brought about by tortious conduct upon his part was not unreasonable. [Citations.] From the time the airplane started to fall, the opportunity for action was very limited, and, if cutting the ignition was wrong, it was an error in judgment....[T]he evidence is not sufficient to justify one in concluding that there is an accepted general opinion or practice with relation to the advisability of cutting off the ignition when a dive or spin

begins as against maintaining...speed and endeavoring to right the machine, so that the failure to do one or the other cannot be termed negligent and is nothing more than a permissible exercise of judgment.

3. *Creators of Emergencies.* An instruction on sudden emergency generally is not available where the crisis is of the defendant's own making. *See* Burns v. Martin, 589 So. 2d 147, 149 (Ala. 1991) (holding it reversible error to give a sudden-emergency instruction in a case in which the defendant's "wanton" act created the emergency); Illey v. Hatley, 693 S.W.2d 506, 510 (Tex. Ct. App. 1985) (before the defendant believed the plaintiff was drawing a gun, the defendant had participated in various acts of highway misconduct and had led a contingent of cars to a vacant gas station where the harm occurred). *Cf.* Lockhart v. List, 665 A.2d 1176 (Pa. 1995) (it was error to refuse a sudden-emergency instruction where the evidence did not clearly and unequivocally indicate that the plaintiff was operating her vehicle at an unsafe speed before crashing into a garbage truck blocking the road on a sharp curve). *See also* Restatement, Third, of Torts: Liability for Physical Harm (Basic Principles) §9 (Tent. Draft No. 1, 2001) (articulating a different path to "the same result").

4. *Competence.* "Competence is...the ability or capacity of the individual to use care." Restatement, Second, of Torts §298 Comment a. One can hardly be held negligent for failure to have more competence than one actually has. However, an actor's competence, or lack of it, may be the key fact in determining whether it was reasonable for the actor to attempt an activity. A law professor is not negligent simply because she lacks the skills of a surgeon, but if she attempts to take out a colleague's appendix with a paring knife, her lack of competence will be most relevant in the ensuing litigation.

The Restatement notes the need for beginners to attempt activities before they become good at them; were it otherwise, no one could attain competence; Restatement, Second, of Torts §299 Comment d. Nevertheless, the beginner's lack of skill may necessitate special precautions, so that it may be negligent to attempt one's first bicycle ride on a crowded street.

An emergency may well justify an attempt to do something despite incompetence. As the Restatement points out, it may be better for an unskilled layperson to give a badly injured person first aid than to let the victim die. Restatement, Second, of Torts §299 Comment e.

5. *Medical Care in Emergencies.* Good Samaritan statutes typically provide that volunteers who render aid at the scene of an accident are liable only for conduct more blameworthy than ordinary negligence. *See* Chapters 8 and 9. Some "tort reform" legislation has extended the same protection to professionals in the emergency-room context.

TEX. CIV. PRAC. & REM. CODE §74.153
(Westlaw 2004)

In a suit...against a physician or health care provider for injury to or death of a patient arising out of the provision of emergency medical care in a hospital emergency department or obstetrical unit or in a surgical suite immediately following the evaluation or treatment of a patient in a hospital emergency department, the claimant bringing the suit may prove that the treatment or lack of treatment by the physician or health care provider departed from accepted standards of medical care or health care only if the claimant shows by a preponderance of the evidence that the physician or health care provider, with wilful and wanton negligence, deviated from the degree of care and skill that is reasonably expected of an ordinarily prudent physician or health care provider in the same or similar circumstances.

6. *Ethics in Law Practice: Emergency Legal Work.* In general, a lawyer must not undertake to provide legal services in a field in which the lawyer is not competent. However:

> A lawyer need not necessarily have special training or prior experience to handle legal problems of a type with which the lawyer is unfamiliar.... A lawyer can provide adequate representation in a wholly novel field through necessary study. Competent representation can also be provided through the association of a lawyer of established competence in the field in question.

> In an emergency a lawyer may give advice or assistance in a matter in which the lawyer does not have the skill ordinarily required where referral to or consultation or association with another lawyer would be impractical. Even in an emergency, however, assistance should be limited to that reasonably necessary in the circumstances, for ill considered action under emergency conditions can jeopardize the client's interest.

Model Rules of Professional Conduct Rule 1.1 Comments 2 & 3 (2003).

b. Physical Disabilities

Generally. Hill v. City of Glenwood, 100 N.W. 522 (Iowa 1904) addressed the question of whether a person's physical handicaps are relevant to the determination of whether that individual has acted reasonably. In *Hill*, a blind man had been injured in an accident on a public sidewalk. Regarding the issue of contributory negligence, the court said that a blind person need not exercise a higher degree of care than a sighted person, but merely the ordinary care that would be exercised by a person who is blind. In other words, the physical handicap was a relevant circumstance, but it did not change the standard of care.

A similar approach is applied if, for example, a person is deaf, or unusually short, or lacks a sense of smell, or is ill. *See* Restatement, Third, of Torts: Liability for Physical Harm §11(a) (Tent. Draft No. 1, 2001) ("If an actor has a physical disability, the actor's conduct is negligent if it does not conform to that of a reasonably careful person with the same disability").

Intoxication. In Davies v. Butler, 602 P.2d 605 (Nev. 1979), plaintiff's decedent died after drinking a large quantity of alcohol during initiation into a social drinking club. In addressing a contributory negligence issue, Chief Justice Mowbray wrote:

> The court instructed the jury, over appellants' objection that "[i]ntoxication is no excuse for failure to act as a reasonably prudent person would act. A person who is intoxicated or under the influence of intoxicating liquor is held to the same standard of care as a sober person."

> While ordinarily the statement is an accurate summary of the law, the courts have refused to apply the basic rule strictly, at least as to the inebriate's duty to protect himself, if "when the liquor was furnished [plaintiff's decedent] was incapable of acting like a reasonable man." [Citations.]

>   ....

> Where intoxication is involuntary, such as in the "highly unusual case in which one believes that he is drinking tea is plied with liquor, and so becomes

disabled," the standard of conduct to which the actor must conform is that of a reasonable man under a like disability. Restatement, Second, of Torts, *supra*, at 19. Where, however, the intoxication...results from deliberate drinking with knowledge of what is being consumed..., the policy of the law has refused to make any allowance for the resulting disability....

....There was evidence in this case from which the jury could have concluded that at some point decedent's further drinking was "involuntary," and no longer "deliberate drinking with knowledge of what is consumed, so that the result is deliberately risked."

The instruction "practically takes from the consideration of the jury the [plaintiffs'] theory of the case," *i.e.*, that decedent did not *voluntarily* consume a lethal dose of alcohol, and thus it was prejudicial error....

In addition to being no excuse for negligence, voluntary intoxication may be evidence of more-serious wrongdoing. *See* Williams v. Crist, 484 N.E.2d 576 (Ind. 1985) (driving a motor vehicle while intoxicated is "wanton and wilful misconduct *per se*") (plurality opinion).

Illness. What if a person who is sick falls asleep at the wheel and has an accident after taking an over-the-counter medication bearing a label warning users that drowsiness may result and that they should not operate machinery? *See* Restatement, Third, of Torts: Liability for Physical Harm (Basic Principles) §11(b) (Tent. Draft No. 1, 2001) ("If an actor engages in substandard conduct because of sudden incapacitation or loss of consciousness brought about by physical illness, this conduct constitutes negligence only if the sudden incapacitation or loss of consciousness was reasonably foreseeable to the actor").

c. Religious Beliefs

Williams v. Bright

Supreme Court of New York, Appellate Division
658 N.Y.S.2d 910 (App. Div.), *appeal dismissed*,
686 N.E.2d 1368 (N.Y. 1997)

WALLACH, Justice.

Plaintiff Robbins was a passenger in an automobile driven by her 70-year-old father on an upstate highway. An eyewitness saw the car veer off the road at about 65 miles per hour and turn over....There was circumstantial evidence that the driver...had fallen asleep at the wheel. This was conduct that the jury found to be both negligent and a proximate cause of the accident. On this appeal, defendants, who include the lessors of the vehicle, do not seriously contest liability; the main issue is the trial court's treatment of plaintiff Robbins' alleged failure to mitigate damages due to her religious beliefs as a Jehovah's Witness....

...[A] party who claims to have suffered damage by the tort of another is bound "to use reasonable and proper efforts to make the damage as small as practicable" [citation], and if an injured party allows the damages to be unnecessarily enhanced, the incurred loss justly falls upon him [citation].

Plaintiff Robbins suffered a severely damaged left hip, as well as a painful injury to her right knee. Her own expert testified that if these injuries were not alleviated by well-recognized and universally accepted surgical procedures, her prognosis was for a wheelchair-bound life....Moreover, all the experts agreed that the surgical intervention available to this plaintiff...offered her the prospect of a good recovery and a near normal life. However, Robbins, a devout Jehovah's Witness, presented proof...that she was obliged to refuse these recommended surgeries because her church prohibits the blood transfusions they would necessarily entail.

...[T]he New York pattern jury instruction on the subject of damage mitigation refers to the actions of "a reasonably prudent person" (PJI 2:325) and measures the duty to mitigate in accordance with that standard.[2] Although the trial court acquainted the jury with the existence of that standard, it charged that in this case the standard to be applied was something very different (our emphasis added):

> You have to accept as a given that the dictates of her religion forbid blood transfusions.
>
> And so you have to determine...whether she...*acted reasonably as a Jehovah's Witness* in refusing surgery which would involve blood transfusions.
>
> Was it reasonable for her, not what you would do or your friends or family, *was it reasonable for her given her beliefs*, without questioning the validity or the propriety of her beliefs?

In abandoning the "reasonably prudent person" test in favor of a "reasonable Jehovah's Witness" standard, over defendants' objection, the trial court perceived the issue as involving this plaintiff's fundamental right to the free exercise of her religion, protected by the First Amendment of the United States Constitution and article I (§3) of our State Constitution. The First Amendment prohibits any law "respecting an establishment of religion, or prohibiting the free exercise thereof." Essentially, the court held that if the jury were permitted to assess this plaintiff's refusal to accept additional surgery without total deference to her religious beliefs, it would unlawfully restrain "the free exercise" of her Jehovah's Witness faith and would thus be constitutionally prohibited. In effect, this plaintiff's religious beliefs were held, as a matter of law, to relieve her of any legal obligation to mitigate damages under the same standard required of all other persons similarly situated who do not share similar religious convictions.

....Virtually all of the handful of jurisdictions to have considered the question have adopted the test of the reasonably prudent person instead of the formulation employed here. (*See, e.g.,* Munn v. Algee, 924 F.2d 568 [5th Cir], *cert. denied* 502 US 900; Corlett v. Caserta, 204 Ill. App. 3d 403, 413–414, 562 N.E.2d 257, 263; Shorter v. Drury, 103 Wash. 2d 645, 659, 695 P.2d 116, 124, *cert. denied* 474 U.S. 827; *see also*, Nashert & Sons v. McCann, 460 P.2d 941 [Okla].)

In our view, the analysis of the trial court contained many flaws. The first error was in defining the fundamental issue as whether any jury verdict could be permitted to conflict with this plaintiff's "religious belief that it may be better to suffer present pain than to be barred from entering the Kingdom of Heaven")....[T]his is not the question that should have been presented; to put it in this manner inevitably skews the result.

---

2. "A person who has been injured is not permitted to recover for damages that could have been avoided by using means which a reasonably prudent person would have used to (cure the injury, alleviate the pain)....If you find that the plaintiff is entitled to recover in this action, then in deciding the nature and permanence of her injury and what damages she may recover for the injury, you must decide whether in refusing to have an operation the plaintiff acted as a reasonably prudent person would have acted under the circumstances."

No one suggests that the State, or, for that matter, anyone else, has the right to inter-fere with that religious belief. But the real issue here is whether the consequences of that belief must be fully paid for here on earth by someone other than the injured believer....

...[T]he State...[has] a compelling interest in assuring that the proceedings before its civil tribunals are fair, and that any litigant is not improperly advantaged or disad-vantaged by adherence to a particular set of religious principles. The State also has a compelling interest...to extend equal protection of the law to every person....

     ....

....The trial court's instruction to the jurors on mitigation directed them to pass upon the reasonableness of plaintiff Robbins' objection, on religious grounds, to a blood transfusion. The fallacy in this instruction was that the jury never received any evidence pertaining to the rationale of her religious convictions, nor how universally accepted they may have been by members of her faith....The charge thus created a sham inquiry....Let us recall, the jurors were told that they must ask themselves whether this plaintiff's refusal to accept a blood transfusion was reasonable, "given her beliefs, *without questioning the validity*" of those beliefs (emphasis added). Having thus removed from the jury's consideration any question as to the validity (that is to say, the reasonableness) of plaintiff Robbins' religious convictions, the court effectively directed a verdict on the issue.

Of course, the alternative—the receipt of "expert" testimony on this subject—pre-sents an even worse prospect. Such evidence, if any conflict developed, would present a triable issue as to whether the conviction against transfusions was heretical—or ortho-dox—within the Jehovah's Witness faith.

The State may not endorse religion or any particular religious practice [citation]. The trial court, in accepting the sincerity of plaintiff Robbins' beliefs as a given and ask-ing the jury to consider the reasonableness of her actions only in the context of her own religion, effectively provided government endorsement to those beliefs. American courts have no business endorsing or condemning the truth or falsity of anyone's reli-gious beliefs....

     ....

An extraordinary example of the perils of [deciding what religious practices are "rea-sonable"] is the recent Minnesota case of Lundman v. McKown (530 N.W.2d 807, 828, *cert. denied* 516 U.S. 1099), where damages were awarded against a Christian Scientist stepfather who blocked conventional treatment that, to a medical certainty, would have saved a young child's life. Here was a healthy 11-year-old boy who succumbed to a sud-den onset of juvenile diabetes, a disease that is easily diagnosable and treatable by con-ventional medical practice. Instead, his mother and stepfather enlisted the services of Christian Science practitioners who provided only "spiritual treatment." The child's condition deteriorated rapidly, and he died three days later. There was evidence that a shot of insulin administered as late as two hours before death could have saved him. A wrongful death action was commenced by the child's natural father and older sister against the mother and stepfather, the various spiritual practitioners and the Christian Science Church itself. A jury awarded compensatory damages against all defendants in the amount of $5.2 million (reduced on post-trial motion to $1.5 million), and $9 mil-lion in punitive damages against the church.

The Minnesota Court of Appeals overturned the verdict against the church and its officials, but upheld the portion of the award against the mother, stepfather and local practitioners. In reaching that conclusion, the appellate court allowed itself to become deeply entangled in ecclesiastical matters regarding the tenets of the Christian Science faith. The trial court, in awarding damages against the mother and stepfather, had applied the reasonable person standard of care. The Court of Appeals ruled, to the contrary, that the proper standard was that of the "reasonable Christian Scientist", but then went on to hold, as a matter of law, that a new trial was not warranted because the reasonable Christian Scientist would necessarily have concluded (as did the jury under the reasonable person standard) that the life-or-death interest of the child should have prevailed and dictated conventional medical treatment (530 N.W.2d, supra, at 828). In other words, the appellate court undertook to evaluate the reasonableness of various practices and tenets of the Christian Science faith.... We should firmly decline to follow that rarely trodden and perilous path.

....

...[W]e take note of an obvious problem with strict adherence to the pattern jury instruction that is provided as a general guide (see, n. 2, supra). We conclude that the unmodified application of that formulation would work an injustice in this case.... It seems apparent to us that a person in plaintiff Robbins' position must be permitted to present to the jury the basis for her refusal of medical treatment; otherwise, the jury would simply be left with the fact of her refusal, without any explanation at all. Once such evidence is (as it should be) received, the court is called upon to instruct the jurors as to how such evidence should affect their deliberations. Addressing this issue, we hold that the pattern jury instruction must be supplemented here with the following direction:

> In considering whether the plaintiff acted as a reasonably prudent person, you may consider the plaintiff's testimony that she is a believer in the Jehovah's Witness faith, and that as an adherent of that faith, she cannot accept any medical treatment which requires a blood transfusion. I charge you that such belief is a factor for you to consider, together with all the other evidence you have heard, in determining whether the plaintiff acted reasonably in caring for her injuries, keeping in mind, however, that the overriding test is whether the plaintiff acted as a reasonably prudent person, under all the circumstances confronting her.

The so-called "reasonable believer" charge (Pomeroy, *Reason, Religion, and Avoidable Consequences: When Faith and the Duty to Mitigate Collide*, 67 N.Y.U. L. Rev. 1111, 1145–1147 [1992]) has found some support in other jurisdictions (Lange v. Hoyt, 114 Conn. 590, 159 A. 575; Christiansen v. Hollings, 44 Cal. App. 2d 332, 112 P.2d 723).... [W]e reiterate that the court is not to permit the introduction of any "theological" proof, by way of either expert or lay testimony, as to the validity of religious doctrine, nor should the court issue any instructions whatsoever on that score.

....

Accordingly, the judgment...should be reversed, on the law and the facts, without costs, and the matter remanded for new trial on damages alone.

NARDELLI and TOM, JJ., concur with WALLACH, J.

ROSENBERGER, Justice (dissenting).

I respectfully dissent and would affirm the judgment appealed. The Trial Judge charged the jury in a manner more favorable to the defendants than the opinion and holding in United States v. Ballard (322 U.S. 78), quoted and cited by the majority, would require.

....

....The pattern jury instruction as to the legal doctrine of avoidable consequences, or the duty to undertake reasonable efforts to minimize consequential damages, though neutral on its face, would have been discriminatory as applied to a practicing Jehovah's Witness whose religion forbids the acceptance of blood transfusions [citation].

The trial court's adapted charge reveals that it appropriately created an instruction that meets the State's interest in minimizing tort damages to those reasonably incurred, in the situation of an incidental burden placed upon plaintiff's practice of her religious beliefs as a Jehovah's Witness (*see*, United States v. Ballard, *supra*;....)....

The charge in this case did not take the issue of whether Mrs. Robbins acted reasonably away from the jury. The Trial Judge instructed this jury at least five times that whether she acted reasonably in refusing surgery was a matter to be decided by them. In doing so, the court gave an instruction more favorable to the defendants than was proper under the standard set forth by the Supreme Court of the United States in United States v. Ballard (*supra*).

The sincerity and good faith of the plaintiff's beliefs were not contested at trial or on appeal by the defendants. Realistically, they could not have been successfully challenged. The evidence showed that she stated that she would refuse blood transfusions in conformity with her religious belief at her first contact with a physician after the accident. She maintained her resolve even upon being informed that it could cost her her life. Nonetheless, the Trial Judge in his charge instructed the jury to consider her sincerity and good faith, when he told the jurors that "from the evidence, you may or may not conclude that the observance of her religion was very important to her." There was no exception to this portion of the charge, which was in conformity with United States v. Ballard (*supra*).

....

The jury charge was in conformity with our tort system, allowing for an assessment of the actual situation of a victim of negligence, rather than assigning a certain value to a designated injury [citation]. The concept of the "eggshell plaintiff" has not been limited to physical infirmities [citation].

....

This plaintiff should not be subjected to the intrusiveness and indignity of having the reasonableness of her religious beliefs examined and determined by a jury. This basic protection is afforded her by not one, but two constitutions.

d. Age

Goss v. Allen

Supreme Court of New Jersey
360 A.2d 388 (N.J. 1976)

SULLIVAN, J.

....

On February 21, 1972, plaintiff, an experienced skier, was serving as a first aid advisor on the ski patrol at the Mad River Glen ski resort in Vermont. The facility includes a beginners' slope which near its end makes an abrupt left turn. The accident occurred some 60 feet beyond the end of the slope in a flat area where plaintiff and a friend happened to be standing taking pictures....

Defendant...was a beginning skier who had limited cross-country skiing experience but had never attempted a downhill run. Nor had he ever been to Mad River Glen before. Upon arrival, defendant was sent to the beginners' slope.... [D]efendant confined his first run to the lower portion of the slope. He walked a quarter of the way up the hill and started to ski down, successfully completing the comparatively short run of 30 feet or so until he came to the abrupt left turn. In attempting to negotiate the turn, defendant lost control over his momentum and direction. He saw the two girls ahead of him but because of the short distance remaining, his efforts to regain control and his lack of experience, he did not call out until he was almost upon the girls. Plaintiff...was struck and knocked down by defendant.

....

The trial court charged the jury that the standard of care applicable in the case was not the same degree of care required of an adult, but rather that degree of care which a reasonably prudent person of that age (defendant was 17 years of age) would have exercised under the same or similar circumstances....

...[T]he jury in answer to an interrogatory submitted to it found the defendant not negligent.

...[T]he Appellate Division reversed and remanded for a new trial finding plain error in the charge....

The Appellate Division determination that defendant...should be held to the standard of care required of an adult was premised on its conclusion that skiing is an activity which may be dangerous to others and is normally undertaken only by adults, and for which adult qualifications are required. [Citation.] We find nothing in the record to support this conclusion. We think it judicially noticeable that skiing as a recreational sport, save for limited hazardous skiing activities, is engaged in by persons of all ages. Defendant's attempt to negotiate the lower end of the beginners' slope certainly cannot be characterized as a skiing activity that as a matter of law was hazardous to others and required that he be held to an adult standard of conduct. [Citations.]

We recognize that certain activities engaged in by minors are so potentially hazardous as to require that the minor be held to an adult standard of care. Driving a motor vehicle, operating a motor boat and hunting would ordinarily be so classified. However, as to the activities mentioned New Jersey law requires that the minor must be licensed and must first demonstrate the requisite degree of adult competence. [Citation.]

We find that the applicable standard of care, correctly charged by the trial court, was that generally applicable to minors. [Citations.] The required standard is that of a reasonable person of like age, intelligence and experience under like circumstances. [Citations.] Among those circumstances, of course, would be the nature of the activity in which the minor was engaged.

Most of the cases which apply this standard have been concerned with the minor's contributory negligence and not primary negligence. It has been suggested that a different standard might well apply where the minor's conduct causes injury to others. *See* Schulman, "*The Standard of Care Required of Children,*" 37 Yale L.J. 618, 619 (1928).... We think that a rational basis exists for applying the same standard whether the issue involves a question of contributory negligence of a child or primary negligence. Moreover, to hold otherwise would further complicate an already difficult area of tort law....

The Appellate Division, while it decided the case on the ground heretofore discussed, also criticized the trial court's application of the standard applicable to children to a 17-year-old person, pointing out that by...[statute] every person in this State 18 or more years of age is deemed to be an adult. The Appellate Division could see little sense in holding an 18-year-old person to one standard of care and applying a lesser standard to one 17 years of age.

However, this problem will exist no matter where the line is drawn, whether it be at 10, 14, or 18 years. Since it has to be drawn somewhere, it is not unreasonable to fix it at the age of legal maturity—now 18 in this State—holding those under that age and capable of negligence to the standard of care required of a reasonable person of like age, intelligence and experience under like circumstances....

....

The judgment of the Appellate Division is reversed and the judgment of the trial court in favor of defendant is hereby reinstated.

SCHREIBER, J. (dissenting).

....

To the injured party, his loss is the same irrespective of the wrongdoer's date of birth and it is inequitable and unjust that a minor should not be expected to exercise the same degree of care as the mythical reasonable and prudent person, at least when engaged in adult activities. The majority's proposition unnecessarily sanctions the imposition of the burden of young people's hazards on innocent victims....

....

I would affirm the judgment of the Appellate Division.

Notes

1. *Children's Standard.* A child must normally exercise the degree of care that would be observed by children of similar "age, intelligence, and experience." Restatement, Third, of Torts: Liability for Physical Harm (Basic Principles) §10(a) (Tent. Draft No. 1, 2001). The children's standard has been applied to a wide range of activities. *See, e.g.,* Bauman v. Crawford, 704 P.2d 1181 (Wash. 1985) (bicycling); Farm Bureau Ins. Group v. Phillips, 323 N.W.2d 477 (Mich. Ct. App. 1982) (building a fire); Purtle v. Shelton, 474 S.W.2d 123 (Ark. 1971) (hunting animals).

Some courts apply a non-adult standard only to children below 14 years of age. *See* Alpin v. Tew, 839 So. 2d 635 (Ala. 2002) (holding that a 14-year-old child who was injured by fireworks would be held to the general standard for contributory negligence).

2. *Old Enough to Know Better.* Under the children's standard, negligence is not simply a question of what the child "knows." In Plumley v. Birge, 124 Mass. 57 (1878), the court wrote:

> If the [trial] court had ruled that, if the plaintiff was old enough to know that striking the dog would be likely to incite him to bite, he could not recover, it would have been erroneous. This is not the true test. It entirely disregards the thoughtlessness and heedlessness natural to boyhood. The plaintiff may have been old enough to know, if he stopped to reflect, that striking a dog would be likely to provoke him to bite, and yet in striking him may have been acting as a boy of his age would ordinarily act under the same circumstances.

3. *The Dangerous or Adult Activities Exception.* The Restatement provides that a child will be held to an adult standard of care "when the child is engaging in a dangerous activity that is characteristically undertaken by adults." Restatement, Third, of Torts: Liability for Physical Harm (Basic Principles) §10(c) (Tent. Draft No. 1, 2001). "An activity is characteristically engaged in by adults if adults are the primary persons who ordinarily undertake the activity." *Id.* at cmt. f. In addition:

> Even if an activity is characteristically engaged in by adults, if it is not distinctly dangerous it is not covered by Subsection (c). For example, baking a meatloaf, although typically an adult activity, ordinarily is not distinctly dangerous. Accordingly, if a child by misusing a kitchen utensil is injured or injures another while assisting a parent in this activity,... a child standard applies to the evaluation of the child's conduct.

Id. According to the Restatement, "[h]andling firearms is best regarded as a dangerous adult activity."

However, some courts have phrased the exception to the children's rule differently. In Robinson v. Lindsay, 598 P.2d 392 (Wash. 1979), a case arising from a snowmobile accident, the court refused to follow states that couched the exception in terms of children engaging in an activity which is "normally one for adults only." It found that it was preferable to state the exception in terms of whether the activity in which the child was engaged was "inherently dangerous." The court wrote:

> Such a rule protects the need of children to be children but at the same time discourages immature individuals from engaging in inherently dangerous activities. Children will still be free to enjoy traditional childhood activities without being held to an adult standard of care. Although accidents sometimes occur as a result of such activities, they are not generally considered capable of resulting in grave danger to others or to the minor himself....

The phrasing of the exception may be important. Riding a minibike, for example, may be considered "inherently dangerous," but it might not qualify as an activity "characteristically undertaken by adults" or "normally one for adults only."

4. *Presumed Incapacity of Children.* According to the Restatement, a "considerable minority of jurisdictions" take a different approach to addressing the liability of children for negligence.

> Under that approach, for children above 14 there is a rebuttable presumption in favor of the child's capacity to commit negligence; for children between seven and 14, there is a rebuttable presumption against capacity; children under the age of seven are deemed incapable of committing negligence.

Restatement, Third, of Torts: Liability for Physical Harm (Basic Principles) §10 cmt. b (Tent. Draft No. 1, 2001). The third Restatement rejects this minority approach but endorses a rule that "A child who is less than five years of age is incapable of negligence." *Id.* at §10(b). Comment d explains:

> For very young children, moral judgments generally stem from instructions the children have received from their parents or from other external sources.... Moreover, pre-school-age children are commonly accompanied by their parents or other adults as they engage in activities inside and outside the home. These evaluations suggest focusing responsibility for the conduct of such children on parents or those other adults, under appropriate theories of negligent supervision. However, once children reach five and are off for school, those

adults' ability to supervise and control the children's behavior is plainly reduced....Overall, the possibility is slight that the conduct of a child under five is either deserving of moral criticism or is capable of being deterred by the application of tort rules. It is therefore appropriate to simplify tort litigation by adopting a rule that regards children under five as incapable of negligent conduct. It would be quite awkward to have a child under five testifying at trial, or being cross-examined, in a case that seeks to raise an issue of the child's negligence or contributory negligence....

e. Mental Deficiencies

Generally, no allowance is made in the adult standard of care for any mental deficiency of a relatively minor nature. The actor is held to that level of intelligence and stability that would be employed by an ordinary, reasonable person. As Prosser vividly stated:

> The fact that the individual is a congenital fool, cursed with in-built bad judgment, or that in the particular instance the person "did not stop to think," or that the person is merely a stupid ox, or of an excitable temperament which causes him to lose his head and get "rattled," cannot be allowed to protect him from liability. Apart from the very obvious difficulties of proof as to what went on in the person's head,...[t]he harm to his neighbors is quite as great, and may be greater, than if the person had exhibited a modicum of brains....

W. Page Keeton, Dan B. Dobbs, Robert E. Keeton, & David G. Owen, Prosser and Keeton on Torts 176–77 (5th ed. 1984).

As to more-severe mental problems, including those lumped together under the imprecise rubric of "insanity," the rule is largely the same: the actor is not relieved from liability for conduct that does not conform to the standard of the reasonable person under like circumstances. *See* Restatement, Second, of Torts §283B; Restatement, Third, of Torts: Liability for Physical Harm §11(c) (Tent. Draft No. 1, 2001) ("Unless the actor is a child, the actor's mental or emotional disability is not considered").

As the following case and notes suggest, a few jurisdictions have created exceptions to the general rule that mental deficiency is irrelevant.

Breunig v. American Family Ins. Co.

Supreme Court of Wisconsin
173 N.W.2d 619 (Wis. 1970)

[Plaintiff was injured when his truck was struck by an automobile driven on the left side of the highway by Erma Veith. The action was brought against defendant insurance company under a Wisconsin law which permits direct action against a liability insurer. The jury returned a verdict for plaintiff; defendant appealed.]

HALLOWS, Chief Justice.

There is no question that Erma Veith was subject at the time of the accident to an insane delusion which directly affected her ability to operate her car in an ordinarily prudent manner and caused the accident....

....

The psychiatrist testified Mrs. Veith told him she was driving on a road when she believed that God was taking ahold of the steering wheel and was directing her car. She saw the truck coming and stepped on the gas in order to become air-borne because she knew she could fly because Batman does it. To her surprise she was not air-borne before striking the truck, but after the impact she was flying.

. . . .

The psychiatrist testified Erma Veith was suffering from "schizophrenic reaction, paranoid type, acute." He stated that [during the period immediately preceding the accident]...she was not able to operate the vehicle with her conscious mind, and that she had no knowledge or forewarning that such illness or disability would likely occur.

. . . .

The case was tried on the theory that some forms of insanity are a defense to and preclude liability...[for] negligence. [Citation.] We agree. Not all types of insanity vitiate responsibility for a negligent tort. The question of liability in every case must depend upon the kind and nature of the insanity. The effect of the mental illness or mental hallucination must be such as to affect the person's ability to understand and appreciate the duty which rests upon him to drive his car with ordinary care, or if the insanity does not affect such understanding and appreciation, it must affect his ability to control his car in an ordinarily prudent manner. And in addition, there must be an absence of notice or forewarning to the person that he may be suddenly subject to such a type of insanity or mental illness.

. . . .

The policy basis of holding a permanently insane person liable for his tort is:

(1) Where one of two innocent persons must suffer a loss it should be borne by the one who occasioned it; (2) to induce those interested in the estate of the insane person (if he has one) to restrain and control him; and (3) the fear an insanity defense would lead to false claims of insanity to avoid liability....

. . . .

We think the statement that insanity is no defense is too broad when it is applied to a negligence case where the driver is suddenly overcome without forewarning by a mental disability or disorder which incapacitates him from conforming his conduct to the standards of a reasonable man under like circumstances. These are rare cases indeed, but their rarity is no reason for overlooking their existence and the justification which is the basis of the whole doctrine of liability for negligence, *i.e.*, that it is unjust to hold a man responsible for his conduct which he is incapable of avoiding and which incapability was unknown to him prior to the accident.

....All we hold is that a sudden mental incapacity equivalent in its effect to such physical causes as a sudden heart attack, epileptic seizure, stroke, or fainting should be treated alike and not under the general rule of insanity.

. . . .

[Because evidence of past conduct permitted the jury to conclude that Mrs. Veith believed she had a special relationship to God and was the chosen one to survive at the end of the world, and that she could believe that God would take over the direction of her life to the extent of driving her car, the question as to whether she acted negligently was properly left to the jury.]

Judgment affirmed.

Notes

1. *Old Age and Alzheimer's Disease.* Old age, by itself, is not taken into account in determining whether an actor's conduct was negligent. Restatement, Third, of Torts: Liability for Physical Harm §11 cmt. c (Tent. Draft No. 1, 2001). However, a number of cases have concerned Alzheimer's, a disease commonly associated with old age. Gould v. American Family Mut. Ins. Co., 543 N.W.2d 282 (Wis. 1996), involved injuries inflicted on a nurse by an institutionalized patient with Alzheimer's. The court interpreted *Breunig* as a "limited exception" to the general rule that insanity is not a defense to tort liability, and declined "to abandon the long-standing rule in favor of a broad rule adopting the subjective standard for all mentally disabled persons." However, the court found that on the facts of the case public-policy considerations precluded liability. First,

> [the nurse] was not an innocent member of the public unable to anticipate or safeguard against the harm when encountered. Rather, she was employed as a caretaker specifically for dementia patients and knowingly encountered the dangers associated with such employment....
>
> ....
>
> ....Holding...[the patient] negligent under these circumstances places too great a burden on him because his disorientation and potential for violence is the very reason he was institutionalized and needed the aid of employed caretakers....

Second,

> ....[The patient's] relatives did everything they could to restrain him when they placed him in a secured dementia unit of a restricted health care center.... [They did not] need...further inducement [to exercise care].

Third,

> ....To suggest that...[the patient] would "simulate or pretend" the symptoms of Alzheimer's disease over a period of years in order to avoid a future tort liability is incredible.

The court concluded that "a person institutionalized...with a mental disability, and who does not have the capacity to control or appreciate his or her conduct cannot be liable for injuries caused to caretakers who are employed for financial compensation." Other Alzheimer's cases are consistent with *Gould. See, e.g.,* Creasy v. Rusk, 730 N.E.2d 659 (Ind. 2000); Berberian v. Lynn, 809 A.2d 865 (N.J. 2002).

2. *Other Forms of Inability to Control One's Actions.* A few courts hold that if one is unable to *control* one's actions (as opposed to unable to *understand* the nature and consequences of one's acts), liability may not be imposed, even if the deficiency in ability to control results from a condition of long standing. In Padula v. New York, 398 N.E.2d 548 (N.Y. 1979), the court held that certified heroin addicts, who could not resist the temptation to get "high," could not be held to have been contributorily negligent for having ingested a dangerous concoction made from duplicating fluid (which contained a lethal form of alcohol) and Tang. The reach of the *Padula* holding is unclear. Much of the opinion seems simply to say that someone unable to control behavior cannot be held negligent because of that behavior. Another passage in the opinion, however, may limit this holding to "persons in the custody of the state for treatment of a drug problem." The negligence of the state employees in *Padula* consisted of allowing the plaintiffs access to duplicating fluid. To hold the plaintiffs' conduct in drinking that fluid contrib-

utorily negligent would have made the defendants' legal duty to keep the plaintiffs away from the fluid illusory. *Padula* may therefore stand only for the very narrow proposition that the plaintiff's behavior cannot be contributory negligence in a case in which the defendant's duty was to prevent that very behavior. The suggested principle is similar to that invoked in the *Gould* case, above.

3. ***Mental Disability and Contributory Negligence.*** Traditionally, courts held that an actor's mental deficiency could be taken into account in determining whether the actor was contributorily negligent. *See* Stacy v. Jedco Constr., Inc., 457 S.E.2d 875 (N.C. App. 1995) (with respect to contributory negligence, a "person should be held only to the exercise of such care as he was capable of exercising, *i.e.*, the standard of care of a person of like mental capacity under similar circumstances"). Why? In the context of contributory negligence, the issue is not what degree of care an actor must exercise on behalf of others, but what degree of care a person must exercise for self-protection. Thus, the question is not which of two "innocent" individuals should bear a loss, but whether a negligent defendant should escape liability for a loss caused to a mentally deficient plaintiff who is incapable of guarding against such harm. However, the law on this issue is changing. According to the Restatement, Third, of Torts: Liability for Physical Harm § 11 cmt. e (Tent. Draft No. 1, 2001):

> [T]he rule…that a person's mental disabilities shall be disregarded applies in the context of the person's contributory negligence as well as the context of the person's negligence. Restatement Third, Torts: Apportionment of Liability § 3, Comment *a*, concludes that the "[s]tandard for plaintiff's negligence [is the] same as [the] standard for defendant's negligence." The shift in tort doctrine from contributory negligence as a full defense to comparative responsibility as a partial defense weakens whatever arguments there [are that] otherwise might favor a dual standard that would treat the mentally disabled plaintiff more leniently than the mentally disabled defendant. Under comparative responsibility,…even though the plaintiff's mental disability is ignored in considering whether the plaintiff is contributorily negligent at all…that disability can be considered in the course of the more open-ended process of apportioning percentages of responsibility between the plaintiff and the defendant. Accordingly, the plaintiff whose contributory negligence is in part explainable in terms of mental disability can be expected to receive an award that is larger than the awards received by other plaintiffs who engage in seemingly similar acts of contributory negligence.…

4. ***Ethics in Law Practice: Clients with Diminished Capacity.*** Rule 1.14(a) of the Model Rules of Professional Conduct (2003) provides:

> When a client's capacity to make adequately considered decisions in connection with a representation is diminished, whether because of minority, mental impairment or for some other reason, the lawyer shall, as far as reasonably possible, maintain a normal client-lawyer relationship with the client.

The commentary to the Rule adds:

> The fact that a client suffers a disability does not diminish the lawyer's obligation to treat the client with attention and respect…particularly in maintaining communication.

5. ***Amnesia.*** In some jurisdictions, a plaintiff who suffers from amnesia as a result of the defendant's acts is not held to as high a degree of proof in establishing a right to recover as is a plaintiff who can describe the events. The rule does not allow the jury to

presume that the plaintiff exercised due care, nor does it shift the burden of proof to the defendant, but the jury is afforded greater latitude in drawing inferences favorable to the plaintiff. *See, e.g.,* Sawyer v. Dreis & Krump Mfg. Co., 493 N.E.2d 920 (N.Y. 1986) (holding that a claim of amnesia must be supported by expert testimony).

f. Superior Skills or Knowledge

In General. Talent should not be wasted. It is therefore not surprising that the Restatement provides:

> If an actor has skills or knowledge that exceed those possessed by most others, these skills or knowledge are circumstances to be taken into account in determining whether the actor has behaved as a reasonably careful person.

Restatement, Third, of Torts: Liability for Physical Harm §12 (Tent. Draft No. 1, 2001); *cf.* Wilhelm v. Flores, 2003 W.L. 22479211 (Tex. App.) (a beekeeper, who was an entomologist with experience in beekeeping and who knew that an adverse reaction to bee stings could result in death, had a duty to warn a worker who moved bee hives of the dangers of bee stings).

Cases alleging misconduct by professionals typically raise issues relating to special skills and knowledge. They also raise concerns about whether professionals must afford consumers a certain minimum level of care beyond that which would be exhibited by non-professionals under similar circumstances. The Restatement, Second, of Torts provides:

§299A. Undertaking in Profession or Trade

> Unless he represents that he has greater or less skill or knowledge, one who undertakes to render services in the practice of a profession or trade is required to exercise the skill and knowledge normally possessed by members of that profession or trade in good standing in similar communities.

Comment f. Schools of thought.

> Where there are different schools of thought in a profession, or different methods are followed by different groups engaged in a trade, the actor is to be judged by the professional standards of the group to which he belongs. The law cannot undertake to decide technical questions of proper practice over which experts reasonably disagree, or to declare that those who do not accept particular controversial doctrines are necessarily negligent in failing to do so. There may be, however, minimum requirements of skill applicable to all persons, of whatever school of thought, who engage in any profession or trade. Thus any person who holds himself out as competent to treat human ailments must have a minimum skill in diagnosis, and a minimum knowledge of possible methods of treatment. Licensing statutes, or those requiring a basic knowledge of science for the practice of a profession, may provide such a minimum standard.

"While a defendant practicing a profession is entitled to be judged by the standard of care applicable to the professional school to which the defendant belongs, [citation], that standard is not always conclusive proof of due care." United Blood Services v. Quintana, 827 P.2d 509, 520 (Colo. 1992) (instructions erroneously created an irrebuttable presumption that a blood bank's compliance with practices of the blood bank community constituted due care regardless of whether those practices were unreasonably deficient in failing to employ available scientific safeguards).

Professional Malpractice. Negligence by a professional is referred to as professional malpractice, although the term "malpractice" also typically encompasses other forms of liability including breach of fiduciary duties and intentionally tortious conduct. The consequences of subjecting professionals to suit are suggested by the following passage discussing the standards applicable to art experts:

> Malpractice liability is not necessarily a bad thing for a profession. It provides an extra incentive to improve one's skills, maintain high professional standards and make referrals to specialists when the problem exceeds one's own level of competence. Over time, the less capable or less scrupulous members tend to be weeded out. In the field of art assessment, an additional benefit is the development of a clear standard of care that stresses the importance of observable and reportable facts in addition to purely subjective impressions.
>
> Malpractice suits also serve to educate the public about problem areas in the profession that would otherwise remain shrouded in secrecy, and about the availability of legal remedies....
>
> Malpractice exposure is not without its undesirable effects, however. The threat of litigation has had the effect of discouraging candid, unequivocal opinions and encouraging evaluations couched with disclaimers....Members of the public increasingly have difficulty finding a qualified [art] expert to render an opinion under any circumstances, anonymously or otherwise, with or without an exculpatory release. When they do find a willing expert, they pay higher fees because of the additional time required to perform the work more carefully and to document it fully.
>
> A final consequence of malpractice liability is the necessity for malpractice insurance....
>
> Ironically, the availability of malpractice insurance has increased the chances of an art expert being sued for malpractice, because a plaintiff is more likely to incur the expense and uncertainty of a lawsuit if he knows that there are substantial assets available to pay a judgment.[d]

Steven Mark Levy, *Liability of the Art Expert for Professional Malpractice*, 1991 Wis. L. Rev. 595, 650–51.

Malpractice principles have been applied to persons engaged in a wide range of callings, including, among others, physicians, attorneys, accountants, architects, pharmacists, nurses, dentists, pilots, engineers, and social workers. Any trade or profession with identifiable standards, or requiring specialized education, potentially falls within the scope of the rule. *Cf.* Franklin D. Ormsten, Norman B. Arnoff, and Gregg R. Evangelist, *Securities Broker Malpractice and Its Avoidance*, 25 Seton Hall L. Rev. 190, 190 (1994) (arguing that state and federal law and self-regulatory organization rules establish minimally appropriate standards for malpractice actions against brokers).

The following cases consider some basic principles applicable to doctors and lawyers.

---

d. Copyright 1991 by the University of Wisconsin. Reprinted by permission of the Wisconsin Law Review.

g. *Legal Malpractice and Medical Malpractice*

Hodges v. Carter

Supreme Court of North Carolina

80 S.E.2d 144 (N.C. 1954)

Civil action to recover compensation for losses resulting from the alleged negligence of defendants D.D. Topping and H.C. Carter, now deceased, in prosecuting, on behalf of plaintiff, certain actions on fire insurance policies.

On 4 June 1948 plaintiff's drug store building...was destroyed by fire.... [P]laintiff was insured under four policies of fire insurance.... He filed proof of loss with each of the four insurance companies.... The insurance companies severally rejected the proofs of loss, denied liability, and declined to pay any part of the plaintiff's losses....

H.C. Carter and D.D. Topping were at the time attorneys....As they were the ones from whom plaintiff seeks to recover, they will hereafter be referred to as the defendants.

   ....

On 3 May 1949 defendants, in behalf of plaintiff, instituted...four separate actions—one against each of the four insurers. Complaints were filed and summonses were issued....In each case the summons and complaint, together with copies thereof, were mailed to the Commissioner of Insurance of the State of North Carolina. The Commissioner accepted service of summons and complaint in each case and forwarded a copy thereof by registered mail to the insurance company named defendant therein.

Thereafter each defendant made a special appearance and moved to dismiss the action against it for want of proper service of process for that the Insurance Commissioner was without authority, statutory or otherwise, to accept service of process issued against a foreign insurance company doing business in this State.... [T]he judge presiding concluded that the acceptance of service of process by the Insurance Commissioner was valid....Each defendant excepted and appealed. This Court reversed. [Citations.]

On 4 March 1952 plaintiff instituted this action in which he alleges that the defendants were negligent in prosecuting his said actions in that they failed to (1) have process properly served, and (2) sue out alias summonses at the time the insurers filed their motions to dismiss the actions for want of proper service of summons, although they then had approximately sixty days within which to procure the issuance thereof.

   ....

At the hearing in the court below the judge, at the conclusion of plaintiff's evidence in chief, entered judgment of involuntary nonsuit. Plaintiff excepted and appealed.

BARNHILL, Chief Justice.

   ....

Ordinarily when an attorney engages in the practice of the law and contracts to prosecute an action in behalf of his client, he impliedly represents that (1) he possesses the requisite degree of learning, skill, and ability necessary to the practice of his profession and which others similarly situated ordinarily possess; (2) he will exert his best judgment in the prosecution of the litigation entrusted to him; and (3) he will exercise reasonable and ordinary care and diligence in the use of his skill and in the application of his knowledge to his client's cause. [Citations.]

An attorney who acts in good faith and in an honest belief that his advice and acts are well founded and in the best interest of his client is not answerable for a mere error of judgment or for a mistake in a point of law which has not been settled by the court of last resort in his State and on which reasonable doubt may be entertained by well-informed lawyers. [Citations.]

Conversely, he is answerable in damages for any loss to his client which proximately results from a want of that degree of knowledge and skill ordinarily possessed by others of his profession similarly situated, or from the omission to use reasonable care and diligence, or from the failure to exercise in good faith his best judgment in attending to the litigation committed to his care. [Citations.]

When the facts appearing in this record are considered..., it immediately becomes manifest that plaintiff has failed to produce a scintilla of evidence tending to show that defendants breached any duty the law imposed upon them when they accepted employment to prosecute plaintiff's actions against his insurers or that they did not possess the requisite learning and skill required of an attorney or that they acted otherwise than in the utmost good faith.

The Commissioner of Insurance is the statutory process agent of foreign insurance companies doing business in this State, G.S. §58-153, Hodges v. New Hampshire Insurance Co., 232 N.C. 475, 61 S.E.2d 372, and when defendants mailed the process to the Commissioner of Insurance for his acceptance of service thereof, they were following a custom which had prevailed in this State for two decades or more. Foreign insurance companies had theretofore uniformly ratified such service, appeared in response thereto, filed their answers, and made their defense. The right of the Commissioner to accept service of process in behalf of foreign insurance companies doing business in this State had not been tested in the courts. Attorneys generally, throughout the State, took it for granted that under the terms of G.S. §58-153 such acceptance of service was adequate. And, in addition, the defendants had obtained the judicial declaration of a judge of our Superior Courts that the acceptance of service by the Commissioner subjected the defendants to the jurisdiction of the court. Why then stop in the midst of the stream and pursue some other course?

Doubtless this litigation was inspired by a comment which appears in our opinion on the second appeal, Hodges v. Home Insurance Co., 233 N.C. 289, 63 S.E.2d 819. However, what was there said was pure dictum, injected—perhaps ill advisedly—in explanation of the reason we could afford plaintiff no relief on that appeal. We did not hold, or intend to intimate that defendants had been in any wise neglectful of their duties as counsel for plaintiff.

The judgment entered in the court below is affirmed.

Notes

1. *Mere Errors of Judgment.* Courts are divided over whether it is misleading to say (as the *Hodges* court did) that a professional is not liable for a "mere error of judgment." That language has been criticized as improperly suggesting that there is no liability for some negligent errors. *See, e.g., Riggins v. Mauriello,* 603 A.2d 827 (Del. 1992) (abandoning "mere error" language and indicating that a proper instruction in a medical malpractice case should state that "when a physician chooses between appropriate alternative medical treatments, harm which results from the physician's good faith choice of one proper alternative over the other is not malpractice").

2. *No Good-Faith Exception.* The reference to "good faith" in *Hodges* must be read carefully. According to Cosgrove v. Grimes, 774 S.W.2d 662, 664–65 (Tex. 1989):

> There is no subjective good faith excuse for attorney negligence. A lawyer...
> is held to the standard of care which would be exercised by a reasonably pru-
> dent attorney. The jury must evaluate his conduct based on the information
> the attorney has at the time of the alleged act of negligence. In some instances
> an attorney is required to make tactical or strategic decisions. Ostensibly, the
> good faith exception was created to protect this unique attorney work product.
> However, allowing the attorney to assert his subjective good faith, when the
> acts he pursues are unreasonable as measured by the reasonably competent
> practitioner standard, creates too great a burden for wronged clients to over-
> come.... The instruction to the jury should clearly set out the standard for neg-
> ligence in terms which encompass the attorney's reasonableness in choosing
> one course of action over another.

> If an attorney makes a decision which a reasonably prudent attorney *could*
> make in the same or similar circumstance, it is not an act of negligence even if
> the result is undesirable. Attorneys cannot be held strictly liable for all of their
> clients' unfulfilled expectations. An attorney who makes a reasonable decision
> in the handling of a case may not be held liable if the decision later proves to be
> imperfect. The standard is an objective exercise of professional judgment, not
> the subjective belief that his acts are in good faith....

Compare Bain v. Gillispie, 357 N.W.2d 47, 49 (Iowa App.1984) (there is no independent tort for basketball referee "malpractice"; "absent corruption or bad faith...no such
tort exists").

3. *Failure to Consider Debatable Questions.* Although there is no duty to predict the
ultimate resolution of unsettled legal questions, an attorney is obliged "to undertake
reasonable research in an effort to ascertain relevant legal principles and to make an informed decision as to a course of conduct based upon an intelligent assessment of the
problem." Smith v. Lewis, 530 P.2d 589 (Cal. 1975) (imposing liability on an attorney
who, as a result of ignorance, failed to claim that his client had a community property
interest in her husband's vested retirement benefits, even though that right was uncertain and there might have been reasons for forgoing the claim; "there is nothing strategic or tactical about ignorance"); Aloy v. Mash, 696 P.2d 656 (Cal. 1985) (defendant's
reliance on an incomplete reading of a single court decision presented a triable negligence issue; it was irrelevant that the claim the lawyer failed to pursue was determined
to be invalid ten years later in different litigation).

However, there are limits to how far this duty extends. In Darby & Darby, P.C. v. VSI
Int'l, Inc., 739 N.E.2d 744 (N.Y. 2000), a particular theory of insurance coverage had
been rejected in Florida and New York, the two states "most relevant" to the dispute,
and accepted by "only a handful of courts, particularly in California." The court wrote:

> We agree that attorneys should familiarize themselves with current legal de-
> velopments so that they can make informed judgments and effectively counsel
> their clients [citation]. However,...[the attorneys] in this case should not be
> held liable for failing to advise defendants about a novel and questionable the-
> ory pertaining to their insurance coverage [citation]. As one commentator
> noted, "[a] legal malpractice action is unlikely to succeed when the attorney
> erred because an issue of law was unsettled or debatable. The perfect vision
> and wisdom of hindsight is an unreliable test for determining the past exis-

tence of legal malpractice" [citation]. Because plaintiff acted in a manner that was reasonable and consistent with the law as it existed at the time of representation, it had no duty to inform defendants about possible "advertising liability" insurance coverage for their patent infringement litigation expenses.

4. *The "Trial within a Trial" Requirement and Its Limits.* In a legal malpractice action based on negligence, the plaintiff must prove that the defendant's breach of the applicable standard of care resulted in damage.

What this means as to errors in litigation is reasonably clear. If an attorney has failed to take appropriate action within the statute of limitations, the plaintiff ordinarily must establish not only that the deadline was missed, but that had the statute not run the plaintiff would have prevailed in the underlying action. Consequently, the plaintiff is faced with a heavy burden of proof. As to litigation errors, it is often said there must be a "trial within a trial." *See* Orrick Herrington & Sutcliff, LLP v. Superior Ct., 132 Cal. Rptr.2d 658 (Ct. App. 2003) (if malpractice involves negligence in the prosecution or defense of a claim, a case-within-a-case method is properly employed).

Transactional errors may entail a somewhat different approach to proof of causation of damage. Thus, in Viner v. Sweet, 70 P.3d 1046 (Cal. 2003), a case involving legal work relating to the sale of a business, the defendant argued, and the court agreed, that the plaintiffs were required to show that but for the defendant's negligence "(1) they would have had a more advantageous agreement (the "better deal" scenario), or (2) they would not have entered into the transaction...and therefore would have been better off (the "no deal" scenario)."

In addition, it is important to remember that many disputes are resolved by settlement, rather than by litigation, and a settlement may be based on considerations other than the strict legal merits. Thus, some courts have questioned the "trial within a trial" requirement. For example, in Estate of Campbell v. Chaney, 485 N.W.2d 421 (Wis. Ct. App. 1992), the attorneys were allegedly negligent in drafting a prenuptial agreement. As a result, the deceased client's estate was subjected to a claim by the decedent's widow, which it eventually settled. In the ensuing malpractice action, the court held that the estate was not required to prove that the agreement would have been held unenforceable if its validity had been litigated. Rather, the estate could recover if it showed that the negligence caused a weakness in the agreement, that the weakness of the agreement caused the litigation, and that the decision to settle the claim was caused by the weakness in the agreement, rather than by other facts establishing that the widow had a strong claim.

See also Vahila v. Hall, 674 N.E.2d 1164, 1169–70 (Ohio 1997), a case involving representation in various civil, criminal, and administrative proceedings, where the court noted that a "strict 'but for' test" for causation tends to over-protect errant attorneys and require the introduction of "remote and speculative" evidence. While acknowledging that "the requirement of causation often dictates that the merits of the malpractice action depend upon the merits of the underlying case," *Vahila* refused to "endorse a blanket proposition that requires a plaintiff to prove, in every instance, that he or she would have been successful in the underlying matter."

5. *Failure to Appeal.* Errors in litigation are sometimes corrected on appeal. Must a plaintiff demonstrate that an appeal was unsuccessful prior to suing for litigation malpractice? In Hewitt v. Allen, 43 P.3d 345, 348–49 (Nev. 2002), the court wrote:

> If an appeal would be a futile gesture, that is, the appeal would most likely be denied, then litigants should be able to forgo an appeal, or dismiss a pending appeal, without abandoning their legal malpractice actions....

... [T]he defendants in the legal malpractice action are able to assert, as an affirmative defense, that the proximate cause of the damages was not the attorney's negligence, but judicial error that could have been corrected on appeal.... [B]ecause the issue is raised in the context of an affirmative defense, the attorney defendant has the burden of proof to establish that an appeal would have been successful. Finally, whether an appeal is likely to succeed is a question of law to be determined by the trial court.

See also Sturgis v. Skokos, 977 S.W.2d 217, 222 (Ark. 1998) (holding that if an attorney negligently fails to appeal, whether the appeal would have succeeded is a question of law).

6. *Fee Offsets.* If an attorney working on a contingent fee basis negligently causes loss of the claim, should the aggrieved client receive the full value of the claim or the value of the claim minus the contingent fee? Although there is authority to the contrary, most courts refuse to make any reduction. *See* Foster v. Duggin, 695 S.W.2d 526 (Tenn. 1985) ("deduction of... [the malpracticing attorney's anticipated] fee would not fully compensate the client who has incurred additional legal fees in pursuing the malpractice action"; in an appropriate case the attorney may be entitled to a credit for expenses incurred on the client's behalf which ultimately benefitted the client). *See also* Campagnola v. Mulholland, Minion & Roe, 555 N.E.2d 611 (N.Y. 1990) (similar result).

7. *Collectibility.* Some courts also hold that a malpractice plaintiff must prove that the judgment which would have been won, but for the negligence of the defendant, would have been collectible. *See, e.g.,* Taylor Oil Co. v. Weisensee, 334 N.W.2d 27, 29 n.2 (S.D. 1983); Lavigne v. Chase, 50 P.3d 306 (Wash. Ct. App. 2002). Other courts subscribe to the view that because uncollectibility of a judgment should be treated as a matter constituting avoidance or mitigation of the consequences of one's negligent act, it must be pleaded and proved by the defendant as an affirmative defense. *See* Kituskie v. Corbman, 714 A.2d 1027 (Pa. 1998) (expressly rejecting majority rule to the contrary); Jourdain v. Dineen, 527 A.2d 1304, 1306 (Me. 1987) (same).

8. *Liability for Inadequate Settlements.* There is a split of authority as to whether an attorney is liable for negligence resulting in the client's acceptance of an inadequate settlement. Some courts hold that to permit such actions would "create chaos" in the civil litigation system, for lawyers "would be reluctant to settle a case for fear some enterprising attorney representing a disgruntled client will find a way to sue them for something that 'could have been done, but was not.'" Muhammad v. Strassburger, et al., 587 A.2d 1346, 1349 (Pa. 1991) (permitting only actions based on fraudulent inducement of inadequate settlements); *cf.* Schlomer by Bye v. Perina, 485 N.W.2d 399 (Wis. 1992) (no liability for delay which allegedly caused a lesser settlement).

Other courts, recognizing that litigants rely heavily on professional advice when deciding to accept or reject offers of settlement, insist that lawyers advise clients with respect to settlements with the same skill, knowledge, and diligence with which they must pursue other legal tasks. *See* Ziegelheim v. Apollo, 607 A.2d 1298 (N.J. 1992); *see also* Parker v. Wobber v. Miles & Stockbridge, P.C., 756 A.2d 526 (Md. 2000) (permitting contribution and indemnity claims related to allegedly negligent settlement by successor counsel).

9. *Informal Client Relationships.* An attorney owes a duty of care to anyone who becomes a client, even if the relationship is created informally. For example, suppose that during a social event an attorney promises a teacher to "check into" a legal question they have discussed. If the teacher reasonably relies on that promise and the statute of limitations runs before the attorney acts, the attorney is liable even though no lawyer-client

relationship was formally consummated. *See* Restatement, Third, of the Law Governing Lawyers §14 (1998) ("A relationship of client and lawyer arises when: (1) a person manifests to a lawyer the person's intent that the lawyer provide legal services for the person; and…(b) the lawyer fails to manifest lack of consent to do so, and the lawyer knows or reasonably should know that the person reasonably relies on the lawyer to provide the services…").

10. *Prospective Clients.* Lawyers even owe some duties to prospective clients, such as the duty to keep those persons' information confidential. *See* Restatement, Third, of the Law Governing Lawyers §15 (1998).

11. *Lawyers' Liability to Third Parties.* A duty of care may extend to intended third party beneficiaries of the attorney-client relationship, such as those who would benefit under a will or trust drafted by the attorney. *See* Lucas v. Hamm, 364 P.2d 685 (Cal. 1961); *see also* Flaherty v. Weinberg, 492 A.2d 618 (Md. 1985) (whether a mortgagee's attorney owed a duty to the mortgagor was a question of fact). In Meighan v. Shore, 40 Cal. Rptr.2d 744 (Cal. Ct. App. 1995), a lawyer representing a client in a medical malpractice action was negligent in failing to inform the client's wife that she might have a derivative claim for loss of consortium.

A duty may also extend to persons who foreseeably rely on documents provided by an attorney, such as opinion letters. *See* Petrillo v. Bachenberg, 655 A.2d 1354, 1359 (N.J. 1995).

Although until recently "attorneys were only liable to nonclients in narrowly circumscribed situations," today "the potential for liability exists in all areas of law practice." *See generally* Jay M. Feinman, *Attorney Liability to Nonclients*, 31 Tort & Ins. L.J. 735, 736 (1996).

However, some states follow a strict privity approach. *See* Barcelo v. Elliott, 923 S.W.2d 575 (Tex. 1996) (no liability to trust beneficiaries); Taco Bell Corp. v. Cracken, 939 F. Supp. 528 (N.D. Tex. 1996) (litigant had no right to recover from other parties' attorneys).

12. *Doctors' Liability to Third Parties.* In some states, duties to third parties may also be imposed on physicians. *See* Osborne v. U.S., 567 S.E.2d 677 (W. Va. 2002) (holding that the state's medical professional liability act permits a third party to bring suit against a health care provider for foreseeable injuries proximately caused by negligent treatment of a patient); Tenuto v. Lederle Labs., 687 N.E.2d 1300 (N.Y. 1997) (duty to warn parents of risks to their health resulting from vaccination of their child); DiMarco v. Lynch Homes-Chester County, Inc., 583 A.2d 422 (Pa. 1990) (claim stated by third person against doctor who negligently advised a patient with a communicable disease).

But see Schmidt v. Mahoney, 659 N.W.2d 552 (Iowa 2003) (physician who allegedly advised a seizure patient that she could safely operate a car owed no duty to a third party who was seriously injured when the patient suffered a seizure); Johnson v. Fine, 45 P.3d 441 (Okla. Ct. App. 2002) (doctor who failed to warn a patient of a possible drug reaction was not liable for injury and death of the patient's children resulting from an auto accident); Althaus v. Cohen, 756 A.2d 1166 (Pa. 2000) (special nature of the relationship between therapist and child patient in a sexual abuse case precluded recognition of a duty to the parents); Praesel v. Johnson, 967 S.W.2d 391 (Tex. 1998) (treating physicians do not have a common-law duty to third parties to warn epileptic patients not to drive).

13. *Superior Experience.* Courts generally hold that superior experience does not change the applicable standard of care. *See* Fredericks v. Castora, 360 A.2d 696 (Pa. Super. Ct. 1976) (declining to hold experienced truck drivers to a higher standard of

care). *See also* Heath v. Swift Wings, Inc., 252 S.E.2d 526 (N.C. Ct. App. 1979) (instructions erroneously defined negligence by referring to the "ordinary care and caution, which an ordinary prudent pilot *having the same training and experience as... [the defendant]*, would have used in the same or similar circumstances"; instruction should have referred to the minimum standard generally applicable to all pilots).

14. *Scope of Representation.* An attorney's duties to a client generally extend no further than the scope of the representation. *See* Lerner v. Laufer, 819 A.2d 471 (N.J. 2003) (an attorney hired to look over a settlement agreement hammered out by the client was not required to launch a full-blown investigation into whether she could lay claim to more of the marital estate).

15. *Assignment of Legal Malpractice Claims.* Suppose that a lawyer represents a client in the defense of a pending tort claim. If the client believes that the lawyer has committed malpractice during the representation, can the client settle the underlying case by assigning to the adverse party the right to sue the client's attorney for malpractice? Generally, no. *See* Kommavongsa v. Haskell, 67 P.3d 1068 (Wash. 2003) (permitting assignment would risk encouraging collusion with respect to stipulation of damages in the underlying litigation, condone abrupt and shameless shifting of positions, and make lawyers hesitant to accept the defense of defendants who are nearly judgment-proof or underinsured). However, there may be ways for inventive attorneys to surmount the no-assignment rule. *See* William D. Cobb, Jr., *Tactical Considerations in Defending Assigned Legal Malpractice Claims*, 34 St. Mary's L.J. 941 (2003).

Russo v. Griffin
Supreme Court of Vermont
510 A.2d 436 (Vt. 1986)

HILL, Justice.

This is a legal malpractice action. The trial court found for defendants.... We reverse.

.... In 1975, Mr. Russo... [turned over his Rutland, Vermont, paving business] to his two sons,... [Tony and Frank].

In early 1978, Frank entertained thoughts of purchasing a laundromat..., and he entered into discussions with his brother concerning the sale of his interest in the corporation.... [The negotiations culminated in a meeting in the office of Mr. Griffin, a Rutland attorney who in the past had done work for the corporation. Documents were prepared selling Frank's interest in the corporation to Tony.]

....

At no time during the meeting did defendant Griffin inform the corporation or Tony Russo, the sole remaining shareholder, of the desirability of obtaining a covenant not to compete or explain the implications thereof. Three months after the stock transfer, Frank went back into the paving business in Rutland in direct competition with the plaintiff corporation. A properly drafted noncompetition covenant would have prevented this from occurring.

At trial, plaintiff introduced two expert witnesses, both well-respected practicing attorneys from the Burlington area, who testified that defendant Griffin's failure to advise the corporation to exact a covenant not to compete deviated from the standard of care required of attorneys practicing in Vermont at that time. Defendants introduced two similarly qualified Rutland attorneys who testified that defendant Griffin's conduct comported with the standard of care then expected of Rutland attorneys.

The question for determination was clearly whether defendant Griffin's conduct violated the attorney standard of care as it existed at the time of the alleged breach....The [trial] court ultimately chose to accept the testimony of defendants', rather than plaintiff's, expert witnesses on the premise that "those attorneys whose practice primarily was conducted in the Rutland area prior to and during 1978 are more familiar with the standard of care then required of lawyers."

....The court concluded:

> The *standard of care in the Rutland area* in 1978 required of an attorney did not require him to suggest or recommend to a purchasing client that a noncompete agreement be obtained from a seller who is a relative and who has been a business associate for several years, the transaction not being one at arms length. (Emphasis added).

In Hughes v. Klein, 139 Vt. 232, 233, 427 A.2d 353, 354 (1981), this Court held that the standard of care within the legal profession required lawyers to exercise "the customary skill and knowledge which normally prevails at the time and place." We are now asked to reexamine the underlying rationale and continued vitality of the so-called locality rule.

The locality rule...was first applied to the medical profession approximately a century ago when there existed a great disparity between standards of practice in large urban centers and remote rural areas. [Citation.] "The rule was unquestionably developed to protect the rural and small town practitioner, who was presumed to be less adequately informed and equipped than his big city brother." [Citation.]

The shortcomings of the locality rule are well recognized. It immunizes persons who are sole practitioners in their community from malpractice liability and it promotes a "conspiracy of silence" in the plaintiffs' locality which, in many cases, effectively precludes plaintiffs from retaining qualified experts to testify on their behalf. [Citations.] Recent developments in technology and the trend toward standardization have further undermined support for the rule. [Citation.]

According to defendants, the reasoning of the courts which have rejected the locality rule in medical malpractice decisions is inapposite to legal malpractice. We disagree.

> The ability of the practitioner and the minimum knowledge required should not vary with geography. The rural practitioner should not be less careful, less able or less skillful than the urban attorney. The fact that a lower degree of care or less able practice may be prevalent in a particular local community should not dictate the standard of care.

Mallen & Levit, Legal Malpractice §254, at 334 (2d ed. 1981). Defendants correctly note that "knowledge of local practices, rules, or customs may be determinative of, and essential to, the exercise of adequate care and skill." *Id*. To argue this fact in support of continued application of the locality rule, however, is to confuse "the *degree* of 'skill and knowledge' and the relevance of local factors which constitute the *knowledge* required by the standard of care." *Id*. at 337. Although attorneys throughout this state may be required to familiarize themselves with local practices, rules or customs peculiar to their area, the crucial inquiry for malpractice purposes turns not on the substance of the underlying practice, rule, or custom but on whether a reasonable and prudent attorney can be expected to know of its existence and practical applications.

In selecting a territorial limitation on the standard of care, we believe that the most logical is that of the state. *See* Mallen & Levit, *supra*, at 336; *see also* Restatement, Second, of Torts §299A Comment g (1965)(allowance for variations in type of community or degree of skill and knowledge possessed by practitioners therein has seldom been made in legal profession as such variations either do not exist or are not worthy of recognition). In Vermont, the rules governing the practice of law do not vary from community to community but are the same throughout the state. Moreover, in order to practice law in Vermont attorneys must successfully complete the requirements for admission established by this Court and administered by the Vermont Board of Bar Examiners.

....Accordingly, we hold that the appropriate standard of care to which a lawyer is held in the performance of professional services is "that degree of care, skill, diligence and knowledge commonly possessed and exercised by a reasonable, careful and prudent lawyer in the practice of law in this jurisdiction." [Citations.]

Unlike the medical profession, the legal profession has not yet established a certification and licensing process which is national in scope. Mallen, *supra*, §254, at 337. Nevertheless, "[w]hen certain recognized specialties are involved a national standard may be appropriate." *Id.* These "national law" specialties might include federal taxation law, securities law, patent law, and bankruptcy law where the need for uniformity is clearly apparent. *Id.* at 338. Regardless of whether a state or national standard is applied, however, our holding points out the need to advise clients as to the limits of one's professional capabilities and to refer them to specialists in appropriate cases.

> In this case..., the trial court erroneously applied the locality rule in defining the applicable standard of care....Accordingly, the decision of the superior court is reversed and the cause is remanded for a new trial.

....

HAYES, Justice, concurring in part and dissenting in part.

I agree with the majority that the correct standard to which an attorney should be held in the performance of professional services is *not* the standard of his or her locality. If there are only two lawyers in a small town, and both are incompetent, they cannot set a standard of inferiority for a third who comes to town.

I disagree with the Court's holding that the applicable standard of care should be a *state* standard. Doctors in Vermont are required to adhere to standards based upon the medical profession generally. Lawyers should be subject to a similar standard....

....The law schools of today are truly national in legal training. Vermont and almost all other states give a multistate bar examination. Much of our continuing legal education is national in scope....

I would require that the standard of care for Vermont lawyers be based upon the legal profession generally, and I would reject a state or local standard.

Notes

1. *The Locality Rule.* The locality rule still retains a few adherents. *See* Hickson v. Martinez, 707 S.W.2d 919 (Tex. Ct. App. 1985) (reaffirming that a physician must "act as a reasonable and prudent physician in the same or similar community would have acted," but noting that "including the locality rule in the jury charge is unnecessary at

best" because it is a predicate for "admitting expert testimony and thus is a question of law, not fact").

Locality is sometimes treated as a relevant factor, even if it is not the principal determinant of the standard of care. *See* Vergara by Vergara v. Doan, 593 N.E.2d 185 (Ind. 1992) (abandoning the "same or similar" locality rule and holding that a physician must exercise that degree of care, skill, and proficiency exercised by reasonably careful, skillful, and prudent practitioners under the same or similar circumstances considering the locality, advances in the profession, availability of facilities, and whether the doctor is a specialist or general practitioner). *But see* Frank J. Cavico and Nancy M. Cavico, *The Nursing Profession in the 1990s: Negligence and Malpractice Liability*, 43 Clev. St. L. Rev. 557, 574 (1995) (although some courts treat "the community as merely one factor to be taken into consideration," in "most jurisdictions...the 'locality' rule and geographic considerations have been discarded altogether in favor of general, national, professional nursing standards"). *See also* Hall v. Hilbun, 466 So. 2d 856 (Miss. 1985) (defining the standard with reference to "minimally competent physicians in the same specialty or general field of practice throughout the United States, who have available to them the same general facilities, services, equipment, and options").

2. ***Duty to Recommend a Specialist.*** Like other professionals, a lawyer must refer a client to a specialist if, under the circumstances, a reasonably careful lawyer would do so. *See, e.g.*, Horne v. Peckham, 158 Cal. Rptr. 714, 724 (Ct. App. 1979) (general practitioner had a duty to refer a client seeking an irrevocable trust tax shelter to a tax law specialist). *See also* Salazar v. Ehmann, 505 P.2d 387, 389–90 (Colo. Ct. App. 1972) (a chiropractor must refer a patient to a medical doctor when the patient's problem is beyond the limits of chiropractic practice); *but see* Kerkman v. Hintz, 418 N.W.2d 795 (Wis. 1988) (chiropractor has no duty to refer patient to medical doctor).

Care must be exercised in making referrals. *Cf.* Greenberg v. Perkins, 845 P.2d 530 (Colo. 1993) (physician owed patient a duty not to injure her by referring her for testing of a type that would foreseeably result in injury, based on information known to the physician); Barry R. Temkin, *Can Negligent Referral to Another Attorney Constitute Legal Malpractice?*, 17 Touro L. Rev. 639 (2001).

3. ***Malpractice in Criminal Representation.*** Courts generally require a former criminal defendant to prove innocence of the crime charged, and any lesser included offenses, as an element of a malpractice claim alleging that counsel was negligent in conducting the defense. In part, the rule is intended to prevent parties who are "guilty in fact" from "profiting" from their wrongdoing. *See* Peeler v. Hughes & Luce, 909 S.W.2d 494 (Tex. 1995); Bailey v. Tucker, 621 A.2d 108 (Pa. 1993); Glenn v. Aiken, 569 N.E.2d 783 (Mass. 1991); Hicks v. Nunnery, 643 N.W.2d 809 (Wis. 2002). *But see* Shaw v. State, 861 P.2d 566 (Alaska 1993) (guilt is an affirmative defense); Krahn v. Kinney, 538 N.E.2d 1058 (Ohio 1989) (holding that a malpractice plaintiff need not first obtain reversal of criminal charges and noting that if an attorney's alleged negligence affects the plea bargaining process, the injury "is not a bungled opportunity for vindication, but a lost opportunity to minimize...[the accused's] criminal record").

4. ***Educational Malpractice.*** Courts have typically refused to recognize educational malpractice as a cause of action. Although the reasoning differs according to the nature of the claim, the decisions are often based on beliefs that the court system should not interfere in school administrative practices, that imposing negligence liability would subject schools to numerous burdensome claims, that judges and juries should not second-guess teachers on debatable pedagogical questions, and that

whether a student develops reading, writing, and other skills is influenced by many factors beyond the classroom, making it impossible in many cases to establish causation of harm.

Illustratively, courts have denied relief for alleged negligence in allowing a functionally illiterate student to graduate from high school (Peter W. v. San Francisco Unified Sch. Dist., 131 Cal. Rptr. 854 (Ct. App. 1976); Donohue v. Copiague Union Free Sch. Dist., 391 N.E.2d 1352 (N.Y. 1979)); misevaluating and misplacing a learning-disabled student (Hunter v. Board of Educ., 439 A.2d 582 (Md. 1982)); failing to provide remedial education (Meyers v. Medford Lakes Bd. of Educ., 489 A.2d 1240 (N.J. Super. Ct. App. Div. 1985)); failing to retest a child classified as mentally retarded (Hoffman v. Board of Educ., 400 N.E.2d 317 (N.Y. 1979)); and operation of a court reporting program (Finstad v. Washburn Univ. of Topeka, 845 P.2d 685 (Kan. 1993)).

A number of commentators have urged recognition of an educational malpractice action—thus far without much success. *See generally* Thomas G. Eschweiler, Comment, *Educational Malpractice in Sex Education*, 49 S.M.U. L. Rev. 101 (1995) (reviewing theories of liability). The most useful approach may be to distinguish seemingly imponderable cases broadly alleging negligent failure adequately to educate a child from more-manageable disputes asserting specific acts of mistesting or misplacement. *See* B.M. by Burger v. State, 649 P.2d 425 (Mont. 1982) (permitting a claim based on negligent administration of a special education program).

5. *Ethics in Law Practice: Non-Competition Agreements among Attorneys.* Courts will normally enforce a non-competition agreement of the type at issue in *Russo*, provided it is reasonable in terms of time and place. However, different standards apply to the legal profession, and between attorneys non-competition agreements will often be held invalid on ethical grounds.

> The reasons underlying the ethical rule are twofold. On the one hand, it protects the public from having only a restricted pool of attorneys from which to select counsel. On the other, the rule protects attorneys, particularly young practitioners, from bargaining away an important aspect of their right to open offices of their own upon leaving a firm or other employer. These considerations dictate that ordinary commercial standards not be used to evaluate the reasonableness of lawyer restrictive covenants.

Vincent R. Johnson, *Solicitation of Law Firm Clients by Departing Partners and Associates: Tort, Fiduciary, and Disciplinary Liability*, 50 U. Pitt. L. Rev. 1, 111–14 (1988).

6. *Punitive Damages for Malpractice.* If the facts are egregious and therefore establish more than mere negligence (*i.e.*, intentional wrongdoing or recklessness (or in some jurisdictions gross negligence)), punitive damages based on the attorney's misconduct may be recovered in a malpractice action. However, in an unusual decision Virginia has held that punitive damages ordinarily are not available because malpractice claims (including breach of fiduciary duty and constructive fraud), while sounding in tort, are really claims for breach of contract, for which punitive damages may not be awarded. *See* O'Connell v. Bean, 556 S.E.2d 741 (Va. 2002).

7. *Liability for "Lost" Punitive Damages.* May an attorney be held liable for "lost punitive damages"—punitive damages that might have been recovered from a third-person but for the lawyer's malpractice? In Ferguson v. Lieff, Cabraser, Heimann & Bernstein, 135 Cal. Rptr. 2d 46 (Cal. 2003), the court refused to recognize this element of malpractice damages, stating:

> Making a negligent attorney liable for lost punitive damages would not serve a
> societal interest, because the attorney did not commit and had no control over
> the intentional misconduct justifying the punitive damages award.

The court added that permitting recovery of lost punitive damages would also violate the public policy against speculative damages, necessitate an excessively complex standard of proof, and exact a significant social cost in terms of the cost and availability of malpractice insurance.

Boyce v. Brown

Supreme Court of Arizona
77 P.2d 455 (Ariz. 1938)

LOCKWOOD, Judge.

Berlie B. Boyce and Nannie E. Boyce, his wife,...brought suit against Edgar H. Brown,...to recover damages for alleged malpractice by the defendant upon the person of Nannie E. Boyce.... [A]t the close of the evidence for plaintiffs, the court granted a motion for an instructed verdict in favor of the defendant, on the ground that there was no competent testimony that he was guilty of any acts...sufficient, as a matter of law, to charge him with malpractice. Judgment was rendered on the verdict....

....

....The sole question for our consideration...is whether, taking the evidence as strongly as is reasonably possible in support of plaintiffs' theory of the case, as we must do when the court instructs a verdict in favor of defendant, there was sufficient evidence to sustain a judgment in favor of plaintiffs.

....About September 1, 1927, plaintiffs engaged the services of defendant...to reduce a fracture of Mrs. Boyce's ankle. This was done by means of an operation which consisted, in substance, of making an incision at the point of fracture, bringing the broken fragments of bone into apposition, and permanently fixing them in place by means of a metal screw placed in the bone. Defendant continued to attend Mrs. Boyce for three or four weeks following such operation until a complete union of the bone had been established, when his services terminated. There is no serious contention in the record that defendant did not follow the approved medical standard in the treatment of the fractured bone up to this time. No further professional relations existed between the parties until seven years later, in November, 1934, when Mrs. Boyce again consulted him, complaining that her ankle was giving her considerable pain. He examined the ankle, wrapped it with adhesive tape, and then filed the edge of an arch support, which he had made for her seven years before, and which, from use, had grown so thin that the edge was sharp. About a week later he removed the bandage. Her ankle, however, did not improve after this treatment, but continued to grow more painful until January, 1936....At this last-mentioned time she returned to defendant, who again examined the ankle. A few days later she went to visit Dr. Kent of Mesa, who, on hearing the history of the case, and noticing some discoloration and swelling, caused an X-ray of the ankle to be made. This X-ray showed that there had been some necrosis of the bone around the screw. Dr. Kent operated upon Mrs. Boyce, removing the screw, and she made an uneventful recovery, the ankle becoming practically normal.

There are certain general rules of law governing actions of malpractice, which are almost universally accepted by the courts, and which are applicable to the present situation. We state them as follows: (1) One licensed to practice medicine is presumed to possess the degree of skill and learning which is possessed by the average member of the medical profession in good standing in the community in which he practices, and to apply that skill and learning, with ordinary and reasonable care, to cases which come to him for treatment. If he does not…, he is guilty of malpractice. [Citation.] (2) Before a physician or surgeon can be held liable as for malpractice, he must have done something in his treatment of his patient which the recognized standard of good medical practice in the community in which he is practicing forbids in such cases, or he must have neglected to do something which such standard requires. [Citation.] (3)…[T]he standard of medical practice in the community must be shown by affirmative evidence, and, unless there is evidence of such a standard, a jury may not be permitted to speculate as to what the required standard is, or whether the defendant has departed therefrom. [Citations.] (4) Negligence on the part of a physician or surgeon in the treatment of a case is never presumed, but must be affirmatively proven, and no presumption of negligence nor want of skill arises from the mere fact that a treatment was unsuccessful, failed to bring the best results, or that the patient died. [Citation.] (5) The accepted rule is that negligence on the part of a physician or surgeon, by reason of his departure from the proper standard of practice, must be established by expert medical testimony, unless the negligence is so grossly apparent that a layman would have no difficulty in recognizing it. [Citations.] (6) The testimony of other physicians that they would have followed a different course of treatment than that followed by the defendant is not sufficient to establish malpractice unless it also appears that the course of treatment followed deviated from one of the methods of treatment approved by the standard in that community. [Citation.]

With these principles of the law…as a guide, let us consider the record.…Two questions present themselves to us: (a) What was the treatment which defendant gave Mrs. Boyce in November, 1934? and (b) What was the medical standard which he was required to conform to, under all the circumstances, in giving her treatment at that time?.…The evidence does not show that she ever came back to defendant for further treatment in November, 1934, or, indeed, until January, 1936.…The only testimony we have which, in any manner, bears upon medical standards or the proper treatment of Mrs. Boyce in November, 1934, is that of Dr. Kent, who performed the operation on the ankle in January, 1936, and of defendant. The latter testified that he did what was required by Mrs. Boyce's condition as it existed then.…He was asked as to how long prior to that time the screw should have been removed, and stated that he could not answer; that, if the ankle was in the same condition as it was when he operated, he would say that the screw should have been removed, but that it was impossible for him to testify as to when the condition justifying removal arose. He was questioned more fully and answered substantially that his first conclusion, if he had been in the position of defendant, when Mrs. Boyce called on the latter in November, 1934, would have been that arthritis in the ankle joint was causing the pain, but that he would not have been fully satisfied without having an X-ray made of the ankle.…Nowhere, however, did Dr. Kent testify as to what was the proper standard of medical care required at the time defendant treated Mrs. Boyce in 1934, or as to whether, in his opinion, the treatment given deviated from that standard. The nearest he came to such testimony was the statement that he personally would have had an X-ray taken, but he did not say the failure to do so was a deviation from the proper standard of treatment.

Counsel for plaintiffs, in their oral argument, apparently realized the weakness of their evidence on the vital point of what the proper medical standard required in 1934, and based their claim of negligence almost entirely upon the failure of defendant to take an X-ray of Mrs. Boyce's ankle at that time. They urge that this comes within the exception to the general rule, in that a failure to do so is such obvious negligence that even a layman knows it to be a departure from the proper standard. We think this contention cannot be sustained. It is true that most laymen know that the X-ray usually offers the best method of diagnosing physical changes of the interior organs of the body, and particularly of the skeleton, short of an actual opening of the body for ocular examination, but laymen cannot say that in all cases where there is some trouble with the internal organs that it is a departure from standard medical practice to fail to take an X-ray. Such things are costly and do not always give a satisfactory diagnosis, or even as good a one as other types of examination may give. In many cases the taking of an X-ray might be of no value and put the patient to unnecessary expense, and, in view of the testimony in the present case as to the arthritis which Mrs. Boyce had, and which Dr. Kent testified would have been his first thought as to the cause of Mrs. Boyce's pain in 1934, we think it is going too far to say that the failure to take an X-ray of Mrs. Boyce's ankle at that time was so far a departure from ordinary medical standards that even laymen would know it to be gross negligence. Since, therefore, there was insufficient evidence in the record to show that defendant was guilty of malpractice, under the rules of law above set forth, the court properly instructed a verdict in favor of the defendant.

The judgment of the superior court is affirmed.

Notes

1. Parts 1, 2, 3, and 6 of the charge in *Boyce* may be subject to objection. *See* Russo v. Griffin, 510 A.2d 436 (Vt. 1986), *supra* at 282.

See also Johnson v. Riverdale Anesthesia Assoc., 563 S.E.2d 431 (Ga. 2002) (because the "applicable standard of care is that employed by the medical profession generally and not what one individual doctor thought was advisable," it was impermissible to cross-examine an expert about what course he personally would have followed).

2. *"Average" Professional?* Part 1 of the charge refers to the "average" member of the profession. Consider the following:

> Not only would this ["average" standard] put a jury in a predicament as to how to arrive at an "average" but it seems to us that requiring the skill of the "average qualified practitioner" automatically makes approximately one-half of the doctors guilty of malpractice. The question is not one of the "average" or "medium" skill, but of the minimum skill.

Gambill v. Stroud, 531 S.W.2d 945, 950 (Ark. 1976); Hall v. Hilbun, 466 So. 2d 856 (Miss. 1985) ("such concepts as "average" are misleading and should be avoided . . . [for they] suggest that the lower 50 percent of our physicians regularly engage in medical malpractice").

3. *Matters of Common Knowledge.* As noted in the principal case, expert testimony is not necessary if the conduct required of a professional is a matter of common knowledge. *See* Schneider v. Haws, 118 S.W.3d 886 (Tex. App. 2003) (whether the failure to provide a patient with an escort or mechanism capable of safely returning her to the waiting room caused her to strike her head was a matter within the range of general experience and common sense, and therefore no expert testimony was needed); Sherbert v. Alcan Alum. Corp., 66 F.3d 965 (8th Cir. 1995) (expert testimony was not required to establish a breach of the standard of care applicable to a forklift operator because "One does not have to be a physicist to understand that tilting a 6,000 pound pile of slippery material, precariously balanced on the end of a forklift, involves the risk that some of the material will fall").

Some courts have narrowly interpreted this exception to the general rule. *See, e.g.,* Osborn v. Irwin Mem. Blood Bank, 7 Cal. Rptr. 2d 101 (Ct. App. 1992) ("Steps that should have been taken to safeguard the blood supply [from AIDS] in early 1983 are not matters of 'common knowledge'"). But others have been more generous. *See* Baiko v. Mays, 746 N.E.2d 618 (Ohio Ct. App. 2000) (failure of lawyer and accountant to review records and financial books was the type of malpractice that is within the common understanding of a lay jury); Rizzo v. Haines, 555 A.2d 58 (Pa. 1989) ("breach of the duty to investigate, and to inform one's client of, settlement offers does not require expert testimony").

4. *Expert Witnesses.* In legal malpractice actions, expert witnesses routinely rely on the rules relating to lawyer discipline (that is, state ethics codes paralleling the Model Rules of Professional Conduct) as evidence of the standard of care, even though those enactments typically provide that a violation does not automatically create a civil cause of action. The experts consider those provisions in preparing their opinions, and they refer to them on the witness stand. In some states, attorneys litigating malpractice suits may prepare demonstrative evidence, for use as part of the expert's testimony or perhaps in closing argument, showing in enlarged font the text of relevant disciplinary rules. This can be powerful evidence of what type of conduct is required of a lawyer, for disciplinary rules often speak in sharply mandatory terms, using words like "shall" and "shall not." It can be persuasive evidence in a case involving alleged mishandling of client trust funds to be able to point to a large exhibit quoting a disciplinary rule saying, for example, that "Upon receiving funds...a lawyer *shall* promptly notify the client.... *shall* promptly deliver [the funds] to the client...and... *shall* promptly render a full accounting...." *See* Model Rules of Prof. Conduct Rule 1.15 (2003) (emphasis added). However, at least one jurisdiction holds that the mere mention of the disciplinary rules at trial is error. *See* Hizey v. Carpenter, 830 P.2d 646 (Wash. 1992).

In medical malpractice actions, recommendations and warnings on drug manufacturers' package inserts and their annual compilation, the Physician's Desk Reference (PDR), are not by themselves sufficient to establish the standard of care; expert testimony is still required. *See* Morlino v. Medical Ctr., 706 A.2d 721 (N.J. 1998).

5. *Expert Witness Malpractice?* Can an expert witness be sued for malpractice? It is generally agreed that the in-court statements of an expert witness are protected by absolute immunity. Whether that immunity extends to the expert's pre-trial preparations—such as conducting tests or reviewing documents—is a matter of dispute. *See* Douglas R. Richmond, *The Emerging Theory of Expert Witness Malpractice,* 22 Cap. U.L. Rev. 693, 695–708 (1992). While acknowledging that "[c]ourts have generally afforded witnesses absolute immunity from liability linked to their testimony in order to free the judicial process of 'harassment or intimidation,'" and that "precious little on-point authority exists," the author argues that expert witness liability "should mirror the scheme of the potential liability to which trial lawyers are subject."

> There is no question that an attorney's defamatory statement during a judicial proceeding is shielded from subsequent attack under the doctrine of immunity. However, the same attorney remains liable to his or her own client for any acts of malpractice that occur in that very forum.

Id. at 708 (*quoting* Bruce v. Byrne-Stevens & Assoc. Eng'rs, Inc., 776 P.2d 666, 675 (Wash. 1989) (Pearson, J., dissenting)). *See also* LLMD of Mich., Inc. v. Jackson-Cross Co., 740 A.2d 186 (Pa. 1999) (immunity did not bar a malpractice action based on an expert's allegedly negligent performance of mathematical calculations required to determine lost profits); Jeffrey L. Harrison, *Reconceptualizing the Expert Witness: Social Costs, Current Controls, and Proposed Responses*, 18 Yale J. on Reg. 253 (2001) (noting a slight increase in expert witness liability). Only the rare decision has suggested that an expert witness owes a duty to the opposing party. *See* David v. Wallace, 565 S.E.2d 386 (W. Va. 2002) (holding that a "novel approach" of suing the opposing party's experts was not frivolous).

6. ***Ethics in Law Practice: Intimidating Experts.*** In Ky. Bar Assn. v. Mussler, 19 S.W.3d 87 (Ky. 2000), an attorney was publicly reprimanded for telling the opposing side's expert, during a deposition, that his client was filing suit against the expert based on the way in which the expert had conducted a medical examination of the client.

7. ***Hospitals and HMOs.*** Originally, hospitals were free from tort liability under the doctrine of charitable immunity. Since abrogation of that doctrine (*see* Chapter 18), at least three theories have been used to hold hospitals liable for the negligence of a physician. First, *respondeat superior* liability may be imposed if the doctor is employed by the hospital and the negligence occurs within the scope of the doctor's employment. Second, even if a doctor is an independent contractor, many courts hold there is an "ostensible agency" if the patient looks to the institution rather than the individual doctor for care or if the hospital "holds out" the physician as its employee. *See* Capan v. Divine Providence Hosp., 430 A.2d 647 (Pa. Super. Ct. 1980); Hill v. St. Clare's Hosp., 490 N.E.2d 823 (N.Y. 1986). Finally, an increasing number of courts have endorsed the theory of "corporate negligence," under which a hospital may be held liable for failure to review a doctor's treatment of patients or require consultation. *See* Darling v. Charleston Comm. Hosp., 211 N.E.2d 253 (Ill. 1965); Thompson v. Nason Hosp., 591 A.2d 703 (Pa. 1991). *See generally* Judith M. Kinney, *Note: Tort law—Expansion of Hospital Liability Under the Doctrine of Corporate Negligence*, 65 Temple L. Rev. 787 (1992).

The liability of HMOs for personal injury claims depends heavily on applicable statutes, administrative regulations, and contractual provisions. *See generally* Barbara A. Noah, *The Managed Care Dilemma: Can Theories of Tort Liability Adapt to the Realities of Cost Containment?*, 48 Mercer L. Rev. 1219, 1230–32 (1997) (noting that "patients have begun to succeed in pursuing tort claims against managed care organizations," even though "many HMO contracts require patients to settle disputes through internal appeals or arbitration").

8. ***Professional-Layperson Sexual Relations.*** According to one article, "[s]exual misconduct is the leading cause of action against psychologists, representing the greatest expense in defense costs and damages for their insurers." The malpractice theory is that "the patient has given the therapist enormous power by revealing intimate details…, and the therapist has a duty not to abuse that power [by becoming sexually involved with the patient]." Julie Gannon Shoop, *Dangerous Liaisons: Patients Sue Therapists for Sexual Abuse*, Trial, Oct. 1992, at 12–13. *See also* Linda Jorgenson, Rebecca Randles, and Larry Strasburger, *The Furor Over Psychotherapist-Patient Sexual Contact: New Solutions to an Old Problem*, 32 Wm. & Mary L. Rev. 645, 689 (1991) ("Because the major health care organizations have universally condemned intimate sexual contact with a patient, proving a breach of care is generally not difficult…"). *But see* Vallinoto v. DiSandro, 688 A.2d 830 (R.I. 1997) (legal malpractice claim rejected where the client produced no evidence that legal services were traded for sexual favors or that the unprofessional personal relationship harmed the legal representation).

9. ***Statutes Relating to Malpractice.*** As noted in Chapter 4, numerous tort-reform statutes have modified the rules applicable to medical malpractice actions. For example,

a recent statute in Texas (Tex. Civ. Prac. & Rem. Code §74.301 *et seq.* (Westlaw 2003)) limits non-economic damages for a "health care liability claim" to "$250,000 for each claimant, regardless of the number of defendant physicians or health care providers other than a health care institution against whom the claim is asserted or the number of separate causes of action on which the claim is based"(§74.301(a)). The law also imposes strict requirements with respect to expert witnesses and their reports (§74.351). Another provision caps damages in medical malpractice cases resulting in death:

TEX. CIV. PRAC. & REM. CODE §74.303
(Westlaw 2004)

(a) In a wrongful death or survival action on a health care liability claim where final judgment is rendered against a physician or health care provider, the limit of civil liability for all damages, including exemplary damages, shall be limited to an amount not to exceed $500,000 for each claimant, regardless of the number of defendant physicians or health care providers against whom the claim is asserted or the number of separate causes of action on which the claim is based.

(b) When there is an increase or decrease in the consumer price index...the liability limit prescribed in Subsection (a) shall be increased or decreased....

(c) Subsection (a) does not apply to the amount of damages awarded on a health care liability claim for the expenses of necessary medical, hospital, and custodial care received before judgment or required in the future for treatment of the injury.

Statutes also affect other types of malpractice actions. *See, e.g.,* N.J. Stat. Ann. 2a:53A-27 (Westlaw 2004) (requiring the filing of an expert "affidavit of merit" within 60 days of the defendant's answer in all professional malpractice actions against a "licensed person in his profession or occupation"). *See also* Cherie Song, *States Move to Curb Nursing Home Suits*, Nat'l L.J., July 8, 2003 ("[s]tate legislatures across the nation are moving to cap damages in suits against nursing homes").

See also Michael Flynn, *Physician Business (Mal)Practice*, 20 Hamline L. Rev. 333 (1996) (arguing that despite the trend toward tort reform, courts should hold physicians accountable for unscrupulous business practices under state deceptive trade practices laws); Martha Chamallas, *The Architecture of Bias: Deep Structures in Tort Law*, 146 U. Pa. L. Rev. 463, 520 (1998) (discussing a study showing that capping noneconomic damages for pain and suffering and loss of enjoyment of life would have a disparate effect on women because the non-economic portion of the tort award is crucial for women plaintiffs).

10. *How Effective Is the Law of Medical Malpractice?* There is no real doubt that many patients are injured by the carelessness of doctors. The much-discussed "Harvard Study" of medical practices concluded that some 99,000 patients suffered serious injuries while in hospitals in New York State during 1984; 13,000 of them died from those injuries. The findings of a number of other studies are similar. *See generally* Don Dewees, David Duff & Michael Trebilcock, Exploring the Domain of Accident Law, Chapter 3 (1996) (also pointing out that "credible" claims have been made that approximately five percent of American doctors are incompetent). What is disputed is whether medical malpractice litigation has been reasonably successful at holding negligent physicians liable and exonerating doctors in cases in which bad patient outcomes were not caused by physician error. In other words, do judgments and settlements in mal-

practice cases distinguish good doctors, whose patients have had unfortunate outcomes through no fault of the doctors, from butchers, or do they fall largely at random? Assuming that the law does hit the right targets, do physicians and health-care organizations respond to the law in socially desirable ways—for example, by encouraging doctors to use safer procedures, better diagnostic tests, and the like? Does the "customary practice" standard for physician liability discourage untried and dangerous treatments, or does it encourage doctors to stick with old ways of doing things even if better approaches are available? Do doctors perform unnecessary and expensive tests as a sort of insurance against being sued for malpractice? Unfortunately, solid data on these questions are hard to come by.

The Harvard Study of medical malpractice concluded that malpractice is widespread and that the legal results correlate poorly with quality of care: most patients injured by malpractice do not even sue, and most suits that are filed are without merit. One of the study's authors concedes, however, that the tort system "has played a valuable role in stimulating broad-based improvements" in medical care and that the threat of malpractice suits "reduce[s] the danger of negligent injuries occurring"; Paul C. Weiler, Medical Malpractice on Trial 91 (1991).

Even when hard facts are available, it may be difficult to say what the significance of those facts is. For example, it is clear that the high cost of malpractice insurance for obstetricians—who pay much more for malpractice insurance than do most other doctors—has caused many medical students to choose other specialties and has led many general practitioners to refuse to deliver babies. Whether these developments are a good thing (because they encourage only the best doctors to deliver babies) or a bad thing (because they make obstetric care less widely available than it would otherwise be) is unknown.

For detailed discussions of the Harvard study, see Weiler, *supra*, and Paul C. Weiler, Howard H. Hyatt, Joseph P. Newhouse, William G. Johnson, Troyen A. Brennan & Lucian L. Leape, A Measure of Malpractice: Medical Injury, Malpractice Litigation, and Patient Compensation (1993). This study and many others are discussed and cited in Dewees, et al., *supra*.

Scott v. Bradford

Supreme Court of Oklahoma
606 P.2d 554 (Okla. 1979)

DOOLIN, Justice.

This appeal is taken by plaintiffs…from a judgment in favor of defendant rendered on a jury verdict in a medical malpractice action.

Mrs. Scott's physician advised her she had several fibroid tumors on her uterus. He referred her to defendant surgeon. Defendant admitted her to the hospital where she signed a routine consent form prior to defendant's performing a hysterectomy. After surgery, Mrs. Scott experienced problems with incontinence. She visited another physician who discovered she had a vesico-vaginal fistula which permitted urine to leak from her bladder into the vagina. This physician referred her to an urologist who, after three surgeries, succeeded in correcting her problems.

Mrs. Scott, joined by her husband, filed the present action alleging medical malpractice, claiming defendant failed to advise her of the risks involved or of available alternatives to surgery. She further maintained had she been properly informed she would have refused the surgery.

. . . .

The issue involved is whether Oklahoma adheres to the doctrine of informed consent as the basis of an action for medical malpractice, and if so did the present instructions adequately advise the jury of defendant's duty.

Anglo-American law starts with the premise of thoroughgoing self-determination, each man considered to be his own master. This law does not permit a physician to substitute his judgment for that of the patient by any form of artifice. The doctrine of informed consent arises out of this premise.

Consent to medical treatment, to be effective, should stem from an understanding decision based on adequate information about the treatment, the available alternatives, and the collateral risks. This requirement, labeled "informed consent," is, legally speaking, as essential as a physician's care and skill in the *performance* of the therapy. The doctrine imposes a duty on a physician or surgeon to inform a patient of his options and their attendant risks. If a physician breaches this duty, patient's consent is defective, and physician is responsible for the consequences.

If treatment is completely unauthorized and performed without any consent at all, there has been a battery. However, if the physician obtains a patient's consent but has breached his duty to inform, the patient has a cause of action sounding in negligence for failure to inform the patient of his options, regardless of the due care exercised at treatment, assuming there is injury.

. . . .

... [E]arlier decisions seemed to perpetuate medical paternalism by giving the profession sweeping authority to decide unilaterally what is in the patient's best interests....

More recently, in perhaps one of the most influential informed consent decisions, Canterbury v. Spence, 150 U.S. App. D.C. 263, 464 F.2d 772 (D.C. Cir. 1972), *cert. den.,* 409 U.S. 1064, the doctrine [of informed consent] received perdurable impetus. Judge Robinson...emphasized the fundamental concept in American jurisprudence that every human being of adult years and sound mind has a right to determine what shall be done with his own body. True consent to what happens to one's self is the informed exercise of a choice. This entails an opportunity to evaluate knowledgeably the options available and the risks attendant upon each. It is the prerogative of every patient to chart his own course and determine which direction he will take.

The decision in *Canterbury* recognized the tendency of some jurisdictions to turn this duty on whether it is the custom of physicians practicing in the community to make the particular disclosure to the patient. That court rejected this standard and held the standard measuring performance of the duty of disclosure is conduct which is reasonable under the circumstances: "[We can not] ignore the fact that to bind disclosure obligations to medical usage is to arrogate the decision on revelation to the physician alone." We agree. A patient's right to make up his mind whether to undergo treatment should not be delegated to the local medical group. What is reasonable disclosure in one instance may not be reasonable in another. We decline to adopt a standard based on the professional standard. We, therefore, hold the scope of a physician's communications must be measured by his patient's need to know enough to enable him to make an intelligent choice. In other words, full disclosure of all *material risks* incident to treatment must be made. There is no bright line separating the material from the immaterial; it is a question of fact. A risk is material if it would be likely to affect patient's decision. When non-disclosure of a particular risk is open to debate, the issue is for the finder of facts.

This duty to disclose is the first element of the cause of action in negligence based on lack of informed consent. However, there are exceptions creating a privilege of a physician not to disclose. There is no need to disclose risks that either ought to be known by everyone or are already known to the patient. Further, the primary duty of a physician is to do what is best for his patient and where full disclosure would be detrimental to a patient's total care and best interests a physician may withhold such disclosure, for example, where disclosure would alarm an emotionally upset or apprehensive patient. Certainly too, where there is an emergency and the patient is in no condition to determine for himself whether treatment should be administered, the privilege may be invoked.

The patient has the burden of going forward with evidence tending to establish *prima facie* the essential elements of the cause of action. The burden of proving an exception to his duty and thus a privilege not to disclose, rests upon the physician as an affirmative defense.

The cause of action, based on lack of informed consent, ... requires that plaintiff patient would have chosen no treatment or a different course of treatment had the alternatives and material risks of each been made known to him. If the patient would have elected to proceed with treatment had he been duly informed of its risks, then the element of causation is missing. In other words, a causal connection exists between physician's breach of the duty to disclose and patient's injury when and only when disclosure of material risks incidental to treatment would have resulted in a decision against it. A patient obviously has no complaint if he would have submitted to the treatment if the physician had complied with his duty and informed him of the risks. This fact decision raises the difficult question of the correct standard on which to instruct the jury.

The court in Canterbury v. Spence, *supra*, ... permits liability only if non-disclosure would have affected the decision of a fictitious "reasonable patient," even though actual patient testifies he would have elected to forego therapy had he been fully informed.

. . . .

Although the *Canterbury* rule is probably that of the majority, its "reasonable man" approach has been criticized by some commentators as backtracking on its own theory of self-determination. The *Canterbury* view certainly severely limits the protection granted an injured patient. To the extent the plaintiff, given an adequate disclosure, would have declined the proposed treatment, and a reasonable person in similar circumstances would have consented, a patient's right of self-determination is *irrevocably lost*. This basic right to know and decide is the reason for the full-disclosure rule. Accordingly, we decline to jeopardize this right by the imposition of the "reasonable man" standard.

If a plaintiff testifies he would have continued with the proposed treatment had he been adequately informed, the trial is over under either the subjective or objective approach. If he testifies he would not, then the causation problem must be resolved by examining the credibility of plaintiff's testimony. The jury must be instructed that it must find plaintiff would have refused the treatment if he is to prevail.

Although it might be said this approach places a physician at the mercy of a patient's hindsight, a careful practitioner can always protect himself by insuring that he has adequately informed each patient he treats. If he does not breach this duty, a causation problem will not arise.

The final element of this cause of action is that of injury. The risk must actually materialize and plaintiff must have been injured as a result of submitting to the treatment.

Absent occurrence of the undisclosed risk, a physician's failure to reveal its possibility is not actionable.

....

Because we are imposing a new duty on physicians, we hereby make this opinion prospective only, affecting those causes of action arising after the date this opinion is promulgated.

....The instructions objected to did instruct that defendant should have disclosed material risks of the hysterectomy and feasibility of alternatives. Instructions are sufficient when considered as a whole they present the law applicable to the issues....We find no basis for reversal.

Affirmed.

[The opinion of Justice BARNES, concurring in part and dissenting in part, has been omitted.]

Notes

1. *Objective Test.* Most cases have rejected a subjective test in informed consent cases. *See* Ashe v. Radiation Oncology Assoc., 9 S.W.3d 119 (Tenn. 2000) (endorsing the majority objective standard); Pauscher v. Iowa Methodist Med. Ctr., 408 N.W.2d 355 (Iowa 1987) (holding that under the objective test there was no duty to disclose a 1 in 100,000 risk).

2. *Disclosure of Physician's Interests and Experience.* Moore v. Regents of the Univ. of Cal., 793 P.2d 479 (Cal. 1990), extended the informed-consent doctrine to require disclosure of the physician's economic or research interests in the proposed medical procedure. *See also* Howard v. Univ. of Med., 800 A.2d 73 (N.J. 2002) ("a serious misrepresentation concerning the quality or extent of a physician's professional experience...can be material to the grant of intelligent and informed consent").

3. *Disclosure of Life Expectancy.* A physician has no duty as a matter of law to disclose life-expectancy information to a patient, but disclosure may be required under the facts of a particular case. Arato v. Avedon, 858 P.2d 598 (Cal. 1993).

4. *Battery versus Negligence.* In Mink v. University of Chicago, 460 F. Supp. 713 (N.D. Ill. 1978), the court wrote:

> While early cases treated lack of informed consent as vitiating the consent to treatment so there was liability for battery, the modern view "is that the action...is in reality one for negligence in failing to conform to the proper standard, to be determined on the basis of expert testimony as to what disclosure should be made."....
>
> ...[W]e find the analysis of the court in Cobbs v. Grant, 8 Cal.3d 229, 104 Cal. Rptr. 505, 512, 502 P.2d 1, 8 (1972), persuasive:
>
> > The battery theory should be reserved for those circumstances when a doctor performs an operation to which the patient has not consented. When the patient gives permission to perform one type of treatment and the doctor performs another, the requisite element of deliberate intent to deviate from the consent given is present. However, when the patient consents to certain treatment and the doctor performs that treatment but an undisclosed inherent complication with a low probability occurs, no in-

tentional deviation from the consent given appears; rather, the doctor in obtaining consent may have failed to meet his due care duty to disclose pertinent information. In that situation the action should be pleaded in negligence.

See also Ashcraft v. King, 278 Cal. Rptr. 900 (Ct. App. 1991) (surgeon committed battery if patient's consent to an operation was conditioned on the use of family-donated blood and the surgeon intentionally violated that condition). What ramifications does classification of the tort as battery or negligence have for efforts to reach the defendant's malpractice insurance? What about the consequences for defenses, immunities, *respondeat superior*, and punitive damages?

5. *Informed-Consent Statutes.* In some states, the common-law doctrine of informed consent in medicine has been augmented or replaced by statutory developments. For example, Texas has adopted detailed legislation (Tex. Civ. Prac. & Rem. Code §74.101 *et seq.* (Westlaw 2003)) which creates a state Medical Disclosure Panel "to determine which risks and hazards related to medical care and surgical procedures must be disclosed by health care providers or physicians...and to establish the general form and substance of such disclosure." *Id.* at §74.102(a). The making or failure to make specified disclosures creates certain rebuttable presumptions in litigation. *Id.* at §74.106(a). "If medical care or surgical procedure is rendered with respect to which the disclosure panel has made no determination either way regarding a duty of disclosure, the physician or health care provider is under the duty otherwise imposed by law." *Id.* at §74.106(b).

6. *Contributory Negligence in Informed-Consent Cases.* In Brown v. Dibbell, 595 N.W.2d 358 (Wis. 1999), the court held that a patient's contributory negligence could be a defense in an action under the state medical informed-consent statute. The court wrote:

> A patient is usually the primary source of information about the patient's material personal, family and medical histories. If a doctor is to provide a patient with the information required by Wis. Stat. §448.30, it is imperative that in response to a doctor's material questions a patient provide information that is as complete and accurate as possible under the circumstances. We therefore conclude that for patients to exercise ordinary care, they must tell the truth and give complete and accurate information about personal, family and medical histories to a doctor to the extent possible in response to the doctor's requests for information....

However, the court opined that a patient ordinarily could not be found to be contributorily negligent based on failure to ascertain the accuracy or completeness of information presented by the doctor or by reason of choosing one viable mode of medical treatment presented by the doctor over another.

7. *Informed Consent in Legal Malpractice.* Informed consent principles apply as readily in law as in medicine. *See* Sierra Fria Corp. v. Donald J. Evans, P.C., 127 F.3d 175, 179–80 (1st Cir. 1997). In *Sierra*, the court wrote:

> [W]hen a client seeks advice from an attorney, the attorney owes the client "a duty of full and fair disclosure of facts material to the client's interests." [Citation.] This means that the attorney must advise the client of any significant legal risks involved in a contemplated transaction, and must do so in terms sufficiently plain to permit the client to assess both the risks and their potential impact on his situation....

Id. (*citing* Williams v. Ely, 668 N.E.2d 799, 806 (Mass. 1996)). However, the court found that the evidence supported a finding that the law firm repeatedly warned its client of the dangers of consummating a property purchase without a survey, and therefore the client could not later complain when he discovered that the tennis courts, parking spaces, and other assets he thought he had bought were on land belonging to an adjoining complex. *See also* Vincent R. Johnson, *"Absolute and Perfect" Candor to Clients,* 34 St. Mary's L.J., 737, 749 & n. 37 (2003).

8. ***Ethics in Law Practice: Client Decisionmaking.*** Comment 1 to Rule 1.2 of the Model Rules of Professional Conduct (2003) states:

> [T]he client [has] the ultimate authority to determine the purposes to be served by legal representation, within the limits imposed by law and the lawyer's professional obligations.... With respect to the means by which the client's objectives are to be pursued, the lawyer shall consult with the client...and may take such action as is impliedly authorized to carry out the representation.

9. ***Standard of Care for Medical Entities.*** In some suits against an entity, such as hospital or blood bank, it makes sense to frame the standard of care in terms of what would be done by other similar institutions. *See* De Martini v. Alexander Sanitarium, Inc., 13 Cal. Rptr. 564 (Ct. App. 1961) ("that degree of care, skill, and diligence used by hospitals generally"); Osborn v. Irwin Mem. Blood Bank, 7 Cal. Rptr. 2d 101 (Ct. App. 1992) ("'that reasonable degree of skill, knowledge, and care ordinarily possessed and exercised' by other blood banks").

However, in other cases, where the plaintiff simply seeks to hold an entity liable vicariously for the acts of a medical professional, a more precise analysis may be required. *See* Cox v. Flint Bd. Of Hosp. Managers, 651 N.W.2d 356 (Mich. 2002) (a jury instruction substituting "hospital neonatal intensive care unit" for the specific profession or specialities at issue improperly relieved parents of their burden of proof as to hospital's vicarious liability).

10. ***Tortious Breach of Confidentiality.*** The unauthorized disclosure of nonpublic medical information relating to a patient may be actionable under a variety of theories, including invasion of privacy, breach of contract, or violation of statute. Some states simply recognize an independent common-law tort action for breach of confidence in the physician-patient setting. *See* Biddle v. Warren Gen. Hosp., 715 N.E.2d 518 (Ohio 1999).

h. Gender

In tort law, the same standard of care applies to both men and women. However, recent years have seen the emergence of an important school of jurisprudence often described as "Law and Feminism." To simplify a complex subject greatly, feminists are somewhat divided in their approach to such matters as the place of women as participants in the legal system. Years ago, when stereotypes were somewhat more prevalent than today, feminists emphasized similarities between men and women, in opposition, for example, to those who thought that women weren't "tough enough" to be lawyers. Today, some feminist scholars tend to focus upon differences between the ways in which men and women look at the world, in the hope that feminist views will reveal ways in which "male thinking" has (mis)shaped the law.

In *A Lawyer's Primer on Feminist Theory and Tort*, 38 J. Legal Educ. 3 (1988), Professor Leslie Bender argues that negligence law is permeated by traditional male values and perspectives:

Our legal system...is a system that resolves problems through male inquiries formulated from distanced, abstract, and acontextual vantage points, while feminism emphasizes relationships, context, and factual particulars for resolving human problems.

Turning to the reasonable person standard, Professor Bender writes:

It was originally believed that the "reasonable man" standard was gender neutral. "Man" was used in the generic sense to mean person or human being. But man is not generic except to other men. Would men regard a "prudent woman" standard as an appropriate measure of their due care? As our social sensitivity to sexism developed, our legal institutions did the "gentlemanly" thing and substituted the neutral word "person" for "man.".... The language of tort law was neutered, made "politically correct," and sensitized. Although tort law protected itself from allegations of sexism, it did not change its content and character.

....When the standard was written into judicial opinions, treatises, and casebooks, it was written about and by men....When the authors of such works said "reasonable man," they meant "male," "man" in a gendered sense. The legal world that generated the "reasonable man" was predominantly, if not wholly, male....When...[the term] was converted to "reasonable person," it still meant "person who is reasonable by my standards" almost exclusively from the perspective of a male judge, lawyer, or law professor, or even a female lawyer trained to be "the same as" a male lawyer.

Changing the word without changing the underlying model does not work....

....

....If we are wedded to the idea of an objective measure, would it not be better to measure the conduct of a tortfeasor by the care that would be taken by a "neighbor" or "social acquaintance" or "responsible person with conscious care and concern for another's safety"?

Perhaps we have gone astray in tort-law analysis because we use "reason" and caution as our standard of care, rather than focusing on care and concern....

....

....Tort law should begin with a premise of responsibility rather than rights, or interconnectedness rather than separation, and a priority of safety rather than profit or efficiency. The masculine voice of rights, autonomy, and abstraction has led to a standard that protects efficiency and profit; the feminine voice can design a tort system that encourages behavior that is caring about others' safety and responsive to others' needs or hurts, and that attends to human contexts and consequences.[e]

Other feminists have questioned Bender's assumption that negligence standards and cases are always based on a "male" perspective. Professor Margo Schlanger has examined three categories of nineteenth and early twentieth century cases, those involving injuries to women who were car and wagon passengers, those involving injuries to female wagon drivers, and those involving injuries to women getting on and off trains. She writes that:

---

e. Reprinted with permission.

[r]eported decisions in these categories evince common understandings of gender differences courts considered relevant: that wives had less authority than husbands, that women were less competent in the public sphere of transportation than men, and that women were less physically agile than men.... The results of...[the] interplay [between those understandings and tort doctrine] were as complex as gender differences and tort law themselves...[O]ne solid conclusion to be drawn from all three categories is that, as might be expected given the existence of female accident victims and the importance of gender to social ordering, the accusation of erasure of gender difference is incorrect. Far from naively erasing gender by subsuming women into the male category of "reasonable men" or a purportedly neutral, but no less male category of "reasonable persons," courts actually treated gender as an important factor in assessing appropriate standards of care. Neither do the cases support a charge of invariable refusal to take account of women's experience, or of consistent deprecation of women's capabilities. Each of the three categories of opinions serves as a case study of tort law's intricate interaction with gender difference, illuminating the diversity of possible and actual legal approaches to thinking about women's agency, authority, and capabilities. Together, in rhetoric, analysis, and result, they present a world frequently, although not uniformly, friendly to women and their needs.

Margo Schlanger, *Injured Women Before Common Law Courts, 1860–1930*, 21 Harv. Women's L.J. 79 (1998).

Even if the historical background of the reasonable person standard is more complicated than Bender suggests, do Bender's observations shed interesting light on tort law? How would tort law be different if it began with a premise of responsibility, care, and connectedness? For example, would loss of consortium compensation be broader or narrower than it is?

Note

1. *"Masculine" and "Feminine" Thinking?* The proposition that men and women approach many social issues differently is often asserted but has been the subject of little empirical investigation. For an attempt to measure the extent to which the proposition is true, see William J. Turnier, Pamela Johnson Conover & David Lowery, *Redistributive Justice and Cultural Feminism*, 45 Am. U.L. Rev. 1275 (1996). Using regression analysis of polling data, Professors Turnier, Conover, and Lowery attempted to measure the extent to which men and women differ in supporting redistributive taxation and redistributive spending. Their study found women somewhat more supportive than men of redistributive spending measures, but somewhat less supportive than men of redistributive taxation. In both cases, the differences were quite small: factors like age, income level, and political affiliation were as good as or better than sex as predictors of support for redistributive measures. Further empirical work on this important question can be expected.

2. Judge-Made Standards

As noted earlier, one of the disadvantages of allowing the finder of fact to determine on a case-by-case basis whether a particular defendant has exercised reasonable care is that similar cases may give rise to different results. Disparities may arise solely because of differences in the temperaments of juries, or the skills of counsel, or the attractiveness, in the eyes of the jurors, of the parties. Another disadvantage is that a prospective defendant is given no clear notice of what conduct is expected. In addition, when the same fact patterns recur, judicial resources may be wasted in hearing and resolving largely identical suits.

A possible approach to the reasonable care question is for a court, in the context of a given case, to attempt to articulate definite rules of conduct on issues of continuing importance. That is, in abstract terms, a court could rule that "In situation X, it is negligent as a matter of law for a person not to do Y." Theoretically, this rule would then be followed in subsequent cases involving situation X, thereby eliminating the problem of inconsistent results. The existence of the rule would give potential defendants notice of what level of care is expected. It would also encourage out-of-court settlements, because the outcome of litigation under the rule would be more predictable.

The difficulty with this approach is that even apparently similar disputes frequently involve important details which call for a result contrary to the general rule. For example, early in the twentieth century, accidents in which cars had been struck by trains after proceeding across railroad tracks where vision was obstructed were common. Attempting to resolve the matter "once and for all," Justice Oliver Wendell Holmes, in B & O R. Co. v. Goodman, 275 U.S. 66 (1927), wrote: "[I]f a driver cannot be sure otherwise whether a train is dangerously near he must stop and get out of his vehicle...and look." The rule seemed sensible, but in practice it proved unrealistic. Road conditions vary greatly from one place to another, and it is impossible to say with certainty that it is always less dangerous to get out of one's car and reconnoiter than to proceed ahead with caution. The Court's effective repudiation of the *Goodman* rule in Pokora v. Wabash Ry. Co., 292 U.S. 98 (1934), just seven years after its adoption, stands as a lesson that courts should be cautious in articulating inflexible rules to govern varying and complex occurrences.

Suppose the issue is whether the failure of the driver of a car to wear a seat belt was negligent. This may be a matter on which reasonable persons could differ; if so, it seems to fit the model of a factual question. But does it make any sense to try this question again and again, with some factfinders determining that the conduct was negligent and others finding it not negligent? The third Restatement takes the position that this particular issue should be dealt with as a question of law:

> Occasionally...the need for providing a clear and stable answer to the question is so overwhelming as to justify a court in withdrawing the negligence evaluation from the jury. In highway-accident cases, for example, the question continuously arises whether it is contributory negligence not to wear an available seat belt. Granted, the advantages to wearing a seat belt vary to some extent from case to case....Still, the benefits of having the contributory-negligence question settled in advance are of such force as to make it acceptable for a state's highest court to reach a final, general decision as to whether or not wearing seatbelts is...contributory negligence.

Restatement, Third, of Torts: Liability for Physical Harm (Basic Principles) § 8, Comment c.

One well-known example of judicial declaration of the standard of care is Helling v. Carey.

Helling v. Carey

Supreme Court of Washington
519 P.2d 981 (Wash. 1974)

HUNTER, Associate Justice.

This case arises from a malpractice action instituted by the plaintiff..., Barbara Helling.

The plaintiff suffers from primary open angle glaucoma...[,] a condition of the eye in which there is an interference in the ease with which the nourishing fluids can flow out of the eye. Such a condition results in pressure gradually rising above the normal level to such an extent that damage is produced to the optic nerve and its fibers with resultant loss in vision. The first loss usually occurs in the periphery of the field of vision. The disease usually has few symptoms and, in the absence of a pressure test, is often undetected until the damage has become extensive and irreversible.

The defendants..., Dr. Thomas F. Carey and Dr. Robert C. Laughlin, are partners who practice the medical specialty of ophthalmology. Ophthalmology involves the diagnosis and treatment of defects and diseases of the eye.

The plaintiff first consulted the defendants for myopia, nearsightedness, in 1959. At that time she was fitted with contact lenses. She next consulted the defendants in September, 1963, concerning irritation caused by the contact lenses. Additional consultations occurred in October, 1963; February, 1967; September, 1967; May, 1968; July, 1968; August, 1968; September, 1968; and October, 1968. Until the October 1968 consultation, the defendants considered the plaintiff's visual problems to be related solely to complications associated with her contact lenses. On that occasion,...Dr. Carey, tested the plaintiff's eye pressure and field of vision for the first time. This test indicated that the plaintiff had glaucoma. The plaintiff, who was then 32 years of age, had essentially lost her peripheral vision and her central vision was reduced to approximately 5 degrees vertical by 10 degrees horizontal....

After consulting other physicians, the plaintiff filed a complaint against the defendants alleging...that she sustained severe and permanent damage to her eyes as a proximate result of the defendants' negligence....[T]he testimony of the medical experts for both the plaintiff and the defendants established that the standards of the profession for that specialty in the same or similar circumstances do not require routine pressure tests for glaucoma upon patients under 40 years of age. The reason...is that the disease rarely occurs in this age group. Testimony indicated, however, that the standards of the profession do require pressure tests if the patient's complaints and symptoms reveal to the physician that glaucoma should be suspected.

The trial court entered judgment for the defendants following a defense verdict. The plaintiff thereupon appealed to the Court of Appeals, which affirmed....

....

We find this to be a unique case. The testimony of the medical experts is undisputed concerning the standards of the profession for the specialty of ophthalmology....The issue is whether the defendants' compliance with the standard of the profession of ophthalmology, which does not require the giving of a routine pressure test to persons under 40 years of age, should insulate them from liability....

....

The incidence of glaucoma in one out of 25,000 persons under the age of 40 may appear quite minimal. However, that one person, the plaintiff in this instance, is entitled to the same protection, as afforded persons over 40, essential for timely detection of the evidence of glaucoma where it can be arrested to avoid the grave and devastating result of this disease. The test is a simple pressure test, relatively inexpensive. There is no judgment factor involved, and there is no doubt that by giving the test the evidence of glaucoma can be detected. The giving of the test is harmless if the physical condition of the eye permits. The testimony indicates that although the condition of the plaintiff's eyes might have at times prevented the defendants from administering the pressure test, there is an absence of evidence in the record that the test could not have been timely given.

....

... [R]easonable prudence required the timely giving of the pressure test to this plaintiff. The precaution of giving this test to detect the incidence of glaucoma to patients under 40 years of age is so imperative that irrespective of its disregard by the standards of the ophthalmology profession, it is the duty of the courts to say what is required to protect patients under 40 from the damaging results of glaucoma.

We therefore hold, as a matter of law, that the reasonable standard that should have been followed under the undisputed facts of this case was the timely giving of this simple, harmless pressure test to this plaintiff and that, in failing to do so, the defendants were negligent, which proximately resulted in the blindness sustained by the plaintiff for which the defendants are liable.

....

The judgment of the trial court and the decision of the Court of Appeals is reversed, and the case is remanded for a new trial on the issue of damages only.

[The concurring opinion of UTTER, Associate Justice, has been omitted.]

Notes

1. The decision in *Helling* was promptly followed by legislative action. Section 4.24.290 of the Washington Revised Code now provides that in order to prevail in a medical malpractice action, other than an action based on failure to obtain informed patient consent, a plaintiff must:

> prove by a preponderance of the evidence that the defendant or defendants failed to exercise that degree of skill, care and learning possessed by other persons in the same profession....

This statute seems to have been intended to overrule Helling v. Carey. However, in Gates v. Jenson, 595 P.2d 919, 924 (Wash. 1979), a subsequent case involving glaucoma testing, the court reaffirmed the *Helling* view that reasonable prudence may sometimes still require a higher standard of care than is followed by other professionals. The court reasoned that the quoted statute did not abrogate *Helling*. Unlike the original house bill, which would have established the standard of care as that "skill and care practiced by others in the same profession," the final version of the bill defined the standard of care as that "skill, care, and learning possessed" by such persons. *See also* Harris v. Robert C. Groth, M.D., Inc., P.S., 663 P.2d 113 (Wash. 1983) (saying that *Helling* "broke with the traditional medical malpractice rule" and *Gates* "rejected the contention that [Wash. Rev. Code Ann. §4.24.290 (West 1988 & Supp. 1998)] had overruled *Helling*"). If the legislature did not intend to overrule *Helling*, why would it have enacted §4.24.290? In recent years, some legislatures overruling judge-made law have cited the specific decisions meant to be overruled, to reduce the danger of misinterpretation.

2. Some courts hold that a surgeon is negligent as a matter of law if a foreign object, such as a sponge, is left in a patient following an operation, and that expert testimony is not needed to establish the breach of duty. *See* Rudeck v. Wright, 709 P.2d 621 (Mont. 1985) (imposing liability even though the nurse failed to inform the surgeon of the missing sponge and the radiologist failed to detect it).

3. In Maussner v. Atlantic City Country Club, 691 A.2d 826 (N.J. Super Ct. 1997), the court wrote:

> All golf courses have a duty to post a sign that details what, if any, safety procedures are being utilized by the golf course to protect its patrons from lightning. If a particular golf course uses no safety precautions, its sign must inform golfers that they play at their own risk and that no safety procedures are being utilized to protect golfers from lightning strikes.

4. In Antwaun A. v. Heritage Mut. Ins. Co., 596 N.W.2d 456 (Wis. 1999), the court held that, as a matter of common law, a duty to test for lead paint arises whenever the landlord of a residential property constructed before 1978 either knows or should know that there is peeling or chipping paint on the rental property. The court noted that in 1978 the Consumer Products Safety Commission banned the use of lead paint on residential properties, and that since then numerous developments have called attention to the serious health hazards created by lead paint. The court acknowledged that other jurisdictions have held that the age of deteriorating paint does not give rise to a duty to test for lead. However, the court concluded that those decisions in other states were made at a time when the dangers of lead paint were not widely known.

3. Standards Created by Statute

Some statutes expressly provide that a violation gives rise to a tort action for damages. For example, Minn. Stat. §617.245(2) (Westlaw 2003) provides:

> Subd. 2. Cause of action. A cause of action exists for injury caused by the use of a minor in a sexual performance. The cause of action exists against a person who promotes, employs, uses, or permits a minor to engage or assist others to engage in posing or modeling alone or with others in a sexual performance, if the person knows or has reason to know that the conduct intended is a sexual performance.
>
> A person found liable for injuries under this section is liable to the minor for damages....

[I]n Norton v. Wilbur Waggoner Equip. Rental, 394 N.E.2d 403 (Ill. 1979), the statute at issue required any person having charge of the erection of a building to "provide planking or scaffolding" for workers to stand on. It further provided:

> For any injury to person...occasioned by wilful violations of this act...a right of action shall accrue to the party injured, for any direct damages sustained thereby.

There was no question in *Norton* that scaffolding had not been provided—the standard of care had been violated—and that injuries had been sustained by the plaintiff. The court devoted its attention to the question of who was the person "in charge," within the language of the statute.

Whenever a legislative enactment expressly creates a tort cause of action, the court's deliberations will normally be confined to questions of the enactment's applicability to the facts at hand and constitutionality. *See* Harris v. Manor Healthcare Corp., 489 N.E.2d 1374 (Ill. 1986) (upholding against a constitutional challenge a statute giving nursing home residents a cause of action, with enhanced damages, for certain kinds of injuries).

Sexual Abuse Statutes. In Marquay v. Eno, 662 A.2d 272 (N.H. 1995), the court held that a statute requiring any person having reason to suspect that a child has been abused or neglected to report the abuse to the state did not create a private cause of action in favor of abused former students against school employees who allegedly violated the statute's reporting requirement since neither the statute nor the legislative history directly revealed any such legislative intent.

However, some states have sexual abuse statutes that expressly recognize a cause of action against the abuser. For example, the New Jersey law expressly provides:

> b. In any civil action for injury or illness based on sexual abuse, the cause of action shall accrue at the time of reasonable discovery of the injury and its causal relationship to the act of sexual abuse....
>
> ....
>
> h. A plaintiff who prevails in a civil action pursuant to this act shall be awarded damages in the amount of $10,000, plus reasonable attorney's fees, or actual damages, whichever is greater....

N.J. Stat. Ann. §2A:61B-1 (Westlaw 2003).

4. Standards Adopted by Courts Based on Legislation

Some statutes impose standards of care, but do not expressly make those standards applicable to tort cases. For example, laws establishing speed limits typically provide only for criminal sanctions, such a fine payable to the state.

In dealing with this kind of legislative enactment, a court may determine that it will adopt the terms of the statute as embracing the applicable level of care for civil suits. The essential inquiry is whether the statute was intended to protect this class of persons from this type of harm. If so, the court may find it appropriate to say that the statute defines what a reasonable person would do under the circumstances.

Courts taking this approach occasionally find that there is implicit legislative intent to create a standard of care. For example, in Walker v. Bignell, 301 N.W.2d 447 (Wis. 1981), the court held that although a statute requiring municipalities to trim vegetation along the highway did not expressly provide that it could be used as a predicate for civil liability, that was the "necessary implication" of the language of the statute. The statute said that there was a duty to remove vegetation "in order to provide safety to users of the highway." This line of analysis is more a matter of candor than of substance. Rather than take responsibility for adopting the legislature's rule for use in tort cases, the court attributes that decision about tort liability to the legislature. In the one case, the court is saying that the legislation sets the standard because the legislature implicitly intended it to do so, and in the other case, the court acknowledges that the statute sets the standard because the court thinks that is a good idea. Either way, if the statute does not expressly create a cause of action, the essential inquiry is the same: was the law intended to protect this class of persons from this type of harm.

a. In General

Pelkey v. Brennan

Supreme Court of New York, Appellate Division
209 N.Y.S.2d 691 (App. Div. 1961)

GIBSON, Justice.

The infant plaintiff and her father have recovered damages on account of personal injuries sustained as the result of the infant's fall while skating on defendant's roller skating rink, which occurred, according to her version, when she was brushed or struck by an unidentified skater. Contrary to the statute hereinafter discussed, the infant plaintiff, then 13 years old, was permitted to enter and remain at the rink after 7:00 p.m., accompanied only by another girl of the same age.

In our view, plaintiffs failed to establish any common-law negligence on the part of the defendant and recovery can be sustained, if at all, only upon the theory that the accidental injuries may be legally attributed to defendant's conceded violation of...the Penal Law.... It need scarcely be added that the damage sought upon violation of a statute enacted for the protection of a special class must be to the particular interest protected, so that if, in this case, the statute was designed to safeguard children's morals and not for their protection against accidental bodily injury, the rules contended for do not apply.

In our view, physical injury is not within the contemplation of the statute and plaintiffs had the burden of proving negligence and proximate cause as in the ordinary negligence case. Section 484, in substance and so far as here pertinent, makes it a misdemeanor to permit the presence of a child, under 16 years and unaccompanied by a parent or authorized adult, at any of the types of public places there enumerated, "skating rink" being one of them. Section 484-a, applicable to skating rinks only, permits some exceptions under certain conditions. In a number of instances the language of the sections seems clearly to indicate their primary purpose to be the protection of children's morals and good habits and conduct. Secondarily, the statute inhibits late hours prejudicial to school work. When these references are eliminated there remains no indication that accidental injuries are contemplated....

Judgment reversed...and a new trial ordered....

Notes

1. *Wrong Class of Person or Wrong Type of Harm.* See also Remsburg v. Montgomery, 831 A.2d 18 (Md. 2003) (holding that a statute regulating hunting on privately owned land was intended to prevent harm to property, not accidental shooting of a person, and that therefore the statute imposed no duty on a hunting party leader to prevent a member of the group from injuring the owner of the land); Sisk v. Williamson County, 657 N.E.2d 903 (Ill. 1995) (denying recovery to a person who fell from a bridge where weeds

concealed danger because pedestrians were not "intended and permitted" users of rural roads for purposes of a statute requiring local public entities to exercise reasonable care).

Even if a statute is held not to set the standard of care on the ground that it was intended to protect a different class of persons or prevent a different type of harm, negligence may be found under the reasonable-person standard applied to the facts of the case. For example, in De Gregorio v. Malloy, 52 A.2d 195 (Pa. 1947), a police officer escorting an emergency vehicle through heavy traffic was injured while riding on its running board. The court held that the plaintiff's violation of legislation prohibiting persons from hanging onto or riding on the outside of vehicles did not establish contributory negligence, for the statute, entitled "Tampering with vehicles," was intended to prevent injuries to *trespassing persons*. The court nevertheless held that the jury could determine, based on its assessment of the facts, that the plaintiff acted unreasonably and was contributorily negligent.

2. *Safety Statutes and Rescuers.* Safety statutes are often interpreted as not intended to protect professional rescuers from harm. *See* Entwistle v. Draves, 490 A.2d 313 (N.J. Super. Ct. App. Div. 1985) (statute prohibiting tavern brawls and other disorderly conduct was intended to protect general public, not police officers called upon to restore order); Kelly v. Muhs Co., 59 A. 23 (N.J. Sup. Ct. 1904) (ordinance was intended to protect employees of businesses where fires occur, not firefighters).

3. *Assessing Legislative Intent.* In determining whether legislation was intended to protect a particular class of persons from a specific type of harm, a court will look to the language of the statute, including its title, and to the legislative history of the act, including statements by the bill's sponsor, committee findings, and the like. A court often enjoys considerable discretion in making this assessment, and reasonable minds may differ.

For example, in Ney v. Yellow Cab Co., 117 N.E.2d 74 (Ill. 1954), the plaintiff was struck by the defendant's taxi while it was being driven by a thief who had stolen it. Contrary to statute, the cab had been left unattended, with the key in the ignition and the motor running. Upon considering the legislation, the majority concluded that the key-removal provision was intended to protect the public from harm to persons or property, and that there was no reason to think that the legislature had intended to distinguish between harm precipitated by the intervention of a criminal actor and other causes of harm. Taking precisely the opposite view, the dissenter concluded that because there was no direct indication that the legislature had considered the issue of harm occasioned by theft, as opposed to harm caused by negligent or inadvertent operation of a vehicle in which a key had been left, the statute was not intended to prevent the type of accident which had occurred. The case illustrates that conflicting meanings may be attributed to legislative silence.

Stachniewicz v. Mar-Cam Corp.

Supreme Court of Oregon
488 P.2d 436 (Or. 1971)

HOLMAN, Justice.

The patron of a drinking establishment seeks to recover against the operator for personal injuries allegedly inflicted by other customers during a barroom brawl. The jury returned a verdict for defendant. Plaintiff appealed.

From the evidence introduced, the jury could find as follows:

A fight erupted in a bar between a group of persons of American Indian ancestry, who were sitting in a booth, and other customers who were at an adjacent table with plaintiff.

Facts One of plaintiff's friends had refused to allow a patron from the booth to dance with the friend's wife because the stranger was intoxicated. Thereafter, such threats as, "Hey, Whitey, how big are you?" were shouted from the booth at plaintiff and his companion. One of the persons at the table, after complaining to the bartender, was warned by him, "Don't start trouble with those guys." Soon thereafter, those individuals who had been sitting in the booth approached the table and one of them knocked down a person who was talking to a member of plaintiff's party. With that, the brawl commenced.

After a short melee, someone shouted "Fuzz!" and those persons who had been sitting in the booth ran out a door and into the parking lot, with one of plaintiff's friends in hot pursuit. Upon reaching the door, the friend discovered plaintiff lying just outside with his feet wedging the door open.

Plaintiff suffered retrograde amnesia and could remember nothing of the events of the evening. No one could testify to plaintiff's whereabouts at the time the [disturbance occurred] or to the cause of the vicious head injuries which plaintiff displayed when the brawl was ended.

The customers in the booth had been drinking in defendant's place of business for approximately two and one-half hours before the affray commenced.

The principal issue is whether...violations of ORS 471.410(3) and of Oregon Liquor Control Regulation No. 10-065(2) constitute negligence as a matter of law. The portion of the statute relied on by plaintiff reads as follows:

> (3) No person shall give or otherwise make available any alcoholic liquor to a person visibly intoxicated....

The portion of the regulation to which plaintiff points provides:

> (2) No licensee shall permit or suffer any loud, noisy, disorderly or boisterous conduct, or any profane or abusive language, in or upon his licensed premises, or permit any visibly intoxicated person to enter or remain upon his licensed premises.

The trial court held that a violation of either the statute or the regulation did not constitute negligence *per se*. It refused requested instructions and withdrew allegations of negligence which were based on their violation.

A violation of a statute or regulation constitutes negligence as a matter of law when the violation results in injury to a member of the class of persons intended to be protected by the legislation and when the harm is of the kind which the statute or regulation was enacted to prevent. [Citations.] The reason behind the rule is that when a legislative body has generalized a standard from the experience of the community and prohibits conduct that is likely to cause harm, the court accepts the formulation....

However, in addition, it is proper for the court to examine preliminarily the appropriateness of the standard as a measure of care for civil litigation under the circumstances presented. [Citations.] The statute in question prevents making available alcohol to a person who is *already visibly intoxicated*. This makes the standard particularly inappropriate for the awarding of civil damages because of the extreme difficulty, if not impossibility, of determining whether a third party's injuries would have been caused, in any event, by the already inebriated person. Unless we are prepared to say that an alcoholic drink given after visible intoxication is the cause of a third party's injuries as a matter of law, a concept not advanced by anyone, the standard would be one almost impossible of application by a factfinder in most circumstances.

....

The regulation promulgated by the commission is an altogether different matter. The regulation required certain conduct of licensees in the operation of bars....

....

An examination of the regulation discloses that it concerns matters having a direct relation to the creation of physical disturbances in bars which would, in turn, create a likelihood of injury to customers. A common feature of our western past, now preserved in story and reproduced on the screen hundreds of times, was the carnage of the barroom brawl. No citation of authority is needed to establish that the "abuses associated with saloons," which the Liquor Control Act seeks to prevent, included permitting on the premises profane, abusive conduct and drunken clientele (now prohibited by the regulation) which results in serious personal injuries to customers in breach of the bar owner's duty to protect his patrons from harm. We find it reasonable to assume that the commission, in promulgating the regulation, intended to prevent these abuses, and that they had in mind the safety of patrons of bars as well as the general peace and quietude of the community....

....

....We believe it would be fair for the jury to infer, in the circumstances set forth in the statement of the facts, that plaintiff was injured by one of the persons in the booth who had created the disturbance and that the injuries would not have occurred except for defendant's violation of the commission's regulation, as alleged.

The judgment of the trial court is reversed and the case is remanded for a new trial.

Notes

1. *Other Relevant Considerations.* The discussion of the visible-intoxication statute in *Stachniewicz* illustrates that a court may take into account considerations other than class of persons and type of harm in determining whether to adopt a legislative enactment as setting the standard of care. It is important to note, however, that not all courts would conclude, as did the *Stachniewicz* court, that reliance upon such a statute poses serious problems for proving causation. In El Chico Corp. v. Poole, 732 S.W.2d 306, 312–13 (Tex. 1987), the court held that a statute prohibiting a person from selling "an alcoholic beverage to an habitual drunkard or an intoxicated person" imposed on a liquor licensee "a duty to the general public not to serve alcoholic beverages to a person when the licensee knows or should know the patron is intoxicated." Concerning causation, the court wrote:

> [Defendants] argue that any duty premised on the statute fails the cause in fact test, i.e., because the patron is already intoxicated, the cause of the plaintiff's injuries is already present....
>
> [Defendants] misread the [plaintiffs'] cause in fact burden. The plaintiff must prove it is more probable than not that but for the licensee's conduct, the accident would not have occurred....[T]he plaintiff need not exclude all possibility that the accident occurred other than how he alleges, but instead must only prove the greater probability is that the defendant's conduct was a cause of the accident....
>
> All persons who contributed to the injury are liable; the negligence of the one does not excuse the negligence of another....

2. *Exclusive Penalties.* A court may not adopt a statute as setting the civil standard of care if the legislature intended that the specified penalty be the exclusive sanction for an

infraction, or if there is other evidence that the legislature intended to bar use of the statutory standard in tort cases. *See* Pool v. Ford Motor Co., 715 S.W.2d 629 (Tex. 1986) (the lower court erred in relying on two statutes, one of which specifically provided that the presumption of intoxication would not apply in civil actions, and the other of which stated that "maximum or minimum speed limitations shall not be construed to relieve the plaintiff in any action from the burden of proving negligence on the part of the defendant as the proximate cause of an accident"); *cf.* Hoosier v. Landa, 17 Cal. Rptr. 2d 518, 521 (Ct. App. 1993) (rejecting an argument that state and federal gun-control laws are intended only to impose criminal penalties, and finding that a claim was stated against a gun dealer who indirectly and illegally sold the gun with which the plaintiff was shot).

Some statutes expressly state that evidence of a violation of their provisions shall not be admissible in a civil action. *See, e.g.,* Tex. Health & Safety Code §242.017 (Westlaw 2003) (nursing home law).

Other statutes leave the door open for a finding of negligence *per se*. *See* Sanchez v. Galey, 733 P.2d 1234 (Idaho 1986) (joining a majority of courts in finding that the intent of Congress to ensure workplace safety would be best served by holding that a violation of an OSHA regulation is negligence *per se* despite a provision in the act that "Nothing in this chapter shall be construed to...enlarge or diminish or affect...the common law...rights, duties, or liabilities of employers").

3. *Vague Legislation.* A court may decline to embrace a vague statute as setting the applicable standard of care. *See* Hosein v. Checker Taxi Co., Inc., 419 N.E.2d 568 (Ill. App. Ct. 1981) (statute requiring bulletproof shields in taxicabs, which had been declared unconstitutionally vague in a prior criminal action, was too indefinite to establish the standard of care in a negligence case, even though on appropriate facts a court may elect to rely upon constitutionally infirm legislation); Perry v. S.N., 973 S.W.2d 301 (Tex. 1998) (holding that a child abuse reporting statute, which imposed a reporting requirement on any person having "cause to believe" that a child was being abused, was not an appropriate standard for negligence *per se* liability considering that there was no relevant common law duty, the statutory standard was not clearly defined, liability could be significantly disproportionate to the underlying conduct, the statute applied to a broad class of persons, and the connection between the statutory violation and the relevant injury was attenuated).

See also Louisiana-Pacific Corp. v. Knighten, 976 S.W.2d 674 (Tex. 1998), which involved an assured-clear-distance statute that provided:

> The driver of a motor vehicle shall, when following another vehicle, maintain an assured clear distance between the two vehicles, exercising *due* regard for the speed of such vehicles, traffic upon and conditions of the street or highway, so that such motor vehicle can be *safely* brought to a stop without colliding with the preceding vehicle....

(Emphasis added.) The court held that the statute only imposed a duty to exercise reasonable care and was not a proper basis for a negligence *per se* instruction.

4. *Judicial Restraint.* In Bruegger v. Faribault County Sheriff's Dept., 497 N.W.2d 260 (Minn. 1993), the court held that a violation of the Crime Victims Reparations Act (CVRA) did not create a private cause of action against the law enforcement agencies which failed to inform the plaintiffs of their rights to seek reparations. It wrote:

> Principles of judicial restraint preclude us from creating a new statutory cause of action that does not exist at common law where the legislature has

not either by the statute's express terms or by implication provided for civil tort liability.

5. *Statutes Duplicating the Common Law.* According to Restatement, Third, of Torts: Liability for Physical Harm (Basic Principles) §14 cmt. e (Tent. Draft No. 1, 2001):

> Many statutes impose obligations on actors that largely correspond to or codify obligations imposed by negligence law.... Thus a statute might require motorists to drive their vehicles at a "reasonable and prudent" speed, or might prohibit driving the vehicle "carelessly." To find that a person has violated such a statute, the jury would also need to find that the person has behaved negligently. In such situations, the doctrine of negligence *per se* is largely superfluous in ascertaining the person's liability.

See County of Dallas v. Poston, 104 S.W.3d 719 (Tex. App. 2003) (holding that the statutory duty of the operator of a motor vehicle about to enter or cross a highway to yield the right-of-way to an approaching vehicle is not absolute and therefore not a proper basis for a finding of contributory negligence as a matter of law; rather the appropriate inquiry is whether a reasonably prudent driver under the same or similar circumstances would have yielded the right-of-way). *See also* Louisiana-Pacific Corp. v. Knighten, 976 S.W.2d 674 (Tex. 1998) (a statute governing the duty of a driver to the vehicle in front, which required that a driver proceed safely and safely bring a vehicle to a stop, imposed on the driver a duty of reasonable care, and precluded the leading driver from obtaining a negligence *per se* instruction in an action arising out of a rear-end collision involving three vehicles).

Brown v. Shyne

Court of Appeals of New York
151 N.E. 197 (N.Y. 1926)

LEHMAN, J.

The plaintiff employed the defendant to give chiropractic treatment to her for a disease or physical condition. The defendant had no license to practice medicine, yet, he held himself out as being able to diagnose and treat disease, and, under the provisions of the Public Health Law [citation], he was guilty of a misdemeanor. The plaintiff became paralyzed after she had received nine treatments by the defendant. She claims, and upon the appeal we must assume, that the paralysis was caused by the treatment she received. She has recovered judgment in the sum of $10,000 for the damages caused by said injury.

....

At the close of the plaintiff's case the plaintiff was permitted to amend the complaint to allege "that in so treating the plaintiff the defendant was engaged in the practice of medicine contrary to and in violation of the provisions of the Public Health Law...." Thereafter the trial judge charged the jury that they might bring in a verdict in favor of the plaintiff if they found that the evidence established that the treatment given to the plaintiff was not in accordance with the standards of skill and care which prevail among those treating the disease. He then continued:

"....I am going to allow you,...to predicate negligence upon another theory.... [The trial judge then charged the jury that from the violation of the statute they might infer negligence which produced injury to the plaintiff.]"

In so charging the jury...the trial justice...erred.

The provisions of the Public Health Law prohibiting the practice of medicine without a license...are of course intended for the protection of the general public against injury which unskilled and unlearned practitioners might cause....If violation of the statute has no direct bearing on the injury, proof of the violation becomes irrelevant. For injury caused by neglect of duty imposed by the penal law there is civil remedy; but, of course, the injury must follow from the neglect.

Proper formulation of general standards of preliminary education and proper examination of the particular applicant should serve to raise the standards of skill and care generally possessed by members of the profession in the state; but the license to practice medicine confers no additional skill upon the practitioner, nor does it confer immunity from physical injury upon a patient if the practitioner fails to exercise care. Here, injury may have been caused by lack of skill or care; it would not have been obviated if the defendant had possessed a license yet failed to exercise the skill and care required of one practicing medicine. True, if the defendant had not practiced medicine in this state, he could not have injured the plaintiff, but the protection which the statute was intended to provide was against risk of injury by the unskilled or careless practitioner, and, unless the plaintiff's injury was caused by carelessness or lack of skill, the defendant's failure to obtain a license was not connected with the injury....

....Even a skilled and learned practitioner who is not licensed commits an offense against the state; but against such practitioners the statute was not intended to protect, for no protection was needed, and neglect to obtain a license results in no injury to the patient and, therefore, no private wrong....In order to show that the plaintiff has been injured by defendant's breach of the statutory duty, proof must be given that defendant in such treatment did not exercise the care and skill which would have been exercised by qualified practitioners within the state, and that lack of skill and care caused the injury....

....Evidence of defendant's training, learning, and skill and the method he used in giving the treatment was produced at the trial, and upon such evidence the jury could base finding either of care or negligence, but the absence of a license does not seem to strengthen inference that might be drawn from such evidence, and *a fortiori* would not alone be a basis for such inference....

....

For these reasons the judgment should be reversed, and a new trial granted, with costs to abide the event.

[The dissenting opinion of CRANE, J., is omitted.]

Notes

1. *Licensing Statutes.* Brown v. Shyne has been followed by nearly all courts. In principle, the absence of a license to drive a car or to practice a profession shows nothing about whether the car was driven carefully or the profession practiced acceptably. *See generally* Charles O. Gregory, *Breach of Criminal Licensing Statutes in Civil Litigation*, 36 Cornell L.Q. 622 (1951). Legislatures are, of course, free to differ. N.Y. C.P.L.R. §4504 (Westlaw 2003) now provides that the absence of a license to practice medicine shall be "*prima facie* evidence" of negligence in a medical-malpractice action.

Note that the defendant in Brown v. Shyne was not a lawyer undertaking surgery for the fun of it; he was a chiropractor, perhaps doing the things chiropractors normally do. Licensing statutes reflect not only judgments about professional competence, but also the outcomes of jurisdictional disputes between competing professional groups.

According to Restatement, Third, of Torts: Liability for Physical Harm (Basic Principles) §14 cmt. h (Tent. Draft No. 1, 2001):

> [I]n many cases, the immediate reason for the person's lack of a license is unrelated to the state's general safety purpose. For example, a motorist may lack a license only because of a failure to file for license renewal. If this motorist is involved in an accident, the lack of a license has no bearing on the motorist's likely negligence. Similarly, a physician may lack a license in a state only because the physician has not yet satisfied the state's residency requirement....
>
> In other cases, however, this general assessment does not pertain. If, for example, a person operates a motorcycle in a way that suggests a lack of skill, and if the evidence shows that the person does not have a license to operate a motorcycle because the person has failed the test that assesses skills, then, depending on the jurisdiction's evidence rules, the lack of the license may be admissible as tending to show the person's negligent unskillfulness. If a property owner has installed a furnace without securing a permit required by a city ordinance, and if the evidence indicates that the inspector would not have issued the permit because of the furnace's capacity for emitting dangerous gases, then the person who suffers physical harm on account of such emissions can show that the owner's violation of the permit-requiring ordinance is negligence *per se*. The absence of a license in such a case is a proxy for the owner's violation of the city's substantive safety standards that are enforced through the licensing process.

The Restatement cites no cases using the absence of a license as a proxy for a finding of negligence.

2. *Revenue-Raising Statutes.* Many licensing statutes are intended to raise revenue, rather than promote safety, and are therefore not appropriate predicates for establishing negligence. *See* Inland Steel v. Pequignot, 608 N.E.2d 1378 (Ind. Ct. App. 1993).

b. Unexcused Violations of Statute

Martin v. Herzog
Court of Appeals of New York
126 N.E. 814 (N.Y. 1920)

CARDOZO, J.

The action is one to recover damages for injuries resulting in death. Plaintiff and her husband, while driving toward Tarrytown in a buggy on the night of August 21, 1915, were struck by the defendant's automobile coming in the opposite direction. They were thrown to the ground, and the man was killed. At the point of the collision the highway makes a curve....Negligence is charged against the defendant, the driver of the car, in that he did not keep to the right of the center of the highway. [Citation.] Negligence is charged against the plaintiff's intestate, the driver of the wagon in that he was traveling without lights. Highway Law, §329a, as amended by Laws 1915, c. 367....The jury found...[defendant] delinquent and his victim blameless....

We agree with the Appellate Division that the charge to the jury was erroneous and misleading....In the body of the charge the trial judge said that the jury could consider the absence of light "in determining whether the plaintiff's intestate was guilty of contributory negligence in failing to have a light upon the buggy as provided by law. I do not mean to say that the absence of light necessarily makes him negligent, but it is a fact for your consideration." The defendant requested a ruling that the absence of a light on the plaintiff's vehicle was "*prima facie* evidence of contributory negligence." This request was refused, and the jury were again instructed that they might consider the absence of lights as some evidence of negligence, but that it was not conclusive evidence. The plaintiff then requested a charge that "the fact that the plaintiff's intestate was driving without a light is not negligence in itself," and to this the court acceded. . . .

We think the unexcused omission of the statutory signals is more than some evidence of negligence. It *is* negligence in itself. Lights are intended for the guidance and protection of other travelers on the highway. Highway Law, §329a. By the very terms of the hypothesis, to omit, willfully or heedlessly, the safeguards prescribed by law for the benefit of another that he may be preserved in life or limb, is to fall short of the standard of diligence to which those who live in organized society are under a duty to conform. . . .

. . . . A rule less rigid has been applied where the one who complains of the omission is not a member of the class for whose protection the safeguard is designed. [Citations.] Some relaxation there has also been where the safeguard is prescribed by local ordinance, and not by statute. [Citations.] Courts have been reluctant to hold that the police regulations of boards and councils and other subordinate officials create rights of action beyond the specific penalties imposed. This has led them to say that the violation of a statute is negligence, and the violation of a like ordinance is only evidence of negligence. An ordinance, however, like a statute, is a law within its sphere of operation, and so the distinction has not escaped criticism. . . .

. . . . [Here, the jurors] were allowed to "consider the default as lightly or gravely" as they would . . . Jurors have no dispensing power, by which they may relax the duty that one traveler on the highway owes under the statute to another. It is error to tell them that they have. The omission of these lights was a wrong, and, being wholly unexcused, was also a negligent wrong. No license should have been conceded to the triers of the facts to find it anything else.

We must be on our guard, however, against confusing the question of negligence with that of the causal connection between the negligence and the injury. . . .

We think, however, that evidence of a collision occurring more than an hour after sundown between a car and an unseen buggy, proceeding without lights, is evidence from which a causal connection may be inferred between the collision and the lack of signals. . . .

There may, indeed, be times when the lights on a highway are so many and so bright that lights on a wagon are superfluous. If that is so, it is for the offender to go forward with the evidence, and prove the illumination as a kind of substituted performance. The plaintiff asserts that she did so here. She says that the scene of the accident was illumined by moonlight, by an electric lamp, and by the lights of the approaching car. Her position is that, if the defendant did not see the buggy thus illumined, a jury might reasonably infer that he would not have seen it anyhow. We may doubt whether there is any evidence of illumination sufficient to sustain the jury in drawing such an inference; but the decision of the case does not make it necessary to resolve the doubt, and so we leave it open. . . .

. . . .

The order of the Appellate Division should be affirmed, and judgment absolute directed on the stipulation in favor of the defendant, with costs in all courts.

[The dissenting opinion of HOGAN, J., addressed chiefly to the issue of causation, is omitted.]

Notes

1. *Procedural Effect of Unexcused Violations of Statute.* There are three views as to the procedural effect of evidence establishing an unexcused violation of a standard-setting statute: negligence *per se*; *prima facie* negligence; and some evidence of negligence.

(a) Some states hold that an unexcused violation of statute is negligence *per se* (negligence "in itself"). The unexcused violation conclusively establishes that the defendant breached a duty of reasonable care to the plaintiff; the only issues remaining for the jury are causation, defenses, and damages. *See generally* Restatement, Third, of Torts: Liability for Physical Harm (Basic Principles) §14 (Tent. Draft No. 1, 2001) (discussing statutory violations as negligence *per se*).

(b) Other states hold that proof of a violation of a standard-setting statute is *prima facie* negligence. The evidence of the violation raises a presumption of negligence, and if the presumption is not rebutted by proof of an excuse or other evidence of reasonable care, a breach of duty is established, in which case, again, the only issues remaining for the jury are causation, defenses, and damages.

(c) A few states take the position that proof of a violation of a standard-setting statute is only some evidence of negligence which the jury can either accept or reject. Thus, even after the violation is established, the jury must still decide the question of negligence, as well as issues related to causation, defenses, and damages.

Courts endorsing the negligence *per se* or *prima facie* negligence rules sometimes treat violation of a legislative enactment emanating from an inferior tribunal (for example, an ordinance passed by city council, rather than a statute passed by the legislature) as merely some evidence of negligence.

According to *Martin*, which rule is subscribed to in New York? Is the same view followed in Michigan? *See* Zeni v. Anderson, 243 N.W.2d 270 (Mich. 1976), *infra* at 317.

2. *See* Jones v. Southwestern Newspapers Corp., 694 S.W.2d 455 (Tex. Ct. App. 1985) (driving on the left side of the road to deliver newspapers is negligence *per se*).

c. Excused Violations of Statute

Ranard v. O'Neil

Supreme Court of Montana
531 P.2d 1000 (Mont. 1975)

HASWELL, Justice.

. . . .

...[P]laintiff was struck and injured by an automobile driven by defendant. The incident occurred on a Helena city street at approximately 9:00 p.m. The street was snow packed and icy; it was illuminated by street lights.

Plaintiff, whose eighth birthday was on the day following the accident, was on his way home from a boxing lesson. His instructor had driven plaintiff and his brother to the street in front of their home, double-parking across from their home. The brother, who was a year older than plaintiff, ran across the street, followed almost immediately by the younger boy.

As plaintiff reached the middle of the street, he saw defendant's headlights, stopped, and then ran in an attempt to avoid being struck. Defendant, upon seeing the boy, applied her brakes but was unable to avoid hitting him....

Plaintiff, in a deposition taken some eight and one-half months after the accident, admitted that he had not looked before he ran into the path of defendant's vehicle. Although he admitted that he knew he should check for traffic, he said that he had just forgotten.

....

Following discovery, the district court granted defendant's motion for summary judgment, on the ground...[that plaintiff was contributorily negligent].

....

...[D]efendant asserts that plaintiff violated Montana statutes regulating the conduct of pedestrians, and therefore he was contributorily negligent, as a matter of law. Her argument is that section 32-2178, R.C.M. 1947, sets the standard for determining the care which must be exercised by *any* pedestrian. That section provides, in pertinent part:

> (a) Every pedestrian crossing a roadway at any point other than within a marked crosswalk or within an unmarked crosswalk at an intersection shall yield the right of way to all vehicles upon the roadway.

That statute makes no express exceptions for anyone, and certainly not for children. Pedestrians are defined as "any person afoot" and persons include "every natural person." [Citation.]

Authorities recognize the inconsistency inherent in a standard which imposes adult guidelines on children who violate statutes, but applies a lesser-than-adult standard to a child's conduct outside statutory regulation. *See* Prosser, Law of Torts, 4th ed. §36, n.13.

2 Restatement of Torts 2d, §288A, p. 32 uses this language:

> (1) An excused violation of a legislative enactment or an administrative regulation is not negligence.

> (2) Unless the enactment or regulation is construed not to permit such excuse, its violation is excused when

> (a) the violation is reasonable because of the actor's incapacity.

This illustrative comment in §288A is particularly pertinent here:

> 2. A statute provides that pedestrians shall not step into the street without looking in both directions for approaching traffic. A, a boy eight years of age, dashes into the street without looking, in pursuit of a ball. A's violation of the statute may be found not to be negligence if his conduct was reasonable for a child of similar age, intelligence, and experience.

The statutory violation may thus be excused if the plaintiff lacked the capacity for compliance.

The summary judgment for defendant is vacated. The case is remanded to the district court for further proceedings.

Note

1. Some courts hold that even if a child of the same age, intelligence, maturity, and experience would have complied with the law, the violation of the statute by the child in question is only evidence of negligence, not negligence *per se*. Bauman by Chapman v. Crawford, 704 P.2d 1181, 1185 (Wash. 1985) (citing other cases).

Zeni v. Anderson
Supreme Court of Michigan
243 N.W.2d 270 (Mich. 1976)

WILLIAMS, Justice.

....

The accident which precipitated this action occurred one snowy morning, March 7, 1969, when the temperature was 11 degrees F, the sky was clear and the average snow depth was 21 inches. Plaintiff Eleanor Zeni, then a 56-year-old registered nurse, was walking to her work at the Northern Michigan University Health Center in Marquette. Instead of using the snow-covered sidewalk, which in any event would have required her to walk across the street twice to get to her job, she traveled along a well-used pedestrian snowpath, with her back to oncoming traffic.

Defendant Karen Anderson, a college student, was driving within the speed limit in a steady stream of traffic on the same street. Ms. Anderson testified that she had turned on the defroster in the car and her passenger said she had scraped the windshield. An eyewitness whose deposition was read at trial, however, testified that defendant's windshield was clouded and he doubted that the occupants could see out. He also testified that the car was traveling too close to the curb and that he could tell plaintiff was going to be hit.

....

Ms. Zeni's injuries were serious.... She has retrograde amnesia and therefore, because she does not remember anything from the time she began walking that morning until sometime after the impact, there is no way to determine whether she knew defendant was behind her....

Testimony at trial indicated that it was common for nurses to use the roadway to reach the Health Center, and a security officer testified that in the wintertime it was safer to walk there than on the one sidewalk. Apparently, several days before the accident, Ms. Zeni had indeed fallen on the sidewalk. Although she was not hurt when she fell, the Director of University Security was hospitalized when he fell on the walk.

Defendant, however, maintained plaintiff's failure to use that sidewalk constituted contributory negligence because, she said, it violated M.C.L.A. §257.655; M.S.A. §9.2355, which requires:

> Where sidewalks are provided, it shall be unlawful for pedestrians to walk upon the main traveled portion of the highway. Where sidewalks are not provided, pedestrians shall, when practicable, walk on the left side of the highway facing traffic which passes nearest.

.... [Although the trial court instructed the jury on this point, the jury found against the defendant. The intermediate appellate court reversed and remanded on other grounds. The Supreme Court granted leave to appeal.]

In a growing number of states, the rule concerning the proper role of a penal statute in a civil action for damages is that violation of the statute which has been found to apply to a particular set of facts establishes only a *prima facie* case of negligence, a presumption which may be rebutted by a showing on the part of the party violating the statute of an adequate excuse under the facts and circumstances of the case. The excuses may not necessarily be applicable in a criminal action, since, in the absence of legislatively-mandated civil penalties, acceptance of the criminal statute itself as a standard of care in a civil action is purely discretionary. [Citation.]

Michigan cases...have almost consistently adopted a rebuttable presumption approach, even though the language of the statute is not written in terms of a presumption.

    ....

...[One] attraction of this approach is that it is fair. "If there is sufficient excuse or justification, there is ordinarily no violation of a statute and the statutory standard is inapplicable." [Citation.] It would be unreasonable to adhere to an automatic rule of negligence "where observance would subject a person to danger which might be avoided by disregard of the general rule." [Citation.]

The approach is logical. Liability without fault is not truly negligence, and in the absence of a clear legislative mandate to so extend liability, the courts should be hesitant to do so on their own. Because these are, after all, criminal statutes, a court is limited in how far it may go in plucking a statute from its criminal milieu and inserting it into the civil arena. The rule of rebuttable presumption has arisen in part in response to this concern, and in part because of the reluctance to go to the other extreme and in effect, discard or disregard the legislative standard.

    ....

We have not...chosen to join that small minority which has decreed that violation of a statute is only evidence of negligence. In view of the fairness and ease with which the rebuttable presumption standard has been and can be administered, we believe the litigants are thereby well served and the Legislature is given appropriate respect.

    ....

An accurate statement of our law is that when a court adopts a penal statute as the standard of care in an action for negligence, violation of that statute establishes a *prima facie* case of negligence, with the determination to be made by the finder of fact whether the party accused of violating the statute has established a legally sufficient excuse. If the finder of fact determines such an excuse exists, the appropriate standard of care then becomes that established by the common law. Such excuses shall include, but shall not be limited to, those suggested by the Second Restatement of Torts, §288A, and shall be determined by the circumstances of each case.

In the case at bar, moreover, the statute itself provides a guideline for the jury, for a violation will not occur when it is impracticable to use the sidewalk or to walk on the left side of a highway. This is ordinarily a question for the finder of fact, [citation], and thus the statute itself provides not only a legislative standard of care which may be accepted by the court, but a legislatively mandated excuse as well.

...[W]e find the jury was adequately instructed as to the effect of the violation of this particular statute on plaintiff's case....

    ....

....The Court of Appeals is reversed and the trial court is affirmed. Costs to plaintiff.

[The dissenting opinions of LINDEMER and COLEMAN, JJ., have been omitted.]

Notes

1. Section 288A of the second Restatement, referred to in the principal case, has been supplanted by Restatement, Third, of Torts: Liability for Physical Harm (Basic Principles) §15 (Tent. Draft No. 1, 2001), which reads as follows:

> An actor's excused violation of a statute is not negligence. A violation is excused when:
>
> > (a) the violation is reasonable because of the actor's childhood, physical disability, or physical incapacitation;
> >
> > (b) the actor exercises reasonable care in attempting to comply with the statute;
> >
> > (c) the actor neither knows nor should know of the factual circumstances that render the statute applicable;
> >
> > (d) the actor's violation of the statute is due to the confusing way in which the requirements of the statute are presented to the public; or
> >
> > (e) the actor's compliance with the statute would involve a greater risk of physical harm to that person or to others than noncompliance.

In addition, "there may be further excuses worthy of recognition." *Id.* at cmt. g. Furthermore,

> [I]t is useful to set forth circumstances that do not count as an excuse. The violation of a statute is not excused by the fact that the person sincerely or reasonably believes that the requirement set by the statute is excessive or unwise; nor is it an excuse if the person is unaware or ignorant of the statutory requirement; nor is it an excuse if there is a custom to depart from the statutory requirement.

Id. at cmt. a.

2. *Excuse Based on Emergency.* In Lockhart v. List, 665 A.2d 1176 (Pa. 1995), the plaintiff collided with a truck stopped in the roadway on a sharp curve. The defendant argued that the plaintiff had violated the statutory assured-clear-distance-ahead rule by failing to drive a speed that would enable her to stop in time to avoid a collision. The trial court erred by refusing to instruct the jury that a sudden emergency could provide an excuse for the violation.

3. *Statutes Permitting No Excuse.* Comment c to Restatement, Second, of Torts §288A points out that some statutes have been interpreted as admitting of no excuses for violations, even when applied in tort cases. An example is a statute prohibiting the employment of children under a certain age in occupations involving dangerous machinery.

d. Compliance with Statute

Montgomery v. Royal Motel

Supreme Court of Nevada
645 P.2d 968 (Nev. 1982)[f]

MANOUKIAN, Justice.

On January 10, 1978, appellants Helen and Kenneth Montgomery rented a room at respondent Royal Motel, a fourteen unit building in Las Vegas. On February 1, the Montgomerys had just returned to their motel room when they were assaulted and robbed by an unknown assailant. The door to their room was not self-locking, but was equipped with an operable deadbolt latch. The door was not locked when the assault occurred, although the Montgomerys customarily locked the door immediately upon entry.

The trial court granted respondent's motion for summary judgment upon respondent's presentation of evidence of a Las Vegas municipal ordinance, 4-10-2, "Housing Security Standards," which the trial court found set the applicable standard of conduct for the motel proprietors. The ordinance requires deadbolt locks, but not self-locking doors at units such as those at respondent's motel.

The main issue confronting us is whether the trial court erred in its determination that, as a matter of law, respondent motel met the required standard of conduct in protecting its guests from criminal acts of third parties by complying with the ordinance.

The ordinance...applies to motels with individual entrances such as the Royal. Appellants contend, however, that the ordinance establishes only a minimum standard of conduct and that reasonably prudent conduct might require additional precautions under the circumstances (i.e., a self-locking door), raising a question of fact for the jury.

    ....

We recognize that the standard of conduct defined by a legislative enactment is usually a minimum standard and that special circumstances may support a finding of negligence, despite compliance, if a reasonable person would have taken additional precautions. [Citations.] But when the facts pose a "normal" situation, within that contemplated by the enactment, "it may be found, and can be ruled as a matter of law, that the actor has done his full duty by complying with the statute...." Prosser on Torts, §36 (4th ed. 1971). [Citation.]

In the affidavits in opposition to the motion for summary judgment, the Montgomerys failed to present facts which would indicate that the case posed special circumstances requiring affirmative action beyond the requirements of the ordinance. So far as appears, the proprietor had no reason to suspect that an attacker was near the premises, there was no showing of a history of prior similar incidents, nor were the Montgomerys deceived by the door's appearance. [Citations.]

    ....

We affirm the judgment below.

---

f. Subsequent to publication, this opinion was withdrawn. Before the case was reargued, the appeal was dismissed pursuant to a stipulation of the parties. The withdrawn opinion appears to state good law.—Eds.

Notes

1. *Compare Montgomery with* Medlar v. Mohan, 409 S.E.2d 123 (Va. 1991). There, in a case arising from an intersection collision, the plaintiff argued that the trial court erred in submitting the issue of her contributory negligence to the jury because "she was traveling no faster than the speed limit…[and] had a green light." Answering this contention, the court wrote:

> "[A] green light is [not] an unqualified command to a motorist to move in the direction indicated under any and all circumstances. It is only a command to do so in the exercise of reasonable care…." [Citation.] "The mere fact that one vehicle has the right of way over another at a street intersection does not relieve the driver thus favored from the duty of keeping a reasonable lookout and otherwise exercising ordinary care to avoid a collision." [Citations.] Thus, "[t]he duty of maintaining a proper lookout requires the favored driver to be on the alert for a motorist who attempts to drive through the intersection from an intersecting street on a red light." [Citation.] In the present case,…we think it was a jury issue whether Medlar failed to maintain a proper lookout….

2. *Refusal to Violate a Statute.* Can a person be found negligent for refusing to violate a statute? According to the Restatement, no. Section 16 of Restatement, Third, of Torts: Liability for Physical Harm (Basic Principles) (Tent. Draft No. 1, 2001), provides:

> (a) An actor's compliance with a pertinent statute, while evidence of non-negligence, does not preclude a finding that the actor is negligent…for failing to adopt precautions in addition to those mandated by the statute.

> (b) If the actor's adoption of a precaution would require the actor to violate a statute, the actor cannot be found negligent for failing to adopt that precaution.

Amplifying subsection (b), comment g states:

> If, for example, an administrative agency, exercising powers delegated by statute, prohibits a railroad from installing a certain form of warning device at a highway crossing, the railroad cannot be found negligent for not providing that device. If a statute requires pedestrians or bicyclists to walk or ride with traffic, it would be wrong to find a pedestrian or bicyclist guilty of contributory negligence because of expert testimony that it is safer to walk or ride facing traffic. If traffic is flowing at 80 miles per hour on a highway whose statutory speed limit is 55 miles per hour, the motorist who chooses to drive at 55 may by doing so significantly disturb traffic flow in a way that could foreseeably lead to an accident; even so, that motorist cannot be found negligent for declining to drive at an illegal speed.

3. *Regulatory Agency Approval and Compliance with Agency-Prescribed Standards.* Closely related to compliance with statute is the question whether following the standards of a regulatory agency should insulate the defendant from liability for negligence. Many writers have argued that such standards should control. Juries are not themselves experts on industry standards, and expert testimony may not make up for this deficiency, as an "expert" can be found to testify, for a fee, to almost any conceivable technical proposition. In theory, administrative agencies are supposed to base their standards on expertness. However, there are good reasons to think that standards promulgated by regulatory agencies may be seriously defective. The following criticisms of agency expertness are directed in large part at warnings on consumer products, but the analysis applies to other kinds of safety regulation as well.

[One author]...proposes barring recovery in tort where a product which causes harm has been placed on the market with regulatory agency approval or where an allegedly defective warning conforms to agency-prescribed standards. Aside from the fact that to so hold would remove important incentives for manufacturers to improve many products, this plan for short-circuiting the ordinary channels of judicial review is subject to criticism on at least four grounds. To a greater or lesser extent, each of these arguments goes to the central issue of whether the final word on product safety and accident compensation should reside in a regulatory agency.

    ....

First, regulatory agencies—such as those which license or regulate new drugs, medical devices, aircraft, nuclear power, and a wide range of consumer products—all operate on limited budgets. History demonstrates that they are frequently underfunded and lack the personnel and other resources that are needed to set standards effectively or to evaluate thoroughly the applications and products which they are called upon to review. These budgetary limitations, coupled with often "staggering workloads," counsel caution, to say the least, in according conclusive status to agency determinations concerning which products may be used or purveyed and what warnings must be given. An affirmative decision by an agency to permit the use or sale of a product may more accurately reflect a scarcity of regulatory resources than a thoroughly considered judgment that a product is harmless or that it would be unfair to hold the purveyor liable for resulting injuries. Similarly, an agency's lack of dispatch in revoking previously conferred approval for marketing of a product may be more a function of budgetary constraints than of doubt as to the validity of new evidence tending to demonstrate the unsoundness of a prior decision.

    ....

In contrast to the dearth of resources available to regulatory bodies, personal injury attorneys representing injured individuals often enjoy both the contingent-fee incentive and the financial wherewithal necessary to promote a full exploration of questions relating to product safety through litigation. Potential liability provides regulated firms with good reason to vigorously defend their practices, thus ensuring a sharp, adversarial presentation of relevant arguments in court. To slam the courthouse door preemptively on all cases where regulatory approval has been obtained would in many instances preclude a proper resolution of important issues never before fully considered.

This is not to suggest that regulatory agencies play an unimportant role in the advancement of public safety or that courts should freely disregard their findings. Indeed, regulatory determinations may make substantial contributions to product quality control, and at least where the process is adequately funded and working well, agency findings are entitled to some degree of deference. Nevertheless, the competence of regulatory agencies is sufficiently variable, and budgetary limitations are frequently so severe, that there is good reason for not according regulatory agency approval or compliance with agency-prescribed warnings the status of an irrebuttable defense to tort liability.

    ....

Second, unlike courts, regulatory agencies frequently are the object of direct and indirect lobbying by special interests which may affect not only the nature of applicable standards, but the extent of their enforcement. The representatives of commercial enterprises, in many instances, endeavor to persuade agency decision-makers of the merits of a position through advocacy that is neither objective nor balanced in its presentation of the relevant facts. The risk of distortion of the decision-making process is serious because managers in regulated industries often have close working relationships with regulatory officials. In contrast, the interests of the victims of product defects may go largely unchampioned by persons outside of the regulatory agency, since public interest lobbies "rarely have the legal staffs or war chests of a well-heeled business lobby."

The risk that agency determinations may unfairly favor the interests of the companies seeking regulatory approval are all the more ominous in view of the revolving door between government work and the private sector, which tempts agency employees to render decisions which may enhance their own employment chances with the same regulated firms they are charged with overseeing.

. . . .

Third, administrative agencies, far more than courts, are subject to political pressures. When a new Administration comes into power at the federal level, its political agenda has an impact on the entire range of agency actions, from enforcement of pollution laws, to approval of vaccines and food additives, to disposal of toxic chemicals. The chances of an abrupt, and perhaps ill-considered, change in administrative course with respect to product safety are not insubstantial—and this despite the fact that many would argue that rights of individuals to compensation for injuries should depend on principles more lasting than the results of the latest election. Similar political pressures might, in theory, also imperil tort judgments rendered by the judicial branch. All federal judges, and many state judges, however, are permitted to serve long terms of office under conditions which permit them to enjoy a substantial degree of independence and insulation from political pressure. Moreover, the discretion of judges is procedurally constrained by principles or procedures not necessarily applicable at the administrative level, such as due process, *stare decisis*, and the right to trial by jury....

. . . .

Finally, [a]...proposal that the duty of a potential defendant to warn consumers of product dangers should extend no further than compliance with agency-prescribed warnings is ill-conceived on at least two accounts. First, as courts have frequently recognized, "The warnings required by such agencies may be only minimal in nature." Where that is the case, and the manufacturer or supplier has reason to know of greater dangers not included in the prescribed warning, the only sound course for minimizing accidents and preventing the wasting of human and material resources is to require disclosure of the added dangers to otherwise unknowing consumers....

Second, even where an agency-prescribed warning is adequate to insure disclosure of all dangers which would ordinarily be encountered, the warning may be eroded or even nullified by the over-promotion of the product through a vigorous sales program that may persuade the user to disregard warnings.

Again, the better course is to evaluate the adequacy of a warning in light of the surrounding circumstances—with due deference paid to the extent of the disclosures required by regulatory agencies.

Vincent R. Johnson, *Liberating Progress and the Free Market From the Specter of Tort Liability*, 83 Nw. U. L. Rev. 1027, 1048–54 (1989) (footnotes omitted). *See* United Blood Servs. v. Quintana, 827 P.2d 509 (Colo. 1992) (a blood bank's compliance with FDA recommendations and national guidelines was some evidence of care to prevent the spread of AIDS, but not conclusive on that issue, and therefore it was error to exclude expert testimony intended to show that screening and testing procedures were unreasonably deficient).

e. Defenses to Liability Based on Statute

Seim v. Garavalia

Supreme Court of Minnesota
306 N.W.2d 806 (Minn. 1981)

SHERAN, Chief Justice.

.... Shannon Marie Seim, two days from her seventh birthday, called upon defendant's six-year-old son Scott. Tied to a tree in the backyard was defendant's dog, Hollow. The dog was friendly and had no history of growling or snapping...[and] had just received some table scraps....Encountering Hollow, Shannon decided to pet him and asked Scott if he bit. Although Scott said "no," Shannon asked him to pet Hollow first. Scott...petted him, at which time Hollow barked. Shannon...then petted him on top of his head....Hollow jumped up, knocked her down, and bit her in the face...[causing injuries which will leave permanent scars].

Plaintiffs subsequently initiated an action based upon the provisions of Minn. Stat. §347.22 (1980). This statute states that:

> If a dog, without provocation, attacks or injures any person who is peaceably conducting himself in any place where he may lawfully be, the owner of the dog is liable in damages to the person so attacked or injured to the full amount of the injury sustained....

....[The] District Court Judge...directed a verdict in favor of plaintiffs on the issue of statutory liability, [but]...submitted the question of...contributory negligence to the jury. The jury returned a verdict apportioning 50% of the negligence to the minor plaintiff and 50% to the defendant. [A judgment for plaintiffs was entered in an amount equal to one-half of their damages.]....We reverse and remand this case to the district court with directions to restore the full verdict of $2,325.50....

The statute at issue...permits a person attacked by a dog to recover damages simply by proving that the statute has been violated. If the elements set forth by the statute are satisfied, the legislature has decided to impose liability without fault, or strict liability, upon the owner of the dog. The question arises, therefore, whether the statutory strict liability of the defendant under Minn. Stat. §347.22 (1980) may be compared with the ordinary negligence of the minor plaintiff under Minn. Stat. §604.01 (1980)....

[The court then discussed §604.01, a 1978 comparative fault statute which significantly broadened the scope of an earlier comparative negligence law and included "strict tort liability" in its definition of fault.]

... [R]esolution of this case requires an understanding of what types of tort liability may arise due to the violation of a statute and the defenses that may be asserted in such instances.

Negligence *per se* is a form of ordinary negligence that results from violation of a statute....Such statutes are often penal statutes that do not provide for a civil action. The statute is said to express a policy for the protection of a certain class of persons. *See* Minn. Stat. §126.20 (1980) (requiring protective eye glasses when operating machinery); *id.* §609.675 (requiring owners of refrigerators to detach door before abandoning); *id.* §624.21 (outlawing the sale of fireworks). Thus, to violate the statute is to deviate from the standard of care owed to another. [Citation.] But, as pointed out by Prosser, negligence *per se* is not liability *per se*. "[T]here remain [the defenses of] assumption of risk, contributory negligence and proximate cause....In short, such 'negligence *per se*' is merely ordinary negligence, whose existence is established by proof of the violation, but which once proved does not differ in its legal consequences from negligence at common law."....

A second type of tort liability that may be created by statute is strict liability....

....

... [S]tatutory strict liability...is distinct from negligence *per se* for two reasons. First, a statutory strict liability statute purports to create a basis for recovery where none would otherwise exist while statutes forming the basis of a negligence *per se* action are often penal and do not expressly provide for a civil action. For example, the statute at issue in this case states that the owner of a dog is "liable in damages" if certain conditions exist. Minn. Stat. §347.22 (1980). In contrast, *id.* §624.21 merely prohibits the sale of fireworks. Although the latter statute provides for no civil liability, the legislature has established a policy that, if deviated from, may constitute negligence. Second, violation of a strict liability statute, by itself, renders the violator liable without any showing of fault. In the case of negligence *per se*, violation of the statute is a form of fault that may evidence negligence.

This court has previously considered the categorization of the statute at issue in this case. In Lavalle v. Kaupp, 240 Minn. 360, 61 N.W.2d 228 (1953), violation of the statute was viewed as imposing strict liability and not negligence....

The preceding analysis appears to answer the question of what defenses are permitted in a statutory strict liability case.... [B]ecause of the specific inclusion of "strict tort liability" in the comparative fault statute's definition of fault, the comparative fault statute requires the comparison of plaintiff negligence with defendant statutory strict liability. Thus...it may be argued that even though the minor plaintiff did not provoke the dog as a matter of law, she may have been negligent and that this negligence should be permitted to mitigate respondent's damages.

The above discussion would mandate affirmance in this case except for an additional factor. No consideration has yet been given to another doctrine that developed contemporaneously with the law of statutory strict liability and negligence *per se*—absolute liability. The doctrine of absolute liability is applicable when the legislature, by enacting a particular statute, intends to preclude certain defenses and place the entire responsibility for the injury upon the individual who violated the statute. The doctrine of absolute liability was recognized before enactment of the comparative negligence statute with reference to negligence *per se* in Dart v. Pure Oil Co., 223 Minn. 526, 27 N.W.2d 555 (1947). In *Dart*, the court recognized the existence of an exceptional class of statutes that, by legislative design, do not permit the defense of contributory negligence when it is found that the statute "was intended...for the protection of a limited class of persons from their inability to protect themselves." [Citation.] Types of statutes included in this category are child labor statutes, statutes for the protection of intoxicated persons, and statutes prohibiting sale of dangerous articles to minors. [Citation]; *see* Restatement (Second) of Torts §483, Comment c (1965).

In Lavalle v. Kaupp,...[*supra*], the court indicated that the legislature intended the statute at issue in the instant case to leave the owner of a dog "with the strict liability of an insurer."....*Lavalle* indicates that in 1953 this statute was equivalent to absolute liability except for the statutory defenses of provocation and failure to peaceably conduct oneself in any place where one may lawfully be.

It may be argued that both absolute liability based upon negligence *per se* and absolute statutory strict liability were abolished by the comparative negligence statute and its successor, the comparative fault statute. For assistance in resolving this difficult question of statutory construction, we look for guidance to the Uniform Comparative Fault Act, which provided a model for the 1978 Minnesota statute. [Citation.] The comments to the Uniform Act state that "[a] tort action based on violation of a statute is within the coverage of the Act if the conduct comes within the definition of fault and unless the statute is construed as intended to provide for recovery of full damage irrespective of contributory fault." [Citation.] Because the principle of absolute liability is based upon legislative intent, the comparative fault statute did not necessarily abolish absolute liability....

Although section 347.22 was not enacted to protect a limited class of persons unable to protect themselves, we hold that the legislature intended to impose absolute liability upon a violator of the law for two reasons. First this court in the *Lavalle* case indicated that the statute placed the entire responsibility of injury due to a dog bite upon the dog's owner if the elements of the statute were met. Thus, except for the defenses already built into the law, recovery is insured in all cases....Second, the [comment to section 1 of the] Uniform Comparative Fault Act...states that statutes that are "construed as intended to provide for recovery of *full damage* irrespective of contributory fault," are not covered by the Uniform Act. [Citation.] The statute at issue in this case states that the "owner of the dog is liable in damages to the person so attacked or injured *to the full amount of the injury sustained*." [Citation.] The similarity of language between the comment to the Uniform Act and the statute at issue herein provides a compelling reason to conclude that section 347.22 was meant to provide absolute statutory strict liability. Our application of the absolute liability doctrine during this era of comparative fault recognizes the principle that the legislative body that enacted the comparative fault statute has the authority to carve out or preserve exceptions to the statute in the interest of public policy. We reverse and remand with directions to restore the full jury verdict.

. . . .

Reversed and remanded with directions.

Notes

1. *Statutes Intended to Protect Class Members from Inability to Protect Themselves.* *See also* Zerby v. Warren, 210 N.W.2d 58 (Minn. 1973) (retailer who sold glue to a minor in violation of statute was absolutely liable for the death of another minor who intentionally sniffed the glue; assumption of risk and comparative negligence were no defense); *but see* District of Columbia v. Brown, 589 A.2d 384 (D.C. 1991) (elevator

safety law was not intended to protect persons from their own negligence, and therefore recovery was barred for the death of a 19-year-old, 320-pound former football player who was contributorily negligent as a matter of law when he drove his shoulder against an elevator door in a public housing project and fell into the shaft).

2. *Worker-Safety Legislation.* In actions based on violations of worker-protection statutes, such as those requiring adequate worksite lighting or safety devices, the defenses of contributory negligence and assumption of the risk are typically not available. *See, e.g.,* Wren v. Sullivan Elec. Co., 797 F.2d 323 (6th Cir. 1986); Zimmer v. Chemung County Performing Arts, Inc., 482 N.E.2d 898 (N.Y. 1985).

D. Special Standards of Care

Terms like "slight negligence" and "gross negligence" have sometimes been used for the purpose of varying the negligence standard of care. In general, however, courts have eschewed gradations in the negligence standard, for while such distinctions are theoretically possible, they often prove impractical in application. The question of whether a party's negligence is slight, ordinary, or gross can be highly fact-specific, time-consuming, and subject to dispute on appeal. To avoid devoting disproportionate judicial resources to inquiries which have no precedential value, courts tend to distinguish negligence only from such other broad categories of tort liability as intentional harm, recklessness, and strict-liability conduct. With slight exaggeration, one court commented:

> Care does not increase or diminish by calling it names. We think the abstract concept of reasonable care is in itself quite difficult enough to grapple with and apply in our law without our courts gratuitously conferring honorary degrees upon it. There is only *one* degree of care in the law, and that is the standard of care which may reasonably be required or expected under all the circumstances of a given situation....

Spence v. Three Rivers Bldrs. & Masonry Supply, 90 N.W.2d 873, 878 (Mich. 1958). However, legislatures have shown a greater propensity to subdivide the negligence category or invent terms having no established meaning in the common law of torts (see the reference to "heedlessness" in the statute discussed in Whitworth v. Bynum, 699 S.W.2d 194 (Tex. 1985)).

Common Carriers and Bailees. It is sometimes said that a common carrier will be held liable for slight negligence, and that a gratuitous bailee will be liable only for gross negligence. *See* Fowler V. Harper, Fleming James, Jr., & Oscar S. Gray, The Law of Torts §§16.13–16.14 (2d ed. 1986); Andrews v. United Airlines, Inc., 24 F.3d 39, 40–41 (9th Cir. 1994) (because a common carrier owes "both a duty of utmost care and the vigilance of a very cautious person towards [its] passengers," there was a genuine issue of material fact as to whether the airline had done "everything technology permits and prudence dictates" to protect passengers from harm caused by baggage falling from overhead compartments). *But see* Bethel v. N.Y. City Transit Auth., 703 N.E.2d 1214 (N.Y. 1998) (holding that "the rule of a common carrier's duty of extraordinary care is no longer viable" and that "a common carrier is subject to the same duty of care as any other potential tortfeasor—reasonable care under all of the circumstances").

Automobile Guest Statutes. Legislatures have sometimes immunized classes of defendants from suits based on ordinary negligence, imposing liability only for aggravated levels of misconduct. For example, persistent lobbying by insurance companies led to the passage of automobile guest statutes in more than half of the states between 1920 and 1970. While they differed in their language, these statutes generally provided that the owner or operator of a car was liable to a non-paying passenger only for aggravated misconduct that in some way exceeded ordinary negligence. Eventually such laws came under attack, and they were held unconstitutional or legislatively repealed. As suggested in Whitworth v. Bynum, 699 S.W.2d 194 (Tex. 1985), courts frequently found that neither of the two justifications traditionally offered to support such statutes — (1) protection of hospitality and (2) prevention of collusive lawsuits — constituted a rational basis for differential treatment. Regarding hospitality, courts tended to say that there was no valid reason to distinguish between automobile guests and other types of guests, and that exposure to liability for ordinary negligence would not deter hospitality because automobile insurance is widely available, often compulsory, and would spread a loss so that it would not fall heavily on the driver or owner. As to preventing collusive claims against insurance companies, courts generally held that guest statutes were over-inclusive and irrational because they barred not only the few fraudulent claims but the great majority of valid ones as well.

One possible response to the judicial invalidation of an automobile guest statute was for an insurance company to redraft its contracts to exclude coverage for suits by family members. *But see* National County Mut. Fire Ins. Co. v. Johnson, 879 S.W.2d 1 (Tex. 1993) (holding that a family member exclusion in an automobile policy was invalid up to the level of minimum coverage mandated by the compulsory insurance statute).

Obsolete Statutes. The cases invalidating automobile guest statutes may perhaps be best understood as judicial attempts to grapple with apparently obsolete statutes that restricted tort liability in the face of a strong trend favoring compensation of accident victims and spreading of losses. According to conventional wisdom, a court faced with an out-of-date statute has essentially no options other than to apply it as written, hold it unconstitutional, or attempt to force, sometimes disingenuously, a more functional interpretation. However, there is some support (at least in academic circles) for the view that other avenues of judicial action may be available. *See* Guido Calabresi, A Common Law for the Age of Statutes (1982). For example, if a court thinks that a statute no longer fits the legal landscape and in all likelihood would not be repassed, it may be better to act in a manner that will facilitate, rather than preclude, legislative reconsideration. Thus, rather than holding an automobile guest statute to be unconstitutional, a court might consider attempting to break the legislative inertia on the subject by, for example, (1) applying the law to the instant case, but criticizing it on policy grounds; (2) applying the law to the instant case, but raising doubts whether it will survive constitutional scrutiny in future cases; or perhaps even (3) declining to enforce the law unless it is repassed by the legislature. (The last option is a radical alternative; the first two alternatives are not, and have plenty of precedent.) In each instance, the idea would be for the court to exercise its common-law expertness in determining when a rule is outdated and to then act in a way which best facilitates reconsideration and perhaps revision of the obsolete rule. Whether courts should exercise such powers is a subject of much debate.

In Franklin v. Hill, 444 S.E.2d 778 (Ga. 1994), the court struck down as an unconstitutional violation of the Georgia Constitution's equal protection clause an 1863 statute which imposed liability only upon men by giving parents a cause of action for seduction of their unmarried daughter. Justice Sears-Collins, in a concurring opinion, stated:

I write separately to urge a new method for reviewing the validity of statutes that focuses not on the application of traditional constitutional and interpretive principles but rather on what, in many cases, would be the less strained approach of examining whether the statute has become obsolete since its enactment.

Citing Calabresi's book for support, the Justice would have affirmed the trial court's grant of summary judgment for the defendant because the statute had become obsolete, "thus forcing the General Assembly to reexamine the tort of seduction in view of modern day concepts." *Id.* at 783.

Chapter 6

Proving Negligence

"The burden of proving negligence is on the party alleging it, and merely establishing that an accident happened does not prove it." Macfie v. Kaminski, 364 N.W.2d 31 (Neb. 1985) (skidding of a car without more does not prove negligence).

A. Evidence of Custom

The T.J. Hooper

United States Court of Appeals for the Second Circuit
60 F.2d 737 (2d Cir. 1932)

L. HAND, Circuit Judge.

The barges No. 17 and No. 30, belonging to the Northern Barge Company, had lifted cargoes of coal at Norfolk, Virginia, for New York in March, 1928. They were towed by two tugs of the petitioner, the 'Montrose' and the 'Hooper,' and were lost off the Jersey Coast on March tenth, in an easterly gale. The cargo owners sued the barges under the contracts of carriage; the owner of the barges sued the tugs under the towing contract, both for its own loss and as bailee of the cargoes.... [T]he judge found that all the vessels were unseaworthy; the tugs, because they did not carry radio receiving sets by which they could have seasonably got warnings of a change in the weather which should have caused them to seek shelter in the Delaware Breakwater en route. He therefore entered an interlocutory decree holding each tug and barge jointly liable to each cargo owner, and each tug for half damages for the loss of its barge. The petitioner appealed, and the barge owner appealed and filed assignments of error.

....

The weather bureau at Arlington broadcasts two predictions daily, at ten in the morning and ten in the evening. Apparently there are other reports floating about, which come at uncertain hours but which can also be picked up. The Arlington report of the morning read as follows: "Moderate north, shifting to east and southeast winds, increasing Friday, fair weather to-night." The substance of this, apparently from another source, reached a tow bound north to New York about noon, and, coupled with a falling glass, decided the master to put in to the Delaware Breakwater in the afternoon. The glass had not indeed fallen much and perhaps the tug was over cautious; nevertheless, although the appearances were all fair, he thought discretion the better part of valor. Three other tows followed him, the masters of two of which testified. Their decision was in part determined by example; but they too had received the Arlington report or its equivalent, and though it is doubtful whether alone it would have turned the scale, it is plain that it left them in an indecision which needed little to be resolved on the side of prudence; they preferred to take no chances, and chances they believed there were....

Moreover, the "Montrose" and the "Hooper" would have had the benefit of the evening report from Arlington had they had proper receiving sets. This predicted worse weather....The master of the "Montrose" himself, when asked what he would have done had he received a substantially similar report, said that he would certainly have put in....Taking the situation as a whole, it seems to us that these masters would have taken undue chances, had they got the broadcasts.

They did not, because their private radio receiving sets, which were on board, were not in working order. These belonged to them personally, and were partly a toy, partly a part of the equipment, but neither furnished by the owner, nor supervised by it. It is not fair to say that there was a general custom among coastwise carriers so to equip their tugs. One line alone did it; as for the rest, they relied upon their crews, so far as they can be said to have relied at all. An adequate receiving set suitable for a coastwise tug can now be got at small cost and is reasonably reliable if kept up; obviously it is a source of great protection to their tows. Twice every day they can receive these predictions, based upon the widest possible information, available to every vessel within two or three hundred miles and more. Such a set is the ears of the tug to catch the spoken word, just as the master's binoculars are her eyes to see a storm signal ashore. Whatever may be said as to other vessels, tugs towing heavy coal laden barges, strung out for half a mile, have little power to manoeuvre, and do not, as this case proves, expose themselves to weather which would not turn back stauncher craft. They can have at hand protection against dangers of which they can learn in no other way.

Is it then a final answer that the business had not yet generally adopted receiving sets? There are, no doubt, cases where courts seem to make the general practice of the calling the standard of proper diligence; we have indeed given some currency to the notion ourselves. [Citations.] Indeed in most cases reasonable prudence is in fact common prudence; but strictly it is never its measure; a whole calling may have unduly lagged in the adoption of new and available devices. It never may set its own tests, however persuasive be its usages. Courts must in the end say what is required; there are precautions so imperative that even their universal disregard will not excuse their omission. [Citation.] But here there was no custom at all as to receiving sets; some had them, some did not; the most that can be urged is that they had not yet become general. Certainly in such a case we need not pause; when some have thought a device necessary, at least we may say that they were right, and the others too slack....We hold the tugs therefore because had they been properly equipped, they would have got the Arlington reports. The injury was a direct consequence of this unseaworthiness.

Decree affirmed.

Notes

1. *What Was the Custom in The T.J. Hooper?* Judge Hand was wrong in thinking that there was no generally followed custom with regard to receivers: nearly all tugs carried them. One reason why the trial judge in *The T.J. Hooper* ruled that the T.J. Hooper and the Montrose were unseaworthy was that 90 percent of coastwise tugs carried radio receivers; 53 F.2d 107 (S.D.N.Y. 1931). Judge Hand may have been misled by the fact that many of the receivers belonged to the captains of the tugs, rather than to the tugs' own-

ers. To say that there was no custom of having receivers because the captains, rather than the owners, often provided the radios makes no more sense than to say that it is customary for automobile repairs to be done without wrenches on the ground that mechanics, rather than the garages which employ them, usually provide hand tools.

What determines whether the employee or the employer provides the tools needed to do a job? (Hint: the relative wealth of the parties should have nothing to do with the matter—if doing a job requires $100 worth of equipment a month and labor costing $1000, the employer can either (1) pay an employee $1000 and provide the $100 in equipment, or (2) pay $1100 to an employee who brings equipment along.)

Suppose that (1) both tugboat owners and their customers (who are also professionals in the shipping business) decide that the benefit of having radio receivers does not justify their cost, and (2) a judge whose nautical experience is confined to the Staten Island Ferry thinks receivers are worth their cost. How likely is it that the judge is right and the professionals wrong? Note that cases like *The T.J. Hooper* are not cases in which any of the harm will fall on persons who are not parties to the transaction in question. One can easily understand why a business might fail to take cost-justified precautions to prevent harm to outsiders. But no business owner has an incentive to refuse to pay $100 for something that would provide more than $100 in benefits to the owner or to the business's customers. To be sure, the owner of one particular business may be bad at making the proper estimates. But the failure of *any* proprietor in a particular line to adopt a particular precaution that has long been available suggests strongly that the precaution is not cost-justified.

For an exhaustive analysis of the relationship between custom and negligence and of *The T.J. Hooper, see* Richard A. Epstein, *The Path to The T.J. Hooper: The Theory and History of Custom in the Law of Tort*, XXI J. Legal Stud. 1 (1992).

Low v. Park Price Co.

Supreme Court of Idaho
503 P.2d 291 (Idaho 1972)

DONALDSON, Justice.

The defendant-respondent, Highway Motor Company, dba Park Price Motors, operates an automobile repair garage in Pocatello, Idaho. On December 2, 1969, Cal Dale Low, the son of plaintiff-appellant Dale K. Low, brought the latter's car to the respondent's garage for repairs. In order to make these repairs, it was necessary to remove the engine from the appellant's car. Having removed the engine, the respondent stored the car in an unfenced area between the garage and an adjacent street. While the vehicle was stored in this location, its transmission disappeared. On or about December 18, the respondent told the appellant that the transmission had been stolen. Exactly when and by whom the transmission was removed are facts which remain unknown.

The respondent disclaimed any obligation to compensate the appellant for the loss of his transmission. The appellant then commenced this action for conversion and, in the alternative, for negligence. The parties stipulated that the lost transmission had a reasonable market value of five hundred dollars.... [T]he respondent admitted its status as "bailee" of the appellant's automobile. After a nonjury trial, the district court entered judgment in favor of the respondent garage owner and denied the appellant car owner's motion for a new trial. This appeal followed.

....As a bailee for hire, a repair garage operator is required to exercise ordinary or reasonable care to protect vehicles entrusted to his custody for repairs or servicing....

....

....While courts are ordinarily reluctant to impose upon defendants the duty of proving the non-existence of negligence, an exception is justified in bailment cases....

In its defense at trial, the respondent-bailee introduced testimony as to the currently prevailing custom and usage regularly observed by other service garages in the area.... As a general rule, the customs of the community, or of others under like circumstances, are factors to be taken into account in determining whether conduct is negligent. Restatement (Second) of Torts §295A (1965). We do not think this is one of the extreme cases where it may be said that the defendant's practices, or those customarily adhered to by others similarly situated, are negligent as a matter of law. Therefore, the evidence of custom was properly admitted in this case. But the appellant further contends that the trial court erroneously reasoned that simply *because* the respondent had adhered to the customary practices among garage owners in the area, the respondent was, for that reason — and for that reason only — not negligent. "In determining whether conduct is negligent, the customs of the community, or of others under like circumstances, are factors to be taken into account, *but are not controlling where a reasonable man would not follow them.*" *Id.* (emphasis added). In other words, "custom or usage does not determine ordinary care, but the standard is what a reasonably prudent man under like circumstances would do." [Citation.] Or, as Justice Holmes succinctly stated the rule: "What usually is done may be evidence of what ought to be done, but what ought to be done is fixed by a standard of reasonable prudence, whether it usually is complied with or not." [Citations.] A good summary of the law is contained in comments b and c to §295A of the Restatement (Second) of Torts (1965):

> b. *Relevance of Custom.* Any such custom of the community in general, or of other persons under like circumstances, is always a factor to be taken into account in determining whether the actor has been negligent. Evidence of the custom is admissible, and is relevant, as indicating a composite judgment as to the risks of the situation and the precautions required to meet them, as well as the feasibility of such precautions, the difficulty of any change in accepted methods, the actor's opportunity to learn what is called for, and the justifiable expectation of others that he will do what is usual, as well as the justifiable expectation of the actor that others will do the same. If the actor does what others do under like circumstances, there is at least a possible inference that he is conforming to the community standard of reasonable conduct; and if he does not do what others do, there is a possible inference that he is not so conforming. In particular instances, where there is nothing in the situation or in common experience to lead to the contrary conclusion, this inference may be so strong as to call for a directed verdict, one way or the other, on the issue of negligence. Thus, even in the absence of any applicable traffic statute, one who drives on the right side of a private way is under ordinary circumstances clearly not negligent in doing so, and one who drives on the left side is under ordinary circumstances clearly negligent.

> On the same basis, evidence of the past practices of the parties to the action in dealing with each other is admissible, and relevant, as indicating an understood standard of conduct, or the reasonable expectation of each party as to what the other will do.

> c. *When Custom [Is] Not Controlling.* ... Customs which are entirely reasonable under the ordinary circumstances which give rise to them may become quite unreasonable in the light of a single fact in the particular case. It may be

negligence to drive on the right side of the road, and it may not be negligence to drive on the left side when the right side is blocked by a dangerous ditch. Beyond this, customs and usages themselves are many and various. Some of them are the result of careful thought and decision, while others arise from the kind of inadvertence, neglect, or deliberate disregard of a known risk which is associated with negligence. No group of individuals and no industry or trade can be permitted, by adopting careless and slipshod methods to save time, effort, or money, to set its own uncontrolled standard at the expense of the rest of the community. If the only test is to be what has always been done, no one will ever have any great incentive to make any progress in the direction of safety. It follows, therefore, that whenever the particular circumstances, the risk, or other elements in the case are such that a reasonable man would not conform to the custom, the actor may be found negligent in conforming to it; and whenever a reasonable man would depart from the custom, the actor may be found not to be negligent in so departing....

... [W]e note that since the respondent has shown that it has done what others do under like circumstances, there is at least an inference that it is conforming to the community's idea of reasonable behavior. Prosser on Torts, *supra* at 169; *see* Restatement (Second) Torts, *supra* §295A, comment b. Where there is nothing in the evidence or in common experience to lead to a contrary conclusion, the inference arising from conformity to custom may be so strong that the issue of negligence may be determined as a matter of law. [Citations.] We conclude that this is such a case.... [E]ven though the burden of persuasion is on the respondent-bailee, in this case the bailee proved, by a preponderance of the evidence, its freedom from negligence.

....

Judgment affirmed. Costs to respondent.

Notes

1. *See generally* Restatement, Third, of Torts: Liability for Physical Harm (Basic Principles) §13 (Tent. Draft No. 1, 2001) (discussing custom).

2. **Social Customs.** *See* Bouton v. Allstate Ins. Co., 491 So. 2d 56, 58 (La. Ct. App. 1986) (in finding that trick-or-treaters were not negligent in frightening a homeowner, the court noted that "society encourages children to transform themselves into witches, demons, and ghosts, and play a game threatening neighbors into giving them candy").

3. **Industry Customs and Practices.** In Ray v. American Natl. Red Cross, 696 A.2d 399, 407 (D.C. 1997), a suit involving HIV-contaminated blood, the court held that an instruction which "focused the jury's attention almost exclusively on the evidence concerning industry practice" and, at least initially, "'defined' the standard of care in terms of industry custom and practice" was erroneous. The standard was "what [a] reasonable and prudent blood bank[ ] would do under the same or similar circumstances."

B. Circumstantial Evidence

There are two chief categories of evidence, direct and circumstantial, and evidence falling within either class may be used to prove the defendant's negligence and other issues in a tort action. Direct evidence is evidence which tends directly to support a finding of a fact in issue, such as eyewitness testimony that the defendant's vehicle was traveling in the wrong lane. Circumstantial evidence, in contrast, is evidence not of a disputed fact, but of one or more other facts from which the existence or non-existence of the fact in issue may reasonably be inferred. For example, evidence of skid marks may be used to prove circumstantially that the defendant's car was traveling faster than the speed limit.

The strength of either type of evidence will vary according to the particular facts, including the credibility of the witnesses providing the evidence and the presence of corroborating facts. It is a serious mistake to think that direct evidence is always more persuasive than circumstantial evidence, for while eyewitness testimony from a credible source is valuable evidence, it often pales in comparison to such circumstantial evidence as footprints, fingerprints, or traces of blood. Eyewitness testimony that the defendant chopped off the plaintiff's foot is worthless if the plaintiff shows up in court with two perfectly functioning feet.

1. Constructive Notice

Goddard v. Boston & M.R. Co.

Supreme Judicial Court of Massachusetts
60 N.E. 486 (Mass. 1901)

Action by Wilfred H. Goddard against the Boston & Maine Railroad Company for personal injuries received by falling upon a banana skin lying upon the platform at defendant's station at Boston. The evidence showed that plaintiff was a passenger who had just arrived, and was about the length of the car from where he alighted when he slipped and fell. There was evidence that there were many passengers on the platform. Verdict directed for defendant, and plaintiff excepts....

    ....

HOLMES, C.J.

The banana skin upon which the plaintiff stepped and which caused him to slip may have been dropped within a minute by one of the persons who was leaving the train. It is unnecessary to go further to decide the case.

Exceptions overruled.

Note

1. *See* Kennedy v. Wal-Mart Stores, 733 So. 2d 1188 (La. 1999) (holding that a customer who produced evidence that a large puddle of water was in an area within view of the customer service podium and that it was raining on the evening in question failed to prove constructive notice because there was "absolutely no evidence as to the length of time the puddle was on the floor").

It is important to keep in mind the demands of the preponderance of the evidence standard. *See* Threlkeld v. Total Petroleum, Inc., 211 F.3d 887 (5th Cir. 2000) ("if a plaintiff cannot prove facts to establish that it is more likely than not that the dangerous condition existed long enough that a proprietor should have known of its presence, there is simply no basis for recovery").

Anjou v. Boston Elevated Ry. Co.

Supreme Judicial Court of Massachusetts
94 N.E. 386 (Mass. 1911)

Action by Helen G. Anjou against the Boston Elevated Railway Company. Verdict
was directed for defendant....

....

RUGG, J.

The plaintiff arrived on one of defendant's cars on the upper level of the Dudley
Street terminal; other passengers arrived on same car, but it does not appear how many.
She waited until the crowd had left the platform, when she inquired of one of defendant's uniformed [employees] the direction to another car. He walked along a narrow
platform, and she, following a few feet behind him toward the stairway he had indicated, was injured by slipping upon a banana peel. It was described by several who examined it in these terms: It "felt dry, gritty, as if there were dirt upon it," as if "trampled
over a good deal," as "flattened down, and black in color," "every bit of it was black,
there wasn't a particle of yellow," and as "black, flattened out and gritty." It was one of
the duties of [employees] of the defendant, of whom there was one at this station all the
time, to observe and remove whatever was upon the platform to interfere with the
safety of travelers. These might have been found to be the facts.

The inference might have been drawn from the appearance and condition of the banana peel that it had been upon the platform a considerable period of time, in such position that it would have been seen and removed by the [employees] of the defendant if
they had been reasonably careful in performing their duty. Therefore there is something
on which to base a conclusion that it was not dropped a moment before by a passenger,
and Goddard v. Boston & Maine R.R., 179 Mass. 52, 60 N.E. 486, and Lyons v. Boston
Elevated Railway Co., 204 Mass. 227, 90 N.E. 419, are plainly distinguishable. The
obligation rested upon the defendant to keep its station reasonably safe for its passengers. It might have been found that the platform was suffered to remain in such condition as to be a menace to those rightfully walking upon it. Hence there was evidence of
negligence on the part of the defendant, which should have been submitted to the jury.
[Citations.]

....

Judgement for the plaintiff for $1250 with costs.

Notes

1. *Discoloration.* Courts may differ as to what inferences may be drawn from relatively similar sets of facts, and minor differences in factual detail may precipitate different results. In Joye v. Great Atlantic and Pacific Tea Co., 405 F.2d 464 (4th Cir. 1968),
the plaintiff slipped on a banana which was "brown in color, having dirt and sand on
it." Noting that "[t]here was dirt on the floor near the banana, and that the banana was
sticky around the edges," the court held that the evidence was insufficient to present a
jury issue as to constructive notice. "[T]he jury could not tell whether the banana had
been on defendant's floor for 30 seconds or 3 days." In contrast, in J.C. Penney Co., Inc.
v. Chavez, 618 S.W.2d 399, 401 (Tex. Civ. App. 1981), the court upheld a judgment in a
slip-and-fall case where the evidence established that the banana on which the plaintiff

slipped was "discolored, 'gooey' and 'black with yellow stripes.'" In *Chavez*, a bystander testified that "the banana peel looked like it was several hours old." Does such testimony assist the trier of fact?

2. ***Proximity and Opportunity to Discover.*** How can you prove constructive notice of a clear liquid, such as water, which does not discolor with age? Some courts seem to hold that proximity to the site of the danger is a basis for concluding that the danger should have been discovered and remedied. For example, in Thoma v. Cracker Barrel Old Country Store, 649 So. 2d 277, 278–79 (Fla. Dist. Ct. App. 1995), the court reversed a grant of summary judgment for the defendant, observing:

> The area of the fall was in clear view of Cracker Barrel employees, since they traversed it regularly on their way in and out of the kitchen. If a jury were to believe Thoma's description of the liquid as covering an area 1 foot by 2 feet, it might also be convinced that Cracker Barrel employees, in the exercise of due diligence, should have noticed the liquid before the accident. No one except Cracker Barrel employees were seen to carry food or beverage in the area of the fall, and the manager of the restaurant would not have expected customers to move around carrying food or drinks.

However, other courts hold that:

> An employee's proximity to a hazard, with no evidence indicating how long the hazard was there, merely indicates that it was *possible* for the premises owner to discover the condition, not that the premises owner reasonably *should* have discovered it....Without some temporal evidence, there is no basis upon which the factfinder can reasonably assess the opportunity the premises owner had to discover the dangerous condition.

Wal-Mart Stores, Inc. v. Reece, 81 S.W.3d 812 (Tex. 2002). *Reece* found insufficient evidence of constructive notice of a clear-liquid spill even though an employee of the defendant was only five to eight feet from the plaintiff at the time she slipped and fell. The plaintiff presented no evidence to show what had caused the spill or how long it had been present.

3. ***Absence of Inspection.*** The absence of an inspection is sometimes relevant to the issue of constructive notice. In Ortega v. K-Mart Corp., 114 Cal Rptr. 2d 470 (Cal. 2001), the court held that evidence that a supermarket operator had not inspected the aisle where a patron slipped on a puddle of milk for at least 15 to 30 minutes, and that the milk could have been on the floor for as long as two hours, permitted an inference that the dangerous condition had existed long enough for it to be discovered by the owner. The court noted, quoting an earlier case:

> "The exact time the condition must exist before it should, in the exercise of reasonable care, have been discovered and remedied, cannot be fixed, because, obviously, it varies according to the circumstances. A person operating a grocery and vegetable store in the exercise of ordinary care must exercise a more vigilant outlook than the operator of some other types of business where the danger of things falling to the floor is not so obvious."

4. ***Prior Occurrence.*** A jury sometimes may infer constructive notice of a dangerous condition from evidence of similar dangers on previous occasions. In Beach Bait & Tackle v. Bull, 82 S.W.3d 663 (Tex. Ct. App. 2002), the court held that because there was evidence that water seeping under a wall had previously caused water to be present at the location where the plaintiff fell, the jury could conclude that the defendant knew

that there would be water on the floor in that location after it rained. *See also* Nicholson v. St. Anne Lanes, Inc., 483 N.E.2d 291 (Ill. App. Ct. 1985) (bartender previously observed soap on the restroom floor and knew that the small bars of soap used by the defendant could create a potentially dangerous condition).

2. Mode of Operation

Corbin v. Safeway Stores, Inc.

Supreme Court of Texas
648 S.W.2d 292 (Tex. 1983)

SPEARS, Justice.

Gary Corbin sued Safeway Stores, Inc. ("Safeway") for damages resulting from personal injuries he suffered when he slipped on a grape and fell in a Safeway produce aisle. The trial court granted Safeway's motion for directed verdict, and the court of appeals affirmed.... We reverse... and remand the cause for a new trial.

In October 1977 Gary Corbin slipped on a grape or grapes directly in front of the self-service grape bin in a Safeway produce aisle and fell on the store's green linoleum tile floor. While sprawled on the floor, he noticed several ruptured and discolored grapes lying around him. He saw no mat or other floor covering of any kind in the area where he fell. As a result of the fall, Corbin injured... his right knee....

At trial, a store manager trainee and a district manager of Safeway testified that company policy required each store to keep large non-skid, non-slip walk-off mats in front of the grape display. According to these two employees, the reason for this requirement was that Safeway recognized that customers frequently either knock grapes off their stems or drop them, creating a great risk that someone will subsequently step on a slippery grape peel and fall on the linoleum floor.... The mats were considered necessary because store employees were unable adequately to supervise the floor to ensure that it remained free of grapes.

. . . .

.... To recover from Safeway,... Corbin had the burden to prove (1) that Safeway had actual or constructive knowledge of some condition on the premises; (2) that the condition posed an unreasonable risk of harm to Corbin; (3) that Safeway did not exercise reasonable care to reduce or to eliminate the risk; and (4) that Safeway's failure to use such care proximately caused Corbin's personal injuries.

Corbin claimed at trial that there were three dangerous conditions in Safeway's store. First, he alleged that the presence on the floor of the specific grape on which he slipped posed an unreasonable risk of harm and that Safeway had constructive knowledge of that risk. Safeway does not deny the unreasonableness of that risk, but contends Corbin produced no proof of the requisite constructive knowledge. We agree. Corbin's testimony that the grapes lying around him were discolored and ruptured does not tend to prove that the grapes had been on the floor a sufficient time to impute knowledge of their location to Safeway. The aging and discoloration may just as likely have occurred before as after the grapes fell, and the rupturing could have been caused during or soon before Corbin's accident....

Second, Corbin claimed that the floor was dangerous because it was excessively dirty and littered. He introduced evidence that this Safeway store has a history of letting its floors become filthy and that the last time Safeway had swept the floor on which he fell was more than eight hours before his fall. This evidence, however, would not support a finding that the dirty floor proximately caused Corbin's fall, since he testified that he slipped on a grape, not on dirt or other slippery matter.

Finally, Corbin alleged that Safeway's chosen self-service method for displaying green grapes in an open, slanted bin above a green linoleum tile floor resulted in an unreasonable risk of customers falling on grapes that have fallen or been knocked to the floor. Safeway admitted that at the time of Corbin's fall it knew of this unusually high risk associated with its grape display. It argues, however, that it is not obligated to protect customers from the acts of other customers in causing grapes to fall to the floor, regardless of whether those acts are foreseeable. Safeway believes the only duty it owes its customers with respect to the prevention of these kinds of falls is to pick up whatever objects it finds or should find on the floors of the store. We do not agree.

In all negligence actions, the foreseeability of the harmful consequences resulting from the particular conduct is the underlying basis for liability. Thus, Corbin's right to recover from Safeway depends on his showing Safeway's knowledge of the foreseeable harm of some course of conduct or method of operation. He is not required to prove one particular instance of negligence or knowledge of one specific hazard, as Safeway contends. [Citation.]

....

....There was...evidence that no mat was in front of the grape display at the time Corbin fell. Furthermore, Safeway acknowledges that it took no other action, such as bagging the grapes, warning customers, or conducting frequent inspections, to minimize this hazard. Under these circumstances, because reasonable minds could conclude that Safeway did not use reasonable care to take some preventive measure against a foreseeable harm, the question of its negligence was for the jury to decide.

....

Safeway also argues that if the directed verdict is not upheld, this court will be penalizing Safeway for its diligence in instituting the limited use of the walk-off mats as a company-wide safety measure. This argument reflects a misunderstanding of the basis for negligence liability. Safeway's liability to Corbin depends on its knowledge of store conditions posing risks to customers and the failure to act reasonably in response to those risks, not on the failure to comply with a company policy. If reasonable store conduct includes the use of mats or other floor coverings or even warnings in front of a particular display, then Safeway may be held liable for not using them, regardless of whether company policy requires them.

Many states now recognize that a storekeeper may be held liable for any dangerous premises condition about which he should be aware, not just for specific objects left on the floor by customers....Accordingly, we reverse the judgment of the court of appeals and remand this cause to the trial court for a new trial.

Notes

1. *Foreseeability of Danger.* To similar effect is Jasko v. Woolworth Co., 494 P.2d 839 (Colo. 1972), where plaintiff was injured after slipping on a piece of pizza:

> The practice of extensive selling of slices of pizza on waxed paper to customers who consume it while standing creates the reasonable probability that food will

drop to the floor. Food on a terrazzo floor will create a dangerous condition. In such a situation, notice to the proprietor of the specific item on the floor need not be shown.

The basic notice requirement springs from the thought that a dangerous condition, when it occurs, is somewhat out of the ordinary....However, when the operating methods of a proprietor are such that dangerous conditions are continuous or easily foreseeable, the logical basis for the notice requirement dissolves....

See also Owens v. Publix Supermarkets, Inc., 802 So. 2d 315 (Fla. 2001) (recognizing the continued viability of the "mode of operation theory," and stating "If the evidence establishes a specific negligent mode of operation such that the premises owner could reasonably anticipate that dangerous conditions would arise as a result of its mode of operation, then whether the owner had actual or constructive knowledge of the specific transitory foreign substance is not an issue"); Hammond v. Wal-Mart Stores, Inc., 971 F.2d 158 (8th Cir. 1992) (store employees working with slippery advertising signs left them unattended; store had presumptive knowledge of the dangerous condition created by the signs when they fell into the aisle, regardless of how long they had been in the aisle).

But see Wal-Mart Stores, Inc. v. Diaz, 109 S.W.3d 584 (Tex. Ct. App. 2003) (store's policy of allowing customers to carry drinks in store did not alone establish negligence).

2. ***Easing Plaintiff's Burden.*** Juries are notoriously unsympathetic to slip-and-fall cases. To address that issue, the court in *Owens, supra,* took the usual and controversial step of creating a presumption.

[O]nce the plaintiff establishes that he or she fell as a result of a transitory foreign substance, a rebuttable presumption of negligence arises. At that point, the burden shifts to the defendant to show by the greater weight of evidence that it exercised reasonable care in the maintenance of the premises under the circumstances.

802 So. 2d at 330. *See also* Lanier v. Wal-Mart Stores, Inc., 99 S.W.3d 431 (Ky. 2003) (similar; holding that issues of causation and notice are to be treated not as elements of the customer's case, but as affirmative defenses of the business proprietor).

As a result of lobbying, the decision in *Owens* was quickly superseded by an act of the legislature, which provides:

In any civil action for negligence involving...a transitory foreign object or substance on business premises, the claimant shall have the burden of proving that:

....

(b) The person or entity in possession or control of the business premises acted negligently by failing to exercise reasonable care in the maintenance, inspection, repair, warning, or mode of operation of the business premises. Actual or constructive notice of the transitory foreign object or substance is not a required element of proof to this claim. However, evidence of notice or lack of notice offered by any party may be considered together with all of the evidence....

Fla. Stat. Ann §768.0710 (Westlaw 2003).

C. *Res Ipsa Loquitur*

1. In General

Definitions and Examples. The Latin phrase *res ipsa loquitur* means "the thing speaks for itself." In tort law, *res ipsa loquitur* evidence is one form of circumstantial evidence which may satisfy the plaintiff's burden of proof on the issues of breach of duty and causation.

Under the *res ipsa loquitur* doctrine, facts establishing the special nature of the accident and the defendant's relationship to it may justify a jury's decision that the defendant more likely than not was negligent. Although authorities vary in articulating the requirements of the doctrine, all agree that the event giving rise to the harm must be of the type which does not ordinarily occur in the absence of negligence. In addition, there must be other facts which make it fair to conclude that the defendant was a legal cause of the event giving rise to the injuries.

There is reason to think that negligence was more likely that not the cause of the accident if a car falls off of a jack (Cramer v. Mengerhausen, 550 P.2d 740, 743 (Or. 1976)), or leaves the highway without apparent reason (Merchants Fast Motor Lines v. State, 917 S.W.2d 518 (Tex. Ct. App. 1996)), or detaches from a tow truck (Imig v. Beck, 503 N.E.2d 324 (Ill. 1986)); or if a riding mower turns over (Conaway v. Roberts, 725 S.W.2d 377 (Tex. Ct. App. 1987)); or a patient suffers a broken toe during a hemorrhoidectomy (Martin v. Petta, 694 S.W.2d 233 (Tex. Ct. App. 1985)), or falls out of bed despite restraining devices (Keyes v. Tallahassee Mem. Reg. Med. Ctr., 579 So. 2d 201 (Fla. Dist. Ct. App. 1991)); or an atomic simulator causes an unexpected explosion (Jenkins v. Whittaker Corp., 785 F.2d 720 (9th Cir. 1986)); or a light fixture falls from the ceiling (Anderson v. Service Merchandise, 485 N.W.2d 170 (Neb. 1992)).

> On the other hand there are many accidents which, as a matter of common knowledge, occur frequently enough without anyone's fault. A tumble downstairs,…an ordinary slip and fall,…a fire of unknown origin, will not in themselves justify the conclusion that negligence is the most likely explanation; and to such events *res ipsa loquitur* does not apply.

W. Page Keeton, Dan B. Dobbs, Robert E. Keeton, & David G. Owen, Prosser and Keeton on Torts 246 (4th ed. 1984).

Expert testimony is frequently used to assist the jury in determining whether harm was more likely than not caused by negligence. *See* States v. Lourdes Hosp., 792 N.E.2d 151 (N.Y. 2003) (alleged negligence by anesthesiologist in positioning a patient's arm during surgery).

See also Chism v. Campbell, 553 N.W.2d 741 (Neb. 1996) (because uncontroverted facts established that a fixed percentage of patients under general anesthesia will suffer damage to the teeth even in the absence of negligence and that there is simply no way in which to prevent such an occurrence, the doctrine was inapplicable as a matter of law); Trans. Amer. Holding v. Market-Antiques, 39 S.W.3d 640 (Tex. App. 2000) (in an action for damages caused by a fire in a neighboring store, plaintiffs were not entitled to *res ipsa loquitur* instruction because none of their experts testified that such a fire cannot begin without negligence and plaintiffs failed to show general knowledge of that proposition).

Procedural Effect. What is the value of having a *res ipsa loquitur* case? The procedural effect of *res ipsa loquitur* evidence varies from jurisdiction to jurisdiction. In general, there are three views: (1) In some states, if the jury finds from the evidence that the requirements of the doctrine have been met, it must find for the plaintiff unless the defendant introduces evidence to rebut a finding of negligence (that is, a presumption shifts the burden of going forward with evidence). (2) In a few of these states, the jury will be told that the defendant has the burden of proving that it was not negligent if the plaintiff establishes the elements of the doctrine (that is, a presumption shifts both the burden of going forward with evidence and the burden of persuasion). (3) In most jurisdictions, however, establishing the elements of *res ipsa* normally creates only a "*prima facie* case" of negligence, a permissible inference of negligence. This means that the evidence allows the plaintiff's case to go to the jury, but the jury may still find as a fact that the defendant was not negligent.

The Third Restatement endorses the permissible-inference view of *res ipsa loquitur* evidence. *See* Restatement, Third, of Torts: Liability for Physical Harm (Basic Principles) §17 (Tent. Draft No. 1, 2001) ("It may be inferred that the defendant has been negligent when the accident causing the plaintiff's physical harm is a type of accident that ordinarily happens because of the negligence of the class of actors of which the defendant is the relevant member").

Common Sense and Necessity. In one sense, the *res ipsa loquitur* doctrine is nothing more than common sense. It recognizes that it is appropriate to draw conclusions from circumstantial evidence.

> Surely judges and juries are capable of drawing conclusions from circumstantial evidence without the aid of a doctrine with a Latin name. However, the doctrine, by focusing on the likelihood of the essential components of the plaintiff's case, provides a logical framework for approaching circumstantial evidence. As such, it is a powerful antidote to an unfortunate judicial hesitancy to accept circumstantial evidence.

Stephen A. Spitz, *From Res Ipsa Loquitur to Diethylstilbestrol: The Unidentified Tortfeasor in California*, 65 Ind. L.J. 591 (1990).

In a different sense, *res ipsa loquitur* is a rule of necessity, for without it the plaintiff would often be unable to establish the defendant's negligence. Some courts hold that the doctrine is not available to a plaintiff who has access to conventional kinds of evidence of what went wrong. *See* Davies v. Butler, 602 P.2d 605 (Nev. 1979), *supra* at 135, (a *res ipsa loquitur* instruction was properly refused in a wrongful-death action in which nondefendant observers were present at every point in the events leading to the death and were fully available to testify); Ewen v. Baton Rouge Gen. Hosp., 378 So. 2d 172 (La. Ct. App. 1979) (doctrine inapplicable because plaintiffs failed to show absence of direct evidence to explain the activities leading to their son's death during cosmetic surgery).

Res ipsa loquitur is inapplicable if a plaintiff offers expert testimony that purports to furnish a complete explanation of the specific cause of an accident. *See* Dover Elevator Co. v. Swann, 638 A.2d 762 (Md. 1994) (the doctrine could not be used in a case involving an elevator's misleveling because the plaintiff's expert fully explained that the contacts were "burned," which caused the elevator to either "overshoot" or "stall" in the leveling zone).

a. Control

Mobil Chemical Co. v. Bell

Supreme Court of Texas
517 S.W.2d 245 (Tex. 1974)

McGEE, Justice.

This is a common law damage suit for personal injuries sustained by Edward L. Bell and J. A. Hurley, employees of an independent contractor constructing a large chemical plant for Mobil Chemical Company, when acetic acid escaped from a portion of the plant already completed and turned over to Mobil. A jury failed to find that Mobil was guilty of specific acts of negligence but answered *res ipsa loquitur* issues favorably to the plaintiffs. Based on these findings, judgment was entered that each plaintiff recover $12,000 from Mobil. The court of civil appeals has held...that the *res ipsa* theory was improperly submitted to the jury and has reversed and remanded for a new trial....

As in any *res ipsa* case, the particular facts surrounding the event are extremely important. This case involves a plant being constructed to manufacture terephthalic acid [TPA]....[As part of the manufacturing process, a liquid compound was pumped into a mechanism called "Unit A" and was subjected to great pressure. To avoid clogging in a "relief valve," the unit incorporated two "rupture disks." If a disk ruptured, a positive reading was to register on a pressure gauge to inform the operator to take the appropriate steps. The pressure gauge was connected to the main assembly by a pipe incorporating a fitting called "Valve A."]

....

Shortly after noon on April 4, 1966 a pressure surge caused the pressure in the feed line to exceed 850 p.s.i. At this time the pressure relief mechanism worked perfectly—the discs ruptured, the relief valve relieved the pressure, and the pressure gauge indicated that the discs were ruptured. Mobil maintenance personnel then replaced the discs, bled the acetic acid out of the relief mechanism, and continued the commissioning process. Just before 5:00 P.M., April 5, 1966 the feed line was again overpressured. This time, however, the pressure relief mechanism failed and acetic acid under high pressure spurted...into the atmosphere, creating both a danger to personnel and a fire hazard. As soon as he realized where the leak was, Jerry Griffith, Mobil's process superintendent, put on protective equipment, crawled out on the feed line and stopped the leak by closing Valve A.

Plaintiffs Bell and Hurley were employees of C.F. Braun and were working on Unit B of the plant at a point some 70 feet from the rupture. Both were exposed to strong acetic acid vapor and suffered respiratory damage for which they seek recovery. They alleged specific acts of negligence in failing to either have the pressure gauge in place or close Valve A and in the alternative pleaded *res ipsa loquitur*. The jury failed to find that the specific acts of negligence were committed and these findings have not been attacked on appeal. The jury did find, however, that Mobil failed to use ordinary care in maintaining the plant and that such failure was a proximate cause of the incident in question....

....

...[I]t is helpful to focus on exactly what is encompassed within the doctrine of *res ipsa loquitur*. The phrase, meaning "the thing speaks for itself," was used by Pollock, C.B., in discussing a barrel of flour which fell from the defendant's window, Byrne v. Boadle, 2

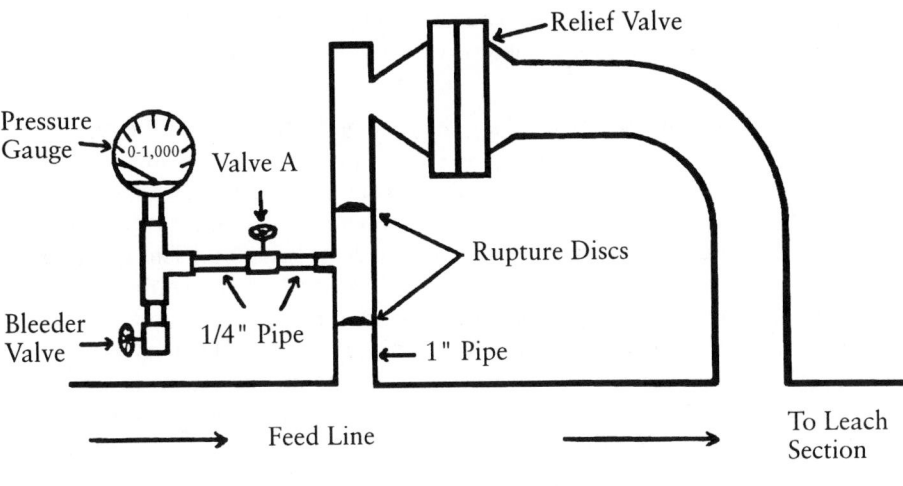

Diagram of Unit A.

H. & C. 722, 159 Eng. Rep. 299 (Ex. 1863), and has come to signify that in certain limited types of cases the circumstances surrounding an accident constitute sufficient circumstantial evidence of the defendant's negligence to support such a fact finding. [Citation.] These cases are those in which the circumstances surrounding the event are such that the mere occurrence of the accident supports reasonable inferences that there was negligence involved and that the defendant was the negligent party. [Citations.]

The *res ipsa* doctrine is applicable when two factors are present: (1) the character of the accident is such that it would not ordinarily occur in the absence of negligence; and (2) the instrumentality causing the injury is shown to have been under the management and control of the defendant. [Citations.] The first factor is necessary to support the inference of negligence and the second factor is necessary to support the inference that the defendant was the negligent party. [Citation.] As such the "control" requirement is not a rigid rule that the instrumentality must have always been in the defendant's possession or even that it must have been in the defendant's control at the time of the injury. [Citation.] It is sufficient if the defendant was in control at the time that the negligence inferable from the first factor probably occurred, so that the reasonable probabilities point to the defendant and support a reasonable inference that he was the negligent party. [Citation.] The possibility of other causes does not have to be completely eliminated, but their likelihood must be so reduced that the jury can reasonably find by a preponderance of the evidence that the negligence, if any, lies at the defendant's door. [Citation.]

In Texas it is well settled that *res ipsa loquitur* is simply a rule of evidence whereby negligence may be inferred upon proof of the factors stated above. [Citations.] Texas courts have quoted with approval the following language of the U.S. Supreme Court in Sweeney v. Erving, 228 U.S. 233, 240, 33 S. Ct. 416, 418, 57 L. Ed. 815 (1913):

> In our opinion, *res ipsa loquitur* means that the facts of the occurrence warrant the inference of negligence, not that they compel such an inference; that they furnish circumstantial evidence of negligence when direct evidence of it may be lacking, but it is evidence to be weighed, not necessarily to be accepted as sufficient; that they call for explanation or rebuttal, not necessarily that they

require it; that they make a case to be decided by the jury.... When all the evidence is in, the question for the jury is whether the preponderance is with the plaintiff.

... [T]he effect of successfully invoking the *res ipsa* doctrine is that the plaintiff can survive no-evidence procedural challenges—he has produced some evidence of the defendant's negligence. He is in the same position as any other plaintiff who has made out a case for the jury.... [I]t is the rare *res ipsa* case where the defendant is in danger of a directed verdict if he chooses not to explain the accident. [Citation.] This is because the inferences to be drawn from the circumstances of the accident are within the province of the jury, not the court. Only in extraordinary circumstances does the mere occurrence of the accident so strongly compel a conclusion that the defendant was negligent that the jury could not reasonably find otherwise. [Citations.] Of course, in any case the defendant may, if he chooses, produce evidence to lessen the impact of the plaintiff's circumstantial evidence. [Citation.]

In order to rely on the *res ipsa* doctrine, the plaintiff must produce evidence from which the jury can conclude, by a preponderance of the evidence, that both the "type of accident" and "control" factors are present. This is not so much a rule of law as it is a rule of logic— unless these factors are present, the jury cannot reasonably infer from the circumstances of the accident that the defendant was negligent. In a great many cases the plaintiff can rely upon a general knowledge to prove the accident in question is the type of accident which does not ordinarily happen in the absence of negligence. [Citation.] However, expert testimony on this factor is clearly admissible and may be necessary to the plaintiff's case....

....

....Both lower courts have held that the facts of this case raise the *res ipsa* doctrine. We agree. The facts show that the entire plant was designed as a closed system so that acid vapors would not be released into the atmosphere. The relief mechanism was included to prevent the same sort of occurrence as happened here. It is true that this was a new plant just being started up. However, we are not dealing with a minor leak of the type that can hardly be avoided with new equipment, but a violent rupture spewing acid 30 feet into the air. It seems reasonable to infer that due care could have prevented the accident. And since Mobil had accepted the Unit only after extensive tests, had been in control of the equipment for at least two weeks, and had been performing additional tests and maintenance, it is reasonable to infer that if negligence was involved, Mobil was the negligent party. From the circumstances of the accident, a jury could reasonably decide that Mobil's negligence probably caused the accident and the resulting injuries. We conclude that Plaintiffs Bell and Hurley made out a *res ipsa* case....

The [defendant's second argument is] that Mobil's rebutting evidence completely negated the plaintiff's *res ipsa* case and made it unreasonable to infer that Mobil's negligence caused the accident. Mobil's evidence consisted primarily of testimony by Marvin Fannin, a chemical engineer with Mobil, who saw the equipment after the accident. He testified that the quarter inch pipe broke between Valve A and the pressure gauge, which caused the acid to spew out horizontally. He theorized that the pipe might have broken because (1) it was defectively manufactured, (2) the metal crystallized when threads were cut improperly, or (3) the metal crystallized when the pipe was overly tightened upon installation. He explained that the pipe could have been further weakened by operational vibrations until it was so weak that it broke under the sudden pressure.

While the jury was certainly entitled to believe this explanation, it was not compelled to.... [T]he jury could still reasonably infer from the circumstances of the accident that the accident was probably caused by Mobil's negligence. Therefore, we hold that the trial court did not err in submitting the *res ipsa* issues to the jury. [Citations.]

. . . .

Since…this case will be [re-tried]…we think it appropriate to further express our views…with respect to cases, such as this one, tried on alternate theories of specific negligence and *res ipsa loquitur*.

First, it should be noted that a plaintiff does not necessarily lose the right to rely on the *res ipsa* doctrine by pleading specific acts of negligence. "The purpose of pleading is to apprize opposing parties of the exact grounds of complaint against them, so that they may prepare to meet the issues thus made." [Citation.] If a plaintiff pleads specific acts of negligence only, his proof is limited to those specific acts but may consist of circumstantial evidence, including the circumstances of the accident if the inferences reasonably arising from such circumstances are relevant to the specific acts alleged. However, if the plaintiff's pleading gives fair notice that he is not relying solely on specific acts but instead intends to also rely on any other negligent acts reasonably inferable from the circumstances of the accident, his proof is not limited to the specific acts alleged. [Citations.]

Likewise, proof of specific acts of negligence does not necessarily make the *res ipsa* doctrine inapplicable since proof of specific acts is not necessarily inconsistent with inferences of other facts. Of course, if the evidence, whether introduced by the plaintiff or the defendant, conclusively establishes the facts surrounding the accident, then there is no room for inferences and the *res ipsa* doctrine is not applicable. [Citations.] But where the evidence is inconclusive, the plaintiff is still entitled to rely on any inferences that are consistent with the evidence. [Citations.]

. . . .

A final question to be considered is whether the trial court should give an instruction about *res ipsa loquitur* in an appropriate case….

….In some cases the inferences arising from the circumstances of the accident are so apparent that no special instruction is necessary. In other cases it is sufficient to give the jury a circumstantial evidence instruction to instruct them that acts of negligence can be proved both by direct evidence and by inferences from other facts proved. Finally, there are some cases in which it is helpful to give the jury a more specialized *res ipsa* instruction to the effect that if they find the two required factors, they are entitled, but not compelled, to infer that the defendant was negligent.

… [W]e believe that if the same evidence is presented at retrial of the instant case… [a]mong the definitions in the forepart of the charge, the trial court may include an explanation of *res ipsa loquitur* similar to the following:

> You are instructed that you may infer negligence by a party but are not compelled to do so, if you find that the character of the accident is such that it would ordinarily not happen in the absence of negligence and if you find that the instrumentality causing the accident was under the management and control of the party at the time of the negligence, if any, causing the accident probably occurred.

This general instruction may require variations under the particular circumstances of individual cases.

. . . .

[The concurring opinion of DANIEL, J., is omitted.]

Notes

1. *Exclusive Control.* The key question is who was in control at the time the negligence more likely than not occurred. In Wright v. Carter, 622 N.E.2d 170 (Ind. 1993), the fact that a piece of wire that a radiologist had inserted into the patient's breast prior to surgery to aid a surgeon remained in her body after surgery raised an inference of negligence against the surgeon and hospital, but not against the radiologist. Before the end of the operation, the radiologist had finished his work and departed, and the patient was under the exclusive control of the surgeon when the fragment was left behind.

In some instances, the evidence is too weak to permit an inference that the defendant was the responsible person. For example, in Kmart Corp. v. Bassett, 769 So. 2d 282 (Ala. 2000), the court said that *res ipsa loquitur* could not be used to impose liability on a business owner for harm caused by a malfunctioning automatic door because the malfunction could have occurred because the doors were defective or because the company that serviced the doors had been negligent, and expert testimony was insufficient to show that automatic doors do not malfunction unless a premises owner fails to use reasonable care to keep them in safe condition.

However, there is authority that a plaintiff does not have to rule out all other possible causes of harm. *See* Newell v. Westinghouse Elec. Corp., 36 F.3d 576 (7th Cir. 1994) (fact that a building owner had the ability to control an elevator, whose doors slammed shut on the plaintiff, did not preclude reliance on *res ipsa loquitur* in an action against a contractor that had an exclusive elevator maintenance agreement, absent evidence that the building owner actually interfered with the elevator); Tompkins v. Northwestern Union Trust Co., 645 P.2d 402 (Mont. 1982) (fact that a third party was responsible for maintaining an aircraft which crashed did not foreclose application of *res ipsa loquitur* to show negligence on the part of the pilot).

In some cases, even a loosely interpreted "exclusive control" requirement may preclude recovery. For example, in Dermatossian v. New York City Transit Auth., 492 N.E.2d 1200 (N.Y. 1986), a passenger on a city bus brought suit to recover for injuries allegedly sustained when he stood up and struck his head on a grab handle which projected straight down from the ceiling, instead of at the customary angle of about 45 degrees. The court, while recognizing that the exclusive control requirement should not be "literally" applied as a "fixed, mechanical or rigid rule," held that a *res ipsa loquitur* case was not made out, for the "grab handle was continuously available for use by defendant's passengers" and the "proof did not exclude the chance" that the handle had been damaged by one of the passengers. Thus, as in many cases, the question was really whether the defendant, more likely than not, had control at the time the negligence probably occurred. The facts could not establish that probability.

2. *Control by the Plaintiff.* The fact that the plaintiff exercised some control over the harmful instrumentality does not necessarily preclude reliance on the doctrine. *See* Giles v. City of New Haven, 636 A.2d 1335 (Conn. 1994) (evidence that an elevator operator controlled the elevator's movement and its chain's sway did not prevent the operator from relying on *res ipsa loquitur* to assert a claim against the elevator company for negligence in inspecting, maintaining, and repairing the elevator compensation chain).

3. *Rebuttal Evidence.* As *Bell* suggests, the defendant's introduction of evidence of due care does not ordinarily preclude the plaintiff from successfully invoking *res ipsa loquitur*. In Cox v. Northwest Airlines, 379 F.2d 893 (7th Cir. 1967), plaintiff's husband was killed when the plane on which he was a passenger went down over the ocean.

The evidence of due care to which appellant allude[d] concern[ed] its maintenance records and procedures with respect to the aircraft involved; the qualified and certified status, and the competence, of the operating personnel of the aircraft and of the dispatcher; the safety training received by the crew; and the evidence that the flight was properly dispatched and the weather normal.

In affirming a finding of liability, the court held that the doctrine of *res ipsa loquitur* was correctly applied to the case.

See also Roberts v. Weber & Sons, Inc., 533 N.W.2d 664, 669 (Neb. 1995) (although the defendant introduced evidence that the pen from which cattle had escaped was constructed of the "sturdiest and most expensive materials," the court held that a truck driver who collided with the cattle could rely on *res ipsa loquitur* because "cattle would not ordinarily escape... [from a] state-of-the-art cattle pen in the absence of negligence").

b. *Greater Access to Information*

Mahowald v. Minnesota Gas Co.

Supreme Court of Minnesota
344 N.W.2d 856 (Minn. 1984) (en banc)

KELLEY, Justice.

On the morning of February 26, 1977, the home of Alice and Michael Kannegieter exploded.... Investigation revealed that a natural gas main pipe located in the right-of-way in front of the Kannegieter residence had fractured, causing natural gas to leak into the home.

....

In November 1970, Minnesota Gas Company (Minnegasco) installed a gas main in the right-of-way.... The main was installed at a depth of 42 inches, exceeding the depth required by federal regulations and company policy.... There is no evidence in the record that the line was improperly installed.

Pursuant to Minnegasco's ownership and obligation to maintain its gas lines, periodic leak checks were performed on the line in compliance with federal requirements. No leaks in the gas line were ever detected prior to the 1977 explosion.

No further construction occurred in the area of the gas line until 1974 when Barbarossa and Sons was hired by the City of Prior Lake to install water and sewer lines in... the development in which the Kannegieter residence was to be located. On April 30, 1974, Barbarossa struck and severed a gas main with a backhoe. The strike was reported to and repaired by Minnegasco.

On May 15, 1974, Barbarossa again struck a gas main. The pipe was scraped and bent a distance of approximately 16 feet from where the explosion-causing fracture eventually occurred. Minnegasco was notified of the hit and sent a repairman to the site. Because the pipe itself was not physically damaged, the pipe was wrapped with special tape, sealed, and reburied.

....

In addition... other entities apparently engaged in excavating or other digging activities in the street. These entities were not named as defendants and... include telephone, electric, and landscaping companies.

Alice and Michael Kannegieter and their two children moved into their newly built home...in September 1976. On Saturday morning, February 26, 1977, Alice went to the garage to start the family car, while Michael gathered the children in the family room. Alice placed her key into the car's ignition. The house exploded causing its total destruction.

....

...[T]he case was submitted to the jury under a theory of negligence only. The jury found both...[Barbarossa and Minnegasco] not negligent and set damages at $110,850.

....

....Appellants, in the alternative, urge us to hold that the trial court erred in refusing to submit a *res ipsa loquitur* instruction. Moreover, they contend the doctrine should apply to both the utility and Barbarossa....

The burden of proving that a natural gas company was negligent in the operation of its gas distribution system is indeed onerous. That is true, in part at least, because the gas company does not have complete exclusive control over its distribution lines located on public right-of-ways. Activities, of which the gas company frequently has no notice, are normally taking place on streets over which the company has no meaningful control. Here, for example, the city laid water and sewer lines in proximity to the gas lines; contractors tapped those mains to make service connections; either the city or the developer reduced the street grade after installation of the gas mains; and the city contracted for street servicing....

In declining to submit a *res ipsa loquitur* instruction in this case, the trial court felt that one element necessary before that rule is applicable was missing—to wit, exclusive control....[4]

....In ordinary parlance, "exclusive control" connotes that no other person or entity had any control over the instrumentality which caused the damage. If viewed in that light, Minnegasco did not have "exclusive control" during the 7 years preceding the explosion. Nevertheless, some jurisdictions, including Minnesota, in natural gas explosion cases have found such "exclusive control" where the gas distributor has the non-delegable responsibility to maintain and inspect its mains in the public streets at all times. As pointed out by Professor Prosser, a rigid adherence to the literal meaning of "exclusive control" could be pernicious and misleading unless control is seen as a flexible term. W. Prosser, Law of Torts §39, at 218–21 (4th ed. 1971). Really what we are considering in a determination of whether *res ipsa loquitur* applies is the shifting of the burden of proof to someone who is responsible for the instrumentality that caused the damage. In a gas explosion case such as here, the gas distributor is responsible for the reasonable inspection and maintenance of its lines. It is this responsibility for its gas line that constitutes the type of control that establishes this element allowing the application of *res ipsa loquitur*....In somewhat similar contexts, other courts have shifted the burden of proof where the plaintiff was blameless but the instrumentality causing the harm could not be readily identified or was not exclusively in control of a charged defendant, although the person charged was responsible to see the instrumentality was not negligently used so as to cause harm to others. *See, e.g.,* Summers v. Tice, 33 Cal. 2d 80, 199 P.2d 1 (1948)

---

4. We note the *res ipsa loquitur* issue raised in appellants' brief differs from the issue presented to the trial court and in their prehearing conference statements to this court. In those documents, the appellants sought only a *res ipsa loquitur* instruction as to Minnegasco. On appeal we address only issues presented to the trial court. [Citation.]

[*infra* at p. 386]. Likewise, a bailee has the burden of proving that personal property damaged while entrusted to him was not caused by his fault whether or not, at the time of the damage, the bailee was in actual physical control. [Citation.]

In the ordinary course of events, natural gas does not escape from gas mains in public streets so as to cause explosion. When it does so escape and does result in an explosion, an inference of fault on the part of the gas distribution company is justifiable. Even though the gas company may be faultless, in view of its superior knowledge of the gas distribution system, its access and opportunity to identify persons acting in the vicinity of the gas mains, its inspection and control over the mains, and its responsibility for the safety of the persons and property in the community, the gas company should have the obligation to show it was not negligent or to establish who was. [Citation.] As between the gas company and the person who sustains injury to person or property, the gas company is by far in a better position to make that showing. In essence, this is the rationale of *res ipsa loquitur*: to allow a plaintiff to get to the jury by allowing the jury, in an appropriate case, to draw an inference of negligence on the part of the gas company.

. . . .

. . . . Had the plaintiffs had the advantage of the *res ipsa loquitur* instruction, the jury could have concluded that plaintiffs had met their burden of proof. Therefore, we reverse and remand for a new trial against Minnegasco only.

Reversed and remanded.

[The dissenting opinion of Justice TODD is omitted.]

c. *Res Ipsa* and Plaintiff's Conduct

It was once said that for *res ipsa loquitur* to apply, the plaintiff had to prove that the negligence which caused the injury was more likely than not attributable to the defendant, rather than to the plaintiff or some third person. This meant that *res ipsa loquitur* was inapplicable in any case involving contributory negligence. The advent of comparative negligence and comparative fault has necessitated modification of the old rule, for under comparative principles fault on the part of the plaintiff no longer always requires a denial of recovery. In one typical decision, Montgomery Elevator Co. v. Gordon, 619 P.2d 66 (Colo. 1980), the court held that under comparative negligence a *res ipsa loquitur* plaintiff is required to show only that the "defendant's inferred negligence was, more probably than not, *a cause* [not *the cause*] of the injury, . . . even though plaintiff's negligent acts or omissions may also have contributed to the injury." *See also* Giles v. City of New Haven, 636 A.2d 1335 (Conn. 1994).

How is the jury to compare the negligence of the defendant with that of the plaintiff in order to reduce damages to an appropriate level? The jury, by definition, is unaware in a *res ipsa loquitur* case of precisely what the defendant did wrong. The court in *Montgomery Elevator Co.* was not seriously troubled by the question:

> [T]he jury will know the general nature of the breach of duty committed by the defendant, such as the general failure to keep an elevator in good working condition. Since the process of comparison of negligence lacks scientific precision, the ruling should not result in an additional undue burden on the jury.

The theory appears to be that a rough allocation of damages is better than no allocation at all. Presumably the plaintiff will not complain, since otherwise reliance upon the *res ipsa loquitur* doctrine might be barred. And the defendant may well not suffer, since in the absence of specific details evidencing wantonness of conduct, the jury may be reluctant to judge the defendant severely.

2.   Multiple Defendants

Ybarra v. Spangard
Supreme Court of California
154 P.2d 687 (Cal. 1944)

GIBSON, Chief Justice.

This is an action for damages for personal injuries alleged to have been inflicted on plaintiff by defendants during the course of a surgical operation. The trial court entered judgment of nonsuit as to all defendants and plaintiff appealed.

On October 28, 1939, plaintiff consulted defendant Dr. Tilley, who diagnosed his ailment as appendicitis, and made arrangements for an appendectomy to be performed by defendant Dr. Spangard at a hospital owned and managed by defendant Dr. Swift. Plaintiff entered the hospital, was given a hypodermic injection, slept, and later was awakened by Drs. Tilley and Spangard and wheeled into the operating room by a nurse whom he believed to be defendant Gisler, an employee of Dr. Swift. Defendant Dr. Reser, the anesthetist, also an employee of Dr. Swift, adjusted plaintiff for operation, pulling his body to the head of the operating table....Dr. Reser then administered the anesthetic and plaintiff lost consciousness. When he awoke early the following morning he was in his hospital room attended by defendant Thompson, the special nurse, and another nurse who was not made a defendant.

Plaintiff testified that prior to the operation he had never had any pain in, or injury to, his right arm or shoulder, but that when he awakened he felt a sharp pain about half way between the neck and the point of the right shoulder....The pain did not cease... and after his release from the hospital...[he] developed paralysis and atrophy of the muscles around the shoulder....

[Two doctors testified for the plaintiff that the injury was of a traumatic origin.]

....

Plaintiff's theory is that the foregoing evidence presents a proper case for the application of the doctrine of *res ipsa loquitur*, and that the inference of negligence arising therefrom makes the granting of a nonsuit improper. Defendants'...main defense may be briefly stated in two propositions: (1) that where there are several defendants, and there is a division of responsibility in the use of an instrumentality causing the injury, and the injury might have resulted from the separate act of either one of two or more persons, the rule of *res ipsa loquitur* cannot be invoked against any one of them; and (2) that where there are several instrumentalities, and no showing is made as to which caused the injury or as to the particular defendant in control of it, the doctrine cannot apply. We are satisfied...that these objections are not well taken....

....

The present case is of a type which comes within the reason and spirit of the doctrine more fully perhaps than any other. The passenger sitting awake in a railroad car at the time of a collision, the pedestrian walking along the street and struck by a falling object or the debris of an explosion, are surely not more entitled to an explanation than the unconscious patient on the operating table....Without the aid of the doctrine a patient who received permanent injuries of a serious character, obviously the result of someone's negligence, would be entirely unable to recover unless the doctors and nurses in attendance voluntarily chose to disclose the identity of the negligent person and the facts establishing liability. [Citation.] If this were the state of the law of negligence, the courts, to avoid gross injustice, would be forced to invoke the principles of absolute liability, irrespective of negligence, in actions by persons suffering injuries during the course of treatment under anesthesia. But we think this juncture has not yet been reached, and that the doctrine of *res ipsa loquitur* is properly applicable to the case before us.

The condition that the injury must not have been due to the plaintiff's voluntary action is of course fully satisfied under the evidence produced herein; and the same is true of the condition that the accident must be one which ordinarily does not occur unless some one was negligent....

The argument of defendants is simply that plaintiff has not shown an injury caused by an instrumentality under a defendant's control, because he has not shown which of the several instrumentalities that he came in contact with while in the hospital caused by the injury; and he has not shown that any one defendant or his servants had exclusive control over any particular instrumentality. Defendants assert that some of them were not the employees of other defendants, that some did not stand in any permanent relationship from which liability in tort would follow, and the different functions performed by each, they could not all be liable for the wrong, if any.

We have no doubt that in a modern hospital a patient is quite likely to come under the care of a number of persons in different types of contractual and other relationships with each other. For example, in the present case it appears that Drs. [Swift], Spangard and Tilley were physicians or surgeons commonly placed in the legal category of independent contractors; and Dr. Reser, the anesthetist, and defendant Thompson, the special nurse, were employees of Dr. Swift and not of the other doctors. But we do not believe that either the number or relationship of the defendants alone determines whether the doctrine of *res ipsa loquitur* applies. Every defendant in whose custody the plaintiff was placed for any period was bound to exercise ordinary care to see that no unnecessary harm came to him and each would be liable for failure in this regard. Any defendant who negligently injured him, and any defendant charged with his care who so neglected him as to allow injury to occur, would be liable. The defendant employers would be liable for the neglect of their employees; and the doctor in charge of the operation would be liable for the negligence of those who became his temporary servants for the purpose of assisting in the operation.

....

It may appear at the trial, that, consistent with the principles outlined above, one or more defendants will be found liable and others absolved, but this should not preclude the application of the rule of *res ipsa loquitur*. The control at one time or another, of one or more of the various agencies or instrumentalities which might have harmed the plaintiff, was in the hands of every defendant or of his employees or temporary servants. This, we think, places upon them the burden of initial explanation. Plaintiff was rendered unconscious for the purpose of undergoing surgical treatment by the defendants; it is manifestly unreasonable for them to insist that he identify any one of them as the person who did the alleged negligent act.

. . . .

. . . [I]f we accept the contention of defendants herein, there will rarely be any compensation for patients injured while unconscious. A hospital today conducts a highly integrated system of activities, with many persons contributing their efforts. . . . The number of those in whose care the patient is placed is not a good reason for denying him all reasonable opportunity to recover for negligent harm. It is rather a good reason for re-examination of the statement of legal theories which supposedly compel such a shocking result.

We do not at this time undertake to state the extent to which the reasoning of this case may be applied to other situations in which the doctrine of *res ipsa loquitur* is invoked. We merely hold that where a plaintiff receives unusual injuries while unconscious and in the course of medical treatment, all those defendants who had any control over his body or the instrumentalities which might have caused the injuries may properly be called upon to meet the inference of negligence by giving an explanation of their conduct.

The judgment is reversed.

Notes

1. At a second trial, each defendant (except the owner of the hospital) gave evidence and denied seeing anything which could have produced the injury to plaintiff's arm and shoulder. The trial court found that this did not overcome the inference of negligence raised by the doctrine of *res ipsa loquitur*, and found against all defendants. The judgment was affirmed: Ybarra v. Spangard, 208 P.2d 445 (Cal. Ct. App. 1949).

2. *Joint Control.* Ybarra is the seminal decision on whether *res ipsa loquitur* may be invoked against multiple defendants, and it has often been cited by subsequent decisions. Many of the cases have involved operating-room injuries. *See, e.g.*, Swierczek v. Lynch, 237 Neb. 469, 466 N.W.2d 512 (1991) (*res ipsa loquitur* was applicable to alleged negligence of hospital, oral surgeon, and nurse anesthetist). However, the doctrine has been applied to multiple defendants in other contexts, with joint control of the risk often being a key issue. *See* Jackson v. H.H. Robertson Co., Inc., 574 P.2d 822 (Ariz. 1978) (negligence action for construction site accident was properly maintainable against two subcontractors under *res ipsa loquitur*; employees of both defendants had control of the dangerous instrumentality at "times close enough to the accident" to permit an inference of negligence that one or both defendants caused the harm); Barb v. Farmers Ins. Exch., 281 S.W.2d 297 (Mo. 1955) (*res ipsa loquitur* applied to a landlord and tenant who shared control of a passageway where falling boxes struck and injured the plaintiff); Meny v. Carlson, 77 A.2d 245 (N.J. 1950) (plaintiff injured in a scaffolding fall could invoke *res ipsa loquitur* against the partnership which supplied and the corporation which assembled the defective scaffolding; whether there was joint control was a jury question); Schroeder v. City & County Savings Bank, Albany, 57 N.E.2d 57 (N.Y. 1944) (*res ipsa loquitur* applied to three defendants who were in joint control of a barricade that collapsed); Bond v. Otis Elevator Co., 388 S.W.2d 681 (Tex. 1965) (doctrine applied to co-defendants who jointly controlled an elevator that plummeted). *See also* Whitby v. One-O-One Trailer Rental Co., 383 P.2d 560 (Kan. 1963) (injured plaintiff, who had been asleep in a towed car that overturned when the hitch failed, could bring a *res ipsa loquitur* action against both the lessor and lessee of the towing equipment); Bronz v. St. Jude's Hosp. Clinic, 402 S.E.2d 263, 267 (W. Va. 1991) ("where

there is divided control over the instrumentality causing the injury, the plaintiff is required to introduce 'evidence from which it is reasonable to infer that more likely than not the cause of the fall was one for which the defendant was responsible'").

See generally Restatement, Third, of Torts: Liability for Physical Harm (Basic Principles) §17 cmt. f (Tent. Draft No. 1, 2001), stating that:

> In limited circumstances,...a group approach to *res ipsa loquitur* is supportable. If two parties have an ongoing relationship pursuant to which they share responsibility for a dangerous activity, and if an accident happens establishing the negligence of one of the two, imposing *res ipsa loquitur* liability on both is proper.

3. ***Independent Multiple Forces.*** The ruling in *Ybarra* appears to be grounded in part on the fact that the defendants all stood in an integrated relationship as professional colleagues and all had some responsibility for the plaintiff's safety. In cases in which the defendants are strangers to one another—as when a pedestrian injured in a collision sues the drivers of two cars independently involved in the crash—invocation of the doctrine has generally not been allowed, even if at least one of the defendants must have been negligent. *See* Dean v. Young, 636 N.E.2d 745, 747 (Ill. Ct. App. 1994) ("in a situation involving divided responsibility—[such as]...a collision between two automobiles resulting in injury to a third party—*a res ipsa loquitur* instruction is inappropriate"; neither party was in exclusive control of the instrumentalities).

See also Unwin v. Campbell, 863 F.2d 124 (1st Cir. 1988) (*res ipsa loquitur* not applicable to a case in which officers from several state and local police departments quelled a disturbance at a prison; "[u]nlike *Ybarra*, the defendants here...[were] not the individuals who were immediately responsible for plaintiff's care"); Wellman v. Faulkner, 715 F.2d 269 (7th Cir. 1983) (relying on the same rationale in declining to presume that senior prison officials were responsible for various violations of prisoners' rights).

Of course, even if evidence is insufficient to establish joint control on the part of multiple defendants, it may show that one of the defendants had exclusive control and therefore is subject to *res ipsa loquitur*. *See* Anderson v. Service Merchandise Co., Inc., 485 N.W.2d 170 (Neb. 1992) (holding, in an action by a customer who was struck by a falling light fixture, that a lighting contractor did not have sufficient control over store's lighting system to permit application of *res ipsa loquitur*, but that store operator was in "exclusive control" of store premises and therefore subject to doctrine).

4. Although decisions such as *Montgomery Elevator Co.*, 619 P.2d 66 (Colo. 1980), indicate that the availability of the doctrine should not ordinarily be conditioned upon the plaintiff's freedom from fault in comparative negligence (and, presumably, comparative fault) states, is it appropriate for a court to consider the plaintiff's behavior in deciding whether the doctrine should be liberally interpreted to encompass "extraordinary" situations, such as those involving multiple defendants? The pre-comparative negligence ruling in *Ybarra* appears to have placed some weight on the plaintiff's freedom from fault, and decisions expanding other rules of tort law have frequently noted that in those cases the plaintiff was blameless and at least one of the defendants must have been at fault. *See* Summers v. Tice, 199 P.2d 1 (Cal. 1948), *infra* at p. 386, and Sindell v. Abbott Lab., 607 P.2d 924 (Cal. 1980), *infra* at p. 389.

5. ***Tort Reform and Res Ipsa Loquitur.*** Some states have limited the use of *res ipsa loquitur* in certain types of cases, such as those involving medical malpractice. *See, e.g.*, Tex. Rev. Civ. Stat. Ann. art. 4590i §7.01 (Westlaw 2003) (limiting doctrine to those types of cases in which it had been applied prior to August 29, 1977).

D. Disposing of Unfavorable Evidence

The best evidence that a defendant has acted negligently may be contained in the defendant's files, or may consist of the condition of a vehicle or other piece of property belonging to the defendant. In these cases, the defendant has every incentive to destroy or alter the evidence. Altering the evidence for the purpose of misleading a factfinder is plainly fraudulent, and may well subject the defendant to criminal as well as civil sanctions. Destroying evidence is a more-complex matter: the law cannot require every person who might possibly be sued for negligence to keep forever all documents or objects that a plaintiff might someday find useful.

One possible response to the problem of evidence retention in tort cases is to create another tort—the tort of "spoliation of evidence."

Trevio v. Ortega
Texas Supreme Court
969 S.W.2d 950 (Tex. 1998)

ENOCH, Justice, delivered the opinion of the Court, in which PHILLIPS, Chief Justice, and GONZALEZ, HECHT, SPECTOR, OWEN, ABBOTT and HANKINSON, Justices, join.

The issue in this case is whether this Court should recognize an independent cause of action for intentional or negligent spoliation of evidence by parties to litigation.[1]....

In 1988, Genaro Ortega, individually and as next friend of his daughter, Linda Ortega, sued Drs. Michael Aleman and Jorge Trevio and McAllen Maternity Clinic for medical malpractice. Ortega alleged that the defendants were negligent in providing care and treatment during Linda's birth in 1974.[2] Discovering that Linda's medical records from the birth had been destroyed, Ortega then sued Dr. Trevio in a separate suit for intentionally, recklessly, or negligently destroying Linda Ortega's medical records from the birth.

....Here, Ortega claims that Trevio had a duty to preserve Linda's medical records and that destroying the records materially interferes with Ortega's ability to prepare his medical malpractice suit. Ortega explains that Aleman, the attending physician, testified that he has no specific recollection of the delivery and, therefore, the missing medical records are the only way to determine the procedures used to deliver Linda. Because the medical records are missing, Ortega's expert cannot render an opinion about Aleman's, the Clinic's, or Trevio's negligence.

....The court of appeals reversed the trial court's dismissal order and held that Texas recognizes an independent cause of action for evidence spoliation. [Citation.]

This Court treads cautiously when deciding whether to recognize a new tort. [Citations.] While the law must adjust to meet society's changing needs, we must balance that adjustment against boundless claims in an already crowded judicial system. We are especially averse to creating a tort that would only lead to duplicative litigation, encour-

---

1. Whether we recognize a cause of action for spoliation of evidence by persons who are not parties to the underlying lawsuit is not before the Court, and therefore we do not consider it.

2. At the time of submission, this case was still pending in district court.

aging inefficient relitigation of issues better handled within the context of the core cause of action.... A number of jurisdictions that have considered the issue have been hesitant to recognize an independent tort for evidence spoliation for a variety of different reasons. [Citations.][3]

Evidence spoliation is not a new concept. For years courts have struggled with the problem and devised possible solutions. Probably the earliest and most enduring solution was the spoliation inference or *omnia praesumuntur contra spoliatorem*: all things are presumed against a wrongdoer. [Citations.] In other words, within the context of the original lawsuit, the factfinder deduces guilt from the destruction of presumably incriminating evidence.

This traditional response to the problem of evidence spoliation properly frames the alleged wrong as an evidentiary concept, not a separate cause of action. Spoliation causes no injury independent from the cause of action in which it arises....

Even those courts that have recognized an evidence spoliation tort note that damages are speculative. [Citations.] The reason that the damages inquiry is difficult is because evidence spoliation tips the balance in a lawsuit; it does not create damages amenable to monetary compensation.

Our refusal to recognize spoliation as an independent tort is buttressed by an analogous line of cases refusing to recognize a separate cause of action for perjury or embracery.[4] Like evidence spoliation, civil perjury and civil embracery involve improper conduct by a party or a witness within the context of an underlying lawsuit. A number of courts considering the issue have refused to allow the wronged party to bring a separate cause of action for either perjury or embracery. [Citations.] These decisions rely on public policy concerns such as ensuring the finality of judgments, avoiding duplicative litigation, and recognizing the difficulty in calculating damages. [Citations.] Similarly, recognizing a cause of action for evidence spoliation would create an impermissible layering of liability and would allow a plaintiff to collaterally attack an unfavorable judgment with a different factfinder at a later time, in direct opposition to the sound policy of ensuring the finality of judgments.

...[W]hen spoliation occurs, there must be adequate measures to ensure that it does not improperly impair a litigant's rights.... It is simpler, more practical, and more logical to rectify any improper conduct within the context of the lawsuit in which it is relevant.... Trial judges have broad discretion to take measures ranging from a jury instruction on the spoliation presumption to, in the most egregious case, death penalty sanctions. [Citations.] As with any discovery abuse or evidentiary issue, there is no one remedy that is appropriate for every incidence of spoliation; the trial court must respond appropriately based upon the particular facts of each individual case.

---

3. Courts in more than twenty states have considered the issue, but the courts of only six states have recognized a cause of action for negligent or intentional spoliation. *See* Hazen v. Municipality of Anchorage, 718 P.2d 456, 463 (Alaska 1986) (intentional); Velasco v. Commercial Bldg. Maintenance Co.,...[215 Cal. Rptr. 504, 506 (Cal. Ct. App. 1985)] (negligent); Smith v. Superior Court,... [198 Cal. Rptr. 829, 832–33 (Cal. Ct. App. 1984)] (intentional); Bondu v. Gurvich, 473 So. 2d 1307, 1312–13 (Fla. Dist. Ct. App. 1984) (negligent); Callahan v. Stanley Works,...[703 A.2d 1014, 1017–19 (1997)] (negligent); Coleman v. Eddy Potash, Inc.,...[905 P.2d 185, 189 (1995)] (intentional); Smith v. Howard Johnson Co.,...[615 N.E.2d 1037 (1993)] (intentional). [Ed. note: The California Supreme Court rejected *Velasco* and *Smith* in Cedars-Sinai Med. Ctr. v. Superior Court, 954 P.2d 511 (Cal. 1998).]

4. Embracery is "[t]he crime of attempting to influence a jury corruptly to one side or the other." Black's Law Dictionary 522 (6th ed. 1990).

Ortega also argues that the failure to maintain Linda's medical records violated a statutory duty to maintain such records as required by section 241.103(b) of the Texas Health and Safety Code. Assuming without deciding that such a duty exists and that there was a breach of that duty, it does not necessarily follow that an independent cause of action arises. Nor does a cause of action necessarily arise from a party's obligation to comply with the rules of discovery.... [O]bligations not to destroy evidence arise in the context of particular lawsuits; consequently, spoliation is best remedied within the lawsuit itself, not as a separate tort.

We reverse the court of appeals' judgment and render judgment that Ortega take nothing.

BAKER, Justice, concurring.

....

...[C]ourts have been hesitant to apply remedies for spoliation....Accordingly, I believe it appropriate to review what remedies are available...and when the remedies should be applied.

....

When a party believes that another party has improperly destroyed evidence, it may either move for sanctions or request a spoliation presumption instruction....

Upon a spoliation complaint, the threshold question should be whether the alleged spoliator was under any obligation to preserve evidence. A party may have a statutory, regulatory, or ethical duty to preserve evidence....

Other jurisdictions have held that there is also a common law duty to preserve evidence....

....While there is no question that a party's duty to preserve relevant evidence arises during pending litigation, courts have been less clear about whether a duty exists prelitigation....A party should not be able to subvert the discovery process and the fair administration of justice simply by destroying evidence before a claim is actually filed....

....Courts that have imposed a prelitigation duty to preserve evidence have held that once a party is on "notice" of potential litigation a duty to preserve evidence exists. [Citations.] Most courts have not elaborated on the concept of notice. But, a few courts have determined that a party is on notice of potential litigation when the litigation is reasonably foreseeable. [Citations.]

....

...[I]n spoliation cases a party should be found to be on notice of potential litigation when, after viewing the totality of the circumstances, the party either actually anticipated litigation or a reasonable person in the party's position would have anticipated litigation....

....A party that is on notice of either potential or pending litigation has an obligation to preserve evidence that is relevant to the litigation. "While a litigant is under no duty to keep or retain every document in its possession...it is under a duty to preserve what it knows, or reasonably should know, is relevant in the action, is reasonably calculated to lead to the discovery of admissible evidence, is reasonably likely to be requested during discovery, [or] is the subject of a pending discovery sanction.".....

....

If the trial court finds that a party has a duty to preserve evidence, it should then decide whether the party breached its duty. Parties need not take extraordinary measures to preserve evidence; however, a party should exercise reasonable care in preserving evidence. [Citation.]

Some courts have allowed sanctions or the presumption only for intentional or bad faith spoliation. [Citations.]

Because parties have a duty to reasonably preserve evidence, it is only logical that they should be held accountable for either negligent or intentional spoliation....

A spoliator can defend against an assertion of negligent or intentional destruction by providing other explanations for the destruction. For example, if the destruction of the evidence was beyond the spoliator's control or done in the ordinary course of business, the court may find that the spoliator did not violate a duty to preserve evidence. Importantly though, when a party's duty to preserve evidence arises before the destruction or when a policy is at odds with a duty to maintain records, the policy will not excuse the obligation to preserve evidence. [Citation.]

. . . .

Though a party may have improperly spoliated evidence, the nonspoliating party may not be entitled to a remedy....A party is entitled to a remedy only when evidence spoliation hinders its ability to present its case or defense. [Citations.]

Courts should look to a variety of factors in deciding whether destroying evidence has prejudiced a party. Most importantly, courts should consider the destroyed evidence's relevancy....

Additionally, courts should consider whether the destroyed evidence was cumulative of other competent evidence...and whether the destroyed evidence supports key issues in the case....

. . . .

Once a court finds that evidence has been improperly spoliated and that the nonspoliating party was prejudiced by the spoliation, the court should decide what sanction to apply....

....Important factors for the trial court to weigh include the degree of the spoliator's culpability and the prejudice the nonspoliator suffers....

The most severe sanction for evidence spoliation is to dismiss the action or render a default judgment.... [C]ourts have found that a dismissal or default judgment is justified when a party destroys evidence with the intent to subvert discovery. [Citations.] Thus, courts can dismiss an action or render a default judgment when the spoliator's conduct was egregious, the prejudice to the nonspoliating party was great, and imposing a lesser sanction would be ineffective to cure the prejudice. [Citations.]

Another effective sanction is excluding evidence or testimony. Courts generally use this sanction when the spoliating party is attempting to admit testimony or evidence adduced from the destroyed evidence....Understandably, it will be extremely difficult for the nonspoliating party to defend against the spoliating party's allegations without being able to inspect the evidence. Thus, in some instances, it is proper for courts to exclude the spoliating party's evidence.

In addition to sanctions,...trial courts may submit a spoliation presumption instruction....

Depending on the severity of prejudice resulting from the particular evidence destroyed, the trial court can submit one of two types of presumptions. [Citation.] The first and more severe presumption is a rebuttable presumption. This is primarily used when the nonspoliating party cannot prove its *prima facie* case without the destroyed evidence. [Citations.] The trial court should begin by instructing the jury that the spoliating party has either negligently or intentionally destroyed evidence and, therefore, the jury should presume that the destroyed evidence was unfavorable to the spoliating party on the particular fact or issue the destroyed evidence might have supported. Next, the court should instruct the jury that the spoliating party bears the burden to disprove the presumed fact or issue. [Citations.] This means that when the spoliating party offers evidence rebutting the presumed fact or issue, the presumption does not automatically disappear. It is not overcome until the fact finder believes that the presumed fact has been overcome by whatever degree of persuasion the substantive law of the case requires. [Citation.]

...[B]y shifting the burden of proof, the presumption will support the nonspoliating party's assertions and is some evidence of the particular issue or issues that the destroyed evidence might have supported. The rebuttable presumption will enable the nonspoliating party to survive summary judgment....

The second type of presumption is less severe. It is merely an adverse presumption that the evidence would have been unfavorable to the spoliating party. [Citations.] The presumption itself has probative value and may be sufficient to support the nonspoliating party's assertions. [Citation.] However, it does not relieve the nonspoliating party of the burden to prove each element of its case. [Citation.] Therefore, it is simply another factor used by the factfinder in weighing the evidence.

...Ortega can move for sanctions or request a spoliation presumption in the underlying malpractice action. If he shows that Dr. Trevio had a duty to preserve evidence, Dr. Trevio violated that duty, and the destruction prejudiced Ortega's ability to bring suit, the trial court can remedy the spoliation.

Notes

1. *See generally* Bart S. Wilhoit, Comment, *Spoliation of Evidence: The Viability of Four Emerging Torts*, 46 U.C.L.A. L. Rev. 631 (1998).

2. *Sanctions Rather Than Independent Actions.* Many decisions have found that spoliation is better addressed through sanctions than by allowing a separate cause of action. *See, e.g.,* Martino v. Wal-Mart Stores, Inc., 835 So. 2d 1251 (Fla. Dist. Ct. App. 2003) (a patron could not recover against a store for spoliation of evidence, based on the store's failure to preserve a videotape and a shopping cart that allegedly caused her injury, because the store was a defendant in the underlying negligence action and numerous sanctions were already available).

3. *Examples of Sanctions.* See Allstate Ins. Co. v. Sunbeam Corp., 53 F.3d 804 (7th Cir. 1995) (insurer's destruction of material evidence, which would have "shed light upon" the cause of a fire, warranted dismissal of a subrogation claim); Sponco Mfr., Inc. v. Alcover, 656 So. 2d 629 (Fla. Dist. Ct. App. 1995) (a default judgment on the issue of liability was appropriate because, despite a lack of evidence that a manufacturer's destruction of an allegedly defective ladder was willful, the plaintiff's expert testified that without the ladder the plaintiff could not proceed against the manufacturer or other defendants). *But see* Wal-Mart Stores v. Johnson, 106 S.W.3d 718 (Tex. 2003) (because patrons failed to show that the store disposed of a plastic reindeer that fell on one of the patrons after it knew, or should have known, that there was a substantial chance of litigation, it was reversible error for the trial court to give a spoliation instruction).

4. *Spoliation by Third Parties.* Boyd v. Travelers Ins. Co., 652 N.E.2d 267 (Ill. 1995), addressed the question whether a person not a party to the underlying lawsuit may be held liable for spoliation of evidence. There, after an employee was injured when a heater exploded, the employer's workers' compensation insurer took possession of the damaged heater and lost it. The employee sued the insurer, alleging that its negligence impaired his ability to bring a products liability action against the manufacturer of the heater. The court held that an action for negligent spoliation was available under existing negligence principles without creating a new tort and that the employee should be allowed to try that claim concurrently with the claim against the manufacturer.

> A single trier of fact would be in the best position to resolve all the claims fairly and consistently. If a plaintiff loses the underlying suit, only the trier of fact who heard the case would know the real reason why. This factor is important because a spoliator may be held liable in a negligence action only if its loss or destruction of the evidence caused a plaintiff to be unable to prove the underlying suit.

In contrast, Smith v. Atkinson, 771 So. 2d 429 (Ala. 2000), agreed that an action for spoliation by a third party could be stated under ordinary negligence principles, but endorsed a very different procedural approach. The court stated that the third-party spoliation claim did not need to be joined with the underlying claim and that the plaintiff did not even need to "file an action pursuing the underlying cause of action and be denied recovery," provided the plaintiff could show that the lost or destroyed evidence was so important that its absence would have kept the plaintiff's underlying claim from surviving a motion for summary judgment.

Some courts have refused to permit actions for third-party spoliation. *See* Dowdle Butane Gas Co. v. Moore, 831 So. 2d 1124 (Miss. 2002) (refusing to recognize an independent action for either first-party or third-party intentional spoliation because "the costs to defendants and courts would be enormous, particularly from the risks of erroneous determinations of liability due to the uncertainty of the harm and from the extraordinary measures required to preserve for indefinite periods items for the purpose of avoiding potential spoliation liability in future litigation"); Fletcher v. Dorchester Mut. Ins. Co., 773 N.E.2d 420 (Mass. 2002) (holding that in the absence of an agreement or a subpoena duces tecum, a non-party ordinarily does not have a duty to preserve evidence "merely because that item may be of use to others in pending or anticipated litigation").

5. *Spoliation of Testimonial Evidence.* The spoliation doctrine does not apply to testimonial evidence. In Loomis v. Ameritech Corp., 764 N.E.2d 658 (Ind. Ct. App. 2002), the court rejected a spoliation claim against attorneys who allegedly induced a witness to sign a false affidavit. The court wrote:

> Physical evidence is readily capable of being evaluated in terms of being exclusively possessed and being made unavailable, destroyed, or altered. Testimonial evidence does not lend itself to being similarly evaluated.
>
>   ....
>
>   ....Nothing prevents the...[plaintiffs] from having...[the witness] testify about witnessing...[the] signing of the release....
>
>   ....Expanding spoliation of evidence to allow a party to sue opposing attorneys when a witness changes his or her testimony, even if the change in testimony is alleged to be a result of misconduct, would be untenable. Such a policy could discourage attorneys from interviewing witnesses for fear that if a witness changes his or her testimony it could give rise to a suit based upon spoliation....

6. *Belated Evidence of Spoliation.* In Davis v. Wal-Mart Stores, Inc., 756 N.E.2d 657 (Ohio 2001), the court held that claims for spoliation of evidence may be brought after the primary action has been concluded only when evidence of spoliation is not discovered until after the termination of the primary action.

7. *Ethics in Law Practice: Destruction of Evidence.* A lawyer may be reprimanded, suspended, or disbarred for destroying evidence. Rule 3.4 of the Model Rules of Professional Conduct (2003) states:

A lawyer shall not:

(a) unlawfully obstruct another party's access to evidence or unlawfully alter, destroy or conceal a document or other material having potential evidentiary value. A lawyer shall not counsel or assist another person to do any such act; [or]

(b) falsify evidence, counsel or assist a witness to testify falsely, or offer an inducement to a witness that is prohibited by law....

Presumably, the word "unlawfully," as used in subparagraph (a), includes any conduct that violates federal or state criminal laws or tort standards governing alteration, destruction, or concealment of evidence.

Draft of reports by expert witnesses may be discoverable, at least where they reflect data and other information considered by the expert in forming an opinion. *See* Fed. R. Civ. Proc. 26(a)(2)(B) (2003). "Consequently, ordering experts to destroy drafts and notes is generally sanctionable." Gregory P. Joseph, *Expert Spoliation*, Nat. L.J. Feb. 3, 2003, at B7. Note, however, that there may be an important difference between an expert's disclosing what has been considered in forming an opinion and the expert's determination of how to phrase that opinion. According to some courts, it is an open question "whether a testifying expert is required to retain, and a party is required to disclose, the drafts prepared solely by that expert while formulating the proper language in which to articulate that experts' own, ultimate opinion arrived at by the expert's own work or those working at the expert's personal direction." Trigon Ins. Co. v. U.S., 204 F.R.D. 277, 283 (E.D. Va. 2001) ("there are cogent reasons which militate against such a requirement").

In addition to discipline and other sanctions, attorneys are subject to tort liability based on spoliation. If the attorney's failure to preserve evidence harms the client, the lawyer may be sued for malpractice. *Cf.* Murray v. Farmers Ins. Co., 796 P.2d 101 (Idaho 1990) (recovery denied because jury found that clients would probably not have achieved a favorable outcome in their products liability case). In addition, "[i]f an attorney actively participates in spoliation [of evidence by a client], or gives open or veiled advice designed to aid spoliation, the attorney and client are jointly liable as tortfeasors." Steffen Nolte, *The Spoliation Tort: An Approach to Underlying Principles*, 26 St. Mary's L.J. 351, 391 (1995). Query: Can a lawyer be held liable for failing to advise a client of the legal obligation to preserve evidence?

Chapter 7

Factual Causation

A. An Overview of Causation

Williams v. Steves Industries, Inc.
Supreme Court of Texas
699 S.W.2d 570 (Tex. 1985)

ROBERT M. CAMPBELL, Justice.

....

On July 30, 1981, Mrs. Williams was driving her car on a four-lane segment of Interstate 35 in Austin. Her two children were riding in the back seat. The car ran out of gas and stalled in one of the center lanes. Mrs. Williams restarted the car but continued only a short distance before it stalled again. There was testimony the car was hidden from the view of approaching traffic by shadows of an overpass. Robinson, who was driving an eight-ton equipment repair truck owned by Steves Industries, hit Mrs. Williams' car from behind. Mrs. Williams and her children were injured and the children died from those injuries. [Mrs. Williams and her husband sought to recover from Steves Industries for personal injuries and wrongful death based on a theory of negligent entrustment. As to the issue of comparative negligence:]

.... Renee Williams traveled only five miles from her home when her car stalled. After the accident, a fireman at the scene checked the gas tank for a possible fire hazard, but found no gasoline. A wrecker service employee drained the tank through a hole in the gas tank and less than a cupful of gasoline ran out of the tank....

The jury found Renee Williams negligent for failing to have enough gasoline in her car to make the trip, and found her negligence to be a proximate cause of the accident. The jury also found that her negligence contributed twenty-five percent to the collision. Renee Williams does not attack the negligence finding but contends that as a matter of law her negligence was not a proximate cause of the accident. The two elements of proximate cause are cause in fact and foreseeability. [Citation.] We will consider each element separately.

The first issue, therefore, is whether there is some evidence that Mrs. Williams' negligence was a cause in fact of the accident. If a negligent act or omission is a substantial factor in bringing about the injury and without which no harm would have occurred, the act or omission is a cause in fact of the injury.... Had Mrs. Williams had enough gasoline in her car to make her trip, her car would not have stalled in the middle of Interstate 35. A jury could infer that had the car not stalled in the middle of the highway,

Robinson would not have collided with it. Thus, we find some evidence that Mrs. Williams' negligence was a cause in fact of the accident.

....."Foreseeability means that the actor, as a person of ordinary intelligence, should have anticipated the dangers that his negligent act created." [Citation.] Furthermore, the actor need only anticipate an injury of the same general character as the actual injury:

> [I]t is not required that the particular accident complained of should have been foreseen. All that is required is "that the injury be of such a general character as might reasonably have been anticipated; and that the injured party should be so situated with relation to the wrongful act that injury to him or to one similarly situated might reasonably have been foreseen." [Cite omitted.]

Carey v. Pure Distributing Corp., 133 Tex. 31, 124 S.W.2d 847, 849 (1939)....

On the day of the accident Mrs. Williams knew the route she was taking; therefore, she knew that she would be traveling on a high traffic section of an interstate highway. The jury found that she knew or should have known that she did not have enough gas to make the trip. The jury could reasonably conclude that a person of ordinary intelligence would anticipate that if his car ran out of gas it might stall on the highway and that a stalled car on a highly traveled section of an interstate highway would create a danger of another vehicle colliding with it. Thus, there is some evidence of foreseeability.

We affirm the judgment of the court of appeals.

[The dissenting opinion of Justice RAY, relating to punitive damages, is omitted.]

Notes

1. *Burden of Proof.* In nearly every tort action—whether based on intentional wrong-doing, failure to exercise care, or strict liability—the plaintiff must prove causation.

2. *Two-Step Inquiry.* As *Williams* indicates, the issue of causation involves a two-step inquiry. The first step asks whether in fact there was a connection between the allegedly tortious conduct and the plaintiff's injury. One way (but not the only way) to meet this requirement is to show that "but for" the defendant's conduct the harm would not have occurred.

The second step in the causation analysis concerns the fairness of imposing liability for harm in fact caused by the defendant. That is, notwithstanding the fact that the defendant played a substantial role in the plaintiff's injury, it may be unfair to impose liability. This determination is sometimes framed in terms of foreseeability, on the belief that it is fair to hold a defendant responsible for those consequences of conduct which could have been foreseen, and unfair to impose liability for results which could not have been anticipated. While foreseeability plays a large role in the second step of the causation analysis, Chapter 8 will show that, in appropriate cases, other considerations may be taken into account.

The terms "cause in fact" or "factual causation" are often used to refer the first step in the causation analysis, and "proximate causation" often denotes the second step. This book follows that terminology. Chapter 7 deals with factual causation. The difficult subject of proximate causation is considered in Chapter 8. Note, however that some authorities, such as *Williams*, use "proximate causation" to describe the overall two-step inquiry.

3. *"Cause in Fact" and "Proximate Cause."* In everyday speech, "cause" is used to indicate responsibility. If *A* drives too fast, slides off the road, and strikes *B*, most observers would say that *A*'s conduct "caused" the accident, and that the conduct of *B*,

who was walking along minding her own business, did not cause the accident. This way of discussing the problem is not suitable for legal analysis. The problem is that it is too conclusory: on the facts given, it may well make sense to hold *A* liable for *B*'s injuries, but lawyers and judges must be able to say specifically what it was about *A*'s conduct— and *B*'s—that requires *A* to pay. Simply saying "*A* caused the accident" will not do, because to say that is to state the conclusion that *A* should be responsible, not to justify it. Most cases like the one described here will indeed be cases in which *A* is liable to *B*, because in most cases like this *A* was negligent. But if *A*'s speeding resulted from a sudden and unforeseeable seizure, *A* will not be liable.

As a simple illustration of the role of "but-for causation" or "cause in fact" in the law of negligence, suppose that the plaintiff is struck by a speeding hit-and-run driver and that the plaintiff sues the defendant. If the factfinder determines that the defendant was not the driver who struck the plaintiff, the case is over—even if the defendant was negligent. (Suppose, for instance, that the evidence shows that the defendant was speeding on a street ten miles from the scene of the accident.) Many tort cases turn primarily on issues like this: was it the defendant whose car hit the plaintiff; was it the defendant who made the defective product that injured the plaintiff; was it the defendant who set off the explosion that knocked down the plaintiff's barn?

Every accident has countless "causes" in the but-for sense, and so "but-for causation" can never be, in itself, the sole reason for holding a defendant liable. Suppose, for example, that the plaintiff, while walking to church one morning, is run down by a drunken driver. The driver's conduct is obviously a "but-for cause" of the accident. But so is the *plaintiff's* conduct—but for the plaintiff's decision to go to church that morning, the accident would not have happened. Similarly, if the person from whom the defendant bought the car had not sold the car to the defendant the accident would not have happened, so that person's conduct is a "but-for cause" of the accident. So is the church's decision to have a service that morning, or to have it at ten rather than at ten thirty, for if the service had not been held, or had been held at a different time, the plaintiff would not have been in position to be struck by the defendant's car. Causation, in the but-for sense, is normally required if the defendant is to be liable. But causation in the but-for sense is *never* enough, by itself, to establish liability. "Only those causes attributable to tortious conduct are legally relevant in determining liability and apportioning liability for plaintiff's harm." Restatement, Third, of Torts: Liability for Physical Harm (Basic Principles) §28 cmt. c (Tent. Draft No. 3, 2003).

B. The Traditional Rules of Factual Causation

1. *Sine Qua Non*: The "But For" Test

Reynolds v. Texas and Pacific Railway Co.

Supreme Court of Louisiana
1885 W.L. 6364, *1 (La.)

FENNER, J.

The plaintiff and his wife claim damages of the defendant company for injuries suffered by the wife and caused by the alleged negligence of the company.

....

The mode of getting from the depot to the [railroad] cars was as follows: passengers went down a stairway of several steps, which ran parallel to the track and led to a lower platform....

....Although both the east and west-bound trains customarily stopped at this station in the night-time, no stationary lights were provided for the depot platform or the steps. There was no moon on this night....The lights in the rooms of the station could have shed no light on the bottom of the steps....After an attentive study of the evidence, we clearly concur in the conclusion of the district judge that there was no sufficient light....

The train was behind time. Several witnesses testify that passengers were warned to "hurry up." Mrs. Reynolds, a corpulent woman, weighing two hundred and fifty pounds, emerging from the bright light of the sitting-room, which naturally exaggerated the outside darkness, and hastening down these unlighted steps, made a misstep in some way and was precipitated beyond the narrow platform in front and down the slope beyond, incurring the serious injuries complained of.

Upon what grounds does the company claim exemption from liability?

....

2nd. It contends that, even conceding the negligence of the company in the above respect, it does not follow that the accident to plaintiff was necessarily caused thereby, but that she might well have made the misstep and fallen even had it been broad daylight. We concede that this is possible, and recognize the distinction between *post hoc* and *propter hoc*. But where the negligence of the defendant greatly multiplies the chances of accident to the plaintiff, and is of a character naturally leading to its occurrence, the mere possibility that it might have happened without the negligence is not sufficient to break the chain of cause and effect between the negligence and the injury....The whole tendency of the evidence connects the accident with the negligence.

....

Judgment affirmed.

Notes

1. *Jury Question.* Normally, it is a question of fact for the jury to determine, based on common experience, whether a particular course of conduct is such as to multiply the chances of injury and thus justify a finding of factual causation. However, if the matter is beyond the ken of the ordinary juror, expert testimony is needed to guide the finder of fact. *See* Dodge-Farrar v. American Cleaning Services Co., Inc., 54 P.3d 954 (Idaho Ct. App. 2002) (holding that the causal relationship between an employee's slip and fall and immediate symptoms in the ankle, knee, and back (such as pain, swelling, and the inability to sit, stand, or walk without assistance) was within the usual and ordinary experience of the average person, but that expert testimony was necessary to establish that the fall caused permanent ankle deformity).

Expert testimony is normally necessary in cases involving medicine and other sciences. *See, e.g.,* Money v. Manville Corp. Asbestos Disease Comp. Trust Fund, 596 A.2d 1372 (Del. 1991) (the fact that plaintiffs had been exposed to defendants' products containing asbestos and suffered from an asbestos-related disease did not permit the jury to infer causation without expert testimony).

For a detailed discussion of whether the failure to take precautions is the cause of an injury, see David A. Fischer, *Causation in Fact in Omission Cases*, 1992 Utah L. Rev. 1335.

2. *Causation Based on Circumstantial Evidence.* If direct evidence is unavailable, circumstantial evidence may establish factual causation. *See* Havner v. E-Z Mart Stores, Inc., 825 S.W.2d 456 (Tex. 1992) (a jury's finding that a convenience store's negligently deficient security system was a cause in fact of an employee's abduction and murder by an unknown assailant was supported by circumstantial evidence that negated the possibility that the employee voluntarily left the store, and by a police investigation that produced no evidence indicating that the employee had been murdered by an acquaintance); In re Brooklyn Navy Yard Asbestos Litig., 971 F.2d 831 (2d Cir. 1992) (evidence that asbestos-containing products made by the defendants were used interchangeably throughout a large shipyard, that the environment was extremely dusty with asbestos fibers, and that plaintiffs or their decedents were exposed to asbestos fibers there, was sufficient to establish causation of plaintiffs' injuries; "to require precision of proof would impose an insurmountable burden"); McCarley v. West Quality Food Service, 960 S.W.2d 585, 587 (Tenn. 1998) (where the plaintiff consumed both bacon and chicken, either of which could have contained the bacteria that made the plaintiff ill, the plaintiff's testimony that the chicken "looked strange, and 'didn't taste right,'" supported an inference that the chicken was the source of the bacteria; therefore it was error to take the case from the jury and grant summary judgment for the defendant on the ground that there was insufficient evidence to prove causation).

3. *Causation Based on Breach of Statute.* The breach of a statutory duty itself may give rise to an inference that an injury was the proximate result of the violation. *See, e.g.,* Lucas v. Hesperia Golf & Country Club, 63 Cal. Rptr. 189, 196 (Ct. App. 1967) (failure to have a lifeguard on duty at a swimming pool) and cases cited therein.

Kramer Service, Inc. v. Wilkins
Supreme Court of Mississippi
186 So. 625 (Miss. 1939)

GRIFFITH, Justice.

Appellant was and is the owner and operator of a large hotel. About 5:30 o'clock P.M. on January 15, 1935, one Clockey registered as a guest and was given a room, to which he was conducted by a bellboy....

Soon after entering the room, Clockey discovered that...the transom [could not be] lowered so as to give ventilation. The reason...was that there was a break in the glass thereof....

....

About two hours later appellee came to Clockey's room in response to...[a] telephone message, and when the business conference was concluded appellee was in the act of leaving the room. When he opened the door,...the broken piece of the transom fell striking appellee upon the head. Three wounds were thus made upon appellee's head, one of which was a jagged abrasion on the temple.

....There is...competent evidence to the effect that the condition of unrepair...had existed for a sufficient length of time to charge appellant with responsible notice thereof, and that the condition was such that a reasonably prudent and careful operator should have foreseen the fall of the broken glass and an injury thereby as a likelihood of appreciable weight and moment. [Citation.] There is no reversible error in the record on the issue of liability....

But there is plain and serious error in the matter of the amount of the damages. The wound on the temple did not heal, and some months after the injury appellee was advised by his local physician to visit a specialist in skin diseases, which he did...about two years after the injury, and it was then found that at the point where the injury occurred to appellee's temple, a skin cancer had developed, of which a cure had not been fully effected at the time of the trial....

Appellee sued for a large sum in damages,...contending that the cancer resulted from the stated injury; and the jury evidently accepted that contention, since there was an award by the verdict in the sum of twenty thousand dollars. Appellant requested an instruction to the effect that the cancer or any prolongation of the trouble on account thereof should not be taken into consideration by the jury, but this instruction was refused.

Two physicians or medical experts, and only two, were introduced as witnesses.... One testified that it was possible that a trauma such as appellee suffered upon his temple, could or would cause a skin cancer at the point of injury, but that the chances that such a result would ensue from such a cause would be only one out of one hundred cases. The other testified that there is no causal connection whatsoever between trauma and cancer, and went on to illustrate that if there were such a connection nearly every person of mature age would be suffering with cancer....

It seems therefore hardly to be debatable but that appellant was entitled to the requested instruction as regards the cancer; and since, except as to that element, the verdict could not have been large, the verdict and judgment must be reversed on the issue of the amount of the damages.

There is one heresy in the judicial forum which appears to be Hydra-headed, and although cut off again and again, has the characteristic of an endless renewal. That heresy is that proof that a past event possibly happened, or that a certain result was possibly caused by a past event, is sufficient in probative force to take the question to a jury. Such was never the law in this state, and we are in accord with almost all of the other common-law states. Nearly a half century ago,...Chief Justice Campbell said in Railroad v. Cathey, 70 Miss. 332, 337, 12 So. 253: "It is not enough that negligence of the employer and injury to the employee coexisted, but the injury must have been caused by the negligence....'Post hoc ergo propter hoc' is not sound as evidence or argument. Nor is it sufficient for a plaintiff seeking recovery for alleged negligence by an employer towards an employee to show a possibility that the injury complained of was caused by negligence. Possibilities will not sustain a verdict. It must have a better foundation."

    ....

Taking the medical testimony in this case in the strongest light in which it could be reasonably interpreted in behalf of the plaintiff, this testimony is that as a possibility a skin cancer could be caused by an injury such as here happened, but as a probability the physicians were in agreement that there was or is no such a probability.

...[A]fter long and anxious years of research the exact cause of cancer remains unknown....If, then, the cause be unknown to all those who have devoted their lives to a study of the subject, it is wholly beyond the range of the common experience and observation of judges and jurors, and in such a case medical testimony when undisputed, as here, must be accepted...; otherwise the jury would be allowed to resort to and act upon nothing else than the proposition post hoc ergo propter hoc, which, as already mentioned, this Court has long ago rejected as unsound....

    ....

Affirmed as to liability; reversed and remanded on the issue of the amount of the damages.

Notes

1. *Failure to Prove Factual Causation. See* Turpin v. Merrell Dow Pharmaceuticals, Inc., 959 F.2d 1349 (6th Cir. 1992) (at most, studies demonstrated only a possibility, not a probability, that the drug Bendectin caused birth defects in human babies); Saporta v. State, 368 N.W.2d 783 (Neb. 1985) (in an action by a schizophrenic patient who walked away from a state mental hospital and threw himself in front of a truck, a judgment for the state was affirmed because there was evidence to support a finding that the patient would not have been found even if appropriate search procedures had been followed upon discovery of the patient's absence); Grain Dealers Mut. Ins. Co. v. Porterfield, 695 S.W.2d 833 (Ark. 1985) (the negligent failure of a school district to ground a stadium press box electrical system was not a proximate cause of the death of a welder who used an extension cord with the grounding prong snipped off and plugged the cord into the receptacle upside down, thereby reversing the polarity).

2. *Multiple "but for" Causes.* As shown earlier, an accident may, indeed *must,* have more than one "but for" cause, and so more than one defendant may be liable for an injury. In a case in which one defendant was negligent in leaving his truck parked in the road, and the other defendant was negligent in failing to take evasive measures to avoid hitting it, both actions were factual causes of the injuries sustained by a passenger in the second vehicle. But for the negligence of each defendant, the accident would not have occurred. Hill v. Edmonds, 270 N.Y.S.2d 1020 (App. Div. 1966).

Saelzler v. Advanced Group 400

California Supreme Court
23 P.3d 1143 (Cal. 2001)

CHIN, J.

....

...[P]laintiff Marianne Saelzler was an employee of Federal Express. Defendants were owners of the Sherwood Apartments, a 28-building, 300-unit apartment complex located on a several-acre site in Bellflower. Plaintiff came to the complex in midafternoon to deliver a package to a resident. As she entered through one of the many gated entrances to the premises, she saw two young men loitering outside a security gate that had been propped open. While walking across the grounds she saw another young man already on the premises.

Plaintiff's attempt to deliver the package proved unsuccessful because the resident was not at home. When plaintiff returned down a walk path with the package in hand, the three men confronted her.... Then the three of them beat her and attempted to rape her, inflicting serious injuries. After assaulting plaintiff, her assailants fled and were never apprehended.

Plaintiff's complaint alleged that defendants, knowing that dangerous persons frequented their premises, nonetheless failed to maintain the premises in a safe condition, failed to provide adequate security, and failed to warn others of the unsafe conditions. Defendants moved for summary judgment on the basis that plaintiff was unable to establish any substantial causal link between defendants' omissions and plaintiff's injury.

Plaintiff offered no evidence showing the identity of her assailants, whether they were gang members, whether they trespassed on defendants' property to assault her, or whether they were tenants of the building who were permitted to pass through the security gates. Similarly, plaintiff submitted no evidence showing that the propped-open security gate was actually broken or otherwise not functioning properly, or whether her assailants entered through the gate or themselves broke it and entered....

As the trial court found, plaintiff presented evidence that defendants knew of frequent recurring criminal activity on the premises of their 28 building apartment complex. The community of Bellflower was itself a high-crime area, with considerable juvenile gang activity occurring both on and off defendants' premises....

Defendants' security manager acknowledged that during the year preceding the assault on plaintiff, several nighttime assaults, and actual or attempted rapes, occurred on the premises....

    ....

Plaintiff observes that police officers advised both defendants' apartment manager and the head of the security firm they employed that they should hire *daytime* as well as nighttime security patrols. Plaintiff filed a lengthy declaration from a security expert, Robert Feliciano.... His qualifications included service as Director of Police and Safety for the Housing Authority of Los Angeles County, as well as advanced education in public safety and several years in law enforcement. At the time he made his declaration, he was a full-time instructor in criminal justice and police science at a community college. Feliciano expressed the opinion "that this attack...would not have occurred had there been daytime security and a more concerted effort to keep the gates repaired and closed...."

The trial court granted summary judgment for defendants, finding plaintiff had failed to show defendants' breach of duty to safeguard her was a proximate cause of her assault....

A majority of the Court of Appeal reversed, concluding that plaintiff's showing was sufficient to raise a triable causation issue for the jury. In summary, the majority held, relying primarily on commonsense and ordinary experience, that defendants' "complete absence of required security measures" by itself reasonably could be deemed a contributing cause of any criminal activity in the area.

The Court of Appeal majority also held that defendants' failure to provide additional security justified shifting the burden of proof to defendants, for purposes of their summary judgment motion, to conclusively establish the absence of a causal relation between their breach of duty and the assault on plaintiff by showing this particular assault would have occurred even if reasonable security measures had been taken....

Finally, according to the Court of Appeal majority, the testimony of plaintiff's expert, opining that the assault on plaintiff would not have occurred but for the lack of daytime security measures, was "both admissible and credible" on the causation issue.

    ....

Plaintiff admits she cannot prove the identity or background of her assailants. They might have been unauthorized trespassers, but they also could have been tenants of defendants' apartment complex, who were authorized and empowered to enter the locked security gates and remain on the premises. The primary reason for having functioning security gates and guards stationed at every entrance would be to exclude *unauthorized* persons and trespassers from entering. But plaintiff has not shown that her assailants were indeed unauthorized to enter. Given the substantial number of incidents and disturbances involving defendants' own tenants, and defendants' manager's statement that a juvenile gang was "headquartered" in one of the buildings, the assault on plaintiff could well have been made by tenants having authority to enter and remain on the premises. That being so, and despite the speculative opinion of plaintiff's expert, she cannot show that defendants' failure to provide increased daytime security at each entrance gate or functioning locked gates was a substantial factor in causing her injuries. [Citations.] Put another way, she is unable to prove it was "more probable than not" that additional security precautions would have prevented the attack. ([Citation]; *see* Prosser & Keeton, Torts, *supra*, § 41, p. 269 [plaintiff must show it more likely than not defendant's conduct was cause in fact of the result; "mere possibility of such causation is not enough"]; Rest.2d Torts, § 433B, com. a, p. 442.)

. . . .

Plaintiff also argues in favor of the Court of Appeal majority's practical approach to the causation issue. . . . [T]he majority held that common sense and common experience should lead us to conclude that a defendant's "complete absence of required security measures" is necessarily a "contributing cause of most crimes occurring on that property." Defendants observe, of course, that the evidence fails to show any such complete absence of security, as defendants provided, among other things, nighttime roving security patrols and regular daytime inspections to repair broken gates.

More fundamentally, we hesitate to adopt a rule of common sense that seemingly would prevent summary judgment on the causation issue *in every case* in which the defendant failed to adopt increased security measures of some kind. . . .

. . . [T]o demonstrate actual or legal causation, the plaintiff must show that the defendant's act or omission was a "substantial factor" in bringing about the injury. [Citations.] In other words, plaintiff must show some substantial link or nexus between omission and injury. Under the Court of Appeal's "common sense" rule, the defendants' omission itself would constitute the missing link.

. . . .

. . . [I]n a given case, direct or circumstantial evidence may show the assailant took advantage of the defendant's lapse (such as a failure to keep a security gate in repair) in the course of committing his attack, and that the omission was a substantial factor in causing the injury. Eyewitnesses, security cameras, even fingerprints or recent signs of break-in or unauthorized entry, may show what likely transpired at the scene. In the present case no such evidence was presented. . . .

. . . .

Plaintiff also urges us to adopt the Court of Appeal's novel approach of shifting the proof burden on the causation issue to defendants. . . .

We think such a drastic shifting of the proof burden is unjustified by either the evidence in this case or prior statutory and case law. First, and contrary to the Court of Appeal's hyperbole, the evidence discloses no flagrant failure in this case. As we have seen, most of the assaults and similar incidents of crime plaintiff has cited occurred during the night, and the record indicates defendants did provide extensive nighttime security. Moreover, plaintiff's own evidence showed that defendants at least attempted to keep all security gates in working order, performing regular inspections and repairs.

But again, even assuming a triable issue existed regarding the extent or reasonableness of defendants' security efforts, even a flagrant failure to provide such measures would not justify shifting to defendants the burden of conclusively proving the absence of causation. No matter how inexcusable a defendant's act or omission might appear, the plaintiff must nonetheless show the act or omission caused, or substantially contributed to, her injury. Otherwise, defendants might be held liable for conduct which actually caused no harm, contrary to the recognized policy against making landowners the *insurer* of the absolute safety of anyone entering their premises. [Citations.]

Indeed, the Court of Appeal's burden-shifting approach seems directly contrary to the state's summary judgment statute, which provides that a defendant meets its burden of showing that a cause of action has no merit "if that party has shown that one or more elements of the cause of action...cannot be established...."....

In short, plaintiff cannot prove that defendants' omissions were a substantial factor in causing her injuries, and no proper basis exists for shifting the burden of proof on that issue to defendants. Plaintiff has had ample opportunity, through pretrial discovery, to marshal evidence showing that defendants' asserted breach of duty actually caused her injuries. The evidence at hand, however, merely shows the speculative possibility that additional daytime security guards and/or functioning security gates might have prevented the assault. Plaintiff's evidence is no less speculative because she offered a security expert's testimony. Because he was equally unaware of the assailants' identities, his opinion regarding causation is simply too tenuous to create a triable issue whether the absence of security guards or functioning gates was a substantial factor in plaintiff's assault.

The judgment of the Court of Appeal is reversed with directions to affirm the award of summary judgment in defendants' favor.

GEORGE, C.J., BAXTER, J., and BROWN, J., concur.

[The dissenting opinion of KENNARD, J., in which WERDEGAR, J., concurred, and dissenting opinion of WERDEGAR, J., in which MOSK, J., and KENNARD, J., concurred, are omitted.]

Note

1. *No Speculation.* "[S]ome suspicion linked to other suspicion produces only more suspicion, which is not the same as some evidence" and "an inference stacked only on other inferences is not legally sufficient evidence." Marathon Corp. v. Pitzner, 106 S.W.3d 724, 728 (Tex. 2003).

Pitzner was a suit to recover for catastrophic injuries sustained by an electrician who did not remember what happened when he fell from a roof while working on air conditioning equipment that violated various building and mechanical codes. There was a screw driver with a burnt tip on the ground near the body of the electrician, and an expert testified the most likely scenario was that the electrician must have come into contact with the high voltage wire on the defectively installed equipment and was shocked, causing him to tumble backwards over the edge of the roof. However, there was also evidence that electricians often carry with them screwdrivers with burnt tips to use when they need to short a circuit. A ladder that was used by the electrician to access the roof was missing. Also, the plaintiff had suffered various injuries to his head, which could have been caused by the fall or may have resulted from a struggle with an attacker (which is what the parmedic and physician, but not the police, thought). The court concluded that there was no evidence that made one scenario more likely than another, and that the expert's opinion was mere speculation. The court reversed a judgment of almost $8 million dollars and ordered that the plaintiff take nothing for his "devastating" injuries.

See Southwest Key Program, Inc. v. Gil-Perez, 81 S.W.3d. 269 (Tex. 2002) (no liability for an allegedly negligent failure to provide protective equipment to a boy participating in an amateur football game because plaintiff's expert said only that it was a matter of "speculation" whether those precautions would have prevented the knee injury); Friedman v. Safe Sec. Services, Inc., 765 N.E.2d 104 (Ill. App. Ct. 2001) (holding that an expert's testimony that a breach of the standard of care caused the plaintiff's harm was speculative and inadmissible because the expert's opinion assumed that the attacker entered the building after the security guard began duty, though there was no foundation for that assumption).

See also Jojos Restaurants, Inc. v. McFadden, 117 S.W.3d 279 (Tex. App. 2003) (holding that there was no evidence that having security personnel in a restaurant parking lot could have prevented a drive-by shooting).

2. *Causation in Toxic-Tort Cases.* Tort cases involving exposure to toxic substances raise difficult issues relating to proof of factual causation, including whether a substance is generally capable of causing a particular disease and, if so, whether the exposure to the substance caused the plaintiff in particular to contract the disease. In adjudicating toxic-tort cases, some courts have been inclined to place heavy reliance on scientific evidence developed in group (epidemiological) studies.

Proof of causation in toxic-exposure cases is beyond the scope of a basic course in torts. However, this subject is extensively addressed in Restatement, Third, of Torts: Liability for Physical Harm (Basic Principles) §28 Cmt. c (Tent. Draft No. 3 2003). The Restatement warns that:

> Courts…should be cautious about adopting specific "scientific" principles, taken out of context, to formulate bright-line legal rules or conclude that reasonable minds cannot differ about factual causation.

It notes that:

> [M]ost courts have appropriately declined to impose a threshold requirement that a plaintiff always must prove causation with epidemiologic evidence.…

The Restatement opines that for a number of reasons:

> [R]eliance on a threshold increase in risk or a doubling in incidence in a group study to meet the requirement of sufficient proof of specific causation is usually inappropriate.…

Comment c was developed by the American Law Institute in consultation with the National Academy of Sciences and prominent epidemiologists.

2. Independently Sufficient Causes and Related Problems

If several senators simultaneously stab Caesar on the steps of the Senate, none is a but-for cause of Caesar's death. Should each of the assailants escape liability? Not surprisingly, the answer is no.

> The "but for" rule serves to explain the vast majority of cases wherein a causation instruction is required. However, there is one type of situation in which

it fails. If two or more causes concur to bring about an event, and any one of them, operating alone, would have been sufficient to cause the identical result, some other test is needed. In such cases it is quite clear that each cause has in fact played so important a part in producing the result that responsibility should be imposed upon it; and it is equally clear that neither can be absolved from that responsibility upon the ground that the identical harm would have occurred without it, or there would be no liability at all.

Rudeck v. Wright, 709 P.2d 621, 628 (Mont. 1985).

Anderson v. Minneapolis, St. P. & S.S.M. Ry. Co.
Supreme Court of Minnesota
179 N.W. 45 (Minn. 1920)

[Plaintiff's property was destroyed by fire. The destruction was caused by either (a) a bog fire which resulted from the negligence of the defendant, (b) a fire of independent and uncertain origin which was sweeping through the Northeastern part of the state, or (c) a fire which resulted from the combining of the fire caused by the defendant with the fire of independent origin.]

LEES, C.

....Plaintiff had a verdict. The appeal is from an order denying a motion in the alternative for judgment notwithstanding the verdict or for a new trial.

[The defendant contends that the following jury instruction was error:]

If the plaintiff was burned out by some fire other than the bog fire, which other fire was not set by one of the defendant's engines, then, of course, defendant is not liable....

If you find that other fires not set by one of defendant's engines mingled with one that was set by one of the defendant's engines, there may be difficulty in determining whether you should find that the fire set by the engine was a material or substantial element in causing plaintiff's damage. If it was, the defendant is liable; otherwise, it is not....

If you find that the bog fire was set by the defendant's engine, and that some greater fire swept over it before it reached the plaintiff's land, then it will be for you to determine whether the bog fire...was a material or substantial factor in causing plaintiff's damage. If it was, the defendant is liable. If it was not, defendant is not liable....

....

The following proposition is stated in defendant's brief and relied on for reversal:

If plaintiff's property was damaged by a number of fires combining, one being the fire pleaded, and the others being of no responsible origin, but of such sufficient or superior force that they would have produced the damage to plaintiff's property regardless of the fire pleaded, then defendant was not liable.

This proposition is based on Cook v. Minneapolis, St. P. & S.S.M. Ry. Co., 98 Wis. 624, 74 N.W. 561....If the *Cook* case merely decides that one who negligently sets a fire is not liable if another's property is damaged, unless it is made to appear that the fire was a material element in the destruction of the property, there can be no question about the soundness of the decision. But if it decides that if such fire combines with another of no responsible origin, and after the union of the two fires they destroy the property, and either fire independently of the other would have destroyed it, then, irrespective of whether the first fire was or was not a material factor in the destruction of the property, there is no liability, we are not prepared to adopt the doctrine as the law of this state....

....

We find no error requiring a reversal, and hence the order appealed from is affirmed.

Notes

1. *The "Two Fires" Cases and but-for Causation.* In cases in which two fires merge and the combined fire destroys the plaintiff's property, the negligent conduct of the person who started one of the fires may or may not be a cause of the harm in a "but for" sense. Consider the following hypothetical cases:

Case (1): Denise negligently starts a small fire in the woods. If this had been the only fire at that time, the fire department could easily have handled it and the plaintiff's property would not have been destroyed. However, the fire set by Denise merges with a much larger fire. The larger fire could not have been stopped by the fire department. The merged fire burns the plaintiff's house to the ground. Denise's negligence is not a but-for cause of the loss of the plaintiff's house, and she will not be liable for the loss. If the other fire was negligently set, that negligence is a but-for cause of the loss.

Case (2): Darryl negligently sets a small fire, which merges with one negligently set by Donald. The fire department could have handled either fire alone, but the combined fire is too much for the department's resources, and the plaintiff's house burns. Darryl's negligence is a but-for cause of the damage, as "but for" that negligence the house would not have burned, so Darryl is liable. For the same reason, Donald's negligence is a but-for cause of the damage, so Donald is also liable.

Case (3): Donna and David, acting independently, negligently set large fires. Each fire, by itself, is too much for the fire department; they merge, and the merged fire destroys the plaintiff's house. In this case, neither the negligence of Donna nor that of Darryl is a but-for cause of the harm. If, for example, Donna had not set a fire, the plaintiff's house would have burned, so Donna's negligence is not a *sine qua non.* Similar reasoning shows that David's negligence was not a but-for cause of the harm. Nevertheless, both Donna and David are liable for the harm: this is like a case in which two persons, acting independently but at the same time, shoot the plaintiff in the head. This situation is often described as involving "independently sufficient causes."

2. *The "Substantial Factor" Test for Causation.* There is no doubt that both negligent defendants are liable to the plaintiff in most cases of independently sufficient causes, despite the absence of but-for causation. There has, however, been controversy as to how juries in these cases should be instructed. One possibility is simply to tell the jury that both defendants are liable if the jury finds that each defendant's negligence was an independently sufficient cause of the harm. Another is to dispense with any instruction on but-for cause in these cases and to instruct the jury that it may find the defendant liable if the defendant's negligence was a "substantial factor" in producing the harm. For very different views of the utility of the "substantial factor" approach, compare Prosser

and Keeton, Torts §41, at 267–268 (5th ed 1984), with David W. Robertson, *The Common Sense of Cause in Fact*, 75 Texas L. Rev. 1765 (1997). Prosser & Keeton find the "substantial factor" approach "an improvement over the 'but for' rule" for the "special class of cases" like Case (3), above. They point out that the "substantial factor" charge also allows the jury to exonerate some defendants, as when a negligent defendant tosses a single match into a raging forest fire; Prosser & Keeton at 267. Professor Robertson, conceding that substantial factor yields the right result in some cases, observes that, "[i]n a looser and potentially confusing usage, the substantial factor test is treated as more or less interchangeable with the but-for test; in this usage, courts seem to feel that it is appropriate to shift to the substantial factor vocabulary whenever the but-for test is proving difficult to work with for whatever reason"; Robertson, *supra*, at 1776. For a judicial opinion expressing a preference for explaining to the jury that the defendant is liable in "independently sufficient cause" cases over charging the jury that they can find liability if the defendant's negligence was a "substantial factor," see Rudeck v. Wright, 709 P.2d 621 (Mont. 1985).

In Mitchell v. Gonzalez, 819 P.2d 872 (Cal. 1991), a pattern jury instruction asking whether the injury would not have occurred but for the defendant's conduct was discontinued in favor of one asking whether the defendant's conduct was a substantial factor in bringing about the harm. However, in Viner v. Sweet, 70 P.3d 1046 (Cal. 2003), the same court made clear:

> In so holding, *Mitchell* did not abandon or repudiate the requirement that the plaintiff must prove that, *but for* the alleged negligence, the harm would not have happened. On the contrary, *Mitchell* stated that jury instructions on causation in negligence cases should use the "substantial factor" test articulated in the Restatement Second of Torts (Restatement), and *Mitchell* recognized that "the 'substantial factor' test subsumes the 'but for' test."....
>
> The text of Restatement section 432 demonstrates how the "substantial factor" test subsumes the traditional "but for" test of causation. Subsection (1) of section 432 provides: "Except as stated in Subsection (2), the actor's negligent conduct is *not a substantial factor* in bringing about harm to another *if the harm would have been sustained even if the actor had not been negligent.*".... Subsection (2) states that if "two forces are actively operating...and each of itself is sufficient to bring about harm to another, the actor's negligence may be found to be a substantial factor in bringing it about."
>
> Thus, in Restatement section 432, subsection (1) adopts the "but for" test of causation, while subsection (2) provides for an exception to that test. The situation that the exception addresses has long been recognized, but it has been given various labels, including "concurrent independent causes," [citation], "combined force criteria," [citation], and "multiple sufficient causes" (Rest. 3d Torts, Liability for Physical Harm (Basic Principles) (Tent. Draft No. 2, Mar. 25, 2002) §27, com. b, p. 70).

The *Viner* court held that because the transactional legal malpractice action before it did not involve concurrent independent causes, the plaintiffs had to satisfy the but-for test and show that it was more likely than not that they would have obtained a more favorable result absent the malpractice. *See also* Callahan v. Cardinal Glennon Hosp., 863 S.W.2d 852, 860 (Mo. 1993) (en banc) (but-for test applies to all cases except those involving two independently sufficient torts); Williams v. Steves Indus., Inc., 699 S.W.2d 570 (Tex. 1985), *supra* at 363 (test is whether the negligence was "a *substantial factor* in bringing about the injury and *without which no harm would have occurred*"; emphasis added); Gerst v. Marshall, 549 N.W.2d 810, 817 (Iowa 1996) (regardless of "[w]hether it would be prudent to eliminate the substantial factor test...a plaintiff...[must] meet the traditional but-for test of causation in fact"). The third Restatement rejects the "substantial factor" approach on the ground that it "has...not withstood the test of time, proving confusing and being misused," Restatement, Third, of Torts: Liability for Physical Harm (Basic Principles) (Tent. Draft No. 2, 2002), § 26, cmt j.

3. *Concurrence with Destructive Natural Forces.* In addition to cases of independently sufficient tortious cause (discussed in the preceding note), a case in which some courts may find a "substantial factor" instruction appropriate is this:

> Case (4): Doris negligently sets a large fire. This fire alone would be enough to overwhelm the fire department and destroy the plaintiff's house. The fire merges with another large fire, which was set by a lightning strike, without fault on anyone's part.

This is a difficult case. As in Case (3), above, Doris's negligence was not a but-for cause of the fire. Unlike Case (3), holding that Doris is not liable would not entail leaving a loss caused by the actions of two negligent people on the innocent plaintiff. (In Case (3), if the defendants were held not liable, the plaintiff would be worse off than if one defendant had stayed home that day instead of cooking hot dogs in the woods. In this case, the plaintiff would not have been worse off if Doris had stayed home.) Would the *Anderson* court approve of a "substantial factor" charge in this case? If the facts (in a "what happened" sense) are known, should juries be allowed to hold some defendants liable and to exonerate others, or should the law provide an answer? The *Cook* decision, cited in *Anderson*, holds that the defendant is not liable in a case like this. See also Kingston v. Chicago & N.W. Ry., 211 N.W. 913 (Wis. 1927), holding the known negligent defendant liable when the fires are "of comparatively equal rank" and the other fire seems to have been "set by some human agency," though its exact origins are unknown.

Section 27 of the Restatement, Third, of Torts: Liability for Physical Harm (Basic Principles) (Tentative Draft No. 2, 2002) deals with the independently sufficient cause problem by saying:

> When an actor's tortious conduct is not a factual cause of physical harm...only because another causal set exists that is also sufficient to cause the physical harm at the same time, the actor's tortious conduct is a factual cause of the harm.

Under the Restatement's approach as applied to the two-major-fires case, it does not matter whether the fire not set by the defendant is of tortious or natural origins. The comments to § 27 give no reason for selecting this particular rule.

4. *Joint and Several Liability.* In cases in which more than one defendant is liable for the destruction of the plaintiff's house, the plaintiff does not get a double recovery. In some states, the defendants will be jointly and severally liable, which means that the plaintiff can collect from either, or partly from both, but is not entitled to more than the total loss. If one defendant pays more than an appropriate share of the damages, that defendant may be entitled to recover the excess from the other tortfeasor. In other states, joint and several liability has been abolished and each tortfeasor will be liable only for a portion of the total harm. These matters are examined in Chapter 17.

3. The "Loss of a Chance" Rule

Alberts v. Schultz

Supreme Court of New Mexico
975 P.2d 1279 (N.M. 1999)

FRANCHINI, Chief J.

Dee and Mildred Alberts...brought a medical malpractice action for the amputation of Dee's right leg below the knee....

Dee had a history of peripheral vascular disease, which is a chronic progressive narrowing of the blood vessels which restricts the flow of blood to a particular area of the body. On July 14, 1992, he went to his primary care physician, Dr. Russell C. Schultz, with symptoms including severe pain in his right foot. He described pain in the absence of any activity or exercise, an affliction known as "rest pain," which is an acknowledged sign of impending gangrene that could lead to the amputation of the affected limb. Dr. Schultz noted that Dee's right foot was a "dusky" color. However, Dr. Schultz did not order an arteriogram, a diagnostic test that assists in evaluating the condition of blood vessels, and he did not conduct a motor sensory examination.

Dee specifically requested a referral to Dr. Gopal Reddy, a vascular surgeon who had previously examined his condition. Dr. Schultz apparently gave Dee the impression that Dr. Reddy was on vacation....The Alberts allege, and Dr. Schultz disputes, that he declined to refer Dee to a specialist other than Dr. Reddy....

It was not until thirteen days later, on July 27, 1992, that Dee saw Dr. Reddy....Dr. Reddy immediately sent him to the hospital. That same day, following an arteriogram, several procedures were performed unsuccessfully. The following day, bypass surgery was attempted. Dee's leg showed no improvement and on August 1, 1992, his right leg was amputated below the knee.

The Alberts brought a medical malpractice action...against Dr. Schultz and Dr. Reddy for negligence resulting in the amputation of Dee's right leg below the knee.... They claimed Dr. Schultz...failed to make a timely referral to a specialist. They further asserted that Dr. Reddy...had failed to perform the appropriate diagnostic tests and treatments. The Alberts argued that the thirteen-day delay before Dr. Reddy's intervention decreased the probability that the leg could be saved.

The Alberts' case was supported by the testimony of Dr. Max Carlton Hutton, a vascular surgeon. Dr. Hutton...testified that in his opinion Dr. Schultz should have performed motor and sensory exams and should have immediately ordered an arteriogram on Dee when he saw him on July 14, and should not have allowed nearly two weeks to pass before Dee could be seen by a vascular surgeon. Dr. Reddy, according to Dr. Hutton, was negligent in not performing motor and sensory exams, and in not doing a bypass immediately on July 27. Dr. Hutton noted that in cases such as Dee's, even the passage of six hours can make the difference between success and failure.

Dr. Hutton's testimony was based on the presumption Dee's leg could have been saved if specific arteries in his leg were suitable candidates for bypass surgery. However, in his testimony, he could not establish this presumption with certainty because the medical records were incomplete regarding the specific arteries in question....Dr. Hutton could not pinpoint...a time when earlier intervention would have changed the outcome. In Dr. Hutton's opinion "the probability that Mr. Alberts' leg could have been saved decreased significantly," because of the inaction of both physicians. Nevertheless, Dr. Hutton testified that he could not state to a reasonable degree of medical probability that immediate use of the motor and sensory exams, the arteriogram, and the bypass would have increased the chances of saving Dee's leg.

The trial court granted partial summary judgment in favor of the defendants, because the Alberts could not establish to a reasonable degree of medical probability that the physicians' conduct proximately caused the amputation of Dee's leg....However, the trial court found that there was an issue of fact about whether the allegedly negligent conduct of either or both defendants may have increased the risk that Dee's leg would have to be amputated. The trial court certified that issue for interlocutory appeal. As phrased by the trial court, this issue poses two questions: (1) whether New Mexico should recognize a patient's claim that...a health giver's negligence has resulted in the loss of a chance for a better result; and (2) if New Mexico does recognize loss of chance, whether the Alberts could recover under such claim. The Court of Appeals certified the case to us....

....

Generally, the fact pattern in a lost-chance claim begins when a patient comes to a health giver with a particular medical complaint. We will refer to "[t]he illness, disorder, discomfort, pain, fear, etc. that is the main reason for the patient's seeking medical help" as the "presenting problem." [Citation.] The problem may be a sudden injury or illness, or it may be a malady that the patient has suffered over a long period of time. *See, e.g.,* Delaney v. Cade, 255 Kan. 199, 873 P.2d 175, 177–83 (1994) (sudden injury;...approving loss-of-chance claim for victim who claimed she suffered permanent paralysis after automobile accident, because of delay in transferring her to a facility that was equipped to properly treat her injuries); Wendland v. Sparks, 574 N.W.2d 327, 328–33 (Iowa 1998) (long term illness; even though patient had only 10% chance of leaving hospital, permitting loss-of-chance claim for patient being treated for several ailments including cancer of the plasma cells, and who suffered cardiorespiratory arrest while in hospital and was not revived by physician). A claim for loss of chance is predicated upon the negligent denial by a health-care provider of the most effective therapy for a patient's presenting medical problem. The negligence may be found in such misconduct as an incorrect diagnosis, the application of inappropriate treatments, or the failure to timely provide the proper treatment....

The essence of the patient's claim is that, prior to the negligence, there was a chance that he or she would have been better off with adequate care. *See* John D. Hodson, Annotation, *Medical Malpractice: "Loss of Chance" Causality,* 54 A.L.R.4th 10, § 2(a), at 17 (1988) (stating that in such cases patients must present "expert testimony that if proper treatment had been given, better results would have followed"). Because of the negligence, this chance has been lost.... [U]nder the lost-chance theory, the patient may seek recovery even if the chance of a favorable outcome prior to the negligence was very slim. [Citation.] Every patient has a certain probability that he or she will recover from the presenting medical problem. The probability of recovery may be high — more than fifty percent; or the prognosis may be more bleak — less than fifty percent. Whether great or small, there is *some* chance that the person will recover. Under the loss-of-chance theory, the health provider's malpractice has obliterated or reduced those odds of recovery that existed before the act of malpractice. The patient with a greater-than-fifty-percent chance of recovery is deprived of a more promising outcome. The patient with a slim chance is deprived of the opportunity to beat the odds. Where there was once a chance of a better result, now there is a lesser or no chance. *See Delaney,* 873 P.2d at 178 (citing Joseph H. King, Jr., *Causation, Valuation, and Chance in Personal Injury*

Torts Involving Preexisting Conditions and Future Consequences, 90 Yale L.J. 1353, 1354 (1981)); [citation].

Ultimately, the patient may suffer the consequences of the presenting medical problem. However, under the lost-chance theory, the patient does not allege that the malpractice caused his or her entire injury. Rather, the claim is that the health care provider's negligence reduced the chance of avoiding the injury actually sustained. *See* Herber v. Johns-Manville Corp., 785 F.2d 79, 82 (3d Cir. 1986). Thus, it is that chance in and of itself— the lost opportunity of avoiding the presenting problem and achieving a better result— that becomes the item of value for which the patient seeks compensation. [Citation.]

Some of the resistance that this concept has received from other courts seems, in part, to be caused by the very terms by which it is named. The idea of a "lost chance" raises the concern that the claim is for something indeterminate, if not completely unreal. Some courts seek to clarify the theory by use of the term "increased risk of harm."....As used by this theory, the word "chance" connotes an opportunity for a better result that is measured by the same kinds of statistical probabilities that are familiar to both physicians and courts of law....[W]e believe that, when considering compensation for injuries under this theory, malpractice that reduces the probability that a patient will recover from the presenting problem is equivalent to malpractice that increases the probability that the patient will suffer the effects of that problem. Scafidi v. Seiler, 119 N.J. 93, 574 A.2d 398, 410 (1990) (Handler, J., concurring) (stating that the concept is equally understandable whether called "lost chance" or "increased risk"). *But see* United States v. Anderson, 669 A.2d 73, 75–76 (Del. 1995) (distinguishing between "increased risk" and "lost chance").

....

...[T]he loss-of-chance concept is not an unprecedented departure from traditional theories of recovery....It is certainly not a theory that we have ever expressly abrogated. Loss of chance is conceptually related to well-established theories of recovery in New Mexico tort law, such as failure to diagnose, [citation]; comparative negligence, [citation]; enhancement of a preexisting condition, [citation]; and failure to inform about a condition so that the condition remains untreated, [citation]. Loss of chance is not a new cause of action so much as a logical extension of existing probable cause analysis.

....

The basic test for establishing loss of chance is no different from the elements required in other medical malpractice actions, or in negligence suits in general: duty, breach, loss or damage, and causation. [Citations.] *Loss of chance differs from other medical malpractice actions only in the nature of the harm for which relief is sought.*

....Because the issues raised in lost-chance actions are, in virtually every case, "beyond the province of lay persons," the plaintiff will almost always establish these elements through expert testimony. [Citation.]

....

In New Mexico, as in most jurisdictions, healthcare providers are "under the duty to possess and apply the knowledge and to use the skill and care ordinarily used by reasonably well-qualified [health care providers] practicing under similar circumstances, giving due consideration to the locality involved."....

....

A healthcare provider who breaches this duty of skill and care is negligent. [Citations.] A critical issue in most lost-chance actions is not whether the defendant owed the patient a duty, but whether that duty was breached by the defendant's failure to timely or properly diagnose the presenting problem and follow an appropriate course of treatment. [Citation.]

....

...[I]t is the injury alleged, that separates a lost-chance claim from other medical malpractice actions. The injury is the lost opportunity of a better result, not the harm caused by the presenting problem. It is not the physical harm itself, but rather the lost chance of avoiding the physical harm. [Citation.] As we explain below, the causal connection between the negligence and the resultant injury must be medically probable.

....

It must be emphasized that the injury—the lost chance—is not in any way speculative. It is manifested by actual physical harm. This claim must not be confused with cases in which, as a result of the tortious conduct of one party, another party suffers exposure to something harmful, which may, in the future lead to an injury. Loss of chance does not involve prognostication about future injury or harm. *See Perez*, 805 P.2d at 592 ("Of course, the plaintiff or injured person cannot recover merely on the basis of a decreased chance of survival or of avoiding a debilitating illness or injury; the plaintiff must in fact suffer death or debilitating injury before there can be an award of damages."). Rather, the patient must present evidence that the harm for which he or she originally sought treatment—the presenting medical problem—was in fact made worse by the lost chance. [Citation.]

....

We see no reason at this time to limit lost-chance claims to those cases in which the chance of a better result has been utterly lost. Denying compensation for the diminution—as opposed to the loss—of a chance may lead to unreasonable hairsplitting. "Evidence of the physical progression of the patient's disease during a negligent delay in diagnosis or treatment may be sufficient to establish that the plaintiff was 'injured' by the delay." [Citation.] It is possible that trial courts may conclude in some cases that the diminished chance of a better result is of negligible significance. *See, e.g., Wollen*, 828 S.W.2d at 685 n. 3 (limiting loss-of-chance recovery "to those cases in which the chance of recovery lost was sizeable enough to be material, which must be so found by the jury"). The cost of litigating such actions will no doubt discourage claims that are insignificant. [Citation.]

....

If the Alberts had brought a claim under an ordinary medical malpractice negligence theory, the injury alleged would be the loss of Dee's leg below the knee. They cannot sustain such a claim, however, because his preexisting condition—peripheral vascular disease—precludes proof to a reasonable degree of medical probability that the doctors' negligence proximately caused the loss of the leg below the knee. In contrast, Dee can submit evidence that he had a chance—even if it was a small chance—of being cured of the presenting problem of rest pain and possible impending gangrene. He can be compensated if he can demonstrate, to a reasonable degree of medical probability, a causal link between the doctor's negligence and the loss of that chance.

....

There are many theories as to the calculation of pecuniary damages for loss of chance. We conclude that damages should be awarded on a proportional basis as determined by the percentage value of the patient's chance for a better outcome prior to the negligent act....

In loss-of-chance cases, most courts apportion damages by valuing the chance of a better result as a percentage of the value of the entire life or limb. [Citations.] For example, the value of a patient's fifty-percent chance of survival is fifty percent of the value of their total life. If medical malpractice reduced that chance of survival from fifty to twenty percent, that patient's compensation would be equal to thirty percent of the value of their life....

The valuation of life, limb, and lost chances is necessarily imprecise. Just as causation is proved by probabilities, the value of the loss must be established by fair approximations, based on the kinds of proof that courts commonly use when making such determinations....

   ....

When loss of chance, as set forth in this opinion, is applied to the facts of this case, the Alberts' claim must fail. The Alberts have not established the causation element in their negligence claim. They have not demonstrated, to a reasonable degree of medical probability, that the alleged negligence of Dr. Schultz and Dr. Reddy proximately caused Dee to lose the chance of saving his leg.

...[A] lost-chance claim may be conceived of as the loss of a window of time. The loss of time is the essence of the Alberts' claim. They argue that there was a brief time, beginning on July 14, 1992, during which the proper medical intervention would have saved Dee's leg....

Unfortunately, the Alberts cannot...show, to a reasonable degree of medical probability, that timely and proper medical intervention would have saved Dee's leg. Specifically, they cannot show that a bypass on July 14, 1992, would have precluded the amputation; nor can they show that Dee was a suitable candidate for a bypass on that date; nor can they show that Dee was a suitable candidate for a bypass on July 27, 1992, when Dr. Reddy finally saw him, but that he became unsuitable by the next day when the bypass was actually performed.

The evidence the Alberts presented to support their lost-chance claim was based on incomplete medical records and unsupported assumptions. Dr. Hutton, the Alberts' expert, based his opinion on inadequately verified and speculative assumptions concerning Dee's condition.... [H]e testified that bypass surgery would have had a strong chance of being successful *if* Dee's leg had exhibited "a good saphenous vein." However, Dr. Hutton stated no authoritative conclusions about the integrity of Dee's saphenous vein. In fact, he unequivocally stated that the medical records were incomplete, that certain information that would have credibly established Dee's suitability for surgery was not available. Thus Dr. Hutton stated that, *if* he had available "better arteriograms," he "would find *probably*" a particular artery to be suitable for bypass surgery. Without proof that Dee's leg possessed at least one vein or artery that was suitable for bypass surgery, the Alberts cannot validly contend that the failure to timely perform a bypass caused the leg to deteriorate....

The burden of proving reasonable medical probability rests with the plaintiff, and a causal connection between the alleged act of malpractice and the plaintiff's loss or damages cannot be substantiated by arguments based upon conjecture, surmise, or speculation....

   ....

We recognize the legitimacy of the lost-chance concept in New Mexico....However, in this specific case, the Alberts are not entitled to compensation under that theory because they did not prove that the alleged malpractice proximately caused Dee's lost chance for a better result.

BACA and SERNA, JJ., concur.

PETRA J. MAES, Justice (Dissenting).

....

....Plaintiff's expert, Dr. Hutton, testified to a reasonable degree of medical probability that the success rate of the bypass procedure would be greater than 90 percent. The testimony raises a genuine issue of material fact.

....Granted, the opinions and reports upon which Dr. Hutton relied do not perfectly establish the condition of every inch of Plaintiff Alberts' leg. However, that is not the standard in New Mexico for the reliability of expert opinions....

> ....Causation exists within a reasonable medical probability when a qualified medical expert testifies as to his opinion concerning causation and, in the absence of other reasonable casual [sic] explanations, it becomes more likely than not that the injury was a result of its action. [Citations.]

....

I believe Dr. Hutton's testimony met this test. For example, based on the lack of any mention of distal occlusions of the peroneal and posterior tibial artery in Dr. Winterkorn's report, *Dr. Hutton infers that there were none.* His opinion that either of these arteries would have been suitable for a bypass is based on this inference. [Citation.]

His opinion is not impermissible speculation; it is a reasonable inference from known facts. [Citations.]

....

....I would conclude that the plaintiff has shown a genuine issue of material fact concerning the failure to timely perform the bypass which caused increased risk of harm to the plaintiff's leg. For these reasons, I would reverse the summary judgment and remand this case to the district court for further proceedings.

Notes

1. The article by Professor King noted in *Alberts*, has been quoted and debated by many courts. *See also* Joseph H. King, Jr., *"Reduction of Likelihood" Reformulation and Other Retrofitting of the Loss-of-a-Chance Doctrine*, 28 U. Memphis L. Rev. 491 (1998); David A. Fischer, *Tort Recovery for Loss of a Chance*, 36 Wake Forest L. Rev. 605 (2001) (exploring non-arbitrary limiting principles that would permit courts to use loss of a chance outside of the medical context without fear that the doctrine will expand into a general theory of probabilistic causation).

The recent decisions have been deeply divided. *Compare* U.S. v. Cumberbatch, 647 A.2d 1098 (Del. 1994) (loss of a chance is not actionable), Kramer v. Lewisville Mem'l Hosp., 858 S.W.2d 397 (Tex. 1993) (same), *and* Jones v. Owings, 456 S.E.2d 371 (S.C. 1995) (same), *with* Jorgenson v. Vener, 616 N.W.2d 366 (S.D. 2000) (loss of a chance is actionable); Delaney v. Cade, 873 P.2d 175 (Kan. 1994) (same), *and* Roberts v. Ohio Permanente Med. Group, 668 N.E.2d 480 (Ohio 1996) (same).

2. *"Loss of a Chance" and Deterrence.* Compare two rules: (1) negligent defendants must pay full damages to victims who would have had a better than 50-percent chance of survival, but for the negligence, and (2) in all cases, negligent defendants pay according to the chance the plaintiff has lost, so that a plaintiff whose lost chance of survival was 70 percent gets a 70-percent recovery, and so on. On an overall basis, the amount a

defendant should expect to pay under either of these rules should be roughly the same. Indeed, even on an *individual* basis, payments under either rule should be similar, as most cases are settled, not tried, and the greater the plaintiff's chances of convincing a jury that the chance of survival was high, the greater the settlement value of the plaintiff's case, under either rule.

If, however, the loss-of-a-chance rule comes into play only for plaintiffs whose chance was 50 percent or less, with other plaintiffs getting full recovery, the loss-of-a-chance rule will increase the amount defendants will pay, and in theory this will over-deter them. Similarly, if plaintiffs with less than a 50 percent chance of survival recover nothing, and other plaintiffs recover only the chance they have lost, the rules will produce under-deterrence.

The use of the loss-of-a-chance doctrine is a recent development. In other contexts, however, the victim's chance of survival has long been taken into account. For example, the damages assessed in a wrongful-death case in which the defendant's wrongdoing plainly caused the death are, in a sense, damages for the decedent's "loss of a chance of survival." The decedent's life expectancy—which fixes the number of years which the decedent would have had a 50–50 chance of living—is routinely used to calculate wrongful-death damages. For a dramatic instance of taking the victim's chance of survival into account, see Dillon v. Twin State Gas & Elec. Co., 163 A. 111 (N.H. 1932) (damages for death by electrocution were reduced to reflect the pre-existing fact that at the time the decedent touched the defendant's wires he had lost his balance and begun to fall from a bridge, and the fall would certainly have killed him). *See also* McCahill v. New York Transp. Co., 94 N.E. 616 (N.Y. 1911) (damages reduced to reflect the fact that premature death might have otherwise resulted from the decedent's preexisting alcoholism). What is new about the loss-of-a-chance cases is not the use of estimates of survival in tort cases, but rather their use in cases in which the defendant's negligence may not have harmed the plaintiff at all.

3. *"Loss of a Chance" and Statistics.* In Fennell v. Southern Maryland Hosp., 580 A.2d 206 (Md. 1990), a case which refused to recognize damages for loss of a chance in a survival action, the court wrote:

> Because loss of chance recovery is based on statistical probabilities, it might be appropriate to examine the statistical probabilities of achieving a "just" result with loss of chance damages. In Brennwald, *Proving Causation in "Loss of a Chance" Cases: A Proportional Approach*, 34 Cath. U. L. Rev. 747, 779 n. 254 (1985), the author, citing Orloff and Stedinger's article *A Framework for Evaluating the Preponderance-of-the-Evidence Standard*, 131 U. Pa. L. Rev. 1159 (1983), attempted to analyze statistically the errors produced using traditional tort recovery as compared to the errors produced by loss of chance recovery.
>
> To compare the two rules, assume a hypothetical group of 99 cancer patients, each of whom would have had a 33 1/3% chance of survival. Each received negligent medical care, and all 99 died. Traditional tort law would deny recovery in all 99 cases because each patient had less than a 50% chance of recovery and the probable cause of death was the pre-existing cancer not the negligence. Statistically, had all 99 received proper treatment, 33 would have lived and 66 would have died; so the traditional rule would have statistically produced 33 errors by denying recovery to all 99.
>
> The loss of chance rule would allow all 99 patients to recover, but each would recover 33 1/3% of the normal value of the case. Again, with proper care 33 patients would have survived. Thus, the 33 patients who statistically would have survived with proper care would receive only one-third of the appropriate

recovery, while the 66 patients who died as a result of the pre-existing condition, not the negligence, would be overcompensated by one-third. The loss of chance rule would have produced errors in all 99 cases.

Re-defining loss of chance of survival as a new form of damages so that the compensable injury is not the death, but is the loss of chance of survival itself, may really be an exercise in semantics. Loss of chance of survival in itself is not compensable unless and until death ensues. Thus, it would seem that the true injury is the death.

While we should not award damages if there is no injury, the logical extension of the loss of chance damages theory arguably should allow loss of chance damages for negligence, even when the patient miraculously recovers.

For example, if a doctor negligently treats a person with a 40% chance of recovery and the doctor's negligence reduces the patient's chance of recovery to only 10%, whether the patient lives or dies, the doctor's negligence cost the patient a 30% loss of chance of survival. If the patient dies, the probable cause of death was the pre-existing disease or injury; it is unlikely that the negligence caused the death. If the patient lives, the negligence clearly did not cause the death. In both scenarios, there was negligence resulting in a 30% loss of chance of survival.

If courts are going to allow damages solely for the loss of chance of survival, logically there ought to be recovery for loss of chance regardless of whether the patient succumbs to the unrelated pre-existing medical problem or miraculously recovers despite the negligence and unfavorable odds.

Since loss of chance damages are only permitted when the patient dies, it is also arguable that, when we strip away the rhetoric, damages are really being awarded for the possibility that the negligence was a cause of the death....

Another factor weighing against adoption of a loss of chance damages approach is its practical application in civil jury trials. Probabilities and statistical evidence comprise a substantial portion of the evidence submitted to the trier of fact in loss of chance actions. This evidence will generally be in the form of opinions based on statistics that show chance of survival of other individuals similarly situated to the victim. The use of statistics in trials is subject to criticism as being unreliable, misleading, easily manipulated, and confusing to a jury. When large damage awards will be based on the statistical chance of survival before the negligent treatment, minus the statistical chance of survival after the negligent treatment, times the value of the lost life, we can imagine the bewildering sets of numbers with which the jury will be confronted, as well as the difficulties juries will have in assessing the comparative reliability of the divergent statistical evidence offered by each side.

Is the court's reasoning sound? Consider the claim that, in the case of the 99 cancer patients, the loss-of-a-chance rule will "produce[] errors in all 99 cases," while the traditional rule will produce errors in only 33 cases. So what? Under ideal circumstances, defendants will pay exactly the right amount of damages under the loss-of-a-chance rule, and will pay nothing under the traditional rule, so the loss-of-a-chance rule works much better when we look only at defendants. From the plaintiffs' point of view, it may be true in some sense that all 99 plaintiffs get "the wrong amount" under the loss-of-a-chance rule, which undercompensates some of them and overcompensates the rest, but plaintiffs would clearly prefer the loss-of-a-chance rule to a rule of no recovery. The "number of errors," standing alone, is a meaningless figure. To illustrate, consider whether it would make sense for the courts to take resources away from trying capital cases and devote them to minor traffic offenses if the result were ten more capital cases decided erroneously with better results in fifty traffic cases.

Responding to the majority's reasoning in *Fennell*, Judge Adkins wrote in dissent:

> Tort law is not about mathematical niceties; it has to do with fairness to fault-free victims who have suffered harm by reason of the tortious acts or omissions of others. It is a basic principle of our tort system that those who can prove they have been so harmed should be compensated. Why should we reject that principle when the harm is loss of a chance of survival that is less than 51%.

4. *Damages for "Loss of a Chance."* As to valuing the lost chance, compare the approach discussed in *Alberts* with Smith v. State Dept. of Health & Hosp., 676 So. 2d 543 (La. 1996) (the factfinder should make a subjective determination of the value of the lost chance without going through the illusory exercise of setting a value for a wrongful death or survival claim and then reducing that amount by some percentage).

5. *Legal Malpractice and Other Contexts.* Recall that, in cases involving *legal* malpractice, the victim must establish that the malpractice caused a loss (*see* Chapter 5). Is a loss-of-a-chance rule any less desirable for legal malpractice cases than for medical-malpractice cases? *See* Erik M. Jensen, Note, *The Standard of Proof of Causation in Legal Malpractice Cases*, 63 Cornell L. Rev. 666 (1978); Daugert v. Pappas, 704 P.2d 600 (Wash. 1985) (declining to apply loss-of-a-chance principles to legal malpractice action).

See also Hardy v. Southwestern Bell Telephone Co., 910 P.2d 1024 (Okla. 1996) (refusing to extend the loss-of-a-chance doctrine to ordinary negligence cases, such as where negligence causes a 911 emergency system to fail and prevents aid from being summoned for a heart attack victim, because the trier of fact would "have no more than mere conjecture as to what damages plaintiff suffered by reason of defendant's action").

The Restatement, noting that loss-of-a-chance has been "almost universally limited" to cases of medical malpractice and that the doctrine's expansion into other areas would be a reform "of potentially enormous scope," takes no position on the issue of expansion; Restatement, Third, of Torts: Liability for Physical Harm (Basic Principles) (Tent. Draft No. 2, 2002), §26, cmt. n.

C. Modifications of the Traditional Approach

1. Multiple Fault and Alternative Liability

Summers v. Tice
Supreme Court of California, In Bank
199 P.2d 1 (Cal. 1948)

CARTER, Justice.

. . . .

. . . [P]laintiff and the two defendants were hunting quail on the open range. Each of the defendants was armed with a 12 gauge shotgun loaded with shells containing 7½ size shot. Prior to going hunting plaintiff discussed the hunting procedure with defendants, indicating that they were to exercise care when shooting and to "keep in line." . . . .

....There is evidence that both defendants, at about the same time or one immediately after the other, shot at a quail and in so doing shot toward plaintiff who was uphill from them, and that they knew his location. That is sufficient [evidence] from which the trial court could conclude that they acted with respect to plaintiff other than as persons of ordinary prudence....

....

The problem presented in this case is whether the judgment against both defendants may stand. It is argued by defendants that...there is not sufficient [evidence] to show which defendant was guilty of the negligence which caused the injuries—the shooting by Tice or that by Simonson....

...[I]t is clear that the court...determined that the negligence of both defendants was the legal cause of the injury—or that both were responsible. Implicit in such finding is the assumption that the court was unable to ascertain whether the shots were from the gun of one defendant or the other or one shot from each of them. The one shot that entered plaintiff's eye was the major factor in assessing damages and that shot could not have come from the gun of both defendants. It was from one or the other only.

It has been held that where a group of persons are on a hunting party, or otherwise engaged in the use of firearms, and two of them are negligent in firing in the direction of a third person who is injured thereby, both of those so firing are liable for the injury suffered by the third person, although the negligence of only one of them could have caused the injury. [Citations.] The same rule has been applied in criminal cases [citation] and both drivers have been held liable for the negligence of one where they engaged in a racing contest causing an injury to a third person. [Citation.] These cases speak of the action of defendants as being in concert as the ground of decision, yet it would seem they are straining that concept....

"...The real reason for the rule that each joint tortfeasor is responsible for the whole damage is the practical unfairness of denying the injured person redress simply because he cannot prove how much damage each did, when it is certain that between them they did all; let them be the ones to apportion it among themselves. Since, then, the difficulty of proof is the reason, the rule should apply whenever the harm has plural causes, and not merely when they acted in conscious concert...." (Wigmore, Select Cases on the Law of Torts, §153)....   *Rule*

When we consider the relative position of the parties and the results that would flow if plaintiff was required to pin the injury on one of the defendants only, a requirement that the burden of proof on that subject be shifted to defendants becomes manifest. They are both wrongdoers—both negligent toward plaintiff. They brought about a situation where the negligence of one of them injured the plaintiff, hence it should rest with them each to absolve himself if he can. The injured party has been placed by defendants in the unfair position of pointing to which defendant caused the harm. If one can escape the other may also and plaintiff is remediless. Ordinarily defendants are in a far better position to offer evidence to determine which one caused the injury. This reasoning has recently found favor in this Court. In a quite analogous situation this Court held that a patient injured while unconscious on an operating table in a hospital could hold all or any of the persons who had any connection with the operation even though he could not select the particular acts by the particular person which led to his disability. Ybarra v. Spangard, 25 Cal. 2d 486, 154 P.2d 687, 162 A.L.R. 1258. There the Court was considering whether the patient could avail himself of *res ipsa loquitur*, rather than where the burden of proof lay, yet the effect of the decision is that plaintiff has made out a case when he has produced evidence which gives rise to an inference of negligence which was the proximate cause of the injury. It is up to defendants to explain the cause of the injury. It was there said: "If the doctrine is to continue to serve a useful purpose, we should not forget that 'the particular force and justice of the rule, regarded as a presumption throwing upon the party charged the duty of producing evidence, consists in the circumstance that the chief evidence of the true cause, whether culpable or innocent, is practically accessible to him but inaccessible to the injured person.'" [Citation.] Similarly in the instant case plaintiff is not able to establish which of defendants caused his injury.

. . . .

The judgment is affirmed.

Notes

1. *Alternative Liability.* The rule of "multiple fault and alternative liability" set forth in *Summers* has been embodied in Restatement, Third, of Torts: Liability for Physical Harm (Basic Principles) §28(b) (Tent. Draft No. 2, 2002):

> When the plaintiff sues all of two or more defendants whose tortious conduct exposed the plaintiff to a risk of harm and proves that the tortuous conduct of one or more defendants caused the plaintiff's harm but cannot reasonably prove which of the defendants caused the harm, the burden of proof, including both production and persuasion, on factual causation is shifted to the defendants.

2. *Policy Basis.* According to the Restatement, the reason underlying the rule is that:

> as between two culpable defendants and an innocent plaintiff, it is preferable to put the risk of error on culpable defendants rather than on the innocent plaintiff.

Restatement, Third, of Torts: Liability for Physical Harm (Basic Principles) (Tent. Draft No. 2, 2002), §28, cmt. f. Section 28 provides for liability even in cases in which more than two defendants have acted negligently. It requires, however, that all negligent defendants be joined, at least if all of them are subject to the court's jurisdiction and not immune from liability. The joinder requirement is based on a concern that the party actually responsible could escape liability if fewer than all the persons who acted tortiously are made defendants.

Discussing Summers v. Tice and the rule of alternative liability, the New York Court of Appeals has said:

> The central rationale for shifting the burden of proof in such a situation is that without this device both defendants will be silent and plaintiff will not recover; with alternative liability, however, defendants will be forced to speak, and reveal the culpable party, or else be held jointly and severally liable themselves. Consequently, use of the alternative liability doctrine generally requires that the defendants have better access to information than does the plaintiff, and that all possible tortfeasors be before the court [citations]. It is also recognized that alternative liability rests on the notion that where there is a small number of possible wrongdoers, all of whom breached a duty to the plaintiff, the likelihood that any one of them injured the plaintiff is relatively high, so that forcing them to exonerate themselves, or be held liable, is not unfair [citation].

Hymowitz v. Eli Lilly and Co., 539 N.E.2d 1069, 1074 (N.Y. 1989).

Although *Summers* has been widely cited with approval, at least one court has declined to follow it on nearly identical facts. *See* Leuer v. Johnson, 450 N.W.2d 363 (Minn. Ct. App. 1990).

3. *Requirement of Multiple Fault.* The alternative liability rationale is applicable only where all of the defendants are shown to have acted tortiously. Illustration 6 to the Restatement, Third, of Torts: Liability for Physical Harm (Basic Principles) (Tent. Draft No. 2, 2002), § 28 provides:

> Reed, a pedestrian, was injured by a sofa that was negligently or intentionally thrown from an upper-story hotel room during the celebration of an NCAA basketball championship. Reed sues all of the occupants of the 47 rooms from which the sofa might have been thrown. Reed must prove which of the defendants was responsible for throwing the sofa; the burden shifting provided in this subsection is not available to Reed in his suit because he has not shown that the occupants of each of the 47 rooms acted tortiously.

See also Garcia v. Joseph Vince Co., 148 Cal. Rptr. 843, 846–47 (Ct. App. 1978) (alternative liability theory inapplicable in suit against two saber manufacturers, where plaintiff was unable to identify which of the two had produced the defective weapon which injured him because it had been commingled with other sabers after the accident).

2. Market-Share Liability and Enterprise Liability

Sindell v. Abbott Laboratories

Supreme Court of California
163 Cal. Rptr. 132 (Cal. 1980)

MOSK, Justice.

...[M]ay a plaintiff, injured as the result of a drug administered to her mother during pregnancy, who knows the type of drug involved but cannot identify the manufacturer of the precise product, hold liable for her injuries a maker of a drug produced from an identical formula?

Plaintiff Judith Sindell brought an action against eleven drug companies and Does 1 through 100, on behalf of herself and other women similarly situated. The complaint alleges as follows:

Between 1941 and 1971, defendants were engaged in the business of manufacturing, promoting, and marketing diethylstilbestrol (DES),...a synthetic compound of the female hormone estrogen. The drug was administered to plaintiff's mother...for the purpose of preventing miscarriage. In 1947, the Food and Drug Administration authorized the marketing of DES as a miscarriage preventative, but only on an experimental basis....

DES may cause cancerous vaginal and cervical growths in the daughters exposed to it before birth, because their mothers took the drug during pregnancy. The form of cancer from which these daughters suffer...manifests itself after a minimum latent period of 10 or 12 years. It is a fast-spreading and deadly disease, and radical surgery is required to prevent it from spreading. DES also causes adenosis, precancerous vaginal and cervical growths which may spread to other areas of the body....

In 1971, the Food and Drug Administration ordered defendants to cease marketing and promoting DES..., and to warn physicians and the public that the drug should not be used by pregnant women because of the danger to their unborn children.

During the period defendants marketed DES, they knew or should have known that... there was a grave danger after varying periods of latency it would cause cancerous and precancerous growths in the daughters of the mothers who took it, and that it was ineffective to prevent miscarriage. Nevertheless, defendants continued to advertise and market the drug.... They failed to test DES for efficacy and safety; the tests performed by others, upon which they relied, indicated that it was not safe or effective....

. . . .

The first cause of action alleges that defendants were jointly and individually negligent....

. . . .

Defendants demurred to the complaint... [T]he trial court sustained the demurrers of these defendants without leave to amend on the ground that plaintiff did not and stated she could not identify which defendant had manufactured the drug responsible for her injuries. Thereupon, the court dismissed the action. This appeal involves only five of [the]... defendants named in the complaint.

. . . .

... [A]s a general rule, the imposition of liability depends upon a showing by the plaintiff that his or her injuries were caused by the act of the defendant or by an instrumentality under the defendant's control....

There are, however, exceptions to this rule.... The first of these theories, classically illustrated by Summers v. Tice (1948) 33 Cal.2d 80, 199 P.2d 1, places the burden of proof of causation upon tortious defendants in certain circumstances. The second basis of liability emerging from the complaint is that defendants acted in concert to cause injury to plaintiff. There is a third and novel approach to the problem, sometimes called the theory of "enterprise liability," but which we prefer to designate by the more accurate term of "industry-wide" liability, which might obviate the necessity for identifying the manufacturer of the injury-causing drug. We shall conclude that these doctrines, as previously interpreted, may not be applied to hold defendants liable under the allegations of this complaint. However, we shall propose and adopt a fourth basis for permitting the action to be tried, grounded upon an extension of the *Summers* doctrine.

. . . .

Defendants assert that... [the principles of Summers v. Tice, 199 P.2d 1 (Cal. 1948), *supra* at 386, and Ybarra v. Spangard, 154 P.2d 687 (Cal. 1944), *supra* at 352] are inapplicable here. First, they insist that a predicate to shifting the burden of proof under *Summers-Ybarra* is that the defendants must have greater access to information regarding the cause of the injuries than the plaintiff, whereas in the present case the reverse appears.

. . . .

In *Summers*, the circumstances of the accident themselves precluded an explanation of its cause. To be sure, *Summers* states that defendants are "[o]rdinarily... in a far better position to offer evidence to determine which one caused the injury" than a plaintiff [citation], but the decision does not determine that this "ordinary" situation was present. Neither the facts nor the language of the opinion indicate that the two defendants, simultaneously shooting in the same direction, were in a better position than the plaintiff to ascertain whose shot caused the injury. As the opinion acknowledges, it was impossible for the trial court to determine whether the shot which entered the plaintiff's eye came from the gun of one defendant or the other. Nevertheless, burden of proof was shifted to the defendants.

Here, as in *Summers*, the circumstances of the injury appear to render identification of the manufacturer of the drug ingested by plaintiff's mother impossible by either plaintiff or defendants, and it cannot reasonably be said that one is in a better position than the other to make the identification....

    ....

It is important to observe, however, that while defendants do not have means superior to plaintiff to identify the maker of the precise drug taken by her mother, they may in some instances be able to prove that they did not manufacture the injury-causing substance. In the present case, for example, one of the original defendants was dismissed from the action upon proof that it did not manufacture DES until after plaintiff was born.

... [T]he fact defendants do not have greater access to information which might establish the identity of the manufacturer of the DES which injured plaintiff does not per se prevent application of the *Summers* rule.

Nevertheless, plaintiff may not prevail in her claim that the *Summers* rationale should be employed to fix the whole liability for her injuries upon defendants, at least as those principles have previously been applied. There is an important difference between the situation involved in *Summers* and the present case. There, all the parties who were or could have been responsible for the harm to the plaintiff were joined as defendants. Here, by contrast, there are approximately 200 drug companies which made DES, any of which might have manufactured the injury-producing drug.

Defendants maintain that, while in *Summers* there was a 50 percent chance that one of the two defendants was responsible for the plaintiff's injuries, here since any one of 200 companies which manufactured DES might have made the product which harmed plaintiff, there is no rational basis upon which to infer that any defendant in this action caused plaintiff's injuries, nor even a reasonable possibility that they were responsible.

....While we propose, *infra*, an adaptation of the rule in *Summers* which will substantially overcome these difficulties, defendants appear to be correct that the rule, as previously applied, cannot relieve plaintiff of the burden of proving the identity of the manufacturer which made the drug causing her injuries.

[The court next held that there was no concert of action among the defendants within the meaning of that doctrine. *See infra* pp. 406–14, discussing concerted action.]

    ....

A third theory upon which plaintiff relies is the concept of industry-wide liability, or according to the terminology of the parties, "enterprise liability." This theory was suggested in Hall v. E. I. Du Pont de Nemours & Co., Inc. (E.D.N.Y. 1972) 345 F. Supp. 353. In that case, plaintiffs were 13 children injured by the explosion of blasting caps in 12 separate incidents which occurred in 10 different states between 1955 and 1959. The defendants were six blasting cap manufacturers, comprising virtually the entire blasting cap industry in the United States, and their trade association. There were, however, a number of Canadian blasting cap manufacturers which could have supplied the caps. The gravamen of the complaint was that the practice of the industry of omitting a warning on individual blasting caps and of failing to take other safety measures created an unreasonable risk of harm, resulting in the plaintiffs' injuries. The complaint did not identify a particular manufacturer of a cap which caused a particular injury.

The court reasoned as follows: there was evidence that defendants, acting independently, had adhered to an industry-wide standard with regard to the safety features of blasting caps, that they had in effect delegated some functions of safety investigation and design, such as labeling, to their trade association, and that there was industry-wide cooperation in the manufacture and design of blasting caps. In these circumstances, the evidence supported a conclusion that all the defendants jointly controlled the risk. Thus, if plaintiffs could establish by a preponderance of the evidence that the caps were manufactured by one of the defendants, the burden of proof as to causation would shift to all the defendants. The court noted that this theory of liability applied to industries composed of a small number of units, and that what would be fair and reasonable with regard to an industry of five or ten producers might be manifestly unreasonable if applied to a decentralized industry composed of countless small producers.

        ....

We decline to apply this theory in the present case. At least 200 manufacturers produced DES; *Hall*, which involved 6 manufacturers representing the entire blasting cap industry in the United States, cautioned against application of the doctrine espoused therein to a large number of producers. [Citation.] Moreover, in *Hall*, the conclusion that the defendants jointly controlled the risk was based upon allegations that they had delegated some functions relating to safety to a trade association. There are no such allegations here....

        ....

If we were confined to the theories of *Summers* and *Hall*, we would be constrained to hold that the judgment must be sustained. Should we require that plaintiff identify the manufacturer which supplied the DES used by her mother or that all DES manufacturers be joined in the action, she would effectively be precluded from any recovery. As defendants candidly admit, there is little likelihood that all the manufacturers who made DES at the time in question are still in business or that they are subject to the jurisdiction of the California courts. There are, however, forceful arguments in favor of holding that plaintiff has a cause of action.

In our contemporary complex industrialized society, advances in science and technology create fungible goods which may harm consumers and which cannot be traced to any specific producer. The response of the courts can be either to adhere rigidly to prior doctrine,...or to fashion remedies to meet these changing needs....

The most persuasive reason for finding plaintiff states a cause of action is that advanced in *Summers*: as between an innocent plaintiff and negligent defendants, the latter should bear the cost of the injury. Here, as in *Summers*, plaintiff is not at fault in failing to provide evidence of causation, and although the absence of such evidence is not attributable to the defendants either, their conduct in marketing a drug the effects of which are delayed for many years played a significant role in creating the unavailability of proof.

From a broader policy standpoint, defendants are better able to bear the cost of injury resulting from the manufacture of a defective product. As was said by Justice Traynor in Escola [v. Coca Cola Bottling Co., 150 P.2d 436 (1944)], "[t]he cost of an injury and the loss of time or health may be an overwhelming misfortune to the person injured, and a needless one, for the risk of injury can be insured by the manufacturer and distributed among the public as a cost of doing business." (24 Cal.2d p. 462, 150 P.2d p. 441; *see also* Rest.2d Torts, §402A, com. c, pp. 349–350.) The manufacturer is in the best position to discover and guard against defects in its products and to warn of harmful effects; thus, holding it liable for defects and failure to warn of harmful effects will provide an incentive to product safety. [Citation.] These considerations are particularly significant where medication is involved, for the consumer is virtually helpless to protect himself from serious, sometimes permanent, sometimes fatal, injuries caused by deleterious drugs.

Where, as here, all defendants produced a drug from an identical formula and the manufacturer of the DES which caused plaintiff's injuries cannot be identified through no fault of plaintiff, a modification of the rule of *Summers* is warranted....

...[W]e hold it to be reasonable in the present context to measure the likelihood that any of the defendants supplied the product which allegedly injured plaintiff by the percentage which the DES sold by each of them for the purpose of preventing miscarriage bears to the entire production of the drug sold by all for that purpose. Plaintiff asserts in her briefs that Eli Lilly and Company and 5 or 6 other companies produced 90 percent of the DES marketed. If at trial this is established to be the fact, then there is a corresponding likelihood that this comparative handful of producers manufactured the DES which caused plaintiff's injuries, and only a 10 percent likelihood that the offending producer would escape liability.

If plaintiff joins in the action the manufacturers of a substantial share of the DES which her mother might have taken, the injustice of shifting the burden of proof to defendants to demonstrate that they could not have made the substance which injured plaintiff is significantly diminished....

The presence in the action of a substantial share of the appropriate market also provides a ready means to apportion damages among the defendants. Each defendant will be held liable for the proportion of the judgment represented by its share of that market unless it demonstrates that it could not have made the product which caused plaintiff's injuries. In the present case, as we have seen, one DES manufacturer was dismissed from the action upon filing a declaration that it had not manufactured DES until after plaintiff was born. Once plaintiff has met her burden of joining the required defendants, they in turn may cross-complaint against other DES manufacturers, not joined in the action, which they can allege might have supplied the injury-causing product.

Under this approach, each manufacturer's liability would approximate its responsibility for the injuries caused by its own products. Some minor discrepancy in the correlation between market share and liability is inevitable; therefore, a defendant may be held liable for a somewhat different percentage of the damage than its share of the appropriate market would justify. It is probably impossible, with the passage of time, to determine market share with mathematical exactitude. But just as a jury cannot be expected to determine the precise relationship between fault and liability in applying the doctrine of comparative fault [citation] or partial indemnity [citation], the difficulty of apportioning damages among the defendant producers in exact relation to their market share does not seriously militate against the rule we adopt....

We are not unmindful of the practical problems involved in defining the market and determining market share, but these are largely matters of proof which properly cannot be determined at the pleading stage of these proceedings....

The judgments are reversed.

BIRD, C. J., and NEWMAN and WHITE, JJ., concur.

RICHARDSON, Justice, dissenting.

...[T]he majority adopts a wholly new theory which contains these ingredients: The plaintiffs were not alive at the time of the commission of the tortious acts. They sue a generation later. They are permitted to receive substantial damages from multiple defendants without any proof that any defendant caused or even probably caused plaintiff's injuries. Although the majority purports to change only the required burden of proof by shifting it from plaintiffs to defendants, the effect of its holding is to guarantee that plaintiffs will prevail on the causation issue because defendants are no more capable of disproving factual causation than plaintiffs are of proving it. "Market share" liability thus represents a new high water mark in tort law. The ramifications seem almost limitless.... In my view, the majority's departure from traditional tort doctrine is unwise.

....

The fact that plaintiffs cannot tie defendants to the injury-producing drug does not trouble the majority for it declares that the *Summers* requirement of proof of actual causation by a named defendant is satisfied by a joinder of those defendants who have *together* manufactured "*a substantial percentage*" of the DES which has been marketed. Notably lacking from the majority's expression of its new rule, unfortunately, is any definition or guidance as to what should constitute a "substantial" share of the relevant market.... [T]he answer, presumably, is anyone's guess.

Much more significant, however, is the consequence of this unprecedented extension of liability. Recovery is permitted from a handful of defendants *each* of whom *individually* may account for a comparatively small share of the relevant market, so long as the *aggregate* business of those who have been sued is deemed "substantial." In other words, a particular defendant may be held proportionately liable *even though mathematically it is much more likely than not that it played no role whatever in causing plaintiff's injuries*....

....

[I]t is readily apparent that "market share" liability will fall unevenly and disproportionately upon those manufacturers who are amenable to suit in California. On the assumption that no other state will adopt so radical a departure from traditional tort principles, it may be concluded that under the majority's reasoning those defendants who are brought to trial in this state will bear effective joint responsibility for 100 percent of plaintiffs' injuries despite the fact that their "substantial" aggregate market share may be considerably less. This undeniable fact forces the majority to concede that, "a defendant may be held liable for a somewhat different percentage of the damage than its share of the appropriate market would justify." [Citation.] With due deference, I suggest that the complete unfairness of such a result in a case involving only five of two hundred manufacturers is readily manifest.

....The injustice inherent in the majority's new theory of liability is compounded by the fact that plaintiffs who use it are treated far more favorably than are the plaintiffs in routine tort actions....

The majority attempts to justify its new liability on the ground that defendants herein are "better able to bear the cost of injury resulting from the manufacture of a defective product." [Citation.] This "deep pocket" theory of liability, fastening liability on defendants presumably because they are rich, has understandable popular appeal and might be tolerable in a case disclosing substantially stronger evidence of causation than herein appears. But as a general proposition, a defendant's wealth is an unreliable indicator of fault, and should play no part, at least consciously, in the legal analysis of the problem. In the absence of proof that a particular defendant caused or at least probably caused plaintiff's injuries, a defendant's ability to bear the cost thereof is no more pertinent to the underlying issue of liability than its "substantial" share of the relevant market. A system priding itself on *"equal* justice under law" does not flower when the *liability* as well as the *damage* aspect of a tort action is determined by a defendant's wealth. The inevitable consequence of such a result is to create and perpetuate two rules of law—one applicable to wealthy defendants, and another standard pertaining to defendants who are poor or who have modest means. Moreover, considerable doubts have been expressed regarding the ability of the drug industry, and especially its smaller members, to bear the substantial economic costs (from both damage awards and high insurance premiums) inherent in imposing an industry-wide liability. [Citation.]

....

....It seems to me that liability in the manner created by the majority must inevitably inhibit, if not the research or development, at least the dissemination of new pharmaceutical drugs. Such a result...is wholly inconsistent with traditional tort theory.

....

Given the grave and sweeping economic, social, and medical effects of "market share" liability, the policy decision to introduce and define it should rest not with us, but with the Legislature which is currently considering not only major statutory reform of California product liability law in general, but the DES problem in particular....

I would affirm the judgments of dismissal.

CLARK and MANUEL, JJ., concur.

....

Notes

1. *Absence of Evidence Attributable to Defendant.* If the absence of evidence of causation is the direct and foreseeable result of the defendant's negligence, the burden of proof on the issue of causation may shift to the defendant. Haft v. Lone Palm Hotel, 478 P.2d 465 (Cal. 1970), was an action for damages by the survivors of a father and son who had drowned in the defendant's swimming pool. State statutes required motels either (1) to have a lifeguard on duty, or (2) to post a sign saying that no lifeguard was on duty. The defendant did neither, and so plainly was negligent. But did the defendant's negligence "cause" the drownings? As the victims were the only users of the pool, it must have been obvious to them that there was no lifeguard, so a "no lifeguard" sign would surely not have helped. But if the defendant had complied with the statutes by hiring a lifeguard, the decedents probably would not have drowned. The court ruled that the defendant's negligence (in the form of having no lifeguard) prevented there being anyone to witness the drownings and report how they had occurred, so that the burden of proving that the defendant's statutory violations did not cause the drownings was on the defendant.

If the statute in question had simply required that all pools have a lifeguard, *Haft* would have been a fairly routine case. The court's opinion passes lightly over the difficulties raised by the fact that the defendant could have complied with the statute by posting a sign. It seems most unlikely that the presence of a sign that would have told the father something he could see with his own eyes would have prevented the drowning. The court repeatedly described the negligence in question as failure to have a lifeguard.

In *Sindell*, the court expressly declined to follow *Haft* on the ground that while plaintiff "alleged that... [defendants] produced a defective product with delayed effects and without adequate warnings, the difficulty or impossibility of identification result[ed] primarily from the passage of time rather than from their allegedly negligent acts of failing to provide adequate warnings."

2. *Required Percentage for Market-Share Liability*. In a case subsequent to *Sindell* against a single manufacturer of DES, the California Supreme Court held that the manufacturer's 10 percent share of the national market was an insufficient predicate for shifting the burden of proof on the issue of causation from the injured party to the manufacturer. Murphy v. E. R. Squibb & Sons, Inc., 710 P.2d 247 (Cal. 1985). The court did not say what percentage would have been sufficient, although it did note that:

> a major reason why shifting the burden of proof... was warranted in *Summers* was that... there was a 50 percent chance that one of the defendants was responsible for the injury.

3. *Asbestos, Lead Paint, Guns, Tobacco, and Breast Implants*. Attempts to invoke market-share liability usually involve mass-marketed products, such as asbestos, lead-based paint, and tobacco.

A number of cases have held that market-share liability is inappropriate for asbestos litigation. Some courts have based their decision on that fact that asbestos, unlike DES, is not a fungible product. Marshall v. Celotex Corp., 660 F. Supp. 772 (E.D. Mich. 1987). Other courts have relied on different grounds. In Gaulding v. Celotex Corp., 772 S.W.2d 66 (Tex. 1989), the asbestos which allegedly caused the decedent's death was contained in a home-made vanity cabinet. In rejecting the claim based on market-share liability against the five asbestos manufacturers who allegedly "dominated the market," the court wrote:

> Based on the particular facts of this case, we will not apply market share liability or any variation of it. It is undisputed that the asbestos board to which Gaulding was exposed was purchased at a salvage yard. There is no way to know whether this product was initially sold in Texas or whether it was placed into the stream of commerce someplace far away.... [T]he practical impossibility of determining where or when the product was marketed makes insurmountable the problem of identifying the defendants' relevant market shares. We conclude that no variation of market share liability could be applied rationally and fairly on the facts of this case. We express no opinion on the question of fungibility in this case.

Similarly, in Santiago v. Sherwin Williams Co., 3 F.3d 546 (1st Cir. 1993), the court held that a plaintiff who was allegedly exposed to lead paint when she was a child could not recover from paint manufacturers under market-share liability because the plaintiff was unable to pinpoint with any degree of precision when the injury-causing paint was applied. Manufacturers' contributions to the lead-paint market varied significantly over a 60-year period. *See also* Skipworth v. Lead Indus. Ass'n, Inc., 690 A.2d 169 (Pa. 1997) (rejecting market-share and alternative liability in a suit against entities that manufactured lead paint over a 100-year period); Brenner v. American Cyanamid Co., 699 N.Y.S.2d 848 (App. Div. 1999) (holding that market-share liability did not apply to a lead poisoning case against the manufacturers of white lead carbonate because lead pigments other than white lead carbonate were used in lead-based paint, plaintiffs could not determine when lead-based paint was applied to their apartment, and manufacturers of white lead carbonate were not in exclusive control of risk posed by lead-based paint).

In Hamilton v. Beretta U.S.A. Corp., 750 N.E.2d 1055 (N.Y. 2001), a products liability action, the court held that handgun manufacturers do not owe a duty of reasonable care in the marketing and distribution of their handguns to persons injured or killed through the use of illegally obtained handguns. The court further opined that market-share liability would not apply to such a case:

> Unlike DES, guns are not identical, fungible products. Significantly, it is often possible to identify the caliber and manufacturer of the handgun that caused injury to a particular plaintiff. Even more importantly—given the negligent marketing theory on which plaintiffs tried this case—plaintiffs have never asserted that the manufacturers' marketing techniques were uniform. Each manufacturer engaged in different marketing activities that allegedly contributed to the illegal handgun market in different ways and to different extents. Plaintiffs made no attempt to establish the relative fault of each manufacturer, but instead sought to hold them all liable based simply on market share.

See also Matter of New York State Silicone Breast Implant Litigation, 631 N.Y.S.2d 491 (Sup. Ct. 1995), *aff'd without op.*, 650 N.Y.S.2d 558 (App. Div. 1996) (market share theory would not be extended to silicone breast implants because implants were not fungible); Sanderson v. Int'l Flavors and Fragrances, Inc., 950 F. Supp. 981 (C.D. Cal. 1996) (alternative liability and market-share liability were inapplicable to an action involving exposure to aldehydes in fragrance products).

In 1994, Florida enacted a statute which created a form of market-share liability applicable to tobacco companies. The Act applies only to claims made by the state, not to private plaintiffs. *See* Fla. Stat. Ch. 409.910 (Westlaw 2003). Arguably, market-share liability is appropriate in this context "[b]ecause harm to the State from smoking-related illness is independent of the individual identities of Medicaid smokers, [and therefore] it is unnecessary, even if feasible, to determine which brand of cigarettes was smoked by each Medicaid patient." Note, 108 Harv. L. Rev. 525, 529 (1994). Liability for tobacco-related injuries is discussed more fully in Chapter 15.

4. *Enterprise Liability.* In refusing to embrace enterprise liability, the Texas Supreme Court said in Gaulding v. Celotex Corp., 772 S.W.2d 66 (Tex. 1989):

> Enterprise liability as embodied in *Hall* has been rejected by virtually all other jurisdictions that have considered this concept. [Citations.] The prominent reason for declining recovery under this theory is its limited application to cases which involve only a small number of manufacturers in a highly centralized industry....

See also Hurt v. Philadelphia Housing Auth., 806 F. Supp. 515 (E.D. Pa. 1992) (rejecting enterprise liability in a suit against a relatively small number of manufacturers of lead-based paints, because plaintiffs failed to allege the delegation of safety responsibility to a trade association).

Hymowitz v. Eli Lilly and Co.
Court of Appeals of New York
539 N.E.2d 1069 (N.Y. 1989)

WACHTLER, C.J.

Plaintiffs in these appeals allege that they were injured by the drug diethylstilbestrol (DES) ingested by their mothers during pregnancy. They seek relief against defendant DES manufacturers. While not class actions, these cases are representative of nearly 500 similar actions pending in the courts in this State; the rules articulated by the Court here, therefore, must do justice and be administratively feasible in the context of this mass litigation. With this in mind, we now resolve the issue twice expressly left open by this Court, and adopt a market share theory, using a national market, for determining liability and apportioning damages in DES cases in which identification of the manufacturer of the drug that injured the plaintiff is impossible (*see,* Kaufman v. Lilly & Co., 65 N.Y.2d 449, 456; Bichler v. Lilly & Co., 55 N.Y.2d 571, 580). We also hold that the Legislature's revival for one year of actions for injuries caused by DES that were previously barred by the statute of limitations (*see,* L. 1986, ch. 682, §4) is constitutional under the State and Federal Constitutions.

. . . .

. . . [E]xtant common law doctrines, unmodified, provide no relief for the DES plaintiff unable to identify the manufacturer of the drug that injured her. This is not a novel conclusion; in the last decade a number of courts in other jurisdictions also have concluded that present theories do not support a cause of action in DES cases. Some courts, upon reaching this conclusion, have declined to find any judicial remedy for the DES plaintiffs who cannot identify the particular manufacturer of the DES ingested by their mothers (*see,* Zafft v. Lilly & Co.,. . . [676 S.W.2d 241 (Mo. 1984) (en banc)]; Mulcahy v. Lilly & Co.,. . . [386 N.W.2d 67 (Iowa 1986) (stating that any change in the law to allow for recovery in non-identification DES cases should come from the legislature)]. Other courts, however, have found that some modification of existing doctrine is appropriate to allow for relief for those injured by DES of unknown manufacture (*e.g.,* Sindell v. Abbott Labs.,. . . [607 P.2d 924 (Cal. 1980)]; Collins v. Lilly & Co.,. . . [342 N.W.2d 37 (Wis. 1984)]; Martin v. Abbott Labs.,. . . [689 P.2d 368 (Wash. 1984)].

We conclude that the present circumstances call for recognition of a realistic avenue of relief for plaintiffs injured by DES. . . .

Indeed, it would be inconsistent with the reasonable expectations of a modern society to say to these plaintiffs that because of the insidious nature of an injury that long remains dormant, and because so many manufacturers, each behind a curtain, contributed to the devastation, the cost of injury should be borne by the innocent and not the wrongdoers. This is particularly so where the legislature consciously created these expectations by reviving hundreds of DES cases. Consequently, the ever-evolving dictates of justice and fairness, which are the heart of our common-law system, require formation of a remedy for injuries caused by DES [citations].

We stress, however, that the DES situation is a singular case, with manufacturers acting in a parallel manner to produce an identical, generically marketed product, which causes injury many years later, and which has evoked a legislative response reviving previously barred actions. Given this unusual scenario, it is more appropriate that the loss be borne by those that produced the drug for use during pregnancy, rather than by those who were injured by the use, even where the precise manufacturer of the drug cannot be identified in a particular action. We turn then to the question of how to fairly and equitably apportion the loss occasioned by DES, in a case where the exact manufacturer of the drug that caused the injury is unknown.

....

The past decade of DES litigation has produced a number of alternative approaches to resolve this question. Thus, in a sense, we are now in an enviable position; the efforts of other courts have provided examples for contending with this difficult issue, and enough time has passed so that the actual administration and real effects of these solutions now can be observed. With these useful guides in hand, a path may be struck for our own conclusion.

....

A...basis for liability, tailored...closely to the varying culpableness of individual DES producers, is the market share concept. First judicially articulated by the California Supreme Court in Sindell v. Abbott Labs. (*supra*), variations upon this theme have been adopted by other courts (*see*, Collins v. Lilly & Co., *supra*; Martin v. Abbott Labs., *supra*). In Sindell v. Abbott Labs. (*supra*), the Court synthesized the market share concept by modifying the Summers v. Tice (*supra*) alternative liability rationale in two ways. It first loosened the requirement that all possible wrongdoers be before the court, and instead made a "substantial share" sufficient. The court then held that each defendant who could not prove that it did not actually injure plaintiff would be liable according to that manufacturer's market share. The court's central justification for adopting this approach was its belief that limiting a defendant's liability to its market share will result, over the run of cases, in liability on the part of a defendant roughly equal to the injuries the defendant actually caused (*id*. at 612).

In the recent case of Brown v. Superior Court (44 Cal. 3d 1049), the California Supreme Court resolved some apparent ambiguity in Sindell v. Abbott Labs., and held that a manufacturer's liability is several only, and, in cases in which all manufacturers in the market are not joined for any reason, liability will still be limited to market share, resulting in a less than 100% recovery for a plaintiff. Finally, it is noteworthy that determining market shares under Sindell v. Abbott Labs. proved difficult and engendered years of litigation. After attempts at using smaller geographical units, it was eventually determined that the national market provided the most feasible and fair solution, and this national market information was compiled (*see*, In re Complex DES Litigation, No. 830/109 Cal. Super. Ct.).

Four years after Sindell v. Abbott Labs., the Wisconsin Supreme Court followed with Collins v. Lilly & Co. (116 Wis. 2d 166). Deciding the identification issue without the benefit of the extensive California litigation over market shares, the Wisconsin court held that it was prevented from following *Sindell* due to "the practical difficulty of defining and proving market share" (*id*. at 189). Instead of focusing on tying liability closely to the odds of actual causation, as the *Sindell* court attempted, the *Collins* court took a broader perspective, and held that each defendant is liable in proportion to the amount of risk it created that the plaintiff would be injured by DES. Under the *Collins* structure, the "risk" each defendant is liable for is a question of fact in each case, with market shares being relevant to this determination (*id*. at 191, 200). Defendants are allowed, however, to exculpate themselves by showing that their product could not have caused the injury to the particular plaintiff (*id*., at 198).

The Washington Supreme Court, writing soon after Collins v. Lilly & Co., took yet another approach (*see*, Martin v. Abbott Labs., 102 Wash. 2d 581). The *Martin* court first rejected the *Sindell* market share theory due to the belief (which later proved to be erroneous in Brown v. Superior Court [*supra*]) that California's approach distorted liability by inflating market shares to ensure plaintiffs of full recovery (*id.*, at 601). The *Martin* court instead adopted what it termed "market share alternative liability," justified, it concluded, because "[e]ach defendant contributed to the *risk* of injury to the public, and consequently, the risk to individual plaintiffs" (*id.*, at 604).

Under the Washington scheme, defendants are first allowed to exculpate themselves by proving by the preponderance of the evidence that they were not the manufacturer of the DES that injured plaintiff. Unexculpated defendants are presumed to have equal market shares, totaling 100%. Each defendant then has the opportunity to rebut this presumption by showing that its actual market share was less than presumed. If any defendants succeed in rebutting this presumption, the liability shares of the remaining defendants who could not prove their actual market share are inflated, so that the plaintiff received a 100% recovery (*id.*, at 605–606). The market shares of defendants is a question of fact in each case, and the relevant market can be a particular pharmacy, or county, or state, or even the country, depending upon the circumstances the case presents [citation].

Turning to the structure to be adopted in New York, we heed both the lessons learned through experience in other jurisdictions and the realities of the mass litigation of DES claims in this State. Balancing these considerations, we are led to the conclusion that a market share theory, based upon a national market, provides the best solution. As California discovered, the reliable determination of any market smaller than the national one likely is not practicable. Moreover, even if it were possible, of the hundreds of cases in the New York courts, without a doubt there are many in which the DES that allegedly caused injury was ingested in another State. Among the thorny issues this could present, perhaps the most daunting is the spectre that the particular case could require the establishment of a separate market share matrix. We feel that this is an unfair, and perhaps impossible burden to routinely place upon the litigants in individual cases.

Nor do we believe that the Wisconsin approach of assessing the "risk" each defendant caused a particular plaintiff, to be litigated anew as a question of fact in each case, is the best solution for this State. Applied on a limited scale this theory may be feasible, and certainly is the most refined approach by allowing a more thorough consideration of how each defendant's actions threatened the plaintiff. We are wary, however, of setting loose, for application in the hundreds of cases pending in this State, a theory which requires the factfinder's individualized and open-ended assessment of the relative liabilities of scores of defendants in every case. Instead, it is our perception that the injustices arising from delayed recoveries and inconsistent results which this theory may produce in this State outweigh arguments calling for its adoption.

Consequently, for essentially practical reasons, we adopt a market share theory using a national market. We are aware that the adoption of a national market will likely result in a disproportion between the liability of individual manufacturers and the actual injuries each manufacturer caused in this State. Thus our market share theory cannot be founded upon the belief that, over the run of cases, liability will approximate causation in this State (*see*, Sindell v. Abbott Labs., *supra* at 612). Nor does the use of a national market provide a reasonable link between liability and the risk created by a defendant to a particular plaintiff (*see*, Collins v. Lilly & Co., *supra*; Martin v. Abbott Labs., *supra*). Instead, we choose to apportion liability so as to correspond to the overall culpability of each defendant, measured by the amount of risk of injury each defendant created to the public at large. Use of a national market is a fair method, we believe, of apportioning defendants' liabilities according to their total culpability in marketing DES for use during pregnancy. Under the circumstances, this is an equitable way to provide plaintiffs with the relief they deserve, while also rationally distributing the responsibility for plaintiffs' injuries among defendants.

To be sure, a defendant cannot be held liable if it did not participate in the marketing of DES for pregnancy use; if a DES producer satisfies its burden of proof of showing that it was not a member of the market of DES sold for pregnancy use, disallowing exculpation would be unfair and unjust. Nevertheless, because liability here is based on the overall risk produced, and not causation in a single case, there should be no exculpation of a defendant who, although a member of the market producing DES for pregnancy use, appears not to have caused a particular plaintiff's injury. It is merely a windfall for a producer to escape liability solely because it manufactured a more identifiable pill, or sold only to certain drugstores. These fortuities in no way diminish the culpability of a defendant for marketing the product, which is the basis of liability here.

Finally, we hold that the liability of DES producers is several only, and should not be inflated when all participants in the market are not before the court in a particular case. We understand that, as a practical matter, this will prevent some plaintiffs from recovering 100% of their damages. However, we eschewed exculpation to prevent the fortuitous avoidance of liability, and thus, equitably, we decline to unleash the same forces to increase a defendant's liability beyond its fair share of responsibility.

. . . .

The constitutionality of the revival statute remains to be considered (*see*, L. 1986, ch. 682, §4). This section revives, for the period of one year, actions for damages caused by the latent effects of DES, tungsten-carbide, asbestos, chlordane, and polyvinylchloride. Defendants argue that the revival of barred DES claims was unconstitutional as a denial of both due process and equal protection, under the State and Federal Constitutions (*see* N.Y. Const. art. 1, §§6, 11; U.S. Const., 14th Amend., §1). We are concerned here only with the constitutionality of the statute as it pertains to DES....

The Federal Due Process Clause provides very little barrier to a State Legislature's revival of time-barred actions (*see*, Chase Securities Corp. v. Donaldson, 325 U.S. 304). In *Chase*, the United States Supreme Court upheld the revival of a time-barred action, stating that Statutes of Limitation "represent a public policy about the privilege to litigate...the history of pleas shows them to be good only by legislative grace and to be subject to a relatively large degree of legislative control" (*id.*, at 314). [The court then found that doctrinal limitations imposed by state law did not bar revival of DES claims.]

. . . .

Defendants also argue that the revival statute violates equal protection, because the Legislature designated only five substances for revival, including DES, while instituting a prospective only discovery rule for other substances. Defendants claim that this categorization is without sufficient basis, and that it is the result of a "political compromise." But most, if not all legislation is the product of some compromise, so that this objection surely is no basis for finding the revival statute unconstitutional. Instead, here we must proceed on the presumption that the law is constitutional, and will hold otherwise only if it is established that the distinction drawn has no reasonable basis [citations]. Moreover, because defendants allege no impairment of a fundamental right, the

Legislature has substantial leeway in making classifications in this area of "economics and social welfare" [citations].

As it pertains to DES, surely the revival statute has a rational basis, and the Legislature acted within its broad range of discretion in enacting the law. The number of DES-caused injuries was relatively well known by the Legislature, which allowed for the ramifications of revival of DES claims, such as the effect on insurance interests, and the other costs, to be reasonably predicted [citation]. Furthermore, it was also well known, particularly after Fleishman v. Lilly & Co. (*supra*), that DES victims were prejudiced under current law. This, we believe, is enough of a basis for the Legislature to revive DES claims now, and wait as to other substances until it is felt that these substances present a problem suitable for resolution. The Legislature does not violate equal protection by providing a rationale piecemeal remedy for what may be a larger problem (Williamson v. Lee Optical, 348 U.S. 483).

Accordingly, in each case the order of the Appellate Division should be affirmed, with costs, and the certified question answered in the affirmative.

[The opinion of MOLLEN, J., concurring in part and dissenting in part, has been omitted. Arguing that it is "no more and no less than a basic principle of tort law... [that] a plaintiff may not recover for his or her injuries from a defendant who could not have caused those injuries," Judge Mollen would have permitted defendants to escape liability by proving that they did not produce or market the pill ingested by the plaintiff's mother. He would also have imposed joint and several liability upon defendants unable to exculpate themselves.]

[ALEXANDER, TITONE, and HANDCOCK, JJ., concurred with WACHTLER, C.J. MOLLEN, J., concurred and dissented. SIMONS, KAYE, and BELLACOSA, JJ., took no part.]

Notes

1. *Factors Relevant to Market-Share Liability.* Comment c to §11 of the Restatement, Third, of Torts: Products Liability, says with respect to market-share liability:

> In deciding whether to adopt a rule of proportional liability, courts have considered the following factors: (1) the generic nature of the product; (2) the long latency period of the injury; (3) the inability of plaintiffs to discover the identity of the defendant even after exhaustive discovery; (4) the clarity of the causal connection between the defective product and the injury suffered by plaintiffs; (5) the absence of medical or environmental factors that could have caused or materially contributed to the injury; and (6) the availability of sufficient "market share" data to support a rational apportionment of liability....

2. *Third-Generation Liability.* Recognizing the "dangers of overdeterrence... [and] the possibility that research will be discouraged or beneficial drugs withheld from the market," the court in Enright v. Eli Lilly & Co., 570 N.E.2d 198, 204 (N.Y. 1991), refused to permit a third-generation DES suit by the granddaughter of a woman who had ingested the drug. Grover v. Eli Lilly & Co., 591 N.E.2d 696 (Ohio 1992), refused to allow an action by a DES-grandson because liability does not extend to persons who were never exposed to the drug, either directly or *in utero*. Does the reasoning of *Grover* make sense? Suppose a doctor negligently prescribes a drug which causes *A* to have a seizure while driving, and *B* is injured in the ensuing crash. *B* has been injured by the

drug, though without being "exposed to" it, and would certainly have a claim against the doctor.

Some courts hold that ordinary tort principles governing causation provide adequate protection against liability for injuries with attenuated connections to defendants' actions. *See also* Squibb v. Lloyd's & Companies, 241 F.3d 154 (2d Cir. 2001) (holding that an insured's excess policies covered claims based on injuries suffered by grandchildren of women who ingested DES during pregnancy).

3. *Other Applications of Market-Share Liability. See* Conley v. Boyle Drug Co., 570 So. 2d 275 (Fla. 1990) (applying a variation of market-share liability to DES cases); Ray v. Cutter Labs., 754 F. Supp. 193 (M.D. Fla. 1991) (extending market share liability to negligence actions for AIDS infections resulting from contaminated blood products); Smith v. Cutter Biological, Inc., 823 P.2d 717,728 (Haw. 1991) (applying market-share liability, calculated on the basis of a national market, to blood factor products).

Judicial creativity in dealing with the issue of factual causation has inspired legislative innovations, such as the Illinois Drug Dealer Liability Act, Ill. Comp. Stat. Ch. 740, §57/1-85 (Westlaw 2003).

> Illinois became the fifth state to enact legislation establishing [in addition to civil forfeiture]...civil rights of action against drug dealers. The Drug Dealer Liability Act imposes liability on all persons in the state who "knowingly participate[ ] in the illegal drug market" for any damage caused by drug users. The Act draws upon a theory of market liability to allow for the recovery of damages from any drug dealer in the "market," even absent proof that the dealer sold the particular injury-causing drugs.

Comment, 109 Harv. L. Rev. 699, 699 (1996) (noting that liability is not limited in proportion to market share and criticizing the law as neither rational nor just).

See generally Restatement, Third, of Torts: Liability for Physical Harm (Basic Principles) §28 cmt. o (Tent. Draft No. 2, 2002).

4. *Collective Justice and Mass Torts.* In tort law, the prevailing paradigm for accident compensation is a highly individualized process. An injured party is entitled to a "day in court" during which the story of the accident will be told, including the many details of the exact injuries sustained. So, too, the defendant has a right to have the factfinder focus specifically on its conduct. Liability may not be imposed unless there is evidence establishing *this* defendant's responsibility to *this* particular plaintiff, and, even then, the amount of damages will be tailored to the facts of the case. When viewed against that paradigm, cases like *Sindell* and *Hymowitz* appear to be startling departures from the usual rules of the game. In fact, however, accident compensation is often less individualized or fact specific than the paradigm might suggest. Such pervasive features of accident law as workers' compensation systems, class action procedures in tort suits involving many parties, and statutory capping of damages all depart, to a greater or lesser extent, from any highly individualized models of litigation or compensation. There may in some situations be a stronger public interest in achieving justice on a system-wide basis than in according particularized treatment to individual cases, especially when practical considerations make individualized decisionmaking infeasible. Another example of the law's interest in what may loosely be termed "collective justice" is the National Childhood Vaccine Injury Compensation Program, discussed *supra* at p. 26 n. 4.

Some of the foregoing examples are concerned with what are called "mass torts": events, products, or practices that give rise to large numbers of claims, such as hotel fires, industrial accidents, collapsing buildings, and defective consumer goods. The 1995 bombing of the federal building in Oklahoma City, and the September 11, 2001, attacks on the World Trade Center quickly come to mind. An emerging body of literature explores the question whether these cases differ qualitatively, as well as quantitatively, from traditional tort litigation, and, if so, how the law should respond to such demands. *See* Linda Mullenix, Mass Tort Litigation (1996); Glen O. Robinson & Kenneth S. Abraham, *Collective Justice in Tort Law*, 78 Va. L. Rev. 1481 (1993); Jack B. Weinstein, *Preliminary Reflections on Law's Reaction to Disaster*, 11 Colum. J. Envtl. L. 1 (1986); Kenneth Abraham, *Individual Action and Collective Responsibility: The Dilemma of Mass Tort Reform*, 73 Va. L. Rev. 845 (1987); David Rosenberg, *Class Actions for Mass Torts: Doing Justice by Collective Means*, 62 Ind. L.J. 561 (1987); David Rosenberg, *The Causal Connection in Mass Exposure Cases: A "Public Law" Vision of the Tort System*, 97 Harv. L. Rev. 851 (1984).

Viewed as part of the law's interest in achieving collective justice, cases like *Sindell* and *Hymowitz* are less surprising than they may seem at first glance. It should be noted, however, that a number of recent decisions have been hostile to attempts to vary the usual trial paradigm. *See, e.g.*, Cimino v. Raymark Indus., Inc., 151 F.3d 297 (5th Cir. 1998) (rejecting a novel trial plan that used sampling to calculate damages in aggregate asbestos litigation).

5. *The September 11th Victim's Compensation Fund of 2001*. In the wake of the September 11, 2001, attack on the World Trade Center in New York City, Congress established a Victim's Compensation Fund.

> The VCF accomplishes two main objectives. First, as originally intended, the VCF limits airline liability. Second, it provides a unique means of compensating victims outside the normal realm of tort law.

> .... The VCF limits the liability of the airlines in two distinct ways. First, Congress expressly limited airline liability for all claims to the amount of the airlines' liability insurance, estimated at $1.5 billion, for each of the four flights. The second way in which the VCF limits airline legal expense is by requiring those who make claims under the Fund to waive their right to sue the airlines. Subsequent legislation in November 2001 expanded the scope of protection not only to airlines, but also to airports, aircraft manufacturers, and certain other potential targets of claimants. However, victims were expressly granted the right to sue the terrorists. The VCF also vests exclusive jurisdiction over civil lawsuits by victims in the U.S. District Court for the Southern District of New York.

> .... VCF's other objective provides "compensation to any individual (or relatives of a deceased individual) who was physically injured or killed as a result of the terrorist-related aircraft crashes of September 11, 2001." The VCF allows victims or their families to make a compensation claim, and, within 120 days, the claimant will receive notification of the award....

> The essential trade-off is that victims and their families waive their right to sue anyone other than the terrorists....[A] claimant may recover [from the Fund] without proving negligence....

Patrick J. Keating, Kevin R. Sutherland, Gerald V. Cleary III, and Timothy J. Walsh, *Recent Developments in Aviation and Space Law*, 38 Tort Trial & Ins. Prac. L.J. 205 (2003).

6. *Problem: Statistical Evidence and the Case of the Blue Bus*. Consider the following hypothetical from Laurence H. Tribe, *Trial by Mathematics: Precision and Ritual in the Legal Process*, 84 Harv. L. Rev. 1329, 1340–41 (1971):

Mrs. Smith was driving on a public street and was forced off the road by a negligently driven bus. She is able to testify that the bus was blue, but is unable to describe the bus to any greater extent. Blue Bus Co. owns and operates 80% of the blue buses operating in the town. Mrs. Smith files a negligence action against Blue Bus Co. alleging the foregoing. Does she recover?

See the analysis in Stephen A. Spitz, *From Res Ipsa Loquitur to Diethylstilbestrol: The Unidentified Tortfeasor in California*, 65 Ind. L.J. 591, 629–36 (1990).

7. *Ethics in Law Practice: Expenses of Suit and Frivolous Litigation.* The lawyer for a plaintiff harmed by a product manufactured by an unknown producer faces practical and ethical barriers, as well as doctrinal obstacles, to suing every manufacturer in an effort to shift the burden of proof on causation. To begin with, lawsuits are expensive. Typically, the more parties there are, the greater the expenses. In personal-injury litigation, such essential disbursements as medical examination fees, filing costs, expert witness fees, and transcription of depositions are often advanced by the plaintiff's attorney on a contingent basis. This arrangement is ethically permissible in most states (*see* Model Rules of Professional Conduct Rule 1.8(e)(1) (2003)), and it is usually a matter of necessity, for few victims have the cash that it takes to litigate a claim.[a] If the suit is unsuccessful, the amounts contingently advanced by the attorney are never recovered, and if the legal work was on a contingent fee basis, the attorney is paid nothing for time spent on the suit. In routine cases, expenses can easily amount to a thousand dollars or more. In mass tort litigation, out-of-pocket expenses can run into the hundreds of thousands or millions of dollars, and the resulting temptation for the attorney to litigate the case in a way which ensures the recovery of those advances may create serious conflicts of interest between client and attorney. *See* Vincent R. Johnson, *Ethical Limitations on Creative Financing of Mass Tort Litigation*, 54 Brook. L. Rev. 539 (1988) (discussing the novel and ethically impermissible arrangement used to fund the Agent Orange litigation, the then-largest mass tort claim in history).

In addition, in many states, and in the federal courts, attorneys are personally subject to sanctions, including monetary penalties, for representing clients in frivolous litigation, including claims based on insufficient investigation of the facts. For example, in Albright v. The Upjohn Co., 788 F.2d 1217 (6th Cir. 1986), lawyers named as defendants multiple pharmaceutical companies involved in the manufacture, sale, and distribution of a drug that allegedly caused the plaintiff's injuries. The court held that the attorneys were subject to sanctions for failure to conduct a sufficient prefiling investigation to identify as defendants only those companies involved in the manufacture of brands known to have been ingested by the plaintiff. During the last decade or so, a voluminous body of precedent on frivolous litigation has emerged.

---

a. A case in point is Helen Palsgraf, the unsuccessful plaintiff in the most famous tort case of all time, Palsgraf v. Long Island R.R. Co., 162 N.E. 99 (N.Y. 1928), *supra* at 238. Palsgraf was a Brooklyn janitor. Her annual salary was $416. At the time of trial, an outstanding bill for $70 in medical care was three years past due. Not counting attorneys' fees and expert witness fees, the cost of litigating her case through three courts was at least $350. "It is improbable to the point of implausibility" that Helen Palsgraf had cash on hand to finance her case. John T. Noonan, Persons and Masks of the Law 125, 144 (1976).

D. Liability Based on Concerted Action

Herman v. Wesgate

Supreme Court of New York, Appellate Division
464 N.Y.S.2d 315 (App. Div. 1983)

MEMORANDUM:

Plaintiff was injured while a guest at a stag party to celebrate the impending marriage of defendant Thomas Hauck. The party was held on board a barge owned by defendants Donald Wesgate and Thomas Rouse. Following a three-hour cruise, the barge was anchored near the shoreline of Irondequoit Bay. The depth of the water off the bow of the barge was approximately two feet. Several guests began "skinny dipping" and, within a brief period of time, some in the party began to throw others still clothed off the bow into the water. Two or more individuals escorted plaintiff to the bow of the barge where, unwillingly, he went overboard. Trauma to his head or neck resulted in injury to his spinal cord.

. . . .

It was improper to grant the motions [for summary judgment, etc.] of defendants John Hauck and James Hauck. Plaintiff's complaint alleges concerted action by all of the defendants.

"Concerted action liability rests upon the principle that '[a]ll those who, in pursuance of a common plan or design to commit a tortious act, actively take part in it, or further it by cooperation or request, or who lend aid or encouragement to the wrongdoer, or ratify and adopt his acts done for their benefit, are equally liable with him' (Prosser, Torts [4th ed.], §46, at p. 292; *see also*, Restatement, Torts 2d, §876). An injured plaintiff may pursue any one joint tort-feasor on a concerted action theory [citations]. Such tort-feasor may, in turn, seek contribution from others who acted in concert with him...." [Citation.]

Here, the conduct of the defendants alleged to be dangerous and tortious is the pushing or throwing of guests, against their will, from the barge into the water. Liability of an individual defendant will not depend upon whether he actually propelled plaintiff into the water; participation in the concerted activity is equivalent to participation in the accident resulting in the injury [citation].

Whether codefendants acted in concert is generally a question for the jury [citation]. The complaint states a cause of action against each of the defendants and the record presents questions of fact as to whether defendants John Hauck and James Hauck acted in concert with the other defendants. Thus summary judgment should not have been granted [citation].

Order unanimously modified and as modified affirmed with costs.

Halberstam v. Welch

United States Court of Appeals for the District of Columbia Circuit
705 F.2d 472 (D.C. Cir. 1983)

WALD, Circuit Judge.

Linda S. Hamilton appeals a judgment...that she is civilly liable, as a joint venturer and coconspirator, for the killing of Michael Halberstam by Bernard C. Welch, Jr....

. . . .

Patricia Wald

This case arises out of the shocking climax to a coldly efficient criminal campaign that had confounded, frustrated, and ultimately terrorized the Washington area. We are asked to determine the civil liability of the passive but compliant partner to this rampage that left widowed the wife of one of the community's most eminent physicians. As a result of Welch's innumerable burglaries over the course of five years, he and Hamilton acquired a fortune....

Hamilton first met Welch in October 1975, when Welch walked up to her in an apartment parking lot and asked her for a date. Hamilton stated that this was the first and only time she saw Welch with a gun....

In 1976, Hamilton and Welch moved to a rented house in Falls Church, Virginia. Hamilton, still employed at this time, gave Welch her salary in cash to invest for her in gold coins. Welch had no outside employment, and spent most days at home managing investments. He would leave the house four or five times each week between 5:00 p.m. and 5:30 p.m., and return between 9:00 p.m. and 9:30 p.m. This routine continued throughout the five years Hamilton lived with Welch. Hamilton stated that she never accompanied Welch on these evening expeditions....

Soon Welch's "investments" bore fruit. In April 1978,...Welch and Hamilton purchased a house in Minnesota for $102,000....

In 1979, the couple built a home in Great Falls, Virginia, valued at $1,000,000....

Meanwhile, a different kind of refinement was taking place in the garage. With Hamilton's knowledge, Welch installed a smelting furnace in the garage and used it to melt gold and silver into bars. He then sold the ingots to refiners in other states. Hamilton typed transmittal letters for these sales....She also...did the secretarial work for Welch's "business." The buyers of Welch's goods made their checks payable to her, and she deposited them in her own bank accounts. She kept the records on these asymmetrical transactions—which included payments coming in from buyers, but no money going out to the sellers from whom Welch had supposedly bought the goods....

....Hamilton's individual tax returns for 1978 and 1979...took deductions, per Welch's instructions, for "cost of goods sold and/or operations" in 1978 and 1979 of $498,770.87 and $360,000, respectively—despite the absence of any evidence of payouts for such goods....

....

Prosser notes that "[t]he original meaning of 'joint tort' was that of vicarious liability for concerted action...." W. Prosser, Law of Torts §46, at 291 (4th ed. 1971). His illustration portrays a standard situation that involved this "joint tort": combined action by tortfeasors on the scene together—"one might have battered the plaintiff, while another imprisoned him, and a third stole his silver buttons." Id. (footnote omitted). Each was responsible for the others' actions.

Over time, courts applied the principle of vicarious liability for concerted action to less obvious situations.... The two variations significant here are (1) *conspiracy, or concerted action by agreement*, and (2) *aiding-abetting, or concerted action by substantial assistance*. These two bases of liability correspond generally to the first two subsections in the Restatement (Second) of Torts §876....

....A list of the separate elements of civil conspiracy includes: (1) an agreement between two or more persons; (2) to participate in an unlawful act, or a lawful act in an unlawful manner; (3) an injury caused by an unlawful overt act performed by one of the parties to the agreement; (4) which overt act was done pursuant to and in furtherance of the common scheme. [Citation.]

The element of agreement is a key distinguishing factor for a civil conspiracy action. Proof of a tacit, as opposed to explicit, understanding is sufficient to show agreement.... "It is only where means are employed, or purposes are accomplished, which are themselves tortious, that the conspirators who have not acted but have promoted the act will be held liable." [Citation.]

Aiding-abetting includes the following elements: (1) the party whom the defendant aids must perform a wrongful act that causes an injury; (2) the defendant must be generally aware of his role as part of an overall illegal or tortious activity at the time that he provides the assistance; (3) the defendant must knowingly and substantially assist the principal violation.... "Advice or encouragement to act operates as a moral support to a tortfeasor and if the act encouraged is known to be tortious it has the same effect upon the liability of the adviser as participation or physical assistance." [Citation.]

In practice, liability for aiding-abetting often turns on how much encouragement or assistance is substantial enough. The Restatement suggests five factors in making this determination: "the nature of the act encouraged, the amount of assistance given by the defendant, his presence or absence at the time of the tort, his relation to the other [tortfeasor] and his state of mind." Id.

The prime distinction between civil conspiracies and aiding-abetting is that a conspiracy involves an agreement to participate in a wrongful activity....

....

[The court discussed several cases from other jurisdictions dealing with civil conspiracy.]... [S]ince in most cases the court will have to infer a conspiracy from indirect evidence, it must initially look to see if the alleged joint tortfeasors are pursuing the same goal—although performing different functions—and are in contact with one another.... The easiest situation in which to draw the inference of agreement is where the parties are on the scene together at the same time performing acts in support of one another.... Mutually supportive activity by parties in contact with one another over a long period suggests a common plan.

....

...[O]nce the conspiracy has been formed, all its members are liable for injuries caused by acts pursuant to or in furtherance of the conspiracy. A conspirator...need not even have planned or known about the injurious action, as in the case of...[a] getaway driver..., so long as the purpose of the tortious action was to advance the overall object of the conspiracy.

....[The court discussed aiding-abetting cases].

....Rael v. Cadena, 93 N.M. 684, 604 P.2d 822 (1979), involved a person who had given verbal encouragement ("Kill him!" and "Hit him more!") to an assailant....The court...found...that the fact of encouragement was enough to create joint liability for the battery. Mere presence at the scene, it noted, would not be sufficient for liability.

Suggestive words may also be enough to create joint liability when they plant the seeds of action and are spoken by a person in an apparent position of authority. In Cobb v. Indian Springs, Inc., 258 Ark. 9, 522 S.W.2d 383 (1975), a security guard allegedly urged a younger motorist with a new car to "run [the car] back up here and see what it will do." [Citation.] The driver then struck the plaintiff while trying to avoid a pedestrian during his high-speed "test run." The court held...that a jury could have found the guard's encouragement substantial because he had first proposed the trial drive and because his position of authority gave his suggestion extra weight....

Vicarious liability can of course be based on acts of assistance as well as words of encouragement. And the contributing activity itself need not be so obviously nefarious as cheering a beating or prodding someone to drive recklessly. Keel v. Hainline, 331 P.2d 397 (Okl. 1958) [supra at 49], involved students throwing erasers at one another in a classroom.... The court found that a student who had only aided the throwers by retrieving and handing erasers to them was still liable for the injury....

....

The facts of... [American Family Mut. Ins. Co. v. Grim, 440 P.2d 621 (Kan. 1968)]—a break-in to pilfer soft drinks by four boys, two of whom jerry-rigged torches that caused substantial fire damage—also raise an interesting question of the permissible extent of liability.... The Grim court...pointed out that...: "[A] person who encourages another to commit a tortious act may also be responsible for other foreseeable acts done by such other person in connection with the intended act."... [T]he Grim court noted that "the need for adequate lighting could reasonably be anticipated [and] torches served that purpose." 440 P.2d at 626. Thus, the boy who had not used a torch, nor even expected one to be lighted, could be liable for the damage caused by the torches because their employment was foreseeable.

....Duke v. Feldman, 245 Md. 454, 226 A.2d 345 (1967), involved an allegation that a woman was liable for civil assault because she had aided and assisted her husband, who had struck the plaintiff....Evidence that she was merely present at or took pleasure in the assault and battery would not be enough to create liability. The plaintiff's evidence of her involvement—consisting of the defendant's awareness of her husband's previous threats to plaintiff; her contemporaneous request to her husband to get their downpayment back from the plaintiff; her observation of the incident; and driving her husband away—was found insufficient to go to the jury....

....

As for the second issue in aiding-abetting, the extent of liability, the test from *Cobb* and *Grim* appears to be that a person who assists a tortious act may be liable for other reasonably foreseeable acts done in connection with it. While this language is slightly different from that found in civil conspiracy cases—where a conspirator is liable for acts pursuant to, in furtherance of, or within the scope of the conspiracy—we are not sure that it is a distinction that makes a practical difference....

....

....It is the inferences the trial judge drew from those facts that are in contention on appeal....First, the district court found that Hamilton "knew full well the purpose of [Welch's] evening forays and the means" he used to acquire their wealth. [Citation.] Second, the district court inferred an agreement—that "[she] was a willing partner in his criminal activities." *See id.* Third, the district court pointed to various acts by Hamilton (*e.g.*, typing transmittal letters for the ingot sales, handling the payments and accounts, maintaining all financial transactions solely in her name), [citation], and concluded that they were performed knowingly to assist Welch in his illicit trade....

...[W]e do not find these inferences to be impermissible....

....

The district court relied on the same three factual inferences to conclude that Hamilton was liable as a coconspirator. [Citation.] We agree....The only remaining issue, then, is whether Welch's killing of Halberstam during a burglary was an overt act in furtherance of the agreement. We believe it was...Welch was trying to further the conspiracy by escaping after an attempted burglary, and he killed Halberstam in his attempt to do so. The use of violence to escape apprehension was certainly not outside the scope of a conspiracy to obtain stolen goods through regular nighttime forays and then to dispose of them....

....

The district court also concluded that Hamilton was liable as a "joint venturer." The...court basically relied on the theory that we have labeled aiding-abetting. We have summarized its elements as follows: (1) the party the defendant aids must perform a wrongful act that causes an injury; (2) the defendant must be generally aware of his role as part of an overall illegal or tortious activity at the time he provides the assistance; and (3) the defendant must knowingly and substantially assist the principal violation.

Welch fulfilled the first of these three elements by killing Halberstam during the course of a burglary. The district court's conclusions that Hamilton knew about and acted to support Welch's illicit enterprise establish that Hamilton had a general awareness of her role in a continuing criminal enterprise. The second element is thus satisfied. Finally, the district court also justifiably inferred that Hamilton assisted Welch with knowledge that he had engaged in illegal acquisition of goods. The only remaining issue, then, is whether her assistance was "substantial."

Applying the Restatement's five factors, we look first at the *nature of the act assisted*, here a long-running burglary enterprise, heavily dependent on aid in transforming large quantities of stolen goods into "legitimate" wealth. Hamilton's assistance was indisputably important to this laundering function....Second, although the *amount of as-*

sistance Hamilton gave Welch may not have been overwhelming as to any given burglary in the five-year life of this criminal operation, it added up over time to an essential part of the pattern.

Third, Hamilton was admittedly not *present at the time* of the murder or even at the time of any burglary. But as we noted above, the success of the tortious enterprise clearly required expeditious and unsuspicious disposal of the goods, and Hamilton's role in that side of the business was substantial.

Fourth, the significance of Hamilton's *relation to the tortious actor* requires a careful balancing. We are understandably wary of finding a housemate civilly liable on the basis of normal spousal support activities. Even though Hamilton's assistance surely transcended performing household chores for Welch, we must be cautious not to overemphasize the relationship. Hence, we accord it a low priority in our calculus.

... [T]he fifth factor, the *defendant's state of mind* assumes a special importance in this case.... Hamilton's continuous participation reflected her intent and desire to make the venture succeed; it was no passing fancy or impetuous act. Finally, the *duration of the assistance* has strongly influenced our weighing of Hamilton's assistance.... In sum, we find that Hamilton's assistance was indeed substantial enough to justify liability on an aider-abettor theory.

... [W]e agree with the district court that Hamilton's assistance to Welch's illegal enterprise should make her liable for Welch's killing of Halberstam.... [I]t was a natural and foreseeable consequence of the activity Hamilton helped Welch to undertake. It was not necessary that Hamilton knew specifically that Welch was committing burglaries. Rather, when she assisted him, it was enough that she knew he was involved in some type of personal property crime at night—whether as a fence, burglar, or armed robber made no difference—because violence and killing is a foreseeable risk in any of these enterprises. [Citations.]

....

Affirmed.

[BORK and SCALIA, Circuit Judges, concurred.]

Notes

1. *Aiding-and-Abetting.* Some form of liability for concerted action is imposed in all jurisdictions. A single course of conduct may constitute both civil conspiracy and aiding-and-abetting, but, as the principal case indicates, the theories are distinguishable.

An example of aiding-and-abetting is Price v. Halstead, 355 S.E.2d 380 (W. Va. 1987) (holding that an allegation that passengers directly participated and encouraged a driver to continue to drink and smoke marijuana when he was already visibly intoxicated stated a cause of action).

A "person who bribes an agent of a principal has 'aided and abetted' the agent in the breach of the agent's fiduciary duty of loyalty to the principal." *See* Franklin Med. Assoc. v. Newark Pub. Schools, 828 A.2d 966, 975–76 (N.J. Super. Ct. App. Div. 2003). (Breach of fiduciary duty is a tort; see Chapter 11.)

2. *Civil Conspiracy.* Civil conspiracy requires specific intent to agree to accomplish an unlawful purpose or to accomplish a lawful purpose by unlawful means. Merely proving that there was joint intent to engage in conduct that resulted in injury is not sufficient to establish a cause of action. In Juhl v. Airington, 936 S.W.2d 640 (Tex.

1996), the court held that allegations by a police officer that he had suffered injuries while he was attempting to physically remove anti-abortion demonstrators who had blocked access to a health clinic were insufficient to state a claim for civil conspiracy against other demonstrators because the officer's pleadings alleged only that the other demonstrators had been negligent.

See also Brown v. Birman Managed Care, Inc., 42 S.W.3d 62 (Tenn. 2001) (holding that if a former husband's employers conspired with him to intentionally reduce his income so that he could avoid paying the full amount of child support, they could be liable to his former wife for fraud, even though the fraudulent representations on which the former wife relied were made only by the former husband).

3. *Conscious Parallel Activity.* Bichler v. Lilly & Co., 436 N.E.2d 182 (N.Y. 1982), was an action by a DES daughter against a single manufacturer of the drug based on a concerted-action theory. The suit alleged that even if the defendant did not produce the dosages of the drug consumed by the plaintiff's mother, it was liable for the plaintiff's injuries because it had acted in concert with the manufacturer who did. In seeking government approval to market DES, all manufacturers had relied upon the same negligently performed studies and had requested permission to make the same strength tablet. The jury was instructed based on a theory of concerted action which substituted proof of conscious parallel activity by the manufacturers for the usual common-law requirement of an actual agreement between actors to act tortiously. Because the defendant did not object to the instruction, the modified-concerted-action theory became the law of the case, and liability was imposed.

In Hymowitz v. Eli Lilly and Co., 539 N.E.2d 1069, 1076 (N.Y. 1989), *supra* at 398, the court repudiated the conscious-parallel-activity theory of concerted action liability, writing:

> Now given the opportunity to assess the merits of this theory, we decline to adopt it as the law of this State. Parallel behavior, the major justification for visiting liability caused by the product of one manufacturer upon the head of another under this analysis, is a common occurrence in industry generally. We believe, therefore, that inferring agreement from the fact of parallel activity alone improperly expands the concept of concerted action beyond a rational or fair limit; among other things, it potentially renders small manufacturers, in the case of DES and in countless other industries, jointly liable for all damages stemming from the defective products of an entire industry....

Other courts have taken similar positions. Consequently, concerted-action claims are generally unsuccessful in product liability actions. *See* Rastelli v. Goodyear Tire & Rubber Co., 591 N.E.2d 222 (N.Y. 1992) (tire manufacturer was not subject to concerted-action liability with rim manufacturers; evidence showed that rim manufacturers engaged in parallel activities such as lobbying and failing to recall rims likely to explode under pressure).

4. *First Amendment Concerns Bearing on Liability Relating to Groups.* May civil liability be imposed merely because an individual belonged to or supported a group, some members of which committed tortious acts? Probably not.

In Chavers v. Gatke Corp., 132 Cal. Rptr. 2d 198 (Ct. App. 2003), a former automobile and truck mechanic and his spouse sought to hold a manufacturer of friction brake products liable on concerted-action theories based on allegations that the manufacturer participated in a conspiracy with other manufacturers to conceal a study that reported the harmful effects of products containing asbestos. The court rejected the plaintiffs' arguments, writing:

"[t]o impose liability without a finding that the [defendant] authorized—either actually or apparently—or ratified unlawful conduct would impermissibly burden the rights of political association that are protected by the First Amendment." [Citation.] It is necessary...to show that "'the group itself possessed unlawful goals and that the individual held a specific intent to further those illegal aims.'" [Citation.]

We are skeptical that the record here satisfies such an exacting constitutional standard, requiring as it would evidence that Gatke, a minor player contributing about $250 a year to the Saranac Laboratory research investigations, possessed the specific intent to promote the sale of asbestos products made by its competitors. The testimony that was produced at trial tended to show that Gatke sought access to the Saranac Laboratory report in order to assist its defense of workers compensation claims filed against it in Massachusetts.... [R]equiring a manufacturer "to stand trial for civil conspiracy and concert of action predicated solely on its exercise of its First Amendment freedoms could generally chill the exercise of the freedom of association by those who wish to contribute to, attend the meetings of, and otherwise associate with trade groups and other organizations that engage in public advocacy and debate."

Similarly, in Boim v. Quranic Literacy Institute, 291 F.3d 1000 (7th Cir. 2002), the decedent was killed by members of a militant Palestinian organization while waiting at a bus stop in Israel's West Bank. His parents sued two U.S.-based non-profit organizations for tort damages. The court held that First Amendment right of free association did not prohibit imposition of civil liability against organizations under a federal statute providing a civil cause of action for those injured by an act of international terrorism for directing funds to terrorist groups for the purpose of funding terrorist activities. However, an aiding-and-abetting claim, the court said, would require proof that the organizations knew about the terrorist group's illegal operations and provided aid to the terrorist group with the intent to facilitate those illegal activities.

5. *Joint Enterprise Doctrine.* One form of concerted action is the "joint enterprise," which is discussed in the Comment to §491 of the Restatement, Second, of Torts:

> b. ....A "joint enterprise" is in the nature of a partnership, but is a broader and more inclusive term. In a partnership, there is a more or less permanent business arrangement, creating a mutual agency between the partners for the purpose of carrying on some general business dealings, so that the acts of one are to be charged against the others. A joint enterprise includes a partnership, but it also includes less formal arrangements for cooperation, for a more limited period of time and a more limited purpose. It includes an undertaking to carry out a small number of activities or objectives, or even a single one, entered into by members of the group under such circumstances that all have a voice in directing the conduct of the enterprise. The law then considers that each is the agent or servant of the others, and that the act of any one within the scope of the enterprise is to be charged vicariously against the rest. While it is by no means impossible that the principle may be applied to other activities, the very great majority of the decisions applying it have involved the use of motor vehicles.

> c. The elements which are essential to a joint enterprise are commonly stated to be four: (1) an agreement, express or implied, among the members of the group; (2) a common purpose to be carried out by the group; (3) a community

of pecuniary interest in that purpose, among the members; and (4) an equal right to a voice in the direction of the enterprise, which gives an equal right of control....

See Texas Dep't of Transp. v. Able, 35 S.W.3d 608 (Tex. 2000) (governmental entity held liable under joint enterprise doctrine for negligence in the operation and maintenance of a public transportation system).

Some cases reject the Restatement's suggestion that the community of interest necessary for a joint enterprise must be of a business or pecuniary nature. *See* Pittman v. Frazer, 129 F.3d 983 (8th Cir. 1997) (a finding of contributory negligence based on joint enterprise by a couple was upheld where a car belonging to a woman's parents was driven by her lover directly into the path of a train while the couple was returning from a secluded area on private property); Neal v. J.B. Hunt Transport, Inc., 805 S.W.2d 643, 645 (Ark. 1991) (unmarried couple returning from hospital after collecting family member).

Other cases strictly apply the "community of pecuniary interest" requirement, and there it may be difficult to establish a joint enterprise. In St. Joseph Hosp. v. Wolff, 94 S.W.3d 513 (Tex. 2002), the court held that a common business or pecuniary interest is not sufficient to establish a joint enterprise. Rather, to establish a "community of pecuniary interest" there must be a monetary interest common among the members of the group that is "shared without special or distinguishing characteristics." The court ruled that a joint enterprise did not exist between a teaching hospital that sponsored medical residency program and a foundation that employed and was training a surgical resident when he negligently treated a patient. The evidence showed that the parties did not share any income from residency program's operations at the hospital, as the foundation billed for the residents' services and kept all the revenue.

6. ***Ethics in Law Practice: Assisting Unlawful Conduct.*** "A lawyer shall not counsel a client to engage, or assist a client, in conduct that the lawyer knows is criminal or fraudulent...." Model Rules of Prof. Conduct Rule 1.2(d) (2003). Such conduct may give rise to civil liability, as well as discipline. *See* Morganroth & Morganroth v. Norris, McLaughlin & Marcus, 331 F.3d 406 (3d. Cir. 2003) ("when a complaint alleges that an attorney has knowingly and intentionally participated in a client's unlawful conduct to hinder, delay, and/or fraudulently obstruct the enforcement of a judgment of a court, the plaintiff has stated a claim...for creditor fraud against the attorney").

E. Incitement

As Herman v. Wesgate, 464 N.Y.S.2d 315 (App. Div. 1983), *supra* at 406, pointed out, citing Prosser, those who "lend aid or encouragement to the wrongdoer," are liable for the harm the wrongdoer does. As applied to someone who urges the defendant to punch the plaintiff in the mouth, this notion is not at all troublesome. But liability for "incitement" is a concept that, if not carefully limited, may clash with principles such as free speech. Suppose, for example, that a newspaper denounces "greedy slumlords," giving examples of wealthy tenement owners whose tenants live in wretched conditions, and an irate reader beats a landlord senseless. One doubts that the newspaper would, or should, be liable. It is well known that dramatic crimes often lead to the commission of similar, "copycat" crimes, yet it has never been thought that those who report the original crimes are liable to the victims of the later ones.

Relevant Variables. In thinking about whether one person, who has said something orally or in writing, should be held liable because of that statement for harm caused by another, it is useful to focus on three variables. First, the defendant's level of culpability. Presumably, a mere lack of care (negligence) will be less likely than conscious indifference to a known risk of harm (recklessness) or knowing advocacy of a harmful result (intentionally tortious conduct) to give rise to liability. Second, it is important to consider whether the defendant's statement is protected under the First Amendment. If so, it may be difficult or impossible to impose liability. Indeed, in Brandenburg v. Ohio, 395 U.S. 444 (1969), the Supreme Court held that the First Amendment right to freedom of speech includes the right to advocate lawlessness, at least in the abstract. Finally, foreseeability plays a role. Liability ordinarily will not be imposed for harm that is unforeseeable, or for harm which, although foreseeable, is too attenuated in time or space for it to be fair to hold the defendant responsible.

Culpability. A leading case imposing liability for incitement is Weirum v. RKO General, Inc., 539 P.2d 36 (Cal. 1975), holding the owner of a radio station liable for the death of a motorist who was killed when a car driven by a teenager forced her off the road. The teenager was trying to win a $25 cash prize by being the first to locate one of the station's disc jockeys, "The Real Don Steele," who was driving from place to place in the Los Angeles area. The station broadcast information about Steele's location and destination and urged its listeners to try to find him. Holding that the record justified the jury in finding that the station's contest created a foreseeably "grave danger" to those on the roads, as bored teenagers would likely drive unsafely in an attempt to win the prize, the court upheld a verdict finding the station negligent. The defendant argued that this holding would make anyone who advertised limited quantities of desirable items liable for the negligence of others, as when a sports fan is injured while rushing to purchase a ticket to the big game. In response, the court observed:

> The giveaway contest was no commonplace invitation to an attraction available on a limited basis. It was a competitive scramble in which the thrill of the chase to be the one and only victor was intensified by the live broadcast which accompanied the pursuit.

Weirum is in many respects a high water mark in the law of incitement. The defendant was held liable for mere negligence on based oral statements that caused an unknown driver to act in a way that caused harm to an unknown person in a manner that was only loosely foreseeable.

Braun v. Soldier of Fortune Magazine, 968 F.2d 1110 (11th Cir. 1992), and Rice v. The Paladin Enterprises, Inc., 128 F.3d 233 (4th Cir. 1997), involved more egregious facts, and it is easier to see why liability was imposed. In *Braun,* the defendant published an advertisement offering services as a "gun-for-hire," with "all jobs considered." The court held that the survivors of the victim who was murdered by the person who placed the ad stated a valid claim against the magazine.

In *Rice,* suit was brought by the survivors of three people murdered by a hit man hired by the father of one of the victims, who wanted his son killed so that he would get the money the son had received in a personal-injury settlement. The hit man had learned his trade by reading "Hit Man," a book published by the defendant, which gave very detailed instructions on how to murder people in a variety of ways and which glorified the career of being a professional killer (one's first murder, according to the book, would "verify your manhood"). In a stipulation of facts which the court termed "extraordinary," the defendant acknowledged that it had intended, in publishing the book, "to provide assistance to murderers and would-be murderers which would be used by them 'upon receipt,' and that it in fact assisted Perry [the man who had killed the victims] in particular in the commission of the murders."

Freedom of Speech. The *Weirum* court, *supra*, failed see any constitutional obstacle to the imposition of liability in case involving the contest to find the disc jockey. The court wrote simply:

> Defendant's contention that the giveaway contest must be afforded the deference due society's interest in the First Amendment is clearly without merit. The issue here is civil accountability for the foreseeable results of a broadcast which created an undue risk of harm to decedent. The First Amendment does not sanction the infliction of physical injury merely because achieved by word, rather than act.

Other courts would have been more troubled about First Amendment concerns.

For example, in Herceg v. Hustler Magazine, Inc., 814 F.2d 1017 (5th Cir. 1987), the defendant published an article, called *Orgasm of Death*, describing the practice of auto-erotic asphyxia and warning that the reader should not attempt the practice (which was said to be described for "educational reasons"). The parents of a fourteen-year-old, who read the article, tried the technique, and died, failed to state a cause of action against the magazine.

> If the shield of the first amendment can be eliminated by proving after publication that an article discussing a dangerous idea negligently helped bring about a real injury simply because the idea can be identified as "bad," all free speech becomes threatened. An article discussing the nature and danger of "crack" usage—or of hang gliding—might lead to liability just as easily....Mere negligence...cannot form the basis of liability under the incitement doctrine any more than it can under [the law of libel].

The court held that for liability to arise, the plaintiffs had to establish that the publication went beyond mere advocacy and amounted to incitement, and that the incitement was directed toward producing imminent action. The court found that under no fair reading could the article be seen as advocacy, let alone incitement, for it repeatedly warned the reader against engaging in the practice it described.

The *Rice* court, in holding that the claim had been stated against the publisher of "Hit Man," also implicitly recognized that the constitution imposes a high barrier to recovery. It cited cases holding that the First Amendment does not protect speech that is criminal aiding and abetting, "at least where, as here, the defendant has the specific purpose of assisting and encouraging commission of such conduct and the alleged assistance and encouragement takes a form other than abstract advocacy."

Because the facts of *Rice* were so extreme, it is hard to know how willing the court might have been to impose liability for aiding and abetting on less outrageous facts. For example, one can find publications, aimed at paintball enthusiasts, giving detailed instructions on how to make a silencer for a paintball gun. (One of your editors has made one.) Such a silencer can be used as easily on a real gun as on a paintball gun, as those who publish this information know. If someone considering murder obtains these instructions, follows them, and uses a silenced gun to commit a murder, would the First Amendment protect the publisher?

In many cases, the First Amendment has been found to bar recovery against one who allegedly made statements that led to a harmful result. *See* Sanders v. Acclaim Entertainment, Inc., 188 F. Supp. 2d 1264 (D. Col. 2002) (violent movie and video games that allegedly led to the shooting at Columbine high school were not directed to inciting or producing imminent lawless action and thus were protected by the First Amendment); Walt Disney Prods., Inc. v. Shannon, 276 S.E.2d 580 (Ga. 1981) (holding that the First Amendment barred an action against the creators of a children's television program for injuries sustained when a child sought to reproduce a sound effect demonstrated on the program by rotating a BB inside an inflated balloon); Zamora v. Columbia Broadcasting Sys., 480 F. Supp. 199 (S.D. Fla. 1979) (where a complaint alleged that a minor became involuntarily addicted to and subliminally intoxicated by extensive viewing of television violence and, as a result, shot and killed an 83-year-old neighbor, a cause of action was barred by the First Amendment).

Unforeseeability of the Injurer, the Conduct, or the Victim. Courts generally have been unwilling to impose liability on an aiding and abetting theory against sellers of goods or media defendants in cases involving harm to unknown persons. For example:

James v. Meow Media, Inc., 300 F.3d 683 (6th Cir. 2002). Companies that produced or maintained video games, movies, and Internet websites which allegedly desensitized a student to violence, causing him to shoot and kill three classmates, did not owe duty of care to the classmates under a theory that their games, movies, and Internet sites gave student "psychological tools" to commit such murders. Even if the ideas and images conveyed by such products could be deemed to be tools for the student's criminal acts, the companies did not know that the student existed and were not aware of his particular idiosyncrasies that made their products particularly dangerous in his hands.

Waller v. Osborne, 763 F. Supp. 1144 (M.D. Ga. 1991), *aff'd without op.* 958 F.2d 1084 (11th Cir. 1992). The creators of a song which allegedly contained subliminal messages did not engage in culpable incitement to commit suicide. There was no evidence that the music was directed toward any particular person or group or likely to cause imminent acts of suicide, and the First Amendment barred claims for negligence, nuisance, fraud, and invasion of privacy.

Winter v. G.P. Putnam's Sons, 938 F.2d 1033 (9th Cir. 1991). The publisher of a mushroom encyclopedia was not liable to plaintiffs who relied on the book's erroneous advice while gathering wild mushrooms and became critically ill, requiring liver transplants.

Sakon v. PepsiCo Inc., 553 So. 2d 163 (Fla. 1989). A soft-drink manufacturer breached no duty by broadcasting a commercial portraying youths engaged in a sporting activity which could be dangerous if not done by skilled persons under proper conditions. The accident, which occurred when a 14-year-old boy attempted the same stunt (lake jumping on a bicycle) and broke his neck, was not a foreseeable consequence of the advertising.

However, where the publication of material has posed a risk of harm specifically to the plaintiff, a number of courts have imposed liability. For example:

S & W Seafoods v. Jacor Broadcasting, 390 S.E.2d 228 (Ga. 1990). A restaurant manager stated a claim for intentional infliction of mental distress against a radio station on which a talk show host urged listeners to confront the manager with rude gestures and spit on him.

Hyde v. City of Columbia, 637 S.W.2d 251 (Mo. Ct. App. 1982). A newspaper could be held liable for negligent publication of a crime victim's name and address while her abductor was still at large. *But see* Orozco v. Dallas Morning News, Inc., 975 S.W.2d 392 (Tex. Ct. App. 1998) (newspaper had no duty to refrain from publishing the street name and block number of a criminal suspect's address and thus could not be held liable on a negligence theory for the retaliatory shooting of the suspect's family members on the day of the publication of the article; the likelihood of injury was outweighed by the social utility of crime reporting).

Times Mirror Co. v. Superior Court (Doe), 244 Cal. Rptr. 556 (Ct. App. 1988). The defendant published the name of the witness to a murder, with the almost-inevitable result.

Professor Andrew B. Sims offers a detailed discussion of this subject in *Tort Liability for Physical Injuries Allegedly Resulting from Media Speech: A Comprehensive First Amendment Approach*, 34 Ariz. L. Rev. 231 (1992).

Chapter 8

Proximate Causation

A. Introduction

A Question of Policy. Even if the defendant's conduct was unreasonable and was a factual cause of the plaintiff's injuries, it may be undesirable to impose liability on the defendant. Consider, for example, a case in which the defendant has negligently injured the plaintiff, inflicting minor injuries. While taking a bus to the doctor's office for treatment of those injuries, the plaintiff suffers serious injuries in a collision between the bus and a truck. Although the defendant's negligence was a factual cause of the injuries the plaintiff sustained in the bus accident—"but for" the defendant's negligence, the plaintiff would not have been on the bus and so would not have been injured when the bus hit the truck—it is inconceivable that the defendant would be held liable for those injuries. Holding the defendant liable for all harms that result, in a "but for" sense, from negligence or other wrongdoing could lead to liability wildly disproportionate to the defendant's fault, and the intervening events may make it seem unjust to hold the defendant responsible. In this case, any court would say that the defendant's negligence was not the "proximate cause" of the injuries sustained on the bus.

The use of the term "proximate cause" to draw judicial lines beyond which liability will not be extended can be seen as an instrument of fairness and policy; some scholars have suggested that it has nothing at all to do with "cause." On the other hand, cases in which proximate cause is lacking are always cases in which the defendant is relieved of liability because of something about the way in which the defendant's conduct caused the injury. The language of causation therefore seems suitable for use in discussing this matter.

Limiting liability for harm caused in fact by the defendant's negligence to harm "proximately caused" serves an important economic function, as well as comporting with the sense that liability should not be greatly disproportionate to fault. This matter will be explored further below.

Terminology. The term "proximate causation" is often used to describe an inquiry quite distinct from that entailed in finding "factual causation," although some authorities have used "proximate cause" to denote the overall inquiry into both factual connection and the fairness of imposing liability. *See, e.g.*, Williams v. Steves Indus., Inc., 699 S.W.2d 570 (Tex. 1985), *supra* p. 363. Others, in an attempt to distinguish the policy determination of whether liability should attach from the "factual causation" inquiry into whether there is an actual cause and effect relationship, have avoided the use of the term "proximate causation" altogether. For example, the Restatement, Second, of Torts speaks simply in terms of whether "there is . . . [a] rule of law relieving the actor from liability." (§431.) The Restatement, Third, of Torts: Liability for Physical Harm (Basic Principles) (Tent. Draft No. 3, 2003) at p.1, rejects the term "proximate cause" as "an especially poor one to describe the idea to which it is connected." In place of "proximate cause," the new Restatement speaks of rules concerning the "scope of liability" for tortious conduct.

"Proximate," Not "Proximity." Proximate causation frequently has little to do with "proximity" in the ordinary sense of the word. Only in the rarest of instances has the law sought to define the scope of liability based solely on physical distance. The classic example of such an approach is the "New York Fire Rule." Originally, the rule held that one who negligently starts a fire is liable for the destruction of the first building it reaches, not the second or any other. Ryan v. New York Cent. R.R. Co., 35 N.Y. 210 (1866). Mindful of the fact that the first building may be on the defendant's own land, the rule was later modified to allow recovery by the first other landowner to whose property the fire spread. Webb v. Rome, W. & O. R. Co., 49 N.Y. 420 (1872); Homac Corp. v. Sun Oil Co., 180 N.E. 172 (N.Y. 1932). Other jurisdictions have rejected the rule, which is not surprising in view of the fact that distance is only one of the many considerations which may bear on the question of whether it makes sense to limit liability. *See also* Mitchell v. Gonzales, 819 P.2d 872, 878 (Cal. 1991) (disapproving use of the term "proximate causation" in jury instructions because it may cause jurors "to focus improperly on the cause that is spatially or temporally closest to the harm").

"Sole Proximate Cause." There can be more than one proximate cause of harm. However, defense attorneys often argue that something other than their clients' conduct was the sole proximate cause of the plaintiff's loss and that therefore their clients should not be held liable. There is nothing wrong with this strategy for avoiding liability, except when it leads a court or jury to believe erroneously that as a matter of law (rather than a matter of fact) there can be only one proximate cause of harm. In most states, "[t]here is no requirement that a . . . proximate cause . . . be the sole cause, the last act, or the one nearest to the injury." McClenahan v. Cooley, 806 S.W.2d 767, 775 (Tenn. 1991). *See generally*, John G. Phillips, *The Sole Proximate Cause "Defense": A Misfit in the World of Contribution and Comparative Negligence*, 1997 Trial Law. Guide 198. However, the concept sometimes appears in statutes. *See* First Assembly of God v. Texas Utilities, 52 S.W.3d 482, 489 (Tex. App. 2001) (indicating that under a state statutory tariff, a utility was not liable for a church fire unless the utility's negligence was the "sole proximate cause" of the harm). The Restatement says that the term is confusing and should be avoided. Restatement, Third, of Torts: Liability for Physical Harm (Basic Principles) §34 Cmt. f (Tent. Draft No. 3, 2003).

Direct Causation versus Foreseeability. The legal system could embrace the opposite of a limit based on proximity and follow what might be called a "direct causation" approach. Under such a rule, liability would be imposed whenever there is a direct connection between the negligence of the defendant and the injury to the plaintiff. Thus, unless the thread of causation between the negligent act and the resulting harm is broken by the intervention of some new cause, liability would attach, no matter how bizarre or unexpected the harm might seem to the negligent actor. The famous *Polemis* decision, studied by generations of torts students, appears to subscribe to this view. In Re Arbitration Between Polemis and Furness, Withy & Co., Ltd., 3 K.B. 560 (Court of Appeal 1921).

In *Polemis*, a ship hand negligently knocked a plank into the hold of a ship which was carrying benzine and petrol in cases. It might have been expected that the falling of the plank would have dented the ship or crushed part of its contents, or have struck a person walking below, causing damage within a relatively limited sphere. Instead, the plank unexpectedly struck a spark, which in turn ignited petroleum vapor that had collected in the hold, and the resulting fire completely destroyed the vessel. Although the arbitrators found that "the spark could not reasonably have been anticipated from the falling of the board," Bankes, L.J., wrote that "given the damage as a direct result of... [the] negligence, the anticipations of the person whose negligent act has produced the damage appear...to be irrelevant." More pointedly, Scrutton, L.J., said:

> To determine whether an act is negligent, it is relevant to determine whether any reasonable person would foresee that the act would cause damage; if he would not, the act is not negligent. But if the act would or might probably cause damage, the fact that the damage it in fact causes is not the exact kind of damage one would expect is immaterial, so long as the damage is in fact directly traceable to the negligent act, and not due to the operation of independent causes having no connection with the negligent act, except that they could not avoid its result. Once the act is negligent, the fact that its exact operation was not foreseen is immaterial.

Liability was imposed for the loss of the entire ship.

The direct-causation approach has had some influence in American jurisprudence, particularly in cases concerning liability for harm caused by intentional conduct (*see* William L. Prosser, *Transferred Intent*, 45 Tex. L. Rev. 650, 658-61 (1967)). Indeed, courts often state the test for proximate causation in terms that sound very much like a direct-causation inquiry. For example, in Cleveland v. Rotman, 297 F.3d 569, 573 (7th Cir. 2002) the court wrote:

> A proximate cause is one that produces an injury through a natural and continuous sequence of events unbroken by any effective intervening cause.

However, many American courts interpret the test as requiring, at least in some cases, a measure of foreseeability with respect to the consequences that resulted from the defendant's acts. *Wagon Mound No. 1*, which follows, identifies some of the considerations underlying this practice.

("Wagon Mound No. 1")
Overseas Tankship (U.K.) Ltd. v. Morts Dock & Engineering Co., Ltd.
Privy Council
[1961] A.C. 388

[The freighter Wagon Mound, owned by the defendants, carelessly discharged a large quantity of furnace oil into Sydney Harbor. The oil was carried by wind and tide to plaintiffs' wharf (Morts Dock), about 600 feet away, where workmen were using welding equipment. Some cotton waste or a rag on a piece of floating debris beneath the wharf was set on fire by falling molten metal. The oil then caught fire, and the conflagration seriously damaged the wharf. The trial judge specifically found that the defendant's employees did not know, and could not have been expected to know, that the furnace oil was capable of being set on fire when spread on water. A judgment was ren-

no foreseeability (i.e. no prox cause)

dered for the plaintiffs on the ground that the damage to the wharf was the direct result of the negligent escape of the oil. The Supreme Court of New South Wales affirmed. The case was appealed to the Privy Council.]

The judgment of their Lordships was delivered by VISCOUNT SIMONDS....

....The trial judge held that apart from damage by fire the [plaintiffs] had suffered some damage from the spillage of oil in that it had got upon their slipways and congealed upon them and interfered with their use of the slips. He said:

> The evidence of this damage is slight and no claim for compensation is made in respect of it. Nevertheless it does establish some damage, which may be insignificant in comparison with the magnitude of the damage by fire, but which nevertheless is damage which, beyond question, was a direct result of the escape of the oil.

It is upon this footing that their Lordships will consider the question whether the [defendants] are liable for the fire damage....

....

...[T]he authority of *Polemis* has been severely shaken though lip-service has from time to time been paid to it. In their Lordships' opinion it should no longer be regarded as good law. It is not probable that many cases will for that reason have a different result, though it is hoped that the law will be thereby simplified, and that in some cases at least palpable injustice will be avoided. For it does not seem consonant with current ideas of justice or morality that for an act of negligence, however slight or venial, which results in some trivial foreseeable damage the actor should be liable for all consequences however unforeseeable and however grave, so long as they can be said to be "direct." It is a principle of civil liability, subject only to qualifications which have no present relevance, that a man must be considered to be responsible for the probable consequences of his act. To demand more of him is too harsh a rule, to demand less is to ignore that civilized order requires the observance of a minimum standard of behavior.

...[I]f it is asked why a man should be responsible for the natural or necessary or probable consequences of his act...the answer is that...he ought to have foreseen them. Thus it is that...in different judgments in the same case and sometimes in a single judgment liability for a consequence has been imposed on the ground that it was reasonably foreseeable or alternatively on the ground that it was natural or necessary or probable. The two grounds have been treated as coterminous, and so they largely are. But, where they are not, the question arises to which the wrong answer was given in *Polemis*. For, if some limitation must be imposed upon the consequences for which the negligent actor is to be held responsible—and all are agreed that some limitation there must be—why should that test (reasonable foreseeability) be rejected which, since he is judged by what the reasonable man ought to foresee, corresponds with the common conscience of mankind, and a test (the "direct" consequence) be substituted which leads to nowhere but the never ending and insoluble problems of causation....

....

...[T]here can be no liability until the damage has been done. It is not the act but the consequences on which tortious liability is founded. Just as...there is no such thing as negligence in the air, so there is no such thing as liability in the air. Suppose an action brought by A for damage caused by the carelessness (a neutral word) of B, for example a fire caused by the careless spillage of oil....It is vain to isolate the liability from its content and to say that B is or is not liable and then to ask for what damage he is liable.

For his liability is in respect of that damage and no other. If, as admittedly it is, B's liability (culpability) depends on the reasonable foreseeability of the consequent damage, how is that to be determined except by the foreseeability of the damage which in fact happened—the damage in suit?....

....Their Lordships have already observed that to hold B liable for consequences however unforeseeable of a careless act, if, but only if, he is at the same time liable for some other damage however trivial, appears to be neither logical nor just. This becomes more clear if it is supposed that similar unforeseeable damage is suffered by A and C but other foreseeable damage, for which B is liable, by A only. A system of law which would hold B liable to A but not to C for the similar damage suffered by each of them could not easily be defended. Fortunately, the attempt is not necessary. For the same fallacy is at the root of the proposition. It is irrelevant to the question whether B is liable for unforeseeable damage that he is liable for foreseeable damage, as irrelevant as would the fact that he had trespassed on Whiteacre be to the question whether he had trespassed on Blackacre. Again suppose a claim by A for damage by fire by the careless act of B. Of what relevance is it to that claim that he has another claim arising out of the same careless act? It would surely not prejudice his claim if that other claim failed: it cannot assist it if it succeeds. Each of them rests on its own bottom and will fall if it can be established that the damage could not reasonably be foreseen.

....As Denning, L.J. said in King v. Phillips, [1953] 1 Q.B. 429 at p. 441, there can be no doubt since Bourhill v. Young that the test of *liability for shock* is foreseeability of *injury by shock*. Their Lordships substitute the word "fire" for "shock" and endorse this statement of the law.

....

Their Lordships humbly advise Her Majesty that this appeal should be allowed, and the [plaintiffs'] action so far as it related to damage caused by the negligence of the [defendants] be dismissed with costs.... [A nuisance claim was remitted.]

Notes

1. *Foreseeability of What?* Although foreseeability is a major consideration in determining whether the defendant's lapse is the proximate cause of the plaintiff's injury, the concept cannot be used mechanically. Indeed, were the plaintiff required to prove that one standing in the position of the defendant would reasonably have foreseen in precise detail the sequence of events and the extent of harm to be sustained, liability would be denied in a great many cases in which the defendant's conduct is blameworthy. The specific contours of any accident—whether the plaintiff landed on his head, or twisted her right ankle, for instance—are almost always unforeseeable in some sense. What the law requires is not that the defendant could have foreseen, precisely, everything that happened, but simply that the plaintiff fall, at least generally, within the class of persons endangered by the defendant's conduct (*see* Palsgraf v. Long Island R.R. Co., 162 N.E. 99 (N.Y. 1928), *supra* at 238) and that the broad outlines of the harm be foreseeable, though not the specific details or the manner of the occurrence (*see* Merhi v. Becker, 325 A.2d 270 (Conn. 1973), *infra* at 437). Foresight of a remote possibility of harm may be sufficient not only to trigger a duty of care (*see* Gulf Refining Co. v. Williams, 185 So. 234 (Miss. 1938), *supra* at 246), but also to establish proximate causation, if the gravity of the threatened harm is great and the cost of adequate precautions is minimal (*see* Wagon Mound No. 2, 1 A.C. 617 (1967), *infra* at 425). The full extent of the resulting

harm need not be foreseen if the damage that ensues, though other and greater than expected, is of the same general sort which is anticipated and demands precautions (*see Kinsman No. 1*, 338 F.2d 708 (2d Cir. 1964), *infra* at 439).

2. *Proximate Causation as a Jury Question.* The issue of proximate causation is normally for the jury. Thus, in Marshall v. Nugent, 222 F.2d 604 (1st Cir. 1955), the court wrote:

> When an issue of proximate cause arises in a borderline case, as not infrequently happens, we leave it to the jury with appropriate instructions. We do this because it is deemed wise to obtain the judgment of the jury, reflecting as it does the earthy viewpoint of the common man—the prevalent sense of the community—as to whether the causal relation between the negligent act and the plaintiff's harm which in fact was a consequence of the tortious act is sufficiently close to make it just and expedient to hold the defendant answerable in damages. That is what the courts have in mind when they say the question of proximate causation is one of fact for the jury....
>
> In dealing with these issues of negligence and proximate causation, the trial judge has to make a preliminary decision whether the issues are such that reasonable men might differ on the inferences to be drawn. This preliminary decision is said to be a question of law, for it is one which the court has to decide, but it is nevertheless necessarily the exercise of judgment on the facts, just as an appellate court may have to exercise a judgment on the facts, in reviewing whether the trial judge should or should not have left the issue to the jury. [Citations.]

3. *Proximate Causation as a Question of Law.* A court will decide the issue of proximate causation as a matter of law if reasonable minds cannot differ. Thus, in Shideler v. Habiger, 243 P.2d 211, 215 (Kan. 1952), the court wrote:

> [I]t may be said as a matter of law that the allegations of the petition that the driver of an automobile who violates the traffic laws and collides with another vehicle which veers into an electric light pole and breaks it off so that it falls with the wires it carries, and the stress of those wires causes another pole to break off below the ground and an employee of the light company [the alleged rescuer] climbs the latter pole and is injured by its fall, discloses a series of facts which would occur so infrequently that the injury to the person of the climber of the pole may not be said to be the natural and probable result of the negligence of the driver.

Because proximate cause is a very difficult concept, hard to explain to a jury in a brief charge, the doctrine's practical importance may lie more in the courts' ability to override a verdict on proximate-cause grounds than in its effect on the outcomes of jury deliberations. Nearly all of the proximate-cause cases in this book are cases in which the court holds that the defendant's negligence either was or was not the proximate cause of the plaintiff's injuries as a matter of law.

4. *Passage of Time.* The passage of time figures into the assessment of proximate causation, and at some point so much time has passed, and so many developments have occurred, that it becomes unfair to impose liability. In Cleveland v. Rotman, 297 F.3d 569, 574 (7th Cir. 2002), a widow argued that bad tax advice had caused her husband to commit suicide. Rejecting the negligence claim, the court wrote:

> Even assuming that Rotman's allegedly erroneous advice precipitated the audit, Cleveland was aware of the impending audit for almost a year before taking his

life. Given the significant time lapse between the allegedly triggering event and Cleveland's suicide, as well as Cleveland's history of depression which had its origins in events that preceded his relationship with Rotman — including the loss of his legal practice, his disbarment, the confiscation of his assets and income, and his mounting debt — Cleveland's suicide did not follow Rotman's advice through a natural and continuous sequence of events unbroken by any effective intervening cause.

("Wagon Mound No. 2") Overseas Tankship (U.K.) Ltd. v. Miller Steamship Co.

Privy Council
1966 [1967] 1 A.C. 617

[The fire which consumed Morts Dock in Wagon Mound No. 1 also destroyed two ships moored at the dock. The owners of those vessels commenced this action, based on nuisance and negligence, against the owners of the Wagon Mound. The trial court, Walsh, J., found as follows:

(1) Reasonable people in the position of the officers of the Wagon Mound would regard the furnace oil as very difficult to ignite upon water. (2) Their personal experience would probably have been that this had very rarely happened. (3) If they had given attention to the risk of fire from the spillage, they would have regarded it as a possibility, but one which could become an actuality only in very exceptional circumstances. (4) They would have considered the chances of the required exceptional circumstances happening whilst the oil remained spread on the harbor waters as being remote. (5) I find that the occurrence of damage to the plaintiff's property as a result of the spillage not reasonably foreseeable by those for whose acts the defendant would be responsible. (6) I find that the spillage of oil was brought about by the careless conduct of persons for whose acts the defendant would be responsible.... (8) Having regard to those findings, and because of finding (5), I hold that the claim of each of the plaintiffs, framed in negligence, fails.

A judgment for the defendants was affirmed by the Supreme Court of New South Wales. The plaintiffs appealed to the Privy Council.]

The judgment of the Board was delivered by LORD REID.

. . . .

It is...necessary to turn to the respondents' submission that the trial judge was wrong in holding that damage from fire was not reasonably foreseeable. In *The Wagon Mound (No. 1)*, the finding upon which the Board proceeded was that of the trial judge: "The defendant did not know and could not reasonably be expected to have known that [the oil] was capable of being set afire when spread on water." In the present case the evidence led was substantially different from the evidence led in *The Wagon Mound (No. 1)* and the findings of Walsh, J. are significantly different. This is not due to there having been any failure by the plaintiff in *The Wagon Mound (No. 1)* in preparing and presenting their case. The plaintiffs there were no doubt embarrassed by a difficulty which does not affect the present plaintiffs. The outbreak of the fire was consequent on the act of the manager of the plaintiffs in *The Wagon Mound (No. 1)* in resuming oxy-acetylene welding and cutting while the wharf was surrounded by this oil. So if the plaintiffs in the former case had set out to prove that it was foreseeable by the engineers of the

Wagon Mound that this oil could be set alight, they might have had difficulty in parry-
ing the reply that this also must have been foreseeable by their manager. There would
have been contributory negligence and at that time contributory negligence was a complete defense in New South Wales.

    ....

    In *The Wagon Mound (No. 1)* the Board were not concerned with degrees of foresee-
ability because the finding was that the fire was not foreseeable at all.... But here the
findings show that some risk of fire would have been present to the mind of a reasonable man in the shoes of the ship's chief engineer....

    ....

    ... [I]t does not follow that, no matter what the circumstances may be, it is justifi-
able to neglect a risk of such a small magnitude. A reasonable man would only neglect
such a risk if he had some valid reason for doing so, e.g., that it would involve considerable expense to eliminate the risk. He would weigh the risk against the difficulty of
eliminating it.

    ....

    In the present case there was no justification whatever for discharging the oil into
Sydney Harbor. Not only was it an offence to do so, but it involved considerable loss financially. If the ship's engineer had thought about the matter, there could have been no
question of balancing the advantages and disadvantages. From every point of view it
was both his duty and his interest to stop the discharge immediately.

    It follows that in their Lordship's view the only question is whether a reasonable man
having the knowledge and experience to be expected of the chief engineer of the Wagon
Mound would have known that there was a real risk of the oil on the water catching fire
in some way: if it did, serious damage to ships or other property was not only foreseeable but very likely....

    .... The findings show that he ought to have known that it is possible to ignite this
kind of oil on water, and that the ship's engineer probably ought to have known that
this had in fact happened before. The most that can be said to justify inaction is that he
would have known that this could only happen in very exceptional circumstances. But
this does not mean that a reasonable man would dismiss such a risk from his mind and
do nothing when it was so easy to prevent it. If it is clear that the reasonable man would
have realized or foreseen and prevented the risk, then it must follow that the appellant is
liable in damages....

    ....

[The appeal of the ship owners was allowed.]

B. Result Within the Risk

1. In General

    Under the *Wagon Mound* decisions, the defendant is not liable for harms that were
not reasonably foreseeable. This principle seems to make sense, and a "foreseeability"
test is often invoked in proximate-cause opinions. Foreseeability cannot be the whole

story, however, as there are some cases in which the defendant plainly should not be liable even for some foreseeable harms. Consider an example from the Restatement in which the defendant negligently leaves a loaded pistol lying on a table, where it is found by a child. If the child shoots someone, the defendant will be liable: the risk that the child will shoot someone is just what makes the defendant's conduct negligent. But suppose the child shoots nobody, but accidentally drops the pistol on a playmate's toe: should the defendant be liable for that injury? If "foreseeability" is the test, the answer must be "yes," as this kind of accident is just as foreseeable as a shooting. Yet the risk of injury from having the pistol dropped on a toe is not one of the risks that makes the defendant's conduct negligent (assuming that it would not have been negligent to leave a heavy but non-lethal object, such as a toy gun, where a child could find it). Therefore, there should be no liability. Restatement, Second, Torts, §281, Illus. 3.

The pistol example shows that the foreseeability view of proximate cause is only a partial explanation: unforeseeable consequences are not proximately caused by the conduct in question, but neither are some foreseeable consequences. What unforeseeable consequences (like the fire in *Wagon Mound No. 1*) and the foreseeable consequences that are not proximately caused by the defendant's negligence (like the pistol's being dropped on a toe) have in common is this: neither consequence resulted from one of the risks that made the defendant's conduct negligent. An approach to proximate cause that asks whether those risks that made the defendant's behavior negligent included the risk that led to the plaintiff's injuries explains many proximate-cause cases better than simply asking whether the result was "foreseeable." The case that follows provides both an illuminating illustration of the "result within the risk" approach to proximate cause and an example of the tendency of many courts to talk of "foreseeability" as well as (sometimes instead of) results and risks.

Di Ponzio v. Riordan

Court of Appeals of New York
679 N.E. 2d 616 (N.Y. 1997)

TITONE, Judge.

. . . .

Defendant United Refining Co. (URC) owns and operates a self-service filling station in Rochester. According to the complaint allegations and summary judgment submissions, the injury-producing accident occurred on defendant's premises on April 15, 1991. At about 1:00 P.M. on that date, plaintiff Richard Di Ponzio drove into defendant's gas station, exited his car and began to fill his tank with fuel. At approximately the same time, defendant Michael Riordan drove his car into the gas station, stopped opposite plaintiff's vehicle and, without turning off his engine, began pumping gas into his vehicle. Riordan stated during his deposition testimony that the pavement was relatively level and that he placed his console gearshift in the park position.

Riordan took about five minutes to pump gas into his car and then went inside the gas station's storefront enclosure to pay the attendant for his fuel. He left his vehicle running because he had been experiencing problems with the carburetor and was afraid that he would not be able to restart the vehicle if he turned its ignition off. When he exited the store and began walking toward the car, he noticed that it was moving backward toward the rear of plaintiff's vehicle, where plaintiff was still pumping gas. Riordan moved toward the vehicle, but he was unable to reach it in time to stop it from striking plaintiff. Plaintiff, who was pinned between the two cars, suffered a fractured leg.

Plaintiff and his spouse subsequently commenced the present personal injury action against Riordan and URC. Plaintiffs' theory against defendant URC was that it had been negligent in failing to properly train its attendants and that its attendants had been negligent in failing to comply with URC rules requiring that customers be warned to turn off their engines while fueling their vehicles. In support of their claim, plaintiffs cited information obtained during discovery that URC attendants were not supposed to allow customers to pump gas while their engines were running and that the attendants had the ability to turn off a particular pump in the event that a customer refused to comply. They also relied on deposition testimony that on the day of the accident URC's attendants had deliberately turned down the sound on an intercom system that would otherwise have enabled them both to hear the sound of Riordan's engine and to admonish him to turn it off.

Following discovery, defendant URC moved for summary judgment dismissing the complaint on several grounds, including...the lack of a proximate causal relationship between its alleged negligence, if any, and the accident and the unforeseeability of the accident. Supreme Court denied the motion, holding that...the questions of foreseeability and proximate cause should be resolved by the fact finder.

On URC's appeal, the Appellate Division reversed and dismissed the complaint against URC....

    ....

In this case, the focus of the inquiry is on the foreseeability of the risk. Foreseeability of risk is an essential element of a fault-based negligence cause of action because the community deems a person at fault only when the injury-producing occurrence is one that could have been anticipated (Prosser and Keeton, Torts §31, at 169-170, and n 15 [5th ed]). Further, although virtually every untoward consequence can theoretically be foreseen "with the wisdom born of the event" [citation], the law draws a line between remote possibilities and those that are reasonably foreseeable because "[n]o person can be expected to guard against harm from events which are...so unlikely to occur that the risk...would commonly be disregarded" (Prosser and Keeton, op. cit., §31, at 170; [citation]).

A related problem...is the need to analyze the relationship between the risk created by the actor's conduct and the actual occurrence that caused the harm. It is often said that plaintiffs need not demonstrate the foreseeability of the precise manner in which the accident occurred or the precise type of harm produced in order to establish the foreseeability component of their tort claims [citations]. This principle is sometimes mistakenly cited to support an argument that a careless act should lead to liability even though the injury-producing accident itself occurred in an unexpected manner. Such arguments, however, are misguided to the extent that they fail to recognize the analytically important distinction between the concept of risk or hazard and the concept of harm.

The Restatement (Second) of Torts is useful in clarifying this often misconstrued principle. As is explained in §281, comment e, conduct is considered negligent when it tends to subject another to an unreasonable risk of harm arising from one or more particular foreseeable hazards [citation]. When the person is harmed by an occurrence resulting from one of those hazards, the negligent actor may be held liable. In contrast, where the harm was caused by an occurrence that was not part of the risk or recognized hazard involved in the actor's conduct, the actor is not liable (*see, id.,* comment f). The following example taken directly from the Restatement provides a useful illustration of the point:

"A gives a loaded pistol to B, a boy of eight, to carry to C. In handing the pistol to C the boy drops it, injuring the bare foot of D, his comrade. The fall discharges the pistol, wounding C. A is subject to liability to C, but not to D" (*id.*, comment f, illustration 3, at 7).

As this hypothetical fact pattern makes clear, where an individual breaches a legal duty and thereby causes an occurrence that is within the class of foreseeable hazards that the duty exists to prevent, the individual may be held liable, even though the harm may have been brought about in an unexpected way. On the other hand, no liability will result when the occurrence is not one that is normally associated with such hazards. Significantly, the kind and number of hazards encompassed within a particular duty depend on the nature of the duty (*see, id.*, comment e).

The gist of plaintiffs' claim is that defendant URC's servants were negligent in failing to monitor its customers' conduct and, more specifically, in failing to require Riordan to turn off his vehicle's engine despite having had the means and obligation to do so. Assuming without deciding that URC had a duty to control its customer's conduct in this manner [citation], the existence of such a duty would not aid plaintiff Di Ponzio's case, since his injuries did not arise from the occurrence of any of the foreseeable hazards that the duty would exist to prevent.

When a vehicle's engine is left running in an area where gasoline is being pumped, there is a natural and foreseeable risk of fire or explosion because of the highly flammable properties of the fuel. Indeed, the local ordinance plaintiffs cite as one source of support for the existence of a duty to direct gas station patrons to turn off their engines is, in fact, contained within the City of Rochester Fire Prevention Code, whose stated purpose is to safeguard against "the hazards of fire and explosions" [citation]. It is this class of foreseeable hazards that defines the scope of the URC's purported duty.

The occurrence that led to plaintiff's injury was clearly outside of this limited class of hazards. Plaintiff was injured because the parking gear of another customer's car inexplicably failed and the unattended vehicle, which had rested stationary on a level surface for more than five minutes, suddenly began to move backwards, pinning plaintiff between its rear bumper and the bumper of his own car. Because this type of accident was not among the hazards that are naturally associated with leaving a car engine running during the operation of a gas pump, the alleged misconduct of URC's employees does not give rise to liability in tort. Indeed, plaintiff's position in this case is analogous to that of the child whose foot was injured by the plummeting pistol in the Restatement hypothetical. Moreover, while plaintiff's accident may have been an indirect consequence of the station attendant's failure to direct Riordan to turn off his engine, the accident was, at most, a remote possibility at the time the conduct in question occurred and thus was not a foreseeable consequence of the attendant's inaction, even though the risk may now readily be perceived through hindsight (*see,* Prosser and Keeton, op. cit., §31, at 170 ["It is not enough that everyone can see now that the risk was great, if it was not apparent when the conduct occurred"]). Accordingly, as a matter of law defendant URC had no cognizable legal duty to protect against the injury-producing occurrence and plaintiff's cause of action based on URC's own alleged negligence was properly dismissed.

. . . .

Accordingly, the order of the Appellate Division should be affirmed, with costs.

KAYE, C.J. and BELLACOSA, SMITH, LEVINE and CIPARICK, JJ. concur.

WESLEY, J., taking no part.

Order affirmed, with costs.

Notes

1. *"Result within the Risk" and the Third Restatement.* The third Restatement whole-heartedly adopts the result-within-the-risk approach to proximate cause (which the Restatement insists on calling "scope of liability"):

> § 29. Limitations on Liability for Tortious Conduct
>
> An actor is not liable for harm different from the harms whose risks made the actor's conduct tortious.
>
> § 30. Risk of Harm Not Increased by Tortious Conduct
>
> An actor is not liable for harm when the tortious aspect of the actor's conduct did not increase the risk of harm.

Restatement, Third, of Torts: Liability for Physical Harm (Basic Principles) (Tent. Draft No. 3, 2003). Comment e to § 29 presents the rationale for the Restatement's approach:

> Limiting liability to harm arising from the risks created by tortious conduct has the virtue of relative simplicity. It also provides a more refined analytical standard than a foreseeability standard or an amorphous direct-consequences test. Furthermore,... [it] imposes limits on liability by reference to the reasons for holding an actor liable for tortious conduct in the first place. The risk standard appeals to intuitive notions of fairness and proportionality by imposing liability for the harms resulting from risks created by the actor's conduct, but for no others. It also provides sufficient flexibility to accommodate any fairness concerns raised by the specific facts of a case.

2. *"Result within the Risk" and Statutory Violations.* One kind of case in which the result-within-the-risk analysis is routinely applied is that in which the defendant's conduct violates a statute that has a particular purpose. Suppose, for instance, that the defendant has parked illegally in front of a fire hydrant. If the plaintiff's building catches fire and burns to the ground because the defendant's car keeps the fire department from getting to the hydrant, the defendant should be liable. But if a skateboarder trips and hits her head on the car—an accident that would not have happened if the car had not been in that particular place—the defendant's negligence would not be a proximate cause of the harm: it is illegal to park in front of hydrants because this increases the risks of fire, not because a skateboarder may fall against a car in that particular spot. A famous English case, Gorris v. Scott, L.R. 9 Ex. 125 (1874), was brought by the owner of sheep which had washed overboard in a storm while being carried on the defendant's ship. If the sheep had been in pens, as required by an order issued pursuant to the Contagious Diseases (Animals) Act of 1869, they would not have been lost. The court, finding it "perfectly clear" that the act was a disease-prevention measure, denied recovery.

Consider again the problem of the defendant whose conduct is perfectly proper, except that he is engaging in an activity requiring a license, which the defendant does not have (Brown v. Shyne, *supra*, p. 311). Suppose that an unlicensed driver, who is in fact driving very carefully, runs over a pedestrian who has fainted and fallen in front of her car. It is quite clear that the defendant is not liable for the pedestrian's injuries, even though the defendant's actions violated a law that was enacted as a safety measure. One way to analyze this problem is to say that the statute, although a "safety statute" in a sense, is not a statute that prescribes a standard of care: the defendant was observing all of the standards of care required of drivers (paying attention to traffic, staying in her lane, not speeding, and so on). Her actions were therefore not negligent, because they created no excessive risk of harm, even though they were illegal. Another way to explain the result is to invoke proximate cause. The reason for licensing statutes is to keep incompetent drivers off the road. If a particular driver, though involved in an accident, was driving competently, the harm in question was not the kind of harm the licensing statute was adopted to prevent. (Compare a case in which the defendant, driving very carefully to a bank the defendant intends to rob, hits a pedestrian who stumbles in front of his car. The defendant's illegal conduct will not make him liable to the pedestrian.)

3. *Negligent Medical Treatment.* A fairly common situation involves a plaintiff who is tortiously injured, and whose injuries are aggravated by the negligence of the plaintiff's physician. It is generally agreed that the defendant is liable for all of the harm, including that attributable to the negligent treatment. As the Indiana Court of Appeals put it in Whitaker v. Kruse, 495 N.E.2d 223 (Ind. Ct. App. 1986), "[s]ince he put the injured person in the position of needing medical services, the tort-feasor is liable for any additional injury resulting from the medical treatment."

If medical misconduct is so extraordinary that it can no longer be thought of as a risk inherent in the necessity of submitting to medical treatment, the antecedent tortfeasor will not be liable for the aggravation of the plaintiff's injuries. *See* Restatement, Third, of Torts: Liability for Physical Harm (Basic Principles) (Tent. Draft No. 3, 2003), § 35, cmt. c: "The actor is not subject to liability for enhanced harm caused by extraordinary or unusual acts that create risks of harm different from those normally created by efforts to render aid." The line is to be drawn somewhere between ordinary negligence on the one hand and intentionally inflicted injury on the other, but beyond that generalization, its precise location is unclear. *See* W. Page Keeton, Dan B. Dobbs, Robert E. Keeton, & David G. Owen, Prosser and Keeton on Torts 309-10 (5th ed. 1984). Some decisions involving other intervening causes suggest that a reckless intervening act, like an intentional one, will break the chain of causation. *See, e.g.,* Boltax v. Joy Day Camp, 490 N.E.2d 527 (N.Y. 1986) (trespasser's reckless act of diving into the shallow end of a pool absolved the defendant of liability for alleged negligence in maintenance of the pool).

Suppose that, instead of suffering additional injuries because of negligent medical treatment, the victim of negligence is injured while driving to the doctor's office for treatment. This case, as we have seen, is a classic example of an injury that would not be regarded as proximately caused by the original tortfeasor's conduct. The difference cannot be that medical malpractice is more easily "foreseeable" than a traffic accident: traffic accidents are everyday occurrences. A result-within-the-risk analysis makes sense of these results. One of the risks created by negligent driving is the risk that whatever injuries others sustain will be aggravated by improper care, so that kind of harm is "within the risk." On the other hand, while it is certainly foreseeable that a victim of negligence may be injured while driving to see a doctor, that further risk is no greater than the risks of driving the plaintiff would have encountered anyway. It would therefore seem odd to say that one of the reasons why it is negligent to drive carelessly is that this may lead to further injuries while the plaintiff is driving to the doctor's office. (Contrast a case in which the victim's injuries are very serious, so the ambulance taking the victim to the hospital drives at 90 miles an hour and, because of its high speed, crashes.)

See Lear Siegler, Inc. v. Perez, 819 S.W.2d 470 (Tex. 1991) (plaintiff would not have been at the place where the collision occurred at the time it occurred if a flashing arrow manufactured by the defendant had not malfunctioned, but the defendant was not liable for injuries sustained by the plaintiff, who was struck by a van driven by a driver who had fallen asleep, because the defendant's conduct did no more than furnish a condition that made the plaintiff's injury possible).

4. ***Problem: Negligent Entrustment.*** Pete has a tendency to drink heavily, as his friend Dave well knows. Pete borrows Dave's car so that, as he tells Dave, he can "go to the tavern tonight and get plowed with the guys." If Pete should get drunk and, as a result, injure a pedestrian while driving home, Dave would be liable for the pedestrian's injuries. If, on the way to the tavern, while sober, Pete drives negligently and injures Paula, is Dave liable to Paula? It is, of course, quite foreseeable that someone to whom a car has been lent may drive carelessly even when sober: nearly everybody drives carelessly some of the time. (Assume that the state in question does not have an "owner liability" law. These laws make the owners of motor vehicles liable for the negligent driving of anyone using their cars with permission.)

5. ***Other Examples.*** In Barr v. Jacobson, 795 So. 2d 1244 (La. Ct. App. 2001), a child was injured when she stepped in a hole in the ground after an auto accident. In finding that the driver's alleged breach of duty was not a legal cause of the injuries from the misstep, the court wrote:

> [T]he duty of reasonable care in the operation of motor vehicles was not designed to protect automobile passengers involved in an accident from all conceivable harms. We find that the danger of stepping into holes located off of the roadway while embarking on a second trip to observe other vehicles or persons involved, out of curiosity or personal interest, six or seven minutes after the accident, is simply not within the scope of this duty.

In Lodge v. Arett Sales Corp., 717 A.2d 215 (Conn. 1998), an alarm company and alarm servicer, who negligently caused transmission of a false fire alarm, were not liable to firefighters who were injured during an accident precipitated by negligent maintenance and failure of the brakes on the responding fire engine. The court found that the harm suffered by firefighters was not reasonably foreseeable, and imposing liability on alarm companies for harm they could not have anticipated and over which they had no control would not serve any legitimate objective of the law.

6. ***Culpability and Scope of Liability.*** *See* Restatement, Third, of Torts: Liability for Physical Harm (Basic Principles) §33(b) (Tent. Draft No. 3, 2003) ("An actor who intentionally or recklessly causes physical harm is subject to liability for a broader range of harms than the harms for which that actor would be liable if acting negligently").

7. ***References.*** For a thorough historical study of proximate cause, see Patrick J. Kelley, *Proximate Cause in Negligence Law: History, Theory, and the Present Darkness*, 69 Wash. U.L.Q. 49 (1991). Works dealing with the relationship between risk and result include Robert E. Keeton, *Legal Cause and the Law of Torts* (1963), and Warren A. Seavey, *Principles of Torts*, 56 Harv. L. Rev. 72, 90-93 (1942).

2. Policy and Proximate Cause

One way to look at the "proximate cause" restriction on plaintiffs' recoveries is to see it as denying recovery when the defendant's negligence was not the sort of misconduct that tends to lead to the kind of harm that resulted. For example, suppose that a tree falls on a speeding car, injuring a passenger.[a] The driver's speeding is negligent because it creates an excessive risk that the car may slide off the road on a sharp corner, or that the driver may not be able to stop in time if vehicles ahead slow down or change lanes. The reason for calling the driver's conduct negligent has nothing to do with threats from falling trees. Indeed, speeding may reduce the danger of being hurt by falling trees: the faster one drives, the less time one spends on the road and under the trees. Therefore, although the excessive speed was a "but for" cause of the accident—the speed happened to put the car in position to be hit by the tree—it was not a proximate cause of the accident. Similarly, recall the second Restatement's example of the defendant who negligently leaves a loaded pistol where a six-year-old can find it: the reason it is negligent to leave loaded weapons around has to do with the dangers of gunshot wounds, not with objects being dropped on toes, so the defendant is liable for shootings but not if the child drops the pistol on someone's toe.

Economic Analysis: Avoiding Over-Deterrence. Looking at tort law from the point of view of deterrence, the examples above show that a proximate-cause rule is essential to prevent the law from over-deterring conduct that can cause injuries. Consider, for instance, the question of how much the law should deter drivers from exceeding the speed limit by five miles an hour on uncrowded interstate highways. The answer is: a bit, but not very much. Speed saves time and money, though it causes some harm. If the law makes those who exceed the speed limit liable for all of the additional accidents that can be expected to result from this small increase in speed, it gives those drivers just the right incentive. Those for whom getting to their destination quickly is very important will accept the risk; those for whom it isn't will not. But now suppose that these drivers are liable not only for the harms done in accidents predictably caused by their excessive speed, but also for any accident in which they were involved while speeding—even if the only contribution of speed to the accident was that it happened to put the car in the place where the accident occurred, as in the falling-tree hypothetical. Now, drivers will (in theory) know that if they exceed the speed limit, even by a very small amount, they will be liable for any accident that happens. This imposes a burden quite disproportionate to the harm one would foresee from the conduct, and so would have too great a deterrent effect.

The argument above can be restated in a more general way. Proper deterrence requires making those who contemplate dangerous conduct liable for all of the increased harm that occurs whenever that dangerous conduct is undertaken. Making actors liable for more than that over-deters. Without a doctrine of proximate cause to limit liability, the prospective penalty for any conduct that a factfinder might find negligent would be far in excess of the additional harm one can foresee as resulting from the conduct.

As another illustration of both proximate cause and of the economic rationale for the doctrine, consider a case in which *A* is driving her friend *B* to the airport. They are somewhat late for the flight, so *A* speeds. The law should deter *A* somewhat from doing this, as *A*'s speeding creates a danger for other users of the highway. But if the highway is empty, the road is dry, the weather is clear, and it is important for *B* to make her

---

a. This example is adapted from one in Prosser and Keeton on Torts, §41, which in turn comes from Berry v. Sugar Notch Borough, 43 A. 240 (Pa. 1899), in which the vehicle was a trolley.

plane, speeding may be the economically sensible thing to do. If *A* knows that she will be liable for any accident of the sort the rule against speeding is designed to prevent, she is in a position to make an intelligent choice. But suppose there were no doctrine of proximate cause. Now, *A*'s speeding would make her liable for all of the consequences of *B*'s catching her plane on time, so that, for example,

(1) If *B*'s plane crashes, *A* would be liable for *B*'s injuries ("but for" *A*'s speeding, *B* would have missed the plane and so would not have been hurt).

(2) If *B*, driving a rental car in the city to which she flew, ran over a pedestrian, *A* would be liable for the pedestrian's injuries ("but for" *A*'s speeding, *B* would have missed the plane and would not have been driving her rental car the next day).

If anyone who speeds could be held liable for every harm that could be traced to the speeding in a "but for" sense, potential liability for speeding would greatly exceed the harm that the speeding could be expected to cause.

Cases involving defendants who are vicariously liable, such as employers, illustrate the need for limiting liability. In Edwards v. Honeywell, Inc., 50 F.3d 484, 490 (7th Cir. 1995), holding that a fire-alarm service's negligence did not breach a duty to a firefighter who died fighting a fire, Judge Posner observed:

[T]he arguments in favor of the...limitation are twofold. The first arises from the fact that a corporation or other enterprise does not have complete control over its employees, yet it is strictly liable under the principle of *respondeat superior* for the consequences of their negligent acts committed in the scope of their employment. It is not enough to say to the enterprise be careful and you have nothing to fear. The carelessness of its employees may result in the imposition of a crushing liability upon it. In order to know how many resources (in screening new hires and in supervising and disciplining workers after they are hired) to invest in preventing its employees from being careless, the employer must have some idea, some foresight, of the harms the employees are likely to inflict....

The second argument...is that the defendant may not be in the best position to prevent a particular class of accidents, and placing liability on it may merely dilute the incentives of other defendants....

For an economic analysis of proximate cause much more complete and rigorous than that presented here, see Steven Shavell, *An Analysis of Causation and the Scope of Liability in the Law of Torts*, IX J. Legal Stud. 463 (1980).

Fairness. While the above analysis focused on deterrence, and so was an "economic" explanation of proximate cause, much the same sort of analysis can be made in terms of "fairness." A common-sense notion of justice is that the penalty for wrongful behavior should not be disproportionate to the seriousness of the misbehavior. Without a doctrine of proximate cause, the most trivial lapses could subject an actor (and sometimes the actor's employer) to massive liability, just because the lapse happened to contribute, in an unforeseeable and minor way, to a serious accident (as by putting the actor on a particular road at a particular time). A law of torts without proximate cause would often impose liability wildly disproportionate to the seriousness of an actor's wrongdoing. Here, as in so many other areas, an analysis of a problem in economic terms ("deterrence") can be restated in terms of everyday notions of fairness. Proximate cause was developed by courts quite ignorant of and mostly indifferent to economics. That it serves an important economic goal illustrates that ordinary notions of justice often tend to promote efficiency as well.

3. The "Eggshell Skull" Doctrine

McCahill v. New York Transp. Co.
Court of Appeals of New York
94 N.E. 616 (N.Y. 1911)

HISCOCK, J.

One of the appellant's taxicabs struck respondent's intestate on Broadway, in the city of New York, in the night time under circumstances which permitted the jury to find that the former was guilty of negligence and the latter free from contributory negligence. As a result of the accident the intestate was thrown about 20 feet, his thigh broken and his knee injured. He immediately became unconscious, and was shortly removed to a hospital, where he died on the second day thereafter of delirium tremens. A physician testified that the patient when brought to the hospital "was unconscious or irrational rather than unconscious.... He rapidly developed delirium tremens.... I should say with reasonable certainty the injury precipitated his attack of delirium tremens...." And, again, that in his opinion "the injury to the leg and knee hurried up the delirium tremens." He also stated: "He might have had it (delirium tremens) anyway. Nobody can tell that." Of course, it is undisputed that the injuries could not have led to delirium tremens except for the pre-existing alcoholic condition of the intestate, and under these circumstances the debatable question in the case has been whether appellant's negligence was, legally speaking, the proximate cause of intestate's death. It seems to me that it was....

.... There can be no doubt that the negligent act directly set in motion the sequence of events which caused death at the time it occurred. Closer analysis shows that the real proposition urged by the appellant is that it should not be held liable for the results which followed its negligence, either, first, because those results would not have occurred if intestate had been in a normal condition; or, secondly, because his alcoholism might have caused delirium tremens and death at a later date even though appellant had not injured him. This proposition cannot be maintained in either of its branches which are somewhat akin.

The principle has become familiar in many phases that a negligent person is responsible for the direct effects of his acts, even if more serious, in cases of the sick and infirm as well as in those of healthy and robust people, and its application to the present case is not made less certain because the facts are somewhat unusual and the intestate's prior disorder of a discreditable character. [Citations.] The principle is also true, although less familiar, that one who has negligently forwarded a diseased condition, and thereby hastened and prematurely caused death, cannot escape responsibility, even though the disease probably would have resulted in death at a later time without his agency. It is easily seen that the probability of later death from existing causes for which a defendant was not responsible would probably be an important element in fixing damages, but it is not a defense....

I think the judgment should be affirmed, with costs.

[The concurring opinion of VANN, J., is omitted.]

Notes

1. *The "Eggshell Skull" Doctrine.* The rule underlying *McCahill*—which is often invoked by reference to a person with an eggshell skull who suffers greater than normal injuries from a blow to the head—is uniformly endorsed. It holds that once a plaintiff suffers any foreseeable physical injury, even a trivial one, the defendant is liable for all physical consequences, even unforeseeable injuries, so long as they do not stem from superseding causes. *Cf.* Juisti v. Hyatt Hotel Corp., 94 F.3d 169, 171 (4th Cir. 1996). In reinstating an action by a hotel guest who suffered a collapsed lung while fleeing a building when a fire alarm went off, the *Juisti* court wrote:

> The question of proximate cause...is not whether the hotel's negligence in setting off the alarm could reasonably be expected to cause the plaintiff's specific injury, but whether such negligence could reasonably be expected to cause the plaintiff any injury.

2. *Aggravation of Pre-Existing Conditions.* As the principal case illustrates, an accident which produces physical injury by precipitating the development of a latent condition or by aggravating a pre-existing condition may be a proximate cause of the injury. *See also* Tobin v. Steisel, 475 N.E.2d 101 (N.Y. 1985) (psychological disability resulting from explosion); Miley v. Landry, 582 So. 2d 833 (La. 1991) (psychosis triggered by auto accident). The defendant must take the plaintiff "as is." *See* Restatement, Third, of Torts: Liability for Physical Harm (Basic Principles) §31 (Tent. Draft No. 3, 2003) ("When an actor's tortious conduct causes harm to a person that, because of the person's preexisting physical or mental condition or other characteristic, is of a greater magnitude or different type than might reasonably be expected, the actor is nevertheless subject to liability for all such harm to the person").

3. *"Eggshell Skulls" and Proximate Cause.* At first glance, the doctrine of the *McCahill* case seems inconsistent with standard proximate-cause doctrine, for the defendant is held liable, under *McCahill,* even for results that could not easily have been foreseen. Yet both doctrines are similar in one respect: They tend to make the amount of damages actually paid by negligent defendants (as a whole) approximately equal to the amount of harm done by those defendants. Without a doctrine like that of *McCahill,* potential injurers would be seriously underdeterred. To illustrate, suppose that the average amount of harm done to the victims of a particular kind of accident is $100,000. This is the average of the harms done to individual victims, which may range from a low of $1.00 (for a handful of very resilient victims) to a high of $1,000,000 (for the rare victim with an "eggshell skull"). Proper deterrence requires that a potential injurer's expected liability be $100,000. If there were no "eggshell skull" doctrine, so that those injurers whose victims suffered $1,000,000 in damages had to pay only the expected damages of $100,000 or so, the average damage payment would be less than the average harm of $100,000. In a sense, holding injurers liable for all of the harm suffered by unusually sensitive victims makes up for the benefits that some injurers get when their victims turn out to be unusually hardy.

Although the eggshell-skull doctrine can lead to liability for harms not easily foreseeable, it seems consistent with a result-within-the-risk analysis. One of the reasons for taking precautions against striking pedestrians with a car is surely that some pedestrians may be unusually fragile. Even a very unlikely result may be "within the risk" created by dangerous behavior. (For a further illustration of this point, see *Kinsman No. 1, infra* at p. 439.)

4. *Problem: The Delicate Football Player.* Moose, a large, strong, and athletic highschool student had an unusually weak joint in his knee. Neither he nor anyone else

knew of this condition until Moose was tackled by Tom in the first football game of the season. Because of the weak joint, Moose's knee sustained serious, permanent injuries. Is Tom liable for those injuries?

4. Manner of Occurrence and Kind and Extent of Harm

Merhi v. Becker

Supreme Court of Connecticut
325 A.2d 270 (Conn. 1973)

BOGDANSKI, Associate Justice.

The plaintiff, Ronald Merhi, brought this action in four counts to recover damages for personal injuries....From a verdict and judgment rendered against it, Local 1010 has appealed to this court....

Local 1010 contends (1) that the jury could not reasonably have found that the defendant was negligent in discharging its duty of care toward those attending the picnic and (2) that even if the jury found the defendant negligent, it could not reasonably have found that its negligence was the proximate cause of the plaintiff's injuries.

There was evidence from which the jury could find the following facts: On July 21, 1962, the plaintiff, a member of Local 1010, attended an outdoor picnic planned and sponsored by the defendant Local 1010 for the benefit of its union members and their guests....[A]pproximately 500 people attended.

The committee designated by the union to be in charge of the picnic decided to have three or four policemen on duty at the grounds and a member of the committee was paid by the union to hire the policemen. In fact, however, only one person was assigned to police the grounds and he was not a regular member of any police force, normally worked in a shop, and was sixty years of age. On the morning of the picnic, the chairman of the committee determined that more police protection was needed. No additional police, however, were obtained.

The admission price entitled the patrons to all the food and beer they desired. Some of the union members brought their own liquor. The tenor of the picnic became noisy and inharmonious. Many men and women went swimming in the pool with their clothes on. Richard Becker testified that during the day he had more than five beers and "it could have been more than a thousand." Everyone had been drinking quite a bit. Becker was involved in two fights during the picnic, one with John Keiper, a member of the committee sponsoring the picnic....

Becker was not arrested, evicted or escorted from the grounds after his physical involvement with Keiper. About a half-hour later Becker went to his car which was parked in the picnic area, drove the car into the area of the picnickers, aimed and steered it in the direction of Keiper, but struck and injured the plaintiff instead.

....

....On the evidence, the jury could properly find that the defendant Local 1010 had failed to perform its duty to provide adequate police protection or otherwise to control the activities of its beer drinking guests, especially after the earlier outbreak of fisticuffs.

. . . .

. . . . The defendant Local 1010, nevertheless, further contends that even if the jury did find it was negligent, it could not have found its negligence was the cause of the plaintiff's injuries because no person in the defendant's position, knowing what it knew or should have known, could have anticipated that the harm of the nature suffered by the plaintiff was likely to result.

"If the . . . [defendant's] conduct is a substantial factor in bringing about harm to another, the fact that the . . . [defendant] neither foresaw nor should have foreseen the extent of the harm or the manner in which it occurred does not prevent him from being liable." Restatement (Second), of Torts §435(1). Neither foreseeability of the extent nor the manner of the injury constitutes the criteria for deciding questions of proximate cause. The test is whether the harm which occurred was of the same general nature as the foreseeable risk created by the defendant's negligence. [Citations.] Here, the jury could have found that the events at the picnic fulfilled the test for proximate cause; that the inadequate policing of a large crowd served alcoholic beverages all day created the foreseeable risk that boisterous and angry occurrences might result in injury to bystanders, and that this risk became more obvious once the brawls involving Becker occurred. Consequently, no matter how one characterizes the exact nature of Becker's action in harming the plaintiff, the jury could reasonably have found that it constituted an instance of the general kind of harm that the defendant's negligence would cause, i.e., harm to patrons from inadequately deterred raucous, violent conduct.

. . . .

We conclude therefore, that the verdict of the jury is clearly supported by the evidence and the law and that the court properly denied the motion to set aside the verdict.

There is no error.

In this opinion the other judges concurred.

Note

1. The weight of authority agrees with the principal case that an unforeseeable difference in manner of occurrence will not preclude a finding of proximate causation if the harmful end result was foreseeable. However, the analysis in some cases appears to be at odds with the rule.

For example, in City of Bishop v. South Texas Elec. Coop., Inc., 577 S.W.2d 331 (Tex. Civ. App. 1979), a fire truck was destroyed at the site of a grass fire when its pumping equipment unexpectedly failed and its engine died and would not restart. Although the court found that the party responsible for the fire "should have known that firefighters and their equipment would respond to the fire" and that "a fire truck . . . [could become] immobilized in the area of the fire because of hidden tree stumps, bailing wire, or ground ruts," it refused to impose liability for damage to the truck. The court found that "[n]othing short of prophetic ken . . . could have anticipated the happening of the combination of events which resulted in the truck's destruction." The decision places more emphasis on foreseeability of minor detail than do most reported opinions. Interestingly, many cases would have reached the same result under the rule that no duty of care is owed to a professional rescuer. *See* Chapter 16.

("Kinsman No. 1") Petition of Kinsman Transit Co.

United States Court of Appeals for the Second Circuit
338 F.2d 708 (2d Cir. 1964)

[The Buffalo River flows through Buffalo from east to west, with many bends and turns, until it empties into Lake Erie. About a mile from the mouth, the City of Buffalo maintains a bridge at Michigan Avenue. The Shiras, owned by Kinsman Transit Co., was improperly moored at a dock operated by the Continental Grain Company, about three miles upstream from the Michigan Avenue Bridge. The river, which was about 200 feet wide, moved rapidly and was full of floating ice. Because the Shiras, which was more than 400 feet in length, extended considerably beyond the length of the dock near a turn in the river, ice and debris accumulated between the ship and the dock. As a result of the pressure, the mooring lines began to part, and a "deadman," to which a mooring cable was attached, pulled out of the ground, the judge finding that it had not been properly constructed or inspected. Careening downstream, the Shiras struck another ship, the Tewksbury, which had been properly moored. The Tewksbury broke loose, and the two ships continued to move with the current. Several frantic telephone calls were made to have the bridge raised. However, because one crew had left early, and another was late arriving on duty, the bridge was just beginning to be raised when the ships crashed into its center. Ice jammed behind the wreckage which fell into the river; the river backed up; and property along the banks was flooded as far upstream as the Continental dock. On the claims for the property damage, the trial court held that Kinsman, Continental, and the City of Buffalo were liable for negligence. All three appealed.]

FRIENDLY, Circuit Judge.

   ....

...[A] ship insecurely moored in a fast flowing river is a known danger not only to herself but to the owners of all other ships and structures down-river and to persons upon them. No one would dream of saying that a shipowner who "knowingly and wilfully" failed to secure his ship at a pier on such a river "would not have threatened" persons and owners of property downstream in some manner. The shipowner and the wharfinger in this case having thus owed a duty of care to all within the reach of the ship's known destructive power, the impossibility of advance identification of the particular person who would be hurt is without legal consequence. [Citations.] Similarly the foreseeable consequences of the City's failure to raise the bridge were not limited to the Shiras and the Tewksbury. Collision plainly created a danger that the bridge towers might fall onto adjoining property, and the crash of two uncontrolled lake vessels, one 425 feet and the other 525 feet long, into a bridge, over a swift ice-ridden stream, with a channel only 177 feet wide, could well result in a partial damming that would flood property upstream....

   ....

...[A]ll the claimants here met the *Palsgraf* requirement of being persons to whom the actors owed a "duty of care".... But this does not dispose of the alternative argument that the manner in which several of the claimants were harmed particularly by flood damage was unforeseeable....

So far as concerns the City, the argument lacks factual support. Although the obvious risks from not raising the bridge were damage to itself and to the vessels, the danger of a fall of the bridge and of flooding would not have been unforeseeable under the circumstances to anyone who gave them thought. And the same can be said as to the failure of

Kinsman's shipkeeper to ready the anchors after the danger had become apparent. The exhibits indicate that the width of the channel between the Concrete Elevator and the bridge is at most points less than two hundred fifty feet. If the Shiras caught upon a dock or vessel moored along the shore, the current might well swing her bow across the channel so as to block the ice floes, as indeed could easily have occurred at the Standard Elevator dock where the stern of the Shiras struck the Tewksbury's bow. At this point the channel scarcely exceeds two hundred feet, and this was further narrowed by the presence of the Druckenmiller moored on the opposite bank. Had the Tewksbury's mooring held, it is thus by no means unlikely that these three ships would have dammed the river. Nor was it unforeseeable that the drawbridge would not be raised since, apart from any other reason, there was no assurance of timely warning. What may have been less foreseeable was that the Shiras would get that far down the river, but this is somewhat negated both by the known speed of the current when freshets developed and by the evidence that, on learning of the Shiras' departure, Continental's employees and those they informed foresaw precisely that.

Continental's position on the facts is stronger. It was indeed foreseeable that the improper construction and lack of inspection of the "deadman" might cause a ship to break loose and damage persons and property on or near the river—that was what made Continental's conduct negligent. With the aid of hindsight one can also say that a prudent man, carefully pondering the problem, would have realized that the danger of this would be greatest under such water conditions as developed during the night of January 21, 1959, and that if a vessel should break loose under those circumstances, events might transpire as they did. But such *post hoc* step by step analysis would render "foreseeable" almost anything that has in fact occurred; if the argument relied upon has legal validity, it ought not to be circumvented by characterizing as foreseeable what almost no one would in fact have foreseen at the time.

The effect of unforeseeability of damage upon liability for negligence has recently been considered by the Judicial Committee of the Privy Council, Overseas Tankship (U.K.) Ltd. v. Morts Dock & Engineering Co. (*The Wagon Mound [No. 1]*), [*supra*, p. 421]. The Committee there disapproved the proposition, thought to be supported by Re Polemis and Furness, Withy & Co. Ltd., [1921] 3 K.B. 560 (C.A.) "that unforeseeability is irrelevant if damage is 'direct.'" We have no difficulty with the result of *The Wagon Mound*, in view of the finding that the appellant had no reason to believe that the floating furnace oil would burn [citations]. On that view the decision simply applies the principle which excludes liability where the injury sprang from a hazard different from that which was improperly risked [citation]. Although some language in the judgment goes beyond this, we would find it difficult to understand why one who had failed to use the care required to protect others in the light of expectable forces should be exonerated when the very risks that rendered his conduct negligent produced other and more serious consequences to such persons than were fairly foreseeable when he fell short of what the law demanded. Foreseeability of danger is necessary to render conduct negligent; where as here the damage was caused by just those forces whose existence required the exercise of greater care than was taken—the current, the ice, and the physical mass of the Shiras, the incurring of consequences other and greater than foreseen does not make the conduct less culpable or provide a reasoned basis for insulation. [Citation.] The oft encountered argument that failure to limit liability to foreseeable consequences may subject the defendant to a loss wholly out of proportion to his fault seems scarcely consistent with the universally accepted rule that the defendant takes the plaintiff as he finds him and will be responsible for the full extent of the injury even though a latent susceptibility of the plaintiff renders this far more serious than could reasonably have been anticipated. [Citation.]

The weight of authority in this country rejects the limitation of damages to consequences foreseeable at the time of the negligent conduct when the consequences are "direct," and the damage, although other and greater than expectable, is of the same general sort that was risked. [Citations.] Other American courts, purporting to apply a test
of foreseeability to damages, extend that concept to such unforeseen lengths as to raise
serious doubt whether the concept is meaningful....

We see no reason why an actor engaging in conduct which entails a large risk of small
damage and a small risk of other and greater damage, of the same general sort, from the
same forces, and to the same class of persons, should be relieved of responsibility for the
latter simply because the chance of its occurrence, if viewed alone, may not have been
large enough to require the exercise of care. By hypothesis the risk of the lesser harm was
sufficient to render his disregard of it actionable; the existence of a less likely additional
risk that the very forces against whose action he was required to guard would produce
other and greater damage than could have been reasonably anticipated should inculpate
him further rather than limit his liability. This does not mean that the careless actor will
always be held for all damages for which the forces that he risked were a cause in fact.
Somewhere a point will be reached when courts will agree that the link has become too
tenuous—that what is claimed to be consequence is only fortuity. Thus, if the destruction of the Michigan Avenue Bridge had delayed the arrival of a doctor, with consequent
loss of a patient's life, few judges would impose liability on any of the parties here, although the agreement in result might not be paralleled by similar unanimity in reasoning;
perhaps in the long run one returns to Judge Andrews' statement in *Palsgraf*, 248 N.Y. at
354-355, 162 N.E. at 104 (dissenting opinion). "It is all a question of expediency,...of fair
judgment, always keeping in mind the fact that we endeavor to make a rule in each case
that will be practical and in keeping with the general understanding of mankind." It
would be pleasant if greater certainty were possible, [citation], but the many efforts that
have been made at defining the *locus* of the "uncertain and wavering line," 248 N.Y. at 354,
162 N.E. 99, are not very promising; what courts do in such cases makes better sense than
what they, or others, say. Where the line will be drawn will vary from age to age; as society
has come to rely increasingly on insurance and other methods of loss-sharing, the point
may lie further off than a century ago. Here it is surely more equitable that the losses from
the operators' negligent failure to raise the Michigan Avenue Bridge should be ratably
borne by Buffalo's taxpayers than left with the innocent victims of the flooding; yet the
mind is also repelled by a solution that would impose liability solely on the City and exonerate the persons whose negligent acts of commission and omission were the precipitating
force of the collision with the bridge and its sequelae. We go only so far as to hold that
where, as here, the damages resulted from the same physical forces whose existence required the exercise of greater care than was displayed and were of the same general sort
that was expectable, unforeseeability of the exact developments and of the extent of the
loss will not limit liability. Other fact situations can be dealt with when they arise.

[Affirmed as to liability, but modified as to damages.]

[The opinion of MOORE, J., concurring and dissenting, has been omitted.]

Note

1. *See also* Restatement, Third, of Torts: Liability for Physical Harm (Basic Principles) §29 Cmt. o (Tent. Draft No. 3, 2003) ("If the harm that occurs is within the scope
of the risk, the defendant is liable for all such harm caused, regardless of its extent").

("Kinsman No. 2") Petition of Kinsman Transit Co.
United States Court of Appeals for the Second Circuit
388 F.2d 821 (2d Cir. 1968)

[The background facts are the same as in *Kinsman No. 1*, 338 F.2d 708 (2d Cir. 1964), *supra*. The action was commenced by the owners of wheat stored aboard a ship berthed in the Buffalo harbor below the bridge, for transportation expenses incurred because the ship could not be moved to the shipper's grain elevators located above the bridge, and for storage costs and the purchase of replacement wheat.]

IRVING R. KAUFMAN, Circuit Judge.

. . . .

. . . [We] conclude that recovery was properly denied on the facts of this case because the injuries to [the shippers] were too "remote" or "indirect" a consequence of defendants' negligence.

Numerous principles have been suggested to determine the point at which a defendant should no longer be held legally responsible for damages caused "in fact" by his negligence. [Citations.] Such limiting principles must exist in any system of jurisprudence, for cause and effect succeed one another with the same certainty that night follows day and the consequences of the simplest act may be traced over an ever-widening canvas with the passage of time. In Anglo-American law, as Edgerton has noted, "except only the defendant's intention to produce a given result, no other consideration so affects our feeling that it is or is not just to hold him for the result so much as its foreseeability." [Citation.]

When the instant case was last here, we held—although without discussion of the [claims of these shippers]—that it was a foreseeable consequence of the negligence of the city of Buffalo and Kinsman Transit Company that the river would be dammed. It would seem to follow from this that it was foreseeable that transportation on the river would be disrupted and that some would incur expenses because of the need to find alternative routes of transportation or substitutes for goods delayed by the disaster. . . .

On the previous appeal we stated aptly: "somewhere a point will be reached when courts will agree that the result has become too tenuous—that what is claimed to be consequence is only fortuity." [Citation.] We believe that this point has been reached with [these] claims. . . . The instant claims occurred only because the downed bridge made it impossible to move traffic along the river. Under all the circumstances of this case, we hold that the connection between the defendants' negligence and the claimants' damages is too tenuous and remote to permit recovery. . . .

In the final analysis the circumlocution whether posed in terms of "foreseeability," "duty," "proximate cause," "remoteness," etc. seems unavoidable. . . . We return to Judge Andrews' frequently quoted statement in Palsgraf v. Long Island R.R. [*supra* at p. 238]: "It is all a question of expediency. . . of fair judgment, always keeping in mind the fact that we endeavor to make a rule in each case that will be practical and in keeping with the general understanding of mankind."

Affirmed.

Notes

1. *Grounds for Denying Recovery.* Perhaps the rule applied in *Kinsman No. 2* should be viewed a special case, rather than as an application of ordinary doctrines of proximate cause. Ignoring the highly unusual circumstance that led to the accident in the *Kinsman* cases, *Kinsman No. 2* seems a routine illustration of the principle that those whose accidents cause economic harms because of delays caused by traffic tie-ups and the like are not responsible for those particular harms. A speeding driver who causes a crash is liable to those injured in the crash, but not to someone who is prevented from getting to a key business meeting on time because the road was blocked for an hour. The idea may be that people who conduct their businesses in such a way that they become vulnerable to delays should bear the consequences of all delays, including those that happen to result from someone's negligent driving. This cannot be an application of foreseeability principles, as it is just as foreseeable that a bad accident will tie up traffic as that it may cause personal injuries and property damage. One possible reading of *Kinsman No. 2* is to focus on the nature of the harm, namely purely economic harm rather than property damage or personal injury. In general, in American tort law, there is no liability for negligent interference with economic interests. *See* Restatement, Second, of Torts §766C.

In Walker v. Bignell, 301 N.W.2d 447 (Wis. 1981), the Wisconsin Supreme Court, quoting an earlier case and discussing the issues of duty and proximate causation, suggested that recovery may be denied on any of several grounds:

> (1) The injury is too remote from the negligence; or (2) the injury is wholly out of proportion to the culpability of the negligent tort-feasor; or (3) in retrospect it appears too highly extraordinary that the negligence should have brought about the harm; or (4) because allowance of recovery would place too unreasonable a burden on the negligent tort-feasor; or (5) because allowance of recovery would be too likely to open the way for fraudulent claims; or (6) allowance of recovery would enter a field that had no sensible or just stopping point.

See also Judge Andrews' dissent in Palsgraf v. Long Island R.R. Co., 162 N.E. 99 (N.Y. 1928), *supra* at p. 240, setting forth seven somewhat-similar factors relevant to proximate causation.

2. *No-Duty Versus No-Proximate Causation.* A determination that liability should not attach may be expressed by stating that the defendant is under "no duty" to exercise care on behalf of the plaintiff or that the defendant's conduct, even if negligent, is not a "proximate cause" of the plaintiff's injuries. The difference may be important. The question of duty is always one for the court, and its decision on that issue carries with it precedential force and governs subsequent cases. The issue of proximate causation, in contrast, is normally a factual question for the jury, and carries no precedential weight, save for a limited range of cases in which the court holds that there was, or was not, proximate cause "as a matter of law."

C. Intervening and Superseding Causes

An intervening force (sometimes called intervening cause or intervening act) is a force which comes into play after the negligence of the defendant, and which participates along with the defendant's negligence in causing injury to the plaintiff.

A superseding cause is the type of intervening force which breaks the chain of proximate causation between the defendant's negligence and the plaintiff's harm and thus absolves the defendant of legal responsibility. Not all intervening forces qualify as superseding causes.

1. End Results within the Risk

Derdiarian v. Felix Contracting Corp.

Court of Appeals of New York
414 N.E.2d 666 (N.Y. 1981)

[Felix Contracting Corporation had excavated a work site in the street while installing an underground gas main. Plaintiff Derdiarian, an employee of a subcontractor, was injured while sealing a gas main at the site, and sued Felix.]

COOKE, Chief Judge.

....

On the afternoon of November 21, 1973, defendant James Dickens suffered an epileptic seizure and lost consciousness, allowing his vehicle to careen into the work site and strike plaintiff with such force as to throw him into the air. When plaintiff landed, he was splattered over his face, head and body with 400 degree boiling hot liquid enamel from a kettle struck by the automobile. The enamel was used in connection with sealing the gas main. Although plaintiff's body ignited into a fire ball, he miraculously survived the incident.

At trial, plaintiff's theory was that defendant Felix had negligently failed to take adequate measures to insure the safety of workers on the excavation site....

....

To support his claim of an unsafe work site, plaintiff called as a witness Lawrence Lawton, an expert in traffic safety. According to Lawton, the usual and accepted method of safeguarding the workers is to erect a barrier around the excavation. Such a barrier, consisting of a truck, a piece of heavy equipment or a pile of dirt, would keep a car out of the excavation and protect workers from oncoming traffic. The expert testified that the barrier should cover the entire width of the excavation. He also stated that there should have been two flagmen present, rather than one, and that warning signs should have been posted advising motorists that there was only one lane of traffic and that there was a flagman ahead.

....Felix now argues that plaintiff was injured in a freakish accident, brought about solely by defendant Dickens' negligence, and therefore there was no causal link, as a matter of law, between Felix' breach of duty and plaintiff's injuries.

The concept of proximate cause, or more appropriately legal cause, has proven to be an elusive one, incapable of being precisely defined to cover all situations. [Citations.] This is, in part, because the concept stems from policy considerations that serve to place manageable limits upon the liability that flows from negligent conduct....

Where the acts of a third person intervene between the defendant's conduct and the plaintiff's injury, the causal connection is not automatically severed. In such a case, liability turns upon whether the intervening act is a normal or foreseeable consequence of the situation created by the defendant's negligence. [Citations.] If the intervening act is extraordinary under the circumstances, not foreseeable in the normal course of events, or independent of or far removed from the defendant's conduct, it may well be a superseding act which breaks the causal nexus. [Citations.] Because questions concerning what is foreseeable and what is normal may be the subject of varying inferences, as is the question of negligence itself, these issues generally are for the fact finder to resolve.

....

...[I]n the present case, we cannot say as a matter of law that defendant Dickens' negligence was a superseding cause which interrupted the link between Felix' negligence and plaintiff's injuries. From the evidence in the record, the jury could have found that Felix negligently failed to safeguard the excavation site. A prime hazard associated with such dereliction is the possibility that a driver will negligently enter the work site and cause injury to a worker. That the driver was negligent, or even reckless, does not insulate Felix from liability. [Citations.] Nor is it decisive that the driver lost control of the vehicle through a negligent failure to take medication, rather than a driving mistake. [Citation.] The precise manner of the event need not be anticipated. The finder of fact could have concluded that the foreseeable, normal and natural result of the risk created by Felix was the injury of a worker by a car entering the improperly protected work area. An intervening act may not serve as a superseding cause, and relieve an actor of responsibility, where the risk of the intervening act occurring is the very same risk which renders the actor negligent.

In a similar vein, plaintiff's act of placing the kettle on the west side of the excavation does not, as a matter of law, absolve defendant Felix of responsibility. Serious injury, or even death, was a foreseeable consequence of a vehicle crashing through the work area. The injury could have occurred in numerous ways, ranging from a worker being directly struck by the car to the car hitting an object that injures the worker. Placement of the kettle, or any object in the work area, could affect how the accident occurs and the extent of injuries. That defendant could not anticipate the precise manner of the accident or the exact extent of injuries, however, does not preclude liability as a matter of law where the general risk and character of injuries are foreseeable.

....

...[T]he order of the Appellate Division should be affirmed, with costs.

Notes

1. *Independent Force.* Some courts talk in terms of the "independence" of the intervening cause and say that in order to be a superseding cause, "an intervening cause must operate independently of any other act." Wehner v. Weinstein, 444 S.E.2d 27, 33 (W. Va. 1994). *See* Martinez v. Martinez, 553 S.W.2d 211, 215 (Tex. Civ. App. 1977), in which the plaintiff was blinded in one eye by a "bottle rocket" ignited by the defendant. The court held that the malfunctioning of the rocket was not "a new and intervening cause" which precluded proof of proximate causation, for there was evidence to support a finding that the defendant "should have anticipated that danger to others was created by his act."

See also Kimble v. Mackintosh Hemphill Co., 59 A.2d 68 (Pa. 1948) (stating that "Even if, with an extraordinary wind or storm there is concurring negligence, the party chargeable with it will be relieved from liability if the wind or storm is so overwhelming in character that it would...[have] itself produced the injury complained of, independently of negligence if there were negligence").

2. Is *Derdiarian* consistent with the result-within-the-risk approach to proximate cause? What risks make it negligent to fail to erect a barrier around an excavation? Suppose that Derdiarian had been hurt not by a car that went out of control but by a stray bullet fired by a police officer at a fleeing suspect. If a barrier would have kept this shot from hitting Derdiarian, would Felix be liable?

3. *Problem: The Loose Lid.* Suppose an automobile lessor supplies a car with a defective latch on the trunk lid. While the car is in motion, the lid springs open. The lessee, upon stopping to make repairs, is injured by the negligent driving of a third person. Is the lessor liable for the injuries?

2.   Foreseeable Intervening Acts

The following case, though instructive, was erroneously decided. Wherein lies the error?

Huddleston v. City of Charleston
Appellate Court of Illinois
495 N.E.2d 82 (Ill. App. Ct. 1986)

Justice WOMBACHER delivered the Opinion of the Court:

Plaintiff Linda Huddleston, special administrator for the estate of Ernest Neal, Jr. appeals the grant...of directed verdicts in favor of all defendants. We affirm.

On May 14, 1982, plaintiff's decedent was a passenger on a motorcycle being driven by Robert Hildebrand, who is not a party to this action. Deputy William Powell of the Coles County Sheriff's Department, driving west on Route 316, observed the motorcycle traveling eastbound at 103 m.p.h. Powell turned in pursuit and informed the Sheriff's Department. Powell gave chase for over six miles, using his siren and his flashing lights. Powell eventually lost sight of the motorcycle, partially because of traffic.

Deputy Sheriff Donald Jenkins, a defendant here, was also on duty that day. He heard Powell's broadcast and prepared to intercept the motorcycle....He parked his car diagonally on Route 316, blocking parts of both lanes....

Charleston Police Officer Henry Pauls, another defendant, also heard the broadcast and proceeded to assist in the chase. He pulled his car onto the south shoulder of Route 316, blocking 2 to 3 feet of the eastbound lane. Pauls' car was 142 to 150 feet east of Jenkins'. When Pauls parked his car, he was informed by police radio that the motorcycle was one half mile from his location.

As the motorcycle came around the curve, it was traveling approximately 90 m.p.h. The motorcycle passed Jenkins' car, moved into the westbound lane as it neared Pauls' car, veered toward the north, and hit the soft shoulder after it passed Pauls' police car. Hildebrand lost control of the motorcycle, and plaintiff's decedent was thrown from the motorcycle and killed.

....

....The trial judge found that there was no evidence presented as to the proximate cause. Plaintiff's post trial motion was denied. She brings this appeal.

....

An intervening and efficient cause is a new and independent force which breaks the causal connection between the original wrong and the injury and it- self becomes the direct and immediate cause of the injury. [Citations.] The in- tervention of independent concurrent or intervening forces will not break the causal connection if the intervention of such forces was, itself, probable and foreseeable. [Citations.]

It is clear that the driving of Hildebrand constituted nothing less than gross negli- gence. He drove over 80 m.p.h. for almost the entire six miles. This was on a road that was under repair. Hildebrand also drove down the center line of this two lane road in order to pass eastbound traffic and to avoid being hit by oncoming west- bound traffic. Hildebrand was also not licensed to drive a motorcycle, nor was his motorcycle registered.

Hildebrand's reckless disregard for his own safety, the safety of his passenger, the safety of other drivers, his disregard for the various licensing rules, and his engaging in a high speed police chase, evidences such negligence that it is clear that his actions were the original wrong. We must thus examine defendant's intervening conduct to deter- mine if it broke the causal connection.

Holding

The test that should be applied in all cases determining the question of proximate cause is whether the first wrongdoer might have reasonably antici- pated the intervening cause as a natural and probable result of the first party's own negligence. [Citation.]

[Citation.]

Applying the above test, we find as a matter of law that Hildebrand should have reason- ably anticipated the actions of the defendant officers in creating a roadblock. In a high speed chase, it would be unreasonable to believe, given today's radio communications, that only one squad car would be used. This is especially so given Hildebrand's driving, his knowledge that he was being chased, and his partial success in eluding the first officer. A method to stop Hildebrand was needed. He did not respond to the siren and flashing lights. We find it highly improbable that he would have responded to an officer holding out his hand signaling "stop." Hildebrand should have anticipated some type of roadblock....

....

Plaintiff also argues that...the defendant officers negligently set up the roadblock, and the defendant County negligently instructed Deputy Jenkins in the proper proce- dures for roadblocks. The officers' conduct was reasonably foreseeable. As such, their conduct could not be the proximate cause of the accident. We will not examine issues relating to standard of care if plaintiff cannot show proximate cause. [Citations.]

....

...[T]he judgment of the circuit court...is hereby affirmed.

Notes

1. *Contrast Huddleston with* Travis v. City of Mesquite, 830 S.W.2d 94 (Tex. 1992) (holding that an action was stated against police officers on similar facts because they are not exempt from the usual rules of proximate causation).

2. *High-Speed Chases and the Constitution.* The Supreme Court has held that a po- lice department's engaging in an unreasonably dangerous high-speed chase does not vi-

olate the federal constitutional rights of those endangered by the activity; County of Sacramento v. Lewis, 523 U.S. 833 (1998). The victims' remedies in these cases are therefore state-law tort actions, not actions in federal courts for violations of their constitutional rights. In recent years lawyers have tried to turn a variety of tort cases into constitutional cases, with little success so far. For another example, see DeShaney v. Winnebago County Dep't of Social Services, 489 U.S. 189 (1989).

Why would a plaintiff's lawyer try to turn a run-of-the-mill tort action into a constitutional claim, especially when that claim is, as in *Lewis*, questionable? One possibility is that successful plaintiffs in constitutional-tort cases recover lawyers' fees as well as damages, though this explanation has been questioned; Stewart J. Schwab & Theodore Eisenberg, *Explaining Constitutional Tort Litigation: The Influence of the Attorney Fees Statute and the Government as Defendant*, 73 Cornell L. Rev. 719 (1988).

3. *"Normal" Consequences.* In the context of intervening cause, the requirement of foreseeability often means nothing more than that the intervening force was a "normal" consequence of the defendant's conduct—"normal" not in the sense that it was usual or customary, but in the sense that it was not bizarre or extraordinary. *See* Restatement, Second, of Torts §443 and Comment b.

4. *Negligence That Has "Run Its Course."* In some intervening-causation cases, courts have focused upon whether the risks created by the initial tortfeasor had "run their course" or "come to rest" prior to the intervening act. If so, the original negligence is not a proximate cause of the plaintiff's injuries.

Compare Union Pump Co. v. Allbritton, 898 S.W.2d 773 (Tex. 1995) (injuries were not proximately caused by the manufacturer of a pump which caught fire because at the time the plaintiff, who was still in firefighting gear, fell off a wet pipe rack, the fire had been extinguished and the forces generated by the fire had "come to rest"), *with* Henry v. Houston Lighting & Power Co., 934 S.W.2d 748 (Tex. Ct. App. 1996) (injury to rescuer was proximately caused by negligent damage to pipe because the dangerous gas leak had not been repaired when the plaintiff was injured while fleeing the scene when another worker yelled "fire").

In Marshall v. Nugent, 222 F.2d 604 (1st Cir. 1955), the plaintiff Marshall had been a passenger in a car belonging to Harriman, which was forced off the road by the negligent driving of defendant Socony's employee, Prince. While the others attempted to return the car to the road, plaintiff walked to the crest of the hill to warn oncoming traffic, and in the process was struck by a third vehicle driven by Nugent, which skidded out of control on the snow-covered pavement. In affirming a judgment against Socony, Chief Judge Magruder wrote:

> Plaintiff Marshall was a passenger in the oncoming Chevrolet car, and thus was one of the persons whose bodily safety was primarily endangered by the negligence of Prince, as might have been found by the jury, in "cutting the corner" with the Socony truck. . . . Though this particular act of negligence was over and done with when the truck pulled up alongside of the stalled Chevrolet without having actually collided with it, still the consequences of such past negligence were in the bosom of time, as yet unrevealed.

> If the Chevrolet had been pulled back onto the highway, and Harriman and Marshall, having got in it again, had resumed their journey and had had a collision with another car five miles down the road, in which Marshall suffered

bodily injuries,...the courts would no doubt conclude, "as a matter of law," that Prince's earlier negligence in cutting the corner was not the "proximate cause" of this later injury received by the plaintiff. That would be because the extra risks to which such negligence by Prince had subjected the passengers in the Chevrolet car were obviously entirely over; the situation had been stabilized and become normal, and, so far as one could foresee, whatever subsequent risks the Chevrolet might have to encounter in its resumed journey were simply the inseparable risks, no more and no less, that were incident to the Chevrolet's being out on the highway at all. But in the case at bar, the circumstances under which Marshall received the personal injuries complained of presented no such clear-cut situation.

...[T]he extra risks created by Prince's negligence were not all over at the moment the primary risk of collision between the truck and the Chevrolet was successfully surmounted....It is true, the Chevrolet car was not owned by the plaintiff Marshall, and no doubt, without violating any legal duty to Harriman, Marshall could have crawled up onto the snowbank at the side of the road out of harm's way and awaited there, passive and inert, until his journey was resumed. But the plaintiff, who as a passenger in the Chevrolet car had already been subjected to a collision risk by the negligent operation of the Socony truck, could reasonably be expected to get out onto the highway and lend a hand to his host in getting the Chevrolet started again.... Marshall was therefore certainly not an "officious intermeddler"....The injury Marshall received by being struck by the Nugent car was not remote, either in time or place, from the negligent conduct of defendant Socony's servant, and it occurred while the traffic mix-up occasioned by defendant's negligence was still persisting, not after the traffic flow had become normal again. In the circumstances presented we conclude that the district court committed no error in leaving the issue of proximate cause to the jury for determination.

5. *Efforts to Escape Injury.* A tortfeasor may be liable for injuries sustained by another in an effort to escape threatened harm, if such measures are based on a well-grounded belief that harm will otherwise occur. *See* Palmer v. Warren St. Ry. Co., 56 A. 49 (Pa. 1903) (leap from path of vehicle); Lehner v. Pittsburgh Rys. Co., 72 A. 525 (Pa. 1909) (jump from careening street car). Moreover, consistently with the standard of care for emergencies, a person who places another in a dangerous situation cannot escape responsibility for an injury merely because the victim, in fright, frenzy, or panic, adds to the danger by an act which in a later serene moment of contemplation may seem to have been unwise. *See* Stebner v. Y.M.C.A., 238 A.2d 19, 21 (Pa. 1968) (Musmanno, J.) (wrist cut on glass during attempt to escape from negligently locked steam room).

6. *Conditions versus Causes.* Courts have sometimes endeavored to draw a distinction between actionable "causes" and nonactionable "conditions." For example, in Lear Siegler, Inc. v. Perez, 819 S.W.2d 470, 472 (Tex. 1991), the court held that legal cause is not established if the defendant's conduct or product does no more than furnish the condition that makes the plaintiff's injury possible. *See also* Bonham v. Texas Dept. of Crim. Justice, 101 S.W.3d 153 (Tex. App. 2003) (holding that a correctional facility's layout was not a proximate cause of a guard's sexual assault of an inmate because "it was, at most, a condition that made the guard's intervening intentional act possible"). According to one commentator:

The "condition versus cause" doctrine is nothing more than the special application of the intervening cause rule when the passive negligence of one party results in an injury produced by the subsequent active negligence of another.

Terence B. Kelly, *Condition Versus Cause: A Doctrine Whose Time Has Passed?*, 84 Ill. Bar J. 138 (1996). The dichotomy's focus on passivity, rather than on foreseeability, has been controversial. "[T]he 'condition versus cause' doctrine has been criticized by scholars and rejected by most jurisdictions." *Id.*

7. *Unforeseeable Criminal or Intentionally Tortious Acts.* Unforeseen criminal or intentionally tortious conduct precludes a finding of proximate causation, even though the plaintiff's injuries are of a type that were, or could have been, anticipated. According to Comment b to §442B of the Restatement, Second, of Torts:

> The reason usually given by the courts is that in such a case the third person had deliberately assumed control of the situation, and all responsibility for the consequences of his act shifted to him.

From a different perspective, one might say that intentionally tortious or criminal conduct so differs in degree, if not in kind, from other types of intervening forces that it is unfair to hold the original actor responsible. Without this exception to the general rule, there would be a very substantial risk of imposing liability disproportionate to fault. *See generally* Restatement, Third, of Torts: Liability for Physical Harm (Basic Principles) §34 Cmt. e (Tent. Draft No. 3, 2003) (discussing unforeseeable, unusual, or highly culpable intervening acts).

In Gaines-Tabb v. ICI Explosive USA, Inc., 160 F.3d 613 (10th Cir. 1998), victims of a terrorist bombing brought a class action against the manufacturer of ammonium nitrate that was sold as fertilizer and was allegedly used to construct a bomb that destroyed a federal building in Oklahoma City. The court found that the terrorist's act was a superseding cause precluding negligence liability on part of the manufacturer.

See also Roach v. Dental Arts Lab., Inc., 79 S.W.3d 265 (Tex. App. 2002) (borrower's act of loaning out a borrowed car in exchange for crack cocaine was unforeseeable and therefore a superseding cause precluding liability against the owner of the car on a negligent entrustment theory).

8. *Foreseeable Criminal or Intentionally Tortious Acts.* A *foreseeable* criminal or intentionally tortious intervening act does not preclude a finding of proximate causation. *See* Herrera v. Quality Pontiac, 73 P.3d 181 (N.M. 2003) (jury could find that harm was proximately caused where "Defendant, leaving the car unlocked, unattended, and with the key in the ignition, could have reasonably foreseen...intervening theft of the vehicle, as well as...[thief's] subsequent criminal and negligent operation of it"); Haselhorst v. State, 485 N.W.2d 180 (Neb. 1992) (criminal acts of sexual abuse by a foster child were not a superseding cause because the likelihood of that behavior was what made the defendant's conduct negligent).

In Nixon v. Mr. Property Management Co., Inc., 690 S.W.2d 546 (Tex. 1985), a young girl was abducted, taken across the street into an abandoned, dilapidated apartment complex, and raped. In an action against the complex, based on its negligent failure to comply with a city ordinance regarding maintenance of buildings, the court held that the criminal acts of the abductor did not prevent a finding of proximate causation. During the prior two years, 34 crimes had been committed in the apartments. Although there had been no rapes, there had been crimes involving violent harm to persons, and thus it was foreseeable that another crime of violence might occur. It was important to the

Nixon court that there was evidence that the abductor proceeded directly to the vacant building. If the building had been used as a place for the crime only as a last resort after other plans had failed, the case might have turned out differently, for it would have been difficult to establish that the dilapidation of the vacant building (*i.e.*, the alleged negligence of the defendant) substantially increased the chance that someone would be raped.

9. *The "Prior Similar Incidents" Rule.* Some jurisdictions hold that, in the absence of prior similar incidents, an occupier of land is not bound to anticipate the criminal acts of third parties, especially if the assailant was a complete stranger to both the occupier and the victim and the criminal act resulting in the injury came about precipitately. *See* Rosensteil v. Lisdas, 456 P.2d 61 (Or. 1969); Shipes v. Piggly Wiggly St. Andrews, Inc., 238 S.E.2d 167 (S.C. 1977).

In criticizing the "prior similar incidents," the California Supreme Court said in Isaacs v. Huntington Mem. Hosp., 695 P.2d 653 (Cal. 1985):

> First, the rule leads to results which are contrary to public policy. The rule has the effect of discouraging landowners from taking adequate measures to protect premises which they know are dangerous. This result contravenes the policy of preventing future harm. Moreover, under the rule, the first victim always loses, while subsequent victims are permitted recovery. Such a result is not only unfair, but is inimical to the important policy of compensating injured parties....

> Second, a rule which limits evidence of foreseeability to prior similar criminal acts leads to arbitrary results and distinctions. Under this rule, there is uncertainty as to how "similar" the prior incidents must be to satisfy the rule. The rule raises a number of other troubling questions. For example, how close in time do the prior incidents have to be? How near in location must they be?....

> Third, the rule erroneously equates foreseeability of a particular act with previous occurrences of similar acts.... "The mere fact that a particular kind of an accident has not happened before does not...show that such accident is one which might not reasonably have been anticipated."....

> Finally, the "prior similar incidents" rule improperly removes too many cases from the jury's consideration. It is well established that foreseeability is ordinarily a question of fact.

See also Seibert v. Vic Regnier Builders, Inc., 856 P.2d 1332 (Kan. 1993) (endorsing "totality of the circumstances" rule rather than "prior similar incidents" rule). *But see* Ann M. v. Pacific Plaza Shopping Ctr., 863 P.2d 207 (Cal. 1993) (a landlord's duty to hire security guards can rarely, if ever, be proven in the absence of prior similar incidents of violent crime on the landlord's premises).

3. Special Applications of the Rules on Intervening and Superseding Causes

a. Rescuers

The rules governing intervening and superseding causes find frequent application in cases involving rescuers. To deal with these cases, a special body of rules — the "rescue doctrine" — has emerged.

Altamuro v. Milner Hotel, Inc.

United States District Court for the Eastern District of Pennsylvania
540 F. Supp. 870 (E.D. Pa. 1982)

McGLYNN, District Judge.

This is a diversity case brought by Doris E. Altamuro, administratrix of the estate of her husband, Joseph S. Altamuro, against the defendant, Milner Hotel, Inc. ("Hotel"), for damages for the death of her husband resulting from the inhalation of fumes and carbon monoxide while attempting to rescue residents of the Hotel during a three-alarm fire....

....

Plaintiff's case against the defendant, Milner Hotel, is based principally on the "rescue doctrine,"....

Perhaps the most quoted articulation of this doctrine was that by then New York Court of Appeals [Judge] Cardozo:

> Danger invites rescue. The cry of distress is the summons to relief. The law does not ignore these reactions of the mind in tracing conduct to its consequences. It recognizes them as normal. It places their effects within the range of the natural and probable. The wrong that imperils life is a wrong to the imperiled victim; it is a wrong also to his rescuer. The state that leaves an opening in a bridge is liable to the child that falls into the stream, but liable also to the parent who plunges to its aid.... The risk of rescue, if only it not be wanton, is born of the occasion. The emergency begets the man. The wrongdoer may not have foreseen the coming of the deliverer. He is accountable as if he had....

Wagner v. International Railway Co., 232 N.Y. 176, 180, 133 N.E. 437, 438 (1921). Twenty-one years earlier, the Pennsylvania Supreme Court stated:

> A rescuer—one who, from the most unselfish motives, prompted by the noblest impulses that can impel man to deeds of heroism, faces deadly peril— ought not to hear from the law words of condemnation of his bravery, because he rushed into danger, to snatch from it the life of a fellow creature imperiled by the negligence of another; but he should rather listen to words of approval, unless regretfully withheld on account of the unmistakable evidence of his rashness and imprudence.
>
> ....
>
> ....The law has so high a regard for human life, that it will not impute negligence to an effort to preserve it, unless made under such circumstances as to constitute rashness in the judgment of prudent persons....One who imperils his own life for the sake of rescuing another from imminent danger is not chargeable, as a matter of law, with contributory negligence; and, if the life of the rescued person was endangered by the defendant's negligence, the rescuer may recover for the injuries which he suffered from the defendant in consequence of his intervention.

Corbin v. City of Philadelphia, 195 Pa. 461, 468-472, 45 A. 1070, 1072-1074 (1900) (citations omitted). In applying the rescue doctrine, I must first determine the negligence *vel non* of the Milner Hotel.

....

Here, the fire at The Milner Hotel...originated in the defective television set in Room 706. The defective condition of the television was known to the Hotel through its employee, Jennings, who nevertheless left the set plugged in, unattended and with the power switch in the "on" position....[G]iven the substantial risk of fire..., Jennings' conduct clearly amounted to negligence and his negligence was a substantial factor in placing the lives of the Hotel guests in peril....Of course, Jennings' negligence is imputed to his employer under the doctrine of *respondeat superior*. [Citation.]

That a fire in a ten-story hotel presents an imminent danger to the residents cannot be gainsaid....

....

Defendant Hotel argues that since Altamuro's death occurred after the firemen ordered all civilians out of the Hotel and because it can be inferred from the evidence that the deceased heard the command by his conduct in immediately leaving the Hotel, then his final rescue effort was so unreasonable as to preclude recovery by his administratrix. The test...is whether the rescuer "acted with due regard for his own safety, or so rashly and imprudently" as to bar recovery. [Citation.] The court stated that "where another is in great and imminent danger, he who attempts a rescue may be warranted, by surrounding circumstances, in exposing his limbs or life to a very high degree of danger. In such a case, he should not be charged with the consequences of errors of judgments resulting from the excitement and confusion of the moment...." 195 Pa. at 472, 45 A. at 1074....Thus the standard of care for a rescuer is not to act rashly or imprudently.

In any event, Pennsylvania has abolished the defense of contributory negligence and has replaced it with comparative negligence....[T]he instant case clearly falls within the literal language of Act, which states that the Act is to be applied to "*all actions* brought to recover damages for negligence resulting in death or injury to person or property...." [Citation.] Courts in other jurisdictions have applied their comparative negligence schemes in similar circumstances, holding that if "the trier of fact finds that the rescue is unreasonable or unreasonably carried out the factfinder should then make a comparison of negligence between the rescuer and the one whose negligence created the situation to which the rescue was a response." [Citations.] While I believe Pennsylvania courts would reach a similar result, it is not necessary for me to decide the issue because I find that Altamuro did not act rashly, imprudently or so unreasonably as to constitute negligence on his part under the rescue doctrine.

There is no dispute that during the initial phase of the fire, Altamuro busied himself warning guests at the Hotel of the fire, and later he assisted Officer Markowski in helping people out of the building. The last time Altamuro was seen alive was when he left the Hotel after the firemen ordered all civilians out of the building. There was no evidence as to how Altamuro got back into the building. What prompted his return can only be surmised but, having been successful in two prior missions to the upper floors of the Hotel, I am not convinced that it was unreasonable for him to conclude that he could successfully complete another mission without unduly imperiling his own safety even though he disobeyed the order of the firemen by returning to the building.

....

....Plaintiff is entitled to judgment in her favor and against defendant The Milner Hotel, Inc. in the amount of $396,373.

....

Notes

1. *Policy Basis of the Rescue Doctrine.* The law encourages persons to render aid in emergencies. It does this by modifying the usual tort rules so that a rescuer will be less readily held liable for mistakes and more readily able to recover for injuries sustained in the rescue efforts. The rescue doctrine therefore attempts to balance the need to encourage rescue against the need to guard against creating unacceptable risks of further harm.

2. *Scope of the Rescue Doctrine.* Although rescue cases typically involve three different actors—the person who creates the peril, the endangered victim, and the rescuer—the doctrine applies just as readily to those situations where the victim has been endangered by personal lack of care and there is no third-party tortfeasor. *But see* Struempler v. Estate of Kloepping, 626 N.W.2d 564 (Neb. 2001) (refusing to apply the rescue doctrine to a two-party case where a neighbor injured her back while helping an elderly invalid who had fallen from his wheelchair).

The rescue doctrine is not a single rule, but rather a matrix of rules which encompass at least five distinct issues, two of which concern the ability of the victim to recover from the creator of the peril or the rescuer for injuries arising from the intervention, and three of which relate to the ability of the rescuer to recover from the creator of the peril or a third person for injuries sustained in the course of the rescue effort:

(a) *Superseding Cause.* Normal rescue efforts, even if negligent, do not break the chain of proximate causation. The initial tortfeasor can be liable to the victim for injuries arising from the rescuer's intervention. *See* Restatement, Third, of Torts: Liability for Physical Harm (Basic Principles) §35 (Tent. Draft No. 3, 2003) ("An actor whose tortious conduct is a factual cause of physical harm to another is subject to liability for any enhanced harm suffered due to the efforts of third persons to render aid reasonably required by the other person's injury, so long as the enhanced harm arises from a risk that inheres in the effort to render aid"). In contrast, abnormal rescue efforts which are so extraordinary as to be no longer a part of the risks inherent in the original wrongdoing are sufficient to constitute a superseding cause.

(b) *Rescuer's Liability to the Victim and Good Samaritan Laws.* A rescuer whose careless intervention injures the person in peril may be liable for the harm. The emergency nature of the circumstances will be taken into account in determining whether the rescuer was in fact negligent. *See* Restatement, Second, of Torts §296. Some Good Samaritan statutes limit the liability of rescuers to cases of aggravated misconduct. *See, e.g.,* Alaska Stat. §09.65.090(a) and (d) (Westlaw 2003) (permitting liability for gross negligence, recklessness, or intentional misconduct). The Texas statute, which has parallels in many other states, provides:

TEX. CIV. PRAC. & REM. CODE §74.151
(Westlaw 2004)

(a) A person who in good faith administers emergency care...is not liable in civil damages for an act performed during the emergency unless the act is wilfully or wantonly negligent.

(b) This section does not apply to care administered:

(1) for or in expectation of remuneration....or

(2) by a person who was at the scene of the emergency because he or a person he represents as an agent was soliciting business or seeking to perform a service for remuneration.

(c) *Injuries Sustained by Rescuers as a Result of Rescue Efforts.* As *Altamuro* indicates, one who places another in danger may also be held liable for injuries sustained by a rescuer. Thus, the duty of care owed by the tortfeasor to the victim extends to potential rescuers, and the policies underlying this rule normally cannot be frustrated by claims of lack of proximate causation. *See* Restatement, Third, of Torts: Liability for Physical Harm (Basic Principles) §32 (Tent. Draft No. 3, 2003) ("the scope of an actor's liability includes harm to a person resulting from that person's efforts to aid another or another's property imperiled by the actor's tortuous conduct, so long as the harm arises from a risk that inheres in the effort to provide aid"); Leaders v. Dreher, 169 N.W.2d 570 (Iowa 1969) (injuries which plaintiff sustained while chasing defendant's sow off plaintiff's land were proximately caused). *But see* Govich v. North American Sys., Inc., 814 P.2d 94 (N.M. 1991) (holding that whether negligence precipitating a rescue was a proximate cause of the rescuer's injuries would be established under the usual rules of proximate and intervening causation, not by reliance on the fiction that rescuers are always foreseeable); McCoy v. American Suzuki Motor Corp., 961 P.2d 952 (Wash. 1998) (a fact issue as to whether it was foreseeable that a rescuer would be injured by a hit-and-run driver after he stopped to aid passengers in an overturned vehicle precluded summary judgment in a products liability action against the manufacturer of the vehicle).

A victim who has placed only himself or herself in danger owes a similar duty of care to potential rescuers. *See* Provenzo v. Sam, 244 N.E.2d 26 (N.Y. 1968) (intoxicated motorist held liable to rescuer who was struck by car while attempting to come to his aid after an accident). "By extension, a person does not have a duty toward her potential rescuers when the person does not create the situation that necessitates the rescue." Allen v. Albright, 43 S.W.3d 643 (Tex. App. 2001) (holding that a woman whose house was fire bombed was not liable to a rescuer even if the woman's decision to remain in a burning house and run from her rescuers contributed to the rescuer's injury).

(d) *Defenses Based on the Rescuer's Conduct. Altamuro* held that "the standard of care for a rescuer is not to act rashly or imprudently." As these imprecise terms suggest, there has been some uncertainty about the circumstances under which an injured rescuer's failure to exercise care will preclude or reduce recovery of damages that would otherwise be available. Some courts appear to hold that a rescuer will be barred from recovery only by recklessness, while others indicate that contributory negligence is a defense. §472 of the Restatement, Second, of Torts endorses the latter view.

The widespread abrogation of the contributory-negligence doctrine and the consequent adoption of comparative negligence and comparative fault systems have lessened the stakes with respect to classification of disqualifying fault on the part of the rescuer. Still, states continue to differ in their approach to the question. *Compare* Rosell v. Central West Motor Stages, Inc., 89 S.W3d 643 (Tex. App. 2002) (rescue doctrine could not be used to relieve a rescuer of contributory negligence and, in light of adoption of comparative negligence and abolition of all-or-nothing doctrines, it was proper for the court to refuse to instruct the jury the conduct of a rescuer is not negligent unless the rescuer acts rashly or recklessly), *with* Ouellette v. Carde, 612 A.2d 687 (R.I. 1992) (rescue doctrine survives the adoption of comparative negligence and those principles apply only if the rescuer's actions were "rash and reckless," for the comparative negligence doctrine "does not fully protect the rescue doctrine's underlying policy of promoting rescue").

In many jurisdictions, the defense of assumption of the risk has been merged with the defense of contributory negligence under rules of comparative negligence or comparative fault. *See* Chapter 16. However, even traditional assumption of the risk was generally held to constitute no bar to recovery by an injured rescuer. *See* In re Consolidated Coal Co., 296 F. Supp. 837 (W.D. Pa. 1968) (plaintiff did not assume the risk of injury by jumping into turbulent waters to rescue bathers). The cases reasoned that there was no "voluntary" confrontation of the danger because the rescuer had been left no other reasonable course.

(e) *Injuries to Rescuers Arising from Another's Negligence during the Rescue.* Injuries to a rescuer may result not merely from the extant dangers to which the rescuer has chosen to respond or from the rescuer's failure to exercise care, but from the negligent conduct of another which occurs after the rescue has begun. For example, a rescuer standing in the road to warn oncoming motorists of a fallen tree may be struck by a negligently driven car. Under ordinary principles having nothing to do with the rescue doctrine, the negligent driver may be liable to the injured rescuer for the injuries arising from the crash, even though the creator of the peril may also be held responsible for those same injuries. *See* Hammonds v. Haven, 280 S.W.2d 814 (Mo. 1955). In these actions, however, the rescue doctrine is relevant to the issue of defenses if the doctrine is seen as enlarging the scope of actions which a rescuer may take without being barred from recovery by allegedly unreasonable conduct. *But see* Hutton v. Logan, 566 S.E.2d 782 (N.C. Ct. App. 2002) (holding that the rescue doctrine has no applicability to a third-party defendant who had nothing to do with the original peril).

3. *Requirements of the Rescue Doctrine.* In order for the rescue doctrine to apply, there must be (1) a risk of imminent peril to the person or (perhaps) property of another and (2) an act of intervention in response to the peril by the purported rescuer. In addition, if the action is against the creator of the peril, the plaintiff must (3) establish that the peril resulted from the creator's tortious conduct.

4. *Apparent Imminent Peril.* The standard for determining the imminence of the peril is an objective one. The peril need only be apparent, not actual. Thus, the Court of Appeals of New York has said:

> [T]o have been a reasonable course of conduct at the time, it is of no import that the danger was not as real as it appeared.... It is conceded that something more than a mere suspicion of danger to the life of another is requisite before the doctrine should be implemented.

Provenzo v. Sam, 244 N.E.2d 26 (N.Y. 1968).

The objective of the rescue doctrine is to dispel the would-be rescuer's doubts and tip the scales in favor of intervention when there is a need for prompt action. If harm is not imminent, the reason for the rule ceases, and the benefits of the doctrine will not be available. *See* Trapp v. Vess, 847 So. 2d 304 (Ala. 2002) (a passing motorist who helped to pull a car out of the ditch could not recover for his own injuries under the rescue doctrine because there was no imminent peril); Snellenberger v. Rodriguez, 711 S.W.2d 138 (Tex. Ct. App. 1986) (officer suffered heart attack while helping to control crowd after an auto accident); Miller v. Carter, 346 So. 2d 748 (La. Ct. App. 1977) (motorist, who could not see if anything was wrong, backed up on bridge to determine why another car had been parked with its trunk lid open); Hawkins v. Palmer, 188 P.2d 121 (Wash. 1947) (man injured while lifting victim onto stretcher a considerable length of time after victim was discovered); Stevenson v. Delahaye, 310 So. 2d 651 (La. Ct. App. 1975) (man injured while consoling accident victims after flares had been set and a crowd had gathered).

5. *Intervention versus Investigation.* In Barnes v. Geiger, 446 N.E.2d 78 (Mass. App. Ct. 1983), the court held that the rescue doctrine does not extend to those who are injured while running to the scene of an accident to see what happened. The court wrote:

> Danger invites rescue; accidents invite onlookers. It is not reasonable that the rescue doctrine be extended to all who run to the scene of a calamity to see what happened and on the chance that they might be able to do some good.

In Lambert v. Parrish, 492 N.E.2d 289, 291 (Ind. 1986), the rescue doctrine was held inapplicable to the claim of a husband who, after being told that his wife had been injured a block away, slipped on a patch of ice and sustained back injuries while running to the crash site. The court said:

> [A] rescuer must in fact attempt to rescue someone.... [Husband's] only attempt was to reach the scene of the accident. He exerted no physical activity to facilitate the rescue of his wife from the consequences of the allegedly tortious act.

See also Kinchen v. Missouri Pacific R. Co., 678 F.2d 619, 625 (5th Cir. 1982) (the rescue doctrine did not apply where the plaintiff was injured while crossing railroad tracks in an effort to investigate an alleged theft of his employer's equipment).

Until the would-be rescuer does something to distinguish himself from a curiosity-seeker, it is largely a matter of speculation whether assistance will be forthcoming. However, if there is good reason to believe that aid would have been given if the rescuer had reached the victim, the rescue doctrine should apply. Would it make sense to consider such factors as the "rescuer's" relationship to the victim, proximity to the peril, and contemporaneous observation of the developing crisis? In many states, those factors determine whether a tortfeasor will be held liable for negligently causing emotional distress to a "bystander." *See* Chapter 11.

6. *Responding to a Peril of One's Own Making.* Until recently, it was universally held that the benefits of the rescue doctrine could not be invoked by one whose negligence contributed to the creation of the peril. *See, e.g.,* Nelson v. Pendelton, 198 S.E.2d 593 (Va. 1973) (baby sitter failed to secure door to basement stairs and later fell while trying to rescue a small child who had started down the steps). With the advent of comparative negligence and comparative fault, the old rule, which was rooted in the absolute bar of contributory negligence, has come under scrutiny. There is now precedent indicating that the rescuer's contribution to the creation of the peril will not necessarily bar reliance on the rescue doctrine, but will be taken into account in determining whether compensation is available under comparative principles. *See* Zimny v. Cooper-Jarrett, Inc., 513 A.2d 1235 (Conn. App. Ct. 1986).

7. *Professional Rescuers.* Ordinarily, the rescue doctrine does not apply to firefighters and other professional rescuers. See the discussion of the "firefighter's rule" in Chapter 16.

8. *Problem: Triple Trouble.* Several years ago, a grocery store tabloid carried an article which read as follows:

> The 18th hole meant triple trouble for golfer Mike Megala. As he walked toward the tee at Seven Springs Golf Course in Pittsburgh, Pennsylvania, he was beaned by a stray ball.

Then an ambulance taking him to nearby McKeesport Hospital was hit by a car.

The car driver and two attendants were injured, so they joined Megala…in a second ambulance, but a few miles down the road, it was hit by another car.

In all, seven people required medical treatment.

Is the golfer liable? To whom? For what?

b. Victim Suicide

Involuntary Suicide. The most dramatic example of an intervening act by the victim of tortious conduct is suicide. The early American common law dealt with such matters sternly, perhaps because of the puritanical sense of self-determination and rugged individualism that contributed to the shaping of many areas of the law. *See* Roscoe Pound, The Spirit of the Common Law 36-37 (1912). If the victim retained any capacity to know what he or she was doing, recovery for the death was denied. As explained in McGuire v. Almy, 8 N.E.2d 760, 762 (Mass. 1937):

> [T]he rule was laid down that where an accident causes insanity, and while insane the victim takes his own life, the causal connection between the accident and the death is broken by the voluntary act of the insane person, if he entertains the purpose of causing his death and understands the physical effect of his acts, *even though his mind is so far impaired that he can no longer form sound judgments or weigh the reasons which should induce him to refrain from the act*; but the causal connection is not broken if the act results from uncontrollable impulse, delirium or frenzy without conscious volition.

(Emphasis added.) Cases still say that "[n]egligence actions for the suicide of another will generally not lie since the…suicide is considered a deliberate intervening act exonerating the defendant from legal responsibility." Krieg v. Massey, 781 P.2d 277 (Mont. 1989) (landlord not liable for failure to prevent suicide of tenant). "But employing superseding cause to bar a plaintiff's recovery based on the plaintiff's conduct is difficult to reconcile with modern notions of comparative responsibility." Restatement, Third, of Torts: Liability for Physical Harm (Basic Principles) §34 Cmt. c (Tent. Draft No. 3, 2003).

Irresistible Suicide. Some decisions take a less-stringent position. They hold that even if the victim was conscious, life may have been made so physically and mentally painful that the victim may have been deprived of any real choice in the matter. These courts recognize that beyond a certain point it is unrealistic to expect the ordinary person to be heroic. One jurisdiction has articulated its position in terms of a type of irresistible-impulse test. In Fuller v. Preis, 322 N.E.2d 263 (N.Y. 1974), head injuries suffered as a result of the defendant's negligence caused the decedent to become constantly depressed, physically unsteady, unable to continue his practice of surgery, and subject to epileptic seizures that became progressively more frequent and severe. The court held that although suicide notes demonstrated that the decedent, who took his own life, "obviously knew what he was doing and intended to do what he did," the pivotal issue was whether, because of mental derangement, he was "incapable of resisting the impulse to destroy himself." Finding that there was evidence to support a determination of irresistible impulse, the court affirmed the judgment for the decedent's estate.

Unforeseeable Suicide. If the risk of suicide is unforeseeable, it will almost certainly prevent a finding that the death was proximately caused by the negligence of another.

See Perez v. Lopez, 74 S.W.3d 60 (Tex. App. 2002) (child did not do or say anything that would have led locksmiths to believe that the child was suicidal when they removed a trigger lock on a rifle and returned the rifle to the child); Scoggins v. Wal-Mart Stores, Inc., 560 N.W.2d 564 (Iowa 1997) (a minor's suicide with ammunition he purchased from a store was a "superseding cause," as matter of law, that relieved store from liability for negligent sale of ammunition, because clerk had no reason to believe that the minor was suicidal).

Doctors and Suicide by their Patients. A risk unforeseeable to an ordinary person may be foreseeable to a person with expertise. Not surprisingly, medical professionals may fall within that category, in which case foreseeable suicide will not break the chain of proximate causation. *See* Bramlette v. Charter-Medical-Columbia, 393 S.E.2d 914 (S.C. 1990) (holding that a doctor's negligence was a proximate cause of a depressed patient's suicide because the doctor had a duty to prevent the suicide, which was foreseeable); McNamara v. Honeyman, 546 N.E.2d 139 (Mass. 1989) (similar); Tomfohr v. Mayo Found., 450 N.W.2d 121 (Minn. 1990) (similar).

Attorneys and Suicide by Clients. Courts may find that while some defendants should be liable for another's foreseeable suicide, others should not. In McPeake v. William T. Cannon, Esq., P.C., 553 A.2d 439 (Pa. Super. Ct. 1989), an attorney was allegedly negligent in representing a client who was charged with burglary, rape, indecent assault, and corrupting the morals of a minor. When a guilty verdict was returned at the trial, the client jumped from the fifth floor of the courthouse. The suicide was foreseeable because the client had threatened to kill himself if he was found guilty, but the attorney was not held liable for the death of the former client. The court reasoned that an attorney is not required to protect a client against suicidal tendencies because lawyers have no ability to identify or treat that kind of problem. Moreover, to impose a risk of liability would discourage attorneys from representing "a sizeable number of depressed or unstable criminal defendants," and would therefore defeat the important goal of making legal counsel available to those who need it. *See also* Cleveland v. Rotman, 297 F.3d 569 (7th Cir. 2002) (similar). These cases illustrate that just as there are limits on the role of foreseeability in proximate-causation analysis generally, an intervening action may still be considered a superseding cause even though it is foreseeable.

Suicide in Jail. Is it foreseeable that a prison inmate will commit suicide? Empirical evidence shows that suicide among inmates is many times more likely that among the general population, particularly during the early days of confinement. However, courts sometimes go to great lengths to hold that prisons are not liable for suicide committed by prisoners. *See* Jutzi-Johnson v. United States, 263 F.3d 753 (7th Cir. 2001) (holding that there was no evidence that a prisoner was a suicide risk merely because he displayed symptoms of a possible psychiatric disturbance that might be called "bizarre" behavior); Harvey v. Nichols, 581 S.E.2d 272 (Ga. Ct. App. 2003) (holding that an inmate's suicide was an unforeseen act that was not caused by failure of detention officers to conduct regular surveillance of his cell).

4. Relationship to Comparative Principles

Like many now-abrogated common-law principles—for example, the 100% bar of contributory negligence, the 100% bar of implied assumption of the risk, and the total exception to contributory negligence called "last clear chance" (see Chapter 16)—the rule on superseding causation is an all-or-nothing determination, which, if satisfied, totally overlooks the negligence of one of the parties to an accident. The question arises as to whether the adoption of comparative principles requires the abandonment of the superseding causation rules. "[T]he need for aggressive use of superseding cause to absolve a tortfeasor from liability has subsided in light of the modification of joint and several liability [see Chapter 17] and the trend [in a minority of states] toward permitting comparative responsibility to be apportioned among negligent and intentional tortfeasors." Restatement, Third, of Torts: Liability for Physical Harm (Basic Principles) §34 Cmt. c (Tent. Draft No. 3, 2003)

However, change is slow. In Exxon v. Sofec, Inc., 517 U.S. 830 (1996), the Supreme Court held that the proximate causation requirement, and related superseding-cause doctrine, are applicable in admiralty, notwithstanding the Court's adoption of the comparative-fault principle.

Control Techniques, Inc. v. Johnson

Supreme Court of Indiana
762 N.E.2d 104 (Ind. 2002)

BOEHM, Justice.

This case deals with the relationship between the Comparative Fault Act and the common law tort doctrine of superseding or intervening cause. The requirement of causation as an element of liability for a negligent act includes the requirement that the consequences be foreseeable. A superseding cause that forecloses liability of the original actor is, by definition, not reasonably foreseeable by a person standing in the shoes of that actor. Accordingly, the doctrine of superseding cause is simply an application of the larger concept of causation. Because an instruction on superseding cause would only further clarify proximate cause, the trial court's failure to give a separate jury instruction on superseding cause was not reversible error.

    ....

John Johnson sustained serious burns to his arms and face...while measuring the voltage of a circuit breaker at the LTV Steel Plant....A jury awarded him $2,000,000 and allocated eighty percent liability to Meade Electric Co., Inc., which installed the breaker, fifteen percent to Johnson, and five percent to Control Techniques, Inc. (Control), which designed and built the circuit breaker. Control was thus ordered to pay $100,000, representing its five percent of the total.

    ....Essentially, Control contended that Meade's method of installing the breaker was a superseding cause of the accident that foreclosed any liability Control may have had from the breaker's design and manufacture. The Court of Appeals concluded that the instructions on fault causation adequately covered the subject. [Citation.] We essentially agree....

    ....

The plaintiffs argue, and the Court of Appeals agreed, that the doctrine [of superseding causation] has been incorporated into Indiana's Comparative Fault Act, which allocates damages among the parties according to their respective negligence.[b] They argue that the need for the doctrine is obliterated because a defendant is liable only for

---

b. Not all states hold that the adoption of comparative fault abolishes joint and several liability. — Eds.

the amount of damages traceable to his or her conduct and that a simple jury instruction on proximate cause is sufficient....

The Comparative Fault Act...went into effect in 1985. [Citation.] Some version of comparative fault has been adopted by statute in well over half of the fifty states, and several other jurisdictions have adopted comparative fault principles by judicial decisions.

...[W]e conclude that the doctrines of causation and foreseeability impose the same limitations on liability as the "superseding cause" doctrine. Causation limits a negligent actor's liability to foreseeable consequences. A superseding cause is, by definition, one that is not reasonably foreseeable. As a result, the doctrine in today's world adds nothing to the requirement of foreseeability that is not already inherent in the requirement of causation.

....

...[I]n order to be liable for a plaintiff's injury, the harm must have been reasonably foreseeable by the defendant, in this case the original negligent actor. This is the case if there is only one negligent act or omission and it is equally true in the case of a negligent act or omission followed by a "superseding" act or omission. These propositions were valid both before and after the adoption of the Comparative Fault Act. [Citation.]

...[C]omparative fault abolished the harsh common law rule that a plaintiff contributorily negligent to any degree was barred from all recovery.... [T]he Act did not change the standard for imposing liability. Rather, it changed the apportionment of the damages flowing from that liability. Enactment of comparative fault preserved the requirement of proximate cause as a requirement of liability.

Under the Comparative Fault Act, liability is to be apportioned among persons whose fault caused or contributed to causing the loss in proportion to their percentages of "fault" as found by the jury. [Citation.] As a result, the jury is first required to decide whether an actor's negligence was a proximate cause of the plaintiff's injury. To say there is a "superseding cause" foreclosing one actor's liability is to say that the superseding event was not reasonably foreseeable to that actor. This is simply another way of saying, in comparative fault terms, that the original actor did not cause the harm and receives zero share of any liability.

Here, the trial court refused Control's jury instruction on intervening cause, which is drawn verbatim from Indiana Pattern Jury Instructions Civil 5.41 (2d ed. 2000):

> An intervening cause is an action by a third party or agency that breaks the causal connection between the defendant's alleged negligence and the plaintiff's injury. This intervening cause then becomes the direct cause of the injury.
>
> If you decide that the injury to the plaintiff would not have occurred without the action of the third party or agency, then the plaintiff cannot recover from the defendant.[3]
>
> However, if you find that the defendant acted negligently and could have reasonably foreseen the actions of the third party or agency, then the defendant can still be liable for the defendant's injuries.

....

---

3. Because we conclude that this instruction was properly refused for other reasons, we reserve judgment on the issue of whether the second paragraph is a correct statement of law. However, we note that this paragraph arguably injects an erroneous "but for" test into the causation analysis.

.... There is evidence in the record to support the giving of an instruction on superseding cause. However, to the extent that this instruction is a correct statement of the law, the substance of it was covered in the court's final instruction number 17: "'Proximate cause' is that cause which produces injury complained of and without which the result would not have occurred. That cause must lead in a natural and continuous sequence to the resulting injury."

Trial courts may properly elect to give an instruction on this doctrine if they conclude it would aid the jury in determining liability. However, this call is better left to the discretion of the trial courts, as they are in the best position to determine whether an instruction on superseding cause is useful. It was not error to instruct only on causation.

....

We conclude that the adoption of the Comparative Fault Act did not affect the doctrine of superseding cause, but on the facts presented here the trial court did not commit reversible error in refusing to instruct the jury on the doctrine.... The judgment of the trial court is affirmed.

SHEPARD, C.J., and SULLIVAN and RUCKER, JJ., concur.

DICKSON, J., dissents with separate opinion [which has been omitted].

Notes

1. *Abrogation of Superseding Causation. Compare Control Techniques with* Barry v. Quality Products, Inc., 820 A.2d 258 (Conn. 2003). In *Barry*, the court unanimously abandoned the superseding cause doctrine—at least in a limited range of cases:

> [T]he doctrine of superseding cause no longer serves a useful purpose in our jurisprudence when a defendant claims that a subsequent negligent act by a third party cuts off its own liability for the plaintiff's injuries. We conclude that under those circumstances, superseding cause instructions serve to complicate what is fundamentally a proximate cause analysis. Specifically, we conclude that, because our statutes allow for apportionment among negligent defendants; *see* General Statutes §52-572h; and because Connecticut is a comparative negligence jurisdiction; General Statutes §52-572o; the simpler and less confusing approach to cases, such as the present one, where the jury must determine which, among many, causes contributed to the plaintiffs' injury, is to couch the analysis in proximate cause rather than allowing the defendants to raise a defense of superseding cause.

> ....

> ...[I]t is inconsistent to conclude simultaneously that all negligent parties should pay in proportion to their fault, as §52-572h requires, but that one negligent party does not have to pay its share because its negligence was somehow "superseded" by a subsequent negligent act....

> Moreover, it is no longer necessary to utilize doctrines that aid fact finders in making policy decisions regarding how to assign liability among various defendants and the plaintiff because those decisions already are inherent in our modern scheme of comparative negligence and apportionment. Thus, under the approach we adopt herein, the question to be answered by the fact finder is whether the various actors' allegedly negligent conduct was a cause in fact and a proximate cause of the plaintiff's injury in light of all the relevant circum-

stances. If found to be both, each actor will be liable for his or her proportionate share of the plaintiff's damages.

The *Barry* decision is limited in scope. The court noted that:

> Our conclusion that the doctrine of superseding cause no longer serves a useful purpose is limited to the situation in cases, such as the one presently before us, wherein a defendant claims that its tortious conduct is superseded by a subsequent negligent act or there are multiple acts of negligence. Our conclusion does not necessarily affect those cases where the defendant claims that an unforeseeable intentional tort, force of nature, or criminal event supersedes its tortious conduct.

Id. at 267, n. 16.

2. *See generally* Michael D. Green, *The Unanticipated Ripples of Comparative Negligence: Superseding Cause in Products Liability and Beyond,* 53 S.C. L. Rev. 1103 (2002).

D. Shifting Responsibility

The doctrine of "shifting responsibility" is a conceptual counterpart to the doctrine of "intervening cause." It focuses on omissions, rather than actions, which occur subsequent to the initial tortfeasor's conduct, and it determines whether those omissions break the chain of proximate causation.

Normally, once the defendant has negligently created a risk of harm to the plaintiff, it is irrelevant that a third person fails to prevent the harm. The third party's omission is not ordinarily viewed as a superseding cause. *See* Restatement, Second, of Torts §452. Thus, *X*'s failure to stop and render aid to an auto accident victim will not limit a negligent hit-and-run driver's liability to the victim. This is true even if *X* could have acted without personal risk or inconvenience, and even if *X*'s conduct violates a statutory duty to stop and render aid. *Id.*, Illus. 4. *See also* Osborne v. U.S., 166 F. Supp. 2d 479 (S.D. W. Va. 2001) (the failure of an auto parts store employee to notify authorities of a driver's impaired condition and of a police officer to arrest the driver were not intervening causes that absolved a physician of liability relating to negligent prescription of addictive medications); NKC Hosps., Inc. v. Anthony, 849 S.W.2d 564 (Ky. Ct. App. 1993) (the negligence of a primary care physician in failing to diagnose a ruptured appendix after a patient was readmitted to the hospital was not a superseding cause relieving the hospital from liability for its negligence in connection with the patient's prior admission and discharge).

In extraordinary circumstances, however, the burden of preventing harm to the plaintiff may "shift" from an antecedent tortfeasor to a third person. In these cases, the third person's failure to prevent the harm is a superseding cause which relieves the original tortfeasor of liability for any harm incurred subsequent to the shifting of the responsibility. The following cases illustrate the principle and its applications.

Goar v. Village of Stephen

Supreme Court of Minnesota
196 N.W. 171 (Minn. 1923)

STONE, J.

Action for personal injuries caused by electrical burns, wherein plaintiff had a verdict against both defendants, the Village of Stephen, a municipal corporation, and Minnesota Electric Distributing Company....

Each defendant moved separately in the alternative for judgment notwithstanding the verdict or a new trial. The motions were denied upon condition that plaintiff consent to a reduction of the $12,500 verdict to $8,500. She so consented but both defendants have appealed.

While in her own home in Stephen, plaintiff was injured on August 10, 1922, by a high voltage current, for the escape of which, from its proper conductors into the Goar dwelling, one or both of the defendants is responsible. For convenience, we refer to the parties as plaintiff, the Village and the Company.

[The Company, as an independent contractor, undertook to reconstruct an electricity distribution system for the Village. The contract provided in part: "The contractor shall guarantee all apparatus and appliances...to be free from defects of any kind for a period of one year from date of acceptance, and shall make all repairs...free of charge." As part of the reconstruction, the company installed a transformer pole, with a complicated arrangement of wires, near plaintiff's home. Two of the wires were negligently placed too close together and, as a result of "the more or less constant but sometimes none too gentle breezes that play over the Red River Valley," the wires eventually wore through. Approximately seventeen and one-half months after completion of the reconstruction by the company, and the acceptance of the work by the Village, a 2,300 volt current was sent into the Goar residence, severely injuring the plaintiff. On appeal, the Minnesota Supreme Court found the evidence of the village's negligent failure to inspect and maintain adequate to support liability.]

....

It does not follow, however, that the Company is liable, even though it was negligent in the manner indicated. That initial negligence was followed by the serious and wrongful inaction of the Village. Before the verdict against the Company can be sustained, we must resolve against it the question as to whether the negligence of the Village was a new agency severing causal connection between the Company's negligence and plaintiff's hurt; or whether, on the other hand, such negligence simply concurred with that of the Company so as to charge both defendants.

....

In such a case, the contractor has a right to rely upon the owner's assuming, immediately upon his acceptance of the work, the duty of inspection and maintenance, which confessedly was not performed here. If it had been, the plaintiff would not have been injured for the fact that the original clearance was lessening and growing dangerous would have been discovered before the insulation was worn through. It took a year and a half of neglect, and the consequent freedom of the elements to work their will, before any injury resulted.

Not only was the Village in exclusive control, and, in consequence, the only agency upon which rested the burden of inspection and maintenance, but the Company was deprived, upon its delivery of the plant to the Village, of the opportunity and means of protecting the property from deterioration, and itself from resulting liability.

While the law of contract does not help us, the presence in the case of the contract is a fact to which proper reference may be made, and which may be given its appropriate place with the other facts. One of the facts established by the contract is that the Village, by the guaranty clause, assumed the duty, as between the two, of notifying the Company of any defect in the plant which it could be required to make good. As between the defendants, then, the Company has a much better standing than the Village. They could, by contract, adjust their reciprocal duties to suit themselves. The duty so allocated to the Village was not performed. As against the Company, it has no complaint, because, it must be assumed, had the decreasing clearance between the two wires been called to the Company's attention, the condition would have been rectified.

How serious and long continued must such obvious neglect be in order to become an independent cause of injury? Is there no limit of time beyond which a contractor will cease to be liable, with the owner, for an injury which could not have happened but for the negligence of the latter?

If the Company is liable in this case, there is no rule of law which would prevent the same result were the accident to occur ten years later....

Our examination of the problem and the authorities...leads us to the conclusion, and we so hold, as a matter of law, that, under the circumstances of this case, the negligence of the Village was an independent producing agency of such character, that it broke the causal connection between the negligence of the Company and plaintiff's injury, and thereby became the proximate cause of the latter.

....

...[W]here there has been such a lapse of time as we have here, and there is a duty, clear and affirmative, on the part of the purchaser, to inspect and maintain as against that sure deterioration which is bound to follow from ordinary use, and a complete failure of the performance of duty, but for which the accident could not have happened, such failure becomes the proximate and not merely a concurring cause.

....

On the appeal of the Village there must be an affirmance, and on that of the Company, a reversal....

So ordered.

Notes

1. *Contractual Shifting of Responsibility.* In Torres v. Texas Dept. of Transp., 88 S.W.3d 768 (Tex. App. 2002), an agreement appeared to pass to the city the obligation to maintain street lights installed by the city, relieving the state from maintenance duties. However, the evidence failed to show that the street light in question was subject to that agreement, and therefore it was improper to grant summary judgment to the state on the ground that it owed no duty to maintain the light.

2. *See* Kent v. Commonwealth, 771 N.E.2d 770 (Mass. 2002) (holding that a board's decision to parole an inmate pursuant to an INS deportation warrant shifted the duty to

prevent harm to the INS, which could lawfully be relied on to safely perform the responsibilities it had assumed, and that therefore the parole decision was not a proximate cause of injuries to a police officer who was shot by the released inmate eight years later); Braun v. New Hope Twp., 646 N.W.2d 737 (S.D. 2002) (holding that the lapse of time, the independent statutory duty of a township to erect guards and maintain appropriate signs warning of washouts, and the affirmative performance of that duty in an allegedly negligent manner were superseding causes that relieved farmers of their liability for breaking the warning sign, and thus liability for a motorist's injuries shifted to the township).

Balido v. Improved Machinery, Inc.

California Court of Appeal
105 Cal. Rptr. 890 (App. Ct. 1973)

[In 1965, Juana Balido's right hand was crushed when a plastic injection molding press closed as she was adjusting an insert. The press had been manufactured in 1951 by defendant Improved Machinery, Inc., sold to defendant Paper Mate in 1953, and resold by Paper Mate to Balido's employer, Olympic Plastics Company, in 1958. Following the sale of the machine to Paper Mate, Improved learned that operators of similar presses were being injured and that a California industrial safety order required that comprehensive safety devices be installed. Improved notified Olympic of this fact and offered to install the safety devices for $500. Olympic did not accept this offer. Had the safety mechanisms been installed, plaintiff would not have been injured. The trial court rendered a judgment in favor of all three defendants. Plaintiff appealed.]

FLEMING, Associate Justice.

....

Olympic. The trial court properly granted a nonsuit in favor of Olympic. The California Workmen's Compensation Law makes the right to recover workmen's compensation the exclusive remedy of an employee against his employer for personal injuries....

....

Paper Mate. The trial court likewise correctly entered judgment of nonsuit in favor of Paper Mate. The only evidence concerning Paper Mate, the prior owner of the press, showed it had been warned of the press's safety deficiencies and had installed a hydraulic safety limit switch before selling the press to Olympic.

....

Improved....

There remain for consideration the negligence, warranty, and strict liability counts against Improved. The theory of these counts is that Improved negligently and deficiently designed, manufactured, and sold a press whose inadequate safety devices made it unreasonably dangerous to operate. Although separate counts for negligence, warranty, and strict liability have been pleaded, we view them as stating a single cause of action, in that the complaint seeks damages for personal injuries caused by deficiencies in the design of a manufactured product....

....

....For purposes of nonsuit Improved conceded deficient design of the press. Moreover, from the first year of manufacture Improved had been put on notice that this model press might be causing injuries attributable to inadequate safety controls. The product was an item of capital equipment sold to a small market and a limited number of customers, and its continuing superintendence did not present the difficulties associated with such mass consumer products as automobiles, refrigerators, and washing machines. To the contrary, Improved kept track of this particular press at all times through repair and maintenance records. We cannot say this is one of those extreme cases that would require a trial court to rule as a matter of law that passage of time had broken the causation between deficiency and injury and terminated the manufacturer's liability. We conclude, therefore, that passage of time did not justify the nonsuit but rather presented a question for the trier of fact.

. . . . The second factor relied upon by the trial court to support the nonsuit was the series of warnings given the owner of the press by its manufacturer. The court viewed the owner's disregard of these warnings as a superseding cause of the injury that legally relieved Improved from liability for its antecedent deficient design. The court concluded that Olympic's continued use of the press after it had been warned of the press's safety deficiencies constituted a superseding cause of the injury that cut off Improved's liability for deficient design. . . . Olympic's knowing disregard of the industrial safety order, the trial court said, introduced an unforeseeable element that amounted to a legally superseding cause of the accident.

In this second aspect of the case the basic question is whether as a matter of law the obligation of the original wrongdoer has been replaced by that of a third-party wrongdoer. On the shift of responsibility from one wrongdoer to another, Restatement 2d Torts, §452(2), comment f, has this to say: "It is apparently impossible to state any comprehensive rule as to when such a decision [shift of duty] will be made. Various factors will enter into it. Among them are the degree of danger and the magnitude of the risk of harm, the character and position of the third person who is to take the responsibility, his knowledge of the danger and the likelihood that he will or will not exercise proper care, his relation to the plaintiff or to the defendant, the lapse of time, and perhaps other considerations. The most that can be stated here is that when, by reason of the interplay of such factors, the court finds that full responsibility for control of the situation and prevention of the threatened harm has passed to the third person, his failure to act is then a superseding cause, which will relieve the original actor of liability."

. . . .

The basic question is whether the court should pass on superseding cause as matter of law or the jury should do so as matter of fact. . . . [W]e conclude that the extent to which designers and manufacturers of dangerous machinery are required to anticipate safety neglect presents an issue of fact. . . .

. . . .

As a general proposition it can be said that a manufacturer who has taken all reasonable steps to correct its error may succeed in absolving itself from future liability. An example of the manufacturer's ability to terminate its liability for deficient design is found in the leading case of Ford Motor Co. v. Wagoner (1946), 183 Tenn. 392, 192 S.W.2d 840, 842, 164 A.L.R. 371, where an automobile manufacturer discovered a defect in a hood catch and distributed an auxiliary catch to its dealers with instructions to install the catch on defective automobiles at no cost. The owner of an automobile with the defective catch refused to have the auxiliary catch installed, and a subsequent owner of the vehicle was injured in an accident caused by the defect. The court held that the original owner's refusal to accept free repair of the defect amounted to an independent superseding cause of the accident that cut off the manufacturer's liability. (*See*, Rest. 2d Torts, §452, Illustration 10.) Similarly in Rekab, Inc. v. Frank Hrubetz & Company (1971) 261 Md. 141, 274 A.2d 107, the court found that a manufacturer of Ferris wheels did all that was reasonably possible to correct a deficiency in the design of one of his products when he notified the customer of the deficiency, shipped free replacement parts, and offered free installation of the new parts.

....

Improved relies heavily on E.I. Du Pont De Nemours & Co. v. Ladner (1954) 221 Miss. 378, 73 So. 2d 249, and Nishida v. E.I. Du Pont De Nemours & Co. (5th Cir. 1957) 245 F.2d 768, two cases involving a chemical manufacturer's warning to a processor of soybean meal that use of the manufacturer's chemical in the processing of soybean meal made the meal dangerous for cattle. In spite of this explicit warning the soybean processor continued to sell its existing stock of soybean meal as cattle feed, and dairy herds of purchasers of the cattle feed were injured. In both cases the court viewed the conduct of the soybean processor as a superseding cause of the injury to the dairy herds and absolved the chemical manufacturer from liability. We find these cases readily distinguishable from that bench in that the hazards they presented did not involve danger to human life and limb.

In the present case a trial of fact might have concluded that Improved had not done everything reasonably within its power to prevent injury to Balido. [Citation.] Improved warned Olympic on several occasions that the press did not meet California industrial safety standards, but offered to conform the press to those standards only at a cost of $500. *Quaere*: Should Improved have reasonably anticipated that a purchaser of a second-hand press would ignore its warnings of inadequate safety devices and refuse to spend money to purchase additional safety equipment? In our view this question remained open for decision by the trier of fact, and hence the judgment of nonsuit was improper.

The judgment for Olympic and Paper Mate is affirmed. The judgment for Improved is affirmed on the fourth cause of action for willful misconduct and reversed on the first, second, and third cause[s] of action.

....

ROTH, P.J., concurs.

COMPTON, Associate Justice (concurring and dissenting).

I concur in affirming the judgment of non-suit as to Paper Mate and Olympic. I would also affirm the judgment as to Improved.

....

Stultz v. Benson Lumber Co., 6 Cal.2d 688, 59 P.2d 100, appears to be controlling. There the defendant negligently furnished defective lumber to plaintiff's employer, who used it to build a scaffolding, knowing that the lumber was defective and unsafe for the use to which it was put. This conduct by the employer was held a superseding cause of plaintiff's injury, which terminated defendant's liability.

In our case, Improved furnished defectively designed machinery to the plaintiff's employer, who intentionally continued to use the machinery after having been directly advised that the machinery did not comply with the industrial safety law. The difference between scaffolding and machinery is not such as to alter the legal principle. Both scaffolding and machinery are dangerous to life and limb when they are defectively designed or constructed.

....

Applying this concept to the situation in which Improved found itself upon discovery of the defective design of its machine, compels the holding that its action in notifying Olympic terminated its liability. Olympic's conduct became the superseding cause of the injury, and the trial court correctly granted a nonsuit in favor of Improved.

Notes

1. *Shifting Responsibility: Relevant Factors.* Among the many factors relevant to the issue of whether there has been a shift of responsibility from the defendant to a third person are:

- the existence of a contract between the defendant and the third person purporting to define their obligations;
- the magnitude of the threatened harm;
- the character and position of third person and that party's ability to take remedial action;
- the likelihood that the third person will act to prevent that harm, including such considerations as expense, inconvenience, and exposure to, or immunity from, legal liability;
- the third person's relationship to the plaintiff; and
- the lapse of time.

See generally Restatement, Second, of Torts §452 and Comments.

See also Springmeyer v. Ford Motor Co., 71 Cal. Rptr. 2d 190 (Cal. Ct. App. 1998) (whether a prior owner's failure to replace a fan blade in response to a recall was a superseding cause of an accident was a question for the jury).

2. *Foreseeability of the Omission.* In addressing the subject of proximate causation, some decisions place great weight on whether a subsequent omission was foreseeable, For example, in Gracyalny v. Westhinghouse Elec. Corp., 723 F.2d 1311, 1323 (7th Cir. 1983), the court wrote:

> [W]here a plaintiff is injured by a manufacturer's product, the intervening negligence of the plaintiff's employer [the purchaser] does not insulate the manufacturer from liability unless the employer's acts or omissions are unforeseeable.

Because there was evidence that the employer was confused about which circuit breaker remedial parts were to be installed, the foreseeability of the lapse was a question of fact rendering summary judgment inappropriate.

See also National Health Labs. v. Ahmadi, 596 A.2d 555 (D.C. 1991) (negligent failure to discover a medical test error was not necessarily unforeseeable or extraordinary, and therefore it was not a superseding cause as a matter of law.

3. *Shifting Responsibility and Duty.* It is possible to talk about shifting responsibility in terms of duty, rather than proximate causation. For example, in First Assembly of God v. Texas Utilities, 52 S.W.3d 482, 492 (Tex. App. 2001), the court discussed a statutory tariff which provided that "the Customer assumes full responsibility for electric energy at the point of delivery." The court held that the utility did not have a duty to check equipment "downstream" to insure that it was installed and maintained properly.

4. Does the doctrine of shifting responsibility survive the adoption of comparative negligence or comparative fault?

Chapter 9

Limited Duty:
Failure to Act

In many negligence cases, the element of "duty" poses no problem. Under the rule of Palsgraf v. Long Island Railroad Co., 162 N.E. 99 (N.Y. 1928), *supra* at 238, if there is a "risk reasonably to be perceived," there is a "duty to be obeyed." Thus, in the usual case, a person conducting an activity plainly has a duty to use reasonable care to prevent it from causing foreseeable harm.

However, in a few areas, the law takes a different approach. As discussed in this chapter, the law of torts does not, in general, require someone to protect others against injuries inflicted by third parties, or to aid them when they are in need. For example, one may spend the evenings at home, without risk of legal liability, even though there is a dangerous intersection nearby, and even though one might be able to prevent harm by going to that intersection and helping pedestrians cross the street. Furthermore, the common law has traditionally said that possessors of land owe trespassers and even social guests only limited duties of care; this subject will be explored in Chapter 10. Finally, a variety of cases present serious problems of allocating responsibility, of distinguishing meritorious claims from fraudulent ones, or of determining appropriate measures of recovery even if a wrong has plainly been done. One response to those problems is to adopt rules to the effect that defendants are not liable for certain kinds of harms that they have negligently caused. These rules are sometimes (but not always) called "limited duty" or "no-duty" rules. Chapters 11, 12, and 13 will examine three of these situations: negligent infliction of emotional distress, negligence involving alcohol-related injuries, and negligence relating to conception, pregnancy, birth, and adoption.

A. The Traditional Rule of No Liability for Nonfeasance

In general, there is no duty to render assistance to another who is in peril, no matter how easily aid might be furnished, and regardless of whether the failure to act is inadvertent or intentional. This was the law a hundred years ago, and, in the absence of an exception, it is still the rule today.

Johnson v. Minnesota

Supreme Court of Minnesota
553 N.W.2d 40 (Minn. 1996)

ANDERSON, Justice.

....

.... At approximately 12:00 p.m. on Independence Day... 1991, Scott Edward Stewart was released from Minnesota's maximum security prison in St. Cloud and told to report to 180 Degrees, a halfway house located in Minneapolis, Minnesota. Stewart's parole agreement stated that he was to report directly to 180 Degrees and to telephone his supervising agent within 24 hours of his release. Stewart did neither; instead, he engaged in an eight-day crime spree.

During this crime spree, Stewart abducted [Melissa] Johnson at gunpoint... [on] July 9. He forced Johnson into his car and drove her to the outskirts of the city, where he raped [and murdered her]....

[Johnson's family sued the state, the county, and the halfway house. The district court granted the defendants' motions to dismiss, and the court of appeals reversed in relevant part. The opinion of the court of appeals stated that "Agents at the St. Cloud facility did not contact 180 Degrees on July 5 to find out whether Stewart had arrived. Nor did 180 Degrees contact the corrections facility to find out why Stewart had not arrived." (536 N.W.2d at 331.)]

....

The state and the county, along with 180 Degrees,... argue that they had no duty to control Stewart and determine his whereabouts when Stewart failed to arrive at 180 Degrees or to telephone Lamb [Stewart's supervising agent] as instructed... Because the state and county are protected by statutory immunity and their agents by official immunity, we need not reach the issue of whether they had a duty to control Stewart or to immediately issue a warrant. Our focus is limited to 180 Degree's duty to control Stewart.

....

The fact that an actor realizes or should realize that action on his part is necessary for another's aid or protection does not of itself impose upon the actor a duty to take such action. Restatement (Second) of Torts §314 (1965) (Restatement). Under fundamental principles of tort law,

> There is no duty so to control the conduct of a third person as to prevent him from causing physical harm to another unless
>
> (a) a special relation exists between the actor and the third person which imposes a *duty* upon the actor *to control* the third person's conduct, or
>
> (b) a special relation exists between the actor and the other which gives rise to the other a right to protection.

Restatement §315 (emphasis added).... [S]uch "special relationships exist between parents and children, masters and servants, possessors of land and licensees, common carriers and their customers, or people who have *custody* of a person with dangerous propensities." 289 N.W.2d 479, 483-84 (Minn.1979) (emphasis added).

Restatement §319 also states:

> One who *takes charge* of a third person whom he knows or should know to
> be likely to cause bodily harm to others if not controlled is under a duty to ex-
> ercise reasonable care to control the third person to prevent him from doing
> such harm.

(Emphasis added.)

180 Degrees argues that it had no legal "duty to control" Stewart under Restatement
§315, that it did not have "custody" of Stewart..., and that it did not "take charge" of
him pursuant to Restatement §319....

....

We find no basis in the case law nor in this court's treatment of relevant provisions of
the Restatement to impose a legal duty on 180 Degrees under the facts and circumstances
of this case.... 180 Degrees neither had custody of Stewart nor had entered into a special
relationship with him due to his failure to arrive at the halfway house.... 180 Degrees had
no "ability to control" Stewart due to his failure to arrive at the halfway house. [Citation.]
Stewart's release from prison without supervision was an initial and virtually irremedia-
ble relinquishing of control such that 180 Degrees cannot be held to have a legal duty to
"reassert" control over him. We reverse the court of appeals and hold that, under the facts
and circumstances of this case, 180 Degrees had no legal duty to control Stewart.

....

Reversed.

Notes

1. *General Rule: No Duty to Act. See* Remsburg v. Montgomery, 831 A.2d 18 (Md.
2003) (a hunting party leader had no duty protect a property owner from actions of his
adult son, a hunting party member, who accidentally shot and injured the property
owner); Entex v. Gonzalez, 94 S.W.3d 1 (Tex. App. 2002) (a utility had no duty to inspect a customer's wiring or appliances before supplying natural gas); Murillo v. Sey-
mour Ambulance Assn., 823 A.2d 1202 (Conn. 2003) (a hospital had no duty to prevent
the plaintiff from fainting and breaking her jaw when she said she was about to pass out
while watching a needle being inserted into her sister's arm); A.H. Belo Corp. v. Corco-
ran, 52 S.W.3d 375 (Tex. App. 2001) (a television station and reporter who interviewed
a mother and her abducted child in a secret location owed no duty to the father to reveal the location of the child); San Benito Bank & Trust Co. v. Landair Travels, 31
S.W.3d 312 (Tex. App. 2000) (an employer that was the victim of embezzlement by an
employee owed no duty to the employee's next employer to report the crime to authorities or to warn the next employer about it); Rhodes v. Illinois Cent. Gulf R.R., 665
N.E.2d 1260 (Ill. 1996) (a railroad had no duty to aid an injured person discovered in
an unmanned station); Fiala v. Rains, 519 N.W.2d 386 (Iowa 1994) (a woman was not
liable for failing to warn a friend of her disgruntled boyfriend's violent propensities);
Cramer v. Mengerhausen, 550 P.2d 740 (Or. 1976) (a customer had no duty to warn
auto mechanic that a car was about to slip off a jack); Bishop v. City of Chicago, 257
N.E.2d 152 (Ill. App. Ct. 1970) (an airport operator had no duty to dispatch rescuers to
aid survivors of a plane which crashed into water short of the runway).

The Restatement illustrates the rule with this example:

> A sees B, a blind man, about to step into the street in front of an approach-
> ing automobile. A could prevent B from so doing by a word or touch without

delaying his own progress. *A* does not do so, and *B* is run over and hurt. *A* is under no duty to prevent *B* from stepping into the street, and is not liable to *B*.

Restatement, Second of Torts, §314 Illus. 1.

Wisconsin, which does not employ no-duty rules, reaches the same result on public policy grounds. *See* Rockweit v. Senecal, 541 N.W.2d 742 (Wis. 1995) (family friend was not liable for campfire accident that injured child).

2. *Policy.* The Restatement explains the no-duty-to-act rule on the historical ground that the courts were once so busy handling cases of active misconduct that they could not be troubled to hold nonfeasance actionable, and it points out that many inroads on the rule have been made in recent years. While there may be some truth to this explanation, it is worth noting that, even today, no one has ever advocated applying the usual "reasonableness" test to *all* cases of nonfeasance. Many writers have suggested that someone who could *easily* prevent serious harm at little cost should be liable for failure to do so, so that *A*, in the Restatement's example, would be liable to *B*. But few writers have proposed that every pedestrian hit by a car should be able to recover from anyone who might "reasonably" have foreseen and prevented the accident. For example, suppose that as *B* was about to step into the street *C* was walking by. Preoccupied with business matters, *C* did not notice *B*'s danger, and so did nothing. However "unreasonable" *C*'s inattentiveness, few people think that *B* should be able to get a verdict against *C*. (Compare a case in which *C*'s inattentiveness while driving caused *C*'s car to hit *B*: that is a routine negligence case.)

Complete abrogation of the no-duty rule would often subject dozens, or even hundreds, of persons near an accident to the risk of a lawsuit. It is worth remembering that "reasonableness" is much easier to assume in hypothetical cases than to determine in the real world. Limiting liability to those actually involved in an accident keeps many non-meritorious cases out of court, though perhaps at the cost of barring some good cases as well.

3. *Misfeasance and Nonfeasance.* There is no liability for "nonfeasance," absent special circumstances. In contrast, "misfeasance" readily gives rise to liability. Defining the distinction between "misfeasance" (such as recklessly driving a car) and "nonfeasance" (such as failing to prevent a blind person from stepping into the street) is extraordinarily difficult. Fortunately, recognizing and applying the distinction seldom presents serious problems. For instance, suppose that *A*, driving along with the car's cruise control set at 45 miles an hour, does nothing upon seeing *B* asleep in the road ahead and so runs over *B*. An argument that *B* should not recover because *A*'s negligence consisted entirely of the "nonfeasances" of failing to step on the brakes and failing to turn the steering wheel would be ludicrous, though ingenious. *See* Restatement, Third, of Torts: Liability for Physical Harm (Basic Principles) §37 (Preliminary Draft No. 4, 2003) (the relevant question is "whether the actor's *entire conduct* created a risk of physical harm").

Some cases do present difficult issues, however. For example, suppose that the operator of a parking garage knows that drivers sometimes speed out of the garage after paying, endangering pedestrians. The operator could reduce this danger inexpensively by installing a barrier like those at railroad crossings to force drivers to stop at the edge of the sidewalk. If it does nothing, and a pedestrian is hurt, has the operator (1) designed and operated a dangerous parking facility (misfeasance) or (2) failed to protect pedestrians against dangerous drivers (nonfeasance)? For one answer, see Pulka v. Edelman, 358 N.E.2d 1019 (N.Y. 1976), holding that the garage had no duty to protect pedestrians against this kind of harm. The court viewed the case as raising the issue of whether the garage had a duty to control the conduct of its customers after they left its premises. How could an attorney frame the issue in representing the plaintiff?

4. *Compare Johnson with* Dudley v. Offender Aid & Restoration, 401 S.E.2d 878 (Va. 1991) (halfway house had a duty to exercise reasonable care to control a felon so as to prevent him from causing harm to persons foreseeably accessible to the felon during his hours at large).

B. Qualifications and Exceptions

1. Duties Based on the Defendant's Relationship to the Victim or the Injurer

A key fact in most of the no-duty cases described above is that the victim, the defendant, and the person who caused the harm were strangers. The law has long held that some persons have duties either to protect certain others from being harmed or to prevent persons in their custody from causing harm. The captain of a ship cannot sail on, ignoring the cries of a passenger who, through no fault of the captain's, has fallen overboard. A father who knows that his child likes to stab smaller children cannot sit idly by while the child invites a playmate to come in and see some hunting knives. This section looks at cases in which the no-duty rule may be overridden because of the defendant's relationship with the victim or with the person who caused the harm.

De Vera v. Long Beach Public Transportation Co.

Court of Appeal of California
225 Cal. Rptr. 789 (Ct. App. 1986)

DANIELSON, Associate Justice.

Defendant Long Beach Public Transportation Company appeals from a judgment awarding plaintiff Federico De Vera $17,500 as damages for injuries he sustained when another motor vehicle ran into the rear end of defendant's bus. The fundamental question presented by defendant's appeal is whether a common carrier owes a duty to its passengers to investigate an accident caused by a third party for the purpose of facilitating a claim by the passenger against the third party tortfeasor. We hold that it does, and affirm the judgment.

....

Plaintiff sustained injuries when a bus owned and operated by defendant was rear-ended by a vehicle owned and operated by a third party. He filed a complaint alleging... that defendant, through its employees, "negligently lost or failed to obtain the identity of the motor vehicle and its driver... [involved in the collision," and that as] a proximate result... plaintiff has been deprived of pursuing a claim against the driver of the other motor vehicle and other related parties....

....

....The carrier's duty is described in Civil Code §2100, which provides: "A carrier of persons for reward must use the utmost care and diligence for their safe carriage, must provide everything necessary for that purpose, and must exercise to that end a reasonable degree of skill." This standard is set forth in ... [the instruction] which was given to the jury.

....

.... We find no case, and plaintiff cites none, in which a carrier's duty has been held to extend beyond the duty to protect its passengers from physical harm and to see that they are cared for if injured. According to the Restatement, "A common carrier is under a duty to its passengers to take reasonable action ... (a) to protect them against unreasonable risk of physical harm, and ... (b) to give them first aid after it knows or has reason to know that they are ill or injured, and to care for them until they can be cared for by others." (Rest. 2d Torts, §314A.)....

In the case at bench, we are asked to recognize an expanded duty on the part of the carrier to assist its passengers in pursuing civil litigation against third parties who cause them harm. The term "duty" is "only an expression of the sum total of those considerations of policy which lead the law to say that the particular plaintiff is entitled to protection." [Citations.] "The existence of 'duty' is a question of law. [Citation.] '[L]egal duties are not discoverable facts of nature, but merely conclusory expressions that, in cases of a particular type, liability should be imposed for damage done.' [Citation.]"....

"[I]n considering the existence of 'duty' in a given case several factors require consideration including 'the foreseeability of harm to the plaintiff, the degree of certainty that the plaintiff suffered injury, the closeness of the connection between the defendant's conduct and the injury suffered, the moral blame attached to the defendant's conduct, the policy of preventing future harm, the extent of the burden to the defendant and consequences to the community of imposing a duty to exercise care with resulting liability for breach, and the availability, costs, and prevalence of insurance for the risk involved. [Citations.]' [Citations.] When public agencies are involved, additional elements include 'the extent of [the agency's] powers, the role imposed upon it by law and the limitations imposed upon it by budget;....' [Citations.]"

When we apply the relevant considerations of policy we find that they militate strongly in favor of a finding of duty. A carrier can readily foresee the possibility of harm to its passengers by reason of its failure to collect and preserve information concerning a motorist involved in an accident with the carrier's vehicle, in that the passengers could be foreclosed, as was plaintiff, from recovery against such a motorist for any injuries they sustained in the accident. The duty to collect and preserve accident-related information imposes no undue burden upon a carrier, which would presumably, as did defendant, have a procedure in place for the reporting of accidents by its drivers, if only for its own benefit.

Conversely, absent such a duty on the part of the carrier, each passenger would be obliged to alight from the carrier's vehicle and seek the requisite information for himself or herself. Such a practice would be unwieldy, unduly time-consuming, and possibly even dangerous. It would also require the cooperation of the carrier's driver in waiting for passengers to collect the information, a process that could seriously interfere with the carrier's schedule.

We hold that, following an accident between its vehicle and that of another, a common carrier has a duty to collect and preserve information concerning the other vehicle and its driver for use by the carrier's passengers in future civil litigation.

....

The judgment and order are affirmed.

Notes

1. *Invitors.* A duty of care has frequently been found to exist where the plaintiff was a guest on the defendant's land at the time the need for assistance arose. *See, e.g.,* L.S. Ayres & Co. v. Hicks, 40 N.E.2d 334, *reh'g denied,* 41 N.E.2d 195 (Ind. 1942) (child injured on department store escalator); *see also* Depue v. Flateau, 111 N.W. 1 (Minn. 1907) (traveling salesman fell ill after joining family for dinner).

However, there are limits to how much an invitor must do on behalf of an invitee. *See* Atcovitz v. Gulph Mills Tennis Club, Inc., 812 A.2d 1218 (Pa. 2002) (tennis club did not owe a duty to acquire and maintain an automated external defibrillator on its premises for emergency use to mitigate injuries from heart attacks); Lee v. GNLV Corp., 22 P.3d 209 (Nev. 2001) (holding that a restaurant owed a duty to a choking invitee to act reasonably, but had no duty to administer the Heimlich maneuver).

To the extent that the duty obliges a possessor to protect invitees from the criminal acts of third parties, the duty is derived from the principle that a party who has the "'power of control or expulsion' is in the best position to protect against the harm." Exxon Corp. v. Tidwell, 867 S.W.2d 19, 20 (Tex. 1993). *Cf.* Butcher v. Scott, 906 S.W.2d 14 (Tex. 1995) (beneficial owner of property was not in control of house when child was sexually abused, so owed no duty to child).

In Graves v. Warner Bros., 656 N.W.2d 195, 202-03 (Mich. Ct. App. 2002), the estate of a homicide victim filed a wrongful death suit against the producers of a television talk show following the victim's appearance on the show and subsequent murder by another guest. The other guest had allegedly been "ambushed" by the producers, who intentionally withheld information that the true topic of the show was same-sex crushes. The victim revealed his crush on the other guest on the show, and though the two departed from the show on amicable terms, three days later the other guest murdered the victim. The court held that the only special relationship that ever existed between defendants and the victim was that of business invitor and invitee. Any duty that the defendants owed to protect the victim from harm ended three days prior to the murder, and therefore a $29 million verdict in the wrongful death action was reversed. (An earlier decision by the state high court, MacDonald v. PKY, Inc., 628 N.W.2d 33 (Mich. 2001), had dramatically limited the duty of businesses to invitees by holding that there is no duty to anticipate or prevent criminal acts by third parties and that the only duty is to respond to a situation occurring on the premises by expediting involvement of the police. In *MacDonald,* the plaintiff had alleged that the defendant was negligent in failing to provide security at a concert, screen the crowd for intoxicated individuals, or stop the performance when it should have known that continuing the performance would incite the crowd.)

2. *Educational Institutions.* The relationship between a school and its students imposes certain obligations on the institution. *See, e.g.,* Stanton v. Univ. of Maine, 773 A.2d 1045 (Me. 2001) (a university owed a duty to a 17-year-old student-athlete, as a business invitee attending a pre-season soccer program, to advise the student of steps she could take to improve her personal safety; the student was sexually assaulted by a companion she had admitted to her dormitory); Mirand v. City of N.Y., 637 N.E.2d 263 (N.Y. 1994) (school liable for failure to take adequate measures in light of death threat by one student against another); Marquay v. Eno, 662 A.2d 272 (N.H. 1995) (school employees who have supervisory responsibility over students, and who know or should know of sexual abuse of a student, are subject to liability if their level of supervision is unreasonable).

Do the duties of school personnel extend beyond the official class day or beyond the campus? *Compare* Fazzolari v. Portland Sch. Dist., 734 P.2d 1326 (Or. 1987) (whether a high school was negligent in not protecting students who arrived at the school before morning classes was a question for the jury), *with* Young v. Salt Lake City Sch. Dist., 52 P.3d 1230 (Utah 2002) (because a school district did not have custody of an elementary school student at time he was injured when struck by a vehicle in a crosswalk while riding his bicycle to a mandatory parent-teacher-student conference after school had adjourned for the day, the district had no duty to inform him of dangerous conditions or provide a crossing guard or warning light; the student was not participating in school-sponsored event, but was simply traveling to one). *See also* Boyd v. T.C.U., 8 S.W.3d 758 (Tex. App. 1999) (a university owed the plaintiff student no duty to control, supervise, or discipline its adult student athletes during an event that was not organized or sponsored by university and that was held at off-campus location, and did not have a duty to provide the student with a safe environment while he was at an off-campus bar).

In Kleinknecht v. Gettysburg College, 989 F.2d 1360 (3d Cir. 1993), a lacrosse player suffered a cardiac arrest during practice and died. The court held that a college has a duty to be reasonably prepared to handle medical emergencies arising from intercollegiate contact sports. *Compare Kleinknecht with* Dillon v. Keatington Racquetball Club, 390 N.W.2d 212 (Mich. Ct. App. 1986) (club had no duty to adult members to supervise a game of "Walleyball" to make sure it was played in a safe manner).

3. *Wardens and Prisoners.* A warden is obliged to exercise reasonable care to prevent harm to a prisoner. An unusual application of this rule may be found in State v. Tidwell, 735 S.W.2d 629 (Tex. App. 1987). Plaintiff was arrested by two game wardens for hunting squirrels out of season. On the way back to town, the wardens saw a large rattlesnake on the road, and plaintiff, who was intoxicated, told the officers: "Hell, turn around, I'll catch that snake.... I have caught snakes all my life." The wardens turned the car around and parked within twenty feet of the snake. Plaintiff jumped out, caught the snake, was bitten, and spent two weeks in intensive care. The court upheld a judgment against the wardens and the state, which the jury had reduced by 40% to make allowance for the plaintiff's contributory negligence.

4. *Family Members.* One would expect that a duty to act will be imposed on close family members. However, there is little precedent, in part because of once-strong, but now diminished, intra-family immunities (discussed in Chapter 18). *See* Lundman v. McKown, 530 N.W.2d 807 (Minn. App. 1995) (stepfather owed a duty of care to child whose afflictions were treated by "spiritual means"); Cain v. Cain, 870 S.W.2d 676 (Tex. Ct. App. 1994) (duty to prevent son-in-law from raping niece, both of whom lived in defendant's house).

Some cases have reached surprising results. *See* Lauritzen v. Lauritzen, 874 P.2d 861 (Wash. Ct. App. 1994) (no special relationship exists between a husband, as driver, and his wife, as passenger, requiring husband to exercise reasonable care to protect wife from a third party's criminal attack); *see also* In re Marriage of J.T., 891 P.2d 729 (Wash. Ct. App. 1995) (no legal duty to disclose extramarital sexual relations to one's spouse).

Beyond the nuclear family, how far should the duty to act extend? *See* Chastain v. Fuqua Indus., Inc., 275 S.E.2d 679 (Ga. Ct. App. 1980) (aunt had no duty to warn 11-year-old nephew of loose seat on riding mower).

5. *Incest.* Issues relating to the duty to act arise when one parent knows or suspects that the other parent is sexually abusing a child. *See* Barbara A. Michaels, *Is Justice Served? The Development of Tort Liability Against the Passive Parent in Incest Cases*, 41 St. Louis U.L.J. 809, 844 (1997) ("viable actions...have recently begun to emerge").

6. *Social Companions.* In Farwell v. Keaton, 240 N.W.2d 217, 222 (Mich. 1976), the court imposed a duty on a 16-year-old to seek medical attention for a friend, with whom he had been out drinking and who had been injured in a fight with other boys. As between "companions on a social venture," there is an implicit "understanding that one will render assistance to the other when he is in peril if he can do so without endangering himself." Later cases have narrowly interpreted *Farwell.*

7. *Churches.* Sex-related cases involving allegations that a church has acted negligently often turn on issues relating to foreseeability of abuse and opportunity to control the abuser. In Willams v. Pentecostal Church Int'l, 115 S.W.3d 612 (Tex. App. 2003), the court held that a district church organization owed no duty to prevent a local church leader from sexually abusing children within the local church. Although church officials had general knowledge about the risk of sexual abuse of minors in church programs, and had instituted preventive measures at its youth camps, the particular church leader's alleged conduct was not foreseeable to the district organization, which had no knowledge of any prior allegations of sexual molestation by the leader. The organization also had no right to control the leader's activities.

In some instances, the injury has too little to do with the church to support an action for negligence. In Napieralski v. Unity Church, 802 A.2d 391 (Me. 2002), the court wrote:

> Napieralski is a life insurance agent. She attended Unity Church....Reverend Kenneth Williamson, a member of the clergy at Unity Church, approached Napieralski about obtaining life insurance. Napieralski agreed to meet him at his home that was owned by Unity Church. Napieralski alleges that Williamson "forced her to perform sexual acts...." Napieralski further alleges that Unity Church "knew or should have known that before Plaintiff was sexually assaulted by Williamson, he had engaged in inappropriate sexual behavior with at least two other women who attended the church,"....

Napieralski filed suit against the Church for negligence....

> ....

> We have not recognized the tort of negligent supervision in Maine....

> Even if we were disposed to recognize a cause of action for negligent supervision, it would be problematic at best to undertake recognition of that tort in this case....

> The facts here involve contact between adults for the purpose of addressing a private, personal matter unrelated to the business or function of the Unity Church. The contact occurred at the residence of the individual who was allegedly negligently supervised. Recognizing a cause of action for negligent supervision, and extending it to such facts, would go far beyond the scope of any traditional negligent supervision action. Such an interpretation would suggest that employers should become the guarantors of their employee's good conduct in private matters merely because the initial contact with the employee occurred in the regular course of business.

> We decline to adopt such an extension of the law. The fact that this misconduct is alleged to have occurred at an employer-owned residence makes no difference in this analysis. Where an employer does provide a residence for employees, it is very different from the employer's premises....The employee retains rights of privacy and quiet enjoyment in the residence that are not subject to close supervision or domination by the employer. [Citation.]

Napieralski does not allege that Reverend Williamson was engaged in the Church's business, that she was attending any type of religious event with him, or that her presence at his home pertained to church-related matters. Indeed, the only fact alleged in her complaint connecting the Reverend's actions to the Church is the allegation that Napieralski met the Reverend "[a]s a result of her attending Unity Church." On these facts, we decline Napieralski's invitation to adopt an expansive view of the tort of negligent supervision.

8. *Care Facilities.* In Texas Home Mgt., Inc. v. Peavy, 89 S.W.3d 30 (Tex. 2002), the survivors of a victim who was shot and killed by a patient on family leave from court-mandated residence at an intermediate care facility for the mentally retarded sued the facility's management company. The court held that the company had sufficient control over the patient to create a special relationship imposing a duty on the company to use reasonable care in determining whether the patient should be allowed to continue unsupervised home visits.

Kline v. 1500 Massachusetts Ave. Apartment Corp.
United States Court of Appeals for the District of Columbia Circuit
439 F.2d 477 (D.C. Cir. 1970)

WILKEY, Circuit Judge.

The appellee apartment corporation states that there is "only one issue presented for review...whether a duty should be placed on a landlord to take steps to protect tenants from foreseeable criminal acts committed by third parties." The District Court as a matter of law held that there is no such duty. We find that there is....

....

The appellant, Sarah B. Kline, sustained serious injuries when she was criminally assaulted and robbed at approximately 10:15 in the evening by an intruder in the common hallway of an apartment house...with approximately 585 individual apartment units....At the time the appellant first signed a lease a doorman was on duty at the main entrance twenty-four hours a day, and at least one employee at all times manned a desk in the lobby....

By mid-1966, however, the main entrance had no doorman, the desk in the lobby was left unattended much of the time, the 15th Street entrance was generally unguarded..., and the 16th Street entrance was often left unlocked all night. The entrances were allowed to be thus unguarded in the face of an increasing number of assaults, larcenies, and robberies being perpetrated against the tenants in and from the common hallways of the apartment building....

....

In this jurisdiction, certain duties have been assigned to the landlord because of his *control* of common hallways, lobbies, stairwells, etc., used by all tenants in multiple dwelling units....

While [a prior case] dealt with a physical defect in the building leading to plaintiff's injury, the rationale as applied to predictable criminal acts by third parties is the same. The duty is the landlord's because by his control of the areas of common use and common danger he is the only party who has the *power* to make the necessary repairs or to provide the necessary protection.

As a general rule, a private person does not have a duty to protect another from a criminal attack by a third person. We recognize that this rule has sometimes in the past been applied in landlord-tenant law, even by this court. Among the reasons for the application of this rule to landlords are: judicial reluctance to tamper with the traditional common law concept of the landlord-tenant relationship; the notion that the act of a third person in committing an intentional tort or crime is a superseding cause of the harm to another resulting therefrom; the oftentimes difficult problem of determining foreseeability of criminal acts; the vagueness of the standard which the landlord must meet; the economic consequences of the imposition of the duty; and conflict with the public policy allocating the duty of protecting citizens from criminal acts to the government rather than the private sector.

But the rationale of this very broad general rule falters when it is applied to the conditions of modern day urban apartment living, particularly in the circumstances of this case. The rationale of the general rule exonerating a third party from any duty to protect another from a criminal attack has no applicability to the landlord-tenant relationship in multiple dwelling houses. The landlord is no insurer of his tenants' safety, but he certainly is no bystander. And where, as here, the landlord has notice of repeated criminal assaults and robberies, has notice that these crimes occurred in the portion of the premises exclusively within his control, has every reason to expect like crimes to happen again, and has the exclusive power to take preventive action, it does not seem unfair to place upon the landlord a duty to take those steps which are within his power to minimize the predictable risk to his tenants.

....

...[I]nnkeepers have been held liable for assaults which have been committed upon their guests by third parties, if they have breached a duty which is imposed by reason of the innkeeper-guest relationship....

....

Other relationships in which similar duties have been imposed include landowner-invitee, businessman-patron, employer-employee, school district-pupil, hospital-patient, and carrier-passenger. In all, the theory of liability is essentially the same: that since the ability of one of the parties to provide for his own protection has been limited in some way by his submission to the control of the other, a duty should be imposed upon the one possessing control (and thus the power to act) to take reasonable precautions to protect the other one from assaults by third parties which, at least, could reasonably have been anticipated....

....

...[I]t would be well to state what is *not* said by this decision. We do not hold that the landlord is by any means an insurer of the safety of his tenants. His duty is to take those measures of protection which are within his power and capacity to take, and which can reasonably be expected to mitigate the risk of intruders assaulting and robbing tenants. The landlord is not expected to provide protection commonly owed by a municipal police department; but as illustrated in this case, he is obligated to protect those parts of his premises which are not usually subject to periodic patrol and inspection by the municipal police....

....

The landlord is entirely justified in passing on the cost of increased protective measures to his tenants, but the rationale of compelling the landlord to do it in the first place is that he is the only one who is in a position to take the necessary protective measures for overall protection of the premises, which he owns in whole and rents in part to individual tenants.

Reversed and remanded to the District Court for the determination of damages.

[MacKINNON, J., dissented.]

Notes

1. *Economic Analysis: Tort, Contract, and Apartment Security.* If a landlord expressly promises to provide security measures and fails to do so, the landlord is plainly liable for harm that results. And liability may also be clear even if the promise is not spelled out in words: If Kline had moved into a building featuring security measures, which had then been discontinued without notice, it would have been pretty clear that her contract with the landlord called for the latter to continue the normal level of security for the duration of the lease. The cases involving hotels may illustrate this principle: the hotel guest is surely entitled to assume that ordinary security precautions will be taken. Tort law comes into play only when the parties' agreement does not expressly or implicitly call for security measures and the tenant then sues because those measures were not taken. This may happen when a tenant rents an apartment in a building lacking the kind of security more-expensive apartment buildings employ. Or, as in the *Kline* case, a building that once had first-rate security may change to one that does not, and the tenant nevertheless renews the lease.

As the *Kline* court recognizes, the cost of security measures taken by landlords will be borne by tenants. Since this is so, is there any need for the law of torts to impose on landlords and tenants higher costs than they bargained for? Is it now illegal in the District of Columbia for landlords to rent apartments in buildings lacking the kinds of security measures that well-to-do tenants routinely insist upon?

An apparent belief of many judges (and legislators) is that, by imposing higher standards than those that emerge from market transactions, they can make poor tenants better off. Bearing in mind that those tenants will inevitably pay the costs of the benefits the courts give them, this may not be the case. If extra security would cost $30 a month for each apartment in a building, and if tenants value the extra security at $30 or more, there seems to be no need for courts to require that the security be offered. If tenants value the extra security at less than the $30 they will have to pay for it, the courts are making them worse off—by their own standards, though perhaps not by the courts'—when the security measures are mandated. Would poor people who must buy cars be better or worse off if a law were passed prohibiting the sale of any car more than four years old or with more than 50,000 miles on the clock?

2. *Common-Area Liability. Kline* is a leading case on landlords' duty to provide adequate security for common areas. A number of cases have reached the same result. *See, e.g.,* Trentacost v. Brussel, 412 A.2d 436 (N.J. 1980) (alternative grounds of conventional negligence and implied warranty of habitability); Johnston v. Harris, 198 N.W.2d 409 (Mich. 1972) (based on Restatement, Second, of Torts §§302B, 448, and 449). *See also* O'Hara v. Western Seven Trees Corp. Intercoast Mgt., 142 Cal. Rptr. 487 (Ct. App. 1978) (landlord may be liable for an assault in a tenant's apartment if failure to take precautions to safeguard common areas contributed substantially to the tenant's injuries). As summarized by one writer, "Today, in virtually every jurisdiction, landlords have some duty to protect their tenants from the criminal activities of

strangers." B.A. Glesner, *Landlords As Cops: Tort, Nuisance & Forfeiture Standards Imposing Liability on Landlords for Crime on the Premises*, 42 Case W. Res. L. Rev. 679, 790 (1992).

3. *Off-Premises Dangers.* A lessor's duty to provide safe common areas may necessitate some consideration of off-premises dangers. In Calkins v. Cox Estates, 792 P.2d 36 (N.M. 1990), an eight-year-old boy was killed when he was struck by an automobile on a frontage road in the vicinity of the apartment complex where he lived. The child had reached that location by crossing through a hole in a playground fence which the lessor had allowed to fall into disrepair. In addressing the issue of duty, Justice Baca wrote for a divided court:

> Respondent chose to erect a fence and he reaped the economic benefits from providing a fenced play area at the complex.... Every landlord is not required, as a matter of law, to fence in his property or to insure the safety of his tenants' children. However, when a landowner undertakes to provide a common area for the use of his tenants, he undertakes to maintain it in a reasonably safe condition....
>
> ....
>
> ....The scope of the landlord's duty... is to maintain the common areas of his property in a reasonably safe condition. However, injury resulting from a breach of that duty need not occur on the property for the lessor to be liable, if the breach proximately causes the harm....

4. *Condominium Associations.* Some courts have held that condominium associations are subject to the same duties as landlords. *See* Frances T. v. Village Green Owners Ass'n, 723 P.2d 573 (Cal. 1986) (failure to provide adequate lighting in common area).

5. *Employers.* An employer has a common-law duty to provide employees with a reasonably safe workplace. *See* Widera v. Ettco Wire and Cable Corp., 611 N.Y.S.2d 569 (App. Div. 1994).

The opinion in *Kline* recognizes, as many courts do, that employers have a duty to protect their employees from foreseeable criminal attacks. *See, e.g.*, Guerrero v. Memorial Med. Ctr. of E. Tex., 938 S.W.2d 789 (Tex. Ct. App. 1997) (acknowledging rule, but holding that no duty arose because it was unforeseeable that husband would murder wife on employer's premises). However, there are cases to the contrary. In Dupont v. Aavid Thermal Tech., Inc., 798 A.2d 587 (N.H. 2002), the court held that the employment relationship is not the type of "special" relationship that gives rise to a broad duty on an employer's part to protect employee from foreseeable crimes. The court wrote:

> In the end, we believe that the general duty to protect citizens from criminal attacks is a government function, which private sector employers should not be required to shoulder merely because of their status as employers.

However, the court recognized in dicta a more specific duty on employers to protect employees from criminal attacks when an employer has unreasonably created a condition of employment that foreseeably enhances risk of criminal attack. Further, the court held that there is a duty on an employer's part to protect an employee from an imminent danger of serious harm. A claim was stated on that ground because there were allegations that supervisors of the plaintiff, who was shot to death in the parking lot by a co-worker, saw the co-worker become increasingly agitated, then escorted the plaintiff and the co-worker outside without warning the plaintiff that the co-worker was armed or calling the police.

A startling decision is Habich v. Crown Central Petrol. Corp., 642 So. 2d 699, (Ala. 1994), a case involving a female employee working the night shift at a convenience store, who was required to go to the storage room to get merchandise for restocking, but was not permitted to lock the front door while doing so. While on duty alone, she was raped and abducted by an intruder. The court held that the plaintiff had failed to prove that the attack was foreseeable *or* that there was a special relationship between the parties. What is more foreseeable than an attack on a lone convenience store employee in an unlocked building at 3 a.m.? In the words of Judge Wilkey in *Kline*, who was "the only one…in a position to take the necessary protective measures for overall protection of the premises"? On similar facts, some cases have reached a different result than *Habich. See* Morris v. Krauszer's Food Stores, 693 A.2d 510 (N.J. Super. Ct. 1997) (because attack at convenience store was reasonably foreseeable, there was a duty to protect employees). Of course, a suit against an employer may have to surmount claims of workers' compensation immunity.

See also Wise v. Complete Staffing Services, Inc., 56 S.W.3d 900 (Tex. App. 2001) (stating that there is no "expanded duty" on an employer to require an "unlimited background check" of all employees); Madley v. The Evenings News Ass'n, 421 N.W.2d 682 (Mich. Ct. App. 1988) (no special relationship which would give rise to a duty to warn of the hazards of crossing a street existed between a newspaper and an independent-contractor carrier).

6. ***Threats Posed by Children.*** A parent may have a duty to exercise care to control a child. In Linder v. Bidner, 270 N.Y.S.2d 427 (Sup. Ct. 1966), the defendants' son, an 18-year-old, had assaulted and injured the plaintiff, a young child. The court refused to dismiss the complaint against the parents, since it alleged that they had knowledge of their son's propensity for mistreating younger children and that they had failed to avail themselves of the opportunity to control their child. *But see* Childers v. A.S., 909 S.W.2d 282 (Tex. Ct. App. 1995) (mother of a minor child, of whose prior sexual activities the mother was aware, owed no duty to the child's friend or the friend's parents to prevent the minor child from harming the friend by inappropriate sexual contacts, where all sexual acts between the minor child and friend took place in the friend's home, outside the presence and supervision of the minor's parents and without their knowledge).

While a parent will generally not be held liable for rearing an incorrigible child, a parent who fails to exercise due care in the face of knowledge of specific dangerous habits is subject to liability. By analogy to this rule on parental duty, Hoff v. Vacaville Unified Sch. Dist., 968 P.2d 522 (Cal. 1998), held that school personnel who neither knew nor reasonably should have known that a particular student had a tendency to drive recklessly owed no duty to an off-campus non-student who was injured by a car exiting the school parking lot.

Compare Linder with Nova Univ. v. Wagner, 491 So. 2d 1116 (Fla. 1986), holding a university which operated a residential center for children with behavioral problems liable when two residents of the center ran away and, several days later, killed one child and injured another. Interestingly, the opinion did not limit liability to cases in which the harm resulted from a specific dangerous propensity known to the defendant.

What about the obligations of divorced or separated parents? In K.H. v. J.R., 826 A.2d 863 (Pa. 2003), the court held that parents of a minor child who was injured when another minor child shot him in the abdomen with a BB gun could not recover against shooter's father for negligent supervision, even though father had legal custody and shared physical custody of the shooter, had purchased the BB gun, and had agreed to allow the shooter to take it to his mother's home, because the shooter was in the mother's custody at time of the shooting. The court reasoned:

> [O]ne's status as a legal custodian is not, in and of itself, dispositive in establishing the ability and the opportunity to control.... [T]he fact that... [the father] was aware of the BB gun and agreed to allow... [his son] to take it to his mother's home does not alter the absence of evidence demonstrating ability and opportunity to control....Moreover, considering the difficulty and emotion that often attend custody arrangements, imposing a duty to supervise upon a non-custodial parent would unnecessarily interject additional tension into the domestic relations arena.

How should adult children be treated? *Compare* Silberstein v. Cordie, 474 N.W.2d 850 (Minn. Ct. App. 1991) (action stated against parents for allegedly failing to control their schizophrenic 27-year-old son who lived with the parents at the time he committed a murder), *with* Villacana v. Campbell, 929 S.W.2d 69 (Tex. Ct. App. 1996) (parents had no duty to control the conduct of adult child who committed murder, even though he was living in their home), *and* Grover v. Stechel, 45 P.3d 80 (N.M. Ct. App. 2002) (a mother's payment of her adult son's living expenses at the time of son's assault on the victim did not fit into any recognized special relationship so as to impose a legal duty on the mother to control her adult son, who was using drugs).

7. ***Threats Posed by a Spouse.*** There is authority that a woman who has actual knowledge or "special reason to know" that her husband is engaging in sexually abusive behavior against a particular person has a duty of care to take reasonable steps to prevent or warn of the harm. *See* J.S. v. R.T.H., 714 A.2d 924 (N.J. 1998) (abuse of neighbors' daughters). If, in such a case, the husband can be sued for committing the sexual abuse, what difference does it make that the husband's wife can be sued for negligent failure to act?

8. ***Threats Posed by Other Relatives and Friends.*** *See* Bell & Hudson, P.C. v. Buhl Realty Co., 462 N.W.2d 851 (Mich. App. 1990) (no duty to prevent brother from committing shotgun massacre in a law office); Sierocki v. Hieber, 425 N.W.2d 477 (Mich. Ct. App. 1998) (roommate's relationship with driver did not create a duty to use reasonable care to prevent a collision with a pedestrian).

Remsburg v. Docusearch, Inc.

Supreme Court of New Hampshire
816 A.2d 1001 (N.H. 2003)

DALIANIS, J.

...[T]he United States District Court...certified to us the following...[question] of law:

...[D]oes a private investigator or information broker who sells information to a client pertaining to a third party have a cognizable duty to that third party with respect to the sale of the information?

....

....Docusearch, Inc. and Wing and a Prayer, Inc. (WAAP) jointly own and operate an Internet-based investigation and information service known as Docusearch.com. Daniel Cohn and Kenneth Zeiss each own 50% of each company's stock....

On July 29, 1999,...Liam Youens contacted Docusearch through its Internet website and requested the date of birth for Amy Lynn Boyer....Youens provided Docusearch his name, New Hampshire address, and a contact telephone number. He paid the $20 fee by credit card....The next day, July 30, 1999, Docusearch provided Youens with the birth dates for several Amy Boyers, but none was for the Amy Boyer sought by Youens. In response, Youens e-mailed Docusearch inquiring whether it would be possible to get better results using Boyer's home address, which he provided. Youens gave Docusearch a different contact phone number.

Later that same day, Youens again contacted Docusearch and placed an order for Boyer's social security number (SSN), paying the $45 fee by credit card. On August 2, 1999, Docusearch obtained Boyer's social security number from a credit reporting agency...and provided it to Youens....The next day, Youens placed an order with Docusearch for Boyer's employment information, paying the $109 fee by credit card, and giving Docusearch the same phone number he had provided originally....On August 20, 1999, having received no response to his latest request, Youens placed a second request for Boyer's employment information, again paying the $109 fee by credit card....

With his second request for Boyer's employment information pending, Youens placed yet another order for information with Docusearch on September 6, 1999. This time, he requested a "locate by social security number" search for Boyer. Youens paid the $30 fee by credit card, and received the results of the search—Boyer's home address—on September 7, 1999.

On September 8, 1999, Docusearch informed Youens of Boyer's employment address. Docusearch acquired this address through a subcontractor, Michele Gambino, who had obtained the information by placing a "pretext" telephone call to Boyer in New Hampshire. Gambino lied about who she was and the purpose of her call in order to convince Boyer to reveal her employment information. Gambino had no contact with Youens, nor did she know why Youens was requesting the information.

On October 15, 1999, Youens drove to Boyer's workplace and fatally shot her as she left work. Youens then shot and killed himself. A subsequent police investigation revealed that Youens kept firearms and ammunition in his bedroom, and maintained a website containing references to stalking and killing Boyer as well as other information and statements related to violence and killing.

>   ....

All persons have a duty to exercise reasonable care not to subject others to an unreasonable risk of harm....

In situations in which the harm is caused by criminal misconduct, however, determining whether a duty exists is complicated by the competing rule "that a private citizen has no general duty to protect others from the criminal attacks of third parties." [Citation.] This rule is grounded in the fundamental unfairness of holding private citizens responsible for the unanticipated criminal acts of third parties, because "[u]nder all ordinary and normal circumstances, in the absence of any reason to expect the contrary, the actor may reasonably proceed upon the assumption that others will obey the law." [Citation.]

In certain limited circumstances, however, we have recognized that there are exceptions to the general rule where a duty to exercise reasonable care will arise. [Citation.] We have held that such a duty may arise because: (1) a special relationship exists; (2) special circumstances exist; or (3) the duty has been voluntarily assumed. *Id*. The special circumstances exception includes situations where there is "an especial temptation and opportunity for criminal misconduct brought about by the defendant." [Citation.]

This exception follows from the rule that a party who realizes or should realize that his conduct has created a condition which involves an unreasonable risk of harm to another has a duty to exercise reasonable care to prevent the risk from occurring....

Thus, if a private investigator or information broker's (hereinafter "investigator" collectively) disclosure of information to a client creates a foreseeable risk of criminal misconduct against the third person whose information was disclosed, the investigator owes a duty to exercise reasonable care not to subject the third person to an unreasonable risk of harm. In determining whether the risk of criminal misconduct is foreseeable to an investigator, we examine two risks of information disclosure implicated by this case: stalking and identity theft.

It is undisputed that stalkers, in seeking to locate and track a victim, sometimes use an investigator to obtain personal information about the victims. [Citation.]

Public concern about stalking has compelled all fifty States to pass some form of legislation criminalizing stalking. Approximately one million women and 371,000 men are stalked annually in the United States. [Citation.] Stalking is a crime that causes serious psychological harm to the victims, and often results in the victim experiencing posttraumatic stress disorder, anxiety, sleeplessness, and sometimes, suicidal ideations. [Citation.] Not only is stalking itself a crime, but it can lead to more violent crimes, including assault, rape or homicide. [Citations.]

Identity theft, *i.e.*, the use of one person's identity by another, is an increasingly common risk associated with the disclosure of personal information, such as a SSN. [Citation.] A person's SSN has attained the status of a quasi-universal personal identification number. [Citation.] At the same time, however, a person's privacy interest in his or her SSN is recognized by state and federal statutes...which prohibits the release of SSNs contained within drivers' license records. [Citations.] "[A]rmed with one's SSN, an unscrupulous individual could obtain a person's welfare benefits or Social Security benefits, order new checks at a new address on that person's checking account, obtain credit cards, or even obtain the person's paycheck." [Citation.]

Like the consequences of stalking, the consequences of identity theft can be severe. The best estimates place the number of victims in excess of 100,000 per year and the dollar loss in excess of $2 billion per year. [Citation.] Victims of identity theft risk the destruction of their good credit histories. This often destroys a victim's ability to obtain credit from any source and may, in some cases, render the victim unemployable or even cause the victim to be incarcerated. [Citation.]

The threats posed by stalking and identity theft lead us to conclude that the risk of criminal misconduct is sufficiently foreseeable so that an investigator has a duty to exercise reasonable care in disclosing a third person's personal information to a client. And we so hold. This is especially true when, as in this case, the investigator does not know the client or the client's purpose in seeking the information.

....

Remanded.

NADEAU and DUGGAN, JJ., concurred.

Note

1. *Identity Theft.* In Huggins v. Citibank, 585 S.E.2d 275 (S.C. 2003), the court, citing similar decisions in New York and Missouri, declined to recognize the tort of negli-

gent enablement of imposter fraud. The court held that "The relationship, if any, between credit card issuers and potential victims of identity theft is far too attenuated to rise to the level of a duty between them." The plaintiff had alleged that the defendant banks had issued credit cards to an imposter without investigating, verifying, or corroborating the applicant's claimed identity.

Peck v. Counseling Service of Addison County, Inc.
Supreme Court of Vermont
499 A.2d 422 (Vt. 1985)

HILL, Justice.

Plaintiffs-appellants appeal from a judgment…that found…The Counseling Service of Addison County, Inc. (hereinafter Counseling Service) not liable in negligence…, and dismissing the plaintiff's cause of action with prejudice.…

.…During the night of June 27, 1979, John Peck, age twenty-nine, son of the plaintiffs, set fire to the plaintiffs' barn. The barn, located 130 feet from the plaintiffs' house, was completely destroyed. At the time of this incident, John Peck was an outpatient of the Counseling Service, under the treatment of one of defendant's counselor-psychotherapists.… [After a fight with his father,] John told his therapist that he "wanted to get back at his father." In response to a question by the therapist about how he would get back at his father, John stated, "I don't know, I could burn down his barn." After the therapist and John discussed the possible consequences of such an act, John, at the request of the therapist, made a verbal promise not to burn down his father's barn. Believing that John would keep his promise, the therapist did not disclose John's threats to any other staff member…or to the plaintiffs.

    ….

.…Following the trial, the court…dismissed the case with prejudice because it determined that under current Vermont law there was no basis to find that the defendant owed a duty to take actions to protect the plaintiffs.

The plaintiffs argue that the defendant, by and through its employees, knew or should have known, in accordance with the prevailing standards of the mental health profession, that John Peck represented an unreasonable risk of harm to them. Plaintiffs further contend that by its failure "to take steps that were reasonably necessary to protect" the plaintiffs, the defendant breached a duty of care owed to them.

Generally, there is no duty to control the conduct of another in order to protect a third person from harm. Restatement (Second) of Torts §315 (1965).…

Defendant contends that the relationship between a community mental health agency and a voluntary outpatient does not give rise to a duty to protect third persons because of the absence of control over the outpatient. [Citations.]

Whether or not there is actual control over an outpatient in a mental health clinic setting similar to that exercised over institutionalized patients, the relationship between a clinical therapist and his or her patient "is sufficient to create a duty to exercise reasonable care to protect a potential victim of another's conduct." Tarasoff v. Regents of the University of California, 17 Cal. 3d 425, 435, 551 P.2d 334, 343, 131 Cal. Rptr. 14, 23 (1976). Vermont already recognizes the existence of a special relationship between a physician and a patient that imposes certain legal duties on the physician for the benefit of third persons. Physicians, health officials and health institutions are required, in patient cases of venereal and other contagious diseases, to warn others in order to protect the public health. [Citation.] We see no reason why a similar duty to warn should not exist when the "disease" of the patient is a mental illness that poses an analogous risk of harm to others. [Citation.]

....Defendant also argues that a duty to take action...should not be imposed...because a therapist is no better able than anyone else to predict future violent behavior. [Citation.] This Court recognizes the difficulty of predicting whether "a particular mental patient may pose a danger to himself or others. This factor alone, however, does not justify barring recovery in all situations. The standard of care for [mental] health professionals adequately takes into account the difficult nature of the problem facing [them]." [Citation.]

Defendant states that John's therapist, acting as a reasonably prudent counselor, "concluded in good faith that John Peck would not burn his parent's [sic] barn." The trial court nonetheless found that the therapist was negligent, and did not act as a reasonably prudent counselor, because her good faith belief was based on inadequate information and consultation. Sufficient evidence was presented to the court to support this finding.

Plaintiffs' psychiatric expert testified that, given (1) John's past history of impulsive assaultive behavior, (2) his medical treatment for the control of epilepsy, (3) the possibility of a brain disorder, associated with epilepsy, that increasingly diminished John's capacity for exercising good judgment, and (4) his past alcohol abuse, all of which were known to the therapist, the failure to reveal John's threat was inconsistent with the standards of the mental health profession. The evidence also revealed that at the time of John's threat the therapist was not in possession of John's most recent medical history. The Counseling service did not have a cross-reference system between its therapists and outside physicians who were treating the medical problems of its patients. Nor did the Counseling Service have any written policy concerning formal intrastaff consultation procedures when a patient presented a serious risk of harm to another. The defendant's own expert testified that a therapist cannot make a reasonable determination of a patient's propensity for carrying out a threatened act of violence without knowledge of the patient's complete medical history.

Our decision today requires only that "the therapist...exercise 'that reasonable degree of skill, knowledge, and care ordinarily possessed and exercised by members of [that professional specialty] under similar circumstances.'" [Citation.] Once a therapist determines, or, based on the standards of the mental health professional community, should have determined that his or her patient poses a serious risk of danger to another, then he or she has the duty to take whatever steps are reasonably necessary to protect the foreseeable victim of that danger. "...[I]n each instance the adequacy of the therapist's conduct must be measured against the traditional negligence standard of the rendition of reasonable care under the circumstances."....

Defendant also argues that the therapist could not lawfully have warned the plaintiffs of John's threat because of the physician-patient privilege against disclosure of confidential information. [Citation.] We are aware of the crucial role that confidentiality performs between therapist and patient in establishing and maintaining the "tenuous therapeutic alliance." [Citation.] Defendant points out that the legislature has specified certain "public policy" exceptions to the physician-patient privilege, see, e.g., 33 V.S.A. §§683-684 (Supp. 1984) (report of child abuse), 13 V.S.A. §4012 (disclosure of gunshot wounds), 18 V.S.A. §§1152-1153 (report of abuse of the elderly) and that a therapist's duty to disclose the risk of harm posed by his or her patient to a foreseeable victim is not a recognized legislative exception. Given this, defendant argues that this Court is preempted from finding a duty-to-warn exception to the physician-patient privilege. The statutory exceptions to the physician-patient indicate to this Court, however, that the privilege is not sacrosanct and can properly be waived in the interest of public policy under appropriate circumstances. A mental patient's threat of serious harm to an identified victim is an appropriate circumstance under which the physician-patient privilege may be waived. This exception to the physician-patient privilege is similar to that recognized in the attorney-client relationship when a client informs an attorney of his or her intent to commit a crime. Code of Professional Responsibility, 12 V.S.A., App. IX, DR 4-101(C)(3) (attorney may reveal client's intent to commit a crime). However, "the therapist's obligations to his patient require that he not disclose a confidence unless such disclosure is necessary to avert danger to others, and even then that he do so discretely, and in a fashion that would preserve the privacy of his patient to the fullest extent compatible with the prevention of the threatened danger."....

....

Cause remanded for entry of judgment consistent with this opinion and the findings of the trial court.

....

BILLINGS, Chief Justice, dissenting.

....

....It is scientifically recognized that it is impossible to predict future violent behavior. The professional's duty is to the patient, and not to others....Here the evidence discloses that...the counselor in good faith did not believe there was any threat to person or property by the patient, and so no duty arises. [Citation.]

The issues here present an important social problem. If the common law requirements of the duty to warn, the foreseeability of harm, and ability to control are not warranted or necessary, that is for the legislature to decide.

Notes

1. **Tarasoff** *and the Duties of Mental-Health Professionals.* A leading decision on the liability of psychotherapists for harm done by their patients is Tarasoff v. Regents of the Univ. of Calif., 551 P.2d 334 (Cal. 1976). Dr. Lawrence Moore, a psychologist, had, according to the complaint, been told by one of his patients, Prosenjit Poddar, that Poddar intended to kill Tatiana Tarasoff. Dr. Moore called the police, who were unable to detain Poddar because he had not committed a crime; Moore did not notify Tatiana (who was then in Brazil) or her parents. After Tatiana returned from Brazil, Poddar killed her. The California Supreme Court held that the "special relationship" between Poddar and Dr. Moore required Moore to take reasonable care to protect Tatiana.

The *Tarasoff* opinion said not only that a doctor who *knows* that a patient would cause harm has a duty to the potential victims, but also that a psychotherapist has a duty to make "reasonable" predictions about the dangerous tendency of his patients and to warn potential victims when appropriate. Because predicting dangerousness is far from easy, California psychotherapists were quite concerned about that aspect of the opinion. The California legislature then enacted the following statute.

CAL. CIV. CODE §43.92
(Westlaw 2004)

(a) There shall be no monetary liability on the part of, and no cause of action shall arise against, any person who is a psychotherapist...[for] failing to warn of and protect from a patient's violent behavior or failing to predict and warn of and protect from a patient's violent behavior except where the patient has communicated to the psychotherapist a serious threat of physical violence against a reasonably identifiable victim or victims.

(b) If there is any duty to warn and protect under the limited circumstances specified above, the duty shall be discharged by the psychotherapist['s] making reasonable efforts to communicate the threat to the victims or victim and to a law enforcement agency.

What result in *Peck* if Vermont had adopted a statute like California's? What result in *Tarasoff* itself under the California statute?

Restatement, Third, of Torts: Liability for Physical Harm (Basic Principles) §42 Cmt. f Reporters' Note (Council Draft No. 4, 2003) observes:

> Virtually all courts confronting the issue have decided that mental-health professionals owe some affirmative duty to third parties with regard to patients who are recognized as posing dangers....The vast majority of...states in which a *Tarasoff* duty has been judicially imposed have subsequently enacted statutes that codify the duty...to provide greater clarity or limits to the judically-imposed duty.
>
> ....
>
> Some courts have declined to adopt a duty beyond warning....
>
> Some courts and statutes require a specific threat by the patient or actual knowledge by the mental-health professional of the patient's danger to another....
>
> Some courts and statutes have limited any warning obligation to those who are specifically identified by the patient. Others couch the limitation as those who are "readily identifiable"....
>
> The duty...is applicable to all mental-health professionals who act in a relationship with a mental patient.

But see Thapar v. Zezulka, 994 S.W.2d 635 (Tex. 1999) (holding that a psychiatrist has no duty to warn a victim or the victim's family because that duty would conflict with a confidentiality statute that barred disclosure); Nasser v. Parker, 455 S.E.2d 502 (Va. 1995) (holding that there is no duty unless the defendant has "taken charge" of the patient, which means more than accepting the patient for the purpose of providing prolonged treatment, prescribing medication, and arranging the patient's admission to a hospital); Boynton v. Burglass, 590 So. 2d 446 (Fla. Dist. Ct. App. 1991) (expressly rejecting *Tarasoff*).

2. *Duty to Prevent Suicide.* What if the threat of harm is not to a third person but only to the well-being of the one making the threat? In Eisel v. Board of Educ., 597 A.2d 447 (Md. 1991), the court, under a *Tarasoff* analysis which recognized the strong public interest in preventing youth suicide, held that school counselors have a duty to use reasonable means to attempt to prevent suicide when they are on notice of a child or adolescent student's suicidal intent. *See also* Wyke v. Polk County Sch. Bd., 129 F.3d 560, 571 (11th Cir. 1997) (holding that "when a child attempts suicide at school and the

school knows of the attempt, the school can be found negligent in failing to notify the child's parents or guardian").

However, warning and prevention are two different matters, and many courts have been reluctant to impose a duty to prevent suicide. In *Donaldson v. YWCA*, 539 N.W.2d 789 (Minn. 1995), the court concluded that a YWCA "lodging house" owed no duty to prevent residents from committing suicide. The court reasoned:

> Here, the relationship between the YWCA and Robarge [the decedent] bore little resemblance to the caretaking relationship of a hospital toward its patients or the custodial relationship between a jail and its inmates. Unlike hospitals or jails, the YWCA did not have custody or control of Robarge. Robarge did not entrust her health to the YWCA, and the YWCA did not accept the responsibility to care for her or to protect her from self-inflicted harm. The YWCA did not provide medical services or have expertise treating mental health problems.... Simply put, the YWCA was not in a position to protect Robarge from committing suicide and Robarge had no reasonable expectation that the YWCA would protect her from committing suicide. Moreover, the YWCA did nothing to deprive Robarge of normal opportunities for self-protection....

See also Lee v. Corregedore, 925 P.2d 324 (Haw. 1996) (counselors do not have duty to prevent suicides of noncustodial clients, regardless of whether suicides are foreseeable); Webstad v. Stortini, 924 P.2d 940, 947 (Wash. Ct. App. 1996) (host had no duty to prevent guest, with whom host had been romantically involved, from committing suicide because he did not create her dependent condition; there is no "legal duty to immediately summon aid whenever a person has reason to suspect that another person may be attempting suicide").

3. *Lawyers and Clients Who Make Threats.* What if Peck had told his lawyer, rather than his doctor, of his proposal to burn his father's barn? Rule 1.6 of the American Bar Association's Model Rules of Professional Conduct (2004) provides:

> (a) A lawyer shall not reveal information relating to the representation of a client unless the client gives informed consent...or the disclosure is permitted by paragraph (b).

> (b) A lawyer may reveal information relating to the representation of a client to the extent the lawyer reasonably believes necessary:

> (1) to prevent reasonably certain death or substantial bodily harm....

Not surprisingly, there has been disagreement within the legal profession about where the line between confidentiality and the protection of third parties should be drawn, and several states have rules that differ from Rule 1.6 in some respects. For example, Rule 1.05(e) of the Texas Disciplinary Rules of Professional Conduct (2004) provides:

> When a lawyer has confidential information clearly establishing that a client is likely to commit a criminal or fraudulent act that is likely to result in death or substantial bodily harm to a person, the lawyer *shall* reveal the confidential information to the extent reevaluation reasonably appears necessary to prevent the client from committing the criminal or fraudulent act. [Emphasis added.]

The preamble to the Texas ethics rules, like similar language in the ethics codes of many other states, indicates that the rules do not set standards for civil liability, and that a "[v]iolation of a rule does not give rise to a private cause of action [or] create a presumption that a legal duty to a client has been breached."

In Hawkins v. King County Dept. of Rehab. Services, 602 P.2d 361 (Wash. Ct. App. 1979), the court concluded that an attorney's "obligation to warn, when confidentiality would be compromised to the client's detriment, must be permissive at most, unless it appears beyond a reasonable doubt that the client has formed a firm intention to inflict serious personal injuries on an unknowing third person." Because the attorney received no information that his client planned to assault anyone, but only that he was mentally ill and likely to be dangerous to himself and others, there was no common-law duty on the part of the attorney to warn or disclose.

4. *Physicians and Patients.* See Van Horn v. Chambers, 970 S.W.2d 542, 547 (Tex. 1998) (a physician-patient relationship is not "special," so a physician who transferred a patient from a critical care unit to a private room on an unsecured floor could not be liable to hospital employees for injuries sustained while trying to subdue the patient when he became violent).

5. *Duty to Provide a Reference?* In an attempt to avoid being sued for defamation by disgruntled former employees, some employers have adopted policies of not providing references for anyone. Under these "no comment" policies, employers refuse to furnish information about former employees, other than dates of employment and rank. This practice makes it difficult for potential employers to obtain important data relevant to employment decisions, and may advance the interests of "bad" employees (about whom the damning truth will not be known), while harming "good" employees (about whom favorable information will also not be disclosed).

To ameliorate these difficulties, some persons favor placing a *Tarasoff*-type duty on a former employer to disclose information, in response to a request, about any danger a former employee may pose to a new employer or anyone who could foreseeably be harmed as a result of the new employment. *See* Janet Swerdlow, *Negligent Referral: A Potential Theory of Employer Liability*, 64 S. Cal. L. Rev. 1645, 1671 (1991). There is authority to the contrary. For example, in Cohen v. Wales, 518 N.Y.S.2d 633 (App. Div. 1987), a child injured by a school teacher sued the teacher's former employer for recommending the teacher for hire even though it had charged the teacher with sexual misconduct. The court refused to recognize the claim because the child could potentially recover from both the teacher and the teacher's new employer: "The mere recommendation of a person for potential employment is not a proper basis for asserting a claim of negligence where another party is responsible for the actual hiring."

2. Liability Based on Defendant's Involvement in an Accident

La Raia v. Superior Court
Supreme Court of Arizona, En Banc
722 P.2d 286 (Ariz. 1986)

FELDMAN, Justice.

....

....Ms. La Raia (plaintiff) resided in an apartment project owned and operated by the real parties in interest, Friedkin/Becker, Inc. (defendant). Plaintiff had problems with roaches and asked the apartment manager to arrange for pest control service. Rather than calling the contract pest control company, the manager authorized the janitor, who was unlicensed and untrained, to spray plaintiff's apartment. He did so while plaintiff was away at work. Never having sprayed indoors before, he apparently saturated everything with pesticide. When she returned to her apartment, plaintiff noticed an overpowering, pungent odor....

Plaintiff became ill and asked the apartment manager for a list of the chemicals in the spray. The manager provided her with a partial list of the contents which omitted all toxic items. Thus, when plaintiff conveyed the information to her doctor and the pest control board, she was informed that none of the chemicals was toxic. Believing it was safe, plaintiff then reentered her apartment, only to become more seriously ill. Her condition worsened and she was hospitalized....

Staff from the poison control center telephoned the apartment manager to ask what chemicals had been used. Before returning the call..., the manager ascertained that the pesticide can which the janitor had used was marked with a skull and crossbones and was "for outside use only." She also learned that the product had been used by mistake. The manager instructed the janitor to take the can and dispose of it off the property. She then had the janitor bring a different pesticide from the maintenance room. This product...was approved for indoor use but was not the spray used in plaintiff's apartment. The manager copied the list of ingredients...and gave that list to the poison control center.

> ....

After moving back to her apartment, plaintiff awoke every morning feeling nauseated, chilled and weak....She was continually tired and found it impossible to work full time at her job. She finally moved into a new apartment..., but was forced to throw away most of her possessions as they reeked of the pesticide.

Plaintiff sued for negligence....

Having learned the full story of what occurred, plaintiff filed a motion for leave to amend. The proposed second amended complaint...labeled the counts in question... as "Intentional Spoliation of Evidence," no doubt referring to the destruction of the pesticide can containing labeled ingredients. The trial judge denied the motion....

> ....

The tort of intentional spoliation of evidence has been recognized by case law in California. Smith v. Superior Court, 151 Cal. App.3d 491, 198 Cal. Rptr. 829 (1984).... [However, there] is no need to invoke esoteric theories or recognize some new tort.... [T]he remedy for the problem before us is well within the realm of existing tort law....

Assuming plaintiff's allegations are true, defendant certainly acted wrongfully. However, no wrong is actionable unless the putative defendant owed a duty to the party injured....

Traditionally, tort law has been hesitant to impose a duty to render aid or assistance to those in peril....The law did not require us

> ...to play the part of Florence Nightingale and bind up the wounds of a stranger who is bleeding to death, or to prevent a neighbor's child from hammering on a dangerous explosive, or to remove a stone from the highway where it is a menace to traffic,...or even to cry a warning to one who is walking into the jaws of a dangerous machine. The remedy in such cases is left to the "higher law" and the "voice of conscience" which, in a wicked world, would seem to be singularly ineffective either to prevent the harm or to compensate the victim.

W. Prosser & W. Keeton, *supra*, §56 at 375 (citations omitted).

....

Over the years, numerous exceptions have been made to the common law doctrine that there is no duty to assist those in peril. Among the exceptions are the duty of innkeepers and owners of real property to render assistance to guests or invitees. *See* Restatement (Second) of Torts §314A (1965). Arguably, these exceptions are applicable to the facts presented by the case at bench. Even more on point, however, is the principle that where the defendant created the danger the law imposes a duty to do what is reasonable to extricate the plaintiff.

Duty to Aid Another Harmed By Actor's Conduct

> If the actor knows or has reason to know that by his conduct, whether tortious or innocent, he has caused such bodily harm to another as to make him helpless and in danger of further harm, the actor is under a duty to exercise reasonable care to prevent such further harm.

Restatement [(Second) of Torts] §322.

We formally adopt this as the law in Arizona, although the principles are not new and have been used previously in this state. *See* Maldonado v. Southern Pacific Transportation Company, 129 Ariz. 165, 168, 629 P.2d 1001, 1004 (App. 1981). *Maldonado* applied §322 to a situation in which it was alleged that defendant negligently jerked a train car, causing plaintiff to fall under the wheels and become severely injured. Defendant then refused to aid plaintiff and may have hindered those who came to his assistance. The court of appeals found that in the absence of prior case law, it would apply Restatement [(Second) of Torts] §322. That situation is closely analogous to the one before us. In the present case, we need say only that because defendant poisoned plaintiff it had a duty to minimize the resulting harm after it discovered what had occurred.

....Certainly, providing correct information as to the nature of the poison when requested by plaintiff and her doctors was well within the bounds of what could reasonably be expected, especially since defendant had that information at hand. In failing to provide it, and intentionally providing false information, defendant...caused a new or further injury to the plaintiff.

....

We hold, therefore, that plaintiff has stated a cause of action against defendant for the exacerbation of her injuries....

....

...[T]he case is remanded....

Notes

1. *See* Restatement, Third, of Torts: Liability for Physical Harm (Basic Principles) §40 (Council Draft No. 4, 2003) ("When an actor's earlier conduct, even though not tortious, materially contributes to creating a continuing risk of physical harm, the actor has a duty to exercise reasonable care to prevent the harm or to minimize the extent of any harm that does occur").

2. *See also* Conant v. Rodriguez, 828 P.2d 425 (N.M. Ct. App. 1992) (entity which furnished erroneous polygraph results to an employer, leading to plaintiff's discharge, owed a duty to plaintiff to advise the employer of the error).

3. *Instrumentalities.* The rule is the same if the harm is caused not by an action on the part of the defendant, but by an instrumentality under its control. *See* L.S. Ayres & Co. v. Hicks, 40 N.E.2d 334, *reh'g denied*, 41 N.E.2d 195 (Ind. 1942) (department store, which unreasonably delayed stopping an escalator in which a six-year-old child's fingers were caught, held liable for aggravation of injuries).

Rocha v. Faltys

Texas Court of Appeals
69 S.W.3d 315 (Tex. App. 2002)

BEA ANN SMITH, Justice.

Appellants Julia Rocha and George Rocha Sr., individually and as representatives for the Estate of George Rocha Jr. (the Rochas), appeal the trial court's order granting summary judgment in favor of...[appellee] Michael Faltys....

This case arises out of a tragic accident that occurred on April 26, 1998. At the time of the accident, George Rocha Jr. was a twenty-one-year-old junior at Southwestern University in Georgetown and a member of Pi Kappa Alpha fraternity. On April 25, 1998, George and his friend Faltys (a former suitemate who was also a member of the fraternity) attended a crawfish boil at the fraternity house. George consumed some beer at the crawfish boil, which officially ended at 6:00 p.m.; an informal open house followed for some period of time. Around 2:45 a.m. on April 26, George and Faltys, accompanied by three co-eds from Southwestern, went to a local swimming spot on the San Gabriel River called the "Blue Hole." At the Blue Hole, Faltys and George climbed to the top of some cliffs that overlook the river. Faltys dove into the river from the cliffs and then, according to appellants, encouraged George to do the same. George, who was unable to swim, also jumped from the cliffs but began floundering as soon as he hit the water. Despite the efforts of Faltys and other students to save George, he drowned.

...[T]he Rochas filed suit for wrongful death arising out of the alleged negligence of Faltys....

....

....It is fundamental that the existence of a legally cognizable duty is a prerequisite to all tort liability....Generally, a person is under no legal duty to control the conduct of another, even if the person has the ability to do so, unless there exists a special relationship between them. [Citation.]

....

The Rochas...argue that Faltys, by taking George to the top of the cliff and encouraging him to jump off the cliff while he was intoxicated, created a dangerous situation, thus giving rise to a duty to prevent George's death. It is a basic principle of legal responsibility that "individuals should be responsible for their own actions and should not be liable for others' independent misconduct." [Citation.] However, if a "party negligently creates a situation, then it becomes his duty to do something about it to prevent injury to others if it reasonably appears or should appear to him that others in the exercise of their lawful rights may be injured thereby." [Citation.]

Faltys's act of taking George to the top of the cliffs, in and of itself, does not give rise to a legal duty. Simply taking George, an adult man, to the location where George could choose to engage in an allegedly dangerous activity does not constitute negligent creation of a dangerous situation. The fact that George was intoxicated does not affect this analysis. It has been long-recognized at common law that an individual who chooses to consume alcohol maintains the ultimate power over his situation and thus the obligation to control his own behavior. [Citation.] To impose a legal duty on Faltys because George had consumed alcohol would be contrary to this principle.

The Rochas also allege, however, that Faltys negligently created a dangerous situation by encouraging George to jump from the cliff when he knew George could not swim. None of the parties have identified any Texas case suggesting that an adult encouraging another adult to engage in a dangerous activity can give rise to a legal duty. We are unable to locate any such precedent....In holding that Faltys's actions did not create a duty, we do not decide whether encouragement could ever give rise to a duty but only that on these facts a duty did not arise.

The "encouragement" alleged to create a duty in the instant case was implicit encouragement at most. It consisted of Faltys's suggestion to George that they jump off the cliff at the Blue Hole and Faltys's showing George a purportedly safe location on the cliffs from which to jump into the water. However, there is no evidence that Faltys actively encouraged, urged, pressured, forced, or coerced George into jumping from the cliff. Rather, Faltys told George that he did not have to jump if he did not want to; George decided to jump from the cliff. Under these facts we decline to impose a legal duty on Faltys for negligently creating a dangerous situation.

. . . .

....When a young man dies at such a young age, one cannot avoid a feeling of sadness. But while the events leading to George's death were tragic and unfortunate, on these facts his friend Faltys did not have a legal duty such that a cause of action for negligence can be maintained....Therefore, we affirm the trial court's summary judgment.

3. Voluntarily Assumed Duties

Coffee v. McDonnell-Douglas Corp.

Supreme Court of California
503 P.2d 1366 (Cal. 1972)

SULLIVAN, Justice.

In this action for damages for personal injuries defendant McDonnell-Douglas Corporation appeals from a judgment entered upon a jury verdict in favor of plaintiff and from an order denying defendant's motion for a judgment notwithstanding the verdict.

Plaintiff Robert Coffee, after retiring from the United States Air Force in January 1966, applied for a position as a pilot with defendant, a manufacturer of aircraft. Defendant corporation required each of its pilot applicants to undergo a pre-employment physical examination to establish his physical fitness for the job....[P]laintiff underwent a physical examination at defendant's Long Beach medical clinic. Among other things, the examination consisted of a review of plaintiff's medical history, extensive X-rays, urinalysis, an electrocardiogram and a blood test. Coffee, examined by Dr. Gray, one of defendant's doctor-employees, was told that the examination could not be completed until the results of the X-rays and laboratory tests were received, about one week later. However, Dr. Gray signed the examination form on the day of the examination indicating that Coffee was qualified for duties as a pilot, with the understanding that medical approval would be withdrawn if the laboratory tests or X-rays produced any negative results.

... [P]laintiff was informed by Mr. Heimerdinger, the chief pilot in flight operations for defendant, that he had passed the physical examination and that he was acceptable for employment as a pilot. On August 9, 1966, Coffee began work.

Seven months later, on March 9, 1967, plaintiff collapsed from exhaustion after returning from an extended flight for defendant. He was admitted to the Long Beach Naval Hospital where he remained for approximately 10 days. Dr. Snyder, a hematologist, examined him and found that he had severe anemia, his kidney function was impaired, and that the bone structure of his ribs and skull had deteriorated significantly. Plaintiff's condition was diagnosed as multiple myeloma, a disease commonly referred to as cancer of the bone marrow. Dr. Snyder informed plaintiff that he had three to six months to live unless he responded to drug therapy.

Plaintiff responded favorably to the ensuing medical treatment. Initially he received several blood transfusions. He also began the daily use of drugs which caused nausea and resulting weight loss. Because the drugs prescribed made him more susceptible to infection, he also contracted hepatitis. By the fall of 1967, his condition was described as in a state of remission and the nausea stopped. At the time of the trial in November 1970, his condition was still in remission and he had been able to return to work for defendant.

Plaintiff commenced the instant action against McDonnell-Douglas and its three doctor-employees (Waters, Gray, and Ruetman) alleging that defendants required plaintiff to undergo a pre-employment physical examination to determine whether or not he was physically fit to be a test pilot and that defendants performed the physical examination negligently in that they either "knew or should have known of his true condition [i.e., multiple myeloma] and negligently failed to disclose" it, or that they were so negligent in the performance of the examination that they failed to discover the presence of the disease. As a proximate result of defendants' negligence, plaintiff averred, his "disease progressed and became aggravated and spread because plaintiff was without medical treatment," thereby reducing his life expectancy, lessening his resistance to other diseases, weakening his bone structure and causing loss of wages.

[Plaintiff's evidence showed that, pursuant to McDonnell-Douglas's usual policy, the blood-test report was filed without having been examined by a doctor. An evaluation of the report would have disclosed plaintiff's condition, and while prompt treatment would not have made the condition curable, it would have reduced his suffering.]

    ....

An employer generally owes no duty to his prospective employees to ascertain whether they are physically fit for the job they seek, but where he assumes such duty, he is liable if he performs it negligently. [Citations.] The obligation assumed by an employer is derived from the general principle expressed in §323 of the Restatement, Second, of Torts, that one who voluntarily undertakes to perform an action must do so with due care.[6]

---

6. Restatement, Second, of Torts, §323, states: "One who undertakes, gratuitously or for consideration, to render services to another which he should recognize as necessary for the protection of the other's person or things, is subject to liability to the other for physical harm resulting from his failure to exercise reasonable care to perform his undertaking, if [¶] (a) his failure to exercise such care increases the risk of such harm, or [¶] (b) the harm is suffered because of the other's reliance

In the case at bench, defendant, in conformity with its policy that all prospective employees undergo a physical examination, required plaintiff to take such an examination in order to ascertain if he was physically fit to perform the duties of a test pilot. Having assumed the duty to examine plaintiff, defendant also assumed the duty to conduct and complete the examination with due care.

Defendant, however, contends that the duty of an employer, within the context of a pre-employment physical examination, is a limited one; that defendant had no duty to *discover* diseased conditions in plaintiff; and, that even if it had the duty to *disclose known* results, defendant's conduct did not constitute a breach of such duty. More specifically, defendant argues, to impose on employers a "duty to discover" would "ignore the purposes" of pre-employment physical examinations and would "place an undue and unreasonable burden on prospective employers screening possible employees."

We agree that defendant did not breach a duty "to disclose" known results of the examination. We have found no evidence in the record establishing that any of the doctor-employees had actual knowledge of the contents of the blood test report showing, among other things, an abnormally high sedimentation rate and thus indicating the presence of an inflammatory condition. Obviously, having no knowledge of the results of the blood test, defendant's doctor-employees who examined plaintiff were at no time under a duty to make a disclosure.

However, we think defendant has misconceived the issue crucial in this case when it asserts that it had no duty "to discover." The question presented here is not whether defendant has assumed the duty "to discover" diseased conditions; rather, the question is whether the relationship between the parties was such that plaintiff was entitled to legal protection against the wrongful conduct of the defendant. Such a relationship was formed here when defendant undertook, although voluntarily, to examine plaintiff so as to ascertain his physical fitness for duties as a pilot.

Defendant insists that the imposition of a duty "to discover" is an "undue burden." However, it has been said that an employer has failed to exercise due care when it fails "to disclose" diseased or dangerous conditions revealed in a physical examination. [Citations.] Yet, defendant in effect argues that if an employer fails to perform an examination with due care and thereby fails "to discover" the presence of such a condition, he should not be held liable. In other words, defendant's liability would be limited by the commission of its negligent acts. We cannot approve of such a result.

At the same time we do not say that an employer, once having required a prospective employee to submit to a physical examination in order to ascertain his fitness for the job, assumes an absolute obligation to discover any diseased conditions. In our view the proper test is this: whether the employer in such instance is liable for not discovering the disease depends upon whether or not in the light of all of the circumstances he conducted and completed the examination with due care. Included among the relevant circumstances is the purpose of the examination.

In the matter before us, the purpose of the physical examination was to determine plaintiff's physical fitness as a pilot. In order to examine prospective pilots properly, defendant decided it was essential to take a blood sample and subject it to analysis. The blood test report, indicating an inflammatory condition in plaintiff, was never seen by defendant's medical employees because of a corporate procedure allowing the

---

upon the undertaking."

....

report to be filed without evaluation. The question posed, already answered by the jury in the affirmative, was whether in the exercise of due care, defendant "should have known" of the results of the blood test. [Citation.] Viewed in this context, the failure "to discover" the inflammatory condition in plaintiff was the consequence of defendant's own negligence.

....

....The judgment is affirmed....

WRIGHT, C.J., and McCOMB, PETERS, TOBRINER, MOSK, and BURKE, JJ., concur.

Notes

1. *Choosing to Act. See* Union Park Mem. Chapel v. Hutt, 670 So. 2d 64, 66 (Fla. 1996) (funeral director has no duty to orchestrate a funeral procession, but upon undertaking to do so assumes at least a minimal duty to exercise good judgment to ensure safety of procession members); Golden Spread Council, Inc. v. Akins, 926 S.W.2d 287 (Tex. 1996) (council's affirmative act of recommending a scoutmaster created duty to use reasonable care in light of information the council had received about the scoutmaster's alleged prior conduct with other boys); Budden v. United States, 963 F.2d 188 (8th Cir. 1992) (defendant, who provided some weather information in response to a pilot's request, had a duty to provide accurate and complete information); Maussner v. Atlantic City Country Club, 691 A.2d 826 (N.J. Super Ct. 1997) (when a golf course has taken steps to protect golfers from lightning strikes, it must use reasonable care to implement its safety precautions properly). The *Maussner* court wrote:

> [I]f a golf course builds shelters, it must build lightning-proof shelters; if a golf course has an evacuation plan, the evacuation plan must be reasonable and must be posted; if a golf course uses a siren or horn system, the golfers must be able to hear it and must know what the signals mean; and if the golf course uses a weather forecasting system, it must use one that is reasonable under the circumstances.

But see Petersen v. U.S. Reduction Co., 641 N.E.2d 845 (Ill. Ct. App. 1994) (by devising strike plan in which incidents that occurred during a truckers' strike at a manufacturing plant would be reported through chain of command, the manufacturer did not voluntarily undertake to warn replacement drivers of threats to shoot those drivers; the manufacturer's adoption of the strike plan was for its own purposes, not for benefit of replacement drivers).

2. *Scope of the Undertaking.* Some undertakings impose no duties to do anything more than the defendant actually did. Thus:

- the Postal Service's reassignment of a mail carrier (known by co-workers as "Lester the Molester") to a desk job pending investigation of sexual abuse charges did not amount to voluntary assumption of a duty to protect local children from the mail carrier upon reassignment, LM v. United States, 344 F.3d 695 (7th Cir. 2003);

- an employer's provision of a sleeping facility for its employees did not create a duty to third parties to make sure employees got enough sleep before leaving work in a car, McNeil v. Nabors Drilling USA, Inc., 36 S.W.3d 248 (Tex. App. 2001);

- a person who called the police did not undertake a duty to rescue an injured stranger, Rhodes v. Illinois Cent. Gulf R.R., 665 N.E.2d 1260, 1273 (Ill. 1996);

- a premises owner, merely by placing a safety employee on the work site, does not incur a duty to an independent contractor's employees to intervene and ensure that they safely perform their work, Koch Refining Co. v. Chapa, 11 S.W.3d 153 (Tex. 1999);

- a laboratory which correctly communicated drug test results had no duty to warn a prospective employer or job applicant of possible causes of positive results, such as eating poppy seeds, SmithKline Beecham Corp. v. Doe, 903 S.W.2d 347 (Tex. 1995);

- a hotel that requested patrons to keep a snowmobile track clear of debris did not have a duty to clear the track, Brunsfeld v. Mineola Hotel & Restaurant, 456 N.E.2d 361 (Ill. App. Ct. 1984).

In Homer v. Pabst Brewing Co., 806 F.2d 119 (7th Cir. 1986), an employee who fell ill at work was treated in the plant infirmary and sent home. While driving home, he lost consciousness and was injured. The court held that the employer's duty to keep its employees safe and well at work did not extend to determining whether employees could safely drive home. *Compare Homer with* Otis Eng'g Corp. v. Clark, 668 S.W.2d 307 (Tex. 1983), *infra* at 627 (employer who sent drunken employee home was liable for resulting auto-accident deaths).

3. *Assumed Duty to Third Parties?* Sometimes the defendant plainly owes a duty to one person, and the issue is whether failure to perform that duty creates liability to a third person who was injured as a result. For example, suppose that an architect or engineer owes a client a duty to detect and stop inadequate construction of a building. If the building collapses because of unsafe construction, injuring a passer-by, is the architect or engineer liable to that person? For differing views, see Associate Engineers, Inc. v. Job, 370 F.2d 633 (8th Cir. 1966) (liable); McGovern v. Standish, 357 N.E.2d 1134 (Ill. 1976) (not liable). *See also* Graham v. Freese & Nichols, Inc., 927 S.W.2d 294 (Tex. Ct. App. 1996) (the fact that engineering firm expressed concerns about safety to general contractor and issued stop-order related to quality of work at site created no duty to injured employee of general contractor).

Restatement, Second, of Torts §324A states:

> One who undertakes, gratuitously or for consideration, to render services to another which he should recognize as necessary for the protection of a third person or his things, is subject to liability to the third person for physical harm resulting from his failure to exercise reasonable care to protect his undertaking, if
>
> (a) his failure to exercise reasonable care increases the risk of such harm, or
>
> (b) he has undertaken to perform a duty owed by the other to the third person, or
>
> (c) the harm is suffered because of the reliance of the other or the third person upon the undertaking.

In Alder v. Bayer Corp., 61 P.3d 1068 (Utah 2002), hospital technicians brought an action against a manufacturer of an x-ray processing machine, alleging that they suffered illness from chemical exposure caused by the manufacturer's negligent installation and servicing of the machine. The court, relying on §324A, held there was a duty of care running from manufacturer to the technicians, arguably on all three grounds.

See also Sharpe v. St. Luke's Hosp., 821 A.2d 1215 (Pa. 2003) (hospital that contracted with an employer to perform drug testing owed an employee a duty of reasonable care with regard to collection and handling of her urine specimen); Duncan v. Afton, Inc., 991 P.2d 739 (Wyo. 1999) (similar); Webb v. T.D., D.C., 951 P.2d 1008 (Mont. 1997) (physician who performed independent examination of worker at request of her employer's workers' compensation carrier owed a duty to worker to exercise ordinary care to discover conditions posing imminent danger to worker's physical or mental well-being and to take reasonable steps to communicate such conditions to the worker); Snyder v. American Assoc. of Blood Banks, 676 A.2d 1036 (N.J. 1996) (trade association that set standards for blood banks, but which had no immediate connection with the donor or recipient, owed duty of care to recipient of HIV-tainted blood); Merrick v. Thomas, 522 N.W.2d 402 (Neb. 1994) (merit commission owed duty not only to sheriff, but also to job applicant, to score test accurately); King v. National Spa and Pool Inst., 570 So. 2d 612 (Ala. 1990) (trade association that voluntarily issued diving-board standards owed a duty of care to persons who could be injured by a diving board manufactured by a company relying upon the standards).

4. *Contagious Diseases.* If a doctor gives erroneous advice about a communicable disease to a patient, and as a result a third person, whose health was likely to be threatened by the patient, contracts the disease, the third person may sue the doctor. *See* DiMarco v. Lynch Homes-Chester County, Inc., 583 A.2d 422 (Pa. 1990) (hepatitis); *cf.* Lemon v. Stewart, 682 A.2d 1177 (Md. App. 1996) (rule recognized, but a cause of action was not stated because the plaintiffs were not sexual or needle-sharing partners of the person the defendants had failed to inform about being HIV-positive).

5. *Genetic Screening.* Katherine Brokaw, *Genetic Screening in the Workplace and Employers' Liability*, 23 Colum. J. L. & Soc. Prob. 317, 341-45 (1990), states that if an employment physical includes genetic screening tests, the physician's duty includes disclosure of information to a patient who suffers from or is vulnerable to a genetic disorder. She opines that potentially "enormous" tort liability will discourage employers from attempting to use genetic screening for discriminatory purposes.

6. *Suppliers of Chattels.* Restatement, Second, of Torts §392 provides;

> One who supplies to another, directly or through a third person, a chattel to be used for the supplier's business purposes is subject to liability to those for whose use the chattel is supplied, or to those whom he should expect to be endangered by its probable use, for physical harm caused by the use of the chattel in the manner for which and by person for whose use the chattel is supplied
>
> (a) if the supplier fails to exercise reasonable care to make the chattel safe for the use for which it is supplied, or
>
> (b) if he fails to exercise reasonable care to discover its dangerous condition or character, and to inform those whom he should expect to use it.

In Heinz v. Heinz, 653 N.W.2d 334 (Iowa. 2002), a farm laborer who was injured when his arm became entangled in a speed jack brought a negligence action against the farmer (his brother). The court held that the farmer was a supplier of a chattel within the meaning of §392 and therefore owed a duty of care to the laborer with respect to the condition of the chattel.

7. *Problem: The Auto Club.* An auto club tow truck fails to locate the disabled vehicle it has been sent to assist. While waiting for assistance, the driver is fatally injured by a drunken driver whose van plows into the disabled car. Is the auto club liable for the death?

Johnson v. Souza

Superior Court of New Jersey, Appellate Division
176 A.2d 797 (N.J. 1961)

CONFORD, S.J.A.D.

Plaintiff, a social visitor of defendants, was injured when she fell down the icy front steps of their home upon leaving....

Plaintiff's testimony was to the following effect:...When she entered the house she told defendant Mrs. Souza "that their steps were starting to ice up." Thereupon the latter, in plaintiff's presence, told her daughter "Cele" to "go down the cellar and get the rock salt and put it on the steps." Cele said she would do so, and left the room a "few times" during the approximate hour or so that plaintiff was there. In going from the premises, plaintiff "took one step," slid, and injured herself. At the time, the steps were "a sheet of ice."

In the pretrial order, plaintiff claimed: "defts. had knowledge of the treacherous condition of the front steps of the home and voiced their intention to perform certain acts to safeguard plaintiff, when she left the premises, but they negligently failed to do so effectively or at all." The trial court in dismissing the action stated that the defendant Mrs. Souza could not be charged with negligence in relation to telling her daughter to put rock salt on the steps. "She did nothing...so she did no negligent act." The court was not impressed with the argument submitted on behalf of plaintiff to the effect that: "It seems to me that this telling her daughter to do this in the presence of the plaintiff is every indication that it would be done....It tended to build up a sense of false security in the mind of the plaintiff."

It is our conclusion that a jury question was presented insofar as the liability of the female defendant was concerned on the theory of inferable reliance by plaintiff on the gratuitous undertaking by defendant to assure plaintiff's safety in traversing the slippery steps....

Where the defendant has gratuitously undertaken to do an act or perform a service recognizably necessary to another's bodily safety and there is reasonable reliance thereon, the defendant will be liable for harm sustained by the other resulting from his failure to exercise reasonable care to carry out the undertaking. Restatement, Torts, §325, p. 881 (1934), [citations].

In the present case a jury might not unreasonably infer reliance by plaintiff upon the undertaking of Mrs. Souza to eliminate or reduce the hazard of slipperiness on the front steps before she left the house. [Citations.] On that hypothesis, Mrs. Souza would be liable for the consequences of the default of her daughter, whom she made her agent for the purpose, on the principle of respondeat superior....

....

Reversed and remanded for a new trial.

Notes

1. **Promises without Action.** Abresch v. Northwestern Bell Tel. Co., 75 N.W.2d 206 (Minn. 1956), held that although the telephone company has no duty to pass on messages in emergencies, it will be liable if it agrees to pass on a request for help and fails to

do so. The plaintiff, whose building was burning, had asked the operator to call the fire department. The court pointed out that the victim who relies on the operator's promise to call the fire department will pass up other opportunities to get help.

In Pucalik v. Holiday Inns, Inc., 777 F.2d 359 (7th Cir. 1985), the defendant had promised its security guards that it would correct unsafe conditions and defects in the security system at its hotel. It never made the promised corrections, and a guard was killed by an intruder. The court upheld a judgment against the hotel.

See also Long v. Broadlawns Med. Ctr., 656 N.W.2d 71 (Iowa. 2002) (promise to call a wife on the date the defendants discharged her husband from psychiatric care; he later murdered her); Texas Drydock, Inc. v. Davis, 4 S.W.3d 919 (Tex. App. 1999) (promise to provide non-skid tape for a cherry picker's elevated surfaces); Marsallis v. LaSalle, 94 So. 2d 120 (La. Ct. App. 1957) (promise to confine cat to determine whether it was rabid).

2. *Termination of Efforts to Assist.* Aid, once begun, need not be continued forever; a doctor who administers first-aid to an accident victim and sees the victim taken to a hospital need not continue treating the victim until recovery. But premature discontinuance of rescue efforts may violate a duty, especially if the truncated efforts leave the victim worse off than if no rescue had been attempted. Partial rescue efforts may leave the victim worse off for any of several reasons. For example, others may have been discouraged from rendering aid, the rescuer may have placed the victim in a position of greater danger or rendered improper assistance, or the victim may have been encouraged by the rescuer to reduce personal efforts to remedy the situation.

In Parvi v. City of Kingston, 362 N.E.2d 960 (N.Y. 1977), city police officers picked up two intoxicated, noisy men. The officers left the men on an abandoned golf course near a highway; they wandered onto the highway and were struck by a car. Refusing to "speculate" on the question whether the officers had a duty to arrest the men in the first place, the court held that, once the men were in custody, the officers had a duty to care for their safety.

When beginning and then stopping a rescue leaves the victim worse off than if no rescue had been attempted, the plaintiff's case is strong. What if a would-be rescuer begins rescue efforts and then unreasonably stops, leaving the victim no worse off than if rescue had never been attempted? The *Parvi* court, quoting the Restatement, said:

> if the actor has succeeded in removing the other from a position of danger to one of safety, he cannot change his position for the worse by unreasonably putting him back into the same peril, or a new one.

Thus, one supposes, a boater who sees a drowning swimmer need not pull the swimmer into the boat, but, having done so, cannot throw him back. This outcome is consistent with the policy underlying the no-duty rule. The rationale for the rule is that an unlimited duty to prevent harm threatens to impose liability on anyone near an accident victim. Once a would-be rescuer has actually undertaken to furnish help, this argument loses its force.

See Brownsville Med. Ctr. v. Gracia, 704 S.W.2d 68 (Tex. Ct. App. 1985) (a hospital which began to prepare a child for surgery, but terminated those efforts and transferred the child to another hospital upon learning that the parents lacked financial resources, was held liable for the child's death eight days later without surgery).

If discontinuance of rescue efforts is reasonable, no action will lie. In Bowman v. City of Baton Rouge, 849 So. 2d 622 (La. Ct. App. 2003), the court held that an EMS dispatcher did not owe a duty to continue to interrogate a 911 caller or to send an emergency vehicle after being advised that there was no further emergency).

3. *Problem: The Ring Buoy.* Emilio, a swimmer, is rendered totally helpless by stomach cramps. Betty, the only other person in sight, throws him a ring-buoy, and pulls him half the distance to shore, then terminates her rescue efforts. If Emilio drowns, is Betty liable for the death?

4. Negligent Entrustment

McKenna v. Straughan

Court of Appeal of California
222 Cal. Rptr. 462 (Ct. App. 1986)

KINTNER, Associate Justice.

....

On July 29, 1982, Cherie Straughan, the defendants' daughter, drove her car onto the wrong side of the road and hit [Pamela] McKenna head-on, causing McKenna extensive damages and personal injuries. Cherie was driving under the influence of alcohol at the time and was charged with a felony and convicted of a related criminal charge.

McKenna saw Mrs. Straughan almost every Saturday for several months prior to the accident when McKenna did her hair at the beauty shop. McKenna presented evidence the Straughans knew their daughter Cherie had a serious alcohol problem, had been in and out of eight recovery homes and was still drinking. Cherie lived with her parents since she had wrecked her previous car. Mrs. Straughan knew Cherie had a history of driving while intoxicated. Just before the car was purchased, McKenna had urged the Straughans not to give a car to Cherie because of her drinking problem. Mrs. Straughan told McKenna she and her husband were buying Cherie a car shortly before the accident because they did not want to be bothered driving Cherie to her Alcoholics Anonymous meetings. McKenna said "Why give her another one? That's like giving a six year old a loaded gun and telling them [sic] not to use it." A car was purchased with Cherie as the registered owner and William Straughan, Cherie's father, as the registered lienholder 10 days before the accident in question.

....

McKenna sued the Straughans, alleging they were negligent in entrusting or supplying the car to Cherie knowing she was an incompetent and unfit driver.... McKenna also claimed she was entitled to punitive damages because Cherie voluntarily became intoxicated before driving and because the Straughans recklessly and wantonly supplied the car to Cherie knowing she was an unfit driver....

....

After hearing, the court granted the Straughans' motion for summary judgment, finding "there [was] no material issue of fact regarding the custody, control or in the required sense, the supplying of the automobile."....

McKenna appeals....

....

The Straughans argue that...McKenna cannot state a cause of action for negligent entrustment because they never owned or controlled the vehicle which Cherie drove at the time of the accident.

....

....The [trial] Court, apparently...decided in favor of the Straughans because liability should not be extended to "an individual who loans money and ends up [as] the lienholder in such a transaction."

The trial court correctly stated the general rule. In a commercial context, acting solely as a lender without more does not subject the lender to liability. [Citations.] Whether there is "more" turns on the facts of a particular case and the application of the criteria laid down in Biakanja v. Irving (1958) 49 Cal. 2d 647, 650, 320 P.2d 16. [Citations.] Those criteria include the foreseeability of harm to the injured party, the degree of certainty that the plaintiff suffered injury, the closeness of the connection between the defendant's conduct and the injury suffered, the moral blame attached to the defendant's conduct and the policy of preventing future harm. [Citations.]

Here, there can be no question on the foreseeability of harm. The plaintiff herself described the risk as being similar to "giving a six year old a loaded gun." There is also no question that McKenna was injured and that absent the Straughans' decision to make a car available to their daughter, Cherie would not have possessed what in her hands was a dangerous instrumentality. The incident occurred 10 days after the Straughans advanced the funds.

In terms of moral responsibility, there is no functional difference between the Straughans giving their daughter the keys to a car or giving her funds specifically to acquire one. Arguably, the Straughans who loaned money to their daughter so she could have permanent use of a car are more culpable than if they had merely allowed her to borrow their car for temporary use. In effect, they gave their daughter a weapon which she was able to use at any and all times regardless of her condition. [Citations.] Imposing potential liability on the Straughans serves the important public policy of protecting the public from intoxicated drivers who cause needless and tragic deaths and injuries on the highways. Our holding has no effect upon the typical financial transaction in which an automobile is financed through a bank or commercial lender since we are not suggesting a lender has an affirmative duty to investigate the driver's condition before advancing funds. [Citations.]

Because we conclude the Straughans' status as lienholder does not preclude their liability on a negligence theory, we reverse the summary judgment to permit a resolution in trial of the factual issues presented.

Notes

1. A similar analysis was applied in Vince v. Wilson, 561 A.2d 103 (Vt. 1989). The court held that whether a relative, who provided funding for the purchase of vehicle despite knowledge that the purchaser had no driver's license, had failed the driver's test several times, and had abused alcohol and other drugs, was liable for negligent entrustment was for the jury to determine. The court further ruled that a similar question was presented as to the liability of the auto sale corporation and the salespersons, because there was evidence that the relative told them that the purchaser lacked a license and had repeatedly failed the test. *But see* Zedella v. Gibson, 650 N.E.2d 1000, 1003 (Ill. 1995) (holding that a father's co-signing of a loan for his son

to buy a car did not amount to negligent entrustment, because entrustment must be defined with reference to the right to control the property in question, and co-signing the loan did not give the father "an exclusive or superior right of control over the vehicle").

2. *Negligent Entrustment.* Section 390 of the Restatement, Second, of Torts provides:

> One who supplies...a chattel for the use of another whom the supplier knows or has reason to know to be likely because of his youth, inexperience, or otherwise, to use it in a manner involving unreasonable risk of physical harm to himself and others whom the supplier should expect to share in or be endangered by its use, is subject to liability for physical harm resulting to them.

See Rios v. Smith, 744 N.E.2d 1156 (N.Y. 2001) (a father who negligently entrusted all-terrain vehicles to his minor son was subject to liability to another minor who was injured); Ross v. Glaser, 559 N.W.2d 331 (Mich. App. 1996) (a father was liable for giving a handgun to his mentally impaired son, who used it to kill a neighbor); Williams v. Bumpass, 568 So. 2d 979 (Fla. Dist. Ct. App. 1990) (absence of a legal or possessory right to the firearm did not preclude liability for negligent entrustment).

3. *"Entrusting" a Chattel to Its Owner.* Some cases hold that to be held liable for negligent entrustment, the defendant must have a superior right to the chattel, and therefore a person with temporary possession of a vehicle cannot be held liable for returning it to its owner. *See* De Blanc v. Jensen, 59 S.W.3d 373 (Tex. App. 2001) (no liability even though the defendants' son had two previous DWIs and the defendant father held a lien on the truck).

4. *Furnishing Alcohol.* Suppose Cherie Straughan had had her own car all along, and that her parents had given her a bottle of gin. The question of liability for furnishing alcohol to someone who becomes intoxicated and then injures someone presents special difficulties, which are addressed in Chapter 12.

5. *Stolen Cars.* Suppose a defendant leaves the keys in the ignition of a parked car. Joyriding teenagers then steal the car and run down the plaintiff. Is the defendant liable? Many statutes or ordinances prohibit motorists from leaving their keys in their cars, but these statutes do not necessarily answer the duty question, as their purpose may be primarily to prevent theft, rather than to prevent injuries by thieves. The courts are divided on the question. *Compare* Richards v. Stanley, 271 P.2d 23 (Cal. 1954) (Traynor, J.) (no liability, because no duty to protect bystanders against harm done by thieves), *with* Ross v. Hartman, 139 F.2d 14 (D.C. Cir. 1943) ("both negligence and causation are too clear...for submission to a jury").

Hamilton v. Beretta U.S.A. Corp.

Court of Appeals of New York
750 N.E.2d 1055 (N.Y. 2001)

WESLEY, J.

In January 1995 plaintiffs—relatives of people killed by handguns—sued 49 handgun manufacturers in Federal court alleging negligent marketing, design defect, ultrahazardous activity and fraud....

Plaintiffs asserted that defendants distributed their products negligently so as to create and bolster an illegal, underground market in handguns, one that furnished weapons to minors and criminals involved in the shootings that precipitated this lawsuit....

.... [There was a jury verdict in favor of some of the plaintiffs against some of the defendants on the negligent marketing claim.]

On appeal, the Second Circuit certified the following question[] to us:

"(1) Whether the defendants owed plaintiffs a duty to exercise reasonable care in the marketing and distribution of the handguns they manufacture?...."....

Plaintiffs argue that defendant-manufacturers have a duty to exercise reasonable care in the marketing and distribution of their guns based upon four factors: (1) defendants' ability to exercise control over the marketing and distribution of their guns, (2) defendants' general knowledge that large numbers of their guns enter the illegal market and are used in crime, (3) New York's policy of strict regulation of firearms and (4) the uniquely lethal nature of defendants' products.

According to plaintiffs, handguns move into the underground market in New York through several well-known and documented means including straw purchases (a friend, relative or accomplice acts as purchaser of the weapon for another), sales at gun shows, misuse of Federal firearms licenses and sales by non-stocking dealers (i.e., those operating informal businesses without a retail storefront). Plaintiffs further assert that gun manufacturers have oversaturated markets in states with weak gun control laws (primarily in the Southeast), knowing those "excess guns" will make their way into the hands of criminals in states with stricter laws such as New York, thus "profiting" from indiscriminate sales in weak gun states....

....

The threshold question in any negligence action is: does defendant owe a legally recognized duty of care to plaintiff? Courts traditionally "fix the duty point by balancing factors, including the reasonable expectations of parties and society generally, the proliferation of claims, the likelihood of unlimited or insurer-like liability, disproportionate risk and reparation allocation, and public policies affecting the expansion or limitation of new channels of liability"....

Foreseeability, alone, does not define duty—it merely determines the scope of the duty once it is determined to exist [citations]. The injured party must show that a defendant owed not merely a general duty to society but a specific duty to him or her, for "[w]ithout a duty running directly to the injured person there can be no liability in damages, however careless the conduct or foreseeable the harm" [citation]. That is required in order to avoid subjecting an actor "to limitless liability to an indeterminate class of persons conceivably injured by any negligence in that act"....

The District Court imposed a duty on gun manufacturers "to take reasonable steps available at the point of * * * sale to primary distributors to reduce the possibility that these instruments will fall into the hands of those likely to misuse them"....

A duty may arise...where there is a relationship either between defendant and a third-person tortfeasor that encompasses defendant's actual control of the third person's actions, or between defendant and plaintiff that requires defendant to protect plaintiff from the conduct of others. Examples of these relationships include master and servant, parent and child, and common carriers and their passengers.

The key in each is that the defendant's relationship with either the tortfeasor or the plaintiff places the defendant in the best position to protect against the risk of harm. In addition, the specter of limitless liability is not present because the class of potential plaintiffs to whom the duty is owed is circumscribed by the relationship.

...[Here, the] pool of possible plaintiffs is very large—potentially, any of the thousands of victims of gun violence. Further, the connection between defendants, the criminal wrongdoers and plaintiffs is remote, running through several links in a chain consisting of at least the manufacturer, the federally licensed distributor or wholesaler, and the first retailer. The chain most often includes numerous subsequent legal purchasers or even a thief. Such broad liability, potentially encompassing all gunshot crime victims, should not be imposed without a more tangible showing that defendants were a direct link in the causal chain that resulted in plaintiffs' injuries, and that defendants were realistically in a position to prevent the wrongs....

Plaintiffs make two alternative arguments in support of a duty....The first arises from a manufacturer's "special ability to detect and guard against the risks associated with [its] products [and] warrants placing all manufacturers, including these defendants, in a *protective relationship with those foreseeably and potentially put in harm's way by their products*" [citation]. Plaintiffs predicate the existence of this protective duty—particularly when lethal or hazardous products are involved—on foreseeability of harm and our products liability cases such as MacPherson v. Buick Motor Co., 217 N.Y. 382, 111 N.E. 1050.

As we noted earlier, a duty and the corresponding liability it imposes do *not* rise from mere foreseeability of the harm [citation]. Moreover, none of plaintiffs' proof demonstrated that a change in marketing techniques would likely have prevented their injuries. Indeed, plaintiffs did not present any evidence tending to show to what degree their risk of injury was enhanced by the presence of negligently marketed and distributed guns, as opposed to the risk presented by all guns in society [citation].

The cases involving the distribution or handling of hazardous materials, relied upon by plaintiffs, do not support the imposition of a duty of care in marketing handguns. The manufacturer's duty in each case was based either on a products liability theory—that is, the product was defective because of the failure to include a safety feature—or on a failure to warn....Here, defendants' products are concededly not defective—if anything, the problem is that they work too well. Nor have plaintiffs asserted a defective warnings claim or presented sufficient evidence to demonstrate that defendants could have taken reasonable steps that would have prevented their injuries. Likewise, this case can hardly be analogized to those in which a duty has been imposed upon owners or possessors of hazardous substances to safeguard against unsupervised access by children [citations].

Plaintiffs also assert that a general duty of care arises out of the gun manufacturers' ability to reduce the risk of illegal gun trafficking through control of the marketing and distribution of their products. The District Court accepted this proposition and posited a series of structural changes in defendants' marketing and distribution regimes that might "reduce the risk of criminal misuse by ensuring that the first sale was by a responsible merchant to a responsible buyer" [citation]. Those changes, and others proposed by plaintiffs that a jury might reasonably find subsumed in a gun manufacturer's duty of care,[3] would have the unavoidable effect of eliminating a significant number of lawful sales to "responsible" buyers by "responsible" Federal firearms licensees (FFLs) who would be cut out of the distribution chain under the suggested "reforms." Plaintiffs,

---

3. For example, limiting the volume of sales in states with weak gun controls to insure against circulation of the oversupply to strong gun control states such as New York; restricting distribution entirely to established retail stores carrying stocks of guns; franchising of retail outlets; and barring distribution to dealers who sell at unregulated gun shows [citation].

however, presented no evidence, either through the testimony of experts or the submission of authoritative reports, showing any statistically significant relationship between *particular classes* of dealers and crime guns. To impose a general duty of care upon the makers of firearms under these circumstances because of their purported ability to control marketing and distribution of their products would conflict with the principle that any judicial recognition of a duty of care must be based upon an assessment of its efficacy in promoting a social benefit as against its costs and burdens [citation]. Here, imposing such a general duty of care would create not only an indeterminate class of plaintiffs but also an indeterminate class of defendants whose liability might have little relationship to the benefits of controlling illegal guns [citation].

Finally, plaintiffs and the District Court identify an alternative basis for imposing a duty of care here under the negligent entrustment doctrine, arising out of the firearms manufacturers' authority over "downstream distributors and retailers" to whom their products are delivered [citation]. The owner or possessor of a dangerous instrument is under a duty to entrust it to a responsible person whose use does not create an unreasonable risk of harm to others [citations]; Restatement (Second) of Torts § 390. The duty may extend through successive, reasonably anticipated entrustees [citation]. There are, however, fatal impediments to imposing a general duty of care here under a negligent entrustment theory.

The tort of negligent entrustment is based on the degree of knowledge the supplier of a chattel has or should have concerning the entrustee's propensity to use the chattel in an improper or dangerous fashion. Gun sales have subjected suppliers to liability under this theory [citations]. Of course, without the requisite knowledge, the tort of negligent entrustment does not lie (*see,* Earsing v. Nelson, 212 A.D.2d 66, 629 N.Y.S.2d 563 [dismissing a negligent entrustment claim against the manufacturer of a BB gun because a dealer's knowledge of the individual's ability to use the gun safely could not be imputed to the manufacturer]).

The negligent entrustment doctrine might well support the extension of a duty to manufacturers to avoid selling to certain distributors in circumstances where the manufacturer knows or has reason to know those distributors are engaging in substantial sales of guns into the gun-trafficking market on a consistent basis. Here, however, plaintiffs did not present such evidence. Instead, they claimed that manufacturers should not engage in certain broad categories of sales. Once again, plaintiffs' duty calculation comes up short. General statements about an industry are not the stuff by which a common-law court fixes the duty point. Without a showing that specific groups of dealers play a disproportionate role in supplying the illegal gun market, the sweep of plaintiffs' duty theory is far wider than the danger it seeks to avert.[6]

. . . .

Federal law already has implemented a statutory and regulatory scheme to ensure seller "responsibility" through licensing requirements and buyer "responsibility" through background checks. While common-law principles can supplement a manufacturer's statutory duties, we should be cautious in imposing novel theories of tort liabil-

---

6. [Citing 15 cases from other states and "two notable exceptions" which involved different theories of negligent marketing.]

ity while the difficult problem of illegal gun sales in the United States remains the focus of a national policy debate....

In sum, analysis of this State's longstanding precedents demonstrates that defendants—given the evidence presented here—did not owe plaintiffs the duty they claim; we therefore answer the first certified question in the negative.

....

Chief Judge KAYE and Judges SMITH, LEVINE, CIPARICK, ROSENBLATT and GRAFFEO concur.

5. Statutes Relating to Rescue

Minnesota and Vermont have adopted legislation requiring some persons to render emergency assistance. Here is the Minnesota statute, which combines a duty-to-rescue statute with a "good Samaritan" statute that limits liability.

Minn. Stat. Ann. §604A.01
(Westlaw 2004)
Good Samaritan Law

Subd. 1. Duty to assist. A person at the scene of an emergency who knows that another person is exposed to or has suffered grave physical harm shall, to the extent that the person can do so without danger or peril to self or others, give reasonable assistance to the exposed person. Reasonable assistance may include obtaining or attempting to obtain aid from law enforcement or medical personnel. A person who violates this subdivision is guilty of a petty misdemeanor.

Subd. 2. General immunity from liability.

(a) A person who, without compensation or the expectation of compensation, renders emergency care, advice, or assistance at the scene of an emergency or during transit to a location where professional medical care can be rendered, is not liable for any civil damages..., unless the person acts in a willful and wanton or reckless manner.... This subdivision does not apply to a person rendering emergency care, advice, or assistance during the course of regular employment, and receiving compensation or expecting to receive compensation for rendering the care, advice, or assistance.

(b) For the purposes of this section, the scene of an emergency is an area outside the confines of a hospital or other institution that has hospital facilities, or an office of a person licensed to practice one or more of the healing arts under chapter 147, 147A, 148, 150A, or 153....

(c) For the purposes of this section, "person" includes a public or private nonprofit volunteer firefighter, volunteer police officer, volunteer ambulance attendant, volunteer first provider of emergency medical services, volunteer ski patroller, and any partnership, corporation, association, or other entity.

(d) For the purposes of this section, "compensation" does not include payments, reimbursement for expenses, or pension benefits paid to members of volunteer organizations.

(e) For purposes of this section, "emergency care" includes providing emergency medical care by using or providing an automatic external defibrillator,[a] unless the person on whom the device is to be used objects....

Notes

1. Contrast subdivision 1 of the Minnesota statute with Vt. Stat. Ann. Tit. 12, §519(a) (Westlaw 2004), which provides:

> Any person who knows that another is exposed to grave physical harm shall, to the extent that the same can be rendered without danger or peril to himself or without interference with important duties owed to others, give reasonable assistance to the exposed person unless that assistance or care is being provided by others.

See also Swenson v. Waseca Mut. Ins. Co., 653 N.W.2d 794 (Minn. Ct. App. 2002) (a motorist who was providing roadside assistance to an injured snowmobiler by attempting to drive her to the hospital was immune from liability for negligent driving under the Good Samaritan law, and that protection was not lost by reason of a *de minimis* delay occasioned by planned indirect route to the hospital).

2. **Doctors and Accident Victims.** It is widely believed—though it may not be true—that many doctors rendering aid to accident victims have been sued for negligence in rendering that aid. "Good Samaritan" legislation typically bars negligence actions against doctors who furnish help gratuitously in emergencies.

3. Legislation may also impose a duty to act in more-limited situations. Consider the Virginia statute relating to forest fires (Va. Code Ann. §10.1-1139 (Westlaw 2004)):

> Any forest warden...shall have the authority to summon as many able-bodied persons between eighteen and fifty years of age as may, in his discretion, be reasonably necessary to assist in extinguishing any forest fire....Any person summoned by a forest warden to fight a forest fire shall be paid at the rate of pay provided in the Department of Forestry wage scale for fire fighting....

> Any person summoned who fails or refuses to assist in fighting the fire, unless the failure is due to physical inability or other valid reason, shall be guilty of a Class 4 misdemeanor.

4. If a person violates a statutory duty to render aid, should the one harmed by that failure be permitted to sue the offender for negligence based upon violation of the statute? That is, may a court hold that the statute sets the standard of care for a civil cause of action? Would it make a difference whether the legislation contains a provision similar to one in the Vermont statute which provides, "a person who wilfully violates... this section shall be fined not more than $100.00"? Vt. Stat. Ann. Tit. 12, §519(c) (Westlaw 2004).

---

a. Automatic external defibrillators (AEDs) employ a series of small electrical shocks to help restore normal heart rhythms. To encourage the use of such equipment outside of health care facilities, Congress passed the Cardiac Arrest Survival Act of 2000, which, within limits, immunizes from liability for negligence persons who acquire, use, or attempt to use AEDs. *See* 42 U.S.C. §238q (Westlaw 2004).—Eds.

5. *Emergency Medical Treatment and Active Labor Act.* The EMTALA is a federal law that requires hospitals receiving Medicare funds to provide appropriate medical screening to all persons who come to an emergency room seeking medical assistance and to render the services that are necessary to stabilize the patient's condition. *See* Correa v. Hospital San Fran., 69 F.3d 1184 (1st Cir. 1995).

6. *Leaving the Scene.* Many if not all states prohibit those involved in a motor-vehicle accident from leaving the scene. Some of these statutes also require the rendering of assistance to anyone injured in the accident. For example, the Tex. Transp. Code §550.023 (Westlaw 2003) provides:

Duty to Give Information and Render Aid

> The operator of a vehicle involved in an accident resulting in the injury or death of a person or damage to a vehicle that is driven or attended by a person shall:
>
> ....
>
> (3) provide any person injured in the accident reasonable assistance, including transporting or making arrangements for transporting the person to a physician or hospital for medical treatment if it is apparent that treatment is necessary, or if the injured person requests the transportation.

7. *A Feminist Perspective on No-Duty-to-Rescue Cases.* In *A Lawyer's Primer on Feminist Theory and Tort*, 38 J. Legal Educ. 3, 33-36 (1988),[b] Professor Leslie Bender writes:

> One of the most difficult areas in which questions of duty and the standard of care arise is the "no duty to rescue" case. The problem is traditionally illustrated by the drowning-stranger hypothetical....
>
> Each year that I teach torts I watch again as a majority of my students initially find this legal "no duty" rule reprehensible. After the rationale is explained and the students become immersed in the "reasoned" analysis, and after they take a distanced, objective posture informed by liberalism's concerns for autonomy and liberty, many come to accept the legal rule that intuitively had seemed so wrong to them. They are taught to reject their emotions, instincts, and ethics, and to view accidents and tragedies abstractly, removed from the social and particularized contexts, and to apply instead rationally derived universal principles and a vision of human nature as atomistic, self-interested, and as free from constraint as possible.
>
> How would this drowning-stranger hypothetical look from a new legal perspective informed by a feminist ethic based upon notions of caring, responsibility, interconnectedness, and cooperation? If we put abstract reasoning and autonomy aside momentarily, we can see what else matters. In defining duty, what matters is that someone, a human being, a part of us, is drowning and will die without some affirmative action. That seems more urgent, more imperative, more important than any possible infringement of individual autonomy by the imposition of an affirmative duty....
>
> The drowning stranger is not the only person affected by the lack of care. He is not detached from everyone else. He no doubt has people who care about him—parents, spouse, children, friends, colleagues; groups he participates

---

b. Reprinted with permission.

in—religious, social, athletic, artistic, political, educational, work-related; he may even have people who depend upon him for emotional or financial support. He is interconnected with others. If the stranger drowns, many will be harmed. It is not an isolated event with one person's interests balanced against another's. When our legal system trains us to understand the drowning-stranger story as a limited event between two people, both of whom have interests at least equally worth protecting,...we take a human situation and translate it into a cold, dehumanized algebraic equation. We forget that we are talking about human death or grave physical harms and their reverberating consequences when we equate the consequences with such things as one person's momentary freedom not to act. People are decontextualized for the analysis, yet no one really lives an acontextual life....

If instead we impose a duty of acting responsibly with the same self-conscious care for the safety of others that we would give our neighbors or people we know, we require the actor to consider the human consequences of her failure to rescue. Even though it is easier to understand the problem if we hone it down to "relevant facts," which may include abstracting the parties into letter symbols (either A and B or P and D) or roles (driver and passenger), why is it that "relevant facts" do not include the web of relationships and connected people affected by a failure to act responsibly with care for that person's safety?....

The "no duty" rule is a consequence of a legal system devoid of care and responsiveness to the safety of others. We certainly could create a duty to aid generated from a legal recognition of our interconnectedness, an elevated sense of the importance of physical health and safety, a rejection of the act/omission dualism, and a strong legal value placed on care and concern for others rather than on economic efficiency or individual liberty. The duty to act with care for another's safety, which under appropriate circumstances would include an affirmative duty to act to protect or prevent harm to another, would be shaped by the particular context. One's ability to aid and one's proximity to the need would be relevant considerations. Whether one met that duty would not be determined by how a reasonable person would have acted under the circumstances but by whether one acted out of a conscious care and concern for the safety, health, and well-being of the victim in the way one would act out of care for a neighbor or friend....This seemingly minor change would transform the core of negligence law to a human, responsive system....

C. Abrogation of the General Rule

Soldano v. O'Daniels

Court of Appeal of California
190 Cal. Rptr. 310 (Ct. App. 1983)

ANDREEN, Associate Justice.

Does a business establishment incur liability for wrongful death if it denies use of its telephone to a good Samaritan who explains an emergency situation occurring without and wishes to call the police?

This appeal follows a judgment of dismissal of the second cause of action of a complaint for wrongful death upon a motion for summary judgment.... Both briefs on appeal adopt the defense averments:

> This action arises out of a shooting death occurring on August 9, 1977. Plaintiff's father [Darrell Soldano] was shot and killed by one Rudolph Villanueva....

> Plaintiff alleges that on the date of the shooting, a patron of Happy Jack's Saloon came into the Circle Inn and informed a Circle Inn employee that a man had been threatened at Happy Jack's. He requested the employee either call the police or allow him to use the Circle Inn phone to call the police. That employee allegedly refused to call the police and allegedly refused to allow the patron to use the phone to make his own call. Plaintiff alleges that the actions of the Circle Inn employee were a breach of the legal duty that the Circle Inn owed to the decedent.

....

There is a distinction, well rooted in the common law, between action and nonaction. [Citation.] It has found its way into the prestigious Restatement Second of Torts (hereafter cited as "Restatement"), which provides in §314:

> The fact that the actor realized or should realize that action on his part is necessary for another's aid or protection does not itself impose upon him a duty to take such action.

.... The distinction between malfeasance and nonfeasance, between active misconduct working positive injury and failure to act to prevent mischief not brought on by the defendant, is founded on "that attitude of extreme individualism so typical of Anglo-Saxon legal thought." [Citation.]

Defendant argues that the request that its employee call the police is a request that it *do* something. He points to the established rule that one who has not created a peril ordinarily does not have a duty to take affirmative action to assist an imperiled person. [Citation.] It is urged that the alternative request of the patron from Happy Jack's Saloon that he be allowed to use defendant's telephone so that he personally could make the call is again a request that the defendant do something—assist another to give aid....

The refusal of the law to recognize the moral obligation of one to aid another when he is in peril and when such aid may be given without danger and at little cost in effort has been roundly criticized. Prosser describes the case law sanctioning such inaction as a "refus[al] to recognize the moral obligation of common decency and common humanity" and characterizes some of these decisions as "shocking in the extreme.... Such decisions are revolting to any moral sense. They have been denounced with vigor by legal writers." (Prosser, Law of Torts (4th ed. 1971) §56, pp. 340-341, fn. omitted.)....

Francis H. Bohlen, in his article *The Moral Duty to Aid Others as a Basis of Tort Liability*, commented:

> Nor does it follow that because the law has not as yet recognized the duty to repair harm innocently wrought, that it will continue indefinitely to refuse it recognition. While it is true that the common law does not attempt to enforce all moral, ethical, or humanitarian duties, it is, it is submitted, equally true that all ethical and moral conceptions, which are not the mere temporary manifestations of a passing wave of sentimentalism or puritanism, but on the contrary, find a real and permanent place in the settled convictions of a race and become part of the normal habit of thought thereof, of necessity do in time color the judicial conception of legal obligation....

. . . .

As noted in *Tarasoff v. Regents of University of California*,...[551 P.2d 334 (1976)], the courts have increased the instances in which affirmative duties are imposed not by direct rejection of the common law rule, but by expanding the list of special relationships which will justify departure from that rule. For instance, California courts have found special relationships in *Ellis v. D'Angelo* (1953) 116 Cal. App. 2d 310, 253 P.2d 675 (upholding a cause of action against parents who failed to warn a babysitter of the violent proclivities of their child), *Johnson v. State of California* (1968) 69 Cal. 2d 782, 73 Cal. Rptr. 240, 447 P.2d 352 (upholding suit against the state for failure to warn foster parents of the dangerous tendencies of their ward), *Morgan v. County of Yuba* (1964) 230 Cal. App. 2d 938, 41 Cal. Rptr. 508 (sustaining cause of action against a sheriff who had promised to warn decedent before releasing a dangerous prisoner, but failed to do so). [Citation.]

And in *Tarasoff*...[the] court held the patient-therapist relationship was enough to create a duty to exercise reasonable care to protect others from the foreseeable result of the patient's illness.

Section 314A of the Restatement lists other special relationships which create a duty to render aid, such as that of a common carrier to its passengers, an innkeeper to his guest, possessors of land who hold it open to the public, or one who has a custodial relationship to another. A duty may be created by an undertaking to give assistance. (*See* Rest. 2d Torts, *supra*, §321 et seq.)

Here there was no special relationship between the defendant and the deceased. It would be stretching the concept beyond recognition to assert there was a relationship between the defendant and the patron from Happy Jack's Saloon who wished to summon aid. But this does not end the matter.

It is time to re-examine the common law rule of nonliability for nonfeasance in the special circumstances of the instant case.

. . . .

[The court then discussed state legislation relating to rescue efforts (including provisions indemnifying citizens for injuries and damages sustained in crime suppression efforts, requiring phone users to yield party lines in emergencies, and establishing a 911 number for emergency calls) and quoted language from federal reports about the importance of citizen involvement in crime prevention.]

The above statutes...[and] quotations...demonstrate that "that attitude of extreme individualism so typical of Anglo-Saxon legal thought" may need limited re-examination in the light of current societal conditions and the facts of this case to determine whether the defendant owed a duty to the deceased to permit the use of the telephone.

We turn now to the concept of duty in a tort case. The Supreme Court has identified certain factors to be considered in determining whether a duty is owed to third persons. These factors include:

> "the foreseeability of harm to the plaintiff, the degree of certainty that the plaintiff suffered injury, the closeness of the connection between the defendant's conduct and the injury suffered, the moral blame attached to the defendant's conduct, the policy of preventing future harm, the extent of the burden to the defendant and consequences to the community of imposing a duty to exercise care with resulting liability for breach, and the availability, cost, and prevalence of insurance for the risk involved." (*Rowland v. Christian* (1968) 69

Cal. 2d 108, 113, 70 Cal. Rptr. 97, 443 P.2d 561; *cf.* Raymond v. Paradise Unified School Dist. (1963) 218 Cal. App. 2d 1, 8-9, 31 Cal. Rptr. 847.)

We examine those factors in reference to this case. (1) The harm to the decedent was abundantly foreseeable; it was imminent. The employee was expressly told that a man had been threatened. The employee was a bartender. As such he knew it is foreseeable that some people who drink alcohol in the milieu of a bar setting are prone to violence. (2) The certainty of decedent's injury is undisputed. (3) There is arguably a close connection between the employee's conduct and the injury: the patron wanted to use the phone to summon the police to intervene. The employee's refusal to allow the use of the phone prevented this anticipated intervention. If permitted to go to trial, the plaintiff may be able to show that the probable response time of the police would have been shorter than the time between the prohibited telephone call and the fatal shot. (4) The employee's conduct displayed a disregard for human life that can be characterized as morally wrong: he was callously indifferent to the possibility that Darrell Soldano would die as the result of his refusal to allow a person to use the telephone. Under the circumstances before us the bartender's burden was minimal and exposed him to no risk: all he had to do was allow the use of the telephone. It would have cost him or his employer nothing. It could have saved a life. (5) Finding a duty in these circumstances would promote a policy of preventing future harm. A citizen would not be required to summon the police but would be required, in circumstances such as those before us, not to impede another who has chosen to summon aide. (6) We have no information on the question of the availability, cost, and prevalence of insurance for the risk, but note that the liability which is sought to be imposed here is that of employee negligence, which is covered by many insurance policies. (7) The extent of the burden of the defendant was minimal, as noted.

The consequences to the community of imposing a duty, the remaining factor mentioned in Rowland v. Christian, *supra*, is termed "the administrative factor" by Professor Green in his analysis of determining whether a duty exists in a given case. [Citation.] The administrative factor is simply the pragmatic concern of fashioning a workable rule and the impact of such a rule on the judicial machinery. It is the policy of major concern in this case.

As the Supreme Court has noted, the reluctance of the law to impose liability for nonfeasance, as distinguished from misfeasance, is in part due to the difficulties in setting standards and of making rules workable. (Tarasoff v. Regent of University of California, *supra*, [citation].)

Many citizens simply "don't want to get involved." No rule should be adopted which would require a citizen to open up his or her house to a stranger so that the latter may use the telephone to call for emergency assistance. As Mrs. Alexander in Anthony Burgess' A Clockwork Orange learned to her horror, such an action may be fraught with danger. It does not follow, however, that use of a telephone in a public portion of a business should be refused for a legitimate emergency call. Imposing liability for such a refusal would not subject innocent citizens to possible attack by the "good Samaritan," for it would be limited to an establishment open to the public during times when it is open to business, and to places within the establishment ordinarily accessible to the public. Nor would a stranger's mere assertion that an "emergency" situation is occurring create the duty to utilize an accessible telephone because the duty would arise if and only if it were clearly conveyed that there exists an imminent danger of physical harm. (*see* Rest. 2d Torts, *supra*, §327.)

Such a holding would not involve difficulties in proof, overburden the courts or unduly hamper self-determination or enterprise.

A business establishment such as the Circle Inn is open for profit. The owner encourages the public to enter, for his earnings depend on it. A telephone is a necessary adjunct to such a place. It is not unusual in such circumstances for patrons to use the telephone to call a taxicab or family member.

. . . .

We conclude that the bartender owed a duty to the plaintiff's decedent to permit the patron from Happy Jack's to place a call to the police or to place the call himself.

It bears emphasizing that the duty in this case does not require that one must go to the aid of another. That is not the issue here. The employee was not the good Samaritan intent on aiding another. The patron was.

It would not be appropriate to await legislative action in this area. The rule was fashioned in the common law tradition, as were the exceptions to the rule. [Citation.] To the extent this opinion expands the reach of §327 of the Restatement, it represents logical and needed growth, the hallmark of the common law. It does not involve the sacrifice of other respectable interests.

. . . .

The possible imposition of liability on the defendant in this case is not a global change in the law. It is but a slight departure from the "morally questionable" rule of nonliability for inaction absent a special relationship. It is one of the predicted "inroads upon the older rule." (Rest. 2d Torts, *supra*, §314, com. c.) It is a logical extension of Restatement §327 which imposes liability for negligent interference with a third person who the defendant knows is attempting to render necessary aid. However small it may be, it is a step which should be taken.

We conclude there are sufficient justiciable issues to permit the case to go to trial and therefore reverse.

FRANSON, Acting P.J., and STANTON, J., concur.

Notes

1. *Preventing Aid.* The *Soldano* court noted that the facts of that suit almost fell within Restatement, Second, of Torts §327, which provides that an individual who knows that a third person is ready to give aid to another, and negligently prevents the third person from doing so, is subject to liability for harm caused by the absence of the aid. Section 327 is contained in topic 8 of the Restatement, "Prevention of Assistance by Third Persons." The scope note to that topic provides that an

> actor can prevent a third person from rendering aid to another in many ways including the following: first, by so injuring the third person as to make him incapable of giving aid; second, by interfering with his efforts to give aid; third, by injuring or destroying the usefulness of a thing which the third person is using to give aid or by otherwise preventing him from using it; fourth, by obstructing the third person's access to the other.

Of course, intentional prevention of assistance may also give rise to liability. *Id.* at §326.

2. *Child Abuse.* See Mary Kate Kearney, *Breaking the Silence: Tort Liability for Failing to Protect Children from Abuse*, 42 Buff. L. Rev. 405 (1994) (arguing that current tort law does not adequately protect children and that an adult who knows or should know of on-going child abuse should have an affirmative duty to take reasonable steps to protect the child).

D. The Public-Duty Rule

Governments routinely undertake to protect members of the public from harm. Police and fire protection come immediately to mind; less-obvious examples include weather forecasting (of great importance to the safety of the crews of fishing boats), air-traffic control, the installation and maintenance of traffic lights and signs, and the inspection of food.

The question of how much protection of a particular kind is enough is quintessentially legislative and executive. A city's decision to spend more on traffic-law enforcement instead of buying new fire trucks will save some lives (motorists') at the cost of others (fire victims'). Allowing all of those whose injuries might have been prevented by greater efforts in some safety area to get to a jury against the relevant government agency would soon bankrupt all governments. It would also present factfinders with issues they cannot reasonably be expected to decide: the question whether it was "unreasonable" for a city to spend three times as much on police protection as on fire prevention is not one any sensible society would entrust to juries or judges. It is therefore quite clear that a plaintiff whose only claim is that a government agency should have devoted more resources to preventing the kind of harm the plaintiff suffered has no case.

The inability of the courts to evaluate all government decisions involving safety does not mean, however, that governments can never be liable for conduct relating to safety. If a police officer on the way to interview a suspect drives negligently and runs down the plaintiff, the city will be liable (assuming that municipal immunity has been waived). It will be no defense that tight budgets required the city to hire inexperienced drivers for the police force.

The extreme cases are therefore clear: inadequate performance of specific tasks like driving a car will render a government liable; inadequate decisions about what safety precautions should be taken will not. The difficulties arise in between these extremes, as in the following opinion.

Riss v. City of New York
Court of Appeals of New York
293 N.Y.S.2d 897 (N.Y. 1968)

BREITEL, Judge.

This appeal presents, in a very sympathetic framework, the issue of the liability of a municipality for failure to provide special protection to a member of the public who was repeatedly threatened with personal harm and eventually suffered dire personal injures for lack of such protection. The facts are amply described in the dissenting opinion and no useful purpose would be served by repetition....

   . . . .

... [This] case involves the provision of a governmental service to protect the public generally from external hazards and particularly to control the activities of criminal wrongdoers. [Citations.] The amount of protection that may be provided is limited by the resources of the community and by a considered legislative-executive decision as to how those resources may be deployed. For the courts to proclaim a new and general duty of protection in the law of tort, even to those who may be the particular seekers of protection based on specific hazards, could and would inevitably determine how the limited police resources of the community should be allocated and without predictable limits....

Before such extension of responsibilities should be dictated by the indirect imposition of tort liabilities, there should be a legislative determination that that should be the scope of public responsibility [citation].

....

When one considers the greatly increased amount of crime committed throughout the cities..., it is easy to see the consequences of fixing municipal liability upon a showing of probable need for and request for protection. To be sure these are grave problems at the present time, exciting high priority activity on the part of the national, State and local governments, to which the answers are neither simple, known, or presently within reasonable control. To foist a presumed cure for these problems by judicial innovation of a new kind of liability in tort would be foolhardy indeed and an assumption of judicial wisdom and power not possessed by the courts.

....

... [T]here is no warrant in judicial tradition or in the proper allocation of the powers of governments for the courts, in the absence of legislation, to carve out an area of tort liability for police protection to members of the public....

Accordingly, the order of the Appellate Division affirming the judgment of dismissal should be affirmed.

KEATING, Judge (dissenting).

....

Linda Riss, an attractive young woman, was for more than six months terrorized by a rejected suitor well known to the courts of this State, one Burton Pugach. This miscreant, masquerading as a respectable attorney, repeatedly threatened to have Linda killed or maimed if she did not yield to him: "If I can't have you, no one else will have you, and when I get through with you, no one else will want you." In fear for her life, she went to those charged by law with the duty of preserving and safeguarding the lives of the citizens and residents of this State. Linda's repeated and almost pathetic pleas for aid were received with little more than indifference.... On June 14, 1959 Linda became engaged to another man. At a party held to celebrate the event, she received a phone call warning her that it was her "last chance." Completely distraught, she called the police, begging for help, but was refused. The next day Pugach carried out his dire threats... by having a hired thug throw lye in Linda's face. Linda was blinded in one eye, lost a good portion of her vision in the other, and her face was permanently scarred. After the assault the authorities concluded that there was some basis for Linda's fears, and for the next three and one-half years, she was given around-the-clock protection.

No one questions the proposition that the first duty of government is to assure its citizens the opportunity to live in personal security. And no one who reads the record of Linda's ordeal can reach a conclusion other than that the City of New York, acting through its agents, completely and negligently failed to fulfill this obligation to Linda.

Linda has turned to the courts of this State for redress, asking that the city be held liable in damages for its negligent failure to protect her from harm. With compelling logic, she can point out that, if a stranger, who had absolutely no obligation to aid her, had offered her assistance, and thereafter Burton Pugach was able to injure her as a result of the negligence of the volunteer, the courts would certainly require him to pay damages. (Restatement, 2d, Torts §323). Why then should the city, whose duties are imposed by law and include the prevention of crime...not be responsible?....

Linda's reasoning seems so eminently sensible that surely it must come as a shock to her and to every citizen to hear the city argue and to learn that this court decides that the city has no duty to provide police protection to any given individual. What makes the city's position particularly difficult to understand is that, in conformity to the dictates of the law, Linda did not carry any weapon for self-defense (former Penal Law, §1897). Thus, by a rather bitter irony she was required to rely for protection on the City of New York which now denies all responsibility to her.

It is not a distortion to summarize the essence of the city's case here in the following language: "Because we owe a duty to everybody, we owe it to nobody." Were it not for the fact that this position has been hallowed by much ancient and revered precedent, we would surely dismiss it as preposterous....

The foremost justification repeatedly urged for the existing rule is the claim that the State and the municipalities will be exposed to limitless liability....

The fear of financial disaster is a myth. The same argument was made a generation ago in opposition to proposals that the State waive its defense of "sovereign immunity." The prophecy proved false then, and it would now....No municipality has gone bankrupt because it has had to respond in damages when a policeman causes injury through carelessly driving a police car or in the thousands of other situations where, by judicial fiat or legislative enactment, the State and its subdivisions have been held liable for the tortious conduct of their employees. Thus, in the past four or five years, New York City has been presented with an average of some 10,000 claims each year. The figure would sound ominous except for the fact the city has been paying out less than $8,000,000 on tort claims each year and this amount includes all those sidewalk defect and snow and ice cases about which the courts fret so often....Certainly this is a slight burden in a budget of more than six billion dollars (less than two tenths of 1%) and of no importance as compared to the injustice of permitting unredressed wrongs to continue to go unrepaired. That Linda Riss should be asked to bear the loss, which should properly fall on the city if we assume, as we must, in the present posture of the case, that her injuries resulted from the city's failure to provide sufficient police to protect Linda is contrary to the most elementary notions of justice.

....

Another variation of the "crushing burden" argument is the contention that, every time a crime is committed, the city will be sued and the claim will be made that it resulted from inadequate police protection. Here...too the underlying assumption of the argument is fallacious because it assumes that a strict liability standard is to be imposed and that the courts would prove completely unable to apply general principles of tort liability in a reasonable fashion in the context of actions arising from the negligent acts of police and fire personnel. The argument is also made as if there were no such legal principles as fault, proximate cause or foreseeability, all of which operate to keep liability within reasonable bounds. No one is contending that the police must be at the scene of every potential crime or must provide a personal bodyguard to every person who walks into a police station and claims to have been threatened. They need only act as a reasonable man would under the circumstances. At first there would be a duty to inquire. If the injury indicates nothing to substantiate the alleged threat, the matter may be put aside.... If, however, the claims prove to have some basis, appropriate steps would be necessary.

. . . .

It is also contended that liability for inadequate police protection will make the courts the arbiters of decisions by the Police Commissioner in allocating his manpower and his resources. We are not dealing here with a situation where the injury or loss occurred as a result of a conscious choice of policy made by those exercising high administrative responsibility after a complete and thorough deliberation of various alternatives. There was no major policy decision taken by the Police Commissioner to disregard Linda Riss' appeal for help because there was absolutely no manpower available to deal with Pugach. This "garden variety" negligence case arose in the course of "day-by-day operations of government". . . .

More significant, however, is the fundamental flaw in the reasoning behind the argument alleging judicial interference. It is a complete oversimplification of the problem of municipal tort liability. What it ignores is the fact that indirectly courts are reviewing administrative practices in almost every tort case against the State or a municipality, including even decisions of the Police Commissioner. Every time a municipal hospital is held liable for malpractice resulting from inadequate record-keeping, the courts are in effect making a determination that the municipality should have hired or assigned more clerical help or more competent help to medical records or should have done something to improve its recordkeeping procedures so that the particular injury would not have occurred. Every time a municipality is held liable for a defective sidewalk, it is as if the courts are saying that more money and resources should have been allocated to sidewalk repair, instead of to other public services.

The situation is nowise different in the case of police protection. . . .

. . . .

. . . . In other words, all the courts do in these municipal negligence cases is require officials to weigh the consequences of their decisions. If Linda Riss' injury resulted from the failure of the city to pay sufficient salaries to attract qualified and sufficient personnel, the full cost of that choice should become acknowledged in the same way as it has in other areas of municipal tort liability. Perhaps officials will find it less costly to choose the alternative of paying damages than changing their existing practices. That may be well and good, but the price for the refusal to provide for an adequate police force should not be borne by Linda Riss and all the other innocent victims of such decisions.

What has existed until now is that the City of New York and other municipalities have been able to engage in a sort of false bookkeeping in which the real costs of inadequate or incompetent police protection have been hidden by charging the expenditures to the individuals who have sustained often catastrophic losses rather than to the community where it belongs, because the latter had the power to prevent the losses.

Although in modern times the compensatory nature of tort law has generally been the one most emphasized, one of its most important functions has been and is its normative aspect. It sets forth standards of conduct which ought to be followed. The penalty for failing to do so is to pay pecuniary damages. At one time the government was completely immunized from this salutary control. This is much less so now, and the imposition of liability has had healthy side effects. In many areas, it has resulted in the adoption of better and more considered procedures just as workmen's compensation resulted in improved industrial safety practices. To visit liability upon the city here will no doubt have similar constructive effects. . . .

... [A]lthough "sovereign immunity," by that name, supposedly died...it has been revived in a new form. It now goes by the name "public duty."

....

The [public-duty] rule is Judge made and can be judicially modified. By statute, the judicially created doctrine of "sovereign immunity" was destroyed. It was an unrighteous doctrine, carrying as it did the connotation that the government is above the law. Likewise, the law should be purged of all new evasions, which seek to avoid the full implications of the repeal of sovereign immunity.

....

....A few examples of the actions of the police should suffice to show the true state of the record. Linda Riss received a telephone call from a person who warned Linda that Pugach was arranging to have her beaten up. A detective learned the identity of the caller....When Linda requested that Pugach be arrested, the detective said he could not do that because she had not yet been hurt. The statement was not so. It was and is a crime to conspire to injure someone. True there was no basis to arrest Pugach then, but that was only because the necessary leg work had not been done. No one went to speak to the informant, who might have furnished additional leads. Linda claimed to be receiving telephone calls almost every day. These calls could have been monitored for a few days to obtain evidence against Pugach. Any number of reasonable alternatives presented themselves....

... [W]ith actual notice of danger and ample opportunity to confirm and take reasonable remedial steps, a jury could find that the persons involved acted unreasonably and negligently....The order of the Appellate Division should be reversed and a new trial granted.

....

[FULD, C.J., and BURKE, SCILEPPI, BERGAN, and JASEN, JJ., concurred with BREITEL, J.]

Notes

1. *Inadequate Police and Fire Protection.* It is still the rule in many states that there is no duty to provide police protection to a particular individual in the absence of facts establishing a special relationship between the governmental defendant and the plaintiff. *See* Zimmerman v. Village of Skokie, 697 N.E.2d 699, 702 (Ill. 1998) (stating, incidental to discussion of a "special duty" exception, that "[t]he public duty rule is a long-standing precept which establishes that a governmental entity and its employees owe no duty of care to individual members of the general public to provide governmental services, such as police and fire protection"); King v. Northeast Security, Inc., 790 N.E.2d 474, 478-79 (Ind. 2003) (recognizing that a government unit is immune from liability "where a city or state fails to provide adequate police protection to prevent crime" and stating that "[t]o say the governmental entity is immune for acts or omissions in described areas is the functional equivalent of asserting the entity has no duty to anyone in carrying out those activities"); Mullin v. Municipal City of South Bend, 639 N.E.2d 278, 283 (Ind. 1994) (indicating that "[a] foreseeable plaintiff with a foreseeable injury is not, standing alone, sufficient to establish a private duty of a governmental entity"); Stone v. N.C. Dept. of Labor, 495 N.E.2d 711 (N.C. 1998) (holding that the rule precluded workers who were injured

in a plant fire from recovering based on the alleged negligence of a state department in failing to inspect a plant before the fire); Ohio Dept. of Rehab. and Correction, 728 N.E.2d 428 (Ohio Ct. App. 1999) (relying on the public-duty rule in finding no liability for a death allegedly caused by the negligent release and supervision of a parolee); Am. Jur. 2d Munic. & State Tort Liability §88, *The Public Duty Doctrine* (2003) (stating that the public-duty rule "provides a defense independent of sovereign immunity").

"Because courts narrowly apply the special relationship exception, the police rarely owe a duty to a domestic violence victim." Sue Ellen Schuerman, *Establishing a Tort Duty for Police Failure to Respond to Domestic Violence*, 34 Ariz. L. Rev. 355, 369 (1992).

The "public-duty rule" has been applied in other contexts. *See* Stratmeyer v. U.S., 67 F.3d 1340 (7th Cir. 1995) (holding that, under Indiana law, the U.S. was not liable for a U.S.D.A. veterinarian's failure to quarantine a herd of diseased cattle). *See also* Hernandez v. City of Hartford, 30 F. Supp. 2d 268 (D. Conn. 1998) (stating in an action for negligent infliction of emotional distress involving alleged failure to accommodate a complicated pregnancy under the Americans with Disabilities Act, that, under Connecticut law, a "negligence action against a local governmental entity cannot be predicated on the breach of a general duty owed to the public").

2. *Firsthand Observation.* Cases in which a public officer merely knows of a risk of harm to an individual may be distinguished from those where an officer actually witnesses the infliction of harm. In Crosland v. New York Transit Auth., 498 N.E.2d 143 (N.Y. 1986), hoodlums jumped the turnstiles at a subway stop and savagely attacked a group of students, one of whom died from the wounds he sustained. The complaint alleged that several transit authority workers witnessed the incident and, in violation of internal rules, did nothing to summon aid. Distinguishing cases in which recovery was denied to persons attacked at stations where no police were present, the court held that a motion to dismiss was properly denied.

3. *Voluntary Governmental Assumption of Duty.* In Florence v. Goldberg, 375 N.E.2d 763 (N.Y. 1978), a city was sued by the mother of a first-grader who was struck by a taxicab while returning from school. The complaint alleged that the police department's failure to provide a substitute for a school crossing guard who had called in sick constituted negligence. A crossing guard had been on duty at the intersection for more than two weeks, leading the mother to conclude that she did not need to arrange for someone to provide a similar service. The court stated:

> [W]here a municipality assumes a duty to a particular person or class of persons, it must perform that duty in a nonnegligent manner, notwithstanding that absent its voluntary assumption of that duty, none would have otherwise existed....

See also Schultz v. Foster-Glocester Reg. Sch. Dist., 755 A.2d 153 (R.I. 2000) (allegedly negligent failure to train, supervise, instruct, equip, and treat an injured member of a cheerleading team); Nelson v. Salt Lake City, 919 P.2d 568 (Utah 1996) (allegedly negligent failure by a city to maintain a fence between a park and a river).

4. *Statutory Duties.* Liability may also be imposed when the police violate a statutory duty to take action. *See* Calloway v. Kinkelaar, 659 N.E.2d 1322, 1330 (Ill. 1995) (holding that, in an action for civil damages under the Domestic Violence Act, whether the facts establish a "special duty exception to the public duty immunity is legally irrelevant"); Nearing v. Weaver, 670 P.2d 137, 143 (Or. 1983) (plaintiff stated a claim for statutory liability under the Abuse Prevention Act).

In some states, statutory tariffs govern a utility's relationship with its customers and have the force and effect of law. *See* First Assembly of God v. Texas Utilities, 52 S.W.3d 482 (Tex. App. 2001) (holding that a utility company was not liable for fire damages to a church sanctuary that occurred following repairs because the applicable tariff limited liability to cases where the utility's negligence was the sole proximate cause of the damages, and here the damages were also caused by an initial lightning strike and bad wiring inside the church).

5. *Special Relationships.* A plaintiff can avoid the obstacle to recovery posed by the public-duty rule by establishing that there was a special relationship between the plaintiff and the governmental defendants. The following decision illustrates one type of special-relationship case.

Sorichetti v. City of New York

Court of Appeals of New York
482 N.E.2d 70 (N.Y. 1985)

ALEXANDER, Judge.

This action was commenced against the City of New York (City) by Dina Sorichetti, an infant, and her mother, Josephine Sorichetti, to recover damages resulting from injuries inflicted on Dina by her father, Frank Sorichetti. Plaintiffs' theory of recovery is that the City, through the New York City Police Department, negligently failed to take Frank Sorichetti into custody or otherwise prevent his assault upon his daughter after being informed that he may have violated a Family Court order of protection and that he had threatened to do harm to the infant. Special Term denied a pretrial motion by the City to dismiss the complaint for failure to state a cause of action [citation], and the Appellate Division affirmed [citation].

A jury thereafter returned a verdict in plaintiffs' favor in the amount of $3,000,000 for the infant and $40,000 for the mother. The Appellate Division modified by ordering a new trial on damages unless Dina Sorichetti stipulated to reduce her award to $2,000,000 [citation]. The infant so stipulated and judgment was entered in the reduced amount....

....

Josephine and Frank Sorichetti were married in 1949, and had three children, the youngest being Dina, who was born in 1969. It appears that Frank drank excessively and that the couple's relationship was quite stormy, with Frank becoming violent and abusive when under the influence of alcohol. In January 1975, Josephine obtained an order of protection in Family Court following a particularly violent incident in which her husband had threatened her and punched her in the chest so forcefully as to send her "flying across the room." The order recited that Frank was "forbidden to assault, menace, harass, endanger, threaten or act in a disorderly manner toward" Josephine. By June 1975, Frank's drinking and abusiveness had intensified. Consequently, Josephine moved out of their residence and took her own apartment. Upon her return in early July to obtain her personal belongings, Frank attacked her with a butcher knife, cutting her hand, which required suturing, and threatened to kill her and the children. The police were summoned....A second order of protection was issued....

Frank's drinking and violent behavior continued, however, and in September 1975, Josephine served divorce papers on him. Frank became enraged and proceeded to destroy the contents of their apartment. He broke every piece of furniture, cut up clothes belonging to his wife and Dina, threw the food out of the refrigerator and bent every knife and fork. The police from the 43rd precinct were summoned, but they refused to arrest Frank because "he lived there."

Family Court entered a third order of protection that also ordered Frank Sorichetti to stay away from Josephine's home. During the ensuing months, Frank continued to harass his wife and daughter, following them in the mornings as they walked to Dina's school and threatening that they "were Sorichettis" and were going to "die Sorichettis," and that he was going to "bury them." Josephine reported these incidents to the 43rd precinct....

On November 6, 1975, Josephine and Frank appeared in Family Court where the order of protection was made final for one year. Included in the order was a provision granting Frank visitation privileges with his daughter each weekend from 10:00 a.m. Saturday until 6:00 p.m. Sunday. It was agreed that Dina would be picked up and dropped off at the 43rd precinct. As required by Family Court Act §168, the order also recited that: "[T]he presentation of this Certificate to any Peace Officer shall constitute authority for said Peace Officer to take into custody the person charged with violating the terms of such Order of Protection and bring said person before this Court and otherwise, so far as lies within his power, to aid the Petitioner in securing the protection such Order was intended to afford."

On the following weekend, Josephine delivered Dina to her husband in front of the 43rd precinct at the appointed time. As he walked away with the child, Frank turned to Josephine and shouted, "You, I'm going to kill you." Pointing to his daughter, he said, "You see Dina; you better do the sign of the cross before this weekend is up." He then made the sign of the cross on himself. Josephine understood her husband's statements and actions to be a death threat, and she immediately entered the police station and reported the incident to the officer at the desk....

At 5:30 p.m. the following day, Sunday, Josephine returned to the station house. She was distraught, agitated and crying....She showed the officer the order of protection and related the threats made the previous morning....The officer testified that he told Josephine that if "he didn't drop her off in a reasonable time, we would send a radio car out."

The officer referred Josephine to Lieutenant Leon Granello, to whom she detailed the prior events. He dismissed the protective order as "only a piece of paper" that "means nothing" and told Josephine to wait outside until 6:00. At 6:00 p.m., Josephine returned to the Lieutenant who told her, "why don't you wait a few minutes....Maybe he took her to a movie. He'll be back. Don't worry about it." Josephine made several similar requests, but each time was told "to just wait. We'll just wait."....

    ....

....Josephine...continued to plead that the officer take immediate action. The Lieutenant again told Josephine "Let's just wait." At 7:00, the Lieutenant told Josephine to leave her phone number and to go home, and that he would call her if Sorichetti showed up. She did as suggested.

....Between 6:55 and 7:00 p.m., Sorichetti had attacked the infant repeatedly with a fork, a knife and a screwdriver and had attempted to saw off her leg....The infant plaintiff was hospitalized for 40 days and remains permanently disabled. Frank Sorichetti was convicted of attempted murder, and is currently serving a prison sentence.

    ....

A municipality cannot be held liable for injuries resulting from a failure to provide adequate police protection absent a special relationship existing between the municipality and the injured party....In the context of police protection, a different rule "could and would inevitably determine how the limited police resources of the community should be allocated and without predictable limits" [citation].

In several extraordinary instances, a special relationship has been found which imposes a duty on a municipality to provide reasonable police protection to an individual. For example, in Schuster v. City of New York, 5 N.Y.2d 75, 180 N.Y.S.2d 265, 154 N.E.2d 534, the City was held liable when a citizen collaborated with the police in the arrest of a dangerous fugitive and was thereafter denied protection after he received death threats, which were successfully carried out. Similarly, in De Long v. County of Erie (60 N.Y.2d 296, 469 N.Y.S.2d 611, 457 N.E.2d 717, *supra*), we imposed a special duty of care on a municipality toward a woman who called 911 for police assistance, was told that assistance would be forthcoming, and in reliance on this assurance exposed herself to danger that resulted in her death.

A key element in each of these cases...is some direct contact between agents of the municipality and the injured party.

In the present case, we hold that a special relationship existed between the City and Dina Sorichetti which arose out of (1) the order of protection; (2) the police department's knowledge of Frank Sorichetti's violent history, gained through and verified both by its actual dealings with him, the existence of the order of protection, and its knowledge of the specific situation in which the infant had been placed; (3) its response to Josephine Sorichetti's pleas for assistance on the day of the assault; and (4) Mrs. Sorichetti's reasonable expectation of police protection.

In enacting Family Court Act §168, the Legislature intended to encourage police involvement in domestic matters, an area in which the police traditionally have exhibited a reluctance to intervene [citations]. The statute does not evince a legislative determination that the scope of municipal tort liability attendant upon traditional governmental activities, such as police protection, should be extended to an entire class....When presented with an order of protection, a police officer is not mandated to make an arrest. Nonetheless, such presentation along with an allegation that the order has been violated, obligates the officer to investigate and take appropriate action.

The issuance of a protective order creates a situation quite unlike that presented in *Riss*, 22 N.Y.2d 579, 293 N.Y.S.2d 897, 240 N.E.2d 860, supra in several respects. The order evinces a preincident legislative and judicial determination that its holder should be accorded a reasonable degree of protection from a particular individual. It is presumptive evidence that the individual whose conduct is proscribed has already been found by a court to be a dangerous or violent person and that violations of the order's terms should be treated seriously. Significantly, the class of potential victims to whom a duty to investigate might arise is necessarily limited by the terms of the order.

....

The fact that an injury occurs because of a violation of an order of protection does not in itself create municipal liability. An arrest may not be warranted in each case, and the failure of the police to take such action will not alone be determinative of the reasonableness of their conduct. But when the police are made aware of a possible violation, they are obligated to respond and investigate, and their actions will be subject to a "reasonableness" review in a negligence action.

.... These circumstances are significantly different from those in *Riss*, 22 N.Y.2d 579, 293 N.Y.S.2d 897, 240 N.E.2d 860, *supra* wherein the assailant, who was unknown to the police, was seemingly a citizen in good standing who, up until the attack, had done nothing to indicate a likelihood that he would make good on his threats. Sorichetti, by contrast, was no mere "unfavored swain" who apparently would be satisfied by voicing hollow "predications of dire results to the object of [his] attentions" [citation].

Aside from their awareness of the threatmaker's violent propensity, a critical factor in the creation of a special duty of protection herein is the police officers' conduct toward Josephine on the evening of November 9th. When she first approached the frontdesk officer at 5:30, Josephine was told that if Sorichetti did not arrive within a reasonable time the police would send a patrol car out. Thereafter, the Lieutenant told Josephine to "wait outside" until 6:00, creating the clear impression that at that time, when Sorichetti's failure to return would be a violation of the order of protection, some action would be taken. From this point on, the police repeatedly told Josephine to "wait awhile longer," never dispelling the notion that they would provide assistance at some reasonable time, until she was finally told at 7:00 to "go home." Josephine, in her helpless and distraught state, had no alternative but to seek the assistance of the police to assure her daughter's safety [citation]. The passage of time was critical inasmuch as the assault did not take place until approximately 6:55.

Thus, in this respect also, this case is unlike *Riss* [citation] wherein the police made clear to the victim that they would provide no assistance based on the assailant's threats alone. Under the circumstances presented on this appeal, we hold that a special relationship existed between the police and Josephine and her six-year-old daughter such that the jury could properly consider whether the police conduct satisfied the duty of care owing to Dina.

....

Order affirmed, with costs.

Notes

1. *Compare Sorichetti with*: Solomon v. City of New York, 489 N.E.2d 1294 (N.Y. 1985) (by promulgating and enforcing regulations prohibiting bicycle riding in an area of a park where a park patron was struck, the city did not assume a special relationship toward the patron to protect the latter from the prohibited activity); Caldwell v. City of Philadelphia, 517 A.2d 1296 (Pa. Super. Ct. 1986) (officer had no special relationship to an injured pedestrian; no liability for failure to obtain identification of the motorist who left the scene); Kircher v. City of Jamestown, 543 N.E.2d 443 (N.Y. 1989) (no liability for officer's failure to call in a witness's report of an abduction as promised, absent direct contact between the victim and the police and justifiable reliance by the victim on assurances of protection that would create a "special relationship"; in *Sorichetti*, relaxation of the direct-contact requirement was justified by the existence of the protective order).

2. *Reliance on Assurances*. A number of states hold that reliance upon governmental assurances of action will support a claim based on non-action. For example, in City of Rome v. Jordan, 426 S.E.2d 861, 863 (Ga. 1993), the court required the following elements for imposition of a private duty on governmental defendants:

(1) an explicit assurance by the municipality, through promises or actions, that it would act on behalf of the injured party;

(2) knowledge on the part of the municipality that inaction could lead to harm; and

(3) justifiable and detrimental reliance by the injured party on the municipality's affirmative undertaking.

See also Cuffy v. City of New York, 513 N.Y.S.2d 372 (N.Y. 1987) (same test as in *Rome*, except that direct contact between the city and injured party is required); Mullin v. Municipal City of South Bend, 639 N.E.2d 278, 284 (Ind. 1994) ("Not only must the harm to the injured party be foreseeable, the relationship between the governmental entity and the injured person must be such that the governmental entity has induced the injured person justifiably to rely…"; no liability because the city gave no assurance that an ambulance would be dispatched to the fire immediately); Tipton v. Town of Tabor, 567 N.W.2d 351 (S.D. 1997) (for purposes of the special-duty rule, parents and a child who was mauled by caged, privately owned wolfdog hybrids did not reasonably rely on the city and county, causing them to forgo self-precaution, despite the licensing of the animals and an investigation of the pen; the parents arrived in the town only minutes before the attack and no representations had been made to them about the safety of the hybrids caged in a neighbor's yard); Lauer v. City of N.Y., 733 N.E.2d 184 (N.Y. 2000) (holding that a medical examiner who failed to correct an erroneous autopsy report about a child that led to a homicide investigation against the child's father did not have a "special relationship" with the father so as to render the city liable to the father for negligent infliction of emotional distress because the medical examiner assumed no affirmative duty upon which the father could justifiably have relied and the father alleged no personal contact with medical examiner and there was no indication that the medical examiner knew that the father, or anyone else, had become a suspect in case).

However, there is authority that:

> a promise and reliance thereon are [not] indispensable elements of a special relationship. Such a relationship has also been found when the conduct of a police officer, in a situation of dependency, results in detrimental reliance on him for protection… [by] lulling the injured parties into a false sense of security and perhaps preventing other assistance from being sought.

Souza v. City of Antioch, 62 Cal. Rptr. 2d 909, 918-19 (Cal. Ct. App. 1997) (police had duty to exercise reasonable care when they took exclusive control of hostage situation).

3. *Public Duty and the Constitution.* The Supreme Court held in DeShaney v. Winnebago County Dep't of Social Services, 489 U.S.189 (1989), that an agency's negligent failure to protect a child from a savage beating by his father did not deprive the child of his right to liberty under the Fourteenth Amendment. The agency had taken the child into temporary custody, but later released him to his father and did virtually nothing to protect him. The Court noted that the agency's negligence could make it liable in tort under state law, but held that the Fourteenth Amendment Due Process Clause "is phrased as a limitation of the State's power to act, not as a guarantee of certain minimal levels of safety and security." The *DeShaney* decision leaves to the state courts and legislatures the question of the extent to which agencies are to be held liable for their failure to protect the public. Had the case gone the other way, the federal courts would have had a major role in shaping this body of law.

4. *Public Utilities.* Policy considerations comparable to those described in *Riss* may apply to actions against public utilities, such as electric companies and water companies, for harms caused by the companies' failure to provide services. For example, in Strauss v. Belle Realty Co., 482 N.E.2d 34 (N.Y. 1985), the New York Court of Appeals

held that an electric company could not be held liable to someone who fell on stairs that were unlit because of a blackout caused by the company's negligence. The court's main concern seems to have been preventing "crushing exposure to liability." The accident in question took place during a 25-hour blackout of New York City. *Compare* Weinberg v. Dinger, 524 A.2d 366 (N.J. 1987), holding that private water companies which negligently failed to provide water under sufficient pressure to operate fire hydrants could be liable to owners of property that burned. The *Weinberg* court limited its holding to uninsured or under-insured property owners. Therefore, in New Jersey, fire losses resulting from inadequate water pressure fall on the property owner's fire-insurance company to the extent of the insurance coverage, but on the water company to the extent of any excess. In effect, *Weinberg* abolishes the collateral-source rule for this particular class of accidents.

5. ***Volunteer Fire Departments.*** The tort liability of volunteer fire departments and their firefighters is governed by statute in many states. *See, e.g.*, Tex. Civ. Prac. & Rem. Code §78.103-104 (Westlaw 2003) ("A volunteer fire department is...liable for damages...only to the extent that a county providing the same or similar services would be liable...and...entitled to the exclusions, exceptions, and defenses applicable to a county under...statutory or common law").

6. ***Abrogation of the Public-Duty Rule.*** In Wallace v. Ohio Dept. of Commerce, 773 N.E.2d 1018 (Ohio 2002), the court reviewed the state's prior decisions, which had broadly endorsed the public-duty rule. The court then abrogated the rule in a particular context by holding that the rule was incompatible with the express language of a statutory provision requiring that the state's liability in the Court of Claims be determined "in accordance with the same rules of law applicable to suits between private parties." In negligence suits against the state, the court held, the Court of Claims must determine the existence of a legal duty using conventional tort principles that would be applicable if the defendant were a private individual or entity. In reaching its decision, the court summarized the law nationally by stating that "even though a handful of states have rejected the public-duty rule as a bar to government liability,[c] a majority of jurisdictions that have considered the question apply the doctrine in some form.[d]"

7. ***Judicial Threat and Legislative Response.*** In Jean v. Commonwealth, 610 N.E.2d 305 (Mass. 1993), the court announced its intention to abolish the public-duty rule at

---

c. With regard to rejection of the public-duty rule, the *Wallace* court cited cases from Alaska (1976), Arizona (1982), Colorado (1986), Florida (1979), Louisiana (1990), Massachusetts (1993) [*see* note 7 *infra*], Nebraska (1986), New Hampshire (1993), New Mexico (1984), Oregon (1979), Wisconsin (1976), and Wyoming (1986). 773 N.E.2d at 1024 n. 5.

d. With regard to adherence to the public-duty rule, the *Wallace* court cited cases from California (1983), Connecticut (1982), District of Columbia (1983), Hawaii (1999), Iowa (2001), Kansas (1986), Minnesota (1979), Missouri (1988), Nebraska (1992), New York (1987), Rhode Island (1989), South Carolina (1999), South Dakota (1997), Utah (1991), Washington (1983), and West Virginia (1989). The court added:

"Five other states—Georgia, Indiana, Michigan, North Carolina, and Vermont—have applied the public-duty rule in a more limited fashion. The supreme courts in Georgia and Indiana have expressly declined to apply the public-duty rule beyond the context of police and emergency services. [Citations.] Similarly, the Michigan Supreme Court recently refused to extend the public-duty rule beyond cases involving the alleged failure of a police officer to protect a plaintiff from a third person's criminal acts. [Citation.]. The North Carolina Supreme Court has embraced the public-duty rule in suits against the state but has declined to extend it to suits against municipalities. [Citations.] The Vermont Supreme Court has apparently drawn the same distinction as North Carolina. [Citations.]" 773 N.E. 2d at 1024 n. 6.

the first opportunity after the end of the legislative session, thereby allowing the legislature time to make appropriate arrangements. The legislature responded that same year by amending the law that waives sovereign immunity.

MASS. STAT. 258 §§2-10
(Westlaw 2004)

§ 2 Public employers shall be liable for injury or loss of property or personal injury or death caused by the negligent or wrongful act or omission of any public employee while acting within the scope of his office or employment, in the same manner and to the same extent as a private individual under like circumstances...

....

§ 10 The provisions of sections one to eight, inclusive, shall not apply to:....

(h) any claim based upon the failure to establish a police department or a particular police protection service, or if police protection is provided, for failure to provide adequate police protection, prevent the commission of crimes, investigate, detect or solve crimes, identify or apprehend criminals or suspects, arrest or detain suspects, or enforce any law, but not including claims based upon the negligent operation of motor vehicles, negligent protection, supervision or care of persons in custody, or as otherwise provided in clause (1) of subparagraph (j).

....

(j) any claim based on an act or failure to act to prevent or diminish the harmful consequences of a condition or situation, including the violent or tortious conduct of a third person, which is not originally caused by the public employer or any other person acting on behalf of the public employer. This exclusion shall not apply to:

(1) any claim based upon explicit and specific assurances of safety or assistance, beyond general representations that investigation or assistance will be or has been undertaken, made to the direct victim or a member of his family or household by a public employee, provided that the injury resulted in part from reliance on those assurances. A permit, certificate or report of findings of an investigation or inspection shall not constitute such assurances of safety or assistance....

How would the plaintiffs in *Riss* and *Sorichetti* have fared under the Massachusetts law?

Chapter 10

Limited Duty: Premises Liability

A. The Traditional Categories: Trespassers, Licensees, and Invitees

The early development of the common law was in many respects strongly individualistic. *See* Roscoe Pound, The Spirit of the Common Law 36-37 (1921). Consistently with that philosophy, the law developed rules which granted possessors of land great scope within which they could do as they pleased, free of most worries of tort liability to those injured by a condition of the property or an activity carried on there. *See* Francis Bohlen, Studies in the Law of Torts 163 (1926). During the late nineteenth and early twentieth centuries, the law developed a rigid system that classified persons on land as "trespassers," "licensees," or "invitees." A person's status determined the duty of care owed by the landowner, or by an occupier of land (such as a tenant), toward that person.

Trespassers—persons present without a privilege or the consent of the possessor—were afforded the least protection; licensees—those present with consent, but for their own purposes—were entitled to somewhat greater care; and invitees—persons present on the land at the possessor's invitation and for the possessor's benefit—were owed the usual tort duty of reasonable care under the circumstances. In premises-liability litigation, proper categorization of the injured person's status became a question of pre-eminent importance.

In recent years, some state supreme courts have rejected the traditional approach to premises liability, treating the plaintiff's status as merely one factor to be considered in determining whether the defendant behaved reasonably. However, many states retain the traditional approach, and in some of the states in which the courts have rejected it, the legislatures have enacted statutory protections for landowners.

1. Trespassers

Bonney v. Canadian National Railway Co.

United States Court of Appeals for the First Circuit
800 F.2d 274 (1st Cir. 1986)

LEVIN H. CAMPBELL, Chief Judge.

Plaintiff-appellee Cheryl Bonney brought a tort action seeking damages for the death of her husband, Rodney Bonney, which resulted from his attempt to rescue a 15-year-

533

old trespasser who fell from a railroad bridge under the control of defendant-appellant Canadian National Railway Company (the "Railway"). The Railway now appeals from the judgment entered against it....

....

The railroad bridge, leased to the Railway, spans the Androscoggin River between Lewiston and Auburn, Maine. The bridge is a concrete and steel structure, approximately 410 feet long, with tracks about 50 feet above the surface of the river. The tracks sit on railroad ties which are spaced several inches apart and which extend about three feet on either side of the tracks. Apart from widely spaced steel supports, there is nothing on the sides of the ties to prevent a pedestrian from falling off the bridge into the river below.

While there is a bridge designed for cars and pedestrians a short distance down the river, residents in the area frequently used the railroad trestle as a shortcut....The Railway had been aware of this practice for decades. At times, the Railway had placed "No Trespassing" signs on the bridge. The signs, however, were often removed by vandals, and none was posted the day of the accident. In 1969, the Railway made an unsuccessful attempt to secure enforcement of existing Maine laws forbidding trespass on railroad property. Since then, the Railway has made no effort to prevent pedestrian traffic on the bridge.

On the night of April 6, 1981, 15-year-old Jonathan Thibodeau attempted to return from Auburn to his home in Lewiston via the railroad bridge....The light was so dim that Thibodeau's companion, Mark Sheink, could not see whether anything was written on the trestle. Upon reaching the bridge, Thibodeau told Sheink that he was going to ride his bicycle across the bridge with the tires outside the rails. Sheink warned him not to do so, telling Thibodeau would die if he attempted such a ride. Nonetheless, Thibodeau rode off ahead. Sheink soon heard a "cathump" and, after a pause, a splash. He then heard Thibodeau's cries for help from the river below.

Sheink ran to a nearby store for help. The first police officer to arrive, Rodney Bonney, swam out in an attempt to rescue Thibodeau. Subsequently, another officer, realizing that Officer Bonney and Thibodeau were in distress, swam out to assist them. Officer Bonney pushed Thibodeau toward the second officer who tried, unsuccessfully, to bring Thibodeau back to shore. Both Thibodeau and Officer Bonney drowned.

....

If...defendant violated a duty to Thibodeau, its liability may be extended for the rescuer's benefit, on the theory that defendant's tortious conduct created the situation which invited the rescue attempt, and that the attempt was a foreseeable consequence of defendant's actions....

Under Maine law,...a landowner owes no duty of care to a trespasser; its duty is simply to refrain from "wanton, wilful, or reckless acts." [Citations.] The district court ruled that the Railway's "failure to take anything beyond token measures to prevent injury to pedestrians" evinced such a "callous indifference to a known condition of extreme danger to the public" as to violate even the minimum duty owed to trespassers. On appeal, defendant argues that the simple failure to make its premises safe for trespassers does not rise to the level of wanton misconduct forbidden under Maine law. We agree.

In reaching its conclusion that the Railway's failure to act constituted wanton misconduct in this case, the district court relied on a Maine case which defined "wanton misconduct" in the context of an automobile accident as "a reckless disregard of danger to others," Blanchard v. Bass, 153 Me. 354, 358, 139 A.2d 359 (1958), as well as W. Prosser, The Law of Torts §34, at 184-85 (4th ed. 1971) (defining reckless acts as "highly unreasonable conduct, or an extreme departure from ordinary care, in a situation where a high degree of danger is apparent"). Holding under this standard that the Railway's failure to act displayed "a reckless disregard of danger to others," the court emphasized that the Railway had known "for decades" that the bridge was heavily used by pedestrians of all ages, especially children, and by bicyclists. Witnesses, including five for the railroad, testified that the traffic across the bridge was heavy, from twenty to fifty people on a "busy day," including "winos" and young adults coming from bars at night. Moreover, the court found that the bridge was clearly unsafe for pedestrian use: there were no guardrails, the spaces between the ties were irregular, making it easy to lose one's footing, and protruding between every few ties were large nuts-and-bolts that made walking even more treacherous....

But while we accept the above findings, we do not read Maine case law as supporting a determination that the Railway's "failure to take anything beyond token measures to prevent injury to pedestrians" rose to the level of a "reckless act" violative of a *landowner's* duty towards trespassers. The *Blanchard* definition of "wanton misconduct" was not made in the context of a Maine trespass case, where a defendant normally owes no duty of care to a trespasser. Rather the *Blanchard* definition was tailored to an automobile accident case where the court could properly ask whether defendant's actions in causing a car accident rose to the level of wanton misconduct (or whether he was simply negligent), since defendant had in any event a duty to exercise due care in the operation of his car. Here, the dangerous condition of the bridge being open and obvious, *see infra*, the landowner owed no duty to a trespasser to keep its premises reasonably safe. Absent a duty to act affirmatively, we are reluctant to hold the Railway liable for failure to act under the "reckless disregard of dangers to others" standard in *Blanchard* and Prosser. Applying that standard to trespass cases would, we believe, improperly expand and transform the very limited duty towards trespassers that Maine imposes on landowners.

A trespasser in Maine is deemed to enter at his own risk, and "must take the premises as they are in fact, and he assumes all risk of injury from their condition." [Citations.] Except in special circumstances not applicable here, a landowner is not required to use due care to maintain its premises reasonably safe for the benefit of trespassers. [Citations.] This is particularly true where, as here, the dangerous condition of the land is open and obvious, and fully appreciated by the trespasser. [Citation.]

Moreover, we do not view the particular circumstances of this case (the Railway's long-time knowledge of frequent pedestrian use, the clear dangerousness of the bridge, and the feasibility of making the bridge safer) as differing from those in other trespasser cases so markedly as to have required the Railway to take affirmative measures to prevent injury to trespassers on its bridge....

That it was feasible, as the district court found, for the Railway to have made the bridge safer (by either erecting a barrier gate or installing handrails) does not warrant a finding of liability under Maine law. Even if the effort required of a landowner to make its land less dangerous is minimal, Maine courts have placed the responsibility for protection of trespassers on the person who unlawfully intrudes:

> [W]hat logical reason is there for saying that one, young or old, who is wrongfully upon the premises, can hold the owner to the expenditure of any money, or the submission to any degree of inconvenience, for his protection? We can

think of none. We think there is no reason except the sentimental one, and that
is not the basis of a legal obligation.

Nelson v. Burnham & Morrill Co., 114 Me. 213, 219, 95 A. 1029, 1032 (1915) (emphasis in original).

....

A final issue is whether the Railway owed Bonney an independent duty as a foreseeable rescuer, even though the Railway did not violate any duty to the person Bonney sought to rescue....

Plaintiff argues that this court should...recognize an independent duty to rescuers under Maine law on the grounds that "[b]y keeping its bridge in a dangerous condition, (the Railway) created a likely and *foreseeable* risk of harm to potential rescuers who would be called to the scene." (Emphasis added.) We decline to do so....

All American courts of which we know have so far rejected the concept of an independent duty to a rescuer without an underlying tortious act to the person actually placed in peril....

....

The judgment of the district court is reversed, and the case is remanded with directions to dismiss the complaint.

Note

1. *Trespassers: The General Rule.* In states adhering to some form of the "categories," a "landowner owes a trespasser only a duty to refrain from wilful and wanton conduct." In Blakely v. Camp Ondessonk, 38 F.3d 325 (7th Cir. 1994), a teenager sneaked into a Catholic camp for a cliffside beer party and was injured when she fell. The court held that the defendant diocese, which had previously discouraged trespassing, was not liable because it was unaware of the girl's presence and there were no traps or other conditions on the property intended to harm trespassers.

Humphrey v. Twin State Gas & Electric Co.

Supreme Court of Vermont
139 A. 440 (Vt. 1927)

POWERS, J.

[The defendant corporation's electric transmission line was washed out by a flood. Having obtained permission from one Thomas, the defendant effected a temporary repair by stringing its wires on poles and trees across Thomas's wood lot. A wire tie installed by the defendant's servants to hold the line broke, and the line sagged until it touched a barbed wire fence, charging the fence with a deadly electric current. Plaintiff, while hunting on Thomas's land, came in contact with the fence and was severely injured. At trial, the court granted the defendant's motion for a directed verdict. The Supreme Court assumed for purposes of decision that plaintiff was a trespasser.]

....

[Being a trespasser, plaintiff could recover nothing from Thomas for his injuries.]....
Thomas owed him no duty to keep the premises safe for his unlawful use. The defendant takes the position that, so far as the plaintiff's rights go, it stands in Thomas' posi-

tion and can make the same defense that he could; that it owed the plaintiff no duty, and consequently any negligence proved against it is not actionable so far as the plaintiff can assert. Many cases sustaining this doctrine are to be found in the books.... However, upon careful consideration, we are unwilling to follow them. Traced to its source, the rule exempting a landowner from liability to a trespasser injured through the condition of the premises, is found to have originated in an over-zealous desire to safeguard the right of ownership as it was regarded under a system of landed estates, long since abandoned, under which the law ascribed a peculiar sanctity to rights therein. Under the feudal system as it existed in Western Europe during the Middle Ages, the act of breaking a man's close was an invasion of exaggerated importance and gravity. It was promptly resented. It was under this system that the action of trespass *quare clausum* developed—beginning as a penal process, and so criminal in essence, and finally becoming a means of redressing a private wrong. Happily, in these more neighborly times, trespasses merely technical in character are usually overlooked or excused, unless accompanied with some claim of right. The object of the law being to safeguard and protect the various rights in land, it is obviously going quite far enough to limit the immunity to the one whose rights have been invaded. Nor does logic or justice require more.

A trespass is an injury to the possession; and, as it is only he whose possession is disturbed who can sue therefor, so it should be that he, alone, could assert the unlawful invasion when suit is brought by an injured trespasser. One should not be allowed "to defend an indefensible act" by showing that the party injured was engaged in doing something which, as to a third person, was unlawful....

Reversed and remanded.

Notes

1. *Persons Acting for the Possessor's Benefit.* The Restatement opines that the protections afforded by the traditional premises-liability categories can be invoked only by a possessor or by one who was acting for the benefit of the possessor at the time the hazard was created. *See* Restatement, Second, of Torts §§ 383-86.

2. *Exceptions to the General Rule.* The caselaw presents several standard exceptions to the general rule that the occupier of land has no duty to keep the land safe for trespassers:

(a) *"Discovered Trespassers."* Once a landowner discovers someone on the land, a duty arises to take reasonable care for that person's safety, including a duty to warn the trespasser of concealed artificial conditions which create danger. A trespasser is not an outlaw. *See* Sheehan v. St. Paul & Duluth Ry. Co., 76 F. 201 (7th Cir. 1896). In some states, the duty to a discovered trespasser is only to refrain from "willful and wanton" conduct, a standard which, in practice, may not mean anything fundamentally different from ordinary care. For example, in Frederick v. Philadelphia Rapid Transit Co., 10 A.2d 576 (Pa. 1940), the plaintiff's presence on the defendant's subway tracks was disclosed by a tripper device on the first car of a slow-moving train when the device came in contact with the plaintiff's body. After a cursory inspection, the train was moved forward, severing the plaintiff's legs. The court held that even assuming that the plaintiff, who had involuntarily fallen to the tracks, was owed no greater duty than a trespasser, the jury could find in his favor. "Wanton negligence," the court wrote, is the "fail[ure] to use ordinary and reasonable care to avoid injury to a trespasser after his presence has been ascertained." There was evidence that the search conducted by the defendant's employees was not as exhaustive as the circumstances warranted.

But see Rhodes v. Illinois Cent. Gulf R.R., 665 N.E.2d 1260, 1268-69 (Ill. 1996), recognizing a duty to use reasonable care to avoid injury to a trespasser who had been discovered in "a place of danger," but ruling that only a duty to refrain from wilful and wanton injury is owed to trespassers generally, even if their presence has been discovered. The defendant's employees had discovered the plaintiff's decedent, Carl Rhodes, sleeping in a warming house. The trial court erred in ruling that the discovery required the defendant to use reasonable care to protect Rhodes even if he was a trespasser.

(b) *Constant Trespass on a Limited Area.* According to §§ 334 and 335 of the second Restatement, one who knows or should know that trespassers constantly intrude upon a limited area must conduct dangerous activities with reasonable care for the safety of those trespassers, and must take reasonable steps to warn them of dangerous artificial conditions created by the owner if the trespassers are unlikely to discover the conditions for themselves.

(c) *The Attractive-Nuisance Doctrine.* It is one thing to say that an adult, or even a teenager, who decides to go onto someone else's land must assume whatever risks that activity entails; it is quite another matter to hold that landowners have no duty of care to trespassing children, particularly if the dangerous condition is one children are likely to find attractive. The following opinion illustrates the "attractive-nuisance" doctrine.

Banker v. McLaughlin

Supreme Court of Texas
208 S.W.2d 843 (Tex. 1948)

TAYLOR, Justice.

James McLaughlin brought this suit against H. F. Banker to recover damages for the death of his minor son (five years and ten months old.) The trial court awarded judgment in plaintiff's favor on the jury's verdict for $15,200. The Court of Civil Appeals, under the view that the award was excessive, caused a remittitur to be filed which reduced the judgment to $6,000....

The child met his death on June 19, 1945, by drowning in a large hole, or pit, of water on Forest Park Subdivision, a homesite addition which Mr. Banker, the owner... was in the process of developing and marketing....

....

....The pertinent findings were to the effect that the premises (while especially attractive to children) were *dangerous* to children, such as James McLaughlin, Jr.; that children of tender years, as defendant knew or should have known, played about and swam in the pit; *that defendant was negligent* in failing to inclose it prior to June 19, 1945, and in failing to fill it up, or drain it, within a reasonable time; *and that these acts of negligence were proximate causes, respectively, of the child's death; and that plaintiff was not guilty of contributory negligence in not keeping the child away from the pool.*

....

At the time the child was drowned about 50 families (40 of which had small children) were living in Forest Park Subdivision; and numerous children were living in contiguous group settlements. In response to plaintiff's written request Mr. Banker filed... the following admissions: "Defendant...does admit that prior to June 19, 1945, some people had bought lots in this subdivision, none of which were located *in the immediate vicinity of the pool of water*...; [that...] no warning sign or devices were placed in or near such pit or hole to warn persons of its presence; [and that] H. F. Banker *took no precautions whatsoever to prevent children of immature years from playing about or swimming in said pit or hole...."*

....

The utility of the pool to the owner was negligible after he ceased excavating there for dirt for street grading purposes. His testimony was that the pool was of "no further use" except that "it remained there for the future"; that it would be there as a reservoir for persons "who might purchase the adjoining land"; that it had never "been used for irrigation"; and that "I had nothing to irrigate." He had no cattle or other stock to water there. When asked if he "wanted it for water at the time he built it" his reply was, "I never had occasion to use it"; and that he "let it remain full of water" (that period was "eight or nine months").

Mr. Banker's own testimony indicates also that the expense necessary to be incurred, if any, to eliminate the danger would have been small, if not trivial. As indicated by his filed admissions, he did not endeavor to eliminate the dangerous condition he had created; nor did he erect any warning devices, or any "keep out" signs at the pool, or any "keep off" signs on the premises in its immediate vicinity....

While there was substantial proof of the inherent attractiveness of the place we, under our view of the case as properly one of negligence, *are concerned primarily with the dangerous condition created by petitioner on his open premises* and the fact that the dangerous features of the condition could have been eliminated at small expense without interfering with the owner's marketing of the homesites. The element of attraction is important only in so far as it may mean that the presence of children was to be anticipated.

The excavation was from 5 to 8 feet deep *"at the very shallowest place."* (Emphasis ours.) It appears that soon after its use as a dirt supply had been discontinued it filled up with water so that its depth would not be ascertained by children unless (contrary to the nature of children) they are of such mature years and experience that they would measure the depth (as the average adult who could not swim would do) before entering the water.

....

The following features of the facts and circumstances of the case are determinative of the correctness of the action of the Court of Civil Appeals in affirming the trial court's judgment: (a) the place where the condition was maintained was one upon which the possessor knew or should have known that small children would likely frequent the place and play about it; (b) the condition was one of which the possessor knew, or should have known, involved an unreasonable risk of death or serious bodily harm to such children; (c) the child, because of its tender years, did not realize the risk involved in going into the pool; and (d) the utility, if any, to Mr. Banker of eliminating the danger was slight as compared to the probability of injury resulting therefrom. See in this connection, Restatement, Torts, § 339 and 36 A.L.R. p. 294.

....

The Supreme Court of this state took early recognition that the so-called "attractive-nuisance doctrine" had its origin in the turntable cases; and that when children of tender years came upon the premises by virtue of their unusual attractiveness, the legal effect was that of an implied invitation to do so. Such child was regarded, not as a trespasser, but as being rightfully on the premises. We quote from the *Duron* case as follows [7 S.W.2d 869]: "The theory of liability under the attractive nuisance doctrine is that, where the owner maintains a device or machinery on his premises of such an un-usually attractive nature as to be especially alluring to children of tender years, *he thereby impliedly invites such children to come upon his premises, and, by reason of such invitation, they are relieved* from being classed as trespassers, but are in the attitude *of being rightfully on the premises.* Under such circumstances, the law places upon the owner of such machinery or device the *duty of exercising ordinary care* to keep such ma-chinery in reasonably safe condition for their protection, if the *facts are such as to raise the issue that the owner knew, or in the exercise of ordinary care ought to have known, that such* children were likely or would probably be attracted by the machinery, and thus be drawn to the premises by such attraction." (Emphasis ours.)

....

....Also pertinent is the following excerpt from Prosser on Torts (1941) under the subheading "Trespassing Children"; "Accordingly two-thirds of the American courts have developed a doctrine, which has been sadly miscalled by the name of 'attractive nuisance,' making the occupier of land liable for conditions on it which are highly dan-gerous to trespassing children. This doctrine, which has aroused endless discussion, is surrounded by no little confusion.... *The better authorities now agree that the element of 'attraction' is important only in so far as it may mean that the trespass is to be anticipated, and that the basis of liability is merely the foreseeability of harm to the child....*" (Empha-sis ours.)

....

We...affirm the judgment of the Court of Civil Appeals....

[The dissent of Justice FOLLEY is omitted.]

Notes

1. *Children and Known or Obvious Dangers.* According to Comment j to Restate-ment, Second, of Torts § 339:

> [t]here are many dangers, such [as] those of fire and water,...which under ordinary conditions may reasonably be expected to be fully understood and appreciated by any child of an age to be allowed at large. To such conditions the rule stated in this Section ordinarily has no application, in the absence of some other factor creating a special risk that the child will not avoid the dan-ger, such as the fact that the condition is so hidden as not to be readily visible, or a distracting influence which makes it likely that the child will not discover or appreciate it.

See Carmona Irrigation Co. v. Hagerman, 957 P.2d 44 (N.M. 1998) (interpreting this comment as not creating a blanket immunity for cases involving water). In Bonney v. Canadian Natl. Ry. Co., 800 F.2d 274 (1st Cir. 1986), *supra* at 533, the court wrote:

> Plaintiff argues that even if the Railway did not have a duty towards adult trespassers to make the bridge safe for pedestrian use, it had a special responsi-bility towards minors who trespass. In Jones v. Billings, 289 A.2d 39 (Me. 1972), the Maine court adopted § 339 of the Restatement (Second) of Torts (1977), which establishes a duty of reasonable care as to highly dangerous con-ditions on land involving "an unreasonable risk of death or serious bodily harm" *if the trespasser is a child who, because of his youth, fails to discover or ap-preciate the condition or risk.* But here, even assuming a 15-year-old qualifies as

a child for the purposes of § 339, Thibodeau clearly knew and understood the danger of riding his bicycle across the bridge at night. Eight months before, a classmate of his had died after falling off a nearby railroad bridge (under the control of a different railroad) while bicycling across it; Thibodeau knew of this accident. Moreover, his family as well as his friend, Mark Sheink, had warned him on the night of the accident not to ride across the railroad bridge. The limited exception under § 339 does not apply. *See* Restatement § 339, comment m (noting that the purpose of a landowner's duty under § 339 is *not* to protect children from their own immature recklessness in the face of known and appreciated danger).

See also Kessler v. Mortenson, 16 P.3d 1225 (Utah 2000) (applying the attractive-nuisance doctrine to a case where a six-year-old child was injured by falling through a hole in a floor at a residential construction site, but noting that homebuilders will not become liable automatically for all on-site accidents to children); McKinney v. Hartz & Restle Realtors, Inc., 510 N.E.2d 386 (Ohio 1987) (declining to adopt the attractive-nuisance doctrine and noting that the dangers caused by a moving train would be apparent even to young children; the plaintiff was four years old).

2. *Natural Conditions.* Recognizing that an "attractive nuisance" need neither attract the child nor be a "nuisance" (as to which, see Chapter 20), and that courts often refuse to apply the doctrine to risks created by natural conditions, the Restatement section on this subject (§ 339) eschews the term "attractive nuisance" in favor of the inelegant but descriptive title, "Artificial Conditions Highly Dangerous to Trespassing Children."

3. At least one court has said that a "child" under the Restatement rule may be as old as 16 or 17. *See* Puskey v. Western Mass. Elec. Co., 489 N.E.2d 1025 (Mass. App. Ct. 1986).

2. Licensees and Invitees

Trespassers are easily defined: they are persons on the land without permission and without a privilege. Persons present with the owner's permission or with a privilege are either "licensees" or "invitees"; the latter is a confusing term because those invited to enter may well be "licensees" rather than "invitees." According to the Restatement, Second, of Torts § 332 Comment a:

> "Invitee" is a word of art, with a special meaning in the law. This meaning is more limited than that of "invitation" in the popular sense. . . . A social guest may be cordially invited, and strongly urged to come, but he is not an invitee. . . . Invitees are limited to those persons who enter or remain on land upon an invitation which carries with it an implied representation, assurance, or understanding that reasonable care has been used to prepare the premises, and make them safe for their reception. Such persons fall generally into two classes: (1) those who enter as members of the public for a purpose for which the land is held open to the public; and (2) those who enter for a purpose connected with the business of the possessor. The second class are sometimes called business visitors. There are many visitors, such as customers in shops, who may be placed in either class.

The term "licensee" includes (according to comment h):

> 1. One whose presence upon the land is solely for his own purposes, in which the possessor has no interest, and to whom the privilege of entering is

extended as a mere personal favor to the individual, whether by express or tacit consent or as a matter of general or local custom.

2. The members of the possessor's household, except boarders or paying guests and servants, who, as stated in § 332, Comments i and j, are invitees.

3. Social guests.... The explanation usually given by the courts for the classification of social guests as licensees is that there is a common understanding that the guest is expected to take the premises as the possessor himself uses them, and does not expect and is not entitled to expect that they will be prepared for his reception, or that precautions will be taken for his safety, in any manner in which the possessor does not prepare or take precautions for his own safety, or that of the members of his family. This has not gone without criticism....

Invitees are owed the ordinary duty of reasonable care. While the duty owed licensees varies somewhat from state to state, the traditional approach is that the owner of the property owes them a duty to refrain from actively endangering them and to warn them of concealed hazards known to the owner. *Cf.* Olson v. Sanitary & Improvement Dist. No. 177, 557 N.W.2d 651, 657 (Neb. 1997) (the danger of diving into shallow water is not a hidden danger of which there is a duty to warn a licensee). Importantly, a possessor has no duty to a licensee to inspect the property to make sure it is safe.

Carter v. Kinney

Supreme Court of Missouri, En Banc
896 S.W.2d 926 (Mo. 1995)

ROBERTSON, Judge.

　....

Ronald and Mary Kinney hosted a Bible study at their home for members of the Northwest Bible Church. Appellant Jonathan Carter, a member of the Northwest Bible Church, attended the early morning Bible study at the Kinney's home on February 3, 1990. Mr. Kinney had shoveled snow from his driveway the previous evening, but was not aware that ice had formed overnight. Mr. Carter arrived shortly after 7:00 a.m., slipped on a patch of ice in the Kinneys' driveway, and broke his leg. The Carters filed suit against the Kinneys.

The parties agree that the Kinneys offered their home for the Bible study as part of a series sponsored by their church; that some Bible studies took place at the church and others were held at the homes of church members; that interested church members signed up for the studies on a sheet at the church, which actively encouraged enrollment but did not solicit contributions through the classes or issue an invitation to the general public to attend the studies; that the Kinneys and the Carters had not engaged in any social interaction outside of church prior to Mr. Carter's injury, and that Mr. Carter had no social relationship with the other participants in the class. Finally, the parties agree that the Kinneys received neither a financial nor other tangible benefit from Mr. Carter in connection with the Bible study class.

They disagree, however, as to Mr. Carter's status. Mr. Carter claims he was an invitee; the Kinneys say he was a licensee....

.... The trial court sustained the Kinneys' summary judgment motion on the ground that Mr. Carter was a licensee and that the Kinneys did not have a duty to a licensee with respect to a dangerous condition of which they had no knowledge....

....

As to premises liability, "the particular standard of care that society recognizes as applicable under a given set of facts is a question of law for the courts.".....

....

The Kinneys' motion for summary judgment characterizes Mr. Carter as a social guest....

....

A social guest is a person who has received a social invitation....[S]ocial guests are but a subclass of licensees. The fact that an invitation underlies a visit does not render the visitor an invitee for purposes of premises liability law....

It does not follow from this that a person invited for purposes not strictly social is perforce an invitee....[A]n entrant becomes an invitee when the possessor invites with the expectation of a material benefit from the visit or extends an invitation to the public generally. [Citation.] Absent the sort of invitation from the possessor that lifts a licensee to invitee status, the visitor remains a licensee as a matter of law.

The record shows beyond cavil that Mr. Carter did not enter the Kinneys' land to afford the Kinneys any material benefit.... The record also demonstrates that the Kinneys did not "throw open" their premises to the public in such a way as would imply a warranty of safety. The Kinneys took no steps to encourage general attendance by some undefined portion of the public; they invited only church members who signed up at church. They did nothing more than give permission to a limited class of persons — church members — to enter their property.

Mr. Carter's response to the Kinneys' motion for summary judgment...says that he did not intend to socialize with the Kinneys and that the Kinneys would obtain an intangible benefit, albeit mutual, from Mr. Carter's participation in the class.... But taking Mr. Carter's statement of the facts as true in all respects, he argues a factual distinction that has no meaning under Missouri law. Human intercourse and the intangible benefits of sharing one's property with others for a mutual purpose are hallmarks of a licensee's permission to enter. Mr. Carter's factual argument makes the legal point he wishes to avoid: his invitation is not of the sort that makes an invitee. He is a licensee.

....

[The court declined to abolish the distinction between licensees and invitees.]

The judgment of the trial court is affirmed.

COVINGTON, C.J., and HOLSTEIN, BENTON, THOMAS, and LIMBAUGH, JJ., concur. PRICE, J., concurs in result.

Notes

1. *Social Guests.* Treating social guests as licensees may have originated from a feeling that guests who sue their hosts are ungrateful — compare the discussion of automobile guest statutes in Chapter 5.

See Knorpp v. Hale, 981 S.W.2d 469 (Tex. App. 1998) (the boyfriend of a landowner's daughter, who died as a result of injuries sustained while cutting down a tree on the property, was a social guest and thus a licensee, rather than an invitee; he had been invited to attend a bonfire and had not been expecting payment for cutting the tree, which he volunteered to do).

At least one court has decided to treat social guests as invitees. *See* Burrell v. Meads, 569 N.E.2d 637 (Ind. 1991) (treating social guests as licensees "simply does not comport with modern social practices…[for it] is customary for possessors to prepare as carefully, if not more carefully, for social guests as for business guests"). As discussed below, a number of states have abolished the legal distinction between invitees and licensees, thus obviating concerns about how social guests are classified.

2. *Family Members.* Members of the possessor's family are usually treated as licensees. *But see* McClure v. Rich, 95 S.W.3d 620 (Tex. App. 2003) (holding that there was an issue of material fact as to whether the homeowners' daughter-in-law was an invitee rather than a licensee because there was evidence that the only reason she was on the property was to help the homeowners move into the house, which provided the homeowners with an economic benefit).

3. *Salespersons and Loiterers.* Unsolicited salespersons and persons loitering at places of business have often been considered licensees, and not trespassers, on the theory that their presence has been consented to by reason of the possessor's failure to object to what is customary in the community. A failure to object to another's entry or remaining on land may constitute consent, at least when the possessor's lack of willingness could be manifested without considerable trouble or expense. *See generally* Restatement, Second, of Torts § 330 Comments c to g.

4. *Premises Liability versus Ordinary Negligence.* Suppose a social guest is poisoned by a meal negligently prepared by his host. Is the guest's ability to recover limited by his being a "mere licensee"? Almost certainly not: this is an ordinary negligence case, and the fact that the negligence happened to occur on the defendant's property should be irrelevant. The special limited-duty rules for occupiers of land are rules limiting the occupier's duty to keep the land safe, they are not a license to engage in actively negligent behavior. See, for example, Haugh v. Jones & Laughlin Steel Corp., 949 F.2d 914 (7th Cir. 1991), in which the defendant, whose employees negligently injured the plaintiff, sought to invoke a special Indiana rule of limited duty to business invitees. Judge Richard Posner said:

> The argument…has been immensely confused by [defendant's] insistence on invoking the intricate rules of tort liability of landowners….The question in the present case, however, is not whether [defendant] provided a safe place for [plaintiff's employer] to perform the services for which it had been hired….[The negligence of which plaintiff complains is] negligence by employees of [defendant], to which the site of the accident and hence [defendant's] status as a landowner is irrelevant and its duty of care simply the duty that everyone has (prima facie) to avoid a careless act that injures another person….

As a further illustration of the point, suppose that the defendant is speeding on an icy road near her house, and that her car goes out of control, slides off the road, and injures two pedestrians—one on the sidewalk and the other, a trespasser, taking a shortcut across the defendant's front lawn. As the case does not involve unsafe conditions on the land, both pedestrians should be able to sue the defendant for ordinary negligence. The purpose of the rules creating limited duty to trespassers and licensees would not call for limited duty in the circumstances of this accident.

See also Morgan v. Perlowski, 508 N.W.2d 724, 727 (Iowa 1993) (claim by social guest against host for injuries received when the guest was assaulted by a third person while attending a party at the host's residence was not a premises-liability case, but rather was governed by general principles of negligence).

5. *Police, Firefighters, and Rescuers.* Police officers and firefighters coming onto the defendant's property in the course of their duties are usually on the land for the owner's benefit. However, at least some of the policy arguments for not holding landowners responsible for keeping their property safe for use by licensees apply to cases in which the person injured is a police officer chasing a burglar or a firefighter trying to save the owner's home: the plaintiff's presence on the property cannot readily be anticipated by the owner. Furthermore, nearly all police officers and firefighters receive medical and disability benefits for on-the-job injuries. And some courts have observed that the very nature of the plaintiff's occupation requires facing dangers, so that the risks in question have been "assumed." Therefore, the traditional approach—sometimes called "the firefighter's rule"—has been to treat firefighters and police officers as licensees. *See also* Lechuga v. Southern Pac. Transp. Co., 949 F.2d 790 (5th Cir. 1992) (border patrol agent was licensee).

Allen v. Albright, 43 S.W.3d 643 (Tex. App. 2001), held that a non-professional rescuer was not converted from a licensee to an invitee when a woman whose house had been fire bombed cried for help. The rescuer was merely an "implied licensee."

But see Sims v. Giles, 541 S.E.2d 857 (S.C. Ct. App. 2001) (an electric company "meter reader" was an invitee, not a licensee).

6. *Implied Invitations.* An implied invitation may extend to a person whose presence is reasonably required to achieve the goal for which another person has been expressly invited onto the property. *See* Dabney v. Wexler-McCoy, Inc., 953 S.W.2d 533, 536 (Tex. Ct. App. 1997) (if a repairman has an express invitation to enter and reasonably requires the assistance of a second person, the second person's presence constitutes an entry pursuant to an implied invitation).

Campbell v. Weathers

Supreme Court of Kansas
111 P.2d 72 (Kan. 1941)

WEDELL, Justice.

. . . .

. . . . Plaintiff had been a customer of the defendant lessee for a number of years. On Sunday morning, June 4, 1939, . . . plaintiff entered the place of business operated by the defendant lessee, as a cigar and lunch business. He spent probably fifteen or twenty minutes in the front part of the building and then started for the toilet [which was located down a dimly lighted hallway in the back part of the building]. He stepped into . . . [an] open trap door in the floor of the hallway [and was injured]. . . .

. . . .

[The trial court sustained the defendant lessee's demurrer to the evidence, and plaintiff appealed.]

The first issue to be determined is the relationship between plaintiff and the lessee. Was plaintiff a trespasser, a licensee or an invitee? . . . . A part of the answer is contained in the nature of the business the lessee conducted. It is conceded lessee operated a business which was open to the public. . . . Plaintiff had been a customer of the lessee for a number of years. . . . He stopped at the lessee's place of business whenever he was in town. He had used the hallway and toilet on numerous occasions, whenever he was in town, and had never been advised that the toilet was not intended for public use. . . . He saw no signs which warned him not to use the hallway or toilet. . . .

....

....That the public had a general invitation to be or to become lessee's customers cannot be doubted....Appellant was an invitee not only while in the front part of the place of business where the lunch counter was located but while he was on his way to the toilet....The mere fact appellant had received no special invitation or specific permission on this particular occasion to use the toilet did not convert him into a mere licensee....

Can we say, as a matter of law, in view of the record in this particular case, appellant had no implied invitation to use the toilet simply because he had not made an actual purchase before he was injured?...[D]oes the evidence...compel such a ruling on the demurrer? We think it does not....

The evidence of lessee's own employee was that the toilet was not regarded as a private toilet....In a densely populated business district such a privilege may have constituted a distinct inducement to bring not only old customers like appellant, but prospective customers into lessee's place of business....

....But we need not rest our conclusion that appellant was an invitee upon the fact that, according to the unqualified evidence, not only customers but everybody was permitted to use the toilet.

....It is common knowledge that business concerns invest huge sums of money in newspaper, radio and other mediums of advertising in order to induce regular and prospective customers to frequent their place[s] of business and to examine their stocks of merchandise. They do not contemplate a sale to every invitee....Shall courts say, as a matter of law, that such guests are not invitees until they actually make a purchase? We think the mere statement of the question compels a negative answer. Manifestly this does not imply that a trespasser or a mere licensee who enters the premises on a personal errand for the advancement of his own interest or benefit is entitled to the protection due to an invitee....

> An invitee is one who is either expressly or impliedly invited onto the premises of another in connection with the business carried on by that other....If one goes into a store with the view of then, or at some other time, doing some business with the store, he is an invitee. [Citation.]

....

Of course, if it appears that a person had no intention of presently or in the future becoming a customer he could not be held to be an invitee, as there would be no basis for any thought of mutual benefit. [Citation.]

....

....The order sustaining the demurrer of the lessee is reversed.

Notes

1. *Business Invitees.* Business visitors are "invitees" by anybody's definition. Some cases applying the business-invitee test have broadened the test considerably by finding a possible financial benefit to the landowner whenever possible. For instance, New York, Chicago & St. Louis R.R. v. Mushrush, 37 N.E. 954 (Ind. Ct. App. 1894), had held that a railroad's duty of reasonable care to its passengers extended also to those who came to meet passengers or to see them off. *See also* McIntosh v. Omaha Public Schools, 544 N.W.2d 502 (Neb. 1996) (a high school student who paid no fee was an "invitee" of a

public school when he was injured while participating in two-week spring football clinic conducted as part of school's physical education program; "[t]he invitation was of a business nature for the mutual advantage of both parties...[because] a public school is...in the business of providing academic and physical fitness").

2. *Public Invitees.* Some courts go further than the business-invitation test and hold that a defendant who invites the public onto land owes the usual duty of reasonable care to any member of the public who accepts the invitation, even though the defendant expected no financial gain. One kind of case in which the public-invitee standard has been used is that in which someone attending a religious service is injured because of negligent maintenance of the premises. In Fleischer v. Hebrew Orthodox Congregation, 504 N.E.2d 320 (Ind. Ct. App. 1987), the court adopted the public-invitee test in order to "ensure that a duty of reasonable care is imposed whenever it is appropriate."

3. *Encouragement to Enter.* Comment d to §332 of the Restatement, Second, of Torts points out that land has not been held "open to the public" just because the owner permits members of the public to use the land for their own purposes. The owner must indicate in some way that the public is encouraged to use the land:

> When a landowner tacitly permits the boys of the town to play ball on his vacant lot, they are licensees only; but if he installs playground equipment and posts a sign saying that the lot is open free to all children, there is then a public invitation, and those who enter in response to it are invitees.

4. *Scope of Invitation.* The Restatement points out that an invitee whose activities exceed the scope of the invitation may become a trespasser or licensee:

> [O]ne who goes into a shop which occupies part of a building, the rest of which is used as the possessor's residence, is a trespasser if he goes into the residential part of the building without the shopkeeper's consent; but he is a licensee if the shopkeeper permits him to go to the bathroom, or invites him to pay a social call.

Restatement, Second, of Torts §332 Comment l. *See also* Whelan v. Van Atta, 382 S.W.2d 205 (Ky. 1964) (customer given permission to use a toilet became a licensee, and so could not recover for injuries sustained in a fall into an unlit stairwell, since the defendant did not know the light was out); Webb v. Snow, 132 P.2d 114 (Utah 1942) (amusement park patron who was aware that only the west tracks of a ride were open ceased to be a licensee or invitee upon proceeding down the east tracks for the purpose of entreating employees to open them).

B. Rejection and Reinstatement of the Traditional Approach

1. Abrogation

Rowland v. Christian
Supreme Court of California
443 P.2d 561 (Cal. 1968)

PETERS, Justice.

Plaintiff appeals from a summary judgment for defendant Nancy Christian....

[Plaintiff was a social guest in Ms. Christian's apartment. He asked to use the bathroom, and while there was injured when a cracked handle on the cold water sink faucet broke, severing tendons and nerves in his hand. The defendant had known for two weeks that the handle was cracked, had complained to the building manager, but did not say anything to the plaintiff about its condition. It was not clear from the pleadings whether the crack was obvious or concealed. Unlike the majority of jurisdictions, California had never adopted a rule requiring a possessor to warn a licensee of known latent defects.]

....

....Although it is true that some exceptions have been made to the general principle that a person is liable for injuries caused by his failure to exercise reasonable care in the circumstances, it is clear that...no such exception should be made unless clearly supported by public policy. [Citations.]

A departure from this fundamental principle involves the balancing of a number of considerations; the major ones are the foreseeability of harm to the plaintiff, the degree of certainty that the plaintiff suffered injury, the closeness of the connection between the defendant's conduct and the injury suffered, the moral blame attached to the defendant's conduct, the policy of preventing future harm, the extent of the burden to the defendant and consequences to the community of imposing a duty to exercise care with resulting liability for breach, and the availability, cost, and prevalence of insurance for the risk involved. [Citations.]

One of the areas where this court and other courts have departed from the fundamental concept that a man is liable for injuries caused by his carelessness is with regard to the liability of a possessor of land for injuries to persons who have entered upon that land. It has been suggested that the special rules regarding liability of the possessor of land are due to historical considerations stemming from the high place which land has traditionally held in English and American thought, the dominance and prestige of the landowning class in England during the formative period of the rules governing the possessor's liability, and the heritage of feudalism. [Citation.]

....

In refusing to adopt the rules relating to the liability of a possessor of land for the law of admiralty, the United States Supreme Court stated: "The distinctions which the common law draws between licensee and invitee were inherited from a culture deeply rooted to the land, a culture which traced many of its standards to a heritage of feudalism. In an effort to do justice in an industrialized urban society, with its complex economic and individual relationships, modern common-law courts have found it necessary to formulate increasingly subtle verbal refinements, to create subclassifications among traditional common-law categories, and to delineate fine gradations in the standards of care which the landowner owes to each. Yet even within a single jurisdiction, the classifications and subclassifications bred by the common law have produced confusion and conflict. As new distinctions have been spawned, older ones have become obscured. Through this semantic morass the common law has moved, unevenly and with hesitation, towards 'imposing on owners and occupiers a single duty of reasonable care in all circumstances.'"....

....

There is another fundamental objection to the...distinctions based upon the status of the injured party as a trespasser, licensee, and invitee. Complexity can be borne and confusion remedied where the underlying principles governing liability are based upon proper considerations. Whatever may have been the historical justifications for the common law distinctions, it is clear that those distinctions are not justified in the light of our modern society and that the complexity and confusion which has arisen is not due to difficulty in applying the original common law rules—they are all too easy to apply in their original formulation—but is due to the attempts to apply just rules in our modern society within the ancient terminology.

...[I]t is apparent that the classifications of trespasser, licensee, and invitee, the immunities from liability predicated upon those classifications, and the exceptions to those immunities, often do not reflect the major factors which should determine whether immunity should be conferred upon the possessor of land....

...[A]lthough the foreseeability of harm to an invitee would ordinarily seem greater than the foreseeability of harm to a trespasser, in a particular case the opposite may be true. The same may be said of the issue of certainty of injury. The burden to the defendant and consequences to the community of imposing a duty to exercise care with resulting liability for breach may often be greater with respect to trespassers than with respect to invitees, but it by no means follows that this is true in every case. In many situations, the burden will be the same, i.e., the conduct necessary upon the defendant's part to meet the burden of exercising due care as to invitees will also meet his burden with respect to licensees and trespassers. The last of the major factors, the cost of insurance, will of course, vary depending upon the rules of liability adopted, but there is no persuasive evidence that applying ordinary principles of negligence law to the land occupier's liability will materially reduce the prevalence of insurance due to increased cost or even substantially increase the cost.

Considerations such as these have led some courts in particular situations to reject the rigid common law classifications and to approach the issue of the duty of the occupier on the basis of ordinary principles of negligence. [Citations.] And the common law distinctions after thorough study have been repudiated by the jurisdiction of their birth. (Occupiers' Liability Act, 1957, 5 and 6 Eliz. 2, ch. 31.)

A man's life or limb does not become less worthy of protection by the law nor a loss less worthy of compensation under the law because he has come upon the land of another without permission or with permission but without a business purpose. Reasonable people do not ordinarily vary their conduct depending upon such matters, and to focus upon the status of the injured party as a trespasser, licensee, or invitee in order to determine the question whether the landowner has a duty of care, is contrary to our modern social mores and humanitarian values. The common law rules obscure rather than illuminate the proper considerations which should govern determination of the question of duty.

It bears repetition that the basic policy of this state set forth by the Legislature in § 1714 of the Civil Code is that everyone is responsible for an injury caused to another by his want of ordinary care or skill in the management of his property. The factors which may in particular cases warrant departure from this fundamental principle do not warrant the wholesale immunities resulting from the common law classifications, and we are satisfied that continued adherence to the common law distinctions can only lead to injustice or, if we are to avoid injustice, further fictions with the resulting complexity and confusion. We decline to follow and perpetuate such rigid classifications. The proper test to be applied to the liability of the possessor of land in accordance with § 1714 of the Civil Code is whether in the management of his property he has acted as a reasonable man in view of the probability of injury to others, and, although the plaintiff's status as a trespasser, licensee, or invitee may in the light of the facts giving rise to such status have some bearing on the question of liability, the status is not determinative.

...[W]hen we view the matters presented on the motion for summary judgment as we must, we must assume defendant Miss Christian was aware that the faucet handle was defective and dangerous, that the defect was not obvious, and that plaintiff was about to come in contact with the defective condition, and under the undisputed facts she neither remedied the condition nor warned plaintiff of it. Where the occupier of land is aware of a concealed condition involving in the absence of precautions an unreasonable risk of harm to those coming in contact with it and is aware that a person on the premises is about to come in contact with it, the trier of fact can reasonably conclude that a failure to warn or to repair the condition constitutes negligence....

....

The judgment is reversed.

BURKE, Justice (dissenting).

....In determining the liability of the occupier or owner of land for injuries, the distinctions between trespassers, licensees and invitees have been developed and applied by the courts over a period of many years. They supply a reasonable and workable approach to the problems involved, and one which provides the degree of stability and predictability so highly prized in the law. The unfortunate alternative, it appears to me, is the route taken by the majority in their opinion in this case; that such issues are to be decided on a case by case basis under the application of the basic law of negligence, bereft of the guiding principles and precedent which the law has heretofore attached by virtue of the relationship of the parties to one another.

Liability for negligence turns upon whether a duty of care is owed, and if so, the extent thereof. Who can doubt that the corner grocery, the large department store, or the financial institution owes a greater duty of care to one whom it has invited to enter its premises as a prospective customer of its wares or services than it owes to a trespasser seeking to enter after the close of business hours and for a nonbusiness or even an antagonistic purpose? I do not think it unreasonable or unfair that a social guest (classified by the law as a licensee, as was plaintiff here) should be obliged to take the premises in the same condition as his host finds them or permits them to be. Surely a homeowner should not be obliged to hover over his guests with warnings of possible dangers to be found in the condition of the home (e.g., waxed floors, slipping rugs, toys in unexpected places, etc.). Yet today's decision appears to open the door to potentially unlimited liability despite the purpose and circumstances motivating the plaintiff in entering the premises of another, and despite the caveat of the majority that the status of the parties may "have some bearing upon the question of liability...," whatever the future may show that language to mean.

In my view, it is not a proper function of this court to overturn the learning, wisdom and experience of the past in this field. Sweeping modifications of tort liability law fall more suitably within the domain of the Legislature, before which all affected interests can be heard and which can enact statutes providing uniform standards and guidelines for the future.

I would affirm....

McCOMB, J., concurs.

Note

1. In Sheets v. Ritt, Ritt & Ritt, Inc., 581 N.W.2d 602 (Iowa 1998), a decision abolishing the distinction between invitees and licensees, the court summarized the state of the law as follows:

A number of jurisdictions have followed California, abandoning all classifications, including that of trespasser. *See* Smith v. Arbaugh's Restaurant, Inc., 469 F.2d 97 (D.C. Cir. 1972); Webb v. City & Borough of Sitka, 561 P.2d 731 (Alaska 1977); Mile High Fence Co. v. Radovich, 175 Colo. 537, 489 P.2d 308 (1971)[a]; Pickard v. City & County of Honolulu, 51 Haw. 134, 452 P.2d 445 (1969); Cope v. Doe, 102 Ill.2d 278, 80 Ill. Dec. 40, 464 N.E.2d 1023 (1984) (only with regard to child entrants); Cates v. Beauregard Elec. Coop., Inc., 328 So. 2d 367 (La. 1976); Limberhand v. Big Ditch Co., 218 Mont. 132, 706 P.2d 491 (1985); Moody v. Manny's Auto Repair, 110 Nev. 320, 871 P.2d 935 (1994); Ouellette v. Blanchard, 116 N.H. 552, 364 A.2d 631 (1976); Basso v. Miller, 40 N.Y.2d 233, 386 N.Y.S.2d 564, 352 N.E.2d 868 (1976); Mariorenzi v. Joseph DiPonte, Inc., 114 R.I. 294, 333 A.2d 127 (1975). *But see* Tantimonico v. Allendale Mut. Ins. Co., 637 A.2d 1056 (R.I. 1994) (restoring status category of trespasser).

A number of states have abolished the distinctions between licensees and invitees but retain special duties regarding trespassers.[b] *See* Wood v. Camp, 284 So. 2d 691 (Fla. 1973) (treating all those invited onto property equally and distinguishing between invited and uninvited licensees); Jones v. Hansen, 254 Kan. 499, 867 P.2d 303 (1994); Poulin v. Colby College, 402 A.2d 846 (Me. 1979); Baltimore Gas & Elec. Co. v. Flippo, 348 Md. 680, 705 A.2d 1144 (1998); Mounsey v. Ellard, 363 Mass. 693, 297 N.E.2d 43 (1973); Peterson v. Balach, 294 Minn. 161, 199 N.W.2d 639 (1972); Heins v. Webster County, 250 Neb. 750, 552 N.W.2d 51 (1996); Ford v. Board of County Comm'rs, 118 N.M. 134, 879 P.2d 766 (1994); O'Leary v. Coenen, 251 N.W.2d 746 (N.D. 1977); Ragnone v. Portland Sch. Dist. No. 1J, 291 Or. 617, 633 P.2d 1287 (1981); Hudson v. Gaitan, 675 S.W.2d 699 (Tenn. 1984); Antoniewicz v. Reszcynski, 70 Wis. 2d 836, 236 N.W.2d 1 (1975); Clarke v. Beckwith, 858 P.2d 293 (Wyo. 1993). Illinois eliminated distinctions of licensee and invitee by statute in 1984. *See* 740 Ill. Comp. Stat. 130/2 (West 1996).

Since 1968 at least twelve states have declined to abolish the distinctions. McMullan v. Butler, 346 So. 2d 950 (Ala. 1977); Baldwin v. Mosley, 295 Ark. 285, 748 S.W.2d 146 (1988); Morin v. Bell Court Condominium Ass'n, 223 Conn. 323, 612 A.2d 1197 (1992); Bailey v. Pennington, 406 A.2d 44 (Del. 1979); Mooney v. Robinson, 93 Idaho 676, 471 P.2d 63 (1970); Kirschner v. Louisville Gas & Elec. Co., 743 S.W.2d 840 (Ky. 1988); Astleford v. Milner Enters., Inc., 233 So. 2d 524 (Miss. 1970); Carter v. Kinney, 896 S.W.2d 926 (Mo. 1995); DiGildo v. Caponi, 18 Ohio St. 2d 125, 247 N.E.2d 732 (1969); Lohrenz v. Lane, 787 P.2d 1274 (Okla. 1990); Tjas v. Proctor, 591 P.2d 438 (Utah 1979); Younce v. Ferguson, 106 Wash. 2d 658, 724 P.2d 991 (1986).[c]

---

a. In 1990, the Colorado legislature reinstated the distinctions. *See* Colo. Rev. Stat. §13-21-115(3) (1996).—Eds.

b. *See also* Nelson v. Freeland, 507 S.E.2d 882 (N.C. 1998) (similar); Mallet v. Pickens, 522 S.E.2d 436 (W. Va. 1999) (similar).—Eds.

c. *See also* Alexander v. Medical Assoc. Clinic, 646 N.W.2d 74 (Iowa 2002) (stating that the "common law standard [for trespassers] is just as viable today as it was a century ago"); Hall v.

2. Recreational Use Statutes

Judicial decisions abolishing the traditional categories have encouraged legislation to protect landowners against some kinds of claims. A particular concern of legislatures has been suits against owners of rural land, often for "failure to warn," by hikers, motor-cyclists, and the like who are sometimes trespassers and sometimes licensees who have been permitted, though not invited, to use the land. Most states have enacted "recre-ational use" statutes in an attempt to protect landowners against the threat of liability. Here is the California version:

California Civil Code § 846
(Westlaw 2004)
Duty of care or warning to persons entering property for recreation;
Effect of permission to enter

An owner of any estate or any other interest in real property, whether possessory or nonpossessory, owes no duty of care to keep the premises safe for entry or use by others for any recreational purpose or to give any warning of hazardous conditions, uses of, structures, or activities on such premises to persons entering for such purpose, except as provided in this section.

A "recreational purpose," as used in this section, includes such activities as fishing, hunting, camping, water sports, hiking, spelunking, sport parachuting, riding, includ-ing animal riding, snowmobiling, and all other types of vehicular riding, rock collect-ing, sightseeing, picnicking, nature study, nature contacting, recreational gardening, gleaning, hang gliding, winter sports, and viewing or enjoying historical, archaeologi-cal, scenic, natural, or scientific sites.

An owner of any estate or any other interest in real property, whether possessory or nonpossessory, who gives permission to another for entry or use for the above purpose upon the premises does not thereby (a) extend any assurance that the premises are safe for such purpose, or (b) constitute the person to whom permission has been granted the legal status of an invitee or licensee to whom a duty of care is owed, or (c) assume responsibility for or incur liability for any injury to person or property caused by any act of such person to whom permission has been granted except as provided in this section.

This section does not limit the liability which otherwise exists (a) for willful or mali-cious failure to guard or warn against a dangerous condition, use, structure or activity; or (b) for injury suffered in any case where permission to enter for the above purpose was granted for a consideration other than the consideration, if any, paid to said landowner by the state, or where consideration has been received from others for the same purpose; or (c) to any persons who are expressly invited rather than merely per-mitted to come upon the premises by the landowner.

Nothing in this section creates a duty of care or ground of liability for injury to per-son or property.

Cagle, 773 So. 2d 928 (Miss. 2000) (McRae, J., concurring) (arguing that the distinction between invitees and licensees should be abolished). — Eds.

Notes

1. *The Contours of Recreational-Use Immunities.* Although the California statute and others like it cover persons with an interest in any land, some courts have read the statutes as applying only to accidents on rural land, so that the survivors of a trespassing motorcyclist killed while riding on the asphalt parking lot of a racetrack, which was closed for the winter, could sue the owner of the track for ordinary negligence; Michalovic v. Genesee-Monroe Racing Ass'n, 436 N.Y.S.2d 468 (App. Div. 1981).

Another argument available to plaintiffs is that their particular activities were not listed in the statute; *e.g.* Minn. Fire & Cas. Ins. Co. v. Paper Recycling of La Crosse, 627 N.W.2d 527 (Wis. 2001) (crawling through stacks of baled paper at a recycling facility while lighting matches and starting a fire was not a "recreational" activity); Lucero v. Richardson & Richardson, Inc., 39 P.3d 739 (N.M. Ct. App. 2001) (the phrase "or any other recreational purpose" in a statute limiting liability to persons engaged in hunting, fishing, trapping, camping, hiking, sightseeing, or any other recreational use, did not extend to organized team sports such as Little League baseball).

However, many statutes cover a broad range of conduct. *See* City of Bellmead v. Torres, 89 S.W.3d 611 (Tex. 2002) (sitting on a swing at a public park).

Even if even the recreational activity in question falls within the scope of the statute, the possessor may be held liable for certain forms of aggravated misconduct. *But see* Bird v. Economy Brick Homes, Inc., 498 N.W.2d 408 (Iowa 1993) (placement of a wire cable across an access road was not "wilful" failure to guard against a dangerous condition for purposes of an exception to a recreational use statute).

2. *Problem: Thieves and Birdwatchers.* Suppose that two persons are injured while trespassing on the defendant's rural land. One is a thief, who was on his way to break into the defendant's house; the other is a birdwatcher, who wandered onto the land to get a better look at a woodpecker. Under California law, which plaintiff has the better case?

3. *Other Statutory Restrictions.* A statute in Hawaii releases owners and operators of inherently risky recreational activities from liability as long as the patron is fully aware of the risk and signs a written waiver. *See* Haw. Rev. Stat. §663-1.54 (Westlaw 2003).

A California statute, prompted in part by the belief that the decision in Rowland v. Christian had given rise to a need "to address the increasing number of attempts by criminals injured in the course of their crimes to demand compensation from their intended victims," bars suits by those injured while attempting to commit certain enumerated felonies. *See* Cal. Civ. Code §847 (Westlaw 2003).

C. Lessors and Lessees

Defining "Possessor." Because possessors of land may be subject to liability for injuries that occur on the land, it is sometimes important to precisely identify who qualifies as a possessor. According to the Restatement:

A possessor of land is

(a) a person who is in occupation of the land with intent to control it or

(b) a person who has been in occupation of land with intent to control it, if no other person has subsequently occupied it with intent to control it, or

(c) a person who is entitled to immediate occupation of the land, if no other person is in possession under Clauses (a) and (b).

Restatement, Second, of Torts §328E.

In Coleman v. Hoffman, 64 P.3d 65 (Wash. Ct. App. 2003), the court held that a mortgagee that merely collected rents after a landlord's default on a loan was not a "mortgagee in possession," and thus, a tenant could not recover for common law premises liability against the mortgagee, absent any other indicia of control that a land-lord would normally exhibit, such as leasing, making repairs, paying bills, making management decisions, and receiving and responding to tenant complaints. However, there was sufficient evidence to preclude summary judgment in favor of another mortgagee who exercised control by undertaking plumbing repairs and paying utility bills at the time a child was injured by falling through a rotted balcony railing in a common area.

Matthews v. Amberwood Associates Ltd. Partnership, Inc.

Court of Appeals of Maryland
719 A.2d 119 (Md. 1998)

ELDRIDGE, Judge.

. . . .

Shelly Morton leased apartment A-1. . . . The apartment building was managed by the defendant Monocle Management, Ltd. and owned by the defendant . . . [Amberwood]. . . .

. . . Morton kept her boyfriend's dog, a pit bull named Rampage, in her apartment. Sometimes she kept the dog chained outside, on the grounds of the apartment complex. The dog was not normally aggressive toward persons when Morton was present, but, when she was absent, Rampage would attempt to attack people in his vicinity. . . . [S]everal employees of the defendants testified about dangerous encounters involving the dog, that the dog was "vicious," and that the incidents involving the dog were reported to the defendants' resident manager or the manager on duty.

. . . .

On February 9, 1994, Shanita Matthews and her 16-month-old son Tevin Williams visited Morton. . . . Morton was called away from the apartment. Shortly after Morton left the apartment, Rampage attacked Tevin. Rampage grabbed Tevin by the neck and was shaking him back and forth. Matthews was unable to free Tevin from Rampage's jaws. . . .

. . . .

. . . Tevin died from his injuries.

. . . .

The jury found Amberwood and Monocle liable. . . .

. . . [T]he Court of Special Appeals reversed . . . , holding that . . . the defendants owed no duty to the social invitees of a tenant. [Citation.]

. . . .

. . . . The plaintiffs contend that Rampage constituted a known dangerous condition upon the property and that the defendants retained control over the presence of the pit bull within the leased premises through the "no pets" clause in the lease. Thus, the plaintiffs argue that the defendants had a duty of care to protect Matthews and her son from that extremely dangerous animal.

...[W]hether a landlord owes a duty to his or her tenants and their guests with respect to dangerous or defective conditions on the property, of which the landlord has notice, depends upon the circumstances presented. In a multi-unit facility, the landlord ordinarily has a duty to maintain the common areas in a reasonably safe condition....

....

On the other hand, the duty which a landlord owes to a tenant, and the tenant's guests, within the tenant's apartment or other leased premises, is constrained by the general common law principle

> "[t]hat where property is demised, and at the time of the demise it is not a nuisance, and becomes so only by the act of the tenant while in his possession, and injury happens during such possession, the owner is not liable...." Owings v. Jones, 9 Md. 108, 117-118 (1856).

[Citation.]. Thus, a landlord is not ordinarily liable to a tenant or guest of a tenant for injuries from a hazardous condition in the leased premises that comes into existence after the tenant has taken possession. [Citation.]

...[T]his principle, that a landlord is not responsible for dangerous conditions in the leased premises, is not absolute and has exceptions. For example, where a landlord agrees to rectify a dangerous condition in the leased premises, and fails to do so, he may be liable for injuries caused by the condition. [Citations.] If a landlord, although not contractually obligated to do so, voluntarily undertakes to rectify a dangerous or defective condition within the leased premises, and does so negligently, the landlord is liable for resulting injuries. [Citations.] Defective or dangerous conditions in the leased premises which violate statutes or ordinances may also be the basis for a negligence action against the landlord. [Citations.]

....

The principal rationale for the general rule...is that the landlord "has parted with control," [citation]. Moreover,...a common thread running through many of our cases involving circumstances in which landlords have been held liable (*i.e.*, common areas, pre-existing defective conditions in the leased premises, a contract under which the landlord and tenant agree that the landlord shall rectify a defective condition) is the landlord's ability to exercise a degree of control over the defective or dangerous condition and to take steps to prevent injuries arising therefrom. [Citations.]

....

Turning to the case at bar,...tenant Morton did not have exclusive control over the leased premises because the lease gave the landlord a degree of control. The landlord retained control over the presence of a dog in the leased premises by virtue of the "no pets" clause in the lease. The lease plainly stated that breach of the "no pets" clause was a "default of the lease."[4] Such a default would enable the landlord to bring a breach of lease action to terminate the tenancy pursuant to...the Real Property Article. Even before bringing such an action, the landlord, when it first received notice of the dangerous

---

4. At trial a manager employed by the defendants testified that a procedure for the notification of tenants that they were in breach of their lease was in place and that the use of pre-printed forms enabled such notification to be carried out in less than ten minutes.

incidents involving Rampage, could have informed Morton that harboring the pit bull was in violation of her lease, could have told her to get rid of the aggressive animal, and could have threatened legal action if she failed to do so. If the landlord had taken these steps, it would have been likely that Morton would have gotten rid of the pit bull, particularly because she did not own him....The record in this case, however, shows that the landlord did nothing....[5]

   ....

In addition to the landlord's control..., the foreseeability of the harm supports the imposition of a duty on the landlord....Numerous employees of the defendant testified that they knew of the pit bull, were afraid of the pit bull, witnessed attacks by the dog, and were unable to carry out their duties, both in the leased premises and in the common areas, because of the presence of the pit bull.

   ....The extreme dangerousness of this breed, as it has evolved today, is well recognized. "Pit bulls as a breed are known to be extremely aggressive and have been bred as attack animals.."....The "Pit Bull's massive canine jaws can crush a victim with up to two thousand pounds (2,000) of pressure per square inch—three times that of a German Shepard or Doberman Pinscher." [Citation.]. *See also* Hearn v. City of Overland Park,... [772 P.2d 758 (Kan. 1989)] ("pit bull dogs represent a unique public health hazard... [because] [o]f the 32 known human deaths in the United States due to dog attacks... [in the period between July 1983 and April 1989], 23 were caused by attacks by pit bull dogs")....

   ....

We do not hold that a landlord's retention in the lease of some control over particular matters in the leased premises is, standing alone, a sufficient basis to impose a duty upon the landlord which is owed to a guest on the premises. This Court has employed a balancing test to determine whether a duty of reasonable care should be imposed in particular circumstances....In the instant case, the various policy considerations that need to be weighed are the general understanding that a tenant is primarily in control of the leased premises and the sanctity of a tenant's home, including her ability generally to do as she sees fit within the privacy thereof, against the public safety concerns of permitting that same tenant to harbor an extremely dangerous animal that will foreseeably endanger individuals inside and outside the walls of the leased premises, the degree of control maintained by the landlord, the landlord's knowledge of the dangerous condition, and the landlord's ability to abate the condition. We, like the majority of courts addressing this issue in other states, believe that the balance should be struck on the side of imposing a duty on the landlord which is owed to guests on the premises.

One of the leading cases in this area is Uccello v. Laudenslayer, 44 Cal. App. 3d 504, 118 Cal. Rptr. 741 (1975). There, a tenant's dog inflicted serious injury upon a social

---

   5. The defendants also assert that it is not certain "that the landlord would have been successful with an eviction procedure before February of 1994, when the attack occurred." [Citation.] If the landlord had promptly instituted an eviction proceeding, however, the landlord would have done what it could and thus would have fulfilled its duty even if the legal proceeding did not result in the tenant's eviction before February 9, 1997. Furthermore, the testimony indicated that the defendants received reports of the incidents involving Rampage for a considerable period of time before the attack. One witness stated that he reported incidents to the managers for a two month period.

   Pursuant to Maryland [law]...possession of the leased premises may be restored to the landlord in less than forty-five days after notice is given to a tenant that she is in breach of her lease.

   ....

guest while the guest was in the kitchen of the leased premises. The California court held "that a duty of care arises when the landlord has actual knowledge of the presence of the dangerous animal and when he has the right to remove the animal by retaking possession of the premises.".…

The New York courts have also addressed the issue.…In Strunk v. Zoltanski,…[468 N.E.2d 13 (N.Y. 1984)], the court was faced with a "situation in which the landlord, by leasing the premises to the owner of the dog, could be found…to have created the very risk which was reasonably foreseeable and which operated to injure the plaintiff." [Citation.] Thus, the court held that the landlord was liable because the landlord had an opportunity to act affirmatively prior to letting the property. The *Strunk* court stated, however, that "with respect to the liability of a landlord whose tenant comes into possession of the animal after the premises has been leased," in order to "establish liability it must be shown that the landlord had knowledge of the vicious propensities of the dog and had control of the premises or other capability to remove or confine the animal.…" [Citations.]

    ….

    ….*See also* Annotation, *Landlord's Liability to Third Person for Injury Resulting from Attack on Leased Premises by Dangerous or Vicious Animal Kept by Tenant,* 87 A.L.R.4th 1004, 1012 (1991) ("The general rule regarding the liability of a landlord to a third person for an attack by a tenant's animal on the leased premises appears to be that the landlord is not liable unless the landlord had knowledge of the animal's presence and its dangerous tendencies, and had control of the premises or otherwise had the ability to eliminate the danger by having the animal removed or confined").

    ….

[Reversed and remanded with instructions to affirm the judgment of the trial court in relevant part.]

[The dissenting opinion of RODOWSKY, Judge, has been omitted.]

CHASANOW, Judge, dissenting, in which CATHELL, Judge, joins.

    ….The legal issue in this case is whether a landlord should have to pay over five million dollars solely because the landlord did not make a futile attempt to evict a tenant whose dog barked and growled at maintenance men trying to enter the dog's residence when its owner was not home.

    …[A]ffirming this five million dollar judgment…may ultimately have severe repercussions for lessees with dogs. Landlords wishing to avoid multimillion dollar lawsuits may be forced to initiate eviction proceedings to terminate leases whenever a tenant's dog acts aggressively toward maintenance personnel who attempt to enter the tenant's dwelling when the tenants are not home, and I doubt very many dogs would not bark and growl at a stranger trying to enter a dwelling when the dog's owner is absent.…

    ….

    ….I respectfully dissent.

Notes

1. *Compare Matthews with* Batra v. Clark, 110 S.W.3d 126 (Tex. App. 2003) (a landlord who did not have actual knowledge of a pit bull's vicious propensities did not owe a duty of care to a neighbor girl).

2. *Lessors Not in Possession: General Rule.* The general rule, that a lessor who has parted with possession is not liable for dangerous conditions on the leased premises, finds broad application. *See, e.g.,* Clauson v. Kempffer, 477 N.W.2d 257 (S.D. 1991) (landlord had no duty to motorcyclist to warn him of a smooth wire fence strung across a road on the leased premises by tenants or to ensure that the fence was safely constructed); Brownsville Nav. Dist. v. Izaguirre, 829 S.W.2d 159 (Tex. 1992) (trailer overturned while parked on muddy soil; landlord had no duty to warn about the risks posed by "plain dirt"). However, as the notes below indicate, there are several exceptions. *See generally* Restatement, Second, of Torts §§ 355-362.

3. *Common Areas.* A lessor may be liable for harm that occurs in a common area that is under the lessor's control. *See* Jackson v. Ray Kruse Constr. Co., 708 S.W.2d 664 (Mo. 1986) (landlord was liable for failing to install parking lot speed bumps to reduce the risk posed by speeding bicyclists); *but see* Texas Real Estate Holdings, Inc. v. Quach, 95 S.W.3d 395 (Tex. App. 2002) (landlords, who allegedly provided negligent security, could not have foreseen the violent carjacking that occurred in the apartment complex parking lot in which the tenants were shot and their van was stolen, and thus, the landlords were under no duty to provide additional security to prevent the crime).

In Stokes v. Lyddy, 815 A.2d 263 (Conn. App. Ct. 2003), a tenant's pit bull dog escaped from the apartment, left the premises, and bit the plaintiff who was walking on a nearby public sidewalk. The court held that the landlords owed no duty under a theory of premises liability to protect the plaintiff from the attack because it did not occur within any common area under the landlords' control. In addition, the landlords had no duty to keep a dangerous condition on the leased premises from causing harm to persons outside the property because, under the second Restatement, that kind of liability arises only if at the time of the lease the lessor consented to the activity or knew it would be carried on. In *Stokes*, the tenants did not own a dog when the lease began and did not seek permission from the landlords to keep a dog in the apartment.

4. *Admission of the Public.* According to Section 359 of the Restatement, a lessor may be liable when premises are leased for purposes involving admission of the public, and the lessor has reason to expect that the lessee will admit the public without correcting an unreasonably dangerous situation. In Johnson County Sheriff's Posse, Inc. v. Endsley, 926 S.W.2d 284 (Tex. 1996), the court held that, even assuming the applicability of that section, dirt containing small rocks was, as a matter of law, not an unreasonably dangerous condition for which a rodeo arena lessor could be held liable to a spectator for injuries he sustained when hit in the eye by a rock or clump of dirt kicked into the air by a horse during a barrel race held by tenants.

5. *Negligent Repairs.* In Borders v. Roseberry, 532 P.2d 1366 (Kan. 1975), the plaintiff, a social guest of the tenant, slipped on the icy steps of a single-family dwelling and was injured. The ice had allegedly formed because the landlord had negligently failed to install gutters on the house when he repaired the roof, despite his promise to the tenant to do so. The court held that the exception to the general rule of no liability relating to negligent repairs was of no avail to the plaintiff because that comes into play only when the tenant lacks knowledge of the dangerous condition. In *Borders*, the tenant had full knowledge of the dangerous, icy condition on the steps created by the absence of gutters.

6. *Promised Repairs.* A landlord who promises to install or repair a lock on a rental apartment to prevent criminal entry, and who fails to do so, may be liable to the tenant for losses sustained. *See* Braitman v. Overlook Terrace Corp., 346 A.2d 76 (N.J. 1975); Warner v. Arnold, 210 S.E.2d 350 (Ga. Ct. App. 1974). If a landlord is liable to a tenant

for failing to install a lock, should the landlord be liable to a guest of a tenant who is harmed by the same action?

7. *Abrogation.* A few jurisdictions have abolished the general rule of non-liability of landlords and have substituted in its stead a reasonable-care standard. For example, in Pagelsdorf v. Safeco Ins. Co. of Am., 284 N.W.2d 55 (Wis. 1979), the plaintiff, a social guest of a tenant, was injured when he fell through a dry-rotted balcony railing while helping to move furniture. In a suit against the landlord, the court, relying on the same policies which supported its earlier abrogation of the status distinctions relating to the liability of possessors, held that the suit could be maintained because a landlord owes to a tenant or anyone on the premises with the tenant's consent a duty of ordinary care. Presumably, the factors relevant to the issue of liability would include whether the defect was obvious or latent, whether the defendant had access to the premises to inspect or make repairs, and the gravity and likelihood of the threatened harm. In Wisconsin, *Pagelsdorf* has been "limited to situations dealing with property maintenance issues and defects in the premises." *See* Malone v. Fons, 580 N.W.2d 697, 703 (Wis. 1998) (no liability for bite caused by tenant's dog, despite "no pets" rule which landlord failed to enforce).

Other decisions which have jettisoned limited-duty rules in favor of holding lessors to a duty of reasonable care under the circumstances include: Newton v. Magill, 872 P.2d 1213 (Alaska 1994); Cummings v. Prater, 386 P.2d 27 (Ariz. 1963); Rosales v. Stewart, 169 Cal. Rptr. 660 (Ct. App. 1980); Mansur v. Eubanks, 401 So. 2d 1328 (Fla. 1981); Stephens v. Stearns, 678 P.2d 41 (Idaho 1984); Turpel v. Sayles, 692 P.2d 1290 (Nev. 1985); Young v. Garwacki, 402 N.E.2d 1045 (Mass. 1980); Sargent v. Ross, 308 A.2d 528 (N.H. 1973); Stephenson v. Warner, 581 P.2d 567 (Utah 1978); Favreau v. Miller, 591 A.2d 68 (Vt. 1991). *But see* Ortega v. Flaim, 902 P.2d 199 (Wyo. 1995) (declining to abandon traditional rules governing landlord liability).

8. *Strict Liability of Lessors.* California at one time held that a landlord in the business of leasing buildings was strictly liable for harm to a tenant caused by a hidden defect on a leased premises. *See* Becker v. IRM Corp., 698 P.2d 116, 123 (Cal. 1985). *Becker* was reversed by Peterson v. Superior Ct., 899 P.2d 905 (Cal. 1995), where the court wrote:

> A hotel guest reasonably can expect that the hotel owner diligently will inspect the hotel room for defects and will correct any defects discovered. But the guest cannot reasonably expect that the owner will correct defects of which the owner is unaware and that cannot be discerned by a reasonable inspection. The duty of an innkeeper, therefore, like the duty of a landlord, does not support an action for strict liability.

D. The Demands of Reasonable Care for Possessors

Saying that the possessor of land owes someone a duty of ordinary care—either because the plaintiff is an invitee or because the state has abolished the traditional distinctions in favor of a "reasonable care to everyone" standard—does not automatically solve all problems: one must still determine what ordinary care requires. This issue relating to *what* the possessor must do, rather than to *who* may complain, often presents troublesome questions. Sometimes decisions are surprising, and they underline the importance of the scope-of-duty issue.

In Alfaro v. Wal-Mart Stores Inc., 210 F.3d 111 (2d Cir. 2000), a wheelchair-bound customer, who waited 10 to 15 minutes for a clerk to return, was injured while trying to retrieve merchandise from shelves. The appellate court reversed a trial court judgment in favor of the plaintiff, stating *per curiam*:

> We are unpersuaded by Alfaro's argument...that Wal-Mart assumed a specific duty to assist him in a timely manner when its employee told him to wait while she found someone who could help him. According to Alfaro's testimony at trial, he and the employee spoke for several minutes about paint and paint supplies. By Alfaro's own admission, however, he never asked the employee for assistance in retrieving paint from the shelves, let alone informed her that he might need such assistance. Moreover, when the employee left and promised to find someone who could help Alfaro, it was only because she could not answer his questions about "gloves and latex." Thus, to the extent that she promised anything to Alfaro, it was to find someone who could answer his questions about "gloves and latex," not to find someone who would help him retrieve paint from the shelf. The employee's failure to return to Alfaro may amount to a breach of good business practice, but it does not, under New York law, constitute a breach of any legal duty sufficient to support Alfaro's claim of negligence.
>
> ...[W]e are confident that the New York Court of Appeals would hold that Wal-Mart's alleged breach in this case—failing to assist Alfaro in a timely manner—was beyond the scope of its legal duties. Absent proof that Wal-Mart stored its paint cans in an unreasonably unsafe manner, or otherwise failed to "maintain [its] property in a reasonably safe condition," [citation], there is no basis for finding that Wal-Mart's alleged breach fell within the scope of its general legal duties to Alfaro as a business invitee. [Citations.] If Alfaro could not safely retrieve the paint from the shelf without assistance, as apparently was the case, it was his obligation to seek help or to await the return of his cousin... — not Wal-Mart's obligation to assist him.

The law only requires possessors to exercise ordinary care. Stacking boxes with cans to a height above a customer's head will not support a cause of action when the cans fall while a customer is reaching for them, absent evidence that the boxes were stacked in a defective manner or that the display had become rickety. *See* Garvin v. Bi-Lo, 541 S.E.2d 831 (S.C. 2001).

1. Ill and Injured Invitees

In Hovermale v. Berkeley Springs Moose Lodge, 271 S.E.2d 335 (W. Va. 1980), a Moose Lodge member collapsed to the floor while having a drink and, at the bartender's direction, was taken to his car by two patrons to "sleep it off." The car remained in the parking lot overnight, and the member's body was discovered the following evening. He died of a heart attack a few hours after being placed in the car. In discussing the duty of care owed by the Lodge to the decedent, the court wrote:

> [T]he trial judge defined the legal status of Hovermale as an invitee. As such, the agents, employees, servants and membership of the Moose owed

to him an ordinary degree of care.... A definition of reasonable and ordinary care in this circumstance is best set out in the Restatement (Second) of Torts, § 314A (1965) which states that a possessor of lands open to the public is under a duty to those members of the public who enter in response to its invitation to give them first aid after it knows or has reason to know that they are ill or injured, and to care for them until they can be cared for by others.

...[In] Lloyd v. S.S. Kresge Co., 85 Wis. 2d 296, 270 N.W.2d 423 (1978)... the plaintiff was doing business at the defendant's store when she was informed by store employees it was closing time and she would have to leave. She informed the employees she had developed a cold and a fever and asked if she could stand between the exit door and the inner door while she waited for her ride. She further explained to them there was a possibility she would be chilled to the bone unless she could stand in the foyer. The employees insisted she leave while they closed the store.... Subsequently, she brought suit to recover damages she allegedly suffered as a result of exposure to the elements. The trial court granted the defendant's motion for summary judgment.... The Wisconsin court cited [the] Restatement standard and reversed the lower court....

The rule is not new. In...Depue v. Flateau, 100 Minn. 299, 111 N.W. 1 (1907), the...plaintiff, who was transacting business during dinner at a farmhouse some distance from his own, fell violently ill and collapsed on the floor. The defendants refused to permit him to stay at their farm and instead, placed him in his wagon and started the horses drawing it toward his home. The plaintiff was found the next morning in an advanced state of ill health due to exposure. The court held that since he was an invitee, the defendants owed him a duty, upon discovering his illness, to exercise reasonable care in their own conduct not to expose him to danger by sending him away from their house.... We conclude... that the trial court correctly instructed the jury....

2. Known or Obvious Dangers

There is no duty to warn an invitee or take other precautions with respect to a known or obvious danger, unless there is reason to anticipate harm despite the knowledge or obviousness of the danger. *See* Restatement, Second, of Torts § 343A. Consequently, if the plaintiff will be distracted by other matters, or will forget because of a lapse of time, or will have visibility blocked, or will find it necessary to encounter the dangerous condition, there is a duty to take precautions to avoid the harm. *See also* Restatement, Third, of Torts: Liability for Physical Harm (Basic Principles) §18(a) (Tent. Draft No. 1, 2001) (discussing negligent failure to warn).

In some cases, an exception to the general no-duty-to-warn rule applies. *See* Smith v. Wal-Mart Stores, Inc., 967 S.W.2d 198 (Mo. Ct. App. 1998) (store should have anticipated that water on the vestibule floor would cause harm to invitees even if it was open and obvious); Bertrand v. Alan Ford, Inc., 537 N.W.2d 185 (Mich. 1995) (there was a fact question as to whether a garage breached its duty by not installing a guardrail along steps used by invitees); Klopp v. Wackenhutt Corp., 824 P.2d 293 (N.M. 1992) (an airline owed passenger a duty to use ordinary care to protect her from tripping over the base of a security station while she was preoccupied with recovering her jewelry); Ward v. K Mart, 554 N.E.2d 223 (Ill. 1990) (a store's duty encompassed risk that customers carrying large bulky items would collide with five foot tall concrete post near the exit).

In other cases, the general rule governs. *See* Lilya v. Greater Gulf State Fair, Inc., 855 So. 2d 1049 (Ala. 2003) (no duty to warn fairgoer of possible harm from riding a mechanical bull); McGuire v. New Orleans City Park Imp. Ass'n, 835 So. 2d 416 (La. 2003) (a jogger, who had previously jogged the route and who had observed golfers on day he was injured, should have anticipated the risk of encountering golf balls and, thus, the park operator owed no duty to provide additional warnings); Wal-Mart Stores, Inc. v. Miller, 102 S.W.3d 706 (Tex. 2003) (because a licensee had actual knowledge that the stairway was slippery, the defendant had no duty to warn or make safe); Earnsberger v. Griffiths Park Swim Club, 2002 W.L. 1626126 (Ohio Ct. App.) (a reduction of spring in a diving board was open and obvious); Gatheridge v. Strata Corp., 119 F.3d 710 (8th Cir. 1997) (an owner owed no duty to warn a swimmer of the danger of diving into shallow water); Miranda v. Home Depot, Inc., 604 So. 2d 1237 (Fla. Dist. Ct. App. 1992) (store had no duty to guard against an injury that occurred when a customer reached through a ladder to retrieve merchandise and then, forgetting her stance, withdrew in a manner which caused her injury); Paschal v. Rite Aid Pharmacy, 480 N.E.2d 474 (Ohio 1985) (no breach of duty to a customer who, while using crutches, slipped on a puddle caused by snow tracked in by other customers).

Of course, disputes arise over what is obvious. *See* Phelps v. Hotel Mgt., Inc., 925 P.2d 891 (Okl. 1996) (there was a fact issue as to whether a glass bowl containing a seasonal display which extended into the seating area of a bench was an open and obvious danger).

The known-danger rule applies to persons less privileged than invitees. *See* Doe v. Brainerd Intl. Raceway, Inc., 533 N.W.2d 617, 622 (Minn 1995) (a raceway had no duty to prevent harm to a minor trespasser which occurred as a result of her involvement in a wet t-shirt contest).

The rule has been invoked in contexts other than premises liability. *See* Salinas v. General Motors Corp., 857 S.W.2d 944, 950 (Tex. Ct. App. 1993) (car manufacturers have no duty to warn elderly drivers about the known risks of driving while impaired or incompetent, or to warn car dealers about the known risks of selling cars to incompetent drivers).

Should the open-or-obvious danger rule be merged into a comparative-fault analysis that allows injured plaintiffs to get to the jury, but then requires a reduction in damages based upon the fault of the plaintiff in not guarding against the open or obvious danger? *See* Tharp v. Bunge Corp., 641 So. 2d 20, 25 (Miss. 1994) (in an action by an inspector who was injured while jumping from a landing onto sloping ground below, the trial judge "erred in construing the open and obvious defense as a complete bar when it really is only a mitigation of damages on a comparative negligence basis").

Warning Signs. Not surprisingly, posting a warning sign will often be insufficient to fulfill the obligation of due care. In Wilk v. Georges, 514 P.2d 877 (Or. 1973), a nursery posted a sign advising customers to watch their step and disclaiming liability for injuries. The court held that the sign did not preclude an action against the nursery for injuries sustained on a slippery wooden walkway by a woman who was "looking and glancing" at Christmas trees, because a slip-and-fall accident was easily foreseeable despite the sign. *See also* Restatement, Third, of Torts: Liability for Physical Harm (Basic Principles) §18(b) (Tent. Draft No. 1, 2001):

Even if the defendant adequately warns of the danger that the defendant's conduct creates, the defendant can fail to exercise reasonable care by failing to adopt further precautions to protect against the danger if it is foreseeable that despite the warning some risk of harm will remain.

However, in some circumstances, a sign may be required. *See* Maussner v. Atlantic City Country Club, Inc., 691 A.2d 826 (N.J. Super Ct. 1997) (all golf courses have a duty to post a sign that details what, if any, safety procedures are being used to protect its patrons from lightning).

3. Protection against Crime

As prior chapters suggest, the possessor of land may owe a duty to protect customers (and others) from foreseeable criminal attacks. *See* Early v. N.L.V. Casino Corp., 678 P.2d 683 (Nev. 1984) (evidence presented fact issues as to whether casino was liable for patron's beating in a restroom); *but see* Williams v. Cunningham Drug Stores, Inc., 418 N.W.2d 381 (Mich. 1988) (merchant's duty of reasonable care does not include providing armed, visible security guards to deter criminal acts of third parties). And there may be a duty to warn of the possibility of attack as well. *Compare* Peterson v. San Francisco Comm. Coll. Dist., 685 P.2d 1193 (Cal. 1984) (college which knew of prior attacks in a parking lot was liable for failure to warn students of danger), *with* Hayes v. California, 521 P.2d 855 (Cal. 1974) (no duty to warn students of risk of attack on a beach at night: warnings would be both unnecessary, since the risk of violent crime is well known, and "disquieting").

The case which follows addresses the somewhat different question whether protection of an invitee requires a possessor of land to accede to a criminal's demands.

Boyd v. Racine Currency Exchange, Inc.

Supreme Court of Illinois
306 N.E.2d 39 (Ill. 1973)

RYAN, Justice.

Plaintiff's complaint was dismissed... for failure to state a cause of action. The appellate court reversed and remanded the cause to the circuit court. [Citation.] We granted leave to appeal.

This is a wrongful death action against Racine Currency Exchange and Blanche Murphy to recover damages for the death of plaintiff's decedent during an attempted armed robbery. The facts surrounding that event... are: The plaintiff's husband, John Boyd, was present in the Racine Currency Exchange on April 27, 1970, for the purpose of transacting business. While he was there, an armed robber entered and placed a pistol to his head and told Blanche Murphy, the teller, to give him the money or open the door or he would kill Boyd. Blanche Murphy was at that time located behind a bulletproof glass window and partition. She did not comply with the demand but instead fell to the floor. The robber then shot Boyd in the head and killed him.

. . . .

It is fundamental that there can be no recovery in tort for negligence unless the defendant has breached a duty owed to the plaintiff. [Citation.] The plaintiff contends that a business proprietor has a duty to his invitees to honor criminal demands when failure to do so would subject the invitees to an unreasonable risk....

....

We are aware of only two cases which have discussed issues similar to the one with which we are faced here — whether a person injured during the resistance to a crime is entitled to recover from the person who offered the resistance. In Genovay v. Fox, 50 N.J. Super. 538, 143 A.2d 229, *rev'd on other grounds*, 29 N.J. 436, 149 A.2d 212, a plaintiff who was shot and wounded during the robbery of a bowling alley bar claimed that the proprietor was liable because instead of complying with the criminal demand he stalled the robber and induced resistance by those patrons present. The plaintiff was shot when several patrons attempted to disarm the bandit. The court there balanced the interest of the proprietor in resisting the robbery against the interest of the patrons in not being exposed to bodily harm and held that the complaint stated a cause of action. The court stated: "The value of human life and of the interest of the individual in freedom from serious bodily injury weigh sufficiently heavily in the judicial scales to preclude a determination as a matter of law that they may be disregarded simply because the defendant's activity serves to frustrate the successful accomplishment of a felonious act and to save his property from loss." [Citation.] The court held that under the circumstances it was for the jury to determine whether defendant's conduct was reasonable.

In Noll v. Marian, 347 Pa. 213, 32 A.2d 18, the court held that no cause of action existed. The plaintiff was present in a bank when an armed robber entered and announced "It's a holdup. Nobody should move." The bank teller, instead of obeying this order, dropped down out of sight. The gunman then opened fire and wounded the plaintiff. The court held that even though the plaintiff might not have been injured if the teller had stood still, the teller did not act negligently in attempting to save himself and his employer's property.

In Lance v. Senior, 36 Ill. 2d 516, 224 N.E.2d 231, this court noted that foreseeability alone does not result in the imposition of a duty. "The likelihood of injury, the magnitude of the burden of guarding against it and the consequences of placing the burden upon the defendant, must also be taken into account." [Citation.]

In the present case an analysis of those factors leads to the conclusion that no duty to accede to criminal demands should be imposed. The presence of guards and protective devices do not prevent armed robberies. The presence of armed guards would not have prevented the criminal in this case from either seizing the deceased and using him as a hostage or putting the gun to his head. Apparently nothing would have prevented the injury to the decedent except a complete acquiescence in the robber's demand, and whether acquiescence would have spared the decedent is, at best, speculative. We must also note that the demand of the criminal in this case was to give him the money or open the door. A compliance with this alternate demand would have, in turn, exposed the defendant Murphy to danger of bodily harm.

If a duty is imposed on the Currency Exchange to comply with such a demand the same would only inure to the benefit of the criminal without affording the desired degree of assurance that compliance with the demand will reduce the risk to the invitee. In fact, the consequence of such a holding may well be to encourage the use of hostages for such purposes, thereby generally increasing the risk to invitees upon business premises. If a duty to comply exists, the occupier of the premises would have little choice in determining whether to comply with the criminal demand and surrender the money or to refuse the demand and be held liable in a civil action for damages brought by or on behalf of the hostage. The existence of this dilemma and knowledge of it by those who are disposed to commit such crimes will only grant to them additional leverage to enforce their criminal demands. The only persons who will clearly benefit from the imposition of such a duty are the criminals. In this particular case the result may appear to be harsh and unjust, but, for the protection of the future business invitees, we cannot afford to extend to the criminal another weapon in his arsenal.

For these reasons we hold that the defendants did not owe to the invitee, Boyd, a duty to comply with the demand of the criminal.

Accordingly, the judgment of the appellate court will be reversed, and the judgment of the circuit court of Cook County will be affirmed.

. . . .

[The dissenting opinion of Justice GOLDENHERSH is omitted.]

Notes

1. *See also* Kentucky Fried Chicken v. Superior Ct., 927 P.2d 1260 (Cal. 1997) (no duty to patron to comply with armed robber's unlawful demand); Bence v. Crawford Sav. and Loan Ass'n, 400 N.E.2d 39 (Ill. App. Ct. 1980) (no duty to plaintiff's decedent to activate an electronic door buzzer system to allow robbers to exit). *But see* Helms v. Church's Fried Chicken, Inc., 344 S.E.2d 349 (N.C. Ct. App. 1986) (evidence presented factual issues as to whether an employee, who stated in loud voice to one customer "when you leave call the police we are being robbed," negligently increased the risk to customers, precluding summary judgment).

2. *Parties Held by One's Children.* What if the children of a possessor hold a party that gets out of hand and some of the guests are injured? Is the possessor liable? In Dynas v. Nagowski, 762 N.Y.S.2d 745 (App. Div. 2003), the court wrote:

> Landowners have "a duty to control the conduct of third persons on their premises when they have the opportunity to control such persons and are reasonably aware of the need for such control" [citations]. Ordinarily, landowners who are not present at the time of the harmful conduct by others and have neither notice of nor control over such conduct are under no duty to protect others from its consequences

In *Dynas,* the parents were away on a camping trip at the time the party was held by their two adult children. The parents neither requested nor directed that their sons host the party, which was in no way for the parents' benefit. They were not involved in the planning of the party and gave no direction concerning the manner in which it was to be conducted, except (according to one witness) to say "keep it small." The court held that it was error not to grant the father's motion for summary judgment in an action by an injured guest because, even if the parents consented to the hosting of the party, the sons were not acting as the agents of the parents with respect to the party, and therefore the father could not be held liable as a principal for the sons' failure to exercise control at the event.

See also Comeau v. Lucas, 455 N.Y.S.2d 871 (App. Div. 1982) (holding that there was an issue of fact whether the defendant parents had failed to exercise due care in allowing their 16-year-old daughter to host the party while they were out of the country "despite knowing that beer would be served; that a rock band was engaged; and that many of the guests would be under 18 years of age"; the court further concluded that the daughter was the agent of her parents and was liable for the breach of a duty owed by her parents).

4. Duties to Persons Outside the Premises

a. Persons "Invited" onto the Land of Another

Individuals who treat another's property as their own may be held liable if their invitees are injured on that property. For example, in Holiday Inns, Inc. v. Shelburne, 576 So. 2d 322 (Fla. Dist. Ct. App.), *appeal dismissed* 589 So. 2d 291 (Fla. 1991), the court held that the defendants owed a duty of reasonable care not only to patrons who parked on their premises, but also to those who parked on adjacent lots in accordance with the instructions of security guards. *See also* Hopkins v. Fox & Lazo Realtors, 625 A.2d 1110 (N.J. 1993) (real estate broker has a duty to insure through reasonable inspection and warning the safety of prospective buyers and visitors who tour an open house); Wal-Mart Stores, Inc. v. Alexander, 868 S.W.2d 322 (Tex. 1993) (a lessee exercised control over a ramp area by a constructing ramp, even though the lease covered only the interior of the building).

Orthmann v. Apple River Campground, Inc.

United States Court of Appeals for the Seventh Circuit
757 F.2d 909 (7th Cir. 1985)

POSNER, Circuit Judge.

Owen Orthmann, age 19, was rendered a quadriplegic when he dove into the Apple River near the village of Somerset, Wisconsin, and his head struck a rock on the shallow bottom.... Orthmann brought this diversity suit... against the village and against eight firms that comprise the Floater's Association. Members of the association rent inner tubes for floating down the river to tourists like Orthmann, who was injured when he interrupted his float to go on shore to do some diving. The district judge granted the motion of the members of the Floater's Association... to dismiss the complaint for failure to state a claim, and the village's motion for summary judgment....

  ....

[The court held that the plaintiff's failure to file a notice of claim with the city, as required by statute, precluded any action against it.]

  .... [T]he complaint alleges that... [the remaining] defendants—a campground, a restaurant, and other businesses in Somerset—joined together in a commercial venture (the "Floater's Association") to promote innertubing on the Apple River. On the day of the accident Orthmann rented an inner tube from the campground, where he had camped the night before. The floater is supposed to float down a four-mile stretch of the river and when he comes to the end return on a bus hired by the defendants; the rental fee that Orthmann paid the campground included the bus ride. The defendants own most of the land on both sides of this stretch of the river and take various measures to keep the river clean, such as providing litter bins on the banks. The place where Orthmann dove from, however, was owned not by any of the defendants but by a family named Montbriand. A tree on the property had grown out over the river and kids liked to dive off it, but when Orthmann arrived the queue for the tree was too long and he decided to dive off the bank instead. The water was cloudy, and was reflecting the sun, so that Orthmann couldn't see the bottom, but he was reassured by the fact that he had seen other people dive into the river in the same area without incident.

If the accident had occurred while Orthmann was in the inner tube, there would be no doubt that the complaint should not have been dismissed on the pleadings. One who invites another to engage in a sporting activity for a fee owes him a duty of care. Of course, if the hazard was obvious, or so inseparable a part of the sport that it was a risk assumed by engaging in it, or if the defendants had no reason to know of the hazard (maybe some trespasser had dropped the rock into the river the night before the accident), they might well escape liability....

It is true that only one defendant (the campground) dealt directly with Orthmann, leaving unclear the role of the other seven members of the Floater's Association. But the complaint alleges—not implausibly in light of the name of the association—that floating was a joint venture of the Association's members; and whatever the ultimate truth of this allegation, it is enough to prevent a member from getting the complaint dismissed.... This is not to say that a restaurant which contributed to the cost of a flyer advertising floating, in the hope of getting business from floaters, would be liable as a joint tortfeasor for the torts of the firms actually engaged in renting inner tubes or launching sites. The restaurant would lack the "equal right to a voice in the direction of the enterprise" that is an element of the joint-enterprise doctrine. [Citations.] But if the restaurant was a joint venturer in floating, it could not escape liability just by not dealing face-to-face with the floater who came to grief. [Citations.]

We can take the analysis a step further, and assert with some confidence that if the defendants (or perhaps just one of them, if they were joint venturers) had owned the Montbriand property, with its popular tree, the complaint would withstand a...motion [to dismiss]. Although the mere fact that you invite people into a part of your property for a fee does not make them business invitees on the rest of the property, [citation], we are supposing a situation in which an enterprise trying to make a profit out of floating knows that its customers, while floating down the river, pass by land owned by the enterprise that is conveniently and enticingly fitted with a natural diving board, and that some of these customers land and dive from the tree and the surrounding property. Floating is a summer sport. (Orthmann was injured in July.) A brochure of the Floater's Association shows as one would expect that floaters are young and wear bathing suits. Nothing is more natural than that some of them—maybe many of them—should combine floating with swimming, including diving from a tree invitingly adapted to such use. On these assumptions there would be an implied invitation to the enterprise's customers to use the tree and surrounding land for diving into the river, and the enterprise would be prima facie liable if through its negligence a customer was injured while doing so. [Citation.]

...[E]ven if we could say that Orthmann was negligent as a matter of law, this would not authorize dismissal of the complaint, since contributory negligence is not longer a complete defense in Wisconsin, unless the victim's negligence is greater than the injurer's. Wis. Stat. § 895.045.

....

What makes this case more difficult than our hypothetical variants is that the defendants do not own the property from which Orthmann dove. But according to an affidavit of one of the Montbriands..., shortly after the accident the defendants came on the Montbriands' land without asking their permission, and cut the tree down. The affidavit also states that the Montbriands had seen the defendants cleaning and maintaining the banks of the river on the Montbriands' land. It is possible to infer that the defendants, though they did not own the Montbriand property, treated it as if they did—the cutting down of the tree after the accident being a dramatic assertion of a right normally associated with ownership or at least (which is all that is necessary, as we are about to see) possession.

This is not to say that the defendants could be held liable, under any tort theory we know, if their customers just strayed onto someone else's property and got injured there. This is not because the defendants could not prevent such injuries; they might be able to prevent them quite cheaply and effectively by a warning sign, just as we have assumed that they might have been able to prevent an accident caused by an object that they were not authorized to remove from the river. It is because the law just has not yet imposed on landowners who invite the public onto their property the duty of inspecting their neighbors' property to see whether any of their customers may be wandering onto it, and endangering themselves by doing so. [Citation.] Since a landowner has no right to inspect his neighbor's lands, let alone to correct dangerous conditions on them, little would be accomplished, in general, by making him liable for those conditions along with the neighbors. And though one can think of exceptions—cases where the landowner knows of the condition without having gone on his neighbor's land, and can correct it at trivial cost, as with a warning sign—the law has not seen fit to impose such liability. But if the landowner treats the neighbor's property as an integral part of his, the lack of formal title is immaterial. Whoever controls the land is responsible for its safety....

....Suppose an amusement park when it built its parking lot had encroached on a neighbor's land, and a customer of the amusement park was injured by a pothole in the part of the lot that the amusement park actually did not own (not yet having acquired it by operation of the doctrine of adverse possession) or have any right to occupy. The amusement park could not escape liability by pointing out that the hazard was not actually on its property. *See, e.g.,* Merkel v. Safeway Stores, Inc., 77 N.J. Super. 535, 540-41, 187 A.2d 52, 55 (1962), where a grocery store was held liable for an injury resulting from its failure to remove snow and ice from a public sidewalk that "was the means of ingress and egress provided by defendant for its customers." [Citations.]

....

...[W]hile the judgment in favor of the Village of Somerset is affirmed..., the judgment in favor of the other defendants is reversed and the case is remanded for further proceedings consistent with this opinion....

Note

1. *Adjacent Highways and Neighboring Premises.* Some courts hold that a duty of reasonable care extends "beyond the business premises *when it is reasonable for the invitees to believe* the invitor controls premises adjacent to his own *or where the invitor knows his invitees customarily use* the adjacent premises in connection with the invitation." Ember v. B.F.D., Inc., 490 N.E.2d 764 (Ind. Ct. App., 1986) (emphasis added); *but see* Frampton v. Hutcherson, 784 N.E.2d 993 (Ind. Ct. App. 2003) (homeowners were not liable for negligence to a pedestrian who was injured on a sidewalk in front of their home because the sidewalk was owned by the city, which contrary to an ordinance never gave the homeowners notice of any obligation to make repairs).

See also Mulraney v. Auletto's Catering, 680 A.2d 793 (N.J. 1996) (recognizing duty to undertake reasonable safeguards to protect customers from dangers posed by crossing an adjoining highway to an area neither owned nor controlled by the proprietor, but which the proprietor knows or should know its customers will use for parking). *But see* Rhudy v. Bottlecaps Inc., 830 A.2d 402 (Del. 2003) (a business that advertised the availability of nearby free public parking was not liable for harm caused at that location by a robber because the business did not control the lot or increase the risk of harm to patrons parking there).

b. Hazards after Leaving

A possessor's duty to an invitee may extend to warning, at least, of hazards the invitee may face upon leaving the property.

Mostert v. CBL & Associates

Supreme Court of Wyoming
741 P.2d 1090 (Wyo. 1987)

BROWN, Chief Justice.

....

...Gerrit (Dutch) and Kay Mostert and their daughter, Kumi Maria, were patrons of appellee American's Frontier Six Theatres (AMC) located in the Frontier Mall complex owned by appellee CBL & Associates (CBL), in Cheyenne, Wyoming.

During the evening, Cheyenne experienced a severe thunderstorm which caused the National Weather Service, civil defense authorities, and local law enforcement officials to issue severe thunderstorm, flash flood and tornado warnings. As the storm became progressively worse, local emergency management officials demanded that citizens stay indoors in a safe area and off the streets to avoid being injured or killed. Appellees were aware of the severity of the...storm; were aware of the National Weather Service, civil defense, and local law enforcement warnings, as well as the severe flooding occurring in Cheyenne during the movie. However, the Mostert family never became aware of the warnings or severity of the storm because they were inside AMC's theatre, and they and other patrons attending the movie were not warned.

After the movie, the Mosterts left the theatre through an exit leading directly into the parking lot.... [A]t some point on the road the Mosterts' vehicle was struck by flood waters. In an attempted escape, Kumi Maria drowned. Thereafter, a complaint was filed, alleging negligence and/or willful, wanton and reckless conduct on the part of both appellees.

....The action against AMC was dismissed.

....An order granting CBL a summary judgment was entered....

....

Appellant alleges that the trial court erred when it dismissed the complaint against AMC....

....

...[W]e limit our discussion to duty....

Historically, landowners owed no duty to warn or take action to prevent harm to invitees where the risks involved were outside their premises. However, the imprecise term "duty" has no simple definition that is applicable in all circumstances. One commentator has said:

"....Changing social conditions lead constantly to the recognition of new duties. No better general statement can be made than that the courts will find a duty where, in general, reasonable persons would recognize it and agree that it exists." Prosser & Keeton on Torts, sec. 53, pp. 357-359 (5th ed. 1984).

....The judge's function in a duty determination involves complex considerations of legal and social policies....Consequently,...the imposition and scope of a legal duty is dependent not only on the factor of foreseeability [citation] but involves other considerations, including the magnitude of the risk involved in defendant's conduct, the burden of requiring defendant to guard against that risk, and the consequences of placing that burden upon the defendant.... [Citation.]

....

The court in Bielski v. Schulze, 16 Wis.2d 1, 114 N.W.2d 105, 110 (1962), said:

....Inherent in the common law is a dynamic principle which allows it to grow and to tailor itself to meet changing needs within the doctrine of stare decisis, which, if correctly understood, was not static and did not forever prevent the courts from reversing themselves or from applying principles of common law to new situations as the need arose. If this were not so, we must succumb to a rule that a judge should let others "long dead and unaware of the problems of the age in which he lives, do his thinking for him." Mr. Justice Douglas, *Stare Decisis*, 49 Columbia Law Review 735, 736....

....

Based upon the foregoing and upon balancing a number of factors, we find it appropriate to depart from the traditional rule that a landowner has no duty to warn an invitee of risks off the landowner's premises.

In determining AMC's duty to appellants, as business visitor-invitees,...a court must balance numerous factors when determining the existence of duty in each particular case. Those factors are as follows:

....(1) [t]he foreseeability of harm to the plaintiff, (2) the closeness of the connection between the defendant's conduct and the injury suffered, (3) the degree of certainty that the plaintiff suffered injury, (4) the moral blame attached to the defendant's conduct, (5) the policy of preventing future harm, (6) the extent of the burden upon the defendant, (7) the consequences to the community and the court system, and (8) the availability, cost and prevalence of insurance for the risk involved. Tarasoff v. Regents of University of California, 17 Cal. 3d 425, 131 Cal. Rptr. 14, 551 P.2d 334, 342, 83 A.L.R.3d 1166 (1976). [Citation.]

....We now relate these circumstances to the eight factors set out....

1. The foreseeability factor—AMC was aware of a severe thunderstorm and the presence of tornadoes and flash flooding outside the mall and in the vicinity. It was also aware that the storm became progressively worse and that city officials had demanded that citizens stay off the streets to avoid injury.

2. The closeness factor—the injury suffered by appellants was not remote. Kumi Marie Mostert drowned only minutes after AMC's dereliction in not informing theatre patrons.

3. The degree of certainty factor (that plaintiff had suffered injury)—the injury suffered by the Mostert family was the greatest possible injury—the death of Kumi Marie.

4. The moral blame factor—the Mostert family was a business invitee of AMC and unaware of the storm. AMC was aware of the storm, flooding and attendant dangers. AMC was aware that city officials had demanded that citizens stay off the streets to avoid injury. Despite this superior knowledge, AMC did nothing to warn its patrons.

5. The policy of preventing future harm factor—a rule that business managers have a duty to pass on knowledge to invitees regarding off-premises dangers may reduce injury in the future. If businesses understand they have this duty, they would likely tell patrons what they know about off-premises risks.

6. The burden on defendant factor—the burden of passing AMC's superior knowledge on to patrons regarding the flood appears to be minimal. Theatres find a simple way to pass on to patrons all kinds of information. While we cannot assess the financial costs to AMC, we do not foresee them to be overly excessive. Moreover, the chance of a natural disaster is rare.

7. The consequences to community and courts factor—the consequences of a "duty rule" on the community and court system is a neutral factor.

8. The insurance factor—we do not know the cost of insurance or its availability for the risk involved here. Even if insurance were not available, that single factor should not be dispositive of this case.

Although we have not found a case directly on point, there are some cases that address off-premises risks.

. . . .

In Piedalue v. Clinton Elementary School District No. 32, Mont., 692 P.2d 20, 22-23 (1984), the court said:

> . . . .
>
> . . . [I]t has been held that the duty of an occupier of premises [extends] beyond the premises to the entrances into and exits from such premises and it is his duty to warn his customers of hidden hazards upon, around or beyond his premises, if he would reasonably expect use of an adjacent area by his customer in connection with the invitation. . . .

. . . .

We conclude that appellee AMC owed the Mostert family an affirmative duty to exercise reasonable or ordinary care for their safety which includes an obligation to advise them of off-premises danger that might reasonably be foreseeable. We are not suggesting by our determination that AMC had a duty to restrain its patrons or even a duty to advise them what to do. The duty as we see it is only to reveal what AMC knew to its customers.

. . . .

In this case CBL showed from affidavits and depositions. . . [that] the Mosterts were on the premises exclusively controlled by AMC. CBL had no right or duty as landlord to enter the theatre and warn AMC's patrons about weather conditions. Yet, an employee of CBL reported the thunderstorms to each tenant, including AMC. Additionally, the Mosterts left the theatre through a doorway controlled by AMC directly into the parking lot. . . .

. . . .

The general rule is that the owner or occupier of real property owes a duty to business visitor-invitees to maintain the premises in a reasonably safe condition. . . .

However, when real property is leased to a tenant, the duty to maintain shifts to the lessee....

...[W]e find no breach of duty by CBL to inform or warn the Mostert family of the off-premises dangers. Appellee CBL's conduct fell within the community standards of reasonable conduct. Assuming that injury because of the storm and flood was foreseeable, we do not find that appellee CBL possessed necessary control of the premises or had an opportunity to warn the Mosterts....Finally, because of practical considerations, we find that if this court were to impose liability on a landlord for injuries sustained off the landlord's property, as in this case, it would be difficult to place any practical limitation upon such liability. Extending liability under the circumstances here upon a landlord stretches the legal theory of duty too far. A landlord cannot be expected to be an absolute insurer of the safety of each and every person who enters upon property which is exclusively in the possession and control of his tenant.

....

Accordingly, we reverse and remand to the trial court as to appellee AMC and affirm as to appellee CBL.

[THOMAS, J., filed an opinion, concurring in part and dissenting in part, which has been omitted.]

CARDINE, Justice, concurring and dissenting, with whom THOMAS, Justice, joins.

....

....I concur in the decision of the court affirming summary judgment as to CBL but dissent with respect to reversal of the dismissal of AMC.

....

....This court, apparently adopting a philosophy that holds that for every misfortune that befalls man there must be a third party who should pay, undertakes to overrule all of the common law and to legislate what it thinks best for society....The court suggests support from cases cited as precedent that are not precedent at all, ignoring established law to find a duty where none exists....

A few courts have held that the duty of a possessor of business premises may extend to an area off the premises which is used by the possessor's invitees for immediate ingress and egress to the premises. *E.g.*, Banks v. Hyatt Corp., 722 F.2d 214, *reh. denied* 731 F.2d 888 (5th Cir. 1984) (entrance way to hotel four feet from door); Ollar v. Spakes, 269 Ark. 488, 601 S.W.2d 868 (1980) (dangerous property must be adjacent); Piedalue v. Clinton Elementary School Dist. No. 32, Mont., 692 P.2d 20 (1984) (ditch next to driveway); Annot., 39 A.L.R.3d 579 (1971). But not a single jurisdiction has required a business possessor to warn his invitees of known dangers beyond the area of immediate ingress or egress. [Citations.]

The court has not cited a single case in which a possessor of land has been held liable for failing to warn his invitees of dangerous conditions on land not under the possessor's control....

The court...seeks to buttress the opinion by incorrectly considering as support... key policy factors....Although I seriously question the propriety of considering these policy factors in finding a duty in this case, a review of those factors proves interesting and suggests a result different from that reached by the majority.

1. Foreseeability of harm to the plaintiff. The theatre was not warned of flooding. Would it have foreseen that a patron would drive onto Del Range Boulevard, running

six inches of water and crowded with hundreds of cars, and drive two miles down the road into deepening water and finally into a flooded creek bed and this accident result? I think not.

2. The closeness of the connection between the defendants' conduct and the injury suffered. I would conclude that the place of this accident being more than two miles from the theatre, the defendants' conduct was remote from the injury suffered.

3. The degree of certainty that plaintiffs suffered injury is not questioned.

4. The moral blame attached to defendants' conduct. It cannot be claimed that the theatre owners deliberately withheld information to cause harm to plaintiffs. Severe weather warnings, thunderstorms, hail, tornadoes, blizzards and ice are commonplace in Wyoming. It is doubtful that a warning would have made any difference, especially in light of the fact that hundreds of cars were travelling on Del Range Boulevard and all over Cheyenne.

5. The fifth consideration is a policy of preventing future harm. In light of what has been said in paragraph four, it is doubtful that this policy would be affected.

6. The extent of the burden upon the defendants. The extension of liability by the decision of this court is mind boggling. In the future, it will apply to every business in the mall, every business in Cheyenne, every person having any business relationship with another. It will subject persons to potential liability for injuries from accidents that occur two miles, ten miles, perhaps hundreds of miles from the business because of blizzard conditions, road closures, icing, heavy rains, tornadoes, even perhaps construction work of which the business may be aware. The business proprietor will have no control over the premises where the accident occurs, no ability or right to remedy any defect, and no control over the actions or risks undertaken by his customer.

7. The consequences to the community and the court system. It has long been a practice to join as a party defendant every person with any potential liability for injuries suffered in an accident. Thus, in an auto accident, it has been common for suit to be filed against not only the drivers of the cars involved but the city for posting of warning or traffic signs, the state of Wyoming for construction on its highways, the manufacturer of the car for defective design, and manufacturers of component parts of the cars. Now I expect we will see mall owners and businesses also joined as parties for failure to warn in all accidents in which weather is in any way involved.

8. The availability, cost, and prevalence of insurance for the risk involved. It is doubtful whether insurance exists for this kind of liability, but if it does exist, it will be exceedingly expensive. When the theatre must pay expensive insurance premiums to cover these claims, the money must come from somewhere. The only place it can come from is theatre tickets. We have seen the cost of ski lift tickets ascend from $12.00 to $35.00 in just a few seasons. It is not unreasonable to believe that the cost of theatre tickets might double or triple if theatre owners might be held liable for accidents that result from rain storms or blizzard conditions ten, twenty, or thirty miles away from the theatre after the patrons have left to return home.

Balancing all of the above factors, it seems that the journey upon which this court now embarks in expanding liability is not justified by the review of factors to determine effect and not in the best interest of society.

. . . .

I would affirm.

URBIGKIT, Justice, specially concurring.

The night was dark, the rains came; some say a one-in-a-hundred years flood it was to have been. Within the theater, exposed only to make believe of the silver flicks, the audience was unwarned of the anger of nature outside displayed.

Who knew? Shopping center management knew, and told shop owners. Theater management knew, but perforce told not one among its paying patrons who otherwise were not to be forewarned. Then as the film expired in make believe, by the side door with reality they were extruded as an audience endangered by ignorance contributed to by missing information designedly withheld.

....

One would think that with warning afforded, opportunity to at least listen to the car radio, or telephone to their homes, the life that was lost in a flooded road nearby might have been saved. I see this as a subject for jury review. The issue was not off-premises liability for the theater. I perceive a duty of host to business invitee to communicate his knowledge of facts unknown to the patron of unusual and unexpected exit-time danger. The home of knowledge and needed communication was in the theater, and it was there that the tort occurred, if it did. It simply does not matter whether the clear and obvious danger inculcated in this duty to advise arises from a gunfight adjacent to the north door, a tornado about to arrive, or, as here, flooded conditions on shopping center access roadways.

Whether the plaintiff would have proceeded differently if he had been told what the shopping center and theater management knew is not here disclosed. The child later to drown in the flooded road was denied avoidance opportunity which would have existed if available information had not been withheld.

....I believe a jury should consider whether the zone of duty responsibilities of a host to a business invitee...could be denied without legal responsibility. The issue may be incompletely characterized as a duty to warn, rather than, as I perceive it, a societal duty as a reasonable care obligation of notification to your guest if you know and he does not what may constitute a recognizable departure danger. This is the "tell them what you know" care standard.

....

Notes

1. *Off-Premises Injuries. Compare Mostert with* Walton v. Spindle, 484 N.E.2d 469 (Ill. App. Ct. 1985), holding a tavern owner not liable for injuries sustained outside the tavern in a fight which began in the tavern, and which the bartender did not stop. The court said that the plaintiff's theory, if carried to its logical conclusion, would render the defendant liable if the plaintiff's assailant had followed him home and attacked him there.

Compare Udy v. Calvary Corp., 780 P.2d 1055 (Ariz. 1989) (landlord could be liable for injuries to a child which occurred beyond the boundaries of the landlord's property where the child's parents had repeatedly asked the landlord to erect a fence to keep their small children off a busy street), *with* Kuzmicz v. Ivy Hill Park Apts., Inc., 688 A.2d 1018 (N.J. 1997) (landlord did not owe a duty to tenants to protect them from criminal assaults on a city-owned vacant lot located between the complex and a shopping center, either by warning them of the risks of assault on the lot, or by making more exhaustive efforts to mend the fence that separated the complex from the lot, in which a hole allowing passage had been cut).

2. ***Duties to "Outsiders."*** What about a possessor's duty to those who have never been on the land at all? Active negligence by the possessor will of course give rise to liability. It is no defense to a negligence claim to say that the negligence took place on the defendant's land, and so a landowner who negligently causes an explosion will be liable to a neighbor whose house is knocked down. In Salevan v. Wilmington Park, Inc., 72 A.2d 239 (Del. Super. Ct. 1950), a ballpark operator was held liable for injuries to a pedestrian because it had failed to erect a barrier high enough to keep fly balls from regularly being hit into an adjacent street.

Generally speaking, possessors are said to have no duty to protect their neighbors from dangers arising from natural conditions, so that if rocks fall from a cliff, the possessor is not liable to those on whom they fall. California has gone the other way. In Sprecher v. Adamson Co., 636 P.2d 1121 (Cal. 1981), a landslide shoved some of the defendant's land against that of the plaintiff, who lived downhill from the defendant. The defendant had done nothing to cause the landslide. The California Supreme Court held that "possession alone" creates a duty to exercise care to protect one's neighbors, and held that the trial court had erred in granting the defendant's motion for summary judgment. A dissenting opinion noted that the plaintiff had pointed to nothing which the defendant might reasonably have done to prevent the landslide.

One fairly widespread exception to the rule of "no liability for failure to prevent harm from natural causes" involves trees in urban areas. The risk of harm from falling trees in an urban area is large, and urban landowners usually have so few trees that they can be expected to know when they are dangerous and take precautions. Accordingly, the urban landowner who unreasonably fails to have a dead tree or a rotting branch removed will in many states be liable to one on whom the tree falls. Some courts have been unwilling to distinguish urban trees from rural trees, or trees planted by the defendant (or a preceding owner) from trees which grew naturally, and have applied ordinary negligence principles to all falling-tree cases. *See, e.g.,* Ivancic v. Olmstead, 488 N.E.2d 72 (N.Y. 1985). Factors relevant to determining whether reasonable care has been exercised include the age and size of the tree, its exposure to the wind, the visibility of dead leaves and branches, discolored bark, and the likely proximity and frequency of persons traveling in the vicinity.

3. ***Persons Straying onto Land.*** Not only do possessors owe certain duties to persons outside their properties, they may also have a duty to anticipate and guard against harm to persons straying a short distance onto private land. It is generally agreed that there may be liability for having a dangerous trap near the boundary of the property, such as a concealed pit, against which an entrant cannot exercise self-protection. If, however, the condition is not a trap, there is a divergence of opinion as to whether the possessor may be held liable. In Hayes v. Malkan, 258 N.E.2d 695 (N.Y. 1970), the plaintiff was injured when the car in which he was riding struck a utility pole located on private property a few inches inside the boundary line. Because the dangerous condition was a "visible, sizeable, above-the-surface structure," concerning which travelers could be expected to take precautions, the court held that the complaint against the defendant should have been dismissed. Any other result, the court wrote, would "impose an intolerable burden upon a property owner" by requiring that person "to remove every tree, fence, post, mailbox or name sign located on his property in the vicinity of the highway."

Compare Hayes with McMillan v. State Highway Comm., 393 N.W.2d 332 (Mich. 1986), which held that a utility company owes a duty of reasonable care to the occupant of a vehicle which leaves the road and strikes a utility pole located on the median. The relevant factors were found to include the location of the pole, its proximity to the roadway, the configuration of the roadway, whether the utility company had notice of prior accidents, and whether alternative, less-dangerous locations existed.

Some decisions suggest that possessors may count upon others exercising care, at least in some circumstances. *See also* City of McAllen v. De La Garza, 898 S.W.2d 809 (Tex. 1995) (in an action for the wrongful death of an intoxicated passenger, whose intoxicated driver fell asleep or blacked out, causing the vehicle to enter a caliche pit abutting the road, the court held that the pit owner had no duty to protect those not traveling with reasonable care on the adjoining highway); Ziemba v. Mierzwa, 566 N.E.2d 1365 (Ill. 1991) (landowner owed no duty to warn a passing bicyclist of a hidden driveway which posed no danger to the bicyclist absent negligence on the part of a truck driver who pulled out of the driveway without looking: "the defendant had a right to expect that the truck driver would check for oncoming traffic").

4. *Streets and Sidewalks.* At common law, a municipality is normally required to maintain its streets and sidewalks in reasonably safe condition for the amount and kind of travel which may be fairly expected upon them. The municipality is not required to keep all thoroughfares in perfect condition, and slight inequalities in level or other minor defects are to be expected and are not actionable. *Cf.* Larson v. City of Chicago, 491 N.E.2d 165 (Ill. App. Ct. 1986) (roller skating on a sidewalk was a foreseeable use and therefore a cause of action was stated).

Chapter 11

Limited Duty: Negligent Infliction of Severe Emotional Distress

No area of tort law is more unsettled than compensation for negligent infliction of emotional distress. The decisions continually restate the criteria for recovery, and there are often substantial differences in the requirements, or their interpretation, from one jurisdiction to the next, and within any one jurisdiction at different times.

The law of negligent infliction of emotional distress must face two special concerns: the need to guarantee the genuineness of claims and the need to limit the scope of liability to manageable bounds. Genuineness is a problem here, as it is with all forms of redress for mental harm, because the inner workings of the human mind are difficult to fathom. In the absence of corroboration for the plaintiff's story, there is a substantial risk of falsification. Restricting the scope of liability is important because requiring defendants who are merely negligent (not recklessly or intentionally tortious) to pay for all mental suffering caused by minor lapses could often result in liability disproportionate to fault and exhaust a defendant's resources without regard to whether the most-serious claims were compensated.

If genuineness can be established, and if reasonable lines can be drawn to limit the scope of liability, courts will award compensation, but only if there is proof that the plaintiff suffered serious harm of a type that could reasonably have been anticipated under the circumstances.

A. Serious and Genuine Harm

Lewis v. Westinghouse Electric Corporation

Appellate Court of Illinois
487 N.E.2d 1071 (Ill. App. Ct. 1985)

JIGANTI, Presiding Justice.

.... Lucille Lewis sought damages from the defendants, Westinghouse Elevator Co.... and the Chicago Housing Authority (CHA), for the negligent infliction of emotional distress. The defendants moved to dismiss the plaintiff's complaint for failure to state a cause of action. The trial court granted the motion....

The plaintiff is a resident at one of the apartments owned by the defendant CHA. The defendant Westinghouse maintains and services the elevators.... On August 16, 1983, the plaintiff entered the elevator on the first floor and rode it to the 16th floor. As she attempted to exit the elevator, however, the elevator stalled and the doors remained closed. The elevator remained in this position for approximately 40 minutes. The plaintiff alleges that during that time she was in danger of "suffocation and serious physical harm." In addition plaintiff alleges that as a result of the incident she suffered an unstable angina and aggravation of her coronary arteriosclerotic heart disease and hypertension.

....

...[W]e find that the plaintiff did not have a reasonable fear for her own safety. Whether a fear is reasonable is determined by the objective standard of whether a particular incident would produce fear in the person of ordinary sensibilities. [Citation.] In this case the elevator merely stalled and the doors failed to open. This is not a case such as Bass v. Nooney Co. (Mo. 1983), 646 S.W.2d 765, where water began to rise in the elevator so that the party reasonably feared drowning. Apprehensive or uncomfortable it may have been for the plaintiff, but, absent something more, the incident in this case was not one which produces fear of suffocation.

....

...[I]n making that judgment we are mindful of the admonition of the Illinois Supreme Court in a case involving an intentional infliction of emotional distress. [Citation.] In *Knierim* the court stated that "[i]ndiscriminate allowance of actions for mental anguish would encourage neurotic overreactions to trivial hurts, and the law should aim to toughen the psyche of the citizen rather than pamper it." Knierim v. Izzo (1961), 22 Ill.2d. 73, 85, 174 N.E.2d 157, 164.

...."[Trial judges...should] not permit litigation to enter the field of trivialities and mere bad manners." [Citation.]

It might be argued that this is not a neurotic overreaction to a trivial hurt since the plaintiff has alleged a resulting physical injury, aggravation of her angina condition. However, the *Knierim* court favorably commented on the case of Slocum v. Food Fair Stores of Florida, Inc. (Fla. 1958), 100 So. 2d 396, in which the plaintiff suffered a heart attack as a result of an aggravation of a preexisting condition. The Florida court found that there was no cause of action because the defendant's conduct must cause distress to a person of "ordinary sensibilities." The finding of the Florida court, in which the Illinois Supreme Court agreed, was that this was not a person of ordinary sensibilities. We judge that to be the situation in this instance.

....

The order of the trial court is affirmed.

....

[The dissenting opinion of Justice LINN is omitted.]

Notes

1. *Ordinary Sensibilities.* Is the "ordinary sensibilities rule" discussed in *Lewis* reconcilable with the "eggshell skull" doctrine (*See*, pp. 436, *supra*)?

2. *Foreseeability of Emotional Distress. Compare Lewis with* Friedman v. Merck & Co., 131 Cal. Rptr. 2d 885 (Cal. Ct. App. 2003), where a job applicant, who was a strict, ethical vegan, filed negligence actions against drug test distributors alleging that he suffered serious emotional, and subsequent physical, injuries when he discovered that a tu-

berculosis test he submitted to as part of a condition of offered employment contained animal products. In addressing the negligent infliction of emotional distress claim, the court wrote:

> [E]ven if, as alleged, defendants, the distributors of the TB test, knew plaintiff was a strict ethical vegan, it was not reasonably foreseeable that their negligence in responding to the prospective employer's inquiry would likely cause plaintiff to suffer *serious* emotional distress. Plaintiff alleges the defendants knew that the inquiry was being made on behalf of a prospective employee who, as a vegan, would not submit to a TB test containing animal products. It was reasonably foreseeable, under these circumstances, that plaintiff would be upset upon subsequently learning the TB test did in fact contain cow serum. However, it was not reasonably foreseeable plaintiff would suffer *serious* emotional harm. There is no allegation defendants knew who plaintiff was or the strength of his ethical beliefs.... Defendants' undertaking was not of a personal nature involving an unavoidable risk of *serious* emotional trauma. Defendants did not voluntarily undertake any duty that encompassed plaintiff's emotional tranquility. A corporation responding to an inquiry as to the contents of its product is materially unlike: a physician undertaking to deliver a child; a therapist agreeing to treat a patient; a mortuary contracting to provide burial services; or a doctor telling a patient to advise her husband that she has syphilis. The circumstances of this case do not support a conclusion that defendants, by voluntarily responding to the inquiry, assumed a duty to exercise care for plaintiff's emotional condition.

3. *Fear of AIDS, Cancer, or Other Diseases.* Many courts hold that emotional distress damages for fear of contracting a disease, such as AIDS, can be recovered from a negligent defendant only if the plaintiff was exposed to the disease. *See* Majca v. Beekil, 701 N.E.2d 1084 (Ill. 1998) (a complaint alleging that dental student was infected with HIV at time he provided treatment failed to state a cause of action for fear of contracting AIDS, in the absence of an allegation that the patients were actually exposed to HIV); K.A.C. v. Benson, 527 N.W.2d 553 (Minn. 1995) (patient who did not allege that she was actually exposed to HIV was not, as a matter of law, in the zone of danger and could not recover for negligent infliction of emotional distress).

Of course the critical question is whether "exposed" means (a) that the defendant had the disease, (b) that the circumstances were such that the disease might have been transmitted, (c) that it is probable that the plaintiff will develop the disease, or (d) that the plaintiff in fact contracted the disease. Courts appear to differ in answering this question. *Compare* Johnson v. West Va. Univ. Hosp., 413 S.E.2d 889 (W. Va. 1991) (where the defendant hospital negligently failed to advise a security officer that an unruly patient had AIDS, and the patient bit the officer after biting himself, the court upheld a $1.9 million award, distinguishing cases that had denied recovery on the ground that they involved only suspicion, rather than evidence, of exposure); *with* Potter v. Firestone Tire & Rubber Co., 863 P.2d 795 (Cal. 1993) (damages for fear of cancer in a negligence action are allowed only if the fear stems from a knowledge which is corroborated by reasonable medical and scientific opinion that it is more likely than not that cancer will develop in the future due to the toxic exposure). As in many areas of tort law, the Texas courts adhere to the most strict position. In Temple-Inland Forest Products Corp. v. Carter, 993 S.W.2d 88 (Tex. 1999), the court held that workers who were exposed to asbestos, but who did not then have an asbestos-related disease, could not recover damages for fear of developing such a disease in the future. The court wrote:

A person exposed to asbestos can certainly develop serious health problems, but he or she also may not. The difficulty in predicting whether exposure will cause any disease and if so, what disease, and the long latency period characteristic of asbestos-related diseases, make it very difficult…to evaluate which exposure claims are serious and which are not. This difficulty in turn makes liability unpredictable, with some claims resulting in significant recovery while virtually indistinguishable claims are denied altogether. Some claimants would inevitably be overcompensated when, in the course of time, it happens that they never develop the disease they feared, and others would be undercompensated when it turns out that they developed a disease more serious even than they feared. Also, claims for exposure could proliferate because in our society…"contacts, even extensive contacts, with serious carcinogens are common."…If recovery were allowed in the absence of present disease, individuals might feel obliged to bring suit for such recovery prophylactically, against the possibility of future consequences from what is now an inchoate risk. This would exacerbate not only the multiplicity of suits but the unpredictability of results.

The court allowed the possibility that other cases involving some other dangerous or toxic element might warranted a different outcome. *See also* Brzoska v. Olson, 668 A.2d 1355 (Del. 1995) (damages for emotional distress are recoverable only if underlying physical injury is shown). The United States Supreme Court has addressed similar issues arising under the Federal Employers' Liability Act, a statute governing compensation for injuries to railroad workers. *See* Metro-North Commuter R.R. Co. v. Buckley, 521 U.S. 424 (1997) (employee could not recover under the FELA for negligently inflicted emotional distress unless and until he manifested symptoms of asbestosis); Norfolk & Western Ry. Co. v. Ayers, 538 U.S. 135 (2003) (a plaintiff who has asbestosis, but not cancer, can recover damages for fear of cancer under the FELA without proof of physical manifestations of the claimed emotional distress, if the plaintiff proves the alleged fear is genuine and serious).

In proving exposure, the plaintiff may be aided by a presumption arising from spoliation of evidence. In South Cent. Reg. Med. Ctr. v. Pickering, 749 So. 2d 95 (Miss. 1999), the court held that where the defendant has allowed or caused the best evidence of exposure to HIV or another communicable disease to be destroyed, despite the fact that defendant had notice that an issue existed regarding that evidence, a rebuttable presumption of actual exposure arises in favor of the plaintiff. In that case, the defendant bears the burden of proving that the instrument which came into contact with the plaintiff as a result of defendant's negligence did not contain or carry a disease causing agent.

Some courts do not require exposure. *See* Madrid v. Lincoln County Med. Ctr., 923 P.2d 1154 (N.M. 1996), in which the plaintiff was negligently allowed to come into contact with bodily fluids that might have been, but were not, HIV-positive.

What if a doctor negligently diagnoses a patient as having AIDS or HIV? *Compare* Chizmar v. Markie, 896 P.2d 196 (Alaska 1995) (permitting recovery of emotional distress damages without proof of physical injury), *with* Heiner v. Moretuzzo, 652 N.E.2d 664 (Ohio 1995) (holding that a patient was not entitled to recovery for emotional distress since she never faced actual physical peril as a result of the alleged negligence).

If recovery for fear of AIDS is permitted even if the plaintiff has not in fact contracted the disease, some courts hold that damages should be limited to the "window of anxiety" that occurs before the plaintiff is able to determine with reasonable medical certainty that there has been no infection. *See* Faya v. Almarz, 620 A.2d 327 (Md. 1993). However, in John Doe v. Paul Arts, M.D., 823 A.2d 855 (N.J. Super. App. Div. 2003), the court held, in an action where the plaintiff was negligently informed that he was HIV-positive, that the trial judge did not err in charging a jury that it could consider alleged damages from the distress that occurred even after the patient knew that he was negative, because such distress was an element of post-traumatic stress disorder.

4. *Ways of Establishing Genuineness.* In an action for *intentional* infliction of emotional distress (*see* Chapter 2), the genuineness of the plaintiff's claim may be inferred from both the defendant's mental state and the egregious nature of the conduct. The defendant's desire to cause emotional distress or substantial certainty that distress would result suggests that the plaintiff's claim is not fabricated. Also, it is well known that "extreme and outrageous" conduct is likely to produce in others adverse mental reactions.

In an emotional distress action based on *negligence*, those guarantees of genuineness are not present. The underlying conduct need be only unreasonable (that is, negligent), and intent need not be shown. Not surprisingly, a number of courts have imposed specific requirements that must be met in negligent-emotional-distress cases as a way of excluding claims for which genuineness is hard to determine.

(a) *The Impact Rule.* In the early twentieth century, the law generally required a negligent-emotional-distress plaintiff to present evidence of physical impact or injury. Unless the plaintiff suffered such harm, a claim could not succeed. There was no duty to refrain from negligently inflicting emotional harm which was unaccompanied by physical trauma.

Most states no longer regard impact as essential. *But see* Bader v. Johnson, 732 N.E.2d 1212, 1221-22 (Ind. 2000) (indicating that Indiana continues to adhere to a modified impact rule). However, proof of physical impact or injury is still generally sufficient to secure an award if other requirements are met. *See* Restatement, Second, Torts § 47 Comment b; Deutsch v. Shein, 597 S.W.2d 141 (Ky. 1980) (physician's act in negligently exposing pregnant woman to X-rays was sufficient physical contact to support a claim for mental suffering).

Emotional distress damages that accompany compensation for an impact that causes physical injury are often referred to as "parasitic damages," in the sense that they attach to the award for the physical harm.

(b) *Physical Consequences.* The rigidity of the physical-impact requirement, and its potential for denying recovery in cases where justice appeared to dictate a contrary result, led some courts to seize upon rather trivial impacts, such as a slight jolt, a minor blow, or dust in the eye (*see* W. Page Keeton, Dan B. Dobbs, Robert E. Keeton, & David G. Owen, Prosser and Keeton on Torts (5th ed. 1984)) to justify an award. Many jurisdictions now allow proof of physical consequences or manifestations resulting from mental distress to substitute for physical impact. *See, e.g.,* Daley v. LaCroix, 179 N.W.2d 390 (Mich. 1970) (claim was adequately supported by testimony that explosion caused son to be nervous and mother to be irritable, lose weight, and unable to perform household duties); Champion v. Gray, 478 So. 2d 17 (Fla. 1985) (recognizing an exception to the impact rule where a mother was overcome by grief and dropped dead upon seeing her daughter's dead body following an auto accident). *See also* Brown v. Matthews Mortuary, Inc., 801 P.2d 37 (Idaho 1990) (holding that son could not recover for distress allegedly resulting from mortuary's negligent loss of cremated remains of his father absent physical manifestations of injury).

(c) *Invasion of Particular Kinds of Rights.* Some courts have awarded compensatory damages for mental anguish unaccompanied by physical injury or physical consequences where the defendant's invasion of a legal right is, by its very nature, likely to provoke serious emotional distress. The cases have frequently involved facts similar to those which, if accompanied by intent, would have been sufficient to state a claim for assault or false imprisonment, since in such instances "a disagreeable emotional experience would normally be expected to be inextricably intertwined with the nature of the deliberate wrong committed, thereby lending credence to a claim for mental disturbance." Charlie Stuart Oldsmobile, Inc. v. Smith, 357 N.E.2d 247 (Ind. Ct. App. 1976), *modified on rehearing* 369 N.E.2d 947 (Ind. Ct. App. 1977) (citing cases). *See also* Johnson v. Super Save Markets, Inc., 686 P.2d 209 (Mont. 1984) (as a result of the defendant's negligence, the plaintiff was improperly arrested for failure to pay his debts).

(d) *No Special Requirements.* A growing number of decisions have dispensed altogether with special tests for genuineness, relying instead upon the usual factfinding processes for exposing fraudulent claims, such as cross-examination and jury evaluation of witness demeanor. Thus, in Johnson v. Ruark Obstetrics, 395 S.E.2d 85, 97-98 (N.C. 1990), the court said:

> Where...a plaintiff [who observed injury to another] has established that he or she has suffered severe emotional distress as a proximate result of the defendant's negligence, the plaintiff need not allege or prove any physical impact, physical injury, or physical manifestation of emotional distress in order to recover on a claim for negligent infliction of emotional distress.
>
> ....
>
> ...[O]ur trial courts have adequate means available to them for disposing of improper claims for negligent infliction of emotional distress and for adjusting excessive or inadequate verdicts.

See also Sacco v. High Country Ind. Press, Inc., 896 P.2d 411, 425 (Mont. 1995) (a cause of action arises if "serious or severe emotional distress to the plaintiff was the reasonably foreseeable consequence of the defendant's negligent act or omission"); Jones v. Howard University, Inc., 589 A.2d 419 (D.C. App. 1991) (patient who was subjected to x-rays and surgery before being diagnosed as pregnant could recover for serious and verifiable mental distress suffered as a result of her fear that the procedures had injured her or her unborn twins, without proof of physical injuries or physical manifestations); Paugh v. Hanks, 451 N.E.2d 759 (Ohio 1983) (saying that a physical injury manifestation requirement ignores advances in medicine and psychiatry). *See also* Folz v. New Mexico, 797 P.2d 246 (N.M. 1990) (a person who witnesses firsthand the fatal injury of a family member can recover for negligent infliction of mental distress without proof of physical manifestations or physical injuries).

5. *Attorneys Who Negligently Cause Distress.* Courts have been reluctant to hold attorneys liable for negligently causing mental distress to clients. However, there is authority that liability may be imposed if the lawyer's malpractice results in a loss of the client's liberty. *See* Holt v. Rowell, 850 So. 2d 474 (Fla. 2003) (in a malpractice action based on a lawyer's mishandling of a document that led to his client's ten-day incarceration, the impact rule did not bar an award of emotional distress damages); Wagenmann v. Adams, 829 F.2d 196 (1st Cir. 1987) (court-appointed attorney failed to take any action on behalf of client confined for evaluation in a psychiatric hospital; client's release was later procured by a second attorney who secured a dismissal of criminal charges against the client).

6. *Distress Resulting from Damage to Property.* Most courts hold that negligent harm to property, by itself, is an insufficient predicate for an award of mental-distress damages, at least when the damage occurs outside of the plaintiff's presence. *See* Dobbins v. Washington Suburban Sanitary Comm., 658 A.2d 675 (Md. 1995) (no recovery for emotional distress where property damage occurred on two occasions when defendant's water pipes burst); Charlie Stuart Oldsmobile, Inc. v. Smith, 357 N.E.2d 247 (Ind. Ct. App. 1976), *modified on rehearing* 369 N.E.2d 947 (Ind. Ct. App. 1977) (no recovery for distress resulting from repeated damage to an auto during several attempts to obtain repairs); In re Air Crash Disaster Near New Orleans, 764 F.2d 1084 (5th Cir. 1985) (no recovery for distress where house had to be bulldozed after being doused with jet fuel). *But see* Paugh v. Hanks, 451 N.E.2d 759 (Ohio 1983) (claim for negligent infliction of mental distress was stated by owners, whose house was located directly across from an exit ramp, against motorists whose vehicles collided on various occasions with the house).

In Rodrigues v. Hawaii, 472 P.2d 509 (Haw. 1970), a new house was flooded with six inches of water on the day the plaintiffs were to move in, causing extensive damage to the house and furnishings. The flood was allegedly caused by the state's negligence in failing to provide for proper highway drainage. "Mr. Rodrigues reported that he was 'heartbroken' and 'couldn't stand to look at it' and Mrs. Rodrigues testified that she was 'shocked' and cried because they had waited fifteen years to build their own home." The court awarded a modest $2500 for mental suffering, in addition to other damages for repairs, labor, and loss of occupancy. The decision in *Rodrigues* was later superseded by a statute that allows recovery for serious emotional distress arising solely from damage to property or material objects only if it results in "physical injury or mental illness." *See* Haw. Stat. Ann. §663-8.9 (Westlaw 2002). *See also* Erlich v. Menezes, 981 P.2d 978 (Cal. 1999) (holding that emotional distress damages, even though foreseeable, were not recoverable by homeowners for mere negligent performance of a contract to construct a house, where breach did not cause physical injury and the alleged emotional distress arose solely from property damage).

Cases involving mere negligence are distinguishable from intentional torts, and it is not surprising that a large number of courts have awarded mental anguish damages if the defendant intentionally interfered with the plaintiff's chattels or realty. *See, e.g.,* Smith & Gaston Funeral Directors v. Wilson, 79 So. 2d 48 (Ala. 1955) (trespass and desecration of grave site); Grandeson v. International Harvester Credit Corp., 66 So. 2d 317 (La. 1953) (trespassory repossession of refrigerator); Fredeen v. Stride, 525 P.2d 166 (Or. 1974) (conversion of dog).

B. Some Special Cases

One area in which many courts have been willing to award damages for negligently inflicted emotional distress involves the death (or the erroneously reported death) of someone close to the plaintiff. When a funeral director carelessly botches the ceremony, dumping the decedent's remains beside the road, or when a telegraph company carelessly and erroneously informs the plaintiff that a loved one has died, there is reason to conclude that the distress the plaintiff claims is genuine and serious. Furthermore, cases like this seldom give rise to significant financial losses, so limiting recovery to out-of-pocket damages might seriously under-deter misconduct by those responsible for this kind of harm.

Johnson v. New York
Court of Appeals of New York
334 N.E.2d 590 (N.Y. 1975)

BREITEL, Chief Judge.

... [T]he issue is whether the daughter of a patient in a State hospital, falsely advised that the patient, her mother, had died, may recover from the State for emotional harm....

Claimant and her aunt, Nellie Johnson, since deceased, had filed a claim against the State for funeral expenses incurred, emotional harm and punitive damages. The Court of Claims awarded claimant $7,500 for funeral expenses undertaken on the false information, and for emotional harm. It denied her punitive damages, and dismissed the aunt's claim for insufficiency.... The Appellate Division modified, limiting the daughter's award to her pecuniary losses of $1,658.47, and otherwise affirmed as to both claimants. The aunt's estate, unlike the daughter, took no further appeal to this court.

There should be a reversal....

Claimant's mother, Emma Johnson, had been a patient in the Hudson River State Hospital since 1960. On August 6, 1970, another patient, also named Emma Johnson died. Later that day, the hospital sent a telegram addressed to Nellie Johnson of Albany, claimant's aunt and the sister of the living Emma Johnson. The telegram read:

> [Regret to inform you of death of Emma Johnson. Please notify relatives make burial arrangements have undertaker contact hospital before coming for body. Hospital wishes to study all deaths for scientific reasons. Please wire post mortem consent.
>
> —Hudson River State Hospital]

In accordance with the instructions in the telegram, claimant was notified of her mother's death by her aunt. An undertaker was engaged; the body of the deceased Emma Johnson was released by the hospital and taken to Albany that night. A wake was set for August 11, with burial the next day. In the interim claimant incurred expenses in preparing the body for the funeral, and in notifying other relatives of her mother's death.

On the afternoon of the wake, claimant and her aunt went to the funeral home to view the body. After examining the body, both claimant and her aunt remarked that the mother's appearance had changed. Nellie Johnson also expressed doubt that the corpse was that of her sister Emma. Thereafter the doubts built up, and upon returning that evening for the wake, claimant, in a state of extreme distress, examined the corpse more closely and verified that it was not that of her mother. At this point, claimant became "very, very, hysterical," and had to be helped from the funeral chapel.

The hospital was called, and the mistake confirmed. Claimant's mother was alive and well in another wing of the hospital.... Upon the trial it appeared that the hospital had violated its own procedures and with gross carelessness had "pulled" the wrong patient record.

After this incident, claimant did not work in her employment for more than 11 days. She complained of "[r]ecurrent nightmares, terrifying dreams of death, seeing the cof-

Charles D. Breitel

fin...difficulty in concentrating, irritability, inability to function at work properly, general tenseness and anxiety." Her psychiatrist testified that "She appeared to be somewhat depressed, tremulous. She seemed to be under a considerable amount of pressure. She cried easily when relating events that occurred. I thought that she spoke rather rapidly and obviously perspiring." Both her psychiatrist and that of the State agreed that, as a result of the incident, claimant suffered "excessive anxiety," that is, anxiety neurosis....

....In the absence of contemporaneous or consequential physical injury, courts have been reluctant to permit recovery for negligently caused psychological trauma, with ensuing emotional harm alone. [Citations.] The reasons for the more restrictive rule were best summarized by Prosser [citation]: "The temporary emotion of fright, so far from serious that it does no physical harm, is so evanescent a thing, so easily counterfeited, and usually so trivial, that the courts have been quite unwilling to protect the plaintiff against mere negligence, where the elements of extreme outrage and moral blame which have had such weight in the case of the intentional tort are lacking." Contemporaneous or consequential physical harm, coupled with the initial psychological trauma, was, however, thought to provide an index of reliability otherwise absent in a claim for psychological trauma with only psychological consequences.

There have developed, however, two exceptions. The first is the minority rule permitting recovery for emotional harm resulting from negligent transmission by a telegraph company of a message announcing death....

The second exception permits recovery for emotional harm to a close relative resulting from negligent mishandling of a corpse [citation]. Recovery in these cases has ostensibly been grounded on a violation of the relative's quasi-property right in the body. [Citations.] It has been noted, however, that in this context such a "property right" is little more than a fiction; in reality the personal feelings of the survivors are being protected [citation].

In both the telegraph cases and the corpse mishandling cases, there exists "an espe-cial likelihood of genuine and serious mental distress, arising from the special circum-stances, which serves as a guarantee that the claim is not spurious" (p. 330). Prosser notes that "[t]here may perhaps be other such cases" (p. 330; *see* Neiman v. Upper Queens Med. Group, City Ct., 220 N.Y.S.2d 129, 130, in which plaintiff alleged emo-tional harm due to negligent misinformation by a laboratory that his sperm count indi-cated sterility; and defendant's motion for judgment on the pleadings was denied). The instant claim provides an example of such a case.

….The consequential funeral expenditures and the serious psychological impact on claimant of a false message informing her of the death of her mother, were all within the "orbit of the danger" and therefore within the "orbit of the duty" for the breach of which a wrongdoer may be held liable (Palsgraf v. Long Is. R.R. Co., 248 N.Y. 339, 343, 162 N.E. 99, 100). Thus, the hospital owed claimant a duty to refrain from such con-duct, a duty breached when it negligently sent the false message. The false message and the events flowing from its receipt were the proximate cause of claimant's emotional harm. Hence, claimant is entitled to recover for that harm, especially if supported by objective manifestations of that harm.

….In this case,…the injury was inflicted by the hospital directly on claimant by its negligent sending of a false message announcing her mother's death. Claimant was not directly harmed by injury caused to another; she was not a mere eyewitness of or by-stander to injury caused to another. Instead, she was the one to whom a duty was di-rectly owed by the hospital, and the one who was directly injured by the hospital's breach of that duty….

Moreover, not only justice but logic compels the further conclusion that if claimant was entitled to recover her pecuniary losses she was also entitled to recover for the emo-tional harm caused by the same tortious act. The recovery of the funeral expenses stands only because a duty to claimant was breached. Such a duty existing and such a breach of that duty occurring, she is entitled to recover the proven harmful consequences proxi-mately caused by the breach….[R]ecovery for emotional harm to one subjected directly to the tortious act may not be disallowed so long as the evidence is sufficient to show causa-tion and substantiality of the harm suffered, together with a "guarantee of genuineness"….

Order reversed with costs, and case remitted…for further proceedings in accordance with the opinion herein.

Notes

1. *See also* Wilson v. Ferguson, 747 S.W.2d 499 (Tex. Ct. App. 1988) (where a funeral director abandoned a coffin and body at an improperly prepared gravesite, and ignored the family's request for help in correcting the problem, emotional distress damages were awarded without proof of physical injury or physical manifestations).

2. *Dead Bodies.* The Restatement, Second, of Torts, § 868, recognizes a tort for inter-ference with dead bodies:

> One who intentionally, recklessly or negligently removes, withholds, mutilates or operates upon the body of a dead person or prevents its proper interment or cremation is subject to liability to a member of the family of the deceased who is entitled to the disposition of the body.

Comment a to § 868 states:

The technical basis of the cause of action is the interference with the exclusive right of control of the body, which frequently has been called by the courts a "property" or a "quasi-property" right. This does not, however, fit very well into the category of property, since the body ordinarily cannot be sold or transferred, has no utility and can be used only for the one purpose of interment or cremation. In practice the technical right has served as a mere peg upon which to hang damages for the mental distress inflicted upon the survivor; and in reality the cause of action has been exclusively one for the mental distress....

See Akins Funeral Home, Inc. v. Miller, 2003 W.L. 22221246 (Ala.) (permitting recovery of a substantial emotional distress damages resulting from unwanted cremation in a suit alleging negligence, wantoness, and tort of outrage). *But see* Roach v. Stern, 675 N.Y.S.2d 133 (App. Div. 1998) (outrageous remarks by a radio personality and his guest about the cremated remains of the decedent did not interfere with the decedent's siblings' decision to cremate the body).

3. *Otherwise-Compelling Facts.* Part of the appeal of a rule allowing recovery of mental-distress damages in cases involving death is that creating that kind of liability does not threaten to open the courts to mental-distress claims generally. That is, recovery can be allowed in this particular kind of case without undue concern that anyone frightened by someone's negligence will be able to get to a jury. However, death cases are not the only ones in which the defendant's misconduct and the plaintiff's suffering are so apparent that recovery seems appealing, and so some courts have created other categories of liability.

In Hagan v. Coca-Cola Bottling Co., 804 So. 2d 1234 (Fla. 2001), consumers who drank a beverage that appeared to contain a used condom sued for emotional distress based on fear of contracting AIDS. The court held that a plaintiff need not prove the existence of a physical injury in order to recover damages for emotional injuries caused by the consumption of a contaminated food or beverage.

The plaintiff in Rowe v. Bennett, 514 A.2d 802 (Me. 1986), sought treatment at a health service for problems in her relationship with her homosexual companion of three years. During the course of the treatment, plaintiff's therapist secretly became emotionally involved with plaintiff's companion, and the two later started living together. The court held that the patient could maintain an action for negligent infliction of mental distress, notwithstanding the absence of physical contact because the plaintiff was "extremely vulnerable" to mental harm.

See also Doe Parents No. 1 v. State Dept. of Educ., 58 P.3d 545 (Haw. 2002) (holding that the action of the state in negligently placing students in an environment where they were left unsupervised with a teacher who was an accused child molester, without undertaking any reasonable effort to ascertain whether it could have been anticipated that the teacher would molest again, warranted recognition of an exception to general requirement that a plaintiff seeking redress solely for emotional distress must establish a predicate physical injury to a person).

4. *Problem: Mis-Scoring the Bar Exam.* In May 2003, the National Conference of Bar Examiners announced to bar officials in 48 states that the scores of law students who took the test in February were being recalculated because one question had been mis-scored as a result of a "keying error." This was the first such problem in the 31 years since the Multistate Bar Exam was first administered. In some jurisdictions, applicants were sent letters saying that the revised scores would be used to determine admission to

practice. As a result of the error, some students who had been told they had passed had actually failed; some who had been told that they failed actually passed; and others, who had been correctly told that they passed or failed, worried or hoped that they would be told that the result was in fact different. Some students, who had passed the bar with scores providing a comfortable margin of safety, worried about the predicament of classmates teetering at the precipice of the necessary minimum. Does anyone have a claim for negligent infliction of emotional distress?

C. Distress Occasioned by Harm to Another

James v. Lieb
Supreme Court of Nebraska
375 N.W.2d 109 (Neb. 1985)

WHITE, Justice.

....

....A garbage truck owned by the defendant Watts Trucking Service, Inc., and driven by its employee, John Milton Lieb,...backed into the intersection of 50th and Spaulding Streets, through a stop sign, and hit and ran over Demetria, killing her. Gregory helplessly watched the entire incident. As a result of witnessing his sister's peril, Gregory became physically ill and suffered, and will continue to suffer, mental anguish and emotional distress.

....

....Based upon our prior holding in Fournell v. Usher Pest Control Co., 208 Neb. 684, 305 N.W.2d 605 (1981), the trial court dismissed the petition. To the extent that *Fournell* is in conflict with this opinion, it is expressly overruled....

....

....The issue of first impression presented to us in this case is whether and under what circumstances a bystander may recover for negligent infliction of emotional distress. The term "bystander" throughout this opinion refers to those persons who are not immediately threatened with physical injury nor placed in fear for their own safety by the defendant's negligence.

Under the "zone of danger" rule followed by this court in *Fournell*, other jurisdictions have allowed bystanders to recover for emotional distress only if they (1) were within a physical "zone of danger," (2) feared for their own safety, and (3) suffered physically manifested mental or physical injuries as a result of this fear. [Citations.] However, other "zone of danger" jurisdictions have allowed bystanders to recover damages for "fear for the safety of another," so long as the plaintiff was also at personal risk. [Citations.] The latter view is in accordance with Restatement (Second) of Torts §436 (1965), which would allow recovery when a family member is within the zone of danger but his or her emotional distress arises from fear for another's safety.

....

The "zone of danger" rule in general has been defended as a more rational means of determining liability than the "impact" rule which it replaced and which was abandoned by this court in Rasmussen v. Benson, 133 Neb. 449, 275 N.W. 674 (1937)....

Advocates of the "zone of danger" rule also argue that it provides workable, reasonable limits to the liability of a potential defendant. [Citation.] "Under the zone-of-danger rule the courts and juries can objectively determine whether plaintiffs were within the zone of danger. Furthermore, plaintiffs can be cross-examined regarding whether their fear was for themselves or for another." [Citation.] The "zone of danger" rule is currently followed by several jurisdictions. [Citation.]

However, in 1968 the California Supreme Court became the first jurisdiction to abolish the "zone of danger" rule and allow a bystander to recover for negligently inflicted emotional distress in its now landmark decision of Dillon v. Legg, 68 Cal.2d 728, 441 P.2d 912, 69 Cal. Rptr. 72 (1968). Since that time, a growing number of jurisdictions have taken another look at this tort and have either adopted or modified the *Dillon* approach and allowed bystander recovery for negligent infliction of emotional distress. [Citing decisions from Connecticut, Hawaii, Iowa, Maine, Massachusetts, Michigan, Mississippi, Montana, New Hampshire, New Jersey, New Mexico, Ohio, Pennsylvania, Rhode Island, and Texas.]

In *Dillon* the plaintiffs, a mother and daughter, both witnessed an accident in which another daughter was struck and killed by a negligent driver. Arguably, the sister of the victim was within the zone of danger; her mother was not. In the view of the California Supreme Court, the facts of *Dillon* illustrated the fallacy of the "zone of danger" rule, which would deny recovery to one plaintiff, the mother, and allow recovery to the daughter. In the court's view, relief for the trauma equally suffered by both plaintiffs upon the apprehension of the child's death should not be based on the happenstance of a few yards. *Dillon, supra.*

. . . .

The interest worthy of legal protection presented by bystander cases such as the one before us was best described by the New Jersey Supreme Court when it adopted *Dillon*:

> [T]he interest assertedly injured is more than a general interest in emotional tranquility. It is the profound and abiding sentiment of parental love. The knowledge that loved ones are safe and whole is the deepest wellspring of emotional welfare. Against that reassuring background, the flashes of anxiety and disappointment that mar our lives take on safer hues. No loss is greater than the loss of a loved one, and no tragedy is more wrenching than the helpless apprehension of the death or serious injury of one whose very existence is a precious treasure.

Portee v. Jaffee, 84 N.J. 88, 97, 417 A.2d 521, 526 (1980). We find the profound and abiding love for one's sibling to be no less significant.

In its analysis the *Dillon* court reversed its position on the concept of a limited duty precluding liability to a plaintiff outside the zone of physical danger. According to the court, "the chief element in determining whether defendant owes a duty or an obligation to plaintiff is the foreseeability of the risk["]. . . .

While recognizing that "no immutable rule" could establish the defendant's duty for every future case, the court suggested the following "guidelines" as aids in resolution of bystander claims:

> (1) Whether plaintiff was located near the scene of the accident as contrasted with one who was a distance away from it. (2) Whether the shock resulted from a direct emotional impact upon plaintiff from the sensory and contemporaneous observance of the accident, as contrasted with learning of the acci-

dent from others after its occurrence. (3) Whether plaintiff and the victim were closely related, as contrasted with an absence of any relationship or the presence of only a distant relationship.

[Citation.]

.... While these guidelines have also been called arbitrary, [citation], we believe the *Dillon* approach based upon the reasonable foreseeability of the harm to be a more logical and just method of determining a defendant's liability than the artificial boundaries of recovery drawn by the "zone of danger" rule.

....

We adopt the foreseeability approach of *Dillon*, with the following comments and modifications.

First, of the three *Dillon* factors the relationship between the plaintiff and victim is the most valuable in determining foreseeability, and therefore the most crucial....

To satisfy this factor we choose not to require a relationship within a certain degree of consanguinity, as the Iowa Supreme Court did. Barnhill v. Davis, 300 N.W.2d 104 (Iowa 1981). Rather, we will require that there be a marital or intimate familial relationship between the plaintiff and the victim.

This particular facet of *Dillon* was sharply criticized by the court in Tobin v. Grossman, 24 N.Y.2d 609, 615, 249 N.E.2d 419, 420, 301 N.Y.S.2d 554, 558 (1969):

> But foreseeability, once recognized, is not so easily limited. Relatives, other than the mother, such as fathers or grandparents, or even other caretakers, equally sensitive and as easily harmed, may be just as foreseeably affected. Hence, foreseeability would, in short order, extend logically to caretakers other than the mother, and ultimately to affected bystanders.

We believe this fear is unfounded. For if we require, as Professor Leibson suggests, "evidence of a close relationship between the plaintiff and the victim, one in which there was a strong bond between the two, it will be apparent that, in most cases involving relatives other than immediate family members, the evidence will not be sufficient to establish such a relationship." [Leibson, *Recovery of Damages for Emotional Distress Caused by Physical Injury to Another*, 15 J. Fam. L. 163, 198 (1977).] The explanation for this insufficiency, according to Leibson, lies in the nature of our modern families. Today the extended family often has limited involvement in day-to-day activities of other family members and relatives and, therefore, would not typically possess the strong bond necessary to meet the test.

Our holding would not eliminate aunts, uncles, and grandparents from the class of potential plaintiffs, but would place upon them a heavier burden of proving a significant attachment.

Second, we address the factor that plaintiff's shock result from a "sensory and contemporaneous observance of the accident." No other aspect of the *Dillon* decision has drawn more attention than this factor. We agree with the observation of the Montana Supreme Court that if a "plaintiff is required to experience actual sensory perception of the accident, the requirement of proximity is necessarily satisfied." [Citation.] It has been suggested that the requirements of physical proximity and "contemporaneous observation" impugn the integrity of the *Dillon* approach and that *Dillon* has merely replaced the arbitrary spatial boundary of the "zone of danger" rule with an arbitrary temporal boundary. [Citation.]

It is true in cases such as the one before us that the contemporaneous observation guideline would serve to assure the minds of a jury that the emotional injury is serious.

However, if a sufficiently close relationship exists, the psychological reaction of the plaintiff in many cases could be the same or perhaps worse upon the hearing of the loss. [Citation.]

Rather, this guideline is in effect a policy consideration concerning the extent of the defendant's liability. As one court has stated, "Without such perception, the threat of emotional injury is lessened and the justification for liability is fatally weakened. The law of negligence, while it redresses suffering wrongfully caused by others, must not itself inflict undue harm by imposing an unreasonably excessive measure of liability." [Citation.]

We believe that the Massachusetts Supreme Court has a better perspective on this criterion. The determination of liability for the injury sustained "depends on a number of factors, such as where, when, and how the injury to the third person entered into the consciousness of the claimant, and what degree there was of familial or other relationship...." Dziokonski v. Babineau, 375 Mass. 555, 568, 580 N.E.2d 1295, 1302 (1978).

> A plaintiff who rushes onto the accident scene and finds a loved one injured has no greater entitlement to compensation for that shock than a plaintiff who rushes instead to the hospital. So long as the shock follows closely on the heels of the accident, the two types of injury are equally foreseeable.

[Citation.]

In addition to proving a sufficiently close relationship, we hold that the emotional trauma, the foreseeable harm to be redressed, must result from either death or serious injury to the victim. While minor injuries to a loved one may trigger emotions of sorrow and anxiety, these emotions pale in comparison to the profound grief, fright, and shock experienced following an accidental death or serious injury. [Citations.]

Before concluding, we must also address the further requirement of a cause of action for emotional distress in Fournell v. Usher Pest Control Co., 208 Neb. 684, 305 N.W.2d 605 (1981), that plaintiff must evidence some concurrent physical injury resulting from the emotional trauma. Other courts adopting the *Dillon* approach, to a certain degree, have retained this feature of the "zone of danger" rule. [Citations.] We now reject this requirement....

Ostensibly, the problem in this area is of proving to a jury that a reasonable person in the position of the bystander plaintiff has suffered a compensable injury. While physical manifestation of the psychological injury may be highly persuasive, such proof is not necessary given the current state of medical science and advances in psychology. There are primarily three problems with this requirement: (1) It is overinclusive, since it could possibly lead to recovery for trivial claims of mental distress accompanied by physical symptoms; (2) It is underinclusive, since serious distress is arbitrarily deemed not compensable if not accompanied by physical symptoms; and (3) It encourages extravagant pleadings and distorted testimony. [Citations.]

In reaching our decision we are not unmindful of the several policy arguments advanced against the cause of action we have adopted. Typically, opponents of expanding liability in this area contend that (1) bystander recovery will inundate the courts with fictitious injuries and fraudulent claims; (2) courts will be deluged with a flood of litigation; (3) bystander recovery will unduly burden defendants with undue liability; and (4) once recognized, liability cannot reasonably be restrained. Each of these arguments have been adequately reflected by other courts. [Citations.] We add the following comments.

First, even courts opposed to recognizing this cause of action have acknowledged that the fear of fraudulent claims alone is an insufficient reason to deny all such claims. [Citation.] Furthermore, the "zone of danger" rule also carries with it the risk of fraudulent claims. "It is not hard to imagine plaintiffs and their attorneys falsely alleging that the claimant was in some small way injured by the defendant's negligence, or was within the zone of danger in order to present a valid cause of action." [Citation.] Also, it is not unlikely that under a "zone of danger" rule plaintiffs would carefully draft pleadings so as to vaguely present a factual question that the plaintiff was also in peril. *Leibson, supra.*

Second, taking California as an example, experience shows that its courts have not been overwhelmed with litigation in this area. [Citation.]

Third, the "dollars and cents" argument that society cannot afford the costs that will ensue from recognizing liability for the demonstrable injury of emotional distress naturally resulting from defendant's negligent act has been aptly dispelled. [Citation.] The possibility of increased insurance costs alone should not deny recovery for an otherwise valid claim.

Finally, we are not delayed by the specter that recognizing a cause of action for bystander recovery will naturally entail liability to every acquaintance of the victim. As we have emphasized, the class of bystanders limited to those with a marital or intimate familial status will sufficiently circumscribe the defendant's liability.

. . . .

[Reversed and remanded for further proceedings.]

[The concurring opinion of Chief Justice KRIVOSHA has been omitted.]

CAPORALE, Justice, dissenting.

. . . .

Contrary to the view of the majority, the "dollars and cents" argument has not been dispelled, at least not for me. The harsh reality is that there are societal costs to compensating for accidents; the greater the number of elements of damage, the greater are those costs. *See* G. Calabresi, The Costs of Accidents, A Legal and Economic Analysis 22, 23, 26, 27, 215-25 (1977). I find nothing in the record before us, or the majority opinion, which deals with those arguments other than the bald assertion that they have been "aptly dispelled." . . . .

. . . .

BOSLAUGH and HASTINGS, JJ., join in this dissent.

Notes

1. *The Foreseeability View.* Although the foreseeability approach to negligent infliction of severe emotional distress has a growing number of adherents, it has been interpreted differently by various courts. Some cases, such as *James*, hold that the three criteria set out in Dillon v. Legg are flexible guidelines. *See, e.g.,* Johnson v. Ruark Obstetrics, 395 S.E.2d 85 (N.C. 1990) ("[f]actors to be considered"). Other cases treat those same criteria as indispensable prerequisites to recovery. *See, e.g.,* Kinard v. Augusta Sash & Door Co., 336 S.E.2d 465 (S.C. 1985). In *Kinard*, the court stated the elements of a "bystander" action as follows:

   (a) the negligence of the defendant must cause death or serious physical injury to another;

   (b) the plaintiff bystander must be in close proximity to the accident;

   (c) the plaintiff and the victim must be closely related;

(d) the plaintiff must contemporaneously perceive the accident; and

(e) the emotional distress must both manifest itself by physical symptoms capable of objective diagnosis and be established by expert testimony.

Regardless of whether the *Dillon* criteria are treated as indispensable or merely useful, courts generally agree that the issue to which they pertain is foreseeability. However, California, the birthplace of *Dillon*, no longer phrases the inquiry in terms of foreseeability. Initially, the California courts had interpreted *Dillon* liberally. Archibald v. Braverman, 79 Cal. Rptr. 723 (Ct. App. 1969), had held that the contemporaneous-observance requirement was satisfied when a mother came upon her child moments after he had been injured in an explosion, and Nazaroff v. Superior Ct., 145 Cal. Rptr. 657 (Ct. App. 1978), had held that a mother stated a cause of action where she arrived on the scene in time to see her missing child being pulled out of a neighbor's pool. But Thing v. La Chusa, 771 P.2d 814 (Cal. 1989), overruled *Archibald* and *Nazaroff*, rejecting "foreseeability" because of the importance of "certainty in the law" and the need to limit recovery by some means, however arbitrary. Under *Thing*, the plaintiff must be closely related to the victim and must be present at the scene of the injury and aware of the injury while it is occurring.

2. *The Presence and Observation Requirements.* A number of cases have addressed the issues of bystander presence and contemporaneous observation, and the results are inconsistent. *Compare* Hegel v. McMahon, 960 P.2d 424 (Wash. 1998) (family member who did not observe accident may recover for emotional distress caused by observing injured relative at accident scene before there is substantial change in relative's condition or location), Zell v. Meek, 665 So. 2d 1048 (Fla. 1995) (direct perception of immediate aftermath of the accident may warrant recovery), *and* Masaki v. General Motors Corp., 780 P.2d 566 (Haw. 1989) (recovery permitted where parents were not present at the scene of the accident, but went immediately to the hospital and were told that their son would never walk again), *with* Fineran v. Pickett, 465 N.W.2d 662 (Iowa 1991) (recovery denied to parents and sisters who arrived at accident scene within five minutes and witnessed injured bicyclist's unconscious seizure prior to death). *Compare* Haselhorst v. State, 485 N.W.2d 180 (Neb. 1992) (parents permitted to recover from state for distress they suffered upon learning that their foster child had sexually abused their four minor children outside of their presence, where the state negligently placed the 15-year-old foster child with the family without disclosing his history of violence), *with* Schurk v. Christensen, 497 P.2d 937 (Wash. 1972) (recovery denied against neighbors for distress resulting from the neighbors' son's sexual molestation of plaintiffs' daughter outside of their presence, even though neighbors had recommended their son as a babysitter without disclosing his dangerous propensities).

3. *The Relationship Requirement.* In Dunphy v. Gregor, 642 A.2d 372 (N.J. 1994), the court held that "familial relationship," of the kind required to permit a bystander to recover for emotional distress suffered upon witnessing injury to another, is not necessarily limited to relationships of marriage or blood. A woman who was engaged to and cohabiting with an automobile accident victim was held to have a cause of action. In Graves v. Estabrook, 818 A.2d 1255 (N.H. 2003), the court held that the fiancee of a motorcyclist who was killed in an accident stated a claim for negligent infliction of emotional distress against the motorist involved in the accident. The fiancee had lived with the motorist for seven years prior to witnessing the accident.

See also Laura M. Raisty, *Bystander Distress and Loss of Consortium: An Examination of the Relationship Requirements in Light of Romer v. Evans,* 65 Fordham L. Rev. 2647, 2648 (1997) ("no court has held that a homosexual relationship satisfies the relationship requirements for loss of consortium or bystander distress").

In Rabideau v. City of Racine, 627 N.W.2d 795 (Wis. 2001), the court held that the owner of a companion dog, who observed a city police officer shoot and kill her dog, was not related to the victim in a way that would support a claim for negligent infliction of emotional distress. *See also* Harabes v. Barkery, Inc., 791 A.2d 1142 (N.J. Super. Ct. Law Div. 2001) (holding that public-policy considerations prevent dog owners from recovering for negligent infliction of emotional distress and loss of companionship damages in connection with the loss of a dog).

4. *The Zone-of-Danger View.* The "zone of danger" theory may deny damages in cases that are very sympathetic. *See, e.g.,* Whetham v. Bismark Hosp., 197 N.W.2d 678 (N.D. 1972) (recovery denied to a mother who watched helplessly from her bed as her newborn child was dropped on a tile floor by a hospital employee, causing the child's skull to fracture); Washington v. John T. Rhines Co., 646 A.2d 345 (D.C. App. 1994) (wife's claim for mishandling husband's corpse was dismissed because wife was not within zone of danger); Carlson v. Illinois Farmers Ins. Co., 520 N.W.2d 534 (Minn. Ct. App. 1994) (denying recovery to plaintiff who witnessed death of her best friend); Boucher v. Dixie Med. Ctr., 850 P.2d 1179 (Utah 1992) (denying recovery to parents who observed son before and after a coma from which he awakened as a brain-damaged quadriplegic).

As to the meaning of "zone of danger," consider Harper v. Illinois Cent. Gulf R.R., 808 F.2d 1139 (5th Cir. 1987). The court there held that a mother and her son, who were evacuated from their home after a train derailment caused two major explosions over a mile away, were not within the zone of danger since they were "never in any immediate danger of personal injury" and the evacuation was merely a precautionary measure.

Zone-of-danger jurisdictions generally require evidence that the plaintiff feared for his or her personal safety. *See, e.g.,* Grube v. Union Pac. R. Co., 886 P.2d 845 (Kan. 1994) (judgment reversed where there was no evidence that an engineer, who was involved in a train-automobile accident, feared for personal safety). However, there are decisions to the contrary. *See, e.g.,* Garrett v. City of New Berlin, 362 N.W.2d 137 (Wis. 1985) (sister who saw her brother run over by a police car was within the zone of danger, even though she never feared for her safety, because she was a member of the group the officer was pursuing, not merely a bystander).

5. *Primary Victims v. Bystanders.* Where a claim is based on negligence which directly endangered the plaintiff, rather than someone else, courts generally have little problem with the scope of protection issue. *See, e.g.,* Corgan v. Muehling, 574 N.E.2d 602, 608 (Ill. 1991) (zone-of-danger rule did not apply to a patient who stated a cause of action for negligent infliction of mental distress arising from the defendant psychologist's engaging in sexual relations with her during treatment). Plaintiff, as the primary victim, is within the class entitled to bring suit, and analysis tends to focus on the genuineness of the claim. However, in some instances, it may be difficult to determine whether the plaintiff is a primary victim, as opposed to someone asserting bystander rights.

For example, in Johnson v. Jamaica Hosp., 467 N.E.2d 502 (N.Y. 1984), alleged negligence on the part of a hospital nursery resulted in the abduction of the plaintiff's newborn infant daughter and her absence for four and one-half months. The dissenter argued that the parents were not members of some large, undifferentiated class, and that the mental anguish they suffered was not a mere byproduct of an invasion of the child's rights. Rather, the defendant's negligence directly interfered with the parents' rights to custody of the child, and therefore the parents should have been permitted to sue for their resulting mental suffering. The majority concluded, however, that there was no direct duty running to the parents, and therefore analyzed the case under the "zone of danger" rule applicable to bystanders in that jurisdiction. In denying liability, the majority noted:

> That sound policy reasons support...[this] decision is evident here, for to permit recovery by the infant's parents for emotional distress would be to invite open-ended liability for indirect emotional injury suffered by the families in every instance where the very young, or very elderly, or incapacitated persons experience negligent care or treatment.

A useful contrast is Burgess v. Superior Court, 831 P.2d 1197 (Cal. 1992). The court there held that a mother who suffered emotional distress as a result of negligent injury to her child during labor was not a bystander, but rather a direct victim who could recover for the damages in a professional negligence action without satisfying the criteria of Dillon v. Legg and its progeny. The court wrote:

> Any negligence during delivery which causes injury to the fetus and resultant emotional anguish to the mother...breaches a duty owed directly to the mother.
>
> ....
>
> ...[T]he class of potential plaintiffs in these cases is clearly limited.... [T]here is no possibility, much less a spectre, of unlimited liability presented by these unique cases.

Id. at 1203-08. The decision in Burgess was based in part on Marlene F. v. Affiliated Psychiatric Medical Clinic, Inc., 770 P.2d 278 (Cal. 1989), holding that a psychotherapist who sexually molested minor children he was treating could be liable to the children's mothers, whom he was also treating. The court ruled that the therapist's conduct breached his duty of care to the mothers, as well as to the children.

In Perry-Rogers v. Obasaju, 723 N.Y.S.2d 28 (App. Div. 2001), a couple sought damages for emotional harm after their embryo was mistakenly planted in another woman's uterus. The court held that they stated a viable medical malpractice claim based on breach of a direct legal duty, and therefore it was not necessary to show that they feared for their personal safety.

D. Relationship to Other Actions

1. Loss of Consortium

Lozoya v. Sanchez
Supreme Court of New Mexico
66 P.3d 948 (N.M. 2003)

MINZNER, Justice.

....

This case arises from two automobile collisions in which Ubaldo and Osbaldo Lozoya, father and son, were traveling together.... The first of these collisions took place on June 21, 1999.... The other vehicle was driven by Defendant Diego Sanchez....

At the scene of the accident, neither of the Lozoyas complained of any injuries. Ubaldo began to experience pain shortly thereafter, however, in one of his arms, head, and legs. Father and son visited Presbyterian Occupational Medical Clinic eight days later. The doctor found that Ubaldo was experiencing tenderness in his neck and back, but that his range of motion in these areas was "pretty close to normal." An x-ray showed what appeared to be a compression of one of Ubaldo's vertebrae that "looked like it was old," but the doctor believed that the soreness Ubaldo was experiencing was a result of the accident. Ubaldo visited the same doctor again about a week later, and the doctor decided that Ubaldo could return to work on a light duty basis.

....

Ubaldo continued to experience pain....Ubaldo was presented with the options of either enduring the pain as it existed, taking medication, having "epidural blocks" performed, or surgery. Ubaldo decided that he did not want the injections or surgery.

On April 18, 2000, approximately ten months after the first accident, Ubaldo and Osbaldo were involved in another collision as they were driving toward a job site. They were driving on Interstate 40, near the "Big- I" interchange when they were again rear-ended by another vehicle. This time, the other vehicle involved was a dump truck operated by Defendant Philip McWaters. The collision took place during the morning rush hour. The impact of the McWaters vehicle pushed the Lozoya vehicle into the vehicle in front of it, driven by Christine Sotelo, who testified at trial.

Ms. Sotelo testified that prior to the accident, the truck driven by Osbaldo had been following her very closely. She tried to communicate that to him. He backed off a little bit, but then she was rear-ended by Osbaldo's vehicle that had been rear-ended by the McWaters vehicle during the stop-and-go traffic of the rush hour....

Evidence was also presented that Ubaldo had back problems prior to the accidents....

....

At the time of the first accident, Ubaldo lived in a domestic partnership with Sara Lozoya, although they were not married. They had, however, "been together" for over 30 years. They had three children together....For fifteen years they had lived together in a home that they had purchased. They carried the same last name, and had filed joint tax returns since at least 1997. They were formally married after the first accident, but before the second one [which involved Mr. McWaters], in November 1999.

Ubaldo testified that prior to the accidents, he and Sara had a happy relationship, which included going out dancing, and visiting friends together. Sara testified that they had an intimate relationship, and that they made decisions together. After the first accident, the relationship changed dramatically because Ubaldo became depressed. They could not socialize nearly as much because of the pain that Ubaldo experienced. Ubaldo would stay in bed quite a bit. Their sexual relationship also diminished. After the second accident, the relationship worsened further.

....

Sara brought a loss of consortium claim against both Mr. Sanchez and Mr. McWaters. The district court did not allow the jury to consider such a claim as against Mr. Sanchez, however, because she was not married to Ubaldo at the time. The district court did allow the jury to consider Sara's loss of consortium claim against Mr. McWaters, because Sara and Ubaldo had been married during the interim between the two collisions. The jury did not award Sara damages for this claim because it found that Mr. McWaters was not negligent. Sara claims that the district court erred by not allowing the jury to consider her loss of consortium claim against Mr. Sanchez and his employer.

New Mexico courts did not recognize actions for loss of consortium, spousal or otherwise, until 1994, when this Court decided Romero v. Byers, 117 N.M. 422, 872 P.2d 840 (1994)....

... [W]e held that it is foreseeable that a surviving spouse would experience emotional distress as a result of injury to or death of a victim of negligent conduct. The law should impose a duty upon the tortfeasor toward that surviving spouse....

While this Court was the last in the nation to recognize that a spouse may bring a cause of action for loss of consortium, [citation], we were the first in the nation to recognize that a grandparent may bring such a claim in certain circumstances as well. *See* Fernandez v. Walgreen Hastings Co.,... [968 P.2d 774 (N.M. 1998)]. In that case, we applied the same definition of duty for loss of consortium purposes, and held that "it can be foreseeable that negligently causing the death of a twenty-two month old child will cause emotional distress to a grandparent who had a close familial relationship with the child." [Citation.]

....Plaintiffs now ask us to decide whether the same rationales that led us to extend a cause of action for loss of consortium in those situations should apply here. At the outset, we note that no other State in the union currently allows unmarried cohabitants to recover for loss of consortium. We are not without guidance, however, because many courts have wrestled with this issue and considered the various implications for extending the cause of action in this situation. The only state court decision we have found that allowed this type of claim, Butcher v. Superior Court,... [188 Cal. Rptr. 503 (Ct. App.1983)], *overruled by* Elden v. Sheldon,...758 P.2d 582 (Cal. 1988)], has served as a springboard for academic discussion of this issue, *see, e.g.,* Barbara J. Cox, *Alternative Families: Obtaining Traditional Family Benefits Through Litigation, Legislation and Collective Bargaining,* 15 Wis. Women's L.J. 93, 133-37 (2000), as well as thorough and thoughtful analysis by the judiciary across the country, *see, e.g.,* Trombley v. Starr-Wood Cardiac Group, PC, 3 P.3d 916, 922-23 (Alaska 2000)....

....There are reasonable arguments on both sides....

....

Defendants are correct in their assertion that limiting the field of potential claimants to those with a legal relationship to the victim would serve as a convenient and easily applied line-drawing mechanism for courts. This is perhaps the most significant reason that many courts allow only spouses to make a loss of consortium claim....Defendants point out, "[o]ne would also envision that the injured person has cousins, co-workers, drinking buddies and softball team members who may lose his society, companionship and guidance. For that matter, the dead or injured person may have been having an affair with his married neighbor, who also may suffer a loss of consortium." By only allowing those who are legally married, or familial caretakers to recover, courts would have an easy way for us to dispose of many claims. Ease of administration, however, does not necessarily further the interests of justice....Of course, the State has a continuing interest in protecting the legal interest of marriage as well....[But allowing] an unmarried partner to recover for loss of consortium neither advances nor retracts from that interest. It is doubtful that anyone would choose to marry simply because they would not be allowed to bring a future loss of consortium claim otherwise.

In Dunphy v. Gregor, 136 N.J. 99, 642 A.2d 372 (1994), the Supreme Court of New Jersey considered whether a woman who was engaged to and cohabited with the victim of an automobile accident could recover against the defendant for negligent infliction of emotional distress ("NIED"). NIED is a claim that is often considered by courts at the same time as a claim for loss of consortium, and the same policies are implicated by broadening the field of potential claimants for each. [Citation.] The *Dunphy* court observed that a "marital or intimate, familial relationship between the plaintiff and the injured person" was a required basis for recovery on an NIED claim. [Citation.] When confronted with the same argument made here that a legal relationship provides an easy line-drawing mechanism, the court responded:

> ....

> ...[T]he sound assessment of the quality of interpersonal relationships is not beyond a jury's ken and...courts are capable of dealing with the realities, not simply the legalities, of relationships to assure that resulting emotional injury is genuine and deserving of compensation.

Id. at 378. We agree....It is appropriate that the finder of fact be allowed to determine, with proper guidance from the court, whether a plaintiff had a sufficient enough relational interest with the victim of a tort to recover for loss of consortium.

Next, Defendants argue that to extend a cause of action for loss of consortium in the present case would be to extend the benefits of marriage to Sara, without requiring her to undertake the burdens of marriage, implying that somehow Sara would be unfairly taking advantage of her position. Specifically, Defendants point out that Sara did not commit to giving her income and property to the community, under NMSA 1978, §40-3-8(B) (1999); she did not commit to paying Ubaldo's debt, under NMSA 1978, §40-3-11 (1995); she did not commit to leaving a share of her estate to Ubaldo when she dies, under NMSA 1978, §45-2-301 (1995); she did not have to pay income taxes jointly; and she could have left the relationship any time she wanted without going through the process of a divorce.

Defendants are correct in all of these assertions. What Defendants do not recognize is that almost all of these burdens have a corresponding benefit that Sara also did not receive when she was not married to Ubaldo. Because she was not married to Ubaldo, she had no legal claim to require *him* to give to the community his property acquired during the marriage, or to require him to pay her debts, or to require him to leave her a portion of his estate. Further, she did not have the benefit of the security that a marriage brings, because Ubaldo could have left without a divorce just as easily as she could....Availability of a cause of action for loss of consortium is not a benefit of marriage, any more than it could be a benefit of being a familial caretaker. It is a method of compensation for one who has suffered the loss of a significant relational interest. By extending a cause of action for loss of consortium, this Court is not giving Sara the benefits of marriage without the burdens. We reject any implication that we are enabling Sara to take unfair advantage of the legal system by providing that she may be able to recover for loss of consortium, without paying the "price" of marriage.

...Defendants claim that we would be, in effect, recognizing common law marriage by allowing the claim to proceed. Defendants are correct that this State has not recognized common law marriage after we decided In re Gabaldon's Estate, 38 N.M. 392, 34 P.2d 672 (1934). "For a marriage to be valid, it must be formally entered into by contract and solemnized before an appropriate official."....Our holding today in no way alters this State's nonrecognition of common law marriage. We do think, however, that if a couple were to satisfy the elements of a common law marriage, as it exists in other states, this would be a great indication that the couple would have a significant enough relationship to warrant a claim for loss of consortium.

....

Finally, Defendants argue that allowing unmarried couples to recover for loss of consortium would create an impractical and unworkable cause of action. This would only be true if this Court does not do its duty of providing sufficient guidance to lower courts when determining whether a claim should be allowed. We think that the criteria set forth in *Dunphy* help greatly in this regard. Claimants must prove an "intimate familial relationship" with the victim in order to recover for loss of consortium. *Dunphy*, 642 A.2d at 377. "Persons engaged to be married and living together may foreseeably fall into that category of relationship...." [Citation.]

Of course, not everyone who is engaged to be married, living together, or assuming the roles of husband and wife (common law or not) will be entitled to recover. The claimant must prove a close familial relationship with the victim. [Citation.] Courts should presume that such a relationship exists if the couple fits into one of the above categories, but a myriad of factors should be considered to determine whether the relationship was significant enough to recover.

> That standard must take into account the duration of the relationship, the degree of mutual dependence, the extent of common contributions to a life together, the extent and quality of shared experience, and...whether the plaintiff and the injured person were members of the same household, their emotional reliance on each other, the particulars of their day to day relationship, and the manner in which they related to each other in attending to life's mundane requirements.

[Citation.] By adopting this standard for determining whether an intimate familial relationship exists for loss of consortium purposes, we are putting no additional burden on the finder of fact. Even if the claimant and the victim are actually married, all of this information would need to be weighed when determining the amount of damages anyway. *See Romero*, 117 N.M. at 424-27, 872 P.2d at 842-45 (defining the elements of a claim for loss of consortium).

  ....

...[W]e think that further limits are appropriate. First, a person can only have an intimate familial relationship with one other person at any one time. That is to say, if a person is married to a different person than the victim of the tort, the claim will be barred. In the case of claims by unmarried cohabitants, the relationship between the claimant and the victim must be demonstrated to be committed and exclusive. [Citation.] Second, the burden of proving that an intimate familial relationship existed will be on the claimant, with a presumption that this exists if the parties were engaged, married, or met the general test for common law marriage....

...[W]e cannot deny that Ubaldo and Sara enjoyed a relationship that was very similar, if not identical, to that of the typical married couple, or that a reasonable jury could so find. They had lived together in a house that they owned together for at least fifteen years. They had three children whom they raised together. They carried the same last name, and they generally enjoyed spending time with one another and participating in social events as a couple. Further, their intent to be committed to one another indefinitely is evidenced by their marriage shortly after the first accident, despite Ubaldo's debilitating injuries.[6]

...[I]t seems clear that a reasonable jury could find that Ubaldo and Sara would have met the test for common law marriage.... They held themselves out as a married

---

6. We recognize that there was little evidence of any household services performed by Ubaldo, but this is a separate and independent claim for loss of consortium. *See* UJI 13-1810 NMRA 2003.

couple. Further, they testified as to their mutual dependence on each other in their day to day lives. Every single factor we have enunciated for determining whether they had an intimate familial relationship also appears to cut in their favor. We believe that the evidence presented demonstrates that Sara may be able to present a cognizable claim for loss of consortium. She should therefore be allowed to present this claim to the jury.

....

.... We therefore... remand for a new trial....

WE CONCUR: PETRA JIMENEZ MAES, Chief Justice, PATRICIO M. SERNA, RICHARD C. BOSSON, and EDWARD L. CHAVEZ, Justices.

Note

1. In the case of cohabitants, if actions for both negligent infliction of emotional distress and loss of consortium are permitted, does either action have significant advantages over the other?

2. Breach of Fiduciary Duty

The tort of negligent infliction of emotional distress must be carefully limited, as nearly everyone does things that cause others distress. To take one of countless possible examples, no one but lawyers would gain if the parties to a love affair gone sour could sue for damages, however real the distress they feel. In some cases, however, the existence of a special relationship between the parties may justify imposing a special duty on one of those parties to avoid hurting the other. Consider the following opinion.

F.G. v. MacDonell

Supreme Court of New Jersey
696 A.2d 697 (N.J. 1997)

POLLOCK, J.

This appeal presents two issues. The first issue is whether a parishioner's allegation of an inappropriate sexual relationship between a clergyman and the parishioner states a cause of action when the relationship occurs while the clergyman is providing pastoral counseling to the parishioner. Second, we must decide whether the parishioner may maintain a cause of action against another clergyman who allegedly publicized in a sermon and a letter the relationship with the first clergyman.

....

Because the appeal arises on defendants' motion for judgment on the pleadings..., we assume the truth of the allegations of the complaint....

In 1992, MacDonell was the rector at both All Saints and an affiliated church, St. Luke's Episcopal Church, in Haworth. Harper was the assistant rector at both churches in 1993. In January 1994, following MacDonell's retirement, Harper succeeded MacDonell as rector. F.G. was a parishioner at All Saints in 1992-93.

From April 1992 until the end of 1993, F.G. consulted MacDonell for counseling. Aware that F.G. was vulnerable, MacDonell nonetheless induced her to engage in a sexual relationship with him. Although the complaint does not describe details of the relationship, it apparently did not involve sexual intercourse.

.... The Law Division dismissed Counts I, II, III, and IX, which respectively allege negligent pastoral counseling, negligent infliction of emotional distress, and breach of fiduciary duty by MacDonell, as well as breach of fiduciary duty by Harper. The Appellate Division reversed and remanded the matter to the Law Division. The purpose of the remand was to permit F.G. to prove her claims against defendants for clergy malpractice and breach of their fiduciary duty.

We believe that a claim for breach of fiduciary duty provides the more appropriate form of relief than does clergy malpractice. An action for breach of a clergyman's fiduciary duty permits the parishioner to recover monetary damages without running the risk of entanglement with the free exercise of religion. Consequently, we modify the judgment of the Appellate Division by allowing F.G.'s claim for breach of fiduciary duty against MacDonell, and, subject to a hearing on entanglement with church doctrine, allowing a similar claim against Harper.

....

The threshold issue is whether the First Amendment to the United States Constitution shields a member of the clergy from a claim for inappropriate sexual conduct with a parishioner who has consulted the clergy member for pastoral counseling.... The free exercise of religion does not permit members of the clergy to engage in inappropriate sexual conduct with parishioners who seek pastoral counseling.

....

... [T]he record supports the inference that MacDonell's alleged misconduct was not an expression of a sincerely held religious belief, but was an egregious violation of the trust and confidence that F.G. reposed in him.

The First Amendment does not insulate a member of the clergy from actions for breach of fiduciary duty arising out of sexual misconduct that occurs during a time when the clergy member is providing counseling to a parishioner. Thus, without impinging on the First Amendment, courts can resolve a claim that a member of the clergy has committed sexually inappropriate conduct in the course of pastoral counseling.

....

The next question concerns the nature of the duty that defendants owed to F.G. The Appellate Division held that defendants owed F.G. a duty of care, that they breached that duty, and that she could maintain a cause of action for "clergy malpractice." In so concluding, the Appellate Division acknowledged that F.G.'s claim presented an issue of first impression in New Jersey, and that no other court in the United States had yet recognized a clergy-malpractice claim. [Citations.] Deterring other courts has been the concern that a clergy-malpractice claim will entangle courts with the First Amendment's protection of the free exercise of religion. [Citations.]

Several problems inhere in a claim for clergy malpractice. First, such a claim requires definition of the relevant standard of care. Defining that standard could embroil courts in establishing the training, skill, and standards applicable for members of the clergy in a diversity of religions with widely varying beliefs. [Citation.] Furthermore, defining such a standard would require courts to identify the beliefs and prac-

tices of the relevant religion and then to determine whether the clergyman had acted
in accordance with them. [Citations.] The entanglement could restrain the free exercise of religion.

Concerns about religious entanglement have led some courts also to deny claims for
breach of fiduciary duty....We conclude, however, that courts can adjudicate F.G.'s
claim for breach of fiduciary duty without becoming entangled in the defendants' free
exercise of their religion.

The essence of a fiduciary relationship is that one party places trust and confidence
in another who is in a dominant or superior position. A fiduciary relationship arises
between two persons when one person is under a duty to act for or give advice for the
benefit of another on matters within the scope of their relationship. Restatement (Second) of Torts § 874 cmt. a (1979); *see* In re Stroming's Will, 224, 79 A.2d 492 (App.
Div.), certif. denied, 8 N.J. 319 (1951) (stating essentials of confidential relationship
"are a reposed confidence and the dominant and controlling position of the beneficiary
of the transaction"); Blake v. Brennan, 61 A.2d 916 (Ch. Div. 1948) (describing "the
test [as] whether the relationship between the parties were of such a character of trust
and confidence as to render it reasonably certain that the one party occupied a dominant position over the other"); Bogert, Trusts and Trustees 2d § 481 (1978) (stating
"the exact limits of the term 'fiduciary relation' are impossible of statement. Depending
upon the circumstances of the particular case or transaction, certain business, public
or social relationships may or may not create or involve a fiduciary character"). The
fiduciary's obligations to the dependent party include a duty of loyalty and a duty to
exercise reasonable skill and care. Restatement (Second) of Trusts §§ 170, 174 (1959).
Accordingly, the fiduciary is liable for harm resulting from a breach of the duties imposed by the existence of such a relationship. Restatement (Second) of Torts § 874
(1979).

Trust and confidence are vital to the counseling relationship between parishioner
and pastor. By accepting a parishioner for counseling, a pastor also accepts the responsibility of a fiduciary. Often, parishioners who seek pastoral counseling are troubled
and vulnerable. Sometimes, they turn to their pastor in the belief that their religion is
the most likely source to sustain them in their time of trouble. The pastor knows, or
should know of the parishioner's trust and the pastor's dominant position.

Several jurisdictions have recognized that a clergyman's sexual misconduct with a
parishioner constitutes a breach of a fiduciary relationship. [Citations.] We find the
rationale of those cases to be persuasive.... [In Moses v. Episcopal Diocese of Colorado, 863 P.2d 310 (Col. 1993), the court] considered the case of a parishioner who
entered into a sexual relationship with an associate priest during a counseling relationship. 863 P.2d at 314. The Court found sufficient evidence for the jury to conclude that the defendants, an Episcopalian [sic] bishop and the diocese, owed a fiduciary duty to the plaintiff and that they had breached that duty by failing to provide
the parish with personnel files indicating that the priest had psychological problems.
Id. at 315.

Unlike an action for clergy malpractice, an action for breach of fiduciary duty does
not require establishing a standard of care and its breach. *Moses, supra,* 863 P.2d at 321,
n.13. Establishing a fiduciary duty essentially requires proof that a parishioner trusted
and sought counseling from the pastor. A violation of that trust constitutes a breach of
the duty.

....

Ordinarily, consenting adults must bear the consequences of their conduct, including sexual conduct. In the sanctuary of the church, however, troubled parishioners should be able to seek pastoral counseling free from the fear that the counselors will sexually abuse them....

F.G.'s complaint essentially alleges that MacDonell's sexual misconduct was not so much a failure to adhere to the standards of care applicable to pastoral counseling as it was a violation of F.G.'s trust. But for MacDonell's status as a clergyman, his conduct was unrelated to religious doctrine. Although MacDonell's ultimate goal in counseling F.G. may have been to help her receive assistance from God, his sexual misconduct violated her legal rights. So viewed, F.G.'s claim does not restrict MacDonell's free exercise of religion.

The Appellate Division also reinstated F.G.'s claim for negligent infliction of emotional distress. We likewise conclude that F.G. may maintain her claim for emotional distress arising from MacDonell's breach of his fiduciary duty to her. Our recognition of F.G.'s claim is consistent with the general rule that a claimant who suffers emotional trauma may recover from the tortfeasor who has caused the claimant distress. [Citation.]

F.G.'s claim against Harper presents additional considerations. Basically, F.G. alleges that she consulted Harper for counseling because of MacDonell's inappropriate physical conduct with her and "the possibility of notifying the parishes of All Saints and St. Lukes" about that conduct. F.G. alleges further that Harper induced F.G. "to give consent to the public disclosure, by letter, of [her] name," by his negligent misrepresentation "that this disclosure was for [her] benefit and part of his pastoral care [of her]." According to F.G., Harper breached his fiduciary duty by "exploiting [her] trust and confidence" through his mischaracterization of MacDonell's conduct and the nature of the relationship between him and F.G.

Our review of those allegations begins with the realization that Harper's alleged breaches occurred in sermons and letters to the congregations. Evaluating those sermons and letters might entangle a court in religious doctrine. The question remains whether, without becoming entangled in religious doctrine, a court can adjudicate Harper's alleged breach of his fiduciary duty to F.G. If the trial court can make such a determination by reference to neutral principles, F.G. may maintain her action against Harper. We conclude that the trial court should conduct a hearing to determine whether it can decide F.G.'s allegations by reference to such principles. [Citation.] If so, F.G. may proceed with her action against Harper.

  ....

O'HERN, J., dissenting.

...[T]he majority concludes that because the pastor acknowledges that no tenet of his religion sanctions sexual contact with a congregant, the conduct is a tort. Such reasoning misses the constitutional point entirely. Reverend MacDonell is not asserting that conduct otherwise tortious is protected because it is religious. Rather, F.G. asserts that the conduct is tortious because the defendant is a religious.

It is simply impossible for a court to define the duties of a member of the clergy and impose civil liability therefor. To do so would establish an official religion of the state, something forbidden by the First Amendment.

I must emphasize at the outset that the First Amendment does not protect pedophiles or charlatans wearing religious garb. Members of religious bodies are as liable for worldly wrongs as are any other members of society. A minister, priest or rabbi has no license to steal and no license to commit a sexual offense condemned by law:

It is well settled that clergy may be sued for the torts they commit....

The problem for F.G. is that no law makes it a tort or crime for consenting adults to engage in sexual relationships. [Citation] The only basis for tort liability set forth in plaintiff's complaint is: "During the course of their pastoral care and pastoral counseling relationship there was a breach of the special duty of care which MacDonell owed F.G. as her pastoral care provider and pastoral counselor." Had Alex MacDonell been a neighbor, co-worker, or friend seeking to comfort F.G., no secular law would make his extramarital affair a tort or crime.

No court in the United States has created a tort of clergy malpractice for the simple reason that to do so would require a court to establish a state religion. *See* Carl H. Esbeck, *Tort Claims Against Churches and Ecclesiastical Officers: the First Amendment Considerations*, 89 W. Va. L. Rev. 1 (1986) (explaining that such inquiry would require courts to establish a set of acceptable religions).

....

Even Nally v. Grace Community Church of the Valley, 240 Cal. Rptr. 215 (Ct. App. 1987), once described as "the most celebrated clergy malpractice case," Arlin M. Adams & Charles J. Emmerich, *A Heritage of Religious Liberty*, 137 U. Pa. L. Rev. 1559, 1671 n. 361(1989), was later reversed by the California Supreme Court. 763 P.2d 948 (Cal. 1988)....

Because of the differing theological views espoused by the myriad of religions in our state and practiced by church members, it would certainly be impractical, and quite possibly unconstitutional, to impose a duty of care on pastoral counselors. Such a duty would necessarily be intertwined with the religious philosophy of the particular denomination or ecclesiastical teachings of the religious entity.

[763 P.2d at 960.]

....If there is some general duty on the part of all fiduciaries to refrain from sexual conduct with a client, I assume that trust officers, investment advisors, and real estate agents will be covered by the Court's strictures.

....For this Court now to impose a civil sanction based on violation of the precepts of the Episcopal religion would transgress the principles upon which our nation is founded. Today the Court creates a tort out of a breach of the tenets of one religion— tenets with which there is almost universal agreement. In a future time, breach of the tenets of another religion not so universally accepted might give rise to another type of tort—a result not contemplated by the constitutional framers.

....

...[P]laintiff's complaint against Reverend Fletcher Harper for breach of a pastoral fiduciary duty should be dismissed. I surmise that the Court is temporizing by remanding the matter for further proceedings that can have but one result. *See Hester, supra,* 723 S.W.2d at 553 (holding that to adjudicate claim that divulging confidential communications to church members breached fiduciary duty would force court to judge "the competence, training, methods and content of the pastoral function").

....

Justice GARIBALDI joins in this opinion.

Notes

1. *Breach of Fiduciary Duty.* Section 874 of the Restatement, Second, of Torts provides that a fiduciary is liable for harm resulting from breach of the fiduciary's duties. The comments refer repeatedly to trustees, agents, guardians, executors, and administrators and refer readers to the Restatement, Second, of Trusts for details. It seems likely that this section was drafted with property cases in mind, not negligent infliction of severe emotional distress.

2. *Fiduciary-Duty Claims against Churches.* An opinion that casts doubt on the *F.G.* court's belief that courts can apply "fiduciary duty" law to pastor-parishioner cases without investigating church doctrine or imposing secular standards upon religious bodies is Moses v. Episcopal Diocese of Colorado, 863 P.2d 310 (Col. 1993). The plaintiff, Mary Tenantry, had had an adulterous relationship with her pastor. She sued both the pastor and the Bishop of the diocese for "breach of fiduciary duty." In holding her claims against the Bishop actionable, the Colorado Supreme Court ruled, among other things, that the jury could have found that the Bishop had breached his fiduciary duty by granting her absolution after she discussed with him her fear of losing salvation. According to the court, this conduct could have breached a fiduciary duty to Tenantry by causing her to continue to blame herself for her involvement in the affair.

It is conventional Christian doctrine that adultery is a sin, and that sinners should repent and seek forgiveness. As it is always emotionally distressing to feel guilt, and as most versions of Christianity do their best to induce feelings of guilt for some kinds of behavior, *Moses* seems to hold that clergy who promulgate ordinary Christian teachings can be found to have breached a fiduciary duty if a jury concludes that it was not in the best interest of a parishioner to feel guilty about a particular matter. Consider a line from John Newton's well-known hymn, *Amazing Grace*: " 'Twas grace that taught my heart to fear, and grace my fears relieved." *Moses* can be read as saying that teaching a parishioner's heart to fear—even if followed by an attempt to relieve those fears, as when the Bishop granted Tenantry absolution—can be a tort. Is it possible for a court to handle a case like this without either evaluating the requirements of the parties' faith or holding that clergy must meet "secular" standards, no matter what their churches require? What result on the facts of *Moses* in New Jersey?

In Richelle v. Roman Catholic Archbishop, 130 Cal. Rptr. 601 (Cal. Ct. App. 2003), a case involving a sexual relationship initiated by the defendant pastor, the court wrote:

> [A] pastor may be subject to tort liability for sexually inappropriate and injurious conduct that breaches a fiduciary duty arising out of a confidential relation with a parishioner, provided the alleged injurious conduct was not dictated by a sincerely held religious belief or carried out in accordance with established beliefs and practices of the religion to which the pastor belongs, and there is no other reason the issues cannot be framed for the trier of fact in secular rather than sectarian terms.

The court then affirmed dismissal of the plaintiff's action, reasoning:

> Instead of alleging any of the reasons conventionally relied upon to show that a party to an alleged confidential relation is in a vulnerable position—namely, "advanced age, or youth, or lack of education, or ill health, or mental weakness" [citation]—appellant instead relies on her piety. The theory of the complaint is that Reverend Namocatcat "stood in a…fiduciary relationship

with [appellant] and thus owed her the highest duty of care and good faith…"
merely "by virtue of his position as a Roman Catholic Priest, and as pastor
and priest to [appellant,] a member of his congregation," who was "deeply religious." According to the complaint, Reverend Namocatcat was the regnant
party to the relationship because he knew appellant's piety made her "readily
subject to manipulation and control by a pastor, and her judgment and ability
to resist…his advances [would be] substantially compromised by her religious faith and trust." Appellant's claim that the depth of her religious faith
rendered her vulnerable to Reverend Namocatcat could not be adjudicated
without reference to the nature of her religious beliefs and the doctrines of
her church.

As of this writing, the courts seem to be about evenly divided on whether to allow
claims against clergy for breach of fiduciary duty. *See, e.g.,* Lightman v. Flaum, 761
N.E.2d 1027 (N.Y. 2001) (no breach). No court has yet been willing to call those claims
"clergy malpractice," though whether this makes a difference is uncertain. (As *F.G.*
makes clear—not that it was ever in doubt—clergy are not immune from liability for
conduct that would be tortious if committed by a stranger, such as battery, conversion,
or negligent driving.)

3. *Negligent-Infliction Claims Against Churches.* See Decorso v. Watchtower Bible
and Tract Society of N.Y., Inc., 829 A.2d 38 (Conn. App. 2003). The court held that a
religious corporation's alleged acts and omissions in spiritual counseling of a wife, who
claimed the corporation's elders had told her to stay in an abusive marriage, were protected by the free exercise and establishment clauses of the first amendment. The court
concluded that it could not consider the wife's negligent infliction of emotional distress
count without excessively entangling itself in matters of the Jehovah religion and bur-
dening the free exercise rights of the religious corporation.

4. *Negligent Hiring and Supervision Claims Against Churches.* The First Amendment
ordinarily will not bar claims based on a religious institution's alleged negligence in failing to prevent foreseeable harm based on sexual assault of a minor or adult parishioner
by a member of the clergy. *See* Malicki v. Doe, 814 So. 2d 347 (Fla. 2002).

5. *Legislative Responses.* Some states have created civil or criminal liability by legislation for cases involving sexual relations between pastors and parishioners. For example, Tex. Civ. Prac. & Rem. Code § 81.002 (Westlaw 2003) makes a "mental health services provider" liable to a patient or former patient who suffers physical or emotional
injuries as a result of sexual contact between the provider and the patient. The term
"mental health services provider" includes a member of the clergy; *id.*, § 81.001(2)(4).
Compare Minn. Stat. §§ 609.344 & 609.345 (Westlaw 2003), under which one who is,
or who purports to be, a member of the clergy commits criminal sexual conduct by
engaging in sexual relations, even if consensual, while providing religious or spiritual
advice or counseling. Could a civil cause of action be based on violation of such a
criminal enactment? *See generally* Chapter 5.

In California, licensed professionals are statutorily prohibited from engaging in
sexual misconduct with their clients, but pastoral counselors are expressly exempted
from state licensing requirements. *See* Jacqueline R. v. Household of Faith Family
Church, Inc., 118 Cal. Rptr. 2d 264 (Cal. Ct. App. 2002).

6. *Ethics in Law Practice: Sexual Relations with Clients.* Many states are debating the
need for ethics rules explicitly addressing the issue of sexual relations between lawyers
and clients. The American Bar Association model rule now provides:

MODEL RULES OF PROFESSIONAL CONDUCT
Rule 1.8(j) (Westlaw 2004)

(j) A lawyer shall not have sexual relations with a client unless a consensual sexual relationship existed between them when the client-lawyer relationship commenced.

The disciplinary standard now applicable in New York is more specific:

N.Y. CODE OF PROFESSIONAL RESPONSIBILITY
DISCIPLINARY Rule 5-111 (Westlaw 2004)

A. "Sexual relations" means sexual intercourse or the touching of an intimate part of another person for the purpose of sexual arousal, sexual gratification, or sexual abuse.

B. A lawyer shall not:

1. Require or demand sexual relations with a client or third party incident to or as a condition of any professional representation.

2. Employ coercion, intimidation, or undue influence in entering into sexual relations with a client.

3. In domestic relations matters, enter into sexual relations with a client during the course of the lawyer's representation of the client.

C. DR 5-111 (B) shall not apply to sexual relations between lawyers and their spouses or to ongoing consensual sexual relationships that predate the initiation of the lawyer-client relationship.

D. Where a lawyer in a firm has sexual relations with a client but does not participate in the representation of that client, the lawyers in the firm shall not be subject to discipline under this rule solely because of the occurrence of such sexual relations.

See also Calif. Rule of Prof. Conduct 3-120 (2004). States that have not yet enacted ethics rules specifically addressing the issue of sexual relations ordinarily reach the same result on general principles relating to conflict of interest, competence, and the like. *See also* Debra Cassens Moss, *Lawyer Liable for Coerced Sex*, 79 A.B.A. J. 24 (Feb. 1993) (jury awarded ex-client $225,000 on malpractice claim although representation was otherwise competent).

E. Abrogation of Independent Actions Based on Negligence

Boyles v. Kerr

Supreme Court of Texas
855 S.W.2d 593 (Tex. 1993)

PHILLIPS, Chief Justice.

. . . .

This is a suit for the negligent infliction of emotional distress. We hold that there is no general duty in Texas not to negligently inflict emotional distress. A claimant may recover mental anguish damages only in connection with defendant's breach of some other legal duty....

....

On August 10, 1985, Petitioner Dan Boyles, Jr., then seventeen, covertly videotaped nineteen-year-old Respondent Susan Leigh Kerr engaging in sexual intercourse with him....Kerr testified that she had not had sexual intercourse prior to her relationship with Boyles.

...Boyles arranged with a friend, Karl Broesche, to use the Broesche house for sexual intercourse with Kerr. Broesche suggested videotaping the activity, and Boyles agreed. Broesche and two friends, Ray Widner and John Paul Tamborello, hid a camera in a bedroom before Kerr and Boyles arrived. After setting up the camera, the three videotaped themselves making crude comments and jokes about the activity that was to follow. They left with the camera running, and the ensuing activities were recorded.

Boyles took possession of the tape shortly after it was made, and subsequently showed it on three occasions, each time at a private residence. Although he showed the tape to only ten friends, gossip about the incident soon spread among many of Kerr and Boyles' friends in Houston. Soon many students at Kerr's school, Southwest Texas State University, and Boyles' school, the University of Texas at Austin, also became aware of the story....After [Kerr] confronted him, Boyles eventually admitted what he had done and surrendered the tape to Kerr. No copies had been made.

Kerr alleges that she suffered humiliation and severe emotional distress from the videotape and the gossip surrounding it. At social gatherings, friends and even casual acquaintances would approach her and comment about the video, wanting to know "what [she] was going to do" or "why did [she] do it." The tape stigmatized Kerr with the reputation of "porno queen" among some of her friends, and she claimed that the embarrassment and notoriety affected her academic performance....Eventually, she sought psychological counseling.

Kerr sued Boyles, Broesche, Widner and Tamborello, alleging intentional invasion of privacy, negligent invasion of privacy, and negligent (but not intentional) infliction of emotional distress. Before the case was submitted to the jury, however, Kerr dropped all causes of action except for negligent infliction of emotional distress. The jury returned a verdict for Kerr on that claim, assessing $500,000 in actual damages. The jury also found that all defendants were grossly negligent, awarding an additional $500,000 in punitive damages, $350,000 of which was assessed against Boyles....

Only Boyles appealed to the court of appeals. That court affirmed....

....Kerr claims that we recognized a broad right to recover for negligently inflicted emotional distress in St. Elizabeth Hospital v. Garrard, 730 S.W.2d 649 (Tex. 1987)....

In *Garrard*, a hospital negligently disposed of the Garrards' stillborn baby in an unmarked, common grave without the plaintiffs' knowledge or consent. The Garrards sued for negligent infliction of emotional distress, without alleging that they suffered any physical injury. This Court nonetheless concluded that they had stated a cause of action. We determined that "Texas first recognized the tort of negligent infliction of mental anguish in Hill v. Kimball, 76 Tex. 210, 13 S.W. 59 (1890)." 730 S.W.2d at 652. This tort, we said, had been administered under traditional tort concepts, subject only to a refinement on the element of damages: the mental suffering is not compensable unless it manifests itself physically. *Id.* After determining that the physical manifestation requirement was arbitrary because it "denies court access to persons with valid claims they could prove if permitted to do so," *id.*, we proceeded to abolish it. [Citation.]

....

While the holding of *Garrard* was correct, we conclude that its reasoning was based on an erroneous interpretation of Hill v. Kimball, and is out of step with most American jurisdictions. Therefore, we overrule the language of *Garrard* to the extent that it recognizes an independent right to recover for negligently inflicted emotional distress. Instead, mental anguish damages should be compensated only in connection with defendant's breach of some other duty imposed by law. This was the basis for recovery prior to *Garrard*, which expanded the scope of liability based on a misconstruction of Hill v. Kimball.

In *Hill*, a pregnant woman suffered a miscarriage when she witnessed the defendant severely beating two men in her yard. The woman sued for her physical injuries under negligence, claiming that the emotional trauma of witnessing the beatings produced the miscarriage and that the defendant should have reasonably anticipated the danger to her. The Court found that the plaintiff had stated a cause of action. The basis, however, was the physical injury she had suffered, together with her allegation of foreseeability....

The Court considered only whether the plaintiff could recover for her physical injuries, not whether she could otherwise recover for her emotional distress or mental anguish caused by witnessing the beatings.... In other words, the defendant was negligent if he should have known that he was imposing an unreasonable risk of physical injury to the plaintiff, not if he merely should have anticipated that the plaintiff would suffer emotional distress.

Hill, therefore, did not recognize a cause of action for negligent infliction of emotional distress. It merely recognized the right to recover for physical injuries under standard negligence principles, notwithstanding that the physical injury is produced indirectly through emotional trauma. *Garrard* thus did not merely modify *Hill*, but created an entirely new cause of action.

....

By overruling the language of *Garrard*, we hold only that there is no general duty not to negligently inflict emotional distress. Our decision does not affect a claimant's right to recover mental anguish damages caused by defendant's breach of some other legal duty. *See, e.g.*, Fisher v. Coastal Transp. Co., 149 Tex. 224, 230 S.W.2d 522 (1950) (negligent infliction of direct physical injury); Moore v. Lillebo, 722 S.W.2d 683 (Tex. 1986) (wrongful death); Fisher v. Carrousel Motor Hotel, Inc., 424 S.W.2d 627 (Tex. 1967) (battery); Stuart v. Western Union Tel. Co., 66 Tex. 580, 18 S.W. 351 (1885) (failure of telegraph company to timely deliver death message); Billings v. Atkinson, 489 S.W.2d 858 (Tex. 1973) (invasion of privacy); Leyendecker & Assocs., Inc., v. Wechter, 683 S.W.2d 369 (Tex.1984) (defamation); Pat H. Foley & Co. v. Wyatt, 442 S.W.2d 904 [(Tex. Civ. App. 1969)] (negligent handling of corpse).

Also, our holding does not affect the right of bystanders to recover emotional distress damages suffered as a result of witnessing a serious or fatal accident. Texas has adopted the bystander rules originally promulgated by the California Supreme Court in Dillon v. Legg, [441 P.2d 912, 920 (Cal. 1968)].... The policy concerns that require limiting the emotional distress cause of action in the direct victim case generally do not apply in the bystander case. Before a bystander may recover, he or she must establish that the defendant has negligently inflicted serious or fatal injuries on the primary victim.

We emphasize that we are not broadening a claimant's right to recover mental anguish damages caused by breach of a particular duty; we leave such right unaffected....

We also are not imposing a requirement that emotional distress manifest itself physically to be compensable....

Most other jurisdictions do not recognize a general duty not to negligently inflict emotional distress. Many limit recovery by requiring proof of a physical manifestation. Others allow recovery where the claimant establishes the breach of some independent duty. A few jurisdictions recognize a general right to recover for negligently inflicted emotional distress, but these jurisdictions are squarely in the minority.

We find the experience in California to be instructive. In Molien v. Kaiser Foundation Hospitals, 27 Cal. 3d 916, 167 Cal. Rptr. 831, 838-39, 616 P.2d 813, 820-21 (1980), the California Supreme Court abolished the physical injury requirement, apparently creating an independent cause of action for negligently inflicted "serious" emotional distress. Nine years later, however, the court declared that "the negligent causing of emotional distress is not an independent tort...," Marlene F. v. Affiliated Psychiatric Medical Clinic, Inc., 48 Cal. 3d 583, 257 Cal. Rptr. 98, 101, 770 P.2d 278, 281 (1989), and that damages are recoverable only where there is a "breach of a duty owed the plaintiff that is assumed by the defendant or imposed on the defendant as a matter of law, or that arises out of a relationship between the two." [Citation.] In another case decided shortly after *Marlene F.*, the California Supreme Court further explained as follows:

> [I]t is clear that foreseeability of the injury alone is not a useful "guideline" or a meaningful restriction on the scope of the [negligent infliction of emotional distress] action. The *Dillon* experience confirms, as one commentator observed, that "[f]oreseeability proves too much....Although it may set tolerable limits for most types of physical harm, it provides virtually no limit on liability for nonphysical harm." [citing Rabin, *Tort Recovery for Negligently Inflicted Economic Loss: A Reassessment*, 37 Stan. L. Rev. 1513, 1526 (1985)]....In order to avoid limitless liability out of all proportion to the degree of a defendant's negligence, and against which it is impossible to insure without imposing unacceptable costs on those among whom the risk is spread, the right to recover for negligently caused emotional distress must be limited.

Thing v. La Chusa, [771 P.2d 814, 826-27 (Cal. 1989)].

Last year, the court confirmed that *Molien* should not be relied on as creating an independent tort for negligent infliction of emotional distress, but that recovery may lie "where a duty arising from a preexisting relationship is negligently breached."....

Some courts have recognized an independent cause of action for "serious" or "severe" emotional distress. [Citations.] This standard, however, fails to delineate meaningfully those situations where recovery should be allowed. As one commentator has explained:

> It is difficult to imagine how a set of rules could be developed and applied on a case-by-case basis to distinguish severe from nonsevere emotional harm. Severity is not an either/or proposition; it is rather a matter of degree. Thus, any attempt to formulate a general rule would almost inevitably result in a threshold requirement of severity so high that only a handful would meet it, or so low that it would be an ineffective screen....

Richard N. Pearson, *Liability to Bystanders for Negligently Inflicted Emotional Harm—A Comment on the Nature of Arbitrary Rules*, 34 U. Fla. L. Rev. 477, 511 (1982).

We therefore reverse the judgment of the court of appeals in favor of Kerr on the ground of negligent infliction of emotional distress.

> ....

Kerr cannot recover based on the cause of action under which she proceeded. It may well be, however, that she failed to assert and preserve alternative causes of action because of her reliance on our holding in *Garrard*. We have broad discretion to remand for a new trial in the interest of justice where it appears that a party may have proceeded under the wrong legal theory.... *See generally* Robert W. Calvert, "...*In the Interest of Justice*," 4 St. Mary's L. J. 291 (1972). It is even more appropriate where we have also subsequently given formal recognition to a cause of action which might be applicable to the facts of this case. *See* Twyman [v. Twyman, 855 S.W.2d 619 (Tex. 1993)] (expressly recognizing the tort of intentional infliction of emotional distress). We therefore reverse the judgment of the court of appeals and remand this cause to the trial court for a new trial.

GONZALEZ, Justice. [Concurring opinion on rehearing.]

What happened to Ms. Kerr in this case is grossly offensive conduct which no one should tolerate. As such the law should, and does, provide a remedy. However, as a result of the posturing by the dissenting justices, what has been lost in the shuffle is the pivotal role that insurance played in this case.

> ....

It does not take a rocket scientist to determine why Ms. Kerr's lawyers elected to proceed solely on the tort of negligent infliction of emotional distress....

> ....

In Texas, a homeowners policy covers only accidents or careless conduct and excludes intentional acts. Ms. Kerr's lawyers may have believed that if they obtained a judgment declaring that Boyles' conduct came within the rubric of "negligence" (inadvertence or carelessness), they could tap the homeowners policies owned by the parents of Boyles and the other defendants. Thus, this case has a lot to do with a search for a "deep pocket" who can pay. If the purpose of awarding damages is to punish the wrongdoer and deter such conduct in the future, then the individuals responsible for these reprehensible actions are the ones who should suffer, not the people of Texas in the form of higher insurance premiums for home owners.

> ....

DOGGETT, Justice, dissenting.

> ....

A young woman was found by a jury to have suffered severe emotional distress when her most intimate act was secretly videotaped and displayed to others. To deny her relief, the majority rewrites Texas law and recants the respect for human dignity affirmed by this court in *St. Elizabeth Hospital*.... [T]he majority now declares that in Texas no legal duty necessary to establish negligence arises from nonconsensual, surreptitious videotaping of a woman engaged in sexual intercourse. The rights of Texas women continue to slip away like sand through this majority's fingers.

> ....

....The majority's claim that we have somehow fallen "out of step" with American jurisprudence completely misses the mark. 855 S.W.2d at 595. The only question is whether Texas steps forward as in *St. Elizabeth Hospital* or races backward as the majority insists. Nationally, our prior decision is considered an authority that has provided an example for other states to follow. [Citation.] In the march to justice, Texas should not fear leadership. But rather than leading, today's majority beats a quick retreat. If every such decision of this court is to be erased from the books as being "out of step," Texas is doomed to last place in legal thinking.

And why the rush to retreat? The majority declares with vigor that "judicial resources" would be "strained," [citation], with the insignificant, the trivial, with other mere "intimate" affairs of the heart. 855 S.W.2d at 600. How can anyone view what happened here as just another "instance of rude, insensitive or distasteful behavior"? [Citation.] When a surreptitiously produced videotape of a woman participating in sexual intercourse makes her the focus of public discussion, how can her injury be dismissed as unworthy of protection? How can the majority's purported difficulty in "'distinguish[ing] severe from nonsevere emotional harm,'" *id.* at 600, justify denying relief to Susan Kerr for the humiliation and lifelong disabling psychological disorder she suffered? How can Boyles' conduct be so callously condoned by the majority's announcement that they and other judges are just too busy to handle such matters? [Citation.]

The unwarranted fear of unwarranted claims has been unequivocally rejected by one leading commentator who appropriately declared that: [T]here has long been precedent enough [for emotional injury claims], and no great increase in litigation has been observed. Prosser & Keeton on Torts § 54, at 360....

> ....

....The majority continues to recognize recovery for negligent infliction of emotional distress without evidence of a physical injury for a few previously accepted categories such as the mistreatment of corpses or misdelivery of telegrams....

Greater protection is thus extended to negligent mishandling of the dead than outrageous treatment of the living. Distinctions such as those between abuse to the living, whose parents may not recover for their distress, and abuse of the dead, whose parents may, are "surely no great triumph of logic." [Citation.] One commentator explains that the allowance of damages for mistreatment of corpses derives from little more than the "mysticism or aura of death." Charles E. Cantu, *Negligent Infliction of Emotional Distress: Expanding the Rule Evolved Since Dillon*, 17 Tex. Tech. L. Rev. 1557, 1565 (1986). The law cannot stand on such arbitrary foundations....

> ....

....The law is not irretrievably locked in the days before televisions and videocameras, nor limited to operators of telegraphs and horse-drawn carriages. In refusing to discuss why no duty arises from Boyles' sexual exploitation of Susan Kerr, the majority abdicates its responsibility. Until writings such as today's, our court sought to fulfill its obligation to keep tort law apace with modern times: "The creation of new concepts of duty in tort is historically the province of the judiciary." [Citation.]

> ....

The message of the majority is clear: Don't bother this court to separate injustice from the inconsequential, better to bar both. The cause is now remanded for Susan Kerr to endure the trauma of another trial "in the interest of justice."....

MAUZY and GAMMAGE, JJ., join in this dissenting opinion.

[The supplemental dissenting opinion of Justice DOGGETT on the motion for rehearing, in which Justices GAMMAGE and SPECTOR concurred, has been omitted. The opinion of Justice COOK, concurring and dissenting, has also been omitted.]

Notes

1. On the stated facts, could the plaintiff successfully present a claim under the tort of outrage at a new trial?

2. *See* Fitzpatrick v. Copeland, 80 S.W.3d 297 (Tex. App. 2002) (holding that an automobile passenger who witnessed a tire crash through a car window and kill her friend was not entitled to recover for resulting emotional distress because she did not sustain bodily injury and was not a family member within the rule governing relief to bystanders); Lions Eye Bank of Tex. v. Perry, 56 S.W.3d 872 (Tex. App. 2001) (family members of a decedent whose eyes were removed by an eye bank, contrary to the family's wishes, had no claim for negligent infliction of emotional distress because, absent a contractual relationship, there was no special relationship between the family members and the bank, and the family members were not bystanders to a serious or fatal accident).

3. *Rejection of Negligent Infliction.* See Harris v. Fulton-DeKalb Hosp. Auth., 255 F. Supp. 2d 1347 (N.D. Ga. 2002) (stating that "Georgia law does not recognize a cause of action for the tort of 'negligent infliction of emotional distress'").

4. *Statutory Obstacles.* In Malik v. Carrier Corp., 202 F.3d 97 (2d Cir. 2000), the court held that an employer's obligations under federal law to investigate and remedy claims for sexual harassment precluded an action to hold the company liable to the alleged harasser for negligent infliction of emotional distress based on the conduct of the investigation.

Chapter 12

Limited Duty: Alcohol-Related Injuries

The Common-Law Rule. Traditionally, sellers and donors of alcoholic beverages were not liable to third persons for injuries caused by the drunken behavior of recipients of the alcohol. With little policy analysis, many courts expressed the conclusion of no liability by saying that the proximate cause of the accident was the drinking, not the dispensing, of the intoxicants. *See, e.g.,* Cole v. Rush, 289 P.2d 450 (Cal. 1955). As an application of proximate causation, this approach seems quite odd; the injuries in question are plainly foreseeable, and they are the sort of thing that can naturally be expected to result from furnishing large amounts of liquor to someone who will soon be driving. Moreover, there can be more than one proximate cause: the supplier and the imbiber could both be held liable. In doctrinal terms, rules immunizing those who contribute to harm by furnishing alcohol to injurers seem best categorized as rules exempting the defendant from the usual duty to take reasonable safety precautions.

Today, the liability of those who furnish alcoholic beverages to persons who become intoxicated and injure themselves or others is a very complicated field, with considerable variation from state to state. Much of the law here is statutory.

A. Liability Under Dram Shop Acts

Most states have adopted "dram shop acts," which make some sellers of alcoholic beverages liable to those injured by the buyer's intoxication. Here is the New York statute:

New York General Obligations Law

§ 11-101 (Westlaw 2004)
Compensation for injury caused by the illegal sale of intoxicating liquor

1. Any person who shall be injured...by any intoxicated person, or by reason of the intoxication of any person,...shall have a right of action against any person who shall, by unlawful selling to or unlawfully assisting in procuring liquor for such intoxicated person, have caused or contributed to such intoxication; and in any such action such person shall have a right to recover actual and exemplary damages.

....

Notes

1. *Variations on Statutory Dram-Shop Liability.*

(a) *What is Prohibited?* Because the New York statute is limited to cases in which the selling was "unlawful" (as, for example, when the defendant sells to a minor or to an obviously intoxicated person), liability under that statute is limited to cases of fairly serious misconduct. *Compare* 235 Ill. Comp. Stat. Ann. 5/6-21 (Westlaw 2003), giving a right of action for harm done by an intoxicated person against any licensed seller of liquor "who by selling or giving alcoholic liquor, causes the intoxication." Unlike the New York statute, the Illinois dram shop act limits liability to specified and very low dollar amounts.

(b) *Who May Be Held Liable?* Although the New York statute, unlike those of some states, is not expressly limited to those in the business of selling alcoholic beverages, the courts have tended to construe it as not applying to those who simply give liquor away, even to a minor, and even in a business setting, as when an employer furnishes drinks to its employees. *See* D'Amico v. Christie, 518 N.E.2d 896 (N.Y. 1987); *see also* McGee v. Alexander, 37 P.3d 800 (Okla. 2001) (holding that a hospital that served alcohol at a golf tournament fund-raising event was a social host, rather than a commercial vendor of alcohol for dram-shop-liability purposes, even though the hospital charged participants a $60 entry fee and profits were to benefit the hospital's continuing medical education program). *But see* Born v. Mayers, 514 N.W.2d 687 (N.D. 1994) (holding that the state dram-shop act creates a cause of action against "any person" who knowingly provides alcoholic beverages to an obviously intoxicated person).

(c) *May the Recipient Sue?* It has also been held that the New York dram shop act does not give an illegal drinker who injures himself a cause of action; Marsico v. Southland Corp., 539 N.Y.S.2d 378 (App. Div. 1989). *See also* Lord v. Fogcutter Bar, 813 P.2d 660 (Alaska 1991) (even if the defendant bar violated the dram shop statute by selling alcohol to a drunken customer, who subsequently committed crimes against a third party, the bar was not liable for damages the customer suffered as a result of his imprisonment, because the statute was not intended to protect persons from the consequences of their own intentional, criminal conduct). In states with dram shop laws permitting an injured recipient of alcohol to sue, recovery may be reduced by comparative negligence. *Cf.* Bissett v. DMI, Inc., 717 P.2d 545 (Mont. 1986).

2. *Non-Statutory Liability.*

The California statute making it a misdemeanor to furnish alcohol "to any habitual or common drunkard or to any obviously intoxicated person" expressly provides that those who violate the statute are *not* civilly liable to those injured by the consumer's intoxication; Cal. Bus. & Prof. Code §§ 25602(a)-25602(b) (Westlaw 2003).

However, in many states vendors may be subject to liability at common law in addition to, or instead of, liability under dram-shop statutes. *See, e.g.,* Klingerman v. Sol Corp., 505 A.2d 474 (Me. 1986) (personal representative of decedent who died of alcoholic poisoning had no cause of action against tavernkeeper under dram-shop law, but stated a claim for common-law negligence); Tobin v. Norwood Country Club, Inc., 661 N.E.2d 627, 631 (Mass. 1996) (finding, in "a tort action brought under the general laws of negligence," that a club owed a duty to a minor, even if there was no "hand to hand" selling or furnishing of alcohol by the club to the minor).

Once the statute legislature has entered the field of defining liability for alcohol-related injuries, are courts free to recognize new causes of action? In answering this question, judicial decisions differ widely.

In Daniel v. Reeder, 61 S.W.3d 359 (Tex. 2001), the court held that deference to the legislature was a good reason to hold that an injured guest had no civil cause of action against a host for making alcohol available to guests under the age of eighteen. Justice Craig Enoch wrote:

> [T]he Texas Legislature's enactments in this area caution us against recognizing a new common-law cause of action against social hosts for violating the Code's prohibition against serving alcohol to minors. Not only do the Legislature's actions demonstrate an intent to treat criminal liability separately from civil liability and an intent to treat commercial providers differently from social hosts, but the Legislature has been especially active in this area. The Code now includes over 200 chapters regulating the production, sale, furnishing, consumption, and storage of alcoholic beverages. Notably, the last time we recognized a common-law cause of action against alcohol providers—in that case, against licensed commercial providers for selling alcohol to intoxicated patrons—the Legislature preempted our holding by enacting the Dram Shop Act.

However, three concurring justices opined that:

> Nothing in the Dram Shop Act itself forecloses common-law liability for an adult who provides alcohol to a minor....If the Legislature wanted to foreclose a cause of action for providing alcohol to persons under eighteen, it could have easily written the law so that it would provide the exclusive remedy for providing alcohol to anyone, regardless of age....

In Craig v. Driscoll, 813 A.2d 1003 (Conn. 2003), the court, by a 3-2 margin, held that the Connecticut Dram Shop Act did not so occupy the field of alcohol-related liability as to preclude new recognition of a common-law cause of action for negligence against the purveyor of alcoholic beverages. The state dram-shop law at the time limited recovery to $20,000 per individual or $50,000 in aggregate, and required that written notice of the claim be provided within 60 days and suit commenced within one year. In recognizing a bystander claim against the defendants for negligent and reckless infliction of emotional distress suffered by the mother and brother of the third-person injured by the recipient of the alcohol, the court reasoned:

> [T]he [dram-shop] act covers all sales of liquor that result in an intoxicated person causing injury, irrespective of the bar owner's knowledge or state of mind. The act thereby provides an action in strict liability, both without the burden of proving the element of scienter essential to a negligence action and without the benefit of the broader scope of recovery permitted under such an action. It sets, in essence, a minimum recovery opportunity for persons injured as a result of the sale of liquor to an intoxicated person. By setting a *floor*, however, the legislature did not also intend to be setting a *ceiling*—and we are free, therefore, to exercise our common-law authority to increase the recovery opportunity in circumstances where the state of mind of the bar owner warrants it.
>
> A tort action would provide an avenue to recover full compensation, but only upon establishing the requisite culpability and causation. In this manner, the tort action would supplement, rather than conflict with, the act....
>
>   ....
>
>   ....We conclude...that the act does not...preclude a common-law action in negligence against a purveyor of alcoholic beverages for service of alcoholic liquor to an adult patron who, as a result of his intoxication, injures another.

...We [also] expressly reject the claim that a purveyor who provides alcoholic beverages to an already intoxicated patron or a patron known to him to be an alcoholic cannot, as a matter of law, be the proximate cause of subsequent injuries caused by the intoxicated patron....

Shortly after the decision, the Connecticut legislature amended the dram-shop act to raise the limits on liability to $250,000, either per individual or in aggregate. *See* Conn. Gen. Stat. 30-102 (Westlaw 2003). The legislature also added a sentence to the act which appears to overrule *Craig*. The sentence states:

Such injured person shall have no cause of action against such seller for negligence in the sale of alcoholic liquor to a person twenty-one years of age or older.

Some might regard this development as a rebuke to the majority of justices who voted in favor of the *Craig* decision. However, perhaps those justices achieved their purpose. The decision caused the legislature to reconsider a law that arguably was seriously out of date in terms of the limits it imposed on recovery of damages. Some scholars say that courts, through judicial criticism or otherwise, have an important role to play in persuading legislatures to update obsolete legislation. *See* Guido Calabresi, A Common Law for the Age of Statutes (1982).

3. ***Dram-Shop Liability and Proximate Causation.*** In a rare case, a vendor who negligently provides alcohol to a minor who then injuries a third person may be saved from liability to the third person by lack of proximate causation. *See* Van v. Pena, 990 S.W2d 751 (Tex. 1999) (holding that gang members' criminal conduct, which involved the rape and murder of two girls, was extraordinary in nature and not the type of harm generally associated with furnishing alcohol to minors, and that therefore the conduct was a superseding cause of the girls' injuries and deaths).

Similar causation issues can arise in cases involving social-host liability (discussed below). *See* Nichols v. Dobler, 655 N.W.2d 787 (Mich. Ct. App. 2002) (holding that there was an issue of material fact as to whether a party host's negligence in serving alcohol to a minor proximately caused injuries sustained when the plaintiff was repeatedly hit in the head with a hammer by the minor).

4. ***Casinos and Gambling.*** Does a casino have a duty to refrain from knowingly permitting an invitee to gamble if the patron is visibly intoxicated or under the influence of a narcotic substance? *Compare* GNOC Corp. v. Aboud, 715 F. Supp. 644 (D. N.J. 1989) (yes), *with* Hakimoglu v. Trump Taj Mahal Assoc., 70 F.3d 291 (3rd Cir. 1997) (no). *See also* Merrill v. Trump Ind. Inc., 320 F.3d 729 (7th Cir. 2003) (holding that a casino did not owe a duty to a compulsive gambler to prevent him from gambling).

5. ***Controlled Substances.*** Another New York statute, N.Y. Gen. Oblig. Law § 11-103 (Westlaw 2003), imposes liability similar to that under the state dram shop act for injuries attributable to the illegal sale of controlled substances.

B. Liability of "Social Hosts"

Kelly v. Gwinnell

Supreme Court of New Jersey
476 A.2d 1219 (N.J. 1984)

WILENTZ, C.J.

....

At the trial level, the case was disposed of...by summary judgment in favor of the social host. The record...discloses that defendant Donald Gwinnell, after driving defendant Joseph Zak home, spent an hour or two at Zak's home before leaving to return to his own home. During that time...Gwinnell [allegedly] consumed two or three drinks of scotch on the rocks. Zak accompanied Gwinnell outside to his car, chatted with him, and watched as Gwinnell then drove off to go home. About twenty-five minutes later Zak telephoned Gwinnell's home to make sure Gwinnell had arrived there safely. The phone was answered by Mrs. Gwinnell, who advised Zak that Gwinnell had been involved in a head-on collision. The collision was with an automobile operated by plaintiff, Marie Kelly, who was seriously injured as a result.

....Kelly's expert concluded from...[Gwinnell's .286 percent blood alcohol concentration] that Gwinnell had consumed not two or three scotches...but the equivalent of thirteen drinks; that while at Zak's home Gwinnell must have been showing unmistakable signs of intoxication; and that in fact he was severely intoxicated while at Zak's residence and at the time of the accident.

Kelly sued Gwinnell and...[the Zaks and others]. The Zaks moved for summary judgment, contending that as a matter of law a host is not liable for the negligence of an adult social guest who has become intoxicated while at the host's home. The trial court granted the motion....The Appellate Division affirmed....

The Appellate Division's determination was based on the apparent absence of decisions in this country imposing such liability (except for those that were promptly overruled by the Legislature). [Citation.] The absence of such determinations is said to reflect a broad consensus that the imposition of liability arising from these social relations is unwise. Certainly this immunization of hosts is not the inevitable result of the law of negligence, for conventional negligence analysis points strongly in exactly the opposite direction. "Negligence is tested by whether the reasonably prudent person at the time and place should recognize and foresee an unreasonable risk or likelihood of harm or danger to others." [Citation.] When negligent conduct creates such a risk, setting off foreseeable consequences that lead to plaintiff's injury, the conduct is deemed the proximate cause of the injury....

....Viewing the facts most favorably to plaintiff (as we must, since the complaint was dismissed on a motion for summary judgment), one could reasonably conclude that the Zaks must have known that their provision of liquor was causing Gwinnell to become drunk, yet they continued to serve him even after he was visibly intoxicated....A reasonable person in Zak's position could foresee quite clearly that this continued provision of alcohol to Gwinnell was making it more and more likely that Gwinnell would not be able to operate his car carefully...[and] was likely to injure someone as a result of the negligent operation of his car. The usual elements of a cause of action for negligence are clearly present....[T]he only question remaining is whether a duty exists to prevent such risk or, realistically, whether this Court should impose such a duty.

In most cases the justice of imposing such a duty is so clear that the cause of action in negligence is assumed to exist simply on the basis of the actor's creation of an unreasonable risk of foreseeable harm resulting in injury. In fact, however, more is needed, "more" being the value judgment, based on an analysis of public policy, that the actor owed the injured party a duty of reasonable care. [Citation.] In Goldberg v. Housing Auth. of Newark, 38 N.J. 578, 583, 186 A.2d 291 (1962), this Court explained that "whether a duty exists is ultimately a question of fairness. The inquiry involves a weighing of the relationship of the parties, the nature of the risk, and the public interest in the proposed solution."....

When the court determines that a duty exists and liability will be extended, it draws judicial lines based on fairness and policy. In a society where thousands of deaths are caused each year by drunken drivers,[3] where the damage caused by such deaths is regarded increasingly as intolerable, where liquor licensees are prohibited from serving intoxicated adults, and where long-standing criminal sanctions against drunken driving have recently been significantly strengthened..., the imposition of such a duty by the judiciary seems both fair and fully in accord with the State's policy....

. . . .

The argument is made that the rule imposing liability on licensees is justified because licensees, unlike social hosts, derive a profit from serving liquor. We reject this analysis of the liability's foundation and emphasize that the liability proceeds from the duty of care that accompanies control of the liquor supply. Whatever the motive behind making alcohol available to those who will subsequently drive, the provider has a duty to the public not to create foreseeable, unreasonable risks by this activity.

We therefore hold that a host who serves liquor to an adult social guest, knowing both that the guest is intoxicated and will thereafter be operating a motor vehicle, is liable for injuries inflicted on a third party as a result of the negligent operation of a motor vehicle by the adult guest when such negligence is caused by intoxication. We impose this duty on the host to the third party because we believe that the policy considerations served by its imposition far outweigh those asserted in opposition. While we recognize the concern that our ruling will interfere with accepted standards of social behavior; will intrude on and somewhat diminish the enjoyment, relaxation, and camaraderie that accompany social gatherings at which alcohol is served; and that such gatherings and social relationships are not simply tangential benefits of a civilized society but are regarded by many as important, we believe that the added assurance of just compensation to the victims of drunken driving as well as the added deterrent effect of the rule on such driving outweigh the importance of those other values....

The liability we impose here is analogous to that traditionally imposed on owners of vehicles who lend their cars to persons they know to be intoxicated. [Citations.] If, by lending a car to a drunk, a host becomes liable to third parties injured by the drunken driver's negligence, the same liability should extend to a host who furnishes liquor to a visibly drunken guest who he knows will thereafter drive away.

---

3. From 1978 to 1982 there were 5,755 highway fatalities in New Jersey. Alcohol was involved in 2,746 or 47.5% of these deaths. Of the 629,118 automobile accident injuries for the same period, 131,160, or 20.5% were alcohol related. The societal cost for New Jersey alcohol-related highway deaths for this period has been estimated as $1,149,516,000.00, based on statistics and documents obtained from the New Jersey Division of Motor Vehicles. The total societal cost figure for all alcohol-related accidents in New Jersey in 1981 alone, including deaths, personal injuries and property damage was $1,594,497,898.00. [Citation.] These New Jersey statistics are consistent with nationwide figures. [Citation.]

Some fear has been expressed that the extent of the potential liability may be disproportionate to the fault of the host.... [W]e do not believe that the liability is disproportionate when the host's actions, so relatively easily corrected, may result in serious injury or death....

Given the lack of precedent anywhere else in the country, however, we believe it would be unfair to impose this liability retroactively. [Citations.] Homeowners who are social hosts may desire to increase their policy limits; apartment dwellers may want to obtain liability insurance of this kind where perhaps they now have none....We therefore have determined that the liability imposed by this case on social hosts shall be prospective, applicable only to events that occur after the date of this decision. We will, however, apply the doctrine to the parties before us on the usual theory that to do otherwise would not only deprive the plaintiff of any benefit resulting from her own efforts but would also make it less likely that, in the future, individuals will be willing to claim rights, not yet established, that they believe are just.

....

...[I]f the Legislature differs with us on issues of this kind, it has a clear remedy. [Citations.]

....

....Given the facts before us, we decide only that where the social host directly serves the guest and continues to do so even after the guest is visibly intoxicated, knowing that the guest will soon be driving home, the social host may be liable for the consequences of the resulting drunken driving. We are not faced with a party where many guests congregate, nor with guests serving each other, nor with a host busily occupied with other responsibilities and therefore unable to attend to the matter of serving liquor, nor with a drunken host. [Citation.] We will face those situations when and if they come before us....The fears expressed by the dissent concerning the vast impact of the decision on the "average citizen's" life are reminiscent of those asserted in opposition to our decisions abolishing husband-wife, parent-child, and generally family immunity....Some fifteen years have gone by and, as far as we can tell, nothing but good has come as a result of those decisions.

....

...[T]he dissent's emphasis on the financial impact of an insurance premium increase on the homeowner or the tenant should be measured against the monumental financial losses suffered by society as result of drunken driving. By our decision we not only spread some of that loss so that it need not be borne completely by the victims of this widespread affliction, but, to some extent, reduce the likelihood that the loss will occur in the first place....Does our society morally approve of the decision to continue to allow the charm of unrestrained social drinking when the cost is the lives of others, sometimes of the guests themselves?

If we but step back and observe ourselves objectively, we will see a phenomenon not of merriment but of cruelty, causing misery to innocent people, tolerated for years despite our knowledge that without fail, out of our extraordinarily high number of deaths caused by automobiles, nearly half have regularly been attributable to drunken driving. [Citation.] Should we be so concerned about disturbing the customs of those who knowingly supply that which causes the offense, so worried about their inconvenience, as if they were the victims rather than the cause of the carnage?....

....

We…reverse the judgment in favor of defendants Zak and remand the case to the Law Division for proceedings consistent with this opinion.

[CLIFFORD, SCHRIEBER, HANDLER, POLLOCK and O'HERN, JJ. joined in the majority opinion. The dissent of GARIBALDI, J., is omitted.]

Notes

1. *The Legislative Response.* New Jersey now has the following statutes:

N.J. STAT. ANN. § 2A:15-5.6
(Westlaw 2004)
Exclusive civil remedy for damages in accident involving vehicle
resulting from negligent provision of alcoholic beverages by social host
to person of legal age; conditions for recovery; blood test presumptions

a. This act shall be the exclusive civil remedy for personal injury or property damage resulting from the negligent provision of alcoholic beverages by a social host to a person who has attained the legal age to purchase and consume alcoholic beverages.

b. A person who sustains bodily injury or injury to real or personal property as a result of the negligent provision of alcoholic beverages by a social host to a person who has attained the legal age to purchase and consume alcoholic beverages may recover damages from a social host only if:

(1) The social host willfully and knowingly provided alcoholic beverages either:

(a) To a person who was visibly intoxicated in the social host's presence; or

(b) To a person who was visibly intoxicated under circumstances manifesting reckless disregard of the consequences as affecting the life or property of another; and

(2) The social host provided alcoholic beverages to the visibly intoxicated person under circumstances which created an unreasonable risk of foreseeable harm to the life or property of another, and the social host failed to exercise reasonable care and diligence to avoid the foreseeable risk; and

(3) The injury arose out of an accident caused by the negligent operation of a vehicle by the visibly intoxicated person who was provided alcoholic beverages by a social host.

c. To determine the liability of a social host under subsection b. of this section, if a test to determine the presence of alcohol in the blood indicates a blood alcohol concentration of:

(1) less than 0.10% by weight of alcohol in the blood, there shall be an irrebuttable presumption that the person tested was not visibly intoxicated in the social host's presence and that the social host did not provide alcoholic beverages to the person under circumstances which manifested reckless disregard of the consequences as affecting the life or property of another; or

(2) at least 0.10% but less than 0.15% by weight of alcohol in the blood, there shall be a rebuttable presumption, that the person tested was not visibly intoxicated in the social host's presence and that the social host did not provide

alcoholic beverages to the person under circumstances which manifested reckless disregard of the consequences as affecting the life or property of another.

N.J. Stat. Ann. § 2A:15-5.7 (Westlaw 2004)
Limitation of nonliability of social host

No social host shall be held liable to a person who has attained the legal age to purchase and consume alcoholic beverages for damages suffered as a result of the social host's negligent provision of alcoholic beverages to that person.

N.J. Stat. Ann. § 2A:15-5.8 (Westlaw 2004)
Social hosts or other parties as joint tortfeasors;
responsibility for damages equal to percentage of negligence

… [I]n any case where a social host or any other party to a suit instituted pursuant to the provisions of this act is determined to be a joint tortfeasor, the social host or other party shall be responsible for no more than that percentage share of the damages which is equal to the percentage of negligence attributable to the social host or other party.

2. *Other States' Responses.* Some courts agree with *Kelly*, in whole or in part. *See, e.g.,* McGuiggan v. New England Tel. & Tel. Co., 496 N.E.2d 141 (Mass. 1986) (host may be liable to third parties for injuries caused by drunken driving of an obviously intoxicated adult guest); Langle v. Kurkul, 510 A.2d 1301 (Vt. 1986) (host may be liable for furnishing alcoholic beverages to a visibly intoxicated person who will drive an automobile or to a minor); Ely v. Murphy, 540 A.2d 54 (Conn. 1988) (holding that a minor's consumption of alcohol was not, as a matter of law, an intervening cause that would insulate a social host or other provider of liquor from liability for ensuing injury to the minor or a third party).

However, other courts have refused to hold social hosts liable for injuries caused by their guests, regardless of how negligent the host may have been in furnishing the guest with beverages. *See, e.g.,* Beard v. Graff, 858 S.W.2d 918 (Tex. 1993); Overbaugh v. McKutcheon, 396 S.E.2d 153 (W. Va. 1990).

In some states which have held social hosts liable, the legislature has responded by abolishing liability; see, for example, Cal. Civ. Code § 1714 (Westlaw 2003), which not only abolishes liability based on negligently furnishing alcohol, but also names the California Supreme Court decisions which the legislation was intended to overturn. Several states have created liability as a matter of common law without triggering a legislative response.

In Pennsylvania, social-host liability attaches in cases involving the negligent furnishing of alcoholic beverages to minors, but not to persons of drinking age; Congini by Congini v. Portersville Valve Co., 470 A.2d 515 (Pa. 1983). For an interesting exploration of the extent of this liability, see Fassett v. Delta Kappa Epsilon, 807 F.2d 1150 (3d Cir. 1986), an action following a traffic accident caused by a minor who had become intoxicated at a fraternity party. The court, attempting to discern Pennsylvania law, rejected an argument made by several of the defendants that only those persons who physically hand liquor to a minor can be liable. Instead, liability could attach to anyone whose conduct in "aiding, agreeing or attempting to aid a minor in consuming liquor, did so in substantial fashion." The court refused to dismiss claims against the fraternity's treasurer, whose role in the party consisted of signing the check used to purchase the beverages, against its president, who organized the party, and against the roommates who knowingly allowed their apartment to be used for the party. While the *Fassett* decision may strike the more convivial sort of student as harsh, it may be worth noting that one of the accident victims died and the other was rendered a quadriplegic.

Fassett was a federal court ruling. A later state-court decision made clear that, under Pennsylvania law, a minor cannot be held liable under the social-host doctrine for furnishing alcohol to another minor who is subsequently injured. *See* Kapres v. Heller, 640 A.2d 888 (Pa. 1994). *See also* Panagakos v. Walsh, 749 N.E.2d 670 (Mass. 2001) (holding that a tavern that was sued based on the death of an underaged adult to whom it served alcohol could not assert a claim for contribution against the decedent's underage companions; the companions could not have been held liable for serving alcohol to the decedent, and had no duty to prevent the decedent from suffering the consequences of self-inflicted intoxication).

Compare Wallace v. Wilson, 575 N.E.2d 1134 (Mass. 1991) (mother was not liable for the assault and battery of third persons at her home caused by teenagers who, with the mother's knowledge, brought beer to a party given by her 17-year-old daughter).

C. Other Theories of Liability

The great difficulties of suing a provider of alcohol, in many states, make it desirable for the plaintiff's lawyer to find a basis for a claim that the defendant is responsible on some other ground.

Entrustment. McKenna v. Straughan, 222 Cal. Rptr. 462 (Ct. App. 1986), *supra* at 505, was a case in which furnishing an alcoholic with a car gave rise to an action by a third person based on negligent entrustment. In some jurisdictions, liability under that theory may even extend to cases involving injuries to the person to whom the car was entrusted, and not just to third persons. *See* Casebolt v. Cowan, 829 P.2d 352 (Colo. 1992); *but see* Anderson v. Miller, 559 N.W.2d 29 (Iowa 1997) (estate could not recover for entrustment of a vehicle to a drunken driver if the decedent was the driver).

Assumed Duty. Another possible basis for liability is voluntary assumption of duty (*see* Chapter 9), although the cases on that subject are disturbingly inconsistent. *Compare* McGee v. Chalfant, 806 P.2d 980 (Kan. 1991) (no liability for "merely transporting an intoxicated person to his automobile"), *with* Leppke v. Segura, 632 P.2d 1057 (Colo. Ct. App. 1981) (liability imposed for jump-starting an intoxicated patron's car). *Compare* Venetoulias v. O'Brien, 909 S.W.2d 236 (Tex. Ct. App. 1995) (owner of bar assumed a duty by inducing a patron to drink by taking her keys and promising to provide a ride), *with* Stephenson v. Universal Metrics, Inc., 641 N.W.2d 158 (Wis. 2002).

In *Stephenson*, an employee who agreed to drive a co-worker home after an office party, but who then left without the co-worker, was held not liable to a third person injured in an accident that occurred when the co-worker drove home. The promise had been made in front of a bartender, who had previously refused to serve more drinks to the co-worker, but who thereafter continued to serve him drinks. The court found that the case fit the terms of Restatement, Second of Torts §324A, which imposes a duty in cases of a voluntary undertaking. However, the court declined to impose liability for two reasons. First, a Wisconsin statute provided that "A person is immune from civil liability arising out of the act of procuring alcohol beverages for or selling, dispensing or giving away alcohol beverages to another person." The facts in *Stephenson* did not fall within the statutory exceptions to the general rule of non-liability (forcing another to drink alcohol, misrepresenting that a beverage does not contain alcohol, or providing alcohol to a minor). Second, the court held that public policy precluded the imposition of liability because the injury was "wholly out of proportion to the tortfeasor's culpability," liability would impose an unreasonable burden (to control the promisee), and there was "no sensible stopping point" with respect to this type of liability. Justice Jon P. Wilcox wrote for the majority:

> What happens if conditions change? Would there ever be circumstances under which someone who agrees to drive for an intoxicated person could back out of such an agreement? What if an emergency arose that required the driver to leave? What if the driver were to get sick? Could a designated driver ever transfer the responsibility? What if the intoxicated person was to become disorderly, or assaulted someone? Could the person who agrees to drive be subject to liability for any of the intoxicated person's other negligent acts?

> There could also be effects on those outside of designated drivers. If the intoxicated person calls a cab and the cab driver is late, prompting the intoxicated person to drive—can the driver be held liable? If a company agrees to help arrange rides home from a company function, can they be held liable? Will finding liability in this case allow liability to be extended to party guests who are faced with allowing a clearly intoxicated person to drive home? If no one steps forward and agrees to drive, can they all be held liable?

> These are only a few examples of the extent to which liability might be carried. If we were to hold Kreuser liable under these circumstances, the possibilities for expanding liability would simply have too much potential to grow out of control, and would also threaten to run counter to the legislative enactments regarding immunity.

Duty to Invitees. Even if an establishment is not liable for violation of dram shop laws, it may have a duty to protect its patrons if a fight breaks out. *Cf.* Boone v. Martinez, 567 N.W.2d 508 (Minn. 1997) (no liability because a fight was sudden and unforeseeable).

Public Duty. A municipality may be liable for the negligent failure of its police officers to remove from the highway an intoxicated motorist who subsequently causes injuries to other travelers. *See* Irwin v. Town of Ware, 467 N.E.2d 1292 (Mass. 1984); Kelly Mahon Tullier, *Governmental Liability for Negligent Failure to Detain Drunk Drivers*, 77 Cornell L. Rev. 873, 874 (1992) (increasing number of cases imposing liability).

Intentional Tort. A recipient of the alcohol (or the recipient's survivors) may also be able to state a claim for battery. *See* Davies v. Butler, 602 P.2d 605 (Nev. 1979), *supra* at 135.

Respondeat Superior. An employer may be held liable for drunk driving by an employee within the scope of employment. *See* McNair v. Lend Lease Trucks, Inc., 95 F.3d 325 (4th Cir. 1996) (whether an employer was responsible for a trucker's actions depended upon whether the trucker left the course of his employment by stopping at a lounge and drinking alcohol for over three hours and, if so, whether he returned to the scope of his employment by leaving the lounge and attempting to cross a road to his truck, during which he was involved in an accident with a motorcyclist).

Special Relationship. Garafalo v. Lambda Chi Alpha Frat., 616 N.W.2d 647 (Iowa 2000), suggests that it will be difficult to establish liability for alcohol-related injuries based on duties imposed by some special relationship. In *Garafalo*, a pledge died after consuming excessive quantities of beer and hard liquor. His parents brought a wrongful death action that included claims against the national fraternity, the local chapter of the fraternity, and a fraternity member. The court held that the national fraternity had no duty to protect the 19-year-old pledge from his decision to drink to excess following a big brother/little brother ceremony because the fraternity neither furnished the alcohol, forced the pledge to consume it as part of any recognized fraternal activity, nor exercised control as a custodial institution. The fraternity's members, the court wrote, were "free to make choices about their use and abuse of alcohol." The court further found that the fact that one fraternity member permitted the pledge to lie down on the couch in his room to "sleep it off" was insufficient to establish a special duty running from member to pledge based on allegedly "taking charge" of another who was helpless. The court wrote:

> Reier was not responsible for Garofalo's intoxication. He was not his "big brother." He merely let Garofalo "sleep it off" on his couch. Even if these facts could be stretched to fit the notion of "taking charge," Reier's conduct reveals no breach of that duty. When he left the fraternity house at midnight, Garofalo was intoxicated but conscious. When Reier returned to his room at 3:00 a.m., Garofalo was asleep and snoring. Reier repositioned him on his side, mindful for his safety. When he hurried out the door for an 8:30 a.m. class, Reier glanced at Garofalo, assumed he was asleep and made no attempt to awaken or "revive" him. Although appellants fault this latter omission, we believe the standard urged by appellants is substantially higher than what is required under the Restatement.[a] Given the gratuitous nature of the undertaking, the rule requires only acting in "good faith and with common decency" and relieves the actor from responsibility for "a high standard of diligence and competence, to possess any special skill, or to subordinate his own interests to those of the other." *Id.* cmt. d. Thus Reier... [was] entitled to judgment as a matter of law on this claim.

The court was divided 3–3 on the local fraternity's liability for the death, and therefore summary judgment in favor of the local fraternity was affirmed by operation of law.

Compare Garafalo with Wakulich v. Mraz, 785 N.E.2d 843 (Ill. 2003) (holding that a complaint by the mother of a 16-year-old girl who died after drinking a quart of alcohol at the goading of the defendants stated a cause of action for negligent performance of a voluntary undertaking; the complaint alleged that, after the guest became unconscious, the social hosts placed guest in the family room, observed her vomiting profusely, checked on her periodically, did not seek medical attention, and refused to drive her home or to the hospital).

---

a. Restatement, Second, of Torts §324 provides:
  One who, being under no duty to do so, takes charge of another who is helpless adequately to aid or protect himself is subject to liability to the other for any bodily harm caused to him by
      (a) the failure of the actor to exercise reasonable care to secure the safety of the other while within the actor's charge, or
      (b) the actor's discontinuing his aid or protection, if by so doing he leaves the other in a worse position than when the actor took charge of him.

William W. Kilgarlin

Otis Engineering Corporation v. Clark

Supreme Court of Texas
668 S.W.2d 307 (Tex. 1983)

KILGARLIN, Justice.

This is a wrongful death action instituted by Larry and Clifford Clark against Otis Engineering Corporation after the Clarks' wives were killed in an automobile accident involving an Otis employee, Robert Matheson. At the time of the accident Matheson was not in the course of his employment. The trial court granted Otis' motion for summary judgment. The court of appeals reversed and remanded the cause for trial....

Two questions are presented. First, does the law impose any duty upon Otis under the evidence as developed? Secondly, does such evidence give rise to any genuine issues of material fact?

Matheson...had a history of drinking on the job, and was intoxicated on the night of the accident. At his dinner break that night and on other occasions that day he went to the parking lot, where he allegedly consumed alcoholic beverages in his automobile. Donald Roy was Matheson's supervisor and Rennie Pyle was a co-worker who assisted Matheson on occasion. Pyle testified that he knew of Matheson's drinking problems and that he told Roy on the day of the accident that Matheson was not acting right, was not coordinated, was slurring his words, and that "we need to get him off the machines."... The supervisor testified that he observed Matheson's condition.... When Matheson returned from his dinner break, Roy suggested that he should go home. Roy, as he escorted Matheson to the company's parking lot, asked if he was all right and if he could make it home, and Matheson answered that he could. Thirty minutes later, some three miles away from the plant, the fatal accident occurred.

Dr. Charles S. Petty, the medical examiner, testified that Matheson had a blood alcohol content of 0.268% which indicated he had ingested a substantial quantity of alcohol....

....The testimony indicated the supervisor knew Matheson was in no condition to drive home safely that night. When some night shift employees came to work around 10:30 p.m. and remarked there had been an accident on Belt Line Road, Roy immediately suspected Matheson was involved...knowing that Matheson had to drive on heavily traveled Belt Line Road to reach home....

The Clarks contend that under the facts in this case Otis sent home, in the middle of his shift, an employee whom it knew to be intoxicated. They aver this was an affirmative act which imposed a duty on Otis to act in a non-negligent manner. [Citation.] This action by Otis subjected Matheson and other motorists to the dangers of an accident on the highway.

....The Clarks likewise maintain that Roy had other alternatives which the jury could find to be more reasonable, such as taking Matheson to the nurses' station, giving him a ride home, or calling a taxi, the police, or Matheson's wife....

Otis' motion for summary judgment was granted on the basis that as a matter of law Otis owed no duty to the Clarks....As a general rule, one person is under no duty to control the conduct of another, Restatement (Second) of Torts § 315 (1965), even if he has the practical ability to exercise such control. [Citation.] Yet, certain relationships do impose, as a matter of law, certain duties upon parties. *See e.g.*, Restatement (Second) §§ 316-20....

...[F]actors which should be considered in determining whether the law should impose a duty are the risk, foreseeability, and likelihood of injury weighed against the social utility of the actor's conduct, the magnitude of the burden of guarding against the injury and consequences of placing that burden on the employer. [Citation.]

    ....

Otis contends that, at worst, its conduct amounted to nonfeasance and under established law it owed no duty to the Clarks' respective wives. Otis further says that by imposing liability for the acts of its intoxicated employee, this Court would be judicially creating "dram shop" liability. We disagree. This is not a "dram shop" case. If a duty is to be imposed on Otis it would not be based on the *mere knowledge* of Matheson's intoxication, but would be based on additional factors.

...[W]e do not view this as a case of employer nonfeasance.

What we must decide is if changing social standards and increasing complexities of human relationships in today's society justify imposing a duty upon an employer to act reasonably when he exercises control over his servants. Even though courts have been reluctant to hold an employer liable for the off-duty torts of an employee, "[a]s between an entirely innocent plaintiff and a defendant who admittedly has departed from the social standard of conduct, if only toward one individual, who should bear the loss?"....

...[W]hy should we be reluctant to impose a duty on Otis? As Dean Prosser has observed, "[c]hanging social conditions lead constantly to the recognition of new duties. No better general statement can be made, than the courts will find a duty where, in general, reasonable men would recognize it and agree that it exists." W. Prosser, *supra*, at 327....

Several recent cases in other jurisdictions have extended concepts of duty in the area of employer liability....

An employer was held liable for injuries sustained by third parties in an accident caused by its intoxicated employee in Brockett v. Kitchen Boyd Motor Co., 264 Cal.

App. 2d 69, 70 Cal. Rptr. 136 (1968). The employee, Huff, became intoxicated at a Christmas party given by the motor company. Although Huff was "grossly intoxicated," a representative of the company placed him in his automobile and directed him to drive home. The court recognized that the supplying of alcohol does not ordinarily make the supplier liable to an injured third party, but the affirmative acts of placing him in his car and directing him to drive home imposed a duty on the company to exercise reasonable care. 70 Cal. Rptr. at 139.

Recently, the Supreme Court of Appeals of West Virginia rendered its opinion in Robertson v. LeMaster, 301 S.E.2d 563 (W. Va. 1983). In this case, LeMaster's employer, The Norfolk and Western Railway Company, had required LeMaster to work twenty-seven consecutive hours to remove debris and repair a track damaged by a train derailment. After many complaints by LeMaster that he was tired and wanted to go home, LeMaster's foreman permitted him to do so. LeMaster lived some fifty miles from his place of work, and while driving his car home, fell asleep and was involved in a collision with Robertson, causing injuries to Robertson. The West Virginia court recognized that the railroad company owed no duty to control an employee acting outside of the scope of employment, but stated that such was not the issue in the case, saying "rather it is whether the appellee's conduct prior to the accident created a foreseeable risk of harm." *Id.* at 567. The court concluded that requiring LeMaster to work such long hours and then setting him loose upon the highway in an obviously exhausted condition was sufficient to sustain a cause of action against the railroad. We are persuaded by the logic of the holdings in these three cases.

Therefore, the standard of duty that we now adopt for this and all other cases currently in the judicial process, is: when, because of an employee's incapacity, an employer exercises control over the employee, the employer has a duty to take such action as a reasonably prudent employer under the same or similar circumstances would take to prevent the employee from causing an unreasonable risk of harm to others....

Therefore, the trier of fact in this case should be left free to decide whether Otis acted as a reasonable and prudent employer considering the following factors: the availability of the nurses' aid station, a possible phone call to Mrs. Matheson, having another employee drive Matheson home, dismissing Matheson early rather than terminating his employment, and the foreseeable consequences of Matheson's driving upon a public street in his stuporous condition. As summary judgment proof clearly raises all of these factors questioning the reasonableness of Otis' conduct, a fact issue is present and summary judgment was improper.

For these reasons, we affirm the judgment of the court of appeals and remand to the trial court for determination of the issues.

[The dissenting opinion of MCGEE, J., in which POPE, C.J., and BARROW and CAMPBELL, J.J., joined, is omitted.]

Notes

1. *Failure to Exercise Control.* The ruling in *Otis* addressed an employer's liability for allegedly negligent exercise of control. What if an employer *fails* to exercise control? The answer will depend, at least in part, on what is foreseeable. *Compare* Carroll Air Systems, Inc. v. Greenbaum, 629 So. 2d 914 (Fla. Dist. Ct. App. 1993) (a statute barring liability of one who furnishes alcoholic beverages to a person of lawful drinking age did not preclude an employer from being held liable for punitive damages where its fault

was not in the furnishing of drinks but in not preventing an employee from driving away from a meeting in an intoxicated condition), *with* Duge v. Union Pac. R. Co., 71 S.W.3d 358 (Tex. App. 2001) (holding that an employer had no duty to control the actions of a employee who, after being on the job for 27 hours, caused an accident after leaving the workplace because there was "no indication" that the worker was fatigued; the worker stopped at a gas station and visited with a friend for an hour or more before the accident occurred).

2. *Drinking and Intentional Torts.* Fights are a fairly common result of excessive drinking. The victim of an attack by an intoxicated person almost always has a decent battery action, but this action will not do the victim much good if the defendant is judgment proof. Many otherwise judgment-proof defendants have liability insurance, but that kind of insurance almost always excludes coverage for injuries intentionally inflicted by the insured. In Saba v. Darling, 575 A.2d 1240 (Md. Ct. Spec. App. 1990), the plaintiff dismissed his battery claim after learning that the defendant's insurance would not cover damages for an intentional tort and argued that he had been injured by the defendant's negligence in drinking heavily, as it was foreseeable that heavy drinking could lead to violence. The defendant admitted to a history of fighting when under the influence of alcohol. The court, without much analysis, held that the defendant's conduct, an intentional tort, could not be the subject of a negligence action. Note that, in many states, a third person who had negligently furnished the defendant with alcohol would have been liable to the victim for negligence.

Chapter 13

Torts Involving Conception, Pregnancy, Birth, and Adoption

This chapter examines the important, but somewhat confusing, array of tort actions having to do with unborn children, and with adoption. Actions relating to unborn children include suits for personal injuries suffered by children prior to birth and for the wrongful death of unborn children. They also include actions for "unwanted pregnancy," in cases of negligence resulting in failed contraception, and for "wrongful birth" and "wrongful life," in cases of negligence which deprives parents of information relevant to abortion of a deformed or impaired fetus. Injuries to unborn children are often accompanied by physical harm to the mother or emotional harm to both parents: these claims will also be discussed.

In considering the cases that follow, it is important to pay close attention to:

(1) who is suing (is the action brought on behalf of the child or by the parents on their own behalf?);

(2) what damages the plaintiffs seek (*e.g.*, costs of medical care, compensation for mental suffering, or costs of rearing an unwanted child); and

(3) whether the defendant is alleged to have affirmatively inflicted harm on the child (*e.g.*, by causing a collision with a pregnant woman's vehicle) or deprived the parents of their right not to have children (*e.g.*, through non-disclosure of information relevant to an abortion decision).

Once these matters are clear, it is possible to locate a given set of facts within one or more of the actions dealing with unborn children.

A. Unwanted Pregnancy

McKernan v. Aasheim

Supreme Court of Washington, En Banc
687 P.2d 850 (Wash. 1984)

DIMMICK, Justice.

....

On March 7, 1980, Dr. Glen Aasheim performed a sterilization operation known as a tubal ligation upon Karen McKernan. Despite the operation, Karen became pregnant and gave birth to a healthy, normal child. In February 1983, Karen and her husband

James McKernan filed the present lawsuit, alleging [in part] that Dr. Aasheim performed the tubal ligation negligently.... They alleged the following damages:

> an amount equal to the cost of the tubal ligation procedure, and expenses; an amount equal to the cost of the pregnancy and child birth; an amount for pain and suffering associated with the tubal ligation, pregnancy and child birth; an amount for loss of pleasure associated with the tubal ligation, pregnancy and child birth; an amount for the husband's loss of services and consortium associated with the tubal ligation, pregnancy and child birth; *an amount equal to the costs associated with rearing a child, college education, out of pocket expenses and services of parents, and emotional burdens.*

(Italics ours.)

Dr. Aasheim moved for partial summary judgment dismissing that portion of the McKernans' complaint which sought damages for the cost of rearing and educating a normal, healthy child. The trial court granted the motion....

> ....

Turning to cases from other jurisdictions, we discover the vast majority of courts have held that no damages may be recovered for the cost of rearing and educating a healthy, normal child born as the result of medical malpractice. [Citations.]

These courts have denied recovery of child-rearing costs for a variety of reasons. Many hold that the benefits of joy, companionship, and affection which a healthy child can provide outweigh the costs of rearing that child. [Citations.] This view was well expressed in Public Health Trust v. Brown, [388 So. 2d 1084, 1085-86 (Fla. Dist. Ct. App. 1980)]:

> ... [A] parent cannot be said to have been damaged by the birth and rearing of a normal, healthy child... [I]t is a matter of universally-shared emotion and sentiment that the intangible but all-important, incalculable but invaluable "benefits" of parenthood far outweigh any of the mere monetary burdens involved. Speaking legally, this may be deemed conclusively presumed by the fact that a prospective parent does not abort or subsequently place the "unwanted" child for adoption. On a more practical level, the validity of the principle may be tested simply by asking any parent the purchase price for that particular youngster....

Another common rationale is that recovery of child-rearing costs would be a windfall to the parents and an unreasonable burden on the negligent health care provider. [Citations.] The Wisconsin Supreme Court put it this way:

> To permit the parents to keep their child and shift the entire cost of its upbringing to a physician who failed to determine or inform them of the fact of pregnancy would be to create a new category of surrogate parent. Every child's smile, every bond of love and affection, every reason for parental pride in a child's achievements, every contribution by the child to the welfare and well-being of the family and parents, is to remain with the mother and father.... On the other hand, every financial cost or detriment—what the complaint terms "hard money damages"—including the costs of food, clothing and education, would be shifted to the physician who allegedly failed to timely diagnose the fact of pregnancy. We hold that such result would be wholly out of proportion to the culpability involved....

....Rieck v. Medical Protective Co., *supra* 64 Wis. 2d 514, 518-519, 219 N.W.2d 242 (1974).

Still other courts have denied recovery in order to protect the psyche of the child who is the subject of the action:

> Another problem is the possible harm that can be caused to the unwanted child who will one day learn that he not only was not wanted by his or her parents, but was reared by funds supplied by another person. Some authors have referred to such a child as an "emotional bastard" in a realistic, but harsh, attempt to describe the stigma that will attach to him once he learns the true circumstances of his upbringing.

Boone v. Mullendore, *supra* [416 So. 2d 718, 722 (Ala. 1982)]. [Citation.]

Other reasons for denying recovery of child-rearing costs include the speculative nature of the damages, [citation], and the possibility of fraudulent claims. [Citation.]

A minority line of authority permits recovery of the costs of rearing and educating a healthy, normal child. However, only Ohio currently permits full recovery. Bowman v. Davis, 48 Ohio St. 2d 41, 356 N.E.2d 496 (1976). Other courts allow the parents' damage award to be reduced by the value of the benefits conferred by the parent-child relationship....

Courts adopting the "benefits" rule reject the majority rationale that a healthy, normal child is always more benefit than burden. To hold that the birth of a child can never be an injury, they reason, ignores the fact that millions of persons utilize contraceptive devices and methods for the very purpose of avoiding the birth of a child. [Citations.] Moreover, they note, an individual has a constitutional right to use contraceptive devices and methods to limit the size of his or her family. [Citations.] Complete denial of child-rearing costs on the theory that the birth of a healthy, normal child can never be an injury would, therefore, impair the parents' constitutional right to forego reproduction. [Citation.]

Another rationale for allowing recovery of child-rearing costs is the perceived need to apply strictly that rule of tort law which holds a tortfeasor liable for all damages which he caused. [Citation.] At the same time, however, those courts which have adopted the "benefits" rule have refused to apply the avoidable consequences doctrine, holding that both abortion and adoption are unreasonable means of avoiding or minimizing child-rearing damages, as a matter of law. [Citations.] *But cf.* Sorkin v. Lee, *supra* 78 A.D. 2d at 181-82 (denying child-rearing costs where parents failed to mitigate damages by obtaining abortion).

To recover under the "benefits" rule, the parents of the unplanned child must prove to the jury that the cost of rearing the child outweighs the benefits of parenthood....

We find some of the above cited reasons for denying recovery of child-rearing costs unpersuasive. To being with, we cannot agree that the benefits of parenthood always outweigh the costs of rearing a child. [Citation.] If such were the case, presumably no sterilization operations would be performed. Second, we do not think that recovery may be denied in order to avoid placing an "unreasonable" burden upon health care providers. [Citation.] It is not our place to deny recovery of certain damages merely in order to insulate health care providers from the shock of big tort judgments. Third, the possibility that some parents might bring fraudulent claims is not a sufficient basis for denying recovery. [Citation.] We will not presuppose that courts are so ineffectual and the jury system so imperfect that fraudulent claims cannot be distinguished from the legitimate. [Citation.]

Nevertheless, we are convinced that recovery of child-rearing costs must be denied on other grounds.... [W]hen a parent comes before a court alleging that he or she was damaged by the unplanned birth of a child, the only logical method of determining whether such damage has occurred would be to weigh child-rearing costs against the benefits of parenthood. This, of course, is what the "benefits" rule purports to do.

After careful consideration, however, we have come to the conclusion that the "benefits" rule cannot be applied in this state. Under Washington law, damages may not be recovered unless they are established with reasonable certainty. [Citation.] Uncertainty as to the fact of damage is a ground for denying liability.... Perhaps the costs of rearing and educating the child could be determined through use of actuarial tables or similar economic information. But whether these costs are outweighed by the emotional benefits which will be conferred by that child cannot be calculated. The child may turn out to be loving, obedient and attentive, or hostile, unruly and callous. The child may grow up to be President of the United States, or to be an infamous criminal. In short, it is impossible to tell, at an early stage in the child's life, whether its parents have sustained a net loss or net gain.

....

We base our holding that child-rearing costs may not be recovered on yet another ground. Under the "benefits" rule, parents would be obliged to prove their child was more trouble than it was worth. As one court noted:

> an unhandsome, colicky, or otherwise "undesirable" child would provide fewer offsetting benefits, and would therefore presumably be worth more monetarily in a "wrongful birth" case. The adoption of that rule would thus engender the unseemly spectacle of parents disparaging the "value" of their children or the degree of their affection for them in open court.... [S]uch a result cannot be countenanced.

[Citation.]

Moreover, even if the "benefits" rule were not applied, and parents allowed to sue for the full cost of rearing their unplanned child, the simple fact that the parents saw fit to allege their child as a "damage" to them would carry with it the possibility of emotional harm to the child. We are not willing to sweep this ugly possibility under the rug by stating that the parents must be the one to decide whether to risk the emotional well being of their unplanned child. [Citation.] We therefore hold that to permit recovery of child-rearing costs would violate the public policy of this state. In so holding, we adopt the reasoning of the Arkansas Supreme Court:

> .... Litigation cannot answer every question; every question cannot be answered in terms of dollars and cents. We are also convinced that the damage to the child will be significant; that being an unwanted or "emotional bastard," who will some day learn that its parents did not want it and, in fact, went to court to force someone else to pay for its raising, will be harmful to that child. It will undermine society's need for a strong and healthy family relationship. We have not become so sophisticated a society to dismiss that emotional trauma as nonsense.

Wilbur v. Kerr, 275 Ark. 239, 243-44, 628 S.W.2d 568 (1982).

We have held that child-rearing costs cannot be recovered. This does not mean, however, that health care providers are immunized from all liability resulting from unsuccessful sterilization operations. The McKernans have alleged damages for the expense, pain and suffering, and loss of consortium associated with the failed tubal ligation, pregnancy and childbirth. Dr. Aasheim has conceded in his brief that these damages, if proven, may be recovered. The authorities are in accord. *See* Annot., *Tort Liability for Wrongfully Causing One to be Born*, 83 A.L.R.3d 15, 29-30 (1978). We find that these damages may be established with reasonable certainty, and do not invite disparagement of the child involved. Therefore, we agree that they may be recovered if proven.

Affirmed.

Notes

1. Cases like *McKernan*, in which the child is born healthy, are often called "unwanted pregnancy," "wrongful conception," or "wrongful pregnancy" cases.

2. *Child-Rearing Costs.* Courts remain deeply divided over whether child-rearing costs may be recovered in an unwanted-pregnancy case. In Chaffee v. Seslar, 751 N.E.2d 773, 780 nn.7-9 (Ind. Ct. App. 2001), *rev'd* 786 N.E.2d 705 (Ind. 2003), the intermediate appellate court summarized the state of the law as follows:

> Four jurisdictions adhere to the full recovery rule. *See generally* Custodio v. Bauer, 251 Cal. App.2d 303, 59 Cal. Rptr. 463 (Cal. Ct. App. 1967); Lovelace Med. Ctr. v. Mendez, 111 N.M. 336, 805 P.2d 603 (1991); Zehr v. Haugen, 318 Or. 647, 871 P.2d 1006 (1994); Marciniak v. Lundborg, 153 Wis. 2d 59, 450 N.W.2d 243 (1990)....
>
> Five jurisdictions subscribe to the benefits rule. *See generally* University of Ariz. Health Scis. Ctr. v. Superior Ct., 136 Ariz. 579, 667 P.2d 1294 (1983); Ochs v. Borrelli, 187 Conn. 253, 445 A.2d 883 (1982); Jones v. Malinowski, 299 Md. 257, 473 A.2d 429 (1984); Burke v. Rivo, 406 Mass. 764, 551 N.E.2d 1 (1990); Sherlock v. Stillwater Clinic, 260 N.W.2d 169 (Minn. 1977).
>
> Thirty-one jurisdictions subscribe to the no recovery rule regarding child-rearing expenses, limiting recovery to pregnancy and child-bearing expenses. [Citations to cases from Alabama, Alaska, Arkansas, Delaware, District of Columbia, Florida, Georgia, Illinois, Iowa, Kansas, Kentucky, Louisiana, Maine, Michigan, Missouri, Nebraska, New Hampshire, New Jersey, New York, North Carolina, Ohio, Oklahoma, Pennsylvania, Rhode Island, Tennessee, Texas, Utah, Virginia, Washington, West Virginia, Wyoming.]

In *Chaffee*, the Indiana Supreme Court held that recoverable damages in connection with allegedly negligent sterilization may not include the ordinary costs of raising and educating a normal, healthy child.

Some recent holdings are completely at odds with one another. *Compare* Emercon v. Magendantz, 689 A.2d 409 (R.I. 1997) (if a child suffers from congenital defects, the parents may recover special medical and educational expenses beyond normal child-rearing costs, as well as damages for emotional distress), *with* Williams v. Univ. of Chicago Hosp., 688 N.E.2d 130 (Ill. 1997) (birth of child with a congenital disorder was not a foreseeable consequence of a negligently performed sterilization procedure, and thus the parents may not recover damages for the extraordinary expenses of raising the child).

3. A case can be made for allowing child-rearing costs in some cases, but not others, depending on the parents' reason for not wanting to have another child. Suppose, for instance, that a couple decides on sterilization because they fear that pregnancy would endanger the mother's health or carry a heavy risk that the child will be born with a genetic abnormality. If the sterilization fails, but mother and child do well, the couple

may regard the doctor's error as a blessing. If, by contrast, a couple decides against additional children for financial reasons, a stronger case for a measure of damages that includes the costs of raising the child may be presented. *See* Hartke v. McKelway, 707 F.2d 1544 (D.C. Cir. 1983). Should (or could) courts further refine the distinction by allowing child-rearing costs when the parents' "financial" reason for not wanting more children was concern for their ability to provide for their first several children, but denying that kind of recovery when the parents aim was to spend their money on themselves?

4. *See also* Miceli v. Ansell, Inc., 23 F. Supp. 2d 929 (N.D. Ind. 1998). In a suit by condom users against a condom manufacturer, alleging strict liability, negligence, and breach of warranty in connection with unwanted pregnancy, the court, addressing an issue of apparent first impression, held that pregnancy may constitute a "harm" for purposes of Indiana's products liability statute.

5. *Deception Regarding Paternity.* Questions regarding damages can arise in a case where a former wife misrepresents to her former husband that he is the biological father of her child. In Day v. Heller, 653 N.W.2d 475 (Neb. 2002), the court held that public policy barred a former husband's claims for fraud, restitution, and intentional infliction of emotional distress. In part, the court wrote:

> In effect, Robert is saying, "[Adam]...is not my son; I want my money back." Robert's fraud and assumpsit causes of action focus on the burdens of the parent-child relationship, while ignoring the benefits of the relationship. We do not believe that having a close and loving relationship "imposed" on one because of a misrepresentation of biological fatherhood is the type of "harm" that the law should attempt to remedy.

In addressing the intentional-infliction claim, which it rejected, the court noted that "other courts have reached conflicting conclusions...."

B. Wrongful Birth and Wrongful Life

Smith v. Cote

Supreme Court of New Hampshire
513 A.2d 341 (N.H. 1986)

BATCHELDER, Justice.

....

....Plaintiff Linda J. Smith became pregnant early in 1979. During the course of her pregnancy Linda was under the care of the defendants, physicians who specialize in obstetrics and gynecology....

....

Linda brought her pregnancy to full term. On January 1, 1980, she gave birth to a daughter, Heather B. Smith, who is also a plaintiff in this action. Heather was born a victim of congenital rubella syndrome. Today, at age six, Heather suffers from bilateral cataracts, multiple congenital heart defects, motor retardation, and a significant hearing impairment. She is legally blind, and has undergone surgery for her cataracts and heart condition.

In March 1984 the plaintiffs began this negligence action. They allege that Linda contracted rubella early in her pregnancy and that, while she was under the defendants' care, the defendants negligently failed to test for and discover in a timely manner her exposure to the disease. The plaintiffs further contend that the defendants negligently failed to advise Linda of the potential for birth defects in a fetus exposed to rubella, thereby depriving her of the knowledge necessary to an informed decision as to whether to give birth to a potentially impaired child....

The plaintiffs do not allege that the defendants caused Linda to conceive her child or to contract rubella, or that the defendants could have prevented the effects of the disease on the fetus. Rather, the plaintiffs contend that if Linda had known of the risks involved she would have obtained a eugenic abortion.

....

We recognize that the termination of pregnancy involves controversial and divisive social issues. Nonetheless, the Supreme Court of the United States has held that a woman has a constitutionally secured right to terminate a pregnancy. Roe v. Wade, [410 U.S. 113 (1973)].... Today we decide only whether, given the existence of the right of choice recognized in *Roe*, our common law should allow the development of a duty to exercise care in providing information that bears on that choice.

For the sake of terminological clarity, we make some preliminary distinctions. A wrongful birth claim is a claim brought by the parents of a child born with severe defects against a physician who negligently fails to inform them, in a timely fashion, of an increased possibility that the mother will give birth to such a child, thereby precluding an informed decision as to whether to have the child. *See* Phillips v. United States, 508 F. Supp. 544, 545 n. 1 (D.S.C. 1981). The parents typically claim damages for their emotional distress and for some or all of the costs of raising the child. *Id.* We regard Count I of the plaintiffs' writ as alleging a claim for wrongful birth.

A wrongful life claim, on the other hand, is brought not by the parents of a child born with birth defects, but by or on behalf of the child. The child contends that the defendant physician negligently failed to inform the child's parents of the risk of bearing a defective infant, and hence prevented the parents from choosing to avoid the child's birth. Phillips v. United States, 508 F. Supp. 537, 538 n. 1 (D.S.C. 1980). The child typically claims damages for the extraordinary medical, educational, and institutional costs that it will sustain. We regard Count III of the plaintiffs' writ as a claim for wrongful life.

I. Wrongful Birth: Cause of Action

We first must decide whether New Hampshire law recognizes a cause of action for wrongful birth. Although we have never expressly recognized this cause of action, we have considered a similar claim, one for "wrongful conception." In Kingsbury v. Smith, 122 N.H. 237, 442 A.2d 1003 (1982)...[w]e held that the common law of New Hampshire permitted a claim for wrongful conception, an action "for damages arising from the birth of a child to which a negligently performed sterilization procedure or a negligently filled birth control prescription which fails to prevent conception was a contributing factor." [Citation.] We reasoned that failure to recognize a cause of action for wrongful conception would leave "a void in the area of recovery for medical malpractice" that would dilute the standard of professional conduct in the area of family planning. [Citation.]

In this case, the mother contends that her wrongful birth claim fits comfortably within the framework established in *Kingsbury* and is consistent with well established tort principles. The defendants argue that tort principles cannot be extended so as to accommodate wrongful birth, asserting that they did not cause the injury alleged here, and that in any case damages cannot be fairly and accurately ascertained.

The action for wrongful birth occupies a relatively recent place in the history of tort law. Gleitman v. Cosgrove, 49 N.J. 22, 227 A.2d 689 (1967), is the "fountainhead" for debate in cases of this type. [Citation.] Like the instant case, *Gleitman* involved claims for wrongful birth and wrongful life arising out of the birth of a child suffering from congenital rubella syndrome. The plaintiff mother, who had contracted rubella early in her pregnancy, alleged that the defendant physicians had failed to inform her that the disease might affect her child, and that had she been so informed she would have undergone an abortion.

The trial judge dismissed both the wrongful life and the wrongful birth complaints, and the Supreme Court of New Jersey affirmed. The court first disposed of the child's wrongful life claim, holding that the conduct complained of did not give rise to damages cognizable at law. The court explained that it was legally impossible to weigh "the value of life with impairments against the nonexistence of life itself." [Citation.] Turning to the parents' wrongful birth claim, the court emphasized the analytical difficulty posed by the dual character of the consequences of the defendants' alleged negligence. On the one hand, the defendants arguably had caused the plaintiffs to incur child rearing costs and to undergo emotional distress. On the other, the birth of the child had conferred the intangible benefits of parenthood on the plaintiffs. The court found that this difficulty made it impossible to determine compensatory damages. [Citation.]

The *Gleitman* court also was troubled by the policy implications of recognizing a cause of action for wrongful birth. According to the court, the parents' complaint sought damages for "the denial of the opportunity to take an embryonic life." [Citation.] The court reasoned that to allow such a claim would be to deny the "sanctity of the single human life," *id.*, and that the child's right to live exceeded and precluded the parents' right not to endure financial and emotional injury. [Citation.] The court concluded that the wrongful birth complaint was not actionable because the defendants' conduct did not give rise to damages cognizable at law, and that, even if such damages were cognizable, the "countervailing public policy supporting the preciousness of human life" precluded the claim. *Id.*

Gleitman's influence in wrongful birth cases has considerably diminished during the past two decades. The highest courts of Texas, *see* Jacobs v. Theimer, 519 S.W.2d 846 (Tex. 1975), and Wisconsin, *see* Dumer v. St. Michael's Hospital, 69 Wis. 2d 766, 233 N.W.2d 372 (1975), recognized wrongful birth causes of action in 1975, and three years later the Court of Appeals of New York followed suit. *See* Becker v. Schwartz, 46 N.Y.2d 401, 386 N.E.2d 807, 413 N.Y.S.2d 895 (1978). In 1979 the Supreme Court of New Jersey overruled *Gleitman* on the issue of wrongful birth. *See* Berman v. Allan, 80 N.J. 421, 404 A.2d 8 (1979). Today there is "quite general agreement" that some recovery should be permitted in wrongful birth cases....

Two developments help explain the trend toward judicial acceptance of wrongful birth actions. The first is the increased ability of health care professionals to predict and detect the presence of fetal defects. Science's improved capacity to assess risk factors in pregnant women, as well as the development of "sophisticated biochemical and cytogenic tests for assaying amniotic fluid and maternal and fetal blood," have greatly enhanced the importance of reproductive counseling....

Roe v. Wade, 410 U.S. 113, 93 S. Ct. 705, 35 L. Ed. 2d 147 (1973), and its progeny constitute the second development explaining the acceptance of wrongful birth actions.

[Citation.] In *Roe* the Supreme Court held that the constitutional right of privacy encompasses a woman's decision whether to undergo an abortion. [Citation.] During the first trimester of her pregnancy, a woman may make this decision as she sees fit, free from State interference....[W]e believe that *Roe* is controlling; we do not hold that our decision would be the same in its absence.

....Today, as a result of *Roe* and the advances of science, it is possible for prospective parents (1) to know, well in advance of birth, of the risk or presence of congenital defects in the fetus they have conceived; and (2) to decide to terminate the pregnancy on the basis of this knowledge....

With this background in mind, we turn to the first issue before us: whether New Hampshire recognizes a cause of action for wrongful birth....

The first two elements of a negligence action, duty and breach, present no conceptual difficulties here. If the plaintiff establishes that a physician-patient relationship with respect to the pregnancy existed between the defendants and her, it follows that the defendants assumed a duty to use reasonable care in attending and treating her. [Citation.] Given the decision in Roe v. Wade, we recognize that the "due care" standard, *see* RSA 508:13, may have required the defendants to ensure that Linda had an opportunity to make an informed decision regarding the procreative options available to her....It is a question of fact whether this standard required the defendants, at an appropriate stage of Linda's pregnancy, to test for, diagnose, and disclose her exposure to rubella....If (1) the applicable standard of care required the defendants to test for and diagnose Linda's rubella infection in a timely manner, and to inform her of the possible effects of the virus on her child's health; and (2) the defendants failed to fulfill this obligation; then the defendants breached their duty of due care.

The third element [of a negligence action], causation, is only slightly more troublesome. The defendants point out that proof that they caused the alleged injury depends on a finding that Linda would have chosen to terminate her pregnancy if she had been fully apprised of the risks of birth defects. The defendants argue that this hypothetical chain of events is too remote to provide the basis for a finding of causation.

We do not agree. No logical obstacle precludes proof of causation in the instant case. Such proof is furnished if the plaintiff can show that, but for the defendants' negligent failure to inform her of the risks of bearing a child with birth defects, she would have obtained an abortion....*See* McPherson v. Ellis, 305 N.C. 266, 272-73, 287 S.E.2d 892, 896-97 (1982) (jury in informed consent case may consider plaintiffs' testimony as to what her decision would have been had she been properly informed of risks of operation).

We turn to the final element of a negligence action, injury....

....

The defendants' emphasis on the inherent difficulty of measuring damages is misplaced. An allegation of "injury," an instance of actionable harm, is distinct from a claim for "damages," a sum of money awarded to one who has suffered an injury. We have long held that difficulty in calculating damages is not a sufficient reason to deny recovery to an injured party. [Citation.] Other courts have recognized that the complexity of the damages calculation in a wrongful birth case is not directly relevant to the validity of the asserted cause of action. [Citation.]

We hold that New Hampshire recognizes a cause of action for wrongful birth. Notwithstanding the disparate views within society on the controversial practice of abortion, we are bound by the law that protects a woman's right to choose to terminate

her pregnancy. Our holding today neither encourages nor discourages this practice....
We must...do our best to effectuate the first principles of our law of negligence: to
deter negligent conduct, and to compensate the victims of those who act unreasonably.

II. Wrongful Birth: Damages

We next must decide what elements of damages may be recovered in a wrongful
birth action....

    ....

A. Tangible Losses

The usual rule of compensatory damages in tort cases requires that the person
wronged receive a sum of money that will restore him as nearly as possible to the position he would have been in if the wrong had not been committed. [Citation.] In the
present case, if the defendants' failure to advise Linda of the risks of birth defects
amounted to negligence, then the reasonably foreseeable result of that negligence was
that Linda would incur the expenses involved in raising her daughter. According to the
usual rule of damages, then, Linda should recover the entire cost of raising Heather, including both ordinary child-rearing costs and the extraordinary costs attributable to
Heather's condition.

However, "few if any jurisdictions appear ready to apply this traditional rule of damages with full vigor in wrongful birth cases." [Citation.] Although at least one court has
ruled that all child-rearing costs should be recoverable, Robak v. United States, 658 F.2d
471, 478-79 (7th Cir. 1981), most courts are reluctant to impose liability to this extent.
A special rule of damages has emerged; in most jurisdictions the parents may recover
only the extraordinary medical and educational costs attributable to the birth defects.
[Citation.] In the present case, in accordance with the rule prevailing elsewhere, Linda
seeks to recover, as tangible losses, only her extraordinary costs.

The logic of the "extraordinary costs" rule has been criticized. [Citation.] The rule in
effect divides a plaintiff's pecuniary losses into two categories, ordinary costs and extraordinary costs, and treats the latter category as compensable while ignoring the former
category. At first glance, this bifurcation seems difficult to justify.

The disparity is explained, however, by reference to the rule requiring mitigation of
tort damages. The "avoidable consequences" rule, Restatement (Second) of Torts §918
(1979), specifies that a plaintiff may not recover damages for "any harm that he could
have avoided by the use of reasonable effort or expenditure" after the occurrence of the
tort. Rigidly applied, this rule would appear to require wrongful birth plaintiffs to place
their children for adoption. [Citation.] Because of our profound respect for the sanctity
of the family, [citation], we are loathe to sanction the application of the rule in these
circumstances. If the rule is not applied, however, wrongful birth plaintiffs may receive
windfalls. Hence, a special rule limiting recovery of damages is warranted.

Although the extraordinary costs rule departs from traditional principles of tort
damages, it is neither illogical nor unprecedented. The rule represents an application in
a tort context of the expectancy rule of damages employed in breach of contracts cases.
Wrongful birth plaintiffs typically desire a child (and plan to support it) from the outset. [Citation.] It is the defendants' duty to help them achieve this goal. When the plaintiffs' expectations are frustrated by the defendants' negligence, the extraordinary costs
rule "merely attempts to put plaintiffs in the position they *expected* to be in with defendant's help." [Citation.]....

....Accordingly, we hold that a plaintiff in a wrongful birth case may recover the extraordinary medical and educational costs attributable to the child's deformities, but may not recover ordinary child-raising costs.

Three points stand in need of clarification. First, parents may recover extraordinary costs incurred both before and after their child attains majority. Some courts do not permit recovery of postmajority expenses, on the theory that the parents' obligation of support terminates when the child reaches twenty-one. [Citation.] In New Hampshire, however, parents are required to support their disabled adult offspring. [Citation.]

Second, recovery should include compensation for the extraordinary maternal care that has been and will be provided to the child. Linda alleges that her parental obligations and duties, which include feeding, bathing, and exercising Heather, substantially exceed those of parents of a normal child. One court has ruled that parents "cannot recover for services that they have rendered or will render personally to their own child without incurring financial expense." [Citation.] We see no reason, however, to treat as noncompensable the burdens imposed on a parent who must devote extraordinary time and effort to caring for a child with birth defects....We hold that a parent may recover for his or her ministrations to his or her child to the extent that such ministrations:

(1) are made necessary by the child's condition;

(2) clearly exceed those ordinarily rendered by parents of a normal child; and

(3) are reasonably susceptible of valuation....

Third, to the extent that the parent's alleged emotional distress results in tangible pecuniary losses, such as medical expenses or counseling fees, such losses are recoverable. [Citations.]

B. Intangible Losses

Existing damages principles do not resolve the issue whether recovery for emotional distress should be permitted in wrongful birth cases. Emotional distress damages are not uniformly recoverable once a protected interest is shown to have been invaded. *Compare* Holyoke v. Grand Trunk Ry., 48 N.H. 541, 545 (1869) (plaintiff may recover for actual mental suffering in personal injury case) *with* Crowley v. Global Realty, Inc., 124 N.H. 814, 818, 474 A.2d 1056, 1058 (1984) (plaintiffs cannot recover for emotional distress in claim for negligent misrepresentation).

....

[The court discussed cases which illustrated judicial]...reluctance to permit parents of children injured or killed as a result of negligent conduct to recover for their consequent emotional distress. [Citation.] This reluctance does not stem from uncertainties about the causal relation between the negligent conduct at issue and a parent's distress, or from a failure to appreciate the intensity of the sorrow and anguish that a parent experiences when her child suffers harm. [The cases]...were founded, instead, on a practical consideration: the need to establish a clearly defined limit to the scope of negligence liability in this area. "Every injury has ramifying consequences, like the ripplings of the waters, without end. The problem for the law is to limit the legal consequences of wrongs to a controllable degree."....

....

We also harbor concerns of proportionality....We already have held that a wrongful birth defendant is liable for the pecuniary losses incurred by the parents. Were we additionally to impose liability for parents' emotional distress, we would run the risk of penalizing and overdeterring merely negligent conduct.

We hold that damages for emotional distress are not recoverable in wrongful birth actions. [Citation.]

III. Wrongful Life

The theory of Heather's wrongful life action is as follows: during Linda's pregnancy the defendants owed a duty of care to both Linda and Heather. The defendants breached this duty when they failed to discover Linda's exposure to rubella and failed to advise her of the possible effects of that exposure on her child's health. Had Linda been properly informed, she would have undergone an abortion, and Heather would not have been born. Because Linda was not so informed, Heather must bear the burden of her afflictions for the rest of her life. The defendant's conduct is thus the proximate cause of injury to Heather.

This theory presents a crucial problem, however: the question of injury. It is axiomatic that there is no cause of action for negligence unless and until there has been an injury. [Citation.]....In the present case Heather claims to have had an interest in avoiding "the lifetime of suffering inflicted on [her] by [her] condition." [Citation.] In order to recognize Heather's wrongful life action, then, we must determine that the fetal Heather had an interest in avoiding her own birth, that it would have been best *for Heather* if she had not been born.

This premise of the wrongful life action—that the plaintiff's own birth and suffering constitute legal injury—has caused many courts to decline to recognize the claim. [Citation.] According to the Supreme Court of Texas, the perplexities involved in comparing the relative benefits of life and nonexistence render it "impossible" to decide the question of injury. [Citation.] The notion that nonexistence may be preferable to life with severe birth defects appears to contravene the policy favoring "the preciousness and sanctity of human life." [Citation.] As one court has written,

> [w]hether it is better never to have been born at all than to have been born with even gross deficiencies is a mystery more properly to be left to the philosophers and the theologians. Surely the law can assert no competence to resolve the issue, particularly in view of the very nearly uniform high value which the law and mankind has placed on human life, rather than its absence.

[Citation.]

Moreover, compelling policy reasons militate against recognition of wrongful life claims. The first such reason is our conviction that the courts of this State should not become involved in deciding whether a given person's life is or is not worthwhile. As one commentator has written, "[i]f plaintiff prevails, the result is a formal judicial declaration that it would have been better if plaintiff had not been born." [Citation.] The right to life, and the principle that all are equal under the law, are basic to our constitutional order. N.H. Const. pt. I, arts. 1, 2. To presume to decide that Heather's life is not worth living would be to forsake these ideals.

Our reluctance to decide whether Heather's birth constitutes an injury is not diminished by the evolving "right to die" doctrine. [Citation.] In a right to die case a court may act to protect an individual's right to choose between a natural death and the prolongation of his life by means of extraordinary medical procedures. The court avoids making an objective judgment as to the value of the plaintiff's life; it strives, instead, to protect the individual's subjective will....

The same cannot be said of wrongful life cases....Simply put, the judiciary has an important role to play in protecting the privacy rights of the dying. It has no business declaring that among the living are people who never should have been born.

The second policy reason militating against recognition of Heather's claim is related to the first.

> [L]egal recognition that a disabled life is an injury would harm the interests of those most directly concerned, the handicapped. Disabled persons face obvious physical difficulties in conducting their lives. They also face subtle yet equally devastating handicaps in the attitudes and behavior of society, the law, and their own families and friends. Furthermore, society often views disabled persons as burdensome misfits. Recent legislation concerning employment, education, and building access reflects a slow change in these attitudes. This change evidences a growing public awareness that the handicapped can be valuable and productive members of society. To characterize the life of a disabled person as an injury would denigrate both this new awareness and the handicapped themselves.

[Citation.]

The third reason stems from an acknowledgment of the limitations of tort law and the adjudicative process. Wrongful life actions are premised on the ability of judges and juries accurately to apply the traditional tort concept of injury to situations involving complex medical and bioethical issues. Yet this concept applies only roughly.... In wrongful life cases, however, the finding of injury necessarily hinges upon subjective and intensely personal notions as to the intangible value of life. [Citation.] The danger of markedly disparate and, hence, unpredictable outcomes is manifest.

In deciding whether to recognize a new tort cause of action, we must consider the "defendant's interest in avoiding an incorrect judgment of liability because of the court's incompetence to determine certain questions raised by application of the announced standard." [Citation.] Wrongful life claims present problems that cannot be resolved in a "reasonably sensible, even-handed, and fair" manner from case to case. [Citation.] As Chief Justice Weintraub of the Supreme Court of New Jersey recognized nearly twenty years ago, "[t]o recognize a right not to be born is to enter an area in which no one could find his way." [Citation.]

. . . .

We decline to recognize a cause of action for wrongful life.

. . . .

Remanded.

KING, C.J., did not sit; SOUTER, J., concurred specially; the others concurred.

SOUTER, Justice, concurring:

. . . . The trial court did not ask whether, or how, a physician with conscientious scruples against abortion, and the testing and counselling that may inform an abortion decision, can discharge his professional obligation without engaging in procedures that his religious or moral principles condemn. To say nothing about this issue could lead to misunderstanding.

. . . .

...I do not understand the court to hold, that a physician can discharge the obligation of due care in such circumstances only by personally ordering such tests and rendering such advice. The court does not hold that some or all physicians must make a choice between rendering services that they morally condemn and leaving their profession in order to escape malpractice exposure. The defensive significance, for example, of timely disclosure of professional limits based on religious or moral scruples, combined with timely referral to other physicians who are not so constrained, is a question open for consideration in any case in which it may be raised. [Citations.]

Notes

1. *Terminology.* The distinction between the child's claim and the parents' claim is well established, though not all writers are as careful as the *Smith* court in giving these actions the distinct but misleadingly similar names of "wrongful life" and "wrongful birth."

Some courts have rejected the term "wrongful birth" and treat such claims as just another form of medical malpractice. *See* Bader v. Johnson, 732 N.E.2d 1212 (Ind. 2000). In *Bader*, a physician had failed to inform parents of the results of an ultrasound test that revealed that a fetus would be born with serious birth defects. The court held that the parents stated a cause of action for medical malpractice based on loss of the opportunity and ability to terminate the pregnancy. The court held that the parents could recover (1) hospital and related medical expenses associated with the pregnancy and delivery, (2) costs associated with providing the infant with care and treatment until the child's death at four months of age, (3) lost income, and (4) loss of consortium. However, under Indiana's modified "impact rule," only the mother was permitted to recover emotional-distress damages; the "continued pregnancy and the physical transformation...[the mother's] body underwent" satisfied the "direct impact requirement." The father was "at most...a relative bystander," and therefore not allowed to recover for his emotional distress.

2. *Wrongful Birth.* In wrongful-birth cases, courts often differ as to the elements of damages that may be recovered. *See* Greco v. United States, 893 P.2d 345 (Nev. 1995) (allowing recovery of damages for future extraordinary medical, therapeutic, and custodial costs associated with the child and for emotional damages, but not for loss of companionship); Arche v. United States, 798 P.2d 477 (Kan. 1990) (limiting damages to those costs that would not be incurred but for the child's disability during the child's life expectancy or until the child reaches the age of majority, whichever period is shorter); Keel v. Banach, 624 So. 2d 1022 (Ala. 1993) (defining compensable losses to include any medical and hospital expenses incurred as a result of the physician's negligence, physical pain suffered by the mother, loss of consortium, and mental and emotional anguish of the parents). *But see* Atlanta Obstetrics & Gynecology Group v. Abelson, 398 S.E.2d 557 (Ga. 1990) (declining to recognize an action for "wrongful birth" absent a clear mandate from the legislature).

3. *Causation in Wrongful Birth Cases.* In Provenzano v. Integrated Genetics, 22 F. Supp. 2d 406 (D.N.J. 1998), the court took a different approach in dealing with the causation requirement. It held that under New Jersey law, the issue of proximate causation in wrongful birth cases does not conclusively depend upon whether the

parents would have aborted a fetus with a birth defect, had they been advised of their option to do so. Rather, proximate cause may be established by evidence demonstrating that the defendant's negligence deprived the parents of their right to accept or reject a parental relationship. Could this approach be endorsed by a jurisdiction which has rejected the loss-of-a-chance rule in medical malpractice cases? *See* Chapter 7.

4. *Wrongful Life.* In Kassama v. Magat, 792 A.2d 1102, 1116-17 (Md. 2002), the court refused to permit a wrongful life claim and summarized the law in other jurisdictions as follows:

> It appears, at this point, that 28 States deny recovery for this kind of action— 18 by case law, 10 by statute—but that three, California, New Jersey, and Washington, provide for a limited recovery.

5. *Relationship to Medical Malpractice.* Can casting an action as one for medical malpractice, rather than wrongful birth and wrongful life, surmount obstacles to recovery? Perhaps.

In Shelton v. St. Anthony's Med. Ctr., 781 S.W.2d 48 (Mo. 1989), a woman alleged that she suffered loss of consortium, loss of the right to lead a normal life, and emotional distress as a result of the defendants' negligent failure to advise her that her fetus had congenital defects, thus denying her the right to choose to have an abortion. The Supreme Court of Missouri held that the allegations stated a cause of action for medical malpractice based on the defendants' failure to enable the plaintiff to exercise informed consent with respect to treatment, despite a state statute barring an action for wrongful birth by providing that "[n]o person shall maintain a cause of action or receive an award of damages based on a claim that but for the negligent conduct of another, a child would have been aborted." The alleged harm, the court found, was attributable to the defendants' negligence, regardless of whether plaintiff would have had an abortion.

However, in Paretta v. Medical Officers for Human Reproduction, 760 N.Y.S.2d 639 (Sup. Ct. 2003), recovery was denied. *Paretta* was a medical malpractice action alleging that a physician who performed in-vitro fertilization failed to test the egg donor or the father for cystic fibrosis. The court agreed that the claim on behalf of the child was not one for wrongful life because "[h]ere, by contrast, the Parettas maintain that the defendant doctors were actually responsible for Theresa's conception, had a role in her genetic composition, and combined the sperm and egg both of which carried cystic fibrosis." Nonetheless, the court concluded:

> Theresa,…like any other baby, does not have a protected right to be born free of genetic defects. A conclusion to the contrary, permitting infants to recover against doctors for wrongs allegedly committed during in-vitro fertilization, would give children conceived with the help of modern medical technology more rights and expectations than children conceived without medical assistance. The law does not recognize such a distinction and neither will this Court.

6. *Relation to Wrongful Conception.* The defendants' negligence in *Smith* consisted of failure to diagnose the child's condition. Suppose that the defendant had negligently performed a vasectomy on the father, and the child had been born with a serious and expensive medical condition (not itself related to the defendant's negligence). Would the rationale of the *McKernan* case, 687 P.2d 850 (Wash. 1984), *supra* at 631, deny the parents an award for the child's future medical costs?

C. Prenatal Injuries

Farley v. Sartin

Supreme Court of Appeals of West Virginia
466 S.E.2d 522 (W. Va. 1995)

CLECKLEY, Justice.

.... The issue presented to this Court on appeal is whether the plaintiff can maintain a cause of action under West Virginia's wrongful death statute, W. Va. Code, 55-7-5 (1931),[1] for the death of Baby Farley, who was eighteen to twenty-two weeks of gestation and, at best, of questionable viability in light of the evidence presented to the circuit court.... Upon review, we conclude the plaintiff may maintain his cause of action regardless of viability and, therefore, we reverse the order of the circuit court.

....

On November 6, 1991, the plaintiff's pregnant wife, Cynthia Farley, was killed in an automobile accident she had with the defendant, Billy R. Sartin, who was driving a tractor trailer owned by the defendant, Lee Sartin Trucking Company, Inc.... [According to the only medical testimony in the record, Baby Farley was neither large enough nor developed enough to survive outside the womb.]

The plaintiff filed a wrongful death action as the Administrator of the Estate of Baby Farley. In response, the defendants filed a motion for summary judgment...on the basis that Baby Farley was not viable at the time of death; therefore, the defendants argued Baby Farley was not a "person" under the wrongful death statute.... [T]he circuit court granted summary judgment in favor of the defendants.

....

At common law, there was no cause of action for the wrongful death of a person.... In essence, the cause of action died with the victim, and there was no compensation for the victim's dependents or heirs....

Recognizing the problem with this result, the English Parliament passed the Fatal Accidents Act of 1846, commonly referred to as Lord Campbell's Act. 9 & 10 Vict. c. 93 (1846). This Act permitted recovery of damages by the close relatives of a victim who was tortiously killed.

....

It did not take long...until state legislatures began passing laws similar to Lord Campbell's Act....Currently, every state has created a cause of action for wrongful death....

....

---

1. In relevant part, W. Va. Code, 55-7-5, states:
   "Whenever the death of a person shall be caused by wrongful act, neglect, or default, and the act, neglect or default is such as would (if death had not ensued) have entitled the party injured to maintain an action to recover damages in respect thereof, then, and in every such case, the person who, or the corporation which, would have been liable if death had not ensued, shall be liable to an action for damages, notwithstanding the death of the person injured..."....

....The common law did not permit recovery for prenatal torts in general, [citations], and courts remained hesitant to allow wrongful death actions for unborn children. [Citation.]

....

The argument at common law was that "an unborn child was but a part of the mother, and had no existence or being which could be the subject-matter of injury distinct from the mother, and that an injury to it was but an injury to the mother[.]"....

It was not until 1946 that an American court departed from...[this] approach. In Bonbrest v. Kotz, 65 F. Supp. 138 (D.D.C.1946), the...[court] addressed the question of whether a child could maintain a right of action upon the allegation that she was injured because of professional malpractice when she was taken from her mother's womb....The district court determined that logic and justice require "'that a child, if born alive and viable[,]...should be allowed to maintain an action in the courts for injuries wrongfully committed upon its person while in the womb of its mother.'" [Citation]. To permit otherwise would allow a wrong to be inflicted for which no remedy exists....It is clear from the language and analysis that both the "single entity view" and the no-duty rule were disavowed in *Bonbrest.*

Following *Bonbrest,* "a rapid series of cases, many of them expressly overruling prior holdings, brought about a rather spectacular reversal of the no-duty rule." [Citation.] Indeed, today, every jurisdiction permits recovery for prenatal injuries if a child is born alive. [Citations.] In addition, it generally does not matter whether the injury occurred prior to or after the point of viability. [Citations.]

....

Despite the fact that recovery generally is allowed for prenatal injuries for a child "born alive," courts disagree upon whether they will permit recovery for injuries causing the death of a child *en ventre sa mere.* Although some jurisdictions do not permit a wrongful death action to be maintained for the death of an unborn child,[12] the majority of jurisdictions now do permit a wrongful death action if the unborn child had reached the point of viability.[13] [Citations.]

....

Jurisdictions that originally denied a wrongful death action for a child *en ventre sa mere* did so for a number of reasons that now are rejected by the majority of courts....

....

[One]...reason traditionally given for denying recovery for the wrongful death of a child *en ventre sa mere* is based upon the argument that the Legislature should determine this issue and the courts should not expand the scope of liability beyond what was contemplated when the wrongful death statute was enacted. In response, courts have concluded that it is incumbent upon them to give meaning to the term "person" as used in wrongful death statutes and, in the absence of specific legislative language, that re-

---

12. *See* Chatelain v. Kelley, 322 Ark. 517, 910 S.W.2d 215 (1995); Justus v. Atchison, 19 Cal. 3d 564, 565 P.2d 122, 139 Cal. Rptr. 97 (1977); Hernandez v. Garwood, 390 So. 2d 357 (Fla. 1980); Smith v. Columbus Com. Hosp. Inc., 222 Neb. 776, 387 N.W.2d 490 (1986); Egbert v. Wenzl, 199 Neb. 573, 260 N.W.2d 480 (1977); Giardina v. Bennett, 111 N.J. 412, 545 A.2d 139 (1988); Endresz v. Friedberg, 24 N.Y.2d 478, 301 N.Y.S.2d 65, 248 N.E.2d 901 (1969); Blackman v. Langford, 795 S.W.2d 742 (Tex.1990); Lawrence v. Craven Tire Co., 210 Va. 138, 169 S.E.2d 440 (1969).

13. [Citations to decisions from 32 states and 3 federal courts.]

sponsibility requires courts to supplement the law (*i.e.*, fill in the statutory interstices) regardless of what conclusion is reached....

....

Upon the belief that it was necessary to look beyond the often nonexistent legislative intent, courts have focused much of their attention on the language of the wrongful death statutes, the goals and purposes behind their enactments, and other protections afforded unborn children at common law and by statute. A wrongful death statute, such as W. Va. Code, 55-7-5, see note 1, *supra*, imposes three prerequisites for recovery. First, there must be a death of a "person." Second, the death must "be caused by [the] wrongful act, neglect, or default" of another. [Citation.] Third, the deceased "person" must have been entitled to a cause of action for damages if death had not occurred. In the context of an unborn child, the general question to be asked is whether the unborn child would be able to maintain a cause of action if the unborn child had lived. [Citations.]

As previously stated, every jurisdiction now permits a cause of action for prenatal injuries to a viable unborn child who is born alive. [Citation.] Thus, many courts have determined that if a viable unborn child can maintain a cause of action for injuries sustained if born alive, it only is logical that the phrase "person" within the context of a wrongful death statute should include a viable unborn child who would have been born alive but for the tortious injury inflicted causing death prior to birth. [Citations.]

In addition, wrongful death statutes were enacted to preserve and protect human life by deterring tortious conduct and to provide damages when such conduct results in death. [Citations.] The disparity that results from not permitting a wrongful death action for the death of a viable unborn child while allowing a recovery for injuries if the unborn child is born alive creates the same injustice as existed prior to the enactment of wrongful death statutes. In essence, with no wrongful death cause of action for a viable unborn child, a tortfeasor is given immunity from liability for a greater harm. [Citations.]

....

In West Virginia, we recognized the right of the survivors of a viable unborn child to recover for wrongful death in Baldwin v. Butcher, 155 W. Va. 431, 184 S.E.2d 428 (1971)....

....

...[W]e agree with those jurisdictions that hold a tortious injury suffered by a nonviable child *en ventre sa mere* who subsequently is born alive is compensable and no less meritorious than an injury inflicted upon a viable child who subsequently is born alive. To declare otherwise not only would lead to unjust and inequitable results but also would be contrary to the underlying philosophies of our tort law. In this respect, viability at the time of the injury is "a mere theoretical abstraction" if a child born alive suffers from a pre-viability tort as opposed to a post-viability tort.

Turning to a cause of action for wrongful death, we confront the issue of whether "viability" is the proper line upon which we should permit a cause of action. With the exception of Georgia, which allows recovery after an unborn child is quick in the womb,[20] and Missouri, which found legislative direction to hold a nonviable child is a "person" under its wrongful death statute, we are not aware of any other cases that permit recovery for injury prior to viability unless there is a live birth.... [H]owever, a lack of precedent—standing alone—is an insufficient reason to deny a cause of action....

---

20. ....["Quick" means "capable of moving in its mother's womb."]

In jurisdictions where the viability standard is controlling, the tortfeasor remains un-accountable for the full extent of the injuries inflicted by his or her wrongful conduct. In our judgment, justice is denied when a tortfeasor is permitted to walk away with im-punity because of the happenstance that the unborn child had not yet reached viability at the time of death. The societal and parental loss is egregious regardless of the state of fetal development. Our concern reflects the fundamental value determination of our society that life-old, young, and prospective-should not be wrongfully taken away. In the absence of legislative direction, the overriding importance of the interest that we have identified merits judicial recognition and protection by imposing the most liberal means of recovery that our law permits.

....

....Wrongful death statutes, after all, are designed to provide economic compensa-tion to the surviving family. When a family loses a potential member because of tor-tious conduct, it suffers an injury of the same order as that which occurs when it loses an existing member. The statute allows recovery for the loss of a life that would have provided love and sustenance but for the intervening tort.

...W. Va. Code, 55-7-5, is remedial in nature and should be liberally construed. [Ci-tation.] In light of our previous interpretation of W. Va. Code, 55-7- 5, and the goals and purposes of wrongful death statutes generally, we, therefore, hold that the term "person," as used in this statute and the equivalent language in its counterpart, W. Va. Code, 55-7-6 (1992), encompasses a nonviable unborn child and, thus, permits a cause of action for the tortious death of such child.

We recognize that the closer one gets to the moment of conception, the more sub-stantial becomes the potential for fraudulent claims and for increased difficulties in re-solving some issues of causation and damages. However, those risks are no more of a justification to erect a bar to legitimate claims in this context than they were when we dismissed them as a reason for rejecting claims relating to viable unborn children in *Baldwin*. Moreover, our holding in this case eliminates the need for trial courts to de-cide what often could be an extremely difficult factual question, *i.e.*, whether the fetus was "viable."....

....

Although we have answered the question presented to this Court given the current language in our wrongful death statute, we strongly encourage the Legislature to define the word "person" to deal with future problems that may arise—especially with regard to medical technology that now enables conception outside the mother's womb and pre-conception torts....

....

Reversed and Remanded.

Notes

1. *Wrongful Death of a Fetus.* In Aka v. Jefferson Hosp. Ass'n, Inc., 42 S.W.3d 508 (Ark. 2001), which held that under state law a viable fetus was a "person" within the meaning of the wrongful death statute, the court summarized the law in other jurisdic-tions as follows:

> Thirty-two jurisdictions permit a wrongful-death action on behalf of a viable fetus. (Of those thirty-two jurisdictions, four permit an action for an unviable

fetus (Connecticut, Missouri, South Dakota, and West Virginia).) Four jurisdictions permit an action, even for unviable fetuses, but have a live birth or
stillbirth requirement (Louisiana, Maryland, Oklahoma, and Pennsylvania).
One jurisdiction permits an alternative remedy by allowing an action for damages resulting in stillbirth caused by negligence (Florida). One jurisdiction
noted in dicta that a wrongful-death action might be permitted but declined to
reach the merits on procedural grounds (Utah). Three jurisdictions prohibit an
action for an unborn nonviable fetus but have not reached the issue of whether
a viable fetus may maintain an action (Alaska, Oregon, and Rhode Island).
Four jurisdictions have no case law on the issue (Colorado, Guam, Puerto
Rico, and Wyoming). Only nine jurisdictions, including Arkansas, reject a
wrongful-death action for a viable fetus.

See also 66 Federal Credit Union v. Tucker, 853 So. 2d 104 (Miss. 2003) (permitting a
mother to bring a wrongful death claim for the death of a non-viable fetus).

Some wrongful-death statutes expressly allow recovery for the loss of an "unborn
child." *See* Wiersma v. Maple Leaf Farms, 543 N.W.2d 787 (S.D. 1996). In the absence of
clear language, a court may be reluctant to conclude that the law permits recovery in
such cases. In Bolin v. Wingert, 764 N.E.2d 201 (Ind. 2002), the court held that an unborn child that miscarried as result of injuries sustained by its mother in an automobile
accident did not come within the definition of "child" in the state Child Wrongful Death
Statute. The court noted that three of the four concepts used there to define "child" involved activities engaged in only by living persons; that the definition employed terms
commonly understood to refer only to living persons; that other statutes used explicit
language in extending express protection to unborn children in other contexts; and that
the legislature did not expressly include unborn children within the definition of "child"
in the Child Wrongful Death Statute.

2. *Minority View.* In Endresz v. Friedberg, 248 N.E.2d 901 (N.Y. 1969), the court
embraced the minority view that refuses to permit an action for wrongful death of a
fetus, reasoning:

> The considerations of justice which mandate the recovery of damages by an
> infant, injured in his mother's womb and born deformed through the wrong of
> a third party, are absent where the foetus, deprived of life while yet unborn, is
> never faced with the prospect of impaired mental or physical health.

> In the latter case,... proof of pecuniary injury and causation is immeasur-
> ably more vague than in suits for prenatal injuries....

> Beyond that, since the mother may sue for any injury which she sustained in
> her own person, including her suffering as a result of the stillbirth, and the fa-
> ther for loss of her services and consortium, an additional award to the "distrib-
> utees" of the foetus would give its parents an unmerited bounty and would con-
> stitute not compensation to the injured but punishment to the wrongdoer....

3. *Emotional Distress in Pre-Natal Injury Cases.* In some instances, harm to a pregnant mother will allow her to commence a personal injury action that will include an
award of emotional distress damages relating to the injured fetus. In Smith v. Borello,
804 A.2d 1151 (Md. 2002), the court wrote that:

> The courts in other States are in considerable disagreement over the extent
> to which, and on what theory, a woman who loses an unborn child as the re-
> sult of another's tortious conduct may, as part of her own personal injury ac-

tion, recover for the mental anguish she suffered as a result of the aborted pregnancy and the loss of the child. In States where emotional damages are not allowed generally in the absence of some independent physical injury, the issue, particularly in malpractice cases against obstetricians arising from still-births, has sometimes hinged on whether the plaintiff established the requisite independent physical injury. Courts that have allowed some recovery have relied on different theories in doing so.

Smith held, as a matter of first impression in Maryland, that a pregnant woman who sustains a personal injury as the result of a defendant's tortious conduct and who, as part of that injury, suffers the loss of the fetus may recover, in her own action for personal injuries, for any demonstrable emotional distress that accompanies and is attributable to the loss of the fetus.

See Modaber v. Kelley, 348 S.E.2d 233 (Va. 1986) (holding that injury to an unborn child constituted injury to the mother, and that the mother could recover for the physical injury and mental suffering associated with the stillbirth); Edinburg Hosp. Auth. v. Trevino, 941 S.W.2d 76 (Tex. 1997) (similar).

See also Carey v. Lovett, 622 A.2d 1279 (N.J. 1993) (holding that parents, without attempting to prove any physical injury to themselves, could recover for emotional distress caused by medical malpractice resulting in the premature birth and death of a child).

Note, however, that some cases reach rather harsh results. In Tebbutt v. Virostek, 483 N.E.2d 1142 (N.Y. 1985), a fetus died as a result of an amniocentesis that was alleged to have been performed negligently. The mother was denied recovery of emotional-distress damages relating to the stillbirth of her child. The court reasoned that "parasitic" damages for mental pain and suffering could not be recovered because the mother had alleged no physical injury distinct from that suffered by the fetus, and that the "by-stander" type of emotional-distress damages were not available because the mother had not contemporaneously observed the injury.

4. *Pre-Natal Injuries to Children Born Alive.* Most courts have had no trouble allowing recovery when a child who was injured while *en ventre sa mere* is born alive, but with a handicap attributable to the defendant's negligence.

Some courts have, however, denied recovery when the negligence injured the mother before the child was conceived, but with consequences that affected the child. Defendants' lawyers in these cases sometimes assert that the defendant cannot "logically" have been negligent toward someone who did not yet exist. This argument is remarkable for its complete disregard for any considerations relevant to real-world concerns: negligence that will produce injuries to persons not yet conceived is as undesirable as any other kind of negligence. A somewhat more realistic concern involves the difficulties of proof in at least some of these cases. For a case allowing recovery, *see* Renslow v. Mennonite Hosp., 367 N.E.2d 1250 (Ill. 1977). Plaintiff, whose blood was Rh-negative, was transfused with Rh-positive blood when she was a teenager. This led to her child's being born, years later, with jaundice.

5. *Pre-Natal Injuries Caused by a Child's Mother.* Can a mother be held liable to a child for injuries caused by the mother's unsafe conduct during pregnancy? The issue has been addressed by only a handful of cases. *Compare* Chenault v. Huie, 989 S.W.2d 474 (Tex. App. 1999) (no cause of action based on mother's illegal drug use), *with* National Cas. Co. v. Northern Trust Bank of Fla., 807 So. 2d 86 (Fla. Dist. Ct. App. 2002) (holding, in an auto accident case, that a child had cause of action against her mother

"up to the limits of the insurance coverage"), *and* Bonte v. Bonte, 616 N.E.2d 464 (N.H. 1992) (a claim was stated based on a mother's alleged negligence in failing to use a crosswalk).

6. *No-Fault Compensation.* A few states have enacted legislation which removes certain infant injuries allegedly caused by medical professionals from the tort system and provides no-fault compensation under a scheme modeled on workers' compensation. *See* Va. Code Ann. §38.2-5002 (Westlaw 2003).

D. Wrongful Adoption

Burr v. Board of County Commissioners of Stark City

Supreme Court of Ohio
491 N.E.2d 1101 (Ohio 1986)

Appellees Russell H. and Betty J. Burr, filed a "wrongful adoption" civil action against the Board of County Commissioners of Stark County, the Stark County Welfare Department, Logan Burd, its director, and Winifred M. Schaub, a former employee of the department's adoption division.

....

....Appellees contacted the adoption division of the Stark County Welfare Department in 1964 expressing their desire to adopt a child. Betty Burr is partially disabled, having earlier lost a leg to polio....

...[A]n employee of appellants telephoned the Burrs and told them a seventeen-month-old boy was available for adoption. At appellants' suggestion, the Burrs met the county caseworker, Schaub, in order to be introduced to the child. During this meeting Schaub [had] told the Burrs the infant was borne by an eighteen-year-old unwed mother, that the mother was living with her parents, that the mother was trying to take care of the child and trying to work during the day, that the grandparents were mean to the child, that the mother was going to Texas for better employment, and that she had surrendered the child to appellants for adoption. Russell Burr testified that Schaub represented to them that the child "...was a nice big, healthy, baby boy" who had been born at the Massillon City Hospital. The Burrs decided to proceed with the adoption....

The Burrs testified that during the ensuing years Patrick suffered from a myriad of physical and mental problems. Physical twitching, speech impediment, poor motor skills, and learning disabilities were among Patrick's more apparent problems....He was classified as E.M.R. (educable, mentally retarded) and attended special education classes....

...[B]y high school, Patrick was observed to also suffer from hallucinations....Eventually, Patrick was diagnosed as suffering from Huntington's Disease, a genetically inherited disease which destroys the central nervous system. Movement disorders, delusions and intellectual deterioration are all associated with the disease. The average life expectancy after onset if the disease begins during childhood is 8.5 years. During the course of Patrick's treatment, the Burrs obtained a court order opening the sealed records concerning his background prior to adoption.

....These previously sealed records revealed that Patrick's mother was actually a thirty-one-year old mental patient at the Massillon State Hospital. Patrick had not been born at Massillon City Hospital, but rather was delivered at the state mental institution. The father's identity was unknown, but he was presumed to also have been a mental patient. Patrick's biological mother shared his low intellectual level and also had a speech impediment. She was diagnosed as having a "mild mental deficiency, idiopathic, with psychotic reactions" and was described as "bovine." The "mean" grandparents, the trip to Texas, voluntary placement, and seemingly all other information regarding Patrick other than his age and sex were fabrications. In fact, prior to adoption, he had been placed in two foster homes.

The records also showed that Patrick suffered a fever at birth, and was known by appellants to be developing slowly....Although Patrick's biological mother had not been diagnosed as suffering Huntington's Disease, expert testimony established that Patrick's family background and medical profile made him at risk for disease....

In order to recoup Patrick's medical expenses (in excess of $80,000 for the Huntington's Disease treatment alone), together with other damages, the Burrs commenced this "wrongful adoption" action against appellants.

....The jury returned a verdict in favor of appellees in the sum of $125,000. The court of appeals...affirmed....

....

CELEBREZZE, Chief Justice.

....

We deem that in a civil action captioned "Complaint in Fraud...for Wrongful Adoption," which alleges that adoptive parents were fraudulently misled to their detriment by an adoption agency's material misrepresentations of fact concerning an infant's background and condition, the parents must prove each element of the tort of fraud.

In Cohen v. Lamko, Inc. (1984), 10 Ohio St. 3d 167, 169, 462 N.E.2d 407, we set forth the elements of fraud as:

   (a) a representation or, where there is a duty to disclose, concealment of a fact,

   (b) which is material to the transaction at hand,

   (c) made falsely, with knowledge of its falsity, or with such utter disregard and recklessness as to whether it is true or false that knowledge may be inferred,

   (d) with the intent of misleading another into relying upon it,

   (e) justifiable reliance upon the representation or concealment, and

   (f) a resulting injury proximately caused by the reliance....[Citations.]

...[W]e find that the instant record amply supports the lower courts' decisions that fraud was demonstrated. There was evidence presented that appellants represented to appellees that the infant was a nice, big, healthy baby boy when in fact the welfare agency had test records which indicated...that the child may have low intelligence and was at risk of disease. Appellants further represented that he was born at the Massillon City Hospital; the working mother was an unwed eighteen-year-old who was living with her parents, could not care for her son and voluntarily signed custody to appellants; that the grandparents were mean to the boy; and that the mother was moving to Texas for better employment.

Each of these untrue statements was found to have been affirmatively made with knowledge of its falsity. The representations were material to the adoption transaction and were obviously made with the intention of misleading the Burrs into relying upon them as fact while making their decision whether to adopt.

Both Mr. and Mrs. Burr testified that had they not been lied to regarding Patrick's history, they never would have adopted him. Hence, had they not relied on the representations, their subsequent damages would never have resulted. In short, appellants knew the history was false, intended reliance, and in fact misled the Burrs to their detriment.

Lastly, we find appellees' reliance was justifiable in this case and that their injuries resulted therefrom....

    ....

We find that the judgment and award ($125,000) were appropriate in light of the evidence presented to the jury, medical bills ($81,000), other expenses, and appellees' claimed emotional damage....

... [T]he award appears commensurate with the injuries inflicted and is not so excessive as to be set aside. [Citations.]

    ....

We believe it appropriate to comment briefly concerning the breadth of today's decision. In no way do we imply that adoption agencies are guarantors of their placements. Such a view would be tantamount to imposing an untenable contract of insurance that each child adopted would mature to be healthy and happy.... Adoptive parents are in the same position as, and confront risks comparable to those, of natural parents relative to their child's future.... However, just as couples must weigh the risks of becoming natural parents, taking into consideration a host of factors, so too should adoptive parents be allowed to make their decision in an intelligent manner. It is not the mere failure to disclose the risks inherent in the child's background which we hold to be actionable. Rather, it is the deliberate act of misinforming this couple which deprived them of their right to make a sound parenting decision and which led to the compensable injuries....

Judgment affirmed.

Notes

1. What do the cases in this chapter suggest about how damages should be calculated in a "wrongful adoption" case? Is it relevant whether, as in many states, the law offers the parents the option of annulling the adoption decree?

2. *Culpability in Wrongful-Adoption Cases.* In other areas of the law, there has been a definite tendency to extend the scope of torts based on intentional misrepresentation to negligent misrepresentations and even to strict liability for misrepresentations that could not have been prevented by reasonable care. For example, manufacturers of defective products were once immune even from suits for negligence, though liable for deliberately misleading their customers. Today, as discussed in Chapter 15, manufacturers are often liable for injuries caused by their products even if the manufacturers were not at fault. And the law of misrepresentation generally (Chapter 21) has moved in the same direction, though suits for negligent misrepresentation are still allowed only in special cases, and strict-liability misrepresentation cases are rare. The court's attempt in the last paragraph of the *Burr* opinion to limit the sweep of its decision does not necessarily indicate what the law on this subject will be in future years.

There is growing support for a cause of action based on negligence. *See* McKinney v. State, 950 P.2d 461 (Wash. 1998) (finding a statutory cause of action for negligent failure to comply with adoption agency reporting requirements relating to disclosure of medical and social information about a child); Mohr v. Commonwealth, 653 N.E.2d

1104 (Mass. 1995) (recognizing liability of an adoption agency for both negligent and intentional misrepresentations); Gibbs v. Ernst, 647 A.2d 882 (Pa. 1994) (holding that traditional common-law causes of action grounded in fraud and negligence applied to the adoption setting, but that the defendant agencies did not have a common-law or statutory duty to investigate a child's mental and physical health). Indeed, a negligence action may have some advantages. *See* Zernhelt v. Lehigh County Office of Children and Youth Services, 659 A.2d 89 (Pa. Commw. Ct. 1995) (fraud claim was barred by an immunity statute which did not bar negligence claims).

3. *Fraud on an Unborn Child?* If a company lies to a pregnant mother about workplace safety and the child is then born with defects resulting from the mother's exposure at work to toxic chemicals, can the child sue for fraud? The conventional answer is no. An action for fraudulent misrepresentation ordinarily requires that the plaintiff have relied upon the false statement. (*See* Chapter 21.) However by a 3-2 vote, the court in Ruffing v. Union Carbide Corp., 764 N.Y.S.2d 462 (App. Div. 2003), held that, although there was limited authority on the question, a claim for fraud was stated. One might reason that for purposes of reliance, the mother acts in the place of the child. However, the court relied upon disparate cases for the proposition that "[f]raud…may…exist where a false representation is made to a third party, resulting in injury to the plaintiff."

4. *Wrongful Prolongation of Life.* In Taylor v. Muncie Med. Investors, 727 N.E.2d 466 (Ind. Ct. App. 2000), a patient's estate and adult children brought an action against a nursing home for wrongful prolongation of the patient's life, alleging gross negligence, battery, and other claims. The suit accused a nursing home and two physicians of extending the patient's life for 140 days, despite the fact that she had executed a living will and a "do not resuscitate" form. The court held that there was no need to recognize a new cause of action for "wrongful prolongation of life" because the state Health Care Consent Act permitted a cause of action that would have protected the rights of the family.

Chapter 14

Strict Liability

Liability without Fault. Defendants are sometimes held liable for injuries despite their not having been "at fault" in any sense. When this occurs, the defendants are "strictly liable."

The "strictness" of strict liability lies in the fact that one or more of the usual prerequisites for liability based on fault—typically, proof of unreasonable (or worse) conduct and foreseeability of harm—are dispensed with or modified. As the requirements for recovery become less numerous or less formidable, the liability becomes more strict. There are different varieties of strict liability, and not all are equally exacting. Some authorities have used the term "absolute liability" to refer to the imposition of strict liability under circumstances where the defendant is barred from introducing defenses based on the plaintiff's conduct. *See* Seim v. Garavalia, 306 N.W.2d 806 (Minn. 1981), *supra* at 324. Other sources employ the "absolute liability" label less precisely.

Policy Basis. Although the arguments differ depending on the field, strict liability is sometimes touted as having advantages over negligence as a basis for liability. It has been contended, for example, that strict liability: (1) achieves more-effective deterrence than a negligence standard; (2) that it increases the likelihood that injured persons will be compensated; (3) that it may be effectively employed as a device for spreading losses or shifting losses to "deeper pockets"; (4) that it can be used to ensure that persons who benefit from dangerous activities bear the burden of resulting losses; and (5) that it is easier to apply than the negligence standard. The merit of these contentions is hotly debated.

Opponents of strict liability often note that relieving plaintiffs of the need to prove fault creates a risk that too many cases will be brought, with the result that the costs of resolving claims may outweigh any advantages gained by a rule of strict liability. It has also been urged that strict liability tends to erode the incentives potential victims otherwise have to exercise care on their own behalf. The weight of this concern depends to a considerable extent upon whether a jurisdiction has enacted comparative fault. At common law, assumption of the risk, but not contributory negligence, was a complete defense to a suit for strict liability. Under comparative fault, contributory negligence, assumption of the risk, and other forms of plaintiff misconduct may be raised by a defendant to preclude or reduce recovery under a theory of strict liability. *See generally* Chapter 16.

Categories of Strict Liability. One important and recently developed category of strict liability—the liability of manufacturers and other sellers of products for injuries to consumers caused by defects in those products—will be examined in Chapter 15. This Chapter will examine several older forms of strict liability: (1) liability of employers to injured employees under workers' compensation laws; (2) liability of employers to those injured by the torts of their employees; (3) liability for harm done by certain kinds of animals kept by the defendant; and (4) "traditional strict liability" or, as it is sometimes (misleadingly) called, liability for conducting abnormally dangerous activities.

A. Employer and Employee

1. Workers' Compensation

Every state has adopted workers' compensation statutes, which require most employers to provide compensation for on-the-job injuries suffered by their employees. In many cases, employers provide for this liability by buying insurance, though large employers often find it cheaper to self-insure.

Recovery under workers' compensation is set by statutory schedules, rather than determined by case-by-case inquiries into the amount of harm suffered by the employee. In comparison with tort damages, payments under workers' compensation are usually quite low, especially in cases involving death or serious injury. The thought behind workers' compensation—which was first adopted in most states during the 1910's, following the enactment of statutes in Germany and England in the late 1800's—was to provide employees with the means of paying medical bills and with some measure of compensation for lost wages, not to award recovery for pain and suffering. But an injured worker's right to recover under workers' compensation will often be clear, so the injured person usually need not litigate for years or pay a large portion of any recovery to a lawyer. Problems leading to litigation do arise under workers' compensation, however. For instance, it may not be obvious whether a worker's disability resulted from harm suffered on the job or from some other cause. Recently, claims by former employees for illnesses allegedly caused by on-the-job stress have been much litigated, with mixed results.

Negligence and Recklessness. Workers' compensation is ordinarily an injured employee's exclusive remedy against the employer for failure to exercise care: the statutes bar negligence and recklessness claims relating to injuries arising "in the course of employment." Therefore, although an injured employee may recover from the employer without showing that the employer was negligent, the employee covered by workers' compensation loses the right to sue the employer for negligence. *See, e.g.,* Elliott v. Dugger, 579 So. 2d 827 (Fla. Dist. Ct. App. 1991) (workers' compensation was the exclusive remedy against the state where a correctional officer allegedly ingested blood serum containing the AIDS virus as a result of a co-worker's negligence in supervising an inmate). This immunity affords employers with a considerable measure of protection, and will in some cases reduce the employer's incentive to take safety precautions.

In a small number of instances, negligence on the part of an employer may be actionable because the resulting injury does not occur "in the course of employment," as where negligent structuring of hours of employment causes a fatigued employee to be injured while driving home after the overnight shift. *See* Harrington v. Brooks Drugs, Inc., 808 A.2d 532, 534-35 (N.H. 2002).

Intentional Torts. Workers' compensation laws do not bar suits against an employer for intentional wrongdoing. *See* Turner v. PCR, Inc., 754 So. 2d 683 (Fla. 2000).

Co-Employees. The immunity enjoyed by an employer normally also bars actions against co-employees. *See, e.g.,* La. Rev. Stat. 23:1032 (Westlaw 2003) (barring negligence actions against the "employer, or any principal or any officer, director, stockholder, partner, or employee of such employer or principal"); Tex. Labor Code §408.001 (Westlaw 2003) (barring suits against the "employer or an agent or employee of the employer"). *See also* SOS Staffing Services, Inc. v. Fields, 54 P.3d 761 (Wyo. 2002) (holding that a temporary employee was employed by the temporary employment service provider, not by the company for which the temporary employee worked, and therefore the temporary employee was not entitled to co-employee immunity for injuries suffered by a company employee when the vehicle the temporary employee was driving overturned).

Third-Parties. Parties outside of the employment relationship do not pay workers' compensation premiums and do not enjoy the benefit of workers' compensation immunity. Therefore, in cases involving on-the-job accidents, attorneys representing injured workers are assiduous in searching for blameworthy third parties who can be held liable for the injuries. *See* Brown v. Adair, 846 So. 2d 687 (La. 2003) (outside rehabilitation specialists were "third persons" who were not immune from a malpractice action). As to whether a responsible third party's liability is reduced by the amount of the workers' compensation benefits received by the plaintiff, see the discussion of the collateral-source rule in Chapter 3. As to whether the responsible third party can rely upon comparative-fault principles to limit liability to less than the full amount of the plaintiff's losses, see Chapter 16.

Employer Participation. In all states except Texas, employers must participate in the workers' compensation system. (In Texas, participation is optional, though it is encouraged by laws providing that a non-participating employer may not raise traditional common-law defenses in a suit by an injured employee). However, even where participation is mandatory, there are exceptions. Employers with less than a certain number of employees may not have to subscribe, and the same is true of certain types of employers (e.g., those employing agricultural workers or domestic help).

Many law schools offer a separate course on Workers' Compensation Law, a detailed examination of which is beyond the scope of a basic torts course. The following excerpt from the New York statute shows how workers' compensation is calculated in one state. The schedules typically take into account whether the worker's injury is permanent or temporary and the extent of the injury.

New York Workers' Compensation Law
(Westlaw 2004)

§15. Schedule in case of disability

The following schedule of compensation is hereby established:

1. Permanent total disability. In case of total disability adjudged to be permanent sixty-six and two-thirds per centum of the average weekly wages shall be paid to the employee during the continuance of such total disability. Loss of both hands, or both arms, or both feet, or both legs, or both eyes, or of any two thereof shall, in the absence of conclusive proof to the contrary, constitute permanent total disability. In all other cases permanent total disability shall be determined in accordance with the facts....

2. Temporary total disability. In case of temporary total disability, sixty-six and two-thirds per centum of the average weekly wages shall be paid to the employee during the continuance thereof, except as otherwise provided in this chapter.

3. Permanent partial disability. In case of disability partial in character but permanent in quality the compensation shall be sixty-six and two-thirds per centum of the average weekly wages and shall be paid to the employee for the period named in this subdivision, as follows:

Member lost	Number of weeks' compensation
a. Arm	312
b. Leg	288
c. Hand	244
d. Foot	205
e. Eye	160
f. Thumb	75
g. First finger	46
h. Great toe	38
i. Second finger	30
j. Third finger	25
k. Toe other than great toe	16
l. Fourth finger	15

m. Loss of hearing. Compensation for the complete loss of the hearing of one ear, for sixty weeks, for the loss of hearing of both ears, for one hundred and fifty weeks.

n. Phalanges. Compensation for the loss of more than one phalange of a digit shall be the same as for loss of the entire digit. Compensation for loss of the first phalange shall be one-half of the compensation for loss of the entire digit.

o. Amputated arm or leg. Compensation for an arm or a leg, if amputated at or above the wrist or ankle, shall be for the proportionate loss of the arm or leg.

p. Binocular vision or per centum of vision. Compensation for loss of binocular vision or for eighty per centum or more of the vision of an eye shall be the same as for loss of the eye.

q. Two or more digits. Compensation for loss or loss of use of two or more digits, or one or more phalanges of two or more digits, of a hand or foot may be proportioned to the loss of use of the hand or foot occasioned thereby but shall not exceed the compensation for loss of a hand or foot.

r. Total loss of use. Compensation for permanent total loss of use of a member shall be the same as for loss of the member.

s. Partial loss or partial loss of use. Compensation for permanent partial loss or loss of use of a member may be for proportionate loss or loss of use of the member....

t. Disfigurement....The board may award proper and equitable compensation for serious facial or head disfigurement, not to exceed twenty thousand dollars, including a disfigurement continuous in length which is partially in the facial area and also extends into the neck region as described in paragraph two hereof.

....

u. Total or partial loss or loss of use of more than one member or parts of members. In any case in which there shall be a loss or loss of use of more than one member or parts of more than one member set forth in paragraphs a to t, both inclusive, of this subdivision, but not amounting to permanent total disability, the board shall award compensation for the loss or loss of use of each such member or part thereof, which awards shall run consecutively.

....

w. Other cases. In all other cases in this class of disability, the compensation shall be sixty-six and two-thirds per centum of the difference between his average weekly wages and his wage-earning capacity thereafter in the same employment or otherwise, payable during the continuance of such partial disability, but subject to reconsideration of the degree of such impairment by the board on its own motion or upon application of any party in interest.

....

5. Temporary partial disability. In case of temporary partial disability resulting in decrease of earning capacity, the compensation shall be two-thirds of the difference between the injured employee's average weekly wages before the accident and his wage earning capacity after the accident in the same or other employment.

5-a. Determination of wage earning capacity. The wage earning capacity of an injured employee in cases of partial disability shall be determined by his actual earnings, provided, however, that if he has no such actual earnings the board may in the interest of justice fix such wage earning capacity as shall be reasonable, but not in excess of seventy-five per centum of his former full time actual earnings, having due regard to the nature of his injury and his physical impairment.

2. *Respondeat Superior*

Turning from harms *to* employees to harms inflicted *by* employees, one finds that the doctrine of *respondeat superior* holds employers liable for torts committed by their employees in the scope of their employment. This is a form of strict liability because the plaintiff's right to recover against the employer does not depend on a showing that the *employer* was at fault. The plaintiff must, however, show that the employee committed a tort, and in most cases the tort in question is negligence. Therefore, although employers are "strictly liable" for their employees' torts, this form of strict liability typically requires the plaintiff to show that *someone*—though not the employer—was negligent. So it is not a particularly "strict" form of "strict liability."

In the following case, a court managed to find an employer liable *in tort* for an injury to an employee by applying the doctrine of *respondeat superior* while avoiding the workers' compensation law's denial of a tort cause of action to an employee injured on the job.

Smith v. Lannert

St. Louis Court of Appeals, Missouri
429 S.W.2d 8 (Mo. Ct. App. 1968)

BRADY, Commissioner.

In this action to recover damages for personal injuries allegedly sustained on October 31, 1961, while on Bettendorf-Rapp's premises, plaintiff received a verdict and judgment in the amount of $2,500.00 against Bettendorf-Rapp and the individual defendant. Bettendorf-Rapp was given a judgment in this same amount on its crossclaim against the individual defendant. Both defendants appeal....

....Plaintiff, who at the time of trial was a 36-year-old married female, was employed as a checker in Bettendorf-Rapp's supermarket at the time of the incident....On the day this incident occurred plaintiff began work about 9:00 or 9:30 and in the late afternoon of that day went to Lannert to request time for a break to go to the restroom.... She was told to return to work....Her testimony was Lannert "...told me to get back down to the courtesy checkout and get to work or he would spank me."....Instead of doing so she asked a coemployee for her purse and upon receiving it started for the ladies' room in the employees' lounge. When she got to the door of the employees' lounge someone grabbed her from behind and pushed her into the lounge. She looked around and saw it was Lannert who then bent her over and struck her three times with his open hand on her buttocks....The spanking caused red marks....

She went back to the courtesy counter...and returned to her cash register where she remained for a half hour or so. Her only other conversation with Lannert on this day occurred when he came to check the cash register to see if it balanced. Her testimony was that it did balance and that Lannert told her it was a good thing it did or he would spank her again. Her testimony was that she felt Lannert was trying to joke with her on this occasion but neither she nor Lannert were joking on the earlier occasion when she was struck.

Lannert was called by plaintiff as her witness....His testimony was that he was not perturbed with plaintiff in any way and thought the incident to be entirely in jest since both he and plaintiff were laughing and "kidding around" at the time. In December of 1961 plaintiff told Bettendorf-Rapp's personnel manager what had happened.

Lannert testified he did not consider himself in the course and scope of his duties when he struck plaintiff. It also appeared it was against company policy to lay hands on any employee and Bettendorf-Rapp had received no complaints about Lannert having ever done so prior to this time....

....

[The court held that the plaintiff's action was not barred by the State worker's compensation statute because the "accident did not arise 'in the course of' plaintiff's employment for...she was injured while in the process of disobeying a direct order of her superior and doing an act her employer...had expressly forbidden her to do."]

There is no dispute but that Lannert was an employee of Bettendorf-Rapp and that he intentionally struck plaintiff....The issue is whether there is evidence from which the jury could find Lannert "...was within the scope of his employment by Bettendorf-Rapp, Inc." as submitted in that instruction....

The principle of *respondeat superior* underlies the liability of Bettendorf-Rapp, if any exists. As was stated in Haehl v. Wabash R. Co., 119 Mo. 325, 24 S.W. 737..."'The principal is responsible, not because the servant has acted in his name or under color of his employment, but because the servant was actually engaged in and about his business, and carrying out his purposes....But if his business is done, or is taking care of itself, and his servant, not being engaged in it, not concerned about it, but impelled by motives that are wholly personal to himself, and simply to gratify his own feeling of resentment, whether provoked or unprovoked, commits an assault upon another, when that has and can have no tendency to promote any purpose in which the principal is interested, and to promote which the servant was employed, then the wrong is the purely personal wrong of the servant, for which he, and he alone, is responsible.'" In this connection we are cognizant Bettendorf-Rapp may be held responsible for the assault committed by Lannert even though Lannert acted wantonly and contrary to Bettendorf-Rapp's instructions [citation] provided there is proof the assault was made with intent to promote or further the master's business. [Citation.]

Plaintiff's best evidence shows the employees were entitled to certain rest "breaks" and the jury was entitled to the fair inference these were to be granted at the discretion of the store manager Lannert whom plaintiff's evidence described as having the "full say" over all matters taking place within the store.... [T]he jury could reasonably infer from the evidence Bettendorf-Rapp was interested in maintaining what it deemed to be an adequate work force with which to handle the volume of its business and that this was one of the purposes for which Lannert was employed as store manager. When this inference is considered in the light of Lannert's previous reprimand to plaintiff for taking too much time on an earlier rest break, his refusal to grant permission for another rest break, Lannert's order to plaintiff to return to work, her immediate disobedience of that order, and Lannert's assault upon her following so closely in the sequence of events as to refute any contention but that it was connected therewith, we hold there is evidence from which the jury could find Lannert's act in striking plaintiff was to enforce employee discipline with respect to orders given by the store manager with reference to employee rest breaks, thus promoting Bettendorf-Rapp's purpose of keeping an adequate work force on the floor and maintaining employee discipline.

....We cannot say as a matter of law Lannert abandoned his duties...and indulged in the assault as an individual act.

....

The judgment is affirmed.

Notes

1. *Accord* Rodebush v. Oklahoma Nursing Homes, Ltd., 867 P.2d 1241 (Okla. 1993) (employer held liable for nurse's slapping of an Alzheimer's patient while giving him a bath).

2. **Respondeat Superior**. The rule of *respondeat superior*—meaning "let the master answer" or "look to the one higher up"—is a rule of strict, vicarious liability. In the master and servant context, it provides that if an employee commits a tort while acting within the scope of the employment, the employer will be held accountable, even though the employer's conduct is in no way blameworthy. The application of *respondeat superior* hinges on two questions: (1) whether the tortfeasor is an employee (a "servant" in the older jargon), rather than an independent contractor; and (2) whether, if the tortfeasor is an employee, the tort occurs within the scope of the employment.

3. *Employees versus Independent Contractors*. Subject to certain important exceptions dealing with non-delegable duties (discussed *infra* at pp. 677), a principal is not vicariously liable for the torts of an agent who is an independent contractor, rather than an employee. *See* Restatement, Second, of Torts §409; Restatement, Second, of Agency §250. *See also* Amaya v. Potter, 94 S.W.3d 856 (Tex. App. 2002) (holding that a repairman temporarily doing work at a garage, who was urged to chase after a stolen vehicle, was not an employee, and therefore *respondeat superior* principles did not apply to an accident resulting from the chase).

The critical distinction between employees ("servants") and independent contractors is addressed by §2 of the Restatement, Second, of Agency, which provides:

> (2) A servant is an agent employed by a master to perform service in his affairs whose physical conduct in the performance of the service is controlled or subject to the right to control by the master.

> (3) An independent contractor is a person who contracts with another to do something for him but who is not controlled by the other nor subject to the

other's right to control with respect to his physical conduct in the performance of the undertaking....

Many decisions have emphasized the importance of right to control in determining the status of the tortfeasor. *See, e.g.,* Glenmar Cinestate, Inc. v. Farrell, 292 S.E.2d 366 (Va. 1982) (holding a drive-in theater not liable for a death resulting from an off-duty police officer's negligent direction of traffic because the officer was an independent contractor who chose his own methods and the theater did not reserve the power to direct his activities); Verrett v. Houma Newspapers, Inc., 305 So. 2d 547, 550 (La. Ct. App. 1974) (holding that a carrier delivering newspapers by bicycle was an independent contractor where the publisher did not reserve or retain any right of control over the manner in which carrier made deliveries). *See also* Restatement, Third, of Agency §2.04 Cmt. b (Tent. Draft No. 2, 2001) ("*Respondeat superior* is inapplicable when a principal does not have the right to control the actions of the agent..."); *id*, at §7.07.

The right to control is also relevant to whether one entity will be held vicariously liable for the acts of another. *See* Golden Spread Council, Inc. v. Akins, 926 S.W.2d 287 (Tex. 1996) (holding that the Boy Scouts of America could not be held liable under a *respondeat superior* theory for the alleged negligence of a local council in referring to a potential troop sponsor a scoutmaster who subsequently allegedly molested a scout because the local council was a separate corporate entity and the BSA had no right to control its activities).

However, some cases have minimized the significance of right to control. In Dias v. Brigham Med. Assoc., 780 N.E.2d 447 (Mass. 2002), the court held that vicarious liability could be imposed on a medical group without proof of its right to control a physician's actions. In interrogatory answers, both the allegedly negligent physician and his medical practice group had indicated that the former was employed by the latter. However, the practice group then sought to escape vicarious liability on the ground that it had no right to control the physician's specific treatment decisions. The court wrote:

> In 1969,...this court broadened the scope of liability under the theory of *respondeat superior*, and held that an employer need not control the details of an employee's tasks in order to be held liable for the employee's tortious acts. *See* Konick v. Berke, Moore Co., 355 Mass. 463, 467, 468, 245 N.E.2d 750 (1969).... [T]he employer in the *Konick* case was found to be liable for the employee's automobile accident, even though the employer was unable to control the precise manner and means of the employee's driving....Our *Konick* decision comported with the view of the vast majority of States....
>
> ....
>
> In order to determine whether an employer-employee relationship actually exists, a judge may consider a number of factors. [Citation.] These factors may include, but are not limited to, the method of payment (e.g., whether the employee receives a W-2 form from the employer), and whether the parties themselves believe they have created an employer-employee relationship. While the point is not of import in this case where both BMA and Dr. Schlitzer admit the existence of the employer-employee relationship,...in cases where there is no clear admission of employment, a direction and control analysis may be useful to determine whether the relationship is that of employer-employee as opposed to that of an independent contractor. The right to direct and control the details of an alleged employee's actions "may be very attenuated," but remains an important factor that should be examined when the employer-employee re-

lationship is contested. [Citation.] Once an employer-employee relationship is established, however, any further analysis of the employer's right to direct and control is unnecessary....

However, even courts that talk in terms of a right-to-control requirement take similar factors into account in determining whether *respondeat superior* liability will be imposed. So, in reality, there may be less divergence between the Restatement position, on the one hand, and decisions like the *Dias* opinion, on the other hand, than might first appear. In Limestone Products Distrib., Inc. v. McNamara, 71 S.W.3d 308 (Tex. 2002), the court said that:

> We measure the right to control by considering: (1) the independent nature of the worker's business; (2) the worker's obligation to furnish necessary tools, supplies, and materials to perform the job; (3) the worker's right to control the progress of the work except about final results; (4) the time for which the worker is employed; and (5) the method of payment, whether by unit of time or by the job.

The court concluded that a driver for a limestone supplier was an independent contractor, rather than an employee, at time of the driver's collision with a motorcyclist. Although the supplier told the driver where to pick up and drop off loads, the supplier merely controlled the end sought to be accomplished. The facts showed that driver was free to drive any route he wished; the driver did not work regular hours and did not have to visit the supplier's office on a regular basis; the driver used his own truck and paid for gasoline, repairs, and insurance; the supplier paid the driver by the load when he delivered; the driver received no pay if there was no work; the supplier reported the driver's income on IRS 1099 form rather than a W-2 wage-withholding form; the supplier did not pay the driver for vacation, sick leave, or holidays; and the driver paid his own Social Security and federal income taxes.

In some instances, persons will be classified as employees even though they are paid by an outside source or indirectly compensated. *See* Riverbend Country Club v. Patterson, 399 S.W.2d 382 (Tex. Civ. App. 1965) (holding a country club liable for injuries caused by a caddy, even though caddies were not required to report for work at a particular time and were paid directly by players, because all caddies registered with and were supervised by a caddy master who controlled the work). *See also* Bishop v. Texas A & M Univ., 35 S.W.3d 605 (Tex. 2000) (holding, in an action based on an accidental stabbing during a school play, that professors who acted as faculty advisors to a drama club were employees rather than volunteers, because, even though they were not separately paid for that activity, service as an advisor to a student organization was considered in determining overall compensation).

4. *Temporary Servants.* A person may be held liable for the actions of a "temporary servant." Thus, in some states physicians and nurses who assist in an operation, though employed by the hospital, are held to be temporary servants or agents of the surgeon in charge while the operation is in progress, and liability may be imposed upon the surgeon for their negligent acts under the doctrine of *respondeat superior. See* Swierczek v. Lynch, 237 Neb. 469, 466 N.W.2d 512, 518 (1991).

5. *Ethics in Law Practice: Lawyers as Independent Contractors.* A defense attorney hired by an insurer to represent an insured is an independent contractor who has discretion regarding the day-to-day details of conducting the defense. Accordingly, an insurer is not vicariously liable for the legal malpractice of an independent attorney whom it selected to defend an insured. *See* State Farm Mut. Auto. Ins. Co. v. Traver, 980 S.W.2d 625 (Tex. 1998).

6. *Scope of Employment.* According to the Restatement, Second, of Agency, §228, the conduct of a servant is within the scope of employment, if but only if:

(a) it is of the kind he is employed to perform;

(b) it occurs substantially within the authorized time and space limits;

(c) it is actuated, at least in part, by a purpose to serve the master; and

(d) if force is intentionally used by the servant against another, the use of the force is not unexpectable by the master.

The evolving third Restatement of Agency proposes a somewhat different test for scope of employment:

> An employee acts within the scope of employment when performing work assigned by the employer or engaging in a course of conduct subject to the employer's control. An employee's act is not within the scope of employment when it occurs within an independent course of conduct not intended by the employee to serve any purpose of the employer.

Restatement, Third, of Agency §7.08(2) (Council Draft No. 5, 2003).

"Off-duty" conduct is ordinarily not within the scope of employment. *See* Ginther v. Domino's Pizza, Inc., 93 S.W.3d 300 (Tex. App. 2002) (a pizza delivery driver's actions while driving friends home in a car he used to deliver pizza fell outside scope of his employment where it was undisputed that the driver's shift had ended and he had left work almost two hours earlier); Burroughs v. Massachusetts, 673 N.E.2d 1217 (Mass. 1996) (an off-duty national guard member who served as a bartender at the armory did so voluntarily and was not within the scope of his employment where the work was uncompensated and there was no evidence that superiors had ordered him to provide the services); Haybeck v. Prodigy Services Co., 944 F. Supp. 326, 331 (S.D.N.Y. 1996), *app. dismissed on other grounds*, 116 F.3d 465 (2d Cir. 1997) (the conduct of an employee of an on-line service provider, who failed to disclose his HIV status before having sex outside his place of employment with a customer he met in a company "chat room," was not within the scope of employment even if the employee's "conduct arose in part out of his intent to further the business of [his employer]" by encouraging the plaintiff to use more of the employer's services).

As Smith v. Lannert shows, conduct is not "outside the scope of employment" merely because it violates the rules of employment; one who employs drivers cannot escape liability for their negligence merely by prohibiting them from violating the traffic laws or otherwise driving carelessly. Sometimes, however, conduct may be found to be so far outside the rules set by an employer as to place that conduct beyond the scope of employment. *Compare Smith with* Normand v. City of New Orleans, 363 So. 2d 1220 (La. Ct. App. 1978). In *Normand*, a park commission employee returned to the zoo after working hours to perform an employment task. After completing the task, and in violation of the commission's rules, the employee took a mother and child into the primate night house, an area off limits to the public. The court held that the employee's conduct was such a significant and unpredictable departure from his employment duties, and was so unrelated to service for his employer, as to remove his conduct from the scope of employment.

Conduct that serves no business purpose of the employer ordinarily will not give rise to *respondeat superior* liability. *See* Jones v. Baisch, 40 F.3d 252 (8th Cir. 1994) (leaking of confidential information to friends about a patient's genital herpes, for which the employees were later reprimanded, was not within the scope of employment). In Minyard Food Stores, Inc. v. Goodman, 80 S.W.3d 573 (Tex. 2002), the court held that a manager was not acting within the scope of his employment when he lied about kissing another employee during a workplace misconduct investigation because the statements were not made "in furtherance of the employer's business, and for the accomplishment of the objective for which the employee was employed." The court noted that "[t]here is a critical distinction between defaming someone to one's employer and defaming someone for one's employer."

7. *Intentional Torts within the Scope of Employment.* It is often said that it is harder to establish that an intentional tort, as opposed to negligence, is within the scope of employment. *See* Twardy v. Northwest Airlines, Inc., 2001 W.L. 199567 ((N.D. Ill.) (holding that a flirtatious flight attendant's smacking, kissing, and dumping water on a passenger were not within the scope of employment, so the airline was not liable for battery under *respondeat superior*).

However, "[i]f the intentional tort is committed in the accomplishment of a duty entrusted to the employee, rather than because of personal animosity, the employer may be liable." GTE Southwest, Inc. v. Bruce, 998 S.W.2d 605 (Tex. 1999) (holding an employer liable for outrageous conduct perpetrated over a two-year period in connection with performance of supervisory duties).

8. *Frolic and Detour.* It is possible for an employee to leave the scope of employment, but later return to it. *See, e.g.,* McNair v. Lend Lease Trucks, Inc., 95 F.3d 325 (4th Cir. 1996) (there was a factual dispute over whether a trucker left the course of his employment by stopping at a lounge and drinking alcohol for over three hours and, if so, whether he returned to the scope of his employment by leaving the lounge and attempting to cross the road to his truck when he was struck by a motorcyclist).

9. *Broad Interpretation of Scope of Employment.* In Farmers Ins. Group v. County of Santa Clara, 47 Cal. Rptr. 2d 478, 486-87 (Cal. 1995), the court wrote:

> In California, the scope of employment has been interpreted broadly under the *respondeat superior* doctrine. For example, "[t]he fact that an employee is not engaged in the ultimate object of his employment at the time of his wrongful act does not preclude attribution of liability to an employer." [Citation.] Thus, acts necessary to the comfort, convenience, health, and welfare of the employee while at work, though strictly personal and not acts of service, do not take the employee outside the scope of employment. [Citation.] Moreover, " 'where the employee is combining his own business with that of his employer, or attending to both at substantially the same time, no nice inquiry will be made as to which business he was actually engaged in at the time of injury, unless it clearly appears that neither directly nor indirectly could he have been serving his employer.' ..." [citation]. It is also settled that an employer's vicarious liability may extend to willful and malicious torts of an employee as well as negligence. [Citations.] Finally, an employee's tortious act may be within the scope of employment even if it contravenes an express company rule and confers no benefit to the employer.
>
> ...[However,] "[i]f an employee's tort is personal in nature, mere presence at the place of employment and attendance to occupational duties prior or subsequent to the offense will not give rise to a cause of action against the employer under the doctrine of *respondeat superior*." [Citation.] In such cases, the losses do not foreseeably result from the conduct of the employer's enterprise and so are not fairly attributable to the employer as a cost of doing business.

In *Farmers*, the court held that sexual harassment was not within the scope of employment even though it occurred during work hours in a workplace that could be characterized as traditionally male-dominated.

Other courts have declined to follow California's expansive approach to defining the scope of employment. For example, in O'Toole v. Carr, 815 A.2d 471 (N.J. 2003), the court held that a law firm was not responsible for an auto accident involving one of its partners who was en route to a part-time job as a municipal judge, which the plaintiff argued indirectly benefitted the law firm, although no income from the judgship was paid to the firm. The court wrote:

> [The parties] argue that we should consider the broad articulation of enterprise liability adopted in California, which states that the "'modern and proper basis of vicarious liability of the master is not his control or fault but the risks incident to his enterprise.'" [Citation.] In other words, "'[t]he losses caused by the torts of employees, which as a practical matter are sure to occur in the conduct of the employer's enterprise, are placed upon that enterprise itself, as a required cost of doing business.'" [Citation.]
>
> ... [W]e have thus far declined to adopt that view, retaining instead the Restatement as our vicarious liability standard. Restatement (Second) of Agency §§ 220, 228, 229 (1958). Further, even if we were inclined to adopt the broadest view of enterprise liability, it would not alter the outcome in this case.... Carr's commutation to his job as a municipal court judge is, as a legal matter, unrelated to his law firm activity. Accordingly, the accident could in no event be considered a risk incident to that enterprise.

California's approach to scope-of-employment issues is explored in the next principal case, John R. v. Oakland Unified Sch. Dist.

10. *Deterrence under Negligence and Strict Liability.* Will an employer's willingness to take safety precautions depend upon whether the employer is strictly liable for the negligence of its employees or whether the employer is liable only for its own negligence—such as careless hiring of incompetent employees or failure to train or supervise its employees carefully enough? As a first approximation, at least, it may make no difference at all. If one assumes that neither courts nor employers ever make mistakes about negligence, and that damages are set accurately, both strict liability and negligence should give the employer the same incentive to take safety precautions.

To see why strict liability and negligence may be equivalent with respect to safety measures, consider an employer who is deciding whether to spend an additional $1,000 a year in safety training in order to encourage employees to drive more carefully. Suppose that spending the additional $1,000 each year will, on average, prevent one accident every 10 years, and that the cost of the harm done by one accident is either

(1) $12,000, or

(2) $8,000.

If the employer is strictly liable for harm done by its employees, it has an incentive to spend the $1,000 a year to prevent one $12,000 accident every ten years, as the expected annual saving from spending $1,000 a year is $1,200. But the employer would not want to spend $1,000 a year to prevent a one-in-ten chance of an $8,000 accident. The average annual cost of the latter sort of accident is only $800, so the employer will be better off not spending the $1,000 a year on training and paying an average of $800 a year in damages instead.

What if the standard of care is negligence? Again, the employer's incentive is to spend $1,000 a year on training if the expected annual accident cost is $1,200, but not if it is $800. In this case, if the employer does not spend the $1,000 a year to prevent accidents expected to cost $1,200 a year, the employer will be negligent, and therefore liable. (It is unreasonable not to spend $1,000 to prevent harm of $1,200.) If the expected harm from accidents is only $800 a year, the employer will not be found negligent if the $1,000 is not spent, as reasonable care does not require spending $1,000 to save $800. Therefore, under both negligence and strict liability, the employer has the same incentive to take safety precautions.

Two important qualifications to the above discussion are necessary. First, suppose that it is very hard for outsiders—including potential plaintiffs—to get evidence of the inadequacy of an employer's safety precautions. In that case, strict liability will provide the correct incentive, and negligence will not. For instance, suppose that the employer could prevent harm of $1,000 a year by spending $600 a year, and that the employer knows that even if it doesn't spend the money it has a very good chance of convincing juries that it took all "reasonable" precautions. Under a negligence standard, the employer might not spend the $600 in the hope that it will not be held liable for the $1,000 in harm expected to occur.

Second, even if strict liability and negligence create the same incentive to take safety precautions, they differ in another potentially important way: strict liability increases the costs of conducting an activity which will cause injuries even when that activity is carried on with no negligence. For instance, suppose that an employer of truck drivers estimates the average accident cost per trip to be $30 (all borne by outsiders), and suppose that this cost cannot be reduced further by any cost-effective measures the employer can take. If the standard for the employer's liability is negligence, the employer has an incentive to send a driver out even if the trip will earn the employer only $20. Although the expected harm from the trip—$30—exceeds the employer's benefit—$20—the harm will fall on someone else. If the employer is strictly liable, it will send the employee out only if the trip will earn more than $30.

Because strict liability—unlike negligence—affects activity levels as well as safety precautions, economists who study tort liability often say that strict liability is efficient, and that negligence is not. This is not always true. Consider the matter (examined further in the next chapter) of strict liability for adverse side effects caused by prescription medicine. If the manufacturer of the medicine is liable for all harm done by the medicine, even though that harm could not have been prevented, the manufacturer's costs will be high, and less of the medicine will be used than if the manufacturer were not liable. If, despite its occasional harmful side-effects, the medicine does a great deal of good by curing disease, any reduction in activity level occasioned by strict liability may do more harm than good. (The harm will fall largely upon those too poor to buy the medicine at a price high enough to cover anticipated liability costs.) The "activity level" case for strict liability ignores the possibility that conducting an activity may provide safety benefits on an overall basis even though it does harm in particular cases.

11. *Joinder*. A master and servant, in most jurisdictions, may be joined as defendants in a single suit. *See* Restatement, Second, Agency §217B and Comments and §369C; *see, e.g.*, Shandor v. Lischer, 84 N.W.2d 810 (Mich. 1957) (holding a bartender and his employers liable to a fiddler for personal injuries and damage to his bass viol resulting from a New Year's Eve altercation).

12. *Indemnification of an Employer*. As indicated in the principal case, an employer held liable solely on the basis of *respondeat superior* can seek indemnification for the full

amount of the judgment from the employee whose actions gave rise to the liability. Depending on state procedural rules, the indemnity claim may be asserted against the employee either in the suit by the third person against the employer, or in a separate action. See generally Chapter 17, discussing the liability of joint tortfeasors.

13. *Negligent Hiring.* Even if *respondeat superior* is inapplicable, it may be possible to hold a principal liable for injuries caused by an agent under the doctrine of negligent hiring. This action requires a showing that the principal had actual or constructive notice of the agent's incompetence and that the injury complained of resulted from that incompetence. *See* Ponticas v. K.M.S. Invs., 331 N.W.2d 907 (Minn. 1983) (liability was imposed because an apartment complex was negligent in investigating the background of a manager who raped a tenant; the manager had a history of violent offenses and was given access to a passkey); *cf.* Medlin v. Bass, 398 S.E.2d 460 (N.C. 1990) (where a school principal who perpetrated a sexual assault had performed his official duties in a satisfactory manner for 16 years, and the only rumor relating to his sexual tendencies had been investigated and remained unconfirmed, there was no evidence that the defendant Board of Education knew or could have known of the principal's alleged pedophilic tendencies); Stevens v. Lankard, 254 N.E.2d 339 (N.Y. 1969) (no liability for sodomy of a 13-year-old boy because a routine background check would not have revealed the employee's sodomy conviction in another state); Connes v. Molalla Transp. Sys., Inc., 831 P.2d 1316 (Colo. 1992) (a trucking company had no duty to investigate a driver's non-vehicular criminal background because his employment called for only incidental contact with third persons and drivers were required to stay on interstate highways and sleep in their trucks).

Although liability for negligent hiring or negligent supervision does not require a finding that the employee was acting within the scope of employment when the tortious act occurred, there must be some connection between the plaintiff's injury and the fact of employment. *See* Robertson v. Church of God, Intl., 978 S.W.2d 120 (Tex. Ct. App. 1997) (allegedly negligent hiring and retention of a minister was not a cause in fact of injuries to a massage therapist, whom the minister saw for personal reasons, even though the minister discussed religion and his church work before committing a sexual assault).

Does an employer's liability for negligent hiring end once the employee is discharged? "In many instances it may, but where the employer has created a special relationship whereby his customers admit his employee into their homes, then the employer may be required to give notice or warning to the customer that the employee is no longer employed." Coath v. Jones, 419 A.2d 1249, 1250 (Pa. Super. Ct. 1980).

14. *Vicarious Liability of Partners.* Relations other than employer-employee can give rise to strict liability for the torts of another. One important example is that a member of a partnership is vicariously liable for torts of another partner within the scope of the partnership.

15. *Car Owner Responsibility Laws, the Dangerous-Instrumentality Doctrine, and the Family-Purpose Doctrine.* In some states, the owner of a motor vehicle is liable by statute for the negligence of one who operates the vehicle with the owner's express or implied consent. *See* N.Y. Veh. & Traf. Law §388(1) (Westlaw 2003); Horvath v. Lindenhurst Auto Salvage, Inc., 104 F.3d 540 (2d Cir. 1997) (under New York law, a plaintiff is not required to identify the driver of the vehicle to hold the owner liable, as the driver is presumed to be operating the vehicle with the owner's permission, in the absence of rebuttal evidence). The California statute provides:

CAL. VEHICLE CODE §17150
(Westlaw 2004)

Every owner of a motor vehicle is liable and responsible for death or injury to person or property resulting from a negligent or wrongful act or omission in the operation of the motor vehicle, in the business of the owner or otherwise, by any person using or operating the same with the permission, express or implied, of the owner.

Note that the statute does not impose strict liability. The person using the car must have committed a tort, and the car must have been used with consent.

Some states reach a similar result under a common-law "dangerous-instrumentality doctrine." *See* Toombs v. Alamo Rent-A-Car, Inc., 833 So. 2d 109 (Fla. 2002) (stating that the doctrine "imposes strict vicarious liability upon the owner of a motor vehicle who voluntarily entrusts that motor vehicle to an individual whose negligent operation causes damage to another").

In addition, some states recognize a "family-purpose doctrine" which "subjects the owner of a car to vicarious liability when the owner provides an automobile for the general use by members of the family for non-business purposes." Dan B. Dobbs, The Law of Torts 935 (2000).

John R. v. Oakland Unified School District
Supreme Court of California, In Bank
769 P.2d 948 (Cal. 1989)

ARGUELLES, Justice.

John R.... allegedly was sexually molested by his mathematics teacher while he was at the teacher's apartment participating in an officially sanctioned, extracurricular program. The principal question before us is whether the school district that employed the teacher can be held vicariously liable for the teacher's acts under the doctrine of *respondeat superior*....

...John R. was a ninth grade student....His mathematics teacher...asked John to participate in the school's instructional, work-experience program, under which students received both school credit and monetary payments for assisting teachers by, for example, helping to correct other students' papers....

....Performance of the required work by students at teachers' homes was an option authorized by the district, and the teacher either encouraged or required John to come to his apartment for this purpose. Over the course of many sessions at the teacher's apartment, the teacher sought to develop a close relationship with John as the boy's tutor and counselor, and ultimately endeavored to seduce him. The teacher attempted to convince John that engaging in sex acts with him would be a constructive part of their relationship and, at times, threatened to give John failing grades if John would not go along with his desires and said he would tell people that John had solicited sex from him. On one occasion in February of 1981, the teacher succeeded in pressuring John into sexual acts....

....

John's parents, on behalf of their son and on their own behalf, brought suit against the teacher and the district, alleging that the district was vicariously liable for the teacher's acts and directly liable for its own negligence....

John A. Arguelles

The Court of Appeal reversed...[a trial court] order sustaining the district's demurrer to those causes of action against it premised on a theory of vicarious liability, reasoning that the facts as pleaded by plaintiffs could allow the trier of fact to find the district responsible for the tort of its employee because the teacher's misconduct, although not within or contemplated by his official duties, was made possible by his use, and abuse, of the official, job-created authority he was given over the boy. We granted review....

    ....

....."[A]n employer's liability extends to torts of an employee committed within the scope of his employment...." [Citation.] Whether a tort was committed within the scope of employment is ordinarily a question of fact....(Alma W. v. Oakland Unified School Dist. (1981) 123 Cal. App.3d 133, 138, 176 Cal. Rptr. 287.)

....The question before us here is whether an employer (specifically, a school district) can be held liable for a sexual assault committed by an employee (here, a teacher) on another person (particularly, on a student committed to that teacher's supervision). The natural, initial reaction is "No! Of course not!" A more personal escapade less related to an employer's interests is difficult to imagine. But the question is not so easily disposed of. It is closer than might appear upon first examination....

The courts of other jurisdictions and our own Courts of Appeal have struggled in recent years over whether and how to apply the *respondeat superior* doctrine to the sexual assaults or misconduct of employees. The historical and perhaps still prevailing point of view declines to impose vicarious liability in such circumstances.[7] But the other school

---

7. *See* Jeffrey E. v. Central Baptist Church (1988) 197 Cal. App. 3d 718, 722-724, 243 Cal. Rptr. 128 (church not liable for sexual abuse of minor by Sunday school teacher); Rita M. v. Roman Catholic Archbishop (1986) 187 Cal. App. 3d 1453, 1461, 232 Cal. Rptr. 685 (archbishop not liable for sexual relations between seven priests and minor parishioner); *Alma W., supra,* 123 Cal. App. 3d at pages 143-144, 176 Cal. Rptr. 287 (school district not liable for rape of student by janitor);

of thought has its adherents as well,[8] and what we must decide here is if such liability should be imposed in light of the law of this state and the purposes of the doctrine.

Plaintiffs urge us to take the approach adopted by the Court of Appeal, which looked not to whether a teacher's sexual abuse of a student is foreseeable in the sense that it is characteristic of the job or broadly incidental to a school district's activities [citation], but rather to the nature of the teacher-student relationship. The essence of their argument is that vicarious liability is appropriate when the tort is a consequence of the employer's conferring of official authority on the employee. That is, plaintiffs would have us impose liability on the employer if: (1) there is an official, job-created, hierarchical relationship by which the employee is given authority over a certain, and possibly limited, class of persons; and (2) there is a sufficient nexus between the exercise of that authority and the commission of the tort that it was foreseeable the authority so conferred might be abused to the detriment of the victim.

We recognize that this theory is not without substance...and finds some support in the language of both lines of cases.

. . . .

But although the facts of this case can be made to fit a version of the *respondeat superior* doctrine, we are unpersuaded that they should be or that the doctrine is appropriately invoked here..... "The principal justification for the application of the doctrine of *respondeat superior* in any case is the fact that the employer may spread the risk through insurance and carry the cost thereof as part of his costs of doing business.".... "Three reasons have been suggested for imposing liability on an enterprise for the risks incident to the enterprise: '(1) [I]t tends to provide a spur toward accident prevention; (2) it tends to provide greater assurance of compensation for accident victims[;] and (3) at the same time it tends to provide reasonable assurance that, like other costs, accident losses will be broadly and equitably distributed among the beneficiaries of the enterprises that entail them.'" [Citation.] The first of these three considerations just noted plays little role in the allocation of responsibility for the sexual misconduct of employees generally, and with respect to the unique situation of teachers, indicates that untoward consequences could flow from imposing vicarious liability on school districts. Although it is unquestionably important to encourage both the careful selection of these employees and the close monitoring of their conduct, such concerns are, we think, better addressed by holding school districts to the exercise of due care in such matters and subjecting them to liability only for their own direct negligence in that regard. Applying the doctrine of *respondeat superior* to

---

Boykin v. District of Columbia (D.C. App. 1984) 484 A.2d 560, 562-563 (school district not liable for sexual assault on student by teacher); Bozarth v. Harper Creek Bd. of Ed. (1979), 94 Mich. App. 351, 288 N.W.2d 424, 425 (same); Gambling v. Cornish (N.D. Ill. 1977) 426 F. Supp. 1153, 1155 (municipality not liable for abduction and rape by police officers).

8. *See* Richard H. v. Larry D. (1988) 198 Cal. App. 3d 591, 596, 243 Cal. Rptr. 807 (liability of clinic where psychotherapist consulted by married couple had sexual relations with the wife); White v. County of Orange (1985) 166 Cal. App. 3d 566, 571-572, 212 Cal. Rptr. 493 (liability of county for deputy sheriff's threats to rape motorist); Simmons v. United States (9th Cir. 1986) 805 F.2d 1363, 1368-1371 (liability of federal agency for mental health counselor's sexual involvement with client); Turner v. State (La. App. 1986) 494 So. 2d 1292, 1295-1296 (liability of state for National Guard recruiter's sexual misconduct with applicants); Marston v. Minneapolis Clinic of Psychiatry (Minn. 1982) 329 N.W.2d 306, 310-311 (liability of clinic for therapist's sexual relations with patient); Applewhite v. City of Baton Rouge (La. App. 1979) 380 So. 2d 119, 121-122 (liability of city for policeman's rape of detainee); Lyon v. Carey (D.C. Cir. 1976) 533 F.2d 649, 651 (liability of employer for deliveryman's rape of customer).

impose, in effect, strict liability in this context would be far too likely to deter districts from encouraging, or even authorizing, extracurricular and/or one-on-one contacts between teachers and students or to induce districts to impose such rigorous controls on activities of this nature that the educational process would be negatively affected. Nor is the second consideration—the assurance of compensation for accident victims—appropriately invoked here. The acts here differ from the normal range of risks for which costs can be spread and insurance sought. (*See* Alma W., *supra,....*) The imposition of vicarious liability on school districts for the sexual torts of their employees would tend to make insurance, already a scarce resource, even harder to obtain, and could lead to the diversion of needed funds from the classroom to cover claims.

The only element of the analysis that might point in favor of vicarious liability here is the propriety of spreading the risk of loss among the beneficiaries of the enterprise. School districts and the community at large benefit from the authority placed in teachers to carry out the educational mission, and it can be argued that the consequences of an abuse of that authority should be shared on an equally broad basis. But the connection between the authority conferred on teachers to carry out their instructional duties and the abuse of that authority to indulge in personal, sexual misconduct is simply too attenuated to deem a sexual assault as falling within the range of risks allocable to a teacher's employer. It is not a cost this particular enterprise should bear, and the consequences of imposing liability are unacceptable.

In sum, we believe the Court of Appeal erred in looking mainly to the factual similarities between this case and *White, supra,...* and in failing to consider whether the underlying justifications for the *respondeat superior* doctrine would be served by imposing vicarious liability here. We need not and do not decide whether *White* itself was properly decided or whether the job-created authority theory has any validity in evaluating vicarious liability for the torts of police officers. It suffices here to note that the authority of a police officer over a motorist—bolstered most immediately by his uniform, badge and firearm, and only slightly less so by the prospect of criminal sanctions for disobedience—plainly surpasses that of a teacher over a student. The teacher's authority is different in both degree and kind, and it is simply not great enough to persuade us that vicarious liability should attach here for the teacher's tort. Furthermore, invoking *respondeat superior* here would raise an entirely different specter of untoward consequences, or interference with the purposes for which the authority was conferred in the first place, than might result from the imposition of vicarious liability in the limited context of a police officer's abuse of authority. We doubt that police departments would deprive their officers of weapons or preclude them from enforcing the laws, but we see a significant and unacceptable risk that school districts would be dissuaded from permitting teachers to interact with their students on any but the most formal and supervised basis.

....

....The judgment of the Court of Appeal is reversed insofar as it reversed the trial court's order sustaining the district's demurrer to those claims premised on a theory of vicarious liability under the *respondeat superior* doctrine....

[BROUSSARD, J., concurred. LUCAS, C.J., and PANNELLI, J., concurred in a concurring and dissenting opinion by EAGLESON, J., which did not discuss the *respondeat superior* issue and has been omitted.]

MOSK, Justice, concurring and dissenting.

....

It is my view that the Court of Appeal was entirely correct in its analysis of plaintiffs' claim against the school district....

The case at bench is in analytical symmetry with [White v. County of Orange (1985) 166 Cal. App. 3d 566, 212 Cal. Rptr. 493]....

As in *White*, the teacher, by virtue of the exercise of his official authority, was able to perpetrate the sexual assault. That is, through the use of his authority to administer grades, to assign extracurricular work projects, and, significantly, by utilizing the school-approved work experience program, the teacher procured the student's presence in his home facilitating the opportunity for the assault. In concluding that such pleaded facts would be clearly incident to the teacher's exercise of his official duties, we [should] focus not on whether the school teacher's sexual activity with a student is either "characteristic" or foreseeable, but rather on whether the assault arose out of the exercise of job-created authority over the plaintiff student. It was, therefore, error to sustain the demurrer as to appellants' *respondeat superior* theory....

I would affirm the Court of Appeal judgment in its entirety.

KAUFMAN, Justice, concurring and dissenting.

....I would agree it is the rare case in which a sexual assault by a teacher against a student should give rise to liability on the part of his employing school district. Nevertheless,...this is such a case.

    ....

The determination as to whether an employee committed a tort in the course of his employment turns upon whether or not the act was required by or incident to his duties, or could reasonably be foreseen by the employer in any event. [Citations.] "Foreseeability" in this context must be distinguished from foreseeability as a test for negligence. "In the latter sense 'foreseeable' means a level of probability which would lead a prudent person to take effective precautions, whereas 'foreseeability' as a test for *respondeat superior* merely means that in the context of the particular enterprise an employee's conduct is not so unusual or startling that it would seem unfair to include the loss resulting from it among other costs of the employer's business.".....

A sexual assault by a teacher against a student, indeed a sexual assault by anyone under any circumstances, strikes the normal sensibility as so extreme and abhorrent that it would indeed be "unfair to include the loss resulting from it among other costs of the employer's business.".....

Sadly, however, we have learned that sexual harassment and assaults—in the home as well as the workplace—are not uncommon occurrences. This is a hard truth to accept....

Thus, the courts of this and other jurisdictions have recognized that there are circumstances where an employee's sexual misconduct cannot, in all candor, be deemed so "unusual or startling" that it would be unfair to impose vicarious liability upon the employer. [Citations.]

The case before us falls within this narrow category. The sexual assault by the teacher against the minor occurred in the teacher's home, in the course of an official educational program known as Instructional Work Experience (IWE). The district affirmatively sanctioned IWE work at teachers' homes as an acceptable feature of the program. The assault was further facilitated by the teacher's representations to the minor that a sexual relationship would enhance his educational experience in the IWE program.

The district did not require that a student obtain the written permission of his parents to participate in the IWE program at the teacher's home, nor did it require that other students or adults be present during the home instruction. In effect, the district sanctioned IWE program virtually guaranteed that the teacher could act with impunity, free from the fear of interruption or discovery, fully assured of complete privacy and secrecy. Under these circumstances, it is not so "unusual or startling" that a teacher might seize the opportunity created by the program to make improper sexual advances toward one of his students. Under these circumstances, it is unjust not to require that the district share in the liability for the injuries which resulted.

    ....

The IWE home-instruction program contained none of the usual safeguards incident to most normal extracurricular activities, i.e., a public setting (as opposed to the private seclusion of the teacher's home) and the presence or knowledge of other persons (in contrast to the isolation and secrecy inherent in the IWE program). Such reasonable safeguards would normally act to deter such misconduct, or, failing that, to limit the district's exposure to claims based on vicarious liability.

Indeed, "public policy" militates strongly in favor of vicarious liability in this case. One of the "policy" bases of *respondeat superior* is said to be its tendency to act as a "spur toward accident prevention." [Citation.] If that is the case, and incidents of the nature at issue here are, as I believe, a foreseeable result of such ill-advised programs, then the imposition of vicarious liability in this case might ultimately prove to be an inducement, not a deterrent, to well planned and properly executed extracurricular school programs.

It is further suggested that the underlying purposes of respondeat superior—the assurance of fair compensation for tort victims by spreading the risk of losses through insurance carried by the responsible enterprise as a cost of doing business [citation]—would not be furthered in this case.[2] On the contrary, these considerations amply justify the imposition of vicarious liability....

For these reasons, I would allow plaintiffs to proceed against the district on its claims based on vicarious liability....

Notes

1. ***Sexual Abuse by an Employee.*** *See* Lisa M. v. Henry Mayo Newhall Mem. Hosp., 48 Cal. Rptr. 2d 510 (Cal. 1995) (a hospital technician who sexually molested a pregnant patient while performing an ultrasound examination was, as a matter of law, not acting within the scope of employment). *See also* Medlin v. Bass, 398 S.E.2d 460 (N.C. 1990). In refusing to hold a school board liable for a principal's alleged sexual assault of a student, the *Medlin* court wrote:

> While...[the principal] was exercising authority conferred upon him by...
> [the defendant board of education] when he summoned the minor plaintiff to

---

2. As to the availability of insurance to cover such claims, it is well settled that Insurance Code §533 (insurance for willful acts void as against public policy) does not preclude coverage for liability based upon *respondeat superior* for the intentional torts of an employee. [Citation.] In the rare case where vicarious liability is appropriate, the distribution of costs is clearly consistent with the policy underlying the doctrine of *respondeat superior*. Should the minor or his parents have to bear the expense of psychiatric or psychological treatment in addition to the trauma resulting from the sexual assault?

his office to discuss her truancy problem, in proceeding to assault her sexually he was advancing a completely personal objective. The assault could advance no conceivable purpose of... [the board of education];... [the principal] acted for personal reasons only, and his acts thus were beyond the course and scope of his employment as a matter of law.

2. *Insurance for Damages Caused by Sexual Abuse.* In St. Paul Fire & Marine Ins. Co. v. F.H., 55 F.3d 1420 (9th Cir. 1995), the court held that Alaska public policy did not preclude the availability of insurance coverage for liability based on sexual abuse.

3. *Non-Delegable Duties.* Courts occasionally speak of non-delegable duties, though it is difficult to predict when this concept will be invoked. The term "non-delegable duty" is more a conclusion (that liability will be imposed) than an aid to analysis. The Restatement indicates that a principal will be held vicariously liable for the torts of an independent contractor involving the breach of a non-delegable duty, although it candidly acknowledges that "[f]ew courts have made any attempt to state any general principles as to when the employer's duty cannot be delegated, and it may as yet be impossible to reduce these exceptions to such principles." Restatement, Second, of Torts, note preceding §416.

Despite this disclaimer, the Restatement attempts to articulate a long list of occasions on which a principal cannot shift responsibility for the proper conduct of work to an independent contractor. This rule applies (but is by no means limited) to cases where the contemplated work requires special precautions (§416), is to be done in a public place (§§417 and 418), involves the construction or maintenance of buildings in the principal's possession (§422) or instrumentalities used in highly dangerous activities (§423), is subject to safety requirements imposed by legislation (§424), is itself inherently dangerous (§427), or involves an "abnormally dangerous" activity (§427A). Courts often struggle in attempting to apply these exceptions to the general rule that a principal is not liable for the torts of an independent contractor.

See generally Maldonado v. Gateway Hotel Holdings, L.L.C., 2003 W.L. 22287857 (E.D. Mo.) (a boxing match was an inherently dangerous activity, and therefore a hotel was liable for the negligence of an independent contractor in failing to provide post-fight medical monitoring and an ambulance); Beckman v. Butte-Silver Bow Cty., 1 P.3d 348 (Mont. 2000) (trenching is an inherently dangerous activity because the risks of death or serious bodily injury are well recognized in the construction industry and special precautions are required to prevent a cave-in that could bury a worker); Saiz v. Belen Sch. Dist., 827 P.2d 102 (N.M. 1992) (installation of a high voltage light system at a football stadium was inherently dangerous work); Huddleston v. Union Rural Elec. Ass'n, 841 P.2d 282 (Colo. 1992) (it was for the jury to determine whether the inherently dangerous activity exception applied to a utility which hired a charter airplane service to fly passengers in winter to the Colorado mountains in an unpressurized plane that was uncertified for flights into icy conditions).

4. *Common Carriers and Non-Delegable Duties.* If the relationship between an employer and the plaintiff is deemed to impose on the employer a duty that may not be delegated, the employer may be held liable for an employee's tort that is prompted by purely personal motives and therefore outside of the scope of employment. On this theory common carriers have been held liable to patrons for assaults and robberies perpetrated by their employees, and it has been urged that "similar rulings may be expected as to innkeepers, proprietors of public utilities, and the like." Fowler V. Harper, Fleming James, Jr., & Oscar S. Gray, The Law of Torts §26.9, p. 54 (2d ed. 1986) (collecting

cases). *But see* Adams v. New York City Transit Auth., 666 N.E.2d 216 (N.Y. 1996) (holding that a common carrier is no longer liable in New York for torts of employees falling outside the scope of employment).

5. *Ethics in Law Practice: Non-Lawyer Assistants.* A lawyer may be held liable for the tort of an employee occurring within the scope of the employment. In addition, misconduct by a non-lawyer assistant may subject a lawyer to professional discipline, such as reprimand, suspension, or disbarment. *See, e.g.,* In re Galbasini, 786 P.2d 971 (Ariz. 1990) (six-month suspension based on lawyer's failure to supervise employees who engaged in debt collection in the lawyer's name, improperly solicited clients, and failed to communicate with those clients); In Re Berkos, 444 N.E.2d 150 (Ill. 1982) (attorney suspended for failure to supervise a secretary, despite the attorney's lack of knowledge of the employee's improper interception of client correspondence and other misconduct).

In the Model Rules of Professional Conduct (2003)—which define standards for attorney discipline, not tort liability—Rule 5.3 provides in part:

> With respect to a nonlawyer employed or retained by or associated with a lawyer:
>
> (a) a partner, and a lawyer who individually or together with other lawyers possesses comparable managerial authority in a law firm, shall make reasonable efforts to ensure that the firm has in effect measures giving reasonable assurance that the person's conduct is compatible with the professional obligations of the lawyer;
>
> ...and
>
> (c) a lawyer shall be responsible for conduct of such a person that would be a violation of the Rules of Professional Conduct if engaged in by a lawyer if:
>
> (1) the lawyer orders or, with the knowledge of the specific conduct, ratifies the conduct involved; or
>
> (2) the lawyer is a partner or has comparable managerial authority in the law firm in which the person is employed, or has direct supervisory authority over the person, and knows of the conduct at a time when its consequences can be avoided or mitigated but fails to take reasonable remedial action.

Does the language of subsection (a) impose strict liability or a fault-based standard? What about subsection (c)?

3. Ostensible or Apparent Agency

Baptist Memorial Hospital System v. Sampson

Supreme Court of Texas
969 S.W.2d 945 (Tex. 1998)

PHILLIPS, Chief Justice, delivered the opinion of the Court.

....

On March 23, 1990, Rhea Sampson was bitten on the arm by an unidentified creature that was later identified as a brown recluse spider. By that evening, her arm was swollen and painful, and a friend took her to the Southeast Baptist Hospital emergency room. Dr. Susan Howle, an emergency room physician, examined Sampson, diagnosed an allergic reaction, administered Benadryl and a shot of painkiller, prescribed medication for pain and swelling, and sent her home. Her condition grew worse, and she returned to the Hospital's emergency room by ambulance a little over a day later. This time Dr. Mark Zakula, another emergency room physician, treated her. He administered additional pain medication and released her....About fourteen hours later, with her condition rapidly deteriorating, Sampson went to another hospital and was admitted to the intensive care ward in septic shock. There, her bite was diagnosed as that of a brown recluse spider, and the proper treatment was administered to save her life. Sampson allegedly continues to have recurrent pain and sensitivity where she was bitten, respiratory difficulties, and extensive scarring.

Sampson sued Drs. Howle and Zakula for medical malpractice. She also sued Baptist Memorial Hospital System ("BMHS")....Sampson...alleged that the Hospital was vicariously liable for Dr. Zakula's alleged negligence under an ostensible agency theory. Sampson nonsuited Dr. Howle early in the discovery process. The trial court granted BMHS summary judgment on Sampson's claims of vicarious liability....Sampson appealed only on the vicarious liability theory.

Both parties agree that BMHS established as a matter of law that Dr. Zakula was not its agent or employee. Thus the burden shifted to Sampson to raise a fact issue on each element of her ostensible agency theory, which Texas courts have held to be in the nature of an affirmative defense.[Citations.] Sampson contended that she raised a material fact issue on whether Dr. Zakula was BMHS's ostensible agent. The court of appeals, with one justice dissenting, agreed and reversed the summary judgment....

. . . .

Under the doctrine of *respondeat superior*, an employer is vicariously liable for the negligence of an agent or employee acting within the scope of his or her agency or employment, although the principal or employer has not personally committed a wrong. [Citations.] The most frequently proffered justification for imposing such liability is that the principal or employer has the right to control the means and methods of the agent or employee's work. [Citations.] Because an independent contractor has sole control over the means and methods of the work to be accomplished, however, the individual or entity that hires the independent contractor is generally not vicariously liable for the tort or negligence of that person. [Citations.] Nevertheless, an individual or entity may act in a manner that makes it liable for the conduct of one who is not its agent at all or who, although an agent, has acted outside the scope of his or her authority. Liability may be imposed in this manner under the doctrine of ostensible agency in circumstances when the principal's conduct should equitably prevent it from denying the existence of an agency.[2] [Citation.] Ostensible agency in Texas is based on the notion of estoppel, that is, a representation by the principal causing justifiable reliance and resulting harm. *See* [citation]; Restatement (Second) of Agency § 267; Keeton et al., Prosser and Keeton on the Law of Torts § 105, at 733–34 (5th ed.1984).

Texas courts have applied these basic agency concepts to many kinds of principals, including hospitals. [Citation.] A hospital is ordinarily not liable for the negligence of a physician who is an independent contractor. [Citation.] On the other hand, a

---

2. Many courts use the terms ostensible agency, apparent agency, apparent authority, and agency by estoppel interchangeably. As a practical matter, there is no distinction among them....Regardless of the term used, the purpose of the doctrine is to prevent injustice and protect those who have been misled. [Citation.]

hospital may be vicariously liable for the medical malpractice of independent contractor physicians when plaintiffs can establish the elements of ostensible agency. [Citations.]

    ....

In this case, the court of appeals held that two distinct theories of vicarious liability with different elements are available in Texas to impose liability on a hospital for emergency room physician negligence: agency by estoppel (referred to in this opinion as ostensible agency), based on the Restatement (Second) of Agency section 267, and apparent agency, based on the Restatement (Second) of Torts section 429. [Citation.] Under section 267, the party asserting ostensible agency must demonstrate that (1) the principal, by its conduct, (2) caused him or her to reasonably believe that the putative agent was an employee or agent of the principal, and (3) that he or she justifiably relied on the appearance of agency. Restatement (Second) of Agency § 267 (1958). Although neither party mentioned section 429 in the trial court or in their briefs to the court of appeals, the court of appeals then proceeded to adopt section 429 and hold that under that section, plaintiff had only to raise a fact issue on two elements: (1) the patient looked to the hospital, rather than the individual physician, for treatment; and (2) the hospital held out the physician as its employee. [Citation.] Holding that the plaintiff had established a genuine issue of material fact on each element of this latter affirmative defense, the court reversed and remanded to the trial court for trial on the merits. The court of appeals further suggested that a hospital could do nothing to avoid holding out a physician in its emergency room as its employee because notification to prospective patients in any form would be ineffectual:

> [W]e take an additional step in our analysis to consider whether notice provided in consent forms and posted in emergency rooms can ever be sufficient to negate a hospital's "holding out"....

>   ....

> ....Because we do not believe hospitals should be allowed to avoid such responsibility, we encourage the full leap—imposing a nondelegable duty on hospitals for the negligence of emergency room physicians.

[Citation.] Thus, the court of appeals would create a nondelegable duty on a hospital solely because it opens its doors for business.

We first reject the court of appeals' conclusion that there are two methods, one "more difficult to prove" than the other, to establish the liability of a hospital for the malpractice of an emergency room physician. [Citation.] Our courts have uniformly required proof of all three elements of section 267 to invoke the fiction that one should be responsible for the acts of another who is not in fact an agent acting within his or her scope of authority. As we have explained:

> Apparent authority in Texas is based on estoppel. It may arise either from a principal knowingly permitting an agent to hold herself out as having authority or by a principal's actions which lack such ordinary care as to clothe an agent with the indicia of authority, thus leading a reasonably prudent person to believe that the agent has the authority she purports to exercise....

> A prerequisite to a proper finding of apparent authority is evidence of conduct by the principal relied upon by the party asserting the estoppel defense which would lead a reasonably prudent person to believe an agent had authority to so act.

[Citations.] Thus, to establish a hospital's liability for an independent contractor's medical malpractice based on ostensible agency, a plaintiff must show that (1) he or she had a reasonable belief that the physician was the agent or employee of the hospital, (2) such belief was generated by the hospital affirmatively holding out the physician as its agent or employee or knowingly permitting the physician to hold herself out as the hospital's agent or employee, and (3) he or she justifiably relied on the representation of authority. [Citations.] While a few courts of appeals have referred to section 429, it has never before been adopted in this state by any appellate court. [Citations.] To the extent that the Restatement (Second) of Torts section 429 proposes a conflicting standard for establishing liability, we expressly decline to adopt it in Texas.

Next, we reject the suggestion of the court of appeals quoted above that we disregard the traditional rules and take "the full leap" of imposing a nondelegable duty on Texas hospitals for the malpractice of emergency room physicians. [Citation.] Imposing such a duty is not necessary to safeguard patients in hospital emergency rooms. A patient injured by a physician's malpractice is not without a remedy. The injured patient ordinarily has a cause of action against the negligent physician, and may retain a direct cause of action against the hospital if the hospital was negligent in the performance of a duty owed directly to the patient. [Citations.]

We now examine the record below in light of the appropriate standard. The Hospital may be held liable for the negligence of Dr. Zakula if Sampson can demonstrate that (1) she held a reasonable belief that Dr. Zakula was an employee or agent of the Hospital, (2) her belief was generated by some conduct on the part of the Hospital, and (3) she justifiably relied on the appearance that Dr. Zakula was an agent or employee of the Hospital. [Citation.]

As summary judgment evidence, BMHS offered the affidavit of Dr. Potyka, an emergency room physician, which established that the emergency room doctors are not the actual agents, servants, or employees of the Hospital, and are not subject to the supervision, management, direction, or control of the Hospital when treating patients. Dr. Potyka further stated that when Dr. Zakula treated Sampson, signs were posted in the emergency room notifying patients that the emergency room physicians were independent contractors. Dr. Potyka's affidavit also established that the Hospital did not collect any fees for emergency room physician services and that the physicians billed the patients directly. BMHS presented copies of signed consent forms as additional summary judgment evidence. During both of Sampson's visits to the Hospital emergency room, before being examined or treated, Sampson signed a "Consent for Diagnosis, Treatment and Hospital Care" form explaining that all physicians at the Hospital are independent contractors who exercise their own professional judgment without control by the Hospital. The consent forms read in part:

> I acknowledge and agree that…, Southeast Baptist Hospital,…and any Hospital operated as a part of Baptist Memorial Hospital System, is not responsible for the judgment or conduct of any physician who treats or provides a professional service to me, but rather each physician is an independent contractor who is self-employed and is not the agent, servant or employee of the hospital.

To establish her claim of ostensible agency, Sampson offered her own affidavits. In her original affidavit, she stated that although the Hospital directed her to sign several pieces of paper before she was examined, she did not read them and no one explained their contents to her. Her supplemental affidavit stated that she did not recall signing the documents and that she did not, at any time during her visit to the emergency room, see any signs stating that the doctors who work in the emergency room are not employees of the Hospital. Both affidavits state that she did not choose which doctor would treat her and that, at all times, she believed that a physician employed by the hospital was treating her. Based on this record we must determine if Sampson produced sufficient summary judgment evidence to raise a genuine issue of material fact on each element of ostensible agency, thereby defeating BMHS's summary judgment motion.

Even if Sampson's belief that Dr. Zakula was a hospital employee were reasonable, that belief, as we have seen, must be based on or generated by some conduct on the part of the Hospital. "No one should be denied the right to set up the truth unless it is in plain contradiction of his former allegations or acts." [Citations.] The summary judgment proof establishes that the Hospital took no affirmative act to make actual or prospective patients think the emergency room physicians were its agents or employees, and did not fail to take reasonable efforts to disabuse them of such a notion. As a matter of law, on this record, no conduct by the Hospital would lead a reasonable patient to believe that the treating emergency room physicians were hospital employees.

Sampson has failed to raise a fact issue on at least one essential element of her claim. Accordingly, we reverse the judgment of the court of appeals and render judgment that Sampson take nothing.

Note

1. *See* O'Banner v. McDonald's Corp., 670 N.E.2d 632, 634 (Ill. 1996) (recognizing the principle, but holding that a restaurant patron who was injured when he slipped and fell in restaurant's restroom could not recover on "apparent agency" theory from the restaurant franchisor, as patron failed to show that he actually relied on the alleged apparent agency between the franchisee and franchisor in going to the restaurant).

2. *Manifestations Traceable to the Employer.* Restatement, Third, of Agency §2.03 Cmt. c (Tent. Draft No. 1 2001), the section on apparent authority, states:

> The doctrine…applies to any set of circumstances under which it is reasonable for a third party to believe that an agent has authority, so long as the belief is traceable to manifestations of the principal.…A third party's reasonable understanding of the principal's conduct will reflect general business custom, as well as usage that is particular to the principal's industry and prior dealings between the parties. A belief that results solely from the statements or other conduct of the agent, unsupported by any manifestations traceable to the principal, does not create apparent authority unless, as explained below, the agent's conduct has been directed by the principal. An agent's success in misleading the third party as to the existence of actual authority does not in itself make the principal accountable.
>
> ....
>
> ....If the principal directs the agent to make a statement to a third party about the agent's authority, and the agent's statement of authority is consistent with a reasonable belief on the agent's part about the principal's wishes, the agent's statement to the third party is within the scope of the agent's actual authority....If the third party reasonably believes that the agent is authorized and that the principal has authorized the agent to make the statement, apparent authority is present as well....
>
> ....

.... To establish apparent authority, it is not necessary for the third party to establish fault on the part of the principal.... If apparent authority is present, it is irrelevant that its presence or continued presence eluded the principal's exercise of due care to prevent or defeat it.

3. *Ethics in Law Practice: Lawyers with Apparent Authority. See* Cook v. Brundidge, Fountain, Elliott & Churchill, 533 S.W.2d 751 (Tex. 1976) (stating that if a partner in a law firm was acting within the scope of his apparent authority when he received money and property of the plaintiffs, the law firm would be "bound to make good the loss" from the partner's alleged misapplication of the funds); In re Summit Airlines, Inc., 160 B.R. 911, 919 (Bankr. E.D. Pa. 1993) (holding a law firm liable under agency law for a partner's misappropriation of funds).

4. *Problem: Stealing a Client.* A telephone call to a law firm from a prospective client who saw the firm's television ad is routed by the reception to an associate, who normally handles such calls. Because the prospective client is disabled, the associate goes to her home to discuss providing representation with respect to prosecution of her personal injury claim. The associate gives the woman one of his law firm business cards, but scratches out the phone number and writes down his cell phone number. He tells the woman that it is best always to call him on his cell phone, and to speak with him personally, to insure that her case is handled most efficiently. He directs the woman not to bother calling the general phone number for the law firm.

The associate gives the woman a contract to sign. The contract is not the firm's standard contract, but merely a generic form. The form does not contain the name of the law firm. It merely has a blank for the name of the attorney to be filled in, and the associate has written his name in that blank. The client and the associate both sign the contract.

The associate's intent is to "steal" the client from the law firm and to collect the entire fee that results from the representation. No case file for the client is ever established at the law firm, and no one at the firm ever learns of the relationship with the woman. That is not uncommon, because many prospective clients are not signed up. Because the associate lacks the resources to hire the necessary experts to assist in the preparation of the case, the matter languishes and important deadlines pass, despite the fact that the woman was seriously harmed and is in pain.

When the woman calls the law firm to complain, she learns that no one in the firm, other than the associate, has ever heard of her case. The firm denies that it has any attorney-client relationship with the woman. The woman sues the law firm for malpractice, alleging that the associate acted with apparent authority and that the law firm is therefore responsible for his bungling of the case. The law firm has never had a problem like this before. What result?

4. The Fellow-Servant Rule

The fellow-servant rule holds that, despite the principle of *respondeat superior,* an employer cannot be held liable for harm to an employee which results from the conduct of a fellow worker. The injured employee is deemed to have assumed the risk of a co-employee's negligence by reason of having accepted employment during which negligent conduct might occur. The once-significant effect of the fellow-servant rule has been greatly diminished by the advent of workers' compensation. To the extent that the rule survives, some decisions, such as Buckley v. City of New York, 437 N.E.2d 1088

(N.Y. 1982), have refused to apply it on the ground that it is an unsound departure from the policies of deterrence and spreading of losses than are inherent in the rule of *respondeat superior*. Today, the fellow-servant rule seldom plays a significant role in tort litigation.

B. Harm Inflicted by Animals

Wild versus Domestic. A possessor's liability for harm caused by animals frequently depends upon whether the animal is classified as wild or domestic. In the case of harm done by wild animals, liability is usually strict; liability for harm done by domestic animals is normally based on negligence.

General Princip

Wild Animals (Ferae Naturae). The third Restatement provides:

§ 22. Wild Animals

(a) The owner or possessor of a wild animal is subject to strict liability for physical harm caused by the wild animal.

(b) A wild animal is an animal that belongs to a category which has not been generally domesticated and which is likely, unless restrained, to cause personal injury.

Restatement, Third, of Torts: Liability for Physical Harm (Basic Principles) § 22 (Tent. Draft No. 1, 2001). According to the commentary:

> The wild-animal definition stated in this section...requires that each of two elements be satisfied: that the category of animals is not generally domesticated, and that the category of animals if unrestrained is likely to cause physical injury. For purposes of the first element, the focus is on the status of the category of animals in the United States. Thus an elephant in this country is a wild animal even though it may not be wild in Myanmar, where elephants have long been domesticated and utilized for domestic chores. Most of the lions and tigers that are present in the United States today do not live in the wild, but rather are owned by zoos, circuses, and the like, where they are used for purposes of entertaining and educating human audiences. Despite the prevalence of such ownership, these categories of animals have not been domesticated: they remain capable of surviving on their own. Accordingly, they fall within the first part of the wild-animal definition. The second part of the definition must also be satisfied. It excludes from the wild-animal category many categories of animals that ordinarily live in a state of nature yet which pose no obvious risk of causing substantial personal injury. While lions and tigers plainly do involve such a risk, iguanas, pigeons, and manatees do not, and hence are not wild animals for purposes of this section. Whether a category of animal is or is not wild is an issue for the court to decide....

Id. at cmt. b.

Section 22 turns on ownership or possession of the animal, not ownership or possession of the land on which the animal may be present. "Thus, if a customer brings a rattlesnake into a store, it is the customer and not the store owner who is subject to strict liability if the rattlesnake attacks another customer." *Id.* at cmt. e. As to the rules governing harm that ensues following the escape, theft, or return of wild animals, see Comment e.

If the harm caused by a possessor's wild animal is not the result of a dangerous propensity of the species, as where a wild bear goes to sleep on the highway and is struck by the plaintiff's vehicle, the possessor can be held liable only upon a showing of negligence. *Id.* at cmt. f.

Domestic Animals. At common law, a possessor of a domestic animal is strictly liable for harm which results from an *abnormally* dangerous propensity of the animal of which the possessor knows or has reason to know. Restatement, Second, of Torts §509; Restatement, Third, of Torts: Liability for Physical Harm (Basic Principles) §23 (Tent. Draft No. 1, 2001). The emphasis here is on the abnormality of the danger. Many domestic animals, such as bulls and stallions and other breeding animals, are known to have dangerous propensities. But these tendencies are deemed to be ordinary and necessary incidents of civilized life, since these animals are by custom devoted to the service of mankind. Only if a domestic animal poses an *abnormal* danger will strict liability apply, and in making that determination some courts impose an exacting standard of proof. *See, e.g.,* Duren v. Kunkel, 814 S.W.2d 935 (Mo. 1991) (refusing to find that defendant's bull had a vicious propensity different from other bulls of its breed or class).

Absent clear proof that the possessor was on notice of an abnormal danger, a possessor of a domestic animal will be liable only for negligence—which of course requires evidence that harm was foreseeable. Thus, actual or constructive notice of a domestic animal's dangerousness (whether due to an abnormal propensity or not) is generally a prerequisite to recovery. However, some jurisdictions impose strict liability for unforeseeable dog bites on the theory that the possessor, who enjoys the benefits of having a dog, should also bear the resulting burdens and is in a better position to insure against them. *See* Hossenlopp v. Canon, 329 S.E.2d 438 (S.C. 1985), *supra* at 23.

Despite the frequently recited old saw, a dog or other domestic animal is not "entitled to one free bite." If the possessor has reason to know that the harm may occur, liability for the first bite may be imposed under either a strict liability or negligence theory, depending on the facts.

Only owners or possessors are subject to liability for harm caused by animals. If a person sells a dog to another, and the animal and the money are transferred, the seller owes no duty to a third person who is later injured by the dog. *See* Koepke v. Martinez, 84 S.W.3d 393 (Tex. App. 2002).

Wandering Livestock and Other Animals. According to the third Restatement:

> An owner or possessor of livestock or other animals, except for dogs and cats, that intrude upon the land of another is subject to strict liability for physical harm caused by the intrusion.

Restatement, Third, of Torts: Liability for Physical Harm (Basic Principles) §21 (Tent. Draft No. 1, 2001).

With regard to harm caused to motorists by wandering livestock, a negligence standard may govern or there may be no liability at all. *Compare* Larson-Murphy v. Steiner, 15 P.3d 1205 (Mont. 2000) (holding that livestock owners have a common law duty to exercise control of their livestock to a particular standard of conduct to protect motorists, as foreseeable plaintiffs, against unreasonable risks), *with* Gibbs v. Jackson, 990

S.W.2d 745 (Tex. 1999) (holding that the keeper of a horse had no statutory or common-law duty to prevent the horse from roaming onto a farm-to-market roadway in an area that had not adopted a local stock law). Liability may depend upon whether the plaintiff or defendant is required by local law to erect and maintain a fence for the purpose of preventing harm.

Limits on Strict Liability. According to the third Restatement, the rules on strict liability for harm caused by animals, as well as the rules on strict liability for abnormally dangerous activity (discussed below), are designed largely to protect innocent third persons. Accordingly, these provisions cannot be invoked for the benefit of trespassers or persons who were seeking to secure some benefit from contact with or proximity to the animal or activity in question. *See* Restatement, Third, of Torts: Liability for Physical Harm (Basic Principles) §24(c)and (d) (Tent. Draft No. 1, 2001). Nor do the rules apply to harm not characteristic of the animal or activity or to harm caused by the intentional intervention of a third person. *Id.* at §24(a) & (b). Likewise, strict liability will not be imposed if the defendant maintained ownership or possession of the animal or conducted the activity pursuant to a duty imposed by law. *Id.* at §24(e). Of course, even if strict-liability principles do not apply, the plaintiff may seek to recover for negligence.

Statutory Standards. In many areas, the common law has been supplanted by statutory standards. *See, e.g.,* Bradacs v. Jiacobone, 625 N.W.2d 108 (Mich. Ct. App. 2001) (holding that a guest's conduct in reaching down to pick up a ball she had dropped some two feet from food being eaten by the homeowner's dog was not "provocation" sufficient to relieve the homeowners of liability under dog bite statute); Collins v. Kenealy, 492 N.W.2d 679 (Iowa 1992) (a dog groomer was not a statutory "owner" of a dog left in her temporary care and thus was not precluded from recovery under a strict liability statute). *See also* Sease v. Taylor's Pets, Inc., 700 P.2d 1054 (Or. Ct. App. 1985) (holding that a live pet skunk was a "product" within the meaning of the state products liability statute and that a pet store was subject to strict liability for injuries caused by a skunk it had sold which turned out to be rabid).

C. Abnormally Dangerous Activities

Harm caused by an activity that is "abnormally dangerous" may be governed by a strict-liability standard, rather than by negligence principles.

Yommer v. McKenzie

Court of Appeals of Maryland
257 A.2d 138 (Md. 1969)

SINGLEY, Judge.

Mr. and Mrs. McKenzie, the plaintiffs below, live at Little Crossing in Garrett County. Their immediate neighbors are the defendants, Mr. and Mrs. Yommer, who operate a grocery store and gasoline filling station. On 17 December 1967, Mr. McKenzie noticed a "smell" in his well water which...proved to be caused by the presence of gasoline in the well. McKenzie complained to Yommer, who arranged to have one of his storage tanks removed and replaced in January 1968. However, it was not until the

McKenzies had a filter and water softener installed in April of 1968 that it was possible for them to use the water for cooking and bathing. At the time of the trial of the case in December of 1968 there was testimony that the McKenzies were still bringing drinking water from Grantsville, about a mile distant.

The McKenzies, alleging a nuisance, sued the Yommers for damages and recovered a verdict of $3,500.... The Yommers have appealed....

The thrust of the Yommers' argument is...that the McKenzies failed to show that the damage they sustained was occasioned by the Yommers' negligence in the operation of the filling station....

....

The argument that the McKenzies must prove negligence in order to recover fails to take into account the doctrine of strict liability imposed by the rule of Rylands v. Fletcher which has been adopted by our prior decisions....

Restatement, Torts (1938) §519 at 41 relied on by the Yommers, limits the applicability of the rule of Rylands v. Fletcher to what it terms an "ultrahazardous activity" and incorporates a caveat, "The Institute expresses no opinion as to whether the construction and use of a large tank or artificial reservoir in which a large body of water or other fluid is collected is or is not an ultrahazardous activity." [Citation.] Prosser, Torts, *supra*, §77 at 527, is critical of the ultrahazardous activity concept which

> ...goes beyond the English rule in ignoring the relation of the activity to its surroundings, and falls short of it in the insistence on extreme danger and the impossibility of eliminating it with all possible care. The shift of emphasis is not at all reflected in the American cases, which have laid quite as much stress as the English ones upon the place where the thing is done.

Restatement, Torts 2d,...provides more guidance for us than its predecessor. For the "ultrahazardous activity" test an "abnormally dangerous activity" test has been substituted. The effect of this change is to enlarge the circumstances under which the rule of strict liability will apply. As the Reporter pointed out to the American Law Institute:

> "Ultrahazardous," as it is defined in the old Section, is misleading. There is probably no activity whatever, unless it be the use of atomic energy, which is not perfectly safe if the utmost care is used—which would of course include the choice of an absolutely safe place to carry it on.

[Citation.]

The black letter of new §520 sets out the definition:

Sec. 520. *Abnormally Dangerous Activities*

In determining whether an activity is abnormally dangerous, the following factors are to be considered:

(a) Whether the activity involves a high degree of risk of some harm to the person, land or chattels of others;

(b) Whether the gravity of the harm which may result from it is likely to be great;

(c) Whether the risk cannot be eliminated by the exercise of reasonable care;

(d) Whether the activity is not a matter of common usage;

(e) Whether the activity is inappropriate to the place where it is carried on; and

(f) The value of the activity to the community.

We believe that the present case is clearly within the ambit of this definition. Although the operation of a gasoline station does not of itself involve "a high degree of risk of some harm to the person, land or chattels of others," the placing of a large underground gasoline tank in close proximity to the appellees' residence and well does involve such a risk, since it is not a matter of common usage.[3] The harm caused to the appellees was a serious one, and it may well have been worse if the contamination had not been detected promptly.

Holding

Although there is no evidence of negligence on the part of the Yommers (indeed such a showing is not required as will be discussed below), it is proper to surmise that this risk cannot, or at least was not, eliminated by the exercise of reasonable care.

The fifth and perhaps most crucial factor under the Institute's guidelines as applied to this case is the appropriateness of the activity in the particular place where it is being carried on. No one would deny that gasoline stations as a rule do not present any particular danger to the community. However, when the operation of such activity involves the placing of a large tank adjacent to a well from which a family must draw its water for drinking, bathing and laundry, at least that aspect of the activity is inappropriate to the locale, even when equated to the value of the activity.

In the Reporter's notes concerning the new rule of the Restatement, he is careful to make a distinction which is applicable to this case. While in the first Restatement no position was taken on the issue of the storage of water and other liquids, Restatement, Torts 2d takes a different view:

> The thing which stands out from the cases is that the important thing about the activity is not that it is extremely dangerous in itself, but that it is abnormally so in relation to its surroundings.
>
> ....
>
> The same is true of the storage of gasoline, or other inflammable liquids, in large quantities. In a populated area this is a matter of strict liability.... But in an isolated area it is not.
>
> ....
>
> The same distinction is found in the cases of water stored in quantity, as in a reservoir. Rylands v. Fletcher was a case of a reservoir in Lancashire, which was primarily coal mining country; and the basis of the decision in the House of Lords was clearly that this was a "non-natural" use of the particular land.... Where water is stored in large quantity in [a] dangerous location in a city, there [h]as been strict liability.

Restatement, Torts 2d, *supra*, Note to Institute at 57-58.

We accept the test of appropriateness as the proper one: that the unusual, the excessive, the extravagant, the bizarre are likely to be non-natural uses which lead to strict liability.

....

strict liability & not neg. here

It is apparent to us that the storage of large quantities of gasoline immediately adjacent to a private residence comes within this rule and relieved the McKenzies of the necessity of proving negligence. [Citations.]

---

3. "An activity is a matter of common usage if it is customarily carried on by the great mass of mankind, or by many people in the community.... Gas and electricity in household pipes and wires [are examples of common usage], as contrasted with large gas storage tanks or high tension power lines." Restatement, Torts 2d, *supra*, comment on clause (d) at 65-66.

....

Judgment affirmed; costs to be paid by appellants.

Notes

1. *Must "Abnormally Dangerous Activities" Be Abnormally Dangerous?* Consider the two lists that follow: the first list encompasses some activities that have been held (at least by some courts) to subject the person who conducts them to strict liability; the second list includes activities for which liability is based on negligence.

Strict-Liability Activities:

Storing water in a reservoir. (*See* Rylands v. Fletcher, cited in the *Yommer* opinion.)

Using explosives. (*See, e.g.,* Green v. Ensign-Bickford Co., 595 A.2d 1383 (Conn. App. Ct. 1991) (manufacturer held strictly liable for damages caused by experimentation with a highly explosive chemical).)

Flying an aircraft (with respect to damage done to objects on the ground when the aircraft comes down.) (*See* Restatement, Second, of Torts §520, but note that many jurisdictions do not follow the Restatement on this point. *See also* Guille v. Swan, 19 Johns 381 (N.Y. 1822) (holding the operator of a balloon liable for damage done to crops when the balloon landed, with no showing that the pilot of the balloon was negligent).)

Keeping a wild animal as a pet. (See the text earlier in this chapter.)

Pile driving. (*See* Caporale v. C.W. Blakeslee & Sons, Inc., 175 A.2d 561 (Conn. 1961).)

Conducting a fireworks display. (*See* Klein v. Pyrodyne Corp., 810 P.2d 917, *modified,* 817 P.2d 1359 (Wash. 1991).)

Testing rockets. (*See* Smith v. Lockheed Propulsion Co., 56 Cal. Rptr. 128 (Ct. App. 1967) (vibrations damaged plaintiff's well).)

Dusting crops. (*See* Langan v. Valicopters, Inc., 567 P.2d. 218 (Wash. 1977).)

Disposing of hazardous waste. (*See* Kenney v. Scientific, Inc., 497 A.2d 1310 (N.J. Super. Ct. Law Div. 1985); *contra* Shockley v. Hoechst Celanese Corp., 1993 W.L. 241179 (4th Cir.).)

Fumigating a building. (*See* Old Island Fumigation, Inc. v. Barbee, 604 So. 2d 1246 (Fla. Dist. Ct. App. 1992).)

Activities for Which Liability is Based on Negligence:

Driving an automobile in a city, where small children may run into the street. (*See, e.g.,* Rios v. Sifuentes, 347 N.E.2d 337 (Ill. App. Ct. 1976).)

Selling explosives. (*See, e.g.,* Allen v. Gornto, 112 S.E.2d 368 (Ga. Ct. App. 1959) (negligence claim stated by minor against fireworks vendor).)

Flying an aircraft (with respect to damage done to persons in the aircraft or to persons in other aircraft with which the defendant's aircraft collides). (*See, e.g.,* Farina v. Pan American World Airlines, Inc., 497 N.Y.S.2d 706 (App. Div. 1986) (negligence action by passenger injured in runway accident).)

Keeping a bull on a farm. (*See* Warren v. Davis, 539 S.W.2d 907 (Tex. Civ. App. 1976) (wrongful death action arising from collision between bull and decedent's automobile).)

Drilling and operating natural gas wells. (*See* Williams v. Amoco Prod. Co., 734 P.2d 1113 (Kan. 1987).)

Driving under the influence of alcohol. (*See* Goodwin v. Reilley, 221 Cal. Rptr. 374 (Ct. App. 1985).)

Hauling Steel. (*See* Inland Steel v. Pequignot, 608 N.E.2d 1378 (Ind. Ct. App. 1993).)

Shipping a flammable toxic chemical by rail. (*See* Indiana Harbor Belt Railroad v. American Cyanamid Co., 916 F.2d 1174 (7th Cir. 1990).)

Some reflection on these examples strongly suggests that despite the Restatement's insistence that strict liability applies to those who engage in "abnormally dangerous" activities (or, as the First Restatement put it, "ultrahazardous" activities), the classification here does not turn primarily on levels of danger. As a practical matter, persons face much more danger from their neighbors' and their own automobiles than from leaking reservoirs or hot-air balloons.

2. *An Alternative Formulation: Single-Injurer Accidents.* A better explanation than "abnormal dangerousness" for why some activities are better suited than others for strict liability can be found by considering whether, with respect to a particular activity, the likelihood of an accident turns upon only the defendant's activity level and safety precautions or whether it depends upon the activity levels and safety precautions of both plaintiffs and defendants. In the case of cars striking pedestrians, for instance, the level of accidents depends both on how many people drive and on how many people walk, and upon how careful they are while driving and walking. In other words, both plaintiffs' (pedestrians') and defendants' (drivers') activity levels and safety precautions affect the number of car-pedestrian accidents. By contrast, the amount of harm done to crops from hot-air balloon landings depends almost entirely on the amount of hot-air ballooning that goes on—one would not expect farmers to decide how many beans to plant by taking into account the possibility that errant aviators may alight on their fields.

To put the point somewhat differently, a strict liability standard is appropriate for activities for which the person carrying on the activity is, as a practical matter, the only person in a position realistically to control the amount of harm done by the activity (by taking precautions or by deciding how much of the activity to engage in). A negligence standard, by contrast, is appropriate for activities for which both the potential injurer and the potential victim can take precautions. For instance, when the danger is cars hitting pedestrians, drivers can reduce the chance of harm by not speeding, by keeping a good lookout, and by staying home (especially when the weather is bad). Pedestrians can also affect the likelihood of harm, by refraining from jaywalking, by staying on the sidewalk, and by not walking in dangerous places.

While the analysis above is usually defended by reference to "efficiency" (because the analysis was developed by economists), it also comports with everyday notions of fairness. When the potential problem is damage to a farmer's crops from hot-air balloon landings, one can plausibly say that the balloonist ought to undertake the activity only if willing to compensate those harmed by that activity. This suggests that there is nothing unfair about holding the balloonist strictly liable. But when *A*'s automobile collides at an intersection with *B*'s automobile, one cannot arbitrarily say "this is *A*'s activity, so *A* should be strictly liable"; after all, both *A* and *B* have chosen to engage in an activity that may cause harm to themselves and others. Indeed, it is hard to see how strict liability could be applied to two-car accidents at all, except by holding each driver liable to the other, which would be both unfair and inefficient.

To summarize, strict liability is appropriate for "single-injurer" accidents—accidents for which it is plain that only one of the persons involved was in a position to control the events giving rise to an accident. For that kind of case, strict liability is superior to negligence, for three reasons. First, inquiries into whether someone acted negligently are difficult, and courts will in many cases get it wrong; under strict liability, trials should be much simpler (since the plaintiff's burden will be largely limited to showing causation and damage) and there is less risk that those who should be liable will avoid liability. Second, the increased certainty of liability under a strict liability standard may encourage defendants to settle claims rather than go to court; consequently, the costs of litigation will be reduced. Third, as noted above (p. 668 n. 10), strict liability, unlike negligence, gives potential injurers an incentive to reduce risks by reducing their activity levels, as well as by taking safety precautions. Consider, for instance, a contractor who is about to undertake an excavation project and who must decide whether to do the job quickly, by using dynamite, or slowly, by digging. Suppose that the contractor is quite sure that its employees will be very careful, so that it will not be negligent if it uses dynamite. Suppose also that it knows from experience that there is some chance that blasting, even if very carefully conducted, will cause damage to a neighboring house. Under a negligence standard, the contractor might ignore the risk, figuring that it will not be held liable if harm ensues because it will not be negligent. Under a strict liability standard, the contractor, knowing that it will be held liable if a neighboring house collapses, has an incentive to consider whether some safer but more-expensive method of excavating than blasting might be best.

The analysis above suggests that there will be some cases in which strict liability should not be imposed even on those who engage in an activity which the law characterizes as "abnormally dangerous." Suppose, for instance, that a contractor's blasting has been rattling the walls of neighboring houses all day, and that one of the neighbors stubbornly leaves a Ming vase perched on the edge of a shelf. In this case, the neighbor is in a much better position than the contractor to prevent harm to the vase, so the contractor should not be liable if it falls. On the other hand, if the blasting cracks the neighbor's foundation, the contractor will be liable: the neighbor can hardly be expected to move the house to a safer spot for the duration of the blasting. Consider also the case (*supra* at 685) of the pet bear which falls asleep on the highway and is struck by the plaintiff's car. Here, the plaintiff may have been in a better position than the owner to prevent the harm—maybe the plaintiff was speeding and not keeping a good lookout. A negligence inquiry in cases like this allows imposition of liability on the "cheaper cost avoider." Strict liability typically applies to cases in which it is plain that the "cheaper cost avoider" is the person carrying on the activity.

3. With the foregoing arguments, compare Green v. Ensign-Bickford Co., 595 A.2d 1383 (Conn. App. Ct. 1991) (asserting that "the underlying rationale for strict liability in blasting and pile driving cases is that one acts at his peril when he creates an unavoidable risk of damage").

See also William K. Jones, *Strict Liability for Hazardous Enterprise*, 92 Colum. L. Rev. 1705, 1707-13 (1992). Professor Jones argues that a strict liability standard should be applied to all instances of accidental injury to a stranger by a business entity, "except when (1) the accident is one that typically involves interacting behavior of victim and injurer, or (2) recognition of the strict liability claim will lead to excessive transaction costs."

4. *Strict Liability and Unavoidable Accidents.* Strict liability simplifies the litigation process and makes compensation more certain in cases where the defendant in fact

failed to exercise care. The rule also changes the result that would be reached under a negligence standard in cases of unavoidable accident. Under negligence, unavoidable losses fall on the victim (*see, e.g.,* Cohen v. Petty, 65 F.2d 820 (D.C. Cir. 1933), *supra* at 20); under strict liability, those losses are shifted from the victim to the actor whose conduct caused the loss. This difference is important.

Some supporters of strict liability maintain that holding actors liable for unavoidable losses (including those which are unforeseeable) makes good economic sense. That is, by forcing actors to internalize the burdens placed on society by their activities, the law tends to ensure that no one engages in an endeavor which causes more harm than it is worth. This approach—sometimes called "enterprise liability"—will be examined in Chapter 15.

5. *Cross-subsidization.* Why does it matter whether the cost of an accident properly attributable to a particular activity is borne by that activity or by some other activity? One possible answer rests on concerns of fairness: if *A*'s activity causes harm, it would not be fair, one supposes, to make *B* pay the cost of that harm. But this kind of "fairness" argument carries little weight with many judges, especially when *A* has limited resources, the victim has serious injuries, and *B* has a "deep pocket." In cases like this, many courts employ "risk spreading" to impose liability upon *B* if *B* has some connection, however tenuous, to the accident.

Economists explain the importance of imposing the costs of accidents only upon those whose activities were responsible for the accidents by invoking the concept of cross-subsidization. To illustrate, suppose that automobile manufacturers were held liable for all harms suffered by the owners of their cars—even harms entirely unrelated to driving, as when the owner of a Buick falls down the cellar stairs and suffers serious injuries. What would be wrong with that rule? It would, one supposes, provide a considerable amount of "risk spreading," as the costs of the accident would be borne by all of those who buy cars from General Motors, not just the unfortunate accident victim. And any "unfairness" argument might be countered by announcing the rule in advance, so that General Motors would price its cars so as to take account of the liability.

The case against holding General Motors liable in this hypothetical starts by noting that this kind of liability would make automobiles very expensive. This, by itself, is no argument against liability: there is no basic principle of law or any other discipline which holds that cars should be cheap. The real problem is that holding General Motors liable for this kind of harm raises the price of cars to a point well beyond the actual costs of producing cars. For instance, if the cost of a particular model of car (*including* the costs of accidents attributable to the car's design) is $20,000, and if an additional cost of $30,000 is imposed for completely unrelated accidents, only those for whom having a car is worth more than $50,000 will buy one. This deprives those for whom having a car would provide $40,000 worth of enjoyment from having that enjoyment, even though the car could be produced at a cost of only $20,000. And this is wasteful, or, as the economists say, "inefficient." The phenomenon described here is called "cross-subsidization" because the liability rule in question causes one activity—driving, in this case—to "subsidize" other activities (anything else that might cause an accident).

A point worth noting about the analysis above is that it assumes that car buyers who would have to pay an extra $30,000 for "insurance" would not get $30,000 worth of insurance benefits from their outlays. This is a very plausible assumption: ordinary insurance markets provide opportunities for most people to get most of the insurance they want at a much lower cost than if that insurance were imposed indirectly by making auto manufacturers liable for all harms to car buyers. Note also that the $30,000 estimate is not excessive; indeed, it is probably much too low. The cost of products-liability insurance for manufacturers of small aircraft runs about $300,000 per plane, and that insurance covers only harm to those injured in plane crashes held to result from defects in the aircraft. Realistically, if car manufacturers were held liable for all injuries to car owners, manufacturing cars would become economically impossible. But cross-subsidization does harm even when the activity that pays the subsidy is only cut back, rather than eliminated entirely.

Cross-subsidization causes harm not only by making the subsidizing activity artificially expensive but also by making the subsidized activity artificially cheap. For example, if automobile manufacturers were held liable for accidents caused by blasting, one result would be that too much blasting would go on; since their liability would be picked up at least in part by the auto companies, contractors contemplating blasting would not face the full costs of their activities and so blasting would be artificially cheap.

6. *Problem: Selling Explosives.* If blasting activity conducted by *A* causes harm to *B*, *A* will ordinarily be strictly liable. Should *C*, the company which sold the dynamite to *A*, also be liable? After all, since all dynamite sold is expected to be used, selling dynamite must be as "abnormally dangerous" as using it.

Kent v. Gulf States Utilities Co.

Supreme Court of Louisiana
418 So. 2d 493 (La. 1982)[a]

LEMMON, Justice.

This [is a] case of personal injury by contact with electrical lines....

....

Keith Kent began his employment with Barber shortly before the accident. At the time of his injury the 18-year old employee was making antihydroplaning grooves in the surface of the highway by pulling a metal rake, approximately five feet wide, across the surface of the freshly poured concrete.

The portion of the highway then under construction ran under three high voltage distribution lines, which intersected the highway at an angle. The uninsulated lines, located 25 feet 8 inches above the surface of the ground and 24 feet 8 inches above the surface of the slab, were clearly visible, and everyone on the construction site, including Keith Kent, was aware of them.

The metal rake used by the workers to create grooves had an aluminum handle, which had been extended to a length of 30 feet by screwing together several six foot sections. That length was necessary because of the double width of the concrete roadway (two 13 foot widths) under construction.

---

a. Tort-reform legislation in 1996 imposed significant restrictions on strict liability in Louisiana. *See* Joseph S. Piacun, *The Abolition of Strict Liability in Louisiana: A Return to a Fairer Standard or an Impossible Burden for Plaintiffs?*, 43 Loyola L. Rev. 215, 237-38 (1997) (noting that while "several...areas of strict liability remain," the "limitation of strict liability for ultrahazardous activities...now ranks as one of the most restrictive in the United States"). — Eds.

On the day of the accident Kent and his co-worker, David Jenkins,...began using the "flip-flop" method to transfer the rake back and forth across the slab. In using this method, Kent stood on one side of the slab and pulled the rake, creating the grooves across the concrete. He then returned the rake by holding onto the rake head, raising the handle in the air and letting the rake fall across the slab, where it was caught by Jenkins. Jenkins then pulled the rake across the surface and returned it to Kent in a similar manner.

....

Charles Smith, a cement finisher,...heard the electrical boom caused by the handle's contact with the wire, and then he saw Kent slumped over motionless next to the slab.

It is therefore evident from the testimony that the accident occurred when Kent, while standing very near the overhead lines, raised the rake handle so that it made contact with one of the lines.

....

Plaintiff contends that Gulf States was negligent in failing to take reasonable measures to protect against the foreseeable risk that a person, in contact with the ground or with a grounded object, would come in contact with its wires in the construction area. Plaintiff further urges that we hold Gulf States under some form of absolute or strict liability....

....

[Regarding liability for ultrahazardous activities:]....There are some activities in which the risk may be altogether reasonable and still high enough that the party ought not undertake the activity without assuming the consequences. Such activities include pile driving, storage of toxic gas, blasting with explosives, crop dusting with airplanes, and the like, in which the activity can cause injury to others, even when conducted with the greatest prudence and care. [Citations.]

For these particular activities, Louisiana courts have imposed an *absolute* liability... which virtually makes the enterpriser an insurer. The enterpriser, whether or not negligent in any respect, causes the damage, and the injured party recovers simply by proving damage and causation.

In these cases of absolute liability (or liability without proof of negligence or other fault), liability is imposed as a matter of policy when harm results from the risks inherent in the nature of the activity. The steps taken by the enterpriser to protect others from the inherent risks of the activity are not relevant to the determination of liability.

The activity of driving piles, for example, is likely to cause damage, even when there is no substandard conduct on *anyone's* part. The activity, by its very nature, simply cannot be done without a high degree of risk of injury.

On the other hand, the transmission of electricity over isolated high tension power lines is an everyday occurrence in every parish in this state and can be done without a high degree of risk of injury. And when the activity results in injury, it is almost always because of substandard conduct on the part of either the utility, the victim or a third party.[h]

---

h. It is noteworthy that, in each of the activities placed in this special category by decisions of Louisiana courts, the enterpriser is almost invariably the sole cause of the damage and the victim seldom has the ability to protect himself. No decisions have placed in this category any activities in which the victim or a third person can reasonably be expected to be a contributing factor in the causation of damages with any degree of frequency.

The two activities of driving piles and of transmitting electricity are thus different from the point of view of a policy need to impose absolute liability irrespective of negligence or other fault. Indeed, we have not been directed to any decision from other states in which absolute liability has been imposed on the activity of transmitting electricity for public consumption. [Citation.]

We accordingly conclude that Gulf States should not be held absolutely liable, as an enterpriser engaged in ultrahazardous activities, when its activity of transmitting electricity is a cause-in-fact of injury to another, unless fault was proved on Gulf States' part.

....

[After discussing other issues, the court affirmed the judgment of the court of appeals which held that Kent's conduct barred recovery from Gulf States and that the claims against other defendants had been properly dismissed.]

[The concurring opinions of MARCUS, J., and DENNIS, J., and the dissenting opinion of WATSON, J., are omitted.]

Notes

1. *Abnormally Dangerous Suicide.* An unusual application of the second Restatement rules for abnormally dangerous activities is found in Laterra v. Treaster, 844 P.2d 724 (Kan. 1992). A woman who lived in a duplex committed suicide by allowing her car engine to run in the garage attached to the dwelling. The carbon monoxide fumes seeped into the other half of the duplex, asphyxiating the plaintiff's father, who was sleeping. The court held that this method of committing suicide was such an inherently and abnormally dangerous activity as to make the defendant strictly liable.

2. *A Moribund Theory of Liability?* After reviewing roughly 100 decisions rendered over 35 years, with special emphasis on cases decided after 1980, Professor Gerald W. Boston concludes, in *Strict Liability for Abnormally Dangerous Activity: The Negligence Barrier*, 36 San Diego L. Rev. 597 (1999), that "rarely do plaintiffs succeed in asserting claims for abnormally dangerous activity." He found that "even jurisdictions reflecting the most aggressive application of the doctrine—California, Alaska, and Washington—have indicated a more recent retrenchment." Why was that the case? According to Professor Boston:

> The answer largely resides in the fact that courts reject strict liability because they conclude that the negligence system can function effectively in enforcing safety concerns associated with the activity.
>
> ....
>
> ....While the Restatement (Second) stipulates that all six factors are important,...the decisional reality is different. Courts quote the stipulation, but then proceed to rule that, because the plaintiff cannot demonstrate that due care would not have minimized the danger,...[strict liability is] inapplicable.

3. *Strict Liability by Statute.* In some areas, strict liability is imposed by statute. For example, in some states, proof of fault is not required in actions based on: harm caused by fires originating on a defendant railroad's rights-of-way (*see, e.g.,* Colo. Rev. Stat. §40-30-103 (Westlaw 2003); Me. Rev. Stat. Ann. tit. 23, §7003 (Westlaw 2003); Ohio Rev. Code Ann. §4963.37 (Westlaw 2003); Wyo. Stat. Ann. §37-9-303(a) (Westlaw 2002)); and ground damage inflicted by aircraft (*see, e.g.,* Del. Code Ann. tit. 2, §305 (Westlaw 2003); Haw. Rev. Stat. §263-5 (Westlaw 2002); Vt. Stat. Ann. tit. 5, §479 (Westlaw 2003)).

Examples of strict liability under federal legislation include nuclear accidents (42 U.S.C. §2210(n)(1) (Westlaw 2003)); water pollution clean-up costs (33 U.S.C. §1321(f) (Westlaw 2003)); and improper disposal of hazardous waste (42 U.S.C. §9601-9675 (Westlaw 2003)).

4. The most important recent development in the field of abnormally dangerous activities is the Third Restatement's reformulation of the test for defining such activities.

RESTATEMENT, THIRD, OF TORTS:
LIABILITY FOR PHYSICAL HARM (BASIC PRINCIPLES)
§20 (Tent. Draft No. 1, 2001)

Sec. 20 Abnormally Dangerous Activities

(a) A defendant who carries on an abnormally dangerous activity is subject to strict liability for physical harm resulting from the activity.

(b) An activity is abnormally dangerous if:

(1) the activity creates a foreseeable and highly significant risk of physical harm even when reasonable care is exercised by all actors; and

(2) the activity is not a matter of common usage.

Comment:

....

g. Highly significant risk of physical harm. A risk of physical harm can be highly significant for either or both of two possible reasons. The risk can be highly significant because the likelihood of harm is unusually high, even though the severity of expected harm is no more than ordinary. This is often the case with blasting: the probability of some harm occurring may be quite substantial, even though most of the time the particular harm will be only a moderate amount of property damage. Conversely, there are activities—the operation of a nuclear power plant is an extreme case—where the likelihood of a harm-causing incident when reasonable care is exercised is quite low, but where the severity of harm should there be an incident can be enormous. Both the likelihood of harm and the severity of possible harm should be taken into account in ascertaining whether an activity entails a highly significant risk of physical harm. The absence of a highly significant risk is one of several reasons that courts have been unwilling to impose strict liability for harms caused by leaks from or ruptures in water mains: the likelihood of harm-causing incidents is not especially high, and the level of harm when there is such an incident is generally not severe.... [T]he extent of the risk entailed by the defendant's conduct often depends in significant part on the location at which the defendant engages in its conduct. For example, neither blasting with explosives nor the storage of explosives involves a major risk if the storage or the blasting is done on an uninhabited mountainside, far from property that is of substantial value. On the other hand, blasting with explosives in the midst of a residential area, and even the storage of explosives in such an area, does entail a very substantial risk.

h. Reasonable care as exercised by all actors.... [A] prerequisite for strict liability is not merely a highly significant risk in the defendant's activity overall, but a highly significant risk in that activity even when reasonable care is exercised by the defendant undertaking the activity, and likewise by other actors who contribute to the activity's safety level....

....

....When the conduct of actors other than the defendant has a significant influence on the number of injuries, the defendant cannot fairly be identified as the exclusive cause of the risk, and it becomes more appropriate to assign the liability or loss to whichever actor has departed from the standard of reasonable care. Courts generally have ruled that the transmission of gas through underground lines is not an abnormally dangerous activity, and one reason courts have given for their ruling is that many parties other than the gas company have access to these lines, and hence may be the cause of whatever mishap occurs. As for the companies that engage in the business of manufacturing and selling potentially dangerous products such as toxic substances and handguns, even when these companies exercise reasonable care, the distribution of their products still involves a significant risk of eventual harm. However, that risk can be minimized if the purchasers of products exercise reasonable care and avoid improper use. In large part for this reason, the sale of such products has not been deemed to be an abnormally dangerous activity.

The actors whose practice of reasonable care is relevant under this section include the category of potential victims. The strict-liability rule is designed to protect "the innocent person who suffers harm as a result of" an "unavoidable risk of harm that is inherent" in the defendant's activity. However, an activity is not inherently and unavoidably dangerous if reasonable precautions by potential victims can commonly succeed in avoiding injuries; nor is a class of victims entirely innocent when their own injuries are often due to their own failure to exercise reasonable care. In general, when the accident rate is evidently due to a combination of the conduct choices made by potential defendants and the choices made by potential plaintiffs, both the ethical arguments and the deterrence arguments in favor of strict liability are weakened. As far as the transmission of electricity is concerned, even when reasonable care is exercised by the relevant companies, significant dangers remain; but so long as potential victims likewise exercise reasonable care in avoiding making inappropriate contact with power lines, the likelihood of serious injuries is very low. Similarly, as railroad trains approach highway crossings, significant risks may remain even when the railroads exercise reasonable care. However, if motorists and pedestrians who approach those crossings likewise exercise reasonable care, the likelihood of injuries is minimal. Partly for this reason, neither the transmission of electricity nor the operation of trains through highway crossings has been deemed to be an abnormally dangerous activity. Indeed, of all the activities that courts have found to be abnormally dangerous, there is none in which the accident rate ensuing from the activity is significantly influenced by the degree of reasonableness in the conduct of potential victims.

....

j. Common usage. Even if an activity involves a highly significant risk when reasonable care is exercised, the activity is not abnormally dangerous if it is in common usage. An activity that is normal or usual is not abnormally dangerous....

An activity is plainly of common usage if it is carried on by a large fraction of the people in the community. For example, automobiles are in such general use that their operation is a matter of common usage. Accordingly, at least for this reason, the operation of automobiles is not an abnormally dangerous activity.

On the other hand, the operation of a tank, or another motor vehicle of such size and weight as to be unusually difficult to control safely, is not a usual activity; therefore, the operation of such a vehicle may be abnormally dangerous....

However, activities can be in common use even if they are engaged in by only a limited number of actors. Consider the company that transmits electricity through wires, or distributes gas through mains, to most buildings in the community. The activity itself is engaged in by only one party. Even so, electric wires and gas mains are pervasive within the community. Moreover, most people, though not themselves engaging in the activity, are connected to the activity; electric wires and gas mains reach their homes. Accordingly, the activity is obviously in common usage, and partly for that reason strict liability is not applicable.

....

l. Function of court. Whether the activity is abnormally dangerous is determined by the court....

Chapter 15

Products Liability

A. Historical Background

At the beginning of the twentieth century, "products liability" as a field of law hardly existed. Indeed, it was then often the case that even someone injured by a product which had been negligently manufactured had no cause of action against the manufacturer. Today, in every state, someone who has been hurt by a defective product can recover, often even without showing negligence, from the product's manufacturer. In many jurisdictions the victim will also have a claim against a seller of the product—such as a retailer—again, without a showing of negligence.

A sketch of the development of the law of products liability from "no liability" to its modern form follows. In this particular case, the history of the law has important practical consequences. For example, the tendency of the law to hold *sellers of products* strictly liable exists because one important source of this body of law has been the law of warranty in sales transactions. Warranties typically apply to sales of goods, but not to the performance of services. Furthermore, it seems quite unlikely that this field, which has undergone extensive change over a very short time, will suddenly stop developing. The lawyer faced with a products-liability case cannot assume that last year's law will determine this year's result. To make reasonably accurate judgments about future developments, the lawyer must have a sense of the way in which the law has grown to its present state.

For clarity of presentation, this sketch of the development of the law is divided into two parts: (1) the development of the law from "no liability" to liability based on negligence, and (2) the fusing of negligence law, contract law, and the academic notion of "enterprise liability" into modern products-liability law.

1. From "No Liability" to Negligence

Winterbottom v. Wright, 152 Eng. Rep. 402 (Exchequer 1842), was an action by a driver of a mail coach who alleged that he had been injured when the coach broke down while he was driving it. The defendant had made a contract with the Postmaster-General of England, by which the defendant agreed to provide the coach in question to the Postmaster-General and to keep it in good repair. The court held that the plaintiff's complaint failed to state a cause of action. The defendant's duty to keep the coach in good repair existed only because of the defendant's contract with the Postmaster-General, and the plaintiff was not a party to that contract. The court thought that, because the defendant's duty to keep the coach in good condition existed only because of the contract, no one but a party to the contract could base a claim on the defendant's failure to do what he had promised.

Winterbottom v. Wright was not a "products liability" case in the modern sense: the plaintiff's complaint was that the defendant had failed to perform a service carefully. Nevertheless, the principle that only a party to a contract can complain when the contract is negligently performed prevented those injured by a defendant's negligence in manufacturing a product from recovering from the manufacturer save for the very rare case in which the victim was in "privity of contract" with the manufacturer. Suppose, for example, that *A* manufactured a widget and sold it to *B*, a wholesaler, who then resold it to *C*, a retailer, who sold it to the plaintiff, who was hurt because the widget was negligently made. The manufacturer's only contract was with *B*, the wholesaler, who has not been hurt, and so *Winterbottom* barred recovery.

None of this made a bit of sense: the idea that a contract between *A* and *B* can prevent *A* from being liable to a third party if *A* does something dangerous is absurd on its face. And so, almost from the beginning, courts found ways to get around the doctrine of Winterbottom v. Wright in particularly egregious cases. For example, the defendant in Thomas v. Winchester, 6 N.Y. 397 (1852), negligently placed the wrong label on a bottle of poison and sold it to a druggist, who sold it to the plaintiff, who, misled by the label, consumed it. Holding that products "imminently dangerous to the lives of others" were outside the scope of the *Winterbottom* doctrine, the court allowed the action. In 1909, the New York Court of Appeals ruled that a large coffee urn was "imminently dangerous"; Statler v. George A. Ray Mfg. Co., 88 N.E. 1063 (N.Y. 1909).

Judge Benjamin Cardozo's opinion in MacPherson v. Buick Motor Co., 111 N.E. 1050 (N.Y. 1916), in effect held that *Winterbottom* was no longer the law of New York, though Cardozo's opinion purported simply to apply existing law. The plaintiff was injured when the wooden wheel of his Buick automobile collapsed. The Court of Appeals held that the rule of Thomas v. Winchester applied not only to things that are dangerous in themselves, such as poisons, but also to things that are "reasonably certain to place life and limb in peril when negligently made." As the very definition of negligence involves the creation of an unreasonable risk of harm, this reformulation of the Thomas v. Winchester exception to the rule of Winterbottom v. Wright swallowed the rule, and allowed persons injured by a manufacturer's negligence to recover from the manufacturer.

2. From Negligence to Strict Liability

MacPherson was widely followed, and by mid-century, actions against manufacturers for negligence were routinely allowed. Still, the plaintiff injured by a defective product faced serious obstacles to recovery. For one thing, how was the manufacturer's negligence to be shown? And if the manufacturer could not be sued, the victim was out of luck, for the retailer who sold the product would seldom have been negligent, and so could not be liable under *MacPherson*. Current law generally allows those injured by product defects to recover against "sellers" of products—which includes not only manufacturers but also wholesalers and retailers—without a showing of negligence. This body of law represents the coming together of three developments:

(1) The doctrine of *res ipsa loquitur*, which often allowed plaintiffs to get to the jury against manufacturers without showing specific negligence;

(2) The law of contract warranty, which allowed purchasers of some products—particularly food—to recover in contract against those who had sold them defectively dangerous products; and

(3) The notion of "enterprise liability," advanced by academic lawyers as a sort of compulsory insurance scheme under which those who profited by making and selling products would be liable to all of those injured by the products. As will be seen, enterprise liability is incoherent and almost certainly unwise, but it seems to have encouraged a number of judges to take pro-plaintiff positions in particular cases.

Res Ipsa Loquitur. Consider first the doctrine of *res ipsa loquitur*. A plaintiff who is injured when a new machine falls apart the first time it is used often has a decent argument that the builder of the machine was negligent, and this will typically get the plaintiff to the jury against the manufacturer. (Sometimes, however, the defect may have been introduced by the manufacturer of a component part, in which case the liability of the machine's maker under negligence must be based on inadequate inspection, perhaps a less appealing *res ipsa* case than one in which a single manufacturer produced the entire product.) One argument for holding manufacturers (but not all sellers) strictly liable for injuries caused by product defects is that, in most of the cases, the manufacturer's negligence did cause the defect. And the ability of plaintiffs to get to the jury on a *res ipsa* theory makes the adoption of strict liability for manufacturers seem like a small step, rather than a major restructuring of the law.

Warranty. Today's law of products liability typically holds all sellers of new products, not just manufacturers, strictly liable. For an explanation of this aspect of the law, it is necessary to turn to the law of sales. If *A* goes to *B*'s restaurant and orders a pie, which turns out to be poisoned, it seems eminently sensible to say that *B* has breached a contract to provide *A* with edible food. This liability—like most of contract liability—is strict, so *B* is liable even if *B* was not negligent (as when *B* bought the pie from Grandma *C*'s Pie Company and had no reason to know that there was anything wrong with the pie). Contract, or "breach of warranty," had therefore long provided a sort of strict liability for sellers of defective products. This was, however, a form of strict liability which operated within a very narrow range, because contract liability could traditionally be disclaimed by agreement, and because many of those injured by product defects were not in privity of contract with the defendant.

For a while, it looked as if strict liability would develop by an expansion of contract, through the use of "implied warranties" that the product in question was fit for use, through restrictions on the ability of sellers and buyers to limit the scope of liability, and through expansion of recovery to those who were not in privity of contract with the defendant. This approach reached its high point in the 1960 case of Henningsen v. Bloomfield Motors, Inc., 161 A.2d 69 (N.J. 1960). Helen Henningsen was injured while driving a new Plymouth which her husband, Claus, had bought from Bloomfield Motors. She claimed that the car went out of control, veered to the right, and struck a brick wall. Finding no evidence of negligence by either Bloomfield or Chrysler, the trial court dismissed the negligence claims, leaving the Henningsens with claims for breach of an implied warranty of merchantability, on which the jury ruled in their favor.

Helen Henningsen's claim had two serious shortcomings as a matter of traditional contract law. First, as it was Claus Henningsen who had bought the car, Helen Henningsen had no contract with anyone. Second, the contract of sale limited the manufacturer's obligation under the warranty to replacing defective parts. Nevertheless, the Supreme Court of New Jersey held that she could recover for breach of warranty. Stressing the fineness of the print in which the warranties were presented, the buyer's inability to negotiate a warranty more favorable than Chrysler's standard warranty, and the "grossly unequal" bargaining power of the manufacturer and the buyer, the court held the disclaimer of liability void and allowed Helen Henningsen to recover.

Section 2-316 of the Uniform Commercial Code, some version of which is in force in every state (except Louisiana), allows the sale of goods with no implied warranty that the goods are merchantable, though it requires disclaimers to be clear and, in the case of written disclaimers, conspicuous. If there is a warranty, UCC §2-318 extends implied warranties beyond the buyer and may prohibit some sellers from limiting liability for personal injury.

Today, warranty law is seldom the preferred basis for personal-injury claims resulting from defective products, for several reasons. First, since goods can be sold "as is" (that is, with no warranty at all), the scope of a law of products liability based on warranty is necessarily quite limited. Second, one version of UCC §2-318 limits recovery to the purchaser, members of the purchaser's household, or guests of the purchaser; many product claims involve other kinds of plaintiffs. Third, the UCC contains some technical restrictions on recovery for breach of warranty. But perhaps most important is a recognition that a liability which is imposed by the law, and which the parties to an agreement may not modify even if they want to, is not really a contract remedy at all: contract is about enforcing agreements. Nevertheless, the warranty element of the history of products liability has played a major part in shaping the law. Suppose that a law student is injured while using an Acme Coffee Company coffee maker which she bought from K Mart. If the injury results from a defect in the coffee maker, K Mart will be liable, even if it could not possibly have done anything to detect or prevent the injury. (Assume, for instance, that it bought the machine from a most reputable manufacturer, and that the machine arrived at K Mart in a sealed box and was sold to the student without change.) Holding Acme strictly liable may be justified by pointing out that it was probably the negligence of an Acme employee that caused the defect; holding K Mart liable seems to be mostly a relic of the warranty origins of product-liability law.

Enterprise Liability. The willingness of the courts to expand liability for injuries attributable to products pretty clearly rests in part on a belief that widespread liability is good social policy. To some extent, this belief may rest on an acceptance of the notion of "enterprise liability," the idea that those carrying on an enterprise should be liable for all the harm done by that enterprise. Thus, it is argued, anyone making a living from the manufacture of automobiles should pay for all harm done by the automobiles in question. This notion had considerable currency in the law schools in the 1930s, '40s, and '50s, and traces of it can be found in judicial opinions.

No court has ever endorsed enterprise liability in its full-blown form, and it is likely that none ever will, for the theory, at least as usually presented, is neither coherent nor practicable. For one thing, the task of identifying "the" activity to be held "responsible" for injuries is unpredictable and arbitrary. Suppose, for instance, that Smith buys a car from General Motors so that she can take a vacation from her strenuous job as a reporter. On her way to the Grand Canyon, she hits a pedestrian, through no fault of Smith, General Motors, or the National Park Service. Is "the" activity that injured the pedestrian "manufacturing automobiles," or "driving," or "being a reporter," or "looking at scenery," or "walking"? "But for" any of these "enterprises," the accident would not have happened. Furthermore, the costs of a real enterprise-liability system would be prohibitive without major changes in the way in which damages are calculated. Even fairly modest personal injuries—such as the loss of an arm or leg—can support a multi-million-dollar verdict. If automobile manufacturers (say) were liable for all injuries involving their products, cars would cost hundreds of thousands of dollars, and the manufacture of cars would cease.

One aspect of "enterprise liability theory" often found in judicial opinions is the notion that "risk-spreading" is desirable, and that risk-spreading can be brought about by holding product manufacturers liable in a great many cases. Instead of leaving the loss from an accident to fall on the victim, the manufacturer can pay, and the cost will be reflected in the price of the product. So, instead of (say) the victim's bearing a million-dollar loss, a million customers can pay $1.00 each.

Risk-spreading is often desirable—that is why people buy insurance. It does not follow, however, that risk-spreading is a goal that tort law can sensibly pursue. For one thing, the most expansive possible system of tort liability could not make the private purchase of insurance (or a public equivalent, such as Social Security disability insurance) unnecessary—most people die from causes like sickness, old age, or accidents that are entirely their own fault, causes for which no potential defendant could be found. Whatever "insurance" the tort system provides will therefore be insurance that duplicates coverage many people will buy anyway. In addition, tort damages cover many things for which hardly anyone would buy insurance—pain and suffering and the death of children are examples. Also, those who buy their own insurance and who are also entitled to "tort-insurance" will have, in effect, to buy two policies: their ordinary insurance plus the "policy" they buy whenever they buy a product. These are people who, one presumes, would not buy two policies from an insurance agent, and so one may wonder why it is "good public policy" to make them buy a second, duplicate policy whenever they buy products. If given a choice, few if any buyers would voluntarily buy accident insurance as an optional addition to a product. Since this is so, one may doubt that it is good policy to *make* them buy such insurance. Finally, the "insurance" provided by tort liability is a kind of insurance which may pay claims only after several years of litigation (which the victim is not assured of winning), and which pays as much or more to lawyers, expert witnesses, and others as it does to victims. Nevertheless, the courts are quite fond of the risk-spreading rationale for expanded tort liability.

Justice Roger Traynor's concurring opinion in Escola v. Coca Cola Bottling Co. of Fresno, which follows, is a useful place to begin an examination of modern products-liability law. One thing to ask while reading the opinion is whether the reasons Justice Traynor gives for holding manufacturers liable whenever they sell products with "defects" are limited to that fairly narrow situation. Is the *Escola* concurrence really an argument for products liability, or is it an argument for enterprise liability? Would Justice Traynor favor holding General Motors liable to all pedestrians who are hit by General Motors cars?

Escola v. Coca Cola Bottling Co. of Fresno

Supreme Court of California
150 P.2d 436 (Cal. 1944)

GIBSON, C.J.

[Plaintiff, a waitress, was injured when a bottle of Coca Cola exploded in her hand. She alleged that the defendant, which had bottled and delivered the beverage, was negligent either in failing to detect a defect in the bottle or in putting gas into the bottle at an

Roger J. Traynor

excessive pressure. At trial, the jury returned a verdict for the plaintiff. The Supreme Court of California ruled that the doctrine of *res ipsa loquitur* allowed the case to go to the jury.]

TRAYNOR, J.

I concur in the judgment, but I believe the manufacturer's negligence should no longer be singled out as the basis of a plaintiff's right to recover in cases like the present one. In my opinion it should now be recognized that a manufacturer incurs an absolute liability when an article that he has placed on the market, knowing that it is to be used without inspection, proves to have a defect that causes injury to human beings. MacPherson v. Buick Motor Co., 217 N.Y. 382, established the principle, recognized by this court, that irrespective of privity of contract, the manufacturer is responsible for an injury caused by such an article to any person who comes in lawful contact with it. Sheward v. Virtue, 20 Cal. 2d 410; Kalash v. Los Angeles Ladder Co., 1 Cal. 2d 229. In these cases the source of the manufacturer's liability was his negligence in the manufacturing process or in the inspection of component parts supplied by others. Even if there is no negligence, however, public policy demands that responsibility be fixed wherever it will most effectively reduce the hazards to life and health inherent in defective products that reach the market. It is evident that the manufacturer can anticipate some hazards and guard against the recurrence of others, as the public cannot. Those who suffer injury from defective products are unprepared to meet its consequences. The cost of an injury and the loss of time or health may be an overwhelming misfortune to the person injured, and a needless one, for the risk of injury can be insured by the manufacturer and distributed among the public as a cost of doing business. It is to the public interest to discourage the marketing of products having defects that are a menace to the public. If such products nevertheless find their way into the market it is to the public interest to place the responsibility for whatever injury they may cause upon the manufacturer, who, even if he is not negligent in the manufacture of the product, is responsible for its reaching the market. However intermittently such injuries may occur and however haphazardly they may strike, the risk of their occurrence is a constant risk and a general one. Against such a risk there should be general and constant protection and the manufacturer is best situated to afford such protection.

The injury from a defective product does not become a matter of indifference because the defect arises from causes other than the negligence of the manufacturer, such as negligence of a submanufacturer of a component part whose defects could not be revealed by inspection [citations], or unknown causes that even by the device of *res ipsa loquitur* cannot be classified as negligence of the manufacturer.... In leaving it to the jury to decide whether the inference has been dispelled, regardless of the evidence against it, the negligence rule approaches the rule of strict liability. It is needlessly circuitous to make negligence the basis of recovery and impose what is in reality liability without negligence. If public policy demands that a manufacturer of goods be responsible for their quality regardless of negligence there is no reason not to fix that responsibility openly.

In the case of foodstuffs, the public policy of the state is formulated in a criminal statute. Section 26510 of the Health and Safety Code prohibits the manufacturing, preparing, compounding, packing, selling, offering for sale, or keeping for sale, or advertising within the state, of any adulterated food. Section 26470 declares that food is adulterated when "it has been produced, prepared, packed, or held under insanitary conditions whereby it may have been rendered diseased, unwholesome or injurious to health." The statute imposes criminal liability not only if the food is adulterated, but if its container, which may be a bottle [citation], has any deleterious substance [citation], or renders the product injurious to health. [Citation.] The criminal liability under the statute attaches without proof of fault, so that the manufacturer is under the duty of ascertaining whether an article manufactured by him is safe. People v. Schwartz, 28 Cal. App. 2d Supp. 775. Statutes of this kind result in a strict liability of the manufacturer in tort to the member of the public injured. *See* cases cited in Prosser, Torts, p. 693, note 69.

    ....

The retailer, even though not equipped to test a product, is under an absolute liability to his customer, for the implied warranties of fitness for proposed use and merchantable quality include a warranty of safety of the product.... The courts recognize, however, that the retailer cannot bear the burden of this warranty, and allow him to recoup any losses by means of the warranty of safety attending the wholesaler's or manufacturer's sale to him. [Citations.] Such a procedure, however, is needlessly circuitous and engenders wasteful litigation. Much would be gained if the injured person could base his action directly on the manufacturer's warranty.

The liability of the manufacturer to an immediate buyer injured by a defective product follows without proof of negligence from the implied warranty of safety attending the sale. Ordinarily, however, the immediate buyer is a dealer who does not intend to use the product himself, and if the warranty of safety is to serve the purpose of protecting health and safety it must give rights to others than the dealer....

This court and many others have extended protection according to such a standard to consumers of food products, taking the view that the right of a consumer injured by unwholesome food does not depend "upon the intricacies of the law of sales" and that the warranty of the manufacturer to the consumer in absence of privity of contract rests on public policy. [Citations.] Dangers to life and health inhere in other consumers' goods that are defective and there is no reason to differentiate them from the dangers of defective food products. *See* Bohlen, Studies in Torts, Basis of Affirmative Obligations, American Cases Upon The Liability of Manufacturers and Vendors of Personal Property, 109, 135; Llewellyn, *On Warranty of Quality and Society*, 36 Col. L. Rev. 699, 704, note 14; Prosser, Torts, p. 692.

. . . .

As handicrafts have been replaced by mass production with its great markets and transportation facilities, the close relationship between the producer and consumer of a product has been altered. Manufacturing processes, frequently valuable secrets, are ordinarily either inaccessible to or beyond the ken of the general public. The consumer no longer has means or skill enough to investigate for himself the soundness of a product, even when it is not contained in a sealed package, and his erstwhile vigilance has been lulled by the steady efforts of manufacturers to build up confidence by advertising and marketing devices such as trade-marks. *See* Thomas v. Winchester, 6 N.Y. 397; Baxter v. Ford Motor Co., 168 Wash. 456; Crist v. Art Metal Works, 230 App. Div. 114, *affirmed* 255 N.Y. 624; *see also* Handler, *False and Misleading Advertising*, 39 Yale L.J. 22; Rogers, Good Will, Trade-Marks and Unfair Trading (1914) ch. VI, A Study of The Consumer, p. 65 et seq.; Williston, *Liability For Honest Misrepresentations As Deceit, Negligence Or Warranty*, 42 Harv. L. Rev. 733; 18 Cornell L.Q. 445. Consumers no longer approach products warily but accept them on faith, relying on the reputation of the manufacturer or the trade mark. [Citations.] Manufacturers have sought to justify that faith by increasingly high standards of inspection and a readiness to make good on defective products by way of replacements and refunds. [Citation.] The manufacturer's obligation to the consumer must keep pace with the changing relationship between them; it cannot be escaped because the marketing of a product has become so complicated as to require one or more intermediaries. Certainly there is greater reason to impose liability on the manufacturer than on the retailer who is but a conduit of a product that he is not himself able to test. [Citations.]

put it on the manuf. & not retailer

The manufacturer's liability should, of course, be defined in terms of the safety of the product in normal and proper use, and should not extend to injuries that cannot be traced to the product as it reached the market.

Notes

1. Given the many arguments for expanded liability presented in Justice Traynor's opinion, why should liability be limited to the situations he describes in the last sentence of that opinion? Is "of course" enough of an explanation?

2. *Strict Liability and Economic Incentives to Take Safety Precautions.* As discussed in Chapter 14, a defendant's incentive to take safety precautions should be approximately the same whether liability is strict or is based on negligence. Suppose, for example, that a manufacturer has invested in safety to the point at which an additional $100 of spending on safety will produce only an additional $80 in harm prevention. If liability is based on negligence, the manufacturer will not spend the additional $100, and will not be negligent because of failure to spend that amount since it is not unreasonable to refuse to spend $100 to reduce accident costs by $80. If liability is strict, the manufacturer's incentive is still not to spend the $100; it will be cheaper to pay $80 in damages than to spend $100 on safety.

If negligence on the part of a manufacturer is difficult to establish, even when it oc-curs, strict liability may give better incentives than negligence, as a manufacturer might decide not to spend a reasonable amount on safety in the hope that it will not be held li-able because plaintiffs will be unable to prove negligence. However, this reasoning as-sumes that the manufacturer's customers are irrational. If spending a small amount on precautions will buy a large amount of additional safety, a manufacturer might well de-cide to spend the amount so as to come up with a more-attractive product.

It is theoretically possible that a negligence standard could sometimes provide a greater incentive to take precautions than a strict-liability standard. The basic idea is that some potential defendants may, if subject to a negligence standard, spend extra amounts on safety as a sort of insurance against being erroneously found negligent. The argument depends critically on some key assumptions about the kinds of errors judges and juries make, and no real-world examples are known to exist.

3. Justice Traynor's views in *Escola* prevailed in California in Greenman v. Yuba Power Prods., Inc., 377 P.2d 897 (Cal. 1963), *infra* at 711. Today, all American jurisdic-tions have adopted some form of strict liability in tort for defective products. A widely accepted starting point for discussing the scope of this liability has been §402A of the Restatement, Second, of Torts. (As discussed later, the Restatement, Third, of Torts: Products Liability approaches products liability—especially in "design defect" cases— quite differently. It is important nevertheless to become familiar with the second Re-statement's products-liability provisions, for they reflect the current state of the law in many states and were once the law in virtually all jurisdictions.)

Restatement (Second) of Torts §402A

Special Liability of Seller of Product for Physical Harm to User or Consumer

(1) One who sells any product in a defective condition unreasonably dangerous to the user or consumer or to his property is subject to liability for physical harm thereby caused to the ultimate user or consumer, or to his property, if

(a) the seller is engaged in the business of selling such a product, and

(b) it is expected to and does reach the user or consumer without substantial change in the condition in which it is sold.

(2) The rule stated in Subsection (1) applies although

(a) the seller has exercised all possible care in the preparation and sale of his prod-uct, and

(b) the user or consumer has not bought the product from or entered into any con-tractual relation with the seller.

. . . .

Comment:

a. This Section states a special rule applicable to sellers of products. The rule is one of strict liability, making the seller subject to liability to the user or consumer even though he has exercised all possible care in the preparation and sale of the product.... The rule stated here is not exclusive, and does not preclude liability based upon the al-ternative ground of negligence of the seller, where such negligence can be proved.

. . . .

g. Defective condition. The rule stated in this Section applies only where the product is, at the time it leaves the seller's hands, in a condition not contemplated by the ultimate consumer, which will be unreasonably dangerous to him. The seller is not liable when he delivers the product in a safe condition, and subsequent mishandling or other causes make it harmful by the time it is consumed. The burden of proof that the product was in a defective condition at the time that it left the hands of the particular seller is upon the injured plaintiff; and unless evidence can be produced which will support the conclusion that it was then defective, the burden is not sustained.

Safe condition at the time of delivery by the seller will, however, include proper packaging, necessary sterilization, and other precautions required to permit the product to remain safe for a normal length of time when handled in a normal manner.

. . . .

i. Unreasonably dangerous. . . . The article sold must be dangerous to an extent beyond that which would be contemplated by the ordinary consumer who purchases it, with the ordinary knowledge common to the community as to its characteristics. Good whiskey is not unreasonably dangerous merely because it will make some people drunk, and is especially dangerous to alcoholics; but bad whiskey, containing a dangerous amount of fusel oil, is unreasonably dangerous. Good tobacco is not unreasonably dangerous merely because the effects of smoking may be harmful; but tobacco containing something like marijuana may be unreasonably dangerous. Good butter is not unreasonably dangerous merely because, if such be the case, it deposits cholesterol in the arteries and leads to heart attacks; but bad butter, contaminated with poisonous fish oil, is unreasonably dangerous.

. . . .

Notes

1. *Non-Manufacturer Sellers.* The definition of "one who sells" a product for purposes of strict liability raises a number of problems. Manufacturers are normally "sellers," as they sell their products (though not typically to the ultimate consumer). So are wholesalers and retailers of new products, though a few decisions have held that non-manufacturer sellers who are not responsible for defects should not be strictly liable; *e.g.*, Nichols v. Westfield Indus., Ltd., 380 N.W.2d 392 (Iowa 1985). Several states have adopted legislation to limit the liability of non-manufacturer sellers to cases in which the sellers were negligent. Other legislation is more complex.

Tex. Civ. Prac. & Rem. Code §82.003
(Westlaw 2004)

Liability of Nonmanufacturing Sellers.

(a) A seller that did not manufacture a product is not liable for harm caused to the claimant by that product unless the claimant proves:

(1) that the seller participated in the design of the product;

(2) that the seller altered or modified the product and the claimant's harm resulted from that alteration or modification;

(3) that the seller installed the product, or had the product installed, on another product and the claimant's harm resulted from the product's installation onto the assembled product;

(4) that

(A) the seller exercised substantial control over the content of a warning or instruction that accompanied the product;

(B) the warning or instruction was inadequate; and

(C) the claimant's harm resulted from the inadequacy of the warning or instruction;

(5) that:

(A) the seller made an express factual representation about an aspect of the product;

(B) the representation was incorrect;

(C) the claimant relied on the representation in obtaining or using the product; and

(D) if the aspect of the product had been as represented, the claimant would not have been harmed by the product or would not have suffered the same degree of harm;

(6) that:

(A) the seller actually knew of a defect to the product at the time the seller supplied the product; and

(B) the claimant's harm resulted from the defect; or

(7) that the manufacturer of the product is:

(A) insolvent; or

(B) not subject to the jurisdiction of the court.

Some states provide that a non-manufacturer seller is entitled to indemnity. *See* Tex. Civ Prac. & Rem. Code §82.002(a) (Westlaw 2004) ("A manufacturer shall indemnify and hold harmless a seller against loss arising out of a products liability action, except for any loss caused by the seller's negligence, intentional misconduct, or other act or omission, such as negligently modifying or altering the product, for which the seller is independently liable").

2. *Long-Term Leases.* There is now widespread acceptance of the idea that those who lease products on a long-term basis are "sellers," as there is little practical difference between selling a product and leasing an identical product for a period of several years.

3. *Used Products.* The courts are divided about whether to extend strict liability to commercial sellers of used products. Those favoring the extension tend to emphasize the supposed ability of the sellers to "spread risks." A point worth noting here is that holding commercial sellers strictly liable may well increase the number of dangerous second-hand products in use. To see why, suppose that used-car dealers are able to detect and repair some flaws in the cars they sell, making buying a used car from a dealer a somewhat safer proposition than buying one from an individual seller. If used-car dealers are strictly liable, they will have to raise their prices to cover their expected liability, and this will give individual sellers an edge in the marketplace. As a result, fewer used cars will pass through the hands of dealers, and fewer flaws will be detected before they cause harm. *See* James A. Henderson, Jr., *Extending the Boundaries of Strict Products Liability: Implications of the Theory of the Second Best,* 128 U. Pa. L. Rev. 1036 (1980).

The new products-liability Restatement ordinarily limits the liability of a commercial seller of a used product to harms caused by negligence or by the product's failure to comply with a safety statute or regulation. If, however, the seller's marketing practices would cause reasonable buyers to think that the product in question is as good as new, strict liability for a manufacturing defect may be imposed; Restatement, Third, of Torts: Products Liability §8.

4. *Products versus Services.* Some of those who "sell" products in the ordinary sense of the term have been exempted from strict liability on the ground that they are (at least partly) "providers of services," rather than mere "sellers." For example, pharmacies which sold DES or other harmful drugs have been held not subject to strict liability on the ground that pharmacists, as skilled professionals, provide services; Murphy v. E.R. Squibb & Sons, Inc., 710 P.2d 247 (Cal. 1985). *See also* Bowen v. Niagara Mohawk Power Corp., 590 N.Y.S.2d 628 (App. Div. 1992) (holding, despite contrary authority, that the sale of electricity was a service, not a product, and that strict liability would therefore not be imposed where a house was destroyed by a fire caused by a power surge that overheated the wiring); Cafazzo v. Central Med. Health Services, Inc., 668 A.2d 521 (Pa. 1995) (holding that hospitals and physicians that charge patients for the use of medical devices in connection with providing medical services are not sellers of medical devices and thus may not be held strictly liable for device defects; the primary activity was the provision of medical services).

Does the fact that the seller is an "expert," and thus in a better position than an ordinary retailer or wholesaler to prevent harm, call for reduced, rather than expanded, liability? In *Murphy*, the California Supreme Court gave the following policy justifications for limiting the liability of pharmacies to negligence:

> If pharmacies were held strictly liable for the drugs they dispense, some of them, to avoid liability, might restrict availability by refusing to dispense drugs which pose even a potentially remote risk of harm, although such medications may be essential to the health or even the survival of patients. Furthermore,...the pharmacist [might] select the most expensive product made by an established manufacturer when he has a choice of several brands of the same drug. As [an] amicus brief warns, "Why choose a new company's inexpensive product, which has received excellent reviews in the literature for its quality, over the more expensive product of an established multinational corporation which will certainly have assets available for purpose of indemnification 10, 20, or 30 years down the line?"

Several "tests" have emerged for distinguishing "products" from "services." *See* Charles E. Cantu, *A New Look at an Old Conundrum: The Determinative Test for the Hybrid Sales/Service Transaction Under Section 402A of the Restatement (Second) of Torts*, 45 Ark. L. Rev. 913 (1993).

How should defective computer software be treated? *See* Robin A. Brooks, *Deterring the Spread of Viruses Online: Can Tort Law Tighten the "Net,"* 17 Rev. Litig. 343 (1998).

5. *Blood Shield Laws.* Several states have provided by statute (sometimes called "blood shield laws") that the sale of blood is a service, thus immunizing blood banks and hospitals against strict liability for hepatitis, AIDS, and other conditions transmitted by blood transfusions. *See, e.g.,* Cal. Health and Safety Code §1606 (Westlaw 2003).

6. *Real Estate.* Courts are divided over "whether section 402A extends to entire buildings." Association of Unit Owners v. Dunning, 69 P.3d 788, 801 (Ore. Ct. App. 2003) (holding that condominium buildings were not "products" within the meaning of a state statute governing product liability actions).

B. Manufacturing and Design Defects

Greenman v. Yuba Power Products, Inc.

Supreme Court of California
377 P.2d 897 (Cal. 1963)

TRAYNOR, J.

Plaintiff brought this action for damages against the retailer and the manufacturer of a Shopsmith, a combination power tool that could be used as a saw, drill, and wood lathe. He saw a Shopsmith demonstrated by the retailer and studied a brochure prepared by the manufacturer. He decided he wanted a Shopsmith for his home workshop, and his wife bought and gave him one for Christmas in 1955. In 1957 he bought the necessary attachments to use the Shopsmith as a lathe for turning a large piece of wood he wished to make into a chalice. After he had worked on the piece of wood several times without difficulty, it suddenly flew out of the machine and struck him on the forehead, inflicting serious injuries. About ten and a half months later, he gave the retailer and the manufacturer written notice of claimed breaches of warranties and filed a complaint against them alleging such breaches and negligence.

After a trial before a jury, the court ruled that there was no evidence that the retailer was negligent or had breached any express warranty and that the manufacturer was not liable for the breach of any implied warranty. Accordingly, it submitted to the jury only the cause of action alleging breach of implied warranties against the retailer and the causes of action alleging negligence and breach of express warranties against the manufacturer. The jury returned a verdict for the retailer against plaintiff, and for plaintiff against the manufacturer in the amount of $65,000. The trial court denied the manufacturer's motion for a new trial and entered judgment on the verdict. The manufacturer and plaintiff appeal. Plaintiff seeks a reversal of the part of the judgment in favor of the retailer, however, only in the event that the part of the judgment against the manufacturer is reversed.

Plaintiff introduced substantial evidence that his injuries were caused by defective design and construction of the Shopsmith. His expert witnesses testified that inadequate set screws were used to hold parts of the machine together so that normal vibration caused the tailstock of the lathe to move away from the piece of wood being turned permitting it to fly out of the lathe. They also testified that there were other more positive ways of fastening the parts of the machine together, the use of which would have prevented the accident. The jury could therefore reasonably have concluded that the manufacturer negligently constructed the Shopsmith....

The manufacturer contends, however, that plaintiff did not give it notice of breach of warranty within a reasonable time and that therefore his cause of action for breach of warranty is barred by §1769 of the Civil Code. [The court held that barring recovery in a case like this for failure to give notice would create a "booby-trap for the unwary."]....

....

Moreover, to impose strict liability on the manufacturer under the circumstances of this case, it was not necessary for plaintiff to establish an express warranty....A manufacturer is strictly liable in tort when an article he places on the market, knowing that it is to be used without inspection for defects, proves to have a defect that causes injury to a human being. Recognized first in the case of unwholesome food products, such liability has now been extended to a variety of other products that create as great or greater hazards if defective. [Citations.]

Although in these cases strict liability has usually been based on the theory of an express or implied warranty running from the manufacturer to the plaintiff, the abandonment of the requirement of a contract between them, the recognition that the liability is not assumed by agreement but imposed by law…, and the refusal to permit the manufacturer to define the scope of its own responsibility for defective products (Henningsen v. Bloomfield Motors, Inc., 32 N.J. 358)…make clear that the liability is not one governed by the law of contract warranties but by the law of strict liability in tort. Accordingly, rules defining and governing warranties that were developed to meet the needs of commercial transactions cannot properly be invoked to govern the manufacturer's liability to those injured by its defective products unless those rules also serve the purposes for which such liability is imposed.

We need not recanvass the reasons for imposing strict liability on the manufacturer. They have been fully articulated in the cases cited above. (*See also* 2 Harper and James, Torts, §§28.15-28.16, pp. 1569-1574; Prosser, *Strict Liability to the Consumer*, 69 Yale L.J. 1099; Escola v. Coca Cola Bottling Co., 24 Cal. 2d 453, 461, 150 P.2d 436, concurring opinion.) The purpose of such liability is to insure that the costs of injuries resulting from defective products are borne by the manufacturers that put such products on the market rather than by the injured persons who are powerless to protect themselves. Sales warranties serve this purpose fitfully at best. (*See* Prosser, *Strict Liability to the Consumer*, 69 Yale L.J. 1099, 1124-1134.) In the present case, for example, plaintiff was able to plead and prove an express warranty only because he read and relied on the representations of the Shopsmith's ruggedness contained in the manufacturer's brochure. Implicit in the machine's presence on the market, however, was a representation that it would safely do the jobs for which it was built. Under these circumstances, it should not be controlling whether plaintiff selected the machine because of the statements in the brochure, or because of the machine's own appearance of excellence that belied the defect lurking beneath the surface, or because he merely assumed that it would safely do the jobs it was built to do. It should not be controlling whether the details of the sales from manufacturer to retailer and from retailer to plaintiff's wife were such that one or more of the implied warranties of the sales act arose. [Citation.] "The remedies of injured consumers ought not to be made to depend upon the intricacies of the law of sales." (Ketterer v. Armour & Co., 200 F. 322, 323; Klein v. Duchess Sandwich Co., Ltd., 14 Cal. 2d 272, 93 P.2d 799.) To establish the manufacturer's liability it was sufficient that plaintiff proved that he was injured while using the Shopsmith in a way it was intended to be used as a result of a defect in design and manufacture of which plaintiff was not aware that made the Shopsmith unsafe for its intended use.

. . . .

The judgment is affirmed.

GIBSON, C.J., and SCHAUER, McCOMB, PETERS, TOBRINER, and PEEK, JJ., concurred.

Notes

1. *"Manufacturing Defects" and "Design Defects."* If Greenman's Shopsmith had malfunctioned because the manufacturer had left out a screw, or had accidentally used a screw of the wrong size, the defect would have been a "manufacturing defect." Cases

involving manufacturing defects are usually simple in principle, though proving th
product was defective when it left the manufacturer's hands may be difficult in prac
especially if many years have passed between the time of manufacture and the accid

When a plaintiff complains that a product was defective not because something went wrong in the course of making the particular product involved in the accident, but rather because the design of the product should have been better, the case is typically much more difficult than if a manufacturing defect had been involved. Designers of products can never attain perfect safety: knives cut, and cars hurt those with whom they collide. The issue in a "design defect" case is always in some sense whether the product was "safe enough." This requires the factfinder to compare the actual product with a hypothetical product. For instance, someone hurt in an automobile accident may claim that if the car had been designed differently, the injuries would have been less severe. Even if true, this does not necessarily mean that the product was defective: someone injured in the crash of a small, light, fuel-efficient car does not establish the car's defectiveness by showing that it was not a Cadillac.

2. *The Third Restatement and the Definition of "Defect."* A serious shortcoming of the second Restatement was its attempt to capture in one definition both design and manufacturing defects, which raise very different questions. Sections 1 and 2 of the Restatement, Third, of Torts: Products Liability provide:

§1. Liability of Commercial Seller or Distributor for Harm Caused by Defective Products

One engaged in the business of selling or otherwise distributing products who sells or distributes a defective product is subject to liability for harm to persons or property caused by the defect.

§2. Categories of Product Defect

A product is defective when, at the time of sale or distribution, it contains a manufacturing defect, is defective in design, or is defective because of inadequate instructions or warnings. A product:

(a) contains a manufacturing defect when the product departs from its intended design even though all possible care was exercised in the preparation and marketing of the product;

(b) is defective in design when the foreseeable risks of harm posed by the product could have been reduced or avoided by the adoption of a reasonable alternative design by the seller or other distributor, or a predecessor in the commercial chain of distribution, and the omission of the alternative design renders the product not reasonably safe;

(c) is defective because of inadequate instructions or warnings when the foreseeable risks of harm posed by the product could have been reduced or avoided by the provision of reasonable instructions or warnings by the seller or other distributor, or a predecessor in the commercial chain of distribution, and the omission of the instructions or warnings renders the product not reasonably safe.

Comment:

a. Rationale. The rules set forth in this Section establish separate standards of liability for manufacturing defects, design defects, and defects based on inadequate instructions or warnings. They are generally applicable to most products. Standards of liability applicable to special product categories such as prescription drugs and used products are set forth in separate sections....

The rule for manufacturing defects...imposes liability whether or not the manufacturer's quality control efforts satisfy standards of reasonableness....

....

In contrast to manufacturing defects, design defects and defects based on inadequate instructions or warnings are predicated on a different concept of responsibility. In the first place, such defects cannot be determined by reference to the manufacturer's own design or marketing standards because those standards are the very ones that plaintiffs attack as unreasonable. Some sort of independent assessment of advantages and disadvantages, to which some attach the label "risk-utility balancing," is necessary. Products are not generically defective merely because they are dangerous. Many product-related accident costs can be eliminated only by sacrificing product features that make products useful and desirable. Thus, the various trade-offs need to be considered in determining whether accident costs are more fairly and efficiently borne by accident victims, on the one hand, or, on the other hand, by consumers generally through the mechanism of higher product prices attributable to liability costs imposed by courts on product sellers.

Subsections (b) and (c), which impose liability for products that are defectively designed or sold without adequate warnings or instructions and are thus not reasonably safe, achieve the same general objectives as does liability predicated on negligence. The emphasis is on creating incentives for manufacturers to achieve optimal levels of safety in designing and marketing products. Society does not benefit from products that are excessively safe—for example, automobiles designed with maximum speeds of 20 miles per hour—any more than it benefits from products that are too risky....

3. *Design Cases Not Requiring Proof of a Reasonable Alternative.* In a few special cases, the third Restatement relieves the plaintiff of the obligation of establishing a "reasonable alternative design" to recover on a design-defect theory. If the injury in question occurs in a way that common experience suggests must be attributable to a defect, as when a new car explodes, the plaintiff may, in substance, invoke the doctrine of *res ipsa loquitur*; Restatement, Third, of Torts: Products Liability §3. A product that does not conform to a safety standard imposed by a government is defective for that reason alone; *id.*, §4. And, in a few cases, a product's design may be so "manifestly unreasonable" that sellers will be liable even if no reasonable alternative is available (the Restatement's example is an exploding cigar); *id.*, §2, comment *e*.

Larsen v. General Motors Corp.
United States Court of Appeals for the Eighth Circuit
391 F.2d 495 (8th Cir. 1968)

FLOYD R. GIBSON, Circuit Judge.

....

The plaintiff-appellant, Erling David Larsen, received severe bodily injuries while driving, with the consent of the owner, a 1963 Chevrolet Corvair....A head-on collision, with the impact occurring on the left front corner of the Corvair, caused a severe rearward thrust of the steering mechanism into the plaintiff's head.... [L]iability is asserted against General Motors on an alleged design defect in the steering assembly and the placement or attachment of the component parts of the steering assembly to the structure of the Corvair.[2]

The plaintiff does not contend that the design caused the accident but that because of the design he received injuries he would not have otherwise received or, in the alternative, his injuries would not have been as severe. The rearward displacement of the steering shaft on the left frontal impact was much greater on the Corvair than it would be in other cars that were designed to protect against such a rearward displacement. The plaintiff's complaint alleges (1) negligence in design of the steering assembly; (2) negligent failure to warn of the alleged latent or inherently dangerous condition to the user of the steering assembly placement; and (3) breach of express and implied warranties of merchantability of the vehicle's intended use.

General Motors contends it "has no duty whatsoever to design and manufacture a vehicle...which is otherwise 'safe' or 'safer' to occupy during collision impacts," and since there is no duty there can be no actionable negligence on its part to either design a safe or more safe car or to warn of any inherent or latent defects in design that might make its cars less safe than some other cars manufactured either by it or other manufacturers.

The District Court...rendered summary judgment in favor of General Motors on the basis that there was no common law duty on the manufacturer "to make a vehicle which would protect the plaintiff from injury in the event of a head-on collision" and dismissed the complaint....

....

There is a line of cases directly supporting General Motors' contention that negligent design of an automobile is not actionable, where the alleged defective design is not a causative factor in the accident. The latest leading case on this point is Evans v. General Motors Corp.,...359 F.2d 822 (7 Cir. 1966)....A divided court there held that General Motors in designing an "X" body frame without perimeter support, instead of an allegedly more safe perimeter body frame, was not liable for the death of a user allegedly caused by the designed defect because the defendant's design could not have functioned to avoid the collision. The Court reasoned...:

> A manufacturer is not under a duty to make his automobile accident-proof or fool-proof; nor must he render the vehicle "more" safe where the danger to be avoided is obvious to all. [Citation.] Perhaps it would be desirable to require manufacturers to construct automobiles in which it would be safe to collide, but that would be a legislative function, not an aspect of judicial interpretation of existing law. [Citation.]

> ....

---

2. The plaintiff alleges that the design and placement of the solid steering shaft, which extends without interruption from a point 2.7 inches in front of the leading surface of the front tires to a position directly in front of the driver, exposes the driver to an unreasonable risk of injury from the rearward displacement of that shaft in the event of a left-of-center head-on collision. So positioned it receives the initial impact of forces generated by a left-of-center head-on collision. The unabsorbed forces of the collision in this area are transmitted directly toward the driver's head, the shaft acting as a spear aimed at a vital part of the driver's anatomy.

The intended purpose of an automobile does not include its participation in collisions with other objects, despite the manufacturer's ability to foresee the possibility that such collisions may occur....

A strong dissent was written by Judge Kiley in which he contended that General Motors had a duty in designing its automobile to use such care that reasonable protection would be given a user against death or injuries from foreseeable yet unavoidable accidents.

....

...General Motors concedes on the negligence count that its duty of care extends to designing and constructing an automobile that is reasonably safe for its intended use of being driven on the roads and highways and that contains no latent or hidden defects which could cause an accident and subsequent injuries....Since MacPherson v. Buick Motor Co., 217 N.Y. 382, 111 N.E. 1050, L.R.A. 1916F, 696 (1916), the courts have consistently held a manufacturer liable for negligent construction of an automobile....

The Courts, however, have been somewhat reluctant to impose liability upon a manufacturer for negligent product design in the automotive field. In Gossett v. Chrysler Corp., 359 F.2d 84 (6 Cir. 1966), the Court reversed a judgment based on an alleged defectively designed truck hood latch that allowed the hood to spring open while the vehicle was in motion causing an accident, but did recognize a duty in connection with design, stating:

> The general rule may be stated as follows: "It is the duty of a manufacturer to use reasonable care under the circumstances to so design his product as to make it not accident or foolproof, but safe for the use for which it is intended. This duty includes a *duty to design the product so that it will fairly meet any emergency of use which can reasonably be anticipated.* The manufacturer is not an insurer that his product is, from a design viewpoint, incapable of producing injury." (Emphasis supplied.)

The above statement is in line with the Restatement (Second), Torts, §398 (1965), which reads:

> A manufacturer of a chattel made under a plan or design which makes it dangerous for the uses for which it is manufactured is subject to liability to others whom he should expect to use the chattel or to be endangered by its probable use for physical harm caused by his failure to exercise reasonable care in the adoption of a safe plan or design.

....

Accepting...the principle that a manufacturer's duty of design and construction extends to producing a product that is reasonably fit for its intended use and free of hidden defects that could render it unsafe for such use, the issue narrows on the proper interpretation of "intended use." Automobiles are made for use on the roads and highways in transporting persons and cargo to and from various points. This intended use cannot be carried out without encountering in varying degrees the statistically proved hazard of injury-producing impacts of various types. The manufacturer should not be heard to say that it does not intend its product to be involved in any accident when it can easily foresee, and when it knows that the probability over the life of its product is high, that it will be involved in some type of injury-producing accident. O'Connell in his article "Taming the Automobile," 58 Nw. U. L. Rev. 299, 348 (1963) cites that between one-fourth to two-thirds of all automobiles during their use at some time are involved in an accident producing injury or death.....It should be recognized that the environment in which a product is used must be taken into consideration by the manufacturer. Spruill v. Boyle-Midway, Inc., 308 F.2d 79 (4th Cir. 1962).

....

....No rational basis exists for limiting recovery to situations where the defect in design or manufacture was the causative factor of the accident, as the accident and the resulting injury, usually caused by the so-called "second collision" of the passenger with the interior part of the automobile, all are foreseeable....

We do agree that under the present state of the art an automobile manufacturer is under no duty to design an accident-proof or fool-proof vehicle or even one that floats on water, but such manufacturer is under a duty to use reasonable care in the design of its vehicle to avoid subjecting the user to an unreasonable risk of injury in the event of a collision....

The intended use and purpose of an automobile is to travel on the streets and highways, which travel more often than not is in close proximity to other vehicles and at speeds that carry the possibility, probability, and potential of injury-producing impacts. The realities of the intended and actual use are well known to the manufacturer and to the public and these realities should be squarely faced by the manufacturer and the courts. We perceive of no sound reason, either in logic or experience, nor any command in precedent, why the manufacturer should not be held to a reasonable duty of care in the design of its vehicle consonant with the state of the art to minimize the effect of accidents....

This duty of reasonable care in design rests on common law negligence[5] that a manufacturer of an article should use reasonable care in the design and manufacture of his product to eliminate any unreasonable risk of foreseeable injury.

....

On the issue of strict liability or implied warranty of merchantability for intended use, we make no comment as our holding of sufficiency of counts one and two are dispositive. The doctrine of strict liability is one of policy for the various states and the National Congress, and we do not think there has been a sufficient showing on the Michigan law as respects this point, particularly in the automotive field....

....

For the reasons set forth, we reverse and remand for proceedings not inconsistent with this opinion.

Notes

1. *Larsen* has been widely followed. Of course, a rule of law that manufacturers are liable if their products are not adequately designed does not by itself entitle accident

---

5. The Michigan case of Piercefield v. Remington Arms Company, Inc., 375 Mich. 85, 133 N.W.2d 129 (1965) applied the doctrine of strict liability in tort, and gave effect in a case involving a defective shotgun shell, to an implied warranty that a product is reasonably fit for the use intended. We, however think the duty in this evolving field of the law should and can rest, at this time, on general negligence principles, with each state free to supplement common law liability for negligence with a doctrine of strict liability for tort as a matter of social policy expressed by legislative action or judicial decision....

victims to any recovery—the victim must still establish a "defect" in the product. In the *Larsen* case on remand, the jury returned a unanimous verdict for General Motors after a three-week trial.

2. *Strict Liability and Negligence.* Since the test for whether a product's design is "good enough" almost necessarily involves an inquiry into the "reasonableness" of the design, it may make little difference whether "design-defect" cases are viewed as sounding in negligence or in strict liability. However, some courts have gone to considerable lengths to favor plaintiffs in design-defect cases, in part, perhaps, because of a feeling that the adoption of "strict liability" should give plaintiffs something that negligence would not provide. The next case provides an example.

Barker v. Lull Engineering Co.
Supreme Court of California
573 P.2d 443 (Cal. 1978)

TOBRINER, Acting Chief Justice.

In August 1970, plaintiff Ray Barker was injured at a construction site…while operating a high-lift loader manufactured by defendant Lull Engineering Co. and leased to plaintiff's employer by defendant George M. Philpott Co., Inc. Claiming that his injuries were proximately caused, *inter alia*, by the alleged defective design of the loader, Barker instituted the present tort action.…The jury returned a verdict in favor of defendants, and plaintiff appeals from the judgment entered upon that verdict, contending primarily that in view of this court's decision in Cronin v. J. B. E. Olson Corp. (1972) 8 Cal. 3d 121, 104 Cal. Rptr. 433, 501 P.2d 1153, the trial court erred in instructing the jury.…

    ….

Plaintiff Barker sustained serious injuries as a result of an accident which occurred while he was operating a Lull High-Lift Loader at a construction site. The loader, manufactured in 1967, is a piece of heavy construction equipment designed to lift loads of up to 5,000 pounds to a maximum height of 32 feet. The loader is 23 feet long, 8 feet wide and weighs 17,050 pounds; it sits on 4 large rubber tires which are about the height of a person's chest, and is equipped with 4-wheel drive, an automatic transmission with no park position and a hand brake. Loads are lifted by forks similar to the forks of a forklift.

The loader is designed so that the load can be kept level even when the loader is being operated on sloping terrain. The leveling of the load is controlled by a lever located near the steering column, and positioned between the operator's legs. The lever is equipped with a manual lock that can be engaged to prevent accidental slipping of the load level during lifting.

The loader was not equipped with seat belts or a roll bar. A wire and pipe cage over the driver's seat afforded the driver some protection from falling objects. The cab of the loader was located at least nine feet behind the lifting forks.

On the day of the accident the regular operator of the loader, Bill Dalton, did not report for work, and plaintiff, who had received only limited instruction on the operation of the loader from Dalton and who had operated the loader on only a few occasions, was assigned to run the loader in Dalton's place. The accident occurred while plaintiff was attempting to lift a load of lumber to a height of approximately 18 to 20 feet and to place the load on the second story of a building under construction. The lift was a particularly difficult one because the terrain on which the loader rested sloped sharply in several directions.

Witnesses testified that plaintiff approached the structure with the loader, leveled the forks to compensate for the sloping ground and lifted the load to a height variously estimated between 10 and 18 feet. During the course of the lift plaintiff felt some vibration, and, when it appeared to several coworkers that the load was beginning to tip, the workers shouted to plaintiff to jump from the loader. Plaintiff heeded these warnings and leaped from the loader, but while scrambling away he was struck by a piece of falling lumber and suffered serious injury.

… Plaintiff contended, *inter alia*, that the accident was attributable to one or more design defects of the loader. Defendant, in turn, denied that the loader was defective in any respect, and claimed that the accident resulted either from plaintiff's lack of skill or from his misuse of its product….

Plaintiff's principal expert witness initially testified that by reason of its relatively narrow base the loader was unstable and had a tendency to roll over when lifting loads to considerable heights; the witness surmised that this instability caused the load to tip in the instant case. The expert declared that to compensate for its instability, the loader should have been equipped with "outriggers," mechanical arms extending out from the sides of the machine, two in front and two in back, each of which could be operated independently and placed on the ground to lend stability to the loader. Evidence at trial revealed that cranes and some high lift loader models are either regularly equipped with outriggers or offer outriggers as optional equipment. Plaintiff's expert testified that the availability of outriggers would probably have averted the present accident.

The expert additionally testified that the loader was defective in that it was not equipped with a roll bar or seat belts. He stated that such safety devices were essential to protect the operator in the event that the machine rolled over. Plaintiff theorized that the lack of such safety equipment was a proximate cause of his injuries because in the absence of such devices he had no reasonable choice but to leap from the loader as it began to tip. If a seat belt and roll bar had been provided, plaintiff argued, he could have remained in the loader and would not have been struck by the falling lumber.

In addition, plaintiff's witnesses suggested that the accident may have been caused by the defective design of the loader's leveling mechanism. Several witnesses testified that both the absence of an automatic locking device on the leveling lever, and the placement of the leveling lever in a position in which it was extremely vulnerable to inadvertent bumping by the operator of the loader in the course of a lift, were defects which may have produced the accident and injuries in question. Finally, plaintiff's experts testified that the absence of a "park" position on the loader's transmission, that could have been utilized to avoid the possibility of the loader's movement during a lift, constituted a further defect in design which may have caused the accident.

Defendants, in response, presented evidence which attempted to refute plaintiff's claims that the loader was defective or that the loader's condition was the cause of the accident. Defendants' experts testified that the loader was not unstable when utilized on the terrain for which it was intended, and that if the accident did occur because of the tipping of the loader it was only because plaintiff had misused the equipment by operating it on steep terrain for which the loader was unsuited.[2] In answer to the claim that

---

2. In support of this claim, defendants presented the testimony of Bill Dalton, the regular operator of the loader, who testified that he called in sick on the day of the accident because he knew

the high lift loader was defective because of a lack of outriggers, defendants' expert testified that outriggers were not necessary when the loader was used for its intended purpose and that no competitive loaders with similar height lifting capacity were equipped with outriggers; the expert conceded, however, that a competitor did offer outriggers as optional equipment on a high-lift loader which was capable of lifting loads to 40, as compared to 32, feet. The expert also testified that the addition of outriggers would simply have given the loader the functional capability of a crane, which was designed for use on all terrain, and that an experienced user of a high-lift loader should recognize that such a loader was not intended as a substitute for a crane.

The defense experts further testified that a roll bar was unnecessary because in view of the bulk of the loader it would not roll completely over. The witnesses also maintained that seat belts would have increased the danger of the loader by impairing the operator's ability to leave the vehicle quickly in case of an emergency. With respect to the claimed defects of the leveling device, the defense experts testified that the positioning of the lever was the safest and most convenient for the operator and that the manual lock on the leveling device provided completely adequate protection. Finally, defendants asserted that the absence of a "park" position on the transmission should not be considered a defect because none of the transmissions that were manufactured for this type of vehicle included a park position.

... [D]efendants' witnesses testified that the accident probably was caused by the plaintiff's own inexperience and consequent dangerous actions. Defendants maintained that if the lumber had begun to fall during the lift it did so only because plaintiff had failed to lock the leveling device prior to the lift....

... [T]he jury by a 10 to 2 vote returned a general verdict in favor of defendants. Plaintiff appeals from the judgment entered upon that verdict.

   ....

Plaintiff principally contends that the trial court committed prejudicial error in instructing the jury "that strict liability for a defect in design of a product is based on a finding that the product was unreasonably dangerous for its intended use...." Plaintiff maintains that this instruction conflicts directly with this court's decision in *Cronin*, decided subsequently to the instant trial, and mandates a reversal of the judgment.

The plaintiff in *Cronin*, a driver of a bread delivery truck, was seriously injured when, during an accident, a metal hasp which held the truck's bread trays in place broke, permitting the trays to slide forward and propel plaintiff through the truck's windshield. Plaintiff brought a strict liability action against the seller, contending that his injuries were proximately caused by the defective condition of the truck. Evidence at trial established that the metal hasp broke during the accident "because it was extremely porous and had a significantly lower tolerance to force than a nonflawed aluminum hasp would have had" [citation], and, on the basis of this evidence, the jury returned a verdict in favor of plaintiff.

On appeal, defendant in *Cronin* argued that the trial court had erred "by submitting a definition of strict liability which failed to include, as defendant requested, the element that the defect found in the product be 'unreasonably dangerous.'" [Citation.] Re-

---

that the loader was not designed to make the lifts scheduled for that day, and he was frightened to make lifts in the area where the accident occurred because of the danger involved. Dalton testified that he informed his supervisor that a crane, rather than a high-lift loader, was required for lifts on such sloping ground, but that the supervisor had not agreed to obtain a crane for such lifts.

lying upon §402A of the Restatement, Second, of Torts and a number of California decisions which had utilized the "unreasonably dangerous" terminology in the product liability context, the defendant in *Cronin* maintained that a product's "unreasonable dangerousness" was an essential element that a plaintiff must establish in any product liability action.

...[W]e rejected the defendant's contention, concluding "that to require an injured plaintiff to prove not only that the product contained a defect but also that such defect made the product unreasonably dangerous to the user or consumer would place a considerably greater burden upon him than that articulated in *Greenman*...." ....

. . . .

In attempting to escape the apparent force of *Cronin*'s explicit language, defendants [in the present case] observe that the flawed hasp which rendered the truck defective in *Cronin* represented a manufacturing defect rather than a design defect, and they argue that *Cronin*'s disapproval of the Restatement's "unreasonably dangerous" standard should be limited to the manufacturing defect context. Defendants point out that one of the bases for our rejection of the "unreasonably dangerous" criterion in *Cronin* was our concern that such language, when used in conjunction with the "defective product" terminology, was susceptible to an interpretation which would place a dual burden on an injured plaintiff to prove, first, that a product was defective and, second, that it was additionally unreasonably dangerous. [Citation.] Defendants contend that the "dual burden" problem is present only in a manufacturing defect context and not in a design defect case.

...[D]efendants explain that in a manufacturing defect case, a jury may find a product defective because it deviates from the manufacturer's intended result, but may still decline to impose liability under the Restatement test on the ground that such defect did not render the product unreasonably dangerous. In a design defect case, by contrast, defendants assert that a defect *is defined* by reference to the "unreasonably dangerous" standard and, since the two are equivalent, no danger of a dual burden exists. In essence, defendants argue that under the instruction which the trial court gave in the instant case, plaintiff was not required to prove both that the loader was defective and that such defect made the loader unreasonably dangerous, but only that the loader was defectively designed by virtue of its unreasonable dangerousness.

Although defendants may be correct, at least theoretically, in asserting that the so-called "dual burden" problem is averted when the "unreasonably dangerous" terminology is used in a design defect case simply as a definition of "defective condition" or "defect," defendants overlook the fact that our objection to the "unreasonably dangerous" terminology in *Cronin* went beyond the "dual burden" issue, and was based, more fundamentally, on a substantive determination that the Restatement's "unreasonably dangerous" formulation represented an undue restriction on the application of strict liability principles.

. . . .

...[C]ontrary to defendants' contention, the reasoning of *Cronin* does not dictate that that decision be confined to the manufacturing defect context....

. . . .

Defendants contend, however, that if *Cronin* is interpreted as precluding the use of the "unreasonably dangerous" language in defining a design defect, the jury in all such cases will inevitably be left without any guidance whatsoever in determining whether a product is defective in design or not....

....

.... [O]ur cases have employed two alternative criteria in ascertaining, in Justice Traynor's words, whether there is something "wrong, if not in the manufacturer's manner of production, at least in his product." (Traynor, *The Ways and Meanings of Defective Products and Strict Liability, supra,* 32 Tenn. L. Rev. 363, 366.)

First, our cases establish that a product may be found defective in design if the plaintiff demonstrates that the product failed to perform as safely as an ordinary consumer would expect when used in an intended or reasonably foreseeable manner.... Under this standard, an injured plaintiff will frequently be able to demonstrate the defectiveness of a product by resort to circumstantial evidence, even when the accident itself precludes identification of the specific defect at fault. [Citations.]

As Professor Wade has pointed out, however, the expectations of the ordinary consumer cannot be viewed as the exclusive yardstick for evaluating design defectiveness because "[in] many situations...the consumer would not know what to expect, because he would have no idea how safe the product could be made." (Wade, *On the Nature of Strict Tort Liability for Products, supra,* 44 Miss. L. J. 825, 829.) Numerous California decisions have implicitly recognized this fact and have made clear, through varying linguistic formulations, that a product may be found defective in design, even if it satisfies ordinary consumer expectations, if through hindsight the jury determines that the product's design embodies "excessive preventable danger," or, in other words, if the jury finds that the risk of danger inherent in the challenged design outweighs the benefits of such design. [Citations.]

...[I]n evaluating the adequacy of a product's design pursuant to this latter standard, a jury may consider, among other relevant factors, the gravity of the danger posed by the challenged design, the likelihood that such danger would occur, the mechanical feasibility of a safer alternative design, the financial cost of an improved design, and the adverse consequences to the product and to the consumer that would result from an alternative design. [Citations.]

...[P]ast authorities have generally not devoted much attention to the appropriate allocation of the burden of proof with respect to these matters. [Citations.] The allocation of such burden is particularly significant in this context inasmuch as this court's product liability decisions, from *Greenman* to *Cronin,* have repeatedly emphasized that one of the principal purposes behind the strict product liability doctrine is to relieve an injured plaintiff of many of the onerous evidentiary burdens inherent in a negligence cause of action. Because most of the evidentiary matters which may be relevant to the determination of the adequacy of a product's design under the "risk-benefit" standard—*e.g.,* the feasibility and cost of alternative designs—are similar to issues typically presented in a negligent design case and involve technical matters peculiarly within the knowledge of the manufacturer, we conclude that once the plaintiff makes a prima facie showing that the injury was proximately caused by the product's design, the burden should appropriately shift to the defendant to prove, in light of the relevant factors, that the product is not defective.... [T]he defendant's burden is one affecting the burden of proof, rather than simply the burden of producing evidence....

Thus, to reiterate, a product may be found defective in design, so as to subject a manufacturer to strict liability for resulting injuries, under either of two alternative tests. First, a product may be found defective in design if the plaintiff establishes that the product failed to perform as safely as an ordinary consumer would expect when used in an intended or reasonably foreseeable manner. Second, a product may alternatively be found defective in design if the plaintiff demonstrates that the product's design proximately caused his injury and the defendant fails to establish, in light of the relevant factors, that, on balance, the benefits of the challenged design outweigh the risk of danger inherent in such design.

. . . .

...[C]ontrary to the suggestion of amicus CTLA, an instruction which advises the jury that it may evaluate the adequacy of a product's design by weighing the benefits of the challenged design against the risk of danger inherent in such design is not simply the equivalent of an instruction which requires the jury to determine whether the manufacturer was negligent in designing the product. (*See, e.g.,* Wade, *On the Nature of Strict Tort Liability for Products, supra,* 44 Miss. L.J. 825, 835.) It is true, of course, that in many cases proof that a product is defective in design may also demonstrate that the manufacturer was negligent in choosing such a design. As we have indicated, however, in a strict liability case, as contrasted with a negligent design action, the jury's focus is properly directed to the condition of the product itself, and not to the reasonableness of the manufacturer's conduct. [Citations.]

Thus, the fact that the manufacturer took reasonable precautions in an attempt to design a safe product or otherwise acted as a reasonably prudent manufacturer would have under the circumstances, while perhaps absolving the manufacturer of liability under a negligence theory, will not preclude the imposition of liability under strict liability principles if, upon hindsight, the trier of fact concludes that the product's design is unsafe to consumers, users, or bystanders. [Citation.]

. . . .

The technological revolution has created a society that contains dangers to the individual never before contemplated. The individual must face the threat to life and limb not only from the car on the street or highway but from a massive array of hazardous mechanisms and products. The radical change from a comparatively safe, largely agricultural, society to this industrial unsafe one has been reflected in the decisions that formerly tied liability to the fault of a tortfeasor but now are more concerned with the safety of the individual who suffers the loss. As Dean Keeton has written, "The change in the substantive law as regards the liability of makers of products and other sellers in the marketing chain has been from fault to defect. The plaintiff is no longer required to impugn the maker, but he is required to impugn the product." (Keeton, *Product Liability and the Meaning of Defect* (1973) 5 St. Mary's L.J. 30, 33.)

. . . .

The judgment in favor of defendants is reversed.

Notes

1. *Technology and Safety.* With respect to the court's comments on safety at the end of its opinion, it may be worth noting that (1) life expectancy in modern, "technological" societies is much greater than in agricultural societies, and (2) farming is and has long been one of the most hazardous of occupations.

2. *The Effect of Placing the Burden of Proof on the Defendant.* The plaintiff in Pietrone v. American Honda Motor Co., 235 Cal. Rptr. 137 (Ct. App. 1987), was a passenger on a motorcycle which was hit by a car. Her foot became entangled in the moving spokes of the motorcycle's rear wheel. Although the plaintiff introduced no evi-

dence of any way in which a motorcycle wheel could be designed so as to avoid or reduce the risk of this kind of injury, the California Court of Appeals held that the plaintiff could get to the jury. A dissenting judge argued that the decision encourages lawsuits in which plaintiff's counsel need only allege that an accident occurred and that the plaintiff was injured, thus sparing plaintiff's counsel the usual burdens of investigating the accident and consulting with experts. The great majority of courts continue to require the plaintiff to show that a design was defective.

3. *The Consumer-Expectation Test.* In Soule v. General Motors Corp., 882 P.2d 298 (Cal. 1994), the California Supreme Court held that the consumer-expectation test for the defectiveness of a design should be used only in those few cases in which the everyday experience of consumers gives them a basis for expecting a minimum level of safety from a product. (One of the court's examples was an automobile that exploded while idling at a stop light—not a difficult case under any test.) In complex cases, the common experience of consumers does not provide a reliable basis for evaluating a design. It was therefore error for the trial court to give the jury a consumer-expectation charge in a case involving the crashworthiness of a car, as consumers' everyday experience would not tell them whether a car could reasonably have been designed so that the front wheel did not collapse and crush the floorboard in a serious crash. The Restatement follows *Soule* in limiting the consumer- expectation test to a few special cases. *See* Restatement, Third, of Torts: Products Liability §2(b), under which the basic test for design defect is whether a product is not reasonably safe because the manufacturer did not adopt a reasonable alternative design. Comment g to §2 says

> ...[C]onsumer expectations, standing alone, do not take into account whether the proposed alternative design could be implemented at reasonable cost, or whether an alternative design would provide greater overall safety.

The Restatement retains consumer expectations for some special situations. For example, "[w]hether a fish bone in a commercially distributed fish chowder constitutes a manufacturing defect...is best determined by focusing on reasonable consumer expectations," *id.*, so the question whether the presence in a food product of an ingredient that causes harm depends on whether a reasonable consumer would expect to find the ingredient in the product; Restatement, Third, of Torts: Products Liability, §7. In addition, the Restatement holds sellers of used products strictly liable for manufacturing (and occasionally other) defects in the products only when the seller's marketing practices would cause reasonable buyers to think that the product in question is no riskier than if it were new; *id.*, §8(b).

Wilson v. Piper Aircraft Corp.

Supreme Court of Oregon, In Banc
577 P.2d 1322 (Or. 1978)

HOLMAN, J.

These two products liability cases...are wrongful-death actions brought by the personal representatives of two passengers who died after the crash of a small airplane. The only defendant is Piper Aircraft Corporation, the manufacturer of the aircraft.

The airplane, a Piper Cherokee manufactured in 1966, took off from the Eugene airport on January 22, 1971, with a licensed student pilot at the controls and a qualified instructor in the copilot's seat. Plaintiffs' decedents, Douglas Wilson and Arbie MacDonald, were passengers in the two rear seats. The airplane crashed in the Cascade

Mountains…after entering a cloud.…The only survivor was the instructor, Terry Li-ittschwager, who, at the time of trial, had no memory of the events.…

Plaintiffs' theory was that the crash was caused by engine failure resulting from carburetor icing.…

. . . .

…[P]laintiffs alleged the following design defects: (1) the aircraft was not equipped with an injection type fuel system; (2) the carburetor was not so designed and equipped that it would provide a proper fuel-air mixture under icing conditions; (3) the aircraft was not supplied with an adequate carburetor heating system; and (4) the aircraft was not equipped with a carburetor heat gauge. Defendant contends first that these allegations, regardless of the state of the evidence, do not present a jury question; and second that the evidence was insufficient to justify submitting them to the jury.

…[D]efendant points out that it is undisputed that the design of this model of airplane was specifically approved by the Federal Aviation Administration (FAA) under its statutory authority to set safety standards for aircraft, and that this particular airplane had been issued an FAA certificate of airworthiness. It is defendant's position that the airplane's design could not be dangerously defective since it met the applicable FAA safety standards, and that FAA approval of the design has foreclosed any further inquiry into its adequacy from a safety standpoint.

We have found no support for this position. Neither the applicable statutes themselves, [citations], nor the legislative history [citation] indicates any Congressional intent to provide that FAA approval of either the general model design or the airworthiness of the particular craft is a complete defense to the claim of civil liability for faulty design. Indeed, 49 U.S.C. §1421(a)(1) provides that the FAA design standards are minimum standards only.[a]

We have, in other contexts, refused to hold compliance with statutory or administrative safety standards to be conclusive on the question of tort liability where there is no evidence of a legislative intent that the standards are to be applied for that purpose.…

[However, this]…case presents difficult problems concerning the showing required of a plaintiff in a design defect case. There was evidence from which the jury could find that each of the allegations listed above accurately described the design of the aircraft, that the condition described in each allegation contributed to the likelihood of carburetor ice formation, and that the probable cause of the crash was engine failure caused by carburetor icing. We must consider whether this evidence was sufficient to permit the jury to find that the airplane was dangerously defective. We hold that it was not.

. . . .

….Plaintiff's allegations amount to a contention that an airplane furnished with a standard aircraft engine is defective because an engine of a different type, or with a different carburetor system, would be safer in one particular. It is not proper to submit such allegations to the jury unless the court is satisfied that there is evidence from which the jury could find the suggested alternatives are not only technically feasible but also practicable in terms of cost and the over-all design and operation of the product. It is part of the required proof that a design feature is a "defect" [and the plaintiff is obliged] to present such evidence. In at least some instances in the present case, that requirement has not been met.

---

a. Are there any kinds of standards other than "minimum" standards? — Eds.

We consider…plaintiff's contention that defendant's airplane was defective because it was provided with a carbureted engine rather than an engine with a fuel injection system. There was evidence that carbureted airplane engines are characteristically subject to icing of a kind which can result in engine failure and that fuel injected engines are not nearly so subject to dangerous icing. There was also evidence that, at the time this airplane was manufactured, fuel injected engines of appropriate horsepower were available, and expert testimony that FAA approval of an airplane like this one with a fuel injected engine could probably have been obtained.

There is not, however, any evidence about what effect the substitution of a fuel injected engine in this airplane design would have had upon the airplane's cost, economy of operation, maintenance requirements, over-all performance, or safety in respects other than susceptibility to icing. Plaintiff's own expert witnesses testified that a carbureted engine of the type used in this airplane was, except for its susceptibility to icing, a highly satisfactory, dependable engine. There was also undisputed evidence that 80 to 90 per cent of all small airplanes comparable to this one are manufactured with carbureted engines rather than with fuel injected engines. There was no explanation of why this is the case.

We also think it is significant that both in 1966, when this airplane was manufactured, and at the present time the FAA safety standards disclose that the agency was aware of the carburetor icing problems and provided for them in its regulations and yet determined that the use of carbureted engines was not unduly dangerous. Although we have held that compliance with the FAA safety standards does not preclude the possibility of liability for a design defect, we nevertheless believe that in a field as closely regulated as aircraft design and manufacture, it is proper to take into consideration, in determining whether plaintiffs have produced sufficient evidence of defect to go to the jury, the fact that the regulatory agency has approved the very design of which they complain after considering the dangers involved.

Taking into account all of the evidence, including the FAA determination that this aircraft design included adequate protection against carburetor icing, we hold that plaintiffs did not produce sufficient evidence that a reasonably prudent manufacturer who was aware of the risks of carburetor icing would not have designed this model of aircraft with a carbureted engine, or that substitution of a fuel injected engine was practicable. On this ground alone, defendant is entitled to a new trial.

....

LINDE, J., concurring.

While I join in the court's decision, the relationship between the allegedly defective design of the aircraft and the FAA's certification of that design perhaps deserves additional discussion.

....

It must be kept in mind that this aircraft is alleged to be defective not because it fell short of the safety standards set for its type, but on the ground that these standards provide insufficient safety for the whole series. But once the common-law premise of liability is expressed as a balance of social utility so closely the same as the judgment made in administering safety legislation, it becomes very problematic to assume that one or a sequence of law courts and juries are to repeat that underlying social judgment *de novo* as each sees fit.

....

Notes

1. *Products Liability and Aircraft.* The small-aircraft industry in the United States was eventually destroyed by products-liability litigation. Ironically, in light of the tendency of many courts to insist that they are promoting safety by expanding liability, this made recreational flying, for those who continued to engage in that hobby, much more dangerous than it would otherwise have been. Someone who wanted to buy a lightplane had to buy and assemble a kit—a task requiring considerable skill—or buy a plane 20 or 30 years old (perhaps a rebuilt wreck, which is not a particularly safe form of transportation).

Congress enacted the General Aviation Revitalization Act of 1994 (Pub. L. 103-298, amended by Pub. L. 102, §3(e) (Westlaw 2003)), which provides:

§2. Time Limitations on Civil Actions Against Aircraft Manufacturers

(a) In General.—Except as provided in subsection (b), no civil action for damages for death or injury to persons or damage to property arising out of an accident involving a general aviation aircraft may be brought against the manufacturer of the aircraft or the manufacturer of any component, system, subassembly, or other part of the aircraft, in its capacity as a manufacturer if the accident occurred—

(1) after the applicable limitation period [which is 18 years-eds.] beginning on—

(A) the date of delivery of the aircraft to its first purchaser or lessee, if delivered directly from the manufacturer; or

(B) the date of first delivery of the aircraft to a person engaged in the business of selling or leasing such aircraft; or

(2) with respect to any component, system, subassembly, or other part which replaced another component, system, subassembly, or other part originally in, or which was added to, the aircraft, and which is alleged to have caused such death, injury, or damage, after the applicable limitation period beginning on the date of completion of the replacement or addition.

(b) Exceptions.—…[Exceptions include cases in which the manufacturer knowingly misrepresented or concealed facts in obtaining an airworthiness certificate from the FAA, actions by passengers for the costs of medical or other emergency treatment, actions by a person on the ground injured by the aircraft, and actions under written warranties.]

...

Shortly after the passage of the General Aviation Revitalization Act of 1994, Cessna resumed production of the Cessna 172—a design then some 30 years old. It seems very likely that, if lightplane production had not been interrupted for so long, small-aircraft designs would have improved significantly over the intervening period, just as automobile designs did. In this area, at least, Justice Traynor's hope that expanding the law of products liability would enhance safety (*see Escola*, p. 703, *supra*) seems not to have worked out.

2. *Cost-Benefit Analysis in Products-Liability Cases.* Some writers have questioned the ability of the average jury to make intelligent judgments about the desirability of particular design features. A leading article on this point is James A. Henderson, Jr., *Judicial Review of Manufacturers' Conscious Design Choices: The Limits of Adjudication*, 73 Colum. L. Rev. 1531 (1973), cited in the *Wilson* opinion. Professor Henderson has since

recanted: see James A. Henderson, Jr. & Aaron D. Twerski, *Achieving Consensus on De-fective Product Design*, 83 Cornell L. Rev. 867, 869 (1998) (describing the previous posi-tion as "extreme," though not pointing to any specific flaw in the earlier analysis). Nev-ertheless, most states' versions of design-defect law require factfinders to make judgments about product design.

May a *manufacturer* make a cost-benefit analysis of a proposed design change before deciding whether or not to put it into effect? In Grimshaw v. Ford Motor Co., 174 Cal. Rptr. 348 (Ct. App. 1981), Ford was held liable for punitive damages because it had de-cided not to make changes in the Ford Pinto which would have made the car less sus-ceptible to fire when struck from behind. Ford had prepared a cost-benefit analysis (re-lating to rollover protection, not rear-end crashes) for submission to the National Highway Transportation Safety Bureau, which was considering imposing rollover stan-dards. According to the court of appeals, "[B]y engaging in a cost-benefit analysis bal-ancing human lives and limbs against corporate profits...Ford's institutional mentality was shown to be one of callous indifference to public safety."

Because the figures Ford used to "value" lives were figures appropriate for determining compensation, rather than deterrence, Ford's cost-benefit analysis of the Pinto was grossly inaccurate by modern standards. But the *Grimshaw* decision held Ford liable simply be-cause it had made cost-benefit calculations, not because it had made them badly. Logically, *Grimshaw* and *Barker* cannot both be the law of the same jurisdiction: *Grimshaw* holds that a manufacturer's attempt to determine whether its products are defective will subject the manufacturer to punitive damages even if the products turn out to be adequate. Under *Barker*, if "improving" a product would cost more than the benefits of the improvement, the manufacturer's failure to make the improvement does not render the product defec-tive. As a matter of trial strategy, however, no lawyer would argue simply that the plain-tiff's proposed design would cost too much. In *The Myth of the Ford Pinto Case*, 43 Rutgers L. Rev. 1013, 1038 (1991), Professor Gary T. Schwartz offers this "composite" of the obser-vations of a number of defense lawyers on how to approach juries in design-defect cases:

> There are several kinds of arguments that defense counsel can make which juries are willing to take seriously. One argument is that the design itself is not really improper, in that an alternative design would significantly impair the usefulness of the product itself. In addition, "state of the art" is a liability-limiting idea that adequately speaks to the jury's common sense. You can also argue that the acci-dent was *really* caused by the victim's own faulty conduct, or the faulty conduct of some third party. Here your argument can be strengthened by showing that the product was being misused or used in an abnormal way. When the facts are right, it can also make sense to argue that the victim assumed the risk—that the victim knew what he was getting. However, one argument that you should almost never make is that the manufacturer deliberately included a dangerous feature in the product's design because of the high monetary cost that the manufacturer would have incurred in choosing another design. If you do argue this, you're almost cer-tain to lose on liability, and you can expose yourself to punitive damages as well.

These suggestions seem almost self-evidently sound, yet they lead to the curious con-clusion that the very risk-benefit analysis that *Barker* and the Restatement (Third) make central to the determination of whether a design is defective is an analysis that the de-fense dare not ask the jury to undertake.

A possible alternative to balancing costs and benefits is the "consumer expectations" approach described in Barker v. Lull Eng'g Co., 573 P.2d 443 (Cal. 1978), *supra* at p.

718, though in that case the court advanced this "test" as a supplement to cost-benefit analysis, not a replacement. As noted earlier, the California Supreme Court has abandoned the consumer-expectation approach in complex design cases, a view with which the Third Restatement agrees.

In an attempt to come up with an alternative to asking juries to balance costs and benefits, the Supreme Court of Pennsylvania has held that juries should be instructed that "a manufacturer is effectively a guarantor of his product's safety," and that "the jury may find a defect where the product left the supplier's control lacking any element necessary to make it safe for its intended use or possessing any feature that renders it unsafe for the intended use"; Azzarello v. Black Bros. Co., Inc., 391 A.2d 1020 (Pa. 1978). This instruction is to be given in cases in which the judge concludes that, "under the plaintiff's averment of the facts, recovery would be justified." Apparently, the judge may engage in some sort of cost-benefit calculations before letting a case go to the jury, though in view of the jury's limited role, it seems doubtful that evidence to enable the judge to make an informed judgment would be admissible. Indeed, the Pennsylvania Supreme Court has held that, under the Azzarello test, evidence of industry standards is inadmissible in design-defect cases. That kind of evidence, said the court, might mislead the jury into considering the reasonableness of the design; Lewis v. Coffing Hoist Div., 528 A.2d 590 (Pa. 1987).

C. Failure to Warn

Goins v. The Clorox Co.
United States Court of Appeals for the Sixth Circuit
926 F.2d 559 (6th Cir. 1991)

MARTIN, Jr., Circuit Judge.

Diane Goins, who is the administratrix of her mother Bessie Mae Sheppard's estate, appeals the district court's grant of summary judgment to the defendants, the Clorox Company and Boyle-Midway Household Products, Inc., in this products liability action predicated on Tennessee diversity jurisdiction. We affirm.

On January 23, 1988, Mrs. Bessie Mae Sheppard was visiting the home of her friend, Mrs. Barbara Large, in Lenoir City, Tennessee. While at Mrs. Large's home, Sheppard and Large attempted to clear a clogged drain in the kitchen. Sheppard began this effort because she had some previous experience and had helped her former husband in his plumbing business. The two first attempted to clear the drain using a plunger. When this failed, they poured Drano and Liquid Plumr, a product manufactured by Clorox, into the drain. The drain remained clogged, so they added Sani-Flush, a toilet bowl cleaner manufactured by Boyle-Midway Household Products, Inc. Mrs. Sheppard first sprinkled a small number of Sani-Flush crystals into the drain; a small puff of smoke appeared, prompting Mrs. Large to suggest that they leave the sink alone. Sheppard persisted, however, and while attempting to add a few more crystals she inadvertently allowed a "big glob" of Sani-Flush to enter the drain. A large cloud of grey smoke immediately arose from the drain, burning the lungs of both women and driving them from the house. Mrs. Sheppard, who suffered from a pre-existing respiratory condition, was unable to regain her normal breathing pattern and later died at a local emergency room of cardiac arrest.

....Goins alleges that the defendants proximately caused her mother's death by failing to provide adequate labels or warnings on the packaging of the products at issue. Specifically, she claims that the labels provided were not adequate to appraise the consumer of either the nature or the severity of the risk involved in using the defendants' products. Although the precise language of the labels is impossible to determine because the containers were not available, the district court accepted Goins's submission of photocopied labels of other Liquid Plumber and Sani-Flush containers.

The [trial] court...granted summary judgment to the defendants....The court found that the plaintiff could not carry her burden of showing proximate causation between her mother's injury and the allegedly defective labels because both labels explicitly warned of the danger at issue, (The Liquid Plumr container cautions, "Do not use with toilet bowl cleaners...release of hazardous gases may occur," while the Sani-Flush packaging warns of "harmful fumes"), and because the plaintiff had presented no proof that her mother had ever read those labels. Ms. Goins appeals the grant of summary judgment alleging that the district court erred in not presenting the question of inadequate labeling to jury, claiming that a material question of fact exists as to proximate causation.

....

As we look to Tennessee law on this subject, we find a fairly stiff standard. The plaintiff bears the burden of establishing that a product was in a defective condition or otherwise unreasonably dangerous by reason of the manufacturer's failure to provide an adequate warning informing users of the dangers of that product. [Citations.] Whether a warning is adequate is usually a question for the jury unless reasonable minds could not disagree on the outcome. [Citation.] To be considered adequate, Tennessee requires a warning to be "one calculated to bring home to a reasonably prudent user of the product the nature and the extent of the danger involved in using the product." [Citations.] The Tennessee Products Liability Act of 1978 further provides that:

> Compliance by a manufacturer or seller with any federal or state statute or administrative regulation existing at the time the product was manufactured and prescribing standards for...labeling, warning or instructions for use of a product, shall raise a rebuttable presumption that the product is not in an unreasonably dangerous condition in regard to the matters covered by these standards.

Tenn. Code Ann. §29-28-104 (1980).

As we view Tennessee law, even if a plaintiff is able to establish that a product is unreasonably dangerous by reason of a defective warning, this alone is not enough to establish liability. The plaintiff must also prove that the inadequate labeling proximately caused the claimed injury. Browder v. Pettigrew, 541 S.W.2d 402, 405 (Tenn. 1976). The district court granted summary judgment because it found that plaintiff could not satisfy this second prong of labeling liability. The court did not address the issue of the adequacy of labels themselves. We agree plaintiff has failed to establish that these products were unreasonably dangerous, and need not reach the issue of proximate causation.

Pursuant to Fed. R. Civ. Pro. 56(e), defendants included affidavits with their motions for summary judgment establishing certain facts about the labels included on their products. Boyle-Midway's brief was accompanied by the statement of Richard Carter, Director of Advertising, Toxicology, and Regulatory Affairs for Boyle-Midway. Mr. Carter's affidavit established that the labeling of Sani-Flush is subject to, and controlled by, the provisions of the Federal Insecticide, Fungicide, and Rodenticide Act of

1982, 7 U.S.C. §§136 *et seq.*, as well as by the Environmental Protection Agency. Mr. Carter stated that the warning label included on the Sani-Flush container had been approved by the EPA, and was in full compliance with all applicable federal standards. A similar affidavit was submitted by Clorox in which A. K. Reddy, Manager of the Product Safety and Regulatory Compliance Department of Clorox, stated that Liquid Plumber warning labels are prescribed by, and comply with, the Federal Hazardous Substance Act of 1960, 15 U.S.C. §§1261(p) and 1263(a), and the regulations promulgated thereunder.

The plaintiff introduced no evidence to challenge defendants' compliance with any of these federal regulations. Therefore, as we noted under Tenn. Code Ann. §29-28-104, defendants are entitled to a rebuttable presumption that their products are not unreasonably dangerous.

Having established the existence of the statutory presumption, Rule 56(e) entitles the defendants to summary judgment unless the plaintiff can come forward with sufficient evidence to rebut this presumption. Celotex Corp. v. Catrett, 477 U.S. 317, 322, 91 L. Ed. 2d 265, 106 S. Ct. 2548 (1986) (if movant's motion is properly supported, summary judgment required unless non-movant can "make a showing sufficient to establish the existence of an element essential to that party's case"). Here the plaintiff has failed. There was no fact or opinion submitted which would establish a material issue necessary to rebut the statutory presumption of the adequacy of the Liquid Plumber or Sani-Flush warnings. Rather, plaintiff rested solely upon the allegations in her complaint that those warnings were inadequate. This is insufficient under Rule 56(e) which states:

> an adverse party may not rest upon the mere allegations or denials of the adverse party's pleading; but the adverse party's response, by affidavits or as otherwise provided in this rule, must set forth specific facts showing that there is a genuine issue for trial. If the adverse party does not so respond, summary judgment, if appropriate, shall be entered against the adverse party.

With nothing offered to rebut the evidence offered by defendants, we see no issue of contested fact and affirm.

Notes

1. *Rebuttable Presumption Based on Compliance with Government Requirements.* Many states hold that compliance with government requirements concerning labeling, licensing, or product approval raises a rebuttable presumption that a product is not defective. *See* Perez v. Wyeth Labs. Inc., 734 A.2d 1245 (N.J. 1999) (holding that a rebuttable presumption exists that a manufacturer which complies with FDA labeling and warning requirements has satisfied its duty to warn).

What would the plaintiff in *Goins* have to do to rebut the presumption discussed in that case? A Texas statute addressing the same issue states: "The claimant may rebut the presumption...by establishing that...(1) the mandatory federal safety standards or regulations applicable to the product were inadequate to protect the public from unreasonable risks of injury or damage; or (2) the manufacturer, before or after marketing the product, withheld or misrepresented information or material relevant to the federal government's or agency's determination of adequacy of the safety standards or regulations at issue in the action." Tex. Civ. Prac. & Rem. Code §82.008 (Westlaw 2003).

2. With the principal case, contrast Moran v. Faberge, Inc., 332 A.2d 11 (Md. 1975). The plaintiff, a teenager who was uncertain whether a candle was scented, grabbed a

bottle of cologne and shook it onto the candle to resolve all doubts. Cologne contains alcohol, and the plaintiff was burned. The court held that, although the particular accident may have been "unusual and bizarre," the manufacturer should have foreseen that perfume could be ignited, and upheld a jury verdict for the plaintiff based on the bottle's lack of a warning. The court's examples of accidents that would be "foreseeable" were (1) a woman seated at a dressing table, lighting a cigarette close enough to the top of an open perfume bottle to cause an explosion and (2) the same woman turning suddenly and bumping the bottle with her elbow, splashing cologne on a burning candle.

In response to the spate of "failure to warn" cases in recent years, manufacturers have taken to warning consumers of practically anything that the product could possibly do to them. Whether the several pages of detailed warnings that now accompany new products are routinely read by consumers seems most doubtful (do *you* read all the warnings that accompany the products you buy?). An unfortunate side-effect of the mass of warnings now present because of the tort system is that consumers faced with so much to read may read none of the warnings at all, and they may assume that whatever warnings they do read are mere lawyers' boilerplate, not to be taken seriously. *See* A. D. Twerski, A. S. Weinstein, W. A. Donaher & H. R. Piehler, *The Use and Abuse of Warnings in Products Liability Design — Defect Litigation Comes of Age*, 61 Cornell L. Rev. 495 (1976).

3. *Warnings Never Read.* Some courts hold that a plaintiff who admittedly failed to read an allegedly inadequate warning cannot recover under a failure-to-warn theory. Other courts take a contrary position. For example, in Johnson v. Johnson Chem. Co., Inc., 588 N.Y.S.2d 607 (App. Div. 1992), a consumer was injured in an explosion that occurred when she activated a roach "fogger" near a pilot light in her kitchen. The plaintiff had admittedly failed to read the multiple labels on the can that stated "put out all flames and pilot lights" or words to similar effect. In reversing a grant of summary judgment for the manufacturer, the appellate court wrote:

> It is perhaps difficult to see how a consumer who admittedly does not read the labels on the products he or she uses can reasonably claim to have been injured *because* the text of such label did not give a sufficient warning.
>
> The argument loses its persuasive force, however, once it is understood that the intensity of the language used in the text of a warning is only one of the factors to be considered in deciding whether such warning is adequate. A second factor to be considered is the prominence with which such language is displayed....

4. *"Heeding" Presumptions in Warning Cases.* Products-liability cases talk about two different kinds of heeding presumptions in warning cases: the first is advantageous to the plaintiff when a warning was not given and the second may be advantageous to the defendant when a warning was given.

(a) *For the Advantage of the Plaintiff.* In some states, the plaintiff in a failure-to-warn case is entitled to a rebuttable presumption that if a warning had been given it would have been heeded. The presumption shifts the burden of proof to the defendant on the issue of causation. The presumption is rebuttable by evidence demonstrating that if a warning had been given it would have been disregarded. If the presumption is not rebutted, the failure to warn is presumed to be a proximate cause of the plaintiff's injuries.

In Coffman v. Keene Corp., 628 A.2d 710, 719 (N.J. 1993), the court adopted a heeding presumption, finding that it was consistent with the strict liability public policies of encouraging product safety and easing the burden of proof for persons injured by defective products. The court noted that a "great many jurisdictions have adopted the heeding presumption in failure-to-warn cases."

See also Bunting v. Sea Ray, Inc., 99 F.3d 887 (8th Cir. 1996) (admitting evidence of a drowned boater's blood alcohol level as relevant to the issue of whether he would have heeded an additional warning).

Some courts say that the plaintiff enjoys a presumption that a warning would have been heeded only in a case where no warning was given, and not in a case where a warning that was given but was allegedly inadequate. *See* McLennan v. American Eurocopter Corp., Inc., 245 F.3d 403 (5th Cir. 2001) (Texas law).

(b) *For the Advantage of the Defendant.* Comment j to Restatement, Second, of Torts §402A provided that:

> Where warning is given, the seller may reasonably assume that it will be read and heeded; and a product bearing such a warning, which is safe for use if it is followed, is not in defective condition, nor is it unreasonably dangerous.

This approach has been rejected by many courts as well as by the third Restatement, which says:

> Reasonable designs and instructions or warnings both play important roles in the production and distribution of reasonably safe products. In general, when a safer design can reasonably be implemented and risks can reasonably be designed out of a product, adoption of the safer design is required over a warning that leaves a significant residuum of such risks. For example, instructions and warnings may be ineffective because users of the product may not be adequately reached, may be likely to be inattentive, or may be insufficiently motivated to follow the instructions or heed the warnings. However, when an alternative design to avoid risks cannot reasonably be implemented, adequate instructions and warnings will normally be sufficient to render the product reasonably safe.... Warnings are not, however, a substitute for the provision of a reasonably safe design.

Restatement, Third, of Torts: Products Liability §2 cmt. l (emphasis added). The Reporters' Notes in the third Restatement refer to Comment j in the second Restatement as "unfortunate language" that "has elicited heavy criticism from a host of commentators."

In Uniroyal Goodrich Tire Co. v. Martinez, 977 S.W.2d 328 (Tex. 1998), the court, following the third Restatement, found that the evidence supported the jury's finding that a 16-inch tire that exploded when the plaintiff mechanic attempted to mount it on a 16.5-inch wheel was unreasonably dangerous, even though a prominent warning label attached to the tire warned against mounting it on a 16.5-inch wheel. The facts showed that a redesigned tire would have prevented the accident and that the manufacturer's competitors had previously incorporated the safer design. The court noted that other courts had "overwhelmingly rejected" Comment j to §402A.

5. *Vaccines and Other Pharmaceuticals.* Failure to warn is the principal avenue to recovery for those who claim to have sustained injuries from the side effects of vaccines and other pharmaceutical products. In nearly all cases, vaccines are worth taking, even if they do occasionally produce adverse reactions. Nevertheless, the manufacturers of polio and DPT (whooping cough) vaccines have often been held liable for failure to warn (or to warn strenuously enough) of possible adverse reactions to these vaccines. For instance, the plaintiff in Reyes v. Wyeth Labs., 498 F.2d 1264 (5th Cir. 1974), contracted polio after being vaccinated, perhaps (though this was far from clear) because of the vaccine. There is no question that the risk of polio is much greater for those who are not vaccinated than for those who are, yet the court held that the jury could find both that the vaccine caused the plaintiff's illness and that the plaintiff would not have taken

the vaccine if a warning had been present. *Compare* Givens v. Lederle, 556 F.2d 1341 (5th Cir. 1977), in which the plaintiff's doctor was warned that contracting polio from vaccine might be possible. There, liability was based on the warning's not being strong enough. The plaintiff's doctor had decided that the risk was so small as not to be worth mentioning.

Suppose that the manufacturer of a vaccine does warn of possible side effects in graphic terms, and that the plaintiff, frightened off by the warning, decides not to get vaccinated. If the plaintiff then contracts the disease in question, is there a good claim against the manufacturer on the theory that the warning was defective because it deterred people from using a vaccine that would have protected them? Claims based on overwarning are rare, but not unheard of. In Dimond v. Caterpillar Tractor Co., 134 Cal. Rptr. 895 (Ct. App. 1976), the plaintiff may have been injured by falling rolls of paper after abandoning the safety of the forklift he was operating. (No one knew for sure what had happened, because the plaintiff suffered amnesia, and there were no witnesses to the accident.) The court allowed the plaintiff to get to the jury on the theory that a warning label on the dashboard of the forklift might have caused the plaintiff to think the cab of the lift was less safe than it really was, and so to run from the lift when staying put would have been safer.

In an attempt to protect manufacturers of certain compulsory childhood vaccines from crushing tort liability, Congress enacted the National Childhood Vaccine Injury Act, 42 U.S.C. §§300aa *et seq.* (Westlaw 2003). The Act's no-fault scheme is designed to provide prompt compensation, limited in amount, to victims of vaccine-related injuries.

6. *Expert Testimony in Products Liability Cases.* Suits against drug manufacturers have led to huge increases in the costs of some drugs, and in at least one instance have caused the withdrawal of a product from the market. Bendectin, a drug to prevent morning sickness, was withdrawn from the market in 1983. Before its withdrawal, it had been taken by some 30 million pregnant women. The claims in question were that the drug had caused birth defects in the children of those who took it. Although the consensus among scientists was overwhelmingly that Bendectin had not been shown to cause birth defects, and although the manufacturer won most of the cases (in several instances being granted judgment n.o.v. because of the state of the scientific evidence), the potential exposure and the litigation costs made continued production of Bendectin economically senseless. For a description of the state of the evidence on whether Bendectin caused birth defects and a list of the outcomes of the cases, see Turpin v. Merrell Dow Pharmaceuticals, Inc., 959 F.2d 1349 (6th Cir. 1992) (upholding grant of summary judgment to Merrell Dow because the evidence was insufficient to allow reasonable jurors to find that Bendectin had caused the plaintiff's birth defects).

Many of the pre-1993 Bendectin cases won by the defendant were federal diversity cases in which the plaintiffs were unable to present admissible expert testimony that Bendectin caused birth defects. Under the rule of Frye v. United States, 293 F. 1013 (D.C. Cir. 1923), expert opinion on scientific techniques was admissible only if the techniques were generally accepted in the scientific community. As none of the thirty published studies of Bendectin had found a causal connection between the drug and birth defects, the testimony of the plaintiffs' expert that Bendectin had caused the defects in question was rejected. In Daubert v. Merrell Dow Pharmaceuticals, Inc., 509 U.S. 579 (1993), the Supreme Court held that the *Frye* doctrine had been overruled by the Federal Rules of Evidence, which allow the admission of "all relevant evidence." The Court vacated a court of appeals decision which had affirmed a grant of summary judgment to the defendant in a Bendectin case. Under *Daubert*, scientific testimony may be admissible even if the expert's conclusion contradicts generally accepted scientific beliefs. Trial judges are, however, supposed to determine whether the "reasoning or methodology underlying the testimony is scientifically valid and...whether that reasoning or methodology properly can be applied to the facts in issue" before allowing the testimony. Chief Justice Rehnquist and Justice Stevens, concurring in part, objected that the *Daubert* approach requires trial judges to become "amateur scientists" in deciding what testimony to allow; they too would have rejected the *Frye* rule. On remand, the Ninth Circuit upheld the trial court's grant of summary judgment to Merrell Dow; 43 F.3d 1311 (9th Cir. 1995). The court pointed out that the plaintiff's experts had conducted no studies, had published no scientific papers, and had not explained the methods they used to justify their conclusions that the many studies concluding that Bendectin was safe were flawed. Furthermore, even if the plaintiffs could have made a case that Bendectin was capable of causing birth defects, their experts had not offered any serious attempt to show that Bendectin had caused their injuries.

See also Kumho Tire Co. v. Carmichael, 119 S. Ct. 1167 (1999) (holding that *Daubert's* "gatekeeping" obligation applies not only to "scientific" testimony, but to all expert testimony).

In response to *Daubert, Kumho*, and other cases, the Federal Rules of Evidence were amended, and now provide:

> If scientific, technical, or other specialized knowledge will assist the trier of fact to understand the evidence or to determine a fact in issue, a witness qualified as an expert by knowledge, skill, experience, training, or education, may testify thereto in the form of an opinion or otherwise, if (1) the testimony is based upon sufficient facts or data, (2) the testimony is the product of reliable principles and methods, and (3) the witness has applied the principles and methods reliably to the facts of the case.

Fed. R. Evid. 702 (2003).

7. *Prescription Drugs under the Restatement.* Section 6(c) of the Restatement, Third, of Torts: Products Liability adopts a standard for design defects in cases involving prescription drugs and medical devices which few, if any, products will fail to meet:

> A prescription drug or medical device is not reasonably safe due to defective design if the foreseeable risks of harm posed by the drug or medical device are sufficiently great in relation to its foreseeable therapeutic benefits that reasonable health-care providers, knowing of such foreseeable risks and therapeutic benefits, would not prescribe the drug or medical device for any class of patients.

However, as §6(d) of the Restatement continues to hold drug manufacturers liable for inadequate warnings or instructions, the apparent protections of §6(c) may be largely illusory.

Under the prior Restatement, the analysis of design defect claims relating to prescription drugs focused on Comment k to §402A, which dealt with "unavoidably unsafe products." Some jurisdictions interpreted Comment k as exempting all prescription drugs from strict liability design defect claims. Other courts interpreted Comment k as providing an exemption only to those prescription drugs determined on a case-by-case-basis to be "unavoidably dangerous."

8. *"Learned Intermediary" Doctrine.* The "learned intermediary" doctrine operates as an exception to the manufacturer's duty to warn the ultimate consumer, and shields

manufacturers of prescription drugs from liability if they adequately warn the prescribing physicians of dangers. "The doctrine extends to prescription drugs because, unlike over the counter medications, the patient may obtain the drug only through a physician's prescription, and the use of prescription drugs is generally monitored by a physician." Edwards v. Basel Pharmaceuticals, 933 P.2d 298 (Okla. 1997). There are at least two exceptions to the doctrine: mass immunizations, because there may be no physician-patient relationship, and warnings required by the FDA to be given directly to the consumer.

The learned intermediary doctrine evolved at a time when prescription drugs were not marketed directly to consumers. That situation has changed dramatically, as prescription drugs are now standard fare for television, newspaper, and magazine ads. Although ads often urge consumers to "ask your doctor," some courts now hold that the learned intermediary doctrine does not apply to cases of directly marketed prescription drugs. *See* Perez v. Wyeth Labs. Inc., 734 A.2d 1245 (N.J. 1999).

9. *Problem: Drugs for Expectant Mothers.* You are general counsel to a pharmaceutical company, which has developed a drug that may be taken by millions of pregnant women. Bearing in mind that at least one percent of these women will inevitably give birth to children who are not completely healthy, even if your product is 100-percent safe, would you advise your client to produce the drug? Would it make a difference if use of this drug would save thousands of lives?

10. *Foreign-Language Warnings.* Questions arise as to the adequacy of English-language warnings on products marketed to non-English speaking consumers. In Ramirez v. Plough, Inc., 863 P.2d 167 (Cal. 1993), the court held that manufacturers of non-prescription drugs who conform their product labels to state and federal law (which requires only labels in English) cannot be held liable for failure to warn in a language other than English. The court opined that the issue of foreign-language warnings was more properly one for the legislature than for the judiciary.

11. *Makers of Component Parts.* In Rynders v. E.I. DuPont, De Nemours & Co., 21 F.3d 835 (8th Cir. 1994), the court held that the maker of cartilage replacement implants used to treat temporomandibular joint (TMJ) disorders, rather than the manufacturer of a polymer product incorporated into the implants, had a duty to research and warn consumers about possible dangers associated with implants. The TMJ patients injured by the implants did not claim that the polymers were defective as originally delivered to an implant maker, but rather that the polymer product, as incorporated into the implants, was an inappropriate substance to place in the human body.

12. In Reiff v. Convergent Technologies, 957 F. Supp. 573, 581 (D.N.J. 1997), the court held that a keyboard manufacturer has no duty to warn users of the risks of carpal tunnel syndrome because "a computer keyboard poses no greater threat than does a chair, desk, monitor, or any other component of a work environment." It wrote:

> Products whose use requires physical activity often entail a risk that such use will cause harm—harm not from the product itself but harm from the manner of a product's use. Consider the snow shovel. Each year, hundreds of people suffer heart attacks, strain their backs, and pull various muscles shoveling snow from their driveways. Since any harm posed lies not in the snow shovel but rather in its use in a particular manner, by a particular person with particular physical attributes, the law does not require that snow shovels contain warnings. For the same reasons, the law does not and ought not require that computer keyboards contain warnings relating to a keyboard's use in a particu-

lar way, by a particular person with particular physical characteristics and work habits.

Is this line of reasoning persuasive?

D. Damage to Property

Suppose that, because of a manufacturing defect, the brakes of the plaintiff's car wear out prematurely. Unless this failure is covered by a warranty, the plaintiff should have no claim against the manufacturer: the receipt of a product not as good as one had hoped to get is the sort of thing traditionally governed by contract, not tort. But suppose that, because of the failure, the car crashes into the plaintiff's garage, damaging the car, the garage, and the plaintiff. The plaintiff's personal-injury claim is (by today's standards) an everyday tort claim. So, probably, is the claim for damages to the garage. The claim for damages to the car itself is more questionable.

East River Steamship Corp. v. Transamerica Delaval, 476 U.S. 858 (1986), attempted to draw the line between contract and tort in a property-damage case. A defective component of a turbine, which was supplied to purchasers as part of an integral package, damaged only the turbine itself. The plaintiffs sought damages in tort for the cost of repairs and for lost profits, because statutes of limitations barred contract claims. After reviewing various approaches that have been used to distinguish strict-liability-in-tort claims from breach-of-contract claims, the court held that a manufacturer has no duty under negligence or strict liability to prevent a product from injuring itself. The court reasoned that economic losses can be insured, that commercial situations generally do not involve large disparities of bargaining power, and that the law of warranty provides sufficient protection for the benefits of the bargain.

The Economic-Loss Rule. The legal standard at work in cases like *East River Steamship Corp.* is sometimes referred to as the "economic-loss rule." In a product-defect case, the rule prohibits recovery of damages for economic losses involving harm to the product itself, but recovery of damages for harm caused to "other" property or persons is allowed. *See* Murray v. Ford Motor Co., 97 S.W.3d 888 (Tex. App. 2003) (in a tort action involving a truck that caught fire, the court allowed recovery of $453.25 in damages to other property, but not for the loss of the truck). The economic-loss rule applies to negligence claims, as well as claims based on strict liability.

A product defect which has not caused physical injury ordinarily will not support an action for damages in tort. In Ziegelmann v. DaimlerChrysler Corp., 649 N.W.2d 556 (N.D. 2002), a group of vehicle owners claimed that they were damaged by an automaker's failure to equip its vehicles with a parking brake interlock, which requires the driver to step on the brake before shifting out of park. However, the plaintiffs failed to allege that the defect had caused injury or damage. The court rejected claims for negligence and fraud, noting that economic harm in the form of loss of resale value was too speculative to be actionable.

"The Product Itself." It is often difficult to determine just what constitutes "other" property as opposed to the "product itself." In Jimenez v. Superior Court, 127 Cal. Rptr. 2d 614 (Cal. 2002), the plaintiff alleged that defective windows installed during con-

struction of their mass-produced homes had caused damage to stucco, dry wall, floor coverings, and other parts of the dwellings. The court wrote:

> To apply the economic loss rule, we must first determine what the product at issue is. Only then do we find out whether the injury is to the product itself (for which recovery is barred by the economic loss rule) or to property other than the defective product (for which plaintiffs may recover in tort). Defendant window manufacturers argue that here the "product" is the entire house in which their windows were installed.... We disagree.
>
> ... [T]he economic loss rule does not necessarily bar recovery in tort for damage that a defective product (e.g., a window) causes to other portions of a larger product (*e.g.*, a house) into which the former has been incorporated....
>
> .... We hold only that, under California decisional law, the economic loss rule does not bar a homeowner's recovery in tort for damage that a defective window causes to other parts of the home in which it has been installed.

(The dissenter argued that the majority's holding in *Jimenez* was inconsistent with the United States Supreme Court's treatment of component parts in *East River Steamship Corp.* The tension between the two cases is obvious.)

See also Progressive Ins. Co v. General Motors Corp., 749 N.E.2d 484 (Ind. 2001) (holding that an automobile which caught fire as a result of allegedly defective wiring was to be viewed as a single unit and that therefore there was no damage to "other property" that would support a products-liability claim); Bocre Leasing Corp. v. General Motors Corp., 645 N.E.2d 1195 (N.Y. 1995) (a buyer of a used helicopter could not recover in tort from the engine manufacturer for losses caused by a defect in the engine which resulted in damage only to the helicopter).

Saratoga Fishing Co. v. J.M. Martinac & Co., 520 U.S. 875 (1997), involved a fishing boat that caught fire and sank because of a defectively designed hydraulic system. After the boat had been purchased from the manufacturer, but before the plaintiff had bought it, some equipment had been added to the boat to equip it for fishing. Was "the product itself" the boat as delivered by the manufacturer to the first purchaser, or did it include the equipment added by the first owner? *Saratoga Fishing* held that the added equipment was not part of "the product itself." Justice Scalia, dissenting, argued that this result makes the extent of the seller's liability depend on the often-irrelevant detail of whether the manufacturer sold a fully equipped product or (as in *Saratoga Fishing*) an incomplete product with other features to be added later.

Tort and Contract. What is the difference between tort and contract? Traditionally, tort covers cases in which the parties cannot be expected to agree in advance about the rules that will apply. For instance, it would be absurd to think that motorists and pedestrians could get together in advance of accidents and agree on who should pay what if someone is hit by a car. Contract, by contrast, applies to cases in which the parties can and do deal in advance: if *A* wants *B*'s house, the way to get it is for *A* to agree to buy the house from *B*, not for *A* to sue *B* on the theory that it would be more "reasonable" for *A* to own the house than for *B* to continue to own it. Under this approach, many product-liability cases would be contract cases, as the plaintiff in many of the cases is a buyer of the product. The law, however, leaves questions of whether a product is "good enough" to the law of contract as a rule, but treats the issue as a tort issue when personal injury or (some kinds of) property damage occur. Just why the law has gone in this direction is hard to say. Buyers of products are as much interested in whether the products are likely to hurt them as in whether they will last a long time or perform adequately, yet one of these concerns has become the subject of tort law, while the other is dealt with under the law of contract. Curiously, this question, which is perhaps the most basic problem of product-liability law, has been ignored by the courts, which seem to have thought it self-evident that they should assume responsibility for seeing to it that products are safe enough, while leaving all other aspects of product design to the market.

E. Defenses

1. State-of-the-Art

Beshada v. Johns-Manville Products Corp.

Supreme Court of New Jersey
447 A.2d 539 (N.J. 1982)

PASHMAN, J.

The sole question here is whether defendants in a product liability case based on strict liability for failure to warn may raise a "state of the art" defense. Defendants assert that the danger of which they failed to warn was undiscovered at the time the product was marketed and that it was undiscoverable given the state of scientific knowledge at that time. The case comes to us on appeal from the trial court's denial of plaintiffs' motion to strike the state-of-the-art defense....

....

These six consolidated cases are personal injury and wrongful death actions brought against manufacturers and distributors of asbestos products. Plaintiffs are workers, or survivors of deceased workers, who claim to have been exposed to asbestos for varying periods of time. They allege that as a result of that exposure they contracted asbestosis (a non-malignant scarring of the lungs), mesothelioma (a rare cancer of the lining of the chest, the pleura, or the lining of the abdomen, the peritoneum) and other asbestos-related illnesses.

These cases involve asbestos exposure dating back perhaps as far as the 1930's. The suits are first arising now because of the long latent period between exposure and the discernible symptoms of asbestosis and mesothelioma. [Citation.] Plaintiffs have raised a variety of legal theories to support their claims for damages. The important claim, for purposes of this appeal, is strict liability for failure to warn. Prior to the 1960's, defendants' products allegedly contained no warning of their hazardous nature....

There is substantial factual dispute about what defendants knew and when they knew it. A trial judge in the Eastern District of Texas,... has concluded that "[k]nowledge of the danger can be attributed to the industry as early as the mid-1930's...." [Citation.] Defendants respond, however, that it was not until the 1960's that the medical profession in the United States recognized that a potential health hazard arose from the use of insulation products containing asbestos. Before that time, according to defendants, the danger from asbestos was believed limited to workers in asbestos textile mills, who were exposed to much higher concentrations of asbestos dust than were the workers at other sites, such as shipyards....

We need not resolve the factual issues raised. For purposes of plaintiffs' motion to strike the defense, we assume the defendants' version of the facts. The issue is whether the medical community's presumed unawareness of the dangers of asbestos is a defense to plaintiffs' claims.

....

Our inquiry starts with the principles laid down in Freund v. Cellofilm Properties, Inc., [432 A.2d 925 (N.J. 1981)], Suter v. San Angelo Foundry & Machine Company, [406 A.2d 140 (N.J. 1979)], and Cepeda v. Cumberland Engineering Company, Inc., [386 A.2d 816 (N.J. 1978)]. In *Suter*, we summarized the principle of strict liability as follows:

> If at the time the seller distributes a product, it is not reasonably fit, suitable and safe for its intended or reasonably foreseeable purposes so that users or others who may be expected to come in contact with the product are injured as a result thereof, then the seller shall be responsible for the ensuing damages. [Citation.]

The determination of whether a product is "reasonably fit, suitable and safe" depends on a comparison of its risks and its utility (risk-utility equation).

> Central to this theory is the risk-utility equation for determining liability. The theory is that only safe products should be marketed—a safe product being one whose utility outweighs its inherent risk, provided that risk has been reduced to the greatest extent possible consistent with the product's continued utility. [*Freund*, 87 N.J. at 238, n.1, 432 A.2d 925]

In *Cepeda*, we explained that in the context of design defect liability, strict liability is identical to liability for negligence, with one important caveat: "The only qualification is as to the requisite of foreseeability by the manufacturer of the dangerous propensity of the chattel manifested at the trial—this being imputed to the manufacturer." [Citations.] In so holding, we adopted the explication of strict liability offered by Dean Wade:

> [We should]...assume that the defendant knew of the dangerous condition of the product and ask whether he was then negligent in putting it on the market or supplying it to someone else. In other words, the scienter is supplied as a matter of law, and there is no need for the plaintiff to prove its existence as a matter of fact. Once given this notice of the dangerous condition of the chattel, the question then becomes whether the defendant was negligent to people who might be harmed by that condition if they came into contact with it or were in the vicinity of it. Another way of saying this is to ask whether the magnitude of the risk created by the dangerous condition of the product was outweighed by the social utility attained by putting it out in this fashion. [Wade, *On the Nature of Strict Tort Liability for Products*, 44 Miss. L.J. 825, 834-35 (1973), quoted in *Cepeda*, 386 A.2d 816.]

Stated differently, negligence is conduct-oriented, asking whether defendant's actions were reasonable; strict liability is product-oriented, asking whether the product was reasonably safe for its foreseeable purposes. *Freund*, 87 N.J. at 238.

....

....When plaintiffs urge that a product is hazardous because it lacks a warning, they...[are] saying in effect that regardless of the overall cost-benefit calculation the product is unsafe because a warning could make it safer at virtually no added cost and without limiting its utility....

....

....Defendants argue that the question of whether the product can be made safer must be limited to consideration of the available technology at the time the product was distributed. Liability would be absolute, defendants argue, if it could be imposed on the basis of a subsequently discovered means to make the product safer since technology will always be developing new ways to make products safer. Such a rule, they assert, would make manufacturers liable whenever their products cause harm, whether or not they are reasonably fit for their foreseeable purposes.

....

....Essentially, state-of-the-art is a negligence defense. It seeks to explain why defendants are not culpable for failing to provide a warning. They assert, in effect, that because they could not have known the product was dangerous, they acted reasonably in marketing it without a warning. But in strict liability cases, culpability is irrelevant. The product was unsafe. That it was unsafe because of the state of technology does not change the fact that it was unsafe. Strict liability focuses on the product, not the fault of the manufacturer....

When the defendants argue that it is unreasonable to impose a duty on them to warn of the unknowable, they misconstrue both the purpose and effect of strict liability. By imposing strict liability, we are not requiring defendants to have done something that is impossible. In this sense, the phrase "duty to warn" is misleading. It implies negligence concepts with their attendant focus on the reasonableness of defendant's behavior. However, a major concern of strict liability—ignored by defendants—is the conclusion that if a product was in fact defective, the distributor of the product should compensate its victims for the misfortune that it inflicted on them.

....

The most important inquiry...is whether imposition of liability for failure to warn of dangers which were undiscoverable at the time of manufacture will advance the goals and policies sought to be achieved by our strict liability rules. We believe that it will.

Risk Spreading. One of the most important arguments generally advanced for imposing strict liability is that the manufacturers and distributors of defective products can best allocate the costs of the injuries resulting from those products. The premise is that the price of a product should reflect all of its costs, including the cost of injuries caused by the product. This can best be accomplished by imposing liability on the manufacturer and distributors. Those persons can insure against liability and incorporate the cost of the insurance in the price of the product. In this way, the costs of the product will be borne by those who profit from it: the manufacturers and distributors who profit from its sale and the buyers who profit from its use. "It should be a cost of doing business that in the course of doing that business an unreasonable risk was created." [Citations.]

Defendants argue that this policy is not forwarded by imposition of liability for unknowable hazards. Since such hazards by definition are not predicted, the price of the hazardous product will not be adjusted to reflect the costs of the injuries it will produce. Rather, defendants state, the cost "will be borne by the public at large and reflected in a general, across the board increase in premiums to compensate for unanticipated risks." There is some truth in this assertion, but it is not a bad result.

First, the same argument can be made as to hazards which are deemed scientifically knowable but of which the manufacturers are unaware. Yet it is well established under our tort law that strict liability is imposed even for defects which were unknown to the manufacturer. It is precisely the imputation of knowledge to the defendant that distinguishes strict liability from negligence. [Citation.] Defendants advance no argument as to why risk spreading works better for unknown risks than for unknowable risks.

Second, spreading the costs of injuries among all those who produce, distribute and purchase manufactured products is far preferable to imposing it on the innocent victims who suffer illnesses and disability from defective products. This basic normative premise is at the center of our strict liability rules. It is unchanged by the state of scientific knowledge at the time of manufacture.

Finally, contrary to defendants' assertion, this rule will not cause the price and production level of manufactured products to diverge from the so-called economically efficient level. Rather, the rule will force the price of any particular product to reflect the cost of insuring against the possibility that the product will turn out to be defective.

Accident Avoidance. In *Suter*, we stated:

> Strict liability in a sense is but an attempt to minimize the costs of accidents and to consider who should bear those costs. *See* the discussion in Calabresi & Hirschoff, *Toward a Test for Strict Liability in Torts,* 81 Yale L.J. 1055 (1972), in which the authors suggest that the strict liability issue is to decide which party is the "cheapest cost avoider" or who is in the best position to make the cost-benefit analysis between accident costs and accident avoidance costs and to act on that decision once it is made. *Id.* at 1060. Using this approach, it is obvious that the manufacturer rather than the factory employee is "in the better position both to judge whether avoidance costs would exceed foreseeable accident costs and to act on that judgment." [Suter v. San Angelo Foundry, 406 A.2d 140.]

Defendants urge that this argument has no force as to hazards which by definition were undiscoverable. Defendants have treated the level of technological knowledge at a given time as an independent variable not affected by defendants' conduct. But this view ignores the important role of industry in product safety research. The "state-of-the-art" at a given time is partly determined by how much industry invests in safety research. By imposing on manufacturers the costs of failure to discover hazards, we create an incentive for them to invest more actively in safety research.

. . . .

. . . [W]e conclude that plaintiffs' position . . . will achieve the various policies underlying strict liability. The burden of illness from dangerous products such as asbestos should be placed upon those who profit from its production and, more generally, upon society at large, which reaps the benefits of the various products our economy manufactures. That burden should not be imposed exclusively on the innocent victim. Although victims must in any case suffer the pain involved, they should be spared the burdensome financial consequences of unfit products. At the same time, we believe this position will serve the salutary goals of increasing product safety research and simplifying tort trials.

. . . .

The judgment of the trial court is reversed; the plaintiff's motion to strike the state-of-the-art defense is granted.

Notes

1. *"Risk Spreading."* A few words of elaboration on the *Beshada* court's discussion of "risk spreading" may be in order. If a manufacturer knows before producing a product that sales of the product will generate $5,000,000 in liability, that potential liability will be treated as a "cost" of the product, and the price will be set so as to recover the $5,000,000. If the product cannot be sold at a price that will cover all of its costs, the manufacturer will not produce it. Typically, increasing the price to cover the cost of liability will cause less of the product to be sold than if there were no possible liability. In a sense, then, liabilities predicted when a product is made will be paid, in part, by all of those who buy the product. (In another sense, those who do not buy the product because the price is so high may for that reason bear a burden as well.)

If, as the defendants claimed was the case in *Beshada*, liability is not foreseen when a product is made and sold, the liability, when it is imposed, cannot be passed on to customers in any sense. Suppose, for instance, that Acme Widget Works made and sold Class A widgets years ago, setting prices on the assumption that they could do no harm. It now produces only Class B Widgets, and it has just learned that it will be liable for $5,000,000 in damages caused by Class A widgets. Presumably, the price Acme charges for its Class B widgets is the price that earns it the greatest possible profit on those sales. Its having become liable for $5,000,000 in damages because of Class A widgets does not change the price it will charge for Class B widgets, as changing that price can only reduce its profits (or increase its losses)—recall that the price was set so as to maximize profits on the sale of Class B widgets. To put the point in another way, the manufacturer's liability for harm done by Class A widgets does not increase demand for Class B widgets, and therefore does not enable the manufacturer to sell Class B widgets for a higher price than if it had not been held liable. Therefore, the entire burden of the $5,000,000 liability falls upon Acme (that is, upon its shareholders, creditors, and employees). This is why an unanticipated liability cannot be "passed on" to customers in any sense, as the *Beshada* court recognizes. Note that, in this analysis, "Class A widgets" and "Class B widgets" can be identical products: If a manufacturer learns today that it will be liable for injuries caused by products that it has sold for years, and which it continues to sell, it will price current sales to cover liabilities attributable to the products now being sold, but not liabilities attributable to products sold last year. In other words, knowledge that the manufacturer will be liable for harm done by a product it sold last year does not give the manufacturer the ability to make more money on the products it sells this year.

2. *Beshada Today.* The Supreme Court of New Jersey has refused to apply the *Beshada* rule to cases involving drugs. Feldman v. Lederle Labs., 479 A.2d 374 (N.J. 1984), "restricted" the *Beshada* rule "to the circumstances giving rise to its holding" (apparently, that is, to asbestos cases). What sense can it make to say that state-of-the-art is a defense in cases involving any product other than asbestos? Some plaintiffs have claimed that the asbestos manufacturers really knew all along of the dangers of asbestos, and covered them up. *See also* N.J. Stat. Ann. §2A:58C-1(a) (Westlaw 2003), p. 760, *infra*.

3. *Split of Authority.* Other courts are divided on the admissibility of state-of-the-art evidence. Four states take the position that, at least in some circumstances, a manufacturer is charged with a duty to warn of risks without regard to whether the manufacturer knew or reasonably should have known of the risks. *See* In re Haw. Fed. Asbestos Cases, 960 F.2d 806 (9th Cir. 1992) (applying Hawaii law); Jackson v. Nestle-Beich, Inc., 589 N.E.2d 547 (Ill. 1992); Dambacher v. Mallis, 485 A.2d 408 (Pa. Super. Ct. 1984); Ayers v. Johnson & Johnson Baby Prods. Co., 818 P.2d 1337 (Wash. 1991).

In *Jackson*, plaintiff allegedly broke a tooth on a hard pecan shell while biting into a chocolate-covered pecan-caramel candy. Defendant Nestle argued that manufacturers of certain food products should be exempted from strict liability because of the difficulty of eliminating natural matter, such as nut shells. The Court rejected that contention because it was "essentially an argument for recognizing a state of the art defense in food product cases" and "in Illinois the state of the art has never been a defense to strict products liability." According to the court, "[T]he consumer's reasonable expectation as to the contents of food products, as the gauge of strict liability, adequately balances consumers' interest in defect-free products and such manufacturers' interest in reasonable costs of doing business."

A majority of states permit a state-of-the-art defense. *See, e.g.*, Vassallo v. Baxter Healthcare Corp., 696 N.E.2d 909, 922-23 (Mass. 1998) (reversing prior position); Fibreboard Corp. v. Fenton, 845 P.2d 1168 (Colo. 1993) (admissible to determine whether a product (asbestos) was defective and unreasonably dangerous because of a failure to warn). The *Vassallo* court wrote:

> The thin judicial support for a hindsight approach to the duty to warn is easily explained. The goal of the law is to induce conduct that is capable of being performed. This goal is not advanced by imposing liability for failure to warn of risks that were not capable of being known.

The Restatement endorses a state-of-the-art defense:

> Most courts agree that, for the liability system to be fair and efficient, the balancing of risks and benefits in judging product design and marketing must be done in light of the knowledge of risks and risk-avoidance techniques reasonably attainable at the time of distribution. To hold a manufacturer liable for a risk that was not foreseeable when the product was marketed might foster increased manufacturer investment in safety. But such investment by definition would be a matter of guesswork. Furthermore, manufacturers may persuasively ask to be judged by a normative behavior standard to which it is reasonably possible for manufacturers to conform.

Restatement, Third, of Torts: Products Liability §2, comment a. The Restatement goes on to note that state of the art, in the sense that the defendant's product is the best available at the time of distribution, is not a defense "[if an improved] design could have been practically adopted at the time of sale and if the omission of such a design rendered the product not reasonably safe, the plaintiff establishes [a] defect....; *id.*, §2, comment d. In short, a manufacturer may have an obligation to improve upon even the best existing technology, but may rely on existing scientific knowledge.

In some states, the state-of-the art-defense is embodied in a statute. For example:

FLA. STAT. ANN. §§ 768.1257
(Westlaw 2004)

> In an action based upon defective design, brought against the manufacturer of a product, the finder of fact shall consider the state of the art of scientific and technical knowledge and other circumstances that existed at the time of manufacture, not at the time of loss or injury.

4. *Post-Sale Knowledge.* A manufacturer's post-sale knowledge of hazards arising from modification of its product may support an action for failure to warn, even though the manufacturer could not be held liable for defective design. *See* Liriano v. Hobart Co.,

700 N.E.2d 303 (N.Y. 1998) ("a duty will generally arise where a defect or danger is revealed by user operation and brought to the attention of the manufacturer").

2. Government Contractors

Under some circumstances, parties who contract with the federal government are immune from products-liability claims. In Boyle v. United Technologies Corp., 487 U.S. 500 (1988), the father of a man who drowned in a Marine helicopter crash sued the craft's manufacturer, alleging that the helicopter had been defectively designed because the escape hatch opened outward, instead of inward, and because the escape hatch handle was obstructed by other equipment. The court found that holding government contractors liable for design defects in military equipment under state products-liability law would conflict with federal policy. Therefore, it concluded, state tort principles are displaced if: (1) the government provides precise specifications; (2) the equipment conforms to those specifications; and (3) the supplier warns the government about dangers of which it knows but of which the government is ignorant. The immunity afforded to government contractors is much more extensive than the legal protection given to other manufacturers whose products comply with government-agency standards. A defendant within the latter group enjoys a rebuttable presumption that its product is not defective; a defendant with a product in the former group is wholly immune from liability, if the case falls within the terms of the government-contractor defense.

Notes

1. Recall the facts of Winterbottom v. Wright, 10 M. & W. 109, 152 Eng. Rep. 402 (Exchequer 1842), discussed *supra* at p. 699. The court did not base its opinion in that case on the fact that the defendant's contract was with the government. If it had, would the opinion have become the object of the scorn which it almost universally receives today?

2. *Biomaterials Suppliers.* The Biomaterials Access Assurance Act of 1998 provides those who supply raw materials to medical device manufacturers with relief from liability should the medical device manufacturer be sued in a product liability action, provided the supplier complied with the terms of its contract with the manufacturer. 21 U.S.C.A. §1601.

3. "Misuse" and Other Plaintiff Misconduct

Strictly speaking, there is no such thing as a "misuse" *defense* in products-liability law, but misuse relates to several important issues. Sometimes, showing that the plaintiff "misused" the product amounts to saying that the product was not defective—few products are expected to be completely safe no matter what is done with them—or that the supposed danger was not undisclosed. Occasionally, if the misuse is bizarre enough, a court may rule that the alleged defect was not the "proximate cause" of the plaintiff's injuries. In addition, the best practical way for a seller to defend a products-liability claim may be to show that the accident was in fact the fault of the person who used the product.

Use Not Objectively Foreseeable. A product is not defective if it is reasonably safe for the kind of use that is objectively foreseeable.

As explained by one court:

> Essentially, product misuse contemplates two kinds of conduct. One is the use of a product for an improper purpose. "If, for instance, a plaintiff undertakes to use his power saw as a nail clipper and thereby snips his digits, he will not be heard to complain...."....When a plaintiff is injured while using the product for a purpose that is not objectively foreseeable, the injury does not establish that the product is defective.
>
> The other kind of misuse concerns the manner in which the plaintiff used the product. When, for example, the operator of a high-lift forklift is injured while using the forklift on steep, instead of level, terrain, the emphasis should be on the manner, not the purpose, of the misuse. [Citation.] As comment h of Restatement (Second) of Torts §402A states: "A product is not in a defective condition when it is safe for normal handling or consumption."
>
> ....
>
> ...[W]hen misuse is an issue in a design-defect case, the jury should first determine whether the plaintiff used the product for an objectively foreseeable purpose. If the jury finds that the plaintiff's purpose was not foreseeable, the defendant did not breach any duty owed to the plaintiff. If, however, the jury finds that the plaintiff's purpose was foreseeable, it must then decide whether the product was defective.

Jurado v. Western Gear Works, 619 A.2d 1312 (N.J. 1993).

See Kampen v. American Isuzu Motors, Inc., 157 F.3d 306 (5th Cir. 1998) (plaintiff's use of a jack as the sole support for a car, in contravention of two express warnings, was not a reasonably anticipated use).

Known and Obvious Dangers. Misuse may also relieve the defendant of any duty to protect the plaintiff from harm, as where the plaintiff confronts a danger which is known or obvious. In products liability, as in other areas of the law, there is typically no duty to warn of a known or obvious danger. *See* Coleman v. Cintas Sales Corp., 100 S.W.3d 384 (Tex. App. 2002) (no duty to warn a groundskeeper that a uniform could catch fire because the risk was common knowledge); Bren-Tex Tractor Co, Inc. v. Massey-Ferguson, Inc., 97 S.W.3d 155 (Tex. App. 2002) (no duty to warn buyer of the risk of injury from a rollover in a used tractor that was not equipped with rollover protection system because an average user would recognize the risk); Phillips v. A-Best Prod. Co., 665 A.2d 1167 (Pa. 1995) (no liability for failure to warn a worker who knew of the dangers of silica sand); Caterpillar, Inc. v. Shears, 911 S.W.2d 379 (Tex. 1995) (the dangers of operating a loader without its removable "roll over protective structure" were obvious); Josue v. Isuzu Motors Am., Inc., 958 P.2d 535 (Haw. 1998) (no duty to warn of the dangers of riding unrestrained in an open cargo bed of a pickup truck).

However, even on similar facts, courts may differ as to just what dangers are "obvious." *Compare* Lederman v. Pacific Indus., Inc., 119 F.3d 551 (7th Cir. 1997) (there was no duty to warn because a "reasonable adult...knowing that the pool was shallow in parts, would have recognized the dangers of diving into such a pool at around midnight"); *and* Griebler v. Doughboy Recreational, Inc., 466 N.W.2d 897 (Wis. 1991) (plaintiff confronted an open and obvious danger as a matter of law when he dove headfirst into water of unknown depth); *with* Fleck v. KDI Sylvan Pools, Inc., 981 F.2d 107 (3d Cir. 1992) (the danger of jumping into a pool of unknown depth is not open and obvious).

In Liriano v. Hobart, 170 F.3d 264 (2d Cir. 1999), the court held that even if a product's dangers seem obvious, a manufacturer may still need to provide additional warnings. Judge Guido Calabresi wrote for the court:

> [A] warning can do more than exhort its audience to be careful. It can also affect what activities the people warned choose to engage in. [Citation.] And where the function of a warning is to assist the reader in making choices, the value of the warning can lie as much in making known the existence of alternatives as in communicating the fact that a particular choice is dangerous. It follows that the duty to warn is not necessarily obviated merely because a danger is clear.

> ... [A] warning can convey at least two types of messages. One states that a particular place, object, or activity is dangerous. Another explains that people need not risk the danger posed by such a place, object, or activity in order to achieve the purpose for which they might have taken that risk. Thus, a highway sign that says "Danger-Steep Grade" says less than a sign that says "Steep Grade Ahead—Follow Suggested Detour to Avoid Dangerous Areas."

> If the hills or mountains responsible for the steep grade are plainly visible, the first sign merely states what a reasonable person would know without having to be warned. The second sign tells drivers what they might not have otherwise known: that there is another road that is flatter and less hazardous.... Accordingly, a certain level of obviousness as to the grade of a road might, in principle, eliminate the reason for posting a sign of the first variety. But no matter how patently steep the road, the second kind of sign might still have a beneficial effect....

> .... Even if most ordinary users may—as a matter of law—know of the risk of using a guardless meat grinder, it does not follow that a sufficient number of them will—as a matter of law—also know that protective guards are available, that using them is a realistic possibility, and that they may ask that such guards be used. It is precisely these last pieces of information that a reasonable manufacturer may have a duty to convey even if the danger of using a grinder were itself deemed obvious.

Some courts hold that the open-and-obvious-danger rule is not controlling in cases where it is alleged that a product has a design defect. In Wright v. Brooke Group Ltd., 652 N.W.2d 159 (Iowa. 2002), the court, embracing the third Restatement, held that consumer expectations do not constitute an independent standard for judging the defectiveness of product designs and that therefore the common knowledge of consumers of the health risk associated with smoking did not necessarily preclude liability in a suit filed against various cigarette manufacturers.

Misuse under Comparative Principles. Whether the plaintiff's negligence should reduce recovery under the law of comparative negligence is a much-litigated question which has received a variety of answers. Some of the decisions turn on the language of the relevant comparative-negligence statute; if the statute speaks of recovery in actions "for negligence" or refers to the defendant's "fault" or "wrongful conduct," courts may be inclined to hold the statute inapplicable to products-liability cases. In California, where comparative negligence was created by judicial decision, rather than statute, comparative negligence applies in products-liability cases; Daly v. General Motors Corp., 575 P.2d 1162 (Cal. 1978). The facts of *Daly* provide a nice example of why strict liability for defective products is quite unpopular with manufacturers. The plaintiff's decedent, who was not wearing a seatbelt, hit a highway divider while driving drunk, at a high speed; the claim was that the car was defective because its door lock had an exposed push button, which might have caused the lock to come open during the collision (if it had in fact been locked, which was doubtful).

In many jurisdictions, comparative negligence has now been replaced by comparative fault (sometimes called comparative causation or comparative responsibility). Comparative fault rules generally permit a defendant in a strict liability action (including strict products liability) to introduce evidence of the plaintiff's misconduct (often specifically including "product misuse") for the purpose of reducing or precluding recovery by the plaintiff. *See* Chapter 16.

Notes

1. *Fast Food*. In Pelman v. McDonald's Corp., 237 F. Supp. 2d 512 (S.D.N.Y. 2003), parents brought an action against fast-food corporations and restaurants in connection with their children's over-consumption of fast-food. The court wrote:

> [I]n order to state a claim, the Complaint must allege either that the attributes of McDonalds products are so extraordinarily unhealthy that they are outside the reasonable contemplation of the consuming public or that the products are so extraordinarily unhealthy as to be dangerous in their intended use. The Complaint—which merely alleges that the foods contain high levels of cholesterol, fat, salt and sugar, and that the foods are therefore unhealthy—fails to reach this bar. It is well-known that fast food in general, and McDonalds' products in particular, contain high levels of cholesterol, fat, salt, and sugar, and that such attributes are bad for one.

> ....If a person knows or should know that eating copious orders of super-sized McDonalds' products is unhealthy and may result in weight gain..., it is not the place of the law to protect them from their own excesses. Nobody is forced to eat at McDonalds.... [N]obody is forced to supersize their meal or choose less healthy options on the menu.

> As long as a consumer exercises free choice with appropriate knowledge, liability for negligence will not attach to a manufacturer. It is only when that free choice becomes but a chimera—for instance, by the masking of information necessary to make the choice, such as the knowledge that eating McDonalds with a certain frequency would irrefragably cause harm—that manufacturers should be held accountable. Plaintiffs have failed to allege in the Complaint that their decisions to eat at McDonalds several times a week were anything but a choice freely made and which now may not be pinned on McDonalds.

2. *Modification by the User*. A recurring problem involves a product which is reasonably safe as sold, but which the buyer modifies, as by removing a safety feature. For example, the defendant in Robinson v. Reed-Prentice Division of Package Machinery Co., 403 N.E.2d 440 (N.Y. 1980), sold a plastic molding machine to Plastic Jewel Parts Co. Plastic Jewel cut a hole in the machine's safety gate, allowing the machine's operator to reach into the mold area to remove the finished product. The operator, whose hand was seriously injured when he reached into the mold area, sued the manufacturer. Holding that "[t]he manufacturer's duty...does not extend to designing a product that is impossible to abuse or one whose safety features may not be circumvented," the Court of Appeals denied recovery. Judge Jacob D. Fuchsberg's dissent pointed out that the manufac-

turer knew that the buyer was likely to modify the safety gate and that the plaintiff's experts had testified that the machine could easily have been designed to avoid the dangers that would result from foreseeable modification of the model that was sold.

The Restatement takes the position that cases like *Robinson* should be dealt with by asking whether the product had a defect that proximately caused the plaintiff's injury, rather than by invoking an absolute rule that the manufacturer has no duty to anticipate modifications; Restatement, Third, of Torts: Products Liability, §2, *comment p*; §15, *comment b*. Under that approach, a manufacturer who can anticipate a dangerous modification and who can easily make that modification unnecessary or impossible would be liable. *But see* Jones v. Ryobi, Ltd., 37 F.3d 423 (8th Cir. 1994) (holding that modification by injured operator's employer, not the defect existing when the press was sold, was the sole cause of the operator's injury).

4. Pre-emption by Federal Law

Article VI of the Constitution provides that the laws of the United States "shall be the supreme Law of the Land;...any Thing in the Constitution or Laws of any state to the Contrary notwithstanding." Art. VI, cl. 2. Thus, since our decision in M'Culloch v. Maryland, 17 U.S. (4 Wheat.) 316, 427, 4 L.Ed. 579 (1819), it has been settled that state law that conflicts with federal law is "without effect." Consideration of issues arising under the Supremacy Clause "start[s] with the assumption that the historic police powers of the States [are] not to be superseded by...Federal Act unless that [is] the clear and manifest purpose of Congress." Accordingly, "'[t]he purpose of Congress is the ultimate touchstone'" of pre-emption analysis.

Congress' intent may be "explicitly stated in the statute's language or implicitly contained in its structure and purpose." In the absence of an express congressional command, state law is pre-empted if that law actually conflicts with federal law, or if federal law so thoroughly occupies a legislative field "'as to make reasonable the inference that Congress left no room for the States to supplement it.'"

Cipollone v. Liggett Group, Inc., 505 U.S. 504, 516 (1992) (internal citations omitted).

Geier v. American Honda Motor Co.

Supreme Court of the United States
529 U.S. 861 (2000)

Justice BREYER delivered the opinion of the Court.

This case focuses on the 1984 version of a Federal Motor Vehicle Safety Standard promulgated by the Department of Transportation under the authority of the National Traffic and Motor Vehicle Safety Act of 1966, [citation]. The standard, FMVSS 208, required auto manufacturers to equip some but not all of their 1987 vehicles with passive restraints. We ask whether the Act pre-empts a state common-law tort action in which the plaintiff claims that the defendant auto manufacturer, who was in compliance with the standard, should nonetheless have equipped a 1987 automobile with airbags. We conclude that the Act, taken together with FMVSS 208, pre-empts the lawsuit.

....

In 1992, petitioner Alexis Geier, driving a 1987 Honda Accord, collided with a tree and was seriously injured. The car was equipped with manual shoulder and lap belts which Geier had buckled up at the time. The car was not equipped with airbags or other passive restraint devices.

Geier and her parents, also petitioners, sued the car's manufacturer, American Honda Motor Company, Inc., and its affiliates (hereinafter American Honda), under District of Columbia tort law. They claimed... that American Honda had designed its car negligently and defectively because it lacked a driver's side airbag. App. 3. The District Court... concluded that petitioners' lawsuit... was expressly pre-empted....

The Court of Appeals agreed with the District Court's conclusion but on somewhat different reasoning....

.... We now hold that this kind of "no airbag" lawsuit conflicts with the objectives of FMVSS 208, a standard authorized by the Act, and is therefore pre-empted by the Act.

In reaching our conclusion, we consider three subsidiary questions. First, does the Act's express pre-emption provision pre-empt this lawsuit? We think not. Second, do ordinary pre-emption principles nonetheless apply? We hold that they do. Third, does this lawsuit actually conflict with FMVSS 208, hence with the Act itself? We hold that it does.

....

We first ask whether the Safety Act's express pre-emption provision pre-empts this tort action. The provision reads as follows:

> "Whenever a Federal motor vehicle safety standard established under this subchapter is in effect, no State... shall have any authority either to establish, or to continue in effect, with respect to any motor vehicle or item of motor vehicle equipment[,] any safety standard applicable to the same aspect of performance of such vehicle or item of equipment which is not identical to the Federal standard." [Citation.]

American Honda points out that a majority of this Court has said that a somewhat similar statutory provision in a different federal statute—a provision that uses the word "requirements"—may well expressly pre-empt similar tort actions. [Citation.] Petitioners reply that this statute speaks of pre-empting a state-law "safety *standard*," not a "requirement," and that a tort action does not involve a safety *standard*. Hence, they conclude, the express pre-emption provision does not apply.

We need not determine the precise significance of the use of the word "standard," rather than "requirement," however, for the Act contains another provision, which resolves the disagreement. That provision, a "saving" clause, says that "[c]ompliance with" a federal safety standard "does not exempt any person from any liability under common law." [Citation.] The saving clause assumes that there are some significant number of common-law liability cases to save. And a reading of the express pre-emption provision that excludes common-law tort actions gives actual meaning to the saving clause's literal language, while leaving adequate room for state tort law to operate—for example, where federal law creates only a floor, i.e., a minimum safety standard. *See, e.g.*, Brief for United States as *Amicus Curiae* 21 (explaining that common-law claim that a vehicle is defectively designed because it lacks antilock brakes would not be pre-empted by... a safety standard establishing minimum requirements for brake performance).... The language of the pre-emption provision permits a narrow reading that excludes common-law actions. Given the presence of the saving clause, we conclude that the pre-emption clause must be so read.

....

We have just said that the saving clause *at least* removes tort actions from the scope of the express pre-emption clause. Does it do more? In particular, does it foreclose or limit the operation of ordinary pre-emption principles insofar as those principles instruct us to read statutes as pre-empting state laws (including common-law rules) that "actually conflict" with the statute or federal standards promulgated thereunder? ....

....

Nothing in the language of the saving clause suggests an intent to save state-law tort actions that conflict with federal regulations. The words "[c]ompliance" and "does not exempt," [citation], sound as if they simply bar a special kind of defense, namely, a defense that compliance with a federal standard automatically exempts a defendant from state law, whether the Federal Government meant that standard to be an absolute requirement or only a minimum one. *See* Restatement (Third) of Torts: Products Liability § 4(b), Comment *e* (1997) (distinguishing between state-law compliance defense and a federal claim of pre-emption). It is difficult to understand why Congress would have insisted on a compliance-with-federal-regulation precondition to the provision's applicability had it wished the Act to "save" all state-law tort actions, regardless of their potential threat to the objectives of federal safety standards promulgated under that Act. Nor does our interpretation conflict with the purpose of the saving provision, say, by rendering it ineffectual.... [T]he saving provision still makes clear that the express pre-emption provision does not of its own force pre-empt common-law tort actions. And it thereby preserves those actions that seek to establish greater safety than the minimum safety achieved by a federal regulation intended to provide a floor. [Citation.]

Moreover, this Court has repeatedly "decline[d] to give broad effect to saving clauses where doing so would upset the careful regulatory scheme established by federal law." [Citations.] We find this concern applicable in the present case. And we conclude that the saving clause foresees—it does not foreclose—the possibility that a federal safety standard will pre-empt a state common-law tort action with which it conflicts....

Neither do we believe that the pre-emption provision, the saving provision, or both together, create some kind of "special burden" beyond that inherent in ordinary pre-emption principles—which "special burden" would specially disfavor pre-emption here. [Citation.] The two provisions, read together, reflect a neutral policy, not a specially favorable or unfavorable policy, toward the application of ordinary conflict pre-emption principles. On the one hand, the pre-emption provision itself reflects a desire to subject the industry to a single, uniform set of federal safety standards. Its pre-emption of *all* state standards, even those that might stand in harmony with federal law, suggests an intent to avoid the conflict, uncertainty, cost, and occasional risk to safety itself that too many different safety-standard cooks might otherwise create. [Citations.] This policy by itself favors pre-emption of state tort suits, for the rules of law that judges and juries create or apply in such suits may themselves similarly create uncertainty and even conflict, say, when different juries in different States reach different decisions on similar facts.

On the other hand, the saving clause reflects a congressional determination that occasional nonuniformity is a small price to pay for a system in which juries not only create, but also enforce, safety standards, while simultaneously providing necessary compensation to victims. That policy by itself disfavors pre-emption, at least some of the time. But we can find nothing in any natural reading of the two provisions that would favor one set of policies over the other where a jury-imposed safety standard actually conflicts with a federal safety standard.

Why, in any event, would Congress not have wanted ordinary pre-emption princi-ples to apply where an actual conflict with a federal objective is at stake? Some such principle is needed. In its absence, state law could impose legal duties that would con-flict directly with federal regulatory mandates.... Insofar as petitioners' argument would permit common-law actions that "actually conflict" with federal regulations, it would take from those who would enforce a federal law the very ability to achieve the law's congressionally mandated objectives that the Constitution, through the operation of or-dinary pre-emption principles, seeks to protect....

....

The basic question, then, is whether a common-law "no airbag" action like the one before us actually conflicts with FMVSS 208. We hold that it does.

In petitioners' and the dissent's view, FMVSS 208 sets a minimum airbag standard. As far as FMVSS 208 is concerned, the more airbags, and the sooner, the better. But that was not the Secretary's view. The Department of Transportation's (DOT's) comments, which accompanied the promulgation of FMVSS 208, make clear that the standard de-liberately provided the manufacturer with a range of choices among different passive re-straint devices. Those choices would bring about a mix of different devices introduced gradually over time; and FMVSS 208 would thereby lower costs, overcome technical safety problems, encourage technological development, and win widespread consumer acceptance—all of which would promote FMVSS 208's safety objectives. [Citation.]

....

[The court then recounted the regulatory history relating to seat belts and passive restraints.]

Read in light of this history, DOT's own contemporaneous explanation of FMVSS 208 makes clear that the 1984 version of FMVSS 208 reflected the following significant considerations. First, buckled up seatbelts are a vital ingredient of automobile safety. [Citations.] Second, despite the enormous and unnecessary risks that a passenger runs by not buckling up manual lap and shoulder belts, more than 80% of front seat passen-gers would leave their manual seatbelts unbuckled. [Citation.] Third, airbags could make up for the dangers caused by unbuckled manual belts, but they could not make up for them entirely. [Citations.]

Fourth, passive restraint systems had their own disadvantages, for example, the dan-gers associated with, intrusiveness of, and corresponding public dislike for, nondetach-able automatic belts. [Citations.] Fifth, airbags brought with them their own special risks to safety, such as the risk of danger to out-of-position occupants (usually children) in small cars. [Citations.]

Sixth, airbags were expected to be significantly more expensive than other passive re-straint devices, raising the average cost of a vehicle price $320 for full frontal airbags over the cost of a car with manual lap and shoulder seatbelts (and potentially much more if production volumes were low).... Seventh, the public, for reasons of cost, fear, or physical intrusiveness, might resist installation or use of any of the then-available passive restraint devices....

FMVSS 208 reflected these considerations in several ways. Most importantly, that standard deliberately sought variety—a mix of several different passive restraint sys-tems....[A] mix of devices would help develop data on comparative effectiveness, would allow the industry time to overcome the safety problems and the high produc-tion costs associated with airbags, and would facilitate the development of alternative, cheaper, and safer passive restraint systems. [Citation.] And it would thereby build public confidence....

The 1984 FMVSS 208 standard also deliberately sought a *gradual* phase-in of passive restraints. [Citation.] It required the manufacturers to equip only 10% of their car fleet manufactured after September 1, 1986, with passive restraints. [Citation.] It then increased the percentage in three annual stages, up to 100% of the new car fleet for cars manufactured after September 1, 1989....

   ....

Finally, FMVSS 208's passive restraint requirement was conditional. DOT believed that ordinary manual lap and shoulder belts would produce about the same amount of safety as passive restraints, and at significantly lower costs—*if only auto occupants would buckle up.* [Citation.] Thus, FMVSS 208 provided for rescission of its passive restraint requirement if, by September 1, 1989, two-thirds of the States had laws in place that, like those of many other nations, required auto occupants to buckle up (and which met other requirements specified in the standard)....In the end, two-thirds of the States did not enact mandatory buckle-up laws, and the passive restraint requirement remained in effect.

In sum, as DOT now tells us through the Solicitor General, the 1984 version of FMVSS 208 "embodies the Secretary's policy judgment that safety would best be promoted if manufacturers installed *alternative* protection systems in their fleets rather than one particular system in every car."....

In effect, petitioners' tort action depends upon its claim that manufacturers had a duty to install an airbag when they manufactured the 1987 Honda Accord. Such a state law—*i.e.*, a rule of state tort law imposing such a duty—by its terms would have required manufacturers of all similar cars to install airbags rather than other passive restraint systems, such as automatic belts or passive interiors. It thereby would have presented an obstacle to the variety and mix of devices that the federal regulation sought....Because the rule of law for which petitioners contend would have stood "as an obstacle to the accomplishment and execution of" the important means-related federal objectives that we have just discussed, it is pre-empted. [Citations.]

   ....

The dissent would require a formal agency statement of pre-emptive intent as a prerequisite to concluding that a conflict exists. It relies on cases, or portions thereof, that did not involve conflict pre-emption. [Citations.] And conflict pre-emption is different in that it turns on the identification of "actual conflict," and not on an express statement of pre-emptive intent. [Citations.] While "[p]re-emption fundamentally is a question of congressional intent," [citation], this Court traditionally distinguishes between "express" and "implied" pre-emptive intent, and treats "conflict" pre-emption as an instance of the latter. [Citations.] And though the Court has looked for a specific statement of pre-emptive intent where it is claimed that the mere "volume and complexity" of agency regulations demonstrate an implicit intent to displace *all* state law in a particular area, [citation]—so-called "field pre-emption"— the Court has never before required a specific, formal agency statement identifying conflict in order to conclude that such a conflict in fact exists. Indeed, one can assume that Congress or an agency ordinarily would not intend to permit a significant conflict. While we certainly accept the dissent's basic position that a court should not find pre-emption too readily in the absence of clear evidence of a conflict, [citation], for the reasons set out above we find such evidence here. To insist on a specific expression of agency intent to pre-empt, made after notice-and-comment rulemaking, would be in certain cases to tolerate conflicts that an agency, and therefore Congress, is most unlikely to have intended....

....

The judgment of the Court of Appeals is affirmed.

[The dissenting opinion of Justice STEVENS, in which Justices SOUTER, THOMAS, and GINSBURG joined, is omitted.]

Notes

1. Pre-emption is a major issue in many products-liability cases, and new decisions, by the Supreme Court and lower courts, relating to an ever-increasing number of federal statutes and regulations are continually being reported. For example:

In Sprietsma v. Mercury Marine, 537 U.S. 51 (2002), the Supreme Court held that the Federal Boat Safety Act did not implicitly preempt common-law tort claims arising out of failure to install propeller guards on motorboat engines because the Act did not require the Coast Guard to promulgate comprehensive regulations covering every aspect of recreational boat safety and design or to certify acceptability of every boat subject to its jurisdiction. The Act did not convey a clear and manifest intent to completely occupy the field of safety regulation relating to recreational boats and the Act's goal of fostering uniformity in manufacturing regulations did not justify displacement of state common law remedies.

In Norfolk Southern Ry. Co. v. Shanklin, 529 U.S. 344 (2000), the Supreme Court held that regulations addressing the adequacy of warning devices installed under the Federal Railway-Highway Crossings Program were applicable to all warning devices actually installed with federal funds, and that a widow's action was preempted because the state transportation department had used federal funds for signs installed pursuant to Crossings Program.

2. *Tobacco Litigation: Pre-emption and Economic Analysis.* In Cipollone v. Liggett Group, Inc., 505 U.S. 504 (1992), the Supreme Court held that claims against a cigarette manufacturer were pre-empted by the Public Health Cigarette Smoking Act of 1969 to the extent that the claims were based on the theory that the warnings on cigarette packages should have been stronger. As the act specified the wording that had to be used on the packages, this holding was almost inevitable. Claims based on "express warranties" (which the plaintiff claimed could be found in the defendant's advertisements) were not pre-empted, and neither were claims based on fraudulent misrepresentation, both in advertising and in statements to government agencies. Following the Supreme Court's decision, the plaintiff decided to drop the suit rather than go through another trial.

Prior to *Cipollone*, the history of tobacco-related tort litigation stretched nearly four decades, during which time the tobacco industry paid not a single adverse monetary award. The major obstacle in many tobacco cases is the argument that recovery is barred, in whole or in part, by contributory negligence or assumption of the risk. *See* Note, *Plaintiff's Conduct as a Defense to Claims Against Cigarette Manufacturers*, 99 Harv. L. Rev. 809 (1986).

In recent years, many states have sued the tobacco companies for recovery of the costs of providing medical care under Medicaid for smoking-related illnesses. In an attempt to avoid the argument that smokers have brought their illnesses on themselves by using a product which everyone knows can cause harm, the states have claimed that they are victims of various kinds of bad conduct by the tobacco companies and that they should be allowed to recover even though the defendants would not be liable to the smokers. As a matter of legal doctrine, these cases are highly innovative. For one thing, the claim that states are "injured" because they have had to provide medical care to smokers is questionable. It is clear beyond any doubt that smokers, on the average, incur lower lifetime medical costs than non-smokers, because many smokers die relatively young, before reaching the age at which extremely expensive illnesses such as Altzheimer's disease tend to strike. If everyone were to stop smoking today, total spending on medical care would increase significantly in a few years. (In addition, the Social Security crisis would be greatly worsened if all retirees lived as long as non-smokers typically do.) Furthermore, although the complaints in some of the cases allege that cigarettes are "defective," it is hard to take those claims seriously: the heart of the states' cases is simply the argument that the tobacco companies' products caused illnesses which the Medicaid programs had to treat. If this is a valid theory, those who sell alcohol are liable for hundreds of billions of dollars for treating the victims of drunken driving, beef producers and bakeries are liable for the costs of treating heart-attack victims, automobile manufacturers are liable for the costs of treating accident victims, and so on. Acceptance of these theories would bring manufacturing (and perhaps farming as well) to a standstill. Nevertheless, some of the cases have been settled for very large sums. Part of the defendants' concern may be attributable to the great unpopularity of tobacco in today's society. Furthermore, the litigation by the states is seen as part of a process by which Congress may eventually provide some sort of "settlement," which will provide the government with substantial revenues while ensuring the tobacco industry of its continued survival. The tobacco cases have much more to do with politics than with the law of torts. At least one of the tobacco cases was "settled" for an amount greater than the plaintiff sought in its complaint: something that does not happen in ordinary tort litigation between persons who are truly adversaries.

The Mississippi Product Liability Act precludes all tobacco cases based on products liability. *See* Lane v. R.J. Reynolds Tobacco Co., 853 So. 2d 1144 (Miss. 2003).

3. The question whether federal regulation pre-empts state tort law is a federal question. Even if, as a matter of federal law, federal safety regulations do not pre-empt state law, it is open to a state court to decide that, in light of the extensive federal regulation of a particular kind of product, the state tort law should not lightly allow factfinders to decide that a product meeting the federal standards is defective. Ordinarily, the party that complies with federal standards applicable to the manufacturing or marketing of a product enjoys a rebuttable presumption that the product is not unreasonably dangerous. *See* Wilson v. Piper Aircraft, Inc., 577 P.2d 1322 (Or. 1978), p. 724, *supra*.

F. Policy Issues

1. Liability and Safety

A fair number of judicial opinions in products cases say that expansive liability will make the world safer because manufacturers will respond by making safer products.

This idea cannot be dismissed out of hand; it is certainly true that one consequence of our society's love of litigation is a pervasive attention to safety. Nevertheless, there are many ways in which increased liability can make the world more dangerous. For one thing, the prospect of liability has certainly discouraged the manufacture of some products, in some cases even leading to the withdrawal of products from the market (small aircraft and Bendectin are two examples). When the products in question make life safer, this is clearly a bad thing. The easiest way to reduce the danger of product-liability suits is to continue making the products one has made for the last thirty years or so: expanded liability undoubtedly discourages innovation, and innovation generally leads to more safety, not less.

Even when a product is not withdrawn, the extra costs associated with "safety features" of questionable value and of insuring against expected liability will make the product less widely available than it would have been if liability were not so widespread. This, too, can increase danger, as when consumers continue to use old, worn-out products rather than buying expensive replacements, or when some consumers forgo buying products that would make them better off. Consider, for example, the middle-aged, overweight man who has a heart attack while shoveling snow, and who would have bought a snowblower but for the several hundred dollars added to the cost of every snowblower by the tort system.

An assumption of many courts, so widely shared that it is usually unstated, is that courts must take an active role in product design because market forces will not do the job. Everyday experience may not bear this out. Consider, for example, automobile safety. Today's cars are much safer than those of even ten years ago. Most of the features that make today's cars safer are features introduced by manufacturers seeking increased safety, not features introduced in response to liability. Anti-lock brakes, all-weather tires, intermittent windshield wipers, and general improvements in the reliability of components are examples. Furthermore, it has been contended that the reluctance of American manufacturers to introduce air bags (which came into fairly widespread use in Europe and Japan earlier) was attributable in part to fears of liability (for example, in the rare cases in which air bags deploy accidentally).

For a collection of papers investigating the effects of tort law on safety in various industries, including automobiles, pharmaceuticals, and aviation, *see* Peter W. Huber (ed.), The Liability Maze (Brookings, 1991). *See also*, W. Kip Viscusi, Reforming Products Liability (Harvard University Press, 1991). The main point to note at this stage is that the relationship between liability and safety is extremely complex, and that reading judicial opinions on the subject is quite unlikely to provide one with a realistic sense of how safety can be achieved.

2. Product-Category Liability

One way of making liability even more "strict" than it is now would be to abolish the "defect" requirement entirely, simply making manufacturers of products liable to anyone hurt while using the product. Such a principle has found little, if any, support in the courts. A few courts have, however, held that a jury can decide that a particular product may be defective not because of some feature that might be improved but simply because the dangers of having the product on the market outweigh its utility. Here is one example, followed by the legislation which overruled it.

O'Brien v. Muskin Corp.

Supreme Court of New Jersey
463 A.2d 298 (N.J. 1983)

POLLOCK, J.

Plaintiff, Gary O'Brien, seeks to recover in strict liability for personal injuries sustained because defendant, Muskin Corporation, allegedly marketed a product, an above-ground swimming pool, that was defectively designed and bore an inadequate warning....

O'Brien sued to recover damages for serious personal injuries sustained when he dove into a swimming pool at the home of Jean Henry, widow of Arthur Henry, now Jean Glass. Ultimately, plaintiff sued as defendants not only Muskin Corporation, the manufacturer, but also Kiddie City Inc., the distributor of the pool, charging them with placing a defectively designed pool in the stream of commerce....

... [A]t the close of the plaintiff's case, the trial court determined that he had failed to prove a design defect in the pool. Accordingly,...the court refused to charge the jury on design defect. Instead, the court submitted the case to the jury solely on the adequacy of the warning. [The jury found for the defendant.]

[The Appellate Division ruled that the trial court had erred in taking the design-defect issue from the jury and remanded the case for a new trial.]

....

... [W]e affirm the remand of the matter for a new trial.

....

Muskin, a swimming pool manufacturer, made and distributed a line of above-ground pools. Typically, the pools consisted of a corrugated metal wall, which the purchaser placed into an oval frame assembled over a shallow bed of sand. This outer structure was then fitted with an embossed vinyl liner and filled with water.

In 1971, Arthur Henry bought a Muskin pool and assembled it in his backyard. The pool was a twenty-foot by twenty-four-foot model, with four-foot walls. An embossed vinyl liner fit within the outer structure and was filled with water to a depth of approximately three and one-half feet. At one point, the outer wall of the pool bore the logo of the manufacturer, and below it a decal that warned "DO NOT DIVE" in letters roughly one-half inch high.

On May 17, 1974, O'Brien, then twenty-three years old, arrived uninvited at the Henry home and dove into the pool. A fact issue exists whether O'Brien dove from the platform by the pool or from the roof of the adjacent eight-foot high garage. As his outstretched hands hit the vinyl-lined pool bottom, they slid apart, and O'Brien struck his head on the bottom of the pool, thereby sustaining his injuries.

In his complaint, O'Brien alleged that Muskin was strictly liable for his injuries because it had manufactured and marketed a defectively designed pool. In support of this contention, O'Brien cited the slippery quality of the pool liner and the lack of adequate warnings.

At trial, both parties produced experts who testified about the use of vinyl as a pool liner. One of the plaintiff's witnesses, an expert in the characteristics of vinyl, testified that wet vinyl was more than twice as slippery as rubber latex, which is used to line in-ground pools. The trial court, however, sustained an objection to the expert's opinion about alternative kinds of pool bottoms, specifically whether rubber latex was a feasible liner for above-ground pools. The expert admitted that he knew of no above-ground pool lined with a material other than vinyl, but plaintiff contended that vinyl should not be used in above-ground pools, even though no alternative material was available. A second expert testified that the slippery vinyl bottom and lack of adequate warnings rendered the pool unfit and unsafe for its foreseeable uses.

Muskin's expert testified that vinyl was not only an appropriate material to line an above-ground pool, but was the best material because it permitted the outstretched arms of the diver to glide when they hit the liner, thereby preventing the diver's head from striking the bottom of the pool. Thus, he concluded that in some situations, specifically those in which a diver executes a shallow dive, slipperiness operates as a safety feature....

...[T]he trial court instructed the jury on the elements of strict liability, both with respect to design defects and the failure to warn adequately. The court, however, then limited the jury's consideration to the adequacy of the warning. That is, the court took from the jury the issue whether manufacturing a pool with a vinyl liner constituted either a design or manufacturing defect.

....

Strict liability law, a relatively recent but rapidly growing legal phenomenon, has received uneven treatment from scholars, legislatures and courts. Underlying the various responses is a shared concern about the allocation of the risk of loss upon manufacturers, distributors and others in the stream of commerce for injuries sustained by the public from unsafe products.

....

Although the appropriate standard might be variously defined, one definition, based on a comparison of the utility of the product with the risk of injury that it poses to the public, has gained prominence. To the extent that "risk-utility analysis," as it is known, implicates the reasonableness of the manufacturer's conduct, strict liability law continues to manifest that part of its heritage attributable to the law of negligence....Risk-utility analysis is appropriate when the product may function satisfactorily under one set of circumstances, yet because of its design present undue risk of injury to the user in another situation.

....

...[S]tate-of-the-art evidence...does not constitute an absolute defense apart from risk-utility analysis. *See* Beshada v. Johns-Manville Products Corp., 90 N.J. 191, 202-05 & n. 6, 447 A.2d 539 (1982). The ultimate burden of proving a defect is on the plaintiff, but the burden is on the defendant to prove that compliance with state-of-the-art, in conjunction with other relevant evidence, justifies placing a product on the market. Compliance with proof of state-of-the-art need not, as a matter of law, compel a judgment for a defendant. State-of-the-art evidence, together with other evidence relevant to risk-utility analysis, however, may support a judgment for a defendant. In brief, state-of-the-art evidence is relevant to, but not necessarily dispositive of, risk-utility analysis. That is, a product may embody the state-of-the-art and still fail to satisfy the risk-utility equation.

The assessment of the utility of a design involves the consideration of available alternatives. If no alternatives are available, recourse to a unique design is more defensible. The existence of a safer and equally efficacious design, however, diminishes the justification for using a challenged design.

The evaluation of the utility of a product also involves the relative need for that product; some products are essentials, while others are luxuries. A product that fills a critical need and can be designed in only one way should be viewed differently from a luxury item. Still other products, including some for which no alternative exists, are so dangerous and of such little use that under the risk-utility analysis, a manufacturer would bear the cost of liability of harm to others. That cost might dissuade a manufacturer from placing the product on the market, even if the product has been made as safely as possible. Indeed, plaintiff contends that above-ground pools with vinyl liners are such products and that manufacturers who market those pools should bear the cost of injuries they cause to foreseeable users.

A critical issue at trial was whether the design of the pool, calling for a vinyl bottom in a pool four feet deep, was defective. The trial court should have permitted the jury to consider whether, because of the dimensions of the pool and slipperiness of the bottom, the risks of injury so outweighed the utility of the product as to constitute a defect. In removing that issue from consideration by the jury, the trial court erred. To establish sufficient proof to compel submission of the issue to the jury for appropriate fact-finding under risk-utility analysis, it was not necessary for plaintiff to prove the existence of alternative, safer designs. Viewing the evidence in the light most favorable to plaintiff, even if there are no alternative methods of making bottoms for above-ground pools, the jury might have found that the risk posed by the pool outweighed its utility.

In a design-defect case, the plaintiff bears the burden of both going forward with the evidence and of persuasion that the product contained a defect. To establish a *prima facie* case, the plaintiff should adduce sufficient evidence on the risk-utility factors to establish a defect. With respect to above-ground swimming pools, for example, the plaintiff might seek to establish that pools are marketed primarily for recreational, not therapeutic purposes; that because of their design, including their configuration,...and the use of vinyl liners, injury is likely....

....

Our concurring and dissenting colleague, Justice Schreiber, disagrees with the majority opinion in several respects.... His opinion begins with the correct statement that the imposition of strict liability in a products liability case requires proof of a defect in the product. We depart from our colleague, however, because he believes that proof of a defect through risk-utility analysis is tantamount to absolute, not strict, liability. The majority opinion concludes that risk-utility analysis is one means of proving the existence of a defect. That is, under risk-utility analysis, if the risks outweigh the utility of the product, it is defective.

A second difference between the two opinions is that Justice Schreiber would find that no matter how dangerous a product may be, if it bears an adequate warning, it is free from design defects if there is no known alternative. Under that hypothesis, manufacturers, merely by placing warnings on their products, could insulate themselves from liability regardless of the number of people those products maim or kill. By contrast, the majority concludes that the judicial, not the commercial, system is the appropriate forum for determining whether a product is defective with the resultant imposition of strict liability upon those in the commercial chain.

....

We modify and affirm the judgment of the Appellate Division reversing and remanding the matter for a new trial.

SCHREIBER, J., concurring and dissenting.

Until today, the existence of a defect was an essential element in strict product liability. This no longer is so. Indeed, the majority has transformed strict product liability into absolute liability and delegated the function of making that determination to a jury. I must dissent from that conclusion because the jury will not be cognizant of all the elements that should be considered in formulating a policy supporting absolute liability, because it is not satisfactory to have a jury make a value judgment with respect to a type or class of product, and because its judgment will not have precedential effect.

....

My research has disclosed no case where liability was imposed, utilizing the risk-utility analysis, as a matter of law for an accident ascribable to a product in the absence of a defect (manufacturing flaw, available alternative, or inadequate warning) other than in the absolute liability context....

The purpose of strict product liability is to hold a manufacturer responsible for damages attributable to a failure of the product to perform with reasonable safety. It is not to make the manufacturer an insurer against all losses. Montgomery and Owen, *"Reflections on the Theory and Administration of Strict Tort Liability for Defective Products,"* 27 S.C. L. Rev. 803, 826 (1976). The strict liability policy of encouraging manufacturers to market a safer product is generally inapplicable where the product is unavoidably unsafe. Strict liability arose in part because of a basic presumption that persons not abusing products are not usually injured unless the manufacturer failed in some respect in designing, manufacturing or marketing the product. The strict liability theory was designed to facilitate redress for the injured user or consumer because of the difficulty in proving negligence. This policy is not advanced when imposing absolute liability. *See id.* at 827-28.

....

New Jersey Statutes Annotated §2A:58 C-1, C-3
(Westlaw 2004)

§2A:58C-1. Legislative findings; definitions

a. The Legislature finds that there is an urgent need for remedial legislation to establish clear rules with respect to certain matters relating to actions for damages for harm caused by products....

§2A:58C-3. Defenses

a. In any product liability action against a manufacturer or seller for harm allegedly caused by a product that was designed in a defective manner, the manufacturer or seller shall not be liable if:

> (1) At the time the product left the control of the manufacturer, there was not a practical and technically feasible alternative design that would have prevented the harm without substantially impairing the reasonably anticipated or intended function of the product; or

> (2) The characteristics of the product are known to the ordinary consumer or user, and the harm was caused by an unsafe aspect of the product that is an inherent characteristic of the product and that would be recognized by the ordinary person who uses or consumes the product with the ordinary knowledge

common to the class of persons for whom the product is intended, except that this paragraph shall not apply to industrial machinery or other equipment used in the workplace and it is not intended to apply to dangers posed by products such as machinery or equipment that can feasibly be eliminated without impairing the usefulness of the product; or

(3) The harm was caused by an unavoidably unsafe aspect of the product and the product was accompanied by an adequate warning or instruction as defined in section [2A:58C-4].

b. The provisions of paragraph (1) of subsection a. of this section shall not apply if the court, on the basis of clear and convincing evidence, makes all of the following determinations:

(1) The product is egregiously unsafe or ultra-hazardous;

(2) The ordinary user or consumer of the product cannot reasonably be expected to have knowledge of the product's risks, or the product poses a risk of serious injury to persons other than the user or consumer; and

(3) The product has little or no usefulness....

Notes

1. *Handguns and Ammunition.* Another product which many people consider to carry risks outweighing its utility is the handgun. *See, e.g.,* Andrew Jay McClurg, *Handguns as Products Unreasonably Dangerous Per Se,* 13 U. Ark. Little Rock L.J. 599 (1991). There have been a number of (largely unsuccessful) suits. *See* Halliday v. Sturm, Ruger & Co., Inc., 792 A.2d 1145 (Md. 2002) (declining to impose liability where a gun operated exactly as a consumer would have expected it to operate). *But see* Smith v. Bryco Arms, 33 P.3d 638 (N.M. 2001) (holding that issues of material fact precluded summary judgment claims based on defective design and failure to warn).

In response to heavy lobbying by the National Rifle Association, a majority of states have adopted legislation barring actions by crime victims against the manufacturers of guns. *See* Fox Butterfield, *Gun Industry Is Gaining Immunity Against Suits,* New York Times, Sept., 1, 2002. For example, Montana law now provides:

MONTANA CODE ANN. §27-1-720
(Westlaw 2004)
Liability—defect in design of firearms or ammunition

(1) In a products liability action, no firearm or ammunition may be considered defective in design on the basis that the benefits of the product do not outweigh the risk of injury posed by its potential to cause serious injury, damage, or death when discharged.

(2) For purposes of this section:

(a) the potential of a firearm or ammunition to cause a serious injury, damage, or death when discharged does not make the product defective in design; and

(b) injuries or damages resulting from the discharge of a firearm or ammunition are not proximately caused by its potential to cause serious injury, damage, or death but are proximately caused by the actual discharge of the product.

(3) The provisions of this section do not affect a products liability cause of action based upon the improper selection of design alternatives.

However, in California, a statute which strikingly departs from the national trend now says that principles of negligence apply:

CAL. CIVIL. CODE §1714
(Westlaw 2004)

(a) Everyone is responsible, not only for the result of his or her willful acts, but also for an injury occasioned to another by his or her want of ordinary care or skill in the management of his or her property or person....The design, distribution, or marketing of firearms and ammunition is not exempt from the duty to use ordinary care and skill that is required by this section.....

For a discussion of "product-category" problems, see James A. Henderson, Jr. & Aaron D. Twerski, *Closing the American Products Liability Frontier: The Rejection of Liability Without Defect*, 66 N.Y.U. L. Rev. 1263 (1991).

2. Undesirable products can be prohibited by legislation and by the actions of administrative agencies authorized by statute to bar products. Is allowing juries to decide on a case-by-case basis whether particular products should have been marketed necessary or desirable? Consider the following list of products, none of which is outlawed by legislation or regulation, but all of which are viewed by many people as undesirable: fast automobiles; firearms (especially handguns); alcoholic beverages; cigarettes; motorcycles; mopeds; swimming pools without lifeguards; high-cholesterol food; small automobiles.

It seems likely that most Americans would favor outlawing at least some of these products; many would ban all or most of them if they could. Is there a good reason why a plaintiff injured by one of these products should not have an opportunity to convince a jury that the manufacturer and retailer of the product should have gone into some other line of work?

3. *Product-Category Liability and the Restatement.* The Restatement takes a curiously ambivalent approach to product-category liability. In an example using facts like those of the *O'Brien* case, the Restatement says that the plaintiff has failed to establish a design defect because of the uncontradicted expert testimony that no safer alternative design was feasible; Restatement, Third, of Torts: Products Liability §2, comment d, Illus. 4. However, in comment e to §2, the Restatement concludes (using as its example an exploding cigar) that a product can be found defective if its utility is so low and its risk of injury so high that the product should not have been marketed, even though no feasible alternative is possible. Perhaps the distinction between above-ground swimming pools and exploding cigars rests on the fact that many thousands of people purchase and use above-ground pools, while exploding cigars are rare.

4. *Federal Statutory Reform of Products-Liability law.* Every state has adopted some legislation relating to aspects of the law of products liability. Many of the statutes respond to particular decisions that the legislature thinks went "too far," as illustrated by the New Jersey legislation reproduced above. Because markets for many products are national, state legislation is unlikely to provide manufacturers with enough protection to cause them to change their activities very much. If effective limits on manufacturers' liability are to be enacted, Congress will have to do the job. Bills to reform the law of products liability are introduced in Congress every year; to date, few have passed.

Chapter 16

Defenses Based on Plaintiff's Conduct

A. Traditional Contributory Negligence

1. In General

"Contributory negligence" is unreasonable conduct on the part of the plaintiff which is a contributing proximate cause of the harm which occurs. At common law, proof of contributory negligence normally constituted a total bar to recovery for negligence, regardless of whether the defendant's fault was greater or less than the plaintiff's. Contributory negligence traditionally did not bar recovery based on reckless or intentional wrongdoing or conduct giving rise to strict liability. Under these rules, the task of categorizing the defendant's culpability took on great importance, for compensation to a negligent plaintiff was awarded on an all-or-nothing basis. As discussed below, the scope and import of a defense based on the plaintiff's unreasonable conduct have changed significantly in recent years. Most states have adopted some form of "comparative negligence" or "comparative responsibility" system—usually by statute, but sometimes by judicial decision. Under these systems, a victim's negligence will often reduce, but not eliminate, the victim's recovery against a negligent defendant. *See* note 3, *supra,* at p. 19.

A Difference between Negligence and Contributory Negligence? The Second Restatement distinguished between negligence (conduct creating an undue risk of harm to others) and contributory negligence (conduct creating a risk of harm to the actor):

> An actor is not necessarily required to pursue the same course of conduct for his own protection as is demanded of him for the protection of others. There may be circumstances in which a jury may reasonably conclude that a reasonable man would take more, or less, precaution for the protection of others than for his own safety. Thus the risk of harm to others may be more apparent, or apparently more serious, than the risk of harm to the actor himself; or the actor may have reasonable confidence in his own awareness of the risk, and his ability to avoid it, where he cannot reasonably have such confidence in the awareness and ability of others. He may have undertaken a responsibility toward another which requires him to exercise an amount of care for the protection of the other which he would not be required to exercise for his own

safety.... In the great majority of cases it is probably true that the same conduct will constitute both negligence and contributory negligence, but it does not necessarily follow in all cases.

Restatement, Second, of Torts §464 Comment f.

Section 3 of the Restatement, Third, of Torts: Apportionment of Liability (2000), rejects the distinction:

> Plaintiff's negligence is defined by the applicable standard for a defendant's negligence....

The difference in wording between the second and third Restatements may be less important than it seems at first glance to be. The particular factors listed in the second Restatement's justification for distinguishing between a plaintiff's negligence and the negligence of a defendant in particular cases can be invoked in any case. If, for example, a plaintiff had a particular reason for thinking that a particular course of conduct would not endanger the plaintiff, that fact supports a finding that the plaintiff was not negligent, even if the standard for negligence is simply "reasonable care."

Anticipating the Negligence of Others. Suppose a potential plaintiff (1) knows that others are likely to act negligently, and (2) takes precautions that are "reasonable" if all others act reasonably also, but which will be insufficient if someone else acts negligently. Is the plaintiff's failure to take more precautions contributory negligence? In other words, should the plaintiff be entitled to assume, in taking precautions, that everyone else will take reasonable care as well, or must the plaintiff's reasonable care be care which anticipates and guards against the negligence of others? LeRoy Fibre Co. v. Chicago, Milwaukee & St. Paul Ry., 232 U.S. 340 (1914), involved a fire which started when sparks from a train landed on flax straw stacked by the plaintiff on its own land. The jury found both the railroad and the plaintiff negligent; the plaintiff's negligence supposedly consisted of placing the straw too close to the railroad tracks. The majority ruled that the plaintiff, having stacked the straw on its land in a way that created no danger to anyone off the property, could not be negligent. Justice Holmes, concurring in the result, concluded that the plaintiff's stacking the straw near the tracks could be negligent if the straw was so close as to create a risk of fire from "prudently managed" engines, but not if the only risk was from negligently operated trains.

In cases involving traffic accidents, which do not raise the complicating factor of the plaintiff's rights as a property owner, the *LeRoy Fibre* issue is whether a driver (or pedestrian) can act on the assumption that all other drivers and pedestrians will use reasonable care. Suppose, for instance, that a pedestrian crosses a street without looking for oncoming cars, assuming that they will stop for a red light. If the pedestrian is hit by a driver who runs the light, is the failure to look for traffic contributory negligence? There is surprisingly little authority on this question, perhaps because most of the oversights which can contribute to one's being hurt by a negligent driver could also have contributed to an accident involving someone who was not negligent. Many opinions simply assume that reasonable care can require anticipating that others will be negligent. See, for example, the *Carroll Towing Co.* case, *supra*, p. 247, in which the bargee's absence would have been harmless if everyone else had exercised reasonable care. For an economic analysis of the problem, *see* Mark F. Grady, *Common Law Control of Strategic Behavior: Railroad Sparks and the Farmer*, 17 J. Leg. Studies 15 (1988).

2. Imputed Contributory Negligence

Western Union Tel. Co. v. Hoffman

Supreme Court of Texas
15 S.W. 1048 (Tex. 1891)

HENRY, J.

This suit was brought by August Hoffman for himself, and as next friend of his minor son, Kelly Hoffman, to recover damages caused by the neglect of the defendant to deliver the following telegraphic message: "Spring, Texas, August 6, 1889. To Dr. Dutton, Conroe, Texas: Come on first train. Kelly Hoffman broke his arm. [Signed] HENRY HUGHES." The father of Kelly was away from home when his own son was hurt, and the message was sent by direction of his wife, the mother of the boy. The message was received at Conroe, where Dr. Dutton lived, on the day that it was sent, but was not delivered to him until he inquired for it of the agent of the defendant, on the 15th of the same month. No excuse for the failure to deliver it was offered.

Kelly was 15 years old when he was hurt. His injury was a dislocation of his arm at the elbow. Dr. Dutton was the physician of plaintiff's family, and testified that if the dispatch had been delivered to him he would have responded to it within 24 hours, and would have reset and saved the arm. The testimony shows that the same thing could have been done at any time within a few days after the injury occurred. No other dispatch was sent, and no further effort was made to procure the aid of Dr. Dutton or any other physician. Nothing seems to have been done to remedy the dislocation, and the result followed that, when the wound healed, it left the arm stiff, and permanently disabled. On the 15th day of August — or nine days after the injury occurred — Dr. Dutton happened to be passing by the residence of the parents of the youth, and was seen and called in. He then examined the arm, but did not undertake to treat it. He testified that it was then too late to reset it, and that the attempt to do so would have been attended with great danger to the patient. He was corroborated in this particular by the evidence of another physician.... The defendant pleaded contributory negligence. Upon the verdict of a jury judgment was rendered in favor of the father for $900 and in favor of his son for $4,125....

The only question that we deem it necessary to consider is whether the defense of contributory negligence was made out.... [In view of] the failure to send another message to Dr. Dutton or procure other medical assistance, which would naturally have suggested itself to any person of ordinary prudence and intelligence, we think the evidence clearly shows that the permanent character of the injury must be attributed to a want of proper care upon the part of the parents of the injured boy.... Because of such contributory negligence no verdict should have been rendered in favor of the father of the minor for his own benefit, and the one so rendered should have been set aside upon defendant's motion. [Citations.]

But the negligence of his parents cannot be interposed as a defense to bar a recovery for the benefit of the minor. [Citations.] The contributory negligence that precludes him from a recovery must be that of the minor himself, and whether it existed or not was a question for the jury to decide, taking into their consideration the age and situation of the minor, and all other circumstances connected with the case.... In the case before us it may be well doubted whether a child 15 years old had sufficient experience or discretion to correctly estimate the consequences of the failure to have his injured arm properly treated, especially when his mental and physical condition caused by the injury are considered.... We think the judgment should be affirmed as to the minor, Kelly Hoffman, and reversed, and the cause be remanded, as to the individual judgment in favor of August Hoffman; and it will be so ordered.

Notes

1. *Imputed Contributory Negligence.* Restatement, Third, of Torts: Apportionment of Liability § 5 adopts a "both ways" rule for imputing negligence to a plaintiff. Generally, if negligence would have been imputed had the plaintiff been a defendant, negligence will be imputed to a plaintiff as well. For example, because the negligence of an employee is imputed to the employer under the doctrine of *respondeat superior*, a plaintiff suing for harm done in an accident in which the plaintiff's employee was negligent will be treated as if the plaintiff had been negligent. Cases in which negligence is imputed solely because of ownership of a motor vehicle constitute an exception. Therefore, if A lets B drive A's car, and the car is damaged because both B and a third person, C, were negligent, A may recover in full from C (and B), even if the jurisdiction in question has an owner-liability statute, under which A would be liable to someone injured by B's negligence. Restatement, Third, of Torts: Apportionment of Liability § 5, cmt. c, illus. 6.

Under the "both ways" rule, a parent's negligence is not ordinarily imputed to the parent's child, a spouse's negligence is not imputed to the other spouse, and the negligence of the driver of a vehicle is not imputed to a passenger.

"When a relationship exists in which imputed plaintiff's negligence would otherwise be appropriate, plaintiff's negligence is not imputed from one party of the relationship to another in a suit between them." *Id.* at cmt. d. Thus, if an employee negligently damages an employer's vehicle, imputed negligence will not bar the employer from suing the employee or reduce the employer's recovery.

2. *Wrongful-Death, Survival, and Loss of Consortium.* In cases involving "derivative claims" for damages resulting from a tort against a third person, the Restatement imputes the negligence of the direct victim to the plaintiff; Restatement, Third, of Torts: Apportionment of Liability § 6. Many wrongful-death and survival statutes expressly provide for this result. An exception may exist for cases in which the plaintiff seeks to recover for emotional distress caused by injury to a family member. According to Comment f to § 6 of the Third Restatement, negligence of the direct victim should be imputed in this case as well, but the Reporter's Note to this comment finds "surprisingly little authority" on this particular issue.

3. Last Clear Chance

One of the most important limits on the rule of contributory negligence at common law was the doctrine of last clear chance. The doctrine is thought to have originated in Davies v. Mann, 152 Eng. Rep. 588 (1842), an old English case in which, as the Restatement puts it, "the plaintiff left his ass fettered in the highway, and the defendant ran into it." Restatement, Second, of Torts §479 cmt. a. The doctrine of last clear chance provides that negligence on the part of the plaintiff will not defeat recovery if the defendant (and not the plaintiff), through the exercise of ordinary care, had the last chance to avoid the accident. Because, in *Davies*, the defendant driver of the cart, which was traveling too fast when it hit the animal, had the last clear chance to avoid the harm (*e.g.*, by slowing down and taking other evasive measures), the plaintiff's contributory negligence in leaving the animal in the road was disregarded. Full recovery was permitted.

Under last clear chance, once the defendant has discovered or should have discovered the plaintiff's position of peril, the defendant must have sufficient time and ability to avoid the accident; otherwise the doctrine does not apply. The great body of precedent which emerged to govern the last-clear-chance doctrine is mainly of historical interest today. With the rise of comparative negligence and comparative fault, the need for last clear chance as a palliative for the hardships of the all-or-nothing contributory-negligence rule disappeared. Consequently, most jurisdictions have abolished last clear chance. *See* Prudential Lines, Inc. v. McAllister Bros., Inc., 801 F.2d 616 (2d Cir. 1986) (refusing to continue to apply last clear chance in admiralty). Restatement, Third, of Torts: Apportionment of Liability § 3 provides that "Special ameliorative doctrines for defining plaintiff's negligence are abolished." This provision does away with the doctrine of last clear chance, as well as the doctrine of mitigation of damages.

B. Comparative Negligence

Hilen v. Hays

Supreme Court of Kentucky
673 S.W.2d 713 (Ky. 1984)

LEIBSON, Justice.

The appellant, Margie Montgomery Hilen, was severely injured when the automobile in which she was a passenger was driven into the back of another vehicle and overturned. She sued the driver, appellee Keith Hays. There was no question but that the cause of the accident was the driver's negligent operation of the vehicle. There was a factual dispute as to whether the passenger failed to exercise reasonable care for her own safety by riding with a person whom she knew or should have known to be too intoxicated to drive safely.

At the conclusion of the trial the judge directed a verdict as to appellee's negligence and submitted the case to the jury solely on the issue of appellant's contributory negligence. The jury was given the usual instruction that contributory negligence was a complete bar to any recovery. The appellant objected and tendered an instruction based on the doctrine of comparative negligence, which was refused. The jury found for the appellee and this appeal followed. The Court of Appeals affirmed....

The sole issue before us is whether negligence on the part of the appellant contributing to her injury should be a complete bar to any recovery,...or whether the time has come for us to reject this rule and adopt the doctrine of comparative negligence allocating responsibility for the injury between the parties in proportion to their contributory fault.

    ....

...[T]he contributory negligence rule as it applies to this case is court-made law that bears the imprimatur of neither the Kentucky constitution nor the General Assembly.... Prosser states in the Law of Torts, (4th Ed., 1971), p. 434:

> There never has been any essential reason why the change [to comparative neg-
> ligence] could not be made without a statute by the courts which made the
> contributory negligence rule in the first place....

Having deference to the doctrine of *stare decisis*, the courts of the several states have
been understandably reluctant to abandon contributory negligence as a complete defense notwithstanding the relative merits of the two competing positions. The tendency
was to defer consideration of comparative negligence to the legislatures of the several
states, although there was no statute mandating the traditional rule and thus no question of separation of powers involved....

So the evolution towards comparative negligence began in the various state legislatures first in a trickle and then in an avalanche. The first comparative negligence statute
was enacted in Mississippi in 1910. Wisconsin and Nebraska followed in 1913, South
Dakota in 1941, Arkansas in 1957, Maine in 1964. Following a full-scale public debate
of the relative merits of comparative negligence in textbooks and treatises, twenty-six
more states followed between 1969 and 1983. At present count thirty-two states, Puerto
Rico, and the Virgin Islands have adopted comparative negligence or comparative fault
by statute.

In addition, between 1975 and the present, courts in nine other states have refused to
wait further for their legislatures to act and have adopted comparative negligence by judicial decision. As the Supreme Court of Missouri stated in Gustafson v. Benda, 661
S.W.2d 11 (Mo. 1983):

> We have remained quiescent more than five years while waiting for the legisla-
> ture to act....
>
> ...[L]egislative failure to enact this reform reflects inertia rather than com-
> munity sentiment.

Id. at 14-15.

A comparative negligence bill was introduced at the 1968 session of the Kentucky
General Assembly and a similar bill has been introduced in most, if not all, sessions since
then. Two bills were introduced in 1984 and neither got out of committee. [Citation.]

In broad outline, *stare decisis* directs us to "stand by" our previous decisions unless
there are sound legal reasons to the contrary.... But the doctrine of *stare decisis* does not
commit us to the sanctification of ancient fallacy....

The common law is not a stagnant pool, but a moving stream. [Citation.] It seeks to
purify itself as it flows through time. The common law is our responsibility; the child of
the courts. We are responsible for its direction....

Mr. Justice Sutherland wrote in Funk v. United States, 290 U.S. 371, 54 S. Ct. 212, 78
L. Ed. 369 (1933):

> [T]o say that the courts of this country are forever bound to perpetuate such of
> its rules as, by every reasonable test, are found to be neither wise nor just, be-
> cause we have once adopted them as suited for our situation and institutions at
> a particular time, is to deny to the common law in the place of its adoption a
> "flexibility and capacity for growth and adaptation" which was "the peculiar
> boast and excellence" of the system in the place of its origin.

Citation.]

....

A list of the critics of contributory negligence as a complete bar to a plaintiff's re-covery reads like a tort hall of fame. The list includes, among others, Campbell, Flem-ing, Green, Harper and James, Dreton, Leflar, Malone, Pound and Prosser. In 1953 Prosser wrote:

> The attack upon contributory negligence has been founded upon the obvious injustice of a rule which visits the entire loss caused by the fault of two parties on one of them alone, and that one the injured plaintiff, least able to bear it, and quite possibly much less at fault than the defendant who goes scot-free. No one has ever succeeded in justifying that as a policy, and no one ever will.

[Citation.]

In Li v. Yellow Cab Co., 13 Cal. 3d 804, 119 Cal. Rptr. 858, 532 P.2d 1226 (1975) [the court stated]:

> The essence of that criticism has been constant and clear: the doctrine is in-equitable in its operation because it fails to distribute responsibility in propor-tion to fault.... In a system in which liability is based on fault, the extent of that fault should govern the extent of liability.... [Citation.]

At oral argument... appellee's counsel conceded that the present system creates certain "inequities," claiming that these inequities are supposedly cured by juries acting in disre-gard of their instructions to make comparative findings. Assuming there is any truth to this speculation, it only confirms that the concept of allocating liability proportionate to fault remains "irresistible to reason and all intelligent notions of fairness." [Citation.]

Comparative negligence... eliminates a windfall for either claimant or defendant as presently exists in our all-or-nothing situation where sometimes claims are barred by contributory negligence and sometimes claims are paid in full regardless of contribu-tory negligence such as in cases involving last clear chance or defendant's willful or wan-ton negligence. [Citations.]

The answer to the charge that in a comparative negligence system the claimant recov-ers for his own wrong is that the opposite is true. Even where comparative negligence is applied 100% (the so-called "pure" form of comparative negligence), the claimant who is 95% negligent recovers from the defendant only for that small portion of the injury, 5%, which is fairly attributable to the defendant's fault. In theory, the system is 100% fair.

    ....

    .... To those who speculate that comparative negligence will cost more money or cause more litigation, we say there are no good economies in an *unjust* law.

    ....

Having concluded that contributory negligence as a complete defense in Kentucky should give way to comparative negligence, the next question is what form of compara-tive negligence should be adopted. Although there are variations in the types of compar-ative negligence, the two basic systems are the "modified" form and the "pure form," "modified" meaning "limited" and "pure" meaning "complete." Under the "modified" form, with variations depending on the system, the claimant can recover if his percentage of fault is not equal to or greater than that of the defendant(s). Under the "pure" form, the claimant's recovery is reduced by the amount of fault attributable to him, but he may recover regardless of whether his fault is equal to or greater than that of the defendant(s).

Opponents of the "modified" form of comparative negligence argue that this system encourages appeals on the narrow but crucial issue of whether plaintiff's negligence was equal to or greater than defendant's, and further argue that it does not abrogate contributory negligence but "simply shifts the lottery aspect of the rule to a different ground.".…

In eight of the nine states where comparative negligence has been adopted by judicial decision, the courts have opted for the "pure" form. Only West Virginia has held to the contrary.…

....

In contrast to change by the judiciary where pure comparative negligence has been the overwhelming choice, the majority of state legislatures adopting comparative negligence have favored some modified form. After researching this difference, Prosser concludes:

> "All of these restrictions (modified forms) are obviously the result of compromise between conflicting interests in the legislatures, and smack of political expediency rather than of any reason or logic in the situation." Prosser, Law of Torts, (4th Ed., 1971), 437.

The treatise by Judge Henry Woods, Comparative Fault,… includes an extensive review of both the legislative and judicial experience of our sister states with comparative negligence. Such a review compels us to conclude that the pure form of comparative negligence is preferable over any of the variety of modified forms that have been suggested.…

Henceforth, where contributory negligence has previously been a complete defense, it is supplanted by the doctrine of comparative negligence. In such cases contributory negligence will not bar recovery but shall reduce the total amount of the award in the proportion that the claimant's contributory negligence bears to the total negligence that caused the damages. The trier of fact must consider both negligence and causation in arriving at the proportion that negligence and causation attributable to the claimant bears to the total negligence that was a substantial factor in causing the damages.

....

The final question that remains to be addressed is the application of the present decision to this case and others where contributory negligence is an issue. Other courts that have adopted comparative negligence have all made the doctrine effective to pending cases to some extent. The appellee complains that the rules should not be changed in his case. But unlike contract law the appellee here did not act in reliance on the state of the law at the time of the act, and has no legitimate complaint against the retroactive application of a change. We conclude…that the comparative negligence doctrine shall apply to:

1) The present case;

2) All cases tried or retried after the date of filing of this opinion; and

3) All cases pending, including appeals, in which the issue has been preserved.

The decision of the Court of Appeals and the trial court is reversed, and the within action is remanded to the trial court for proceedings in conformity with this opinion.

[The concurring opinion of Justice LEIBSON and the dissenting opinion of Justice VANCE, in which Justice STEPHENSON joined, are omitted.]

Note

1. Only four states and the District of Columbia retain strict common-law contributory negligence: Alabama (Bergob v. Scrushy, 855 So. 2d 823 (Ala. Ct. Civ. App. 2002));

D.C. (Wingfield v. Peoples Drug Store Inc., 379 A.2d 685, 687 (D.C. 1977)); Maryland (Pippin v. Potomac Electric Power Co., 132 F. Supp. 2d 379, 383 (D. Md. 2001)); North Carolina (Yancey v. Lea, 532 S.E.2d 560, 563 (N.C. Ct. App. 1999)); and Virginia (Litchford v. Hancock, 352 S.E.2d 335, 337 (Va. 1987)).

C. Assumption of the Risk

The second great defense at common law was assumption of the risk. Like contributory negligence, it completely barred recovery by the plaintiff. "In working out the distinction [between contributory negligence and assumption of the risk], the courts...arrived at the conclusion that assumption of risk is a matter of knowledge of the danger and intelligent acquiescence in it, and that to the extent that this can be found recovery will be denied; while contributory negligence is a matter of some fault or departure from the standard of reasonable conduct, however unwilling or protesting the plaintiff may be." Masters v. New York Central R. Co., 70 N.E.2d 898, 903 (Ohio 1947).

1. Introduction

Coleman v. Ramada Hotel Operating Co.
United States Court of Appeals for the Seventh Circuit
933 F.2d 470 (7th Cir. 1991)

CUDAHY, Circuit Judge.

Boisterous rough and tumble sports have long been a source of picnic amusement. The three-legged race, the sack hop and the egg toss seldom fail to evoke hearty guffaws. Most of those who participate in such light-hearted antics escape unscathed, but Peggy Coleman was not so lucky. After fracturing her ankle and tearing a ligament during a company-sponsored recreational outing, Coleman filed this personal injury suit against the owner of the grounds where the unfortunate accident took place, Ramada Hotel Operating Company (Ramada). Coleman attributes her injuries to Ramada's alleged negligence in operating an obstacle course as part of the day's entertainment. The district court granted summary judgment in favor of Ramada because it found that Coleman voluntarily assumed the obvious risks inherent in the activity....

    ....

....One of the events at the picnic—a "mini olympics"—involved a timed obstacle course. To mount a slide backwards was the first hurdle. Participants were instructed to clamber up the slippery slope of an ordinary playground slide and climb down the stairs on the back of the slide. The slide presented no latent danger. Coleman concedes that the slide was in good repair—it was stable and possessed firm handrails. The only risk, then, was that inherent in the reversal of its normal use.

Of her own volition, Coleman competed in this event. After observing her team member ascend the slide before her, Coleman mounted the chute portion of the slide without incident. Carefully grasping the handrails and treading one step at a time, Coleman descended the ladder portion of the slide. Despite her caution, however, Coleman slipped and fell....

Coleman brought suit against Ramada, charging Ramada with breach of its duty of reasonable care towards her in two distinct ways: first, by failing to warn her of the possibility of injury and, second, by failing to provide safe apparatus for the mini olympics. Ramada moved for summary judgment on both claims.

The district court...agreed with Ramada that Illinois imposes no duty to warn of such open and obvious risks. The court relied, however, upon the doctrine of assumption of risk—not the closely-related affirmative defense of contributory negligence—to bar Coleman's second claim, reasoning that any element of negligence in Ramada's decision to include a backward slide in the obstacle course was nullified by Coleman's voluntary choice to engage in an inherently dangerous activity....

[The appeals court held that Ramada was, as a matter of law, not negligent in failing to warn of an obvious danger. It then turned to a discussion of Ramada's assumption-of-the-risk defense to Coleman's claim that Ramada's failure to provide a safer slide presented a negligence question for the factfinder.]

Though distinct in principle, assumption of risk and contributory negligence are often confused and there exists substantial overlap between the two doctrines. Pure assumption of risk consists of voluntary consent to encounter a known risk while pure contributory negligence consists of failure to exercise reasonable care in self-protection. In a large number of real cases, however, the two doctrines are inextricably intertwined. In such cases, the plaintiff's conduct amounts to both assumption of risk and contributory negligence because her acceptance of a known risk is at the same time unreasonable and negligent....

Coleman's conduct...appears to fit into both doctrinal pigeonholes, simultaneously constituting assumption of risk and contributory negligence....

....

This case approaches the paradigmatic instance of assumption of risk: Peggy Coleman elected to take her chances by competing in the mini olympics obstacle course with full knowledge of the hazardous nature of the event. After watching her teammate ascend the first hurdle before her, Coleman mounted the chute portion of the slide and stepped down the ladder, carefully grasping the handrails and treading one step at a time. One who freely chooses to climb up a slide backwards certainly assumes the perils of an inadvertent plunge to the ground. That Coleman was aware of the danger of falling is manifest in the very caution she observed while descending the slide. As Chief Justice Cardozo explained when rejecting the claims of an individual similarly injured by a fall from an amusement park ride aptly termed "The Flopper":

> One who takes part in such a sport accepts the dangers that inhere in it so far as they are obvious and necessary, just as a fencer accepts the risk of a thrust by his antagonist or a spectator at a ball game the chance of contact with the ball.

Murphy v. Steeplechase Amusement Co., 250 N.Y. 479, 482, 166 N.E. 173, 174 (1929). As with "The Flopper," any risks that may have been posed by inclusion of the backwards slide in the obstacle course were overt and inherent in the nature of the activity. Therefore, any misjudgment on Ramada's part in designing the obstacle course was nullified by Coleman's free and informed choice to participate in the event.

Coleman now argues, however, that the doctrine of assumption of risk may be applied only to situations involving an explicit contractual relationship between the parties. Although Illinois courts often proclaim that assumption of risk is limited to cases involving a contractual relationship, they generally construe such a relationship broadly to embrace business invitees. In Provence v. Doolin, 91 Ill. App. 3d at 280, 414 N.E.2d at 793, for example, the Illinois Appellate Court declared that "the defense of assumption of risk is confined to situations where the parties have a contractual or employment relationship" but held that mere payment of a fee for entry upon recreational premises sufficed to create such a contract. The court noted that, although one golfer whose ball strikes and injures another may not assert the defense of assumption of risk, the golf course may raise the defense because of its "contractual relationship" with the injured golfer....

Finally, Coleman asserts that her conduct should not completely bar recovery because it consists solely of secondary implied assumption of risk, a doctrine now merged into the comparative negligence regime. Illinois courts have classified the doctrine of assumption of risk into three categories: express assumption of risk, primary implied assumption of risk and secondary implied assumption of risk. [Citation.]. Express assumption of risk demands an explicit agreement while implied assumption of risk infers willingness to accept a known risk from the conduct of the parties. In primary implied assumption of risk, the plaintiff assumes risks inherent in the nature of the activity while in secondary implied assumption of risk, the plaintiff assumes risks that are created by the defendant's negligence. Only the first two of these forms have survived the advent of comparative negligence in Illinois. Because it is deemed functionally similar to contributory negligence, the third category—secondary implied assumption of risk—has been abolished.... But Coleman's attempt to squeeze herself into the category of secondary implied assumption of risk is of no avail because any risks that she assumed were intrinsic to the activity itself rather than being the product of any negligence on Ramada's part. Whatever danger Coleman faced in mounting the playground slide backwards stemmed from the nature of the activity and not from Ramada's upkeep of the slide. Thus Coleman's conduct amounts to primary implied assumption of risk, which still operates as a complete bar to recovery.

...Coleman's voluntary choice to participate in an inherently risky activity bars her from recovery under Illinois law. Coleman was free to refrain altogether from participation in this hazardous sport had she wished to avert any possible risk of injury. As Chief Justice Cardozo once observed, "The timorous may stay at home." Murphy v. Steeplechase Amusement Co., 250 N.Y. at 483, 166 N.E. at 174. Therefore, the district court's entry of summary judgment in favor of Ramada is

AFFIRMED.

Notes

1. *Is Assumption of the Risk Necessary?* The use of comparative principles to evaluate defenses based on the plaintiff's conduct has been a relatively recent development. Throughout most of America's history, unreasonableness by the plaintiff (contributory negligence) and venturesomeness by the plaintiff (assumption of the risk) were treated as total defenses. It made no difference which label was used to describe the plaintiff's actions; either way the defendant was not liable. This allowed the courts to be somewhat vague about the contours of assumption of the risk. Furthermore, the doctrine was often invoked in cases in which the real ground of the decision seems to have been that the defendant was not negligent. This, too, made no difference because regardless of whether the defendant was not negligent, or whether the plaintiff had assumed the risk, recovery was barred.

For example, it was sometimes said that a spectator at a baseball game "assumed the risk" of being hit by foul balls and so could not recover from those putting on the game.

One might as well have said simply that it is not negligent to play baseball, despite the risk that people will be hurt. Sometimes the plaintiff's knowledge of a danger is relevant to the outcome not because it establishes an affirmative defense but because it shows that the defendant's actions were not unreasonably dangerous. Hitting baseballs in the direction of persons unaware that baseball is being played is negligent; hitting them where they may strike spectators who know what is happening is not. Is *Coleman* just a case of a defendant who was not negligent?

Today, with comparative negligence (or comparative fault) the law in nearly every jurisdiction, it may matter a great deal whether the plaintiff's conduct is labeled "negligence" or "assumption of the risk." This is true if, at least in some cases, assumption of the risk remains a complete defense to liability. Suppose, for instance, that a pedestrian in a hurry dashes across the street in front of a speeding car and is struck by the car. The pedestrian's conduct is negligence, which may reduce the recovery without necessarily eliminating it. The whole point of the comparative-negligence doctrine is to allow some plaintiffs who have acted dangerously to recover damages. Should it be possible to circumvent this policy by calling the plaintiff's conduct "assumption of the risk" and treating that as a total defense? It is almost inconceivable that a court today would deny the plaintiff any recovery by saying that the plaintiff had "assumed the risk."

If negligent assumption of the risk is treated as only a partial defense under comparative principles, how then should *reasonable* assumption of the risk be treated (*e.g.*, a plaintiff injured while entering a building set afire by the defendant's negligence in order to rescue someone)? Presumably, no worse; after all, the latter actor, unlike the former, behaved reasonably.

The discussion above may suggest that the whole notion of assumption of the risk should be abandoned, and in cases in which courts purport to apply that doctrine when all they mean is that the plaintiff was negligent or the defendant was not, abandonment of the doctrine would promote clarity. There are, however, some cases in which the plaintiff's willingness to submit to a risk, whether negligent or not, should preclude any recovery. The principle involved in these cases is freedom of contract: if a plaintiff expressly, or by implication, agrees to run a risk in exchange for getting something from the defendant, the agreement should be enforced, absent some imperfection such as unconscionability, fraud by the defendant, or some other "public policy" making the agreement unenforceable. These situations are examined in the materials that follow.

2. *See generally* Stephen D. Sugarman, *Assumption of Risk*, 31 Valparaiso L. Rev. 833 (1997).

3. *Assumption of the Risk under Comparative Principles.* As *Coleman* indicates, there are at least three different categories of assumption of the risk: (1) express assumption of risk, (2) primary implied assumption of risk, and (3) secondary implied assumption of risk. Most states agree that after the adoption of comparative principles, categories (1) and (2) still fully bar liability, and category (3) is a partial defense that is treated the same as comparative negligence. *See, e.g.,* Anderson v. Ceccardi, 451 N.E.2d 780 (Ohio 1983).

The materials that follow explore these three categories of "assumption of the risk." They should be read with two questions constantly in mind: (1) Are decisions finding that assumption of the risk is not a defense saying anything more than that the plaintiff was not negligent? (2) Are decisions holding that assumption of the risk is a defense saying anything more than that the plaintiff was negligent or that the defendant was not?

Jacob D. Fuchsberg

2. Express Assumption of the Risk

Gross v. Sweet
Court of Appeals of New York
400 N.E.2d 306 (N.Y. 1979)

FUCHSBERG, Judge.

. . . .

Plaintiff Bruce Gross, wishing to learn how to parachute, enrolled in the Stormville Parachute Center Training School, a facility owned and operated by the defendant William Sweet.... [Despite his having informed defendant that several years earlier an orthopedic pin had been inserted into his leg, he was accepted as a student.] As a prerequisite for admission into the course, Gross had to pay a fee and sign a form entitled "Responsibility Release." He was then given the standard introductory lesson, which consisted of approximately one hour of on-land training, including oral instruction as well as several jumps off a two and a half foot table. Plaintiff then was equipped with a parachute and flown to an altitude of 2,800 feet for his first practice jump. Upon coming in contact with the ground on his descent, plaintiff suffered serious personal injuries.

The suit is grounded on negligence, breach of warranty and gross negligence. In the main, plaintiff claims that defendant failed to provide adequate training and safe equipment, violated certain rules and procedures promulgated by the Federal Aviation Administration governing the conduct of parachute jumping schools and failed to warn him sufficiently of the attendant dangers.

Defendant pleaded the release plaintiff had signed and moved for summary judgment, contending that the terms of the release exculpated the defendant from any liability....

....Special Term granted defendant's motion....On plaintiff's appeal from that order, a divided Appellate Division reversed, reinstated the complaint and granted plaintiff's motion to dismiss the affirmative defense....

We begin with the proposition, too well settled to invoke any dispute, that the law frowns upon contracts intended to exculpate a party from the consequences of his own negligence and though, with certain exceptions, they are enforceable, such agreements are subject to close judicial scrutiny. [Citations.] To the extent that agreements purport to grant exemption for liability for willful or grossly negligent acts they have been viewed as wholly void (*see* Restatement, Contracts, §575, 15 Williston, Contracts [3d Jaeger ed.], §1750A, p. 141; [citations]). And so, here, so much of plaintiff's complaint as contains allegations that defendant was grossly negligent, may not be barred by the release in any event. But we need not explore further this possibility for we conclude the complaint in its entirety withstands the exculpatory agreement.

Nor need we consider plaintiff's request that we ignore the release on the grounds that the special relationship of the parties and the public interest involved forbids its enforcement. While we have, for example, had occasion to invalidate such provisions when they were contained in the contract between a passenger and a common carrier [citation], or in a contract between a customer and a public utility under a duty to furnish telephone service [citation] or when imposed by an employer as a condition of employment [citation], the circumstances here do not fit within any of these relationships. And, though we note that a recent statute renders void agreements purporting to exempt from liability for negligence those engaged in a variety of businesses that serve the public (*e.g.*, landlords [General Obligations Law, §5-321]; caterers [§5-322]; building service or maintenance contractors [§5-323]; those who maintain garages or parking garages [§5-325]; or pools, gymnasiums or places of public amusement or recreation [§5-326]), defendant's occupation does not fall within any of these classes either. We also decline, at this point, plaintiff's invitation that we proceed further to consider what effect, if any, the alleged contravention of federal regulations may have on the relationship of the parties or the public interest involved. Such questions need not be reached....

As the cases make clear, the law's reluctance to enforce exculpatory provisions of this nature has resulted in the development of an exacting standard by which courts measure their validity. So, it has been repeatedly emphasized that unless the intention of the parties is expressed in unmistakable language, an exculpatory clause will not be deemed to insulate a party from liability for his own negligent acts. [Citations.] Put another way, it must appear plainly and precisely that the "limitation of liability extends to negligence or other fault of the party attempting to shed his ordinary responsibility" [citation].

Not only does this stringent standard require that the drafter of such an agreement make its terms unambiguous, but it mandates that the terms be understandable as well. Thus, a provision that would exempt its drafter from any liability occasioned by his fault should not compel resort to a magnifying glass and lexicon. [Citation.] Of course, this does not imply that only simple or monosyllabic language can be used in such clauses. Rather, what the law demands is that such provisions be clear and coherent [citation].

By and large, if such is the intention of the parties, the fairest course is to provide explicitly that claims based on negligence are included (*see* Ciofalo v. Vic Tanney Gyms, 177 N.E.2d p. 926 [plaintiff "agreed to assume full responsibility for any injuries which might occur to her in or about defendant's premises, 'including but without limitation, any claims for personal injuries resulting from or arising out of the negligence of' the defendant"]). That does not mean that the word "negligence" must be employed for courts to give effect to an exculpatory agreement; however, words conveying a similar import must appear (*see* Theroux v. Kedenburg Racing Assn., 50 Misc. 2d 97, 99, 269 N.Y.S.2d 789, 792, *aff'd*, 28 A.D.2d 960, 282 N.Y.S.2d 930 [agreement provided for release of liability for any injury "regardless of how such injury... may arise, and regardless of who is at fault...and even if the loss is caused by the neglect or fault of" the defendant]).

We are, of course, cognizant of the fact that the general rule of strict judicial construction has been somewhat liberalized in its application to exoneration clauses in indemnification agreements, which are usually "negotiated at arm's length between...sophisticated business entities" and which can be viewed as merely "allocating the risk of liability to third parties between themselves, essentially through the employment of insurance" [citations]. In such cases, the law, reflecting the economic realities, will recognize an agreement to relieve one party from the consequences of his negligence on the strength of a broadly worded clause framed in less precise language than would normally be required, though even then it must evince the "unmistakable intent of the parties" [citations].

The case before us today obviously does not fit within this exception to the strict legal standard generally employed by the courts of this State under which exculpatory provisions drawn in broad and sweeping language have not been given effect. For example, agreements to release from "any and all responsibility or liability of any nature whatsoever for any loss of property or personal injury occurring on this trip" [citation] or to "waive claim for any loss to personal property, or for any personal injury while a member of [a] club" [citation] have not barred claims based on negligence (*see* Bernstein v. Seacliff Beach Club, 35 Misc. 2d 153, 228 N.Y.S.2d 567). Moreover, in Boll v. Sharp & Dohme (281 App. Div. 568, 121 N.Y.S.2d 20, *aff'd*, 307 N.Y. 646, 120 N.E.2d 836, *supra*), we held not sufficiently unambiguous a release form in which a blood donor was required to agree that defendants were not "in any way responsible for any consequences...resulting from the giving of such blood or from any of the tests, examinations or procedures incident thereto," and further "release[d] and discharge[d] more [defendants] from all claims and demands whatsoever...against them or any of them by reason of any matter relative or incident to such donation of blood." (307 N.Y. p. 647.) The donor was thus allowed to sue in negligence for injuries he sustained when, on the completion of the blood donation, he fainted and fell to the floor.

With all this as background, the language of the "Responsibility Release" in the case before us must be viewed as no more explicit than that in *Boll*. In its entirety, it reads: "I, the undersigned, hereby, and by these covenants, do waive any and all claims that I, my heirs, and/or assignees may have against Nathaniel Sweet, the Stormville Parachute Center, the Jumpmaster and the Pilot who shall operate the aircraft when used for the purpose of parachute jumping for any personal injuries or property damage that I may sustain or which may arise out of my learning, practicing or actually jumping from an aircraft. I also assume full responsibility for any damage that I may do or cause while participating in this sport."

Assuming that this language alerted the plaintiff to the dangers inherent in parachute jumping and that he entered into the sport with apprehension of the risks, it does not follow that he was aware of, much less intended to accept, any *enhanced* exposure to injury occasioned by the carelessness of the very persons on which he depended for his safety. Specifically, the release nowhere expresses any intention to exempt the defendant from liability for injury or property damages which may result from his failure to use due care either in his training methods or in his furnishing safe equipment. Thus, whether on a running reading or a careful analysis, the agreement could most reasonably be taken merely as driving home the fact that the defendant was not to bear any responsibility for injuries that ordinarily and inevitably would occur, without any fault of the defendant, to those who participate in such a physically demanding sport.

In short, instead of specifying to prospective students that they would have to abide any consequences attributable to the instructor's own carelessness, the defendant seems to have preferred the use of opaque terminology rather than suffer the possibility of lower enrollment. But, while, with exceptions not pertinent to this case, the law grudgingly accepts the proposition that men may contract away their liability for negligently caused injuries, they may do so only on the condition that their intention be expressed clearly and in "unequivocal terms" [citation].

Accordingly,…the order of the Appellate Division reversing the grant of summary judgment, reinstating the complaint and dismissing the defense based on the release should be affirmed.

JONES, Judge (dissenting).

....

…[C]ontracts should not be so construed as to make them meaningless and the intent of the parties is to be drawn from the entire instrument, not from the presence or absence of a particular talismanic word or term.…

.…The release…, if construed as not including claims predicated on negligence, releases nothing and is meaningless and a nullity. A more broadly worded exoneration provision would be difficult to imagine.…[C]laims such as the present ones based on ordinary negligence appear to me to be precisely the claims intended by the parties to be included in the language "any and all claims…for any personal injuries or property damage that I may sustain or which may arise out of my learning, practicing or actually jumping from an aircraft."

.…Except as to the cause of action predicated on the alleged claim of gross negligence, I would therefore reverse the order of the Appellate Division.…

COOKE, C.J., and GABRIELLI and WACHTLER, JJ., concur with FUCHSBERG, J.

JONES, J., dissents and votes to reverse in a separate opinion in which JASEN and MEYER, JJ. concur.

Notes

1. *The "Express Negligence Doctrine." See also* Hyson v. White Water Mt. Resorts, 829 A.2d 827 (Conn. 2003) (holding, in a case in which a woman's snowtube went over a cliff at a point where there was no barrier, that a signed release consenting to inherent risks did not bar an action for negligence because an agreement purporting to release or indemnify another prospectively may not be applied to damages arising from that party's negligence in the absence of express language to that effect).

Some courts refer to the rule that a valid pre-accident release must focus the plaintiff's attention on negligence as the "express negligence doctrine." *See* Ethyl Corp. v. Daniel Constr. Co., 725 S.W.2d 705, 706 (Tex. 1987) (holding that the intent of the parties to exculpate the indemnitee from the consequences of its negligence must be specifically stated within the four corners of the contract).

2. ***Strict Construction of Releases.*** Even if a release uses the word "negligence," it may not survive scrutiny by a court. Turnbough v. Ladner, 754 So. 2d 467 (Miss. 1999), involved a negligence claim based on injuries sustained by a scuba-diving student due to the poor planning of a dive by an instructor. The court held that a pre-printed release, which stated that the plaintiff had been thoroughly informed about the risks of decompression sickness and waived liability for injuries resulting from negligence, did not bar an action for harm caused by the instructor's failure to follow basic guidelines. The court wrote:

> The wording of an exculpatory agreement should express as clearly and precisely as possible the *extent* to which a party intends to be absolved from liability. [Citations.] Failing that, we do not sanction broad, general "waiver of negligence" provisions, and strictly construe them against the party asserting them as a defense.

Could any release meeting the *Turnbough* court's standard be drafted?

3. ***Releases Void as against Public Policy.*** In Winterstein v. Wilcom, 293 A.2d 821 (Md. Ct. Spec. App. 1972), the plaintiff, upon entering a race track to compete in the events, signed a release agreeing not to hold the track liable for harm "due to negligence or any other fault." During the race, plaintiff was injured when his car struck a part that had fallen off of another car. In holding that an action against the track for negligence was barred by the release, the court rejected the plaintiff's argument that the agreement violated public policy, saying:

> In Tunkl v. Regents of the University of California,...[383 P.2d 441 (Cal. 1963), the court...] found that "...[The] attempted but invalid exemption involves a transaction which exhibits some or all of the following characteristics. It concerns a business of a type generally thought suitable for public regulation. The party seeking exculpation is engaged in performing a service of great importance to the public, which is often a matter of practical necessity for some members of the public. The party holds himself out as willing to perform this service for any member of the public who seeks it, or at least for any member coming within certain established standards. As a result of the essential nature of the service, in the economic setting of the transaction, the party invoking exculpation possesses a decisive advantage of bargaining strength against any member of the public who seeks his services. In exercising a superior bargaining power the party confronts the public with a standardized adhesion contract of exculpation, and makes no provision whereby a purchaser may pay additional reasonable fees and obtain protection against negligence. Finally, as a result of the transaction, the person or property of the purchaser is placed under the control of the seller, subject to the risk of carelessness by the seller or his agents." [Citation.]

> We note a further refinement. Although the traditional view has been that where the defendant's negligence consists of the violation of a statute, the plaintiff may still assume the risk, there is a growing tendency to the contrary where a safety statute enacted for the protection of the public is violated. The rationale is that the obligation and the right so created are public ones which it is not within the power of any private individual to waive. [Citations.]

In *Winterstein*, the court found it particularly significant that car racing is not an "essential" activity and is not heavily regulated by the state. *See also* Rose v. National Tractor Pullers Ass'n, Inc., 33 F. Supp. 2d 757 (D. Wis. 1998) (a release and waiver of liability signed by a participant in a tractor pull competition was a valid exculpatory contract because the agreement clearly and unambiguously informed the participant that he intended to waive all claims and was limited to a single event on a single day and to occurrences within a restricted area not accessible to general public; the defendant did not engage in reckless conduct, and thereby defeat operation of the exculpatory contract by, at worst, not pursuing safety issues associated with seat belts, roll bars and the risk of rollovers as aggressively as it should have).

However, in Dalury v. S-K-I, Ltd., 670 A.2d 795 (Vt. 1995), the court held that an exculpatory agreement printed on a form signed by the plaintiff, which purported to release the ski area from "any and all liability for personal injury or property damage resulting from negligence, conditions of the premises, operations of the ski area, actions or omissions of employees or agents of the ski area or from my participation in skiing at the area," was void as contrary to public policy.

> Defendants urge us to uphold the exculpatory agreement on the ground that ski resorts do not provide an essential public service. They argue that they owe no duty to plaintiff to permit him to use their private lands for skiing, and that the terms and conditions of entry ought to be left entirely within their control. Because skiing, like other recreational sports, is not a necessity of life, defendants contend that the sale of a lift ticket is a purely private matter, implicating no public interest. [Citation.] We disagree.

> .... The defendants' area is a facility open to the public. They advertise and invite skiers and nonskiers of every level of skiing ability to their premises for the price of a ticket.... Thousands of people ride lifts, buy services, and ski the trails. Each ticket sale may be, for some purposes, a purely private transaction. But when a substantial number of such sales take place as a result of the seller's general invitation to the public to utilize the facilities and services in question, a legitimate public interest arises.

> The major public policy implications are those underlying the law of premises liability....

> The policy rationale is to place responsibility for maintenance of the land on those who own or control it, with the ultimate goal of keeping accidents to the minimum level possible. Defendants, not recreational skiers, have the expertise and opportunity to foresee and control hazards, and to guard against the negligence of their agents and employees. They alone can properly maintain and inspect their premises, and train their employees in risk management. They alone can insure against risks and effectively spread the cost of insurance among their thousands of customers. Skiers, on the other hand, are not in a position to discover and correct risks of harm, and they cannot insure against the ski area's negligence.

> If defendants were permitted to obtain broad waivers of their liability, an important incentive for ski areas to manage risk would be removed with the public bearing the cost of the resulting injuries....

In the medical context, "increasingly, courts are declining to bind complaining patients to the terms of release forms." Martin E. Segal, *Poor Prognosis*, A.B.A. J., Aug. 1997, at 74.

See also Berlangieri v. Running Elk Corp., 76 P.3d 1098 (N.M. 2003) (holding that although a liability release executed by a patron clearly expressed the parties' intention that the patron would not hold the lodge liable for its negligent acts, the release was affected by the public interest as expressed in the Equine Liability Act and was unenforceable against a patron who was injured while horseback riding; the lodge was a business open to the public, did not require patrons to be experienced horseback riders, did not offer the patron a way to purchase additional protection for injuries caused by its employees, and the patron was a novice rider who could not verify that his saddle was mounted properly); Murphy v. North American River Runners, Inc., 412 S.E.2d 504 (W. Va. 1991)(to the extent that an anticipatory release purported to exempt the defendant from tort liability for failure of its whitewater river guide to conform to the statutory standard of care, the release was unenforceable); Richards v. Richards, 513 N.W.2d 118 (Wis. 1994) (a standard form exculpatory contract between a truck driver's employer and the driver's wife that released the employer's liability so that the wife could be a truck passenger was void as against public policy; the contract purported to be a "passenger authorization," did not conspicuously indicate that it would function as a release, was extremely broad, excused intentional, reckless, and negligent conduct by the employer and others, and was not limited to specified time period or vehicle); Chan v. Society Expeditions, Inc., 123 F.3d 1287 (9th Cir. 1997) (contractual provisions relieving the carrier of liability to a cruise ship passenger for injuries occurring while in a tender or launch operating between the ship and shore are void); Kyriazis v. Univ. of West Va., 450 S.E.2d 649 (W. Va. 1994) (anticipatory release that state university students were required to sign as a condition of participating in club sports was against public policy).

4. ***Releases Upheld.*** *Gross* and the cases discussed in the preceding notes illustrate the reluctance of many judges to uphold pre-accident releases. Nevertheless, many courts do uphold releases, especially in cases involving participants in sporting events. If a release is clearly written, if the court is confident that the plaintiff understood what was being signed, and especially if the plaintiff has had some previous experience with the activity, the release may be given effect. An example is Harris v. Walker, 519 N.E.2d 917 (Ill. 1988), a negligence action by a rider who was thrown from a rented horse. Observing that the risk of being thrown from a horse was obvious and that the plaintiff had read and understood the release before signing it, the court ruled that the release, like any other contract, was enforceable. *See also* Clanton v. United Skates of Am., 686 N.E.2d 896 (Ind. App. 1997) (roller skating), in which the plaintiff's awareness of the meaning of the releases he signed every time he skated was shown by his having signed many of the releases under a false name.

Garretson v. United States, 456 F.2d 1017 (9th Cir. 1972), was a negligence action by an injured skier against the owner of the land on which he was skiing, the sponsors of the event in which he was participating, and the event's officials, who had, he alleged, allowed him to ski in unsafe weather conditions. In holding that the release Garretson had signed barred the action, the court pointed out that the language of the release was clear and that Garretson had read and understood it. It found no "public policy" against enforcing the release as a contract. Cases involving releases buried in fine print were distinguishable.

A signed release may be valid even if the plaintiff claims not to have read it. *See* Chauvlier v. Booth Creek Ski Holdings, Inc., 35 P.3d 383 (Wash. Ct. App. 2001) (holding that a release signed by a skier was valid because it was clear and conspicuous and there was no rush to sign it).

5. *Parental Waiver of a Child's Cause of Action.* Compare *Gross* with Scott v. Pacific W. Mt. Resort, 834 P.2d 6 (Wash. 1992). The plaintiff's parents signed a ski school release for their son. The release provided:

> I hereby hold harmless [the ski school and its owner] and any instructor or chaperon from all claims arising out of the instruction of skiing or in transit to or from the ski area. I accept full responsibility for the cost of treatment for any injury suffered while taking part in the program.

Although the language was found to be sufficiently clear to release a claim for negligence, the agreement was void as against public policy because a parent does not have legal authority to waive a child's future cause of action for injuries resulting from a third party's negligence. Consistent with "[n]umerous cases in other jurisdictions," the court reasoned that "[s]ince a parent generally may not release a child's cause of action after injury [without court approval], it makes little, if any, sense to conclude a parent has the authority to release a child's cause of action prior to an injury."

See also Hawkins v. Peart, 37 P.3d 1062 (Utah 2002) (holding a parent's release of a child's claims for negligence void and stating that a related provision, whereby the parent agreed to indemnify the defendant, created an unacceptable conflict of interest between the mother and the child, and was therefore void); Cooper v. Aspen Skiing Co., 48 P.3d 1229 (Colo. 2002) (similar).

In Grimes v. Kennedy Krieger Institute, Inc., 782 A.2d 807 (Md. 2001), the court observed that with respect to nontherapeutic research using minors' "consent to research has been virtually unanalyzed by courts and legislatures." The court held, in a suit involving a study of the effectiveness of lead paint abatement procedures, that a parent cannot consent to the participation of a child in nontherapeutic research if there is any risk of injury or damage to the health of the child.

6. *Ethics in Law Practice: Agreements Limiting Malpractice Liability.* Can a lawyer include a provision in a retainer agreement whereby the client forfeits any right to sue for malpractice? Almost never. Rule 1.8(h) of the Model Rules of Professional Conduct (2003) provides:

> A lawyer shall not:
>
> > (1) make an agreement prospectively limiting the lawyer's liability to a client for malpractice unless the client is independently represented in making the agreement; or
> >
> > (2) settle a claim or potential claim for such liability with an unrepresented client or former client unless that person is advised in writing of the desirability of seeking and is given a reasonable opportunity to seek the advice of independent legal counsel in connection therewith.

An attorney who violates this rule is subject to reprimand, suspension, disbarment, and other sanctions.

3. Primary Implied Assumption of the Risk

Turcotte v. Fell

Court of Appeals of New York
502 N.E.2d 964 (N.Y. 1986)

SIMONS, Judge.

. . . .

Plaintiff Ronald J. Turcotte is a former jockey. Before his injury he had ridden over 22,000 races in his 17-year career and achieved international fame as the jockey aboard "Secretariat" when that horse won the "Triple Crown" races in 1973. On July 13, 1978 plaintiff was injured while riding in the eighth race at Belmont Park, a racetrack owned and operated by defendant New York Racing Association (NYRA). Plaintiff had been assigned the third pole position for the race on a horse named "Flag of Leyte Gulf." Defendant jockey Jeffrey Fell was in the second pole position riding "Small Raja," a horse owned by defendant David P. Reynolds. On the other side of plaintiff, in the fourth position, was the horse "Walter Malone." Seconds after the race began, Turcotte's horse clipped the heels of "Walter Malone" and then tripped and fell, propelling plaintiff to the ground and causing him severe personal injuries which left him a paraplegic.

Plaintiffs, husband and wife, commenced this action against Jeffrey Fell, David P. Reynolds, NYRA and others no longer before the court. . . . [T]hey charge that Fell is liable to them because guilty of common-law negligence and of violating the rules of the New York Racing and Wagering Board regulating "foul riding," that Reynolds is liable for Fell's negligence under the doctrine of *respondeat superior*, and that defendant NYRA is liable because it "negligently failed to water and groom that portion of the racetrack near the starting gate or watered and groomed the same in an improper and careless manner" causing it to be unsafe.

Special Term granted the motions of Fell and Reynolds for summary judgment, holding that Turcotte, by engaging in the sport of horse racing, relieved other participants of any duty of reasonable care with respect to known dangers or risks which inhere in that activity. . . . NYRA subsequently moved for summary judgment and Special Term denied its motion because it found there were questions of fact concerning NYRA's negligent maintenance of the track. On separate appeals, the Appellate Division affirmed, with one Justice dissenting from the order denying NYRA's motion for summary judgment. . . .

It is fundamental that to recover in a negligence action a plaintiff must establish that the defendant owed him a duty to use reasonable care. . . . [W]hile the determination of the existence of a duty and the concomitant scope of that duty involve a consideration not only of the wrongfulness of the defendant's action or inaction, they also necessitate an examination of plaintiff's reasonable expectations of the care owed him by others. This is particularly true in professional sporting contests, which by their nature involve an elevated degree of danger. If a participant makes an informed estimate of the risks involved in the activity and willingly undertakes them, then there can be no liability if he is injured as a result of those risks.

Traditionally, the participant's conduct was conveniently analyzed in terms of the defensive doctrine of assumption of risk. With the enactment of the comparative negligence statute, however, assumption of risk is no longer an absolute defense [citation]. Thus, it has become necessary, and quite proper, when measuring a defendant's duty to a plaintiff to consider the risks assumed by the plaintiff [citations]. The shift in analysis is proper because the "doctrine [of assumption of risk] deserves no separate existence (except for *express* assumption of risk) and is simply a confusing way of stating certain no-duty rules" [citation]....

The risk assumed has been defined a number of ways but in its most basic sense it "means that the plaintiff, in advance, has given his...consent to relieve the defendant of an obligation of conduct toward him, and to take his chances of injury from a known risk arising from what the defendant is to do or leave undone. The situation is then the same as where the plaintiff consents to the infliction of what would otherwise be an intentional tort, except that the consent is to run the risk of unintended injury....The result is that the defendant is relieved of legal duty to the plaintiff; and being under no duty, he cannot be charged with negligence" [citations].

The doctrine has been divided into several categories but as the term applies to sporting events it involves what commentators call "primary" assumption of risk. Risks in this category are incidental to a relationship of free association between the defendant and the plaintiff in the sense that either party is perfectly free to engage in the activity or not as he wishes. Defendant's duty under such circumstances is a duty to exercise care to make the conditions as safe as they appear to be. If the risks of the activity are fully comprehended or perfectly obvious, plaintiff has consented to them and defendant has performed its duty [citations]. Plaintiff's "consent" is not constructive consent; it is actual consent implied from the act of the electing to participate in the activity [citation]. When thus analyzed and applied, assumption of risk is not an absolute defense but a measure of the defendant's duty of care and thus survives the enactment of the comparative-fault statute [citations].

....It would be a rare thing, indeed, if the election of a professional athlete to participate in a sport at which he makes his living could be said to be involuntary. Plaintiff's participation certainly was not involuntary in this case and thus we are concerned only with the scope of his consent.

....Some "of the restraints of civilization must accompany every athlete onto the playing field"....[P]articipants do not consent to acts which are reckless or intentional [citations].

Whether a professional athlete should be held...to have consented to the act or omission of a co-participant which caused his injury involves consideration of a variety of factors including but not limited to: the ultimate purpose of the game and the method or methods of winning it; the relationship of defendant's conduct to the game's ultimate purpose, especially his conduct with respect to rules and customs whose purpose is to enhance the safety of the participants; and the equipment or animals involved in the playing of the game. The question of whether the consent was an informed one includes consideration of the participant's knowledge and experience in the activity generally. Manifestly a professional athlete is more aware of the dangers of the activity, and presumably more willing to accept them in exchange for a salary, than is an amateur.

In this case plaintiff testified before trial to facts establishing that horse racing is a dangerous activity....Plaintiff testified that every professional jockey had experiences when he was not able to keep a horse running on a straight line, or a horse would veer, or jump up on its hind legs, or go faster or slower than the jockey indicated. He further acknowledged that horses in a race do not run in prescribed lanes and it is lawful, under the rules of racing, for horses to move out of their starting lane to other parts of the track provided that the horse does not interfere with other horses when doing so. Indeed, during the course of a race, speeding horses lawfully and properly come within inches of other horses and frequently bump each other. Turcotte conceded that there is a fine line between what is lawful and unlawful in the movement of a horse on the track....Such dangers are inherent in the sport. Because they are recognized as such by plaintiff, the courts below properly held that he consented to relieve defendant Jeffrey Fell of the legal duty to use reasonable care to avoid crossing into his lane of travel.

Plaintiffs nonetheless contend that Fell's alleged violation of 9 NYCRR 4035.2, which prohibits foul riding, is sufficient to sustain their complaint. They assert that the rule is a safety rule and that a participant does not accept or consent to the violation of the rules of a game even though the violation is foreseeable. They rely principally on Hackbart v. Cincinnati Bengals, 601 F.2d 516 [(10th Cir. 1979)], in which the plaintiff was injured when intentionally struck in the neck from behind by an opposing football player after the play was over, and Nabozny v. Barnhill, 31 Ill. App.3d 212, 334 N.E.2d 258 [(1975)], in which the plaintiff, playing goal tender in a high school soccer match, was injured after picking up the ball in a free kick zone when kicked in the head by player on an opposing team (see also, Restatement [Second] of Torts §50 comment b).

The rules of the sport, however, do not necessarily limit the scope of the professional's consent. Although the foul riding rule is a safety measure, it is not by its terms absolute for it establishes a spectrum of conduct and penalties, depending on whether the violation is careless or willful and whether the contact was the result of mutual fault. As the rule recognizes, bumping and jostling are normal incidents of the sport. They are not, as were the blows in *Nabozny* and *Hackbart*, flagrant infractions unrelated to the normal method of playing the game and done without any competitive purpose. Plaintiff does not claim that Fell intentionally or recklessly bumped him, he claims only that as a result of carelessness, Fell failed to control his mount as the horses raced for the lead and a preferred position on the track. While a participant's "consent" to join in a sporting activity is not a waiver of all rules infractions, nonetheless a professional clearly understands the usual incidents of competition resulting from carelessness, particularly those which result from the customarily accepted method of playing the sport, and accepts them. They are within the known, apparent and foreseeable dangers of the sport and not actionable and thus plaintiffs' complaint against defendant Fell was properly dismissed.

....

...[T]he dismissal of the complaint against Fell...mandates dismissal of the complaint against the employer [citations].

The complaint against NYRA should also be dismissed....

NYRA's duty to plaintiff is similarly measured by his position and purpose for being on the track on July 13 and the risks he accepted by being there....

Plaintiffs charge that NYRA was negligent in failing to water the "chute," which leads to the main track, and "overwatering" the main track. Thus, they claim the horses had to run from the dry surface of the chute onto the overly watered, unsafe "cuppy" surface of the main track.[2] Plaintiff testified, however, that "cupping" conditions are common on racetracks and that he had experienced them before at Belmont Park and also at many other tracks. Indeed, he testified that he had never ridden on a track where he had not

---

2. "Cuppiness" is the tendency of wet track surface to stick to the underside of a horse's hoof within the shoe.

observed a cupping condition at one time or another. Thus, Turcotte's participation in three prior races at this same track on the day of his injury, his ability to observe the condition of the track before the eighth race and his general knowledge and experience with cupping conditions and their prevalence establish that he was well aware of these conditions and the possible dangers from them and that he accepted the risk.

. . . .

On the appeal by plaintiffs, order affirmed, etc.

On the appeal by defendant NYRA, order reversed, etc.

Notes

1. *Assumption of the Risk and Athletic Injuries.* As noted previously, spectators at athletic events have sometimes been held to have assumed the risk of being struck by objects leaving the field. *See, e.g.,* Benedetto v. Travelers Ins. Co., 172 So. 2d 354 (La. Ct. App. 1965) (no liability in thrown-bat case). In other cases, those holding sporting events are said to have only a limited duty to provide screening. *See* Benejam v. Detroit Tigers, Inc., 635 N.W.2d 219 (Mich. Ct. App. 2001) (holding that a proprietor satisfied the "limited duty" to erect a screen that protected the most dangerous area of the spectator stands and provided a number of seats in that area sufficient to meet the ordinary demand for protected seats).

The assumption-of-risk line of reasoning has been followed in cases involving injuries to sports officials. *See, e.g.,* Wertheim v. U.S. Tennis Ass'n, Inc., 540 N.Y.S.2d 443 (App. Div. 1989) (umpire struck by a served tennis ball); Cuesta v. Immaculate Conception Roman Cath. Church, 562 N.Y.S.2d 537 (App. Div. 1990) (umpire struck by a baseball).

As for participants in athletic events, consider the Restatement, Second, of Torts §50 ("Apparent Consent") Comment b:

> Taking part in a game manifests a willingness to submit to such bodily contacts or restrictions of liberty as are permitted by its rules or usages. Participating in such a game does not manifest consent to contacts which are prohibited by rules or usages of the game if such rules or usages are designed to protect the participants and not merely to secure the better playing of the game as a test of skill. This is true although the player knows that those with or against whom he is playing are habitual violators of the rules.

How should an injury caused by an offside tackle or clipping in football be treated under this rule? *See id.* §50 Illus. 4-6. Is the Restatement position on habitual violators sound?

Some courts have expressly declined to follow the Restatement's analysis. For example, in Marchetti v. Kalash, 559 N.E.2d 699 (Ohio 1990), a girl broke her leg while playing "kick the can," and sued the playmate who, in violation of the rules, had knocked her down. The court held that individuals assume the ordinary risks inherent in recreational and sports activities and cannot recover for any injury unless it can be shown that the other participant's actions were reckless or intentional. *See also* Jaworski v. Kiernan, 696 A.2d 332 (Conn. 1997) (the only tort duty of a participant in a recreational soccer league was to refrain from reckless or intentional conduct, even though negligent conduct that caused plaintiff's injuries violated league rule); Moser v. Ratinoff, 130 Cal. Rptr. 2d 198 (Ct. App. 2003) (holding that primary assumption of the risk barred recovery for negligence by a participant in a group bicycle race, even though the defendant bicyclist violated statutes).

The great weight of authority on sporting injuries permits recovery only for reckless or intentional harm. *See, e.g.,* Cheong v. Antablin, 946 P.2d 817 (Cal. 1997) (a skier owes a duty to fellow skiers not to injure them intentionally or to act recklessly, but one skier may not sue another for simple negligence); Gyuriak v. Millice, 775 N.E.2d 391 (Ind. Ct. App. 2002) (golfer assumed the risk of being struck by a golf ball as a matter of law and therefore the defendant player did not owe him a duty of care with regard to his tee shot, which was not so reckless as to be totally outside the range of the ordinary activity involved in the sport); Gauvin v. Clark, 537 N.E.2d 94 (Mass. 1989) (college hockey player was not liable for injuries to the other team's player caused by his violation of a safety rule which prohibits "butt-ending" a player with a hockey stick, since the defendant did not act with reckless disregard of safety); Reddell v. Johnson, 942 P.2d 200 (Okla. 1997) (voluntary participants in BB gun "war" assumed risk of being shot in the eye, even though the rules of engagement prohibited aiming above the waist).

The policy underlying these cases is that:

> By eliminating liability for unintended accidents, the doctrine ensures that the fervor of athletic competition will not be chilled by the constant threat of litigation from every misstep, sharp turn, and sudden stop.

Stimson v. Carlson, 14 Cal. Rptr. 2d 670 (Ct. App. 1992) (holding that the risk of being struck by the boom is a fundamental part of sailing, and that failure to call out a course change did not amount to intentional or reckless conduct).

The same rule may apply to noncompetitive sports. *See* Ford v. Gouin, 834 P.2d 724 (Cal. 1992) (ski boat operator, who was at most negligent in steering the boat, was not liable to an injured water skier who was struck in the head by a limb extending over the channel).

In Allen v. Dover Co-Recreational Softball League, 807 A.2d 1274 (N.H. 2002), a woman was injured by an errant throw during a co-recreational slow-pitch tournament. The court declined to say that the defendant could be held liable only for reckless or intentional conduct. Rather, the court said, with respect to negligence, "the only duty the defendants had was not to act in an unreasonable manner that would increase or create a risk of injury outside the range of risks that flow from participation." In finding for the defendants, the court wrote in part:

> While the plaintiffs allege that promulgating and enforcing rules that required batting helmets, a larger, softer softball, or a certain male-female ratio would make the game safer, they do not allege that failing to promulgate and enforce such rules created risks outside the risks ordinarily involved in softball and made the game unreasonably dangerous. Consequently, the plaintiffs' writ does not allege facts that, if true, would show that the defendants breached the duty they owed....

See also Auckenthaler v. Grundmeyer, 877 P.2d 1039 (Nev. 1994) (holding that a negligence standard applied to an action by a horse rider for injuries sustained when another horse kicked her).

Stephen D. Sugarman, *Assumption of Risk*, 31 Valparaiso L. Rev. 833, 877-78 (1997), argues that the use of assumption of the risk to absolve defendants in cases involving sports is more appealing in cases involving organized—especially professional—sports than in informal games. Organized sports have their own ways of controlling misbehavior, and (especially for professionals) their own mechanisms for compensating the victims of injuries; the tort system is not needed so much there as in backyard touch-football games.

A case going quite far in denying recovery to a professional athlete is Maddox v. City of New York, 487 N.E.2d 553 (N.Y. 1985), holding that a professional baseball player who was injured when he slipped on a wet spot in the outfield could not recover against the builders and owners of the stadium even if they had negligently designed and operated the stadium's drainage system. The risks of the game, said the court, "include the risks involved in the construction of the field." Is this persuasive? Would a shopper injured in the collapse of the roof of a store be held to have assumed the risks of the design of the store building?

2. *Skier-Responsibility Laws.* Since the late 1970s, most states with substantial ski industries have enacted laws limiting the liability of a resort to an injured skier. These laws vary in length and substance, but often provide that a ski resort is not liable for injuries resulting from the inherent risks of skiing. For example:

42 Pennsylvania Cons. Stat. Ann. §7102
(Westlaw 2004)

(c) Downhill skiing.

    ....

(2) The doctrine of voluntary assumption of risk as it applies to downhill skiing injuries and damages is not modified by [Pennsylvania's comparative-negligence legislation].

Query: if state common law embraces the doctrine of primary assumption of risk, does it make any difference whether the state has enacted a skier-responsibility law?

A number of skier-responsibility statutes attempt to define inherent risks, at least in part. Thus, Montana law now includes within the risks of skiing: "variations in skiing terrain, including surface and subsurface snow or ice"; "bare spots"; "forest growth on designated trails"; "skiing in an area not designated as a ski trail"; "clearly visible or plainly marked improvements or equipment"; and "avalanches, except on open, designated ski trails." Mont. Code Ann. §23-2-736(4)(a)-(g) (Westlaw 2003). Some states require ski areas to post trail signs in prominent locations listing the inherent risks of skiing and notifying skiers of the operator's limited liability for injuries to skiers.

Skier-responsibility laws bar recovery in many cases. *See* Shukoski v. Indianhead Mt. Resort, Inc., 166 F.3d 848 (6th Cir. 1999) (Michigan act precluded recovery for snowboarder's injuries); Swenson v. Sunday River Skiway Corp., 79 F.3d 204 (1st Cir. 1996) (Maine act barred action for injury sustained while negotiating moguls that were not visible from above). *But see* Murray v. Great Gorge Resort, Inc., 823 A.2d 101 (N.J. Super. Ct. Law Div. 2003) (New Jersey act impliedly contemplates that a ski operator will inspect its slopes and trails, at least on a daily basis, and a fact issue as to whether the resort breached that duty precluded summary judgment).

In Hughes v. Seven Springs Farm, Inc., 762 A.2d 339 (Pa. 2000), the court held that a skier who was traversing an area at the bottom of the mountain toward the ski lift was engaged in "downhill skiing," and therefore could not recover for injuries sustained when struck by another skier, which was an inherent risk of skiing.

The enactment of skier-responsibility laws was the outgrowth of heavy lobbying by the ski industry in the wake of various developments, including the replacement of the traditional contributory negligence defense by comparative principles.

3. *Primary Assumption of the Risk in Employment.* In Hamilton v. Martinelli & Assoc., 2 Cal. Rptr. 3d. 168 (Ct. App. 2003), a probation corrections officer sued a training course business and its owner for negligence and intentional tort after she suffered neck and back injuries while performing a training maneuver during an unarmed defensive tactics course. The court held that the doctrine of primary assumption of risk barred the actions because the officer's injuries were an inherent risk of performing the training maneuver that caused the injuries, and the officer's employment duties, including restraining violent juvenile offenders, entailed the very risk of injury of which she complained.

Minnich v. Med-Waste, Inc.
Supreme Court of South Carolina
564 S.E.2d 98 (S.C. 2002)

Justice PLEICONES.

We accepted the following question on certification from the United States District Court:

> Does the Firefighter's Rule bar an emergency professional, such as a firefighter, police officer, or public safety officer, who is injured as a result of performing his or her duties, from recovering tort-based damages from the party whose negligence caused the injury?

....

The District Court made the following factual findings:

Jeffrey Minnich ("Plaintiff") was employed by the Medical University of South Carolina ("MUSC") as a public safety officer. While working in this capacity, Plaintiff assisted in loading medical waste from the premises of MUSC onto a tractor-trailer truck owned by Defendant Med-Waste, Inc. Plaintiff noticed the unoccupied truck begin to roll forward, toward a public street. Plaintiff ran to the truck, jumped inside, and stopped the truck.

Plaintiff alleges he suffered serious injuries, proximately caused by the acts or omissions of the defendants' employees, for which he seeks to recover damages. The defendants assert that Plaintiff's claims are barred by the firefighter's rule. The firefighter's rule is a common law doctrine that precludes a firefighter (and certain other public employees, including police officers) from recovering against a defendant whose negligence caused the firefighter's on-the-job injury.

....

While a number of states have adopted the firefighter's rule in some form,[3] there is no definitive pronouncement from this Court either adopting or rejecting the rule.

....

The common law firefighter's rule originated in the case of Gibson v. Leonard, 143 Ill. 182, 32 N.E. 182 (1892). There, the Illinois Supreme Court held that a firefighter who entered private property in the performance of his job duties was a licensee, and as such, the property owner owed the firefighter a duty only to "refrain from willful or affirmative acts which are injurious." [Citation.] Practically, this meant that a firefighter,

---

3. *See* Moody v. Delta Western, Inc., 38 P.3d 1139, 1140 n. 2 (Alaska 2002) (counting cases); Waggoner v. Troutman Oil Co., 320 Ark. 56, 894 S.W.2d 913, 914-15 (1995) (counting cases).

injured while fighting a blaze on private property, could not recover tort damages from the property owner whose ordinary negligence caused the fire.[4]

A number of courts reason that police officers and firefighters, aware of the risks inherent in their chosen profession, have assumed those risks. *See e.g.* Armstrong v. Mailand, 284 N.W.2d 343 (Minn.1979) (firefighter assumes all risks of the job); Berko v. Freda, 93 N.J. 81, 459 A.2d 663 (1983) (nature of police work requires officers to recognize inherent dangers; police officer assumes the risks of the job). As such, the firefighter or police officer should not be allowed to recover when injured as a result of confronting these known and accepted risks.

A third rationale advanced is public policy. The Supreme Court of Virginia, in Pearson v. Canada Contracting Co., 232 Va. 177, 349 S.E.2d 106, 111 (1986), cited two fundamental policies in support of that state's firefighter's rule: First, injuries to firemen and policemen are compensable through workers' compensation. It follows that liability for their on-the-job injuries is properly borne by the public rather than by individual property owners. Second, firemen and policemen, unlike invitees or licensees, enter at unforeseeable times and at areas not open to the public. In such situations, it is not reasonable to require the level of care that is owed to invitees or licensees.

Still other courts reason that the public fisc pays to train firefighters and police officers on the ways to confront dangerous situations, and compensates them for doing so. If these public employees were permitted to bring suit against the taxpayers whose negligence proximately caused injury, the negligent taxpayer would incur multiple penalties in exchange for the protection provided by firefighters and police officers. *See* Kreski v. Modern Wholesale Elec. Supply Co., 429 Mich. 347, 415 N.W.2d 178, 187 (1987).

    ....

Not only have courts been unable to agree on a consistent rationale for the rule, they have not been able to agree on the proper parameters for the rule. A number of courts which recognize the firefighter's rule as a viable defense to negligence claims allow recovery for willful and wanton conduct resulting in injury. As one court observed, "a tortfeasor who acts wilfully and wantonly is so culpable that the fireman's rule ought not to preclude the injured officer from suing the egregiously culpable wrongdoer." Miller v. Inglis, 223 Mich. App. 159, 567 N.W.2d 253, 256 (1997).

Courts have allowed police officers and firefighters to recover for injuries resulting from an act of negligence unrelated to the specific reason for which the officer or firefighter was originally summoned. As stated by the Supreme Court of New Jersey:

> The core of the "fireman's rule" is that a citizen's ordinary negligence that occasioned the presence of the public safety officer shall not give rise to liability in damages for the injuries sustained by the officer in the course of the response to duty.... The corollary of the rule is that independent and intervening negligent acts that injure the safety officer on duty are not insulated.

---

4. Those courts relying on premises liability principles to support their firefighter's rule found this rationale problematic. For instance, the Maryland Court of Appeals noted that a rule based on the premises liability theory could be applied only in the landowner context. Flowers v. Rock Creek Terrace Ltd. Partnership, 308 Md. 432, 520 A.2d 361, 366-67 (1987). The court further observed the legal anomaly resulting from a rule based on this rationale: other public employees, such as postmen and building inspectors—who often enter land pursuant to legal authority rather than express invitation of the landowner—were entitled to due care, while their counterparts in the fire and police departments were not. *Id.*

Wietecha v. Peoronard, 102 N.J. 591, 510 A.2d 19, 20-21 (1986) (citation omitted) (Police officers were injured while investigating a traffic accident when drivers negligently hit parked police cars; officers could pursue action against drivers whose negligence occurred subsequent to officers' presence at the scene). *See also* Terhell v. American Commonwealth Assoc., 172 Cal. App.3d 434, 218 Cal. Rptr. 256, 260 (1985) ("Having an unguarded hole in the roof was not the cause of [the firefighter's] presence at the scene, and the firefighter's rule has never been applied to negligence which did not cause the fire."). According to one commentator, all jurisdictions allow recovery under these circumstances. [Citation.]

More recently, a number of state legislatures have acted to limit or abolish the firefighter's rule. For instance, in 1987, only one year after the Virginia Supreme Court's decision in *Pearson, supra,* the Virginia legislature passed a statute providing that:

> An owner or occupant of real property containing premises normally open to the public shall, with respect to such premises, owe to firefighters…and law-enforcement officers who in the performance of their duties come upon that portion of the premises normally open to the public the duty to maintain the same in a reasonably safe condition or to warn of dangers thereon of which he knows or has reason to know, whether or not such premises are at the time open to the public.
>
> An owner or occupant of real property containing premises not normally open to the public shall, with respect to such premises, owe the same duty to firefighters…and law-enforcement officers who he knows or has reason to know are upon, about to come upon or imminently likely to come upon that portion of the premises not normally open to the public….

Va. Code Ann. §8.01-226 (Michie 2001). *See also* Cal. Civil Code § 1714.9 (West 2001) (allowing police officers and firefighters to recover where negligence occurred after negligent party knew of officer's or firefighter's presence, or where negligent act or omission violated statute, or was independent of reason officer or firefighter was summoned); Nev. Rev. Stat. Ann. §41.139 (Lexis L. Publg. 2001) (firefighter or police officer may maintain action for injuries suffered as a result of another's willful acts, as well as for negligent acts occurring after the person who caused the injury knew or should have known of the police officer's or firefighter's presence).

Effectively, the State of New York has statutorily abolished the firefighter's rule…. N.Y. General Obligation Law §11-106 (McKinney 2001). While the New York statute forecloses a tort action against a co-worker or an employer, it virtually eliminates the firefighter's rule as it pertains to all other third-party tortfeasors, and allows police officers and firefighters to recover for ordinary negligence.

New Jersey similarly limits the scope of the firefighter's rule by statute. *See* N.J. Stat. Ann. §2A:62A-21 (West 2001) (whenever any law enforcement officer or firefighter suffers injury while in the discharge of his official duties and that injury is the result of the neglect, wilful omission, or wilful or culpable conduct of any person or entity, other than that law enforcement officer's or firefighter's employer or co-employee, the injured law enforcement officer or firefighter may seek recovery from the person or entity whose neglect, wilful omission, or wilful or culpable conduct resulted in that injury). *See also* Minn. Stat. Ann. §604.06 (West 2001) (the fireman's rule shall not operate to deny any peace officer or public safety officer a recovery in *any action at law* or authorized by statute); Fla. Stat. Ann. §112.182 (West 2001) (common-law firefighter's rule abolished).

. . . .

...[T]hose jurisdictions which have adopted the firefighter's rule offer no uniform justification therefor, nor do they agree on a consistent application of the rule. The legislatures in many jurisdictions which adhere to the rule have found it necessary to modify or abolish the rule. The rule is riddled with exceptions, and criticism of the rule abounds.

Against this backdrop, we answer the certified question in the negative. South Carolina has never recognized the firefighter's rule, and we find it is not part of this state's common law. [Citation.] In our view, the tort law of this state adequately addresses negligence claims brought against non-employer tortfeasors arising out of injuries incurred by firefighters and police officers during the discharge of their duties....The more sound public policy...is to decline to promulgate a rule singling out police officers and firefighters for discriminatory treatment.

TOAL, C.J., MOORE, WALLER and BURNETT, JJ., concur.

Notes

1. *Negligence Liability to Professional Rescuers.* As the principal case suggests, professional rescuers, such as paid firefighters and police officers, have sometimes been treated differently than amateurs. Under the "firefighter's rule," a professional cannot recover from one who negligently creates a crisis for injuries sustained while responding to that crisis.

2. *Policy Basis.* The policy basis for the rule is not entirely clear. It has been suggested that allowing recovery by professional rescuers would subject merely negligent actors to disproportionate liability and would unnecessarily burden the courts with numerous suits involving complex issues. This may sometimes be true, for the fault that gives rise to a fire or other emergency is often trivial. Furthermore, cases involving injuries to professional rescuers may present difficult problems of proof. Yet these conditions do not always obtain, and their presence in some cases hardly justifies overlooking contrary facts. Difficult issues are regularly tried in the courts; absent compelling reasons, the courthouse doors should not be closed to an entire class of cases because some of those disputes may involve hard questions. In matters of proportionality, the preferable course is to examine the facts of each case, not to generalize. However, the firefighter's rule entirely forecloses case-by-case inquiries.

It has also been suggested that the rule is necessary to avoid placing an undue burden on land occupiers to keep their premises safe for the unpredictable entry of firefighters. But because the absence of the rule would result not in strict liability, but only in a duty of reasonable care, this argument is not compelling.

More persuasive is the "consent" rationale. Under this view, the professional is not permitted to recover for injuries caused by risks inherent in a voluntarily chosen profession. *Volenti non fit injuria*—to one who is willing no wrong is done. This principle has ancient lineage, and it runs throughout all of tort law.

Principles of fair and efficient loss allocation have occasionally been invoked to support the firefighter's rule. The courts have reasoned that the costs of injuries which inevitably result to those paid public servants who respond to emergencies are properly borne by the government as an integral expense of providing fire and police protection, since the entire community benefits from the rendition of the services. It has been said that:

The Fireman's Rule... stands for the principle that societal responsibility rather than possible tort recovery is the better, surer, and fairer recourse for a fireman or policeman injured in the line of duty.

Flowers v. Sting Security, Inc., 488 A.2d 523 (Md. 1985). Also, the government, it is argued, is in a good position to spread such losses broadly. However, some authorities have questioned the soundness of the loss-allocation rationale. They have noted that injured firefighters and police officers may be left under-compensated in comparison to other public employees, who not only receive workers' compensation benefits, but retain their rights against third-party tortfeasors.

The firefighter's rule may be sound from an accident-prevention standpoint. It promotes public safety by permitting individuals who may require police or fire department assistance to summon aid without pausing to consider whether they will be held liable for the ensuing consequences. The rule may therefore minimize losses by encouraging prompt requests for professional assistance. It is a well-established economic principle that persons more readily use those services which are free or are available at bargain prices.

3. *Abnormal or Increased Risks.* Even in states adhering to the firefighter's rule, liability has been imposed when the defendant negligently increased the dangers ordinarily confronted by a firefighter, as by failing to warn of a known hidden peril. *See, e.g.,* Shypulski v. Waldorf Paper Products Co., 45 N.W.2d 549, 553 (Minn. 1951) (unstable wall); Jenkins v. 313-321 W. 37th Street Corp., 31 N.E.2d 503, 504-505 (N.Y. 1940) (gasoline).

4. *Intentionally Created Risks.* Virtually all courts hold that the firefighter's rule does not immunize an intentional or reckless wrongdoer from liability to a professional rescuer. *See* Goodwin v. Hare, 436 S.E.2d 605 (Va. 1993) (holding that the rule is inapplicable to intentional torts, since there is no reason to shift financial losses away from the defendant in cases of injuries or damages intentionally inflicted).

5. *Abrogation of the Firefighter's Rule.* As indicated in the principal case, in a number of jurisdictions, the firefighter's rule has been legislatively or judicially repudiated. *See* Christensen v. Murphy, 678 P.2d 1210, 1216-18 (Or. 1984) (legislative abolition of primary and secondary assumption of the risk undercut continued application of the firefighter's rule).

4. Implied Secondary Assumption of Risk

Courts have differed in their articulation of the elements of assumption of the risk. In general, however, it appears that before the doctrine will apply there must be evidence that the plaintiff (1) subjectively appreciated the risk, (2) voluntarily elected to confront it, and (3) manifested a willingness to relieve the defendant of any obligation of care or had no expectation that care would be exercised. When courts speak in these terms, they are probably focusing on secondary implied assumption of the risk.

Marshall v. Ranne

Supreme Court of Texas
511 S.W.2d 255 (Tex. 1974)

POPE, Justice.

Paul Marshall instituted this suit against John C. Ranne seeking damages for injuries sustained when Ranne's vicious hog attacked him.... The jury made findings that plaintiff Marshall was contributorily negligent and also that he voluntarily assumed the risk of the hog. The trial court rendered judgment for the defendant on the verdict. The court of civil appeals...affirmed....We reverse....

....

The only witness to the occurrence was plaintiff. He and defendant...owned neighboring farms....Plaintiff's principal occupation was raising hogs....The hog in question was a boar which had escaped from defendant's farm and had been seen on plaintiff's land during several weeks before the day of the injury. According to plaintiff, defendant's boar had charged him ten to twelve times before this occurrence, had held him prisoner in his outhouse several times, and had attacked his wife on four or five occasions. On the day of the injury plaintiff...saw defendant's boar about a hundred yards behind the barn, but it came no nearer. After feeding his hogs, he went into the house....On emerging from the house, he looked for the boar because, as he testified, he always had to look before he made a move, but he did not see it. He started toward his pickup, and when he was about thirty feet from it, near the outhouse, he heard a noise behind him, turned around and saw the boar charging toward him. He put out his hand defensively, but the boar grabbed it and bit it severely.

Plaintiff testified that the first time the hog had jeopardized his safety was about a week or ten days before he was hurt. He did not shoot the hog because he did not consider that the neighborly thing to do, although he was an expert with a gun and had two available. He made no complaint about the hog to defendant until the day of the injury, when he wrote a note and put it on defendant's gate. The note read:

> John, your boar has gone bad. He is trying to chase me off the farm. He stalks us just like a cat stalks a mouse every time he catches us out of the house. We are going to have to get him out before he hurts someone.

...[T]he evidence does not reveal whether...[the defendant] saw...[the note] before the plaintiff was injured....

....

[There was evidence that the parties had previously discussed the hog's viciousness and that when the defendant visited the plaintiff in the hospital, he told him: "I knew the bugger was mean....Why didn't you kill him?" Based on this evidence, the court, relying on Restatement of Torts §509, held that the defendant was subject to strict liability for the plaintiff's injuries because they resulted from a vicious propensity of the hog of which the defendant should have known. The court further held, based on a draft of Restatement, Second, of Torts §515, that contributory negligence was not a defense to strict liability.]

Plaintiff Marshall does not contend that voluntary assumption of risk is no defense to an action which asserts the defendant's strict liability....Marshall's argument is that he did not, as a matter of law, voluntarily expose himself to the risk of the attack by the hog. The jury found that plaintiff Marshall had knowledge of the vicious propensities of the hog and that it was likely to cause injury to persons, and also found that plaintiff, with knowledge of the nature of defendant's boar hog, voluntarily exposed himself to the risk of attack by the animal. We hold that there was no proof that plaintiff had a free and voluntary choice, because he did not have a free choice of alternatives. He had, instead, only a choice of evils, both of which were wrongfully imposed upon him by the defendant. He could remain a prisoner inside his own house or he could take the risk of reaching his car before defendant's hog attacked him. Plaintiff could have remained inside his house, but in doing so, he would have surrendered his legal right to proceed over his own property to his car so he could return to his home in Dallas. The latter alternative was forced upon him against his will and was a choice he was not legally required to accept. [Citation.] We approve and follow the rule expressed in Restatement (Second) of Torts §496E (1965):

> (1) A plaintiff does not assume a risk of harm unless he voluntarily accepts the risk.

> (2) The plaintiff's acceptance of a risk is not voluntary if the defendant's tortious conduct has left him no reasonable alternative course of conduct in order to

> (a) avert harm to himself or another, or

> (b) exercise or protect a right or privilege of which the defendant has no right to deprive him.

The dilemma which defendant forced upon plaintiff was that of facing the danger or surrendering his rights with respect to his own real property, and that was not, as a matter of law, the voluntary choice to which the law entitled him. [Citations.]

We held in Harvey v. Seale, 362 S.W.2d 310, 313 (Tex. 1962), that a choice afforded a nine-year-old child to cease playing on a porch that her parents held by lease or to risk stepping in a hole was not a voluntary one. We wrote in that case:

> By virtue of her father's lease, she was entitled to be on the front porch of her home without regard to respondent's consent. Respondent was not privileged, therefore, to adopt a "take it or leave it" attitude, and his duty to petitioner was not fully discharged when she learned of the danger. The negligent failure to repair the hole placed her in a position where she was compelled to choose between foregoing her legal right to play on the porch and encountering the risk involved in playing there. If her choice was unreasonable under the circumstance, she was guilty of contributory negligence, but respondent will not be heard to say that she voluntarily exposed herself to the danger....

> ....

> Defendant Ranne argues also that the plaintiff Marshall had yet another alternative, that of shooting the hog. The proof showed that Marshall was an expert marksman and had a gun in his house with which he could have killed the hog. Plaintiff Marshall testified that he was reluctant to destroy his neighbor's animal because he did not know how Ranne would react. We do not regard the slaughter of the animal as a reasonable alternative, because plaintiff would have subjected himself arguably to charges under the provisions of two criminal statutes.

> ....In this case, as a matter of law, the proof shows that plaintiff Marshall did not voluntarily encounter the vicious hog....

> ....

[Reversed, and remanded on the issue of damages.]

Notes

1. *Contributory Negligence or Assumption of the Risk?* As the plaintiff in *Marshall* did nothing wrong, the result of the decision seems plainly correct. Is it true to say, though,

that the plaintiff did not voluntarily run the risk? Or would it be more accurate to say that the plaintiff did voluntarily run the risk, but his running the risk should not be held against him because it was reasonable for him to do so?

Consider a variation on the facts of *Marshall.* Suppose Ranne had come to Marshall's farm with a rifle and offered to shoot the hog. Marshall then insisted that he could handle the hog, and that he didn't want gunfire on his property because it would upset his stock. On hearing this, Ranne went home, and the hog attacked Marshall later that day. Is that a case in which the defense should be allowed?

2. *"Choice of Evils."* For an unusual application of the "no reasonable alternative" rule, see Rush v. Commercial Realty Co., 145 A. 476 (N.J. 1929), where a tenant fell through a bad floor in a detached privy, landed in the accumulation at the bottom, and had to be extricated by use of a ladder. In finding that the woman had not voluntarily assumed the risk of harm, the court wrote:

> Mrs. Rush had no choice, when impelled by the calls of nature, but to use the facilities placed at her disposal by the landlord, to wit, a privy with a trap door in the floor, poorly maintained.... [S]he was not required to leave the premises and go elsewhere.

See also Caldwell v. Ford Motor Co., 619 S.W.2d 534, 540 (Tenn. Ct. App. 1981) (plaintiff did not assume the risk of injury in removing goods from the bed of a burning truck, for the truck manufacturer had no right to force plaintiff to either confront the fire or let the goods burn).

If the lack of alternatives is not attributable to the defendant, the plaintiff's choice may be held to be voluntary. The Restatement, Second, of Torts §496E offers this illustration:

> A is injured in an accident, bleeding badly, and in need of immediate medical attention. Having no other means of transportation, he asks B to drive him to the hospital, knowing that B's car has defective brakes. A assumes the risk of injury caused by the brakes.

Similarly, "a plaintiff who is forced to rent a house which is in obvious dangerous condition because he cannot find another dwelling, or cannot afford another, assumes the risk notwithstanding the compulsion under which he is acting." *Id.* at cmt. b.

3. *Economic Duress and Assumption of the Risk at Work.* An individual who, in the face of an employer's ultimatum or direction, elects to encounter a known dangerous condition, rather than risk losing the job, does not voluntarily assume the risk of injury. *See* Tew v. Sun Oil Co., 407 A.2d 240 (Del. Super. Ct. 1979); Draper v. Airco, Inc., 580 F.2d 91 (3d Cir. 1978) ("To hold that economic duress of this sort does not vitiate... voluntariness...would be to ignore reality").

One occasionally finds sweeping statements that the "trend" of authority is that "assumption of risk in the employment setting is no longer valid." Cremeans v. Willmar Henderson Mfg. Co., 566 N.E.2d 1203 (Ohio 1991); *see also* Carrel v. Allied Products Corp., 677 N.E.2d 795 (Ohio 1997) (explaining that assumption of risk may be a defense against an employee who is injured by a defective product, but that the defense is not available when an employee is required to encounter a risk while performing normal job duties). These assertions must be carefully scrutinized. As *Turcotte* indicated earlier in the chapter, primary assumption of the risk applies to employment contexts. *See also* Crews v. Hollenbach, 751 A.2d 481 (Md. 2000) (declining to recognize primary assumption of the risk, but holding that a gas company worker knew and appreciated the risk of confronting a gas leak, and voluntarily assumed the risk since the danger that he encountered was the very danger that he accepted the risk of confronting when he became an employee of the gas company some twenty years earlier).

4. *"Subjective Appreciation of the Risk."* For a risk to be assumed, it must be subjectively appreciated. In Castello v. County of Nassau, 636 N.Y.S.2d 817 (App. Div. 1996), a case where the risk presented by a protruding home plate was not concealed, the court held that a softball player consciously assumed that risk by his voluntary participation in a softball game. The player admitted that he knew that the third-base side of home plate had been lowered, and had actually stood in the "ditch" next to the protruding corner of the plate. *See also* Anderson v. Ceccardi, 451 N.E.2d 780 (Ohio 1983) (plaintiff used steps that had a hole in the tread portion, over which a board had been placed, despite the fact that he had repeatedly told his landlord that the steps were unsafe).

If the risk in question was not in fact known to the plaintiff, it is not sufficient, for purposes of establishing the defense, that a reasonable person would have appreciated the risk.

5. *"Voluntariness" and Preference for Risk.* The decisions above establish that one cannot "assume a risk" unless that assumption was knowing and voluntary. Do not assume from this that knowingly and voluntarily confronting a risk necessarily establishes the defense. Recall, for example, the case of the pedestrian dashing across a street in front of a speeding car, a case of mere comparative negligence, not assumption of the risk. One approach to distinguishing assumption of the risk from plaintiff's negligence is to say that assumption of the risk requires that the plaintiff have evidenced a willingness to relieve the defendant of liability. The Restatement, Third, of Torts: Apportionment of Liability, §2, Cmt. i, Reporter's Note, invokes the law of implied-in-fact contracts and rules about the scope of defendants' duties to allow a full defense for cases in which a party "clearly and consciously chooses to confront a risk because of an actual preference for the risk," but otherwise treats implied assumption of the risk as simply a form of comparative negligence. Suppose a thrill-seeking teenager runs across a street in front of a speeding car, just for the challenge. Is the teenager's conduct a full defense, or just comparative negligence? Does the answer depend on whether the teenager had a motive in addition to thrill-seeking for crossing the street, as when the teenager was on his way home and would have crossed the street anyway, but chose not to wait for the traffic to pass because of a preference for risk?

Some courts have held that the affirmative defense of assumption of risk does not require proof of consent to relieve the defendant of his obligation of care but merely evidence that the plaintiff knew that nothing would be done to prevent harm from occurring. Suppose, for example, that a contractor leaves a plank straddling a pit that is in the process of being excavated. If, when no one is around, the plaintiff sees the plank, attempts to walk across it, falls, and is injured, the plaintiff has assumed the risk. It may make more sense to say that the plaintiff had no expectation that care would be exercised to protect him from the known, voluntarily encountered danger, than to say that he consented to relieve the defendant of an obligation to exercise care.

6. *Assumption of the Risk at the Supreme Court.* In Washington, D.C., at the Supreme Court, there is a basketball court that is used by justices and members of the court staff. According to the court's newsletter, *The Docket Sheet* (Fall 1994):

> Regulars note the unique structural aspects of the court [which is squeezed into the building above the ceiling of the courtroom and beneath the pitched roof]. The court is 3/4 the size of a regulation basketball court, and with walls only a foot away from the out-of-bounds stripes, it makes for close quarters.

Voices constantly echo off of the walls magnifying the presence of 10 players to stadium levels. Suspended square, plywood boards serve as backboards and vibrate when a "brick" is launched like a clarion call for bad shots. Vent-like protrusions shine light up the walls and towards the ceiling, providing the only sense of Hollywood to a very plain arena. Padding on sharp corners and on the walls provides some protection upon collision.

A sign as one enters the "highest court in the land" reads:

> "All persons use this gym at their own risk. Users assume the risk of the nearness of walls, support columns and stairs to the basketball court."

Is the sign valid? If a user of the court assumes a risk, is this express assumption of the risk, primary implied assumption of the risk, or secondary implied assumption of the risk? Is the bar to liability total or partial?

D. Comparative Fault

The all-or-nothing approach of traditional contributory negligence was an important premise of tort law for more than a century. During that period, other rules were shaped to be consistent with that doctrine—or to react against it. Once contributory negligence began to be supplanted by comparative principles, many questions arose about whether other changes in legal doctrine had to follow. Some of those questions had relatively obvious answers. For example, virtually all courts have held that the doctrine of last clear chance does not survive to adoption of comparative negligence. Other questions have been more subtle, such as whether the endorsement of a comparative approach to accident compensation necessitates changes in the rules on *res ipsa loquitur* (*see* Montgomery Elevator Co. v. Gordon, 619 P.2d 66 (Colo. 1980)), joint and several liability (*see* Chapter 17), liability to rescuers (*see* Altamuro v. Milner Hotel, Inc., 540 F. Supp. 870 (E.D. Pa. 1982), or superseding causation (*see* Control Techniques, Inc. v. Johnson, 762 N.E.2d 104 (Ind. 2002). The following case addresses the question of whether, after the adoption of comparative negligence, unreasonable conduct by the plaintiff can be urged as a defense in actions not based on negligence.

Kaneko v. Hilo Coast Processing

Supreme Court of Hawaii
654 P.2d 343 (Haw. 1982)

OGATA, Retired Justice.

....

[Plaintiff, an ironworker, was injured when the steel girt on which he was standing came loose because it had not been fully welded. In the suit which followed, the jury found for the plaintiff on negligence, warranty, and strict products liability theories. The trial court reduced the award in proportion to the contributory negligence of the plaintiff. On appeal, the defendant manufacturer contested only the strict liability finding. The supreme court held that a prefabricated building was a "product" for the purpose of strict products liability. On the cross-appeal, the plaintiff argued that contributory negligence was no defense to strict liability and that therefore the jury award should not have been reduced.]

We now turn to the principal issue raised in Kaneko's cross-appeal, that is, whether the doctrine of comparative negligence should merge with strict products liability.

As is evident from the vast amount of scholarly comment and case law, we are by no means the first to consider this issue. Other jurisdictions which have addressed the problem have reached varied conclusions on differing rationales.

....

The first objection of those in opposition to the merger of strict products liability and comparative negligence is that the two theories are incapable of being reconciled. They argue that there are both conceptual and semantic difficulties in bringing negligence and strict liability concepts together. "The task of merging the two concepts is said to be impossible, that 'apples and oranges' cannot be compared, and that 'oil and water' do not mix, and that strict liability, which is not founded on negligence or fault is inhospitable to comparative principles." Daly v. General Motors Corp., 20 Cal. 3d 725, 734, 575 P.2d 1162, 1167, 144 Cal. Rptr. 380, 385 (1978).

The Supreme Court of South Dakota, in denying that contributory negligence is a defense in strict products liability, stated in Smith v. Smith, 278 N.W.2d 155 (S.D. 1979), that

> Strict liability is an abandonment of the fault concept in product liability cases. No longer are damages to be borne by one who is culpable; rather they are borne by one who markets the defective product. The question of whether the manufacturer or seller is negligent is meaningless under such a concept; liability is imposed irrespectively of his negligence or freedom from it. Even though the manufacturer or seller is able to prove beyond all doubt that the defect was not the result of his negligence, it would avail him nothing. We believe it is inconsistent to hold that the user's negligence is material when the seller's is not....

Id. at 160.

On the other hand, courts that favor the merger recognize the conceptual and semantic problems between the two principles, but find they are not incompatible. [Citations.]

In a well reasoned opinion, the California Supreme Court in *Daly, supra,* held that comparative negligence should be merged with strict products liability.... The California Supreme Court's rationale can be summed up with their following statement: "Fixed semantic consistency at this point is less important than the attainment of a just and equitable result. The interweaving of concept and terminology in this area suggest a judicial posture that is flexible rather than doctrinaire." [Citations.]

In short, those who oppose the merger believe that negligence and strict liability are different theories and therefore are not compatible. Those jurisdictions that are in favor of the merger argue that fairness and equity are more important than semantic consistency.

We believe that the better reasoned view is that comparative negligence is not incompatible with strict products liability. Our adoption of the theory of strict products liability was premised on equity and fairness and our concern for human safety. The interjection of comparative negligence into strict products liability will reduce an injured plaintiff's award by an amount equal to the degree to which he is culpably and contributorily negligent. Such a system will accomplish a fairer and more equitable result....

The second objection to the application of comparative principles in strict products liability cases is that manufacturers will have less incentive to produce safe products.

This was the view taken by Justice Mosk in his dissenting opinion in *Daly, supra....* The majority, however, viewed the concern as "more shadow than substance." The majority supported their view with two points. First, a manufacturer cannot avoid liability merely because a plaintiff has contributed to his own injury. Secondly, the majority argued that a manufacturer cannot assume that the user of a defective product will be blameworthy. Based on these two points, the majority held that "no substantial or significant impairment of the safety incentives of defendant will occur by the adoption of comparative negligence." [Citation.]

We hold that the majority view in *Daly, supra,* is the better view....

The third major objection to the merger of the two theories is that it will present an impossible task for juries to reconcile the conduct of a plaintiff with the defective product of a defendant.

Some jurisdictions have refused to apply comparative negligence to strict products liability because of a fear of confusing the jury in allocating damages. [Citations.]

    ....

On the other hand, those courts which have merged the two concepts are not persuaded by the argument that jurors would be unable to undertake a fair apportionment of liability. These courts observe that jurors have no difficulty in apportioning awards when using the maritime doctrine of unseaworthiness, a doctrine similar to strict liability, where plaintiff's misconduct is not an absolute bar to recovery, but may be considered in mitigation of damages as justice requires. [Citations.]

Other jurisdictions which have applied comparative negligence principles to strict products liability have dismissed this issue by simply holding that they find no difficulty for jurors if the two theories are merged.

We...hold that jurors will not be confused in determining damages if comparative negligence is merged with strict products liability.

Finding that the major objections of those who oppose the merger of comparative negligence and strict products liability are not persuasive, we conclude that the comparative negligence should be judicially merged with strict products liability.

    ....

The other specifications of error raised in the appeal and the cross-appeal are without merit. We decline to review the merits of the issues raised therein.

[Affirmed.]

Notes

1. *Negligence as a Defense to Strict Liability.* Many states now hold that negligence by the plaintiff is a defense, on a pure or modified basis, in actions based on strict liability. This approach is sometimes referred to as "comparative fault," "comparative causation," or "comparative responsibility." The wording of a jurisdiction's comparative-negligence or comparative-fault statute is always important, but many of these statutes fail to address the issue directly.

2. *Negligence as a Defense to Reckless Conduct.* Most states also hold that a plaintiff's unreasonable conduct should mitigate a defendant's liability for recklessly inflicted harm. *But see* Krivijanski v. Union R. Co., 515 A.2d 933 (Pa. 1986) (holding that comparative negligence should not be applied to cases of willful or wanton misconduct, and

declining to follow decisions endorsing a contrary rule); Burke v. 12 Rothschild's Liquor Mart, 593 N.E.2d 522 (Ill. 1992) (similar).

3. *Comparisons of Negligence and Intentionally Tortious Conduct.* States that have adopted comparative fault often do not include intentionally tortious conduct within the definition of "fault." *See* Whitehead v. Food Max of Miss., Inc., 163 F.3d 265 (5th Cir. 1998). Consequently, a gang member who mugs the plaintiff in a desolate location ordinarily cannot escape or limit liability for battery by arguing that the plaintiff was careless in being alone at the place where the mugging occurred. However, not all intentional torts are equally blameworthy.

> [A] defendant who, while legally hunting wolves, shoots at, hits, and kills plaintiff's dog, which looks exactly like a wolf, has committed an intentional tort. The dog's owner may recover the full value of the dog even though defendant reasonably believed he was shooting a wolf. But what if the dog owner was negligent in releasing his wolf-like dog during wolf-hunting season? Why should this negligence be ignored....
>
> ....
>
> Intentional tort cases in which defendant erroneously thought he had plaintiff's consent may also present situations in which comparative fault should be used....
>
> In other intentional tort cases, defendants are held liable even though they were not morally at fault. Thus, good faith purchasers of stolen goods are converters, and in some jurisdictions private persons who arrest others under the mistaken belief that those arrested have committed a crime are liable for false arrest no matter how reasonable their belief that the arrestee committed the crime....

Gail D. Hollister, *Using Comparative Fault to Replace the All-or-Nothing Lottery Imposed in Intentional Torts Suits in Which Both Plaintiff and Defendant Are at Fault,* 46 Vand. L. Rev. 121, 124-25 (1993). Cases like these suggest that, at least in some circumstances, comparing intentionally tortious conduct with negligence might not be inappropriate.

In Jones v. Thomas, 557 So. 2d 1015 (La. App. 1990), Thomas punched the plaintiff, Jones, in the face, breaking his jaw. The punch followed a ten-minute harangue by Jones in which he shouted curses, obscenities, and racial slurs at Thomas and threatened to kill Thomas's mother and family. The court ruled that comparative fault principles should be used to reduce the plaintiff's damages "[w]here the words or action of a plaintiff in a civil battery action are sufficient to establish provocation...." The appellate court found the trial court's assignment of 90% of the fault to the plaintiff excessive, however, as the provocation was entirely verbal, and reduced the plaintiff's fault to 50 percent.

In addition, if a jurisdiction has adopted comparative fault and abolished joint and several liability (*see* Chapter 17), so that a tortfeasor is to be held liable only for that tortfeasor's percentage of the total fault, it may be necessary to take into account the intentionally tortious conduct of third parties for the purpose of calculating the particular tortfeasor's share of the total fault. *See* Barth v. Coleman, 878 P.2d 319 (N.M. 1994) (bar and bar manager's liability for negligent failure to prevent a fight should have been offset by the percentage of fault attributable to the third-party tortfeasor who intentionally punched the plaintiff in the nose). *But see* Eskin v. Castiglia, 753 A.2d 927, 935 (Conn. 2000) (discussing a state statute prohibiting the apportionment of liability between allegedly negligent tortfeasors and intentional or reckless tortfeasors, among others); Turner v. Jordan, 957 S.W.2d 815 (Tenn. 1997) (holding, in an action by a nurse who was assaulted by mentally ill patient against patient's treating psychiatrist, that the psychiatrist's negligence should not have been compared with the intentional conduct of a nonparty patient in allocating fault).

In Veazey v. Elwood Plantation Associates, Ltd., 650 So. 2d 712 (La. 1994), a tenant, who was raped in her apartment, brought a negligence action against her apartment complex, Southmark. The court wrote:

> First, and foremost, the scope of Southmark's duty to the plaintiff in this case clearly encompassed the exact risk of the occurrence which caused damage to plaintiff. As a general rule, we find that negligent tortfeasors should not be allowed to reduce their fault by the intentional fault of another that they had a duty to prevent. [Citation.]
>
> Second, Southmark, who by definition acted unreasonably under the circumstances in breaching their duty to plaintiff, should not be allowed to benefit at the *innocent* plaintiff's expense by an allocation of fault to the intentional tortfeasor under comparative fault principles. Given the fact that any rational juror will apportion the lion's share of the fault to the intentional tortfeasor when instructed to compare the fault of a negligent tortfeasor and an intentional tortfeasor, application of comparative fault principles in the circumstances presented in this particular case would operate to reduce the incentive of the lessor to protect against the same type of situation occurring again in the future. Such a result is clearly contrary to public policy.
>
> Third, as Dean Prosser has explained it, intentional wrongdoing "differs from negligence not only in degree but in kind, and in the social condemnation attached to it." [Citation.] In our view, this is a correct assessment of the character and nature of the conduct which defendant herein seeks to have the courts compare. Because we believe that intentional torts are of a fundamentally different nature than negligent torts, we find that a true comparison of fault based on an intentional act and fault based on negligence is, in many circumstances, not possible.
>
> In sum, we hold that while Louisiana law is broad enough to allow comparison of fault between intentional tortfeasors and negligent tortfeasors, determination of whether such a comparison should be made must be determined by the trial court on a case by case basis, bearing in mind the public policy concerns discussed herein. We further hold, for the reasons stated herein, that comparison of Southmark's negligence and the rapist's fault in this particular case is not appropriate....

According to the Restatement, Third, of Torts: Apportionment of Liability §1 cmt. c, Reporter's Note:

> Applying comparative responsibility to intentional torts is not the majority rule, but it commands significant support among courts that have addressed the question, especially in cases apportioning damages among defendants. Much of this growing support is in cases involving a comparison of *defendants'* responsibility, not a comparison of a *defendant* with a *plaintiff*. [Citations.]
>
> Some of the support, however, is in cases comparing a *plaintiff's* responsibility with an intentional *defendant's* responsibility. [Citations.]

. . . .

. . . [T]his Restatement does not take a position on whether a plaintiff's negligence is a comparative defense to intentional torts. That issue is left to substantive law. This Restatement does, however, apply its system of comparative responsibility to apportion liability among intentional and negligent defendants.

4. *Some Comparative-Negligence and Comparative-Fault Statutes.* Here is a small collection of legislation on comparative negligence. Examine each statute with these questions in mind:

(1) If the defendant's negligence is 75-percent responsible for an accident causing a $100,000 loss to a plaintiff whose negligence was 25-percent responsible, how much does the defendant have to pay?

(2) Same as (1), except that each party's negligence is equally responsible for the accident.

(3) Same as (1), except that the plaintiff is 90-percent responsible and the defendant 10-percent responsible.

(4) The plaintiff is 40-percent responsible; defendant *A* is 30-percent responsible; and defendant *B* is 30-percent responsible. Plaintiff's loss is $100,000. As a complicating factor, suppose that defendant *B* was not sued because personal jurisdiction could not be obtained.

Do not assume that all of these statutes provide a clear answer to all of the questions raised.

N.Y. Civ. Prac. Law and Rules §1411
(Westlaw 2004)

In any action to recover damages for personal injury, injury to property, or wrongful death, the culpable conduct attributable to the claimant or to the decedent, including contributory negligence or assumption of risk, shall not bar recovery, but the amount of damages otherwise recoverable shall be diminished in the proportion which the culpable conduct attributable to the claimant or decedent bears to the culpable conduct which caused the damages.

Wis. Stat. Ann., §895.045(1)
(Westlaw 2004)

Contributory negligence does not bar recovery in an action by any person or the person's legal representative to recover damages for negligence resulting in death or in injury to person or property, if that negligence was not greater than the negligence of the person against whom recovery is sought, but any damages allowed shall be diminished in the proportion to the amount of negligence attributed to the person recovering. The negligence of the plaintiff shall be measured separately against the negligence of each person found to be causally negligent. . . .

Uniform Comparative Fault Act §§1-2
12 U.L.A. 123 (Westlaw 2004)

Section 1. [Effect of Contributory Fault]

(a) In an action based on fault seeking to recover damages for injury or death to person or harm to property, any contributory fault chargeable to the claimant diminishes proportionately the amount awarded as compensatory damages for an injury attributable to the claimant's contributory fault, but does not bar recovery. This rule applies whether or not under prior law the claimant's contributory fault constituted a defense or was disregarded under applicable legal doctrines, such as last clear chance.

(b) "Fault" includes acts or omissions that are in any measure negligent or reckless toward the person or property of the actor or others, or that subject a person to strict tort liability. The term also includes breach of warranty, unreasonable assumption of risk not constituting an enforceable express consent, misuse of a product for which the defendant otherwise would be liable, and unreasonable failure to avoid an injury or to mitigate damages. Legal requirements of causal relation apply both to fault as the basis for liability and to contributory fault.

Section 2. [Apportionment of Damages]

(a) In all actions involving fault of more than one party to the action, including third-party defendants and persons who have been released under Section 6, the court, unless otherwise agreed by all parties, shall instruct the jury to answer special interrogatories or, if there is no jury, shall make findings, indicating:

(1) the amount of damages each claimant would be entitled to recover if contributory fault is disregarded; and

(2) the percentage of the total fault of all of the parties to each claim that is allocated to each claimant, defendant, third-party defendant, and person who has been released from liability under Section 6. For this purpose the court may determine that two or more persons are to be treated as a single party.

(b) In determining the percentages of fault, the trier of fact shall consider both the nature of the conduct of each party at fault and the extent of the causal relation between the conduct and the damages claimed.

(c) The court shall determine the award of damages to each claimant in accordance with the findings, subject to any reduction under Section 6, and enter judgment against each party liable on the basis of rules of joint-and-several liability. For purposes of contribution under Sections 4 and 5, the court also shall determine and state in the judgment each party's equitable share of the obligation to each claimant in accordance with the respective percentages of fault.

(d) Upon motion made not later than [one year] after judgment is entered, the court shall determine whether all or part of a party's equitable share of the obligation is uncollectible from that party, and shall reallocate any uncollectible amount among the other parties, including a claimant at fault, according to their respective percentages of fault. The party whose liability is reallocated is nonetheless subject to contribution and to any continuing liability to the claimant on the judgment.

E. The "Seatbelt Defense"

The non-use of a seatbelt can greatly increase the chances of injury or the extent of damages incurred in an auto accident. However, courts were initially reluctant to recognize a "seatbelt defense." This is understandable. Seatbelts were first widely available in cars in the 1960s, a time when common-law contributory negligence was still the general rule and any finding of fault on the part of the plaintiff could totally bar recovery.

During the subsequent years much has changed. In particular, comparative principles have replaced the all-or-nothing approach of contributory negligence. The use of seatbelts has become common, and in many circumstances is legally required.

In general, states fall into two camps. In some jurisdictions, often because of compromises attending the enactment of mandatory-seatbelt-use laws, a defense may not be raised based on the plaintiff's non-use of an available seatbelt. For example, the Illinois statute provides:

> (a) Each driver and front seat passenger of a motor vehicle...shall wear a properly adjusted and fastened seat safety belt....
>
> ....
>
> (c) Failure to wear a seat safety belt in violation of this Section shall not be considered evidence of negligence, shall not limit the liability of an insurer, and shall not diminish any recovery for damages arising out of the ownership, maintenance, or operation of a motor vehicle.
>
> (d) A violation of this Section shall be a petty offense and subject to a fine not to exceed $25.

625 Ill. Comp. Stat. Ann. 5/12-603.1 (Westlaw 2003). *See also* Davis v. Knippling, 576 N.W.2d 525 (S.D. 1998) (stating that a "clear majority of states have judicially refused to admit evidence of a plaintiff's nonuse of an available seatbelt as proof of failure to mitigate damages likely to occur in an automobile accident"). In Miller v. Jeffrey, 576 S.E.2d 520 (W. Va. 2002), a state statute which barred admission of seat belt evidence was inapplicable because the accident had occurred on a private road. The court nevertheless held that the evidence of the plaintiff's failure to wear a seatbelt was inadmissible to assess the plaintiff's percentage of fault or to show failure to mitigate damages.

However, other states simply treat seatbelt non-use as just one more form of comparative negligence and to that extent recognize the "seatbelt defense." *See* Law v. Superior Court, 755 P.2d 1135 (Ariz. 1988) (jury could consider non-use in apportioning damages due to "fault" of plaintiffs); Ridley v. Safety Kleen Corp., 693 So. 2d 934 (Fla. 1996) (holding that failure to wear seat belt should be properly raised as an affirmative defense of comparative negligence). The strongest arguments in favor of this position would seem to be that recognizing a seatbelt defense tends to minimize losses by encouraging safe practices, promote individual responsibility, and, where a statute mandates use, fosters respect for the law.

As part of the most recent wave of "tort reform" in Texas, the legislature simply deleted the statutory language that made seatbelt evidence inadmissible. Presumably, this means that attorneys are now free to argue the defense.

Suppose that *A*'s negligent driving destroys *B*'s car, a new Mercedes worth $90,000. When *B* sues *A*, *A* defends on the ground that *B* could have kept the potential loss from an accident low by driving an inexpensive car. This defense would be laughed out of court. Is an argument that one should protect one's bodily integrity by wearing a seatbelt or motorcycle helmet fundamentally different from *A*'s argument in the property-damage case? In each instance, the defendant whose negligence caused the accident seeks relief from part of the liability on the sole ground that different actions by the plaintiff would have made the accident less harmful to the plaintiff.

Removal of Seat Belts. The removal of seatbelts from a vehicle may give rise to a cause of action. Twohig v. Briner, 214 Cal. Rptr. 729 (Ct. App. 1985), held that if the owner or operator of a car removes the seatbelts, a passenger who is thereafter injured may sue on the ground that the owner or operator breached a duty of care by "exposing passengers to increased danger by eliminating their option to 'buckle up' ." In some jurisdictions, an automobile owner has a statutory duty to provide seatbelts for the use of occupants. *See, e.g.,* N.Y. Veh. & Traf. Law §§383 (Westlaw 2003).

See also Dellapenta v. Dellapenta, 828 P.2d 1153 (Wyo. 1992), holding that parents have a common-law duty to buckle the seatbelts of children dependent on adult care, and may be held liable to an injured child for a breach of that duty.

Motorcycle Helmets. The non-use of motorcycle helmets raises issues similar to those relating to the non-use of seatbelts.

Insurance. Injuries resulting from failure to use seatbelts inevitably contribute to the costs of automobile insurance. Would it be desirable to require all drivers to insure themselves, regardless of fault, on, say, the first $30,000 of medical expenses for injuries incurred in accidents involving the non-use of seatbelts?

Chapter 17

Joint Tortfeasors

A. Joint and Several Liability

Chapter 16 dealt with the question whether conduct on the part of a plaintiff reduces the amount for which a defendant may be held liable. This chapter, in large measure, is concerned with the different but related question of whether conduct on the part of other actual or potential defendants reduces a particular defendant's exposure to liability. The answer turns, in the first instance, on the whether the defendant is subject to several liability only or to joint and several liability.

The law on joint and several liability was once reasonably clear and endorsed with widespread uniformity. Today, however, the law is very much in flux. The rule of joint and several liability still governs many types of litigation. But the rise of comparative principles (comparative negligence and comparative fault), and the consequent jurisprudential focus on the policy of limiting liability in proportion to fault, has caused a vigorous re-examination of the traditional rules. With some success, "tort reform" efforts have sought to eliminate joint and several liability in whole or in part. Before advising a client on questions arising in this field, it is essential to consult local law, particularly acts of the legislature.

See Mark Ballard, *17-Front Tort War*, Nat. L.J., May 12, 2003, at 1 ("Tort law battles are being fought in one-third of the states. 'Joint and several liability,' an unlikely sounding war cry, is a major issue in many of them").

1. Definitions

The rule of joint and several liability holds that two or more tortfeasors may be subject to liability for the same harm and may be sued by the plaintiff, together or separately. This does not mean that a plaintiff to whom two tortfeasors (*A* and *B*) are jointly and severally liable for a single judgment can collect in full from each tortfeasor. Rather, the plaintiff can collect in full only once, either all from *A*, or all from *B*, or in part from both. A defendant who pays a disproportionately high amount may be able to recover the excess payment from another tortfeasor under the doctrine — typically statutory — of contribution among joint tortfeasors. And sometimes a tortfeasor who pays a judgment may be entitled to recover the full amount of the judgment from another; this is called "indemnity." An everyday example of indemnity arises when an employer is held liable for an employee's tort under the doctrine of *respondeat superior*. Although the employer is liable to the plaintiff for the full amount of the judgment, it has, in theory at least, the right to recover that payment from the employee who committed the tort. Contribution and indemnity will be examined below.

A useful starting point is American Motorcycle Ass'n v. Superior Ct., 578 P.2d 899 (Cal. 1978). While that decision has been superseded by statute in California, it fairly reflects the common situations in which joint and several liability traditionally arose:

> The "joint and several liability" concept has sometimes caused confusion be-cause the terminology has been used with reference to a number of distinct sit-uations. [Citations.] The terminology originated with respect to tortfeasors who acted in concert to commit a tort, and in that context it reflected the prin-ciple...that all members of a "conspiracy" or partnership are equally responsi-ble for the acts of each member in furtherance of such conspiracy.
>
> Subsequently, the courts applied the "joint and several liability" terminol-ogy to other contexts in which a preexisting relationship between two indi-viduals made it appropriate to hold one individual liable for the act of the other; common examples are instances of vicarious liability between em-ployer and employee or principal and agent, or situations in which joint owners of property owe a common duty to some third party. In these situa-tions, the joint and several liability concept reflects the legal conclusion that one individual may be held liable for the consequences of the negligent act of another.
>
> In the concurrent tortfeasor context, however, the "joint and several liabil-ity" label does not express the imposition of any form of vicarious liability, but instead simply embodies the general common law principle, noted above, that a tortfeasor is liable for any injury of which his negligence is *a* proximate cause. Liability attaches to a concurrent tortfeasor in this situation not because he is responsible for the acts of other independent tortfeasors who may also have caused the injury, but because he is responsible for all damage of which his own negligence was a proximate cause. When independent negligent actions of a number of tortfeasors are each a proximate cause of a single injury, each tort-feasor is thus personally liable for the damage sustained, and the injured per-son may sue one or all of the tortfeasors to obtain a recovery for his injuries; the fact that one of the tortfeasors is impecunious or otherwise immune from suit does not relieve another tortfeasor of his liability for damage which he himself has proximately caused.

Thus, joint and several liability traditionally arose in three situations: first, where in-divisible harm to the plaintiff was legally caused by the tortious actions of two or more actors (*see, e.g., Kinsman No. 1,* 338 F.2d 708 (2d Cir. 1964), *supra* at p. 439); second, where persons acting in concert tortiously caused harm to the plaintiff, regardless of whether that harm was divisible (*see, e.g.,* Herman v. Wesgate, 464 N.Y.S.2d 315 (App. Div. 1983), *supra* at p. 406); third, where liability was imposed by operation of law (*see, e.g.,* Smith v. Lannert, 429 S.W.2d 8 (Mo. Ct. App. 1968) (*respondeat superior*), *supra* at 661; Davey v. Hedden, 920 P.2d 420 (Kan. 1996) (statute providing that a person who furnishes a motor vehicle to a minor is jointly and severally liable for any damages caused by the minor's negligence)).

Although authorities often talk about joint and several liability for negligence, the same rules often apply to liability based on intentional, reckless, and strict liability conduct.

2. Divisibility and Apportionment of Harm

As noted above, whether harm is divisible may determine whether tortfeasors who did not act in concert may be held jointly and severally liable. The Restatement, Third, of Torts: Apportionment of Liability, deals with divisible harms in § 26:

> (a) When damages for an injury can be divided by causation, the factfinder first divides them into their indivisible component parts and separately apportions liability for each indivisible component part....

> (b) Damages can be divided by causation when the evidence provides a reasonable basis for the factfinder to determine:

>> (1) that any legally culpable conduct of a party or other relevant person to whom the factfinder assigns a percentage of responsibility was a legal cause of less than the entire damages for which the plaintiff seeks recovery and

>> (2) the amount of damages separately caused by that conduct.

Otherwise, the damages are indivisible and thus the injury is indivisible....

Elaborating on these rules, the commentary to the Restatement provides in part:

> g. *Indivisible injuries.* Damages are indivisible, and thus the injury is indivisible, when all legally culpable conduct of the plaintiff and every tortious act of the defendants and other relevant persons caused all the damages. Unless the evidence permits the factfinder to determine that damages are divisible, they are indivisible.

If, in a particular case, it is unclear whether damages are divisible, who has the burden of proof? Comment h to the Restatement, Third, of Torts: Apportionment of Liability, § 26, provides that "[a] party alleging that damages are divisible has the burden to prove that they are divisible." As the following opinions show, the burden-of-proof issue may be extremely important.

Michie v. Great Lakes Steel Division, National Steel Corp.

United States Court of Appeals for the Sixth Circuit
495 F.2d 213 (6th Cir. 1974)

EDWARDS, Circuit Judge.

This is an interlocutory appeal from a District Judge's denial of a motion to dismiss filed by three corporations which are defendants-appellants herein....

Appellants' motion to dismiss was based upon the contention that each plaintiff individually had failed to meet the requirement of a $10,000 amount in controversy for diversity jurisdiction set forth in 28 U.S.C.A. §1332 (1970).

.... Thirty-seven persons, members of thirteen families residing near LaSalle, Ontario, Canada, have filed a complaint against three corporations which operate seven plants in the United States immediately across the Detroit River from Canada. Plaintiffs claim that pollutants emitted by plants of defendants are noxious in character and that their discharge in the ambient air violates various municipal and state ordinances and laws. They assert that the discharges represent a nuisance and that the pollutants are carried by air currents onto their premises in Canada, thereby damaging their persons and property. Each plaintiff individually claims damages ranging from $11,000 to

$35,000 from all three corporate defendants jointly and severally. There is, however, no assertion of joint action or conspiracy on the part of defendants.

. . . .

We believe the principal question presented by this appeal may be phrased thus: Under the law of the State of Michigan, may multiple defendants, whose independent actions of allegedly discharging pollutants into the ambient air thereby allegedly create a nuisance, be jointly and severally liable to multiple plaintiffs for numerous individual injuries which plaintiffs claim to have sustained as a result of said actions, where said pollutants mix in the air so that their separate effects in creating the individual injuries are impossible to analyze.

. . . .

In Maddux v. Donaldson, 362 Mich. 425, 108 N.W.2d 33 the Michigan Supreme Court cites Landers v. East Texas Salt Water Disposal Company, 151 Tex. 251, 248 S.W.2d 731, a pollution case. . . . The court indicated that

> . . . [i]t is clear that there is a manifest unfairness in "putting on the injured party the impossible burden of proving the specific shares of harm done by each. . . . Such results are simply the law's callous dullness to innocent sufferers. One would think that the obvious meanness [sic] of letting wrongdoers go scot free in such cases would cause the courts to think twice and to suspect some fallacy in their rule of law."

. . . .

It is the opinion of this court that the rule of *Maddux*, *supra*, and *Landers*, *supra*, cited therein is the better, and applicable rule in this air pollution case.

. . . .

Like most jurisdictions, Michigan has had great difficulty with the problems posed in tort cases by multiple causes for single or indivisible injuries. [Citations.]

. . . .

We believe that the issue was decided in the lengthy consideration given by the Michigan court in the *Maddux* case . . . :

> [I]f the triers of the facts conclude that they cannot reasonably make the division of liability between the tort-feasors, this is the point where the road of authority divides. Much ancient authority, not in truth precedent, would say that the case is now over, and that plaintiff shall take nothing. . . . The conclusion is erroneous. . . . When the triers of the facts decide that they cannot make a division of injuries we have, by their own finding, nothing more or less than an indivisible injury, and the precedents as to indivisible injuries will control. They were well summarized in Cooley on Torts in these words: "Where the negligence of two or more persons concur in producing a single, indivisible injury, then such persons are jointly and severally liable, although there was no common duty, common design, or concert action." Maddux v. Donaldson, 362 Mich. 425, 432-433, 108 N.W.2d 33, 36 (1961). . . .

. . . .

. . . [T]he net effect of Michigan's new rule is to shift the burden of proof as to which one was responsible and to what degree from the injured party to the wrongdoers. The injustice of the old rule is vividly illustrated in an early Michigan case, Frye v. City of

Detroit, 256 Mich. 466, 239 N.W. 886 (1932). There a pedestrian was struck by an automobile, thrown in the path of a street car and struck again. Since his widow could not establish which impact killed him, a verdict was directed against her case.

....

....Like the District Judge, we believe that the Michigan courts would apply the *Maddux* principles to the case at bar. Under *Maddux*, each plaintiff's complaint should be read as alleging $11,000 or more in damages against each defendant....

....

As modified [in regard to punitive damages], the judgment of the District Court is affirmed.

Note

1. *See* Borman v. Raymark Indus., Inc., 960 F.2d 327 (3d Cir. 1992) (holding an asbestos defendant liable for all damages resulting from decedent's disability because the evidence was too speculative to support a jury charge on apportionment of damages between those caused by cigarette smoking and those caused by asbestos exposure).

Bruckman v. Pena
Colorado Court of Appeals
487 P.2d 566 (Colo. Ct. App. 1971)

DWYER, Judge.

....

Plaintiff was injured on July 21, 1964, when the car in which he was riding collided with a truck driven by the defendant Bruckman and owned by the defendant Armored Motors Service. On June 11, 1965, plaintiff was injured in a second collision and certain injuries he had sustained in the first collision were aggravated. This action was commenced on June 25, 1965, and the only defendants named in the action are the owner and driver of the truck involved in the first collision.

[The jury returned a $50,000 verdict in plaintiff Pena's favor.]

In seeking reversal, defendants assert that the court was in error in one of its instructions to the jury....

....The first part of the instruction, which is a proper statement of the law applicable to the case, is as follows:

> If you find that after the collision complained of Plaintiff, William Pena, had an injury which aggravated the ailment or disability received in the collision complained of, the Plaintiff is entitled to recover for the injury or pain received in the collision complained of; but he is not entitled to recover for any physical ailment or disability which he may have incurred subsequent to the collision.

> Where a subsequent injury occurs which aggravated the condition caused by the collision, it is your duty, if possible, to apportion the amount of disability and pain between that caused by the subsequent injury and that caused by the collision.

In addition to this correct statement of the law, the court further instructed the jury:

> But if you find that the evidence does not permit such an apportionment, then the Defendants are liable for the entire disability.

Defendants argue that this last statement in the instruction is in error....

It is the general rule that...the burden of proof is upon the plaintiff to establish that the damages he seeks were proximately caused by the negligence of the defendant. In accordance with this general rule, we hold that the instruction is in error because it permits the plaintiffs to recover damages against the defendants for injuries which the plaintiff received subsequent to any act of negligence on the part of the defendants and from causes for which the defendants were in no way responsible. The instruction erroneously places upon the defendants the burden of proving that plaintiff's disability can be apportioned between that caused by the collision here involved and that caused by the subsequent injury in order to limit their liability to the damages proximately caused by their negligence. Counsel for plaintiffs argues that the rules concerning apportionment of disability announced by our Supreme Court in Newbury v. Vogel, 151 Colo. 520, 379 P.2d 811, should also apply here. In *Newbury*, the Court stated:

> We find the law to be that where a pre-existing diseased condition exists, and where after trauma aggravating the condition disability and pain result, and no apportionment of the disability between that caused by the pre-existing condition and that caused by the trauma can be made, in such case, even though a portion of the present and future disability is directly attributable to the pre-existing condition, the defendant, whose act of negligence was the cause of the trauma, is responsible for the entire damage.

The pre-existing condition in the *Newbury* case was of non-traumatic origin, but the rules there announced also apply where the pre-existing condition was caused by trauma. [Citation.] The reasons for the adoption of the *Newbury* rules are not present here. It is one thing to hold a tort-feasor who injures one suffering from a pre-existing condition liable for the entire damage when no apportionment between the pre-existing condition and the damage caused by the defendant can be made, but it is quite another thing to say that a tort-feasor is liable, not only for the damage which he caused, but also for injuries subsequently suffered by the injured person. We hold that the defendants here cannot be held liable for the plaintiff's subsequent injury and this is so whether or not such damage can be apportioned between the two injuries.

The plaintiffs also rely on the case of Maddux v. Donaldson, 362 Mich. 425, 108 N.W.2d 33, 100 A.L.R. 2d 1. This case involved a chain-type collision, and plaintiff's injuries resulted from successive impacts which to all intents and purposes were concurrent. The court there held that where independent concurring negligent acts have proximately caused injury and damage which cannot be apportioned between the tort-feasors, each tort-feasor is jointly and severally liable for all of the injury and damage. This rule is not applicable where, as here, the second injury or aggravation of the first injury is attributable to a distinct intervening cause without which the second injury or aggravation would not have occurred.

....

Judgments reversed and cause remanded for a new trial on the issues of damages alone.

Notes

1. *See also* Jackson v. Hicks, 738 P.2d 1037 (Utah 1987), granting a new trial because the verdict imposed liability not only for injuries sustained in an auto accident with the defendant, but also for injuries suffered in two subsequent muggings. The court held that the plaintiff had the burden of showing that any subsequent injury might have been reasonably expected to follow from the original tort.

2. *Instructing Jurors on Joint and Several Liability.* There is a split of authority as to whether jurors should be informed about the legal consequences of their answers to questions bearing upon joint and several liability.

3. Effect of Comparative Negligence and Comparative Fault

Before the widespread adoption of comparative negligence and comparative fault, joint tortfeasors were nearly always jointly and severally liable for the full amount of the plaintiff's indivisible injures. For example, if a jury found that a plaintiff's $500,000 injury was caused by both the negligence of another driver and by a defect in the plaintiff's automobile, the other driver and the automobile manufacturer would be jointly and severally liable to the plaintiff for $500,000. This system, like the rule of contributory negligence itself, had the virtue of simplicity and the drawback that a person whose contribution to a misfortune was relatively small might in practice pay all the damages. The adoption of comparative fault, which necessarily involves juries in assigning percentages of responsibility, has led to pressures to take tortfeasors' percentages of responsibility into account in dividing damages among defendants.

American Motorcycle Association v. Superior Court
Supreme Court of California
578 P.2d 899 (Cal. 1978)

TOBRINER, Justice.

Three years ago, in Li v. Yellow Cab Co. (1975) 13 Cal. 3d 804, 119 Cal. Rptr. 858, 532 P.2d 1226, we concluded that the harsh and much criticized contributory negligence doctrine, which totally barred an injured person from recovering damages whenever his own negligence had contributed in any degree to the injury, should be replaced in this state by a rule of comparative negligence, under which an injured individual's recovery is simply proportionately diminished, rather than completely eliminated, when he is partially responsible for the injury.... [W]e explicitly recognized that our innovation inevitably raised numerous collateral issues, "[t]he most serious [of which] are those attendant upon the administration of a rule of comparative negligence in cases involving multiple parties."....The present mandamus proceeding presents such a case, and requires us to resolve a number of the thorny multiple party problems to which Li adverted.

....

...Glen Gregos, a teenage boy, seeks to recover damages for serious injuries which he incurred while participating in a cross-country motorcycle race for novices. Glen's second amended complaint alleges...that defendants American Motorcycle Association

(AMA) and the Viking Motorcycle Club (Viking)—the organizations that sponsored and collected the entry fee for the race—negligently designed, managed, and supervised and administered the race, and negligently solicited the entrants for the race. The second amended complaint further alleges that as a direct and proximate cause of such negligence, Glen suffered a crushing of his spine, resulting in the permanent loss of the use of his legs and his permanent inability to perform sexual functions....

AMA filed an answer....Thereafter, AMA sought leave of court to file a cross-complaint, which purported to state two causes of action against Glen's parents. The first cause of action...asserts that in permitting Glen's entry into the race, his parents negligently failed to exercise their power of supervision over their minor child; moreover, the cross complaint asserts that while AMA's negligence, if any, was "passive," that of Glen's parents was "active." On the basis of these allegations, the first cause of action seeks indemnity from Glen's parents if AMA is found liable to Glen.

In the second cause of action of its proposed cross-complaint, AMA...asks for a declaration of the "allocable negligence" of Glen's parents so that "the damages awarded [against AMA], if any, [may] be reduced by the percentage of damages allocable to cross-defendants' negligence."...[T]he second cause of action is based on an implicit assumption that the *Li* decision abrogates the rule of joint and several liability of concurrent tortfeasors and establishes in its stead a new rule of "proportionate liability," under which each concurrent tortfeasor who has proximately caused an indivisible harm may be held liable only for a portion of plaintiff's recovery, determined on a comparative fault basis.

The trial court...denied AMA's motion for leave to file the cross-complaint....[T]he Court of Appeal...granted a peremptory writ of mandate....

    ....

....Under well-established common law principles, a negligent tortfeasor is generally liable for all damage of which his negligence is a proximate cause; stated another way, in order to recover damages sustained as a result of an indivisible injury, a plaintiff is not required to prove that a tortfeasor's conduct was the sole proximate cause of the injury, but only that such negligence was a proximate cause....

    ....

In the instant case AMA argues that the *Li* decision, by repudiating the all-or-nothing contributory negligence rule and replacing it by a rule which simply diminishes an injured party's recovery on the basis of his comparative fault, in effect undermined the fundamental rationale of the entire joint and several liability doctrine as applied to concurrent tortfeasors....AMA argues that after *Li* (1) there is a basis for dividing damages, namely on a comparative negligence basis, and (2) a plaintiff is no longer necessarily "innocent," for *Li* permits a negligent plaintiff to recover damages. AMA maintains that in light of these two factors it is logically inconsistent to retain joint and several liability of concurrent tortfeasors after *Li*....[W]e cannot accept AMA's argument.

First, the simple feasibility of apportioning fault on a comparative negligence basis does not render an indivisible injury "divisible" for purposes of the joint and several liability rule....[T]he mere fact that it may be possible to assign some percentage figure to the relative culpability of one negligent defendant as compared to another does not in any way suggest that each defendant's negligence is not a proximate cause of the entire indivisible injury.

Second, abandonment of the joint and several liability rule is not warranted by AMA's claim that, after *Li*, a plaintiff is no longer "innocent." Initially, of course, it is by no means invariably true that after *Li* injured plaintiffs will be guilty of negligence. In many instances a plaintiff will be completely free of all responsibility for the accident, and yet, under the proposed abolition of joint and several liability, such a completely faultless plaintiff, rather than a wrongdoing defendant, would be forced to bear a portion of the loss if any one of the concurrent tortfeasors should prove financially unable to satisfy his proportioned share of the damages.

Moreover, even when a plaintiff is partially at fault for his own injury, a plaintiff's culpability is not equivalent to that of a defendant. In this setting, a plaintiff's negligence relates only to a failure to use due care for his own protection, while a defendant's negligence relates to a lack of due care for the safety of others. Although we recognized in *Li* that a plaintiff's self-directed negligence would justify reducing his recovery in proportion to his degree of fault for the accident, the fact remains that insofar as the plaintiff's conduct creates only a risk of self-injury, such conduct, unlike that of a negligent defendant, is not tortious. [Citation.]

Finally, from a realistic standpoint, we think that AMA's suggested abandonment of the joint and several liability rule would work a serious and unwarranted deleterious effect on the practical ability of negligently injured persons to receive adequate compensation for their injuries. One of the principal by-products of the joint and several liability rule is that it frequently permits an injured person to obtain full recovery for his injuries even when one or more of the responsible parties do not have the financial resources to cover their liability. In such a case the rule recognizes that fairness dictates that the "wronged party should not be deprived of his right to redress," but that "[t]he wrongdoers should be left to work out between themselves any apportionment."....

For all of the foregoing reasons, we reject AMA's suggestion that our adoption of comparative negligence logically compels the abolition of joint and several liability of concurrent tortfeasors....[T]he overwhelming majority of jurisdictions which have adopted comparative negligence have retained the joint and several liability doctrine.

....

[The court further held that under the common law equitable-indemnity doctrine a concurrent tortfeasor could obtain partial indemnity from co-tortfeasors on a comparative fault basis.]

Let a peremptory writ of mandate issue directing the trial court (1) to vacate its order denying AMA leave to file its proposed cross-complaint, and (2) to proceed in accordance with the views expressed in this opinion....

....

CLARK, Justice, dissenting.

....

Repudiating the existing contributory negligence system and adopting a system of comparative negligence, this court in Li v. Yellow Cab Co. (1975) 13 Cal. 3d 804, 119 Cal. Rptr. 858, 532 P.2d 1226, repeatedly—like the tolling bell—enunciated the principle that the extent of liability must be governed by the extent of fault....

Now, only three years later, the majority of my colleagues conclude that the *Li* principle is not irresistible after all. Today...they reject it for almost all cases involving multiple parties.

...[T]hey reject it by adopting joint and several liability holding that each defendant—including the marginally negligent one—will be responsible for the loss attributable to his codefendant's negligence. To illustrate, if we assume that the plaintiff is found 30 percent at fault, the first defendant 60 percent, and a second defendant 10 percent, the plaintiff under the majority's decision is entitled to a judgment for 70 percent of the loss against each defendant, and the defendant found only 10 percent at fault may have to pay 70 percent of the loss if his codefendant is unable to respond in damages.

. . . .

Attempting to justify their repudiation of the *Li* principle in favor of joint and several liability, the majority suggest three rationales. First, we are told that the feasibility of apportioning fault on a comparative basis does not "render an indivisible injury 'divisible,'" each defendant's negligence remaining a proximate cause of the entire indivisible injury. [Citation.] The argument proves too much. Plaintiff negligence is also a proximate cause of the entire indivisible injury, and the argument, if meritorious, would warrant repudiation of *Li* not only in the multiple party case but in all cases.

The second rationale of the majority lies in two parts. First, we are told that after *Li* there is no reason to assume that plaintiffs will "invariably" be guilty of negligence. [Citation.] Obviously this is true. The basis of joint and several liability prior to *Li* was that between an innocent plaintiff and two or more negligent defendants, it was proper to hold the defendants jointly and severally liable. The innocent plaintiff should not suffer as against a wrongdoing defendant. [Citations.] Accordingly, it is not unreasonable to reject the *Li* principle when we are comparing the plaintiff's innocence and defendants' negligence. But the issue presented by this case is whether joint and several liability shall be extended to *Li* cases, cases where the plaintiff *by definition* is negligent. While we cannot know whether a plaintiff will be found negligent until trial, we also cannot know whether any given defendant will be found at fault until trial. Since liability is not to be determined until after trial, there is no reason not to deal with the real issue before us whether joint and several liability should be applied in cases where the plaintiff is found negligent—i.e., cases where by definition the plaintiff is "invariably" found negligent.

As a second part of the second rationale for joint and several liability we are told that a plaintiff's culpability is not equivalent to that of a defendant. This obviously is true—this is what *Li* is all about. The plaintiff may have been driving 50 miles in excess of the speed limit while the defendants may have been driving 10 miles in excess. The converse may also be true. But the differences warrant departure from the *Li* principle in toto or not at all.

The majority's third rationale for rejecting the *Li* principle is an asserted public policy for fully compensating accident victims. The majority state that joint and several liability "recognizes that fairness dictates that the 'wronged party should not be deprived of his right to redress,' but that '[t]he wrongdoers should be left to work out between themselves any apportionment....'" [Citation.] The quoted language is not helpful to the majority when the plaintiff is also negligent because he is himself a wrongdoer.

Until today neither policy nor law called for fully compensating the negligent plaintiff. Prior to *Li*, the negligent plaintiff was denied all recovery under the contributory negligence doctrine.... *Li*, of course, repudiated that doctrine replacing it with a policy permitting compensation of the negligent accident victim but only on the basis of comparative fault.... [T]he majority are establishing a new policy both contrary to that existing prior to *Li* and going further than that reflected by the comparative principle enunciated in *Li*.

Conceivably, such a new public policy departing from intelligent notions of fairness may be warranted but, if so, its establishment should be left for the Legislature....

. . . .

Adherence to the *Li* principle that the extent of liability is governed by the extent of fault requires that only a limited form of joint and several liability be retained in cases where the plaintiff is negligent. The issue of joint and several liability presents the problem whether the plaintiff or the solvent defendants should bear the portion of the loss attributable to unknown defendants or defendants who will not respond in damages due to lack of funds.

Consistent with the *Li* principle—the extent of liability is governed by the extent of fault—the loss attributable to the inability of one defendant to respond in damages should be apportioned between the negligent plaintiff and the solvent negligent defendant in relation to their fault. [Citation.] Returning to my 30-60-10 illustration, if the 60 percent at fault defendant is unable to respond, the 30 percent at fault plaintiff should be permitted to recover 25 percent of the entire loss from the 10 percent at fault solvent defendant based on the 3 to 1 ratio of fault between them....

Placing the entire loss attributable to the insolvent defendant solely on the negligent plaintiff or solely on the solvent negligent defendant is not only contrary to the *Li* principle, but also undermines the entire system of comparative fault. If the portion attributable to the insolvent defendant is placed upon the negligent plaintiff, the solvent defendant will attempt to reduce his liability by magnifying the fault of the insolvent defendant. Should the insolvent's portion be placed solely upon the solvent defendant—as done by the majority's application of joint and several liability—the plaintiff will have an incentive to magnify the fault of the insolvent defendant.[5] Because the insolvent—and therefore disinterested—defendant will usually not be present at trial to defend himself, any semblance to comparative fault will be destroyed.

. . . .

[BIRD, C.J., and MOSK, RICHARDSON, MANUEL, and SULLIVAN, JJ., concurred in the majority opinion.]

Notes

1. *Joint and Several Liability Today.* The California Supreme Court's assertion in *American Motorcycle Association* that "the overwhelming majority of jurisdictions which have adopted comparative negligence have retained the joint and several liability doctrine" is no longer true. The Restatement, Third, of Torts: Apportionment of Liability, § 10, cmt. a, says that there is today "no majority rule on this matter," and adds in comment a to § A18 that the number of jurisdictions that retain pure joint and several liability "is dwindling." The matter is today largely statutory, as many jurisdictions have enacted legislation abolishing or modifying joint and several liability. These states include California, which abolished joint and several liability for "noneconomic damages" such as damages for pain and suffering, shortly after the *American Motorcycle Association* decision.

---

5. To illustrate, if plaintiff and the solvent defendant are equally at fault, the amount to be recovered will depend on the extent of fault of the insolvent defendant. If the insolvent defendant is 80 percent at fault, plaintiff will recover 90 percent of his loss but if the insolvent is only 10 percent at fault, recovery will be limited to 55 percent of the loss.

The third Restatement identifies five patterns of liability for multiple tortfeasors, and it devotes a separate "track" to each of these five models. They are:

(a) *Joint and several liability.*

(b) *Pure several liability.* This approach makes each joint tortfeasor liable only for the share of the damages assigned to that defendant by the factfinder. The Restatement takes the position that most intentional tortfeasors should remain jointly and severally liable for an injury even if a jurisdiction has adopted several liability as a general rule. Similarly, tortfeasors who acted in concert remain jointly and severally liable. *See* Restatement, Third, of Torts: Apportionment of Liability, § B18, cmt. a. The same should also be true in cases of vicarious liability; if an employee commits a tort within the scope of employment, the employer and employee will still be jointly and severally liable.

(c) *"Joint and several liability with reallocation."* This system is a variation of joint and several liability in which the liability of an insolvent defendant is reallocated to other parties. In cases where the plaintiff was not at all at fault, this system leads to the same outcomes as joint and several liability: any solvent tortfeasor may pay all the damages. *See generally* Restatement, Third, of Torts: Apportionment of Liability, §§ C18 to C21.

(d) *"Hybrid liability based on threshold percentage of comparative responsibility."* A fairly common statutory approach to the problem of multiple tortfeasors has been to retain joint and several liability for defendants whose wrongdoing was serious, while making "minor" tortfeasors—say those assigned less than ten percent of the responsibility for harm—liable only severally. This approach avoids the perceived problem of the relatively minor tortfeasor's being left with all the liability because the more-reprehensible defendants are insolvent.

(e) *"Hybrid liability based on type of damages."* California's "Proposition 51," discussed in detail in Miller v. Stouffer, 11 Cal. Rptr. 2d 454 (Cal. App. 1992), illustrates this form of liability. Defendants who have caused indivisible harms are jointly and severally liable for harms such as medical expenses and lost wages. For "noneconomic harms" like pain and suffering, however, each defendant is liable only for that defendant's proportionate share of the harm.

2. *Modification.* In many jurisdictions, the traditional rules of joint and several liability have been modified extensively by statute. For example, Texas law contains the following provisions:

TEX. CIV. PRAC. & REM. CODE §§33.002 & 33.013
(Westlaw 2004)

§33.002. Applicability

....

(c) This chapter does not apply to:

(1)....

(2) a claim for exemplary damages included in an action to which this chapter otherwise applies....

§33.013. Amount of Liability

(a) Except as provided in Subsection (b), a liable defendant is liable to a claimant only for the percentage of the damages found by the trier of fact equal to that defendant's percentage of responsibility with respect to the personal injury, property damage, death, or other harm for which the damages are allowed.

(b) Notwithstanding Subsection (a), each liable defendant is, in addition to his liability under Subsection (a), jointly and severally liable for the damages recoverable by the claimant under Section 33.012 with respect to a cause of action if:

(1) the percentage of responsibility attributed to the defendant with respect to a cause of action is greater than 50 percent; or

(2) the defendant, with the specific intent to do harm to others, acted in concert with another person to engage in the conduct described in the following provisions of the Penal Code and in so doing proximately caused the damages legally recoverable by the claimant:

(A) Section 19.02 (murder);

(B) Section 19.03 (capital murder);

(C) Section 20.04 (aggravated kidnaping);

(D) Section 22.02 (aggravated assault);

(E) Section 22.011 (sexual assault);

(F) Section 22.021 (aggravated sexual assault);

(G) Section 22.04 (injury to a child, elderly individual, or disabled individual);

(H) Section 32.21 (forgery);

(I) Section 32.43 (commercial bribery);

(J) Section 32.45 (misapplication of fiduciary property or property of financial institution);

(K) Section 32.46 (securing execution of document by deception);

(L) Section 32.47 (fraudulent destruction, removal, or concealment of writing); or

(M) conduct described in Chapter 31 the punishment level for which is a felony of the third degree or higher.

(c)....

(d) This section does not create a cause of action.

(e) Notwithstanding anything to the contrary stated in the provisions of the Penal Code listed in Subsection (b)(2), that subsection applies only if the claimant proves the defendant acted or failed to act with specific intent to do harm. A defendant acts with specific intent to do harm with respect to the nature of the defendant's conduct and the result of the person's conduct when it is the person's conscious effort or desire to engage in the conduct for the purpose of doing substantial harm to others.

(f) The jury may not be made aware through voir dire, introduction into evidence, instruction, or any other means that the conduct to which Subsection (b)(2) refers is defined by the Penal Code.

3. *Judicial Review of Legislation on Joint and Several Liability.* In 1995, the Illinois legislature enacted sweeping "tort-reform" legislation. The legislation eliminated joint and several liability in actions for death, personal injury, and property damage. The new law provided, however, that if its caps on damages in medical-malpractice cases were held unconstitutional, defendants in those cases would continue to be jointly and severally liable. The Illinois Supreme Court invalidated the damages caps and then held the abolition of joint and several liability unconstitutional as well. The court said that even if a reasonable case for eliminating joint and several liability could be made, that case would apply as strongly to medical-malpractice cases as to others. The legislature's arbitrarily providing different rules for the two kinds of cases therefore violated a state constitutional provision barring "special legislation." Best v. Taylor Machine Works, 689 N.E.2d 1057 (Ill. 1997).

4. *Manufacturers and Joint and Several Liability.* Many potential defendants, particularly manufacturers, have lobbied hard for the elimination or restriction of joint and several liability, usually on the ground that it is unfair to make a defendant whose fault was very slight in comparison to that of another person pay the full cost of the plaintiff's injuries. An everyday example is the plaintiff severely injured in a crash caused by a drunken driver who gets a verdict finding the driver 98-percent responsible for the harm and the manufacturer of the plaintiff's car two-percent responsible, and who then collects in full from the manufacturer because the drunken driver has no assets.

5. *Economic Analysis: Incentives Relating to Joint and Several Liability.* At first glance, it may seem that allowing injured persons to recover in full from any defendant who might have prevented the injury will reduce injuries. Absent joint and several liability, a potential defendant might spend less than the optimal amount on injury prevention, knowing that it will be responsible for only a portion of the plaintiff's costs if something goes awry. For example, someone who might expect to be held ten-percent responsible for a $1,000,000 injury might decide to pay no more than $100,000 to prevent the injury. Under a system of joint and several liability, the same potential defendant should be willing to pay much more to prevent the injury, especially if it knows that other potential defendants are likely to be judgment-proof, so that the entire burden will fall on it. On the other hand, a system that allows joint and several liability encourages plaintiffs to sue as many persons as possible. Potential defendants, knowing this, may assume that much of the financial burden of the harm they cause through their carelessness may be borne by others; when they do, their incentive to exercise care is reduced. Furthermore, the system encourages plaintiffs to draw into litigation all possible defendants who are wealthy or insured, a practice that may deflect attention away from serious wrongdoers and which imposes heavy costs on persons whose connection to the accident was slight, if present at all. For example, it is routine in plane-crash cases for plaintiffs to sue the manufacturer of the airplane involved in the crash, even when it is clear that the crash resulted from gross pilot error.

6. *Problems in Calculating Shares of Fault.* At first glance, applying comparative principles to the liability of defendants may seem simple: a defendant found to be 40-percent responsible for harm would pay 40 percent of the damages, and so on. In practice, however, things are far from being that easy. The Restatement, Third, of Torts: Apportionment of Liability, explores questions like the following in detail.

(a) *Immune Parties.* Suppose that the plaintiff's injuries were caused by the negligence of the plaintiff's employer (not subject to suit because of workers' compensation) and by the defective design of a product; should the product manufacturer's liability be reduced because of the negligence of the employer? That is, can fault be allocated to an immune party? According to some courts, the answer is yes. *See* Taylor v. John Crane Inc., 6 Cal. Rptr. 3d 695 (Cal. App. 2003) (holding in an asbestos-exposure case that fault could be allocated to the Navy, even if it was immune from suit); *but see* Jefferson County Commonwealth Attorney's Office v. Kaplan, 65 S.W.3d 916 (Ky. 2001) (holding that fault in a legal malpractice action could not be apportioned to prosecutors who were immune from suit).

(b) *Intentional Wrongdoers.* What about cases in which some defendants are intentional wrongdoers while others were merely negligent, as when a property owner fails to take reasonable precautions to prevent crimes? Can a portion of the fault be allocated to the intentional wrongdoer? In some instances, the answer is yes, although most states are to the contrary. *See* note 3 *supra* at p. 801. (This is a particularly difficult problem when the plaintiff has been negligent, too, as plaintiff's negligence traditionally does not reduce the plaintiff's recovery from an intentional wrongdoer, though it does reduce or eliminate recovery from negligent defendants.)

(c) *Non-Parties.* Should the tortious conduct of persons whom the victim has not sued or of persons who are judgment-proof reduce the amount the plaintiff can recover from others? In some instances, the answer is yes. *See* Tex. Civ. Prac. & Rem Code §§33.003 and 33.004 (Westlaw 2003) (permitting allocation of fault to a designated third party, even if the party has not been joined); Marier v. Scoggins, 105 S.W.3d 596 (Tenn. Ct. App. 2002) (permitting assignment of fault to an unidentified "phantom" driver).

(d) *Persons Who Have Settled.* In calculating a defendant's portion of the plaintiff's damages, can fault be apportioned to persons who have settled? In some instances, the answer is yes. *See* Smiley v. Corrigan, 638 N.W.2d 151 (Mich. Ct. App. 2002) (permitting a golf instructor to introduce evidence concerning the fault attributable to a driving range and a fellow patron, both of whom had settled with the plaintiff).

Because forms of liability other than joint and several liability in cases involving multiple actors and indivisible harm are fairly new, questions like these have no settled answers in many jurisdictions.

4. Releases from Liability

McMillen v. Klingensmith

Supreme Court of Texas
467 S.W.2d 193 (Tex. 1971)

POPE, Justice.

Joyce Lynn McMillen and husband sued Dr. William Klingensmith and Dr. Henry E. Martinez for negligence in the treatment of Joyce McMillen's injuries which she suffered in an automobile collision with a car driven by William Robert Perkins. Mrs. McMillen and her husband released Perkins from all claims upon his payment of $7,900. The McMillens then instituted suit against the two physicians who moved for summary judgment grounded upon the release. The trial court and the court of civil appeals rendered judgment for the defendant doctors, holding that the release of the original tortfeasor operated to release the subsequent tort-feasors also. [Citation.] We reverse....

    ....

On May 2, 1968, Mrs. McMillen and her husband, upon receipt of $7,900 signed a release which named Perkins only and discharged him

> from any and all actions, causes of action, claims, demands, damages, costs, loss of services, expenses and compensation, on account of, or in any way growing out of, any and all known AND UNKNOWN personal injuries and property damage resulting or to result from the accident that occurred on or about the 2nd day of June, 1967, at or near Clarendon, Texas.

> I/we hereby declare and represent that the injuries sustained are permanent and progressive and that recovery therefrom is uncertain and indefinite, and in making this release and agreement it is understood and agreed that I/we rely wholly upon my/our own judgment, belief and knowledge of the nature, extent and duration of said injuries....

>   ....

> This release contains the ENTIRE AGREEMENT between the parties hereto, and the terms of this release are contractual and not a mere recital.

On May 22, 1969, the McMillens filed suit against Doctors Klingensmith and Martinez.... The legal question presented is whether the McMillens may maintain an action for damages against the doctors for malpractice after releasing from liability the named tortfeasor whose conduct made the services of the doctors necessary.

    ....

The rule that a release of an original tort-feasor also releases a malpracticing physician finds its basis in the broader common-law rule known as the unity of release rule. The unity of release rule is based upon the idea that there is such a unity of the obligation or injury that a release of one is release of all....

The legal basis for the unity of release rule has been challenged by every legal scholar who has examined it. [Citations.]

Underlying much of the criticism is the idea... that there has been a confusion of satisfaction of a claim with release of a cause of action. As expressed by Prosser: "A satisfaction is an acceptance of full compensation for the injury; a release is a surrender of the cause of action, which might be gratuitous, or given for inadequate consideration." [Citation.] Unless the settlement with one of the tort-feasors fully satisfies the injured party, the release of one party should, according to Prosser, release only the tort-feasor who makes the partial settlement.

Those jurisdictions which purport to follow the unity of release rule have, nevertheless, looked with favor upon devices, such as the "covenant not to sue" or a reservation of a cause against others, which are used to skirt the rule. Texas is among those jurisdictions which hold that such devices will save the cause against another tortfeasor when a release would be fatal to it. [Citations.]

These judicial efforts to avoid the harsh common-law rule have also been challenged for their artificial reasoning. They have been declared by the scholars cited above to be less than forthright, judicial fudging, and a trap for the unwary who do not notice in a document such nice distinctions. [Citation.]

Mr. Justice Rutledge, while serving on the court of appeals for the District of Columbia wrote McKenna v. Austin, 77 U.S. App. D.C. 228, 134 F.2d 659, 148 A.L.R. 1253 (1943). He thoroughly examined the foundation and rationale of the unity of release rule. He said that it arose historically by an inappropriate transference of the meta-physics of the property concepts of joint estates and survivorship to the law of obliga-tions independent of property. He summarized the practical reasons for abandoning the rule by saying:

> The rule's results are incongruous. More often than otherwise they are unjust and unintended. Wrongdoers who do not make or share in making reparation are discharged, while one willing to right the wrong and no more guilty bears the whole loss. Compromise is stifled, first, by inviting all to wait for the others to settle and, second, because claimants cannot accept less than full indemnity from one when doing that discharges all. Many, not knowing this, accept less only to find later they have walked into a trap. The rule shortchanges the claimant or overcharges the person who settles.... Finally, it is anomalous in legal theory, giv-ing tortfeasors an advantage wholly inconsistent with the nature of their liability.

The Supreme Court of Alaska, writing in Young v. State, 455 P.2d 889 (Alaska 1969), reviewed the several alternatives which that jurisdiction could adopt, and it chose the path of simplicity. It wrote:

> In our opinion the rule which will bring most clarity to this area of ambigu-ous and conflicting release rules is one under which a release of one tort-feasor does not release other joint tort-feasors unless such tort-feasors are specifically named in the release. We are of the further view that adoption of this rule will insure that the intent of the parties to the release is given effect and will greatly minimize the possibility of any party being misled as to the effect of the release.

The rule is a simple one. Unless a party is named in a release, he is not released. A rule of this type is fairer and easier to apply. It avoids many of the problems arising from the present rule which often requires proof by parol evidence of the releaser's subjective intent at the time the release was executed. With a slight modification we adopt the rule suggested by the Alaska court. We hold that a release of a party or parties named or otherwise specif-ically identified fully releases only the parties so named or identified, but no others. Our holding in this case shall not affect releases presently in existence where it appears from the language of the release and other circumstances that it was the intention of the releaser to release the named parties and other persons generally identified. The release presently be-fore us names only William Robert Perkins and makes no reference to any other parties.

In holding as we do, we preserve the rule that a claimant in no event will be entitled to recover more than the amount required for full satisfaction of his damages....

....

.... The judgments of the courts below are reversed and the cause is remanded for trial.

Notes

1. *Malpractice in Settling Cases.* Allowing a client to release one defendant (rather than giving a covenant not to sue) if the client plans to sue others is as clear a case of legal malpractice as one can imagine, except in states in which the common-law rule has been changed by statute or judicial decision. One suspects that the lawyer who al-lowed McMillen to sign the release, rather than McMillen herself, was the principal beneficiary of the Texas Supreme Court's willingness to change the common-law rule.

2. *Releases under the Uniform Act.* Section 4 of the Uniform Contribution Among Tortfeasors Act, which has been adopted in several states, provides:

A release by the injured person of one joint tortfeasor,... does not discharge the other tortfeasors unless the release so provides; but reduces the claim against the other tortfeasors in the amount of the consideration paid for the release, or in any amount or proportion by which the release provides that the total claim shall be reduced, if greater than the consideration paid.

3. *Releasing Classes.* In Duncan v. Cessna Aircraft Co., 665 S.W.2d 413, 419-20 (Tex. 1984), a suit involving multiple defendants, one tortfeasor settled with the plaintiff and obtained a release. Cessna, a second defendant, claimed that because the release purported to discharge "any other corporations or persons whomsoever responsible" for the accident, the document released Cessna from liability. The court held that in a multiple tortfeasor context:

> the mere naming of a general class of tortfeasors in a release does not discharge the liability of each member of that class. A tortfeasor can claim the protection of a release only if the release refers to him by name or with such descriptive particularity that his identity or his connection with the tortious event is not in doubt.

This approach minimizes the risk that a plaintiff will inadvertently release non-settling wrongdoers.

4. *What Claims Are Released?* In Memorial Med. Ctr. of E. Tex. v. Keszler, 943 S.W.2d 433 (Tex. 1997), a physician who had entered into a settlement in an action he had brought against a hospital after his staff and clinical privileges were revoked subsequently brought a separate action against the hospital, asserting claims based on toxic exposure during his employment. In addressing whether the release signed as part of the initial settlement barred the later action, the court wrote:

> It is true that to release a claim, the releasing document must "mention" it. [Citation.] But the court of appeals holds a claim is not mentioned unless it is specifically enumerated, stating "We find no mention in the preambles of anything related to appellant's present claims for exposure to ethelyne dioxide gas...."
>
> ....
>
> In this case, the parties agreed that Keszler would release all claims "relating to [Keszler's] relationship with [Memorial]." Keszler's claim of ETO exposure, because it is related to his relationship with Memorial, is "mentioned" in the releasing document. The court of appeals erred in holding otherwise.

5. *Release of a Person for Whom Another is Vicariously Liable.* Does the release of a tortfeasor for whose conduct another may be held vicariously liable also release the person on whom liability could be vicariously imposed? Many courts say "no," but there is authority to the contrary. *Compare* Miller v. Grand Union Co., 512 S.E.2d 887 (Ga. 1999) (holding that the release of an employee does not release an employer unless the instrument names the employer), *with* Burke v. Webb Boats, Inc., 37 P.3d 811 (Okla. 2001) (release of a boat operator also released the boat owner who could have been held vicariously liable, even though the owner was specifically excluded in the release).

6. *Fraudulently Procured Settlements.* A tort claimant fraudulently induced to execute a release may rescind the release or bring a separate suit for fraud with damages calculated based on the difference between what the claimant received under the release and the value the claim would have had if there had been no fraud. *See* E.I. DuPont De Nemours and Co. v. Florida Evergreen Folliage, 744 A.2d 457 (Del. 1999).

B. Contribution and Indemnity

Brochner v. Western Insurance Company

Supreme Court of Colorado, En Banc
724 P.2d 1293 (Colo. 1986)

KIRSHBAUM, Justice.

. . . .

The Community Hospital Association (the hospital)...granted staff privileges to Dr. Ruben Brochner in October 1964. Brochner performed numerous craniotomies at the hospital over the next few months. In 1965, after reviews of those craniotomies indicated that tissue samples from many of the patients appeared normal, the hospital's executive committee orally required Brochner to obtain consultations before performing craniotomies if the relevant radiographic evidence did not clearly establish pathology....

In March 1968, the hospital's tissue committee received a report that fourteen of twenty-eight tissue samples taken from Brochner's neurosurgery patients were completely normal and that nine of the remaining fourteen samples indicated only low grade disease. An expert testified at trial that one normal tissue of 100 tissue samples was an acceptable ratio and that two normal tissues out of twenty-eight samples would require investigation.

On November 9, 1968, Brochner performed a craniotomy on Esther Cortez which resulted in injury to Cortez. Cortez later filed a civil action against Brochner and the hospital. She alleged that Brochner negligently diagnosed her..., that the hospital negligently continued Brochner's staff privileges..., and that the hospital negligently allowed Brochner to perform unnecessary surgery. The claim against Brochner was severed, and trial of the claims against the hospital commenced April 3, 1978. Prior to the conclusion of that trial, Cortez and the hospital agreed to a settlement of $150,000. Some time later, Cortez reached a settlement of her suit against Brochner, who was uninsured, for an undisclosed sum.

In 1979, the hospital and its subrogee, Western Insurance Company (Western), filed this indemnity action against Brochner, alleging that Brochner's negligence was the active and primary cause of Cortez' injuries while the hospital's negligence was passive and secondary....[T]he trial court entered judgment for Western and the hospital against Brochner....The Court of Appeals affirmed....

. . . .

Brochner first argues that the adoption of the Uniform Contribution Among Tortfeasors Act, §§13-50.5-101 to -106, 6 C.R.S. (1985 Supp.) (the Act) abrogated the Colorado common law rule of indemnity to the extent such rule is based upon distinctions between primary and secondary fault. We do not agree that the statute *per se* altered the common law doctrine of indemnity. However, we conclude that existence of the Act sufficiently undermines the historical basis for the rule to require its modification.

The common law of Colorado...consistently followed the...rule prohibiting contribution among joint tortfeasors. [Citations.] Recognizing that strict application of this rule sometimes produces unjust results, a rule permitting indemnity between tortfeasors in certain limited circumstances was also incorporated into this jurisdiction's panoply of common law principles. [Citations.]

Contribution and indemnity are analytically quite distinct concepts. The former is based on the equitable notion that one tortfeasor should not be required to pay sums to an injured party in excess of that tortfeasor's proportionate share of the responsibility for the injuries. The latter is grounded in the legal principle that one joint tortfeasor, as indemnitor, may owe a duty of care to another joint tortfeasor, which duty is unrelated to any duty of care owed by the tortfeasors to the injured party. [Citation.] When such duty is established, the indemnitor tortfeasor may be liable to the indemnitee tortfeasor for the entire loss experienced by the latter as the result of payments made to the injured party. [Citation.]

....As initially adopted, our rule required the indemnitor's conduct to be the "sole, proximate and primary cause" of the damages suffered by the injured party. [Citations.] However, in Jacobson v. Dahlberg, 171 Colo. 42, 464 P.2d 298 (1970), this court modified the test for indemnity by eliminating the requirement that the indemnitor's conduct be the sole cause of the injured party's damages and adopting a broader standard requiring only that the indemnitor's conduct be the primary cause of such damages....

....[The] difficulties with definitions and applications of the concepts of active, passive, primary and secondary negligence have been the subject of critical discussion by numerous courts and commentators. [Citations.] These difficulties inevitably have produced great variations in judicial decisions, resulting in a severe lack of predictability and often causing as much inequity as the rule was designed to prevent. As the court in *Missouri Pacific R.R. Co.*, 566 S.W.2d 466 [(Mo. 1978)], observed:

> ....
>
> We have worked ourselves into a situation where indemnity as between tortfeasors is decided on the basis of which one is guilty of "active" and which one guilty of "passive" negligence. "Passive" wins, "active" loses, no matter how great the proportion of fault may have been of the passive tortfeasor.
>
> ....
>
> This is not a sensible way to fix responsibility in indemnity. It comes about by attempting to find a formula by which to excuse one of two joint or concurrent tortfeasors completely when as a practical matter they both are to blame, the true difference between them being only a matter of degree or relativity of fault. With a little ingenuity in phrasing, negligence can be made to be either "active" or "passive" as suits the writer. For example, "driving an automobile with bad brakes" or "running through the stop sign" or "using a defective crane" might be said to be "active" negligence, while "omitting maintenance of brake fluid level" or "neglecting to apply the brakes" or "failing to inspect the crane in order to discover its defectiveness" might be "passive" negligence—these are the same acts or omissions, but the outcome depends not upon the facts, but upon how someone chooses to characterize them.

[Citations.]

Subsequent to this court's decision in...[Ringsby Truck Lines, Inc. v. Bradfield], 193 Colo. 151, 563 P.2d 939 [(1977)], the General Assembly adopted the Act, effective July 1, 1977. This statute abolished the common law prohibition against contribution among joint tortfeasors and established a rule authorizing such contribution based on degrees of relative fault. §13-50.5-102(6) contains the following provision respecting common law principles defining rights and responsibilities among joint tortfeasors:

This article does not impair any right [of] indemnity under existing law. Where one tortfeasor is entitled to indemnity from another, the right of the indemnity obligee is for indemnity and not contribution, and the indemnity obligor is not entitled to contribution from the obligee for any portion of his indemnity obligation.

In addition, §13-50.5-103 provides as follows:

When there is a disproportion of fault among joint tortfeasors, the relative degrees of fault of the joint tortfeasors shall be used in determining their pro rata shares solely for the purpose of determining their rights of contribution among themselves, each remaining severally liable to the injured person for the whole injury as at common law.

The statute thus recognizes that the remedies of indemnity and contribution are in theory mutually exclusive.... [T]he General Assembly's adoption of the principle of contribution among joint tortfeasors invites, if it does not require, reconsideration of the doctrine of indemnity between joint tortfeasors.

Joint tortfeasors are now subject to contribution among themselves based upon their relative degrees of fault. That principle is at odds with the essential characteristic of our present rule of indemnity that, without regard to apportionment of fault, a single tortfeasor may ultimately pay the expense of all injuries sustained by a third party as the result of negligent conduct by two or more tortfeasors. There can be no mistake concerning the intent of the General Assembly to establish the policy of responsibility related to proportionate fault in the context of personal injury litigation.... [The court discussed the legislative history.]

....Application of this principle will prove far more certain in varied factual contexts and will consequently promote more predictability than any continued effort to perpetuate ephemeral distinctions based on primary or secondary negligence concepts. For these reasons we conclude that the doctrine of indemnity insofar as it requires one of two joint tortfeasors to reimburse the other for the entire amount paid by the other as damages to a party injured as the result of the negligence of both joint tortfeasors, is no longer viable, and is hereby abolished.

In this case, the trial court found that the hospital acted negligently and that such negligence was independent of Brochner's negligence. [Citation.] As a joint tortfeasor, the hospital has no right to seek indemnity from Brochner; its sole remedy lies in contribution pursuant to the terms of the Act. §13-50.5-105(1)(b) provides:

When a release or a covenant not to sue or not to enforce judgment is given in good faith to one of two or more persons liable in tort for the same injury or the same wrongful death:

....

It discharges the tortfeasor to whom it is given from all liability for contribution to any other tortfeasor.

....Because both Brochner and the hospital settled with Cortez after... [the effective date of the Act], neither is entitled to contribution from the other.

....

[The discussion of a statute abolishing the doctrine of joint and several liability is omitted.]

The judgment of the Court of Appeals is reversed.

[The dissenting opinion of VOLLACK, J., is omitted.]

Notes

1. *Indemnity and Contribution Distinguished.* Indemnity shifts all the loss from one tortfeasor to another; contribution results in the tortfeasors sharing the loss (sometimes *pro rata*, sometimes in proportion to responsibility). The Restatement, Third, of Torts: Apportionment of Liability, points out in comment d to § 23 that contribution and indemnity are alternatives. If one defendant is entitled to indemnity from another, the question of contribution does not arise. The common-law rule, based on the principle that "the law will not aid a wrongdoer," was that contribution was never allowed; this rule has been abolished in every state.

2. *Cases in Which Indemnity is Allowed.* The Restatement takes the position that indemnity is allowed in only three cases: (1) when agreed to by contract between the indemnitor and the indemnitee; (2) when the indemnitee is liable only vicariously for the indemnitor's tort (as when *respondeat superior* makes an employer liable for the negligence of an employee); and (3) when a product seller, not otherwise at fault, is liable for injuries caused by a defect in a product manufactured by the indemnitor. *See* Restatement, Third, of Torts: Apportionment of Liability, § 22.

The caselaw supports indemnity in other cases, however. Examples include an indemnitee whose negligence allowed the indemnitor, an intentional wrongdoer, to harm the plaintiff, as when a store's lax security precautions allow a mugging. More controversially, some decisions allow a tortfeasor whose negligence was "passive" to obtain indemnity from an "actively negligent" defendant—the approach rejected in *Brochner*.

3. *Indemnity Based on Contract.* Many cases involving a claim to indemnity based on contract pose little problem. If the contract expressly provides for indemnity, it is likely that the document will be enforced as written. For example, in Churchill Forge, Inc. v. Brown, 61 S.W.3d 368 (Tex. 2001), a lease provision requiring a tenant to reimburse a landlord for losses caused by the negligence of any guest or occupant was held to be valid.

However, the mere breach of a contractual duty that does not expressly refer to indemnity may be an insufficient predicate for full indemnity. In Rosado v. Proctor & Schwartz, Inc., 484 N.E.2d 1354 (N.Y. 1985), a sales contract contained a provision requiring the purchaser of a machine to install certain safety devices. The purchaser failed to do so and an employee of the purchaser was seriously injured. The manufacturer of the machine settled with the employee and sought indemnification from the purchaser/employer. In denying relief, the court stated:

> Preventing injuries in the first place is the primary public policy underlying the doctrine of strict products liability. To allow a manufacturer like Proctor, which sells a product…with no safety devices, to shift the ultimate duty of care to others through boilerplate language in a sales contract, would erode the economic incentive manufacturers have to maintain safety and give sanction to the marketing of dangerous, stripped down, machines. This we decline to do.

The court further held that a claim for partial contribution was barred by statute.

4. *Statutory Indemnity.* Some indemnity rights are created by statute. *See* Tex. Civ. Prac. & Rem Code §82.002 (Westlaw 2003) ("A manufacturer shall indemnify and hold harmless a seller against loss arising out of a products liability action, except for any loss

caused by the seller's negligence, intentional misconduct, or other act or omission, such as negligently modifying or altering the product, for which the seller is independently liable"; "'loss' includes court costs and other reasonable expenses, reasonable attorney fees, and any reasonable damages").

5. *The Satisfaction-of-Claim Requirement.* Contribution or indemnity is normally available only to one who has extinguished the liability of the person from whom reimbursement is sought. *See* Fetick v. American Cyanamid Co., 38 S.W.3d 415 (Mo. 2001) (a physician who settled claims against him for administering a vaccine that rendered an infant triplegic had no right to contribution from the vaccine manufacturer and distributor who remained defendants in the infant's suit).

6. *Contribution and Intentional Torts.* It is generally agreed that an intentional tortfeasor may not obtain contribution. *See also* Austro v. Niagara Mohawk Power Corp., 487 N.E.2d 267 (N.Y. 1985), holding that indemnification agreements relating to intentional injury violate public policy and are therefore unenforceable.

7. *Pro Rata versus Proportional Contribution.* There are two basic approaches to calculating contribution. The older *pro rata* approach is a rather crude method of counting heads and dividing. If there are three joint tortfeasors, each one bears one-third of the loss, regardless of their respective degrees of fault. Thus, if *A* satisfies a judgment rendered jointly against *A*, *B*, and *C*, *A* can obtain reimbursement for one-third of that amount from *B*, and the same from *C*.

The modern proportional approach is to award contribution in accordance with the tortfeasors' percentages of the total fault. For example, if *A* satisfies a judgment rendered jointly against *A*, *B*, and *C*, and their respective degrees of fault are 85%, 10%, and 5%, *A* can obtain reimbursement from *B* for 10%, and from *C* for 5%, of the amount paid.

8. *Contribution from Settling Joint Tortfeasors.* May contribution be obtained from a joint tortfeasor who settles with the plaintiff? If so, there is little incentive for a defendant to settle, for doing so does not bring an end to the question of that person's liability. On the other hand, if contribution is not available, other defendants who settle later, or who litigate the case but lose at trial, may be forced to bear a disproportionate part of the total damages paid to the plaintiff.

There are at least three views on this subject, none of which is entirely satisfactory:

(a) Some courts permit an action for contribution against a settling joint tortfeasor.

(b) Other courts deny contribution from a settling joint tortfeasor if the settlement is made in good faith (*see Brochner, supra*; Copper Mt., Inc. v. Poma of Am., Inc., 890 P.2d 100 (Colo. 1995) (interpreting a state law identical to the Uniform Contribution Among Joint Tortfeasors Act, the court held that a settlement is made in "good faith" as long as it is not the product of collusive conduct, regardless of whether the amount reasonably reflects the settling tortfeasor's proportionate share of liability). A non-settling defendant may enjoy a credit against the judgment for amounts previously paid by a settling tortfeasor.

(c) Still other states avoid the issue of contribution by holding that the plaintiff, by settling with a defendant, gives up some portion (determined on a *pro rata* or proportional basis) of the judgment ultimately obtained against non-settling defendants. *See* Tex. Civ. Prac. & Rem Code §33.012 (Westlaw 2003) (reduction equal to each settling person's percentage of responsibility, except in certain health care liability claims, as to which different rules apply). Walton v. Avco Corp., 610 A.2d 454 (Pa. 1992), was a strict-liability action. One defendant settled; then another lost at trial. The court held that the defendant who went to trial had to pay only half of the judgment rendered against it, for, by settling with the one defendant, plaintiff forfeited 50% of the eventual judgment. (*Id.*, at 461 (Papadakos, J., concurring)).

In many states, the issue is controlled by the local version of the Uniform Contribution Among Tortfeasors Act.

Contribution issues do not arise if liability of joint tortfeasors is several, as a system of several liability makes each tortfeasor liable only for an appropriate share of the plaintiff's damages.

9. *Contribution Actions by Settling Joint Tortfeasors.* Many states hold that a tortfeasor who enters into a good faith settlement that extinguishes the liability of other joint tortfeasors may bring an action for contribution. However, there is authority to the contrary.

10. *Contribution Actions Barred by Immunity.* A person immune from suit by the plaintiff may also be immune from a contribution action by a joint tortfeasor. For example, in Shoemake v. Fogel, Ltd., 826 S.W.2d 933 (Tex. 1992), a child drowned in an apartment complex pool. The court held that the doctrine of parental immunity barred a contribution claim by the complex owners and managers against the child's mother, who was allegedly negligent in supervising the youth. *See also* Slater v. Skyhawk Transp. Inc., 77 F. Supp. 2d 580 (D. N.J. 1999) (holding that workers' compensation laws in New Jersey, Michigan, and Virginia all barred contribution claims against employers by third parties defending against claims by injured employees).

Elbaor v. Smith

Supreme Court of Texas
845 S.W.2d 240 (Tex. 1992)

GONZALEZ, Justice.

....

Ms. Smith filed [a medical malpractice] suit against D/FW Medical Center, ACH, Drs. Syrquin, Elbaor, Stephens, and Gatmaitan. Sometime before trial, Ms. Smith entered into Mary Carter agreements with Dr. Syrquin, Dr. Stephens, and ACH.[3] The Mary Carter agreements provided for payments to Ms. Smith of $350,000 from Dr. Syrquin, $75,000 from ACH, and $10 from Dr. Stephens. Under the terms of each agreement, the settling defendants were required to participate in the trial of the case. The agreements also contained pay-back provisions whereby Dr. Syrquin and ACH would be reimbursed all or part of the settlement money paid to Ms. Smith out of the recovery against Dr. Elbaor.

Ms. Smith nonsuited her claim against Dr. Gatmaitan and settled and dismissed her claim against D/FW Medical Center. Dr. Elbaor filed a cross claim against Dr. Stephens, Dr. Gatmaitan, Dr. Syrquin, and ACH. He alleged that in the event he was found liable to Ms. Smith, that he was entitled to contribution from these defendants. Furthermore,

---

3. These agreements acquired their name from a case out of Florida styled Booth v. Mary Carter Paint Co., 202 So. 2d 8, 10-11 (Fla. App. 1967)....

Dr. Elbaor requested that the trial court hold the Mary Carter agreements void as against public policy, and alternatively, to dismiss the settling defendants from the suit. The trial court denied this request. The suit proceeded to trial against Dr. Elbaor and the cross defendants.

At trial, the jury found that Ms. Smith's damages totaled $2,253,237.07, of which Dr. Elbaor was responsible for eighty-eight percent, and Dr. Syrquin for twelve percent. After deducting all credits for Dr. Syrquin's percentage of causation and settlements with other defendants, the trial court rendered judgment against Dr. Elbaor for $1,872,848.62.

. . . .

Although the Mary Carter agreements were not entered into evidence, the trial judge was troubled by them and he took remedial measures to mitigate their harmful effects by reapportioning the peremptory challenges, changing the order of proceedings to favor Dr. Elbaor, allowing counsel to explain the agreements to the jury, and instructing the jury regarding the agreements.

During the trial, the settling defendants' attorneys, who sat at the table with Dr. Elbaor's attorneys, vigorously assisted Ms. Smith in pointing the finger of culpability at Dr. Elbaor. This created some odd conflicts of interest and some questionable representations of fact. For example, although Ms. Smith's own experts testified that Dr. Syrquin committed malpractice, her attorney stated during voir dire and in her opening statement that Dr. Syrquin's conduct was "heroic" and that Dr. Elbaor's negligence caused Ms. Smith's damages. And during her closing argument, Ms. Smith's attorney urged the jury to find that Dr. Syrquin had not caused Ms. Smith's damages. This is hardly the kind of statement expected from a plaintiff's lawyer regarding a named defendant. ACH and Drs. Syrquin and Stephens had remained defendants of record, but their attorneys asserted during voir dire that Ms. Smith's damages were "devastating," "astoundingly high," and "astronomical." Furthermore, on cross examination they elicited testimony from Ms. Smith favorable to her and requested recovery for pain and mental anguish. The settling defendants' attorneys also abandoned their pleadings on Ms. Smith's contributory negligence, argued that Ms. Smith should be awarded all of her alleged damages, and urged that Dr. Elbaor was 100 percent liable.

. . . .

The term "Mary Carter agreement" has been defined in different ways by various courts and commentators....[13] Today we clarify what we mean by the term "Mary Carter agreement." A Mary Carter agreement exists when the settling defendant retains a financial stake in the plaintiff's recovery *and* remains a party at the trial of the case.[14]

---

13. The majority of cases and commentators define "Mary Carter agreement" as one in which the settling defendant possesses a financial stake in the outcome of the case and the settling defendant remains a party to the litigation. [Citations.] Many cases also describe other requisite elements of a Mary Carter agreement, such as secrecy. [Citation.] Other cases and commentators argue that a Mary Carter agreement exists any time the settling defendant possesses a financial interest in the plaintiff's recovery. [Citations.]

14. A Mary Carter agreement does not have to expressly state that the settling defendant must participate in the trial. The participation requirement is satisfied by the mere presence of the settling defendant as a party in the case. Obviously, a Mary Carter agreement would not exist if a settling defendant acquires a financial interest in the outcome of the trial and then testifies at trial as a non-party witness. However, Rule 3.04(b) of the Texas Disciplinary Rules of Professional Conduct prohibits a lawyer from paying or offering to pay a witness contingent upon the content of the testimony of the witness or the outcome of the case. Certainly Rule 3.04(b) mandates that an attorney

Raul Gonzalez

This definition comports with both the present majority view and the original understanding of the term.

....The settling defendant, who remains a party, guarantees the plaintiff a minimum payment, which may be offset in whole or in part by an excess judgment recovered at trial. [Citation.] This creates a tremendous incentive for the settling defendant to ensure that the plaintiff succeeds in obtaining a sizable recovery, and thus motivates the defendant to assist greatly in the plaintiff's presentation of the case (as occurred here). Indeed, Mary Carter agreements generally, but not always, contain a clause requiring the settling defendant to participate in the trial on the plaintiff's behalf.

Given this Mary Carter scenario, it is difficult to surmise how these agreements promote settlement. Although the agreements do secure the partial settlement of a lawsuit, they nevertheless nearly always ensure a trial against the non-settling defendant....Thus, "[o]nly a mechanical jurisprudence could characterize Mary Carter arrangements as promoting compromise and discouraging litigation—they plainly do just the opposite." [Citation.]

....

Many jurisdictions have decided to tolerate the ill effects of Mary Carter agreements, presumably because they believe that the agreements promote settlement. Some have sought to mitigate the agreements' harmful skewing of the trial process by imposing prophylactic protections. Indeed, Texas previously has taken such an approach....[19]

---

has an ethical duty to refrain from making a settlement contingent, in any way, on the testimony of a witness who was also a settling party.

19. The guidelines provided in...[an earlier case] require that Mary Carter agreements: (1) are discoverable; (2) should be fully disclosed "to the trial court before trial or immediately after the agreement is formed"; (3) should be considered by the trial court in allowing jury strikes and ruling

These protective measures generally seek to remove the secrecy within which Mary Carter agreements traditionally have been shrouded. [Citation.]

Justice Spears rightly noted in ... [Scurlock Oil Co. v. Smithwick, 724 S.W.2d 1 (Tex. 1986)] the falsity of the premise upon which the prophylactic protection approach is founded, namely, the promotion of equitable settlements. *Id.* at 8. Mary Carter agreements instead:

> present to the jury a sham of adversity between the plaintiff and one co-defendant, while these parties are actually allied for the purpose of securing a substantial judgment for the plaintiff and, in some cases, exoneration for the settling defendant.

[Citations.] The agreements pressure the "settling" defendant to alter the character of the suit by contributing discovery material, peremptory challenges, trial tactics, supportive witness examination, and jury influence to the plaintiff's cause. [Citation.] These procedural advantages distort the case presented before a jury that came "to court expecting to see a contest between the plaintiff and the defendants [and] instead see[s] one of the defendants cooperating with the plaintiff." [Citation.]

Mary Carter agreements not only allow plaintiffs to buy support for their case, they also motivate more culpable defendants to "make a 'good deal' [and thus] end up paying little or nothing in damages." [Citations.] Remedial measures cannot overcome nor sufficiently alleviate the malignant effects that Mary Carter agreements inflict upon our adversarial system....

> ....

.... The bottom line is that our public policy favoring fair trials outweighs our public policy favoring partial settlements.

This case typifies the kind of procedural and substantive damage Mary Carter agreements can inflict upon our adversarial system. Thus, we declare them void as violative of sound public policy.

> ....

... [A] settling defendant may not participate in a trial in which he or she retains a financial interest in the plaintiff's lawsuit.... Accordingly, we reverse the judgment of the court of appeals and remand this cause to the trial court for further proceedings consistent with this opinion.... [This holding shall be applicable only in the present case, to those cases in the judicial pipeline where error has been preserved, and to those actions tried on or after the date of this opinion].

DOGGETT, Justice, dissenting.

> ....

Although Carole Smith non-suited Dr. Stephens and Dr. Syrquin, they remained as parties because Dr. Elbaor chose to maintain cross-actions against them. The majority remands for perhaps the first trial in Anglo-American jurisprudence in which a named party is denied a right to participate.... The majority denies Dr. Syrquin an opportunity to protect his professional standing by participating at trial. His reputation in the community as a physician has been hereby declared legally worthless, and any effect a jury verdict attributing significant negligence to him may have on hospital privileges, the

---

on witness examination; and (4) should be fully disclosed to the jury at the start of the trial. [Citation.]

cost and availability of malpractice insurance, and their patients is completely ignored.... [T]he majority refuses to recognize a central tenet of our judicial system—those called into court should be allowed to answer.

....

The chief problem associated with a Mary Carter agreement is that a hidden alteration of the relationship of some of the parties will give the jury a misleading and incomplete basis for evaluating the evidence. As is true in so many areas of jurisprudence, secrecy is the first enemy of justice. To address this concern, trial judges have appropriately implemented several procedural safeguards that remove the veil of secrecy from such settlements....

In the instant case the trial court took great care to safeguard procedurally the adversarial nature and fairness of its proceedings. Nothing about the agreements now under attack was hidden from anyone.... At voir dire, the court informed prospective jury members that ACH and Syrquin, by participating in the trial, could recover all or a portion of the amounts paid in settlement to Smith, depending on the size of the verdict. An additional warning was extended regarding the possibility of witness bias arising from the agreements. The implications of the agreements were also explored by various counsel during voir dire.

....The trial cannot be a "sham of adversity," [citation], when the jury, as here, is fully aware of this shift in alliances.... So long as at least two parties with antagonistic interests remain, the likelihood that the truth will emerge is not diminished.

Accordingly, most jurisdictions allow Mary Carter agreements when trial courts implement similar procedural safeguards to those adopted here. [Citations.] In rejecting the full disclosure approach, today's opinion embraces a decidedly minority view accepted in only "a couple of states" that have previously chosen to prohibit such agreements....

....

....The elitist view that ordinary people acting as jurors are incapable of determining the facts after full disclosure has once again prevailed....

MAUZY and GAMMAGE, JJ., join in this dissenting opinion.

Notes

1. *See also* Carter v. Tom's Truck Repair, Inc., 857 S.W.2d 172 (Mo. 1993) (holding that Mary Carter agreements must be reviewed on a case-by-case basis, and noting that "only three states, Texas, Nevada, and Wisconsin, have declared... [them] *per se* invalid); Newman v. Ford Motor Co., 975 S.W.2d 147 (Mo. 1998) (a pretrial agreement between an injured motorist and a truck owner, limiting any liability of the truck owner to the limits of its insurance policy in exchange for its promise not to appeal or employ a particular law firm, was not so unfair to the other defendant as to require disclosure of agreement to the jury, in light of the fact that the agreement did not change the interest of the owner to minimize total damages and its own culpability); Kippenhan v. Chaulk Services, Inc., 697 N.E. 2d 527 (Mass. 1998) (an agreement under which a patient settled his claims against an ambulance service and agreed to pay the ambulance service's insurer a portion of any recovery that he obtained against the manufacturer of a stretcher that collapsed was not a "Mary Carter agreement" because the service did not remain in the case and the settlement was not kept secret).

2. *Ethics in Law Practice: Candor to the Court.* In Gum v. Dudley, 505 S.E.2d 391 (W. Va. 1997), an attorney who jointly represented a tractor trailer's owner and driver in a wrongful death action arising from an auto accident violated his duty of candor by remaining silent when counsel for a codefendant stated in response to an inquiry by the court that no parties had entered into a settlement agreement. In fact, the tractor trailer's owner and driver had settled the former's cross-claim against the latter. Counsel was fully aware of the settlement, so his silence constituted a material misrepresentation that no settlement agreement existed. The court referred the matter to the attorney disciplinary authorities.

Chapter 18

Immunities

In the fairly recent past, a tort claim against one's spouse, or by a minor child against a parent, or against a charitable organization, or against a government body, could seldom be brought with success: the defendants in these cases were "immune" from liability for negligence, as well as for most or all other torts. Today, these immunities have been reduced considerably in scope, and in the case of spousal and parent-child immunities completely eliminated in many states. Sovereign immunity—under which a government cannot be sued without its consent—still survives in all jurisdictions, but most governments have consented, by statute, to suits for many kinds of torts.

A. Family Immunities

Spousal Immunity. The common-law notion that "husband and wife are one" gave rise to the doctrine of "spousal immunity," under which tort actions against one's spouse were prohibited. The doctrine even barred actions based on torts committed before the parties were married, so that if *A* negligently ran down *B*, *B*'s tort claim disappeared if *A* and *B* married before it was brought. The notion that husband and wife were the same person, legally, has long lost whatever appeal it once had, and with its decline spousal immunity has withered. A few states may still retain it; in another decade it will almost certainly have vanished everywhere. The doctrine has no current intellectual or political support. *See, e.g.,* Waite v. Waite, 618 So. 2d 1360 (Fla. 1993) (joining 32 other states in completely abrogating the doctrine); Townsend v. Townsend, 708 S.W.2d 646 (Mo. 1986) (holding that spousal immunity did not bar an action for intentional tort against a husband who shot his wife in the back); Carl Tobias, *Interspousal Tort Immunity in America*, 23 Ga. L. Rev. 359 (1989). *But see* Harry D. Krause, *On the Dangers of Allowing Marital Fault to Re-Emerge in the Guise of Torts*, 73 Notre Dame L. Rev. 1355 (1998).

However, the widespread abrogation of spousal immunity may be of little practical importance. *See* Jennifer Wriggins, *Interspousal Tort Immunity and Insurance "Family Member Exclusions": Shared Assumptions, Relational and Liberal Feminist Challenges*, 17 Wis. Women's L.J. 251 (2002). Professor Wriggins writes:

> [D]e facto interspousal tort immunity persists in the form of insurance exclusions. Insurance companies for decades have included "family member exclusions" in homeowner and automobile liability policies. These exclusions provide that family members can not make claims against the policy. If a wife is injured by her husband, and the wife sues the husband for the injury, the liability policy will not cover the husband for the claim. The injured wife...has a

choice of bringing a claim against her husband where there is no insurance coverage, and not bringing a claim at all. These provisions are ubiquitous in homeowners liability policies and were widespread in automobile policies until fairly recently. The reason for the exclusions…is to protect against collusive suits. Court decisions in both homeowners and automobile contexts have struck some of these exclusions down as against public policy, particularly in the automobile context. An additional common insurance provision, the "intentional acts exclusion," also bars claims for some intentional torts between spouses.

These insurance exclusions have a similar effect to common law interspousal tort immunity.… Family member exclusions and intentional act exclusions in individual liability policies guarantee that lawsuits will only rarely be filed for interspousal injury.… Despite tort compensation for myriad other harms, both physical and psychic, compensation is simply lacking in the area of injury from domestic violence.…

Interspousal immunity has reappeared in a new guise—the guise of private insurance.…

Immunity of Parents from Suits by Unemancipated Minor Children. Like spousal immunity, the once-prevalent doctrine that unemancipated minors could not sue their parents for most torts is fading fast. But unlike spousal immunity, the immunity of parents was based more on policy grounds than upon an absurd legal fiction, and so parental immunity has shown more staying power. *See, e.g.*, Frye v. Frye, 505 A.2d 826 (Md. 1986) (refusing to abrogate parental immunity in negligence cases). Indeed, an occasional decision has extended the doctrine, in qualified form, to new contexts. *See, e.g.*, Mitchell v. Davis, 598 So. 2d 801 (Ala. 1992) (applying the parental-immunity doctrine to claims of simple negligence against foster parents and governmental agencies acting *in loco parentis*); Squeglia v. Squeglia, 661 A.2d 1007 (Conn. 1995) (holding that parental immunity bars actions based on strict liability, as well as negligence); *but see* Wallace v. Smyth, 786 N.E.2d 980 (Ill. 2003) (a residential child-care facility acting *in loco parentis* cannot invoke parental immunity).

One concern with allowing minors to sue their parents for negligence is that the minor's recovery is likely to benefit the parent, as well as the minor, at least in part. For example, suppose that a father negligently injures his daughter, and that the daughter incurs $5000 in medical bills as a result. A $5000 judgment against the father, paid by the father's liability insurer, will in nearly all cases benefit the father rather than the daughter.

Concerns about collusive litigation provide most of whatever support parental immunity retains. The fear is not so much that actions based on entirely fictitious accidents will be brought—that does happen, but it can happen even with persons who are not related, and who stage an imaginary accident to defraud an insurance company. Rather, the concern is that the prospect of financial benefit to the defendant may cause the defendant to "forget" care that was in fact taken or carelessness on the part of the victim. This may be a real problem, but the "immunity" solution throws out many meritorious claims to bar a few that may be less than solid.

Some courts have justified parental immunity by invoking a fear that litigation between parent and child would disrupt family harmony. These courts have sometimes allowed the child's action if the parent has died, as a deceased tortfeasor could hardly be angered by litigation.

Rousey v. Rousey

District of Columbia Court of Appeals
528 A.2d 416 (D.C. 1987)

TERRY, Associate Judge.

Appellee, Doris Rousey, and her eleven-year-old daughter, Cheryl Rousey, were involved in an automobile accident....Cheryl sustained injuries, and through her father, Smith Rousey, she brought suit against her mother, alleging...negligence. Mrs. Rousey, who was insured by Government Employees Insurance Company and represented by its counsel, filed a motion for summary judgment on the ground that parental immunity barred appellant from suing his wife on behalf of their unemancipated daughter. The court granted the motion, and Mr. Rousey appealed to this court.

...A majority of the court *en banc* now concludes...that the parental immunity doctrine is out of date. We decline to adopt it, choosing instead to follow section 895G of the Restatement (Second) of Torts (1979), which in our view sets forth a more appropriate legal standard....

Unlike interspousal immunity, parental immunity was unknown at common law. [Citation.] Interspousal immunity was based on the notion that husband and wife were legally one person, whereas parent and child were never so regarded. Children, unlike wives, were entitled to own property and to enforce their own choses in action, including those in tort; likewise, they were liable as individuals for their own torts. [Citations.]

The notion that a parent might be immune from liability for tortious conduct toward his or her child was not recognized in the United States until 1891, when the Supreme Court of Mississippi refused to permit a suit brought by a child against her mother, alleging that the mother had falsely imprisoned the child in an insane asylum. In ordering the suit dismissed, the court said:

> [S]o long as the parent is under obligation to care for, guide, and control, and the child is under reciprocal obligation to aid and comfort and obey, no such action as this can be maintained. The peace of society, and of the families composing society, and a sound public policy, designed to subserve the repose of families and the best interests of society, forbid to the minor child a right to appear in court in the assertion of a claim to civil redress for personal injuries suffered at the hands of the parent.

Hewellette v. George, 68 Miss. 703, 711, 9 So. 885, 887 (1891). Although the court cited no authority for this proposition, courts in all but eight other states followed Mississippi's lead and adopted some form of parental immunity. [Citation.]

Various reasons have been advanced in support of parental immunity, but the reason most frequently cited by the courts has been the need to preserve domestic tranquility and family unity. [Citations.] Many courts have relied heavily upon the analogy between husband and wife, despite the obvious differences between the husband-wife relationship and the parent-child relationship.... [T]he courts that have adopted parental immunity have never adequately explained why the immunity applies only to suits in tort and not to suits involving property or contract rights. An action to enforce property or contract rights is surely no less adversarial than an action in tort, and in theory, at least, it would present the same threat to family harmony.

....The courts have also expressed concern that parental discipline and control might be compromised if children were permitted to sue their parents. [Citation.] Others believed that an uncompensated tort contributed to peace in the family and respect for the parent. [Citation.] The absurdity of this reasoning, however, becomes plain when the case involves rape, [citation], or a brutal beating, [citations], or when the parent-child relationship has been terminated by death before the suit was filed. [Citation.]

Persistent criticism of the doctrine of parental immunity eventually led to its erosion through the creation of various exceptions to it.[2]...

....

Although the "overwhelming weight of authority" did at one time favor parental immunity, the doctrine began to lose judicial support after a 1963 Wisconsin decision which abolished it entirely except when the allegedly tortious act involved "an exercise of parental authority...[or] ordinary parental discretion with respect to the provision of food, clothing, housing, medical and dental services, and other care." Goller v. White, 20 Wis. 2d 402, 413, 122 N.W.2d 193, 198 (1963). In 1977 the American Law Institute completely rejected general tort immunity between parent and child when it published section 895G of the Restatement (Second) of Torts. That section states:

(1) A parent or child is not immune from tort liability to the other solely by reason of that relationship.

(2) Repudiation of general tort immunity does not establish liability for an act or omission that, because of the parent-child relationship, is otherwise privileged or is not tortious.

Many states have since followed the lead of Goller v. White and the Restatement, so that a substantial majority of states have now abandoned the doctrine in whole or in part. To date eleven states have abrogated it entirely or declined to adopt it; eleven have abrogated it in automobile negligence cases; five have abrogated it in automobile negligence cases in which the parent has liability insurance; and seven have abrogated it except in cases in which the parent's alleged tortious act involves an exercise of parental authority over the child, or ordinary parental discretion with respect to such matters as food, care, and education.

This trend toward abrogation is attributable, in large part, to the prevalence of liability insurance. [Citation.] The availability of insurance relieves the parents of direct financial responsibility for injuries sustained by their children, and thus substantially reduces the possibility that an action for damages will disrupt domestic tranquility or family unity. As the Supreme Judicial Court of Massachusetts wrote...:

When insurance is involved, the action between parent and child is not truly adversary; both parties seek recovery from the insurance carrier to create a fund for the child's medical care and support without depleting the family's other assets. Far from being a potential source of disharmony, the action is more likely to preserve the family unit in pursuit of a common goal—the easing of family financial difficulties stemming from the child's injuries.

[Citations.]

Although there is a possibility that parent and child may conspire to defraud the insurance carrier or that the parent may fail to cooperate with the carrier as required

---

2. *See, e.g.,* Dzenutis v. Dzenutis, 200 Conn. 290, 512 A.2d 130 (1986) (no immunity when child's injury arose out of a business activity conducted by the parent away from the home); Hale v. Hale, 312 Ky. 867, 230 S.W.2d 610 (1950) (no immunity when death of either parent or child terminates the parental relationship); Dunlap v. Dunlap, 84 N.H. 352, 150 A. 905 (1930) (no immunity for intentional or reckless infliction of bodily harm).

under the insurance contract, [citation], that possibility exists to a certain extent in every case; it hardly justifies a "blanket denial of recovery for all minors." [Citations.]

> We constantly depend on efficient investigations and on juries and trial judges to sift evidence in order to determine the facts and arrive at proper verdicts. As part of the fact-finding process, these triers of fact must "distinguish the frivolous from the substantial and the fraudulent from the meritorious." .... Experience has shown that the courts are quite adequate for the task.

[Citation.]

Because there is no controlling precedent on the subject of parental immunity, we need not overrule any prior decisions. Rather, we simply decline to adopt the doctrine of parental immunity as the law of the District of Columbia. We acknowledge that doctrine for what it is: an outdated notion based on faulty premises. We see it as a vestige of an era in which children were without legal protection from the wrongs of their parents, and married women were without legal rights, subordinate to their husbands, all in the name of family harmony....

....We see no reason, moreover, to limit our holding to cases in which the parent-defendant has liability insurance, as some courts have done. There can be no justification for fashioning different rules of law for the insured and the uninsured. [Citation.] The availability of insurance funds to satisfy a judgment should not determine the viability of an action by a child against a parent (or vice versa), nor should the judgment necessarily be limited to the amount of the insurance policy.

....

Reversed and remanded.

[The dissenting opinion of Judge BELSON, in which Chief Judge PRYOR joined, is omitted.]

NEBEKER, Associate Judge, dissenting:

....

In declining to adopt parental immunity, the majority disparages the wisdom of the past which championed the family unit, as if a contrary modern view is obviously superior....

....I view the fact that parental immunity did not exist at common law to be irrelevant because "no American child tortiously injured by his parents had ever sought to recover damages until late in the nineteenth century." [Citation.] It seems that prior to 1891, our social and legal evolution had not "progressed" to the point that a child, or more accurately one in concert with him, could or would consider suing a parent in tort....

....[P]arental immunity is...appropriately considered a judicial response to the latter-day attempt to pit child against parent and other family members. I see rejection of this immunity as part of the pandemic course to expand compensation for injury to yet another outer limit.

....

I note that the majority seems to hope that family discord from offspring suits will be avoided because insurance will eliminate true adversity. It will not; and it will foster collusion. But liability insurance should not serve as the basis for rejecting the doctrine of parental immunity in any event. The majority notes the prevalence of liability insurance as its primary justification for creating new legal rights and duties within the family....

The theory of insurance is that it is supposed to give financial protection against the occurrence of a known risk. Once a type of insurance exists, it is not supposed to encourage the creation of new actions at law. The rationale in this case says, in essence, that because liability insurance exists, this jurisdiction will now create a new class of tort claimants who are eligible to recover because it is hoped most claims will be covered. It would be just as well for the majority to justify its new rule on the hope that suits will not be brought absent insurance coverage.

The whole principle of insurance becomes distorted when the presence of insurance encourages new kinds of liability. As additional types of liability are permitted by the court, the insurance companies must either raise policy premiums or exclude coverage as to that particular risk. This latter approach, which is both logical and lawful, if chosen, would eliminate the very reason for the court's holding in the first place. In the meantime, we encourage collusive suits where no adversity exists, or pit family members against each other in true adversity.

....

.... The threat of a tort suit could shackle a parent and prevent the flexibility needed to exercise parental control. As a child progresses through the more intractable stages of adolescence, a parent's fear of being sued must clearly undermine the exercise of parental authority, and thus the family structure. These concerns loom larger as our society grows more litigious.

I fear the majority has thought precious little of the consequences....

....

I opt for immunity and family unity; so I dissent.

Notes

1. *Aggravated Misconduct.* In states which have not rejected parental immunity entirely, the trend is to permit actions based on wilful misconduct, even if ordinary negligence is not actionable. *See, e.g.,* Herzfeld v. Herzfeld, 781 So. 2d 1070 (Fla. 2001) (parental immunity does not apply to intentional sexual torts); Doe v. Holt, 418 S.E.2d 511 (N.C. 1992) (actions for rape and sexual molestation are not barred); McGee v. McGee, 936 S.W.2d 360 (Tex. Ct. App. 1996) (parental immunity does not preclude actions for intentional or malicious acts, but protects stepfather from liability for negligently providing alcohol and objectionable materials to stepson).

2. *Negligent Supervision of Children.* Some jurisdictions have retained a partial immunity for parents, allowing ordinary tort actions, as when a parent's negligent driving injures a child, but barring actions for "negligent supervision," so that a parent who lets a child play in traffic cannot be sued. The concern here may be that liability for "negligent supervision" can sweep very broadly. For example, almost any accident which a teenager suffers is one which, in theory, could have been prevented by greater parental care in instructing the child about safety precautions. This is especially true if the teenager's own carelessness led to the accident; one can almost always claim that a child's carelessness resulted from parental neglect of some sort. Furthermore, the line between negligent supervision (a bad thing) and encouraging one's children to be independent (a good thing) may be hard to draw.

See Hoppe v. Hoppe, 724 N.Y.S.2d 65 (App. Div. 2001) (holding, despite a bar against suits for negligent supervision, that a son could sue his father for entrusting him with a "nail gun cartridge" and a hammer, which caused injuries when the son struck the cartridge with the hammer, because the injuries were caused by the breach of a duty "owed to the world at large" not to negligently maintain explosives).

3. *Motor-Vehicle Accidents.* More than 30 jurisdictions allow a child to sue a parent for negligent driving. The courts have typically reasoned that, since operation of a car is not an act of parental authority or discretion, permitting suit will not interfere with the complex task of providing guidance to a child. Also, the likely presence of automobile insurance reduces the chances that litigation will produce intra-family strife. *See* Dellapenta v. Dellapenta, 838 P.2d 1153 (Wyo. 1992). *But see* Renko v. McLean, 697 A.2d 468 (Md. 1997). In retaining parental immunity, the court wrote:

> Despite the majority trend,…abrogation is not a panacea.…
>
> In a normal case, liability insurance becomes relevant only after an insured's liability is fixed in an appropriate legal proceeding. Yet as between parent and child, it becomes the *raison d'etre* of the suit. Thus, unlike a true adversarial proceeding, an insurer is forced into the unenviable position of attempting to defend a suit that its insured has every incentive to lose.
>
> This, of course, inevitably leads the trier of fact to realize that the suit targets not the parent or child (to whom immunity would otherwise attach) but rather the insurance company [which may prejudice the assessment of liability].…

Compare Renko with Myers v. Robertson, 891 P.2d 199 (Alaska 1995). Noting that, in an intra-family negligence case, the named defendant may testify in terms that are beneficial to the named plaintiff but disadvantageous to the unnamed insurance company, the court held that to avoid risks of jury confusion and prejudice to any party, the jury should be informed of the insurer's status as the real party in interest.

4. *Policy against Profiting from Wrongdoing.* In Myers v. Robertson, 891 P.2d 199 (Alaska 1995), a child was killed as a result of the alleged negligence of his parents. Had the suit by the child's estate been successful (which it was not), the recovery (which would have been paid by the parents' insurance policy) would have benefitted the parents, since they would have been their son's heirs under the laws of intestacy. Addressing this problem, the court wrote:

> [T]he better policy precludes a negligent party from obtaining any part of a damage award, so that the negligent party will not benefit from his or her wrongdoing.…
>
> …[W]e…believe that any ineligible beneficiaries should be considered to have renounced their right to recover.…Thus,…[the parents] should be considered to have predeceased their son, and the entire award may be distributed to any other existing and eligible statutory heirs.

5. *Relationship of Parental Immunity to Other Issues.* Even if parents are immune from suit, their conduct may bear upon the liability of another party. *See* Sears, Roebuck & Co. v. Huang, 652 A.2d 568 (Del. 1995) (if a parent's negligence is relevant to the minor child's theory of liability, but not actionable, a defendant may introduce evidence to establish that the parent's negligence was a supervening cause of the minor child's injury, in which case the defendant will not be held liable).

B. Sovereign Immunity

Holytz v. City of Milwaukee
Supreme Court of Wisconsin
115 N.W.2d 618 (Wis. 1962)

[This was an action for personal injuries sustained by an infant, together with an action by her father for consequential damages. The infant was injured by a loose trap door covering a water meter pit at a drinking fountain in a playground operated by the defendant.]

GORDON, Justice.

....The trial court found that on the facts alleged in the complaint the city was entitled to invoke the defense of municipal tort immunity....

Historical Background of Tort Immunity

The rule of sovereign immunity developed in this county from an English doctrine and has been applied in the United States far beyond its original conception. The doctrine expanded to the point where the historical sovereignty of kings was relied upon to support a protective prerogative for municipalities. This, according to Professor Borchard, "is one of the mysteries of legal evolution." [Citation.] It would seem somewhat anomalous that American courts should have adopted the sovereign immunity theory in the first place since it was based upon the divine right of kings.

The concept of municipal immunity from tort claims stems from the English case of Russell v. The Men of Devon (1788), 2 T.R. 667, 100 Eng. Rep. 359. That was a case in which an unincorporated county was relieved of liability for damages which were occasioned by the disrepair of a bridge. One of the grounds advanced in the *Men of Devon* case was that immunity was necessary because the community was an unincorporated one and did not have funds to pay for damages. A second reason advanced was "that it is better that an individual should sustain an injury than that the public should suffer an inconvenience." 100 Eng. Rep., p. 362....

The first case in the United States which adopted the doctrine of the *Men of Devon* case was Mower v. Leicester (1812), 9 Mass. 247, in which immunity was granted even though the county was a corporation and had corporate funds....

....

The rules surrounding municipal tort immunity have resulted in some highly artificial judicial distinctions. For example, the municipality may be immune or liable depending upon whether we determine that the particular function involved is "proprietary" or "governmental." Our court held in Christian v. New London (1940), 234 Wis. 123, 290 N.W. 621, that a live wire which carried electricity from a municipal electrical utility to a municipal street light was maintained by the city in a proprietary capacity, but a municipal waterworks which supplied water to be used for fire fighting was operating in a governmental capacity. Highway Trailer Co. v. Janesville Electric Co. (1925), 187 Wis. 161, 204 N.W. 773. The operation of a municipal hospital, although generally a proprietary activity, may have some of its operations classed as governmental. [Citation.]

...

There are probably few tenets of American jurisprudence which have been so unanimously berated as the governmental immunity doctrine....

....

Some of the judicial expressions in other states which have sharply decried the rule of immunity are as follows:

> ....
>
> Little time need be spent in determining whether the strict doctrine of municipal immunity from tort liability should be repudiated. All this is old straw. The question is not "Should we?"; it is "How may the body be interred judicially with non-discriminatory last rites?" No longer does any eminent scholar or jurist attempt justification thereof. [Citation.]
>
> It is almost incredible that in this modern age of comparative sociological enlightenment, and in a republic, the medieval absolutism supposed to be implicit in the maxim, "the King can do no wrong," should exempt the various branches of the government from liability for their torts, and that the entire burden of damage resulting from the wrongful acts of the government should be imposed upon the single individual who suffers the injury, rather than distributed among the entire community constituting the government, where it could be borne without hardship upon any individual, and where it justly belongs. [Citation.]

....

The immunization of municipalities from tort liability has been chipped away by a number of statutes in this state.... [Citing statutes relating to motor vehicle accidents, judgments against public officers, and highway defects.]

Also, the judiciary has engrafted exceptions on the rule of municipal immunity from tort claims. Municipalities are responsible for negligence occurring in the operation of their proprietary activities. [Citations.] Municipalities are also responsible for nuisance whether acting in a governmental or proprietary capacity, as long as the municipality and the injured party did not stand in the relationship of governor to governed. [Citations.] Furthermore, municipalities are responsible for an "attractive nuisance" created in the exercise of a proprietary activity. [Citations.]

....

The defendant argues that any change in the municipal immunity doctrine should be addressed to the legislature. We recognize that earlier decisions of this court contemplated precisely that. [Citations.]

....

We are satisfied that the governmental immunity doctrine has judicial origins. Upon careful consideration, we are now of the opinion that it is appropriate for this court to abolish this immunity notwithstanding the legislature's failure to adopt corrective enactments.

A comparable problem was presented in connection with the charitable immunity doctrine.... However, in Kojis v. Doctors Hospital (1961), 12 Wis. 2d 367, 372, 107 N.W.2d 131, 133, 292, this court concluded that the doctrine with respect to paying hospital patients could be changed by the court as well as by the legislature:

> The defendant insists that if the rule is changed it should be done by the legislature and not by the court. This is upon the theory that questions of public policy are to be determined by the legislature. If that were strictly true then perhaps this court was in error in adopting the doctrine of charitable immunity in

the first place. We do not think that is true. We believe the court was justified in acting as it did in 1917 in view of conditions as they then existed. The rule of *stare decisis*, however desirable from the standpoint of certainty and stability, does not require us to perpetuate a doctrine that should no longer be applicable in view of the changes in present day charitable hospitals....

. . . .

..."We closed our courtroom doors without legislative help, and we can likewise open them."

. . . .

Perhaps clarity will be afforded by our expression that henceforward, so far as governmental responsibility for torts is concerned, the rule is liability—the exception is immunity. In determining the tort liability of a municipality it is no longer necessary to divide its operations into those which are proprietary and those which are governmental....

This decision is not to be interpreted as imposing liability on a governmental body in the exercise of its legislative or judicial or quasi-legislative or quasi-judicial functions....

If the legislature deems it better public policy, it is, of course, free to reinstate immunity....

Another problem which we foresee regarding the scope of this decision is the determination of what public bodies are within the scope of the abrogation of the rule. The case at bar relates specifically to a city; however, we consider that abrogation of the doctrine applies to all public bodies within the state: the state, counties, cities, villages, towns, school districts, sewer districts, drainage districts, and any other political subdivisions of the state—whether they be incorporated or not. By reason of the rule of *respondeat superior* a public body shall be liable for damages for the torts of its officers, agents and employees occurring in the course of the business of such public body.

. . . .

To enable the various public bodies to make financial arrangements to meet the new liability implicit in this holding, the effective date of the abolition of the rule of governmental immunity for torts shall be July 15, 1962.... The new rule shall not apply to torts occurring before July 15, 1962.[a] However, for the reasons set forth in the supplemental opinion in Kojis v. Doctors Hospital (1961), 12 Wis. 2d 367, 373, 374, 107 N.W.2d 131, 292, this decision shall apply to the case at bar.

Order reversed....

[The concurring opinion of Justice CURRIE is omitted.]

Notes

1. *Municipal Immunity.* The *Holytz* opinion is somewhat misleading in suggesting that immunity for municipal governments is a form of sovereign immunity. While municipalities (like other political subdivisions of states) exercise some government functions, they are not "sovereigns"—they cannot, for example, adopt rules of tort liability for themselves or for anyone else. *Cf.* Michigan Coalition for Responsible Gun Owners v. City of Ferndale, 662 N.W.2d 864 (Mich. App. 2003) (holding that a city could not enact and enforce ordinances that made local public buildings gun-free zones). Many

---

a. Ed. note: The opinion in *Holytz* was handed down on June 5, 1962.

states have abolished or limited municipal immunity, sometimes by statute and sometimes, as in *Holytz*, by judicial decision. And judicial abrogation has occasionally been followed by legislative action on the subject.

Sovereign immunity, by contrast, is alive and well: both the federal government and all state governments retain it in some form. However, the federal government and nearly all state governments have adopted statutes which "waive" their sovereign immunity for many kinds of tort claims.

2. *The Federal Tort Claims Act.* The Federal Tort Claims Act, now codified in 28 U.S.C.A. §§1346-2680 and in scattered other provisions, provides, with many exceptions, that the federal government is liable for its torts "in the same manner and to the same extent as a private individual under like circumstances"; 28 U.S.C.A. §2674 (Westlaw 2003). For the most part, the government's liability is determined under state law, as it is usually state law that creates tort liability. However, the federal government cannot be sued in state courts, and jury trial is not available in claims under the FTCA. Punitive damages are not allowed. Also, the federal government may not obtain indemnity from an employee when it is liable under the FTCA. *See* U.S. v. Gilman, 347 U.S. 507 (1954).

The FTCA contains many exceptions to the waiver of sovereign immunity, some of them explicit, others derived largely from caselaw. Generally speaking, the federal government is not liable for intentional torts committed by its employees, and it is not liable for misrepresentation, or for interference with contract rights, or for torts committed in the course of various governmental functions, such as collecting taxes.

A few federal statutes other than the FTCA waive sovereign immunity for particular kinds of cases.

3. *Discretionary-Function Exception to FTCA.* A broad exception to the FTCA waiver of Federal sovereign immunity is the "discretionary function" exception of 28 U.S.C.A. §2680(a) (Westlaw 2003). The idea here is that policy-making is not to be challenged in the courts on the ground that the policy in question was "unreasonable"; compare the somewhat-narrower "public-duty rule" discussed in Chapter 9. *See also* Monzon v. U.S., 253 F.3d 567 (11th Cir. 2001) (failure to warn individual visitors of the danger of rip currents in the surf near a beach adjacent to a national monument was within the discretionary-function exception). For an extension of Federal sovereign immunity to government contractors, *see* Chapter 15.

In considering the reach of this exception, it is important to differentiate the making of a decision from the carrying out of a decision. In Indian Towing v. U.S., 350 U.S. 61, 69 (1955), the court wrote:

> The Coast Guard need not undertake the lighthouse service. But once it exercised its discretion to operate a light..., it was obligated to use due care to make certain that the light was kept in good working order....If the Coast Guard failed in its duty and damage was thereby caused..., the United States is liable under the [FTCA].

In O'Toole v. U.S., 295 F.3d 1029 (9th Cir. 2002), ranch owners claimed they were being harmed by the Bureau of Indian Affairs's negligent maintenance of irrigation canals downstream. The court said:

> The danger that the discretionary function exception will swallow the FTCA is especially great where the government takes on the role of a private landowner. *Cf.* Gotha v. United States, 115 F.3d 176, 179 (3d Cir. 1997) ("[I]f

the word 'discretionary' is given a broad construction, it could almost completely nullify the goal of the [FTCA].”). Every slip and fall, every failure to warn, every inspection and maintenance decision can be couched in terms of policy choices based on allocation of limited resources. As we have noted before in the discretionary function exception context, “[b]udgetary constraints underlie virtually all governmental activity.” [Citation.] Were we to view inadequate funding alone as sufficient to garner the protection of the discretionary function exception, we would read the rule too narrowly and the exception too broadly. Instead, in order to effectuate Congress's intent to compensate individuals harmed by government negligence, the FTCA, as a remedial statute, should be construed liberally, and its exceptions should be read narrowly.

4. *The* Feres *Doctrine.* The *Feres* doctrine bars tort actions involving injuries to military personnel on active duty, even in peacetime. *See* Feres v. United States, 340 U.S. 135 (1950). However, it does not preclude military-related suits against the government when the injured plaintiff is a civilian.

The history and policy basis of the *Feres* doctrine are discussed by Judge Guido Calabresi in Taber v. Maine, 67 F.3d 1029 (2d Cir. 1995). *Taber* was an off-duty serviceman's action against the federal government based on injuries sustained in an automobile accident with another off-duty serviceman who had been drinking on base. The action was not barred by the *Feres* doctrine because the plaintiff's military status was not sufficiently connected to activity in which he was injured.

5. *State Tort Claims Acts.* Any brief description of the extent to which states have waived sovereign immunity would be quite misleading. The subject is largely statutory, and so variations among jurisdictions are wide. *See generally* Note, *Government Tort Liability*, 111 Harv. L. Rev. 2009 (1998).

Discretionary functions are normally immune from liability. *See* Harrison v. Hardin Cty. Comm. Unit Sch. Dist., 758 N.E.2d 848 (Ill. 2001) (principal made a policy decision when he refused a student's request for early dismissal and instead told him to wait for the entire school to be dismissed early because of inclement weather, and thus the school district was entitled to discretionary-act immunity); Texas Dept. of Transp. v. Ramirez, 74 S.W.2d 864 (Tex. 2002) (a roadway median's slope and lack of safety features, such as guardrails, reflect decisions immune under the discretionary-function exception). *See also* Texas Dept. of Transp. v. Garrison, 2003 W.L. 22455092 (Tex. App.) (stating that “once a governmental unit decides to install a particular traffic signal, that decision must be implemented within a reasonable time...[and that the] implementation of a policy decision, unlike the actual decision making, is nondiscretionary”).

6. *Constitutional Barriers.* The Eleventh Amendment immunizes states from suit in federal court by U.S. or foreign citizens.

7. *Constitutional Torts.* A *Bivens* action is a court-created tort action against federal employees individually for injuries caused by their constitutional violations. *See* Bivens v. Six Unknown Named Agents of the Fed. Bureau of Narcotics, 403 U.S. 388, 389 (1971).

A well-known civil rights statute, 42 U.S.C §1983 (Westlaw 2003), exposes individual state and local officials acting “under color of” state law to liability for depriving a citizen of federal constitutional or statutory rights. States are immune from suit under §1983 (*see* Will v. Michigan Dept. of State Police, 491 U.S. 58, 71 (1989)), but municipalities are subject to liability for federal violations if a municipal employee was carrying out an “official policy” or custom of the municipality (*see* Monell v. Department of Soc. Servs., 436 U.S. 658, 663, 690-91 (1978)).

8. *Notice-of-Claim Requirements.* Suits against the government must often comply with strict notice-of-claim requirements. *See, e.g.,* Rivera v. City of Meriden, 806 A.2d 585 (Conn. App. Ct. 2002) (plaintiff failed to provide required notice of highway defect).

C. Official Immunity

Sovereign immunity protects *governments* against being held liable, but it does not shield government officials and employees from liability for their torts, even when they act in furtherance of their duties. Not surprisingly, perhaps, immunities for various kinds of officials have been developed; government could not function if judges could be sued for "negligent" decisions, or if legislators were liable for "unreasonable" votes. Generally speaking, the more discretion an official or employee has, the more "absolute" that employee's immunity, with judges at the top of the scale. But there are always limits; a judge who sanctions contempt of court by shooting the offender dead will, one supposes, be liable to the decedent's survivors, probably on the ground that the judge's act was not "judicial" in nature.

1. Federal Officials and Employees

Barr v. Matteo, 360 U.S. 564 (1959), was a libel action based on a press release. The suit was commenced by government employees against the acting director of the Office of Rent Stabilization. In a plurality decision, the Supreme Court held that the acting director was absolutely immune from liability. Writing for the plurality, Justice Harlan reasoned that official immunity was needed because government officials

> should be free to exercise their duties unembarrassed by the fear of damage suits in respect of acts done in the course of those duties — suits which would consume time and energies which would otherwise be devoted to governmental service and the threat of which might appreciably inhibit the fearless, vigorous, and effective administration of policies of government.

In subsequent cases, a split of authority developed as to whether federal officials and employees were absolutely immune from personal liability in state common-law tort actions for harm that resulted from all activities within the scope of their employment or only those activities that involved the exercise of discretion. Westfall v. Erwin, 484 U.S. 292 (1988), made clear that the immunity of federal government officials and employees extends only to discretionary acts. Justice Thurgood Marshall wrote for the court:

> The purpose of... official immunity is not to protect an erring official, but to insulate the decisionmaking process from the harassment of prospective litigation....
>
> ....
>
> The central purpose of official immunity, promoting effective government, would not be furthered by shielding an official from state-law tort liability without regard to whether the alleged tortious conduct is discretionary in nature. When an official's conduct is not the product of independent judgment, the threat of liability cannot detrimentally inhibit that conduct. It is only when

officials exercise decisionmaking discretion that potential liability may shackle "the fearless, vigorous, and effective administration of policies of government."

Congress then responded to the *Westfall* decision. As described by Judge Reinhard in Pelletier v. Fed. Home Loan Bk. Bd., 968 F.2d 865 (9th Cir. 1992):

> In order to restore immunity to federal employees who perform nondiscretionary functions, Congress enacted the FELRTCA [Federal Employees Liability Reform and Tort Compensation Act], popularly known as the Westfall Act. H.R. Rep. No. 700, 100th Cong., 2d Sess. 3-4 (1988), *reprinted in* 1988 U.S.C.C.A.N. 5945, 5946-47. The FELRTCA amended the FTCA to "remove the potential personal liability of Federal employees for common law torts committed within the scope of their employment, and…instead provide that the exclusive remedy for such torts is through an action against the United States under the Federal Tort Claims Act." [Citation.]
>
> Under the FTCA, an individual who has suffered an injury cognizable in tort as a result of the conduct of a federal employee may bring suit against the United States if that employee was "acting within the scope of his office or employment." *Id.* §§ 1346(b), 2674. The question whether a federal employee whose allegedly tortious conduct is the subject of a lawsuit under the FTCA was "acting within the scope of his office or employment" at the time of the injury is to be answered according to the principles of *respondeat superior* of the state in which the alleged tort occurred. [Citations.]
>
> The FELRTCA accords a right of substitution to any federal employee sued in tort who was "acting within the scope of his office or employment" when the allegedly tortious conduct occurred.…

Id. at 875. Further:

> The FELRTCA provides that "[u]pon certification by the Attorney General that the defendant employee was acting within the scope of his office or employment at the time of the incident out of which the claim arose…the United States shall be substituted as the party defendant."

Id.

In Gutierrez de Martinez v. Lamagno, 515 U.S. 417 (1995), the Court held that the Attorney General's scope-of-employment certifications under the Westfall Act are subject to judicial review.

Federal actors are treated differently if a case involves a "constitutional tort," rather than a common-law tort. As with a §1983 action, an individual defendant in a *Bivens* action is entitled to assert the defense of qualified immunity. "Qualified immunity is not merely a defense to liability, but a shield from suit…[in the sense that a] determination of whether qualified immunity is applicable to any defendant is a matter that is initially determined by the Court as a matter of law." Andrade v. Chojnacki, 65 F. Supp. 2d 431, 452 (W.D. Tex. 1999) (suit by survivors of Branch Davidians).

2. State Officials and Employees

Absolute Immunity. At the state level, it is generally agreed that high officials, such as judges, legislators, and top executive officers, enjoy absolute immunity from suit for actions relating to their official duties.

Some states have extended absolute immunity to lesser officials and employees. *See* Dziubak v. Mott, 503 N.W.2d 771 (Minn. 1993) (holding court-appointed public defenders wholly immune from suit for legal malpractice); Miss. Code Ann. §11-46-7(2) ("no employee shall be held personally liable for acts or omissions occurring within the course and scope of the employee's duties"); Clayton v. Harkey, 826 So. 2d 1283 (Miss. 2002) (surgeon was acting as a state employee and was immune from suit). *But see* State v. Second Jud. Dist. Ct., 55 P.3d 420 (Nev. 2002) (refusing to extend absolute quasi-judicial immunity to every state employee involved in supervising foster children).

Qualified Immunity. Lesser state officials typically have only a "qualified" immunity, which may be lost if the plaintiff can prove that the official acted out of malice—dishonestly, without good faith, or for an improper purpose. *See* Ex Parte Nall & Faulk, 2003 W.L. 21297361 (Ala.) (school coaches were entitled to immunity absent evidence that they acted with malice or wilfulness in hitting balls during a practice session).

Any immunity normally extends only to actions within the official's "discretionary" functions, so that an official who negligently runs down a pedestrian on the way to a government meeting will have no immunity at all. *Compare* Quakenbush v. Lackey, 622 N.E.2d 1284 (Ind. 1993) (police officer was not immune from claim for negligent driving), *with* Ramos v. Tex. Dept. of Pub. Safety, 35 S.W.3d 723 (Tex. App. 2000) (the discretionary duties of an officer administering a driving test continued until the test taker's car was safely parked, and thus the officer was immune from suit for damages caused when the test taker's car lurched forward as the test taker was parking it). *See also* Harris v. McCray, 2003 W.L. 22411209 (Miss.) (holding, in a suit where a player suffered heatstroke, that allegedly negligent acts of a high school football coach were discretionary in nature and therefore both the coach and the school district were immune from suit); Aversano v. Palisades Interstate Pkwy. Com'n, 832 A.2d 914 (N.J. Super. Ct. A.D. 2003) (holding that the duty of public parkway police to call a rescue squad, upon receiving a report that a park user had fallen from a cliff, was "ministerial" rather than "discretionary," and therefore the parkway commission and parkway police were not immune from suit).

State Legislation Limiting the Liability of Governmental Employees. Some states have passed laws capping the liability of "public servants." For example:

TEX. CIV. PRAC. & REM. CODE §108.002 (a) & (b)
(Westlaw 2004)

(a) Except in an action arising under the constitution or laws of the United States, a public servant, other than a provider of health care..., is not personally liable for damages in excess of $100,000 arising from personal injury,[b] death, or deprivation of a right, privilege, or immunity if:

(1) the damages are the result of an act or omission by the public servant in the course and scope of the public servant's office, employment, or contractual performance for or service on behalf of a state agency, institution, department, or local government; and

(2) for the amount not in excess of $100,000, the public servant is covered:

(A) by the state's obligation to indemnify under Chapter 104;

(B) by a local government's authorization to indemnify under Chapter 102;

---

b. Subsection (b) of the statute contains similar provisions relating to property damage.

(C) by liability or errors and omissions insurance; or

(D) by liability or errors and omissions coverage under an interlocal agreement.

Federal Protection for Teachers. The Paul D. Coverdell Teacher Protection Act of 2001, 20 U.S.C.A. §6731 *et seq.* (Westlaw 2003), with various limits, immunizes teachers at public and private elementary and secondary schools that receive federal funds from liability for negligence based on actions within the scope of the teacher's responsibilities undertaken in "efforts to control, discipline, expel, or suspend a student or maintain order or control in the classroom or school."

The Act's limits on teacher liability "[do] not apply to any misconduct that...constitutes a crime of violence...or act of international terrorism...for which the defendant has been convicted in any court;...involves a sexual offense...for which the defendant has been convicted in any court;...involves misconduct for which the defendant has been found to have violated a Federal or State civil rights law; or...where the defendant was under the influence...of intoxicating alcohol or any drug at the time of the misconduct." Nothing in the law affects "any State or local law...pertaining to the use of corporal punishment."

The Act pre-empts state law providing less protection to teachers, unless a State has passed legislation electing to have the Act not apply. Suits based on "willful or criminal misconduct, gross negligence, reckless misconduct, or a conscious, flagrant indifference to the rights or safety of the individual harmed by the teacher" may still be maintained.

Under the act,

> Punitive damages may not be awarded against a teacher in an action brought for harm based on the act or omission of a teacher acting within the scope of the teacher's employment or responsibilities to a school or governmental entity unless the claimant establishes by clear and convincing evidence that the harm was proximately caused by an act or omission of such teacher that constitutes willful or criminal misconduct, or a conscious, flagrant indifference to the rights or safety of the individual harmed.
>
> ....
>
> In any civil action against a teacher, based on an act or omission of a teacher acting within the scope of the teacher's employment or responsibilities to a school or governmental entity...[a] teacher shall be liable only for the amount of noneconomic loss allocated to that defendant in direct proportion to the percentage of responsibility of that defendant...for the harm to the claimant with respect to which that defendant is liable.

State Protection for Teachers. Some states have enacted legislation protecting teachers from tort liability. For example:

TEX. EDUC. CODE §22.0511
(Westlaw 2003)

(a) A professional employee of a school district is not personally liable for any act that is incident to or within the scope of the duties of the employee's position of employment and that involves the exercise of judgment or discretion on the part of the employee, except in circumstances in which a professional employee uses excessive force in the discipline of students or negligence resulting in bodily injury to students.

(b) This section does not apply to the operation, use, or maintenance of any motor vehicle.

(c) In addition to the immunity provided under this section and under other provisions of state law, an individual is entitled to any immunity and any other protections afforded under the Paul D. Coverdell Teacher Protection Act of 2001....

See Kobza v. Kutac, 109 S.W.3d 89 (Tex. App. 2003) (a high school teacher's act of creating a fake newspaper article about a student as a joke, in an attempt to enhance the learning environment by establishing rapport with the student, was within the scope of her duties and therefore the teacher was immune from suit for defamation and other claims).

See also Tex. Educ. Code §22.0517 (Westlaw 2003) ("In an action against a professional employee of a school district involving an act that is incidental to or within the scope of duties of the employee's position of employment and brought against the employee in the employee's individual capacity, the employee is entitled to recover attorney's fees and court costs from the plaintiff if the employee is found immune from liability...").

Other Immunities. Some immunities cover persons who are not government officials; witnesses in court proceedings provide an example. *See* Chapter 22.

D. Charitable Immunity

Albritton v. Neighborhood Centers Association for Child Development

Supreme Court of Ohio
466 N.E.2d 867 (Ohio 1984)

[Alfreda Albritton brought an action, on behalf of herself and her minor child, against the Neighborhood Centers Association for Child Development ("NCA"), a nonprofit corporation. The child was injured while participating at no cost in a Head Start day care program run by NCA. Summary judgment was granted in favor of NCA based on the doctrine of charitable immunity. The court of appeals affirmed.]

WILLIAM B. BROWN, Justice.

....

The critical question is whether the doctrine of charitable immunity retains any validity in Ohio today. The origin of the doctrine in the United States is well documented and needs no repetition here. *See* Avellone v. St. John's Hospital (1956), 165 Ohio St. 467, 469, 135 N.E.2d 410 (60 O.O. 121), *citing* President & Directors of Georgetown College v. Hughes (C.A.D.C. 1942), 130 F.2d 810. Suffice it to say that the rule was originally erroneously adopted in that it derived from *dicta* in two English cases which had already been overruled. Despite such a tenuous inception, the doctrine of charitable immunity spread until it became a concept firmly embedded in American jurisprudence, although not one universally accepted.

However, the "rule" of charitable immunity is, in reality, not a rule at all. In the first place, charitable immunity is an exception to the general principle of liability for tortious conduct. Individuals and entities are ordinarily held responsible for their own legally careless action and for negligent harms inflicted by their agents and employees....

Moreover,...the landscape of charitable immunity has been so pockmarked with exceptions as to be virtually unrecognizable. Immunity for hospitals has been abolished. [Citation.] There is no charitable immunity where the injured plaintiff is not a beneficiary of the defendant charity or where the plaintiff is harmed as a result of the charity's negligence in the selection or retention of an employee. [Citation.] Likewise, a charity is liable where it operates a business enterprise for profit not directly related to the purpose for which the organization was established. [Citation.] Finally, there is no immunity where the plaintiff pays for services rendered by the charity. [Citation.]....Indeed, the very existence of these manifold exceptions militates strongly against all of the policy arguments advanced in favor of retention of the doctrine.

Furthermore, charitable immunity does not, and has not, existed as a "rule" in the nation as a whole. In other jurisdictions charitable immunity survived only in a welter of conflict founded on a kaleidoscope of result and reasoning. [Citation.] There is, consequently, no compelling precedential reason for retention of this doctrine.

This court has previously founded its acceptance of charitable immunity on the theory of public policy. [Citations.] This theory reasons that charities are good and that their purpose, to provide services for intended beneficiaries, should not be defeated by indemnification of tort claimants. As NCA has characterized the rationale, it has been determined that the benefit to society as a whole from protecting charitable organizations outweighs the detriment to any one particular injured individual.

As was discussed in *Avellone*, resolution of such a question involves a balancing of two rights. On the one hand is the right of charitable organizations to any benefit and assistance which society can justly allow them. On the other hand is the right of an individual, injured by the negligence of another, to seek compensation....A careful review of the competing policies...convinces this court that...[charitable immunity] is no longer justified.

In the first place, it is certainly true that a personal injury is no less painful, disabling, costly, or damage producing simply because it was inflicted by a charitable institution rather than by any other party or entity....

...[W]hen an individual is injured or killed through the negligence of a charitable institution there is a strong likelihood that the individual or his or her family will become dependent upon outside support unless recovery may be had. [Citation.] Such support may be met by governmental assistance or may have to be assumed by another charity.

In addition, a policy exempting a charitable organization from having to compensate for harm caused by it is equivalent to requiring an injured individual to make an unwilling contribution to that organization in the amount of the compensation which would be due him had he been injured by a noncharitable entity. [Citation.] Such coerced donations are inimical to the whole concept of charitable donation and service....

At its heart, the whole policy behind charitable immunity rests upon the idea that we do not want to discourage charitable activities or force charities out of business by subjecting them to tort liability. However, as was aptly stated in Flagiello v. Pennsylvania Hospital (1965), 417 Pa. 486, 503, 208 A.2d 193, 201:

"If havoc and financial chaos were inevitably to follow the abrogation of the immunity doctrine,...this would certainly have become apparent in the states where that doctrine is no longer a defense."

As Dean Prosser has indicated, this argument appears to have been concocted in some defense counsel's imagination rather than having been based on experience. Prosser, Law of Torts (4th ed. 1971) 994, §133. Nowhere is there the slightest evidence that the role of charities has been repressed in the overwhelming majority of jurisdictions which have abolished the rule as opposed to the handful which retain some form of immunity. This reality is independent of the existence of liability insurance. In short, charities continue to operate with very little regard as to whether they are immune from tort liability or not.

...[D]emolition of the arguments in favor of charitable immunity has been followed by a deluge of decisions in the same vein. [Citation.] Jurisdictions which have totally abolished charitable immunity now number well over thirty. Apparently, no state continues to grant absolute immunity to charities. Opinion among legal scholars is virtually unanimous that charitable immunity no longer has any valid reason for existence and must go. [Citation.] The Restatement of the Law, Torts 2d (1979) 420, §895E would have the law be that "[o]ne engaged in a charitable, educational, religious or benevolent enterprise or activity is not for that reason immune from tort liability."....

Lastly, NCA contends that if charitable immunity is to be abolished it should be done by the General Assembly and not by the courts....There is no doubt that charitable immunity was judicially created in Ohio....[T]his court not only has the power but the duty and responsibility to evaluate an immunity doctrine in light of reason, logic and the actions and functions of the relevant entities in the twentieth century. It is, therefore, the proper province of this court to correct judicially created doctrines if they are no longer grounded in good morals and sound law. [Citation.]

...[C]haritable immunity is hereby abolished. A charitable organization is subject to liability in tort to the same extent as individuals and corporations....

Judgment reversed and cause remanded.

FRANK D. CELEBREZZE, C.J., and SWEENEY, CLIFFORD F. BROWN and JAMES P. CELEBREZZE, JJ., concur.

LOCHER, Justice, dissenting.

...I feel compelled to dissent to what I feel is an over-broad position adopted by my brethren.

Ohio does not recognize complete charitable immunity. Instead, over the years this court has wisely adopted a case by case formula for retaining or abrogating charitable immunity based upon the policy dictates of the individual factual circumstances....Immunity has been previously retained...for those many charities ministering to the needy, including those...smaller charities balanced precariously on the edge of financial abyss. As government support has continued to diminish, the ranks of the needy have swelled in response. Until today's opinion this court has recognized, as a matter of public policy, that not all charitable organizations could shoulder their burdens and still pay insurance premiums and legal fees in the face of potential negligence liability.

The many exceptions presented by the majority, contrary to their "exception devouring the rule" characterization, are the result of many decades of thoughtful, patient policy analysis by this court. Exceptions have not gobbled the rule; instead, the rule has adapted to the times and to the needs of charities. Now, in a single stroke, the majority has chosen to abolish all charitable immunity based on a narrow factual pattern concerning a governmentally funded charitable organization. This position is squarely against this court's previous posture of judicial restraint.

....

... [T]he majority indulges in legislation.... Today's decision impacts on a wide range of charities not financed by governmental entities and therefore not represented by the parties in interest. Moreover, with less and less governmental support of charities, the facts upon which the majority predicates its new position are more likely to be the exception rather than the rule.

... [T]oday's result can only create an expensive bureaucratic tangle. Volunteerism will be chilled and assistance to the hungry and dispossessed will diminish, in exact degree, to sweeten the coffers of the John Street insurance empires. In this tangle the small but sturdy charity which gives aid to the small towns and communities in this state is engulfed and slowly strangled while the few large, structured, and financially viable charities of the larger cities will survive. The committed and dedicated men and women from all walks of life who give service to charity gain in fraternity and spirit by coming to the aid of those in need. Thus not only will the indigent and downtrodden pay the price for today's decision, but the ethical and moral fiber of what gives worth to the lives of so many citizens, and makes this country great, will be diminished.

....

The sociological studies which might provide an empirical basis for today's sweeping opinion were never presented, never briefed, and never considered because the charity in question was never perceived to be *all* charities.... [N]o mention is made of empirical studies which dispassionately review actual statistics from jurisdictions where immunity has been abolished. Such studies tell a story different than the speculation relied upon by the majority and suggest that when abolition of immunity occurs it is the public which must pay a substantial cost....

I must dissent today not against my fellow justices nor their lofty intentions to aid people injured by charities, but rather against their belief that "bad" law should be broadly and sweepingly eliminated at the expense of charities which never knew such a broad case was before us and never had the opportunity to rebut the presumptions of the majority....

Therefore, I dissent.

HOLMES, Justice, dissenting.

.... I wish to emphasize... the unreality of subjecting all charities, regardless of size and regardless of services performed, to tort liability to the same extent as individuals and corporations....

....

There is a great disparity within charitable organizations, some large, serving on a state or national scale; some small, serving a given neighborhood. Some are admittedly of sizable wealth, most are of modest means, receiving all of their revenue from sources such as United Way and other volunteer fundraising efforts. There is sound reason not to apply tort liability in the same manner and degree to all charitable organizations regardless of the nature of the operation.

There is also sound reason to consider, and fairly conclude, to what extent charitable organizations may be held financially responsible for their torts. Should a monetary judgment against the charity be permitted to completely absorb and annihilate the trust property of the charity? Or should the trust *res* be held exempt from judgment for the benefit of the public at large?

....

LOCHER, J., concurs in the foregoing dissenting opinion.

Notes

1. *What Is a "Charity"?* One reason for abrogating sweeping immunities for all non-profit corporations is that in most states it is easy for persons undertaking a profit-making business to incorporate under their states' not-for-profit corporation statutes. Although not-for-profit corporations cannot pay dividends—indeed, they cannot even issue stock—the organizers of not-for-profit corporations can extract profits by paying themselves high salaries for their work. (Under the federal income tax, organizations which allow private persons to profit from their activities cannot be tax-exempt, but this does not prevent profit-makers from incorporating under not-for-profit corporation statutes without seeking a tax exemption.)

2. *The Effect of Liability Insurance.* The fairly widespread availability of liability insurance has been cited as a reason for doing away with charitable immunity. If the reason for the immunity is to provide an economic benefit to charities, this argument makes little sense. Liability insurance is not free; indeed, if insurance companies are to survive they must collect enough money to cover all their liabilities, and more. On an overall basis, the burden of paying for liability insurance cannot possibly be less than the burden of paying judgments.

Even charities which are immune sometimes buy liability insurance, because of a fear that a court may take away their immunity. Another consideration is noted by Robert E. Keeton & Alan I. Widiss, Insurance Law, §4.8 (1988). Some charities buy liability insurance which allows the insureds to waive their immunity in a particular case. This enables the charity to assert immunity when it thinks that a claim is without merit, while providing for compensation to those with justifiable grievances.

3. *Legislative Restoration of Charitable Immunity.* In many states, immunity for some charitable institutions and their actors has been legislatively restored, at least in part, in recent years. For example, after the New Jersey Supreme Court abolished charitable immunity in Benton v. YMCA, 141 A.2d 298 (N.J. 1958), the state legislature passed the Charitable Immunity Act, reinstating the common-law doctrine as it had been judicially defined. That statute now provides:

N.J. Stat. Ann. §2A:53A-7a
(Westlaw 2003)

a. No nonprofit corporation, society or association organized exclusively for religious, charitable or educational purposes or its trustees, directors, officers, employees, agents, servants or volunteers shall, except as is hereinafter set forth, be liable to respond in damages to any person who shall suffer damage from the negligence of any agent or servant of such corporation, society or association, where such person is a beneficiary, to whatever degree, of the works of such nonprofit corporation, society or association; provided, however, that such immunity from liability shall not extend to any person who shall suffer damage from the negligence of such corporation, society, or association or of its agents or servants where such person is one unconcerned in and unrelated to and outside of the benefactions of such corporation, society or association.

Nothing in this subsection shall be deemed to grant immunity to any health care provider, in the practice of his profession, who is a compensated employee, agent or servant of any nonprofit corporation, society or association organized exclusively for religious, charitable or educational purposes.

   b.... [Relates to nonprofit hospitals].

   c. Nothing in this section shall be deemed to grant immunity to: (1) any trustee, director, officer, employee, agent, servant or volunteer causing damage by a willful, wanton or grossly negligent act of commission or omission, including sexual assault and other crimes of a sexual nature; (2) any trustee, director, officer, employee, agent, servant or volunteer causing damage as the result of the negligent operation of a motor vehicle; or (3) an independent contractor of a nonprofit corporation, society or association organized exclusively for religious, charitable, educational or hospital purposes.

   In O'Connell v. State, 795 A.2d 857 (N.J. 2003), the court ruled that a student was a "beneficiary" under the act and was therefore barred from suing a state college for a slip-and-fall accident. The fact that the college received public funds was irrelevant.

   See also Tex. Civ. Prac. & Rem. Code §§84.001 *et seq* (Westlaw 2003). The Texas statute conditions selected aspects of immunity on the charity's purchase of liability insurance. *See id.* at 84.007(g).

   4. *Caps on Damages against Charities.* In some states, the amount of damages recoverable from a charity has been legislatively capped. *See* Keene v. Brigham and Women's Hosp. Inc., 786 N.E.2d 824 (Mass. 2003) (reducing a $4.1 million malpractice judgment to $20,000).

   5. *Immunity of Volunteers.* In some states where charitable immunity is recognized, a volunteer of a charity is immune from liability to the charity's beneficiaries for negligence while the volunteer was engaged in the charity's work. See the New Jersey statute quoted above. *See also* Moore v. Warren, 463 S.E.2d 459 (Va. 1995). However, this type of immunity may be interpreted so restrictively as to afford volunteers little protection. For example, in Bhatia v. Mehak, Inc., 551 S.E.2d 358 (Va. 2001), the court wrote that "an agent or servant of a charity only shares the charity's immunity from liability if the agent or servant is acting *directly* for the benefit of the charity." *Id.* at 360 (emphasis added). The suit involved the scalding of two children at a religious ceremony as a result of alleged negligence on the part of the employees of a caterer who was providing free refreshments that the minister regarded as "essential" to the religious service. The minister had asked a co-owner of the caterer, who was a devotee of the religion, to arrange for the provision of the food as a donation to the religion. The court held that none of the defendants enjoyed immunity because:

> [The caterer]..., its "co-owners," and its employees were neither acting as agents or servants of the charity in preparing and serving the food and beverages, nor were they directly performing the work of the charity. Instead, they were acting directly for... [the caterer] in preparing and delivering its charitable donation.

   A federal statute, the Volunteer Protection Act of 1997, purports to limit the tort liability of those who volunteer their services to nonprofit organizations and governmental bodies. While the act seems at first glance to make many volunteers immune from suit for torts committed within the scope of their responsibilities, it is so hedged with restrictions and exceptions that it seems largely symbolic. The act confers no immunity for a variety of things, including gross negligence, willful or criminal conduct, reckless misconduct, most motor vehicle accidents, sexual offenses (if the defendant has been convicted), hate crimes, and harms that occurred while the defendant was acting under the influence of "alcohol or any drug." Only volunteers themselves receive protection: the agencies that use their services remain liable. Furthermore, states may enact legislation making the act inapplicable to cases in which all the parties are citizens of that state.

Several states have passed legislation which confers immunities of differing dimensions on various types of volunteers. *See, e.g.,* Ark. Code Ann. §17-95-106 (Westlaw 2002) (creating immunity for volunteer retired physicians who provide services at a low-cost medical clinic); La. Rev. Stat. Ann. §9:2799.5 (Westlaw 2002) (providing immunity to health care providers who provide free services at community clinics.); Md. Code Ann., Cts. & Jud. Proc. §5-425(b) (Westlaw 2003 Reg. Sess.) (conferring immunity on professional engineers who, upon request of state officials, volunteer at the scene of an emergency, disaster, or catastrophic event); Tex. Educ. Code §22.053 (Westlaw 2003) ("A volunteer who is serving as a direct service volunteer of a school district is immune from civil liability to the same extent as a professional employee of a school district..."); W. Va. Code §55-7-19 (Westlaw 2003) (limiting liability of physicians who volunteer for certain athletic events sponsored by a public or private elementary or secondary school).

Some states have passed more broadly applicable statutes that protect volunteers working for a wide range of charities from many types of liability for ordinary negligence occurring within the scope of their duties. *See* Tex. Civ. Prac. & Rem. 84.004 *et seq.* (Westlaw 2003).

6. *Immunity for Mediators.* Theoretically, a legislature can endeavor to encourage any kind of activity by granting tort immunity to potential practitioners. To help ensure the success of mediation as an alternative dispute resolution mechanism, many states have enacted statutes providing mediators with absolute or qualified immunity. *See* Amanda K. Esquibel, *The Case of the Conflicted Mediator: An Argument for Liability and Against Immunity,* 31 Rutgers L.J. 131 (1999).

Chapter 19

Statutes of Limitations

A. Introduction

A tort action must be brought before the applicable statute of limitations has expired. The statutory period begins to run when the cause of action "accrues," which is usually as soon as the plaintiff has suffered damage. For example, the relevant statute begins to run:

- when a credit card holder is denied credit because of an issuer's erroneous negative credit report (Waxler v. Household Credit Services, Inc., 106 S.W.3d. 277 (Tex. App. 2003));

- when a person rightfully in possession of another's property refuses to return it or acts in a manner inconsistent with the rights of the owner (Sharpe v. Roman Cath. Diocese of Dallas, 97 S.W.3d 791 (Tex. App. 2003) (conversion));

- when an accounting client is subject to an assessment by the IRS as a result of negligent preparation of a tax return (Fritz v. Bruner Cox, L.L.P., 756 N.E.2d 740 (Ohio Ct. App. 2001)); or

- when use of a keyboard ultimately causes a repetitive stress injury (Dorsey v. Apple Computers Inc., 936 F. Supp. 89 (E.D.N.Y. 1996) (not when the plaintiff first used the keyboard)).

One reason for having statutes of limitations has to do with accuracy of factfinding. Important evidence may be lost if actions are brought long after the events being litigated took place. Witnesses may die or move away, memories will fade, records may be lost or destroyed. Another consideration relates to the welfare of potential defendants. Without statutes of limitations, those whose conduct may or may not have caused someone harm would be put to considerable and often unnecessary expense. For example, records would have to be kept indefinitely, lest some claim arising out of the distant past be brought. Finally, at least for individual defendants, statutes of limitations may provide some peace of mind. Knowledge that one is potentially subject to litigation arising out of anything one did (or was claimed to have done) at any time in the past would be unsettling for many.

As a rule, statutes of limitations for intentional torts are quite short, sometimes as short as one year. "This is one reason there have been so few tort suits for domestic violence injuries." Jennifer Wriggins, *Domestic Violence Torts*, 75 So. Cal. L. Rev. 121, 169 (2001). Negligence statutes tend to be somewhat longer, though in some states they are as short as two years. Many states have special statutes of limitations for particular kinds of torts. As an example, consider the following New York statute.

New York C.P.L.R. §214
(Westlaw 2003)

The following actions must be commenced within three years:

1. an action against a sheriff, constable or other officer for the non-payment of money collected upon an execution;

2. an action to recover upon a liability, penalty or forfeiture created or imposed by statute, except as provided in §§213 and 215;

3. an action to recover a chattel or damages for the taking or detaining of a chattel;

4. an action to recover damages for an injury to property except as provided in §214-c;

5. an action to recover damages for a personal injury except as provided in §§214-b, 214-c, and 215;

6. an action to recover damages for malpractice, other than medical, dental or podiatric malpractice, regardless of whether the underlying theory is based on contract or tort;

....

Note

1. *Intentional Torts.* In New York, as in many states, the statute of limitations for intentional torts is one year. *See* N.Y. C.P.L.R. §215 (Westlaw 2003). Ordinarily, the victim of an intentional tort knows almost immediately whether there is a claim, so there is little need for a long statute of limitations.

Suppose a physician is sued for failing to disclose the risks of a surgical procedure to a patient. Is this a medical-malpractice claim, for which the New York statute of limitations is two years and six months, or is it a battery, for which the period is one year? In a questionable decision, a New York trial court held that the one-year statute applied; Cox v. Stretton, 352 N.Y.S.2d 834 (Sup. Ct. 1974).

B. Tolling the Statute of Limitations

Discovery Rule. The reasons given above for having statutes of limitations suggest that those statutes should be quite short, and that they should begin to run as soon as the potential defendant does the action complained of. Considerations involving prospective plaintiffs cut the other way, however. If a statute of limitations begins to run as soon as the defendant acts negligently or sells a defective product, the statute may run before the plaintiff even knows of the claim, or even before the plaintiff is injured. Consider, for example, a doctor who leaves a sponge inside a patient during an operation, and suppose that the sponge does no harm for years. If the statute of limitations runs from the time of the negligent conduct, the plaintiff's claim may be lost before the plaintiff has any reason to know that there was a claim. Similarly, if a three-year statute of limitations for making a dangerously defective product begins to run when the product is manufactured or sold, a plaintiff injured by the product five years later would have no claim. The unseemliness of barring actions before they even arise has led many courts to hold that statutes of limitations do not begin to run until the plaintiff has been injured. In some cases, the courts have gone even further and held that the statute is "tolled" until the plaintiff discovers, or at least should reasonably have discovered, the injury. "Tolling" interrupts the running of the statute.

The case which follows illustrates one version of the discovery rule.

Tyson v. Tyson

Supreme Court of Washington, En Banc
727 P.2d 226 (Wash. 1986)

DURHAM, Justice.

The United States District Court for the Western District of Washington has certified the following question of state law to this court: Does the discovery rule, which tolls the statute of limitations until the plaintiff discovers or reasonably should have discovered a cause of action, apply to intentional torts where the victim has blocked the incident from her conscious memory during the entire time of the statute of limitations? We answer that question in the negative.

The plaintiff here alleges that she was the victim of sexual abuse during her childhood. The parties have stipulated to the following facts: Plaintiff Nancy Tyson filed a complaint in the United States District Court…, alleging that her father, the defendant Dwight Robert Tyson, committed multiple acts of sexual assault upon her from 1960 through 1969. Plaintiff, whose birthdate is April 20, 1957, was between 3 and 11 years old at the time of the alleged acts, and was 26 years old at the time she filed the complaint. Plaintiff further alleged that the sexual assaults caused her to suppress any memory of the acts and that she did not remember the alleged acts until she entered psychological therapy during 1983. Plaintiff filed the complaint within 1 year of her recollection of the alleged acts.

    ….

….RCW 4.16.080(2) provides that, in general, an action for personal injury must be brought within 3 years of the time the cause of action accrued. RCW 4.16.100(1) provides that an action for assault and battery must be brought within 2 years. If the person bringing the action is under the age of 18 years at the time the cause of action accrues, the statute of limitations is tolled until the person becomes 18 years old. RCW 4.16.190. Under a literal reading of the limitation statutes, the cause of action accrues when the alleged wrongful act occurs. Ruth v. Dight, 75 Wash. 2d 660, 665, 453 P.2d 631 (1969). Under these rules, the limitation period in this case expired at the latest on April 20, 1978, or 3 years after plaintiff's 18th birthday.…

….The discovery rule provides that a statute of limitations does not begin to run until the plaintiff, using reasonable diligence, would have discovered the cause of action. [Citation.]

Plaintiff claims that the alleged acts of sexual abuse caused her such emotional trauma that she repressed her memory of the events entirely. She asserts that years after the statute of limitations had expired, therapy triggered her knowledge of the abuse and her recognition that the abuse caused emotional problems she was experiencing as an adult. Plaintiff argues that it would be unfair to preclude her claim because she was unable to discover her cause of action during the applicable limitation period.

We recognize that child sexual abuse has devastating impacts on the victim. However, when a person claims emotional injuries resulting from an intentional tort which she has allegedly remembered only after the statute of limitations has expired, we must seriously consider the potential effects on our system of justice.

Statutes of limitation assist the courts in their pursuit of the truth by barring stale claims. A number of evidentiary problems arise from stale claims. [Citations.] As time passes, evidence becomes less available. For example, the defendant might have had a critical alibi witness, only to find that the witness has died or cannot be located by the time the action is brought. Likewise, witnesses who observed the plaintiff's behavior shortly after the alleged act may no longer be available. Physical evidence is also more likely to be lost when a claim is stale, either because it has been misplaced, or because its significance was not comprehended at the time of the alleged wrong. In addition, the evidence which is available becomes less trustworthy as witnesses' memories fade or are colored by intervening events and experiences. Old claims also are more likely to be spurious than new ones. "With the passing of time, minor grievances may fade away, but they may grow to outlandish proportions, too." [Citation.] Thus, stale claims present major evidentiary problems which can seriously undermine the courts' ability to determine the facts. By precluding stale claims, statutes of limitation increase the likelihood that courts will resolve factual issues fairly and accurately.

The discovery rule should be adopted only when the risk of stale claims is outweighed by the unfairness of precluding justified causes of action. [Citation.] In prior cases where we have applied the discovery rule, there was objective, verifiable evidence of the original wrongful act and the resulting physical injury. This increased the possibility that the fact finder would be able to determine the truth despite the passage of time, and thus diminished the danger of stale claims. For example, in Ruth v. Dight, *supra*, we adopted the discovery rule for a medical malpractice action arising from the presence of a foreign substance left inadvertently in a surgical wound. A hysterectomy was performed on the plaintiff in 1944. For a 22-year period following the surgery, plaintiff suffered recurrent abdominal pain. In 1966, plaintiff underwent an exploratory operation during which a sponge was found in her abdomen. After the sponge was removed, her recovery was normal. [Citation.] Thus, there was empirical evidence of the occurrence of the alleged act (the initial surgery) and of the resulting harm (discovery of the sponge). In Ohler v. Tacoma Gen. Hosp., 92 Wash. 2d 507, 598 P.2d 1358 (1979), we applied the discovery rule to a products liability action against an incubator manufacturer for blindness due to excessive administration of oxygen to the plaintiff when she was a premature infant. There was evidence that plaintiff was placed in an incubator for about 16 days and given oxygen. Her blindness was an objective manifestation of the resulting injury. [Citation.] Again, empirical evidence existed of the alleged event and resulting harm. We have also applied the discovery rule to a products liability action for personal injuries resulting from asbestos exposure. Sahlie v. Johns-Manville Sales Corp., 99 Wash. 2d 550, 663 P.2d 473 (1983). There was evidence that the plaintiff had worked around asbestos products for almost 40 years, and he was eventually diagnosed as having asbestosis. [Citation.] The source of plaintiff's injury, continuous exposure to asbestos products, and the resulting harm, asbestosis, were objectively verifiable.

Because of the availability and trustworthiness of objective, verifiable evidence in the above cases, the claims were neither speculative nor incapable of proof. Since the evidentiary problems which the statute of limitations is designed to prevent did not exist or were reduced, it was reasonable to extend the period for bringing the actions.

.... In contrast, in the present case, no empirical, verifiable evidence exists of the occurrences and resulting harm which plaintiff alleges. Her claim rests on a subjective assertion that wrongful acts occurred and that injuries resulted. There is no objective manifestation of these allegations. Rather, they are based on plaintiff's alleged recollection of a memory long buried in the unconscious which she asserts was triggered by psychological therapy.

It is suggested that the subjectivity of plaintiff's claim can be eliminated at trial through the testimony of witnesses such as family, friends, schoolteachers and treating psychologists. However, none of this testimony would provide objective evidence that the alleged acts occurred. First, witnesses who knew the plaintiff at the time of the alleged events would be testifying from their memories of her emotional condition and behavior during that period. This would require witnesses to attempt to recall events which occurred between 17 and 26 years ago. Witnesses' recollections of memories usually become less reliable in a matter of minutes, much less years. Thus, the more time had passed, the less trustworthy such testimony would be.

Second, the testimony of treating psychologists or psychiatrists would not reduce, much less eliminate, the subjectivity of plaintiff's claim. Psychology and psychiatry are imprecise disciplines. Unlike the biological sciences, their methods of investigation are primarily subjective and most of their findings are not based on physically observable evidence. The fact that plaintiff asserts she discovered the wrongful acts through psychological therapy does not validate their occurrence. Recent studies by certain psychoanalysts have questioned the assumption that the analyst has any special ability to help the subject ascertain the historical truth. [Citation.] These studies show that the psychoanalytic process can even lead to a distortion of the truth of events in the subject's past life. The analyst's reactions and interpretations may influence the subject's memories or statements about them. The analyst's interpretations of the subject's statements may also be altered by the analyst's own predisposition, expectations, and intention to use them to explain the subject's problems.... While psychoanalysis is certainly of great assistance in treating an individual's emotional problems, the trier of fact in legal proceedings cannot assume that it will produce an accurate account of events in the individual's past.

....

.... If we applied the discovery rule to ... [actions such as this], the statute of limitations would be effectively eliminated and its purpose ignored. A person would have an unlimited time to bring an action, while the facts became increasingly difficult to determine. The potential for spurious claims would be great and the probability of the court's determining the truth would be unreasonably low.

.... We ... hold that the discovery rule does not apply to an intentional tort claim where the plaintiff has blocked the incident from her conscious memory during the period of the statute of limitations.

DORE, ANDERSEN, CALLOW and GOODLOE, JJ., concur.

GOODLOE, Justice (concurring).

I concur with Justice Durham's majority opinion. I believe the arguments of the dissent are most compelling, however, the end result appears to be subjective judicial policy-making. This is the exclusive province of the Legislature, and the judiciary must not invade it.

PEARSON, Justice (dissenting).

....

Imposition of a statute of limitations generally creates no hardship for plaintiffs because they are aware when they have been wronged. "[W]hen an adult person has a justiciable grievance, he usually knows it and the law affords him ample opportunity to assert it in the courts." [Citation.] However,... in some instances an injured party may not know or be expected to know he has been injured until long after the statute of limitations has cut off his legal remedy. [Citation.] In such instances, it is unfair automatically to foreclose a plaintiff's cause of action.

The decision as to whether it is in fact unfair to foreclose a plaintiff's lawsuit involves a balancing test. The court must balance "the harm of being deprived of a remedy versus the harm of being sued." [Citation.]

We balanced these harms in *Ruth* and applied the discovery rule. We found that the harm to a surgical patient of being deprived of a remedy outweighed the harm to the defendant surgeon of being sued 22 years after he performed allegedly negligent surgery. Our result was based on "fundamental fairness". [Citation.]

The context in *Ruth* was medical malpractice. However, in the 17 years following *Ruth*, both this court and the Court of Appeals have extended the discovery rule to other types of professional malpractice. [Citation.] We have also applied the rule in cases of libel, [citation]; products liability, [citation]; and latent disease, [citation].

....In attempting to prevent...injustice, we have never, contrary to the majority's position, required "objective, verifiable evidence" as a prerequisite to application of the rule. Not one of our discovery rule cases has ever imposed such a requirement. Indeed, the nature of available evidence is simply one factor to be considered in balancing the harm to a defendant of being forced to defend a stale claim with the harm to a plaintiff of being deprived of a remedy. Fundamental fairness, not availability of objective evidence, has always been the linchpin of the discovery rule.

....

Just as I am disturbed by the majority's disregard of the rationale of the discovery rule and criticism of mental health professionals, I am also concerned with the summary manner in which it dismisses the enormous problem of child sexual abuse. A single sentence is offered: "We recognize that child sexual abuse has devastating impacts on the victim." [Citation.]

In reality, the problem warrants a great deal of attention. Indeed, some understanding by this court of the nature of child sexual abuse is essential to our determination of the issue before us. We are asked to determine if fundamental fairness compels us to extend the discovery rule to adults who suffered sexual abuse as children and then repressed that abuse. In reaching our decision, we must understand how and why such repression occurs. It is the repression which gives rise to the need for application of the discovery rule.

Although definitions vary, child sexual abuse can be defined as "contacts or interactions between a child and an adult when the child is being used as an object of gratification for adult sexual needs or desires." [Citation.] It has been estimated that as much as one-third of the population has experienced some form of child sexual abuse. [Citation.] Much of the sexual abuse of children occurs within the family. [Citation.] In one study of 583 cases of child sexual abuse, the offender was a family member in 47 percent of the cases; otherwise, an acquaintance of the child in 42 percent, and a stranger in only 8 percent. [Citation.] Of this high percentage of cases of abuse among family members, it has been estimated that 75 percent involve incest between father and daughter. [Citation.] Both the high incidence of father/daughter incestuous abuse and the special problems of such incest victims have led to much commentary. [Citations.] Because incestuous abuse is so pervasive and because the instant case involves father/daughter incest, I have focused on this type of sexual abuse.

Incestuous abuse begins, in the average case, when the daughter is 8 or 9 years old, although sexual relations and even intercourse may begin even earlier. [Citation.] In order to ensure his daughter's availability to him and provide a cover for his conduct, the father demands secrecy from the child. Often he frightens her into secrecy with threats of harm. [Citation.] Because the victim is thus sworn to secrecy, she is forced to deal with the situation alone. Because she must cope alone, she is likely to internalize her self-blame, anger, fears, confusion, and sadness resulting from the incest. This internalization results in what has been referred to as "accommodation." [Citation.] In accommodating herself to an intolerable situation, the victim often "blocks out" her experience for many years. [Citations.] This "blocking out" is a coping mechanism. A victim will cope in this fashion because "some things are literally so difficult to deal with if remembered that your choices are to go crazy or to forget them." [Citation.]

As the incest victim becomes an adult, she will often begin to exhibit signs of incest trauma. The most common are sexual dysfunction, low self esteem, poor capacity for self protection, feelings of isolation, and an inability to form or maintain supportive relationships. [Citation.] At this time, the daughter may know she is injured. However, until such time as she is able to place blame for the incestuous abuse upon her father, it will be impossible for her to realize that his behavior caused her psychological disorders. [Citation.] Often it is only through therapy that the victim is able to recognize the causal link between her father's incestuous conduct and her damages from incest trauma. [Citation.] Once the victim begins to confront her experiences and link her damages with her father's incestuous conduct, she has taken a step as a survivor of childhood incestuous abuse.

The need for maturity of the survivor before she can confront her childhood incest experience results in a general lack of ability to file suit within the statutory period. [Citation.] As has been seen, the maximum age at which an adult survivor of incest may file suit in this state is 21. Since many survivors are simply incapable of discovering a cause of action by the time they are 21 years old, they are effectively denied a legal remedy unless they are given the benefit of the discovery rule.

. . . .

The purpose behind extending the discovery rule to adult survivors of childhood sexual abuse is not to provide a guaranteed remedy to such plaintiffs. The purpose is to provide an *opportunity* for an adult who claims to have been sexually abused as a child to prove not only that she was abused and that the defendant was her abuser, but that her suffering was such that she did not and could not reasonably have discovered all the elements of her cause of action at an earlier time. The policy behind providing this opportunity has been demonstrated: the nature of child sexual abuse, according to extensive expert commentary, is often so secretive, so humiliating, and so devastating that a victim typically represses the events until the abuse is "discovered" — often through psychotherapy, and often well into adulthood.

For these reasons, I dissent. . . .

DOLLIVER, C.J., and UTTER and BRACHENBACH, JJ., concur.

UTTER, Justice (concurring in dissent).

I agree fully with the well reasoned opinion of Justice Pearson. I write separately to emphasize that the extension of the discovery rule urged by Nancy Tyson is not an issue that should be left to the Legislature. To do so rejects the reasoning adopted by this court in Wyman v. Wallace, 94 Wash. 2d 99, 615 P.2d 452 (1980). It is important for this court to adjust tort law doctrine in response to changes in social values and knowledge. Judicial action is especially appropriate when taken on behalf of individuals who are not organized as a political force and who cannot produce legislative solutions to their problems.

In Wyman v. Wallace, *supra*, we decided that this court does not need to wait for legislative action on matters of common law tort doctrine. We noted in that case that deference to the Legislature is appropriate in some fields; for example, the Legislature is particularly well suited to conduct the fact-finding necessary for economic legislation. [Citation.] However, we concluded that because of its own institutional restraints the Legislature is not always in the best position to modify common law tort doctrine. [Citation.]

This court also has refused to wait for legislative action with respect to application of the statutes of limitations. . . . Under our precedents it is thus within the province of this court to extend the discovery rule to the case of Nancy Tyson.

Increased knowledge and increased public awareness have produced the issue before us. Child abuse has attracted significant attention only since 1962, when the "battered child syndrome" was first defined. Public and professional attention have been directed toward child sexual abuse—incest in particular—for an even shorter period of time. [Citation.] In fact, mental health therapists and other professionals largely denied the prevalence of incestuous abuse until the 1970's. [Citation.] It is only in the past decade or so that professionals have documented the damages of incestuous abuse and the "blocking out" that the trauma of the abuse can cause.

This court cannot rely on the Legislature to extend the discovery rule in response to these recent developments. Legislatures rarely reexamine tort law in light of recent changes. Peck, *The Role of the Courts and Legislatures in the Reform of Tort Law*, 48 Minn. L. Rev. 265, 268-70 (1963). Legislators consider so many issues in so little time that only the most compelling needs can be addressed. [Citation.]

This court also cannot rely on tort victims to bring issues of tort reform to the attention of the Legislature. Tort victims do not constitute a well-organized lobbying group. They are not brought together by a common interest in legislation addressed to the future; instead, each plaintiff usually simply desires redress for past injuries. Peck, *Comments on Judicial Creativity*, 69 Iowa L. Rev. 1, 13 (1983).

In this case, especially, we can hardly expect Nancy Tyson to evoke a response from the Legislature. An adult survivor of child sexual abuse cannot elicit the same public support as a child victim. Survivors with experiences similar to those of Nancy may well be reluctant to reveal their painful experiences by lobbying and testifying at legislative hearings. The public agencies and private groups that represent these individuals do not have the resources to launch such a campaign.

      . . . .

This court should not hesitate to apply the discovery rule on behalf of adult survivors of child sexual abuse who have repressed their memories during the period of the statute of limitations. . . . It is particularly appropriate for this court to take action on behalf of a group that cannot obtain representation in the political process. [Citation.]

For these reasons I concur in the dissenting opinion.

Notes

1. In response to the decision in *Tyson*, the Washington statute was amended to provide as follows:

WASH. REV. CODE ANN. §4.16.340
(Westlaw 2004)

(1) All claims...based on intentional conduct brought by any person for recovery of damages for injury suffered as a result of childhood sexual abuse shall be commenced within the later of the following periods:

(a) Within three years of the act alleged to have caused the injury or condition;

(b) Within three years of the time the victim discovered or reasonably should have discovered that the injury or condition was caused by said act; or

(c) Within three years of the time the victim discovered that the act caused the injury for which the claim is brought:

Provided, That the time limit for commencement of an action under this section is tolled for a child until the child reaches the age of eighteen years.

2. Courts are divided over whether the discovery rule should apply to child-abuse cases. The following rulings are illustrative.

Applicable: Dunlea v. Dappen, 924 P.2d 196 (Haw. 1996); Johnson v. Johnson, 701 F. Supp. 1363 (N.D. Ill. 1988) (Ill. law); Hoult v. Hoult, 792 F. Supp. 143 (D. Mass. 1992) (Mass. law); Sinclair v. Brill, 815 F. Supp. 44 (D. N.H. 1993) (N.H. law); Osland v. Osland, 442 N.W.2d 907 (N.D. 1989).

Inapplicable: Hildebrand v. Hildebrand, 736 F. Supp. 1512 (S.D. Ind. 1990) (Ind. law); Doe v. Maskell, 679 A.2d 1087 (Md. 1996); Lemmerman v. Fealk, 534 N.W.2d 695 (Mich. 1995); Schmidt v. Bishop, 779 F. Supp. 321 (S.D.N.Y. 1991) (N.Y. law); Doe v. Doe, 973 F.2d 237 (4th Cir. 1992) (N.C. law); Bailey v. Lewis, 763 F. Supp. 802 (E.D. Pa. 1991), aff'd, 950 F.2d 722 (3d Cir. 1991) (Pa. law); S.V. v. R.V., 933 S.W.2d 1 (Tex. 1996).

Whether testimony based on "recovered memory" should be relied on has been controversial. For an introduction to the problem, see Review Section Symposium, *Recovered Memory and the Law*, 22 Law & Social Inquiry 651 (1997).

3. ***Liability for Creating False Memories.*** *See* Sawyer v. Midelfort, 595 N.W.2d 423 (Wis. 1999) (permitting a malpractice action by a patient's estate and parents alleging that a psychiatrist and therapist caused the patient to develop false memories of sexual and physical abuse).

4. ***The Discovery Rule and the Continuous-Treatment Exception in Medical-Malpractice Cases.*** The special New York statute of limitations for cases involving medical malpractice provides:

N.Y. C.P.L.R. §214-a
(Westlaw 2004)

Action for medical, dental or podiatric malpractice to be commenced
within two years and six months; exceptions

An action for medical, dental or podiatric malpractice must be commenced within two years and six months of the act, omission or failure complained of or last treatment where there is continuous treatment for the same illness, injury or condition which gave rise to the said act, omission or failure; provided, however, that where the action is based upon the discovery of a foreign object in the body of the patient, the action may be commenced within one year of the date of such discovery or of the date of discovery of facts which would reasonably lead to such discovery, whichever is earlier. For purposes of this section, the term "continuous treatment" shall not include examinations undertaken at the request of the patient for the sole purpose of ascertaining the state of the patient's condition. For the purpose of this section, the term "foreign object" shall not include a chemical compound, fixation device or prosthetic aid or device.

The statute bars some malpractice claims before they even arise, as when a doctor's negligence causes no harm to the plaintiff for several years. *See* Goldsmith v. Howmedica, Inc., 491 N.E.2d 1097 (N.Y. 1986) (plaintiff's cause of action accrued in 1973 when a prosthetic device was implanted, not in 1981 when it malfunctioned, and therefore an action commenced in 1983 was barred by a three-year statute of limitations). C.P.L.R. §214-a was enacted in 1975, in response to physician complaints about large malpractice verdicts.

Note that the New York statute contains a "continuous treatment" exception. Many states have created this kind of exception for medical malpractice cases by judicial decision. The scope of the exception is spectacularly uncertain, and is therefore the subject of a great deal of litigation. *Cf.* Young v. Williams, 560 S.E.2d 690 (Ga. 2002) (refusing to recognize a continuous treatment exception in the absence of statutory authorization).

5. *"Discovered" vs. "Should Reasonably Have Discovered."* Discovery rules vary considerably with respect to what it is that the plaintiff must discover to start the statute running. The possibilities include: (1) that the plaintiff has been injured; (2) that the plaintiff has been injured *by the defendant*; (3) facts that would cause a reasonable person to discover the injury. Consider Miller v. Lakeside Village Condo. Ass'n, 2 Cal. Rptr. 2d 796 (Ct. App. 1991) (plaintiff's action was time-barred before she was ultimately diagnosed as having immune dysregulation because the "delayed discovery doctrine applies only when a plaintiff has not discovered all of the facts essential to the cause of action").

6. *Statutes of Limitations in Sexual Abuse Cases.* Responding in part to increased allegations of sexual abuse by members of the clergy, a few states have extended the statutes of limitations applicable to civil actions involving such misconduct. Consider the following Illinois statute, which also attempts to address precisely what must be discovered for purposes of triggering the discovery rule.

Ill. Comp. Stats. Ann. Ch. 735, Act 5 §13-202.2
(Westlaw 2004)

§13-202.2. Childhood sexual abuse.

    ....

(b)...[A]n action for damages for personal injury based on childhood sexual abuse must be commenced within 10 years of the date the limitation period begins to run under subsection (d) or within 5 years of the date the person abused discovers or through the use of reasonable diligence should discover both (i) that the act of childhood sexual abuse occurred and (ii) that the injury was caused by the childhood sexual abuse. The fact that the person abused discovers or through the use of reasonable diligence should discover that the act of childhood sexual abuse occurred is not, by itself, sufficient to start the discovery period under this subsection (b). Knowledge of the abuse does not constitute discovery of the injury or the causal relationship between any later-discovered injury and the abuse.

....

(d) The limitation periods under subsection (b) do not begin to run before the person abused attains the age of 18 years; and, if at the time the person abused attains the age of 18 years he or she is under other legal disability, the limitation periods under subsection (b) do not begin to run until the removal of the disability.

(d-1) The limitation periods in subsection (b) do not run during a time period when the person abused is subject to threats, intimidation, manipulation, or fraud perpetrated by the abuser or by any person acting in the interest of the abuser....

7. *"Inherently Undiscoverable."* Some courts say that a discovery rule will not be applied to a case unless it involves harm of a type that is inherently undiscoverable. *See* Loguidice v. Metropolitan Life Ins. Co., 336 F.3d 1 (1st Cir. 2003) (refusing to apply a discovery rule because the alleged fraudulent marketing of life insurance as a retirement plan did not involve an inherently unknowable fact; had the plaintiff "looked at the materials in the folder . . . , she would have learned that there was nothing in the folder that could have constituted part of . . . [a] retirement plan"); Bankruptcy Estate of Harrison v. Bell, 99 S.W.3d 163 (Tex. App. 2002) (holding that a discovery rule did not apply to injuries suffered by an attorney who allegedly lost a new client after his former employee referred the client to another firm, since a reasonably diligent attorney would not have remained unaware of a lost client for four years). *See also* Pero's Steak and Spaghetti House v. Lee, 90 S.W.3d 614 (Tenn. 2002) (holding that the discovery rule did not toll the statute on a claim for conversion in the absence of fraud because the law "presumes that property owners know what their assets are and where they are located").

8. *Latent-Disease Cases.* Virtually every jurisdiction applies some form of the discovery rule to latent-disease cases, such as suits resulting from exposure to asbestos, DES, or toxic chemicals. As the U.S. Supreme Court noted in a silicosis case, "no specific date of contact with the [harmful] substances causing the disease can be charged with being the date of injury, inasmuch as the injurious consequences of exposure are the product of a period of time rather than a point of time." Urie v. Thompson, 337 U.S. 163 (1949).

In Childs v. Haussecker, 974 S.W.2d 31 (Tex. 1998), the court noted that requiring the judiciary and defendants to expend their limited resources on premature litigation of speculative claims is neither efficient nor desirable. It held that in the latent occupational disease context, a cause of action does not accrue until a plaintiff's symptoms manifest themselves to a degree or for a duration that would put a reasonable person on notice that he or she suffers from some injury and he or she knows, or in the exercise of reasonable diligence should have known, that the injury is likely work related.

See also Brown v. E.I. Du Pont De Nemours & Co., 820 A.2d 362 (Del. 2003) (holding that the statute of limitations did not begin to run on products liability claims against a fungicide manufacturer, based on children's birth defects that were allegedly caused by their mothers' exposure to the fungicide, until the parents were on notice that the children's defects might have been tortiously caused by the mothers' exposure, as opposed to when the birth defects were first observed).

9. *Tolling Based on Minority, Incompetency, and Fraudulent Concealment.* The discovery rule is only one example of tolling. In most jurisdictions, statutes of limitations are tolled while the plaintiff is a minor. Tort reformers have frequently sought to change this rule. *See, e.g.,* Iowa Code Ann. §614.1(9)(b) (Westlaw 2003) (unless the statutory discovery rule applies, a medical malpractice action brought on behalf of a minor who was under the age of eight years when the malpractice occurred shall be commenced no later than the minor's tenth birthday); Richardson v. Monts, 81 S.W.3d 899 (Tex. App. 2002) (holding statute of limitations tolled until a child reached the age of 14).

Tolling also occurs if the plaintiff is incompetent. *Cf.* Lovelace v. Keohane, 831 P.2d 624 (Okla. 1992) (the plaintiff's multiple personality disorder did not constitute the type of legal disability that tolls the statute of limitations). *But see* Dasha v. Maine Med. Ctr., 665 A.2d 993 (Me. 1995) (even if the defendant hospital's allegedly negligent treatment of the plaintiff's brain deprived the plaintiff of the ability to recognize and timely file a cause of action, the running of the statute was not tolled because the legislature had "clearly...[restricted] the instances in which a medical malpractice action can be filed beyond the general three-year statute of limitations" and the defendant was not equitably estopped from pleading the statute as a bar).

The running of the statute is also tolled if the defendant fraudulently conceals the injury. *See* Santanna Nat. Gas Corp. v. Hamon Operating Co., 954 S.W.2d 885 (Tex. Ct. App. 1997) (affirmative misrepresentations can support fraudulent concealment even in the absence of a duty to disclose); Fager v. Hundt, 610 N.E.2d 246 (Ind. 1993) (fact issue as to whether father concealed material facts regarding his sexual abuse of his daughter).

There are other possibilities. *See* Cal. Civ. Code §48.7(a) (Westlaw 2003) (no person charged by an accusatory pleading with child abuse may bring a defamation action based on such statements while the charges are pending, and the applicable defamation statute of limitations shall be tolled during such period).

10. *Legal Malpractice and the Continuing-Representation Doctrine.* Many courts have also recognized the "continuing representation doctrine," which tolls the statute of limitations in legal malpractice cases while the lawyer continues to represent the plaintiff's interests in the matter in question. According to one court:

> The doctrine "recognizes that a person seeking professional assistance has a right to repose confidence in the professional's ability and good faith, and realistically cannot be expected to question and assess the techniques employed or the manner in which the services are rendered." [Citation.] It is not "realistic to say that the client's right of action accrued before he terminated the relationship with the attorney."

Murphy v. Smith, 579 N.E.2d 165 (Mass. 1991). *See also* Jackson Jordan, Inc. v. Leydig, Voit & Mayer, 633 N.E.2d 627 (Ill. 1994) (law firm was equitably estopped from asserting the statute of limitations as a defense because the firm continually assured the client that its legal position was sound, even after the competitor brought an infringement action).

Note that if the representation has ended, the statute of limitations on a legal malpractice claim arising from negligent representation in a criminal matter is not necessarily tolled while the client pursues a direct appeal or post-conviction relief. *See* Morrison v. Goff, 74 P.3d 409 (Colo. Ct. App. 2003) (recognizing a split of authority and refusing to permit tolling even though the client succeeded in getting his conviction reversed).

11. *Tolling Based on Battered Woman's Syndrome. See* Giovine v. Giovine, 663 A.2d 109 (N.J. Super. Ct. 1995) (statute of limitations for a tort claim incidental to divorce

may be tolled if the plaintiff establishes before trial, by medical, psychiatric or psychological evidence, that the plaintiff suffers from battered woman's syndrome, which caused an inability to take any action to improve or alter the circumstances in the marriage unilaterally).

12. *Tolling Pursuant to Federal Statute.* At least in some circumstances, the statute of limitations governing state tort claims can be tolled by federal legislation. *See* Jinks v. Richland County, S.C., 123 S. Ct. 1667 (2003) (holding constitutional a federal statute which requires tolling of the state statute of limitations on a state-law claim during the period in which a federal cause of action is pending in federal court pursuant to supplemental jurisdiction which is ultimately not exercised).

13. *Contracting around the Statute of Limitations.* Parties may be able to alter the length of the applicable statute of limitations by contract. In Moreno v. Sanchez, 131 Cal. Rptr. 2d 684 (Ct. App. 2003), the court wrote:

> Courts generally enforce parties' agreements for a shorter limitations period than otherwise provided by statute, provided it is reasonable. "Reasonable" in this context means the shortened period nevertheless provides sufficient time to effectively pursue a judicial remedy.

Moreno was an action based on breach of a home inspector's duty of care. The court held that a contractual provision which provided that a one-year limitations period ran from the date of the inspection (as opposed to when the breach was or should have been discovered) was invalid because it unreasonably deprived the plaintiff of the benefits of the discovery rule.

C. Statutes of Repose

Modern technology has, on the whole, increased safety considerably; life expectancy today is much greater than it was even thirty years ago, and very much greater than it was in past centuries. Technology has also, however, created situations in which someone's negligence or other tortious conduct may not lead to an injury for many years. Products that will last for decades may inflict injuries long after their manufacture and sale. Toxic substances like asbestos and DES can lead to injuries which manifest themselves long after the plaintiff's exposure to them.

Many states have enacted "statutes of repose" applicable to particular kinds of claims. *See, e.g.,* Fleck v. KDI Sylvan Pools, Inc., 981 F.2d 107 (3d Cir. 1992) ("improvements to real property"). These statutes resemble statutes of limitations in barring claims after a certain period—generally somewhat longer than the period specified in the statute of limitations—has passed. Unlike statutes of limitations, they are not subject to tolling, and they often begin to run when the activity in question, such as the sale of the product, takes place, rather than at the time the plaintiff is injured. They have been enacted not only because of the concerns that inspire statutes of limitations, but also in response to complaints by certain kinds of defendants—particularly manufacturers, doctors, and builders—that they are being exposed to crushing liability. These statutes are, therefore, to some extent an arbitrary cutoff on liability for reasons involving more than the difficulties raised by the passage of time.

Some statutes of repose are broadly applicable, such as one in Texas relating to defective products:

TEX. CIV. PRAC. & REM. CODE §16.012
(Westlaw 2004)

(b) Except as provided by Subsections (c), (d) [involving latent diseases], and (d-1) [involving actions that accrue before the end of the limitations period], a claimant must commence a products liability action against a manufacturer or seller of a product before the end of 15 years after the date of the sale of the product by the defendant.

(c) If a manufacturer or seller expressly warrants in writing that the product has a useful safe life of longer than 15 years, a claimant must commence a products liability action against that manufacturer or seller of the product before the end of the number of years warranted after the date of the sale of the product by that seller.

See also Fla. Stat. Ann. §95.031(2)(b)-(d) (Westlaw 2003) (defining statutes of repose applicable to products liability actions).

As with all legislation, the reach of a statute of repose is a matter of interpretation. *See, e.g.,* Hyer v. Pittsburgh Corning Corp., 790 F.2d 30 (4th Cir. 1986) (holding that a six-year statute of repose applied to "injuries," but not to "diseases," caused by exposure to asbestos-containing products); Chrysler Corp. v. Batten, 450 S.E.2d 208 (Ga. 1994) (statute permitted a negligent-failure-to-warn claim, but not a negligent-design claim). In addition, the statute must apply to the facts of the case at hand. *See, e.g.,* Hickman v. Carven, 784 A.2d 31 (Md. 2001) (desecration of a graveyard was not an "improvement" of realty, and therefore the statute did not bar an action for concealment of the desecration).

Thompson v. Franciscan Sisters Health Care Corp.

Appellate Court of Illinois
578 N.E.2d 289 (Ill. App. Ct. 1991)

Justice GORMAN delivered the opinion of the Court.

The plaintiff, Lori Ann Thompson, a minor, by Barbara A. Thompson, her mother and next friend, appeals from the dismissal of her medical malpractice complaint by the circuit court. The defendants are Franciscan Sisters Health Care Corporation, doing business as St. Joseph's Medical Center, and physicians T. Christiansen and John J. McLaughlin, as individuals and doing business as Joliet Medical Group, Ltd. The circuit court dismissed the complaint for failure to comply with the statute of limitations for medical malpractice cases, §13-212 of the Code of Civil Procedure (Ill. Rev. Stat. 1989, ch. 110, par. 13-212). We affirm.

On December 31, 1976, plaintiff was born. Complications arose during her birth, and defendants allegedly did not respond to those complications in a timely and proper manner. Plaintiff alleges that due to defendants' negligence she has been permanently and severely damaged. On July 26, 1990, plaintiff filed the present lawsuit. On November 14, 1990, after a hearing on defendants' motions to dismiss, the circuit court dismissed plaintiff's complaint with prejudice for failure to comply with §13-212 of the Code of Civil Procedure. On December 13, 1990, plaintiff filed a notice of appeal.

The issues raised on appeal by the plaintiff are:

(1) whether §13-212(b) unconstitutionally deprives minor victims of medical malpractice of access to court and recovery for damages, in violation of the due process clauses of the Federal and State constitutions;

(2) whether §13-212(b) deprives minor victims of medical malpractice of equal protection of the laws as guaranteed by the Federal and State constitutions;

(3) whether §13-212(b) unconstitutionally restricts free and open access to court for the vindication of the rights of minor victims of medical malpractice, in violation of the first amendment to the Federal constitution and article I, §12 of the State constitution; and

....

Section 13-212(b) of the Code of Civil Procedure (Ill. Rev. Stat. 1989, ch. 110, par. 13-212(b)) states as follows:

> "(b) Except as provided in §13-215 of this Act, no action for damages for injury or death against any physician, dentist, registered nurse or hospital duly licensed under the laws of this State, whether based upon tort, or breach of contract, or otherwise, arising out of patient care shall be brought more than 8 years after the date on which occurred the act or omission or occurrence alleged in such action to have been the cause of such injury or death where the person entitled to bring the action was, at the time the cause of action accrued, under the age of 18 years; provided, however, that in no event may the cause of action be brought after the person's 22nd birthday. *If the person was under the age of 18 years when the cause of action accrued and, as a result of this amendatory Act of 1987, the action is either barred or there remains less than 3 years to bring such action, then he or she may bring the action within 3 years of July 20, 1987.*" (Emphasis added.)

Application of the terms of this statutory provision to the facts of this case indicates that plaintiff had until July 20, 1990, by which to timely file her lawsuit. Since the lawsuit was filed on July 26, 1990, under the terms of this provision it was filed too late.... [W]e will...address the constitutional issues the plaintiff has raised as to §13-212(b).

We note that various challenges to the constitutionality of §21.1 of the Limitations Act..., a precursor of §13-212 of the Code of Civil Procedure, were considered by the Illinois Supreme Court in Anderson v. Wagner (1979), 79 Ill. 2d 295, 402 N.E.2d 560. While *Anderson* involved cases with plaintiffs who were adults at the time the alleged medical malpractice took place, its reasoning can be used in the present case.

We consider first whether application of §13-212(b) violates plaintiff's due process rights. Plaintiff essentially argues that it is fundamentally unfair that a minor's cause of action should ever be barred by the statute of limitations during minority, and that therefore the statute of limitations cannot be so applied without violating the due process clauses of the Federal and State constitutions. Plaintiff has cited no case that has used such broad reasoning to find that application of the statute of limitations had violated one of the due process clauses.

After discussing the so-called medical malpractice insurance crisis of the early 1970's and legislative responses to it, the court in *Anderson* stated:

> "Although such a result—a cause of action barred before its discovery— seems harsh and unfair, the reasonableness of the statute must be judged in light of the circumstances confronting the legislature and the end which it sought to accomplish. We have noted above that various reports, commissions, and authors recommended that the 'long tail' exposure to malpractice claims brought about by the discovery rule be curtailed by placing an outer limit within which a malpractice action must be commenced.... It has not

been demonstrated that the legislative action in establishing the 4-year outer limit within which to file a complaint for medical malpractice is unreasonable. We thus find no due process violation." *Anderson*, 79 Ill. 2d at 312, 402 N.E.2d at 568.

The prior law permitted filing suit 20 years (or sometimes longer) after alleged medical malpractice during childbirth, and it was not unreasonable for the legislature to cut down this "long tail" of liability so as to lend stability to the pricing of medical malpractice insurance for medical personnel involved in childbirths. The reasoning of *Anderson* leads us to conclude that the legislature's reduction of the limitations period to eight years after the wrongful conduct (or three years after the effective date of the amendment) is not unreasonable and does not result in a due process violation.

No authority has been presented to us holding that one or both of the due process clauses require that the statute of limitations protect an injured minor from the failure of a parent or guardian to pursue the minor's interest in a timely fashion. The legislature, when faced with the need to set some reasonable time limits on medical malpractice claims, could reasonably assume that parents and guardians would look after the interests of the affected minors, and it was not a violation of the minors' due process rights for it to make this assumption.

We next consider whether the application of §13-212(b) to the plaintiff denies her equal protection of the laws.... [The court ruled that the legislation, having a rational basis, did not violate equal protection.]

. . . .

Questions regarding the constitutionality of a statute cannot be raised for the first time on appeal. (Brown v. Mason (1985), 132 Ill. App. 3d 439, 442, 477 N.E.2d 61, 64.) The plaintiff did not raise in the circuit court constitutional questions regarding the first amendment of the Federal constitution, nor did she raise there constitutional questions regarding provisions of the State constitution pertaining to access to the courts and special legislation. Therefore she will not be permitted to raise them for the first time on appeal.

For the reasons stated herein, the decision of the circuit court to dismiss the complaint for failure to comply with §13-212 is affirmed.

Affirmed.

Notes

1. ***When Does a Repose Statute Begin to Run?*** Anderson v. Wagner, cited and followed in *Thompson*, was a case in which the statute of repose may have barred an action before the plaintiffs discovered that they had been injured. The importance of a statute of repose in that kind of case is that the statute overrides the discovery rule. Some repose statutes go further, barring claims even before an injury has occurred. For example, if a products-liability statute of repose bars suits filed more than ten years after the product in question was first sold, someone who buys an eleven-year-old defective product and then sustains an injury has no claim against the manufacturer, even if the claim is filed immediately after the injury. *See also* New York C.P.L.R. §214-a (Westlaw 2003).

2. ***Constitutionality of Statutes of Limitations and Repose.*** A few courts have held particular statutes of repose invalid on various federal and state constitutional grounds.

See Kenyon v. Hammer, 688 P.2d 961 (Ariz. 1984) (holding that a medical-malpractice plaintiff had a fundamental state constitutional right to sue for bodily injury and that a statute violated that right by limiting the discovery rule in medical malpractice cases); McCollum v. Sisters of Charity, 799 S.W.2d 15 (Ky. 1990) (medical malpractice statute of repose violated open-courts provisions of state constitution).

3. *Revival of Time-Barred Claims.* Some courts have held that a time-barred claim may be legislatively revived. *See* Hymowitz v. Eli Lilly and Co., 539 N.E.2d 1069 (N.Y. 1989), *supra* at 398. *See also* Roberts v. Caton, 619 A.2d 844 (Conn. 1993) (statutory amendment which extended the statute of limitations for damages caused by sexual assault of a minor could be applied retroactively).

Chapter 20

Interference with Possession or Use of Land: Trespass and Nuisance

A defendant's tortious interference with the plaintiff's possession or use of land is actionable, either as "trespass to land" or as "nuisance." Traditionally, the distinction between trespass and nuisance turned upon whether the defendant's misconduct led to a physical invasion of the plaintiff's land. If the defendant intentionally walked across the land or negligently caused rocks to be thrown upon it, the defendant had committed a trespass. If the defendant tortiously interfered with land without physically invading it, as by negligently or intentionally causing foul odors or loud noises to disturb the plaintiff's use of real property, the tort was nuisance. As cases in this chapter indicate, some jurisdictions, at least in some contexts, no longer distinguish between trespass and nuisance by applying a "physical invasion" test.

In most, if not all, states, neither trespass nor nuisance is an "absolute liability" tort.[a] In order to hold someone liable for either trespass or nuisance, the plaintiff must show that the defendant intentionally interfered with the plaintiff's possession or use of the land, or that the interference was caused by the defendant's failure to exercise care (negligence or recklessness), or that the defendant engaged in an activity—such as blasting—which is subject to strict liability. *See* Fortier v. Flambeau Plastics Co., 476 N.W.2d 593 (Wis. Ct. App. 1991). It is not enough for the plaintiff simply to show that something the defendant did caused an invasion of the plaintiff's interest in the land. For example, suppose that someone's window has been broken by a baseball hit by a child playing on a nearby lot. Is this a "trespass"? On the limited facts given here, there is no way to tell. If the child was trying to hit the defendant's house there is a trespass, based on an intentional invasion. If the child acted unreasonably in playing ball close to a house, there would also be a trespass, based on negligence or recklessness. But if an intentional, reckless, or negligent invasion cannot be shown, there is no trespass (or any other tort): playing baseball is not a strict-liability activity. It is useful to think of trespass and nuisance not as "torts" but rather as kinds of interference with land brought

---

a. At common law, any intentional act by the defendant which led to an invasion of the plaintiff's property was a trespass, even though the defendant did not intend the invasion and was in no way at fault. The Supreme Court rejected this rule in the "Nitroglycerine Case," Parrott v. Wells Fargo & Co., 82 U.S. 524 (1872), in which the defendant's employees used a hammer to open a box which, unknown to them, contained nitroglycerine. The ensuing explosion damaged a building owned by the plaintiffs, who sued the defendant for trespass. The court held that the defendants, not having been at fault, were not liable. State courts have routinely reached a similar result.

about by wrongful conduct. The torts involved in trespass or nuisance cases are intentional misconduct, recklessness, negligence, or strict liability, as the case may be.

Note that some authorities speak of trespass exclusively as an intentional tort, even though they permit an action for damages when negligence causes harm to land. *See, e.g.,* Snow v. City of Columbia, 409 S.E.2d 797 (S.C. Ct. App. 1991) (trespass would not lie where water from a leaking main caused damage to homeowners, but the issue of the city's negligence in installing and maintaining the main should have been submitted to the jury). Other authorities use the term trespass more expansively. *See* State Farm Fire & Cas. Co. v. White-Rodgers Corp., 77 P.3d 729 (Alaska 2003) (holding that a natural gas explosion that destroyed a house, allegedly as a result of a negligently installed and defective gas control product, was trespass upon real property for purposes of the statute of limitations because the label "'trespass' attaches broadly to any alleged interference with a possessor's property rights").

A brief discussion of trespass was set forth *supra* in Chapter 2 at p. 115.

A. Trespass to Land

The formal name for "trespass to land" is "trespass *quare clausum fregit.*" "*Quare clausum fregit*" (often shortened to "q.c.f.") means "because he broke the close." A "close"[b] is an imaginary barrier around the outside edge of someone's real property. By crossing the property line, an intruder "breaks the close."

Gavcus v. Potts
United States Court of Appeals for the Seventh Circuit
808 F.2d 596 (7th Cir. 1986)

FAIRCHILD, Senior Circuit Judge.

   ....

Mr. Gavcus died in March of 1981. Lillian Potts was Mr. Gavcus' daughter by a prior marriage and was a residual beneficiary under her father's will. Lillian's family attended his funeral and left several days afterwards after staying with Mrs. Gavcus in her home. The Potts[es] returned to Mrs. Gavcus' home the day after they left and, in her absence, removed a large quantity of silver coins valued at more than $150,000. The deputy who investigated the removal of the coins contacted Mrs. Potts, who later returned the coins to the sheriff's office. A couple of weeks later, Mrs. Gavcus hired an attorney to get the coins back for her. The attorney initiated a proceeding pursuant to…§968.20 of the Wisconsin Statutes for return of the coins….The circuit court determined that the coins belonged to Mrs. Gavcus individually and ordered their return pursuant to the §968.20 motion. Mrs. Gavcus then brought the suit at bar for damages, including the attorney fees she incurred in the prior litigation.

   ....

Mrs. Gavcus did not claim any physical injury to the real property. The court did allow her to offer evidence of the cost of new locks and the burglar alarm she installed

---

   b. Pronounced like "close" in "please close the door."

after the removal of the coins, and of the amount of attorney's fees incurred in the earlier litigation. Apparently the district court had some doubt as to the propriety of these items of damage and chose to admit the evidence and submit questions concerning those items in a special verdict, and to address the legal questions after the verdict was returned. The appeal arises from the court's determination that these items were not properly recoverable as damages. The jury had awarded by special verdict $3,126 for the cost of locks and a burglar alarm and $12,000 in attorney's fees.

Nominal compensatory damages can be awarded when no actual or substantial injury has been alleged or proved, since the law infers some damage from the unauthorized entry of land. Additionally, compensatory damages can be awarded for actual or substantial injury to realty. These latter damages are generally measured by the cost of restoring the property to its former condition or by the change in value before and after the trespass. Consequential damages can also be recovered for a trespass, since a trespasser is liable in damages for all injuries flowing from his trespass which are the natural and proximate result of it. One such compensable result of a trespass is personal injury to the owner of the land. If a trespass causes mental distress, the trespasser is liable in damages for the mental distress and any resulting illness or physical harm. [Citations.]

The installation of locks and a burglar alarm was not a repair of physical damage, and the cost was not recoverable as compensation for injury to property. Mrs. Gavcus' theory is that the trespass had caused an impairment of her sense of security and that the installation became reasonably necessary on account of that impairment.

We reject the theory, however, for two reasons. Impairment of her sense of security would amount, if anything, to a type of emotional distress. Mrs. Gavcus was not prepared to produce medical or other expert testimony on the subject. Judge Gordon ruled that lay evidence would be inadmissible, and Mrs. Gavcus has not argued the ruling was erroneous. Thus there was a failure of proof as to the nature, extent, and causation of any emotional distress, or cost of required treatment.

Second, assuming that she could have proved that the trespass caused increased nervousness, uneasiness, and worry, she cites no authority, nor was any authority found, which shows that the cost of an improvement to property intended to alleviate distress of that type would be properly allowable as damages.

. . . .

[The court held that the attorney's fees in the earlier action were not recoverable in an action for trespass. The fees, it thought, were incurred because of the dispute as to the ownership of the coins, not because of Mrs. Potts's having trespassed in an effort to obtain the coins. Therefore, the prior litigation and the fees incurred in conducting it were not "a natural and proximate result" of Mrs. Potts's trespass.]

. . . .

Both parties agree that the award of punitive damages could not be sustained unless compensatory damages had been awarded. [Citation.]

The judgment appealed from is affirmed.

Notes

1. *Presumed Damage.* An intentional trespass is actionable even if the plaintiff suffers no actual injury. In addition to the principal case, *see* Dougherty v. Stepp, 18 N.C. 371 (1835). There, defendant had entered on the unenclosed land of the plaintiff, with

a surveyor and chain carriers, and had surveyed a part of it, claiming it as his own, but without marking trees or cutting bushes. The court held that an action for trespass was established: "the law infers some damage; if nothing more, the treading down the grass or herbage, or as here, the shrubbery."

If Hooters and the Olive Garden are adjacent restaurants, and employees from Hooters park in spaces leased to the Olive Garden despite repeated requests not to do so, an action for trespass will lie regardless of whether damage has been caused. *See* General Mills Restaurants, Inc. v. Texas Wings, Inc., 12 S.W.3d 827 (Tex. App. 2000).

2. *Trespassers and Unforeseen Harm.* The law has frequently gone to great lengths to hold intentional tortfeasors liable for unforeseeable results, as is evidenced by the survival of the doctrine of transferred intent (*see* Chapter 2). There are many cases in which trespassers have been assessed damages for harm caused by accidentally started fires and other unforeseeable damage to the defendant's land. *See* William L. Prosser, *Transferred Intent*, 45 Tex. L. Rev. 650, 658-61 (1967).

3. *Mistake.* Many cases of trespass result from disputes over the ownership of land. The defendant's reasonable but mistaken belief that the land belongs to the defendant rather than to someone else does not excuse a trespass. If the law were otherwise, trespass would often not be available to resolve disputes over ownership. Furthermore, the trespasser who removes or destroys part of the real property, such as minerals or trees, is liable to the true owner despite having reasonably believed that the trespasser owned the property.

4. *Trespass to Airspace.* A trespasser need not touch the land in question; building a balcony that overhangs the plaintiff's property is a trespass. In the early days of the common law, the owner's rights in the space above the land were sometimes described by saying, "*cujus est solum, ejus est usque ad coelum*," which means that the landowner owns everything above the surface all the way up to heaven. Until the invention of the airplane, this formulation of the owner's rights did no harm; modern aviation has made change essential.

According to the Restatement, Second, of Torts, §159, flight over land is a trespass only if "it enters into the immediate reaches of the airspace next to the land" or if it "interferes substantially with the...use and enjoyment of [the] land." Under United States v. Causby, 328 U.S. 256 (1946), federal legislation and regulations concerning aviation have made airspace at ordinary flying altitudes a "public highway," and federal law now controls the use of that airspace.

To sum up a complex body of law in a sentence, very low flights over someone's land may be a trespass; higher flights which interfere seriously with land use because of noise or repetitiveness may be nuisances; ordinary flying is neither.

5. *Beneath the Surface.* Seismic testing raises difficult questions about the property rights of mineral owners. *See generally* Harry L. Bloomquist, III, *Geophysical Trespass? The Guessing Game Created by the Awkward Combination of Outmoded Law and Soaring Technology*, 48 Baylor L. Rev. 21 (1996) ("courts have awarded damages for unauthorized geophysical exploration when accompanied by surface entry"). What if the test shooting occurs right outside the plaintiff's boundary line and yields valuable information about mineral deposits, impairing the market value of the plaintiff's property? If this is actionable, should the claim be one for trespass or for some other tort?

6. *Termination of Consent or Privilege.* Rogers v. Board of Road Comm'rs for Kent County, 30 N.W.2d 358 (Mich. 1947), was an action for wrongful death caused by the

defendant's failure to remove the anchor posts for a snow fence it had installed on the decedent's land. The defendant had been given permission to erect the fence, on the understanding that it would be taken down at the end of the winter. Plaintiff's decedent died when a mower he was operating struck the anchor post, throwing him into the mower's moving parts. The court held the defendant's failure to remove the posts a trespass, citing §160 of the Restatement, Second, of Torts:

> A trespass…may be committed by the continued presence on the land of a structure, chattel or other thing which the actor or his predecessor in legal interest therein has placed thereon
>
> (a) with the consent of the person then in possession of the land, if the actor fails to remove it after the consent has been effectively terminated, or
>
> (b) pursuant to a privilege conferred on the actor irrespective of the possessor's consent, if the actor fails to remove it after the privilege has been terminated, by the accomplishment of its purpose or otherwise.

See also Montgomery Ward v. Andrews, 736 P.2d 40 (Colo. Ct. App. 1987) (even if Ward's had a statutory or contractual right to enter the premises of a catalog sales agency to repossess secured property, it exceeded its rights and committed a trespass by changing the locks and keeping the keys for ten days).

7. *Standing.* Because the action for trespass q.c.f. is intended to protect possession of land, it may ordinarily be maintained only by one currently in possession. *See, e.g,* Russell v. American Real Estate Corp., 89 S.W.3d 204 (Tex. App. 2002) (permitting an action by a tenant at sufferance following foreclosure). However, some authorities permit a person entitled to future possession to sue to protect that interest. In Plotkin v. Club Valencia Condo. Ass'n, 717 P.2d 1027 (Colo. Ct. App. 1986), the owner of a condominium that was rented to a tenant was deemed to have constructive possession of the unit's balcony and permitted to sue for trespass. The defendant association had entered the balcony and relocated a storage rack, thus impairing the panoramic view from the unit.

8. *Trespass by Journalists.* Is it a trespass for a journalist to accompany law enforcement officers into a private home after a fire? In Florida Publ'g Co. v. Fletcher, 340 So. 2d 914 (Fla. 1976), the court ruled that a journalist has an implied consent, based on custom and usage, to enter private property after a calamity, if invited by officials. Other courts have ruled that journalists accompanying officials may be liable for trespass, and perhaps other torts as well. *See, e.g.,* Berger v. Hanlon, 129 F.3d 505 (9th Cir. 1997), *judgment vacated on other grounds,* 526 U.S. 808 (1999) (a claim for trespass was stated because law enforcement officers conducting a search were not authorized to invite third parties onto the premises for reasons unrelated to law enforcement; *Fletcher* was irrelevant because it involved a "disaster"); Miller v. NBC, 232 Cal. Rptr. 668, 685 (1986); Prahl v. Brosamle, 295 N.W. 2d 768, 780 (Wis. Ct. App. 1980). *See also* Desnick v. ABC, 44 F.3d 1345, 1351 (7th Cir. 1995) ("there is no journalists' privilege to trespass").

9. *Compensatory Predicate for Punitive Damages.* The penultimate sentence in the *Gavcus* opinion indicates that in some states an award of compensatory damages is an essential predicate for a punitive award. Not all states adhere to that position. In Jacque v. Steenberg Homes, Inc., 563 N.W.2d 154 (Wis. 1997), the court held that nominal damages can support a punitive damages award in a case of intentional trespass to land.

B. Trespass and Private Nuisance

Public Nuisance and Private Nuisance. Nuisance comes in two varieties—"public nuisance" and "private nuisance." This section will compare trespass and "private nuisance," which for present purposes can be thought of as nuisances which affect only the plaintiff, or the plaintiff and a handful of others, as when one's neighbor holds raucous beer parties every weekend with the volume of the music cranked up high. Nuisances not confined in their effects to a few property owners—the wrongful closing of a public road, for example—are "public nuisances," which will be examined in the following section.

"Attractive Nuisance" Distinguished. The "attractive nuisance" doctrine (discussed in Chapter 10) is unrelated to the action for private nuisance. Under the doctrine of attractive nuisance, which is an aspect of the law of premises liability, a landholder may be held liable for injuries to trespassing children caused by artificial conditions on land. *See* Restatement, Second, of Torts §339. The injury-causing condition need not qualify as a "nuisance" in the sense in which that term is used in this chapter in order for relief to be granted under the attractive nuisance doctrine.

1. Trespass and Nuisance Distinguished

a. The Traditional Distinction

Private nuisance and trespass q.c.f. are closely related, for both involve an impairment of another's interests in land. It has traditionally been said that trespass protects a possessor's right to *exclusive possession* of land, while nuisance protects the possessor's interest in *use and enjoyment* of the property. Trespass requires entry above, under, or onto the land in question, but typically does not require that the plaintiff suffer actual damages. Nuisance, in contrast, does not require entry, but substantial harm must be shown. Since a trespassory invasion may result in serious interference with the enjoyment of land, both trespass and nuisance actions may arise from a physical invasion, as where water is diverted onto a neighbor's property (Humphreys-Mexia Co. v. Arsenaux, 297 S.W. 225 (Tex. 1927)), or an encroaching building is erected (Allen v. Virginia Hill Water Supply Corp., 609 S.W.2d 633 (Tex. Civ. App. 1980)). However, not every intrusion amounts to unreasonable interference. *See* Hennessey v. Pyne, 694 A.2d 691, 695 (R.I. 1997) (a single golf ball, hit by the defendant, was "such an isolated incident" that it was "not the type of conduct that nuisance law is intended to remedy").

Unreasonably loud or persistent noises from sources off the land are a fairly common illustration of a nuisance that is not a trespass; the Restatement uses "the defendant's dog howl[ing] under the plaintiff's window night after night" as an example of nuisance. If the dog howls on the plaintiff's land there is a trespass as well; Restatement, Second, of Torts §821D Comment e. Odors can be nuisances, as when the defendant raises cows or pigs in a residential area. So can lights, as when the defendant illuminates a residential neighborhood at night with arc lights.

All of the examples of nuisance given above involved an "invasion" of the plaintiff's property, though not necessarily an invasion by physical objects, as the cases of noise and, perhaps, light,[c] show. But there are cases in which the plaintiff's enjoyment of property can be reduced by conduct which never encroaches on the property itself, as when one's neighbor paints his house plaid, or establishes a house of prostitution, or lets junk accumulate on a vacant lot. Some of these activities have been held to be nuisances (either public or private). However, almost anything one can do will annoy some neighbor, and the courts have been reluctant to find non-invasive conduct to be a nuisance except in cases in which the conduct is manifestly undesirable, as in the prostitution example.

b. Merger of Trespass and Private Nuisance

Bradley v. American Smelting and Refining Co.

Supreme Court of Washington, En Banc
709 P.2d 782 (Wash. 1985)

CALLOW, Justice.

This comes before us on a certification from the United States District Court for the Western District of Washington....

....

...Plaintiffs Michael O. Bradley and Marie A. Bradley, husband and wife, are owners and occupiers of real property....The Bradleys purchased their property in 1978. Defendant ASARCO...operates a primary copper smelter on real property it owns in Rushton....

On October 3, 1983, plaintiffs brought this action against defendant alleging a cause of action for intentional trespass and for nuisance.

Plaintiffs' property is located some 4 miles north of defendant's smelter. Defendant's primary copper smelter (also referred to as the Tacoma smelter), has operated in its present location since 1890....[V]arious gases such as sulfur dioxide and particulate matter, including arsenic, cadmium and other metals, are emitted. Particulate matter is composed of distinct particles of matter other than water, which cannot be detected by the human senses.

....

....[T]he parties stipulate that some particulate emissions of both cadmium and arsenic from the Tacoma smelter have been and are continuing to be deposited on plaintiffs' land. Defendant ASARCO has been aware since...1905 that the wind does, on occasion, cause smelter particulate emissions to blow over Vashon Island where plaintiffs' land is located.

....

....The issues [in this case] present the conflict in an industrial society between the need of all for the production of goods and the desire of the landowner near the manufacturing plant producing those goods that his use and enjoyment of his land not be diminished by the unpleasant side effects of the manufacturing process....

....

....We are asked if the defendant, knowing what it had to know from the facts it admits, had the legal intent to commit trespass.

---

c. We express no opinion here on the relative merits of the wave theory and the particle theory of light.

The Restatement, Second, of Torts, §158 (1965) states:

> One is subject to liability to another for trespass, irrespective of whether he thereby causes harm to any legally protected interest of the other, if he intentionally
>
> (a) enters land in the possession of the other, or causes a thing or a third person to do so, or
>
> (b) remains on the land, or
>
> (c) fails to remove from the land a thing which he is under a duty to remove.

In the comment on clause (a) of §158 at 278 it is stated in part:

> i. *Causing entry of a thing.* The actor, without himself entering the land, may invade another's interest in its exclusive possession by throwing, propelling, or placing a thing, either on or beneath the surface of the land or in the air space above it. Thus, in the absence of the possessor's consent or other privilege to do so, it is an actionable trespass to throw rubbish on another's land.... [I]t is not necessary that the foreign matter should be thrown directly and immediately upon the other's land. It is enough that an act is done with knowledge that it will to a substantial certainty result in the entry of the foreign matter.

.... [S]ection 8A of the Restatement (Second) of Torts says:

> The word "intent" is used...to denote that the actor desires to cause consequences of his act, or that he believes that the consequences are substantially certain to result from it.

....

The defendant has known for decades that sulfur dioxide and particulates of arsenic, cadmium and other metals were being emitted from the tall smokestack. It had to know that the solids propelled into the air by the warm gases would settle back to earth somewhere. It had to know that a purpose of the tall stack was to disperse the gas, smoke and minute solids over as large an area as possible and as far away as possible, but that while any resulting contamination would be diminished as to any one area or landowner, that nonetheless contamination, though slight, would follow....

.... Garratt v. Dailey, 46 Wash. 2d 197, 279 P.2d 1091 (1955) involved a 5-year-old boy who pulled a chair from under an arthritic woman as she was about to sit in it. The court held that to find liability for an intentional tort it had to be found that there was a volitional act undertaken with the knowledge and substantial certainty that reasonably to be expected consequences would follow.

It is patent that the defendant acted on its own volition and had to appreciate with substantial certainty that the law of gravity would visit the effluence upon someone, somewhere.

....

We find that the defendant had the requisite intent to commit intentional trespass as a matter of law.

....

The courts have been groping for a reconciliation of the doctrines of trespass and nuisance over a long period of time and, to a great extent, have concluded that little of substance remains to any distinction between the two when air pollution is involved....

.... Professor Rodgers states:

Trespass is a theory closely related to nuisance and occasionally invoked in environmental cases. The distinction between the two originally was the difference between the old action of trespass and the action on the case: if there was a direct and immediate physical invasion of plaintiff's property, as by casting stones or water on it, it was a trespass; if the invasion was indirect, as by the seepage of water, it was a nuisance.

....

.... Potential problems lurk in the ancient requirements that a trespassory invasion be "direct or immediate" and that an "object" or "something tangible" be deposited upon plaintiff's land. Some courts hold that if an intervening force, such as wind or water, carries the pollutants onto the plaintiff's land, then the entry is not "direct." Others define "object" as requiring something larger or more substantial than smoke, dust, gas, or fumes.

Both of these concepts are nonsensical barriers, although the courts are slow to admit it. The requirement that the invasion be "direct" is a holdover from the forms of action, and is repudiated by contemporary science of causation. Atmospheric or hydrologic systems assure that pollutants deposited in one place will end up somewhere else, with no less assurance of causation than the blaster who watches the debris rise from his property and settle on his neighbor's land.

The insistence that a trespass involve an invasion by a "thing" or "object" was repudiated in the well known (but not particularly influential) case of Martin v. Reynolds Metals Co., [342 P.2d 790 (Or. 1959)], which held that gaseous and particulate fluorides from an aluminum smelter constituted a trespass for purposes of the statute of limitations....

The view recognizing a trespassory invasion where there is no "thing" which can be seen with the naked eye undoubtedly runs counter to the definition of trespass expressed in some quarters. [Citations.] It is quite possible that in an earlier day when science had not yet peered into the molecular and atomic world of small particles, the courts could not fit an invasion through unseen physical instrumentalities into the requirement that a trespass can result only from a *direct* invasion....

Martin is quite right in hastening the demise of the "direct" and "tangible" limitations on the law of trespass....

(Footnotes omitted.) W. Rodgers, Environmental Law §2.13 at 154-57 (1977).

.... We hold that theories of trespass and nuisance are not inconsistent, that the theories may apply concurrently, and that the injured party may proceed under both theories when the elements of both actions are present....

....

When airborne particles are transitory or quickly dissipate, they do not interfere with a property owner's possessory rights and, therefore, are properly denominated as nuisances. [Citations.] When, however, the particles or substance accumulates on the land and does not pass away, then a trespass has occurred. [Citations.] While at common law any trespass entitled a landowner to recover nominal or punitive damages for the invasion of his property, such a rule is not appropriate under the circumstances before us. No useful purpose would be served by sanctioning actions in trespass by every landowner within a hundred miles of a manufacturing plant. Manufacturers would be harassed and the litigious few would cause the escalation of costs to the detriment of the many.... [T]he plaintiff who cannot show that actual and substantial damages have been suffered should be subject to dismissal of his cause upon a motion for summary judgment.

....

....An action for trespass to land must be brought within 3 years of the invasion to the premises....

....The action of the defendant amounts to a continuing trespass which is defined by the Restatement (Second) of Torts §158, comment m as "[a]n unprivileged remaining on land in another's possession." Assuming that a defendant has caused actual and substantial damage to a plaintiff's property, the trespass continues until the intruding substance is removed.... [I]n ruling that actual and substantial damages are required, we find it proper to also require that damages claimed not extend past the 3-year period of limitations.

....

In conclusion, we answer the certified questions as follows:

1. The defendant had the requisite intent to commit intentional trespass.

2. An intentional deposit of microscopic particulates, undetectable by the human senses, gives rise to a cause of action for trespass as well as a claim of nuisance.

3. A cause of action under such circumstances requires proof of actual and substantial damages.

4. The appropriate limitations period for such a trespass is 3 years, but if the trespass continues, suit for damages may be brought for any damages not recovered previously and occurring within the 3-year period preceding suit....

....

Notes

1. After the decision in *Bradley* by the Washington Supreme Court, the case went back to the federal district court, which granted summary judgment for the defendant. The court found that the landowners could not recover for trespass because they had failed to prove actual damage. The evidence showed that arsenic and cadmium deposits were imperceptible to human senses, a health hazard was unproved, and recovery for anxiety unaccompanied by physical symptoms was not permitted. 635 F. Supp. 1154 (W.D. Wash. 1986).

2. *Particulate Trespass. See also* Maddy v. Vulcan Materials Co., 737 F. Supp. 1528 (D. Kan. 1990) (joining the "clear and consistent" case law in other jurisdictions in recognizing that trespass will lie for indirect or intangible invasions, but denying recovery because plaintiffs failed to prove actual damages).

In some jurisdictions, particulate trespass may be actionable without proof of damages. In Stevenson v. E.I. DuPont de Nemours and Co., 327 F.3d 400 (5th Cir. 2003), a case involving the emission of heavy metal particulates, the court opined that Texas courts would so hold and therefore affirmed in part a judgment based on a jury verdict that found that there was no nuisance and no negligence, but that the defendant had committed trespass. "Plaintiffs were not required to show substantial damage to their property," and could recover for diminution in property value.

3. *Injunctive Relief against Trespass.* Cases like *Bradley*, which narrow the distinction between trespass and nuisance, help some plaintiffs by allowing actions that would formerly have been brought in nuisance to take advantage of what may be a longer statute of limitations for trespass. Other plaintiffs, however, may be better off under the traditional rules, because the *Bradley* court's expansive definition of trespass makes it necessary to relax the traditional rule allowing the victim of a threatened future trespass to enjoin intrusions. The idea that anyone on whose land invisible particles have been deposited can enjoin the operation of the factory emitting the particles is so absurd that broadening the definition of trespass entails introducing some sort of "balancing test" in deciding whether an injunction against future trespasses should be issued.

Suppose that the trespass in *Bradley* had consisted of driving trucks across the corner of the plaintiffs' land. This would be a trespass by anybody's definition, and the plaintiffs would have been entitled to enjoin further trespasses under traditional common-law principles. Under *Bradley*, could the defendant now argue with a straight face that its driving across the plaintiffs' land should be enjoined only if the court decides that the harm to the Bradleys outweighs the benefits to the defendant of taking the shortcut? One doubts that a court would go that far. If that is right, perhaps the way to read *Bradley* is as holding, in effect, that nuisances that indirectly or imperceptibly cause trespassory invasions are trespasses for purposes of the statute of limitations, but are still nuisances when the issue is whether to grant an injunction.

In Boomer v. Atlantic Cement Co., 257 N.E.2d 870 (N.Y. 1970), the defendant's cement plant regularly deposited cement dust on the property of nearby residents. This was held to be a nuisance, and under prior New York decisions someone subject to a nuisance resulting in substantial and permanent damage was entitled to enjoin the nuisance. The court was unwilling to enjoin the plant's operation, and instead required the defendant to pay permanent damages to the plaintiffs. These permanent damages purported to compensate the plaintiffs not only for harm done in the past, but also for future harms. Judge Jasen, dissenting, observed that this result had the effect of allowing the defendants to purchase an interest in the plaintiffs' properties—a sort of easement to continue polluting without the plaintiffs' consent.

2. Significant Harm

A finding of nuisance requires proof that the defendant intentionally invaded the plaintiff's interest in land, or that the interference resulted from a failure to exercise care (negligence or recklessness), or from strict liability conduct. Once that predicate has been established, the plaintiff must also show that the harm done was significant. In this respect, the action for private nuisance differs from trespass—at least in its traditional form: *any* trespass is actionable, even if no harm is done.

Section 821F of the Restatement, Second, of Torts provides:

> There is liability for nuisance only to those to whom it causes significant harm, of a kind that would be suffered by a normal person in the community or by property in normal condition and used for a normal purpose.

The commentary to the section states:

c. *Significant Harm.* By significant harm is meant harm of importance, involving more than slight inconvenience or petty annoyance. The law does not concern itself with trifles, and therefore there must be a real and appreciable invasion of the plaintiff's interests before he can have an action for either a public or a private nuisance....

d. *Hypersensitive Persons or Property.* When an invasion involves a detrimental change in the physical condition of land, there is seldom any doubt as to the significant character of the invasion. When, however, it involves only personal discomfort or annoyance, it is sometimes difficult to determine whether the invasion is significant. The standard for the determination of significant character is the standard of normal persons or property in the particular locality....

Thus a hypersensitive nervous invalid cannot found an action for a private nuisance upon...[conduct that] a normal member of the community would regard...as unobjectionable or at most a petty annoyance. This is true also when the harm to the plaintiff results only because of the hypersensitive condition of his land or chattels or his abnormal use of them. Thus an ordinary power line supplying electric current for household use does not create a nuisance when it interferes by induction with highly sensitive electrical instruments operating in the vicinity.

On the other hand, when the invasion is of a kind that the normal individual in the community would find definitely annoying or offensive, the fact that those who live in the neighborhood are hardened to it and have no objection will not prevent the plaintiff from maintaining his action. For example, the noise of a boiler factory next door may be a private nuisance even though the plaintiff and others who live in the vicinity are stone deaf and cannot hear it. The deafness of the plaintiff himself will affect the damages that he can recover, but it does not prevent the existence of a genuine interference with the use and enjoyment of his land as, for example, for the purpose of entertaining guests.

In Langan v. Bellinger, 611 N.Y.S.2d 59 (App. Div. 1994), the court held that the ringing of church bells on an hourly basis, between 8:00 a.m. and 8:00 p.m., and the presentation of carillon concerts at 12 noon and 6:00 p.m., did not constitute nuisance to a resident of a house 250 feet from the church. An acoustical expert testified that the bells made no more noise than passing automobiles, of which 6,500 went by the resident's property each day, and there were affidavits from 15 village residents that the church bells were pleasant.

Unfounded Fears. In Adkins v. Thomas Solvent Co., 487 N.W.2d 715 (Mich. 1992), landowners sought to recover for depreciation in the value of their property resulting from public perception that their land had been subject to groundwater pollution, even though the undisputed testimony showed that the properties were not, and never would be, subject to contamination from the defendant's activities. Ruling that the "boundaries of a traditional nuisance claim should not be relaxed," the court held that the plaintiffs had failed to show any significant interference with the use and enjoyment of their land based on actions by the defendants, so that the plaintiffs could not recover in nuisance.

If the activity in question is operated in a lawful manner and there is no personal injury or property damage, many courts will be reluctant to recognize an action for nuisance based on apprehension of possible harm. In Union Pac. Resources Co. v. Cooper, 109 S.W.3d 557 (Tex. App. 2003), the Coopers granted an oil, gas, and mineral lease to a lessee, who intended to drill a well.

> [I]t was common in the area to encounter hydrogen sulphide gas ("sour gas") when drilling....Sour gas is poisonous and can cause death to people who come into contact with it.

The lessee prepared an evacuation plan, which was approved by the state pursuant to applicable rules, and explained the plan to the Coopers. The Coopers did not wish to live on their property during the drilling and therefore temporarily moved away. No gas was ever detected and it was determined that the well was a dry hole. The court rejected the Coopers' subsequent action for nuisance, stating:

> "If we were to allow a cause of action to persons who have not been harmed, in their land or body, by the lawful operation of an industry, but who are afraid that one day they will be, we would be opening our courts to a potential torrent of litigation...." [Citation.]
>
> ....The uncontroverted evidence showed that even if the sour gas escaped the drilling process three miles underground, it would probably take it a full day to reach the surface....
>
> The only evidence of a possible nuisance which caused the Coopers to leave their home was based on fear, apprehension, and other emotional reactions stemming from what they had been told by Mrs. Cooper's brother [who said "that if they smelled rotten eggs, it was sour gas and they would be sure to die"]. Since no sour gas was ever encountered, no physical harm was shown by the Coopers. Therefore, we conclude that the Coopers presented no evidence which established a viable claim for nuisance.

Interference with Potential Use. For a nuisance to exist, the defendant's conduct need not interfere with the actual, present use of the plaintiff's property; the likelihood of interference with some use to which the property might reasonably be put will suffice. Meat Producers, Inc. v. McFarland, 476 S.W.2d 406, 410 (Tex. Civ. App. 1972), allowed an absentee landlord to recover damages from a cattle feedlot where he produced testimony that the highest and best use of the land was for homesites.

3. Assessing Unreasonableness

A defendant whose conduct has caused significant harm to the plaintiff's use of land may not have committed an actionable nuisance. Before a remedy will be forthcoming, the plaintiff must establish the unreasonableness of the defendant's invasion. The reasonableness question is often, but not always, addressed by "balancing" the competing interests of the plaintiff, the defendant, and, perhaps, "society as a whole."

Social Value of The Defendant's Conduct. Other things being equal, conduct viewed as necessary or useful to the community is much more likely to be held "reasonable," despite an interference with the plaintiff, than blatantly undesirable conduct. So ordinary economic and recreational activities are unlikely to be held nuisances, while illegal activities causing similar harms would be. The illegality question often arises with respect to zoning laws, violation of which may support a finding that an interference with the plaintiff's use of land is unreasonable and therefore a nuisance.

Some legislation expressly defines certain activities as nuisances. *See* Pope v. City of Houston, 559 S.W.2d 905, 907 (Tex. Civ. App. 1977) (ordinance defining "weeds, brush, [and] rubbish" as nuisances); Ga. Stat. Ann. §41-3-1.1 (Westlaw 2003) ("owner of real property who has actual knowledge that substantial drug-related activity is being conducted on such property shall be guilty of maintaining a nuisance"); Cal. Health & Safety Code §11570 (Westlaw 2003) ("Every building or place used for the purpose of unlawfully selling, serving, storing, keeping, manufacturing, or giving away any controlled substance…is a nuisance"). Conduct falling within the terms of such enactments is regarded as having minimal social value, provided the enactment is legally valid. A legislative body may not, however, in the guise of halting injurious conditions, define an otherwise-legal activity as a nuisance, if in fact there is no unreasonable interference with the interests of others. *See* City of Sundown v. Shewmake, 691 S.W.2d 57, 59 (Tex. Ct. App. 1985).

Lawfulness versus Illegality. The defendant's compliance with statutory obligations, while not dispositive, supports a finding of reasonableness. *See* Garland Grain Co. v. D-C Home Owners Improvement Ass'n, 393 S.W.2d 635, 637 (Tex. Civ. App. 1965) (noting, in denying injunction, that a cattle feedlot was periodically inspected by the health department).

Violation of a legislative enactment normally supports a finding of unreasonableness, as where the defendant's conduct violates zoning laws.

However, in some instances violation of the law will be disregarded. *See* Luensmann v. Zimmer-Zampese & Assoc., 103 S.W.3d 594 (Tex. App. 2003) (holding that homeowners residing near a raceway were not entitled to permanent injunctive relief limiting drag racing, even through the drag races caused noise in excess of the 85-decibel-level defined in the disorderly conduct statute, because there was evidence that noise from other nearby sources, including a highway, railroad tracks, a shooting range, and air traffic, exceeded 85 decibels even before the raceway began operations).

The Defendant's Motive. The defendant's reasons for engaging in an activity may support a nuisance finding, especially if the defendant has done something primarily for the purpose of annoying the plaintiff. The classic example is the "spite fence"—a fence erected only to aggravate a neighbor. *See* Hutcherson v. Alexander, 70 Cal. Rptr. 366, 369 (Ct. App. 1968); Brittingham v. Robertson, 280 A.2d 741, 745 (Del. 1971); Hornsby v. Smith, 13 S.E.2d 20, 24 (Ga. 1941). Some older cases were to the contrary. *See* Saddler v. Alexander, 56 S.W. 518, 519 (Ky. 1900); Letts v. Kessler, 42 N.E. 765, 765-67 (Ohio 1896). However, in cases involving less-than-egregious conduct, many courts are inclined to treat motive as irrelevant.

Competing Financial Interests. Courts have sometimes taken financial matters into account, by examining the amounts invested in the activity by the plaintiff or the defendant, and by considering the jobs that would be lost if the defendant should be enjoined. *See* Boomer v. Atlantic Cement Co., 257 N.E.2d 870 (N.Y. 1970).

Aesthetics. The mere unsightliness of a building will not, by itself, cause the structure to be regarded as a nuisance. *See* Houston Gas & Fuel Co. v. Harlow, 297 S.W. 570, 572 (Tex. Civ. App. 1927). Presumably, the reasoning of the courts in this field is not that aesthetic matters are insignificant, but that it would be an unwise expenditure of limited judicial resources to attempt to adjudicate disputes over matters of taste.

Where, however, other factors suggest that the defendant's conduct unreasonably interferes with the interests of the plaintiff, a court may rely upon aesthetic considerations to bolster a finding of unreasonableness.

The Defendant's Manner of Operation. If the defendant's manner of operation is normal and customary, and in accordance with sound scientific and technological principles, courts tend to regard the resulting interference as reasonable. Conversely, a defendant's failure to use technically and economically feasible means of avoiding harm to the plaintiff strongly supports a finding that the resulting interference is unreasonable. *See* Restatement, Second, of Torts §828(c); Guarina v. Bogart, 180 A.2d 557 (Pa. 1962) (a drive-in theater's use of public loudspeakers was enjoined because individual speakers could be installed at a small cost).

The Extent and Character of the Harm. The frequency, duration, and severity of the interference caused by the defendant, and the proximity of the defendant's activities to the site of the disturbance, may be considered by the court in assessing unreasonableness. The number of persons affected by the defendant's conduct is part of this calculation. *See* Brenteson Wholesale v. Public Serv. Co., 803 P.2d 930 (Ariz. Ct. App. 1990) (a utility was entitled to an injunction against use of an airstrip because there was a substantial risk that flights would encroach on the utility's airspace and contact power lines).

The Appropriateness of the Parties' Activities to the Locality. As the U.S. Supreme Court has recognized: "A nuisance may be merely a right thing in the wrong place,— like a pig in the parlor instead of the barnyard." Euclid v. Ambler Realty Co., 272 U.S. 365, 388 (1926). Accordingly, great attention is paid to whether the defendant's activities are suited to the nature of the locality. As Prah v. Maretti, 321 N.W.2d 182 (Wis. 1982), below, indicates, it is also appropriate for a court to consider whether the activities allegedly being interfered with are themselves suited to the locality.

Who Got There First. The assessment of reasonableness is not simply a question of "who got there first." Therefore, it is no bar to a nuisance action that the offending condition existed before the plaintiff acquired or improved the land. Nevertheless, the fact that the plaintiff "came to the nuisance" is given some weight in the balancing process, for the law is reluctant to hold that a newcomer may move into a neighborhood and demand that nearby landowners begin to observe those raised standards of living to which the newcomer intends to become accustomed. *See* Spur Indus. v. Del E. Webb Development Co., 494 P.2d 700 (Ariz. 1972), *infra* at 919.

Prah v. Maretti

Supreme Court of Wisconsin
321 N.W.2d 182 (Wis. 1982)

ABRAHAMSON, Justice.

This appeal...was certified to this court by the court of appeals, [citation], as presenting an issue of first impression, namely, whether an owner of a solar-heated residence states a claim upon which relief can be granted when he asserts that his neighbor's proposed construction of a residence (which conforms to existing deed restrictions and local ordinances) interferes with his access to an unobstructed path for sunlight across the neighbor's property. This case thus involves a conflict between one landowner (Glenn Prah, the plaintiff) interested in unobstructed access to sunlight across adjoining property as a natural source of energy and an adjoining landowner (Richard D. Maretti, the defendant) interested in the development of his land.

The circuit court concluded that the plaintiff presented no claim upon which relief could be granted.... We reverse the judgment of the circuit court and remand the cause to the circuit court for further proceedings.

....

...[T]he plaintiff is the owner of a residence, which was constructed during the years 1978-1979. The...residence has a solar system which includes collectors on the roof to supply energy for heat and hot water and that after the plaintiff built his solar-heated house, the defendant purchased the lot adjacent to and immediately to the south of the plaintiff's lot and commenced planning construction of a home....[P]laintiff... advised the defendant that if the house were built at the proposed location, defendant's house would substantially and adversely affect the integrity of plaintiff's solar system and could cause plaintiff other damage. Nevertheless, the defendant began construction. The complaint...demands judgment for injunctive relief and damages.

    ....

...Plaintiff's home was the first residence built in the subdivision, and although the plaintiff did not build his house in the center of the lot it was built in accordance with applicable restrictions...[P]laintiff requested defendant to locate his home an additional several feet away from the plaintiff's lot line, the exact number being disputed. Plaintiff and defendant failed to reach an agreement on the location of defendant's home before defendant started construction. The Architectural Control Committee and the Planning Commission of the City of Muskego approved the defendant's plans for his home, including its location on the lot. After such approval, the defendant apparently changed the grade of the property without prior notice to the Architectural Control Committee.[2] The problem with defendant's proposed construction, as far as the plaintiff's interests are concerned, arises from a combination of the grade and the distance of defendant's home from the defendant's lot line.

    ....

Although the defendant's obstruction of the plaintiff's access to sunlight appears to fall within the Restatement's broad concept of a private nuisance as a nontrespassory invasion of another's interest in the private use and enjoyment of land, the defendant asserts that he has a right to develop his property in compliance with statutes, ordinances and private covenants without regard to the effect of such development upon the plaintiff's access to sunlight. In essence, the defendant is asking this court to hold that the private nuisance doctrine is not applicable in the instant case and that his right to develop his land is a right which is per se superior to his neighbor's interest in access to sunlight. This position is expressed in the maximum "*cujus est solum, ejus est usque ad coelum et ad infernos*," that is, the owner of land owns up to the sky and down to the center of the earth. The rights of the surface owner are, however, not unlimited. [Citations.]

    ....

...American courts have afforded some protection to a landowner's interest in access to sunlight. American courts honor express easements to sunlight. American courts initially enforced the English common law doctrine of ancient lights, but later every state which considered the doctrine repudiated it as inconsistent with the needs of a developing country....

Many jurisdictions in this country have protected a landowner from malicious obstruction of access to light (the spite fence cases) under the common law private nui-

---

2. There appears to be some dispute over...[whether the defendant built his house at] a grade level not approved by the Board. The specific dispute over this sequence of events is not relevant to this appeal, but suffice it to say that such facts will become relevant to the question of the reasonableness of the defendant's construction in light of our decision that the plaintiff has stated a claim on the issue of private nuisance.

Shirley S. Abrahamson

sance doctrine. If an activity is motivated by malice it lacks utility and the harm it causes others outweighs any social values. [Citation.] This court was reluctant to protect a landowner's interest in sunlight even against a spite fence, only to be overruled by the legislature. Shortly after this court upheld a landowner's right to erect a useless and unsightly sixteen-foot spite fence four feet from his neighbor's windows, [citation], the legislature enacted a law specifically defining a spite fence as an actionable private nuisance. Thus a landowner's interest in sunlight has been protected in this country by common law private nuisance law at least in the narrow context of the modern American rule invalidating spite fences. [Citations.]

This court's reluctance in the nineteenth and early part of the twentieth century to provide broader protection for a landowner's access to sunlight was premised on three policy considerations. First, the right of landowners to use their property as they wished, as long as they did not cause physical damage to a neighbor, was jealously guarded. [Citation.]

Second, sunlight was valued only for aesthetic enjoyment or as illumination. Since artificial light could be used for illumination, loss of sunlight was at most a personal annoyance which was given little, if any, weight by society.

Third, society had significant interest in not restricting or impeding land development. [Citation.] This court repeatedly emphasized that in the growth period of the nineteenth and early twentieth centuries change is to be expected and is essential to property and that recognition of a right to sunlight would hinder property development....

....These three policies are no longer fully accepted or applicable. They reflect factual circumstances and social priorities that are now obsolete.

First, society has increasingly regulated the use of land by the landowner for the general welfare. [Citation.]

Second, access to sunlight has taken on a new significance in recent years. In this case the plaintiff seeks to protect access to sunlight, not for aesthetic reasons or as a source of illumination but as a source of energy. Access to sunlight as an energy source is of significance both to the landowner who invests in solar collectors and to a society which has an interest in developing alternative sources of energy.

Third, the policy of favoring unhindered private development in an expanding economy is no longer in harmony with the realities of our society. [Citation.] The need for easy and rapid development is not as great today as it once was, while our perception of the value of sunlight as a source of energy has increased significantly.

Courts should not implement obsolete policies that have lost their vigor over the course of the years. The law of private nuisance is better suited to resolve landowners' disputes about property development in the 1980's than is a rigid rule which does not recognize a landowner's interest in access to sunlight. As we said in Ballstadt v. Pagel, 202 Wis. 484, 489, 232 N.W. 862 (1930), "What is regarded in law as constituting a nuisance in modern times would no doubt have been tolerated without question in former times."....

....

....Recognition of a nuisance claim for unreasonable obstruction of access to sunlight will not prevent land development or unduly hinder the use of adjoining land. It will promote the reasonable use and enjoyment of land.... That obstruction of access to light might be found to constitute a nuisance in certain circumstances does not mean that it will be or must be found to constitute a nuisance under all circumstances. The result in each case depends on whether the conduct complained of is unreasonable.

....

The circuit court concluded that because the defendant's proposed house was in conformity with zoning regulations, building codes and deed restrictions, the defendant's use of the land was reasonable. This court has concluded that a landowner's compliance with zoning laws does not automatically bar a nuisance claim. Compliance with the law "is not the controlling factor, though it is, of course, entitled to some weight." [Citation.] The circuit court also concluded that the plaintiff could have avoided any harm by locating his own house in a better place. Again, plaintiff's ability to avoid the harm is a relevant but not a conclusive factor. *See* §§826, 827, 828, Restatement (Second) of Torts (1977).

Furthermore, our examination of the record leads us to conclude that the record does not furnish an adequate basis for the circuit court to apply the proper legal principles on summary judgment. The application of the reasonable use standard in nuisance cases normally requires a full exposition of all underlying facts and circumstances. Too little is known in this case of such matters as the extent of the harm to the plaintiff, the suitability of solar heat in that neighborhood, the availability of remedies to the plaintiff, and the costs to the defendant of avoiding the harm. Summary judgment is not an appropriate procedural vehicle in this case when the circuit court must weigh evidence which has not been presented at trial. [Citation.]

....

For the reasons set forth, we reverse the judgment of the circuit court dismissing the complaint and remand the matter to circuit court for further proceedings not inconsistent with this opinion.

....

[The dissenting opinion of Callow, J., is omitted.]

Winget v. Winn-Dixie Stores, Inc.
Supreme Court of South Carolina
130 S.E.2d 363 (S.C. 1963)

LEWIS, Justice.

Plaintiffs instituted this action for damages alleged to have been sustained from the location and operation by the defendants of a grocery supermarket in such a manner as to constitute a nuisance and for an order perpetually restraining the defendants from using the property where the supermarket was located for a retail grocery business or for any other business purpose. The trial of the case resulted in a judgment in favor of the plaintiffs for the sum of $5,000, actual damages, and a denial by the trial judge of injunctive relief. From the judgment entered in favor of the plaintiffs, the defendants have appealed.

....

The business of the defendants is a lawful one and was located in an area which had been zoned by the City of Sumter for retail business and at a location which the Zoning Board determined to be suitable for a retail grocery. The record shows that every requirement of the municipal authorities was met in establishing the business in question, both in the location and the construction of the building. There is no evidence that the building was constructed in such manner as to interfere with the rights of others. Under such circumstances, it cannot be held that the location of the business in the area in question constituted a nuisance.

The fact, however, that one has been issued a license or permit to conduct a business at a particular location cannot protect the licensee who operates the business in such a manner to constitute a nuisance. [Citations.]

....

An owner of property even in the conduct of a lawful business thereon is subject to reasonable limitations. In the operation of such business he must not unreasonably interfere with the health or comfort of neighbors or with their right to the enjoyment of their property....

On the other hand, every annoyance or disturbance of a landowner from the use made of property by a neighbor does not constitute a nuisance. The question is not whether plaintiffs have been annoyed or disturbed by the operation of the business in question, but whether there has been an injury to their legal rights. People who live in organized communities must of necessity suffer some inconvenience and annoyance from their neighbors and must submit to annoyances consequent upon the reasonable use of property by others. [Citation.]

Whether a particular use of property is reasonable and whether such use constitutes a nuisance depends largely upon the facts and no definite rule can be laid down for the determination of the question.... "What is a reasonable use and whether a particular use is a nuisance cannot be determined by any fixed general rules, but depends upon the facts of each particular case, such as location, character of the neighborhood, nature of the use, extent and frequency of the injury, the effect upon the enjoyment of life, health, and property, and the like. A use of property in one locality and under some circumstances may be lawful and reasonable, which under the other circumstances would be lawful, unreasonable, and a nuisance."

....

In...this case, it cannot be properly held that the normal traffic and noise caused by customers going to and from the supermarket would constitute a basis for declaring the operation of the business a nuisance. Of course, the purpose of the business of the defendants is to sell merchandise and in doing so to attract to their store as many customers as possible. It is a natural consequence and incident of the operation of the supermarket that there will be an increase in the number of people visiting the area.

The testimony shows that the store is operated only on week days, opening for business at 8:30 a.m. each day and never closing later than 7:30 p.m. While...the operation of the supermarket has caused an increase in the number of people and automobiles coming into the area, there is nothing to show that there was any mass entrance to or exodus from the store at unreasonable hours. On the contrary, the only reasonable inference from the record is that the traffic to and from the business was the normal traffic of patrons visiting such a grocery store over the usual business day. There is no basis for holding that the normal traffic and noise caused by customers going to and from the supermarket constituted a nuisance.

Neither do we think that the operation of trash trucks and street sweepers in connection with the removal of trash and garbage, under the facts here, can form the basis of a finding of a nuisance. The record shows that the trucks of the City of Sumter went upon the premises of the defendants to remove the trash and garbage which accumulated and that the mechanical street sweeper of the City would occasionally sweep the area surrounding the store. There is nothing to indicate that such acts were other than the usual and normal operations of the City in the gathering and removal of trash and garbage. The noise complained of from the usual operation by the City of its trash trucks and mechanical street sweepers could not be charged to the defendants anymore, than, generally, their operation by the City in collecting trash and garbage at any other business establishment could be attributed to those business owners.

However, with regard to other allegations of the complaint, we think that there was some evidence requiring the submission of those issues to the jury for determination. The record shows that the defendants erected fans on their building in connection with the air conditioning equipment. These fans were so directed as to blow against the trees and shrubbery on plaintiffs' property causing some damage and inconvenience. There was also some testimony that, at least, for a while after opening the supermarket, the floodlights on defendants' lot cast a bright glare over the property of plaintiffs until late at night so as to disturb the plaintiffs in the enjoyment of their home, that obnoxious odors were created from the garbage which accumulated at defendants' store, and that paper and trash from the defendants' garbage was permitted to escape onto plaintiffs' lot to an unusual extent. The record gives rise to a reasonable inference that such acts were not normal or necessary incidents of the operation of the business. We think that the foregoing testimony presented a jury issue and that the trial judge properly refused the defendants' motion for a directed verdict.

....

....[T]he record shows that the acts which would form any basis for damages because of a nuisance in the operation of the business have been largely, if not entirely, discontinued. It was no doubt for this reason that the court ruled that no grounds existed for the issuance of an injunction. Where the acts complained of as constituting a nuisance have been discontinued and their repetition appeared unlikely, it was proper to refuse to issue an injunction.... "The abatement of a nuisance does not affect the right to recover damages for its past existence." 39 Am. Jur. 389, section 128....

.... It is contended that a new trial should be granted because of the refusal of the trial court to strike the testimony of the witness R.E. Graham relative to depreciation in value of the property of the plaintiffs. The witness Graham was asked to give his opinion as to the value of the plaintiffs' property before and after "the moving in of this Winn-Dixie Corporation." In answer to the question, he testified that the property had depreciated in value from about $12,000 to a value of $8,000 "by reason of the Winn-Dixie moving in this property."....

The testimony of the witness Graham related solely to depreciation in value of plaintiffs' property because of the location in the particular locality of defendants' business and was not based upon the particular manner of operation of the supermarket in question. The testimony was irrelevant to any issue in the case and should have been stricken upon the motion of the defendants....

....

Reversed and remanded for a new trial.

Note

1. The opinion which follows approaches the nuisance question in a way that purports to avoid "balancing the equities."

Hughes v. Emerald Mines Corporation

Superior Court of Pennsylvania
450 A.2d 1 (Pa. Super. Ct. 1982)

MONTEMURO, Judge.

The instant action concerns the complaint of landowners that a coal company operating on adjacent property caused the failure of one water-well and the pollution of a second well located on plaintiff-appellees' own land.

....

We affirm the lower court's decision on... [liability], but we reverse the award of $32,500 as excessive, and we remand for more realistic appraisal of actual and consequential damages in view of the testimony of plaintiffs' own witnesses that repair of the wells can be effected at lower cost.

....

The plaintiffs bought this property by a deed dated 1953.... Thereafter they erected a dwelling and drilled a well to supply water. There was a continuous, ample, potable water supply from this well (hereinafter well #1) for some twenty-five years until late May or early June of 1978.

In 1977 the plaintiffs purchased a mobile home and installed it on the property for their son's use. At that time a second well (hereinafter well #2), was drilled, and from its installation until the same period in late May or early June of 1978 the supply was plentiful and potable.

....Defendant owns surface rights in addition to subsurface rights to a portion of the tract contiguous to plaintiffs' property.

In 1975 defendant began to expand its operations into that contiguous portion of the tract. Several airshaft holes were prepared....The airshaft which is the focus of this action is located 540 and 600 feet from defendant's two wells, and is known as "grout hole #4." It was...completed May 29, 1978.

On May 31, 1978, well #1 went dry. Two or three days later, well #2 became polluted. During this same period of time, neighboring properties also experienced similar problems with their wells.

On June 8, 1978 plaintiffs notified an agent of defendant of their problems. Since early June of 1978 the plaintiffs have had a tank installed at their residence and their son-in-law hauls water from his own home to theirs in 55 gallon lots daily. The plaintiffs travel two miles to the home of their son-in-law and daughter to shower, and must now take their laundry to the laundromat twice weekly instead of using the washer in their basement. Water at well #2 can be used to flush the commode in the trailer, but cannot be used for cooking, cleaning, bathing, or drinking....Cost of hauling water, attempted well repair, and laundry amounted to some $7,000....

   ....

This action was tried on the basis of non-trespassory invasion of another's land as set forth in Restatement of Torts, 2d at §822....That section provides as follows:

> One is subject to liability for a private nuisance if, but only if, his conduct is a legal cause of an invasion of another's interest in the private use and enjoyment of land, and the invasion is either:
>
> (a) intentional and unreasonable, or
>
> (b) unintentional and otherwise actionable under the rules controlling liability for negligent or reckless conduct, or for abnormally dangerous conditions or activities.

The instant action was tried on the first of the two theories outlined above: that the act of the coal company was intentional and unreasonable. The Restatement at §825 further defines intentional invasion as follows:

> An invasion of another's interest in the use and enjoyment of land or an interference with the public right is intentional if the actor
>
> (a) acts for the purpose of causing it, or
>
> (b) knows that it is resulting or is substantially certain to result from his conduct.

An intentional invasion becomes unreasonable, according to §826 if:

> (a) the gravity of the harm outweighs the utility of the actor's conduct, or
>
> (b) the harm caused by the conduct is serious and the financial burden of compensating for this and similar harm to others would not make the continuation of the conduct not feasible.

Section 829(a) contributes this analysis of "unreasonableness":

> An intentional invasion of another's interest in the use and enjoyment of land is unreasonable if the harm resulting from the invasion is severe and greater than the other should be required to bear without compensation.

Comments following the section immediately *supra* supply further explanation in pertinent part:

> ...certain types of harm may be so severe as to require a holding of unreasonableness as a matter of law, regardless of the utility of the conduct. This is particularly true if the harm resulting from the invasion is physical in character.... [I]t is apparent that the more serious the harm is found to be, the more likely it is that the trier of fact will hold that the invasion is unreasonable.

> ....

There is no doubt that plaintiffs have suffered a significant harm to use and enjoyment of their property which occurred on or about May 31, 1978.... [The court then concluded that the evidence was sufficient to prove that defendant's activities were the legal cause of the damage sustained.]

> ....

As to "intent," plaintiffs clearly are not contending that the activities of defendant amount to a deliberate plot to ruin their wells. They contend, however, and the jury obviously agreed, that defendant's acts came under the language of §825(b)...and that defendant knew that the grouting injected was substantially certain to injure nearby wells, but nevertheless dug the airshaft and pumped in the grout.

...[W]e do find evidence to support that view: there is agreement that the process itself was specifically for the purpose of sealing off water flow; testimony showed that these two wells were not alone in showing effects from this particular airshaft grouting operation; a witness familiar with both the drilling of wells and the creation of airshafts stated flatly that he had seen this result before as a byproduct of the sealing process. A jury of reasonable persons could deduce that defendant company knew their grouting process would seal off water, that the grout had traveled and destroyed wells in the past, and that in this instance the danger of that happening was indeed so substantial that, in effect, almost all neighboring wells were effected to some degree. Upon review we must agree that the testimony can support intent under the "substantial certainty" rule of §825(b).

> ....

No one is contending that the mining of coal is not a useful activity, and airshafts are a necessary part of that activity as safeguards to the health of miners. "Unreasonable," however, is a term of art, a legal definition rather than a moral judgment on the good sense of a party....

The harm to plaintiffs in the loss of both their wells was undeniably "severe," and we are inclined to agree with the finder of fact that the loss is "greater than they should be required to bear without compensation," "*regardless of the utility of the conduct.*" [Citation.]

Case law further recognizes this principle, and has done so from an early date:

> ...the defendant's right to injure another's land at all, to any extent, is an exception, and *the burden is always upon him to bring himself within it.*

> ....

> Where conflict is irreconcilable, the right to use one's own [land] must prevail, but it can do so without compensation where the resulting damage is *not avoidable at all, or only at such expense as would be practically prohibitory.* [Citation.]

> ....

No testimony was offered to show that this location was the only possible place for an effective airshaft; no discussion of a lack of less destructive methods of waterflow prevention was placed on record; no claim of prohibitive expense in use of other methods or other locations was made.

In short, defendant made no attempt to fulfill its burden to prove that its acts were not avoidable at all or only avoidable at prohibitory expense. Once the plaintiff had met its burden of proof of causation by a preponderance of the evidence, Section 829A and case law agree that the burden shifts to the actor to defend its conduct as "reasonable." Defendant here did not meet its burden, and we affirm the jury's finding of intentional and unreasonable damage to plaintiffs, for which compensation is due.

. . . .

Affirmed as to liability, reversed and remanded as to damages. . . .

PRICE, J., notes dissent.

Notes

1. *Intentional Nuisances Only.* According to §826(b) of the Restatement, Second, of Torts, the test of unreasonableness based upon the feasibility and fairness of paying damages applies only to intentional invasions of the plaintiff's interest. However, the requirement that the invasion be intentional is easily satisfied, for whenever the defendant is placed on notice by another that conduct is causing harm, continuation of the conduct leads to an "intentional" injury. Intent means simply that the defendant desires to produce the result or is "substantially certain" that it will occur as a result of the acts. *See* Restatement, Second, of Torts §8A. By limiting the use of the "alternative" test of unreasonableness to intentionally created nuisances, the Restatement ensures that the defendant has the option of ceasing the offending conduct before being held liable for damages under the test.

Another advantage of establishing that a nuisance was intentionally created is that the defense of comparative negligence will be inapplicable in most states. *See* Vogel v. Grant-Lafayette Elec. Co-op., 548 N.W.2d 829 (Wis. 1996) (holding that a contributory negligence defense could be raised in a nuisance action based on stray electrical voltage on a dairy farm because no continuing invasion occurred so as to render the invasion intentional, for the cooperative immediately and subsequently responded and worked to alleviate problems after it was first notified about the farmers' stray voltage concerns).

2. *See also* Meat Producers, Inc. v. McFarland, 476 S.W.2d 406, 411 (Tex. Civ. App. 1972). In upholding an award of damages, the court reasoned that although the defendant's cattle feedlot was lawful, useful, and appropriately located in a rural area, its continued operation would be unreasonable unless adjoining owners were compensated for the interference with the use of their land.

The Coase Theorem and the Law of Nuisance

Ronald Coase's article *The Problem of Social Cost*, 3 J. L. & Econ. 1 (1960), is the most-cited article on economics ever written. The article deals with the economic principles underlying the law of nuisance, though it has important implications for other legal issues as well. Whether Coase's approach to nuisance questions is one that courts should adopt is doubtful (the paper is addressed primarily to economists, not courts, and it does not purport to give advice to judges except to suggest that they be explicit when making economic judgments). *The Problem of Social Cost* is discussed here not because it provides a recipe for resolving nuisance disputes but because it clarifies the principles underlying nuisance law.

Coase's article makes three distinct but related points about conflicting uses of land:

(1) Problems of conflicting land use cannot be resolved by labeling one of the uses "the cause" of harm to the other user.

(2) If transactions between neighbors whose uses of land conflict were costless, the parties would negotiate an "efficient" solution to the problem no matter which party's use was protected by law.

(3) In principle, when "transaction costs" make it impossible for the parties to a dispute to negotiate a solution, the law should decide the dispute so that the outcome is that which the parties would have bargained for if there were no transaction costs.

The following discussion elaborates on each of these points.

The Futility of "Cause" as a Guide to the Proper Outcome.

In everyday speech, "cause" is often used as a synonym for "ought to be responsible for." Thus, one might say that *A*, whose reckless driving led *A* to run over *B*, has "caused" harm to *B* and so ought to be deterred, or be made to compensate *B*. In the land-use context, it is common to describe a polluter as "causing harm" to the victims of pollution. While the outcomes suggested by these descriptions may well be right, one cannot sensibly *explain* those outcomes by invoking causation. Causation, in the "but for" sense, runs both ways. If defendant's smoking factory makes it impossible for plaintiff to use her house, which sits a block downwind from the factory, *both* defendant's and plaintiff's activities are "causes" (in the but-for sense) of the harm. If defendant had operated a sod farm, rather than a factory, plaintiff's use of her house would have been unimpaired, so defendant's conduct is plainly a "but-for" cause of the harm. But plaintiff's activity is equally a but-for cause of the harm, for if plaintiff had had a blast furnace, rather than a house, on her lot, there would have been no harm. Therefore, to call defendant's factory "the cause of the harm" is simply to say that, under these circumstances, plaintiff's use should be preferred. That conclusion may be correct, but one cannot *justify* the conclusion by invoking "causation."

The law has, for the most part, recognized the impossibility of resolving land-use disputes by invoking but-for cause. Lawyers, perhaps more than the economists whom Coase addressed, have always appreciated that so many things are the "but for" cause of any given harm that it makes no sense to say that anyone who has caused harm, in the but-for sense, must be liable. In the case of the house next to the factory, for example, one would expect a court to hold a defendant who regularly produces clouds of smoke in the middle of a residential suburb liable for creating a nuisance. But if the plaintiff built a house in the middle of the industrial part of town, no court would take seriously the plaintiff's argument that the neighboring factories should be enjoined.

A case which nicely illustrates the futility of approaching the problem of incompatible land uses by invoking causation is Fontainebleau Hotel Corp. v. Forty-Five Twenty-Five, Inc., 114 So. 2d 357 (Fla. Dist. Ct. App. 1959). The owners of the Fontainebleau Hotel proposed to add fourteen stories to their hotel. The addition would have cast a shadow over the pool and cabana of the Eden Roc Hotel, which the plaintiffs owned. The plaintiffs sued to enjoin the building of the addition, claiming that it would cause them harm. And so it would; but granting the injunction would have caused the owner of the Fontainebleau harm by denying it the opportunity to enlarge its building. The question in the case, in Coasean terms, was whether the Fontainebleau would be allowed to harm the Eden Roc or whether the Eden Roc would be allowed to harm the Fontainebleau. A principle of "do no harm to your neighbors" does not help to solve the problem. (The court decided the case in favor of the Fontainebleau by invoking "the universal rule—and the custom followed in this state since its inception—that adjoining landowners have an equal right under the law to build to the line of their respective tracts and to such a height as is desired by them....")

Did the Pennsylvania Superior Court appreciate the reciprocal nature of causation in Hughes v. Emerald Mines Corp., 450 A.2d 1 (Pa. Super. Ct. 1982), *supra* at 899?

Bargaining to Efficient Outcomes.

Suppose that the shadow cast by the Fontainebleau Hotel would cause only the most minor inconvenience to the use of the Eden Roc, and that the Fontainebleau would benefit greatly by being able to build the addition. Would it matter a great deal whether the law gave the Eden Roc the right to enjoin the construction? Perhaps not. One might, as a first approximation, guess that the Eden Roc would get an injunction, resulting in great loss to the Fontainebleau and only little benefit to the Eden Roc. But the parties could bargain around this result; for example, the Fontainebleau might pay the Eden Roc $50,000 to let it build its addition. If the addition were worth millions to the Fontainebleau, and the harm from the shadow would cause only a few hundred dollars' worth of harm to the Eden Roc, both parties would benefit by making this deal. Or suppose that the law gave the Fontainebleau the right to build, that the addition would be worth only $100,000 to the Fontainebleau, and that the harm to the Eden Roc would run in the millions. In that case, an efficient outcome could be achieved, despite the law, by the Eden Roc's paying the Fontainebleau not to build.

Coase showed that, in many cases, assignment of the legal right to one party or the other would not determine the ultimate outcome *if transaction costs are zero.* (Transaction costs are the costs of entering into bargains.) This would occur because, in many cases, the parties could, at no cost, bargain around the outcome supposedly dictated by the legal rule. The principle here extends far beyond disputes between neighbors. If, for example, A has a car which B would like to own, B would not ordinarily seek to have the law changed so that ownership of the car is assigned to him. Instead, he would simply buy the car from A.[d]

Coase has been widely misunderstood by lawyers as having said that it doesn't matter who, in cases involving conflicting uses of land, gets the legal right to use the land as desired, because the parties will simply contract around the legal rule. In fact, as Coase fully appreciated, transaction costs will often be so high that bargaining around the rule will not be economically feasible. For example, suppose that smoke from a factory is annoying the owners of 300 houses, and that the factory has a legal right to emit smoke. Suppose further that being free from smoke would be of more value to the homeowners than the ability to pollute is worth to the owner of the factory. A bargain between the

d. One case in which ultimate ownership of the right may depend on which party has the right in the first place is that in which ownership of the right affects one's wealth in an important way. For example, consider a case in which B could not afford to buy the car from A if A had the right, but in which B would not sell the car to A if B had the right. In this case, the right to the car will stay with whichever party it is assigned to.

homeowners and the factory owner would require, among other things, that the home-owners organize and raise funds to pay the factory to stop polluting. This process would face formidable obstacles (for instance, every homeowner would like to be a "free rider," paying little or nothing in the hope that other homeowners would pay the factory to stop). Even if only two parties are involved, as in the case of the Fontainebleau and the Eden Roc, negotiations may be time-consuming and expensive, as each side argues for the highest or lowest possible price for buying out the other side. (In economic jargon, this is a "bilateral monopoly" problem.) Furthermore, a practice of paying people not to exercise rights to pollute, or to cast shadows, might encourage polluting and shadow-casting by persons hoping to be bought out.

What Should the Law Do?

If we cannot often expect, as a practical matter, to see parties bargaining around common-law land-use rules, why did Coase discuss the outcome that would be reached in a world of zero transaction costs? Because he thought that the theoretically correct solution to land-use questions was for the rights to be assigned in such a way that the outcome was the same as if costless bargaining were possible. For example, if the Fontainebleau's shadow would cause great loss to the owners of the Eden Roc, and if the addition would benefit the Fontainebleau very little, a court could enjoin the building of the addition. If, on the other hand, the shadow would be only a minor inconvenience to the Eden Roc, the court might allow the addition. Other ways of reaching these out-comes are possible. For example, if the benefit to the Fontainebleau of an additional fourteen stories were great, and the harm to the Eden Roc small, a rule requiring the Fontainebleau to pay damages would be efficient, as it would choose to build and pay the damages.

Coase cited many land-use decisions in support of the view that the courts consid-ered the relative values of different uses in deciding what invasions were actionable. He described a number of cases in which the question whether an activity constituted a nuisance turned not just on what the activity was, but where it was conducted. For ex-ample, in Adams v. Ursell, an English case, a fried-fish shop was held to be a nuisance because it was established near houses "of a much better character," but the judge noted that the fish shop, if located elsewhere, might not be a nuisance: "It by no means fol-lows that because a fried fish shop is a nuisance in one place it is a nuisance in another."

For a lawyer, one of the joys of reading *The Problem of Social Cost* is seeing, time after time, cases in which the courts got it right, while pre-Coase economists would have criticized many of the outcomes as "allowing the defendant to harm the plaintiff." Nev-ertheless, one may reasonably doubt whether courts can succeed in mimicking the out-comes of cost-free bargaining in making land-use decisions. For one thing, it seems un-likely in the extreme that courts could consistently make accurate evaluations of the costs and benefits to the parties of different outcomes in close cases. With regard to the problem of shadows, for instance, a "rule" allowing construction when the value of the addition to the owner outweighs the harm done by the shadow to the neighbor would be virtually the antithesis of law. One of the major functions of law is making clear to people what their rights are, so that they can get on with their lives. A rule that one may build without fear of liability for shadows does this. So, too, would legislation restrict-ing building heights to a specified limit.

In practice, a system of case-by-case determinations would lead not only to uncer-tainty but also, one suspects, to decisions based on improper grounds. In the absence of any reliable way of measuring harms and benefits, courts would inevitably resolve disputes according to judges' hunches, political views, or unarticulated beliefs about public policy. Consider, in this regard, the Wisconsin Supreme Court's decision in Prah v. Maretti, 321 N.W.2d 182 (Wis. 1982), *supra* at 893. It is hard to read the opinion without strongly suspecting that the majority believed that solar energy is a "good thing," and that that belief influenced the outcome. Perhaps solar energy is a good thing, or perhaps it is an inefficient form of energy production which wastes resources that might better be used elsewhere. Either way, our system is not one in which judges are supposed to decide cases according to their assumptions about whether solar energy is good or bad.

In the end, the lesson of *The Problem of Social Cost* as applied to nuisance cases may be that there is no alternative to deciding cases not involving physical invasions by asking whether the use in question was an appropriate use of the land, given the surrounding circumstances and relying heavily on traditional notions of what the right to use land means. In traditional trespass cases, as when *A* takes shortcuts across *B*'s property, the only practicable rule is to hold the invasion actionable, despite the theoretical possibility that the result in a particular case is "inefficient" and that transaction costs present obstacles to bargained solutions. We cannot solve land-use problems by holding that every use of land which harms someone else is actionable, but we cannot expect case-by-case cost-benefit analyses to work very well either.

C. Public Nuisance

1. In General

Armory Park Neighborhood Ass'n v.
Episcopal Community Services in Arizona

Supreme Court of Arizona, En Banc
712 P.2d 914 (Ariz. 1985)

FELDMAN, Justice.

On December 11, 1982, defendant Episcopal Community Services in Arizona (ECS) opened the St. Martin's Center (Center) in Tucson. The Center's only purpose is to provide one free meal a day to indigent persons. Plaintiff Armory Park Neighborhood Association (APNA) is a non-profit corporation organized for the purpose of "improving, maintaining and insuring the quality of the neighborhood known as Armory Park Historical Residential District." The Center is located on Arizona Avenue, the western boundary of the Armory Park district. On January 10, 1984, APNA filed a complaint in Pima County Superior Court, seeking to enjoin ECS from operating its free food distribution program. The complaint alleged that the Center's activities constituted a public nuisance....

....

....Before the Center opened, the area had been primarily residential with a few small businesses. When the Center began operating in December 1982, many transients crossed the area daily on their way to and from the Center. Although the Center was only open from 5:00 to 6:00 p.m., patrons lined up well before this hour and often lingered in the neighborhood long after finishing their meal. The Center rented an adjacent fenced lot for a waiting area and organized neighborhood cleaning projects, but the trial judge apparently felt these efforts were inadequate to control the activity stemming from the Center. Transients frequently trespassed onto residents' yards, sometimes urinating, defecating, drinking and littering on the residents' property. A few broke into storage areas and unoccupied homes, and some asked residents for handouts. The number of arrests in the area increased dramatically. Many residents were frightened or annoyed by the transients and altered their lifestyles to avoid them.

. . . .

. . . [T]he trial court granted the preliminary injunction. . . .

A divided court of appeals reversed. . . .

. . . .

Now considered a tort, a public nuisance action originated in criminal law. Early scholars defined public nuisance as "an act or omission 'which obstructs or causes inconvenience or damage to the public in the exercise of rights common to all her Majesty's subjects.'" [Citation.] The sole remedy was criminal prosecution. [Citation.]

Historically, the remedy for a private nuisance was an action "upon the case," as it was an injury consequential to the act done and found its roots in civil law. [Citation.] A private nuisance is strictly limited to an interference with a person's interest in the enjoyment of real property. The Restatement defines a private nuisance as "a nontrespassory invasion of another's interest in the private use and enjoyment of land." [Citation.] A public nuisance, to the contrary, is not limited to an interference with the use and enjoyment of the plaintiff's land. It encompasses any unreasonable interference with a right common to the general public. [Citations.]

We have previously distinguished public and private nuisances. In City of Phoenix v. Johnson, 51 Ariz. 115, 75 P.2d 30 (1938), we noted that a nuisance is public when it affects rights of "citizens as a part of the public, while a private nuisance is one which affects a single individual or a definite number of persons in the enjoyment of some private right which is not common to the public." Id. at 123, 75 P.2d 34. A public nuisance must also affect a considerable number of people. . . .

. . . .

. . . [A] nuisance may be simultaneously public and private when a considerable number of people suffer an interference with their use and enjoyment of land. [Citation.] The torts are not mutually exclusive. . . . However, both because plaintiff did not seek relief under the theory of private nuisance and because that theory might raise standing issues not addressed by the parties, we believe plaintiff's claim must stand or fall on the public nuisance theory alone.

. . . .

Defendant claims that its business should not be held responsible for acts committed by its patrons off the premises of the Center. It argues that since it has no control over the patrons when they are not on the Center's premises, it cannot be enjoined because of their acts. We do not believe this position is supported either by precedent or theory.

In Shamhart v. Morrison Cafeteria Co., 159 Fla. 629, 32 So. 2d 727 (1947), the defendant operated a well frequented cafeteria. Each day customers waiting to enter the business would line up on the sidewalk, blocking the entrances to the neighboring establishments. The dissenting justices argued that the defendant had not actually caused the lines to form and that the duty to prevent the harm to the plaintiffs should be left to the police through regulation of the public streets. The majority of the court rejected this argument, and remanded the case for a determination of the damages. *See, also,* Reid v. Brodsky, 397 Pa. 463, 156 A.2d 334 (1959) (operation of a bar enjoined because its patrons were often noisy and intoxicated; they frequently used the neighboring properties for toilet purposes and sexual misconduct); Barrett v. Lopez, 57 N.M. 697, 262 P.2d 981, 983 (1953) (operation of a dance hall enjoined, the court finding that "mere possibility of relief from another source [police] does not relieve the courts of their responsibilities"); Wade v. Fuller, 12 Utah 2d 299, 365 P.2d 802 (1961) (operation of drive-in café enjoined where patrons created disturbances to nearby residents); McQuade v. Tucson Tiller Apartments, 25 Ariz. App. 312, 543 P.2d 150 (1975) (music concerts at mall designed to attract customers enjoined because of increased crowds and noise in residential area).

Under general tort law, liability for nuisance may be imposed upon one who sets in motion the forces which eventually cause the tortious act....

The testimony at the hearing establishes that it was the Center's act of offering free meals which "set in motion" the forces resulting in the injuries to the Armory Park residents....

....

Since the rules of a civilized society require us to tolerate our neighbors, the law requires our neighbors to keep their activities within the limits of what is tolerable by a reasonable person. However, what is reasonably tolerable must be tolerated; not all interferences with public rights are public nuisances. As Dean Prosser explains, "[t]he law does not concern itself with trifles, or seek to remedy all of the petty annoyances and disturbances of everyday life in a civilized community even from conduct committed with knowledge that annoyance and inconvenience will result."....Our courts have generally used a balancing test in deciding the reasonableness of an interference. [Citation.] The trial court should look at the utility and reasonableness of the conduct and balance these factors against the extent of harm inflicted and the nature of the affected neighborhood. We noted in the early case of MacDonald v. Perry:

> What might amount to a serious nuisance in one locality by reason of the density of the population, or character of the neighborhood affected, may in another place and under different surroundings be deemed proper and unobjectionable. What amount of annoyance or inconvenience caused by others in the lawful use of their property will constitute a nuisance depends upon varying circumstances and cannot be precisely defined.

32 Ariz. 39, 50, 255 P. 494 (1927). [Citation.]

The trial judge did not ignore the balancing test and was well aware of the social utility of defendant's operation. His words are illuminating:

> It is distressing to this Court that an activity such as defendants [sic] should be restrained. Providing for the poor and the homeless is certainly a worthwhile, praiseworthy activity. It is particularly distressing to this Court because it [defendant] has no control over those who are attracted to the kitchen while they are either coming or leaving the premises. However, the right to the comfortable enjoyment of one's property is something that another's activities should not affect, the harm being suffered by the Armory Park Neighborhood and the

residents therein is irreparable and substantial, for which they have no adequate legal remedy.

[Citation.] We believe that a determination made by weighing and balancing conflicting interests or principles is truly one which lies within the discretion of the trial judge. [Citation.] We defer to that discretion here. The evidence of the multiple trespasses upon and defacement of the residents' property supports the trial court's conclusion that the interference caused by defendant's operation was unreasonable despite its charitable cause.

The common law has long recognized that the usefulness of a particular activity may outweigh the inconveniences, discomforts and changes it causes some persons to suffer. We, too, acknowledge the social value of the Center. Its charitable purpose, that of feeding the hungry, is entitled to greater deference than pursuits of lesser intrinsic value. It appears from the record that ECS purposes in operating the Center were entirely admirable. However, even admirable ventures may cause unreasonable interferences. [Citation.] We do not believe that the law allows the costs of a charitable enterprise to be visited in their entirety upon the residents of a single neighborhood. The problems of dealing with the unemployed, the homeless and the mentally ill are also matters of community or governmental responsibility.

....

ECS argues that its compliance with City of Tucson zoning regulations is a conclusive determination of reasonableness. We agree that compliance with zoning provisions has some bearing in nuisance cases. We would hesitate to find a public nuisance, if, for example, the legislature enacted comprehensive and specific laws concerning the manner in which a particular activity was to be carried out. [Citation.] We decline, however, to find that ECS' compliance with the applicable zoning provisions precludes a court from enjoining its activities....

The determination of the type of business to be permitted in a particular neighborhood, therefore, may be left to administrative agencies or legislative bodies. However, the judgment concerning the manner in which that business is carried out is within the province of the judiciary....

....

....ECS argued that there is no criminal violation and that a tort claim for nuisance must be based on such a violation....

....The Restatement states that a criminal violation is only one factor among others to be used in determining reasonableness....

....

We hold, therefore, that conduct which unreasonably and significantly interferes with the public health, safety, peace, comfort or convenience is a public nuisance within the concept of tort law, even if that conduct is not specifically prohibited by the criminal law.

....

The trial court's order granting the preliminary injunction is affirmed. By affirming the trial court's preliminary orders, we do not require that he close the center permanently. It is, of course, within the equitable discretion of the trial court to fashion a less severe remedy, if possible....

Notes

1. *Examples of Public Nuisance.* Typical of the actions based on public nuisance are those involving air and water pollution, obstruction of highways, and the maintenance of facilities prejudicial to health or good morals, such as crack houses.

See Tennessee ex rel. Swann v. Pack, 527 S.W.2d 99 (Tenn. 1975) (snake handling and consumption of strychnine as part of religious services).

2. *No Residual Category of Nuisance.* Although the term "nuisance" is sometimes used imprecisely by lawyers and judges, there is no actionable tort of nuisance outside of the categories of private and public nuisance. Thus, in Mandell v. Pivnick, 125 A.2d 175 (Conn. Super. Ct. 1956), where the plaintiff was struck by a falling awning, a demurrer to his complaint was sustained, for "no where [did] it appear that he was injured in relation to a right which he enjoy[ed] by reason of his ownership of an interest in land" and there was no allegation "that the installation of the awning was dangerous to the public generally." The court noted that, under a proper set of facts, an awning or sign overhanging a public street or sidewalk could constitute a public nuisance, if not properly secured.

3. *Similarities and Differences between Public and Private Nuisance.* Actions for public and private nuisance share a number of requirements. Under each tort, the plaintiff must establish: (1) that the harm results from tortious conduct (*i.e.* failure to exercise care, intentional wrongdoing, or a strict-liability activity); (2) that the harm is significant; and (3) that the invasion is unreasonable under the circumstances.

The main difference between public and private nuisance has to do with standing to sue. Anyone with an interest in land affected by a private nuisance has standing. *See, e.g.,* Graves v. Diehl, 958 S.W.2d 468 (Tex. Ct. App. 1997) (purchasers of property under a contract for a deed had a sufficient interest). However, a plaintiff in a public-nuisance case must show an injury "different in kind" from that suffered by members of the public generally or have a legislative grant of standing. These issues are discussed below.

4. *Public Nuisance and Environmental Law.* According to one article:

> [T]he law of public nuisance has experienced a resurgence recently, particularly in the area of environmental law. Today most claims for money damages for pollution brought under state common laws include a claim for public nuisance. The attempt is being made to apply the law of public nuisance in the environmental area because of perceived benefits that apply to claims for public nuisance such as statute of limitations and measure of damages.

L. Mark Walker and Dale E. Cottingham, *An Abridged Primer on the Law of Public Nuisance*, 30 Tulsa L.J. 355, 355 (1994).

5. *Using Public-Nuisance Law to Fight Crime: Gang Injunctions.* "[L]ocal governments in California have pioneered the use of public nuisance law to obtain sweeping civil injunctions prohibiting suspected gang members from fighting, trespassing, spraying graffiti, and even from engaging in otherwise legal activities such as appearing in public together or carrying pagers or cellular telephones." *See* Matthew Mickle Werdegar, *Enjoining the Constitution: The Use of Public Nuisance Abatement Injunctions Against Urban Street Gangs*, 51 Stan. L. Rev. 409, 409 (1999). Similar crime-fighting tactics have been employed in other states. One advantage for the government is that gang members who know the ropes of the criminal justice system are thrown off bal-

ance by having to deal with a civil injunction process, often without the assistance of counsel. However, gang injunctions raise significant constitutional issues. Moreover, the relevant statutory provisions may make it difficult to build an evidentiary case that will warrant issuance of a gang injunction.

2. Public Nuisance and Products Liability

Among the most dramatic efforts to breath new life into the law of public nuisance has been an array of recent suits relating to the marketing of mass products, such as cigarettes and guns. Lawyers endeavoring to surmount doctrinal obstacles in other areas of the law (such as the necessity of showing that a product is defective under products-liability law) have argued that certain types of products pose a risk to the welfare of the public in general and are therefore actionable under the law of public nuisance. Needless to say, these efforts have been controversial. Courts have been uncertain whether centuries-old doctrine relating to public nuisance can or should be used to address harm caused in modern society by mass-marketed products.

> The tort of public nuisance first burst upon the mass products torts scene as a part of the litigation filed by American states against tobacco companies during the late 1990s. By asserting public nuisance claims, plaintiff states sought to avoid many of the defenses available to tobacco companies against more traditional product tort claims filed by individual victims of tobacco-related illness, such as defenses based on the smoker's own conduct and statutes of limitations. The states' lawsuits against the tobacco companies were settled before courts could address the viability of public nuisance claims in the context of mass products, but the tobacco settlement has inspired states and municipalities and their attorneys to file similar claims against the manufacturers of handguns and lead-pigment.

Donald G. Gifford, *Public Nuisance as a Mass Products Liability Tort*, 71 U. Cinn. L. Rev. 743, 747 (2003). Noting the "strikingly inconsistent" results in court decisions, Professor Gifford concludes that "To allow states and municipalities to hold manufacturers of mass products liable under a public nuisance theory would be to fundamentally alter the nature of the tort."

Judges have been reluctant to use the law of nuisance to address product-related issues. As one court wrote:

> [T]he courts have enforced the boundary between the well-developed body of product liability law and public nuisance law. Otherwise, if public nuisance law were permitted to encompass product liability, nuisance law "would become a monster that would devour in one gulp the entire law of tort."

City of St. Louis v. Cernicek, 2003 W.L. 22533578 (Mo. Cir. Ct.).

But there are startling decisions to the contrary. *See* Ileto v. Glock, Inc., 349 F.3d 1191 (9th Cir. 2003) (holding that victims of a shooting incident perpetrated by an illegal gun purchaser, whose claims rested on the defendants' actions in creating an illegal secondary market, stated claims for public nuisance and negligence under California law against manufacturers, distributors, and dealers of the firearms that were actually fired); City of Cincinnati v. Beretta U.S.A. Corp., 768 N.E.2d 1136 (Ohio 2002) (holding that a city stated a claim for public nuisance against 15 handgun manufacturers, 3 trade associations, and a handgun distributor where it alleged that the defendants man-ufactured, marketed, distributed, and sold firearms in ways that unreasonably inter-fered with public health, welfare, and safety in the city).

One significant obstacle that private individuals face in bringing an action for public nuisance, whether in the products-liability field or otherwise, is the harm-different-in-kind requirement.

NAACP v. Acusport, Inc.

United States District Court for the Eastern District of New York,
271 F. Supp. 2d 435 (E.D. N.Y. 2003)

JACK B. WEINSTEIN, Senior District Judge.

Plaintiff, the National Association for the Advancement of Colored People ("NAACP"), is suing for injunctive relief on its own behalf and that of its individual and potential members in the state of New York. The theory is one of public nuisance under New York state law....

. . . .

....The evidence presented at trial demonstrated that defendants are responsible for the creation of a public nuisance and could—voluntarily and through easily imple-mented changes in marketing and more discriminating control of the sales practices of those to whom they sell their guns—substantially reduce the harm occasioned by the diversion of guns to the illegal market and by the criminal possession and use of those guns. Because, however, plaintiff has failed to demonstrate, as required by New York law, that it has suffered harm different in kind from that suffered by the public at large in the state of New York, the case is dismissed.

. . . .

The law in New York seems to be that public nuisance must be proved by clear and convincing evidence....

. . . .

Since the possibility of a suit brought by a private plaintiff for a public nuisance was first recognized, as early as the sixteenth century, it has been emphasized that no private suit for public nuisance may be brought "unless it be where one man has greater hurt or inconvenience than any other man had, and then he who had more displeasure or hurt, etc., can have an action to recover his damages that he had by rea-son of this special hurt." Y .B. Mich. 27 Hen. 8, f. 26, pl. 10 (1536), *quoted in* William L. Prosser, *Private Action for Public Nuisance,* 52 Va. L. Rev. 997, 1005 (citing this anonymous case as the break away point from the position that public nuisance was a crime and actionable only by the king). A private party bringing an action for public nuisance is acting as a *de facto* private attorney general, suing on behalf of itself as well as the public.

Such a quasi-public action is not appropriate unless the private plaintiff shows some special harm. Prosser succinctly explains this necessity:

> The reasons for the requirement of particular damage have been stated many times. The plaintiff did not and could not represent the king, and the vindica-tion of royal rights was properly left to his duly constituted officers. This is no less true when the rights of the crown have passed to the general public. Defen-

Jack B. Weinstein

dants are not to be harassed, and the time of the courts taken up, with complaints about public matters from a multitude who claim to have suffered.

Prosser, *supra*, at 1007.

While the special harm required in the anonymous case quoted by Prosser is referred to as "greater" or "more" harm, the case law since that time has consistently recognized that a private plaintiff must show not just that it suffered more harm, but that it suffered some particular harm not shared in common with the rest of the public. *See, e.g.,* Callanan v. Gilman, 107 N.Y. 360, 370 (1887) ("It is the undoubted law that the plaintiffs could not maintain this action without alleging and proving that they sustained special damage from the nuisance, different from that sustained by the general public; in other words, that the damage they sustained was not common to all the public living or doing business in Vesey street and having occasion to use the same."); 532 Madison Ave. Gourmet Foods, Inc. v. Finlandia Ctr., 96 N.Y.2d 280, 294 (2001) ("[I]n that the [harm] was common to an entire community and the plaintiffs suffered it only in a greater degree than others, it is not a different kind of harm and the plaintiffs cannot recover for the invasion of a public right.") (quoting Restatement of the Law (Second) of Torts § 821C, cmt. h).

As usually stated, the harm must be different in kind, not just in degree. This is true regardless of the form of the relief requested. [Citations.]

Although it is not necessary that the particular harm alleged be exclusive or unique to a single plaintiff, when the class harmed in the same way "becomes so large and general as to include all members of the public who come in contact with the nuisance... the private action will fail." [Citations.] Physical harm, pecuniary loss, or delay and inconvenience suffered by a private plaintiff may satisfy this requirement, but not when they are so widespread as to affect "a whole community, or a very wide area within it." Prosser, *supra*, at 1015.

Some examples illustrate this requirement. New York courts have found that the harm suffered by commercial fishermen as a result of the pollution of the Hudson River was different in kind from that suffered by the public at large. *See* Leo v. General Elec. Co., 538 N.Y.S.2d 844 (App. Div. 1989). The partial obstruction of a sidewalk, although having an effect on the general public's access, affected the owner of neighboring apartment buildings in a peculiar manner. *See* Graceland Corp. v. Consol. Laundries Corp., 180 N.Y.S.2d 644 (App. Div. 1958), *aff'd*, 6 N.Y.2d 900 (1959).

Particular harm was found not to exist where two law firms sought damages for loss resulting when a labor strike forced the closure of the New York City transit system because "every person, firm and corporation conducting [a] business or profession in the City" suffered damage of a similar kind. Burns Jackson Miller Summit & Spitzer v. Lindner, 59 N.Y.2d 314, 334 (1983). As the New York Court of Appeals pointed out in 532 Madison Ave. Gourmet Foods, Inc. v. Finlandia Ctr., Inc., consolidated cases arising out of several construction disasters in Manhattan that resulted in the closure of the affected areas of the City for significant periods of time, "the hot dog vendor and taxi driver suffered the same kind of injury as the plaintiff law firm. Each was impacted in the ability to conduct business, resulting in financial loss." 96 N.Y.2d 280, 294 (2001). The difference in the degree of that injury was irrelevant to determining whether the private plaintiffs had stated claims for public nuisance. *See id.*

The requirement that a private plaintiff suing for public nuisance demonstrate particular harm different from that suffered by the public at large may be criticized on the ground that it inhibits adequate protection of the public when government authorities can not or will not act. *See, e.g.,* Denise E. Antolini, *Modernizing Public Nuisance: Solving the Paradox of the Special Injury Rule,* 28 Ecology L.Q. 755 (2001). It does cut down potential suits by "busybodies" having no particular interest in abating the nuisance except ideology. It thus stands in somewhat the same shoes as the doctrine of prudence in constitutional Article III standing. New York courts have embraced the doctrine in private suits, preferring in general to rely on public officials such as the Attorney General of the State.

The application of the "harm different in kind" requirement to the facts and issues presented in the instant case...is decisive. The court holds that the extensive and severe harm proven by plaintiff to be suffered by the NAACP, its members, and the African-American community in the state of New York is not "different in kind" as that phrase is defined in the case law. It therefore is not necessary to decide precisely who is a member of and represented in the instant action by the NAACP, and therefore whose "injury" should be considered for the purposes of this third element of a private plaintiff's public nuisance action.

African-Americans do suffer greater harm from illegal handguns for complex socioeconomic and historical reasons. But to say that they suffer a greater amount of harm is not enough under New York law. In order to show the particular harm necessary to have standing to sue for public nuisance as a private plaintiff, the harm suffered must be different in kind. That is not the case here.

It seems almost offensive that, almost a century and a half, after the freeing of the slaves and formal insistence by the courts of full legal equality, African-Americans feel compelled to argue that they must sue to be specially protected on the streets of New York from guns....There is an absolute duty on the part of the government to provide equal protection and safety for all its people. Defendants' moral obligation is no narrower.

....

Since plaintiff has not proved all elements of its cause of action…the case is dismissed.…

Notes

1. *See also* City of Philadelphia v. Beretta USA Corp., 277 F.3d 415 (3d Cir. 2002) (holding that, under the case and controversy clause of the federal constitution, civic organizations lacked standing to sue gun manufacturers on a claim that the gun industry's methods for distributing guns were negligent and a public nuisance, and that the action could not proceed in the absence of participation of the members of the organizations who actually sustained damages).

2. *Remoteness, Intervening Acts, and Deference to the Legislature in Public-Nuisance Actions.* Beyond the harm-different-in-kind requirement, there are other obstacles to nuisance suits against gun manufacturers. In People ex rel Spitzer v. Sturm, Ruger & Co., Inc., 761 N.Y.S.2d 192 (App. Div. 2003), the court held that the alleged conduct of handgun manufacturers, in manufacturing, distributing, and marketing handguns in a manner that knowingly placed a disproportionate number of handguns in the possession of people who used them unlawfully, failed to support a claim by the State for common-law public nuisance. The court found that the harm alleged was far too remote from the corporations' otherwise lawful commercial activity to fairly hold the corporations accountable, and that the corporations' lawful commercial activity, having been followed by harm to person and property caused directly and principally by the criminal activity of intervening third parties, could not be considered a proximate cause of such harm. The court said that the legislature was better equipped than the judiciary to address the problems posed by illegal handguns.

See also Camden County Board of Chosen Freeholders v. Beretta USA Corp., 273 F.3d 536 (3d Cir. 2001) (causal chain too attenuated); Ganim v. Smith & Wesson Corp., 780 A.2d 98 (Conn. 2001) (city and mayor lacked standing because the alleged harm was too indirect and remote).

3. *The Issue of Control in Public-Nuisance Actions.* In nuisance actions against product manufacturers, courts have sometimes focused on whether the defendant had control of the product in question. For example, in Tioga Pub. Sch. Dist. v. U.S. Gypsum Co., 984 F.2d 915 (8th Cir. 1993), the court wrote:

> [C]ourts appear to agree…that nuisance law does not afford a remedy against the manufacturer of an asbestos-containing product to an owner whose building has been contaminated by asbestos following the installation of that product in the building. All of the courts that have considered the issue have rejected nuisance as a theory of recovery in such cases. [Citations.] These courts have noted that liability for damage caused by a nuisance turns on whether the defendant is in control of the instrumentality alleged to constitute a nuisance, since without control a defendant cannot abate the nuisance. Each court found that a defendant who had sold an asbestos-containing material to a plaintiff lacked control of the product after the sale. [Citations.] We believe these decisions are well reasoned.…

However, other courts have minimized the significance of control. *See* In re Starlink Corn Products Liability Litig., 212 F. Supp. 2d 828 (N.D. Ill. 2002) (holding that corn farmers' allegations that pollen from genetically modified (GMO) corn, which was toxic to insects, drifted across property lines and onto their property were sufficient to support public and private nuisance claims against the GMO corn manufacturer).

4. *Harm Different in Kind.* The requirement that the plaintiff's injury differ in kind from the injuries of others means, for example, that an individual may not ordinarily sue to abate an obstruction of a public road (*see* McQueen v. Burkhart, 290 S.W.2d 577 (Tex. Civ. App. 1956)), enjoin the operation of a bawdy house (*see* Coman v. Baker, 179 S.W. 937 (Tex. Civ. App. 1915), *rev'd on other grounds*, 198 S.W. 141 (Tex. 1917)), or close a nude beach (*see* Mark v. Oregon, 974 P.2d 716 (Or. Ct. App. 1999). Were the law otherwise, self-appointed protectors of the public might litigate against many activities they thought undesirable. It is normally the role of government, not busybodies, to keep the highways open and the bawdy houses closed, and to limit nude beaches to appropriate locations.

(a) *Physical Harm.* Physical harm to person or property often qualifies as harm different in kind since physical injuries are rarely sustained by a multitude of persons as a result of the same tortious conduct. *See* George v. City of Houston, 465 S.W.2d 387 (Tex. Civ. App. 1971), *rev'd on other grounds*, 479 S.W.2d 257 (Tex. 1972) (child drowned in polluted pond); Prescott v. Leaf River Forest Products, Inc., 740 So. 2d 301 (Miss. 1999) (holding that interference with the condition of land is sufficient to constitute harm different than that suffered by the public at large, but that the plaintiff group had failed to prove that their property had been affected by water pollution).

(b) *Pecuniary Loss.* Pecuniary losses may also qualify as harm different in kind. *See* Galveston, H. & S.A. Ry. Co. v. De Groff, 118 S.W. 134 (Tex. 1909) (hotel permitted to recover for depreciation in property value and loss of business because of the location of railroad).

(c) *Difference in Kind versus Difference in Degree.* Harm "different in kind" is not equivalent to harm "different in degree"; the test is not simply a search for the most seriously injured plaintiffs. Still, the Restatement indicates that magnitude of interference is not entirely irrelevant. Comment c to §821C of the Restatement, Second, of Torts states:

> Normally there may be no difference in the kind of interference with one who travels a road once a week and one who travels it every day. But if the plaintiff traverses the road a dozen times a day he nearly always has some special reason to do so, and that reason will almost invariably be based upon some special interest of his own, not common to the community....Thus in determining whether there is a difference in the kind of harm, the degree of interference may be a factor of importance that must be considered.

(d) *Policy.* In applying a difficult standard, such as the "harm different in kind" requirement, it is important to look for guidance to the reasons underlying the rule. Some authorities suggest that the rule is intended to protect the defendant from the multiplicity of suits which would follow if everyone could sue for common harm. *See* W. Page Keeton, Dan B. Dobbs, Robert E. Keeton, & David G. Owen, Prosser and Keeton on Torts 646 (5th ed. 1984); Restatement, Second, of Torts §821C cmt. a. This is a weak justification. On the one hand, if the alleged public nuisance does not exist or is not attributable to the defendant, it is unlikely that many persons will go to the trouble and expense of suing the defendant. On the other hand, if a nuisance does exist as a result of the defendant's intentional, negligent, or strict-liability conduct, there is little reason to protect the defendant from liability, for the law ordinarily holds persons responsible for the consequences of their tortious actions. If the defendant has created a nuisance and an injunction is issued, other suits will not be brought to secure the same relief. And to those who argue that multiple actions for damages may subject a defendant to liability disproportionate to fault, the simple answer is that the law should not attempt to address proportionality concerns by using a standard which bars legitimate claims without regard to the magnitude of the defendant's fault or the worthiness of the complaint.

A better justification for the "different in kind" requirement is the fact that it tends to ensure that the state will be a party to legal proceedings significantly affecting the public interest. It does this by precluding private individuals, in many instances, from litigating issues relating to rights common to the public in general. Absent the "different in kind" requirement, "the public policy of...[the] state on...vital matters could be thwarted, without the state having an opportunity to have its side of the controversy presented in a court of justice." Garland Grain Co. v. D-C Home Owners Improvement Ass'n, 393 S.W.2d 635, 640 (Tex. Civ. App. 1965).

Allowing private actions against public nuisances when the "different in kind" requirement is met also performs a "safety valve" function. It permits courts to hear precisely those cases which are unlikely to be championed by the elected representatives of the public—those claims involving atypical injuries which are unlikely to stir enough popular support to secure redress through normal majoritarian channels.

Section 821C of the Restatement, Second, of Torts invited courts to consider whether the harm-different-in-kind requirement should be dispensed with in injunction actions, but that invitation has rarely been accepted. *But see* Akau v. Olohana, 65 Haw. 383 (Haw. 1982) (electing to focus not on whether the injury was shared by the public, but on whether the plaintiff was in fact injured).

5. *Legislative Grants of Standing.* It is open to the legislature to dispense with the "harm different in kind" requirement, and many have done so, at least in certain contexts. Statutes typically confer standing on particular public officials, and, in some states, on ordinary citizens as well. Consider these provisions:

FLORIDA STATUTES ANNOTATED
§§ 60.05 and 823.05 (Westlaw 2004)

§60.05

(1) When any nuisance as defined in §823.05 exists, the Attorney General, state attorney, city attorney, county attorney, or any citizen of the county may sue in the name of the state on his or her relation to enjoin the nuisance, the person or persons maintaining it, and the owner or agent of the building or ground on which the nuisance exists....

§823.05

Whoever shall erect, establish, continue, or maintain, own or lease any building, booth, tent or place which tends to annoy the community or injure the health of the community, or become manifestly injurious to the morals or manners of the people...or any house or place of prostitution, assignation, lewdness or place or building where games of chance are engaged in violation of law or any place where any law of the state is violated, shall be deemed guilty of maintaining a nuisance, and the building, erection, place, tent or booth and the furniture, fixtures and contents are declared a nuisance. All such places or persons shall be abated or enjoined as provided in §§60.05 and 60.06 [dealing with the duty and authority of the court].

See also Tex. Civ. Prac. & Rem. Code §125 (Westlaw 2003).

D. Remedies in Nuisance Cases

Damages. The damages which may be recovered in an action for public or private nuisance typically provide compensation for a broad range of losses, including physical and mental harm to persons and damage to tangible property. The former category includes amounts for physical injury, impairment of health, and personal discomfort, annoyance, and inconvenience. Compensation for harm to property may include, among other things, costs of repair, diminished market value, or lost productivity or rent. Punitive damages may be awarded in an egregious case, subject to the usual limitations.

Permanent versus Temporary Damages. See Bates v. Schneider Natl. Carriers, Inc., 95 S.W.3d 309 (Tex. App. 2002), stating:

> Permanent injuries to land give rise to a cause of action for permanent damages, which are normally measured as the difference in value of the property before and after the injury. Temporary injuries to land give rise to temporary damages, which are the amount of damages that accrued during the continuance of the injury covered by the period for which the action is brought.

Injunctive Relief. A temporary or permanent injunction may be issued where the plaintiff has no adequate remedy at law. In theory, all nuisance cases in which future harm is threatened should entitle the plaintiff to an injunction, as equity regards every tract of land as being unique. In practice, of course, the courts are reluctant to enjoin the conduct of important activities even if landowners are adversely affected. *See* Boomer v. Atlantic Cement Co., 257 N.E.2d 870 (N.Y. 1970).

One need not wait until harm occurs before seeking injunctive relief, though the burden of proving that proposed conduct will constitute a nuisance may be heavy. *See* Sharp v. 251st St. Landfill, Inc., 925 P.2d 546 (Okla. 1996) (neighboring landowners threatened with complete loss of their water supply may apply for injunctive relief without waiting for actual loss).

Self-Help: The Right to Abate a Nuisance. Because resort to the law for monetary or injunctive relief is often slow, expensive, or impractical, authorities recognize that, under appropriate circumstances, an affected individual may act to abate a nuisance without first going to court. This privilege, however, is subject to several qualifications.

First, to encourage the exercise of care by those seeking to take matters into their own hands, the actor is deemed to assume the risk of any mistake about the facts. Thus, the actor gambles that, in a later suit, a trier of fact will not find the exercise of self-help to have been an unreasonable infringement of the rights of others. That the actor honestly and reasonably believed that the condition constituted a nuisance is immaterial to liability if an actual nuisance is not proven.

Second, the means selected to abate the nuisance must not be unnecessarily intrusive or destructive. If the interference with the rights of another exceeds what is warranted by the circumstances, the actor is liable for the excess damage. In addition, entry onto the land of another must be made at a reasonable time and in a reasonable manner, taking into account the degree and extent of the threatened harm and the availability of alternatives. If a request directed to the creator of the nuisance would result in its prompt cessation, a request is prerequisite to self-help. However, if notification is impossible, or if a request has been made and ignored, or if there is reason to believe that the entreaty would be futile, the actor may proceed without making a request.

Third, self-help is permitted only when time is of the essence. Consequently, there is often no right to abate a nuisance which has existed unchanged for a long while. This limitation discourages conduct that would risk a breach of the peace, personal injury, or erroneous interference with property rights under circumstances in which there is time for resort to the courts.

Self-help remedies are allowed, not required. It is no defense to a nuisance action for the defendant to argue that the plaintiff could have used self-help.

Some statutes provide that public representatives may act to halt activities that threaten the health, safety, or welfare of the public without first resorting to legal process.

Spur Industries, Inc. v. Del E. Webb Development Co.

Supreme Court of Arizona, In Banc
494 P.2d 700 (Ariz. 1972)

CAMERON, Vice Chief Justice.

From a judgment permanently enjoining the defendant, Spur Industries, Inc., from operating a cattle feedlot near the plaintiff Del E. Webb Development Company's Sun City, Spur appeals. Webb cross-appeals.... [W]e feel that it is necessary to answer only two questions. They are:

> 1. Where the operation of a business, such as a cattle feedlot is lawful in the first instance, but becomes a nuisance by reason of a nearby residential area, may the feedlot operation be enjoined in an action brought by the developer of the residential area?

> 2. Assuming that the nuisance may be enjoined, may the developer of a completely new town or urban area in a previously agricultural area be required to indemnify the operator of the feedlot who must move or cease operation because of the presence of the residential area created by the developer?

The facts necessary for a determination of this matter on appeal are as follows. The area in question is located in Maricopa County, Arizona, some 14 to 15 miles west of the urban area of Phoenix....

Farming started in this area about 1911....

In 1956, Spur's predecessors in interest, H. Marion Welborn and the Northside Hay Mill and Trading Company, developed feedlots, about ½ mile south of Olive Avenue, in an area between the confluence of the usually dry Agua Fria and New Rivers. The area is well suited for cattle feeding and in 1959, there were 25 cattle feeding pens or dairy operations within a 7 mile radius of the location developed by Spur's predecessors. In April and May of 1959, the Northside Hay Mill was feeding between 6,000 and 7,000 head of cattle and Welborn approximately 1,500 head on a combined area of 35 acres.

In May of 1959, Del Webb began to plan the development of an urban area to be known as Sun City. For this purpose, the Marinette and the Santa Fe Ranches, some 20,000 acres of farmland, were purchased for $15,000,000 or $750.00 per acre. This price was considerably less than the price of land located near the urban area of Phoenix, and...was a factor influencing the decision to purchase the property in question.

....

By December 1967, Del Webb's property had extended south to Olive Avenue and Spur was within 500 feet of Olive Avenue to the north....Del Webb filed its original complaint alleging that in excess of 1,300 lots in the southwest portion were unfit for development for sale as residential lots because of the operation of the Spur feedlot.

Del Webb's suit complained that the Spur feeding operation was a public nuisance because of the flies and the odor which were drifting or being blown by the prevailing south to north wind over the southern portion of Sun City. At the time of the suit, Spur was feeding between 20,000 and 30,000 head of cattle, and the facts amply support the finding of the trial court that the feed pens had become a nuisance to the people who resided in the southern part of Del Webb's development. The testimony indicated that cattle in a commercial feedlot will produce 35 to 40 pounds of wet manure per day, per head, or over a million pounds of wet manure per day for 30,000 head of cattle, and that despite the admittedly good feedlot management and good housekeeping practices by Spur, the resulting odor and flies produced an annoying if not unhealthy situation as far as the senior citizens of southern Sun City were concerned. There is no doubt that some of the citizens of Sun City were unable to enjoy the outdoor living which Del Webb had advertised and that Del Webb was faced with sales resistance from prospective purchasers as well as strong and persistent complaints from the people who had purchased homes in that area.

. . . .

. . . [N]either the citizens of Sun City nor Youngtown are represented in this lawsuit and the suit is solely between Del E. Webb Development Company and Spur Industries, Inc.

. . . .

We have no difficulty . . . in agreeing with the conclusion of the trial court that Spur's operation was an enjoinable public nuisance as far as the people in the southern portion of Del Webb's Sun City were concerned.

§36-601, subsec. A reads as follows:

§36-601. Public nuisances dangerous to public health

A. The following conditions are specifically declared public nuisances dangerous to the public health:

1. Any condition or place in populous areas which constitutes a breeding place for flies, rodents, mosquitoes and other insects which are capable of carrying and transmitting disease-causing organisms to any person or persons.

By this statute, before an otherwise lawful (and necessary) business may be declared a public nuisance, there must be a "populous" area in which people are injured:

. . . [I]t hardly admits a doubt that, in determining the question as to whether a lawful occupation is so conducted as to constitute a nuisance as a matter of fact, the locality and surroundings are of the first importance. (Citations omitted.) A business which is not per se a public nuisance may become such by being carried on at a place where the health, comfort, or convenience of a populous neighborhood is affected. . . . What might amount to a serious nuisance in one locality by reason of the density of the population, or character of the neighborhood affected, may in another place and under different surroundings be deemed proper and unobjectionable. . . . [Citation.]

It is clear that as to the citizens of Sun City, the operation of Spur's feedlot was both a public and a private nuisance. They could have successfully maintained an action to abate the nuisance. Del Webb, having shown a special injury in the loss of sales, had a standing to bring suit to enjoin the nuisance. [Citations.] The judgment of the trial court permanently enjoining the operation of the feedlot is affirmed.

....

A suit to enjoin a nuisance sounds in equity and the courts have long recognized a special responsibility to the public when acting as a court of equity:

§104. Where public interest is involved.

Courts of equity may, and frequently do, go much further both to give and withhold relief in furtherance of the public interest than they are accustomed to go when only private interests are involved. Accordingly, the granting or withholding of relief may properly be dependent upon considerations of public interest.... [Citation.]

In addition to protecting the public interests, however, courts of equity are concerned with protecting the operator of a lawfully, albeit noxious, business from the result of a knowing and willful encroachment by others near his business.

In the so-called "coming to the nuisance" cases, the courts have held that the residential landowner may not have relief if he knowingly came into a neighborhood reserved for industrial or agricultural endeavors and has been damaged thereby:

....

People employed in a city who build their homes in suburban areas of the county beyond the limits of a city and zoning regulations do so for a reason. Some do so to avoid the high taxation rate imposed by cities, or to avoid special assessments for street, sewer and water projects. They usually build on improved or hard surface highways, which have been built either at state or county expense and thereby avoid special assessments for these improvements. It may be that they desire to get away from the congestion of traffic, smoke, noise, foul air and the many other annoyances of city life. But with all these advantages in going beyond the area which is zoned and restricted to protect them in their homes, they must be prepared to take the disadvantages. [Citations.]

And:

... [A] party cannot justly call upon the law to make that place suitable for his residence which was not so when he selected it.... [Citation.]

Were Webb the only party injured, we would feel justified in holding that the doctrine of "coming to the nuisance" would have been a bar to the relief asked by Webb, and, on the other hand, had Spur located the feedlot near the outskirts of a city and had the city grown toward the feedlot, Spur would have to suffer the cost of abating the nuisance as to those people locating within the growth pattern of the expanding city....

....

There was no indication in the instant case at the time Spur and its predecessors located in western Maricopa County that a new city would spring up, full-blown, alongside the feeding operation and that the developer of that city would ask the court to order Spur to move because of the new city. Spur is required to move not because of any wrongdoing on the part of Spur, but because of a proper and legitimate regard of the courts for the rights and interests of the public.

Del Webb, on the other hand, is entitled to the relief prayed for (a permanent injunction), not because Webb is blameless, but because of the damage to the people who have been encouraged to purchase homes in Sun City. It does not equitably or legally follow, however, that Webb, being entitled to the injunction, is then free of any liability to Spur if Webb has in fact been the cause of the damage Spur has sustained. It does not seem harsh to require a developer, who has taken advantage of the lesser land values in a rural area as well as the availability of large tracts of land on which to build and develop a new town or city in the area, to indemnify those who are forced to leave as a result.

Having brought people to the nuisance to the foreseeable detriment of Spur, Webb must indemnify Spur for a reasonable amount of the cost of moving or shutting down. It should be noted that this relief to Spur is limited to a case wherein a developer has, with foreseeability, brought into a previously agricultural or industrial area the population which makes necessary the granting of an injunction against a lawful business and for which the business has no adequate relief.

It is therefore the decision of this court that the matter be remanded to the trial court for a hearing upon the damages sustained by the defendant Spur as a reasonable and direct result of the granting of the permanent injunction. Since the result of the appeal may appear novel and both sides have obtained a measure of relief, it is ordered that each side will bear its own costs.

Affirmed in part, reversed in part, and remanded for further proceedings consistent with this opinion.

Notes

1. *Defenses.* The defenses which may be asserted in a nuisance action depend upon the nature of the tortious conduct on which the action is based. Thus, a plaintiff may not escape the effect of the defense of contributory negligence by recasting a negligence case as a suit for public or private nuisance predicated on negligent interference.

2. *Reference.* For an economic analysis of remedies for trespass and nuisance — including the "purchased injunction" remedy of *Del Webb* — see Guido Calabresi & Douglas Melamed, *Property Rules, Liability Rules, and Inalienability: One View of the Cathedral*, 85 Harv. L. Rev. 1089 (1972).

Chapter 21

Misrepresentation

This chapter examines claims for the harm caused to a plaintiff who relies on a misrepresentation made by the defendant. Every jurisdiction recognizes an action for "deceit," which is based upon the defendant's having defrauded the plaintiff by intentionally (or recklessly) misrepresenting a material[a] fact. In addition, recovery for misrepresentations made negligently, rather than intentionally, is often allowed. As discussed below, claims for negligent misrepresentation are in many ways more limited than for intentional misrepresentation. Furthermore, some jurisdictions impose strict liability for misrepresentations in limited circumstances, so that even entirely innocent misstatements may be actionable. Therefore, this chapter is concerned with three similar but distinct torts: deceit, negligent misrepresentation, and strict liability for inaccurate statements. The discussion begins by examining the law of deceit. Technically speaking, the conduct that gives rise to an action for deceit is "fraud," while the plaintiff's action is called an action for "deceit"; in practice, "fraud" and "deceit" are often used as synonyms.

A. Deceit

1. Intentional or Reckless Misrepresentation

Pleading and Proving Fraud. Fraud cases differ procedurally from other tort cases. Under Rule 9(b) of the Federal Rules of Civil Procedure, a complaint alleging fraud must state "the circumstances constituting fraud...with particularity"; most states have a similar requirement. *See, e.g.,* Martin v. Lancaster Battery Co., 606 A.2d 444 (Pa. 1992). No very persuasive reason for this requirement has ever been advanced. Judge Richard Posner has speculated that the "particularity" requirement may exist because

> Accusations of fraud can do serious damage to the goodwill of a business firm or a professional person. People should be discouraged from tossing such accu-

---

a. Restatement (Second) of Torts §538 provides:
  (1) Reliance upon a fraudulent misrepresentation is not justifiable unless the matter misrepresented is material.
  (2) The matter is material if
    (a) a reasonable man would attach importance to its existence or nonexistence in determining his choice of action in the transaction in question; or
    (b) the maker of the representation knows or has reason to know that its recipient regards or is likely to regard the matter as important in determining his choice of action, although a reasonable man would not so regard it.

sations into complaints in order to induce advantageous settlements or for other ulterior purposes.

Banker's Trust Co. v. Old Republic Ins. Co., 959 F.2d 677 (7th Cir. 1992). Judge Posner concedes that this explanation cannot account for Rule 9(b)'s insistence that mistake, like fraud, must be pleaded with "particularity."

Many jurisdictions say that the burden of persuasion with respect to fraud is higher than the ordinary "preponderance of the evidence" standard. Fraud, it is often said, must be established by "clear and convincing evidence" or by a "clear preponderance of the evidence." Whether these supposedly higher standards differ in practice from the usual "preponderance of the evidence" standard is uncertain. Some courts hold that the higher standard does not apply to the damage element of a deceit action. *See* Kilduff v. Adams, Inc., 593 A.2d 478 (Conn. 1991). And other states reject the higher standard entirely. *See* State v. Alpine Air Prods., 500 N.W.2d 788, 791 (Minn. 1993).

Statutory Actions. One important kind of fraud (which will not be discussed here) is securities fraud. Unlike the common-law fraud with which this chapter is concerned, "securities fraud" is based on federal statutes and regulations. In many cases, securities fraud involves conduct that is not fraudulent in the traditional sense. Securities fraud is examined in detail in courses on corporations and securities regulation.

In addition, virtually every state has enacted some form of statute regulating deceptive trade practices. These laws make it easier for consumers to sue for fraudulent conduct relating to goods or services that may also be actionable under common-law rules. Typically, the statutes permit recovery not only of compensatory damages, but also of attorneys' fees and, on appropriate facts, exemplary damages. Consequently, it is often easier to sue under the deceptive trade practice law, and the potential recovery may be larger. Not surprisingly, complaints alleging common-law fraud often also allege a violation of the state deceptive trade practices act. In law school, deceptive trade practices statutes are usually studied in courses on consumer law or in specialized seminars.

Words, Conduct, and Silence. An actionable misrepresentation may take any of several forms. Oral and written statements are, of course, the most obvious varieties. However, conduct may also create a misrepresentation, as in the case of the defendant who stacks goods so that the bad ones are hidden. *See also* Cadek v. Great Lakes Dragway, Inc., 58 F.3d 1209 (7th Cir. 1995) (track owner misrepresented fire-fighting capability by parking inoperable fire truck near place where drivers signed releases).

Silence, too, may be an actionable misrepresentation—but only if there is a duty to speak.

O'Hara v. Western Seven Trees Corp. Intercoast Management

Court of Appeal of California
142 Cal. Rptr. 487 (Ct. App. 1977)

CHRISTIAN, Associate Justice.

Kim Elizabeth O'Hara appeals from a judgment of dismissal which was rendered after the court sustained a demurrer to her complaint.... Appellant seeks recovery from Western Seven Trees Corporation and others to compensate her for being raped. The complaint alleged two causes of action. The first claimed that respondents, the owners and operators of the apartment complex..., were negligent in failing to provide "adequate security," in misrepresenting the security measures in effect on the premises, in concealing information concerning a man who had raped several female tenants, and in failing to warn plaintiff of the danger of rape. In the second cause of action, for deceit, it was alleged that respondents knowingly misrepresented the safety and security of the complex with the intent to induce appellant to rent an apartment....

....Before April 4, 1975, a Caucasian male had raped several tenants of the Seven Trees Apartments in San Jose. Respondents knew of the crimes, were aware of the conditions indicating a likelihood that the rapist would repeat his attacks, and had been supplied by the local police with composite drawings of the suspect and a general description of his *modus operandi*. On April 4, 1975, respondents assured appellant, a prospective tenant, that the premises were safe and were patrolled at all times by professional guards. Respondents knew these statements were false and disclosed no information concerning the assaults. Appellant, believing and relying upon respondents' representations, was induced to rent an apartment in the complex.

On July 16, 1975, appellant was raped in her apartment; she later identified her assailant as the same person who had been depicted in the composite drawings which had earlier been supplied to respondents and were still in their possession.

....

[The court held that the complaint stated a cause of action for negligence.]

....To state an action for deceit or fraud, a plaintiff must allege a misrepresentation made with knowledge of its falsity and with the intent to defraud, i.e., to induce reliance; the reliance must be justifiable and damages alleged must be a proximate result. [Citations.] The representation usually must be of a fact. Appellant alleged that respondents, with intent to induce her to rent an apartment and with knowledge that their representations were false, stated that the complex was safe and was patrolled 24 hours a day by a security force. The latter representation is one of fact. The claim of safety was at least an opinion made by one with presumed expert knowledge and, thus, can support an action. [Citation.] Also, in the field of products liability, a representation that a product is safe is a statement of fact. [Citation.] Appellant allegedly relied on the assurances and was thus induced to rent an apartment. Since appellant did not know the true facts and since respondents had superior knowledge, the allegations, if proved, would support a finding of justifiable reliance. Causation of the wrong to appellant by respondents' misrepresentations was also alleged.

A deceit action more commonly seeks to recover pecuniary loss. But, "there is no essential reason to prevent a deceit action from being maintained, for intentional misstatements at least, where other types of interests are invaded; and there are a few cases in which it has been held to lie for personal injuries...."....Accordingly, the court in Work v. Campbell (1912) 164 Cal. 343, 128 P. 943, held that a woman could maintain an action for deceit against a defendant whose intentional misrepresentations caused the plaintiff's husband to desert her. "One who by a fraudulent misrepresentation or nondisclosure of a fact that it is his duty to disclose causes physical harm to the person...of another who justifiably relies upon the misrepresentation, is subject to liability to the other." (Rest. 2d, Torts, §557A.) An action may be maintained to recover for physical harm proximately caused by a defendant's deceit.

....

[The court held that if the plaintiff proved that the defendants intentionally misled her in order to advance their pecuniary interest in renting an apartment an award of punitive damages would be appropriate.]

The judgment is reversed with directions to overrule the general demurrer.

Notes

1. *Deceit and Non-Pecuniary Injuries.* Most deceit cases involve losses that are entirely pecuniary, but there is no reason in principle to deny recovery to someone who suffers bodily injury or property damage because of the defendant's misrepresentations. However, some cases involving misrepresentations seem better characterized as actions for battery (as when the plaintiff is fraudulently induced to consent to a harmful contact), or as negligence, than as fraud.

Consider, for example, a case in which the plaintiff is injured when the driver of a car signals to the plaintiff that she can safely pass. If the driver has overlooked an approaching truck and the plaintiff is injured as a result, is the plaintiff's claim one for negligent misrepresentation or is it a simple claim for negligent operation of a motor vehicle? In many cases, of course, characterization of the claim will be unimportant. But suppose the driver is an employee of the federal government. The Federal Tort Claims Act generally allows actions against the government for the negligence of its employees, but it denies recovery for "Any claim arising out of...misrepresentation"; 28 U.S.C. §2680(h) (Westlaw 2003). On the facts of the hypothetical, it seems clear that the policies barring people from suing the government for misrepresentation, but allowing suits for run-of-the-mill motor vehicle accidents, favor recovery.

The Supreme Court has addressed the problem of defining "misrepresentation" under the Federal Tort Claims Act in two cases involving government programs designed to subsidize the purchase of houses. The plaintiff in Neustadt v. United States, 366 U.S. 696 (1961), claimed that an inaccurate appraisal by an employee of the Federal Housing Administration caused him to pay more for a house than it was actually worth. The appraiser had overlooked structural defects in the house. The Court ruled that the Federal Tort Claims Act barred the suit. Then, in Block v. Neal, 460 U.S. 289 (1983), the plaintiff claimed that an inspector who worked for the Farmers Home Administration failed to supervise a builder's construction of a house and told the plaintiff, erroneously, that construction was proceeding properly. The *Block* Court held that the misrepresentation exception did not bar recovery because the claim could be grounded on the employee's negligent supervision of the construction, making the misrepresentations "not essential to plaintiff's negligence claim"; 460 U.S. at 297.

2. *Tort, Contract, and Restitution.* A defendant's fraud can be important for reasons other than providing grounds for a tort action. For example, someone induced by fraud to enter a contract may be excused from performance, and someone whose property has been fraudulently taken by the defendant can recover the property in an action for restitution. In some cases, however, a deceit action may give the plaintiff more than could be obtained by avoiding a contract or by restitution. Suppose, for instance, that D fraudulently induces P to buy Blackacre for $100,000, by telling P that Blackacre contains valuable mineral deposits. If Blackacre really contained those deposits, it would be worth $500,000; its actual value is only $20,000. Restitution or rescission of the contract will get P's $100,000 back (if P returns the land), but an action for deceit will probably allow P to recover the difference between Blackacre's actual value and the $500,000 it would have

been worth if the representations had been true. A tort claim will also be the preferred remedy when the plaintiff was not in privity of contract with the fraudfeasor, or when the plaintiff wants to keep the property in question, or when the plaintiff must sue someone who obtained nothing by making the misrepresentation (as when *A* fraudulently induces *B* to pay $100,000 to *C*, and *B* wants to sue *A* rather than *C*).

In many cases, a complaint will allege claims based on tort, contract, and restitution; the relief awarded will depend on which claims the plaintiff can establish.

Sovereign Pocohontas v. Bond

United States Court of Appeals for the District of Columbia
120 F.2d 39 (D.C. Cir. 1941)

EDGERTON, Associate Justice.

In this action for deceit, the District Court directed a verdict for the defendants. Their alleged misstatements related to the condition of a corporation of which they were officers. There is evidence that they said it was making money, and had made about $800 in the previous quarter and over $3,000 in the preceding year, and that they caused certain financial statements to be sent to plaintiff. Actually the corporation was losing money, and had lost about $86 in the previous quarter and $2,700 in the preceding year, and the financial statements were incorrect.

Defendant Moyer was President, and apparently defendant Bond was Secretary and Treasurer of the corporation. Both were frequently in its office and frequently spoke for it.... There is no evidence that they kept or examined its books, understood bookkeeping, prepared its financial statements, knew whether or not the statements were erroneous, or knew whether or not the corporation had made or was making money. There is evidence that the books were kept by other persons, and no evidence that those persons did not prepare the financial statements.

"The rule is settled that in an action at law where the issue is fraud the party relying upon fraud must show that the misrepresentations asserted were made either with knowledge of their untruth or in reckless disregard of the truth." [Citation.] The evidence would, we think, justify an inference that the defendants made untrue statements of objective fact in reckless disregard of the truth. In the absence of evidence tending to show that they were themselves misled by reasonable or merely negligent reliance on what others told them, a corporation's officers may be regarded as acting recklessly when they make glaringly false statements about its current financial history and condition....

Moreover, the evidence would support an inference that the defendants knowingly made untrue statements of subjective fact. They did not say, "We are informed and believe that the company has been making money." Had they done so, it is not likely that the plaintiff would have relied on what they said. Their alleged statements were positive and unqualified. They purported, by clear implication, to know what they were talking about. Where knowledge is possible, one who represents a mere belief as knowledge misrepresents a fact. "Where a party represents a material fact to be true to his personal knowledge, as distinguished from belief or opinion, when he does not know whether it is true or not, and it is actually untrue, he is guilty of falsehood, even if he believes it to be true, and if the statement is thus made with the intention that it shall be acted upon by another, who does so act upon it to his injury, the result is actionable fraud." [Citation.]

There was evidence that defendant's statements were made for the purpose of inducing plaintiff to refrain from action to collect a debt which defendants' company owed;

that plaintiff did refrain, and also made a further sale to the company, in consequence; and that damage resulted, because the company's condition grew worse and plaintiff was ultimately unable to collect as much as it could have done when the representations were made....Accordingly it was error to direct a verdict for the defendants.

Reversed.

Note

1. *Scienter.* "Scienter"—meaning knowledge of falsity or reckless disregard for the truth—is an element of deceit. According to Restatement, Second, of Torts §526, a misrepresentation is fraudulent (that is, made with scienter), if the maker:

    (a) knows or believes that the matter is not as he represents it to be,

    (b) does not have the confidence in the accuracy of his representation that he states or implies, or

    (c) knows that he does not have the basis for his representation that he states or implies.

2.   Silence and the Duty to Speak

In general, it is still true that "silence is golden." There is ordinarily no duty to disclose information merely because it would be useful, interesting, or important to another person. Thus:

- a reporter had no duty to disclose that he intended to disobey a judge's instruction to the media not to disclose the identity of the plaintiff, a sexual assault victim, who testified following the judge's instruction (Doe v. Associated Press, 331 F.3d 417 (4th Cir. 2003));

- a builder selling a new home had no duty to disclose to the purchaser that a hostile neighbor had raised threatening and abusive objections to the house as an "abominable monolith" (Levine v. The Kramer Group, 807 A.2d 264 (N.J. Super. A.D. 2002)); and

- a bank selling a condominium in a neighborhood that had received a "lot of adverse publicity" had no duty to disclose that a toxic waste problem had been recently cleaned up at a nearby school and had caused difficulty selling the unit (Urman v. S. Boston Sav. Bk., 674 N.E.2d 1078, 1080 (Mass. 1997)).

However, there is an important difference between passive non-disclosure and active concealment. In addition, as the following cases and notes illustrate, there are many occasions when there is a duty to speak, in which case non-disclosure will be actionable.

Weintraub v. Krobatsch

Supreme Court of New Jersey
317 A.2d 68 (N.J. 1974)

JACOBS, J.

....

Mrs. Weintraub owned and occupied a six-year-old Englishtown home which she placed in the hands of a real estate broker (The Serafin Agency, Inc.) for sale. The Krobatsches were interested in purchasing the home, examined it while it was illuminated and found it suitable. On June 30, 1971, Mrs. Weintraub, as seller, and the Krobatsches, as purchasers, entered into a contract for the sale of the property for $42,500. The contract provided that the purchasers had inspected the property and were fully satisfied with its physical condition, that no representations had been made and that no responsibility was assumed by the seller as to the present or future condition of the premises. A deposit of $4,250 was sent by the purchasers to the broker to be held in escrow pending the closing of the transaction. The purchasers requested that the seller have the house fumigated and that was done. A fire after the signing of the contract caused damage but the purchasers indicated readiness that there be adjustment at closing.

During the evening of August 25, 1971, prior to closing, the purchasers entered the house, then unoccupied, and as they turned the lights on they were... "astonished to see roaches literally running in all directions, up the walls, drapes, etc." On the following day their attorney wrote a letter to Mrs. Weintraub... advising that... "the presence of vermin in such great quantities, particularly after the exterminator was done, rendered the house as unfit for human habitation at this time and therefore, the contract is rescinded." On September 2, 1971, an exterminator wrote to Mr. Krobatsch advising that he had examined the premises and that "cockroaches were found to have infested the entire house." He said he could eliminate them for a relatively modest charge by two treatments with a twenty-one day interval but that it would be necessary to remove the carpeting "to properly treat all the infested areas."

Mrs. Weintraub rejected the rescission by the purchasers and filed an action in the Law Division joining them and the broker as defendants. Though she originally sought specific performance she later confined her claim to damages in the sum of $4,250, representing the deposit held in escrow by the broker. The broker filed an answer and counterclaim seeking payment of its commission in the sum of $2,550....At the argument on the motions it was evident that the purchasers were claiming fraudulent concealment or nondisclosure by the seller as the basis for their rescission....[T]heir attorney said: "Your honor, I would point out, and it is in my clients' affidavit, every time that they inspected this house prior to this time every light in the place was illuminated. Now, these insects are nocturnal by nature....By keeping the lights on it keeps them out of sight. These sellers had to know they had this problem. You could not live in a house this infested without knowing about it."

....On appeal, the Appellate Division sustained the [Law Division's] summary judgment in Mrs. Weintraub's favor but disagreed with the Law Division's holding that the broker's claim must await trial....[I]t modified the Law Division's judgment to the end that the purchasers were directed to pay not only the sum of $4,250 to Mrs. Weintraub but also the sum of $2,550 to the broker.

....

Mrs. Weintraub...relies primarily on cases such as Swinton v. Whitinsville Sav. Bank, 311 Mass. 677, 42 N.E.2d 808, 141 A.L.R. 965 (1942)....Swinton is pertinent but, as Dean Prosser has noted (Prosser,...[Torts 696 (4th ed. 1971)]), it is one of a line of "singularly unappetizing cases" which are surely out of tune with our times.

In Swinton the plaintiff purchased a house from the defendant and after he occupied it he found it to be infested with termites. The defendant had made no verbal or written representations but the plaintiff, asserting that the defendant knew of the termites and was under a duty to speak, filed a complaint for damages grounded on fraudulent concealment. The Supreme Judicial Court of Massachusetts sustained a demurrer to the complaint and entered judgment for the defendant. In the course of its opinion, the court acknowledged that "the plaintiff possesses a certain appeal to the moral sense" but concluded that the law has not "reached the point of imposing upon the frailties of human nature a standard so idealistic as this." 42 N.E.2d at 808-809. That was written several decades ago and we are far from certain that it represents views held by the current members of the Massachusetts court. [Citation.] In any event we are certain that it does not represent our sense of justice or fair dealing and it has understandably been rejected in persuasive opinions elsewhere. [Citations.]

In Obde v. Schlemeyer, *supra*, 56 Wash. 2d 449, 353 P.2d 672, the defendants sold an apartment house to the plaintiff. The house was termite infested but that fact was not disclosed by the sellers to the purchasers who later sued for damages alleging fraudulent concealment. The sellers contended that they were under no obligation whatever to speak out and they relied heavily on the decision of the Massachusetts court in *Swinton*. [Citation.] The Supreme Court of Washington flatly rejected their contention, holding that though the parties had dealt at arms length the sellers were under "a duty to inform the plaintiffs of the termite condition" of which they were fully aware. 353 P.2d at 674; *cf.* Hughes v. Stusser, 68 Wash. 2d 707, 415 P.2d 89, 92 (1966). In the course of its opinion the court quoted approvingly from Dean Keeton's article... ["Fraud—Concealment and Non-Disclosure" (1936)] in 15 Tex. L. Rev. 1. There the author first expressed his thought that when Lord Cairns suggested in Peek v. Gurney, L.R. 6 H.L. 377 (1873), that there was no duty to disclose facts, no matter how "morally censurable" (at 403), he was expressing nineteenth century law as shaped by an individualistic philosophy based on freedom of contracts and unconcerned with morals. He then made the following comments which fairly embody a currently acceptable principle on which the holding in *Obde* may be said to be grounded:

> In the present stage of the law, the decisions show a drawing away from this idea, and there can be seen an attempt by many courts to reach a just result in so far as possible, but yet maintaining the degree of certainty which the law must have. The statement may often be found that if either party to a contract of sale conceals or suppresses a material fact which he is in good faith bound to disclose then his silence is fraudulent.

> The attitude of the courts toward nondisclosure is undergoing a change and contrary to Lord Cairns' famous remark it would seem that the object of the law in these cases should be to impose on parties to the transaction a duty to speak whenever justice, equity, and fair dealing demand it....

> ....

...[T]he purchasers here were entitled to withstand the seller's motion for summary judgment. They should have been permitted to proceed with their efforts to establish by testimony that they were equitably entitled to rescind because the house was extensively infested in the manner described by them, the seller was well aware of the infestation, and the seller deliberately concealed or failed to disclose the condition because of the likelihood that it would defeat the transaction. The seller may of course defend factually as well as legally and since the matter is primarily equitable in nature the factual as well as legal disputes will be for the trial judge alone. [Citations.]

If the trial judge finds such deliberate concealment or nondisclosure of the latent infestation not observable by the purchasers on their inspection, he will still be called upon to determine whether, in the light of the full presentation before him, the concealment or nondisclosure was of such significant nature as to justify rescission. Minor conditions which ordinary sellers and purchasers would reasonably disregard as of little or no materiality in the transaction would clearly not call for judicial intervention....

....

Reversed and Remanded.

Notes

1. *See also* Lawson v. Citizens & S. Nat'l Bank, 193 S.E.2d 124 (S.C. 1974) (liability was imposed where a gully was filled with trees and stumps and then covered over with clay and sold to unsuspecting plaintiffs for residential use).

2. ***Problem: The Cracked Block.*** Consider Lindberg Cadillac Co. v. Aron, 371 S.W.2d 651 (Mo. Ct. App. 1963). There, the court held against a defendant who, prior to trading in his old car, had had a service station fill crevices in a cracked motor block with sealer. The defects were not discovered by the plaintiff dealership prior to accepting the car. Would the case have turned out differently if the service station had concealed the cracks without the knowledge of the defendant? Why? If the plaintiff's representative failed to look under the hood, and therefore would not have discovered the cracks even if they had been visible, should plaintiff still be able to recover? Or if only a cursory inspection was made despite the defendant's offer to "take as much time as you like," should the plaintiff now be barred from complaining?

3. ***Reasons for Permitting Non-Disclosure of Material Information.*** Why not simply have a rule that any party to a contemplated transaction must disclose all material information to the other party? One reason is that information is often expensive to acquire; to require everyone having valuable knowledge to give it away free would reduce the incentive to acquire that knowledge in the first place. (Would students go to law school if they had to give their knowledge of the law to clients at no charge?) A standard illustration of this point involves a company which has learned by expensive investigation that a tract of farm land may contain valuable oil deposits. It is not fraud for the company to buy the land from its owner without disclosing the existence of those deposits. (Query: can the oil company's purchasing agent disguise himself as a farmer in negotiating the purchase?) Allowing persons who acquire knowledge to cash in on that knowledge benefits society by making it worthwhile to invest in knowledge. Note that this rationale does *not* justify non-disclosure in a case like *Weintraub*. Homeowners will, in the ordinary course of things, learn of roach infestations, so requiring them to share that kind of knowledge with prospective buyers will not encourage ignorance very much.

Some professions exist almost entirely because their practitioners can use their expertness to make favorable exchanges. Antique dealers, for example, often buy valuable items from sellers who do not realize the value of the objects they are selling. The outcome in any particular case may seem unfair, as when an unsuspecting seller disposes of a $5000 table for $10 at a garage sale. But if this kind of conduct were prohibited, antique experts would have little incentive to attend garage sales, and some valuable antiques would end up as firewood.

4. ***Property Disclosure Laws.*** Since 1985, a majority of states have adopted property disclosure laws which impose on home sellers duties to disclose to buyers a wide range of matters (*e.g.*, asbestos, radon gas, flooding problems, nuisance neighbors, nearby munitions, tree diseases, and deaths on the property). *See, e.g.*, Cal. Civ. Code §1102.1 *et seq.* (Westlaw 2003). Failure to comply with laws of this kind will support an action

in tort. *See* Alexander v. McKnight, 9 Cal. Rptr. 2d 453 (Cal. Ct. App. 1992) (no disclosure of neighborhood noise problems and nuisances).

While such laws normally expand a seller's disclosure obligations, they have sometimes been interpreted as defining the extent of a defendant's disclosure obligations. *Cf.* Nobrega v. Edison Glen Assoc., 772 A.2d 368, 374 (N.J. 2001) (holding that by adopting a statute requiring disclosure of certain types of off-site conditions, the legislature intended to define the entirety of the disclosure duties of sellers of newly-constructed residential real estate, and therefore an action for nondisclosure of a non-specified off-site condition could not be maintained under the state Consumer Fraud Act by purchasers whose claims under the disclosure law were not time-barred).

5. *Half-Truths.* "[O]ne who voluntarily elects to make a partial disclosure is deemed to have assumed the duty to tell the whole truth...even though the speaker was under no duty to make the partial disclosure in the first place." Union Pac. Res. Group, Inc. v. Rhone-Poulenc, Inc., 247 F.3d 574, 584 (5th Cir. 2001).

In Thompson v. Best, 478 N.E.2d 79 (Ind. Ct. App. 1985), the buyer of a house inquired about drainage problems and the seller indicated that the house had previously had problems and that there was a sump pump in the basement. The seller failed to disclose that there was also a second sump pump that had to run continuously and that if for any reason it failed to do so the basement would flood. Within two weeks after the purchase, flooding occurred. The court held that the seller was subject to liability for fraud and stated "[a]s soon as Mr. Best introduced Thompson to the fact of the sump pump and the drainage tiles around the house, it was incumbent upon the Bests to *fully* declare any and all problems associated with their function."

See also Columbia/HCA Healthcare Corp. v. Cottey, 72 S.W.3d 735, 744 (Tex. App. 2002) (partial disclosure about a retirement plan was fraudulent because it failed to indicate that the plan could be rescinded at anytime); Randi W. v. Muroc Jt. Unified Sch. Dist., 929 P.2d 582 (Cal. 1997) (having volunteered information in letters of recommendation praising an employee's character and personality, defendants were obliged to complete the picture by disclosing material facts regarding charges and complaints of the employee's sexual improprieties); Fidelity Mortgage Co. v. Cook, 821 S.W.2d 39, 43 (Ark. 1991) (imposing liability based on failure by a bank to disclose that it lacked the capacity to fund a loan that it had committed to make).

6. *Fiduciary and Confidential Relationships.* A duty to disclose all material facts also arises where the defendant stands in a fiduciary or otherwise trusted relationship to the plaintiff. Such confidential relationships are not limited to purely legal settings, and may be found to exist in situations which are moral, social, domestic, or merely personal. Thus, where the defendant, who was referred to as "uncle" by the plaintiffs and who was the best friend of their deceased father, secured the plaintiffs' signatures on a document which was purportedly a "peace paper" that would prevent other relatives from harassing the plaintiffs, but which secretly deeded the property to the defendant, the court held that a confidential relationship existed and that the deed could be set aside on grounds of fraud. Curl v. Key, 316 S.E.2d 272 (N.C. 1984).

Doctors, lawyers, and certain other professionals are fiduciaries as a matter of law. Other persons may be fiduciaries as a matter of fact. However, because the law of fiduciary obligations is demanding, one would expect courts to be reluctant to characterize a non-professional relationship as fiduciary.

Fiduciary relationships are distinguished from ordinary arms-length commercial relationships (such as the typical relationship between a store and its customers). In fiduciary relationships, there are special reasons (such as necessity of depending on professional expertise) that allow one party to trust another and that oblige the other to act in the interests of the one who relies. In contrast, in ordinary arms-length business relationships, parties must safeguard their own interests and cannot trust others to do that for them. In Pellegrini v. Cliffwood-Blue Moon Joint Venture, Inc., 115 S.W.3d 577 (Tex. App. 2003), the court characterized the relationship between a geophysicist contractor and a joint venture as an arms-length transaction. The joint venture was therefore under no duty to disclose that a particular oil well was not part of the contract and that the geophysicist would earn no royalties therefrom. The geophysicist, the court wrote, "could reasonably be expected to make an investigation, ask questions, draw his own conclusions, and protect his own interests."

In Ho v. University of Texas at Arlington, 984 S.W.2d 672 (Tex. Ct. App. 1998), the court held that because there is no fiduciary relationship between students and professors as a matter of law, and no such relationship arose on the facts of the case, a professor did not have an affirmative duty to tell a student that she would not obtain her doctoral degree if she failed part of the oral dissertation. *See also* Brzica v. Trustees of Dartmouth College, 791 A.2d 990 (N.H. 2002) (holding there was no fiduciary relationship between college trustees and alumni to disclose their intent to use alumni donations to eliminate single-sex fraternities and sororities).

The fiduciary relationship must exist prior to the events that are the basis of the suit. "The fact that one businessman trusts another and relies on another to perform a contract does not give rise to a confidential relationship, because something apart from the transaction between the parties is required." Richter v. Wagner Oil Co., 90 S.W.3d 890, 896 (Tex. App. 2002).

7. *Subsequently Acquired Information.* Suppose a defendant tells the plaintiff something the defendant believes to be true. Later, the defendant learns that the statement was false. Failure to correct the statement can be grounds for a deceit action. For example, in McGrath v. Zenith Radio Corp., 651 F.2d 458 (7th Cir. 1981), the defendants told the plaintiff that he was the "heir apparent" to the presidency of a soon-to-be-acquired subsidiary. Before the plaintiff released his shares of stock to facilitate the acquisition, the defendants learned that there were serious doubts as to whether the plaintiff would ever become president, but failed to disclose that information. In a suit filed by the plaintiff, who was unceremoniously terminated soon after the acquisition, the court upheld a large judgment in his favor.

8. *Information Not Intended to Induce Reliance.* A defendant who makes a false statement to the plaintiff, not expecting the plaintiff to rely on the statement, commits fraud by remaining silent after learning that the plaintiff intends to rely; Restatement, Second, of Torts §551(2)(d).

9. *Facts Basic to the Transaction.* According to the Restatement, §551, a party has a duty to disclose "facts basic to the transaction," the nondisclosure of which would be "so shocking to the ethical sense of the community, and...so extreme and unfair, as to amount to a form of swindling." Restatement, Second, of Torts §551 and Comment l. "Thus a seller who knows that his cattle are infected with tick fever...is not free to unload them on the buyer and take his money, when he knows that the buyer is not aware of the fact...[and] could not easily discover it." *Id.*

In Griffith v. Byers Constr. Co., 510 P.2d 198 (Kan. 1973), the court held that there was a duty to disclose to a buyer of a new home the fact that the saline content of the soil (which was part of an abandoned oil field) would not sustain vegetation. As support, the *Griffith* court cited the Restatement rule, a case which had required disclosure of the existence of a ditch underneath a garage which filled with water at periodic intervals, and a case finding a duty to disclose the fact that houses had been built on filled land susceptible to subsidence.

The Restatement rule on facts "basic to the transaction" has been successfully invoked in cases in which:

- an employer failed to disclose a substantial, known risk that the project for which an employee was being hired would be discontinued in the near future; Berger v. Security Pacific Info. Sys., 795 P.2d 1380 (Colo. Ct. App. 1990); *see also* Pearson v. Simmonds Precision Prod., Inc., 624 A.2d 1134 (Vt. 1993) (similar);

- the purchaser of property and others intended to employ a scheme that would deprive the vendors of their security interest in land; Dewey v. Lutz, 462 N.W.2d 435 (N.D. 1990);

- the seller of cattle failed to disclose that they had not been vaccinated and therefore could never come into the state; Ducheneaux v. Miller, 488 N.W.2d 902 (S.D. 1992).

Note, however, that not only must the fact be basic to the transaction, it must be reasonable to expect disclosure. *See* Schaler Tel. Co. v. Golden Sky Sys., Inc., 298 F.3d 736 (8th Cir. 2002) (holding that the seller of satellite television services had no reason to expect the buyer to disclose its alleged inability to obtain financing for the transaction).

10. *Latent Material Facts Not Reasonably Discoverable.* Even in cases not involving "facts basic to the transaction" there may be a duty to disclose an unknown fact that is material and not reasonably discoverable. This makes sense in light of the reasons underlying the general rule that ordinarily countenances non-disclosure. If the facts are reasonably discoverable, a rule not requiring disclosure creates an incentive for the plaintiffs to protect their own interests by careful investigation and decisionmaking. If, however, the facts are not discoverable, there is nothing to be gained by placing the burden of discovery on the plaintiff: the plaintiff will simply be relegated to making, and bearing the consequences of, a bad decision. Cognizant of these realities, one court wrote, in a typical opinion:

> Where one party to a contract has...knowledge which is not within the fair and reasonable reach of the other party and which he could not discover by the exercise of reasonable diligence...he is under a real obligation to speak, and his silence constitutes fraud.

Wolf v. Brungardt, 524 P.2d 726 (Kan. 1974).

See also Tim v. Clement, 574 N.W.2d 368 (Iowa Ct. App. 1997) (recognizing, in an action based on negligence and breach of contract, that a seller had a duty to purchasers to disclose the presence of underground storage tanks located on an adjacent off-site property owned by the seller because the "defect was a latent one that...[the buyers] had no way of detecting"; such a "duty exists only when the off-site latent defect may materially affect the desirability or market value of the property to be sold"); Quashnock v. Frost, 445 A.2d 121 (Pa. 1982) (duty to disclose hidden termite condition); Stambovsky v. Ackley, 572 N.Y.S.2d 672 (App. Div. 1991) (vendor who had undertaken to inform the public at large about the existence of poltergeists had a duty to inform the purchaser because haunting is not a condition which can and should be ascertained by reasonable inspection of the premises).

11. *Ethics in Law Practice: Disclosure to Clients.* When it comes to attorneys and clients, silence is far from golden. Attorneys must use reasonable care to keep clients informed of all material matters and, under certain circumstances, the duty of disclosure is considerably more demanding and sometimes calls for "absolute and perfect candor." *See* Vincent R. Johnson, *"Absolute and Perfect Candor" to Clients*, 34 St. Mary's L.J. 737 (2003).

3. Statements of Opinion, Prediction, Intention, and Law

It is sometimes said that deceit claims cannot be based on a defendant's expression of an "opinion," as distinct from a statement of "fact." As the following opinion shows, this is an overstatement.

Oltmer v. Zamora

Appellate Court of Illinois
418 N.E.2d 506 (Ill. App. Ct. 1981)

GREEN, Justice.

. . . .

Plaintiffs were a married couple who moved from Independence, Missouri, to the Decatur area. Wishing to buy a home in that area, they contacted the defendant Drobisch firm, who sent their agent, defendant Jones, to plaintiffs. She showed plaintiffs several houses and they eventually purchased one of these homes, that house built and owned by the defendants Zamora. The undisputed evidence at trial showed the house to be 13 to 15 inches higher on its south side than on its north side. The evidence upon which the claim of misrepresentation was based was sharply disputed. Taken most favorably to plaintiffs, . . . it showed: (1) Juanita Jones was an aunt of Elaine M. Zamora but did not disclose this to plaintiffs; (2) Mrs. Jones disparaged several of the houses which she showed to plaintiffs; (3) Mrs. Jones told plaintiffs that Joseph B. Zamora who built the house was a "very reputable" builder and "one of the best in the area" although she knew he had never built any type of structure before; (4) Mrs. Jones had made several inspections of the house but when told by Mr. Oltmer, during the showing of the house, that he felt like he was "walking uphill," responded that could not be so because the house was new; and (5) when measurements confirmed the existence of the sloping nature of the house, Mrs. Jones suggested to plaintiffs that they attempt to sell it and implied that they do so without informing the purchasers of the problem.

. . . .

Defendants emphasize that [to be liable for the tort of misrepresentation] the representation must be as to matters of fact and not of opinion, citing Parker v. Arthur Murray, Inc. (1973), 10 Ill. App. 3d 1000, 295 N.E.2d 487. There, statements by dance hall proprietors to a customer that he had great potential as a dancer made for the purpose of inducing the customer to contract for lessons were as a matter of law held to be insufficiently factual to constitute the basis of fraud. However, we consider determination of whether a statement which might appear to be an opinion is nevertheless to be treated as a statement of fact is more complicated than *Parker* would indicate. The Restatement spoke to the question in the following manner:

Representation of Opinion Implying Justifying Facts

(1) A statement of opinion as to facts not disclosed and not otherwise known to the recipient may, if it is reasonable to do so, be interpreted by him as an implied statement

(a) that the facts known to the maker are not incompatible with his opinion; or

(b) that he knows facts sufficient to justify him in forming it.

(2) In determining whether a statement of opinion may reasonably be so interpreted, the recipient's belief as to whether the maker has an adverse interest is important.

Restatement (Second) of Torts §539 (1965).

The comments to the foregoing state in part...

a.... [W]hen land is bought as an investment, a statement, even by the vendor, that a tenant under a long term lease is a good tenant implies that his conduct has been such that it would not be entirely inappropriate to call him a good tenant. Such a representation is therefore fraudulent if the vendor knows that the tenant has rarely paid his rent except under pressure of legal proceedings, since the vendor is giving a materially false picture of the tenant's conduct.

....

c. The habit of vendors to exaggerate the advantages of the bargain that they are offering to make is a well recognized fact. An intending purchaser may not be justified in relying upon his vendor's statement of the value, quality or other advantages of a thing that he is intending to sell as carrying with it any assurance that the thing is such as to justify a reasonable man in praising it so highly. However, a purchaser is justified in assuming that even his vendor's opinion has some basis of fact and therefore in believing that the vendor knows of nothing which makes his opinion fantastic.

Professor Prosser appears to be in complete agreement. He states:

....There is quite general agreement that such an assertion is to be implied where the defendant holds himself out or is understood as having special knowledge of the matter which is not available to the plaintiff, so that his opinion becomes in effect an assertion summarizing his knowledge.

Prosser, Torts §109, at 726 (4th ed. 1971).

Under the theory of the cited text, a statement by Juanita Jones, that Joseph B. Zamora was a reputable builder who was one of the best in the area when he had never built a structure before the house involved here, would be the basis of a cause of action in misrepresentation. Under §539 of the Restatement (Second) of Torts, and under Prosser, her adverse interest and plaintiffs' unfamiliarity with Zamora, respectively, would be of substantial significance.

The decision in Bergman & Lefkow Insurance Agency v. Flash Cab Co. (1969), 110 Ill. App. 2d 415, 249 N.E.2d 729, is consistent with the texts. An insurance agent assured an official of a taxicab company that a particular insurance carrier was financially sound and capable of carrying their risk. The agent had an interest in the insurance carrier not revealed to the cab company official. Although the statement might appear to have been merely an opinion, it was held to have been a sufficient basis to support a jury determination of fraud after the carrier turned out to have been very unsound financially.... In *Bergman & Lefkow Insurance Agency*, the person making the statement had an undisclosed interest adverse to the recipient of the statement. Here there was evidence that Mrs. Jones had an undisclosed interest adverse to plaintiffs. In both cases the jury could have treated the statement in issue as one of fact.

As the tort of misrepresentation involves fraud, the party claiming fraud is required to prove that element by clear and convincing evidence but it may be proved by either direct or circumstantial evidence. [Citation.] That standard requires evidence stronger than that which merely predominates but does not require proof beyond a reasonable doubt. [Citation.] Whether to believe plaintiffs or Mrs. Jones as to whether she made the claimed statement as to Joseph B. Zamora's reputation as a builder was for the jury. Should the plaintiffs be believed, the jury could properly deem that evidence clear and convincing that Mrs. Jones made a misrepresentation that could be treated as one of fact. Such a determination would be supported by the circumstantial evidence that she (1) disparaged other houses, (2) sharply disagreed with Mr. Oltmer's mention of the possibility that the floor sloped, and (3) when the defect in the house was fully established, inferred to plaintiffs that they should attempt to sell the house without revealing the defect. We conclude that the jury could also have found the evidence to be clear and convincing that Mrs. Jones knew of Joseph B. Zamora's lack of previous experience or was culpably ignorant as to whether he had previous experience and that plaintiffs relied upon her statement in purchasing the house and would not have done so had they known of the defect.

....

Reversed and remanded for a new trial.

Notes

1. *"Puffing."* A common application of the rule that statements of opinion are not actionable concerns "puffing," or "sales talk." The salesperson who tells a customer that a Plymouth is "the best car on the market" has not committed a tort, even if she has just read an issue of Consumer Reports excoriating Chrysler cars in general and Plymouths in particular.

In Vulcan Metals Co. v. Simmons Mfg. Co., 248 F. 853 (2d Cir. 1918), the court held that a manufacturer's statements that vacuum cleaners were "absolutely perfect even in the smallest detail," "the most economical," and "simple, long-lived, easily operated and effective," and that "perfect satisfaction would result" were not actionable, even if the manufacturer knew that they were not true. The privilege to puff does not extend to specific factual claims, however; the *Vulcan Metals* court held that the plaintiff could recover because the defendant had falsely said that the vacuum cleaners in question had never before been offered for sale.

Similar principles appear in other areas of the law. *See* Pizza Hut, Inc. v. Papa John's Int'l, Inc., 227 F.3d 489 (5th Cir. 2000) (the phrase "better ingredients, better pizza," standing alone, was not actionable as unfair competition under the Lanham Act).

2. *Implicit Statements of Fact.* In addition to the discussion in *Oltmer*, see Crown Cork & Seal Co. v. Hires Bottling of Chicago, 371 F.2d 256 (7th Cir. 1967). The plaintiff in that case told the defendant's president that bottling equipment the defendant wanted to buy was "first class equipment," and that buying it would be a "very fine move." The defendant, seeking relief from its contractual obligations on the ground that the plaintiff's fraud had induced it to buy the equipment, claimed

that the equipment was so bad that the defendant could not use it. The court, reversing the District Court's grant of summary judgment to the plaintiff, held that the statements "implied, at least, an assertion of fact that the equipment was capable of producing Hires' goods in marketable condition." The result would have been different "[i]f the deficiency complained of were merely performance which compared unfavorably with other machines with respect to efficiency, economy, or quality of product...."

3. *Exceptions to the No-Reliance-on-Opinion Rule.* Aside from opinions which carry with them implicit statements of fact, a party may reasonably rely and act upon another's expression of opinion in several situations:

(a) *Opinions Stated as Existing Facts.* Where a party states an opinion in the form of an existing fact, the recipient is entitled to rely on the statement. For example, in Westby v. Gorsuch, 50 P.3d 284 (Wash. Ct. App. 2002), an antique dealer told a seller that a ticket from a survivor of the Titanic was worth $500. After purchasing the ticket, the dealer sold it for $100,000. The court affirmed a judgment for the seller, finding unpersuasive the dealer's argument that the misrepresentation did not relate to an existing fact.

Similarly, if a person advances an opinion not honestly or reasonably held, an action may lie. For example, a defendant who told his employees to quote modest figures for additional rent, knowing from several internal memoranda that those were not accurate figures, was held to have made an actionable misrepresentation. *See* Magnaleasing, Inc. v. Staten Is. Mall, 563 F.2d 567 (2d Cir. 1977).

(b) *Special Reasons to Expect Reliance.* Recovery has been allowed in certain cases in which the person expressing the opinion had special reason to expect that the recipient would rely upon the statement:

(i) *Mental Deficiency.* According to the Restatement, this rule has found its chief application where the recipient of the communication suffers from a known lack of intelligence, illiteracy, or unusual credulity or gullibility. One who deliberately seeks to take advantage of such special characteristics "cannot be heard to say that the reliance he sought to induce was not justified because his statement was one of opinion and therefore he should have been distrusted." Restatement, Second, of Torts §542 Comment i.

(ii) *Opinions of "Disinterested" Persons.* A different type of case in which there is special reason to expect reliance is where the one expressing the opinion holds itself out as being a disinterested party rather than an adversary. Courts have readily entertained such actions where the statement was made with the intent or expectation of inducing reliance. In Hanberry v. Hearst Corp., 81 Cal. Rptr. 519 (Ct. App. 1969), the plaintiff slipped and injured herself the first time she wore a new pair of shoes on a vinyl floor. The court permitted an action for negligent misrepresentation against the defendant, which had awarded the shoes its "Good Housekeeping seal of approval" and had said that it had satisfied itself that the products advertised in its magazine, including the shoes, were "good ones."

(iii) *Preventing Investigation.* If the defendant, after expressing an opinion, uses artifice or trickery to prevent further investigation, and so deprives the plaintiff of other sources of information, there is special reason to expect reliance and an action based on a statement of opinion will lie. *See* Garr v. Alden, 102 N.W. 950 (Mich. 1905) (sale of timber); Scheele v. Union Loan & Fin. Co., 274 N.W. 673 (Minn. 1937) (sale of stock).

(c) *Fiduciaries and Other Trusted Persons.* Mere statements of conclusion or opinion, upon which parties dealing at arm's length would not be justified in placing reliance, may give rise to a misrepresentation action if a confidential relationship exists. Such a relationship justifies trust and reliance by the plaintiff. This rule has found support in cases involving:

- Principal and agent: Rogers v. Brummet, 220 P. 362 (Okla. 1923);

- Attorney and client: Rice v. Press, 94 A.2d 397 (Vt. 1953);

- Partners: Teachout v. Van Hoesen, 40 N.W. 96 (Iowa 1878);

- Insurer and insured: Knox v. Anderson, 297 F.2d 702 (9th Cir. 1961);

- Family members: Collins v. Lindsay, 25 S.W.2d 84 (Mo. 1930);

- Close friends: Spiess v. Brandt, 41 N.W.2d 561 (Minn. 1950);

- Past business associates: Pulliam v. Gentry, 268 S.W. 557 (Ky. 1925); and

- Executor and beneficiary: Stephens v. Collison, 94 N.E. 664 (Ill. 1911).

In addition, reliance on opinion is permitted if the speaker has successfully secured the recipient's confidence by stressing common membership in a religious denomination, fraternal order, or social group, or the fact that they were born in the same locality. *See* Restatement, Second, of Torts §542 Comment h.

(d) *Opinions of Persons Purporting to Have Special Knowledge.* In many cases, neither party to a transaction has any business giving special weight to the other party's statements of opinion. For example, a major reason for not allowing deceit actions to be based on "puffing" is that the buyer should normally be as capable as the seller of forming an intelligent opinion about the goods in question. Indeed, buyers should ordinarily give more weight to their own opinions than to sellers' opinions, as buyers well know that sellers stand to profit by making sales, and so are not disinterested. The buyer who later claims to have relied on the seller's assurances that the product was "first rate" or "very good" may well be lying, or at least exaggerating the effect of the seller's representations. If, however, one of the parties to a proposed transaction claims plausibly to have special knowledge or other expertness, the non-expert party's claim to have relied on the other's opinions may be plausible.

In cases in which specialized knowledge or experience is essential to forming an accurate opinion, courts tend to allow a non-expert who relied on an expert's intentionally false representation of opinion to recover in deceit, even without a showing that the opinion impliedly stated facts. For example, according to the Restatement, a jeweler who falsely represents that a diamond is "of the first water" or an antique dealer who falsely claims that a modern imitation is a valuable antique have committed fraud. Restatement, Second, of Torts §542 Comment f. *Cf.* Marcus v. Zenith Travel, Inc., 577 N.Y.S.2d 820 (App. Div. 1991) (traveler stated an action against a travel agent for negligent misrepresentation based on the agent's assurances that a wholesaler would be able to deliver agreed-upon services, after traveler expressed concern over a number of last minute itinerary changes).

Adams v. Gillig

Court of Appeals of New York
92 N.E. 670 (N.Y. 1910)

[Defendant, the prospective buyer of some vacant land in an area devoted exclusively to single family houses, assured plaintiff, the seller, after being questioned, that he would build only single-family dwellings upon his land. The day following the sale, however, he engaged an architect to design a public automobile garage and within two weeks contracted for its erection.]

CHASE, J.

....

It is not claimed on this appeal that the defendant made promises which became a part of the contract, or that the deed could be reformed by including therein restrictive covenants. The rule in regard to including the entire agreement between the parties in the writing does not take away or detract from the general rule by which a contract can always be set aside for fraud affecting the transaction as to a material fact that is not promissory in its nature. Any statement of an existing fact material to the person to whom it is made that is false and known by the person making it to be false and which is made to induce the execution of a contract, and which does induce the contract, constitutes a fraud that will sustain an action to avoid the contract if the person making it is injured thereby.

We have in this case findings by the trial court sustained by the record, which show that the defendant purposely, intentionally, and falsely stated to the plaintiff that he desired to purchase a portion of her vacant lot for the purpose of building a dwelling or dwellings thereon. He must have known that if he thereby induced her to convey to him such portion of the lot and his intention to build a garage thereon was carried out, it would injure her.... The plaintiff relied upon the defendant's honesty and good faith in the purchase, and was apparently willing to take her chances of a subsequent change in his intention, or of his selling the lot to another whose intentions and purposes might be entirely different.

....

Intent is of vital importance in very many transactions.... The intent of a person is sometimes difficult to prove, but it is nevertheless a fact and a material and existing fact that must be ascertained in many cases, and, when ascertained, determines the rights of the parties to controversies. The intent of Gillig was a material existing fact in this case, and the plaintiff's reliance upon such fact induced her to enter into a contract that she would not otherwise have entered into. The effect of such false statement by the defendant of his intention cannot be cast aside as immaterial simply because it was possible for him in good faith to have changed his mind or to have sold the property to another who might have a different purpose relating thereto. As the defendant's intention was subject to change in good faith at any time, it was of uncertain value. It was, however, of some value. It was of sufficient value so that the plaintiff was willing to stand upon it and make the conveyance in reliance upon it....

.... We are of the opinion that the false statements made by the defendant of his intention should under the circumstances of this case be deemed to be a statement of a material, existing fact of which the court will lay hold for the purpose of defeating the wrong that would otherwise be consummated thereby....

....

The judgment should be affirmed, with costs.

Notes

1. *Statements of Intention.* In addition to *Adams*, see Graubard Mollen Dannett & Horowitz v. Moskovitz, 653 N.E.2d 1179 (N.Y. 1995) (a law firm stated a claim by alleg-

ing that the defendant attorney "represented orally to the partnership that he...would act to ensure the future of the firm...when he never intended to do so and indeed was even considering the formation of a new partnership").

2. *Prediction versus Intention.* In McElrath v. Electric Inv. Co., 131 N.W. 380 (Minn. 1911), a summer hotel was leased to the plaintiff. The court held that a deceit action could not be based on an assertion by the defendant that the property "would become an important summer resort," for that prediction rested wholly on conjecture and speculation. But the defendant's representation that a local traction company intended to extend its line past the property was held actionable. What result if the defendant, knowing that the traction company was quite unlikely to extend its line, had predicted that the line would be extended, rather than claiming that the company intended to extend it? Is it possible to make a prediction without at the same time expressing an opinion as to the subject under consideration?

3. *Prediction versus Present Status.* In McConkey v. AON Corp., 804 A.2d 572 (N.J. App. Div. 2002), the plaintiff sued a company for fraudulently inducing him to leave his former employment by making misstatements that the company was not currently engaged in discussions that could result in a merger or other business combination. Shortly after joining the company, the plaintiff lost his job because of a reduction in force that followed the acquisition of the company by another entity. Finding for the plaintiff, the court noted that, by making inquiries into rumors, he was not asking about "future possibilities concerning the restructuring of the company, but was asking...about the present status of the company."

National Conversion Corp. v. Cedar Building Corp.
Court of Appeals of New York.
246 N.E.2d 351 (N.Y. 1969)

BREITEL, Judge.

A former tenant of industrial premises sued its landlords for damages in fraud and for breach of warranty. The landlords counterclaimed for subsequent rents and for use and occupation, and also brought a summary proceeding to recover possession which was consolidated with this action. After a trial without a jury the tenant recovered a judgment for $70,086.81 and defendant landlords appeal, the Appellate Division having affirmed, two Justices dissenting.

There is no dispute that the lease contained a false representation that the demised premises were situated in an unrestricted zone....

. . . .

True, both sides were represented by lawyers. But tenant's testimony is that when it sought an adjournment of the negotiations in order for its lawyer to check whether the premises were located in an unrestricted zone, landlords' lawyer, who was also one of the principals, said that it would not be necessary, that they (landlords) "own the property, and we know the area," that it is in an unrestricted zone, and "We [landlords] guarantee it."....The discussion was resolved only by including the representation in the lease. Tenant contended and proved that it had not actually known of the zoning requirement and had relied on what it was told. This proof, if accepted..., made out a classic instance of fraud in the inducement, for landlords intentionally or recklessly made false representations either as to their knowledge of the facts or the facts themselves....

....

Landlords...contend that only a misrepresentation of law rather than of fact is involved and, therefore, that fraud will not lie. There is no longer any doubt that the law has recognized, even in this State, a sharp distinction between a pure opinion of law which may not, except in unusual circumstances, base an action in tort, and a mixed statement of fact as to what the law is or whether it is applicable....

Most important it is that the law has outgrown the over-simple dichotomy between law and fact in the resolution of issues in deceit. It has been said that "a statement as to the law, like a statement as to anything else, may be intended and understood either as one of fact or one of opinion only, according to the circumstances of the case" (Prosser, op. cit., p. 741). The statements in this case, both before the execution of the lease, and in the body of the lease, exemplify ideally an instance in which the statements are not intended or understood merely as an expression of opinion. Landlords said they knew the premises were in an unrestricted district. This meant that they knew, as a fact, that the zoning resolution did not restrict the use of the particular premises, and tenant so understood it. When coupled with the further fact that tenant's lawyer was persuaded not to verify the status of the premises on the landlords' representation, it is equally clear that tenant understood the statement to be one of fact, namely, what the zoning resolution provided by description, map, and requirements as to the area in question. The misrepresented fact, if it is at all necessary to find misrepresented facts, was what the zoning resolution contained by way of description, map, and requirements, hardly opinions as to the law albeit matters to be found in a law.

....."No presumption exists that all men know the law. The maxim 'a man is presumed to know the law,' is a trite, sententious saying, 'by no means universally true.'.... If ignorance of the law did not in fact exist, we would not have lawyers to advise and courts to decide what the law is."...[I]n the proper circumstances there may indeed be reliance on a fraudulently expressed statement of the law. Arguably, the facts of this case do not require so great a reach, for here the statements were keyed to the underlying data (facts) upon which the applicability of the particular zoning provisions governing the rights of owners and users were to be determined (the law). But, for the reasons indicated, it is not necessary to make the distinction rest on so narrow an analysis.

....

[The discussion of the remaining issues is omitted.]

Accordingly, the order of the Appellate Division should be affirmed, with costs.

Note

1. *Statements about Law and Legality.* The general rule is that an action for misrepresentation cannot be predicated upon statements of law, that is, statements relating to what the law is, what effect it has, or what varieties of conduct are, or are not, legal. The original reasoning underlying this rule seems to have been that because everyone is presumed to know the law, another's statements as to these matters are mere expressions of opinion. *See* Fields v. Life & Casualty Ins. Co. of Tenn., 349 F. Supp. 612 (E.D. Ky. 1972); *see also* Bank of Loretto v. Bobo, 67 So. 2d 77 (Ala. Ct. App. 1953) (opining that the rule is based on the criminal law doctrine that ignorance of the law excuses no one, and that this principle was implanted into civil law in 1802 for no better reason than that plaintiff's counsel could cite no case to the contrary). Today, the general rule has been exten-

sively eviscerated. Of course, even if a statement of law is treated as one of fact, the plaintiff may not rely on the statement if the plaintiff knows that the law is otherwise.

Among the exceptions to the rule denying recovery for reliance on statements of law are the following:

(a) *Statements Intended as Fact.* Courts permit an action for misrepresentation to be predicated on a statement of law intended and understood as an assertion of fact (*see National Conversion, supra*; Restatement, Second, of Torts §525 Comment d and §545 Comments a and b).

In Shafer v. Berger, 131 Cal. Rptr. 2d 777 (Cal. Ct. App. 2003), an attorney hired by an insurance company argued that his statement to a third party about limits on insurance coverage was not a representation of fact, but a non-actionable legal opinion. The court rejected that argument, reasoning that to allow counsel for an insurer to hoodwink the opposition into settling for less by deceiving them about the scope of coverage would seriously undermine the justice system.

(b) *Implicit Statements of Fact.* Actions are permitted for statements of law that carry with them false implicit statements of fact—a matter which depends to some degree on whether the recipient of the communication is familiar with the underlying facts. In Sorenson v. Gardner, 334 P.2d 471 (Or. 1959), the court allowed an action against the seller of a dwelling, who asserted that the house had been constructed in compliance with code requirements, such as those concerning plumbing, building materials, and the location and size of vents. The statement carried with it assertions as to underlying facts, for the recipients were unfamiliar with the relevant data. "[H]ad the plaintiffs been aware of these facts," the misrepresentation would not have been actionable.

Some statements imply that legislation or judge-made law does not exist on a specific subject. *See* Unger v. Eagle Fish Co., 56 N.Y.S.2d 265 (Sup. Ct.), *aff'd*, 58 N.Y.S.2d 332 (App. Div. 1945) (a statement that government authorities had not established any maximum price for fish).

The use of qualifying language may prevent an implicit statement of fact from arising from an expression of legal opinion. *See* Restatement, Second, of Torts §545 Comment d ("I think that my title to this land is good, but do not take my word for it").

(c) *Law of Other Jurisdictions.* Even those who believed that a person could be presumed to know the law never expected persons to know the law of jurisdictions other than their own. Misrepresentation actions may be based on statements concerning the law of states or countries in which the recipient neither resides nor regularly does business. *See* Firemen's Ins. Co. v. Jones, 431 S.W.2d 728 (Ark. 1968); Restatement, Second, of Torts §545 Comment e.

(d) *Actionable Statements of Opinion.* An action for misrepresentation may be based on a statement of law if the statement, though one of opinion, is made under circumstances which render an opinion actionable. *See* Ambrosino v. Rodman & Renshaw, Inc., 635 F. Supp. 968 (N.D. Ill. 1986) (misrepresentation by fiduciary).

4. "Justifiable Reliance"

Recovery for fraud will be allowed only to a plaintiff whose reliance on the statement in question was "justifiable." However, the plaintiff's reliance need not have been "reasonable." Many widely practiced forms of fraud depend for their success upon the victim's gullibility (and, often, greed). The victim who gives his life savings to a confidence trickster who claims to have discovered a way to turn lead into gold has behaved quite unreasonably, yet the defendant's talent for finding gullible victims hardly justifies letting the defendant keep the plaintiff's money.

If "justifiable" reliance need not be "reasonable," what sense is there in insisting that reliance be justifiable? At least part of the answer may be that the requirement serves to deny recovery to plaintiffs who may not in fact have relied at all; who may not even have been defrauded. In other words, "justifiable reliance" is a concept that may be most useful as a means of denying recovery to those whom the court suspects of not having been victims at all. The plaintiff whose story is unworthy of belief, who may be exaggerating or even making up misrepresentations to get out of a contract, is the sort of plaintiff likely to lose on "justifiable reliance" grounds. Consider, in this context, the following opinion, in which (1) the plaintiff's evidence of fraud contained a serious gap, and (2) the court held the plaintiff's reliance not to have been justifiable. Would the case have come out the same way if the court had been sure that the defendant's employee had really lied to the plaintiff?

Williams v. Rank & Son Buick, Inc.

Supreme Court of Wisconsin
170 N.W.2d 807 (Wis. 1969)

On March 19, 1968, respondent and his brother went to appellant's used car lot where they examined a 1964 Chrysler Imperial automobile. While doing so, they were approached by a salesman who permitted them to take the car for a test run. They drove the car for approximately one and one-half hours before returning the car to the appellant's lot. During that time they tested the car's general handling as well as its radio and power windows. According to the respondent, however, it was not until several days after he had purchased the car that he discovered that the knobs marked "AIR" were for ventilation and that the car was not air-conditioned.

At the trial the respondent testified that while examining the car he discussed its equipment with the salesman and was told that it was air-conditioned. He also testified that he relied upon both this representation and an advertisement which read:

> '64 CHRYSLER Imperial 2 door hardtop; silver mist with black vinyl interior; full power, including FACTORY AIR CONDITIONING; there aren't many around like this. See, drive, you'll buy...$1,599.

The appellant's salesman denied making any representations concerning air conditioning and testified that the only equipment discussed with the respondent was the car's vinyl roof. An examination of the record discloses that the advertisement introduced into evidence was dated March 21, 1968, whereas the sales contract signed by both parties was dated March 19, 1968.

Upon these facts the trial court found that the respondent had proven fraud on the part of the appellant and awarded him $150 in damages. The appellant appeals from a circuit court order affirming that judgment....

....

HANLEY, Justice.

....

This court has consistently held that the party alleging fraud has the burden of proving it by clear and convincing evidence....

....

.... [T]here is no question that the advertisement and the alleged oral representation of the salesman were false. The automobile in question was simply not equipped with air conditioning.

....

Appellant's counsel argues that there was no reliance by the respondent and that therefore there was no fraud....

The appellant argues that no reliance could possibly have been placed upon the ad because it did not appear in the newspaper until two days after the automobile was purchased. It is thus contended that the respondent seized upon the error in the ad to seek a reduction in the price previously paid for the automobile.

The respondent, on the other hand, argues that since he saw the ad before purchasing the car the ad must have run for several days prior to the purchase....

We cannot accept respondent's reasoning and are of the opinion that to infer that the ad ran prior to March 19, 1968, is unreasonable. Such evidence is certainly not clear and convincing. Had the ad in fact been placed prior to March 19, 1968, it would have been a simple matter to have introduced such ad, rather than resort to the strained logic now urged upon this court.

....

.... [As to the alleged oral misrepresentation:] Many previous decisions of this court have held that one cannot justifiably rely upon obviously false statements. In Jacobsen v. Whitely (1909), 138 Wis. 434, 436, 437, 120 N.W. 285, 286, the court said:

> .... It is an unsavory defense for a man who by false statements, induces another to act to assert that if the latter had disbelieved him he would not have been injured.... Nevertheless courts will refuse to act for the relief of one claiming to have been misled by another's statements who blindly acts in disregard of knowledge of their falsity or with such opportunity that by the exercise of ordinary observation, not necessarily by search, he would have known. He may not close his eyes to what is obviously discoverable by him....

....

The question is thus whether the statement's falsity could have been detected by ordinary observation....

....

.... The respondent specifically testified that, being a high school graduate, he was capable of both reading and writing. It is also fair to assume that he possessed a degree of business acumen in that he and his brother operated their own business. No fiduciary relationship existed between the parties. They dealt with each other at arms' length. The appellant made no effort to interfere with the respondent's examination of the car, but, on the contrary, allowed him to take the car from the premises for a period of one and one-half hours.

Although the obviousness of a statement's falsity is a question of fact, this court has decided some such questions as a matter of law....

....

No great search was required to disclose the absence of the air conditioning unit since a mere flip of a knob was all that was necessary. If air conditioning was, as stated by the respondent, the main reason he purchased the car, it is doubtful that he would not try the air conditioner.

> It seems plain that, whether the representation in question was made, the [respondent] failed to exercise that care for [his] own protection which was easily within [his] power to exercise, and, under all the circumstances, [he] was not justified in relying upon such a representation, if made. [Citation.]

We conclude that as a matter of law the respondent under the facts and circumstances was not justified in relying upon the oral representation of the salesman....

....

Order reversed.

[The dissenting opinion of Justice WILKIE is omitted.]

Notes

1. *Reliance on Assurances.* Ordinarily, if the defendant makes an affirmative representation, the plaintiff may rely upon its truth and need not investigate, so long as the statement is not obviously false and there are no danger signals calling for inquiry. For example, in Judd v. Walker, 114 S.W. 979 (Mo. 1908), the court held that plaintiff could rely upon the defendant's definite statement as to the acreage of land and was not required to measure the property himself, noting that one need not deal "with [one's] fellow man as if he was a thief or a robber." Similarly, in Fire Ins. Exch. v. Bell, 643 N.E.2d 310 (Ind. 1994), the court found that a victim's attorney had a right to rely on allegedly fraudulent representations made by the liability insurer's attorney that misrepresented policy limits during settlement negotiations.

One possible reading of *Williams* is that a statement that can be checked by the slightest effort — the mere flip of a switch — will be treated as equivalent to a falsehood so obvious that it cannot be actionable. The Restatement suggests that cases like *Williams* should not be read more broadly, for the general rule permitting reliance on another's affirmative statement "applies not only when an investigation would involve an expenditure of effort and money out of proportion to the magnitude of the transaction, but also when it could be made without any considerable trouble or expense." Restatement, Second, of Torts §540 Comment a.

2. *Reliance by Sophisticated Entities.* Most courts hold that the rule a person may rely upon express assurances applies to sophisticated entities, as well as to those less able to protect their own interests. *See* Williams Ford, Inc. v. Hartford Courant Co., 657 A.2d 212 (Conn. 1995) (holding that a claim for negligent misrepresentation can exist between two sophisticated commercial parties with full access to information concerning a business transaction; reliance was a question of fact); Vmark Software, Inc. v. EMC Corp., 642 N.E.2d 587, 595 n. 11 (Mass. Ct. App. 1994) (computer software licensor and licensee). However, there is authority to the contrary. In Lazard Freres & Co. v. Protective Life Ins. Co., 108 F.3d 1531 (2d Cir. 1997), Judge Guido Calabresi wrote:

> According to Protective...Lazard set the whole deal up in such a way that Protective had to rely on Lazard's representations and had to commit itself to purchase the MCC bank debt before it had the opportunity to examine the Scheme Report. It would therefore appear that Protective might have been justified in relying on Lazard's alleged misrepresentations when it orally committed itself to purchase the MCC bank debt....

This conclusion, nevertheless, seems to us to be too simple. As a substantial and sophisticated player in the bank debt market, Protective was under a further duty to protect itself from misrepresentation. It could easily have done so by insisting on an examination of the Scheme Report as a condition of closing. [Citation.]

> [W]here...a party has been put on notice of the existence of material facts which have not been documented and he nevertheless proceeds with a transaction without securing the available documentation or inserting appropriate language in the agreement for his protection, he may truly be said to have willingly assumed the business risk that the facts may not be as represented. Succinctly put, a party will not be heard to complain that he has been defrauded when it is his own evident lack of due care which is responsible for his predicament.

[Citation.] We believe that the failure to insert such language into the contract—by itself—renders reliance on the misrepresentation unreasonable as a matter of law.

3. *Danger Signals Requiring Investigation or Action.* In Greycas, Inc. v. Proud, 826 F.2d 1560 (7th Cir. 1987), a finance company required the applicant for a loan to supply an opinion letter from an attorney containing assurances that there were no prior liens on the machinery that was to secure the loan. The court held that the company could rely upon the attorney's assurances, even though it would not have been hard for it to conduct its own UCC lien search. However, had the opinion letter disclosed the fact that the attorney was the brother-in-law of the loan applicant, that "might have been a warning signal that [the finance company]...could ignore only at its peril."

In Sippy v. Cristich, 609 P.2d 204 (Kan. Ct. App. 1980), water stains on the floor and ceiling of a house clearly suggested that the roof leaked. When the buyers inquired, they were repeatedly assured that the stains antedated appropriate repairs to the roof. Since an inspection of the roof would not easily have revealed whether a leak still existed, the buyer's were justified in their reliance.

4. *Documentary Disclaimers of Reliance.* What if there is language in a contract, order form, or other document stating that the buyer does not rely upon any representations made by the seller? Some courts have held that this language does not automatically preclude an action, but is only one factor for the jury to consider on the reliance issue. *See* First Nat'l Bank v. Brooks Farms, 821 S.W.2d 925 (Tenn. 1991) (imposing liability despite disclaimer). Other courts hold that a cause of action is barred, unless the disclaimer clause relates to matters peculiarly within the knowledge of the seller. *See* Danann Realty Corp. v. Harris, 157 N.E.2d 597 (N.Y. 1959) (applying general rule); *cf.* Yurish v. Sportini, 507 N.Y.S.2d 234 (App. Div. 1986) (applying exception). Should it make a difference whether the disclaimer consists of a "boilerplate" recitation, as opposed to specifically negotiated language? Should the effect of the provision turn upon whether it specifically addresses the matter in issue or is general in nature? What if the plaintiff is a sophisticated commercial entity? Does it make a difference that the language is drafted by the plaintiff, rather than the defendant? *See* Mehaffy, Rider, Windholz & Wilson v. Central Denver Bk., N.A., 892 P.2d 230 (Colo. 1995) (issues of fact existed as to whether "comfort letters" issued by the plaintiff bank disclaimed the bank's reliance on the defendant attorneys' opinion letters).

5. *Comparative Negligence.* If the misrepresentation is intentional, comparative negligence is no defense to an action for deceit.

6. *Time Sequence.* It is important to consider the sequence of events, for detrimental
action that precedes a misstatement obviously was not caused by the misstatement. *See*
Wrights v. Red River Fed. Cr. U., 71 S.W.3d 916, 920 (Tex. App. 2002) (where repair
work was completed four months before a letter was written, the repairs could not have
been done based on any representations in the letter).

7. *No Reliance on Falsity.* A party who has learned that a representation is false cannot rely upon it and then sue for misrepresentation. *See* Richter v. Wagner Oil Co., 90
S.W.3d 890, 896 (Tex. App. 2002).

B. Negligence and Strict Liability

1. Negligence Causing Purely Economic Harm

In the famous case of Derry v. Peek, 14 A.C. 337 (1889), the House of Lords held
that defendants who honestly but unreasonably believed that certain statements they
had made in a prospectus were true were not liable in deceit to those who bought stock
in reliance on those statements. Cases like *Derry* raise the question of whether liability
should extend to situations in which the defendant acts negligently, rather than with
scienter.

In Business Transactions. Most American jurisdictions now allow some actions for
negligent misrepresentation, but only in limited circumstances. The Restatement, for
instance, limits actions for purely economic loss (as opposed to personal injury or
property damage) to cases involving the furnishing of "false information for the
guidance of others in their business transactions," and also says that liability may be
imposed only on those who have a "pecuniary interest" in the transaction in question. *See* Restatement, Second, of Torts §552. Under this approach, someone who
made a careless mistake in passing information to a friend would not be liable if the
friend suffered losses in reliance on the statement. However, an accountant hired to
examine the books of someone proposing to borrow money from the accountant's
client would certainly be liable to the client for negligently misrepresenting the borrower's financial condition. (Whether the accountant would be liable to persons
other than the client who relied on the misstatements will be examined in the next
section.)

In Robinson v. Omer, 952 S.W.2d 423 (Tenn. 1997), an individual who claimed that
he had gotten into trouble after being assured by a friend's lawyer that it was perfectly
legal to videotape the friend's sexual encounters without the consent of the women involved had no claim against the lawyer for negligent misrepresentation. The misinformation was not supplied "for the guidance of others in their business transactions."

For the Benefit of the Recipient. Another example of the reluctance of courts to recognize negligent misrepresentation actions for purely economic harm is Conway v. Pacific Univ., 924 P.2d 818, 824 (Or. 1996). There, a professor brought a negligent misrepresentation action against a university based on the university's alleged assurances that
poor student evaluations would not affect the professor's prospects for attaining tenure.

The court held that the university did not owe a duty to avoid making negligent misrepresentations to the professor:

> [One] way to characterize the types of relationships in which a heightened duty of care exists is that the party who owes the duty has a special responsibility toward the other party. This is so because the party who is owed the duty effectively has authorized the party who owes the duty to exercise independent judgment in the former party's behalf and in the former party's interests. In doing so, the party who is owed the duty is placed in a position of reliance upon the party who owes the duty; that is, because the former has given responsibility and control over the situation at issue to the latter, the former has a right to rely upon the latter to achieve a desired outcome or resolution.
>
> ....
>
> When compared to the types of relationships in which one party has a special responsibility toward the other, however, the relationship between Conway and Pacific University...falls short. Conway did not authorize the university to exercise independent judgment in his behalf, by contract or otherwise, thereby placing him in the position of having a right to rely upon the university. Indeed, at the time of the misrepresentations, both parties were acting in their *own* behalf, each for their own benefit, for the purpose of negotiating a renewal of Conway's contract. In that context, then, the university did not have a special responsibility toward Conway to exercise independent judgment in his behalf and to administer, oversee, or otherwise take care of any of his affairs. Consequently, the parties were not in a special relationship giving rise to a duty of care on the university's part to avoid making negligent misrepresentations to Conway.

Silence versus Affirmative Misstatement. Can silence form the basis for a negligent-misrepresentation action or must there be an affirmative misstatement? Suppose, for example, that a law firm fails to tell its client that the client is doing business with a person who was previously convicted and imprisoned for embezzlement in a case involving a similar transaction. Surely, if the firm knows of the prior felony, it must disclose that information to its client and may be sued for deceit to recover resulting damages, if it fails to do so. But what if the firm does not know, but through the exercise of reasonable care should know, of the prior felony conviction, and fails to make disclosure? Can the firm be sued for negligent misrepresentation?

Some authorities, including Restatement, Second of Torts §552, speak of liability for negligently providing "false information," and thus seem to suggest that there must be some affirmative misstatement. *See also* McCamish, Martin, Brown & Loeffler v. F.E. Appling Interests, 991 S.W.2d 787 (Tex. 1999) (holding that attorneys could be sued for negligently stating that a settlement agreement would be enforceable against the FSLIC). However, other language in the Restatement indicates that, for purposes of misrepresentation, there is no difference between misleading silence and a false statement. For example, Restatement, Second of Torts §551 says that:

> One who fails to disclose to another a fact that he knows may justifiably induce the other to act or to refrain from acting in a business transaction is subject to the same liability to the other as though he had represented the nonexistence of the matter that he has failed to disclose....

This suggests that negligent non-disclosure is actionable, and there is authority that so holds. *See* Agrobiotech, Inc. v. Budd, 2003 WL 22699789 (D. Nev.) ("Pursuant to §551, silence about material facts basic to the transaction, when combined with a duty to speak, is the functional equivalent of a misrepresentation or 'supplying false information' under Restatement § 552").

Measure of Damages. Negligent misrepresentation may also be a narrower cause of action than fraud with respect to the measure of damages. For example, damages may be limited to out-of-pocket losses (as opposed to the benefit-of-the-bargain measure appropriate for fraud[b]). *See* D.S.A., Inc. v. Hillsboro Indep. Sch. Dist., 973 S.W.2d 662 (Tex. 1998).

Comparative Negligence. The plaintiff's negligence will reduce or eliminate liability that is based on negligence, rather than deceit. *See* Gilchrist Timber Co. v. ITT Rayonier, Inc., 696 So. 2d 334 (Fla. 1997). In a suit involving negligent misstatements about zoning restrictions, the *Gilchrist* court held that the plaintiff's comparative negligence was relevant and that it was appropriate to take into account whether the buyer negligently failed to convey to the seller its intent to subdivide the property for residential use and failed to verify the zoning classification set forth in a year-old appraisal contained in materials furnished by the seller.

2. Negligence Causing Physical Harm

If a negligent misrepresentation leads to personal injury or property damage, rather than to the pecuniary loss typical of misrepresentation, the limits discussed above do not come into play. Cases such as that in which a driver "misrepresents" the safety of the road ahead by waving the plaintiff across the street into traffic are probably best viewed as routine negligence cases, not as misrepresentation cases, even though the negligence does involve a misrepresentation.

3. Strict Liability

A handful of cases allow some plaintiffs to recover for misrepresentations on a strict-liability basis. Here is an example.

---

b. Under the benefit-of-the-bargain rule (sometimes called the "contract rule"), the plaintiff receives the difference between the value of the item if it had been as promised and the value of the item as it was received; under the out-of-pocket rule (sometimes called the "tort rule"), damages are measured by subtracting the value of the item received from the amount paid by the plaintiff.

Regardless of which rule is applied in calculating pecuniary damages, consequential damages may also be recovered for such related losses as physical injury, property damage, harm to reputation, or the costs of completing a project or remedying a problem. *See* Vmark Software, Inc. EMC Corp., 642 N.E.2d 587 (Mass. Ct. App. 1994) (licensee of misrepresented computer software was entitled to all damages it had suffered as a proximate result, including the cost of computer equipment which it would not have purchased but for the licensor's misleading representations and the cost of hours fruitlessly spent by the licensee's employees trying to make the defective computer system work).

Some courts permit the recovery of emotional distress damages, if that kind of harm was reasonably foreseeable. *See* Kilduff v. Adams, Inc., 593 A.2d 478 (Conn. 1991).

Richard v. A. Waldman and Sons, Inc.

Supreme Court of Connecticut
232 A.2d 307 (Conn. 1967)

COTTER, Associate Justice.

....

The parties, by written agreement, contracted for the sale and purchase of a lot together with a building....Nine days after the execution of the agreement, the defendant conveyed the real estate to the plaintiffs by warranty deed containing the usual covenants against encumbrances, except those mentioned in the deed, and thereupon the plaintiffs took possession of the property.

At the time of the closing, the defendant delivered to the plaintiffs a plot plan prepared by a registered engineer and land surveyor. This plan showed a sideyard of twenty feet on the southerly boundary of the lot which was in compliance with the minimum requirements for this lot according to the zoning regulations....A permit had previously been granted for the construction of the building...and the survey submitted at the time the defendant made the application indicated that the structure was to be located twenty feet more or less from the southerly property line. Subsequently, a certificate of occupancy was erroneously issued based on the survey submitted by the defendant. Approximately four months after the delivery of the deed to the plaintiffs, the defendant discovered, when it set pins defining the boundaries of the premises, that the southeast corner of the foundation of the plaintiffs' house was only 1.8 feet from the southerly boundary of the lot. At this time, it was found that trespass upon adjoining property occurred in entering and leaving the plaintiffs' back door and stoop. Prior to this discovery, the parties were unaware that there was a violation of the zoning regulations as to sideyard requirements....

....

The defendant claims that "[a]t most, there was an innocent misrepresentation of fact by the defendant." An innocent misrepresentation may be actionable if the declarant has the means of knowing, ought to know, or has the duty of knowing the truth. 23 Am. Jur. 920, Fraud and Deceit, §127.

...[T]he plaintiffs had reasonable grounds upon which to attribute to the defendant accurate knowledge of what it represented as to the location of the structure on the lot. This was a statement of fact about which the defendant, as a developer of residential real estate, had special means of knowledge, and it was a matter peculiarly relating to its business and one on which the plaintiffs were entitled to rely. [Citations.] The defendant was commercially involved in and responsible for the preliminary and final plans for building and locating the structure which was then constructed on the lot by the defendant in a manner which violated the zoning ordinance. Thereafter, the defendant undertook to provide the plaintiffs with a survey and plot plan which erroneously showed a southerly sideyard of twenty feet. Actual knowledge of the falsity of the representation need not be shown under the circumstances, nor must the plaintiffs allege fraud or bad faith. They have alleged all the facts material to support their claim and demand for damages. It is immaterial whether the wrong which can be legally inferred from the facts arises in contract or in tort. The plaintiffs may seek damages resulting from the defendant's misrepresentation and at the same time retain title to the property....It would be unjust to permit the defendant under these circumstances to "retain the fruits of a bargain induced by" a material misrepresentation upon which the plaintiffs relied. [Citations.]

. . . .

There is no error.

In this opinion the other judges concurred.

Notes

1. *Misrepresentations in Sale, Rental, or Exchange Transactions.* The cases imposing strict liability for inaccurate statements of fact typically involve defendants who sold or leased property. *Cf.* Gibson v. Campano, 699 A.2d 68 (Conn. 1997) (disclaimer clause in the real estate contract barred innocent misrepresentation claim relating to termite damage). However, the Restatement, Second, of Torts §552C describes the rule as applying more broadly to "sale, rental or exchange transaction[s]." In some states, a result similar to strict tort liability is achieved by statute. *See, e.g.,* Tex. Bus. & Com. Code Ann. §27.01 (Westlaw 2003) (dispensing with the need to prove scienter in real-estate and stock transactions). As the defendant's misrepresentation of a material fact would allow the plaintiff to rescind the contract in question, the major benefit to plaintiffs of allowing an action "in tort" is to let them keep the property and recover their losses as damages. According to the Restatement, damages are limited to the difference between what the plaintiff gave up and what the plaintiff got in exchange; Restatement, Second, of Torts §552C(2). The principle at work here is that of preventing the defendant's misrepresentations, even though entirely innocent, from enriching the defendant at the plaintiff's expense. Suppose that *A*, relying on a misrepresentation made by *B*, buys property at an inflated price from *C*. If the misrepresentation was fraudulent, *A* could recover from *B*. If it was negligent, *A* could recover from *B* if *B* had a financial interest in the transaction. If it was entirely innocent, *A* could not recover from *B*.

2. *Misrepresentations about Products.* Another example of liability for innocent misrepresentation is found in the products-liability provisions of the Restatement. Under §402B of the Restatement, Second, of Torts, which has been adopted in several jurisdictions, a seller of goods who, by advertising, labeling, or otherwise, misrepresents to the public a material fact is strictly liable to a consumer for physical injury caused by the erroneous statement. Thus, a seller who incorrectly says that a shampoo is safe for use on hair, that glass is shatterproof, or that rope has a certain strength, will be liable for physical injuries resulting to one who could reasonably have been expected to use the product, even though the victim was not the purchaser of the item and the statement was not made intentionally, recklessly, or negligently.

See Ladd v. Honda Motor Co., Ltd., 939 S.W.2d 83 (Tenn. Ct. App. 1996) (in an action by a boy who became paralyzed when he lost control of an all-terrain vehicle, the court held that a manufacturer's advertisements for an entire product line, and not solely for model of ATV used by the plaintiff, could provide a basis for liability based on innocent misrepresentation); Crocker v. Winthrop Labs., 514 S.W.2d 429, 432-33 (Tex. 1974) (holding drug manufacturer liable under §402B for misrepresenting that the drug "was free and safe from all dangers of addiction").

Under the formulation in the second Restatement, liability is limited to physical harm to a person or property and does not extend to economic loss. A tentative draft of the second Restatement also contained a rule paralleling §402B which, under similar circumstances (misrepresentation by "advertising, labels, or otherwise"), would have imposed strict liability for resulting pecuniary losses. The restaters declined to include that rule (§552D) in the final version of the Restatement, Second, of Torts, expressing the view that any such liability was essentially contractual, rather than tortious, in nature. No state ever adopted proposed §552D, except Tennessee, and the rule has since been repudiated in that jurisdiction. *See* First Nat'l Bank v. Brooks Farms, 821 S.W.2d 925 (Tenn. 1991).

As a model, §402B of the second Restatement has now been replaced:

RESTATEMENT, THIRD, OF PRODUCTS LIABILITY §9 (1998)
Liability of Commercial Product Seller or Distributor
for Harm Caused by Misrepresentation

One engaged in the business of selling or otherwise distributing products who, in connection with the sale of a product, makes a fraudulent, negligent, or innocent misrepresentation of material fact concerning the product is subject to liability for harm to persons or property caused by the misrepresentation.

C. Liability to Third Parties

Misleading statements made orally are capable of endless repetition, and those embodied in documents may reach many readers. Consequently, it is important to ask which recipients of a statement have a right to sue if they detrimentally rely upon its content. Beyond the class of persons who the defendant knew would receive and rely upon the statement, the scope of liability is uncertain.

A person who intentionally or recklessly perpetrates a fraud will probably be liable to anyone who suffers losses as a proximate cause of that fraud. That is, in many states, the scope of liability for deceit is defined by foreseeability. *See, e.g.*, Bily v. Arthur Young & Co., 834 P.2d 745, 773 (Cal. 1992) (liability for deceit extends to the class of persons "whom defendant intended or reasonably should have foreseen would rely upon the representation").

Note, however, that some courts have gone to great lengths to indicate that foreseeable reliance is not sufficient to allow a third party to sue for fraud, and that something more is required. *See* Ernst & Young, L.L.P. v. Pac. Mut. Life Ins. Co., 51 S.W.3d 573 (Tex. 2001) (embracing a reason-to-expect reliance standard that requires more than foreseeability). *Cf.* Restatement, Second, of Torts §533 and Comment d ("[I]t is not enough…that the maker of the misrepresentation does recognize, or should recognize, the possibility that the third person to whom he makes it may repeat it for the purpose of influencing the conduct of another. He must…have information that gives him special reason to expect that it will be communicated to others"); Varwig v. Anderson-Behel Porsche/Audi, Inc., 141 Cal. Rptr. 539 (Ct. App. 1977) (sales tax exemption certificate gave seller special reason to know that car would be resold to a consumer).

There is ordinarily no liability to a third person for fraud if the misrepresentation never reaches the third person, because in that case there has been no reliance. *See* Marshall v. Kusch, 84 S.W.3d 781 (Tex. App. 2002) (holding that, because no one told the ultimate purchaser of land that there was no anthrax on the property, the original vendor was not liable to the ultimate purchaser for fraud, even though the vendor had made such a statement to the intermediate purchaser).

Cases involving negligent misrepresentation, rather than deceit, pose an increased risk of imposing liability disproportionate to fault if the class of potential plaintiffs is broad. Consequently, recovery by third parties for negligent misrepresentation has often been much more limited than for misrepresentations intentionally or recklessly made. For purposes of analysis, a distinction should be drawn based on whether or not the negligent statement produces physical harm. If so, liability extends to all foreseeable plaintiffs. *See* Randi W. v. Muroc Jt. Unified Sch. Dist., 929 P.2d 582 (Cal. 1997) (student who was sexually molested was not required to allege that she relied upon the defendant's misrepresentations in a letter of recommendation, but only that her injuries resulted from actions taken by the recipient of the letter in reliance on its contents); Restatement, Second, of Torts §311. In contrast, if purely economic loss (rather than personal injury or property damage) is at issue, different rules apply.

Jaillet v. Cashman

Court of Appeals of New York
139 N.E. 714 (N.Y. 1923)

Appeal, by permission, from a judgment of the Appellate Division of the Supreme Court…, unanimously affirming a judgment in favor of defendant entered upon an order of Special Term sustaining a demurrer to the complaint and granting defendant's motion for judgment on the pleadings. The complaint alleged in substance that the defendant, an unincorporated association, negligently published on its tickers the erroneous report that the United States Supreme Court had decided that stock dividends constituted taxable income; that the plaintiff, a customer in a broker's office having ticker service, believing that this report would depress the value of securities, sold some of his own stock and sold "short" other stock which he did not own; that as a matter of fact the Supreme Court had decided that stock dividends were not taxable, and the defendant corrected its false report 45 minutes after it had been issued; that before this correction the stock market had reacted, and the appellant suffered damages. The Special Term held that the relation of defendant to the public was the same as that of a publisher of a newspaper and that it had no contract or fiduciary relationship for an unintentional mistake in its report.

PER CURIAM. Judgment affirmed, with costs.

Note

1. *"Losses" Involving the Purchase and Sale of Securities.* The plaintiff in *Jaillet* sought damages because he had sold his securities more cheaply than if he (and others) had known the true state of affairs. Note that, for every seller who suffered that kind of loss, someone else (the buyer) had a corresponding gain. If recovery were allowed to every seller, the amount of damages the defendant would have to pay would be considerably more than the total harm caused by the defendant's negligence. This feature distinguishes many "losses" in securities cases from such losses as personal injuries and property damage. When a $1,000,000 building is destroyed, or when an accident victim loses a leg, the world as a whole is poorer by $1,000,000 or one leg. But when someone's negligence causes *A* to lose and *B* to gain $1,000,000, society as a whole is plainly not poorer by $1,000,000. Holding negligent defendants liable for all of the sellers' losses in cases like this, while ignoring the buyers' gains, would over-deter negligence. *See generally* Frank H. Easterbrook & Daniel R. Fischel, *Optimal Damages in Securities Cases*, 52 U. Chi. L. Rev. 611 (1985).

Credit Alliance Corporation v. Arthur Andersen & Co.

Court of Appeals of New York
483 N.E.2d 110 (N.Y. 1985)

JASEN, Judge.

The critical issue common to these two appeals is whether an accountant may be held liable, absent privity of contract, to a party who relies to his detriment upon a negligently prepared financial report and, if so, within what limits does that liability extend.

I

In...["*Credit Alliance*"], plaintiffs are major financial service companies engaged primarily in financing the purchase of capital equipment through installment sales or leasing agreements. Defendant, Arthur Andersen & Co. ("Andersen"), is a national accounting firm. Plaintiffs' complaint and affidavit allege that prior to 1978, plaintiffs had provided financing to L.B. Smith of Virginia ("Smith"), a capital intensive enterprise that regularly required financing. During 1978, plaintiffs advised Smith that as a condition to extending additional major financing, they would insist upon examining an audited financial statement. Accordingly, Smith provided plaintiffs with its consolidated financial statements, covering both itself and its subsidiaries, "For The Years Ended December 31, 1977 and 1976" (the "1977 statements"). These statements contained an auditor's report prepared by Andersen stating that it had examined the statements in accordance with generally accepted auditing standards ("GAAS") and found them to reflect fairly the financial position of Smith in conformity with generally accepted accounting principles ("GAAP"). In reliance upon the 1977 statements, plaintiffs provided substantial amounts in financing to Smith.... [I]n 1979, as a precondition to continued financing, plaintiffs requested and received from Smith the consolidated financial statements "For the Years Ended February 28, 1979 and December 31, 1977" (the "1979 statements"). Again, Andersen's report vouched for its examination of the financial statements and the financial position of Smith reflected therein. Relying upon these certified statements, plaintiffs provided additional substantial financing to Smith.

It is alleged that both statements overstated Smith's assets, net worth and general financial health, and that Andersen failed to conduct investigations in accordance with proper auditing standards, thereby failing to discover Smith's precarious financial condition and the serious possibility that Smith would be unable to survive....Indeed, in 1980, Smith filed a petition for bankruptcy. By that time, Smith had already defaulted on several millions of dollars of obligations to plaintiffs.

In August 1981, plaintiffs commenced this suit..., claiming both negligence and fraud by Andersen....

On Andersen's motion to dismiss the complaint, Special Term...denied Andersen's motion in its entirety. On appeal, the Appellate Division...affirmed....The court concluded that plaintiffs fell within the exception to the general rule that requires privity to maintain an action against an accountant for negligence. Two justices dissented....

....

In...[the second case], the complaint...alleges that plaintiff, European American Bank and Trust Company ("EAB"), made substantial loans to Majestic Electro Industries....

Beginning in 1979,...Majestic Electro retained defendant Strauhs & Kaye ("S & K"), an accounting partnership rendering services in this State, to audit its financial records....EAB relied upon the interim and year-end financial reports prepared by S & K to determine the maximum amounts it was willing to lend. From 1979 through 1982, S & K allegedly, *inter alia*, overstated Majestic Electro's inventory and accounts receivables, and failed to disclose the inadequacy of Majestic Electro's internal recordkeeping and inventory control.

...Majestic Electro filed a petition in bankruptcy. EAB suffered substantial losses from the loans remaining unpaid.

....EAB specifically alleges negligence in that S & K, in performing auditing and accounting services for Majestic Electro, at all relevant times knew that EAB was Majestic Electro's principal lender, was familiar with the terms of the lending relationship, and was fully aware that EAB was relying on the financial statements and inventory valuations certified by S & K. Moreover, it is alleged that representatives of EAB and S & K were in direct communication, both oral and written, during the entire course of the lending relationship between EAB and Majestic Electro, and, indeed, that representatives of EAB and S & K met together throughout this time to discuss S & K's evaluation of Majestic Electro's inventory and accounts receivable and EAB's reliance thereon. The complaint also alleges a second cause of action, merely adding that defendants were "grossly negligent or recklessly indifferent" in performing professional services and that EAB was damaged as a result.

On S & K's motion, Special Term dismissed the complaint holding that, absent a contractual relationship between the parties or an allegation of fraud, the complaint failed to state a cause of action. On appeal, the Appellate Division unanimously reversed and reinstated the complaint, in its entirety....

....

II

In the seminal case of Ultramares Corp. v. Touche, 255 N.Y. 170, 174 N.E. 441, this court, speaking through the opinion of Chief Justice Cardozo more than 50 years ago, disallowed a cause of action in negligence against a public accounting firm for inaccurately prepared financial statements which were relied upon by a plaintiff having no contractual privity with the accountants. This court distinguished its holding from Glanzer v. Shepard, 233 N.Y. 236, 135 N.E. 275, a case decided in an opinion also written by Cardozo nine years earlier. We explained that in *Glanzer*, an action in negligence against public weighers had been permitted, despite the absence of a contract between the parties, because the plaintiff's intended reliance, on the information *directly transmitted* by the weighers, created a bond so closely approaching privity that is was, in practical effect, virtually indistinguishable therefrom. This court has subsequently reaffirmed its holding in *Ultramares* which has been, and continues to be, much discussed and analyzed by the commentators and by the courts of other jurisdictions....Inasmuch as we believe that a relationship "so close as to approach that of privity" (255 N.Y., at pp. 182-183, 174 N.E. 441) remains valid as the predicate for imposing liability upon accountants to non-contractual parties for the negligent preparation of financial reports, we restate and elaborate upon our adherence to that standard today.

The doctrine of privity is said to have had its source in the classic enunciation of its rationale in Winterbottom v. Wright, 10 M & W 109, 152 Eng. Rep. 402. In that case, decided in 1842, the Court of Exchequer held that the defendant, who had failed to keep a mail coach in repair in violation of an agreement made with the purchaser, was not liable to another who suffered injuries while riding in the coach when it collapsed as a result of latent defects. The court ruled that no action could be maintained on defendant's contract because the plaintiff was not a privy thereto. "Unless we confine the operation of such contracts as this to the parties who entered into them," remarked Lord Abinger, "the most absurd and outrageous consequences, to which I can see no limit, would ensue." [Citation.] In concurrence, Baron Alderson added that...: "If we were told that the plaintiff could sue in such a case, there is no point at which such actions would stop. The only safe rule is to confine the right to recover to those who enter into the contract: if we go one step beyond that, there is no reason why we should not go fifty." From *Winterbottom*, the Privity doctrine developed into a general rule prevailing well into the Twentieth Century. [Citations.]

By the time 90 years had passed, however, this court could note in *Ultramares* that the "assault upon the citadel of privity is proceeding in these days apace." [Citation.] We acknowledged that inroads had been made, for example, where third-party beneficiaries or dangerous instrumentalities were involved. [Citation.] Indeed, we referred to this court's holding in MacPherson v. Buick Motor Co., 217 N.Y. 382, 111 N.E. 1050, where it was decided that the manufacturer of a defective chattel—there an automobile—may be liable in negligence for the resulting injuries sustained by a user regardless of the absence of privity—a belated rejection of the doctrine of privity as applied to the facts in *Winterbottom*. Nevertheless, regarding an accountant's liability to unknown parties with whom he had not contracted, the considerations were deemed sufficiently dissimilar to justify different treatment.

Although accountants might be held liable in fraud to nonprivy parties who were intended to rely upon the accountants' misrepresentations, we noted that "[a] different question develops when we ask whether they owed a duty to these to make [their reports] without negligence." (Ultramares Corp. v. Touche, [citation].) Disputing the wisdom of extending the duty of care of accountants to anyone who might foreseeably rely upon their financial reports, Cardozo, speaking for this court, remarked: "If liability for negligence exists, a thoughtless slip or blunder, the failure to detect a theft or forgery beneath the cover of deceptive entries, may expose accountants to a liability in an indeterminate amount for an indeterminate time to an indeterminate class...." [Citation.]

In *Ultramares*, the accountants had prepared a certified balance sheet for their client to whom they provided 32 copies. The client, in turn, gave one to the plaintiff company. The latter, relying upon the misinformation contained in the balance sheet, made loans to the accountants' client who, only months later, was declared bankrupt. This court, refusing to extend the accountants' liability for negligence to their client's lender, with whom they had no contractual privity, noted that the accountants had prepared a report on behalf of their client to be exhibited generally to "banks, creditors, stockholders, purchasers or sellers, *according to the needs of the occasion*." [Citation.] In reciting the facts, we emphasized that: "*Nothing was said as to the persons to whom these [copies] would be shown or the extent or number of the transactions in which they would be used.* In particular there was no mention of the plaintiff, a corporation doing business chiefly as a factor, which till then had never made advances to the [accountants' client], though it had sold merchandise in small amounts. The range of the transactions in which a certificate of audit might be expected to play a part was as indefinite and wide as the possibilities of the business that was mirrored in the summary." [Citation.]

....

By sharp contrast, the facts underlying *Glanzer* bespoke an affirmative assumption of a duty of care to a specific party, for a specific purpose, regardless of whether there was a contractual relationship. There, a seller of beans employed the defendants who were engaged in business as public weighers. Pursuant to instructions, the weighers furnished one copy of the weight certificate to their employer, the seller, and another to the prospective buyer. In reliance upon the inaccurately certified weight, the buyer purchased beans from the seller and, thereby, suffered a loss.

Explaining the imposition upon the weighers of a "noncontractual" duty of care to the buyer, this court held: "We think the law imposes a duty toward buyer as well as seller in the situation here disclosed. The [buyer's] use of the certificates was *not an indirect or collateral consequence* of the action of the weighers. It was a consequence which, to the weighers' knowledge, was the end and aim of the transaction. [The seller] ordered, but [the buyer was] to use. The defendants held themselves out to the public as skilled and careful in their calling. They knew that the beans had been sold, and that on the faith of their certificate payment would be made. *They sent a copy to the [buyer] for the very purpose of inducing action.* All this they admit. In such circumstances, assumption of the task of weighing was the assumption of a duty to weigh carefully for the benefit of all whose conduct was to be governed. We do not need to state the duty in terms of contract or of privity. Growing out of a contract, it has none the less an origin not exclusively contractual. Given the contract and the relation, the duty is imposed by law [citation]." [Citation [emphasis added].]

The critical distinctions between the two cases were highlighted in *Ultramares*, where we explained: "In Glanzer v. Shepard ... [the certificate of weight], which was made out in duplicate, one copy to the seller and the other to the buyer, *recites that it was made by order of the former for the use of the latter.* ... Here was something more than the rendition of a service in the expectation that the one who ordered the certificate would use it thereafter in the operations of his business as occasion might require. Here was a case where *the transmission of the certificate to another was* not merely one possibility among many, but the *'end and aim of the transaction,'* as certain and immediate and deliberately willed as if a husband were to order a gown to be delivered to his wife, or a telegraph company, contracting with the sender of a message, were to telegraph it wrongly to the damage of the person expected to receive it. ... The *intimacy of the resulting nexus* is attested by the fact that after stating the case in terms of legal duty, we went on to point out that ... we could reach the same result by stating it in terms of contract. ... The bond was *so close as to approach that of privity, if not completely one with it.* Not so in the case at hand (*i.e., Ultramares*). No one would be likely to urge that there was a contractual relation, *or even one approaching it,* at the root of any duty that was owing from the (accountants) now before us to the indeterminate class of persons who, presently or in the future, might deal with the (accountants' client) in reliance on the audit. In a word, the service rendered by the defendant in Glanzer v. Shepard was primarily for the information of a third person, *in effect, if not in name, a party to the contract,* and only incidentally for that of the formal promisee." (Ultramares Corp. v. Touche, [citation].)

....

Upon examination of *Ultramares* and *Glanzer* and our recent affirmation of their holdings ... certain criteria may be gleaned. Before accountants may be held liable in negligence to noncontractual parties who rely to their detriment on inaccurate financial reports, certain prerequisites must be satisfied: (1) the accountants must have been aware that the financial reports were to be used for a particular purpose or purposes; (2) in the furtherance of which a known party or parties was intended to rely; and (3) there must have been some conduct on the part of the accountants linking them to that party or parties, which evinces the accountants' understanding of that party or parties' reliance....

We are aware that courts throughout this country are divided as to the continued validity of the holding in *Ultramares*. Some courts continue to insist that a rather strict application of the privity requirement governs the law of accountants' liability except, perhaps, where special circumstances compel a different result....On the other hand, an increasing number of courts have adopted what they deem to be a more flexible approach than that permitted under this court's past decisions....

....[11]

III

In the appeals we decide today, application of the foregoing principles presents little difficulty. In *Credit Alliance*, the facts as alleged by plaintiffs fail to demonstrate the existence of a relationship between the parties sufficiently approaching privity. Though the complaint and supporting affidavit do allege that Andersen specifically knew, should have known or was on notice that plaintiffs were being shown the reports by Smith, Andersen's client, in order to induce their reliance thereon, nevertheless, there is no adequate allegation of either a particular purpose for the reports' preparation or the prerequisite conduct on the part of the accountants. While the allegations state that Smith sought to induce plaintiffs to extend credit, no claim is made that Andersen was being employed to prepare the reports with that particular purpose in mind. Moreover, there is no allegation that Andersen had any direct dealings with plaintiffs, had specifically agreed with Smith to prepare the report for plaintiffs' use or according to plaintiffs' requirements, or had specifically agreed with Smith to provide plaintiffs with a copy or actually did so. Indeed, there is simply no allegation of any word or action on the part of Andersen directed to plaintiffs, or anything contained in Andersen's retainer agreement with Smith which provided the necessary link between them.

By sharp contrast, in *European American*, the facts as alleged by EAB clearly show that S & K was well aware that a primary, if not the exclusive, *end and aim* of auditing its client, Majestic Electro, was to provide EAB with the financial information it required. The prerequisites for the cause of action in negligence, as well as in gross negligence, are fully satisfied. Not only is it alleged, as in *Credit Alliance*, that the accountants knew the identity of the specific nonprivy party who would be relying upon the audit reports, but additionally, the complaint and affidavit here allege both the accountants' awareness of a particular purpose for their services and certain conduct on their part creating an unmistakable relationship with the reliant plaintiff. It is unambiguously claimed that the parties remained in direct communication, both orally and in writing, and, indeed, met together throughout the course of EAB's lending relationship with Majestic Electro, for the very purpose of discussing the latter's financial condition and

---

11. Indeed, certain jurisdictions have unequivocally adopted and applied an unrestricted "foreseeability" rule. [Citations.] A greater number appear to have adopted a rule requiring that the reliant party or his limited class be either known or *actually foreseen* by the accountants. [Citations.] Insamuch as this latter rule deriving from the Restatement (Second) of Torts, §552, does not include an additional requirement for conduct on the part of the accountants linking them to the noncontractual party or parties, we decline to adopt it.

EAB's need for S & K's evaluation. Moreover, it is alleged that S & K made repeated representations personally to representatives of EAB, on these occasions, concerning the value of Majestic Electro's assets.... The parties' direct communications and personal meetings resulted in a nexus between them sufficiently approaching privity... to permit EAB's causes of action.

Finally, disposition of the second cause of action alleged in *Credit Alliance* need not detain us long. The cause of action for fraud repeats the allegations for the negligence cause of action and merely adds a claim that Andersen recklessly disregarded facts which would have apprised it that its reports were misleading or that Andersen had actual knowledge that such was the case. This single allegation of scienter, without additional detail concerning the facts constituting the alleged fraud, is insufficient under the special pleading standards required under CPLR 3016(b), and, consequently, the cause of action should have been dismissed.

Accordingly, in *Credit Alliance* both causes of action should be dismissed [citations], the order of the Appellate Division reversed, with costs, and the certified question answered in the negative. In *European American*, the order of the Appellate Division should be affirmed, with costs, and the certified question answered in the affirmative.

. . . .

Notes

1. In evaluating the *Ultramares* doctrine, consider two ways of reducing the risk that some of the several dozen corporations being audited by an accountant will default on large loans. First, the accountant can (at considerable expense) use great care in auditing all of the corporations. Allowing recovery against negligent accountants to all "foreseeable" plaintiffs encourages this approach (and makes auditing quite expensive). Second, lenders could hire their own auditors to check the books of those to whom they propose to lend (with corporations planning to borrow very large amounts getting the closest scrutiny). If, under *Ultramares*, the lender cannot expect recovery against the corporation's own auditors, it has an incentive to protect itself by doing this.

The economic sense behind the *Ultramares* doctrine is that audits performed at the request of the lender can go into the detail appropriate for the transaction in question. Someone planning to lend $100 would not bother with an audit at all, someone planning to lend $5,000,000 would give the books a very careful going over. If (contrary to *Ultramares*) accountants performing any audit are to be liable to any future lender who relies on the audit's results, the accountants cannot know in advance which of the corporations will take out large loans. What, then, should the accountants do? Auditing every corporation on the assumption that it might borrow millions would be extremely expensive. Much of this expense would be borne by corporations which would not in fact borrow heavily.

The above analysis can be summarized by noting that the lender, rather than the accountant performing a routine audit, is often the "cheaper cost avoider" with respect to the risks of making large loans.

2. In Bily v. Arthur Young & Co., 834 P.2d 745 (Cal. 1992), a case involving the liability of auditors to third parties for negligence, the court summarized existing precedent as follows:

A substantial number of jurisdictions follow the lead of Chief Judge Cardozo's 1931 opinion for the New York Court of Appeals in *Ultramares*, [citation], by denying recovery to third parties for auditor negligence in the absence of a third party relationship to the auditor that is "akin to privity." [Citation.] In contrast, a handful of jurisdictions, spurred by law review commentary, have recently allowed recovery based on auditor negligence to third parties whose reliance on the audit report was "foreseeable." [Citation.]

Most jurisdictions, supported by the weight of commentary…, have steered a middle course based in varying degrees on Restatement, Second, of Torts §552, which generally imposes liability on suppliers of commercial information to third parties who are intended beneficiaries of the information….

The California court overruled lower court decisions which had followed a foreseeability approach, and endorsed the Restatement position. According to §552 of the Restatement, liability for negligent misrepresentation is limited to losses suffered

(a) by the person or one of a limited group of persons for whose benefit and guidance … [the maker of the statement] intends to supply the information or knows that the recipient intends to supply it; and

(b) through reliance upon it in a transaction that he intends the information to influence or knows that the recipient so intends or in a substantially similar transaction.

The *Bily* court distinguished between claims for negligent misrepresentation (which in California are governed by §552), and ordinary claims for negligence, which in that state may be maintained only by an auditor's client, and not by a third person. The point here is important. Unless the plaintiff shows that the substance of the allegedly misstatement was communicated to and relied upon by the plaintiff, the action is not one for misrepresentation, and even more stringent rules may apply.

See also Boykin v. Arthur Andersen & Co., 639 So. 2d 504 (Ala. 1994) (endorsing §552 in an action by a bank's shareholders against its accountants).

3. *Statutes Governing Actions against Accountants.* In some states, the liability of accountants to third parties is governed by statute. For example, the Illinois Public Accounting Act provides (effective July 1, 2004):

IL. ST. CH. 225 §450

(Westlaw 2004)

§§ 30.1. No person … or … entity licensed … under this Act … shall be liable to persons not in privity of contract … for civil damages resulting from acts, omissions, decisions or other conduct in connection with professional services performed by such person … or … entity, except for:

(1) such acts, omissions, decisions or conduct that constitute fraud or intentional misrepresentations, or

(2) such other acts, omissions, decisions or conduct, if such person, partnership or corporation was aware that a primary intent of the client was for the professional services to benefit or influence the particular person bringing the action; provided, however, for the purposes of this subparagraph (2), if such person … or … entity (i) identifies in writing to the client those persons who are intended to rely on the services, and (ii) sends a copy of such writing or similar statement to those persons identified in the writing or statement, then such person … or … entity … may be held liable only to such persons intended to so rely, in addition to those persons in privity of contract.

In addition, some states have enacted legislation which poses another obstacle to tort actions against accountants. *See, e.g.*, La. Rev. Stat. Ann. §37:101 *et seq.* (Westlaw 2002) (establishing mandatory review panels to consider claims for negligence, breach of contract, and breach of fiduciary duty against certified public accountants, and providing that the panel's opinion is admissible as an expert opinion).

4. *Errors in Published Works.* Should liability be imposed if a book contains false factual information which causes injury to a user who relies upon the erroneous information? What if a student following a flawed chemistry text is injured in an explosion? For First Amendment reasons, courts have been extremely reluctant to impose liability. *See, e.g.*, Winter v. G.P. Putnam's Sons, 938 F.2d 1033 (9th Cir. 1991) (no liability for error which caused plaintiffs to eat deadly mushrooms, necessitating liver transplants). *See generally* Roy W. Arnold, Note, *The Persistence of Caveat Emptor: Publisher Immunity from Liability for Inaccurate Factual Information*, 53 U. Pitt. L. Rev. 777 (1992) (arguing that books should be treated as "products" subject to strict liability rules).

5. *Ethics in Law Practice: Misrepresentation.* The ethics codes of most states provide that it is professional misconduct, punishable by disbarment and lesser sanctions, for a lawyer to engage in "conduct involving dishonesty, fraud, deceit or misrepresentation." *See* Model Rules of Professional Conduct Rule 8.4(c) (2003). *See also* Feld's Case, 815 A.2d 383 (N.H. 2002) (an attorney was suspended for one year for knowingly providing false answers to interrogatories in a property dispute).

In Greycas, Inc. v. Proud, 826 F.2d 1560 (7th Cir. 1987), a case holding an attorney liable to a non-client for making false statements in an opinion letter, the court noted that, because the record revealed "serious misconduct," it was forwarding a copy of the opinion to the state commission on attorney discipline for appropriate action.

Some states hold that, because of inherent conflicts of interest, all business transactions between attorney and client are presumptively fraudulent, and that the burden of proving that the transaction was fair and reasonable rests with the attorney. *See* Archer v. Griffith, 390 S.W.2d 735 (Tex. 1965).

D. Special Considerations

Kathleen K. v. Robert B.
California Court of Appeal
198 Cal. Rptr. 273 (Ct. App. 1984)

HASTINGS, Associate Justice.

In this action, plaintiff and appellant Kathleen K. seeks damages because she contracted genital herpes, allegedly by way of sexual intercourse with defendant and respondent Robert B. The trial court granted respondent's motion for judgment on the pleadings based upon failure to state a cause of action. We reverse the judgment.

. . . .

The complaint sets forth four causes of action: (1) negligence (alleging that respondent inflicted injury upon appellant by having sexual intercourse with her at a time when he knew, or in the exercise of reasonable care should have known, that he was a carrier of venereal disease); (2) battery; (3) intentional infliction of emotional distress;

and (4) fraud (alleging that respondent deliberately misrepresented to appellant that he was free from venereal disease, and that appellant, relying on such representations, had sexual intercourse with respondent, which she would not have done had she known the true state of affairs).

In granting respondent's motion for judgment on the pleadings, the trial court relied upon the case of Stephen K. v. Roni L., 105 Cal. App. 3d 640, 164 Cal. Rptr. 618. In *Stephen K.*, the father of a child filed a cross-complaint against the child's mother who had brought a paternity action, claiming that the mother had falsely represented to him that she was taking birth control pills. The father alleged that in reliance upon that misrepresentation, he engaged in sexual intercourse with the mother, resulting in the birth of a child which he did not want. He further alleged that as a proximate result of the misrepresentation, he had become obligated to support the child financially and had suffered emotional distress.

In affirming dismissal of the cross-complaint, the court held that the misrepresentation was not actionable: "The claim of Stephen is phrased in the language of the tort of misrepresentation. Despite its legalism, it is nothing more than asking the court to supervise the promises made between two consenting adults as to the circumstances of their private sexual conduct. To do so would encourage unwarranted governmental intrusion into matters affecting the individual's right to privacy.... We reject Stephen's contention that tortious liability should be imposed against Roni, and conclude that as a matter of public policy the practice of birth control, if any, engaged in by two partners in a consensual sexual relationship is best left to the individuals involved, free from any governmental interference." [Citation.]

After the trial court entered its judgment, the First District Court of Appeal decided the case of Barbara A. v. John G., 145 Cal. App. 3d 369, 193 Cal. Rptr. 422 (hrg. den. September 29, 1983). In *Barbara A.*, a woman who suffered an ectopic pregnancy and was forced to undergo surgery to save her life, which rendered her sterile, brought an action against the man who impregnated her (her former attorney), alleging that she consented to sexual intercourse in reliance on the man's knowingly false representation that he was sterile. The court reversed a judgment on the pleadings in favor of the defendant and held that the complaint stated causes of action for battery and for deceit.

The court distinguished *Stephen K.*, noting that: "In essence, Stephen was seeking damages for the 'wrongful birth' of his child resulting in support obligations and alleged damages for mental suffering. Here, no child is involved; appellant is seeking damages for severe injury to her own body." (145 Cal. App. 3d at pp. 378-379, 193 Cal. Rptr. 422.) We conclude that these same factors distinguish this case from *Stephen K.*, and accordingly hold that *Barbara A.* is controlling here.

... [T]he *Barbara A.* court... [focused] upon the fact that Stephen was alleging an injury which had significant public policy overtones:

> To assess damages against the mother for false representations about birth control would have the practical effect of reducing or eliminating support from the father by way of offset. Erasing much or all of the father's financial support, to the detriment of the child, is clearly against public policy and the statutory mandate.

> Further, we think it is not sound social policy to allow one parent to sue the other over the wrongful birth of their child. Using the child as the damage element in a tortious claim of one parent against the other could seldom, if ever, result in benefit to a child. (145 Cal. App. 3d at p. 379, 193 Cal. Rptr. 422.)

In the present case, as in *Barbara A.*, there is no child involved, and the public policy considerations with respect to parental obligations are absent.

Respondent also argues that it is not the business of courts to "supervise the promises made between two consenting adults as to the circumstances of their private sexual conduct." [Citation.]

Respondent correctly focuses on the constitutional right of privacy as the crux of this case. Courts have long recognized the right of privacy in matters relating to marriage, family and sex [citations], and accordingly have frowned upon unwarranted governmental intrusion into matters affecting the individual's right to privacy. [Citation.] The key word here, however, is *unwarranted*. The right of privacy is not absolute, and in some cases is subordinate to the state's fundamental right to enact laws which promote public health, welfare and safety, even though such laws may invade the offender's right of privacy.... The *Barbara A.* court concluded that the right of privacy "does not insulate a person from all judicial inquiry into his or her sexual relations," and expanded the exceptions to the right of privacy to impose liability upon "one sexual partner who by intentionally tortious conduct causes physical injury to the other." [Citation.]

This is precisely the type of conduct alleged in appellant's complaint....

....

The judgment is reversed.

Note

1. *See also* Miller v. Miller, 956 P.2d 887 (Okla. 1998), which held that a true claim of an existing pregnancy coupled with a false representation that the child is that of the prospective spouse will support an action for fraudulent inducement of marriage. The state's statutory presumption of legitimacy does not bar an action in which the plaintiff is not seeking to delegitimize a child, or to avoid the obligations of parenthood, but rather to obtain damages from an alleged tortfeasor for falsely representing that the plaintiff is the father of the child.

Chapter 22

Defamation

Historical Development. Anglo-American tort law has long allowed many of those injured by false, defamatory statements an action for damages. If the statement in question was written, the action is called "libel"; an action based on oral defamation is for "slander." Libel and slander are ancient torts, complete with peculiar and arcane doctrines and terminology. But in 1964, the Supreme Court began to "constitutionalize" much of the law of defamation by holding that the First Amendment guarantees of freedom of speech and freedom of the press limit the ability of state courts to apply traditional defamation law.

This chapter includes a number of the leading Supreme Court opinions on defamation, as those opinions have overridden the common-law rules to such an extent that a look at the common law alone would be seriously incomplete. Furthermore, although the Supreme Court is interpreting and applying "the Constitution" in its defamation cases, its approach to specific issues consists in large part of deciding where the balance between protection of reputation and freedom of speech and of the press should be struck. This approach closely resembles common-law adjudication, despite its purported basis in the Constitution. Invoking "the Constitution" in these cases gives the Court the power to override state law, but the constitutional basis for the decisions does not much change the way in which a lawyer interprets and applies the opinions. As a practical matter, a lawyer advising a client whether to bring a libel suit against a newspaper which has published false statements injuring the client's reputation will treat the relevant Supreme Court decisions as sources of rules and principles which will apply to the case, just like rules and principles developed under the common law.

A. What Statements Are Defamatory?

1. Harm to Reputation

Not all false statements about the plaintiff give rise to a defamation claim: a statement must injure the plaintiff's reputation to be actionable. A classic description of the kind of statement that is actionable is that the statement must subject the plaintiff to "hatred, ridicule, or contempt." The Restatement, Second, of Torts (§559) defines defamatory statements as those that tend "to harm the reputation of [the victim so] as to lower him in the estimation of the community or to deter third persons from associating or dealing with him."

In a society in which people hold widely divergent views about what kind of behavior is proper, it may be difficult to determine whether a particular statement defames the plaintiff. Consider, for example, a false assertion that the plaintiff is a homosexual, or a communist, or has had an abortion. Not many years ago, any of these statements would pretty clearly have been defamatory. Today, the law must pay considerably more attention than in the past to the question of just who it is who will think badly of the plaintiff if the defendant's false statement is believed.

Grant v. Reader's Digest Ass'n, Inc.

United States Court of Appeals for the Second Circuit
151 F.2d 733 (2d Cir. 1945)

L. HAND, Circuit Judge.

This is an appeal from a judgment dismissing a complaint in libel for insufficiency in law upon its face. The complaint alleged that the plaintiff was a Massachusetts lawyer, living in that state; that the defendant, a New York corporation, published a periodical of general circulation, read by lawyers, judges and the general public; and that one issue of the periodical contained an article...in which the following passage appeared:

> ....In my state the Political Action Committee has hired as its legislative agent one, Sidney S. Grant, who but recently was a legislative representative for the Massachusetts Communist Party.

...[A]lthough the words did not say that the plaintiff was a member of the Communist Party, they did say that he had acted on its behalf, and we think that a jury might in addition find that they implied that he was in general sympathy with its objects and methods. The last conclusion does indeed involve the assumption that the Communist Party would not retain as its "legislative representative" a person who was not in general accord with its purposes; but that inference is reasonable and was pretty plainly what the author wished readers to draw from his words. The case therefore turns upon whether it is libelous in New York to write of a lawyer that he has acted as agent of the Communist Party, and is a believer in its aims and methods.

....A man may value his reputation even among those who do not embrace the prevailing moral standards; and it would seem that the jury should be allowed to appraise how far he should be indemnified for the disesteem of such persons. That is the usual rule. Peck v. Tribune Co.,...[214 U.S. 185]; Restatement of Torts, §559....[T]he opinions at times seem to make it a condition that to be actionable the words must be such as would so affect "right-thinking people"...and it is fairly plain that there must come a point where that is true. As was said in Mawe v. Piggot, Irish Rep. 4 Comm. Law, 54, 62, among those "who were themselves criminal or sympathized with crime," it would expose one "to great odium to represent him as an informer or prosecutor or otherwise aiding in the detection of crime"; yet certainly the words would not be actionable. Be that as it may, in New York if the exception covers more than such a case, it does not go far enough to excuse the utterance at bar. Katapodis v. Brooklyn Spectator, Inc., *supra*, (287 N.Y. 17, 38 N.E.2d 112), following the old case of Moffat v. Cauldwell, 3 Hun. 26, 5 T. & C. 256, held that the imputation of extreme poverty might be actionable; although certainly "right-thinking" people ought not shun, or despise, or otherwise condemn one because he is poor. Indeed, the only declaration of the Court of Appeals (Moore v. Francis, 121 N.Y. 199, 205, 206, 23 N.E. 1127) leaves it still open whether it is not libelous to say that a man is insane....We do not believe, therefore, that we need say whether "right-thinking" people would harbor similar feelings toward a lawyer, because he had been an agent for the Communist Party, or was a sympathizer with its aims and means. It is enough if there be some, as there certainly are, who would feel so, even though they would be "wrong-thinking" people if they did....

....

Judgment reversed; cause remanded.

Notes

1. *The "Whole Publication" Rule.* In determining whether an article or book is defamatory, the writing must be read as a whole. Thus, a statement that a belly dancer sold her time to lonely old men was held not to be libelous in light of other statements that she did so just to sit with them, to be nice to them, and to talk. James v. Gannett Co., Inc., 353 N.E.2d 834 (N.Y. 1976). Similarly, a statement that a political candidate's company was charged with selling obscene books was not defamatory where other expressions, including an explanation by the plaintiff that the accusation was false, absolutely negated the derogatory meaning. Treutler v. Meredith Corp., 455 F.2d 255 (8th Cir. 1972).

Some courts hold that under the "whole publication" rule, headlines, captions, and illustrations are considered along with the body of the text, and thus an obviously erroneous headline or caption, or an otherwise actionable illustration, may be "cured" by accompanying language which corrects the misconception. *See* Ross v. Columbia Newspapers, Inc., 221 S.E.2d 770 (S.C. 1976) (an erroneous headline that the plaintiff was a suspect in the death of his wife was rendered innocuous by the last sentence of the article which said that the wife was in serious condition in the hospital); Reed v. Albanese, 223 N.E.2d 419 (Ill. App. Ct. 1966) (the headline "Reed Jailed for Housing Violations" was remedied by the body of the article, which correctly said that a warrant of arrest was issued in lieu of a fine).

Where, however, oversized headlines are intentionally published to create a false impression, and the reader is reasonably led to an entirely different conclusion than is supported by the facts recited in the story, the headlines may be considered separately for the purpose of determining whether there has been a defamatory communication. Sprouse v. Clay Communication Inc., 211 S.E.2d 674 (W. Va. 1975). Many newspaper readers read *only* the headlines of most articles, so an absolute rule that headlines alone cannot be defamatory would be much too restrictive.

In Kaelin v. Globe Communications Corp., 162 F.3d 1036 (9th Cir. 1998), the National Enquirer published a story, a week after the acquittal of O.J. Simpson, saying (perhaps truthfully) that the police were considering charging Kato Kaelin with perjury. The article appeared on p. 17; its headline, on the cover, said "Cops Think Kato Did It!" Held, Kaelin's defamation claim, based on the inference that readers would naturally draw from the headline, could go forward. A factfinder could conclude that the headline was defamatory, even if the article as a whole was not ("headlines are not...liability-free zones"), and that the publisher acted with "actual malice" (the editor admitted at a deposition that he was concerned that the headline "did not accurately reflect the content of the article"). *See also* Condit v. National Enquirer, Inc., 2002 W.L. 31996127 (E.D. Cal.) (a heading stating that the wife of a former congressman "attacked" her husband's intern, and a subheading "what wife is hiding," were reasonably susceptible of defamatory meanings).

See generally Joseph H. King, Jr., *Defining the Internal Context for Communications Containing Allegedly Defamatory Headline Language*, 71 U. Cinn. L. Rev. 863 (2003).

2. *Ambiguous Statements.* If a statement can be reasonably read in two ways, one of which is defamatory and the other not, most courts hold that the factfinder must determine the sense in which the remark was understood. For example, Belli v. Orlando Daily Newspapers, Inc., 389 F.2d 579 (5th Cir. 1967), held it a jury question whether a prominent lawyer was defamed by a statement that he had "taken" the Florida Bar. *See also* Sprague v. ABA, 2001 W.L. 1450606 (E.D. Pa.) (holding that the term "lawyer-cum-fixer" was capable of two meanings, one of which was defamatory).

If reasonable persons cannot differ about whether a statement is defamatory, the question becomes one of law. *See* Cox Enterprises, Inc. v. Nix, 560 S.E.2d 650 (Ga. 2002) (holding that a newspaper article on lawyer discipline was not defamatory of the plaintiff attorney where it referred to him once (accurately) in the context of a judicial proceeding and distinguished him from other attorneys who were accused of criminal conduct). In Liberty Mut. Fire Ins. Co. v. O'Keefe, 556 N.W.2d 133, 134 (Wis. Ct. App. 1996), an attorney representing a client in a suit against the plaintiff placed an advertisement for evidence which read in part, "If anyone has any information regarding Liberty Mutual Fire Insurance Company's delay or failure to pay claims or losses, please contact the undersigned." The court held that the ad was not defamatory as a matter of law because "there are many legitimate reasons why an insurance company would not immediately pay all claims." Is it correct to say that no reasonable person could understand the ad to be defamatory?

3. *"Mitior Sensus" and the Innocent Construction Rule.* In the sixteenth and seventeenth centuries, the courts of England responded to an avalanche of slander suits by adopting the doctrine of "*mitior sensus,*" under which statements were construed as nondefamatory whenever possible. Under this bizarre doctrine, calling someone a forger was not actionable, as it might have meant only that the plaintiff was a metal-worker.

The doctrine of *mitior sensus* never had much effect in this country, though some Illinois decisions have taken a somewhat-similar approach, even in libel cases (*mitior sensus* applied only to slander). Under the Illinois "innocent construction rule," "words allegedly libelous that are capable of being read innocently must be so read and declared nonactionable as a matter of law"; John v. Tribune Co., 181 N.E.2d 105 (Ill. 1962). A later Illinois case, Chapski v. Copley Press, 442 N.E.2d 195 (Ill. 1982), has been interpreted as requiring that "statements be read in their natural sense, not in the light most favorable to the defendant." Muzikowski v. Paramount Pictures Corp., 322 F.3d 918 (7th Cir. 2003). Some Illinois courts have, however, used a fair amount of ingenuity in finding an innocent construction. Rasky v. Columbia Broadcasting System, Inc., 431 N.E.2d 1055 (Ill. App. Ct. 1981), relied on the dictionary definitions of "landlord" and "slum" to hold that calling someone a "slumlord" might have meant only that he was the landlord of a building located in a slum.

See also Sterling v. Rust Communications, 113 S.W.3d 279 (Mo. Ct. App. 2003) (stating that in determining whether language is defamatory the words must be "stripped of any pleaded innuendo...and construed in their most innocent sense" and given their "plain and ordinarily understood meaning").

4. *Use of Extrinsic Facts to Prove Defamation.* A statement innocent on its face may be defamatory when considered in the light of other facts. In Cassidy v. Daily Mirror Newspapers, Ltd., [1929] 2 K.B. 331, a newspaper article said that a Mr. Cassidy was engaged to a woman whose picture appeared in the paper. In fact, Cassidy was married, though the paper did not know this, and both Cassidy and the woman gave the paper permission to announce their engagement. The court ruled that the article libeled Cas-

sidy's wife because her acquaintances testified that they inferred from the article that Mrs. Cassidy was not in fact married to Cassidy, with whom she was living.

A written statement defamatory on its face is a "libel *per se*"; if knowledge of extrinsic facts turns an apparently harmless written statement into a libel, the statement is a "libel *per quod*." In some jurisdictions, nothing turns on the difference except that the plaintiff in an action for libel *per quod* must establish the extrinsic facts. Some courts have held that plaintiffs in actions for libel *per quod* (unlike plaintiffs seeking damages for libel *per se*) must prove pecuniary damages in order to recover. The question whether plaintiffs in defamation cases are entitled to damages without introducing evidence of actual harm is examined further below.

If a statement, on its face, is not defamatory of the plaintiff, the plaintiff may need to plead facts establishing "colloquium" (that the statement referred to the plaintiff), "inducement" (the predicate for the defamatory meaning), or "innuendo" (the defamatory charge). Consider the words "He's dating Gabriel." On its face, the statement appears innocent. However, if "he" refers to Reynoldo (colloquium), and if Reynoldo is a Roman Catholic priest (inducement), the statement suggests that Reynoldo is unfaithful to his religion (innuendo).

5. ***Untruth without Hatred, Ridicule or Contempt.*** The defendant in Youssoupoff v. Metro-Goldwyn-Mayer Pictures, 50 T.L.R. 581 (C.A. 1934), produced a motion picture in which a character whom the audience might have believed to have been the plaintiff, a Russian princess, was raped by Rasputin. Scrutton, L.J., expressed "great difficulty" in taking seriously the defendant's argument that it was not defamatory to say of "a woman of good character" that she had been raped. Today, it may seem hard to take seriously the argument that such a statement *is* defamatory; the plaintiff was, after all, presented as the victim of a crime, not as a malefactor. Perhaps the problem here arises because the traditional description of the harm in defamation cases as "harm to reputation" is too narrow. A statement like that at issue in *Youssoupoff* may harm the victim not by subjecting her to "hatred, ridicule or contempt" but rather by inviting the public to imagine her as engaging in sexual activities, even if involuntary, and thus making her the subject of unwholesome interest to the pruriently inclined. In other words, *Youssoupoff* might better be regarded as an intentional-infliction-of-emotional-distress case, or perhaps an invasion-of-privacy case, than as a defamation case.

Suppose a false statement causes the plaintiff serious economic harm without injuring the plaintiff's reputation at all. If *A*, as a practical joke, takes out a newspaper advertisement announcing that *B*'s store will be closed for the summer, *B* may lose lots of money without becoming an object of ridicule. The solution to this problem is to allow a tort action other than an action for libel or slander: in this case, most courts would call the tort "interference with prospective economic advantage." For a discussion of this and similar torts, *see* William L. Prosser, *Injurious Falsehood: The Basis of Liability*, 59 Colum. L. Rev. 425.

Whether a misstatement gives rise to defamation or some other kind of action can be important for a variety of reasons. For example, defamation was a strict-liability tort at common law (a rule that has been changed on constitutional grounds, at least in cases brought by public officials, public figures, or private figures suing with regard to matters of public concern, as discussed below). Also, in libel cases (and some slander cases) the plaintiff could recover a large award without having to establish damages; this rule has been limited but not eliminated by the Supreme Court. And statutes of limitations for defamation are typically very short.

2. Assertion of Fact

Hatred, Ridicule or Contempt without Untruth. The plaintiff in Burton v. Crowell Publ'g Co., 82 F.2d 154 (2d Cir. 1936), posed for pictures that were used in an advertisement for Camel cigarettes. In one of the pictures Burton held a saddle, across which lay a white girth. Because of the camera angle, the girth (which was about three feet long) appeared at first glance to be Burton's penis. (While the court does not go into the details of Burton's embarrassment, rumor has it that his friends mercilessly taunted him for some time following the publication of the advertisement.) Judge Learned Hand conceded that the advertisement could not be read as saying anything untrue about the plaintiff, as those who saw it would understand that their initial impression of what it showed was induced by an optical illusion. Nevertheless, because the publication held Burton up to ridicule, it was actionable.

It is easy to picture similar issues arising with respect to digitally altered photographs. However, the result of *Burton* has been called into doubt by later decisions. For example, Hustler Magazine v. Falwell, 485 U.S. 46 (1988), concerned an obscene parody in which the plaintiff, a public figure, was the principal character. It was presented as fiction, and the event described (an incestuous rendezvous in an out-house) was so outlandish that few if any readers could have believed that it had actually taken place. The jury denied recovery on Falwell's libel claim, finding that the parody could not be taken as describing facts, but it awarded him damages for intentional infliction of emotional distress. Relying on defamation precedent, the Supreme Court reversed, ruling that the First Amendment interest in uninhibited debate on public issues precludes a public figure from recovering against a publisher for intentional infliction of emotional distress unless the publication contained a false statement of fact made with knowledge of its falsity or reckless disregard for its truth.

In Milkovich v. Lorain Journal Co., 497 U.S. 1 (1990), a libel action, the Court reiterated its view that statements must be provable as false before liability may constitutionally be imposed. The implication is that a statement devoid of a provably false assertion may not give rise to tort liability.

Defamation by Conduct. Some defamation suits are based on conduct, rather than on written or spoken words. For example, courts have found a cause of action stated where the defendant discharged an employee immediately following a polygraph test (Tyler v. Macks Stores of S.C., Inc., 272 S.E.2d 633 (S.C. 1980)), or duped an unwitting plaintiff into being a contestant on a rigged television game show (Morrison v. National Broadcasting Co., 227 N.E.2d 572 (N.Y. 1967)), or dishonored a merchant's checks (Svendsen v. State Bank of Duluth, 65 N.W. 1086 (Minn. 1896)). However, some courts have declined to recognize a suit for libel or slander based solely on conduct. For example, in Bolton v. Dept. of Human Services, 540 N.W.2d 523, 525-26 (Minn. 1995), a former employee brought an action for defamation based on his former supervisor's accompanying the employee to the exit door, without a spoken word, immediately following the employee's discharge. The court concluded as a matter of law that the plaintiff had not been defamed, stating that:

> In most other states that have allowed an action for defamation by conduct, the behavior has tended to rise to the level of "dramatic pantomime:" that is, an interplay of words and conduct that provide a clearly discernible account of the making of a false statement about the aggrieved to a third party.

The *Bolton* court appears to have been influenced by the fact that even in a defamation suit based on conduct it is necessary to prove a false statement of fact, for it noted the heightened difficulty in a defamatory conduct case of applying applicable legal tests in a suit based on a communication "that can be interpreted by the declarant to have one meaning but to have quite a different one to the recipient."

An employer's mere refusal to talk about a former employee does not constitute defamation. *See* Saucedo v. Rheem Manuf. Co., 974 S.W.2d 117, 122 (Tex. Ct. App. 1998).

3. Truth

Who Has the Burden of Proof? Truth is often said to be a complete bar to liability for defamation, though a Rhode Island case has held that true statements can be actionable if uttered out of "spite or ill will"; Johnson v. Johnson, 654 A.2d 1212 (R.I. 1995) (whether this case is consistent with First Amendment principles limiting defamation actions is doubtful).

At common law, the defendant had the burden of proving that the statement was true. However, the Supreme Court has held that, in some cases, allowing the plaintiff to recover damages without showing that the statements in question were false violates the First Amendment; Philadelphia Newspapers, Inc. v. Hepps, 475 U.S. 767 (1986). The *Hepps* rule applies "at least where a newspaper publishes speech of public concern." Whether the rule will be extended to cases involving non-media defendants or matters not of "public concern" remains to be seen.

In some cases, imposing the burden of proving falsity upon the plaintiff may make it virtually impossible to establish defamation. For example, if the accusation is that the plaintiff short-changes customers whenever it has an opportunity, how can the plaintiff show untruth, as no specific transactions are at issue? Restatement, Second, of Torts §613 cmt. j. However, suits based on broadly stated charges may fail for other reasons. As discussed later in the chapter, statements of opinion that do not imply false facts are not actionable. In Shor Int'l. Corp. v. Eisinger Enterprises, Inc., 2000 W.L. 1793389 (S.D.N.Y.), statements using the words "shoddy goods and dishonest sales and businesses" were held to be non-actionable expressions of opinion that could not be proven true or false. The court wrote: "referring to all of the defendant's practices as dishonest, as opposed to stating that defendant's engaged in dishonest practices on a particular occasion, converts the statement into a hyperbole that cannot be taken as a serious assertion of fact."

Inaccuracies and "Substantial Truth." A trivial inaccuracy in a largely correct account will not give rise to liability if the inaccuracy makes the statement no more derogatory than if it had been entirely true: "Jones murdered his wife at 9:15 last night" is not actionable if in fact Jones murdered his wife at 9:30, or even last week.

In Alleman v. Vermilion Publ'g Corp., 316 So. 2d 837 (La. Ct. App. 1975), a "letter to the editor" said that a doctor had refused to see a seriously injured child in a hospital emergency room because the child was "the patient of the doctor on call." According to the doctor, he refused to provide assistance because another doctor had been contacted and was on route to the hospital. The court held that no action would lie because what was said was substantially true; the doctor had declined to treat the child in the emergency room after being requested to do so by his parents.

See also Steele v. Spokesman-Review, 61 P.3d 606 (Idaho 2002) (holding that a statement in an article that an attorney had relocated from California to Idaho at about same time as members of a white supremacist group was substantially true even though two years separated their moves); Swindall v. Cox Enterprises, Inc., 558 S.E.2d 788 (Ga. Ct. App. 2002) (holding that an editorial's statements that a former Congressman had "lied about drug-money laundering" were substantially true, even though the former Congressman had not been charged with any substantive offenses, because the former Congressman had been convicted of perjury for giving false testimony to a grand jury concealing his involvement in discussions about money laundering); UTV of San Antonio, Inc. v. Ardmore, Inc., 82 S.W.3d 609 (Tex. App. 2002) (holding that a statement that an inspector had found roaches at a daycare center during a follow-up inspection was not more damaging than a more-accurate statement that the inspector had noted allegations by staff members of roaches on a cup, crockpot, and counter, but that no roaches were found on the day of a specific inspection); Provencio v. Paradigm Media, Inc., 44 S.W.3d 677 (Tex. App. 2001) (holding that a post card identifying the plaintiff as a registered sex offender was substantially true, even though the card bore a misleading return address which implied that it had been sent by the government rather than by a news organization).

Except perhaps for cases involving "libel-proof" plaintiffs (*infra* at p. 1002 n. 8), one cannot avoid liability for false, defamatory statements by showing that the plaintiff did something else just as bad. For example, in Kilian v. Doubleday & Co., Inc., 79 A.2d 657 (Pa. 1951), an army officer was falsely accused of permitting the lashing and cursing of prisoners, of ordering a badly wounded soldier on a hike, and of forcing a fingerless patient to be a stretcher bearer. The officer's having been found guilty of permitting atrocities other than these was held to be no defense.

Courts routinely make allowances for the use of technically inaccurate lay terminology. *See* Rouch v. Enquirer & News of Battle Creek, 487 N.W.2d 205 (Mich. 1992) (article using the word "charge" to describe an arrest and booking was not defamatory, even though no formal arraignment had occurred); Rosen v. Capital City Press, 314 So. 2d 511 (La. Ct. App. 1975) (incorrect use of term "narcotics" to encompass depressants and stimulants was not actionable); Restatement, Second, of Torts §581(A) cmt. f ("a charge of theft may be reasonably interpreted as charging any criminally punishable misappropriation, and its truth may be established by proving the commission of any act of larceny").

In determining whether an inaccuracy is minor and irrelevant, many courts ask whether the "gist" or the "sting" of the defamatory charge is justified. *See* Gustafson v. City of Austin, 110 S.W.3d 652 (Tex. App. 2003) (no action was stated where the gist of an e-mailed statement (namely, that a CPR teacher was no longer a valid heart association CPR instructor and his instructor status had been officially revoked by the association) was not substantially worse than the literal truth (namely, that the teacher was no longer a valid heart association CPR instructor, and while he could still teach CPR courses, the courses were not sanctioned by the heart association)).

Omissions. Almost every statement about anything is inaccurate in the sense that it is incomplete; there is usually more to be said about any topic. The question whether an accurate statement is defamatory because it omits facts turns upon whether the omissions substantially distort the account or cause it to convey a false meaning.

Guccione v. Hustler Magazine, Inc.

United States Court of Appeals for the Second Circuit
800 F.2d 298 (2d Cir. 1986)

JON O. NEWMAN, Circuit Judge.

Publishers of pornography are, not surprisingly, often criticized and scorned and, on occasion, may even be libeled. This libel action brought by Robert Guccione, the publisher of *Penthouse* magazine, is noteworthy because the alleged libel was authored not by a righteous crusader against smut but by Larry Flynt, the publisher of *Hustler* magazine. An article printed in *Hustler* in 1983 stated that Guccione "is married and also has a live-in girlfriend, Kathy Keeton." In what the District Court…characterized as a "grudge match," Guccione sued for libel. The undisputed facts disclosed at the trial revealed that Guccione had been notoriously living with Miss Keeton while still married to Muriel Guccione for thirteen of the seventeen years prior to the article's publication, though he and Mrs. Guccione were divorced four years before the article appeared. Guccione emerged from the fray with a judgment in his favor of $1 in nominal damages and $1.6 million in punitive damages.

We must be careful in cases such as this not to accord either the pornographer plaintiff or the pornographer defendant less protection than would be accorded libel litigants who publish more traditional works of literature or journalism. Bearing that point firmly in mind, we conclude, for reasons that follow, that Guccione's claim fails as a matter of law….

….

…Guccione…maintains that because the statement was phrased in the present tense it accused him of committing adultery at the very time the statement was printed, that is, in late 1983, and that the fact of his 1979 divorce rendered the statement false. Guccione concedes that the substantial truth defense permits a certain amount of leeway as to accuracy. He argues, however, that whether the statement at issue was substantially true was a jury question resolved in his favor by a properly instructed jury. We disagree.

The District Court gave the following jury instruction on substantial truth:

> ….If the statement is true or substantially true, it cannot be libelous. It's not necessary of course that a statement be literally true. The test is whether the statement, as it was published, had a different effect on the mind of the reader than the actual literal truth. The facts which are offered to support a claim of substantial truth must be as broad as the alleged libel. Therefore, you have to determine the scope of the alleged libel before you can determine whether or not the statement was substantially true.

632 F. Supp. at 322. To this point, the charge was unexceptional. Unfortunately, however, the next paragraph improperly permitted the jury to disregard the substantial truth defense. The trial judge continued:

> Put another way, if you determine that the libel in question should be read as accusing Guccione of committing adultery only in 1983, the fact that Guccione might have committed adultery at another time is not going to make the statement substantially true. However, if you determine that the libel should only be read as accusing Guccione more generally of being an adulterer, you can then consider the evidence of Guccione's prior actions in relation to this issue of substantial truth.

Id. at 323.

This portion of the instruction permitted the jury to read the alleged libel as accusing Guccione of committing adultery "only" in 1983, in which event the jury was not to consider whether his past adultery made the statement substantially true. Though such a consequence would follow from such a reading of the statement, that reading is not within the range of reasonable interpretations requiring the jury's resolution. The statement was not an allegation of a specific act, like robbing a bank, that might in some circumstances be fairly interpreted either to mean that the act was committed at a time immediately prior to the publication or to mean that commission occurred at some time considerably earlier. The statement about Guccione alleged ongoing relationships—marriage to his wife and cohabitation with his girlfriend. There is not the slightest indication…[that] the statement…may fairly be read to mean that the marriage and the cohabitation existed simultaneously *only* at a moment or brief interval just prior to the article's publication. The statement can be read to mean only that the marriage and the cohabitation existed simultaneously throughout an undefined span of time that included the period immediately prior to publication.

On this reading, the undisputed facts establish the defense of substantial truth as a matter of law. New York law recognizes that an alleged libel is not actionable if the published statement could have produced no worse an effect on the mind of a reader than the truth pertinent to the allegation. [Citation.] The published statement read, "Considering he is married and also has a live-in girlfriend, Kathy Keeton…we wonder if he would let either of them pose nude with a man." Substituting the truth for the false statement yields that following: "Considering that from 1966 to 1979 he was married and also had a live-in girlfriend, Kathy Keeton…we wonder if he would let either of them pose nude with a man." The only difference in effect between the two statements worked in Guccione's favor; as printed, the statement merely points out the fact of his adultery, without calling attention to its duration for thirteen of the preceding seventeen years.

This is not to suggest that every person guilty of even a single episode of marital infidelity has no recourse if, years after the fact, he is accused in print of currently committing adultery. However, the undisputed facts of this case—the extremely long duration of Guccione's adulterous conduct, which he made no attempt to conceal from the general public, and the relatively short period of time since his divorce—make it fair to say that calling Guccione an "adulterer" in 1983 was substantially true. Of course, "former long-time adulterer" would have been more precise. But on the facts of this case, to require such a level of accuracy is unreasonable. The article labels Guccione an adulterer. The average reader would understand that term to include a man who unabashedly committed adultery for thirteen of the last seventeen years and whose adulterous behavior ended only because his wife ultimately divorced him….

    ….

….The judgment of the district court is reversed.

4. Of and Concerning the Plaintiff

To be actionable, a defamatory statement must refer to the plaintiff. But it is not necessary that the plaintiff be specifically named if other facts, such as an illustration or a verbal description, make it possible for the reader to associate the charge with the plaintiff. *See* Poe v. San Antonio Express-News Corp., 590 S.W.2d 537 (Tex. Civ. App. 1979) (summary judgment was denied because some of the plaintiff's acquaintances might have concluded that he was the "mid-fortyish" teacher who allegedly fondled a 14-year-old girl who was seen rushing from a local high school in tears). The test is whether some recipients of the communication reasonably understood the statement as referring to the plaintiff; the fact that not all recipients, or not even a majority, would have drawn that conclusion does not preclude an action.

An interesting set of facts was presented in Harwood v. Bush, 223 So. 2d 359 (Fla. Dist. Ct. App. 1969). There, an allegorical tale of an inquisitive rat with the same name as the plaintiff, a private investigator, was held libelous.

"Group Defamation." The defendants in Neiman-Marcus v. Lait, 13 F.R.D. 311 (S.D.N.Y. 1952), published a book which said that

(1) "Some" of the models at a particular store were call girls;

(2) "The salesgirls" were less expensive and "not as snooty as the models";

(3) "Most" of the male sales staff were homosexuals.

The plaintiffs were all nine of Neiman-Marcus's models, fifteen of its twenty-five salesmen, and thirty of its 382 saleswomen. The court held that false accusations against unspecified members of a small group are actionable by each member of the group, and denied the defendants' motion to dismiss the claims of the models and the male salesclerks. The female clerks' complaint was dismissed, however, because no reasonable reader could conclude from the accusation that any particular clerk was a prostitute. Is the court's approach to the female clerks' complaint convincing? Conceding that the statement, even if believed, would not persuade a reader that any particular clerk was a prostitute, might it not cause readers to think that the chance of any particular clerk's being a prostitute was substantial? Would a false statement that "I have evidence that leads me to think that there is a 20-percent chance that X is a prostitute" defame X?

See also Prince v. Out Publ'g Inc., 2002 W.L. 7999 (Cal. App.). In *Prince*, a party-goer sued the publisher of a gay-oriented magazine and others based on an article which referred to illegal drug use and unsafe sex, which included photographs of the plaintiff and others at "circuit parties." The court held that despite the juxtaposition of the photographs and the text, the plaintiff failed to satisfy the "of and concerning" requirement, reasoning:

> The photographs published in the Article establish that there were many people at the party. In addition, the text refers to parties attended by thousands of people. There is nothing in the text of the Article to suggest that the general statements about illegal drug use and unsafe sex apply to plaintiff.

Defamation in Fiction. It is well known that many works of fiction contain characters and incidents based on fact, despite the common but wildly unbelievable claim often made at the beginning of novels that no character described has any resemblance to any real person. It is therefore possible for passages in a work of fiction to defame someone.

In Bindrim v. Mitchell, 155 Cal. Rptr. 29 (Ct. App. 1979), the defendant, a novelist, attended "therapy" sessions conducted by the plaintiff, who used a technique called "nude marathon." The defendant assured the plaintiff that she had no intention of writing about the nude marathon, and she signed a contract not to "write articles, or in any manner disclose who has attended the workshop or what has transpired." Later, the defendant wrote a novel describing "nude marathon" sessions conducted by a therapist who used obscene language and did other unsavory things that the plaintiff had not done in his sessions. The court upheld a verdict for the plaintiff, ruling that the jury could reasonably have found that readers of the book might think that the incidents described in the book actually took place at the plaintiff's sessions. A dissenting opinion noted the many differences between the plaintiff and the character in the novel. The dissent also pointed out a certain element of bootstrapping in the plaintiff's case: similarities between the plaintiff and the character were used to show that the character represented the plaintiff, while differences were used to establish the untruth of the statements.

See also Muzikowski v. Paramount Pictures Corp., 322 F.3d 918 (7th Cir. 2003) (holding that a Little League baseball coach stated a claim for defamation based on the movie "Hardball" starring Keanu Reeves, because there were many similarities, though the character had a different name, and, unlike the plaintiff, committed theft and lied about being a licensed securities broker).

A defamatory work of fiction is not actionable unless it contains a plausibly believable false statement of fact. Pring v. Penthouse Int'l, Ltd., 695 F.2d 438 (10th Cir. 1982), reversed a $26.5 million judgment in favor of a former Miss Wyoming, who was a baton twirler, based on a story about a baton-twirling Miss Wyoming who performed astounding sexual feats at a nationally televised beauty pageant. The Tenth Circuit based its decision on the unbelievability of the events in the story (*e.g.*, levitation), ruling that no reasonable reader could have understood the story as describing conduct actually engaged in by the plaintiff. *See also* Flip Side, Inc. v. Chicago Tribune Co., 1989 W.L. 2044 (N.D. Ill.) (comic strip could not be interpreted as depicting actual events).

Statements about Ideas. Courts are reluctant to hold that criticism of an idea amounts to defamation of a person who holds the idea. *See* Ezrailson v. Rohrich, 65 S.W.3d 373 (Tex. App. 2001) (holding that a medical research article on an area of medical controversy, which criticized the creative research ideas behind a test to determine the presence of silicone, was not capable of a defamatory meaning as a matter of law).

Entities. An entity, such as a corporation, may be defamed with respect to such institutional characteristics as honesty, efficiency, and credit-worthiness. It is actionable falsely to state that a business has filed bankruptcy. *See* Dun & Bradstreet, Inc. v. Greenmoss Builders, Inc., 472 U.S. 749 (1985).

In Allied Marketing Group, Inc. v. Paramount Pictures Corp., 111 S.W.3d 168 (Tex. App. 2003), the television program *Hard Copy* aired a segment about a sweepstakes scam.

> Paramount intended to use a fictional company name in connection with the...segment and thought that "Sweepstakes Clearing House" was a fictional name. However, unknown to Paramount, Allied had been using the name "Sweepstakes Clearinghouse" since 1984 in connection with a direct mail offer business....

The court held that the show's segment on sweepstakes scams was "of and concerning" the sweepstakes company for purposes of the company's defamation action against the television show, because persons who knew the plaintiff could have concluded that the defamatory matter referred to the plaintiff. The show's fictional company name was identical to that of the real company, the company was actually in the business of conducting sweepstakes contests, one of which was very similar to the show's "scam" sweepstakes, and the show did not indicate to viewers that the show's fictional company did not exist. The court concluded that "[b]ecause the test is based on the reasonable understanding of the viewer of the publication, it is not necessary for the plaintiff to prove that the defendant intended to refer to the plaintiff." The court noted that the program was not an obvious work of fiction.

Defamation of the Dead. It is a well-established rule that the dead cannot be defamed. Of course, it is inherent in the common-law process that even well-established rules can be changed, and, given appealing enough facts, an action for defamation on behalf of a deceased person may someday succeed. Sometimes the relatives and friends of a decedent about whom false statements have been made can make a colorable claim that they have been defamed by statements about the decedent. As the following case shows, the courts have not been eager to accept that argument.

Rose v. Daily Mirror, Inc.
Court of Appeals of New York
31 N.E.2d 182 (N.Y. 1940)

LOUGHRAN, Judge.

The question is whether the complaint in this action states facts sufficient to constitute a cause of action for libel.

The pleading alleges that the plaintiff Anna Rose was the wife of Jack Rose and that the other plaintiffs are their children; that Jack Rose died on May 25, 1939; and that the defendant then published in its newspaper an article of and concerning the deceased Jack Rose wherein he was erroneously identified with one "Baldy Jack Rose," a person described in the article as a self-confessed murderer who had "lived in constant fear that emissaries of the underworld... would catch up with him and execute gang vengeance." This article named the respective plaintiffs as the surviving wife and children of the deceased Jack Rose but made no other direct reference to them.

A motion by the defendant for judgment dismissing the complaint was denied by Special Term. The order of the Special Term was reversed and the motion granted by the Appellate Division....

Defendant does not deny that the publication complained of was a libel on the memory of the deceased Jack Rose. Plaintiffs make no claim of any right to recover for that wrong. They stand upon the position that the publication...tended to subject them in their own persons to contumely and indignity and was, therefore, a libel upon them. It is true that...it has been held that it is a libel to write of a person that a near relative of his was a criminal. [Citations.]

In this State, however, it has long been accepted law that a libel or slander upon the memory of a deceased person which makes no direct reflection upon his relatives gives them no cause of action for defamation....

....

The judgment should be affirmed, with costs.

FINCH, Judge (dissenting).

....To publish that a man was a notorious criminal, and then to say that one of the plaintiffs was his wife and the others his children and so possessed of his blood, would seem to give them a cause of action for damages, just as much as to say that plaintiff had no proper family origin, i.e., was illegitimate. Shelby v. Sun Printing & Pub. Ass'n, 38 Hun. 474, 476, *affirmed* 109 N.Y. 611, 15 N.E. 895. Either of these charges would cause plaintiffs to be held up to ridicule and contempt....

Mere failure to attribute personal fault or misconduct to plaintiffs does not render the publication of defendant any the less libelous. The charge that the plaintiff is illegitimate is not to attribute fault or misconduct to plaintiff, yet plaintiff has a cause of action. There would seem no distinction between such case and the case at bar.

Plaintiffs are not the widow and children of Baldy Jack Rose, as alleged in the publication in question, and Jack Rose was not the despicable criminal whose shameful career was described. A respectable family whose husband and father has just passed away awakes the next morning to find blazoned forth in a morning newspaper that decedent was a notorious criminal, thus blackening the family and all its members. The slightest effort at verification would have shown the falsity of the story. If the law has reached the result of affording no relief here for the damages suffered, it would seem that the matter should be called to the attention of the Legislature.

It follows that the judgment dismissing the complaint should be reversed.

LEHMAN, C. J., and SEARS and LEWIS, JJ., concur with LOUGHRAN, J.

FINCH, J., dissents in opinion in which RIPPEY and CONWAY, JJ., concur.

Judgment affirmed.

Notes

1. Is it libelous of a widow to say in an obituary that her husband was a bachelor?

2. *Statements about Persons Other than the Plaintiff.* To be actionable, a defamatory utterance must reflect adversely on the character of the plaintiff, rather than on someone else. In Wheeler v. New Times, Inc., 49 S.W.3d 471 (Tex. App. 2001), the court held that an article was not defamatory as to a landlord, even though the article alleged that the city was discriminatory in enforcement of ordinances and renewal efforts and that those actions were to the landlord's benefit.

In Sarwer v. Conde Nast Publications, Inc., 654 N.Y.S.2d 768 (App. Div. 1997), the court held that the plaintiff, who was allegedly referred to in a magazine article as a victim of child abuse, did not state a claim for defamation. The 79 statements in the article that were claimed to be defamatory were not about the plaintiff at all, but rather about her family members. Or, if the statements were referable to the plaintiff, they were not susceptible to a defamatory connotation, inasmuch as the effect of article was to leave reader with only sympathy for the plaintiff as a victim of abuse.

5. Publication

If Smith calls Jones a "dirty rotten liar" and no one else hears the statement, Smith has not slandered Jones: defamation requires that the statement be heard or read, and understood, by a third person.

Economopoulos v. A. G. Pollard Co.

Supreme Judicial Court of Massachusetts
105 N.E. 896 (Mass. 1914)

This was an action of tort in three counts...the third count charging defendant with falsely and maliciously charging plaintiff with larceny by words spoken of plaintiff, as follows: "You have stolen a handkerchief from us and have it in your pocket." There was evidence that a clerk of defendant stated in English to plaintiff, a Greek, that he had stolen a handkerchief, and that a Greek clerk stated to plaintiff in Greek that plaintiff had stolen a handkerchief. There was nothing to show that third persons heard the charge, excepting the floor walker.

. . . .

LORING, J.

. . . [T]he judge was right in directing the jury to find the verdict for the defendant because there was no evidence of publication. . . . There was no evidence that anybody but the plaintiff was present when Carrier spoke to the plaintiff in English. There was no publication of this statement made in English, because on the evidence the words could not have been heard by any one but the plaintiff. [Citation.]

Nor was there any evidence of publication of the Greek words spoken by Miralos, for although there was evidence that they were spoken in the presence of others, there was no evidence that any one understood them but the plaintiff. [Citation.]

. . . .

Exceptions overruled.

Notes

1. *Distributors.* Ordinarily, one who repeats a defamatory statement is held to have made a publication of the matter. What about libraries, bookstores, printers, and newspaper deliverers who play a role in disseminating falsehoods originated by others? Are they, too, republishers? Ordinarily not. Such distributors are considered to be mere passive conduits and are subject to liability for statements in the materials they make available only if they knew or had reason to know of the defamatory content. *See, e.g.,* Cubby, Inc. v. CompuServe, Inc., 776 F. Supp. 135 (S.D.N.Y. 1991).

Because the publishers of newspapers and magazines exercise editorial control over the content of their publications, they do not qualify as mere distributors and are held to be publishers of any false statements in those works, regardless of where the libel originated. *See* Flowers v. Carville, 266 F. Supp. 2d 1245 (D. Nev. 2003) (action stated against publisher who allegedly knew that a book contained false defamatory statements about the plaintiff in connection with her alleged affair with a former President).

2. *Defamation on the Internet.* Initially, courts sought to decide whether Internet Service Providers (ISPs) should be treated as publishers of defamatory content posted on their services by others by asking whether the ISP exercised, or purported to exercise, control over content. This had the perverse effect of making ISPs who did nothing to control content generally immune from liability for defamation, while subjecting to the risk of suit those who attempted unsuccessfully to police unsupported gossip and other irresponsible conduct. *See* Stratton Oakmont, Inc. v. Prodigy Serv. Co., 1995 W.L. 805178 (N.Y. Sup. Ct. 1995). The issue has now been resolved by statute.

Under the Communications Decency Act of 1996 (47 U.S.C. sec. 230(c)(1) (Westlaw 2003)), "No provider or user of an interactive computer service shall be treated as the publisher or speaker of any information provided by another information content provider." The CDA has been broadly interpreted to bar defamation and other claims against Internet services. *See, e.g.,* Zeran v. America Online, Inc., 129 F.3d 327 (4th Cir. 1997) (the Act barred negligence claims for unreasonable delay in removing defamatory messages, refusal to post retractions of those messages, and failure to screen for similar postings; the court found the "artfully" pled negligence claims to be "indistinguishable" from "garden variety defamation"); Blumenthal v. Drudge, 992 F. Supp. 44 (D. D.C. 1998) (service provider was immune from defamation liability based on a gossip column, even though the provider paid the columnist, promoted the column as a new source of unverified instant gossip, and had certain editorial rights, including the rights to require changes in or remove content). Of course, the original culpable party who posts defamatory messages on the Internet is subject to liability.

At least in some cases, protection under the CDA extends to web loggers, website operators, and e-mail list editors. *See* Schneider v. Amazon.com, 31 P.3d 37 (Wash. Ct. App. 2001) (holding an online bookseller not liable for defamatory comments posted about an author's books). Immunity is not lost simply because the website operator exercises the option to edit or delete some of the information that has been posted. *See* Ben Ezra, Weinstein, and Co. v. America Online, Inc., 206 F.3d 980 (10th Cir. 2000).

In Batzel v. Smith, 333 F.3d 1018 (9th Cir. 2003), the court held that the operator of an anti-art-theft website, who posted an allegedly defamatory e-mail authored by a third party, and who did no more than select and make minor alterations to the e-mail, could not be considered a content provider subject to liability under the CDA. Further, if the operator could reasonably have concluded that the information was sent to him for posting on the website, he was immunized from liability as a "provider or user of interactive computer services." There was a factual dispute on this point because the operator received the e-mail (which accused the plaintiff, who had an extensive art collection, of being the granddaughter of a Nazi leader) at a different e-mail address, and the message therefore might not have been provided for posting on the listserv.

3. *Anonymous Postings on the Internet.* Many postings on the Internet are anonymous, and therefore plaintiffs who believe they have been defamed by such comments seek to compel ISPs to disclose the identity of the persons behind the pseudonyms. Courts differ in their treatment of these requests. In Dendrite Intl., Inc. v. Doe, No. 3, 775 A.2d 756 (N.J. Super. Ct. App. Div. 2001), the court wrote:

> We offer the following guidelines to trial courts when faced with an application by a plaintiff for expedited discovery seeking an order compelling an ISP to honor a subpoena and disclose the identity of anonymous Internet posters who are sued for allegedly violating the rights of individuals, corporations or businesses. The trial court must consider and decide those applications by striking a balance between the well-established First Amendment right to speak anonymously, and the right of the plaintiff to protect its proprietary interests and reputation through the assertion of recognizable claims based on the actionable conduct of the anonymous, fictitiously-named defendants.

> ... [T]he trial court should first require the plaintiff to undertake efforts to notify the anonymous posters that they are the subject of a subpoena or application for an order of disclosure, and withhold action to afford the fictitiously-named defendants a reasonable opportunity to file and serve opposition to the application. These notification efforts should include posting a message of notification of the identity discovery request to the anonymous user on the ISP's pertinent message board.

> The court shall also require the plaintiff to identify and set forth the exact statements purportedly made by each anonymous poster that plaintiff alleges constitutes actionable speech.

The complaint and all information provided to the court should be carefully reviewed to determine whether plaintiff has set forth a *prima facie* cause of action against the fictitiously-named anonymous defendants. In addition to establishing that its action can withstand a motion to dismiss…, the plaintiff must produce sufficient evidence supporting each element of its cause of action, on a *prima facie* basis, prior to a court ordering the disclosure of the identity of the unnamed defendant.

Finally,….the court must balance the defendant's First Amendment right of anonymous free speech against the strength of the *prima facie* case presented and the necessity for the disclosure of the anonymous defendant's identity to allow the plaintiff to properly proceed.

See also America Online, Inc. v. Nam Tai Electronics, Inc., 571 S.E.2d 128 (Va. 2002) (requiring revelation of identity).

4. *Communications between Agents of the Same Principal.* There is a substantial conflict as to whether intracompany documents or communications can satisfy the publication element of a defamation claim. Some states follow an agency theory and hold that there is no publication, as the corporation is merely communicating with itself. *See* Starr v. Pearle Vision, Inc., 54 F.3d 1548 (10th Cir. 1995) (Oklahoma law). Other states and the Restatement take the contrary position, reasoning that corporate employees remain individuals with distinct personalities and opinions that may be affected by communication of defamatory matter. *See* Restatement, Second, of Torts §577 cmt. i; Bals v. Verduzco, 600 N.E.2d 1353 (Ind. 1992) (labeling the no-publication view an "unacceptable legal fiction"); Staples v. Bangor Hydro-Elec. Co., 629 A.2d 601, 604 (Me. 1993) ("damage to one's reputation within the corporate community may be as devastating as that outside;…the defense of qualified privilege provides adequate protection"); Simpson v. Mars, Inc., 929 P.2d 966 (Nev. 1997) (adopting the Restatement view).

5. *"Compelled" Self-Publication.* In general, there is no actionable publication where a defendant communicates a statement directly to a plaintiff, who then repeats it to a third person. Restatement (Second) of Torts § 577, comment m. However, some states hold that the publication requirement is satisfied by facts showing that an employee was "compelled" to publish a defamatory statement by a former employer to a prospective employer under circumstances where that was foreseeable. *See* Kuechle v. Life's Companion P.C.A., Inc., 653 N.W.2d 214 (Minn. App. 2002) (holding that where the plaintiff was told that the defendant had reported her alleged misconduct to the Nurse's Board, the plaintiff had no reasonable means to avoid self-publishing the statement to a new employer, even though she was not asked the reason for her termination).

Olivieri v. Rodriguez, 122 F.3d 406 (7th Cir. 1997), was a federal constitutional action by a probationary police officer who was discharged without a hearing for harassing female officers. Although the police superintendent who had fired the plaintiff had not disclosed the grounds of his discharge publicly, the plaintiff argued that this was irrelevant, because any police department considering hiring him would ask why he had left his former job. The court, noting the existence of an intercircuit conflict on the issue, rejected the plaintiff's contention, saying:

The [plaintiff's] position resembles the largely discredited doctrine of "compelled republication" or (more vividly) "self-defamation," which allows the victim of a defamation to satisfy the requirement of publication by publishing it himself, for example to prospective employers as in the present case. [Citations] The doctrine is inconsistent with the fundamental principle of mitigation of damages.... The principle of self-defamation, applied in a case such as this, would encourage Olivieri to apply for a job to every police force in the nation, in order to magnify his damages; and to blurt out to each of them the ground of his discharge in the most lurid terms, to the same end. Most states... reject self-defamation as a basis for a tort claim, and it would be odd for federal constitutional law to embrace this principle.

See also Gonsalves v. Nissan Motor Corp., 58 P.3d 1196 (Haw. 2002) (rejecting self-publication).

In some states, legislatures have responded to the issue of "compelled self publication" by passing statutes. Compare the following laws from Colorado and Minnesota:

COLORADO REVISED STATUTES ANNOTATED
§13-25-125.5. Libel and slander—self-publication
(Westlaw 2004)

No action for libel or slander may be brought or maintained unless the party charged with such defamation has published, either orally or in writing, the defamatory statement to a person other than the person making the allegation of libel or slander. Self-publication, either orally or in writing, of the defamatory statement to a third person by the person making such allegation shall not give rise to a claim for libel or slander against the person who originally communicated the defamatory statement.

MINNESOTA STATUTES ANNOTATED
§181.933. Notice of termination
(Westlaw 2004)

Subdivision 1. Notice required.

An employee who has been involuntarily terminated may, within fifteen working days following such termination, request in writing that the employer inform the employee of the reason for the termination. Within ten working days following receipt of such request, an employer shall inform the terminated employee in writing of the truthful reason for the termination.

Subdivision 2. Defamation action prohibited.

No communication of the statement furnished by the employer to the employee under subdivision 1 may be made the subject of any action for libel, slander, or defamation by the employee against the employer.

Does the Minnesota provision mean more than that one cannot bring a defamation action based on truth?

6. *Disclosure by the Plaintiff without Knowledge of the Defamatory Content.* Cases of compelled self-publication involve situations where the plaintiffs are aware of the defamatory content of the information that is communicated. Those types of suits should be distinguished from, and are more difficult than, cases in which plaintiffs unwittingly transmit defamatory messages of whose contents they are unaware. Comment *m* to Restatement, Second, of Torts §577 states the rule for the latter category: "If the defamed person's transmission of the communication to the third person was made... without an awareness of the defamatory nature of the matter and if the circumstances indicated that communication to a third party would be likely, a publication may properly be held to have occurred." The Restatement offers the following illustrations:

10. A writes a defamatory letter about B and sends it to him through the mails in a sealed envelope. A knows that B is blind and that a member of his family will probably read the letter to him. B receives the letter and his wife reads it to him. A has published a libel.

11. A writes a letter to B accusing him of sexual misconduct. The defamatory matter is written in Latin, though A knows that B has no knowledge of Latin. B takes the letter to a Latin teacher to obtain a translation. A has published a libel.

The blackletter rule stated by §577 provides that "publication of defamatory matter" means communication of the matter "intentionally or by a negligent act to one other than the person defamed."

7. *The Single-Publication Rule.* According to §577A of the Restatement, Second, of Torts, any one edition of a book or newspaper, or any one radio or television broadcast, is a single publication, with respect to which only one action may be brought for all damages resulting from the publication. This rule prevents the plaintiff from bringing an action every time a book is sold, and in every jurisdiction in which a sale takes place. It also addresses the concern that, if every sale or reading of a book were a publication, there would be no effective statute of limitations in libel cases. However, the rule also eliminates the possibility of hardship to plaintiffs by allowing the collection of all damages in a single case.

Under this rule, if a book is published in 2006, sold at retail in 2007, and resold second-hand in 2008, the statute of limitations begins to run in 2006. However, if a paperback edition of that book is published in 2009, that event is a separate publication on which the statute starts to run in 2009.

In Altschuler v. University of Pa. Law Sch., 1997 W.L. 129394 (S.D.N.Y. 1997), *aff'd,* 201 F.3d 430 (2d Cir. 1999), the plaintiff asserted that a university had defamed him by putting a false and defamatory grade and other statements on his transcript, which was then released to law firms at various times. In addressing statute of limitations issues, the court wrote:

> The single publication rule does not apply to plaintiff's claims because he does not allege that his law school record and transcript were published to the public in a large, aggregate printing. Rather, he alleges that the law school has allowed professors and administrators to inspect his record "from time to time," and that his transcript has been released to particular law firms where he has applied over a period of time, both before and after his graduation.

See also Stella v. James J. Farley Ass'n, Inc., 122 N.Y.S.2d 322, 330-31 (Sup. Ct. 1953), *aff'd,* 135 N.Y.S.2d 234 (App. Div. 1954) (a distribution of pamphlets by hand was not a "mass publication" to which the single publication rule applied).

The single-publication rule applies to publications on the Internet, because "communications accessible over a public Web site resemble those contained in traditional mass media, only on a far grander scale." Firth v. State, 747 N.Y.S.2d 69, 71 (N.Y. 2002). Does updating the contents of a website constitute a new publication? According to *Firth*:

> The mere addition of unrelated information to a Web site cannot be equated with the repetition of defamatory matter in a separately published edition of a book or newspaper... for it is not reasonably inferable that the addition was made either with the intent or the result of communicating the earlier and separate defamatory information to a new audience.

...[M]any Web sites are in a constant state of change, with information posted sequentially on a frequent basis....Web sites are used by news organizations to provide readily accessible records of newsworthy events as they occur and are reported....A rule applying the republication exception...[to unrelated changes] would either discourage the placement of information on the Internet or slow the exchange of such information, reducing the Internet's unique advantages. In order not to retrigger the statute of limitations, a publisher would be forced either to avoid posting on a Web site or use a separate site for each new piece of information [citation]. These policy concerns militate against a holding that any modification to a Web site constitutes a republication of the defamatory communication itself.

As a practical matter, the statute of limitations for libel in a nationwide publication is that of whatever state has the longest statute of limitations for libel, at least if a substantial number of copies are sold in that state. *See* Keeton v. Hustler Mag., Inc., 465 U.S. 770 (1984), in which the plaintiff sued in New Hampshire because the statute of limitations in every other state had run by the time of the suit. Less than one percent of Hustler's circulation was in New Hampshire, and the plaintiff had no New Hampshire connections.

"[M]any states have passed 'borrowing statutes' that instruct their courts to apply foreign statutes of limitations in certain cases." Flowers v. Carville, 310 F.3d 1118 (9th Cir. 2003).

B. Libel and Slander

Written defamation is libel; oral defamation is slander. The law of libel is in some respects harder on the defendant than the law of slander, so it can matter how a case is classified. Centuries ago, the distinction between oral and written statements may have created a bright-line rule; today, it does not.

Is a radio or television broadcast a libel or a slander, and does the answer depend on whether the person making the remarks in question reads them from a script, or on whether the broadcast is live or taped, or on whether remarks that are aired also appear on the broadcaster's website? And what of defamation that consists of conduct, rather than words, as in Tyler v. Mack's Stores of S.C., Inc., 272 S.E.2d 633 (S.C. 1980), in which the alleged defamation consisted of discharging an employee immediately after a polygraph test?

The only principled (as opposed to historical) ground for treating libel cases differently from slander cases is that written lies tend generally to do more harm than spoken ones. Writing may be almost permanent, and in many cases more people are likely to see a written accusation than to hear a spoken one. Also, those who learn of an accusation may be more inclined to take it seriously if they read it than if they simply hear it. For these reasons, the Restatement, Second, of Torts, §568A, takes the position that defamation by radio or television is libel, since that kind of defamation may well carry the same force as defamation in writing. Some states, however, classify broadcast defamation as slander by statute; *see* Donald H. Remmers, *Recent Legislative Trends in Defamation by Radio*, 64 Harv. L. Rev. 727 (1951).

The main difference between libel and slander is that, at common law, a plaintiff in a libel case could recover damages without proof of any injury.[a] In slander cases, by contrast, the plaintiff ordinarily had to prove special damages, such as lost wages or reduced business income. However, slander is actionable *"per se,"*[b] that is, without proof of damages, if the statement accuses the plaintiff of:

(1) Committing a serious crime;

(2) Having a "loathsome disease" (that is, leprosy or a venereal disease, or perhaps, now, AIDS or SARS);

(3) Being incompetent to practice a chosen business, trade, or profession; or

(4) Being an unchaste woman (the Restatement, not surprisingly, says that this category now covers "serious sexual misconduct" by a plaintiff of either sex).

In certain jurisdictions, statutes make particular types of statements actionable as a matter of law. *See* 740 Ill. Consol. Stat. 145/1 (Westlaw 2003) (false accusations of fornication and adultery). Also, some states, but certainly not all, now treat libel and slander alike, drawing no distinction based on whether the statement is written or oral. *See* Bryson v. News Am. Pubs., Inc., 672 N.E.2d 1207 (Ill. 1996).

The extent to which the common law rules concerning presumed damages survive is a complex question, and the answer is heavily influenced by federal constitutional precedent. As discussed in the following section, the Supreme Court has held that in cases involving matters of "public concern" states may not allow "recovery of presumed or punitive damages, at least when liability is not based on a showing of knowledge of falsity or reckless disregard for the truth"; Gertz v. Robert Welch, Inc., 418 U.S. 323 (1974). However, that limitation does not apply to cases not involving matters of "public concern." *See* Dun & Bradstreet, Inc. v. Greenmoss Builders, Inc., 472 U.S. 749 (1985).

C. Constitutional Considerations

At common law, both libel and slander were strict-liability torts. Recall, for example, the *Cassidy* case, [1929] 2 K.B. 331 (at p. 968 n. 4 above), in which the defendant newspaper had no way of knowing that the information it was publishing was false, or even that the plaintiff existed. The Supreme Court has rewritten this aspect of defamation law so that in most if not all cases there is no strict liability. Moreover, in some cases, even a defendant who has negligently published defamatory material cannot be held liable.

The "constitutionalization" of defamation law began with New York Times v. Sullivan, a case which arose at the "intersection of three dominant themes in modern Amer-

---

a. Some states limited this rule to cases in which the libel, on its face, was defamatory of the plaintiff or to certain types of libelous statements. *See, e.g.,* Lega Siciliana Social Club, Inc. v. St. Germaine, 825 A.2d 827 (Conn. App. Ct. 2003) (holding that a written statement linking a private club to the Mafia was libelous *per se* and therefore it was unnecessary for the plaintiff to prove actual damages).

b. Note that this is a different use of the term *"per se"* than was mentioned above in connection with the discussion of "libel *per se*" (as opposed to "libel *per quod*"). *See* p. 969 *supra*. Consequently, when the words *"per se"* are used, it is necessary to determine whether the phrase means actionable without proof of special damages as opposed to defamatory of the plaintiff without any need to plead and prove additional facts.

ican experience: the power of the federal judiciary, the role of the press as an agent for social change, and the slow and painful struggle of black Americans for legal and social equality." Rodney A. Smolla, Suing The Press: Libel, The Media, & Power 27 (1986). The case involved efforts by southern segregationists to use libel law to levy huge damage awards against the New York Times for running an advertisement supporting Martin Luther King and his struggle for racial justice. The ad, which cost about $4800 and ran in about 650,000 newspapers (fewer than 400 of which were sent to Alabama), contained small factual errors. The plaintiff, a public official not named in the ad, alleged that the errors had defamed him.

In November, 1960, the case was tried in an Alabama courtroom with segregated seating. The air was thick with prejudice, as reflected by the judge's reference to "white man's justice" and the repeated use of the word "nigger" by plaintiff's counsel. Indeed, the atmosphere of racial hatred surrounding the litigation was so intense that the New York Times found it almost impossible to engage a local attorney to represent it. The names and pictures of the jurors were published in the Montgomery papers. When the three-day trial came to an end, television cameras followed the veniremen to the door of the jury room. A verdict for $500,000, the full amount asked for in the complaint, was promptly returned. If the award had been upheld, the effect on the *Times* would have been devastating, for additional suits by other public officials had already been filed throughout Alabama. Exposure of the media to liability under these circumstances threatened to rob the civil rights movement of any support it might find in the press.

As noted in Richard A. Epstein, *Was* New York Times v. Sullivan *Wrong?*, 53 U. Chi. L. Rev. 782, 787 (1986), *New York Times* was seen more as a civil-rights case than as a free-speech or freedom-of-the-press case at the time it was decided. Today's libel cases hardly ever deal with civil rights, but *New York Times* has transformed the law of libel. The case rendered obsolete hundreds of years of legal development and much of the law of libel in every state. Many writers have criticized the Court's holding, and it often seems that no one has anything good to say about the current state of defamation law. Yet *New York Times* has unquestionably achieved cornerstone status in media law, and there is little evidence that it will be abandoned. It may be the most important tort decision ever rendered by an American court.

There is an interesting footnote to the litigation: twenty years after *New York Times* was decided, T. Eric Embry, the Birmingham lawyer who courageously defended the newspaper, was a Justice of the Alabama Supreme Court.

1. Public Officials and Public Figures

New York Times Co. v. Sullivan

Supreme Court of the United States
376 U.S. 254 (1964)

Mr. Justice BRENNAN delivered the opinion of the Court.

We are required in this case to determine for the first time the extent to which the constitutional protections for speech and press limit a State's power to award damages in a libel action brought by a public official against critics of his official conduct.

Respondent L. B. Sullivan is one of the three elected Commissioners of the City of Montgomery, Alabama. [His duties included supervision of the Police Department.]....

He brought this civil libel action against the four individual petitioners, who are Negroes and Alabama clergymen, and against petitioner the New York Times Company, a New York corporation which publishes...a daily newspaper. A jury in the Circuit Court of Montgomery County awarded him damages of $500,000, the full amount claimed, against all the petitioners, and the Supreme Court of Alabama affirmed. [Citations.]

Respondent's complaint alleged that he had been libeled by statements in a full-page advertisement...[relating to the civil rights movement for racial equality.]....

The text appeared over the names of 64 persons, many widely known for their activities in public affairs, religion, trade unions, and the performing arts....

Of the 10 paragraphs of text in the advertisement, the third and a portion of the sixth were the basis of respondent's claim of libel....

. . . .

It is uncontroverted that some of the statements contained in the two paragraphs were not accurate descriptions of events which occurred in Montgomery. Although Negro students staged a demonstration on the State Capitol steps, they sang the National Anthem and not "My Country, 'Tis of Thee."....Although the police were deployed near the campus in large numbers on three occasions, they did not at any time "ring" the campus, and they were not called to the campus in connection with the demonstration on the State Capitol steps, as the third paragraph implied. Dr. King had not been arrested seven times, but only four; and although he claimed to have been assaulted some years earlier in connection with his arrest for loitering outside a courtroom, one of the officers who made the arrest denied that there was such an assault.

[Respondent was not mentioned by name.] On the premise that the charges in the sixth paragraph could be read as referring to him, respondent was allowed to prove that he had not participated in the events described....

. . . .

The trial judge submitted the case to the jury under instructions that the statements in the advertisement were "libelous *per se*" and were not privileged, so that petitioners might be held liable if the jury found that they had published the advertisement and that the statements were made "of and concerning" respondent....

. . . .

Under Alabama law as applied in this case...once "libel *per se*" has been established, the defendant has no defense as to stated facts unless he can persuade the jury that they were true in all their particulars....

. . . .

....The First Amendment, said Judge Learned Hand, "presupposes that right conclusions are more likely to be gathered out of a multitude of tongues, than through any kind of authoritative selection. To many this is, and always will be, folly; but we have staked upon it our all." [Citation.] Mr. Justice Brandeis, in his concurring opinion in Whitney v. California, [274 U.S. 357], gave the principle its classic formulation:

> Those who won our independence believed...that public discussion is a political duty; and that this should be a fundamental principle of American government. They recognized the risks to which all human institutions are subject. But they knew that order cannot be secured merely through fear of punishment for its infractions; that it is hazardous to discourage thought, hope and imagination; that fear breeds repression; that repression breeds hate; that hate

menaces stable government; that the path of safety lies in the opportunity to discuss freely supposed grievances and proposed remedies; and that the fitting remedy for evil counsels is good ones. Believing in the power of reason as applied through public discussion, they eschewed silence coerced by law—the argument of force in its worst form. Recognizing the occasional tyrannies of governing majorities, they amended the Constitution so that free speech and assembly should be guaranteed.

Thus we consider this case against the background of a profound national commitment to the principle that debate on public issues should be uninhibited, robust and wide-open, and that it may well include vehement, caustic, and sometimes unpleasantly sharp attacks on government and public officials. [Citations.] The present advertisement, as an expression of grievance and protest, on one of the major public issues of our time, would seem clearly to qualify for the constitutional protection. The question is whether it forfeits that protection by the falsity of some of its factual statements and by its alleged defamation of respondent.

....As Madison said, "Some degree of abuse is inseparable from the proper use of everything; and in no instance is this more true than in that of the press." [Citation.] In Cantwell v. Connecticut, 310 U.S. 296, the Court declared:

> In the realm of religious faith, and in that of political belief, sharp differences arise. In both fields the tenets of one man may seem the rankest error to his neighbor. To persuade others to his own point of view, the pleader, as we know, at times resorts to exaggeration, to vilification of men who have been, or are, prominent in church or state, and even to false statement. But the people of this nation have ordained in the light of history, that, in spite of the probability of excesses and abuses, these liberties are, in the long view, essential to enlightened opinion and right conduct on the part of the citizens of a democracy.

[The]...erroneous statement is inevitable in free debate, and...it must be protected if the freedoms of expression are to have the "breathing space" that they "need...to survive"....

....

If neither factual error nor defamatory content suffices to remove the constitutional shield from criticism of official conduct, the combination of the two elements is no less inadequate. [The Court then considered the history of the Sedition Act of 1798, which made it a crime to publish defamation against high officers of the United States, and reached the conclusion that it was unconstitutional.]

....What a State may not constitutionally bring about by means of a criminal statute is likewise beyond the reach of its civil law of libel. The fear of damage awards under a rule such as that invoked by the Alabama courts here may be markedly more inhibiting than the fear of prosecution under a criminal statute....Presumably a person charged with violation of [a criminal libel] statute enjoys ordinary criminal-law safeguards such as the requirements of an indictment and of proof beyond a reasonable doubt. These safeguards are not available to the defendant in a civil action. The judgment awarded in this case—without the need for any proof of actual pecuniary loss—was one thousand times greater than the maximum fine provided by the Alabama criminal statute, and one hundred times greater than that provided by the Sedition Act. And since there is no double jeopardy limitation applicable to civil lawsuits, this is not the only judgment that may be awarded against petitioners for the same publication. Whether or not a newspaper can survive a succession of such judgments, the pall of fear and timidity imposed upon those who would give voice to public criticism is an atmosphere in which the First Amendment freedoms cannot survive. Plainly the Alabama law of civil libel is "a form of regulation that creates hazards to protected freedoms markedly greater than those that attend reliance upon the criminal law." [Citation.]

The state rule of law is not saved by its allowance of the defense of truth....A rule compelling the critic of official conduct to guarantee the truth of all his factual assertions—and to do so on pain of libel judgments virtually unlimited in amount—leads to a comparable "self-censorship." Allowance of the defense of truth, with the burden of proving it on the defendant, does not mean that only false speech will be deterred.... Under such a rule, would-be critics of official conduct may be deterred from voicing their criticism, even though it is believed to be true and even though it is in fact true, because of doubt whether it can be proved in court or fear of the expense of having to do so....The rule thus dampens the vigor and limits the variety of public debate. It is inconsistent with the First and Fourteenth Amendments.

The constitutional guarantees require, we think, a federal rule that prohibits a public official from recovering damages for a defamatory falsehood relating to his official conduct unless he proves that the statement was made with "actual malice"—that is, with knowledge that it was false or with reckless disregard of whether it was false or not. An oft-cited statement of a like rule, which has been adopted by a number of state courts, is found in the Kansas case of Coleman v. MacLennan, 78 Kan. 711, 98 P. 281 (1908)....On appeal the Supreme Court of Kansas, in an opinion by Justice Burch, reasoned as follows:

> It is of the utmost consequence that the people should discuss the character and qualifications of candidates for their suffrage. The importance to the state and to society of such discussions is so vast, and the advantages derived are so great that they more than counterbalance the inconvenience of private persons whose conduct may be involved, and occasional injury to the reputations of individuals must yield to the public welfare, although at times such injury may be great. The public benefit from publicity is so great and the chance of injury to private character so small that such discussion must be privileged.

....

We hold today that the Constitution delimits a State's power to award damages for libel in actions brought by public officials against critics of their official conduct. Since this is such an action, the rule requiring proof of actual malice is applicable....

....

...[W]e consider that the proof presented to show actual malice lacks the convincing clarity which the constitutional standard demands, and hence that it would not constitutionally sustain the judgment for respondent under the proper rule of law. The case of the individual petitioners requires little discussion. Even assuming that they could constitutionally be found to have authorized the use of their names on the advertisement, there was no evidence whatever that they were aware of any erroneous statements or were in any way reckless in that regard. The judgment against them is thus without constitutional support.

As to the Times, we similarly conclude that the facts do not support a finding of actual malice. The statement by the Times' Secretary that, apart from the padlocking allegation, he thought the advertisement was "substantially correct," affords no constitutional warrant for the Alabama Supreme Court's conclusion that it was a "cavalier ignoring of the falsity of the advertisement, [from which] the jury could not have but been impressed with the bad faith of The Times, and its maliciousness inferable therefrom." The statement does not indicate malice at the time of the publication; even if the advertisement was not "substantially correct"—although respondent's own proofs tend to show that it was—that opinion was at least a reasonable one, and there was no evidence to impeach the witness' good faith in holding it. The Times' failure to retract upon respondent's demand, although it later retracted upon the demand of Governor Patterson, is likewise not adequate evidence of malice for constitutional purposes. Whether or not a failure to retract may ever constitute such evidence, there are two reasons why it does not here. *First*, the letter written by the Times reflected a reasonable doubt on its part as to whether the advertisement could reasonably be taken to refer to respondent at all. *Second*, it was not a final refusal, since it asked for an explanation on this point—a request that respondent chose to ignore. Nor does the retraction upon the demand of the Governor supply the necessary proof. It may be doubted that a failure to retract which is not itself evidence of malice can retroactively become such by virtue of a retraction subsequently made to another party. But in any event that did not happen here, since the explanation given by the Times' Secretary for the distinction drawn between respondent and the Governor was a reasonable one, the good faith of which was not impeached.

Finally, there is evidence that the Times published the advertisement without checking its accuracy against the news stories in the Times' own files. The mere presence of the stories in the files does not, of course, establish that the Times "knew" the advertisement was false, since the state of mind required for actual malice would have to be brought home to the persons in the Times' organization having responsibility for the publication of the advertisement. With respect to the failure of those persons to make the check, the record shows that they relied upon their knowledge of the good reputation of many of those whose names were listed as sponsors of the advertisement, and upon the letter from A. Philip Randolph, known to them as a responsible individual, certifying that the use of the names was authorized. There was testimony that the persons handling the advertisement saw nothing in it that would render it unacceptable under the Times' policy of rejecting advertisements containing "attacks of a personal character"; their failure to reject it on this ground was not unreasonable. We think the evidence against the Times supports at most a finding of negligence in failing to discover the misstatements, and is constitutionally insufficient to show the recklessness that it is required for a finding of actual malice. [Citations.]

We also think the evidence was constitutionally defective in another respect: it was incapable of supporting the jury's finding that the allegedly libelous statements were made "of and concerning" respondent.... There was no reference to respondent in the advertisement, either by name or official position. A number of the allegedly libelous statements...did not even concern the police.... The statements upon which respondent relies as referring to him are the two allegations that did concern the police or police functions: that "truckloads of police...ringed the Alabama State College Campus" after the demonstration on the State Capitol steps, and that Dr. King had been "arrested...seven times." These statements were false only in that the police had been "deployed near" the campus but had not actually "ringed" it and had not gone there in connection with the State Capitol demonstration, and in that Dr. King had been arrested only four times. The ruling that these discrepancies between what was true and what was asserted were sufficient to injure respondent's reputation may itself raise constitutional problems, but we need not consider them here. Although the statements may be taken as referring to the police, they do not on their face make even an oblique reference to respondent as an individual....

.... The present proposition would sidestep this obstacle by transmuting criticism of government, however impersonal it may seem on its face, into personal criticism, and hence potential libel of the officials of whom the government is composed.... We hold that such a proposition may not constitutionally be utilized to establish that an otherwise impersonal attack on governmental operations was a libel of an official responsible for those operations....

....

The judgment of the Supreme Court of Alabama is reversed and the case is remanded to that court for further proceedings not inconsistent with this opinion.

[The concurring opinions of Justices BLACK and GOLDBERG, both of which would have categorically denied any action for defamation to a public official based on public conduct, are omitted. Justice DOUGLAS joined in both concurring opinions.]

Notes

1. Was there any reason for the jury to presume damage to Sullivan's reputation? Justice Hugo Black, a former Senator from Alabama, noted in his concurring opinion:

> Viewed realistically, this record lends support to an inference that instead of being damaged, Commissioner Sullivan's political, social, and financial prestige has been enhanced by the Times publication.

376 U.S. at 294. *See also* Richard A. Epstein, *Was* New York Times v. Sullivan *Wrong?*, 53 U. Chi. L. Rev. 782, 790 (1986) ("My sense is that tried anywhere outside the deep South, the plaintiff would have been sent packing. The common law was sound; its application was not").

2. *Failure to Retract.* As suggested by *New York Times,* a failure to retract is ordinarily insufficient to establish actual malice because the subsequent conduct does not show the defendant's earlier state of mind. However, if there is independent evidence that the reporter knew at the time of the publication that the article was wrong, and later refused to print a retraction, an action will lie. *See* Golden Bear Distrib. Sys. v. Chase Revel, Inc., 708 F.2d 944 (5th Cir. 1983) (the author of the article had notes showing that she knew the information in her article was wrong).

3. *Actual Malice in Reporting.* In St. Amant v. Thompson, 390 U.S. 727 (1968), the Supreme Court held that relying on a single and perhaps unreliable source without attempting to verify the accuracy of the statement was not "reckless" for purposes of the *New York Times* "actual malice" test. Whether a "reasonable" publisher would have investigated more thoroughly (or at all) is irrelevant. Only defendants who publish with subjective "awareness of probable falsity" are "reckless." The Court observed, however, that a story "based wholly on an unverified anonymous telephone call" or which contains "allegations...so improbable that only a reckless man could have put them in circulation" might be actionable. Under *St. Amant,* there is ordinarily no obligation on the defendant to talk to the subject of the defamatory communication to obtain that person's version of the events described (Rosenbloom v. Metromedia, Inc., 403 U.S. 29 (1971)) or to endeavor to present an objective picture (New York Times Co. v. Connor, 365 F.2d 567, 576 (5th Cir. 1966)).

Moreover, factual inaccuracies alone do not suffice to prove actual malice (Time, Inc. v. Pape, 401 U.S. 279 (1971); Fadell v. Minneapolis Star & Tribune Co., Inc., 557 F.2d 107 (7th Cir. 1977)), nor is recklessness established merely by showing that the reporting in question was speculative or even sloppy (Oliver v. Village Voice, Inc., 417 F. Supp. 235, 238 (S.D.N.Y. 1976)). *See also* Harte-Hanks Communications, Inc. v. Con-

naughton, 491 U.S. 657 (1989) ("a public figure plaintiff must prove more than an extreme departure from professional standards and…a newspaper's motive in publishing
a story—whether to promote an opponent's candidacy or to increase its circulation—
cannot provide a sufficient basis for finding actual malice").

Even the deliberate alteration of quotations will not prove knowledge of falsity, unless the alteration materially changes the meaning of the quotation alleged to be defamatory. *See* Masson v. New Yorker Mag., Inc., 501 U.S. 496 (1991). "That a defendant
publishes statements anticipating financial gain likewise fails to prove actual malice: a
profit motive does not strip communications of constitutional protections." Peter Scalamandre & Sons, Inc. v. Kaufman, 113 F.3d 556, 561 (5th Cir. 1997).

In WJLA-TV v. Levin, 564 So. 2d 383 (Va. 2002), an orthopedist was accused of sexually assaulting his female patients and using inappropriate medical procedures. The
court held that the television station's use of the statements of a physician, which the
station knew the physician had retracted, was sufficient to support a jury finding of actual malice. A $2 million award of presumed damages was upheld.

Because the actual-malice standard makes constitutional protection depend upon
the defendant's state of mind, the focus of the litigation often shifts away from the issue
of whether the defamatory statement was true or false. When that happens, plaintiffs
may find it impossible to clear their names by obtaining rulings on falsity, and the public may never know the truth.

In addition, litigation of the actual-malice issue may be highly disruptive to editorial
processes in suits against media defendants. The publisher's state of mind must normally be inferred from circumstantial evidence. Consequently, plaintiffs routinely seek
discovery of information about such matters as communications between reporters and
editors, facts known but not used in a story, the pressures under which the work was
prepared, and the identity and credibility of the defendant's sources.

4. *"Actual Malice" versus "Express Malice."* "Actual Malice," as defined in *New York
Times* and subsequent cases, is a legal term of art which must be clearly distinguished
from "express" or "common-law" malice. One may utter true statements, just as easily as
those which are false, with spite, ill will, vindictiveness or motives of revenge—that is
to say, with express or common-law malice. A showing that the defendant was actuated
by bad motives is not, by itself, sufficient to satisfy the actual-malice requirement. Proof
of ill will says nothing about whether the defendant knew of, or acted recklessly as to,
the falsity of the defamatory statement.

Jury instructions permitting a finding of actual malice merely upon proof of hatred,
enmity, desire to injure, or the like are constitutionally defective. In discussing the reasoning underlying this position, the Supreme Court observed in Garrison v. State of
Louisiana, 379 U.S. 64, 73-75 (1964), a criminal defamation case:

> [T]he great principles of the Constitution which secure freedom of expression
> in this area preclude attaching adverse consequences to any except the knowing
> or reckless falsehood. Debate on public issues will not be uninhibited if the
> speaker must run the risk that it will be proved in court that he spoke out of
> hatred; even if he did speak out of hatred, utterances honestly believed con-
> tribute to the free interchange of ideas and the ascertainment of truth. Under a
> rule…permitting a finding of [actual] malice based on an intent merely to in-
> flict harm, rather than to inflict harm through falsehood, "it becomes a haz-
> ardous matter to speak out against a popular politician, with the result that the
> dishonest and incompetent will be shielded." [Citation.] Moreover, "[i]n the

case of charges against a popular political figure...it may be almost impossible to show freedom from ill-will or selfish political motives."....

...[O]nly those false statements made with the high degree of awareness of their probable falsity demanded by *New York Times* may be the subject of either civil or criminal sanctions....[The Constitution protects even] vehement, caustic, and sometimes unpleasantly sharp attacks on government and public officials.

Of course, in many instances, evidence of express malice may be coupled with facts showing that the defendant lacked an honest belief in the truth of the statements. In those cases, proof of "malice" in the *New York Times* sense allows the action to go forward; proof of common-law malice may encourage the jury to award a large verdict.

5. ***Honest but Erroneous Beliefs.*** The statement of an erroneous belief which is honestly held, and which has some factual grounding, cannot ordinarily be found to have been uttered with actual malice. *See* Peter Scalamandre & Sons, Inc. v. Kaufman, 113 F.3d 556, 562 (5th Cir. 1997) (assertions that the plaintiff conducted "an illegal haul and dump operation" and that the "people of Texas are being poisoned" were shown at trial to be the defendant's honest beliefs and were not so without basis as to constitute reckless disregard for the truth).

See also Sparks v. Peaster, 581 S.E.2d 579 (Ga. Ct. App. 2003) (holding that a city manager did not act with actual malice when he said that a resident had a serious cocaine habit, because the plaintiff was confrontational and sometimes irrational, and police officers had given the manager reason to believe that the plaintiff had a problem with drugs).

6. ***Clear and Convincing Proof of Actual Malice.*** Although other issues in a defamation action may be controlled by the usual preponderance-of-the-evidence standard, actual malice constitutionally must be established by clear and convincing evidence. *See* Harte-Hanks Communications, Inc. v. Connaughton, 491 U.S. 657, 661 n.2 (1989). This heightened standard of proof applies not only to jury determinations, but to preliminary rulings on motions for summary judgment. *See* Anderson v. Liberty Lobby, Inc., 477 U.S. 242, 255-56 (1986). Consequently, a plaintiff must produce strong evidence of actual malice to survive a defendant's motion for summary disposition—evidence from which actual malice could be found by clear and convincing evidence.

7. ***Judicial Review of Findings on Actual Malice.*** The obstacles posed by the actual-malice and clear-and-convincing-evidence rules are amplified by the fact that a finding of actual malice is not entitled to the deference usually extended to findings of fact. The question whether the evidence supports a finding of actual malice is a question of law, and in determining whether the constitutional standard is satisfied, the trial court and every reviewing court must consider the factual record in full to ascertain whether there is clear and convincing evidence. *See* Bose Corp. v. Consumers U. of the U.S., Inc., 466 U.S. 485 (1984). Since independent review occurs only when the jury finds for the plaintiff, the rule confers its substantial benefits exclusively on defendants. This important procedural rule, and the clear-and-convincing-evidence standard, may do more to provide "breathing space" for free expression than the actual-malice standard itself.

The independent review requirement does not extend to all elements of a defamation cause of action or to all types of defamation cases. *See* Lundell Mfg. Co., Inc. v. ABC, 98 F.3d 351 (8th Cir. 1996) (in a libel case involving a private figure plaintiff, the jury's finding of falsity or substantial truth must be accepted if supported by substantial evidence).

8. ***Public Officials.*** Not all public employees are subject to the "actual malice" requirement of New York Times v. Sullivan. "It is clear...that the 'public official' designa-

tion applies at the very least to those among the hierarchy of government employees who have, or appear to the public to have, substantial responsibility for or control over the conduct of governmental affairs." Rosenblatt v. Baer, 383 U.S. 75, 85 (1966). The test is whether the "position in government has such apparent importance that the public has an independent interest in the qualifications and performance of the person who holds it, beyond the general public interest in the qualifications and performance of all governmental employees." *Id.* at 86.

In practice, courts have often viewed the public official category expansively. For example, police officers, from ordinary patrolman to chief of police, are routinely classified as public officials. *See* Tomkiewicz v. Detroit News, Inc., 635 N.W.2d 36 (Mich. Ct. App. 2001) (holding that a police lieutenant, in an action against a newspaper that erroneously published a photograph identifying him as the police officer who had stalked a former mistress, was a public official because his office afforded him significant authority and control over daily lives of other citizens).

The Restatement makes clear that the actual-malice rule applies to public officials only if the defamatory statement relates to the official's qualifications. "A statement that the governor drinks himself into a stupor at home every night much more clearly affects his qualifications than a statement that a tax assessor keeps a secret collection of pornographic pictures." Restatement, Second, of Torts §580A Cmt. b.

9. *Former Public Officials.* A former public official may be subject to the actual-malice standard if the statement relates to official performance while in office. Rosenblatt v. Baer, 383 U.S. 75 (1966).

10. *Ethics in Law Practice: Criticism of the Judiciary.* Do attorneys enjoy the same free speech rights as members of the general public? Model Rule 8.2 provides that an attorney is not subject to professional discipline (*e.g.*, reprimand, suspension or disbarment), unless a defamatory statement about a judicial officer is made with actual malice:

> A lawyer shall not make a statement that the lawyer knows to be false or with reckless disregard as to its truth or falsity concerning the qualifications or integrity of a judge...or of a candidate for election or appointment to judicial... office.

Model Rules of Professional Conduct Rule 8.2(a) (2003). However, some courts have interpreted Rule 8.2 in a way that clearly departs from constitutional precedent which in all other contexts holds that the actual malice standard requires proof of subjective awareness of probable falsity. In Idaho State Bar v. Topp, 925 P.2d 1113 (Idaho 1996), an attorney, following a hearing conducted amid a "political frenzy" regarding property tax issues, suggested to the media that the judge's immediate ruling on a question was politically motivated. In upholding a public reprimand of the attorney, the court found that Rule 8.2 should be read to impose an objective standard for recklessness and that discipline was warranted because the attorney lacked a reasonable basis for the statement.

Courts differ on the issue of whether discipline may be imposed for attorney criticism of a judge which is not provably false. *Compare* Kentucky Bar Ass'n v. Waller, 929 S.W.2d 181 (Ky. 1996) (holding that truth was no defense in a disciplinary action against an attorney who called a judge a "lying incompetent asshole" because such language promotes disrespect for the law and for the judicial system), *with* Standing Comm. v. Yagman, 55 F.3d 1430 (9th Cir. 1995) (embracing a "reasonable attorney" standard, rather than the subjective *New York Times* actual malice standard, but holding that a lawyer's statements that a federal judge was anti-Semitic, intellectually dishonest, and drunk while on the bench were not proved to be false, or were incapable of being proved true or false, and therefore were protected by the First Amendment).

The constitutional principles applicable to negative statements by judges or judicial candidates during election campaigns are discussed in Vincent R. Johnson, *Ethical Campaigning for the Judiciary*, 29 Tex. Tech. L. Rev. 811, 816-837 (1998).

11. *Public Figures.* The *New York Times* actual-malice requirement was extended to public figures in Curtis Publ'g Co. v. Butts and Associated Press v. Walker, 388 U.S. 130 (1967), and, at least for a brief time, to cases generally involving matters of public interest in Rosenbloom v. Metromedia, Inc., 403 U.S. 29 (1971).

2. Plaintiffs Who Are Not Public Figures

Gertz v. Robert Welch, Inc.
Supreme Court of the United States
418 U.S. 323 (1974)

Mr. Justice POWELL delivered the opinion of the Court.

. . . .

[The family of a youth named Nelson, who was shot and killed by one Nuccio, a police officer later convicted of homicide, retained Elmer Gertz to represent them in civil litigation arising from the death. In this capacity, Gertz attended the coroner's inquest into the boy's death and initiated actions for damages, but he neither discussed Officer Nuccio with the press nor played any part in the criminal proceeding. Notwithstanding petitioner's remote connection with the prosecution of Nuccio, respondent's magazine, an outlet for the views of the John Birch Society, portrayed him as an architect of a plan to "frame" the police officer. Its statements contained serious inaccuracies. The implication that petitioner had a criminal record was false. There was no evidence that he or an organization to which he belonged had taken any part in planning the 1968 demonstrations in Chicago. There was also no basis for the charge that petitioner was a "Leninist" or a "Communist-fronter." And he had never been a member of the "Marxist League for Industrial Democracy" or the "Intercollegiate Socialist Society."]

The managing editor of American Opinion made no effort to verify or substantiate the charges against petitioner. Instead, he appended an editorial introduction stating that the author had "conducted extensive research into the Richard Nuccio Case."....

[The District Court denied defendant's motion to dismiss petitioner's libel action. After the evidence was in, it "ruled in effect that petitioner was neither a public official nor a public figure," and it submitted the issue of damages to the jury, which awarded $50,000. On further reflection the District Court concluded that the New York Times standard applied and entered judgment for defendant notwithstanding the jury verdict. This action was affirmed by the Court of Appeals for the Seventh Circuit, on the basis of Rosenbloom v. Metromedia, Inc., 403 U.S. 29 (1971).]

The principal issue in this case is whether a newspaper or broadcaster that publishes defamatory falsehoods about an individual who is neither a public official nor a public figure may claim a constitutional privilege against liability for the injury inflicted by those statements....

        ....

We begin with the common ground. Under the First Amendment there is no such thing as a false idea. However pernicious an opinion may seem, we depend for its correction not on the conscience of judges and juries but on the competition of other ideas. But there is no constitutional value in false statements of fact. Neither the intentional lie nor the careless error materially advances society's interest in "uninhibited, robust, and wide-open" debate on public issues. [Citation.] They belong to that category of utterances which "are no essential part of any exposition of ideas, and are of such slight social value as a step to truth that any benefit that may be derived from them is clearly outweighed by the social interest in order and morality." [Citation.]

Although the erroneous statement of fact is not worthy of constitutional protection, it is nevertheless inevitable in free debate. As James Madison pointed out in the Report on the Virginia Resolutions of 1798: "Some degree of abuse is inseparable from the proper use of every thing; and in no instance is this more true than in that of the press." [Citation.] And punishment of error runs the risk of inducing a cautious and restrictive exercise of the constitutionally guaranteed freedoms of speech and press....

        ....

The legitimate state interest underlying the law of libel is the compensation of individuals for the harm inflicted on them by defamatory falsehood. We would not lightly require the State to abandon this purpose, for, as Mr. Justice Stewart has reminded us, the individual's right to the protection of his own good name reflects no more than our basic concept of the essential dignity and worth of every human being—a concept at the root of any decent system of ordered liberty.... [Citation.]

Some tension necessarily exists between the need for a vigorous and uninhibited press and the legitimate interest in redressing wrongful injury....

The *New York Times* standard defines the level of constitutional protection appropriate to the context of defamation of a public person. Those who, by reason of the notoriety of their achievements or the vigor and success with which they seek the public's attention, are properly classified as public figures and those who hold governmental office may recover for injury to reputation only on clear and convincing proof that the defamatory falsehood was made with knowledge of its falsity or with reckless disregard for the truth. This standard administers an extremely powerful antidote to the inducement to media self-censorship of the common-law rule of strict liability for libel and slander. And it exacts a correspondingly high price from the victims of defamatory falsehood. Plainly many deserving plaintiffs, including some intentionally subjected to injury, will be unable to surmount the barrier of the *New York Times* test. Despite this substantial abridgment of the state law right to compensation for wrongful hurt to one's reputation, the Court has concluded that the protection of the *New York Times* privilege should be available to publishers and broadcasters of defamatory falsehood concerning public officials and public figures. [Citation.] We think that these decisions are correct.... For the reasons stated below, we conclude that the state interest in compensating injury to the reputation of private individuals requires that a different rule should obtain with respect to them.

....

....The first remedy of any victim of defamation is self-help—using available opportunities to contradict the lie or correct the error and thereby to minimize its adverse impact on reputation. Public officials and public figures usually enjoy significantly greater access to the channels of effective communication and hence have a more realistic opportunity to counteract false statements than private individuals normally enjoy. Private individuals are therefore more vulnerable to injury, and the state interest in protecting them is correspondingly greater.

More important..., there is a compelling normative consideration underlying the distinction between public and private defamation plaintiffs. An individual who decides to seek governmental office must accept certain necessary consequences of that involvement in public affairs. He runs the risk of closer public scrutiny than might otherwise be the case....

Those classed as public figures stand in a similar position. Hypothetically, it may be possible for someone to become a public figure through no purposeful action of his own, but the instances of truly involuntary public figures must be exceedingly rare. For the most part those who attain this status have assumed roles of especial prominence in the affairs of society. Some occupy positions of such persuasive power and influence that they are deemed public figures for all purposes. More commonly, those classed as public figures have thrust themselves to the forefront of particular public controversies in order to influence the resolution of the issues involved. In either event, they invite attention and comment.

Even if the foregoing generalities do not obtain in every instance, the communications media are entitled to act on the assumption that public officials and public figures have voluntarily exposed themselves to increased risk of injury from defamatory falsehood concerning them. No such assumption is justified with respect to a private individual. He has not accepted public office or assumed an "influential role in ordering society." [Citation.] He has relinquished no part of his interest in the protection of his own good name, and consequently he has a more compelling call on the courts for redress of injury inflicted by defamatory falsehood. Thus, private individuals are not only more vulnerable to injury than public officials and public figures; they are also more deserving of recovery.

For these reasons we conclude that the States should retain substantial latitude in their efforts to enforce a legal remedy for defamatory falsehood injurious to the reputation of a private individual. The extension of the *New York Times* test proposed by the *Rosenbloom* plurality [*see* note 11 on p. 995, *supra*] would abridge this legitimate state interest to a degree that we find unacceptable. And it would occasion the additional difficulty of forcing state and federal judges to decide on an *ad hoc* basis which publications address issues of "general or public interest" and which do not—to determine, in the words of Mr. Justice Marshall, "what information is relevant to self-government." [Citation.] We doubt the wisdom of committing this task to the conscience of judges. Nor does the Constitution require us to draw so thin a line between the drastic alternatives of the *New York Times* privilege and the common law of strict liability for defamatory error. The "public or general interest" test for determining the applicability of the *New York Times* standard to private defamation actions inadequately serves both of the competing values at stake. On the one hand, a private individual whose reputation is injured by defamatory falsehood that does concern an issue of public or general interest has no recourse unless he can meet the rigorous requirements of *New York Times*. This is true despite the factors that distinguish the state interest in compensating private individuals from the analogous interest involved in the context of public persons. On the other hand, a publisher or broadcaster of a defamatory error which a court deems unrelated to an issue of public or general interest may be held liable in damages even if it took every reasonable precaution to ensure the accuracy of its assertions. And liability may far exceed compensation for any actual injury to the plaintiff, for the jury may be permitted to presume damages without proof of loss and even to award punitive damages.

We hold that, so long as they do not impose liability without fault, the States may define for themselves the appropriate standard of liability for a publisher or broadcaster of defamatory falsehood injurious to a private individual. This approach...recognizes the strength of the legitimate state interest in compensating private individuals for wrongful injury to reputation, yet shields the press and broadcast media from the rigors of strict liability for defamation....

....

...[W]e endorse this approach in recognition of the strong and legitimate state interest in compensating private individuals for injury to reputation. But this countervailing state interest extends no further than compensation for actual injury. For the reasons stated below, we hold that the States may not permit recovery of presumed or punitive damages, at least when liability is not based on a showing of knowledge of falsity or reckless disregard for the truth.

The common law of defamation is an oddity of tort law, for it allows recovery of purportedly compensatory damages without evidence of actual loss. Under the traditional rules pertaining to actions for libel, the existence of injury is presumed from the fact of publication. Juries may award substantial sums as compensation for supposed damage to reputation without any proof that such harm actually occurred. The largely uncontrolled discretion of juries to award damages where there is no loss unnecessarily compounds the potential of any system of liability for defamatory falsehood to inhibit the vigorous exercise of First Amendment freedoms. Additionally, the doctrine of presumed damages invites juries to punish unpopular opinion rather than to compensate individuals for injury sustained by the publication of a false fact. More to the point, the States have no substantial interest in securing for plaintiffs such as this petitioner gratuitous awards of money damages far in excess of any actual injury.

....It is necessary to restrict defamation plaintiffs who do not prove knowledge of falsity or reckless disregard for the truth to compensation for actual injury. We need not define "actual injury," as trial courts have wide experience in framing appropriate jury instructions in tort actions. Suffice it to say that actual injury is not limited to out-of-pocket loss. Indeed, the more customary types of actual harm inflicted by defamatory falsehood include impairment of reputation and standing in the community, personal humiliation, and mental anguish and suffering.... [T]here need be no evidence which assigns an actual dollar value to the injury.

We also find no justification for allowing awards of punitive damages against publishers and broadcasters held liable under state-defined standards of liability for defamation....Like the doctrine of presumed damages, jury discretion to award punitive damages unnecessarily exacerbates the danger of media self-censorship, but, unlike the former rule, punitive damages are wholly irrelevant to the state interest that justifies a negligence standard for private defamation actions. They are not compensation for injury....In short, the private defamation plaintiff who establishes liability under a less demanding standard than that stated by *New York Times* may recover only such damages as are sufficient to compensate him for actual injury.

....

Notwithstanding our refusal to extend the *New York Times* privilege to defamation of private individuals, respondent contends that we should affirm the judgment below on the ground that petitioner is either a public official or a public figure. There is little basis for the former assertion. Several years prior to the present incident, petitioner had served briefly on housing committees appointed by the mayor of Chicago, but at the time of publication he had never held any remunerative governmental position. Respondent admits this but argues that petitioner's appearance at the coroner's inquest rendered him a "*de facto* public official." Our cases recognize no such concept. Respondent's suggestion would sweep all lawyers under the *New York Times* rule as officers of the court and distort the plain meaning of the "public official" category beyond all recognition. We decline to follow it.

Respondent's characterization of petitioner as a public figure raises a different question....

Petitioner has long been active in community and professional affairs. He has served as an officer of local civic groups and of various professional organizations, and he has published several books and articles on legal subjects. Although petitioner was consequently well known in some circles, he had achieved no general fame or notoriety in the community. None of the prospective jurors called at the trial had ever heard of petitioner prior to this litigation, and respondent offered no proof that this response was atypical of the local population. We would not lightly assume that a citizen's participation in community and professional affairs rendered him a public figure for all purposes. Absent clear evidence of general fame or notoriety in the community, and pervasive involvement in the affairs of society, an individual should not be deemed a public personality for all aspects of his life. It is preferable to reduce the public-figure question to a more meaningful context by looking to the nature and extent of an individual's participation in the particular controversy giving rise to the defamation.

In this context it is plain that petitioner was not a public figure. He played a minimal role at the coroner's inquest, and his participation related solely to his representation of a private client. He took no part in the criminal prosecution of Officer Nuccio. Moreover, he never discussed either the criminal or civil litigation with the press and was never quoted as having done so. He plainly did not thrust himself into the vortex of this public issue, nor did he engage the public's attention in an attempt to influence its outcome. We are persuaded that the trial court did not err in refusing to characterize petitioner as a public figure for the purpose of this litigation.

We therefore conclude that the *New York Times* standard is inapplicable to this case and that the trial court erred in entering judgment for respondent. Because the jury was allowed to impose liability without fault and was permitted to presume damages without proof of injury, a new trial is necessary. We reverse and remand for further proceedings in accord with this opinion.

It is so ordered.

[Justice POWELL'S opinion was joined by STEWART, MARSHALL, BLACKMUN and REHNQUIST, JJ. BLACKMUN, J., stated in a concurrence that he found some difficulties with the majority opinion, but that he joined in it to attain a "definitive ruling." BURGER, C.J., dissented in an opinion which indicated that he disapproved of the requirement of negligence for private defamation. DOUGLAS, J., dissented on the basis of his absolute-privilege theory, and would have at least retained the Rosenbloom rule.

BRENNAN, J., dissented and would have retained the Rosenbloom rule. WHITE, J., dissented and would have retained strict liability for private defamation.]

Notes

1. *Fault as to Falsity in* Gertz *cases.* Virtually all states have accepted *Gertz's* invitation to require only a showing of negligence in cases brought by private persons suing with respect to matters of public concern. *But see* Poyser v. Peerless, 775 N.E.2d 1101 (Ind. Ct. App. 2002) (requiring actual malice).

New Jersey has adopted an interesting variation. It holds that the negligence standard ordinarily applies to defamation actions brought by businesses that do not inherently involve important public interests such as matters of public health or banking. However, even innocuous and prosaic everyday businesses, which are akin to private individuals, must prove actual malice if the defamatory statements allege what would be a violation of the New Jersey Consumer Fraud Act. *See* Turf Lawnmower Repair, Inc. v. Bergen Record Corp., 655 A.2d 417 (N.J. 1995).

2. *Public Figure Status is a Question of Law.* Whether the plaintiff is a public figure for purposes of the defamatory statement is a question of law for the court. In rare cases, the plaintiff will be public figure for all purposes. However, the key question in most cases is simply whether the plaintiff is a public figure with respect to the subject matter of the defamatory statement. Courts have classified as public figures:

> A city resident who was the subject of a feature story where he was quoted acknowledging his political actions on behalf of others and his intention to influence government officials. Sparks v. Peaster, 581 S.E.2d 579 (Ga. Ct. App. 2003).

> A restaurant. Pegasus v. Reno Newspapers, 57 P.3d 82 (Nev. 2002) ("because a restaurant is a place of public accommodation that seeks public patrons, it is a public figure for the limited purpose of a food review or reporting on its goods and services");

> A Holocaust survivor who authorized a biography. Thomas v. L.A. Times Communications, 2002 W.L. 31007420 (9th Cir.).

> A security guard who granted a photo shoot and interviews following the explosion of a bomb at an Olympic venue, but before he became a suspect. Atlanta-Journal Constitution v. Jewell, 555 S.E.2d 175 (Ga. Ct. App. 2001).

> The president of the nation's second largest cooperative, with respect to his innovative policies. Waldbaum v. Fairchild Pubs., Inc., 627 F.2d 1287, 1300 (D.C. Cir. 1980).

> A professional football player, with respect to his physical condition, contractual dispute, and retirement. Chuy v. Philadelphia Eagles Football Club, 595 F.2d 1265, 1280 (3d Cir. 1979) (en banc).

> A woman who was the former girlfriend of Elvis Presley and the wife of a retired football star, concerning her marital status and romantic encounters. Brewer v. Memphis Publ'g Co., 626 F.2d 1238, 1255 (5th Cir. 1980).

> A well-known former U.S. Senate candidate. Williams v. Pasma, 656 P.2d 212, 216 (Mont. 1982) (because the plaintiff had "general fame or notoriety in the community (Montana) and exhibited pervasive involvement in the affairs of society" he was "a public figure as a matter of law," presumably for all purposes).

A Playboy playmate, with respect to allegedly libelous use of a photograph for which she posed. Vitale v. National Lampoon, Inc., 449 F. Supp. 442 (E.D. Pa. 1978).

A college dean, with respect to a controversy relating to his tenure as dean. Byers v. Southeastern Newspaper Corp., Inc., 288 S.E.2d 698 (Ga. Ct. App. 1982).

However, some decisions have construed "public figure" narrowly. *See, e.g.,* Franklin Prescriptions, Inc. v. New York Times Co., 267 F. Supp. 2d 425 (E.D. Pa. 2003) (holding that a pharmacy, which used the Internet for informational purposes only, and did not take orders over the Internet, was not limited purpose public figure in the context of a public controversy about online pharmacies making expensive drugs more accessible).

In Lundell Mfg. Co. v. ABC, 98 F.3d 351 (8th Cir. 1996), the court held that a manufacturer of a garbage recycling machine was not a public figure, for although garbage disposal was a matter of public concern, the manufacturer's entry into a contract for the sale of the machine to a county was not the injection of the manufacturer into a controversy for the purpose of influencing a public issue. Moreover, the defendant network's conduct in televising the issue did not render the manufacturer a public figure.

3. *Self-Help.* Is Justice Powell correct that public figures have greater access to avenues of self-help for correcting defamatory falsehoods? Today, many metropolitan areas have only one newspaper. If a person is defamed by the one newspaper in town, what chance does that person have to rebut the charges?

In *Rosenbloom*, Justice Brennan had written:

> While the argument that public figures need less protection because they can command media attention to counter criticism may be true for some very prominent people, even then it is the rare case where the denial overtakes the original charge. Denials, retractions, and corrections are not "hot" news, and rarely receive the prominence of the original story. When the public official or public figure is a minor functionary, or has left the position that put him in the public eye [citation] the argument loses all of its force....

403 U.S. at 46-47.

4. Justice Powell's opinion in *Gertz* suggests that one who voluntarily enters public life must accept the risk of closer public scrutiny. Does that justify leaving public figures practically without remedy for defamatory falsehoods, as the actual-malice standard and related rules do? Why not hold that the risk of closer public scrutiny justifies more protection for a public official's or public figure's reputation, rather than less?

5. *Defamation in Politics.* Political ads often contain extreme characterizations of an opponent's record. These statements are not exempt from liability. A candidate for public office is a public figure who must prove actual malice in order to recover for defamation. That is a formidable obstacle, but sometimes it can be met.

In Boyce & Isley, PLLC v. Cooper, 568 S.E.2d 893 (N.C. Ct. App. 2002), the successful candidate for attorney general had run a commercial saying that his opponent's law firm had "sued the state" and "charge[d]" the taxpayers an hourly rate of $28,000, "more than a police officer's salary for each hour's work." The ad did not point out that the fee was pursued by the plaintiff's father in a contingent fee class action before the plaintiff joined the firm. The court held that the statements were libelous *per se* because they implied unethical billing practices. Moreover, a claim was stated by all four members of the opponent's law firm and the firm itself. Because the successful candidate refused to pull the ad after demands for discontinuance, there was a basis for finding that the defendant acted with actual malice.

In Flowers v. Carville, 310 F.3d 1118 (9th Cir. 2003), the court held that a claim was stated against former presidential advisors based on their repetition of news reports by CNN that tape recordings made by the plaintiff had been "doctored" or "selectively edited." The court acknowledged that the plaintiff, after conducting discovery, might not be able to prove that the defendants acted with actual malice. "One who repeats what he hears from a reputable news source, with no individualized reason external to the news report to doubt its accuracy, has not acted recklessly." However, here, "[d]efendants were not uninvolved third parties who clearly lacked access to the facts behind the published reports."

6. *The Economic Realities of Defamation Litigation.* Plaintiffs in defamation cases against the media face heavy obstacles. For one thing, large media defendants are "repeat players" in defamation litigation. They therefore have an incentive to defend every case to the hilt. A strong defense not only helps to win the case in question, but also to discourage other victims from bringing suit. Furthermore, proof of the kind of injury suffered in a typical defamation case—mental suffering, loss of respect, and so on—may be difficult. Finally, some victims of defamation sue not because they have suffered heavy damages of a measurable sort, but to clear their names. Victims like this may have trouble in finding lawyers to handle their cases—which are not at all easy to litigate—if their recoveries are limited. As a result, many actions by plaintiffs who are not public officials or public figures may not be worth bringing unless the plaintiff expects to be able to prove actual malice, so as to qualify for damages without proof of actual loss. If so, *Gertz* may leave private-figure plaintiffs with less protection than it seems to at first glance.

7. *Actual Injury versus Special Damages.* "Actual injury," as defined in *Gertz*, differs from the common-law concept of special damages because "actual injury" includes mental suffering. In Terwilliger v. Wands, 17 N.Y. 54 (1858), a man was orally accused of regularly beating a path to the house of his neighbor for the purpose of having sexual intercourse with her while her husband was in prison. The only injury the man proved was that he was so worked up that he could not attend to business; there was no evidence that anyone treated him differently. The court affirmed a judgment for the defendant because the slander did not fall within the four *per se* categories and there was no proof of special damages. (Note that if the suit had been brought by the woman, or if the accusation had been in writing, there would have been no need to prove special damages.)

8. *The "Libel-Proof" Plaintiff.* Because damages in defamation cases are meant to compensate for harm to the plaintiff's reputation, a plaintiff whose reputation was very bad before a particular defamation occurred may be entitled only to nominal damages. If that is the case, there is a serious question as to whether a court should spend limited judicial resources on hearing the action. For instance, the alleged defamation in Wynberg v. National Enquirer, Inc., 564 F. Supp. 924 (C.D. Cal. 1982), was an accusation that the plaintiff had used his "close personal relationship" with a famous actress (Elizabeth Taylor) for personal gain. The court noted that the plaintiff had been convicted five times for such crimes as contributing to the delinquency of minors, bribery, grand theft, and offering the services of prostitutes to police officers, and that these incidents had been widely publicized. Furthermore, "numerous articles" had discussed the ways in which plaintiff had used his relationship with the actress for financial gain. Concluding that the plaintiff was libel-proof, the court granted the defendant's motion for summary judgment.

In Davis v. The Tennessean, 83 S.W.3d 125 (Tenn. Ct. App. 2002), the court held than an inmate, who had been sentenced to 99 years in prison for aiding and abetting a murder, was libel-proof because an article incorrectly reported that he was the one who shot the tavern owner during the course of a robbery. The court noted that:

> A number of jurisdictions have adopted the "libel-proof" doctrine, and it has often been applied in a situation where the plaintiff's complaint is that the publication accused him of the wrong crimes.

See also Lamb v. Rizzo, 242 F. Supp. 2d 1032 (D. Kan. 2003) (prisoner serving three consecutive life terms for murder and kidnapping was libel-proof).

There are two branches to the libel-proof plaintiff doctrine. The "issue-specific" branch considers whether plaintiff's reputation is so bad with respect to the issue in question that the plaintiff is libel-proof on that issue. *Wynberg* is an example of this kind of case. In contrast, the "incremental harm" branch of the doctrine focuses on true statements contained in the allegedly defamatory communication. If the challenged statements harm the plaintiff's reputation far less than the true portions of the communication, an action may be barred because there is little or no incremental harm from the falsehoods. *See* James A. Hemphill, Note, *Libel-Proof Plaintiffs and the Question of Injury*, 71 Tex. L. Rev. 401 (1992).

The "incremental harm" rationale was considered in Masson v. New Yorker Magazine, Inc., 111 S. Ct. 2419, 2436 (1991):

> [W]e reject any suggestion that the incremental harm doctrine is compelled as a matter of First Amendment protection for speech. ... Of course, state tort law doctrines of injury, causation, and damages calculation might allow a defendant to press the argument that the statements did not result in any incremental harm to a plaintiff's reputation.

The defendant's ability to introduce evidence of the plaintiff's bad reputation tends to discourage plaintiffs from bringing defamation actions. If, as is often the case, the plaintiff's goal is to clear a besmirched reputation, the prospect of giving the defendant's lawyer a shot at the plaintiff, in public, may deter even those who can establish defamation. Even if the defendant's evidence of bad character is weak, accusations made at the trial may make a vivid impression on the public. Bringing a defamation action, like shooting at a king, should not be undertaken by those uncertain of success.

Time, Inc. v. Firestone
Supreme Court of the United States
424 U.S. 448 (1976)

Mr. Justice REHNQUIST delivered the opinion of the Court.

Petitioner is the publisher of Time, a weekly news magazine. The Supreme Court of Florida affirmed a $100,000 libel judgment against petitioner which was based on an item appearing in Time that purported to describe the result of domestic relations litigation between respondent and her husband. ...

Respondent, Mary Alice Firestone, married Russell Firestone, the scion of one of America's wealthier industrial families, in 1961. In 1964, they separated, and respondent filed a complaint for separate maintenance in the Circuit Court of Palm Beach County, Fla. Her husband counterclaimed for divorce on grounds of extreme cruelty and adultery. After a lengthy trial the Circuit Court issued a judgment granting the divorce requested by respondent's husband. In relevant part the court's final judgment read:

....

According to certain testimony in behalf of the defendant, extramarital escapades of the plaintiff were bizarre and of an amatory nature which would have made Dr. Freud's hair curl. Other testimony, in plaintiff's behalf, would indicate that defendant was guilty of bounding from one bedpartner to another with the erotic zest of a satyr. The court is inclined to discount much of this testimony as unreliable. Nevertheless, it is the conclusion and finding of the court that neither party is domesticated, within the meaning of that term as used by the Supreme Court of Florida.

....

...Time's staff composed the following item, which appeared in the magazine's "Milestones" section the following week:

[Divorced.] By Russell A. Firestone, Jr., 41, heir to the tire fortune: Mary Alice Sullivan Firestone, 32, his third wife; a onetime Palm Beach schoolteacher; on grounds of extreme cruelty and adultery; after six years of marriage, one son; in West Palm Beach Fla. The 17-month intermittent trial produced enough testimony of extramarital adventures on both sides, said the judge, "to make Dr. Freud's hair curl."

...[R]espondent demanded in writing a retraction from petitioner, alleging that a portion of the article was "false, malicious and defamatory." Petitioner declined to issue the requested retraction.

Respondent then filed this libel action....

....

....Respondent did not assume any role of especial prominence in the affairs of society, other than perhaps Palm Beach society, and she did not thrust herself to the forefront of any particular public controversy in order to influence the resolution of the issues involved in it.

Petitioner contends that because the Firestone divorce was characterized by the Florida Supreme Court as a "cause célèbre," it must have been a public controversy and respondent must be considered a public figure. But in so doing petitioner seeks to equate "public controversy" with all controversies of interest to the public. Were we to accept this reasoning, we would reinstate the doctrine advanced in the plurality opinion in Rosenbloom v. Metromedia, Inc., 403 U.S. 29 (1971) which concluded that the *New York Times* privilege should be extended to falsehoods defamatory of private persons whenever the statements concern matters of general or public interest. In *Gertz*, however, the Court repudiated this position....

Dissolution of a marriage through judicial proceedings is not the sort of "public controversy" referred to in *Gertz*, even though the marital difficulties of extremely wealthy individuals may be of interest to some portion of the reading public. Nor did respondent freely choose to publicize issues as to the propriety of her married life. She was compelled to go to court by the State in order to obtain legal release from the bonds of matrimony....[3]....We hold respondent was not a "public figure" for the purpose of de-

---

3. Nor do we think the fact that respondent may have held a few press conferences during the divorce proceedings in an attempt to satisfy inquiring reporters converts her into a "public figure." Such interviews should have no effect upon the merits of the legal dispute between respondent and her husband or the outcome of that trial, and we do not think it can be assumed that any such purpose was intended. Moreover, there is no indication that she sought to use the press conferences as a

termining the constitutional protection afforded petitioner's report of the factual and legal basis for her divorce.

...[W]e likewise reject petitioner's claim for automatic extension of the *New York Times* privilege to all reports of judicial proceedings. It is argued that information concerning proceedings in our Nation's courts may have such importance to all citizens as to justify extending special First Amendment protection to the press when reporting on such events. We have recently accepted a significantly more confined version of this argument by holding that the Constitution precludes States from imposing civil liability based upon the publication of truthful information contained in official court records open to pubic inspection. Cox Broadcasting Corp. v. Cohn, 420 U.S. 469 (1975).

Petitioner would have us extend the reasoning of *Cox Broadcasting* to safeguard even inaccurate and false statements, at least where "actual malice" has not been established. But its argument proves too much. It may be that all reports of judicial proceedings contain some informational value implicating the First Amendment, but recognizing this is little different from labeling all judicial proceedings matters of "public or general interest," as that phrase was used by the plurality in *Rosenbloom*....

....

....There appears little reason why [private] individuals should substantially forfeit that degree of protection which the law of defamation would otherwise afford them simply by virtue of their being drawn into a courtroom. The public interest in accurate reports of judicial proceedings is substantially protected by *Cox Broadcasting Co., supra*. As to inaccurate and defamatory reports of facts, matters deserving no First Amendment protection [citation], we think *Gertz* provides an adequate safeguard for the constitutionally protected interests of the press and affords it a tolerable margin for error by requiring some type of fault.

[The court then found that the petitioner's argument that the report of the divorce was "factually correct" was refuted by the holding of the Florida court that it was not correct in stating that the divorce was based on a finding of adultery.] The Supreme Court of Florida on appeal concluded that the ground actually relied upon by the divorce court was "lack of domestication of the parties," a ground not theretofore recognized by Florida law. The Supreme Court nonetheless affirmed the judgment dissolving the bonds of matrimony because the record contained sufficient evidence to establish the ground of extreme cruelty. Firestone v. Firestone, 263 So. 2d 223, 225 (1972).

Petitioner may well argue that the meaning of the trial court's decree was unclear, but this does not license it to choose from among several conceivable interpretations the one most damaging to respondent. Having chosen to follow this tack, petitioner must be able to establish not merely that the item reported was a conceivable or plausible interpretation of the decree, but that the item was factually correct....

....Petitioner has argued that because respondent withdrew her claim for damages to reputation on the eve of trial, there could be no recovery consistent with *Gertz*...[In *Gertz*] we made it clear that States could base awards on elements other than injury to reputation, specifically listing "personal humiliation, and mental anguish and suffering" as examples of injuries which might be compensated consistently with the Constitution upon a showing of fault. Because respondent has decided to forgo recovery for injury to

---

vehicle by which to thrust herself to the forefront of some unrelated controversy in order to influence its resolution. *See* Gertz v. Robert Welch, Inc., 418 U.S. 323 (1974).

her reputation, she is not prevented from obtaining compensation for such other damages that a defamatory falsehood may have caused her.

....Several witnesses testified to the extent of respondent's anxiety and concern over Time's inaccurately reporting that she had been found guilty of adultery, and she herself took the stand to elaborate on her fears that her young son would be adversely affected by this falsehood when he grew older. The jury decided these injuries should be compensated by an award of $100,000. We have no warrant for re-examining this determination....

Gertz established, however, that not only must there be evidence to support an award of compensatory damages, there must also be evidence of some fault on the part of a defendant charged with publishing defamatory material. No question of fault was submitted to the jury in this case....

....

...[I]n the absence of a finding in some element of the state court system that there was fault, we are not inclined to canvass the record to make such a determination in the first instance. [Citation] Accordingly, the judgment of the Supreme Court of Florida is vacated and the case remanded for further proceedings not inconsistent with this opinion.

So ordered.

[The concurring opinion of Justice POWELL, and the dissenting opinions of Justices BRENNAN, WHITE, and MARSHALL are omitted.]

Notes

1. *Matters Not of "Public Concern."* In Dun & Bradstreet, Inc. v. Greenmoss Builders, Inc., 472 U.S. 749 (1985), the Court held that a false and defamatory credit report did not involve a matter of "public concern." State libel law, which allowed the plaintiff to recover presumed and punitive damages without proof of actual malice, did not violate the First Amendment as applied in that case.

Unfortunately, *Dun & Bradstreet* provides little guidance for distinguishing matters of private concern from matters of public concern. Indeed, the Court's application of the law to the facts before it seems somewhat counter-intuitive. The credit report had erroneously said that the plaintiff had declared voluntary bankruptcy. Isn't it a matter of public concern whether a business which employs numerous workers and pays taxes is failing? The Court appeared to place weight on the fact that the erroneous credit report was given limited dissemination and that the five subscribers who received the report were contractually precluded from further disseminating its contents. The Court also suggested that the reporting of "objectively verifiable information" deserved less constitutional protection than other kinds of speech, and that market forces gave credit-reporting agencies an incentive to be accurate, "since false credit reporting is of no use to creditors."

It is surprising that *Dun & Bradstreet* drew a distinction between matters of public interest and matters of private concern. In 1971, Rosenbloom v. Metromedia, Inc., 403 U.S. 29, had embraced that distinction in deciding how far to extend the actual-malice standard. However, in 1974, Gertz v. Robert Welch, Inc., 418 U.S. 323, repudiated *Rosenbloom* on the ground that judges should not be called upon to decide what is or is not a matter of public concern. Why was that reasoning not persuasive when *Dun & Bradstreet* was decided in 1985?

Note also that the plurality opinion in *Dun & Bradstreet* was silent on whether the plaintiff in a private-matter action must prove that the defendant acted with some degree of fault as to falsity. Justice White, concurring, thought that *Dun & Bradstreet* had rejected the *Gertz* rule that liability cannot be imposed without fault, as well as the *Gertz* holding on the availability of presumed damages. Justice Brennan, speaking in dissent for four members of the Court, opined that the holding in *Dun & Bradstreet* was narrow and that the parties did not question the requirement of fault to obtain a judgment and actual damages.

2. *Summary: Three Categories.* The Supreme Court's rulings create three categories of defamation cases:

(a) *Actions by Public Officials or Public Figures for Defamation in Respect to Matters of Public Concern (New York Times controls).* The plaintiff must prove actual malice. Presumed and punitive damages are not barred by the Constitution if the requirements of *New York Times* have been met.

(b) *Actions by Private Persons for Defamation in Respect to Matters of Public Concern (Gertz, as modified by Dun & Bradstreet, controls).* The plaintiff must prove that the defendant acted with fault as to the statement's falsity, and recovery is limited to actual injury, unless the plaintiff proves actual malice, in which case, presumed or punitive damages are constitutionally permissible.

(c) *Actions by Anyone for Defamation in Respect to a Matter of Private Concern (Dun & Bradstreet controls).* Whether the plaintiff must prove that the defendant acted with fault as to the falsity of the statement is unclear. Presumed and punitive damages may be awarded without proof of actual malice.

3. *Constitutional Restrictions Imposed by the Religion Clauses.* "Most courts that have considered the question whether the Free Exercise Clause divests a civil court of subject matter jurisdiction to consider a pastor's defamation claims against a church and its officials have answered that question in the affirmative." Cha v. Korean Presby. Ch. of Wash., 553 S.E.2d 511 (Va. 2001) (holding that the trial court lacked subject matter jurisdiction to review such a claim).

But see Lliebenstein v. Iowa Conf. of United Meth. Ch., 663 N.W.2d 404 (Iowa. 2003) (holding that a defamation action by a church member against the church and church officials was not barred by the Establishment Clause because the phrase "spirit of Satan," as used in a widely published letter, had a secular as well as a sectarian meaning, and therefore a factfinder could determine whether the phrase was defamatory without resorting to theological reflection).

3. Retraction Statutes

Some states have enacted "retraction statutes," which limit plaintiffs' remedies in some defamation actions if the defendant publishes a retraction. *See* Mathis v. Cannon, 573 S.E.2d 376 (Ga. 2002) (interpreting state statutes as providing that, because the plaintiff did not request the defendant poster of a defamatory Internet message to issue a retraction, punitive damages were not recoverable). Retraction statutes usually apply only to "media defendants," which have received so much in the way of constitutional protection that at least some retraction statutes no longer serve any purpose.

For example, Fla. Stat. Ann. §770.02 (Westlaw 2003) limits libel plaintiffs' recoveries to actual damages if an erroneous publication or broadcast is properly retracted. The statute applies only if the defendant had "reasonable grounds for believing that the statements...were true." Today, with respect to a matter of public concern, *Gertz* holds that a defendant who had reasonable grounds for believing a statement to be true cannot be held liable even if it does not retract. The *Gertz* decision therefore makes the Florida retraction statute pointless in a wide range of cases. However, because the Supreme Court has never ruled on whether the *Gertz* requirement of fault as to falsity applies to cases in which a private person is suing with respect to a matter of private concern, the Florida statute may retain some significance.

Although the notion of compelled retraction has occasionally been advanced by legal writers, no state presently compels retraction. A forced retraction would often lack the sincerity that is essential to vindication of the defamed individual. *See* Kramer v. Thompson, 947 F.2d 666, 680 (3d Cir. 1991).

4. "Fact" vs. "Opinion"

One may hold and express an unfavorable opinion without becoming liable for defamation, even if airing that opinion harms someone's reputation. However, one cannot insulate a defamatory statement of fact from the law of defamation by casting it as an opinion: "In my opinion, Jones murdered his wife" may be treated as asserting that Jones is a murderer. If so, it is just as actionable as "Jones murdered his wife." However, not all opinions carry with them claims of fact. Recall the discussion in Chapter 21 of how implicit statements of fact are dealt with in the law of misrepresentation.

By the time the following case was decided, all federal circuits and two-thirds of the states had recognized a constitutionally based "opinion" privilege.

Milkovich v. Lorain Journal Co.
Supreme Court of the United States
497 U.S. 1 (1990)

Chief Justice REHNQUIST delivered the opinion of the Court [in which WHITE, BLACKMUN, STEVENS, O'CONNOR, SCALIA, and KENNEDY, JJ., joined].

....

....Petitioner Milkovich, now retired, was the wrestling coach at Maple Heights High School in Maple Heights, Ohio. In 1974, his team was involved in an altercation at a home wrestling match with a team from Mentor High School. Several people were injured. In response to the incident, the Ohio High School Athletic Association (OHSAA) held a hearing at which Milkovich and H. Don Scott, the Superintendent of Maple Heights Public Schools, testified. Following the hearing, OHSAA placed the Maple Heights team on probation for a year and declared the team ineligible for the 1975 state tournament....Thereafter, several parents and wrestlers sued OHSAA in the Court of Common Pleas of Franklin County, Ohio, seeking a restraining order against OHSAA's ruling on the grounds that they had been denied due process in the OHSAA proceeding. Both Milkovich and Scott testified in that proceeding. The court overturned OHSAA's probation and ineligibility orders on due process grounds.

The day after the court rendered its decision, respondent Diadiun's column appeared in the News-Herald. . . . The column bore the heading "Maple beat the law with the 'big lie,'" beneath which appeared Diadiun's photograph and the words "TD Says." The carryover page headline announced ". . . Diadiun says Maple told a lie." The column contained the following passages:

> . . . a lesson was learned (or relearned) yesterday by the student body of Maple Heights High School, and by anyone who attended the Maple-Mentor wrestling meet of last Feb. 8.
>
> A lesson which, sadly, in view of the events of the past year, is well they learned early.
>
> It is simply this: If you get in a jam, lie your way out.
>
> If you're successful enough, and powerful enough, and can sound sincere enough, you stand an excellent chance of making the lie stand up, regardless of what really happened.
>
> The teachers responsible were mainly Maple wrestling coach, Mike Milkovich, and former superintendent of schools, H. Donald Scott.
>
> . . . .
>
> Anyone who attended the meet, whether he be from Maple Heights, Mentor, or impartial observer, knows in his heart that Milkovich and Scott lied at the hearing after each having given his solemn oath to tell the truth.
>
> But they got away with it.
>
> Is that the kind of lesson we want our young people learning from their high school administrators and coaches?
>
> I think not. [Citation.][2]

. . . .

[Milkovich commenced a defamation action against respondents in the county court, alleging that the column accused him of committing the crime of perjury, damaged him in his occupation of teacher and coach, and constituted libel per se. Ultimately, the trial court granted summary judgment for respondents. The Ohio Court of Appeals affirmed, considering itself bound by the state Supreme Court's determination in Superintendent Scott's separate action against respondents that, as a matter law, the article was constitutionally protected opinion.]

The *Scott* court decided that the proper analysis for determining whether utterances are fact or opinion was set forth in the decision of the United States Court of Appeals for the D.C. Circuit in Ollman v. Evans, [750 F.2d 970 (1984)]. [Citation.] Under that analysis, four factors are considered to ascertain whether, under the "totality of circumstances," a statement is fact or opinion. These factors are: (1) "the specific language

---

2. [The entire text of the article was set forth in a footnote. The article included this passage:]

> . . . .
>
> I was among the 2,000-plus witnesses of the meet at which the trouble broke out, and I also attended the hearing before the OHSAA, so I was in a unique position of being the only non-involved party to observe both the meet itself and the Milkovich-Scott version presented to the board.
>
> Any resemblance between the two occurrances [sic] is purely coincidental.
>
> . . . .

used"; (2) "whether the statement is verifiable"; (3) "the general context of the statement"; and (4) "the broader context in which the statement appeared." [Citation.] The court found that application of the first two factors to the column militated in favor of deeming the challenged passages actionable assertions of fact. [Citation.] That potential outcome was trumped, however, by the court's consideration of the third and fourth factors. With respect to the third factor, the general context, the court explained that "the large caption 'TD Says'...would indicate to even the most gullible reader that the article was, in fact, opinion." [Citation.] As for the fourth factor, the "broader context," the court reasoned that because the article appeared on a sports page—"a traditional haven for cajoling, invective, and hyperbole"—the article would probably be construed as opinion. [Citation.]

....

Since the latter half of the 16th century, the common law has afforded a cause of action for damage to a person's reputation by the publication of false and defamatory statements. *See* L. Eldredge, Law of Defamation 5 (1978).

In Shakespeare's Othello, Iago says to Othello:

> Good name in man and woman, dear my lord.
> Is the immediate jewel of their souls.
> Who steals my purse steals trash;
> 'Tis something, nothing;
> 'Twas mine, 'tis his, and has been slave to thousands;
> But he that filches from me my good name
> Robs me of that which not enriches him,
> And makes me poor indeed.

Act III, scene 3. Defamation law developed not only as a means of allowing an individual to vindicate his good name, but also for the purpose of obtaining redress for harm caused by such statements. Eldredge, *supra*, at 5. As the common law developed in this country, apart from the issue of damages, one usually needed only allege an unprivileged publication of false and defamatory matter to state a cause of action for defamation. [Citations.] The common law generally did not place any additional restrictions on the type of statement that could be actionable. Indeed, defamatory communications were deemed actionable regardless of whether they were deemed to be statements of fact or opinion....

However, due to concerns that unduly burdensome defamation laws could stifle valuable public debate, the privilege of "fair comment" was incorporated into the common law as an affirmative defense to an action for defamation. "The principle of 'fair comment' afford[ed] legal immunity for the honest expression of opinion on matters of legitimate public interest when based upon a true or privileged statement of fact." [Citation.] As this statement implies, comment was generally privileged when it concerned a matter of public concern, was upon true or privileged facts, represented the actual opinion of the speaker, and was not made solely for the purpose of causing harm.... Thus under the common law, the privilege of "fair comment" was the device employed to strike the appropriate balance between the need for vigorous public discourse and the need to redress injury to citizens wrought by invidious or irresponsible speech.

....

[The Court discussed its holdings in New York Times Co. v. Sullivan, Curtis Publishing Co. v. Butts, Rosenbloom v. Metromedia, Inc., and Gertz v. Robert Welch, Inc.]

Still later, in Philadelphia Newspapers, Inc. v. Hepps,...[475 U.S. 767 (1986)], we held that "the common-law presumption that defamatory speech is false cannot stand when a plaintiff seeks damages against a media defendant for speech of public concern." [Citation.] In other words, the Court fashioned "a constitutional requirement that the plaintiff bear the burden of showing falsity, as well as fault, before recovering damages."....

We have also recognized constitutional limits on the *type* of speech which may be the subject of state defamation actions. In Greenbelt Cooperative Publishing Assn., Inc. v. Bresler,...[398 U.S. 6 (1970)], a real estate developer had engaged in negotiations with a local city council for a zoning variance on certain of his land, while simultaneously negotiating with the city on other land the city wished to purchase from him. A local newspaper published certain articles stating that some people had characterized the developer's negotiating position as "blackmail," and the developer sued for libel. Rejecting a contention that liability could be premised on the notion that the word "blackmail" implied the developer had committed the actual crime of blackmail, we held that "the imposition of liability on such a basis was constitutionally impermissible—that as a matter of constitutional law, the word 'blackmail' in these circumstances was not slander when spoken, and not libel when reported in the Greenbelt News Review." [Citation.] Noting that the published reports "were accurate and full," the Court reasoned that "even the most careless reader must have perceived that the word was no more than rhetorical hyperbole, a vigorous epithet used by those who considered [the developer's] negotiating position extremely unreasonable." [Citation.] *See also* Hustler Magazine, Inc. v. Falwell,...[485 U.S. 46, 50 (1988)] (First Amendment precluded recovery under state emotional distress action for ad parody which "could not reasonably have been interpreted as stating actual facts about the public figure involved"); Letter Carriers v. Austin,...[418 U.S. 264, 284-286 (1974)] (use of the word "traitor" in literary definition of a union "scab" not basis for a defamation action under federal labor law since used "in a loose, figurative sense" and was "merely rhetorical hyperbole, a lusty and imaginative expression of the contempt felt by union members").

The Court has also determined "that in cases raising First Amendment issues...an appellate court has an obligation to 'make an independent examination of the whole record' in order to make sure that 'the judgment does not constitute a forbidden intrusion on the field of free expression.'"....

Respondents would have us recognize, in addition to the established safeguards discussed above, still another First Amendment-based protection for defamatory statements which are categorized as "opinion" as opposed to "fact." For this proposition they rely principally on the following dictum from our opinion in *Gertz*:

> Under the First Amendment there is no such thing as a false idea. However pernicious an opinion may seem, we depend for its correction not on the conscience of judges and juries but on the competition of other ideas. But there is no constitutional value in false statements of fact. [Citation.]

Judge Friendly appropriately observed that this passage "has become the opening salvo in all arguments for protection from defamation actions on the ground of opinion, even though the case did not remotely concern the question." Cianci v. New Times Publishing Co., 639 F.2d 54, 61 (CA2 1980). Read in context, though, the fair meaning of the passage is to equate the word "opinion" in the second sentence with the word "idea" in the first sentence. Under this view, the language was merely a reiteration of Justice Holmes' classic "marketplace of ideas" concept. *See* Abrams v. United States, 250 U.S.

616, 630, 40 S. Ct. 17, 22, 63 L. Ed. 1173 (1919) (Holmes, J., dissenting) ("[T]he ultimate good desired is better reached by free trade in ideas…the best test of truth is the
power of the thought to get itself accepted in the competition of the market").

Thus we do not think this passage from *Gertz* was intended to create a wholesale
defamation exemption for anything that might be labeled "opinion." *See Cianci, supra,*
at 62, n.10 (The "marketplace of ideas" origin of this passage "points strongly to the
view that the 'opinions' held to be constitutionally protected were the sort of thing that
could be corrected by discussion"). Not only would such an interpretation be contrary
to the tenor and context of the passage, but it would also ignore the fact that expressions of "opinion" may often imply an assertion of objective fact.

If a speaker says, "In my opinion John Jones is a liar," he implies a knowledge of facts
which lead to the conclusion that Jones told an untruth. Even if the speaker states the
facts upon which he bases his opinion, if those facts are either incorrect or incomplete,
or if his assessment of them is erroneous, the statement may still imply a false assertion
of fact. Simply couching such statements in terms of opinion does not dispel these implications; and the statement, "In my opinion Jones is a liar," can cause as much damage
to reputation as the statement, "Jones is a liar." As Judge Friendly aptly stated: "[It]
would be destructive of the law of libel if a writer could escape liability for accusations
of [defamatory conduct] simply by using, explicitly or implicitly, the words 'I think.'"….

Apart from their reliance on the *Gertz* dictum, respondents do not really contend
that a statement such as, "In my opinion John Jones is a liar," should be protected by a
separate privilege for "opinion" under the First Amendment. But they do contend that
in every defamation case the First Amendment mandates an inquiry into whether a
statement is "opinion" or "fact," and that only the latter statements may be actionable.
They propose that a number of factors developed by the lower courts (in what we hold
was a mistaken reliance on the *Gertz* dictum) be considered in deciding which is which.
But we think the "'breathing space'" which "'freedoms of expression require in order to
survive,'" [citation], is adequately secured by existing constitutional doctrine without
the creation of an artificial dichotomy between "opinion" and fact.

Foremost, we think *Hepps* stands for the proposition that a statement on matters of
public concern must be provable as false before there can be liability under state
defamation law, at least in situations, like the present, where a media defendant is involved. Thus, unlike the statement, "In my opinion Mayor Jones is a liar," the statement,
"In my opinion Mayor Jones shows his abysmal ignorance by accepting the teachings of
Marx and Lenin," would not be actionable. *Hepps* ensures that a statement of opinion
relating to matters of public concern which does not contain a provably false factual
connotation will receive full constitutional protection.[7]

Next, the *Bresler-Letter Carriers-Falwell* line of cases provides protection for statements that cannot "reasonably [be] interpreted as stating actual facts" about an individual. *Falwell,* 485 U.S., at 50, 108 S. Ct., at 879. This provides assurance that public debate will not suffer for lack of "imaginative expression" or the "rhetorical hyperbole"
which has traditionally added much to the discourse of our Nation. [Citation.]

The *New York Times-Butts* and *Gertz* culpability requirements further ensure that debate on public issues remains "uninhibited, robust, and wide-open." New York Times,
376 U.S., at 270, 84 S. Ct., at 720. Thus, where a statement of "opinion" on a matter of
public concern reasonably implies false and defamatory facts regarding public figures or

---

7. We note that the issue of falsity relates to the *defamatory* facts implied by a statement….

officials, those individuals must show that such statements were made with knowledge of their false implications or with reckless disregard of their truth. Similarly, where such a statement involves a private figure on a matter of public concern, a plaintiff must show that the false connotations were made with some level of fault as required by *Gertz*. Finally, the enhanced appellate review required by *Bose Corp.* provides assurance that the foregoing determinations will be made in a manner so as not to "constitute a forbidden intrusion of the field of free expression." [Citation.]

We are not persuaded that a separate constitutional privilege for "opinion"…is required to ensure the freedom of expression guaranteed by the First Amendment. The dispositive question in the present case then becomes whether or not a reasonable factfinder could conclude that the statements in the Diadiun column imply an assertion that petitioner Milkovich perjured himself in a judicial proceeding. We think this question must be answered in the affirmative. As the Ohio Supreme Court itself observed, "the clear impact in some nine sentences and a caption is that [Milkovich] 'lied at the hearing after…having given his solemn oath to tell the truth.'" [Citation.] This is not the sort of loose, figurative or hyperbolic language which would negate the impression that the writer was seriously maintaining petitioner committed the crime of perjury. Nor does the general tenor of the article negate this impression.

We also think the connotation that petitioner committed perjury is sufficiently factual to be susceptible of being proved true or false. A determination of whether petitioner lied in this instance can be made on a core of objective evidence by comparing, *inter alia*, petitioner's testimony before the OHSAA board with his subsequent testimony before the trial court. As the *Scott* court noted regarding the plaintiff in that case, "[w]hether or not H. Don Scott did indeed perjure himself is certainly verifiable by a perjury action with evidence adduced from the transcripts and witnesses present at the hearing. Unlike a subjective assertion the averred defamatory language is an articulation of an objectively verifiable event." [Citation.] So too with petitioner Milkovich.

    ….

….The judgment of the Ohio Court of Appeals is reversed and the case remanded for further proceedings not inconsistent with this opinion.

Reversed.

Justice BRENNAN, with whom Justice MARSHALL joins, dissenting.

    ….

The majority does not rest its decision today on any finding that the statements at issue explicitly state a false and defamatory fact. Nor could it. Diadiun's assumption that Milkovich must have lied at the court hearing is patently conjecture. The majority finds Diadiun's statements actionable, however, because it concludes that these statements imply a factual assertion that Milkovich perjured himself at the judicial proceeding. I disagree. Diadiun not only reveals the facts upon which he is relying but he makes it clear at which point he runs out of facts and is simply guessing. Read in context, the statements cannot reasonably be interpreted as implying such an assertion as fact. [Citation.]

    ….

I appreciate this Court's concern with redressing injuries to an individual's reputation. But as long as it is clear to the reader that he is being offered conjecture and not solid information, the danger to reputation is one we have chosen to tolerate in pursuit of "'individual liberty [and] the common quest for truth and the vitality of society as a whole.'"….

….I respectfully dissent.

Notes

1. *Actionable Opinions.* The following are examples of statements which, after *Milkovich*, have been held to raise a triable issue relating to implied defamatory facts:

> Repeated accusations by the host of a call-in talk show that a judge was "corrupt"; Bentley v. Bunton, 94 S.W.3d 561 (Tex. 2002) (even though the host's ravings were often classic soapbox oratory and the host often said that it was his opinion that the judge was corrupt, the host plainly and repeatedly stated that his accusations of corruption were based on objective, provable facts);

> Language in the national directory of a professional organization describing the plaintiff attorney as an "ambulance chaser"; Flamm v. American Assoc. of Univ. Women, 201 F.3d 144 (2d Cir. 2000);

> A supervisor's remark to company officials and other employees that "he had reason to believe" that the plaintiff had sabotaged a computer; Staples v. Bangor Hydro-Elec. Co., 629 A.2d 601 (Me. 1993);

> A statement in a story labeled "fiction" which characterized the plaintiff as a "slut"; Bryson v. News Am. Pubs., Inc., 672 N.E.2d 1207 (Ill. 1996).

2. *Non-Actionable Opinions.* Examples of non-actionable statements include:

> A labor union official describing the union's attorney as "a very poor lawyer"; Sullivan v. Conway, 157 F.3d 1092 (7th Cir. 1998);

> One scholar calling another "a 'crank' for having taken a position that the first scholar considers patently wrongheaded"; Dilworth v. Dudley, 75 F.3d 307, 311 (7th Cir. 1996);

> Referring to the plaintiff as a "lying asshole." Greenhalgh v. Casey, 67 F.3d 299 (6th Cir. 1995) (simple "rhetorical hyperbole" that cannot be interpreted as referring to an actual fact).

In Wilkow v. Forbes, Inc., 241 F.3d 552 (7th Cir. 2001), the court held that it was not defamatory for an author to express opposition to a certain bankruptcy rule and opine that the plaintiff's taking advantage of the rule had caused an inequitable result. Judge Frank Easterbrook wrote:

> [A]n allegation of greed is not defamatory; sedulous pursuit of self-interest is the engine that propels a market economy. Capitalism certainly does not depend on sharp practices, but neither is an allegation of sharp dealing anything more than an uncharitable opinion.

3. *Fully Disclosed Facts.* As expressed by one court:

> [A] statement of opinion based on fully disclosed facts can be punished only if the stated facts are themselves false and demeaning. [Citations.] The rationale behind this rule is straightforward: When the facts underlying a statement of opinion are disclosed, readers will understand they are getting the author's interpretation of the facts presented; they are therefore unlikely to construe the statement as insinuating the existence of additional, undisclosed facts.

Standing Comm. v. Yagman, 55 F.3d 1430, 1439 (9th Cir. 1995).

4. *Imprecise Statements That Are Unverifiable.* A line of cases in Illinois has held that highly unflattering statements were non-actionable statements of opinion because they were not made in any specific factual context and were therefore "too broad, conclusory, and subjective to be objectively unverifiable." Schivarelli v. CBS, Inc., 776 N.E.2d 693,

699 (Ill. App. Ct. 2002) ("the evidence seems to indicate that you're cheating the city"); *see also* Dubinsky v. United Airlines Master Exec. Coun., 708 N.E.2d 441 (Ill. App. Ct. 1999) ("crook"); Hopewell v. Vitullo, 701 N.E.2d 99 (Ill App. Ct. 1998) ("fired because of incompetence").

See also Seelig v. Infinity Broad. Corp., 119 Cal. Rptr. 2d 108 (Ct. App. 2002) (holding that the terms "chicken butt," "local loser," and "big shank" were too vague to be capable of being proven true or false).

In Jefferson County Sch. Dist. v. Moody's Investor's Services, Inc., 175 F.3d 848 (10th Cir. 1999), a school district's bond offering did well at first, but then turned sour when, two hours into the sale, Moody's published an article saying that the outlook on the district's obligation debt was "negative" and that the district was under "ongoing financial pressures" because of the state's underfunding of the school finance act. As a result, the district was forced to re-offer the bonds at a higher interest rate, which caused a loss of more than $750,000. The court held that under the circumstances, including the plaintiff's failure to identify a specific false statement, the vagueness of the phrases "negative outlook" and "ongoing financial pressures" rendered them protected expressions of opinion.

5. *Allowing Readers to Draw Their Own Conclusions.* In Thomas v. L.A. Times Communications, 2002 W.L. 31007420 (9th Cir.), the court held that an article that did not accuse a Holocaust survivor of lying, but which merely contained the views of others that conflicted with the survivor's published statements and permitted readers to draw their own conclusions, did not carry defamatory implications and was not actionable.

6. *State Constitutional Protection.* State constitutional protection of free speech may be more extensive than the protection offered by the federal constitution. The New York Court of Appeals observed in 600 West 115th Street Corp. v. Von Gutfeld, 603 N.E.2d 930 (N.Y. 1992), that federal protections of opinion were narrower than those of the New York constitution, but gave no details, as the defendant's remarks in that case were protected even under the federal test. The court concluded that statements that a proposed restaurant "denigrated" the building, that a lease and "proposition" were fraudulent and "smelled of bribery and corruption," and that the lease was "illegal" could not be the subject of a defamation action because none of the statements implied knowledge of a specific criminal transaction; the statements used figurative language; they were in some respects obviously exaggerated; and they were made at a heated public hearing.

7. *Alleged Sexual Harassment.* In Williams v. Garraghty, 455 S.E.2d 209, 215 (Va. 1995), a prison warden brought a defamation action against a subordinate employee who had submitted a memorandum in which she alleged that the warden was guilty of sexual harassment. The defendant argued that the statements were constitutionally protected expressions of opinion because "[b]y its very nature, sexual harassment is in the eye of the beholder." The court held that supporting statements in the memorandum, relating to an alleged incident at the plaintiff's house and certain "derogatory notes," were clearly factual in nature and therefore could serve as the basis for a defamation suit.

8. *Applying Constitutional Limitations from Defamation to Other Torts.* As noted in the *Milkovich* opinion, Hustler Magazine, Inc. v. Falwell, 485 U.S. 46 (1988), held that a plaintiff cannot circumvent the limitations on recovery that have evolved in defamation cases by casting an action as one for intentional infliction of emotional distress. Other cases have followed a similar line of reasoning. Some of the decisions have involved deception, as where an investigative reporter gains access to truthful information about the plaintiff through the use of false pretenses and then disseminates the information, thereby causing harm to the plaintiff's reputation. The cases generally hold that the

plaintiff is barred from recovering defamation-type damages (harm to reputation and emotional distress) unless the plaintiff proves that the defendant published a false statement of fact with the requisite degree of fault as to falsity.

In 1992, ABC broadcast a story purporting to investigate unhealthful practices at Food Lion stores. The program showed Food Lion employees selling food past its expiration date and engaging in other unpleasant practices. The show was at least partially fraudulent. For example, in one scene purporting to show the sale of tainted food, the Food Lion employee making the sale was actually an ABC employee who had gone to work for Food Lion as part of ABC's investigation. An interview showed a Food Lion worker saying that she had put food out for sale after its expiration date. Food Lion's investigation showed that the employee had immediately told the reporter that her supervisor had seen her do this and had made her throw the food away, but that portion of the interview was edited out of the program. As a result of the broadcast, Food Lion's business fell off sharply, leading to billions of dollars in losses, the closing of eighty-eight stores, and the laying off of more than a thousand employees.

Instead of suing ABC for defamation—a theory under which Food Lion would have had little chance of success because of the *New York Times* line of cases—Food Lion sued for fraud, trespass, violations of a state unfair trade practices act, violation of federal wiretapping statutes, violations of RICO, and other claims. The jury returned a verdict that included $5.5 million in punitive damages (reduced to $315,000 by remittitur). On appeal, the court held that the First Amendment precluded an award of publication damages because the plaintiff was not prepared to offer proof that the broadcast contained a false statement of fact made with actual malice. *See* Food Lion, Inc. v. Capital Cities/ABC, Inc., 194 F.3d 505 (4th Cir. 1999).

In Hornberger v. ABC, Inc., 799 A.2d 566, 597 (N.J. App. Div. 2002), police officers brought an action after three black men acting as "testers" agreed to cruise in an expensive car to find out if police would stop them. The officers stopped the car and were surreptitiously videotaped conducting an unlawful search, and the tape was later broadcast. In turning aside a claim for fraud, the court relied upon *Food Lion* and noted that the damages the plaintiff's sought were "almost entirely for injury to reputation and emotional distress." The court, noted, however, that "[w]hen the damages are non-reputational and do not compensate for injury to the plaintiff's state of mind, First Amendment proscriptions do not preclude recovery on a pre-publication tort, also involving a media-defendant's publication."

To allow a plaintiff whose real grievance is that a story is inaccurate to recover on some theory other than defamation by showing a relatively minor wrongdoing would make the *New York Times* protections largely illusory. On the other hand, *New York Times* can hardly be read as making reporters immune to laws against trespassing, wiretapping, and fraud. For an examination of the problem and a proposed solution, see David A. Logan, *Masked Media: Judges, Juries, and the Law of Surreptitious Newsgathering*, 83 Iowa L. Rev. 161 (1997).

Moldea v. New York Times Co.

United States Court of Appeals for the District of Columbia Circuit
22 F.3d 310 (D.C. Cir. 1994)

HARRY T. EDWARDS, Circuit Judge.

....

In Moldea v. New York Times Co., 15 F.3d 1137 (D.C. Cir. 1994) ("*Moldea (I)*"), this panel was faced with an appeal brought by author and investigative journalist Dan E. Moldea in connection with his defamation action against the New York Times Company, Inc. ("Times"). Moldea's lawsuit alleged that appellee libeled him in a book review.... The review stated that Moldea's book, *Interference: How Organized Crime Influences Professional Football*, ("*Interference*"), was marred by "too much sloppy journalism," and offered a number of examples of the work's alleged journalistic shortcomings. The District Court granted summary judgment in favor of the Times, ruling that the review in question was not actionable as a matter of law because it consisted only of unverifiable statements of the reviewer's opinion, or of statements that no reasonable juror could find to be false. [Citation.] In a 2-1 decision, the panel reversed on the ground that some of the review's characterizations of Moldea's book were potentially actionable because they were verifiable, and could not be held to be true as a matter of law.

After careful consideration of the Times'...petition for rehearing and Moldea's response to that petition, we are persuaded to amend our earlier decision. Unfortunately, that opinion failed to take sufficient account of the fact that the statements at issue appeared in the context of a book review, a genre in which readers expect to find spirited critiques of literary works that they understand to be the reviewer's description and assessment of texts that are capable of a number of possible rational interpretations. While there is no per se exemption from defamation for book reviews, our initial resolution of this case applied an inappropriate standard to judge whether the Times review was actionable.

....

...Moldea alleged that six specific statements in the Times review had defamed him by accusing him of being an incompetent practitioner of his chosen profession, investigative journalism, and by supporting that accusation with false characterizations of his book. We held in *Moldea (I)* that one of these passages was a statement of opinion that implied defamatory facts because it accused Moldea of being an incompetent journalist. That statement read:

> But there is too much sloppy journalism to trust the bulk of this book's 512 pages—including its whopping 64 pages of footnotes.

....*Moldea (I)* went on to hold that the remaining statements Moldea challenged were offered by Eskenazi as factual examples of *Interference*'s alleged "sloppiness," and that "[i]n order for the review to be nonactionable as a matter of law, the Times must show that it offered true facts in support of its judgment that served to support its statement of opinion." [Citation.]

....*Moldea (I)* held...that two of the challenged passages in the Times review were verifiable, and that a reasonable juror could conclude that they were false. First, the review stated:

> Mr. Moldea tells as well of Mr. Namath's "guaranteeing" a victory in Super Bowl III shortly after a sinister meeting in a bar with a member of the opposition, Lou Michaels, the Baltimore Colts' place-kicker. The truth is that the pair almost came to blows after they both had been drinking; and Mr. Namath's well-publicized "guarantee" came about quite innocently at a Miami Touchdown Club dinner when a fan asked him if he thought the Jets had a chance. "We'll win. I guarantee it," Mr. Namath replied.

Second, the review opined that:

[Moldea] revives the discredited notion that Carroll Rosenbloom, the ornery owner of the Rams, who had a penchant for gambling, met foul play when he drowned in Florida 10 years ago.

Our initial opinion in this case concluded that a reasonable juror could find that the Times review had mischaracterized *Interference's* portrayal of each of the foregoing two events. Accordingly, we held that it was error for the trial court to grant summary judgment at so early a stage of this litigation.

....

In contrast to the situation in *Milkovich*, [497 U.S. 1 (1990),] the instant case involves a context, a book review, in which the allegedly libelous statements were evaluations quintessentially of a type readers expect to find in that genre. The challenged statements in the Times review consist solely of the reviewer's comments on a literary work, and therefore must be judged with an eye toward readers' expectations and understandings of book reviews. This would not be the case if, for example, the review stated or implied that *Interference* was a badly written book because its author was a drug dealer. In that situation, this case would parallel *Milkovich*: the reviewer would simply be employing the medium of a book review as a vehicle for what would be a garden-variety libel, and the review would thus potentially be actionable.

There is a long and rich history in our cultural and legal traditions of affording reviewers latitude to comment on literary and other works. The statements at issue in the instant case are assessments of a book, rather than direct assaults on Moldea's character, reputation, or competence as a journalist. While a bad review necessarily has the effect of injuring an author's reputation to some extent—sometimes to a devastating extent, as Moldea alleges is true here—criticism's long and impressive pedigree persuades us that, while a critic's latitude is not unlimited, he or she must be given the constitutional "breathing space" appropriate to the genre. [Citation.]

We believe that the Times has suggested the appropriate standard for evaluating critical reviews: "The proper analysis would make commentary actionable only when the interpretations are *unsupportable by reference to the written work.*" Petition for Rehearing at 8 (emphasis added). This "supportable interpretation" standard provides that a critic's interpretation must be rationally supportable by reference to the actual text he or she is evaluating, and thus would not immunize situations analogous to that presented in *Milkovich*, in which a writer launches a personal attack, rather than interpreting a book. This standard also establishes boundaries even for textual interpretation. A critic's statement must be a rational assessment or account of something the reviewer can point to *in the text,* or *omitted from the text,* being critiqued. For instance, if the Times review [had] stated that *Interference* was a terrible book because it asserted that African-Americans make poor football coaches, that reading would be "unsupportable by reference to the written work," because nothing in Moldea's book even hints at this notion. In such a case, the usual inquiries as to libel would apply: a jury could determine that the review falsely characterized *Interference*, thereby libeling its author by portraying him as a racist (assuming the other elements of the case could be proved).

Our decision to apply the "supportable interpretation" standard to book reviews finds strong support in analogous decisions of the Supreme Court, all decided or reaffirmed after *Milkovich*. These cases establish that when a writer is evaluating or giving an account of inherently ambiguous materials or subject matter, the First Amendment requires that the courts allow latitude for interpretation. For example, in Bose Corp. v. Consumers Union of United States, Inc., 466 U.S. 485, (1984),...a reviewer writing for

Consumer Reports magazine described the experience of listening to music through a pair of stereo speakers: "[I]ndividual instruments heard through the Bose system seemed to grow to gigantic proportions and tended to wander about the room." *Bose*, 466 U.S. at 488.... The Court held that the statements were not actionable, because they were not so obviously false as to sustain a finding of "actual malice."....

....

... [T]his appeal presents a pure question of law, which we review *de novo*: whether Moldea can in fact state a claim for defamation. *Moldea (I)*, 15 F.3d at 1142. In this situation, we must determine as a threshold matter whether a challenged statement is capable of a defamatory meaning; and whether it is verifiable—that is, whether a plaintiff can prove that it is false.... The Times review is... capable of a defamatory meaning insofar as it tends to injure Moldea's reputation as a practitioner of his chosen profession, investigative journalism. The key to this case is the question of verifiability.

Although *Moldea (I)* held that the Times review's statement that *Interference* contained "too much sloppy journalism" was a verifiable assessment of the book, we now recognize that, in the context of a book review, it is highly debatable whether this statement is sufficiently verifiable to be actionable in defamation. Arguably, our decision in *Moldea (I)* failed adequately to heed the counsel of both the Supreme Court and our own precedents that "[w]here the question of truth or falsity is a close one, a court should err on the side of nonactionability."....

However, we need not determine whether "too much sloppy journalism" is verifiable, as the statements that the Times review offers in support of this assessment are supportable interpretations of *Interference*. Thus, even if the review's assertion that the book contains "too much sloppy journalism" is verifiable, that assessment is supported by revealed premises that we cannot hold to be false in the context of a book review....

....

Our initial decision in this case erred by basing its holding on a standard that failed to take into account the fact that the challenged statements appeared in the context of a book review, and were solely evaluations of a literary work. *Moldea (I)* considered whether a reasonable jury *could find* that the challenged statements were false because they mischaracterized *Interference*. *See Moldea (I)*, 15 F.3d at 1146, 1147. Such a standard might be appropriate in the case of an ordinary libel such as that at issue in *Milkovich*, but it is an inappropriate measure of an interpretation of a book. Applying the "supportable interpretation" standard, the correct measure of the challenged statements' verifiability as a matter of law is whether *no reasonable person could find* that the review's characterizations were supportable interpretations of *Interference*. Applying this standard, we hold that the Times review is not actionable in defamation.

....

.... Moldea discusses Rosenbloom's drowning in pages 319 through 326 of his book, closing his account with quoted observations from several of Rosenbloom's friends, who speculate that he was murdered. *Interference* later reveals, on page 360, that Moldea has located previously unknown photographs, taken at Rosenbloom's autopsy, which make clear that he "died in a tragic accident and was not murdered." As we held in *Moldea (I)*, a reasonable jury could conclude that the Times review's characterization of *Interference*'s portrayal of Rosenbloom's death was false, and that the reviewer's account of the book creates the misleading impression that Moldea inadequately investigated this story. *Moldea (I)*, 15 F.3d at 1147-48. However, given that *Interference* does not reveal that Rosenbloom's death was accidental until 35 pages after giving undeniably titillating hints of homicide, we cannot hold that a reviewer could not reasonably suggest that Moldea sought to "revive" the notion that Rosenbloom was murdered in order to build suspense before disproving that theory.

....

....*Moldea (I)*[also] concluded that a reasonable jury could find that Moldea did not describe the meeting [between Namath and Michaels] as a "sinister" rendezvous, but rather made clear that the meeting was "quite accidental and even confrontational." [Citation.] Even applying the "supportable interpretation" standard, this review passage is close to the line. *Interference* not only states that the Namath-Michaels meeting was "accidental," but on the same page quotes Michaels as saying "What we talked about had no relationship to the game," and quotes another player present at the meeting as confirming that "'nothing technical' about the game was discussed."

We are troubled by the "sinister meeting" passage, but are constrained to conclude that it does not give rise to an actionable claim. The review offered at least six observations to support the charge of "sloppy journalism": [five] challenged passages, plus the unchallenged claim that Moldea made several spelling errors. At least five of these observations could not be proved false at trial, either because they are true, are supported opinion, are reasonable interpretations, or are not challenged in this suit. Moldea is left with only the "sinister meeting" passage as a possible basis for his defamation claim, and this is a very weak basis indeed. For one thing, the "sinister meeting" passage is not defamatory on its face, but rather is simply one of the "interpretations offered in support of the review's assessment of Moldea's book. Furthermore, even without the support of the "sinister meeting" passage, the review's assertion that *Interference* is marred by "too much sloppy journalism" is (as a legal matter) "substantially true," and so is not actionable in defamation.

....

Moldea has made a number of allegations in this suit that Gerald Eskenazi's negative review of *Interference* was prompted in part by Eskenazi's allegiance to the National Football League ("NFL"). Moldea alleged in his original brief to this court that Eskenazi has covered the NFL as a correspondent for over thirty years, and that he was therefore biased against *Interference* because he was dependent on the league's goodwill in order to gain access to information necessary to report on its activities. Indeed, Moldea's book predicts that the NFL's "loyal sportswriters" will try to discredit *Interference*. *See Interference* at 25. Even if true, however, these allegations do not make a case for appellant.

Any intelligent reviewer knows at some level that a bad review may injure the author of the book which is its subject. Indeed, some bad reviews may be written with an aim to damage a writer's reputation. There is nothing that we can do about this, at least not without unacceptably interfering with free speech. There simply is no viable way to distinguish between reviews written by those who honestly believe a book is bad, and those prompted solely by mischievous intent. To allow a plaintiff to base a lawsuit on claims of mischief, without some indication that the review's interpretations are unsupportable, would wreak havoc on the law of defamation. [Citation.]

....

....Accordingly, we modify that opinion as indicated herein, and affirm the grant of summary judgment in favor of appellee New York Times Company.

So ordered.

Note

1. *"Supportable Interpretations."* While *Moldea* lets book reviewers relax, the court's narrow reading of what constitutes an "opinion" may encourage future plaintiffs in cases not involving reviews. The court seems to hold that a statement that is a supportable interpretation of an event or a document may lead to a defamation award if a jury finds that the interpretation, although "supportable," was wrong, provided only that the interpretation appears in a less freewheeling context than the book review section of a newspaper. Suppose, for instance, that the defendant sees Smith punching a small, meek-looking man. The defendant goes home and tells his neighbor, "Smith is a bully; I saw him beat up a little guy at the corner of Fourth and Main." If in fact Smith was fending off a small and meek-looking, but vicious, mugger, does Smith have a good defamation claim against the defendant? Should he? *Compare* Time, Inc. v. Firestone, 424 U.S. 448 (1976), *supra* at 1003.

D. Privileges and Defenses

Even if the elements of a libel or slander cause of action are otherwise satisfied, there will be no liability if the defendant's conduct is privileged. Defamation privileges are generally classified as either qualified or absolute, with the classification determining whether and under what circumstances the privilege will arise or will be lost.

1. Absolute Privileges

Absolute privileges are confined to a few relatively well-defined areas in which it can usually be said that the interests to be advanced by unfettered speech are of such paramount importance as to take complete precedence over any interest society may have in allowing compensation of the defamed individual. An absolute privilege gives a statement within its scope complete immunity from liability, no matter what the defendant knew or why the defendant made the statement.

a. Judicial-Proceedings Privilege

A robust, adversarial litigation process is deemed so essential to the American form of government, and depends so heavily on relevant information being brought into court, that virtually all jurisdictions hold that any statement made during judicial proceedings which is in any sense pertinent to the issues before the court is absolutely privileged and may not give rise to liability. *See* Irwin v. Ashurst, 74 P.2d 1127 (Or. 1938) (counsel's statements that plaintiff, a witness, was a "dope fiend," a "lunatic," and "lower than a rattlesnake," held privileged because pertinent to credibility). Any other rule, the courts reason, could deter persons from coming forward with information which, though important to the search for the truth, is not known with certainty to be correct. In construing the judicial proceedings privilege,

> All doubts should be resolved in favor of a finding of pertinency [citation], which is a question of law for the court [citation]. If, however, the defamatory

statements have "no connection whatever with the litigation," then no privilege will attach. [Citation.]

Golden v. Mullen, 693 N.E.2d 385, 389 (Ill. Ct. App. 1998).

The judicial-proceedings privilege applies not only to litigation before courts of general jurisdiction, but to a wide range of public and private hearings involving the exercise of judicial or quasi-judicial powers, as well as the preparation of documents relevant to those proceedings. *See, e.g.,* Henderson v. Wellman, 43 S.W.3d 591 (Tex. App. 2001) (an arbitration hearing is a quasi-judicial proceeding to which the absolute privilege applies); Kelley v. Bonney, 606 A.2d 693 (Conn. 1992) (complaint filed with the state board of education concerning teacher decertification was absolutely privileged).

Statements made before the commencement of judicial proceedings may be absolutely privileged if made in connection with possible litigation and pertinent to that litigation. *See* Collins v. Red Roof Inns, Inc., 566 S.E.2d 595 (W. Va. 2002) (a letter to the attorney for a former employee, who had indicated that judicial proceedings were imminent if the former employee's demands were not met, which allegedly defamed other former employees, was absolutely privileged); Krishnan v. Law Offices of Preston Henrichson, 83 S.W.3d 295 (Tex. App. 2002) (notice letter from attorney about potential malpractice claim); Bell v. Lee, 49 S.W.3d 8 (Tex. App. 2001) (letter threatening defamation action was sent in good faith and therefore privileged, even though claim was later abandoned); Jones v. Clinton, 974 F. Supp. 712 (E.D. Ark. 1997) (statements to media by presidential spokespersons denying alleged sexual relationship and questioning plaintiff's motives were absolutely privileged); Hawkins v. Harris, 661 A.2d 284 (N.J. 1995) (statements made by private investigators of a law firm).

However, at some point the line must be drawn, and a report to the police that a crime has been committed typically enjoys only a qualified privilege. *See* DeLong v. Yu Ent., Inc., 47 P.3d 8 (Ore. 2002).

The judicial-proceedings privilege even provides absolute immunity to certain post-litigation out-of-court statements because an "attorney must be free to discuss with the client the outcome of the litigation, future strategies, if any, and generally respond to inquiries from the client without fear of civil liability." Golden v. Mullen, 693 N.E.2d 385, 390 (Ill. Ct. App. 1998) (privilege protected letter to client, but not letter to client's wife); Cummings v. Kirby, 343 N.W.2d 747 (Neb. 1984) (a statement made to a client at a post-verdict meeting, in an attempt to explain the outcome of a trial, that "everyone in the county thought the client's son was a 'crook,'" was absolutely privileged). However, "[e]ven an 'absolute' privilege does not permit an individual to categorically republish possibly defamatory statements without consequence." Wagner v. Miskin, 660 N.W.2d 593 (N.D. 2003) (upholding a $3 million judgment to a university professor who was defamed on a former student's website following an allegedly quasi-judicial disciplinary hearing).

See also Buckley v. Fitzsimmons, 509 U.S. 259 (1993) (holding, in a constitutional-tort action based on malicious prosecution, that a prosecutor's allegedly false statements, made during the public announcement of an indictment, were entitled to only qualified, not absolute, immunity).

In some states the common-law judicial-proceedings privilege has been supplanted by statute. *See* Cal. Civ. Code sec. 47(b) (Westlaw 2003) (providing an absolute privilege for a publication or broadcast made in any legislative, judicial, or other official proceeding authorized by law).

One consequence of the judicial-proceedings privilege is that no civil remedy is given to a person harmed by perjury. *See* Cooper v. Parker-Hughey, 894 P.2d 1096 (Okl. 1995) (noting in defense of the rule the need for finality in judgments and the possible multiplicity of suits by parties dissatisfied by the outcome of trials).

Note

1. *Ethics in Law Practice: Treatment of Witnesses and Trial Publicity.* Although the judicial-proceedings privilege may prevent an attorney from being held civilly liable for defamation of a witness at trial, rules of ethics limit what an attorney can say about a witness. For example, Rule 3.4(e) of the Model Rules of Professional Conduct (2003) provides:

> A lawyer shall not…in trial, allude to any matter that the lawyer does not reasonably believe is relevant or that will not be supported by admissible evidence.…

In addition, attorneys have special obligations with respect to trial publicity. Model Rule 3.6 (a) (2003) provides:

> A lawyer who is participating or has participated in the investigation or litigation of a matter shall not make an extrajudicial statement that the lawyer knows or reasonably should know will be disseminated by means of public communication and will have a substantial likelihood of materially prejudicing an adjudicative proceeding in the matter.

A lawyer who violates either of these rules is subject to professional discipline, including reprimand, suspension, or removal from the bar.

b. Other Absolute Privileges

An absolute privilege applies to pertinent statements during a legislative proceeding. *See* Riddle v. Perry, (Utah 2002) (holding that a statement of a legislative witness, which implied that the sponsor of a bill had been bribed, was related to the hearing and therefore absolutely privileged, even though both the committee parliamentarian and the legislative witness both acknowledged that the statement was out of order).

Other areas in which courts have found absolute privileges to exist concern legislative proceedings, actions of the executive branch, communications between spouses, publications required by law, and communications consented to by the plaintiff.

Right to Petition the Government. The Petition Clause of the Constitution does not confer upon one who petitions the government absolute immunity from liability for defamation. Rather, the guarantees of the Petition Clause are coextensive with those which have been articulated in First Amendment cases, such as New York Times v. Sullivan. *See* McDonald v. Smith, 472 U.S. 479 (1985) (letters addressed to the President, concerning plaintiff's qualifications to be U.S. Attorney, may give rise to liability if actual malice is proved).

2. Qualified Privileges

A "qualified privilege" entitles the speaker to some degree of immunity from liability for making false statements, but a qualified privilege will be lost if the speaker abuses that immunity. Both the question of when qualified privileges come into play and the matter of what kind of conduct causes a qualified privilege to be lost are usually quite ill defined.

a. Employers

Many qualified privileges cover communications between persons who have some particular need to discuss the plaintiff's affairs. For example, "an employer has a conditional or qualified privilege that attaches to communications made in the course of an investigation following a report of employee wrongdoing." Randall's Food Markets, Inc. v. Johnson, 891 S.W.2d 640, 646 (Tex. 1995). A former employer's statements made in good faith about a former employee to a state workforce commission are qualifiedly privileged because the speaker and the recipient have a common interest. *See* Patrick v. McGowan, 104 S.W.3d 219 (Tex. App. 2003). In addition, comments by one employee about another employee may enjoy a qualified privilege if they are made at a board of directors' corporate grievance hearing (Hagebak v. Stone, 61 P.3d 201 (N.M. Ct. App. 2002)) or are made to management with respect to the other's job performance (Sheehan v. Anderson, 263 F.3d 159 (3d Cir. 2001)).

However, "the statements must be made in good faith." Kuechle v. Life's Companion P.C.A., Inc., 653 N.W.2d 214 (Minn. Ct. App. 2002). In *Kuechle*, the court held that an employer, who said that an employee had been discharged for allegedly violating a direct order, did not have qualified privilege because the employer made only a cursory investigation of the underlying facts, failed to interview the plaintiff, and ignored a supervisor's statement that she had made a request of the plaintiff, rather than given a direct order.

b. Others

Credit-reporting agencies are usually thought to have a qualified privilege with respect to communications to their subscribers.

In theory, a qualified privilege will arise in any situation in which there is good reason for the law to encourage or permit a person to speak or write about someone, even though the speaker is not absolutely sure about the accuracy of the information relayed. In determining whether reasons strong enough to justify a privilege exist, courts typically take into account such factors as:

- the relationship, if any, between the publisher and the recipient;
- the risks, if any, posed to the interests of the publisher, the recipient, or others;
- whether the information was solicited or volunteered;
- the relevance of the information to self-protective action by the publisher or the recipient; and
- whether the plaintiff is alleged to have engaged in wrongful conduct.

c. Loss of a Qualified Privilege

A qualified privilege is defeasible in the sense that the law *does* care about what the defendant knew, who the defendant told, and why the defendant made the statement. A qualified privilege will be lost if the defendant acted with common-law "malice" (in the sense of ill-will, spite, vindictiveness, or revenge) in publishing the defamation. Also, excessive publication may cause a privilege to be lost, so that if *A*, who is privileged to say something to *B*, also tells *C*, *A*'s statements may not be privileged. In addition, at common law, many jurisdictions required that the defendant have acted non-negligently if a statement was to be privileged. The constitutionalization of the law of defamation has made qualified privilege less important than it once was, as in most, if not all cases, libel and slander are no longer strict liability torts. If the plaintiff proves actual malice, there can never be a qualified privilege, because in all jurisdictions a showing of that degree of fault destroys the privilege.

d. Statutes Relating to Former Employees

Statements relating to work present a serious problem for the legal system. Actions based on job recommendations and statements made in connection with the discharge of employees make up a large portion of modern defamation cases. If the plaintiff's employer is asked about the plaintiff's job performance by a prospective new employer, most jurisdictions would say that the employer has a qualified privilege. This may do the employer little good, as qualified privileges can easily be lost, and in any event, the possible existence of a privilege does not prevent a disgruntled employee or former employee from suing. Of course, in certain situations qualified privileges can affect the outcome of cases. *See, e.g.*, Bals v. Verduzco, 600 N.E.2d 1353 (Ind. 1992) (an action by a current employee based on an allegedly defamatory evaluation was barred by qualified privilege); McCoy v. Neiman Marcus Group, Inc., 1997 WL 53124 (N.D. Tex. 1997) (a company did not abuse its qualified privilege by holding a department meeting and explaining to remaining employees that the plaintiff was terminated for fraud and that systems were intact to detect such fraud).

Many employers, fearing defamation suits, have refused to give prospective employers any information about their former employees other than job titles and dates of employment. This harms able employees, who would get good references if employers could comment freely. It may even be dangerous, as when a former employer, fearing litigation, does not disclose a job applicant's history of actual or threatened violence. Many states have tried to encourage disclosure by enacting legislation to make it harder for employees to bring defamation actions. Here is one example.

KANSAS STATUTES ANNOTATED, Chapter 44, Article 1, §44-119a.
(Westlaw 2004)

(a) Unless otherwise provided by law, an employer, or an employer's designee, who discloses information about a current or former employee to a prospective employer of the employee shall be qualifiedly immune from civil liability.

(b) Unless otherwise provided by law, an employer who discloses information about a current or former employee to a prospective employer of the employee shall be absolutely immune from civil liability. The immunity applies only to disclosure of the following:

(1) date of employment;

(2) pay level;

(3) job description and duties;

(4) wage history.

(c) Unless otherwise provided by law, an employer who responds in writing to a written request concerning a current or former employee from a prospective employer of that employee shall be absolutely immune from civil liability for disclosure of the following information to which an employee may have access:

(1) Written employee evaluations which were conducted prior to the employee's separation from the employer and to which an employee shall be given a copy upon request; and

(2) whether the employee was voluntarily or involuntarily released from service and the reasons for the separation....

Note that the Kansas statute covers only information furnished to a prospective employer.

3. The Validity of Releases

Is it possible for a person who provides an employment reference to avoid the risk of being sued for defamation by relying upon a release? To the extent that a release purports to cover knowingly false statements is it void as against public policy? Section 195 of the Restatement, Second, of Contracts says that although one can release another party from liability for negligence, one cannot grant immunity for intentional or reckless torts. In contrast, the Restatement, Second, of Torts §583 provides that "the consent of another to the publication of defamatory matter concerning him is a complete defense to his action for defamation." The courts are divided on this issue. *Compare* Elmer v. Coplin, 485 So. 2d 171 (La. Ct. App. 1986) (waiver that released anyone contacted by bar admission authorities from liability for any information they gave did not preclude defamation claim) and Kellums v. Freight Sales Ctrs., Inc., 467 So. 2d 816 (Fla. Dist. Ct. App. 1985) (clause in employment application that explicitly required applicants to give absolute immunity to any former employer who was contacted was unenforceable), *with* Cox v. Nasche, 70 F.3d 1030 (9th Cir. 1995) (release form signed by applicant afforded absolute privilege against liability for defamation even if statements were made maliciously), Smith v. Holley, 827 S.W.2d 433 (Tex. Ct. App. 1992) (similar); and Rosenberg v. American Bowling Cong., 589 F. Supp. 547 (M.D. Fla. 1984) (plaintiff's consent to communicate results of investigation constituted an absolute immunity).

An employer who is sued for defamatory comments about a current or former employee may be able to escape liability by arguing that the employee who made the statements was not authorized to do so and that the statements were not ratified. *See* David A. Scott, *An Employer's Guide to Defending Workplace Defamation Claims*, 37 So. Tex. L. Rev. 84, 854 (1996); *cf.* Randall's Food Mkts., Inc. v. Johnson, 891 S.W.2d 640, 646 (Tex. 1995) (cosmetician acted independently and outside the scope of her employment by circulating a petition to other employees and customers that the store manager was a deficient administrator and used merchandise without paying for it).

4. Other Privileges

The Reporter's Privilege. Section 611 of the Restatement, Second, of Torts provides:

The publication of defamatory matter concerning another in a report of an official action or proceeding or of a meeting open to the public that deals with a matter of public concern is privileged if the report is accurate and complete or a fair abridgement of the occurrence reported.

Comment i to §611 indicates that "the purpose of the privilege is to protect those who make available to the public information concerning public events that concern or affect the public interest and that any member of the public could have acquired for himself by attending them." Thus, the "reporter," in essence, acts as a conduit for the information. Because it is important in a democracy that persons perform this function, the privilege exists even if the publisher knows that the words repeated are false. *Id.* at Comment a. The privilege is commonly exercised by newspapers, broadcasters, and others who are in the business of reporting the news to the public, but it extends to any person who makes a report, oral or otherwise, to any other person. For example, an expert witness is privileged to repeat the substance of in-court testimony to journalists waiting on the courthouse steps, provided the events have not been illegitimately orchestrated to create a privilege to "report" defamatory statements first uttered in a privileged forum. *See* Rosenberg v. Helinski, 616 A.2d 866 (Md. 1992).

In Friedman v. Israel Labour Party, 957 F. Supp. 701 (E.D. Pa. 1997), the court held that the reporter's privilege extended to fair republication of defamatory official statements about foreign governments.

In a different but related vein, some courts have held that publication to the media of material the media were independently entitled to view cannot provide the basis for a defamation action. Kelley v. Bonney, 606 A.2d 693 (Conn. 1992), held that the judicial-proceedings privilege applied when a complaint was given to a newspaper which could have obtained the document under a freedom-of-information act.

Statutory Privileges. Statutory privileges for employer communications have already been described. Other special privileges have been created by statute. For example, Searcy v. Auerbach, 980 F.2d 609 (9th Cir. 1992), turned upon a California law requiring certain persons to report suspected child abuse to a child protective agency, and additionally providing:

> No child care custodian, health practitioner, employee of a child protective agency, or commercial film and photographic print processor who reports a known or suspected instance of child abuse shall be civilly or criminally liable for any report required or authorized by this article.

The court held that the statute did not bar an action for libel against a psychologist who had advised a divorced father (Michael) of his belief that Michael's child had been sexually abused while in the mother's custody. The privilege did not apply because the information reached California authorities only indirectly (Michael disclosed the information to Texas authorities, who in turn shared it with their California counterparts) and because Michael was not a person to whom disclosure of the report was permitted under the act.

See also, e.g., Tex. Gov't Code Ann. T.2, Subt. G, App. A-1 §15.10 (Westlaw 2003) (creating an absolute privilege relating to complaints to disciplinary authorities about attorney misconduct).

The Neutral-Reportage Privilege. In Edwards v. National Audubon Soc'y, Inc., 556 F.2d 113 (2d Cir. 1977), the New York Times reported that a publication of a prominent conservation group had criticized certain scientists as "paid liars" because of their support of the chemical industry in a controversy over the pesticide DDT. In finding for the newspaper, Chief Judge Kaufman said that even if actual malice had been established (which it was not), a constitutional privilege of neutral republication protected the *Times*. The court ruled that the public interest in being informed about on-going controversies justifies creating a privilege to republish allegations made by a responsible organization against a public figure, if the republication is done accurately and neutrally in the context of an existing controversy.

Some courts have rejected the neutral-reportage privilege (*see, e.g.*, Hogan v. Herald Co., 444 N.E.2d 1002 (N.Y. 1982)), and a few have applied it to private individuals (*compare* Khawar v. Globe Int'l Inc., 965 P.2d 696 (Cal. 1998) (declining to apply the privilege to the case of a private person accused of killing Robert Kennedy, but not deciding or implying whether the privilege applied to statements about public figures), *with* April v. Reflector-Herald, Inc., 546 N.E.2d 466, 469 (Ohio. Ct. App. 1988) (holding that the privilege applies regardless of whether the plaintiff is a public figure or private person)).

The Supreme Court came close to ruling on the privilege in Harte-Hanks Communications, Inc. v. Connaughton, 491 U.S. 657 (1989), but the issue was dropped by the defense on appeal.

Under a neutral-reportage privilege, it would seem fair to require reporters to place readers clearly on notice that the communication concerns disputed charges and is not an assertion of their truth. Responsible reporters will do this on their own; the irresponsible have more than enough protection without giving them an unqualified privilege as well.

Is it desirable to permit the media to print allegations about a public controversy if they believe the allegations to be false? For example, were Senator Joe McCarthy's dubious allegations in the 1950s of communist influence in government agencies news that could not be suppressed or ignored, and which had to be published? Although the neutral reportage privilege has not been widely endorsed, Professor David Anderson opines:

> If the President of the United States baselessly accused the Vice President of plotting to assassinate him…most courts surely would hold that the media could safely report the President's accusation even if they seriously doubted its truth.

Is Libel Law Worth Reforming?, 140 U. Pa. L. Rev. 487, 504 (1991).

5. SLAPP Suits

Persons who become the subject of unfavorable public attention sometimes respond by "slapping" the disseminator of the information with a suit for defamation. This form of retaliation can undoubtedly chill free expression. California and several other states have responded to the problem by passing SLAPP (strategic lawsuit against public participation) statutes which make it relatively easy to dismiss meritless retaliatory defamation charges.

In Dove Audio Inc. v. Rosenfeld, Meyer & Susman, 54 Cal. Rptr.2d 830 (Cal. App. 1996), the son of the late actress Audrey Hepburn asked lawyers to look into why one of his mother's charities had received so little in the way of royalties from one of her audio recordings. The lawyers contacted other celebrities who had participated in the recording and their charities, informing them of the problem and stating an intention to file a complaint with the Attorney General. Dove Audio sued the firm for defamation and tortious interference. Finding that the law firm was immune under both the absolute litigation privilege and the SLAPP statute, the court wrote:

> In general terms, a SLAPP suit is "a meritless suit filed primarily to chill the defendant's exercise of First Amendment rights." [Citation.] Under [Code Civ. Proc.] section 425.16, subdivision (b), "A cause of action against a person arising from any act of that person in furtherance of the person's right of petition or free speech under the United States or California Constitution in connection with a public issue shall be subject to a special motion to strike, unless the court determines that the plaintiff has established that there is a probability that the plaintiff will prevail on the claim."
>
> Subdivision (e) provides: "As used in this section, 'act in furtherance of a person's right of petition or free speech under the United States or California Constitution in connection with a public issue' includes any written or oral statement or writing made before a legislative, executive, or judicial proceeding, or any other official proceeding authorized by law; any written or oral statement or writing made in connection with an issue under consideration or review by a legislative, executive, or judicial body, or any other official proceeding authorized by law; or any written or oral statement or writing made in a place open to the public or a public forum in connection with an issue of public interest."[c]
>
> ....
>
> RM & S's communication raised a question of public interest: whether money designated for charities was being received by those charities. The communication was made in connection with an official proceeding authorized by law, a proposed complaint to the Attorney General seeking an investigation. "The constitutional right to petition...includes the basic act of filing litigation or otherwise seeking administrative action."[Citation.] Just as communications preparatory to or in anticipation of the bringing of an action or other official proceeding are within the protection of the litigation privilege of Civil Code section 47, subdivision (b) [citation], we hold that such statements are equally entitled to the benefits of section 425.16. [Citation.]
>
> ....
>
> ....Once the party moving to strike the complaint makes that threshold showing, the burden shifts to the responding plaintiff to establish a probability of prevailing at trial. Appellant did not, and cannot do so in this case. As we have explained, RM & S's communications were absolutely privileged under Civil Code section 47, subdivision (b). That privilege is applicable to both causes of action alleged by appellant, defamation and interference with economic relationship. [Citation.] The trial court did not err in granting RM & S's special motion to strike under section 425.16.

See also Roberts v. L.A. County Bar Assn., 129 Cal. Rptr. 2d 546 (Ct. App. 2003) (holding that a judicial candidate's claims for breach of contract and fraud, based on a "not qualified" rating, were barred because the candidate failed to show a reasonable probability of success on the merits).

In some states, "unintentional slapping" may trigger statutory rights. *See* Equillon Ent., LLC v. Consumer Cause, Inc., 52 P.3d 685 (Cal. 2002) (holding in a non-defama-

---

c. The terms of the statute were subsequently enlarged by the legislature.

tion suit that a consumer group was not required to demonstrate that an oil company's cause of action was brought with the intent of chilling its exercise of constitutional speech or petition).

E. The Media and the Law of Libel: A Summary

The many constitutional protections for defendants—especially media defendants—in libel cases have made it harder than ever before for plaintiffs to win libel cases against newspapers and broadcasters. In *Libel Law in the Trenches: Reflections on Current Data on Libel Litigation*, 87 Va. L. Rev. 503, 511 (2001), David A. Logan, now Dean of Roger Williams University School of Law, reviewed twenty years of data collected by the Libel Defense Resource Center concerning claims against the media. He concluded that successful pre-trial motions by the media are common, that the number of trials against the media in state and federal courts (only 11 suits in 1999) is "[r]emarkably" low, and that with respect to jury awards, after post-trial motions and appeals are considered, media defendants pay out "less than a nickel on the dollar." Logan opines:

> One could say that the *New York Times/Gertz* constitutional regime has provided the media with something approaching an absolute privilege to defame; a reasonable publisher should worry about having to pay substantial libel damages as much as she worries about being struck by lightning.
>
> ....
>
> ....This means that unless the courts are willing to take the final step and grant the media an absolute immunity from libel liability (something no state or federal court has been willing to do) the costs of obtaining victory—insurance premiums and uninsured litigation costs—may be the only force left that deters irresponsible reporting.

Id. at 520-28.

David A. Anderson, *Is Libel Law Worth Reforming?*
140 U. Pa. L. Rev. 487, 488-90 (1991)[d]

Very few victims of defamation have any hope of remedy under this system. Most have no chance unless, in addition to proving publication of a defamatory statement (1) they can produce before trial clear and convincing proof that the defendant seriously doubted the truth of the defamation; (2) the trial judge, jury, and all reviewing courts independently agree that such proof is clear and convincing; (3) the accusation is not hyperbolic, rhetorical, satirical, or otherwise incapable of sufficiently precise factual content; (4) the plaintiff is able to prove its falsity, perhaps by the clear-and-convincing standard; and (5) the defendant is not neutrally repeating the defamatory accusation of a responsible organization about a matter of public concern.

The plaintiff who survives this gauntlet may still fall victim to common law rules about special damages, state law privileges, retraction statutes, unusually short statutes of limitations, and other peculiar state limitations. What libel law provides today is not a general remedy with exceptions, but a general scheme of nonliability that permits a remedy only in exceptional cases.

....

[Earlier in the article, Professor Anderson observed:]

The remnants of American libel law provide little protection for reputation....

Nonetheless, libel law continues to exact a price from speech. The constitutional protections are designed to, and often do, encourage the media to defame. Outraged juries frequently return six- or seven-figure verdicts. Although such verdicts are usually reversed on appeal, defamation victims continue to sue. While the likelihood of success is minuscule, the amount at issue is usually large, so the media defend vigorously. Because many of the constitutional issues do not lend themselves to preliminary disposition, even the least meritorious cases can require extensive discovery on both sides. Those actions that go to trial often produce plaintiffs' judgments that are eventually reversed on constitutional grounds. Libel law, as modified over the past twenty-five years, produces expensive litigation and occasional large judgments, and therefore continues to chill speech.

As it stands today, libel law is not worth saving. What we have is a system in which most claims are judicially foreclosed after costly litigation. It gives plaintiffs delusions of large windfalls, defendants nightmares of intrusive and protracted litigation, and the public little assurance that the law favors truth over falsehood. If we can do no better, honesty and efficiency demand that we abolish the law of libel.

Much can be said for that course. Since our forebearers abandoned licensing, libel has been the principal legal threat to freedom of the press. Abolishing libel law is the only way to completely eliminate the chilling effect that it exerts on the press. To paraphrase Judge Edgerton, whatever is subtracted from the field of libel is added to the field of free debate. Abolition would leave victims of defamation little worse off than they are today. A few would give up recoveries, but many would be spared the costs, emotional as well as financial, of hopeless litigation. The public would get the benefit of information that is now suppressed by the chill of libel law, and would be disabused of the inferences that may be drawn from a mistaken belief that defamatory falsehoods are generally actionable.

No matter how much it values speech, however, a civilized society cannot refuse to protect reputation. Some form of libel law is as essential to the health of the commonweal and the press as it is to the victims of defamation. Without libel law, credibility of the press would be at the mercy of the least scrupulous among it, and public discourse would have no necessary anchor in truth.

Note

1. Professor Anderson's article goes on to describe the constitutional law of defamation, to examine in detail the harm done by modern libel law, and to propose substantive and procedural reforms. Noting that innovation at the state level has been stifled by

the Supreme Court's preemption of much of the field, and that reform on a less than national basis would provide little comfort to media whose broadcasts and publications cross state lines, he concludes that only the Supreme Court can reform the law of defamation.

Chapter 23

Invasion of Privacy

The law of torts protects a person's interest in life, health, property, and reputation. In 1890, Charles Warren and Louis Brandeis argued that it should also protect privacy:

> . . . . The press is overstepping in every direction the obvious bounds of propriety and of decency. Gossip is no longer the resource of the idle and of the vicious, but has become a trade, which is pursued with industry as well as effrontery. . . . To occupy the indolent, column upon column is filled with idle gossip, which can only be procured by intrusion upon the domestic circle.

Charles D. Warren & Louis D. Brandeis, *The Right to Privacy*, 4 Harv. L. Rev. 193, 196 (1890).

As a glance at the newspapers sold in supermarket checkout lines shows, the law has done virtually nothing about the problem with which Warren and Brandeis were primarily concerned: the publication in newspapers of information about the personal lives of socially prominent persons.[a] Furthermore, what limited protection the law does afford privacy has not been based upon the principal analogy that Warren and Brandeis proposed: common-law copyright.[b] Nevertheless, the Warren and Brandeis article has become a classic in the sense that it is very often cited—probably more often than it is read. And, in a variety of cases, the law does sometimes afford relief for harms that can be characterized as "invasions of privacy."

Prosser classified the "privacy" torts as involving four distinct kinds of invasions. This chapter will use Prosser's categories, which have become standard. They are:

> *Public Disclosure of Private Facts.* This involves the conduct that bothered Warren and Brandeis. While many jurisdictions purport to "recognize" the tort, relatively few cases—some of which are of questionable authority today—have allowed recovery. Any action that allows the award of damages based on dissemination of the truth obviously faces formidable First Amendment obstacles.

> *Intrusion.* In order to obtain private facts to publish, or for other reasons, the defendant may intrude upon the plaintiff's seclusion by peering through windows,

---

a. William L. Prosser, *Privacy*, 48 Cal. L. Rev. 383 (1960), claimed that the Warren & Brandeis article was inspired by unwelcome newspaper coverage of the social activities of Warren, a Boston lawyer, and his wife. Whether this is true in the narrow sense that specific articles about the Warrens led to the article's being written is unclear. Nevertheless, as the quoted excerpt shows, Warren and Brandeis were offended by gossip in general, and by printed gossip in particular.

b. At common law, the creator of an unpublished work, such as a song or a letter, had a right to prevent the publication of that work. In some cases, this right was used to prevent publications which would have embarrassed the writer. Common-law copyright no longer exists in this country; protection of expression is now exclusively a matter of federal copyright law. Note, however, that the copyright statute recognizes a fair-use doctrine, and that that doctrine has helped to shape the law relating to the right-of-publicity form of invasion of privacy discussed later in this chapter.

tapping the plaintiff's phone, opening the plaintiff's letters, or following the plaintiff closely on the street. Warren and Brandeis did not discuss this aspect of privacy, probably because Boston in 1890 was a considerably more civilized place than it is today, despite the deplorable prevalence of gossip in the Boston papers.

False Light. Warren and Brandeis were concerned with the publication of matters they thought to be none of the reader's business; they did not worry much about distortion. But even accurate information can, because of its context, create a misleading and unfavorable impression, as when a picture of the plaintiff, a bystander, appears in connection with a newspaper article about the arrest of criminals. The harm done by this sort of thing is often similar to that done by defamation. One might think that this subject would have developed as a branch of the law of defamation, but it is commonly dealt with as an invasion of privacy.

Appropriation of the Plaintiff's Name or Likeness. Perhaps the healthiest branch of the privacy-tort family is that involving cases in which the defendant uses the plaintiff's name or picture to advertise a product or service, or for other reasons. The plaintiff's right to prevent this—sometimes called the "right of publicity"—is widely recognized. Many of the cases are better seen as involving a "property right" to the plaintiff's identity or public persona than a right to privacy. Indeed, many of the plaintiffs in these cases are celebrities, whose objections are sometimes not to having their names used, but rather to not being paid for the use.

"Only Minnesota, North Dakota, and Wyoming have not yet recognized any of the four privacy torts." Lake v. Wal-Mart Stores, Inc., 582 N.W.2d 231 (Minn. 1998). In some states, privacy categories have been set down in statutory form. *See, e.g.,* R.I. Stat. Ann. 9-1-28.1 (Westlaw 2002).

Prosser's four categories overlap considerably. Suppose, for instance, that a photographer follows the plaintiff, an intensely private person, for days, snapping pictures, and that the pictures are used without the plaintiff's consent to advertise whiskey. This conduct is an appropriation of the plaintiff's likeness; it may put the plaintiff in a false light (as when the plaintiff does not drink); the photographer may have intruded upon the plaintiff's seclusion to get the pictures; and the plaintiff may object to appearing in the press, period. Nevertheless, the categories provide a useful way to organize the cases and statutes.

Constitutional Right of Privacy Distinguished. The tort of invasion of privacy must be clearly distinguished from privacy rights under the United States Constitution. The Constitution limits the power of states to prohibit or regulate certain types of conduct generally involving intimately personal decisions, such as marriage, child rearing, use of contraceptives, or having an abortion. Those limitations are referred to, somewhat unfortunately, as the constitutional right of privacy, but they have little to do with the four causes of action described above. An occasional decision has held that a constitutional right-of-privacy claim will lie for unwarranted disclosure of highly personal or intimate information, but in such a case the analysis differs from the common-law tort action for disclosure of private facts. *See* Sheets v. Salt Lake County, 45 F.3d 1383 (10th Cir. 1995) (recognizing the plaintiff's legitimate expectation of privacy in information in his wife's diary as it pertained to intimate marital matters); *but see* Livsey v. Salt Lake County, 275 F.3d 952 (10th Cir. 2001) (holding that a widow's privacy was not violated by a police officer's revelation of sex-linked details of her husband's death). Note that other constitutional provisions—particularly freedom of speech and freedom of the press—sometimes play an important role in shaping the contours of the four tort actions.

A. Disclosure of Private Facts

Quoting the second Restatement, the court in Cowles Publ'g Co. v. State Patrol, 748 P.2d 597, 602 (Wash. 1988), wrote:

> Every individual has some phases of his life and his activities and some facts about himself that he does not expose to the public eye, but keeps entirely to himself or at most reveals only to his family or to close personal friends. Sexual relations, for example, are normally entirely private matters, as are family quarrels, many unpleasant or disgraceful or humiliating illnesses, most intimate personal letters, most details of a man's life in his home, and some of his past history that he would rather forget. When these intimate details of his life are spread before the public gaze in a manner highly offensive to the ordinary reasonable man, there is an actionable invasion of his privacy, unless the matter is one of legitimate public interest.

Sidis v. F-R Publishing Corp.

United States Court of Appeals for the Second Circuit
113 F.2d 806 (2d Cir. 1940)

CLARK, Circuit Judge.

William James Sidis was the unwilling subject of a brief biographical sketch and cartoon printed in The New Yorker weekly magazine for August 14, 1937.... He brought an action in the district court against the publisher, F-R Publishing Corporation. His complaint stated [a] "cause[] of action" [for] violation of his right of privacy as that right is recognized in California, Georgia, Kansas, Kentucky, and Missouri.... Defendant's motion to dismiss the... "cause[] of action" was granted, and plaintiff has filed an appeal from the order of dismissal....

William James Sidis was a famous child prodigy in 1910. His name and prowess were well known to newspaper readers of the period. At the age of eleven, he lectured to distinguished mathematicians on the subject of Four-Dimensional Bodies. When he was sixteen, he was graduated from Harvard College, amid considerable public attention. Since then, his name has appeared in the press only sporadically, and he has sought to live as unobtrusively as possible. Until the articles objected to appeared in The New Yorker, he had apparently succeeded in his endeavor to avoid the public gaze.

Among The New Yorker's features are brief biographical sketches of current and past personalities. In the latter department, which appears haphazardly under the title of "Where Are They Now?" the article on Sidis was printed with a subtitle "April Fool." The author describes his subject's early accomplishments in mathematics and the widespread attention he received, then recounts his general breakdown and the revulsion which Sidis thereafter felt for his former life of fame and study. The unfortunate prodigy is traced over the years that followed, through his attempts to conceal his identity, through his chosen career as an insignificant clerk who would not need to employ unusual mathematical talents, and through the bizarre ways in which his genius flowered, as in his enthusiasm for collecting streetcar transfers and in his proficiency with an adding machine. The article closes with an account of an interview with Sidis at his present lodgings, "a hall bedroom of Boston's shabby south end." The untidiness of his room, his curious laugh, his manner of speech, and other personal habits are commented upon at length, as is his present interest in the lore of the Okamakammessett Indians. The subtitle is explained by the closing sentence, quoting Sidis as saying "with a grin" that it was strange, "but, you know, I was born on April Fool's Day." Accompanying the biography is a small cartoon showing the genius of eleven years lecturing to a group of astounded professors.

It is not contended that any of the matter printed is untrue. Nor is the manner of the author unfriendly; Sidis today is described as having "a certain childlike charm." But the article is merciless in its dissection of intimate details of its subject's personal life, and this in company with elaborate accounts of Sidis' passion for privacy and the pitiable lengths to which he has gone in order to avoid public scrutiny. The work possesses great reader interest, for it is both amusing and instructive; but it may be fairly described as a ruthless exposure of a once public character, who has since sought and has now been deprived of the seclusion of private life.

    ....

... [W]e are asked to declare that this exposure transgresses upon plaintiff's right of privacy, as recognized in California, Georgia, Kansas, Kentucky, and Missouri. Each of these states except California grants to the individual a common law right, and California a constitutional right, to be let alone to a certain extent. The decisions have been carefully analyzed by the court below, and we need not examine them further. None of the cited rulings goes so far as to prevent a newspaper or magazine from publishing the truth about a person, however intimate, revealing, or harmful the truth may be. Nor are there any decided cases that confer such a privilege upon the press....

All comment upon the right of privacy must stem from the famous article by Warren and Brandeis on *The Right of Privacy* in 4 Harv. L. Rev. 193. The learned authors of that paper were convinced that some limits ought to be imposed upon the privilege of newspapers to publish truthful items of a personal nature. "....The intensity and complexity of life, attendant upon advancing civilization, have rendered necessary some retreat from the world, and man, under the refining influence of culture, has become more sensitive to publicity, so that solitude and privacy have become more essential to the individual; but modern enterprise and invention have, through invasions upon his privacy, subjected him to mental pain and distress, far greater than could be inflicted by mere bodily injury." Warren and Brandeis, *supra* at page 196.

Warren and Brandeis realized that the interest of the individual in privacy must inevitably conflict with the interest of the public in news. Certain public figures, they conceded, such as holders of public office, must sacrifice their privacy and expose at least part of their lives to public scrutiny as the price of the powers they attain. But even public figures were not to be stripped bare. "In general, then, the matters of which the publication should be repressed may be described as those which concern the private life, habits, acts, and relations of an individual, and have no legitimate connection with his fitness for a public office.... Some things all men alike are entitled to keep from popular curiosity, whether in public life or not, while other are only private because the persons concerned have not assumed a position which makes their doings legitimate matters of public investigation." Warren and Brandeis, *supra* at page 216.

It must be conceded that under the strict standards suggested by these authors plaintiff's right of privacy has been invaded. Sidis today is neither politician, public administrator, nor statesman. Even if he were, some of the personal details revealed were of the sort that Warren and Brandeis believed "all men alike are entitled to keep from popular curiosity."

But despite eminent opinion to the contrary, we are not yet disposed to afford to all of the intimate details of private life an absolute immunity from the prying of the press. Everyone will agree that at some point the public interest in obtaining information becomes dominant over the individual's desire for privacy. Warren and Brandeis were willing to lift the veil somewhat in the case of public officers. We would go further, though we are not yet prepared to say how far. At least we would permit limited scrutiny of the "private" life of any person who has achieved, or has had thrust upon him, the questionable and indefinable status of a "public figure." See Restatement, Torts, §867, comments c and d; [citations].

William James Sidis was once a public figure. As a child prodigy, he excited both admiration and curiosity. Of him great deeds were expected. In 1910, he was a person about whom the newspapers might display a legitimate intellectual interest, in the sense meant by Warren and Brandeis, as distinguished from a trivial and unseemly curiosity. But the precise motives of the press we regard as unimportant. And even if Sidis had loathed public attention at that time, we think his uncommon achievements and personality would have made the attention permissible. Since then Sidis has cloaked himself in obscurity, but his subsequent history, containing as it did the answer to the question of whether or not he had fulfilled his early promise, was still a matter of public concern. The article in The New Yorker sketched the life of an unusual personality, and it possessed considerable popular news interest.

We express no comment on whether or not the news worthiness of the matter printed will always constitute a complete defense. Revelations may be so intimate and so unwarranted in view of the victim's position as to outrage the community's notions of decency. But when focused upon public characters, truthful comments upon dress, speech, habits, and the ordinary aspects of personality will usually not transgress this line. Regrettably or not, the misfortunes and frailties of neighbors and "public figures" are subjects of considerable interest and discussion of the rest of the population. And when such are the mores of the community, it would be unwise for a court to bar their expression in the newspapers, books, and magazines of the day.

. . . .

Affirmed.

Notes

1. *Privacy, Truth, and Freedom of the Press.* Even if *Sidis* had gone the other way, current notions of freedom of speech and of the press as applied to the law of torts would, today, give constitutional protection to the article in question. Indeed, the article would probably not be actionable today even if it contained serious inaccuracies, so long as it was not published with "malice" in the sense of knowledge of its falsity or reckless disregard for whether it was true. See the discussion of constitutional protection for defamation in Chapter 22.

At least one state has declined to recognize the private-facts tort because of its potential for conflict with the First Amendment. *See* Hall v. Post, 372 S.E.2d 711 (N.C. 1988); *see also* Doe v. Meth. Hosp., 690 N.E.2d 681 (Ind. 1997) (declining to recognize disclosure actions and noting that "torts involving disclosure of truthful but private facts encounter[] a considerable obstacle in the truth-in-defense provisions of the Indiana Constitution").

2. *Disclosures Relating to Public Figures.* Modern constitutional-law developments in defamation suggest that a "disclosure of private facts" case has a serious

chance of success only if the facts have nothing to do with the plaintiff's conduct as a public figure or with a matter of legitimate public interest. It may be possible to make such an argument in a case involving unconsented disclosure of gay or lesbian sexual orientation. *See* Barbara Moretti, *Note, Outing: Justifiable or Unwarranted Invasion of Privacy? The Private Facts Tort as a Remedy for Disclosure of Sexual Orientation*, 11 Cardozo Arts & Ent. L. Rev. 857, 864 (1993) (arguing that because "outing involves disclosures concerning one's sexual activities, desires, fantasies, or preferences—matters that are essentially private," an action should lie unless the disclosure is clearly linked to some aspect of a person's public life, such as an abuse of governmental power). *Cf.* Guinn v. Church of Christ, 775 P.2d 766 (Okla. 1989) (liability imposed on church elders who revealed intimate details of former member's transgressions).

The facts of Sidis's life were at least newsworthy, and he had once done things to make himself a public figure, though he later regretted those actions. Compare the situation of a rape victim who does not want her name published. It is hard to see any public interest in publishing the victim's name and impossible to find any "consent" on her part—implied or otherwise—to becoming a public figure. Nevertheless, the Supreme Court held in Cox Broadcasting Corp. v. Cohn, 420 U.S. 469 (1975), that publication of the victim's name—which appeared in official records open to the public—was constitutionally protected. Although disclosure of the identity of a rape victim was prohibited by state law, the Court found that by "placing the information in the public domain on official court records, the state must be presumed to have concluded that the public interest was thereby being served." Interestingly, in reaching a similar conclusion in Florida Star v. B.J.F., 491 U.S. 524, 532 (1989), the Court declined an "invitation to hold broadly that truthful publication may never be punished consistent with the First Amendment." Today, it is possible that constitutional protection would be available even if the victim's name is not available from public records.

See also John Doe 2 v. Associated Press, 331 F.3d 417 (4th Cir. 2003) (holding that a reporter was not liable for disclosing the name of a sexual assault victim who testified in open court, even though the judge had instructed reporters not to do so).

3. *Past Conduct.* Melvin v. Reid, 297 P. 91 (Cal. Ct. App. 1931), was an action by a former prostitute who, after her acquittal on a murder charge, led a conventional life. The defendants produced a motion picture about her early life. The court held that the plaintiff's activities had ceased to be a matter of public concern and allowed the action to proceed. The California Supreme Court suggested in Forsher v. Bugliosi, 608 P.2d 716 (Cal. 1980), that *Melvin* might come out differently under current constitutional law. History is, after all, no less deserving than current events of constitutional protection.

The plaintiff in Diaz v. Oakland Tribune, Inc., 188 Cal. Rptr. 762 (Ct. App. 1983), was the president of the student body at her college. The defendant revealed that the plaintiff had once been a man, and had had a sex-change operation before going to college. Although the plaintiff had "waived" her right to privacy about her *public* conduct by seeking to become president of the student body, the court held that this did not "warrant that her entire private life be open to public inspection," especially because the "public arena [she]...entered...is concededly small."

4. *Should a Lawyer Take a "Private-Facts" Case on a Contingent-Fee Basis?* Diane L. Zimmerman, *Requiem for a Heavyweight: A Farewell to Warren and Brandeis's Privacy Tort*, 68 Cornell L. Rev. 291 (1983), concludes that plaintiffs rarely win private-facts cases, although thirty-six jurisdictions recognize their existence. Professor Zim-

merman argues that the contours of the tort are hopelessly vague, that there is often value in circulating facts about private persons, and that commentators who defend the tort have failed to appreciate the extent to which constitutional considerations may apply.

McNamara v. Freedom Newspapers, Inc.

Texas Court of Appeals
802 S.W.2d 901 (Tex. Ct. App. 1991)

BENAVIDES, Justice.

. . . .

The underlying action arises out of the publication by the Newspaper of a photograph taken during a high school soccer game. The photograph in question accurately depicted McNamara and a student from the opposing school running full stride and chasing a soccer ball. The picture further shows McNamara's genitalia which happened to be exposed at the exact moment that the photograph was taken.[1] The photograph was published in conjunction with an article reporting on the soccer game.

. . . .

[McNamara alleged that the defendant invaded his privacy by public disclosure of true private facts.] McNamara argues that the Newspaper could have used one of its other numerous photographs in its article....

. . . .

The uncontroverted facts in this case establish that the photograph of McNamara was taken by a newspaper photographer for media purposes. The picture accurately depicted a public event and was published as part of a newspaper article describing the game. At the time the photograph was taken, McNamara was voluntarily participating in a spectator sport at a public place. None of the persons involved in the publishing procedure actually noticed that McNamara's genitals were exposed.

We hold that because the published photograph accurately depicts a public, newsworthy event, the First Amendment provides the Newspaper with immunity from liability for damages resulting from its publication of McNamara's photograph....

The trial court's judgment is affirmed.

Notes

1. *Expectation of Privacy.* For disclosure to be actionable, there must be a reasonable expectation of privacy. *See* Pontbriand v. Sundlun, 699 A.2d 856 (R.I. 1997) (whether depositors had reasonable expectation of privacy in their bank records and whether disclosure would be offensive to a reasonable person were questions of fact, precluding summary judgment).

---

1. The exposure was apparently caused by McNamara's failure to wear the customary athletic supporter.

2. *Photographs Taken in Public.* Normally, neither intrusion upon seclusion nor a private-facts claim will lie for using photographs of the plaintiff taken in public. The plaintiff has voluntarily chosen to appear in a place visible to others, so taking and using the photographs invades no privacy interest. *See* Prince v. Out Publ'g Inc., 2002 W.L. 7999 (Cal. App.) (pictures depicted a party-goer dancing naked from the waist up on an elevated platform); Floyd v. Park Cities People, Inc., 685 S.W.2d 96 (Tex. Ct. App. 1985) (photo of man on porch published in newspaper). However, if the plaintiff is shown in an embarrassing situation encountered accidentally, use of the photograph may be actionable. *See* Daily Times-Democrat Co. v. Graham, 162 So. 2d 474 (Ala. 1964) (photograph of woman after a rush of air lifted her skirt in "Fun House"); Neff v. Time, Inc., 406 F. Supp. 858 (C.D. Pa. 1976) (photo of football fan with his fly open). The *McNamara* court declined to endorse this view.

3. *Victims.* Many of the cases involve victims of crimes or accidents who are photographed in agony or without their clothes on. Unless the pictures create misleading impressions, thus raising a "false light" claim, the plaintiffs nearly always lose. Anderson v. Fisher Broad. Co., Inc., 712 P.2d 803 (Or. 1986), held that televising pictures of the plaintiff, an accident victim who was bleeding and in pain, was not an invasion of privacy. The plaintiff conceded that showing this footage on the evening news would not have violated his rights, but argued that using the footage in a commercial for a program on emergency medical services did. The court distinguished situations in which the information in question was obtained by trespassing or other wrongful conduct. Compare *Anderson* with Taylor v. KTVB, Inc., 525 P.2d 984 (Idaho 1974), holding that a television station could be held liable for broadcasting a film clip showing plaintiff being arrested and taken from his house in the nude, if it acted with "malice," meaning a purpose of embarrassing or humiliating the plaintiff or recklessness.

See Andrew Jay McClurg, *Bringing Privacy Law Out of the Closet: A Tort Theory of Liability for Intrusions in Public Places*, 73 N.C.L. Rev. 989 (1995) (arguing that expecting to be seen in public and expecting to be photographed for the front page of the paper are not the same thing).

4. *Family Members.* Some courts have held that family members of decedents have a privacy right in records regarding their deceased relatives. *See* Reid v. Pierce County, 961 P.2d 333 (Wash. 1998) (relatives of deceased individuals could maintain an invasion of privacy action against the county based on allegations that county employees had appropriated photographs of the decedents' corpses that were taken by a medical examiner's office and had shown the photographs to others). In Katz v. National Archives & Records Admin., 862 F. Supp. 476, 485-86 (D.D.C.1994), *aff'd*, 68 F.3d 1438 (1995), the court wrote:

> [T]he Kennedy family has a clear privacy interest in preventing the disclosure of both the x-rays and the optical photographs taken during President Kennedy's autopsy....
>
> ...[A]llowing access to the autopsy photographs would constitute a clearly unwarranted invasion of the Kennedy family's privacy.

5. *Non-Private Facts.* In International U. v. Garner, 601 F. Supp. 187 (M.D. Tenn. 1985), employees and union organizers sued police officers who recorded license tag numbers of persons attending union meetings and later disclosed their identity to their employer. The court dismissed a private-facts claim, finding that the information was of legitimate concern to the public and that, in any event, the information was not private because the cars were parked in plain view in front of the meeting hall.

Vassiliades v. Garfinckel's, Brooks Brothers

District of Columbia Court of Appeals
492 A.2d 580 (D.C. 1985)

ROGERS, Associate Judge.

...Mary Vassiliades, sued her plastic surgeon, Csaba Magassy, M.D., and... [Garfinckel's] for invasion of privacy on several theories because the doctor used "before" and "after" photographs of her cosmetic surgery at a Garfinckel's department store presentation and on a television program promoting the presentation....

....The jury returned a verdict of $100,000 against Dr. Magassy for the television presentation and a verdict of $250,000 against Dr. Magassy and Garfinckel's jointly for the department store presentation. After a hearing, the trial court granted defendants' motions for judgment notwithstanding the verdicts....

....

Several months after Mrs. Vassiliades' last postoperative visit, Dr. Magassy was invited by the director of public relations for Garfinckel's to participate in a store promotion during the month of March 1979. He agreed to participate without compensation in a program entitled, "Creams versus Plastic Surgery"....In connection with its promotion and prior to the presentation at Garfinckel's, Garfinckel's arranged to have Dr. Magassy and other participants appear on the "Panorama" television program on WTTG, Channel 5, in Washington, D.C. During his television presentation, Dr. Magassy used slide photographs of several of his patients, including two "before" and two "after" of Mrs. Vassiliades. Although Mrs. Vassiliades' face appeared on the television screen for less than one minute and her name was not mentioned, a former coworker, Beatrice Brooks, recognized her. Mrs. Brooks testified she had not previously known about Mrs. Vassiliades' surgery and after seeing Mrs. Vassiliades' photographs during the television program, she immediately called a friend at work to share this information. The coworker whom Mrs. Brooks called told another employee, Elliott Woo, a neighbor of Mrs. Vassiliades, but he already knew. Three days later Dr. Magassy made a similar presentation at Garfinckel's department store; seventy-nine people were in the audience, but no evidence was presented that anyone there recognized Mrs. Vassiliades' photographs.

Mrs. Vassiliades...testified that when she learned of the disclosure she was "devastated," "absolutely shocked" and "felt terrible" that everyone at her former office knew about her face-lift. She "went into a terrible depression," and did not want to go out in public anymore. She claimed she virtually went into hiding....

....

In its Memorandum Opinion and Judgment the trial court held that the right of privacy is not absolute and that, in balancing the individual's right to be let alone and the public's right to know, there are occasions on which the public right must prevail. We agree. We also agree that the precise boundaries of the public interest may be exceedingly difficult to define, that the subject matter of plastic surgery, as the trial court noted, "at a time when many well-known and highly visible men and women were the objects of news articles about face-lifts and other plastic surgery" was of general public interest, and that a professional presentation with photographs would enhance the public interest in the subject. We disagree, however, with the trial court's conclusions that "reasonable minds could not differ in finding the publication [of Mrs. Vassiliades' photographs] to be of legitimate public interest," and that "certainly, the subject of face-lifts and plastic surgery was no longer a subject calculated to generate offense to persons of ordinary sensibilities." We hold Mrs. Vassiliades was entitled to expect photographs of her surgery would not be publicized without her consent.

. . . .

The Restatement, . . . [Second, of Torts] §652D, recognizes that publicity of a private matter may constitute an invasion of privacy.[1] The drafters contemplated that "any broadcast over the radio, or statement made in an address to a large audience, is sufficient to give publicity" to the private life of a person. *Id.*, comment a. The determinative factor is whether the communication is public as opposed to private. Mrs. Vassiliades offered evidence that, after agonizing over losing her youthful appearance and contemplating plastic surgery for many years, she underwent plastic surgery and kept her surgery secret, telling only family and very intimate friends.

. . . .

. . . . Publicizing the photographs as part of a presentation on plastic surgery communicated private facts about Mrs. Vassiliades' life. The nature of the publicity ensured that it would reach the public. [Citation.] Thus the fact that Mrs. Vassiliades presented only two witnesses who learned of her plastic surgery from the television show and none who saw the store presentation does not defeat her claim. Nor need her name have been mentioned. [Citation.]

. . . . The trial court found that the photographs were not highly offensive because there was nothing "uncomplimentary or unsavory" about them. Although the photographs may not have been uncomplimentary or unsavory, the issue is whether the publicity of Mrs. Vassialiades' surgery was highly offensive to a reasonable person, a factual question usually given to a jury to determine. [Citation.] "The protection afforded to the plaintiff's interest in his privacy must be relative to the customs of the time and place, to the occupation of the plaintiff and to the habits of his neighbors and fellow citizens." [Citation.] The jury was instructed that it had to find the publication highly offensive to a reasonable person in order to establish liability. . . . In view of the evidence presented to the jury, we find no basis to conclude that it did not follow the instruction. [Citations.]

Appellees also contend, and the trial court found, that the publicity was protected because there was a legitimate public interest in the publication. It is a defense to a claim of invasion of privacy that the matter publicized is of general public interest. [Citations.] Moreover, this defense or privilege is not limited to dissemination of news about current events or public affairs, but also protects "information concerning interesting phases of human activity and embraces all issues about which information is needed or appropriate so that that individual may cope with the exigencies of their period." . . . .

Nevertheless, the privilege to publicize matters of legitimate public interest is not absolute. [Citation.] Certain private facts about a person should never be publicized, even if the facts concern matters which are, or relate to persons who are, of legitimate public interest. [Citation.] We thus find persuasive the distinction Mrs. Vassiliades draws between the private fact of her reconstructive surgery and the fact that plastic surgery is a matter of legitimate public interest.

---

1. The Restatement, *supra*, §652D, provides: One who gives publicity to a matter concerning the private life of another is subject to liability to the other for invasion of his privacy, if the matter publicized is of a kind that (a) would be highly offensive to a reasonable person, and (b) is not of legitimate concern to the public.

The conflict between the public's right to information and the individual's right to privacy requires a balancing of the competing interests.... [U]pon balancing the two interests, we hold that Mrs. Vassiliades had a higher interest to be protected. Although Dr. Magassy and Garfinckel's may well have performed a public service by making the presentations about plastic surgery, and the public undoubtedly has an interest in plastic surgery, it was unnecessary for Dr. Magassy to publicize Mrs. Vassiliades' photographs. Publication of her photographs neither strengthened the impact nor the credibility of the presentations nor otherwise enhanced the public's general awareness of the issues and facts concerning plastic surgery. [Citation.] Dr. Magassy's presentations could have been just as informative by using either photographs of other patients or photographs from medical textbooks....We hold, therefore, that Dr. Magassy invaded Mrs. Vassiliades' privacy by giving publicity to private facts and the trial court erred in granting his motion for a judgment notwithstanding the verdict.

This finding of liability does not compel a like result with respect to Garfinckel's. The undisputed evidence is that Dr. Magassy had unqualifiedly assured Garfinckel's that he had obtained his patients' consent. Clear evidence of consent will insulate a party from liability. [Citations.] Thus, the issue is whether Garfinckel's was justified in relying on Dr. Magassy's oral assurance. Garfinckel's decision to ask Dr. Magassy to participate in its program was based on its understanding that he was a reputable professional....Before the television program, Garfinckel's director...asked Dr. Magassy if he had obtained permission from his patients to use the slides. Based on Dr. Magassy's assurance that he had, the director did not inquire about consent prior to the department store presentation. No evidence was presented to suggest that Garfinckel's had any reason to doubt Dr. Magassy's statement.

Under these circumstances, we hold that Garfinckel's was justified in relying on Dr. Magassy's assurances that he had Mrs. Vassiliades' consent and that Mrs. Vassiliades has failed to meet her burden to prove Garfinckel's liability for invasion of her privacy....

....

A plaintiff whose private life is given publicity may recover damages for the harm to her reputation or interest in privacy resulting from the publicity and also for the "emotional distress or personal humiliation...if it is of a kind that normally results from such an invasion and it is normal and reasonable in its extent." Restatement, *supra*, §652H comment b. Actual harm need not be based on pecuniary loss, and emotional distress may be shown simply by the plaintiff's testimony....Because the damages arising from the tort constitute psychic and emotional harm and the tort is defined in terms of the mores of the community, [citation] mental distress lawsuits offer the potential for large verdicts, although little objective evidence is available to test the size of a jury award for mental distress. [Citations.]

Although we hold that Mrs. Vassiliades presented sufficient evidence of an invasion of privacy, it does not necessarily follow that the trial court abused its discretion in ruling that the verdicts were contrary to the weight of the evidence....

The evidence at trial relating to the extent of the injury suffered by Mrs. Vassiliades showed that her photograph was on television for less than 40 seconds, her name was not mentioned and the person in the photograph was referred to only as a patient in her forties. Only one person who saw the television program identified her and that person told one of Mrs. Vassiliades' former coworkers about her surgery. Although most of Mrs. Vassiliades' testimony focused on the television presentation, she also offered evidence that seventy-nine people saw her photograph at the department store presentation. However, her name was not mentioned; only one person at the store presentation knew her, and there was no evidence that anyone recognized her photographs....Mrs. Vassiliades did not offer evidence of the impact of the publicity on the persons who saw her photographs, but only described her own mental and behavioral reactions. Her husband corroborated her behavioral reactions, but no medical evidence was offered to support her claim of severe depression....

...[W]e cannot say the trial court's grant of a new trial was so beyond the range of reason as to require reversal....

Accordingly, the judgment is affirmed in part, reversed in part, and the case is remanded for a new trial on damages to be assessed against Dr. Magassy.

[The concurring opinion of Judge Newman, which argued that "judges should be exceedingly reluctant to set aside jury verdicts," has been omitted.]

Notes

1. *See also* Doe v. Univision Television Group, Inc., 717 So. 2d 63 (Fla. Dist. Ct. App. 1998) (claim stated against a broadcaster who failed to protect the identity of a woman scarred by plastic surgery).

2. *Limited Disclosure and the Publicity Requirement.* Section 652D of the Restatement defines the private-facts tort as consisting of "giving publicity" to offensive private facts not of legitimate concern to "the public." Under this definition, only those communications that "reach[] or are sure to reach, the public" are actionable, so that a letter to a creditor of the plaintiff cannot create liability; Restatement, Second, of Torts §652D Comment a and Illus. 1. *See also* Robins v. Conseco Fin. Loan Co., 656 N.W.2d 241 (Minn. Ct. App. 2003) (a lender's disclosure of an applicant's negative credit rating to one person from whom the applicant intended to make a purchase was not publicity); Eddy v. Brown, 715 P.2d 74 (Okla. 1986) (disclosure to a limited number of co-workers that plaintiff was undergoing psychiatric treatment did not amount to "publicity"); Childs v. Williams, 825 S.W.2d 4 (Mo. Ct. App. 1992) (similar facts and result; the test under the Restatement is whether there has been communication to "so many persons that the matter must be regarded as substantially certain to become one of public knowledge").

Note, however, that a small number of cases hold that "[w]hen a special relationship exists, the public can include one person or small groups such as fellow employees, club members, church members, family or neighbors." *See* Pachowitz v. Le Doux, 666 N.W.2d 88, 96 & n. 9 (Wis. Ct. App. 2003) (citing cases that have so held; declining to state that disclosure to one person or a small group, as a matter of law, fails to satisfy the publicity requirement; and affirming in relevant part a judgment based on disclosure to one person whom the defendant knew had "loose lips"). *See also* Biederman's of Springfield, Inc. v. Wright, 322 S.W.2d 892, 898 (Mo. 1959) (oral publication over a three-day period in a public restaurant with numerous customers present satisfied the publicity requirement). *But see* Swinton Creek Nursery v. Edisto Farm Cr., 514 S.E.2d 126 (S.C. 1999) (rejecting the argument that if information eventually became public, a party who disclosed the information to only one person could be held liable for "sparking the flame" of publicity).

It is not necessary for liability that the facts in question be published in a newspaper or announced on the air. The defendant in Norris v. King, 355 So. 2d 21 (La. Ct. App. 1978), owned a laundromat, which the plaintiff had robbed. On the wall of the laundromat the defendant posted photographs, taken with a hidden camera, of the robbery in progress. Captions identifying the plaintiff and making mildly amusing observations about his impending trial and his ineptness at theft accompanied the pictures. Although the defendant claimed that he took these steps to deter other thefts, the evidence strongly suggested that the actions were taken to induce the plaintiff to pay for the harm he had done. The court held that the defendant's conduct was "unreasonable, coercive action," which overstepped "the bounds of propriety" and was actionable. In Louisiana, at least, the victim of a theft has no more rights than any other creditor when it comes to debt collection.

Query whether the conduct in *Norris* would have been actionable if the defendant had not been found to have engaged in the actions for the purpose of extorting money from the plaintiff. *Norris* may be a sort of tort equivalent to the puzzling crime of blackmail. Blackmailers typically threaten to do things which they have every legal right to do: for example, to disclose the victim's misconduct to the victim's spouse or employer, or to the press. It is the demand for money, not the mere publication or threat of publication, that makes blackmail illegal. If this analysis is sound, the *Norris* court's discussion of whether the information had been made public was beside the point. On blackmail, *see generally* Symposium, *Blackmail*, 141 U. Pa. L. Rev. 1565 (1993).

3. *Disclosure of Confidential Information.* Mere disclosure of confidential information is not necessarily "highly offensive to a reasonable person." *Cf.* Bratt v. IBM, 785 F.2d 352, 359 (1st Cir. 1986) (although revelation that the plaintiff frequently used a confidential open-door process for resolving work-related grievances might have had a negative connotation to some managers, it was "not of such a personal nature that an invasion of privacy" resulted).

Several cases have held that disclosure of confidential information by the plaintiff's physician can be actionable, even though the information was given to only one person. The basis for this kind of action is "breach of a duty of confidentiality," rather than the private-facts tort. Humphers v. First Interstate Bk., 696 P.2d 527 (Or. 1985), upheld a claim against a physician who revealed the identity of the natural mother of a child who had been given up for adoption. The plaintiff in *Humphers* had also pleaded a cause of action for intentional infliction of severe mental distress; this claim was abandoned on appeal. The chief difficulty with the mental-distress claim in a case like *Humphers* is the impossibility of showing that the defendant's actions transcended "the farthest reaches of socially tolerable behavior"; 696 P.2d at 529. The defendant's conduct, though improper, was prompted by a desire to help the child rather than by ill will toward the mother.

4. *Newsworthiness.* In Capra v. Thoroughbred Racing Ass'n, 787 F.2d 463, 464-65 (9th Cir. 1986), a man convicted of fixing horse races provided useful testimony for the government, and was thereafter resettled and given a new identity under the federal witness protection program. His wife and son were accorded similar treatment. Organized crime figures allegedly offered large sums of money for information about the husband's new name and whereabouts. After the wife applied to the racing board for licenses (which would have allowed them to purchase and race horses) in her new name and her son's new name, the board issued a press release disclosing the identity and location of the husband and wife. In a privacy action by the husband, wife, and son, the court applied a three-part standard for newsworthiness:

> [T]he jury [must ordinarily] weigh: (1) the social value of the facts published,
> (2) the depth of the publication's intrusion into ostensibly private affairs, and

(3) the extent to which the party voluntarily assumed a position of public notoriety. [Citations.]

On the record before us, a reasonable jury, applying the three-part standard,
could find that the press release was not newsworthy as to one or more of the
plaintiffs. First, the jury must consider the social value of the facts published in
light of the public's interest in protecting persons willing to testify....While the
federal witness protection program cannot by itself overcome the First Amendment, the program possesses some social values that weight against unlimited
free speech under the general balancing test....Second, the jury must consider
the seriousness of the intrusion caused by the publication. Finally, the jury
must consider the extent to which parties voluntarily exposed themselves to
public notoriety. In this respect,...[the husband], who was convicted, his
wife..., who made the application, and their son Kevin, whose name was
placed on the application, are not all similarly situated.

5. *Damages.* Because there are few successful cases involving disclosure of private
facts, little can be said with confidence about the way in which damages in those cases
are measured. According to Gertz v. Robert Welch, Inc., 418 U.S. 323 (1974), a defamation case, "States may not [constitutionally] permit recovery of presumed or punitive
damages, at least when liability is not based on a showing of knowledge of falsity or
reckless disregard for the truth." Because defamation, which requires proof that the
statements in question were untrue, is usually more reprehensible than making accurate
disclosures, this standard will very likely limit damages in most private-facts cases to actual damages (including mental suffering).

B. Intrusion upon Seclusion

To prevail upon a claim for intrusion upon seclusion, one must establish, first, an intentional interference with one's solitude or seclusion, or prying into one's private affairs or concerns, and second, that the intrusion would be highly offensive to a reasonable person.

Defendant Must Intrude. Intrusion can take many forms. In Tompkins v. Cyr, 202
F.3d 770 (5th Cir. 2000), the court held that anti-abortion activists invaded the privacy
of an abortion-performing physician and his spouse by engaging in each of the following forms of conduct: watching their house from a car parked on a side street and using
binoculars and a camera; using a bull-horn to preach during the demonstrations at the
plaintiffs' home; making repeated and harassing phone calls to the plaintiffs; and rattling their gate while they were eating Thanksgiving dinner.

According to Comment b of §652B of the Restatement, Second, of Torts:

The invasion may be by physical intrusion into a place in which the plaintiff has secluded himself, as when the defendant forces his way into the
plaintiff's room in a hotel or insists over the plaintiff's objection in entering
his home. It may also be by the use of the defendant's senses, with or without mechanical aids, to oversee or overhear the plaintiff's private affairs, as
by...tapping his telephone wires. It may be by some other form of investigation or examination into his private concerns, as by...searching his safe or

his wallet, examining his private bank account, or compelling him by a forged court order to permit an inspection of his personal documents. The intrusion itself makes the defendant subject to liability, even though there is no publication or other use of any kind of the photograph or information outlined.

However, not all forms of annoying conduct constitute actionable intrusions: there generally must be something in the nature of prying into the affairs of the plaintiff. In Dwyer v. American Express Co., 652 N.E.2d 1351 (Ill. Ct. App. 1995), American Express cardholders brought suit based on the defendants' practice of renting information regarding cardholder spending habits. The court held that the plaintiffs failed to state an action for intrusion:

> The alleged wrongful actions involve the defendants' practice of renting lists that they have compiled from information contained in their own records. By using the American Express card, a cardholder is voluntarily, and necessarily, giving information to defendants that, if analyzed, will reveal a cardholder's spending habits and shopping preferences. We cannot hold that a defendant has committed an unauthorized intrusion by compiling the information voluntarily given to it and then renting its compilation.

See also Mayes v. LIN Television of Tex., Inc., 1998 W.L. 665088 (N.D. Tex.) (broadcast of a secretly taped phone conversation with a councilperson did not constitute intrusion into seclusion where the station legally obtained the tape, didn't record the tape, and the tape had already been disseminated to the public by other media organizations).

Compelled disclosure is not the same as intrusion. See Jensen v. State, 72 P.3d 897 (Idaho 2003) (a state requirement that a contractor seeking license renewal disclose any criminal conviction, "even if the conviction was sealed, expunged or the judgment withheld," did not constitute an act of intrusion).

In Allstate Ins. Co. v. Ginsberg, 2003 W.L. 22145227 (Fla.), the court said that for an action to lie there must be intrusion into a *place*. Accordingly, the court held that a supervisor's alleged unwelcome conduct, including physical touching and sexual comments, was not an invasion of privacy. The court noted that:

> the tort of invasion of privacy was not intended to be duplicative of some other tort. Rather, this is a tort in which the focus is the right of a private person to be free from public gaze.

Solitude, Seclusion, or Private Affairs. For an action to lie the plaintiff must reasonably expect solitude, seclusion, or privacy of the matter. See Sabrah v. Lucent Tech., Inc., 1998 W.L. 792503 (N.D. Tex.), *aff'd*, 200 F.3d 815 (5th Cir. 1999) (a claim was stated where defendant's employee opened several packages of plaintiff's mail, including one labeled "private," and removed their contents); Mauri v. Smith, 929 P.2d 307 (Or. 1996) (allegedly unauthorized entry into an apartment by police officers was actionable); *cf.* Hoskins v. Howard, 1998 W.L. 835098 (Idaho) (issue as to whether cordless telephone users had a legitimate expectation of privacy in their telephone conversation precluded summary judgment); People for the Ethical Treatment of Animals v. Bobby Berosini, Ltd., 895 P.2d 1269 (Nev. 1995) (animal trainer had no expectation of privacy backstage while preparing animals for a performance and could not state a privacy claim against a worker who videotaped the trainer striking animals backstage); Remsburg v. Docusearch, Inc., 816 A.2d 1001 (N.H. 2003) (stating that "where a person's work address is readily observable by members of the public, the address cannot be private and no intrusion upon seclusion action can be maintained").

In Swerdlick v. Koch, 721 A.2d 849 (R.I. 1998), the court held that a neighbor did not violate the statutory rights of landowners to be secure from unreasonable intrusions upon their physical solitude or seclusion by photographing activity occurring outside the landowners' residence, maintaining a log of arriving delivery trucks, employees, and other vehicles, and repeatedly requesting the town to conduct inspections for alleged zoning violations in connection with the landowners' operation of a business from their home. The conduct and activity did not fit within the language of the privacy statute, as it all occurred in full public view, although it happened in the vicinity of the landowners' residence.

Suppose that two persons are photographed naked by a friend. A store declines to develop the film, but the subjects of the photograph later learn that store employees circulated copies of the picture. Can they sue for intrusion or for some other privacy tort? These were the facts in Lake v. Wal-Mart Stores, Inc., 582 N.W.2d 231 (Minn. 1998). The court recognized claims for disclosure, appropriation, and intrusion under state law, but declined to opine on the merits of the case.

Intrusion by Inquiry? Does asking questions about the plaintiff constitute actionable intrusion? In Myrick v. Barron, 820 So. 2d 81 (Ala. 2001), a case brought by the well-known president pro tem of the state Senate, the court answered in the negative. It held that an investigation, which resulted only in disclosure of information already known by others, could not support a claim under the wrongful intrusion branch of invasion of privacy. The court reasoned that information that other people know cannot be protected as "private."

See also Dempsey v. Nat. Enquirer, 702 F. Supp. 927 (D. Maine 1988) (reporter's repeated and ongoing attempts to interview the plaintiff were insufficient to support an intrusion action).

Intrusion Statutes. In some jurisdictions, the cause of action for intrusion is statutory. Nebraska law provides:

§20-203. Invasion of privacy; trespass or intrude upon a person's solitude.

Any person, firm, or corporation that trespasses or intrudes upon any natural person in his or her place of solitude or seclusion, if the intrusion would be highly offensive to a reasonable person, shall be liable for invasion of privacy.

Neb. Rev. Stat. §20-203 (Westlaw 2002).

Harkey v. Abate

Court of Appeals of Michigan
346 N.W.2d 74 (Mich. Ct. App. 1984)

KNOBLOCK, Judge.

....

Plaintiff's original complaint…alleged that plaintiff and her daughter were patrons at defendant's roller-skating rink on April 19, 1979, and that, while on the premises, they had utilized the women's restroom provided by defendant for his patrons. Plaintiff thereafter discovered that the defendant had installed see-through panels in the ceiling of the restroom which permitted surreptitious observation from above of the interior, including the separately partitioned stalls. Plaintiff alleged that defendant had personally viewed plaintiff and her daughter while they used the restroom and claimed that defendant's conduct constituted an invasion of their privacy, for which they seek damages.

Defendant moved for summary judgment....The motion was supported by an affidavit of defendant asserting he did not personally view the plaintiff and her daughter as alleged. Plaintiff conceded...that there appeared to be no proof available which would establish that defendant had actually viewed plaintiff and her daughter in the restroom, but she asserted such proof is unnecessary to establish a *prima facie* case of invasion of privacy. The trial court apparently disagreed and granted summary judgment.

....The type of invasion of privacy alleged in this case may be characterized as an "unreasonable intrusion upon the seclusion of another," 3 Restatement of Torts, 2d §652A, p. 376, or more specifically an "[i]ntrusion upon the plaintiff's seclusion or solitude, or into his private affairs." [Citations.] A necessary element of this type of invasion of privacy is, of course, that there be an "intrusion." The issue presented for our resolution is whether the installation of the hidden viewing devices complained of can itself constitute a sufficient wrongful intrusion into the seclusion or solitude of plaintiff and her daughter so as to permit recovery. We hold that it can and that, therefore, the granting of summary judgment was improper.

The Michigan Supreme Court acknowledged the concept of the right of privacy in the early case of De May v. Roberts, 46 Mich. 160, 9 N.W. 146 (1881). In the case, Mrs. Roberts gave birth in her home and the attending physician allowed a young man, who had accompanied him to carry his bags, to remain in the room during the delivery....

....The New Hampshire Supreme Court...confronted an analogous situation where a landlord had secretly installed a listening device in the bedroom of his tenants, enabling him to monitor and record voices and sounds emitting therefrom. Hamberger v. Eastman, 106 N.H. 107, 206 A.2d 239; 11 A.L.R.3d 1288 (1964). The court held that, in spite of the fact that the tenants did not allege the landlord actually utilized the listening device, their complaint adequately stated an action for invasion for privacy.

The installation of viewing devices as alleged by plaintiff is a felony in this state. M.C.L. §750.539d; M.S.A. §28.807(4). Though this statute does not specifically impose civil liability for such conduct,...it does constitute, at a minimum, a legislative expression of public policy opposed to such conduct.

The type of invasion of privacy asserted by plaintiff does not depend upon any publicity given to the person whose interest is invaded, but consists solely of an intentional interference with his or her interest in solitude or seclusion of a kind that would be highly offensive to a reasonable person. 3 Restatement of Torts, 2d, §652B, p. 378. Clearly, plaintiff and her daughter in this case had a right to privacy in the public restroom in question. In our opinion, the installation of the hidden viewing devices alone constitutes an interference with that privacy which a reasonable person would find highly offensive. And though the absence of proof that the devices were utilized is relevant to the question of damage, it is not fatal to plaintiff's case.

....

Reversed and remanded.

J.H. GILLIS, Presiding Judge (dissenting).

I respectfully dissent. Since plaintiff concedes that there appeared to be no proof available which would establish that defendant or anyone else actually used the mirror to view plaintiff and her daughter in the restroom, I fail to see how plaintiff and her daughter have been injured. Installation of the mirror, by itself, was insufficient to harm the plaintiff and her daughter. Any harm to plaintiff and her daughter would arise from use of the mirror to observe them in private acts.

....

I would affirm the decision of the trial judge.

Notes

1. *See also* Carter v. Innisfree Hotel, Inc., 661 So. 2d 1174 (Ala. 1995) (guests who sued a hotel based on alleged "peeping Tom" incident were not required to prove actual identity of the "peeping Tom" or even that anyone had actually spied on them, although the absence of proof of spying might be relevant to the issue of damages).

2. Compare *Harkey* with an earlier decision by a different panel of the same court in Lewis v. Dayton Hudson Corp., 339 N.W.2d 857 (Mich. Ct. App. 1983), which turned aside an invasion of privacy claim based on hidden cameras in the fitting room of a store. "[W]here, as here, signs are clearly posted notifying customers that they are under surveillance while inside the fitting room of a retail establishment, the 'modicum of privacy' the fitting room appears to afford does not include freedom from overhead observation by a store security guard who is of the same sex as the customer."

3. **Intent Required.** Because intrusion is an intentional tort, inadvertent viewing of sexual conduct in a bathroom stall is not actionable. *See* Hougum v. Valley Mem. Homes, 574 N.W.2d 812 (1998).

4. **Telephone Harassment.** Harassment by numerous phone calls at unreasonable hours can support an action for intrusion upon seclusion. *See* Donnel v. Lara, 703 S.W.2d 257 (Tex. Ct. App. 1985). Some cases have involved debt collection. *See, e.g.,* Carey v. Statewide Fin. Co., 223 A.2d 405 (Conn. Cir. Ct. 1966).

5. **Damage.** Some courts hold that an intrusion action requires proof of damage. *See* LaMartiniere v. Allstate Ins. Co., 597 So. 2d 1158 (La. Ct. App. 1992) (peeping over a wall to see furniture that had been stored by suspected arsonists was not actionable because it caused no damage). *But see* Sabrina W. v. Willman, 540 N.W.2d 364 (Neb. Ct. App. 1995) (permitting nominal damages).

6. **Stalking.** Ordinarily, watching or observing another person in a public place is not tortious. "However,...surveillance of an individual on public thoroughfares, where such surveillance aims to frighten or torment a person, is an unreasonable intrusion upon a person's privacy." Summers v. Bailey, 55 F.3d 1564 (11th Cir. 1995). In many states, stalking is now a crime. *See* Dawn A. Morville, *Comment, Stalking Laws: Are They Solutions for More Problems,* 71 Wash. U.L.Q. 921 (1993).

Even so famous a figure as a widow of an American President has been afforded privacy protection. Donald Galella, a freelance photographer, followed Jacqueline Kennedy Onassis and her children constantly, taking pictures, interrupting their activities, bribing doormen to report on their whereabouts, and generally making their lives unpleasant. A federal district court enjoined Galella from engaging in some of these practices. On appeal, the Second Circuit affirmed, but modified the injunction (for example, instead of requiring Galella to stay at least 50 yards from Mrs. Onassis, the modified injunction allowed him to come within 25 feet). Although New York has never recognized a common-law right of privacy, the Second Circuit found support for the District Court's action in New York's statutory prohibition of harassment (a crime) and in its recognition of the common-law tort of intentional infliction of emotional distress. Galella v. Onassis, 487 F.2d 986 (2d Cir. 1973). The court also opined that the New York courts might eventually see the light and recognize invasion of privacy as a tort. Given the scope of intentional infliction of emotional distress, does it matter whether New York treats intrusion upon seclusion as a separate tort?

7. *Information Gathering and Investigative Firms.* *Compare* Johnson v. Stewart, 854 So. 2d 544 (Ala. 2002) (holding that there was insufficient evidence to support an intrusion claim where the defendant provided an investigative firm with only general information already known to others, such as the plaintiffs' address, make and model of their cars, social security numbers, telephone numbers, and license plate numbers), *with* Remsburg v. Docusearch, Inc., 816 A.2d 1001 (N.H. 2003) (holding, in a case where information provided by an Internet search business led to a murder, that "a person whose SSN is obtained by an investigator from a credit reporting agency without the person's knowledge or permission may have a cause of action for intrusion upon seclusion for damages caused by the sale of the SSN, but must prove that the intrusion was such that it would have been offensive to a person of ordinary sensibilities").

The New York Court of Appeals, applying District of Columbia law, held in Nader v. General Motors Corp., 255 N.E.2d 765 (N.Y. 1970), that gathering information "of a confidential nature" by means that are "unreasonably intrusive" can be an invasion of privacy. The court held that interviewing Ralph Nader's acquaintances to obtain personal information was not tortious, nor was causing women to accost Nader with "illicit proposals." Allegations of wiretapping and electronic eavesdropping were held to state a cause of action, however; and keeping the plaintiff under constant surveillance might also be a tort if the surveillance was "overzealous."

In Wolfson v. Lewis, 924 F. Supp. 1413 (E.D. Pa. 1996), the CEO of a health insurer and his family were entitled to a preliminary injunction against television reporters, barring them from violating the family's privacy rights. There was evidence that the reporters had placed the exterior of the family's house under surveillance, with telescopes, zoom lens video cameras, and ultra-sensitive microphones; followed the daughter and son-in-law to work and attempted to film them entering a building; followed the family to Florida, where they went for seclusion; and established a surveillance boat in public waters as close as possible to the CEO's house, for the purpose of forcing the CEO to reconsider an earlier decision not to appear on camera for an interview regarding allegedly high salaries paid to executives of the insurer.

8. *Offensiveness.* A privacy action for intrusion, like one for disclosure, will lie only for an invasion that would be highly offensive to a reasonable person. In Denton v. Chittenden Bank, 655 A.2d 703 (Vt. 1994), the court held that a supervisor did not commit invasion of privacy when he came to an employee's home during a birthday party for the employee's daughter and asked questions, which were overheard by the employee's family and friends, about the employee's physical condition, his doctor, whether he was taking medication, and when he would be coming back to work. Although the questions were unusual and possibly rude, they would not be highly offensive to a reasonable person.

See also Moore v. R.Z. Sims Chevrolet-Subaru, 738 P.2d 852 (Kan. 1987) (unauthorized entry through kitchen doors marked "Employees only," during attempt to repossess a truck, was not an intrusion that a reasonable person would find highly offensive); Froelich v. Werbin, 548 P.2d 482 (Kan. 1976) (no intrusion action against a hospital orderly who obtained a sample of plaintiff's hair in an unobtrusive manner); Deteresa v. ABC, 121 F.3d 460 (9th Cir. 1997) (surreptitious taping was not sufficiently offensive to support privacy claim); Tapia v. Sikorsky Aircraft, 1998 W.L. 310872 (Conn. Super. Ct.) (an inventory of the contents of the plaintiff's locker after he had been suspended from employment because he was fighting in the workplace would not have been highly offensive to a reasonable person).

9. *Categorical Duties versus Reasonable Care.* Why shouldn't the law protect individuals from all unreasonable interferences with their right to be let alone? In *Privacy*, 7 St. Louis Univ. Public L. Rev. 313 (1988), Professor Charles E. Cantu argues that the varying tests for Prosser's four categories should be replaced by a duty of reasonable care under the circumstances, similar to the legal standard imposed in most other fields of tort liability. The argument has respectable antecedents. Section 867 of the first Restatement of Torts (1939) defined an invasion of privacy as follows:

> A person who unreasonably and seriously interferes with another's interest in not having his affairs known to others or his likeness exhibited to the public is liable to the other.

10. *The First Amendment and Intrusion.* Intrusion cases often raise no First Amendment difficulties, for the tort seldom involves speech or other expression. One case raising free-speech concerns is Miller v. NBC, 232 Cal. Rptr. 668 (Ct. App. 1986). There, a television news crew entered an apartment to film the activities of paramedics called to rescue a man who had suffered a fatal heart attack. The film was used on the nightly news without anyone's consent. In finding that the widow had stated claims for trespass, intrusion, and outrage, the court rejected NBC's argument that liability was precluded by its constitutional right to gather news. It found that "the obligation not to make unauthorized entry into the private premises of individuals...does not place an impermissible burden on newsgatherers." Quoting an earlier case, the court wrote:

> [T]he protection extended for newsgathering does not mandate "that the press and its representatives are immune from liability for crimes and torts committed in newsgathering simply because the ultimate goal is to obtain publishable material."

Miller was followed in Shulman v. Group W Productions Co., 955 P.2d 469 (Cal. 1998), allowing the plaintiff to get to a jury on an intrusion claim against the employer of a television cameraman who had videotaped conversations between the plaintiff and a nurse on board a rescue helicopter taking the plaintiff to a hospital after an accident. In contrast, the court held that the plaintiff's claim for disclosure of private facts could not succeed because the facts were newsworthy. As to the distinction between the private-facts claim and the intrusion claim, the court said:

> The broadcast details of Ruth's rescue of which she complains were, as a matter of law, of legitimate public concern because they were substantially relevant to the newsworthy subject of the piece and their intrusiveness was not greatly disproportionate to their relevance. That analytical path is dictated by the danger of the contrary approach; to allow liability because this court, or a jury, believes certain details of the story as broadcast were not important or necessary to the purpose of the documentary, or were in poor taste or overly sensational in impact, would be to assert impermissible supervisory power over the press.
>
> The intrusion claim calls for a much less deferential analysis. In contrast to the broad privilege the press enjoys for publishing truthful, newsworthy information in its possession, the press has no recognized constitutional privilege to violate generally applicable laws in pursuit of material. Nor, even absent an independent crime or tort, can a highly offensive intrusion into a private place, conversation, or source of information generally be justified by the plea that

the intruder hoped thereby to get good material for a news story. Such a justification may be available when enforcement of the tort or other law would place an impermissibly severe burden on the press, but that condition is not met in this case.

In short, the state may not intrude into the proper sphere of the news media to dictate what they should publish and broadcast, but neither may the media play tyrant to the people by unlawfully spying on them in the name of newsgathering. Summary judgment for the defense was proper as to plaintiffs' cause of action for publication of private facts..., but improper as to the cause of action for invasion of privacy by intrusion....

C. False Light

West v. Media General Convergence, Inc.
Supreme Court of Tennessee
53 S.W.3d 640 (Tenn. 2001)

FRANK F. DROWOTA, III, J.

. . . .

This suit arises out of a multi-part investigative news report aired by WDEF-TV 12 in Chattanooga about the relationship between the plaintiffs [Charmaine West and First Alternative Probation Counseling, Inc.] and the Hamilton County General Sessions Court, and in particular, one of the general sessions court judges. Plaintiffs operated a private probation services business, and were referred this business by the general sessions courts. Plaintiffs claim that WDEF-TV defamed them by broadcasting false statements that the plaintiffs' business is illegal. Plaintiff West, in particular, claims that the defendant invaded her privacy by implying that she had a sexual relationship with one of the general session judges; and that the general sessions judges and the plaintiffs otherwise had a "cozy," and hence improper, relationship.

Media General filed a motion to dismiss the plaintiffs' false light invasion of privacy claim. Thereafter, the District Court for the Eastern District of Tennessee certified to this Court the following question of law: Do the courts of Tennessee recognize the tort of false light invasion of privacy, and if so, what are the parameters and elements of that tort?....

. . . .

....Section 652E of the Restatement (Second) of Torts (1977) defines the tort of false light:

One who gives publicity to a matter concerning another that places the other before the public in a false light is subject to liability to the other for invasion of his privacy, if

(a) the false light in which the other was placed would be highly offensive to a reasonable person, and

(b) the actor had knowledge of or acted in reckless disregard as to the falsity of the publicized matter and the false light in which the other would be placed.

A majority of jurisdictions addressing false light claims have chosen to recognize false light as a separate actionable tort. Most of these jurisdictions have adopted either the analysis of the tort given by Dean Prosser or the definition provided by the Restatement (Second) of Torts. [Citations.]

A minority of jurisdictions have refused to recognize false light invasion of privacy. [Citations.] Among these jurisdictions, Virginia, New York, and Wisconsin refused to recognize the common law tort of false light because their state legislatures adopted privacy statutes that do not expressly include the tort.

Perhaps the most significant case upholding the minority view is Renwick v. News and Observer Publishing Co., 310 N.C. 312, 312 S.E.2d 405 (1984). In *Renwick,* the Supreme Court of North Carolina expressed two main arguments for not recognizing the tort of false light invasion of privacy in North Carolina. First, the protection provided by false light either duplicates or overlaps the interests already protected by the defamation torts of libel and slander. [Citation.]. Second, "to the extent it would allow recovery beyond that permitted in actions for libel or slander, [recognition of false light] would tend to add to the tension already existing between the First Amendment and the law of torts in cases of this nature." *Id.* After analyzing the standards of constitutional protection provided by New York Times Co. v. Sullivan, 376 U.S. 254 (1964) and Time, Inc. v. Hill, 385 U.S. 374 (1967), the North Carolina Supreme Court was unwilling to extend protection to plaintiffs under false light partly because of a concern that recognition of the tort "would reduce judicial efficiency by requiring our courts to consider two claims for the same relief which, if not identical, would not differ significantly." [Citation.] Further, the court asserted that "such additional remedies as we *might* be required to make available to plaintiffs should we recognize false light invasion of privacy claims are not sufficient to justify the recognition in this jurisdiction of such inherently constitutionally suspect claims for relief." *Id.* (emphasis in original).

... [W]e agree with the majority of jurisdictions that false light should be recognized as a distinct, actionable tort. While the law of defamation and false light invasion of privacy conceivably overlap in some ways, we conclude that the differences between the two torts warrant their separate recognition. The Supreme Court of West Virginia noted the following differences in Crump v. Beckley Newspapers, Inc.:

> In defamation law only statements that are false are actionable, truth is, almost universally, a defense. In privacy law, other than in false light cases, the facts published are true; indeed it is the very truth of the facts that creates the claimed invasion of privacy.[5] Secondly, in defamation cases the interest sought to be protected is the objective one of reputation, either economic, political, or personal, in the outside world. In privacy cases the interest affected is the subjective one of injury to [the] inner person. Thirdly, where the issue is truth or falsity, the marketplace of ideas furnishes a forum in which the battle can be fought. In privacy cases, resort to the marketplace simply accentuates the injury.

---

5. The facts may be true in a false light claim. However, the angle from which the facts are presented, or the omission of certain material facts, results in placing the plaintiff in a false light. " 'Literal accuracy of separate statements will not render a communication "true" where the implication of the communication as a whole was false.'... The question is whether [the defendant] made "discrete presentations of information in a fashion which rendered the publication *susceptible to inferences* casting [the plaintiff] in a false light." Santillo v. Reedel, 430 Pa.Super. 290, 634 A.2d 264, 267 (1993) (citing Larsen v. Philadelphia Newspapers, Inc., 375 Pa.Super. 66, 543 A.2d 1181 (1988)) (emphasis added). Therefore, the literal truth of the publicized facts is not a defense in a false light case.

173 W. Va. 699, 320 S.E.2d 70, 83 (1984) (quoting Thomas Emerson, *The Right of Privacy and Freedom of the Press*, 14 Harv. C.R.-C.L. L. Rev. 329, 333 (1979)).

With respect to the judicial economy concern expressed by the North Carolina Supreme Court, we find that such concerns are outweighed in this instance by the need to maintain the integrity of the right to privacy in this State.... Certainly situations may exist in which persons have had attributed to them certain qualities, characteristics, or beliefs that, while not injurious to their reputation, place those persons in an undesirable false light.[6] However, in situations such as these, victims of invasion of privacy would be without recourse under defamation law. False light therefore provides a viable, and we believe necessary, action for relief apart from defamation.

The Appellant, and likewise the minority view, predict that recognition of the tort will result in unnecessary litigation, even in situations where "positive" or laudatory characteristics are attributed to individuals. We disagree. Such needless litigation is foreclosed by Section 652E (a) of the Restatement (Second) of Torts which imposes liability for false light only if the publicity is highly offensive to a reasonable person. Comment c to Section 652E notes that the hypersensitive plaintiff cannot recover under a false light claim where the publicized matter attributed to the plaintiff was, even if intentionally falsified, not a seriously offensive misstatement.

> Complete and perfect accuracy in published reports concerning any individual is seldom attainable by any reasonable effort, and most minor errors, such as a wrong address for his home, or a mistake in the date when he entered his employment or similar unimportant details of his career, would not in the absence of special circumstances give any serious offense to a reasonable person.

Restatement (Second) of Torts, § 652E cmt. c (1977). Thus, the "highly offensive to a reasonable person" prong of Section 652E deters needless litigation.[7]

Comment b to Section 652E of the Restatement (Second) of Torts addresses the concern that one publication may result in multiple recoveries. If, in addition to false light, a plaintiff also asserts an alternative theory of recovery under libel, "the plaintiff can proceed upon either theory, or both, *although he can have but one recovery for a single instance of publicity.*" *Id.* (emphasis added).

We must also disagree with the North Carolina Supreme Court that recognition of false light would destabilize current First Amendment protections of speech. In our view, the "actual malice" standard adequately protects First Amendment rights when the plaintiff is a public official, a public figure, or the publicity is a matter of public interest.

---

6. Comment b, Illustration 4 to Section 652E provides such an example:

A is a democrat. B induces him to sign a petition nominating C for office. A discovers that C is a Republican and demands that B remove his name from the petition. B refuses to do so and continues public circulation of the petition, bearing A's name. B is subject to liability to A for invasion of privacy.

7. Illustrations provided in Section 652E of the Restatement (Second) of Torts, (1977), are helpful in understanding the limits of protection provided by false light. Illustration 9 reads:

A is the pilot of an airplane flying across the Pacific. The plane develops motor trouble, and A succeeds in landing it after harrowing hours in the air. B Company broadcasts over television a dramatization of the flight, which enacts it in most respects in an accurate manner. Included in the broadcast, however, are scenes, known to B to be false, in which an actor representing A is shown as praying, reassuring passengers, and otherwise conducting himself in a fictitious manner that does not defame him or in any way reflect upon him. Whether this is an invasion of A's privacy depends on whether it is found by the jury that the scenes would be highly objectionable to a reasonable man in A's position.

This standard was first adopted in a defamation case, New York Times Co. v. Sullivan, 376 U.S. 254 (1964), in which the Court held that public officials may not recover damages for defamatory statements relating to their official duties unless the statement was made with actual malice—knowledge of the falsity of the statement or reckless disregard for the truth of the statement. In Time, Inc. v. Hill, 385 U.S. 374 (1967), the Court extended the actual malice standard to alleged defamatory statements about matters of public interest.[9] In Gertz v. Robert Welch, Inc., 418 U.S. 323 (1974), the Court held that negligence is a sufficient constitutional standard for defamation claims asserted by a private individual about matters of private concern, but the Court has not yet decided which standard applies to false light claims. See Cantrell v. Forest City Publishing Co., 419 U.S. 245 (1974).

In light of the uncertain position of the United States Supreme Court with respect to the constitutional standard for false light claims brought by private individuals about matters of private interest, many courts and Section 652E of the Restatement (Second) of Torts adopt actual malice as the standard for all false light claims. [Citations.] We hold that actual malice is the appropriate standard for false light claims when the plaintiff is a public official or public figure, or when the claim is asserted by a private individual about a matter of public concern. We do not, however, adopt the actual malice standard for false light claims brought by private plaintiffs about matters of private concern. In Memphis Publishing Co. v. Nichols, 569 S.W.2d 412 (Tenn. 1978), this Court adopted negligence as the standard for defamation claims asserted by private individuals about matters of private concern. Our decision to adopt a simple negligence standard in private plaintiff/private matter false light claims is the result of our conclusion that private plaintiffs in false light claims deserve the same heightened protection that private plaintiffs receive in defamation cases. Therefore, when false light invasion of privacy claims are asserted by a private plaintiff regarding a matter of private concern, the plaintiff need only prove that the defendant publisher was negligent in placing the plaintiff in a false light. For all other false light claims, we believe that the actual malice standard achieves the appropriate balance between First Amendment guarantees and privacy interests.

With respect to the parameters of the tort of false light, we conclude that Sections 652F-I of the Restatement (Second) of Torts adequately address its limits. Sections 652F and 652G note that absolute and conditional privileges apply to the invasion of privacy torts, and we hereby affirm that such privileges previously recognized in Tennessee apply to false light claims. Damages are addressed in Section 652H of the Restatement (Second) of Torts (1977), which provides:

> One who has established a cause of action for invasion of his privacy is entitled to recover damages for
>
> (a) the harm to his interest in privacy resulting from the invasion;
>
> (b) his mental distress proved to have been suffered if it is of a kind that normally results from such an invasion; and
>
> (c) special damage of which the invasion is a legal cause.

Consistent with defamation, we emphasize that plaintiffs seeking to recover on false light claims must specifically plead and prove damages allegedly suffered from the inva-

---

9. "[T]he constitutional protections for speech and press preclude the application of the New York statute to redress false reports of matters of public interest in the absence of proof that the defendant published the report with knowledge of its falsity or in reckless disregard of the truth." Time, Inc. v. Hill, 385 U.S. at 387-88.

sion of their privacy. [Citation.] As with defamation, there must be proof of actual damages. [Citation.] The plaintiff need not prove special damages or out of pocket losses necessarily, as evidence of injury to standing in the community, humiliation, or emotional distress is sufficient. [Citation.]

In addition, for purposes of clarification, this Court adopts Section 652I of the Restatement (Second) of Torts (1977) which recognizes that the right to privacy is a personal right. As such, the right cannot attach to corporations or other business entities, may not be assigned to another, nor may it be asserted by a member of the individual's family, even if brought after the death of the individual. Restatement (Second) of Torts §652I cmt. a-c (1977). Therefore, only those persons who have been placed in a false light may recover for invasion of their privacy.

Finally, we recognize that application of different statutes of limitation for false light and defamation cases could undermine the effectiveness of limitations on defamation claims. Therefore, we hold that false light claims are subject to the statutes of limitation that apply to libel and slander, as stated in Tenn. Code Ann. §§28-3-103 and 28-3-104(a)(1), depending on the form of the publicity, whether in spoken or fixed form.

. . . .

Having answered the certified question, the Clerk is directed to transmit a copy of this opinion in accordance with Tennessee Supreme Court Rule 23(8)....

Notes

1. *See* Kolegas v. Heftel Broad. Corp., 607 N.E.2d 201 (Ill. 1992) (holding that a complaint stated a claim for false light based on allegations that the defendants said that the plaintiff and his wife must have been married in a "shotgun wedding," which they were not, and that the plaintiff's wife and child had abnormally large heads as a result of Elephant Man's disease, although their heads were not of abnormal size).

2. *Publicity Requirement.* Since "false light" requires "publicity," a newspaper reporter's alleged report to the IRS regarding a village council member's corporation's tax filings did not support the claim. *See* Andrews v. Stallings, 892 P.2d 611 (N.M. Ct. App. 1995).

3. *False Light and the Media.* A number of cases have allowed persons whose pictures appeared in the press to recover damages if the pictures, together with the stories in question, conveyed an erroneous impression that the plaintiff was a criminal. Leverton v. Curtis Publ'g Co., 192 F.2d 974 (3d Cir. 1951), went even further by holding that creating a misleading impression that the plaintiff was careless is actionable. The plaintiff, a ten-year-old, was injured in a traffic accident in which she was not at fault. The defendant published a picture of the accident to illustrate a story about pedestrian carelessness.

Many of the false-light cases antedate the development of constitutional restrictions on defamation actions. Because "false light" resembles defamation in many respects, one can confidently predict that a case like *Leverton* would not be worth bringing against a media defendant today—even though the Supreme Court has seldom addressed the subject. Courts routinely hold that constitutional limitations that evolved in the field of defamation apply to false light actions. *See, e.g.*, Stien v. Marriott Ownership Resorts, Inc., 944 P.2d 374 (Utah Ct. App. 1997) (if a statement cannot reasonably be taken as factual, the statement does not amount to false light).

4. *The Supreme Court and False Light.* Time, Inc. v. Hill, 385 U.S. 374 (1967), was, on its facts,[c] a false-light case; it involved a magazine article about a play, which was based on a crime in which the plaintiffs had been taken hostage for 19 hours. Although the ordeal ended peacefully, the plaintiffs were depicted as having been subjected to violent and brutal treatment. Noting the differences between false light and defamation, the Court held that both theories required proof of actual malice. The *Time* decision was reaffirmed in Cantrell v. Forest City Publ'g Co., 419 U.S. 245 (1974), a case in which the survivors of a man killed in the Silver Bridge disaster were portrayed as impoverished, and his widow was described as continually wearing a "mask of non-expression." The Court held that there was adequate evidence of actual malice to support the false-light claim. Though acknowledging that its ruling in Gertz v. Robert Welch, Inc., 419 U.S. 323 (1974), *supra* at 995, had modified the constitutional standards applicable to defamation actions, the Court found it unnecessary to address whether, in a false-light action by a private person, a state can set the standard for proving fault as to falsity at the level of ordinary negligence. Thus far, the Supreme Court has never resolved the issue, and few of the twenty or so states recognizing false light have said that negligence will suffice.

The "constitutionalization" of false light does not mean that all false-light claims are hopeless. If, for example, a television program rearranges scenes from an interview to create a seriously misleading impression, the kind of "malice" necessary for maintaining an action against a media defendant can be established. In a much-publicized episode, NBC staged a collision between a Chevrolet truck and a car. The collision appeared to cause the truck to explode. In fact, NBC had rigged the truck with a device to trigger the explosion, and had otherwise altered the fuel system to assure a dramatic picture. General Motors' claim against NBC was settled; the terms of the settlement included an abject on-the-air apology.

5. *Privileges.* The Restatement, Second, of Torts §652G provides that the same absolute and conditional privileges that apply to a defamation action (see Chapter 22) may also defeat a false-light action. *But see* Susan S. v. Israels, 67 Cal. Rptr. 2d 42 (Ct. App. 1997) (holding that litigation relating to judicial or quasi-judicial proceedings did not immunize a criminal defense attorney from liability for invasion of a crime victim's state constitutional right to privacy by reading and disseminating the victim's confidential mental health records, even if the attorney acted to gather evidence for use in a criminal case).

6. *False Light versus Defamation.* Statements which place one in a false light are also often defamatory. It is therefore not surprising that many persons have questioned the necessity of this form of privacy action, or that limits crafted for libel and slander have been applied to false-light suits.

Still, there are cases in which a statement is capable of casting a highly offensive false light that is not defamatory. Consider the classic example of an inferior poem, article, or book attributed to a famous author. The author may be highly offended by the misrepresentation, even though the work is not so bad as to subject the author to the hatred, scorn, or ridicule that is the gist of a defamation action.

In Douglass v. Hustler Mag., 769 F.2d 1128 (7th Cir. 1985), photographs of an actress who had posed nude for *Playboy* were published in *Hustler* without her consent. Following a detailed review of the record, the court concluded that it could not

---

c. Because *Hill* was brought under the law of New York, which does not recognize a common-law right of privacy, the action was not technically one for false light; it was based on a New York statute.

say that it would be irrational for a jury to find that in the highly permissive moral and cultural climate prevailing in late twentieth-century America, posing nude for *Playboy* is consistent with respectability for a model and actress but that posing nude in *Hustler* is not (not yet, anyway), so that to portray Robyn Douglass as voluntarily posing nude for *Hustler* could be thought to place her in a false light even though she had voluntarily posed nude for *Playboy*.

Addressing the differences between defamation and false light, the court wrote:

> Part of Douglass's claim is that *Hustler* insinuated that she is a lesbian; and such a claim could of course be the basis for an action for defamation. But the rest of her claim fits more comfortably into the category of offensive rather than defamatory publicity. The difference is illustrated by Time, Inc. v. Hill,... [385 U.S. 374 (1967)]. *Life* magazine had presented as true a fictionalized account of the ordeal of a family held hostage by escaped convicts. The members of the family were shown being subjected to various indignities that had not actually occurred. The article did not defame the family members in the sense of accusing them of immoral, improper, or other bad conduct, and yet many people would be upset to think that the whole world thought them victims of such mistreatment. The false-light tort, to the extent distinct from the tort of defamation..., rests on an awareness that people who are made to seem pathetic or ridiculous may be shunned, and not just people who are thought to be dishonest or incompetent or immoral. We grant, though, that the distinction is blurred by the fact that a false statement that a woman was raped is actionable as defamation, *see, e.g.*, Youssoupoff v. Metro-Goldwyn-Mayer Pictures, Ltd., 50 Times L. Rep. 581, 584 (C.A.1934), though in such a case the plaintiff is represented to be a victim of wrongdoing rather than a wrongdoer herself.
>
> ....
>
> The question whether [plaintiff]...was also being depicted in a degrading association with *Hustler* invites attention to the difference between libel and false light. It would have been difficult for Douglass to state this claim as one for libel. For what exactly is the imputation of saying (or here, implying) of a person that she agreed to have pictures of herself appear in a vulgar and offensive magazine? That she is immoral? This would be too strong a characterization in today's moral climate. That she lacks good taste? This would not be defamatory. [Citation.] The point is, rather, that to be shown nude in such a setting before millions of people—the readers of the magazine—is degrading in much the same way that to be shown beaten up by criminals is degrading (although not libelous, despite the analogy to being reported to have been raped)....

7. *False Light and Matters of Public Concern.* Some jurisdictions hold that, because false light is a form of invasion of *privacy*, the tort must relate to the *private* affairs of the plaintiff and cannot involve matters of public interest. *See* Godbehere v. Phoenix Newspapers Inc., 783 P.2d 781 (Ariz. 1989).

8. *Rejection of False Light.* Would it be desirable to abolish false light and in its stead expand the definition of defamation to encompass those types of statements which traditionally have not been regarded as defamatory, but which nevertheless place the plaintiff in a highly offensive false light?

A number of states have rejected actions for false light. The Texas Supreme Court re-fused to recognize false light invasion of privacy because defamation encompasses most false light claims and false light "lacks many of the procedural limitations that accompany actions for defamation, thus unacceptably increasing the tension that already exists between free speech constitutional guarantees and tort law." Cain v. Hearst Corp., 878 S.W.2d 577 (Tex. 1994). The court rejected the solution of some jurisdictions—application of the defamation restrictions to false light—because any benefit to protecting nondefamatory false speech was outweighed by the chilling effect on free speech. *See also* Denver Publ'g Co. v. Bueno, 54 P.3d 893 (Colo. 2002) (rejecting false light but indicating that thirty state courts treat it as a viable claim); Lake v. Wal-Mart Stores, Inc., 582 N.W.2d 231, 235-36 (Minn. 1998) (declining to recognize false light and noting that "because of the overlap with defamation and the other privacy torts, a case has rarely succeeded squarely on a false light claim").

D. Unauthorized Use of the Plaintiff's Name or Picture

1. The "Right of Publicity"

Unauthorized use of the plaintiff's name or likeness is referred to as "appropriation" or interference with the "right of publicity." Some courts have differentiated the two terms, saying that the misappropriation involves unauthorized use "to obtain some advantage," while invasion of the right of publicity involves unauthorized use "to obtain a *commercial* advantage." *See* Doe v. TCI Cablevision, 110 S.W.3d 363, 368-69 (Mo. 2003). However, the terms are often used interchangeably.

The tort of appropriation is discussed in Restatement, Second, of Torts §652C (1977), but more recent guidance, limited to the redress of commercial injuries, can be found in the new Restatement, Third, of Unfair Competition §§46-49 (1995). *See generally* Oliver R. Goodenough, *Go Fish: Evaluating the Restatement's Formulation of the Law of Publicity*, 47 S.C. L. Rev. 709 (1996).

Cohen v. Herbal Concepts, Inc.
Court of Appeals of New York
472 N.E.2d 307 (N.Y. 1984)

[Without consent, a mother and child where photographed while bathing, nude, in a stream. The photograph was used to illustrate an advertisement for a consumer product in various magazines. The action was brought against the photographer, the company placing the advertisements, and the publishers of the magazines.]

SIMONS, Judge.

. . . .

Special Term dismissed the privacy actions because it concluded "the identities of the plaintiffs cannot be determined from the picture." . . . [T]he Appellate Division Justices were unanimous for reversal. . . .

....Although the tort has assumed various forms in other jurisdictions (*see* Restatement, Torts 2d, §652A *et seq.*), in New York privacy claims are founded solely upon §§50 and 51 of the Civil Rights Law. The statute protects against the appropriation of a plaintiff's name or likeness for defendants' benefit. Thus, it creates a cause of action in favor of "[a]ny person whose name, portrait or picture is used within this state for advertising purposes or for the purposes of trade without...written consent"....We are concerned in this case with the appropriation of plaintiffs' likenesses. Defendants claim that there has been no wrong because even if the photograph depicts plaintiffs, they are not identifiable from it.

The statute is designed to protect a person's identity, not merely a property interest in his or her "name", "portrait" or "picture", and thus it implicitly requires that plaintiff be capable of identification from the objectionable material itself [citation]. That is not to say that the action may only be maintained when plaintiff's face is visible in the advertising copy. Presumably, by using the term "portrait" the Legislature intended a representation which includes a facial reproduction, either artistically or by photograph, but if we are to give effect to all parts of the statute, it applies also to the improper use of a "picture" of plaintiff which does not show the face. Manifestly, there can be no appropriation of plaintiff's identity for commercial purposes if he or she is not recognizable from the picture and a privacy action could not be sustained, for example, because of the nonconsensual use of a photograph of a hand or a foot without identifying features. But assuming that the photograph depicts plaintiff, whether it presents a recognizable likeness is generally a jury question unless plaintiff cannot be identified because of the limited subject matter revealed in the photograph or the quality of the image. Before a jury may be permitted to decide the issue, to survive a motion for summary judgment, plaintiff must satisfy the court that the person in the photograph is capable of being identified from the advertisement alone and that plaintiff has been so identified.

The sufficiency of plaintiff's evidence...will necessarily depend upon...the quality and quantity of the identifiable characteristics displayed in the advertisement and this will require an assessment of the clarity of the photograph, the extent to which identifying features are visible, and the distinctiveness of those features. This picture depicts two nude persons, a woman and a child, standing in water a few inches deep. The picture quality is good and there are no obstructions to block the view of the subjects. The woman is carrying a small unidentified object in her left hand and is leading the child with her right hand. Neither person's face is visible but the backs and right sides of both mother and child are clearly presented and the mother's right breast can be seen. The identifying features of the subjects include their hair, bone structure, body contours and stature and their posture. Considering these factors, we conclude that a jury could find that someone familiar with the persons in the photograph could identify them by looking at the advertisement. Although we do not rely on the fact, it is also reasonable to assume that...identifiability may be enhanced...in a photograph depicting two persons because observers may associate the two and thus more easily identify them when they are seen together.

The plaintiffs also submitted evidence that they were identified as the persons in defendants' advertisement by Ira Cohen's affidavit in which he stated that while leafing through one of defendants' magazines he "recognized [his] wife and daughter immediately." That was prima facie sufficient [citation].

....

Accordingly, the order of the Appellate Division should be affirmed....

Notes

1. *Newsworthiness.* Language in N.Y. Civ. Rights Law §51 (Westlaw 2003), applied in *Cohen*, provides:

> Any person whose name, portrait, picture or voice is used within this state for advertising purposes or for the purposes of trade without the written consent first obtained...may maintain an equitable action...to prevent and restrain the use thereof; and may also sue and recover damages for any injuries sustained by reason of such use....

The "right of publicity" conferred by this statute (and by statutes in some other jurisdictions[d]) is protected by similar common-law principles in many states.

Although the New York law does not define the terms "advertising" or "trade," the statute has been consistently construed as not applying to publications concerning newsworthy events or matters of public interest.[e] Accordingly, the right of publicity does not prevent the publication of books or articles using the names or pictures of actual people; Meeropol v. Nizer, 560 F.2d 1061 (2d Cir. 1977) (unauthorized biography). Similarly, actual persons and institutions can be given roles in works of fiction. *See* University of Notre Dame du Lac v. Twentieth Century-Fox Film Corp., 207 N.E.2d 508 (N.Y. 1965), involving a motion picture featuring a preposterous college football game. A picture illustrating an article on a matter of public interest is not considered used for purposes of trade or advertising unless it has no relationship to the article or unless the article is an advertisement in disguise.

In Howell v. New York Post, 612 N.E.2d 699 (N.Y. 1993), a trespassing photographer climbed the wall of a psychiatric facility to photograph a woman who had been involved in a highly publicized child abuse case. In the photograph, which was published on the front page of the Post, the woman was shown walking with the plaintiff, whose hospitalization was otherwise a secret. The court held that the plaintiff could not sue either under the privacy statute or for tortious infliction of mental distress based on publication of her image.

Similarly, in Finger v. Omni Publications Int'l, 566 N.E.2d 141 (N.Y. 1990), the unconsented use of a picture of the plaintiffs and their six children to illustrate a segment about caffeine-enhanced fertility was not actionable even though none of the children had been conceived in the manner suggested by the article. The requisite nexus between the article and the photograph was established because the theme of the article—having a large family—was reflected in the picture. The court wrote:

> [T]he "newsworthiness exception" should be liberally applied...not only to reports of political happenings and social trends..., and to news stories and arti-

---

d. There are statutes dealing with interference with the right of publicity in California, Florida, Kentucky, Massachusetts, Nebraska, Nevada, New York, Oklahoma, Rhode Island, Tennessee, Texas, Virginia, and Wisconsin. *See* Restatement, Third, of Unfair Competition §46 Statutory Note (1995).

e. *Cf.* Restatement, Third, of Unfair Competition §47 (1995) provides:
The name, likeness, and other indicia of a person's identity are used "for purposes of trade" under the rule stated in §46 [Appropriation of The Commercial Value of a Person's Identity: The Right of Publicity] if they are used in advertising the user's goods or services, or are placed on merchandise marketed by the user, or are used in connection with services rendered by the user. However, use "for purposes of trade" does not ordinarily include the use of a person's identity in news reporting, commentary, entertainment, works of fiction or nonfiction, or in advertising that is incidental to such uses.

cles of consumer interest such as developments in the fashion world…, but to matters of scientific and biological interest such as enhanced fertility and *in vitro* fertilization as well. Moreover, questions of "newsworthiness" are better left to reasonable editorial judgment and discretion [citation]; judicial intervention should occur only in those instances where there is "'no real relationship'" between a photograph and an article.…

2. ***Uses Incidental to Advertising.*** Interesting questions arise when pictures which have appeared in a publication—as part of a use that does not violate §51 of the New York law and parallel common-law principles—are used to advertise the publication. The plaintiff in Namath v. Sports Illus., 371 N.Y.S.2d 10 (App. Div. 1975), *aff'd*, 352 N.E.2d 584 (N.Y. 1976), was a professional football player, whose picture was used to illustrate an article in Sports Illustrated on the 1969 Super Bowl game. The magazine then used that picture in advertisements seeking subscriptions to Sports Illustrated. The court held that this use did not violate §51. It described the use of the picture in the advertisements as "incidental" to advertising the magazine, and pointed out that the pictures were used to illustrate the magazine's quality and content, not to imply that Namath had endorsed it.

3. ***Commercial Use Other than Advertising.*** Advertising is not the only kind of use barred by §51. For example, marketing clothing or board games with the likeness of a famous person violates that section. *See* Rosemont Ent., Inc. v. Choppy Productions, Inc., 347 N.Y.S.2d 83 (Sup. Ct. 1972), and Rosemont Ent., Inc. v. Urban Sys., Inc., 345 N.Y.S.2d 17 (App. Div. 1973), both involving products exploiting the name of the reclusive billionaire Howard Hughes.

4. ***Non-Commercial Use.*** Common-law rules against appropriation may confer protection against some non-commercial uses of the plaintiff's name or likeness, as where the defendant impersonates the plaintiff to obtain confidential information. *See* Restatement, Second, of Torts §652C cmt. b.

In Hinish v. Meier & Frank Co., 113 P.2d 438 (Or. 1941), the court found an actionable invasion of privacy where the plaintiff's name had been signed, without his consent, to a telegram urging the governor to veto a bill. Would the result have been the same if the message sent by the defendant had simply stated, "Mr. Hinish, too, opposes the bill," and in fact Hinish did oppose the bill and had expressed his opposition to the defendant? The Oregon Supreme Court, in Humphers v. First Interstate Bank, 696 P.2d 527, 532 (Or. 1985), considered this hypothetical and opined that no action would lie, saying, "The false appropriation, not the potential public exposure of Hinish's actual views, constituted the tort." Restatement, Second, of Torts §652C indicates that falsity is not a requirement of an appropriation action. Should it be? Might the conduct in the hypothetical be actionable under some invasion-of-privacy theory other than appropriation of the plaintiff's name?

5. ***Names.*** In the absence of statute, there is no exclusive right to the use of a personal name. One may change one's name to Truman Capote, Betty Ford, or Mother Teresa without risk of liability. However, using a name to appropriate the identity of another, as when one deceptively impersonates an individual, is actionable. Restatement, Second, of Torts §652C cmt. c.

See also Doe v. TCI Cablevision, 110 S.W.3d 363, 368-69 (Mo. 2003) (although a comic book character did not physically resemble the former professional hockey player Tony Twist, and the publication's story line did not attempt to track Twist's life, both shared the same unusual name and tough-guy persona, and there was sufficient evidence to prove that the defendants intended to use the plaintiff's name as a symbol of his identity to obtain a commercial advantage).

6. *Businesses That Sell Information about Persons.* In Remsburg v. Docusearch, Inc., 816 A.2d 1001 (N.H. 2003), the court stated:

> An investigator who sells personal information sells the information for the value of the information itself, not to take advantage of the person's reputation or prestige. The investigator does not capitalize upon the goodwill value associated with the information but rather upon the client's willingness to pay for the information. In other words, the benefit derived from the sale in no way relates to the social or commercial standing of the person whose information is sold. Thus, a person whose personal information is sold does not have a cause of action for appropriation against the investigator who sold the information.

In Dwyer v. American Express Co., 652 N.E.2d 1351 (Ill. Ct. App. 1995), a suit by credit cardholders challenging the defendants' practice of renting information regarding cardholder spending habits, the court wrote:

> [P]laintiffs have not stated a claim for tortious appropriation because they have failed to allege the first element. Undeniably, each cardholder's name is valuable to defendants. The more names included on a list, the more that list will be worth. However, a single, random cardholder's name has little or no intrinsic value to defendants (or a merchant). Rather, an individual name has value only when it is associated with one of defendants' lists. Defendants create value by categorizing and aggregating these names. Furthermore, defendants' practices do not deprive any of the cardholders of any value their individual names may possess.

7. *Benefit to the Defendant.* According to Restatement, Second, of Torts §652C Comment c, "In order that there may be liability..., the defendant must have appropriated to his own use or benefit the reputation, prestige, social or commercial standing, public interest or other values of the plaintiff's name or likeness."

In Moore v. Big Picture Co., 828 F.2d 270 (5th Cir. 1987), the plaintiff's name was used to fill in a blank on a staffing chart prepared in connection with a contract bid. In response to an appropriation claim, the defendant argued that the name had no particular value and was used only as a symbol for someone with qualifications similar to the plaintiff's. The court acknowledged that it would have been an overstatement for the plaintiff to claim that without his name the contract would not have been awarded. However, testimony showed that the plaintiff was a well-known, highly qualified worker in the field. A judgment for the plaintiff was upheld.

8. *Statutory Authorization.* Consent will bar an action for appropriation. The same is true if the transaction in question is authorized by statute. *See* Sloan v. South Carolina Dep't of Pub. Safety, 586 S.E.2d 108 (2003) (a company that purchased driver's license information and photographs pursuant to an fraud-prevention arrangement that was authorized by statute was not liable for appropriation).

9. *Appropriating Identity without Name or Likeness.* Can a phrase be so identified with a person that its's mere use constitutes actionable appropriation? In some cases, yes. In Carson v. Here's Johnny Portable Toilets, Inc., 698 F.2d 831 (6th Cir. 1983), the defendant appropriated neither the name nor the likeness of a famous television personality. Rather, in marketing its products, the defendant used the phrase "Here's Johnny" — the words with which the plaintiff was introduced to TV audiences for years

on his late-night show. The court held that the use of the phrase was so clearly intended to capitalize on Carson's identity, notoriety, and achievements that an action would lie. The dissenter, observing that the appropriation action is intended to encourage creative works and to allow those whose achievements have imbued their identities with pecuniary value to profit from their fame, would have disallowed the action since the phrase was neither created by nor spoken by the plaintiff and was, therefore, not a product of his efforts.

2. Deceased Celebrities

An issue of much recent concern is whether the right of publicity survives the death of the person in question. It is hard to imagine an action being brought by the descendants of George Washington, or Shakespeare, or Attila the Hun for use of depictions of those persons in advertising. But in the case of celebrities who have died more recently, a carefully exploited image may be the estate's most valuable asset. This kind of asset, if available to all comers, may be less valuable than if its use can be controlled by the decedent's heirs. It is an interesting reflection on modern American culture that many of the recent cases involve the right to produce images of Elvis Presley.

State Ex Rel. Elvis Presley International Memorial Foundation v. Crowell
Court of Appeals of Tennessee
733 S.W.2d 89 (Tenn. Ct. App. 1987)

WILLIAM C. KOCH, JR., J.

This appeal involves a dispute between two not-for-profit corporations concerning their respective rights to use Elvis Presley's name as part of their corporate names. The case began when one corporation filed an unfair competition action in the Chancery Court for Davidson County to dissolve the other corporation and to prevent it from using Elvis Presley's name. Elvis Presley's estate intervened on behalf of the defendant corporation. It asserted that it had given the defendant corporation permission to use Elvis Presley's name and that it had not given similar permission to the plaintiff corporation.

The trial court determined that Elvis Presley's right to control his name and image descended to his estate at his death and that the Presley estate had the right to control the commercial exploitation of Elvis Presley's name and image. Thus, the trial court granted the defendant corporation's motion for summary judgment and dismissed the complaint.

The plaintiff corporation has appealed. Its primary assertion is that there is no descendible right of publicity in Tennessee and that Elvis Presley's name and image entered into the public domain when he died....

Elvis Presley's career is without parallel in the entertainment industry. From his first hit record in 1954 until his death in 1977, he scaled the heights of fame and success that only a few have attained....

Elvis Presley was aware of this recognition and sought to capitalize on it during his lifetime. He and his business advisors entered into agreements granting exclusive commercial licenses throughout the world to use his name and likeness in connection with the marketing and sale of numerous consumer items....

Elvis Presley's death on August 16, 1977 did not decrease his popularity. If anything it preserved it....

The demand for Elvis Presley merchandise was likewise not diminished by his death. The older memorabilia are now collector's items. New consumer items have been authorized and are now being sold. Elvis Presley Enterprises, Inc., a corporation formed by the Presley estate, has licensed seventy-six products bearing his name and likeness and still controls numerous trademark registrations and copyrights. Graceland, Elvis Presley's home in Memphis, is now a museum that attracts approximately 500,000 paying visitors a year. Elvis Presley Enterprises, Inc. also sells the right to use portions of Elvis Presley's filmed or televised performances. These marketing activities presently bring in approximately fifty million dollars each year and provide the Presley estate with approximately $4.6 million in annual revenue....

....

The status of Elvis Presley's right of publicity since his death has been the subject of four proceedings in the Federal courts. The conflicting decisions in these cases mirror the difficulty other courts have experienced in dealing with the right of publicity.

The first case originated in Tennessee and involved the sale of pewter statutes of Elvis Presley without the exclusive licensee's permission. The United States District Court recognized Elvis Presley's independent right of publicity and held that it had descended to the Presley estate under Tennessee law. Memphis Development Foundation v. Factors, Etc. Inc., 441 F. Supp. 1323, 1330 (W.D. Tenn. 1977). The United States Court of Appeals for the Sixth Circuit reversed. Apparently without considering Tennessee law, the court held that Tennessee courts would find that the right of publicity would not survive a celebrity's death. Memphis Development Foundation v. Factors, Etc., Inc., 616 F.2d 956, 958 (6th Cir.), cert. denied, 449 U.S. 953, 101 S. Ct. 358 (1980).

[In the second and third cases, the Court of Appeals for the Second Circuit felt obliged to follow *Memphis Development*, although it disagreed with the Sixth Circuit's view of the law. In the fourth case, a federal district court in New Jersey held that Presley's right of publicity survived his death.]

....

The courts in each of these cases recognized the existence of Elvis Presley's right of publicity. All the courts, except [*Memphis Development*], also recognized that this right was descendible upon Elvis Presley's death. The reasoning employed by the United States Court of Appeals for the Sixth Circuit to deny the descendibility of Elvis Presley's right of publicity has not been widely followed. The United States Court of Appeals for the Second Circuit specifically disagreed with it. Factors Etc., Inc. v. Pro Arts, Inc., 652 F.2d 278, 282 (2d Cir. 1981). It has also been consistently criticized in the legal literature.

....

The concept of the right of property is multi-faceted. It has been described as a bundle of rights or legally protected interests. These rights or interests include: (1) the right of possession, enjoyment and use; (2) the unrestricted right of disposition; and (3) the power of testimonial disposition. [Citations.]

In its broadest sense, property includes all rights that have value....

Our courts have recognized that a person's "business," a corporate name, a trade name and the good will of a business are species of intangible personal property. [Citations.]

Tennessee's common law thus embodies an expansive view of property. Unquestionably, a celebrity's right of publicity has value. It can be possessed and used. It can be assigned, and it can be the subject of a contract. Thus, there is ample basis for this Court to conclude that it is a species of intangible personal property.

. . . .

The United States Court of Appeals for the Sixth Circuit appears to believe that there is something inherently wrong with recognizing that the right of publicity is descendible. [Citation.] We do not share this subjective policy bias. Like the Supreme Court of Georgia, we recognize that the "trend since the early common law has been to recognize survivability, notwithstanding the legal problems which may thereby arise." [Citation.]

We have also concluded that recognizing that the right of publicity is descendible promotes several important policies that are deeply ingrained in Tennessee's jurisprudence. First, it is consistent with our recognition that an individual's right of testamentary distribution is an essential right. If a celebrity's right of publicity is treated as an intangible property right in life, it is no less a property right at death. [Citation.]

Second, it recognizes one of the basic principles of Anglo-American jurisprudence that "one may not reap where another has sown nor gather where another has strewn." . . . . This unjust enrichment principle argues against granting a windfall to an advertiser who has no colorable claim to a celebrity's interest in the right of publicity. [Citations.]

Third, recognizing that the right of publicity is descendible is consistent with a celebrity's expectation that he is creating a valuable capital asset that will benefit his heirs and assigns after his death. [Citations.] It is now common for celebrities to include their interest in the exploitation of their right of publicity in their estate. While a celebrity's expectation that his heirs will benefit from his right of publicity might not, by itself, provide a basis to recognize that the right of publicity is descendible, it does recognize the effort and financial commitment celebrities make in their careers. This investment deserves no less recognition and protection than investments celebrities might make in the stock market or in other tangible assets. [Citations.]

Fourth, concluding that the right of publicity is descendible recognizes the value of the contract rights of persons who have acquired the right to use a celebrity's name and likeness. The value of this interest stems from its duration and its exclusivity. If a celebrity's name and likeness were to enter the public domain at death, the value of any existing contract made while the celebrity was alive would be greatly diminished. [Citations.]

Fifth, recognizing that the right of publicity can be descendible will further the public's interest in being free from deception with regard to the sponsorship, approval or certification of goods and services. . . .

Finally, recognizing that the right of publicity can be descendible is consistent with the policy against unfair competition through the use of deceptively similar corporate names. [Citations.]

The legal literature has consistently argued that the right of publicity should be descendible. A majority of the courts considering this question agree. [Citations.] We find this authority convincing and consistent with Tennessee's common law and, therefore, conclude that Elvis Presley's right of publicity survived his death and remains enforceable by his estate and those holding licenses from the estate.[11]

---

11. There is some dispute concerning whether the right of publicity must be exercised while a celebrity is alive in order to render it descendible. We need not decide this question in this case.

While Tennessee's courts are capable of defining the parameters of the right of publicity on a case by case basis, the General Assembly also has the prerogative to define the scope of this right. The General Assembly undertook to do so in 1984 when it enacted Tenn. Code Ann. §47-25-1101 *et seq.* which is known as "The Personal Rights Protection Act of 1984." Tenn. Code Ann. §47-25-1103(a) recognizes that an individual has "a property right in the use of his name, photograph or likeness in any medium in any manner." Tenn. Code Ann. §47-25-1103(b) provides that this right is descendible. Tenn. Code Ann. §47-25-1104(a) & (b)(1) provide that the right is exclusive in the individual or his heirs and assigns until it is terminated. Tenn. Code Ann. §47-25-1104(b)(2) provides that the right is terminated if it is not used after the individual's death.

Our decision concerning the descendibility of Elvis Presley's right of publicity is not based upon Tenn. Code Ann. §47-25-1101 *et seq.* but rather upon our recognition of the existence of the common law right of publicity. We note, however, that nothing in Tenn. Code Ann. §47-25-1101 *et seq.* should be construed to limit vested rights of publicity that were in existence prior to the effective date of the act. To do so would be contrary to Article I, Section 20 of the Tennessee Constitution. A statute cannot be applied retroactively to impair the value of a contract right in existence when the statute was enacted. [Citations.]

      ....

Notes

1. ***Prior Exploitation.*** The question left open in footnote 11 of the court's opinion—whether a right of publicity not exploited during the decedent's lifetime descends to heirs—received a negative answer in Lugosi v. Universal Pictures, 603 P.2d 425 (Cal. 1979).[f] Bela Lugosi, who played Dracula in a well-known motion picture, never sought to cash in on his Dracula image during his lifetime. After Lugosi's death, the owner of the rights to the picture licensed the production of Dracula products which incorporated pictures based on Lugosi's portrayal. The court rejected Lugosi's heirs' claim that this action violated a right of publicity which they had inherited from Lugosi. Because Lugosi himself had not "created" such a right by exploiting his name and image, the right did not exist.

When an actor portrays a fictional character in a motion picture or television production, may the owner of the production license others to use the character's likeness without the actor's consent? Wendt v. Host Int'l, Inc., 125 F.3d 806 (9th Cir. 1997), rehearing en banc denied, 197 F.3d 1284 (1999), says no. George Wendt and John Ratzenberger played "Norm" and "Cliff" on a television show called "Cheers," which was set in a bar. Paramount, which owned the rights to the show, licensed the defendant to create airport bars resembling the bar on the television program. The defendant's bars included robot figures bearing some resemblance to the television characters portrayed by the plaintiffs. The Ninth Circuit ruled that a jury could find that the defendant's use of the robots violated the plaintiffs' right of publicity by appropriating their likenesses if it found that the robots sufficiently resembled Wendt and Ratzenberger. Conceding that they had no rights to the characters, the plaintiffs claimed that the robots' similarities to their own physical characteristics could violate their right of publicity. The court agreed, citing *Lugosi* for the proposition that "an actor...does not lose the right to control the commercial exploitation of

---

There is no dispute in this record that Elvis Presley commercially exploited his right of publicity while he was alive.

    f. In California, rights relating to a deceased personality are now governed by statute. See Cal. Civil Code §4433.1 (Westlaw 2003).

his...likeness by portraying a fictional character," 125 F. 3d at 811. This proposition is certainly true—hiring an actor to play a particular character cannot give a studio the right to use that actor's likeness in any context whatever. On the facts of *Wendt*, though, giving the actor a right of publicity clashes with the studio's unquestioned right to exploit its characters. See Judge Kozinski's dissent from denial of rehearing en banc, 197 F.3d 1285, 1286, observing that the Copyright Act gave Paramount the unquestioned right to produce derivative works (including the bars in question) based on Cheers, and that

> When portraying a character who was portrayed by an actor, it is impossible to recreate the character without evoking the image of the actor in the minds of viewers.

A decision upholding descendibility of the right of publicity without lifetime exploitation is Martin Luther King Ctr. for Soc. Change Inc. v. Am. Heritage Products, Inc., 296 S.E.2d 697, 706 (Ga. 1982). The defendant, without permission, manufactured and sold plastic busts of Dr. King. Rejecting the defendant's argument that commercial exploitation during life was required, the court said:

> The cases which have considered this issue...involved entertainers. The net result of following them would be to say that celebrities and public figures have the right of publicity during their lifetimes (as others have the right of privacy), but only those who contract for bubble gum cards, posters and tee shirts have a descendible right of publicity upon their deaths. [Citation.] That we should single out for protection after death those entertainers and athletes who exploit their personae during life, and deny protection after death to those who enjoy public acclamation but did not exploit themselves during life, puts a premium on exploitation. Having found valid reasons for recognizing the right of publicity during life, we find no reason to protect after death only those who took commercial advantage of their fame.

2. *Inheritability under Statutes.* In states in which the right of publicity is created or recognized by statute, the inheritability of the right is a matter of statutory interpretation. The Tennessee statutes cited in *Elvis Presley* expressly provide that the right to a name or likeness survives for ten years, even if not exploited during the decedent's life. A right exploited by heirs remains in existence for ten years after death or until two years after the exploitation ceases, whichever is later. Tenn. Code Ann. §47-25-1104 (Westlaw 2002). In New York, by contrast, §50 of the Civil Rights Law (N.Y. Civ. Rights Law §50 (Westlaw 2003))—a criminal provision which creates the right of publicity protected civilly by §51, p. 1062, *supra*—grants the right in question to "any living person." It has been held that this language means that once the person in question has died, the right disappears; Pirone v. MacMillan, Inc., 894 F.2d 579 (2d Cir. 1990).

3. Special Constitutional Considerations

Comedy III Productions, Inc. v. Gary Saderup, Inc.
Supreme Court of California
21 P.3d 797 (Cal. 2001)

MOSK, J.

....

In this state the right of publicity is both a statutory and a common law right....

....

Section 990[g] declares broadly that "Any person who uses a deceased personality's name, voice, signature, photograph, or likeness, in any manner, on or in products, merchandise, or goods, or for purposes of advertising or selling, or soliciting purchases of, products, merchandise, goods, or services, without prior consent from the person or persons specified in subdivision (c), shall be liable for any damages sustained by the person or persons injured as a result thereof." (*Id.*, subd. (a).) The amount recoverable includes "any profits from the unauthorized use," as well as punitive damages, attorney fees, and costs. (*Ibid.*)

The statute defines "deceased personality" as a person "whose name, voice, signature, photograph, or likeness has commercial value at the time of his or her death," whether or not the person actually used any of those features for commercial purposes while alive. (§ 990, subd. (h).)

The statute further declares that "The rights recognized under this section are property rights" that are transferable before or after the personality dies, by contract or by trust or will. (§ 990, subd. (b).) Consent to use the deceased personality's name, voice, photograph, etc., must be obtained from such a transferee or, if there is none, from certain described survivors of the personality. (*Id.*, subds. (c), (d).)....

....

The statute provides a number of exemptions from the requirement of consent to use. Thus a use "in connection with any news, public affairs, or sports broadcast or account, or any political campaign" does not require consent. [Citation.] Use in a "commercial medium" does not require consent solely because the material is commercially sponsored or contains paid advertising; "Rather it shall be a question of fact whether or not the use...was so directly connected with" the sponsorship or advertising that it requires consent. [Citation] Finally, subdivision (n) provides that "[a] play, book, magazine, newspaper, musical composition, film, radio or television program" [citation], work of "political or newsworthy value" [citation], "[s]ingle and original works of fine art" [citation], or "[a]n advertisement or commercial announcement" for the above works [citation] are all exempt from the provisions of the statute.

....

Plaintiff Comedy III Productions, Inc. (hereafter Comedy III), brought this action against defendants Gary Saderup and Gary Saderup, Inc. (hereafter collectively Saderup), seeking damages and injunctive relief....

Comedy III is the registered owner of all rights to the former comedy act known as The Three Stooges, who are deceased personalities within the meaning of the statute.

Saderup is an artist with over 25 years' experience in making charcoal drawings of celebrities. These drawings are used to create lithographic and silkscreen masters, which in turn are used to produce multiple reproductions in the form, respectively, of lithographic prints and silkscreened images on T-shirts. Saderup creates the original drawings and is actively involved in the ensuing lithographic and silkscreening processes.

Without securing Comedy III's consent, Saderup sold lithographs and T-shirts bearing a likeness of The Three Stooges reproduced from a charcoal drawing he had made....

---

g. Ed. note: Footnote 1 of the opinion notes that §990 was subsequently renumbered as section 3344.1 of the California Civil Code and the wording of the statute was amended in several respects.

....

...[T]he court found for Comedy III and entered judgment against Saderup awarding damages of $75,000 and attorney fees of $150,000 plus costs. The court also issued a permanent injunction....

Saderup appealed. The Court of Appeal modified the judgment by striking the injunction....

The Court of Appeal affirmed the judgment as thus modified....

....

The right of publicity is often invoked in the context of commercial speech when the appropriation of a celebrity likeness creates a false and misleading impression that the celebrity is endorsing a product. [Citations.] Because the First Amendment does not protect false and misleading commercial speech [citation], and because even nonmisleading commercial speech is generally subject to somewhat lesser First Amendment protection [citation], the right of publicity may often trump the right of advertisers to make use of celebrity figures.

But the present case does not concern commercial speech. As the trial court found, Saderup's portraits of The Three Stooges are expressive works and not an advertisement for or endorsement of a product. Although his work was done for financial gain, "[t]he First Amendment is not limited to those who publish without charge.... [An expressive activity] does not lose its constitutional protection because it is undertaken for profit." [Citation.]

The tension between the right of publicity and the First Amendment is highlighted by recalling the two distinct, commonly acknowledged purposes of the latter. First, " 'to preserve an uninhibited marketplace of ideas' and to repel efforts to limit the ' "uninhibited, robust and wide-open" debate on public issues.' " [Citation.] Second, to foster a "fundamental respect for individual development and self-realization. The right to self-expression is inherent in any political system which respects individual dignity. Each speaker must be free of government restraint regardless of the nature or manner of the views expressed unless there is a compelling reason to the contrary." [Citations.]

The right of publicity has a potential for frustrating the fulfillment of both these purposes. Because celebrities take on public meaning, the appropriation of their likenesses may have important uses in uninhibited debate on public issues, particularly debates about culture and values. And because celebrities take on personal meanings to many individuals in the society, the creative appropriation of celebrity images can be an important avenue of individual expression.... [T]he very importance of celebrities in society means that the right of publicity has the potential of censoring significant expression by suppressing alternative versions of celebrity images that are iconoclastic, irreverent, or otherwise attempt to redefine the celebrity's meaning....

...[S]peech about public figures is accorded heightened First Amendment protection in defamation law.... Giving broad scope to the right of publicity has the potential of allowing a celebrity to accomplish through the vigorous exercise of that right the censorship of unflattering commentary that cannot be constitutionally accomplished through defamation actions.

Nor do Saderup's creations lose their constitutional protections because they are for purposes of entertaining rather than informing.... First, "[t]he line between informing and entertaining is too elusive for the protection of the basic right. Everyone is familiar with instances of propaganda through fiction. What is one man's amusement, teaches another doctrine."....

Nor does the fact that expression takes a form of nonverbal, visual representation re-move it from the ambit of First Amendment protection. In Bery v. City of New York (2d Cir.1996) 97 F.3d 689, the court overturned an ordinance requiring visual artists—painters, printers, photographers, sculptors, etc.—to obtain licenses to sell their work in public places, but exempted the vendors of books, newspapers or other written mat-ter. As the court stated: "....Visual art is as wide ranging in its depiction of ideas, con-cepts and emotions as any book, treatise, pamphlet or other writing, and is similarly entitled to full First Amendment protection...." [Citation.]

....

Nor does the fact that Saderup's art appears in large part on a less conventional av-enue of communications, T-shirts, result in reduced First Amendment protection. As Judge Posner stated in the case of a defendant who sold T-shirts advocating the legaliza-tion of marijuana, "its T-shirts...are to [the seller] what the *New York Times* is to the Sulzbergers and the Ochs—the vehicle of her ideas and opinions."....

But having recognized the high degree of First Amendment protection for noncom-mercial speech about celebrities, we need not conclude that all expression that trenches on the right of publicity receives such protection. The right of publicity, like copyright, protects a form of intellectual property that society deems to have some social utility. "Often considerable money, time and energy are needed to develop one's prominence in a particular field. Years of labor may be required before one's skill, reputation, notoriety or virtues are sufficiently developed to permit an economic return through some medium of commercial promotion...."

The present case exemplifies this kind of creative labor. Moe and Jerome (Curly) Howard and Larry Fein fashioned personae collectively known as The Three Stooges, first in vaudeville and later in movie shorts, over a period extending from the 1920's to the 1940's. [Citation.] The three comic characters they created and whose names they shared—Larry, Moe, and Curly—possess a kind of mythic status in our culture. Their journey from ordinary vaudeville performers to the heights (or depths) of slapstick comic celebrity was long and arduous....

In sum, society may recognize, as the Legislature has done here, that a celebrity's heirs and assigns have a legitimate protectible interest in exploiting the value to be ob-tained from merchandising the celebrity's image, whether that interest be conceived as a kind of natural property right or as an incentive for encouraging creative work....

Although surprisingly few courts have considered in any depth the means of recon-ciling the right of publicity and the First Amendment, we follow those that have in concluding that depictions of celebrities amounting to little more than the appropria-tion of the celebrity's economic value are not protected expression under the First Amendment....

....

It is admittedly not a simple matter to develop a test that will unerringly distinguish between forms of artistic expression protected by the First Amendment and those that must give way to the right of publicity. Certainly, any such test must incorporate the principle that the right of publicity cannot, consistent with the First Amendment, be a right to control the celebrity's image by censoring disagreeable portrayals. Once the celebrity thrusts himself or herself forward into the limelight, the First Amendment dic-tates that the right to comment on, parody, lampoon, and make other expressive uses of the celebrity image must be given broad scope. The necessary implication of this observation is that the right of publicity is essentially an economic right. What the right of publicity holder possesses is not a right of censorship, but a right to prevent others from misappropriating the economic value generated by the celebrity's fame through the merchandising of the "name, voice, signature, photograph, or likeness" of the celebrity. (§ 990.)

Beyond this precept, how may courts distinguish between protected and unprotected expression? Some commentators have proposed importing the fair use defense from copyright law (17 U.S.C. § 107), which has the advantage of employing an established doctrine developed from a related area of the law. [Citations.] Others disagree, pointing to the murkiness of the fair use doctrine and arguing that the idea/expression dichotomy, rather than fair use, is the principal means of reconciling copyright protection and First Amendment rights. [Citations.]

We conclude that a wholesale importation of the fair use doctrine into right of publicity law would not be advisable. At least two of the factors employed in the fair use test, "the nature of the copyrighted work" and "the amount and substantiality of the portion used" (17 U.S.C. § 107(2), (3)), seem particularly designed to be applied to the partial copying of works of authorship "fixed in [a] tangible medium of expression" (17 U.S.C. § 102); it is difficult to understand why these factors would be especially useful for determining whether the depiction of a celebrity likeness is protected by the First Amendment.

Nonetheless, the first fair use factor — "the purpose and character of the use" (17 U.S.C. § 107(1)) — does seem particularly pertinent to the task of reconciling the rights of free expression and publicity.... [T]he central purpose of the inquiry into this fair use factor "is to see, in Justice Story's words, whether the new work merely 'supersede[s] the objects' of the original creation [citations], or instead adds something new, with a further purpose or different character, altering the first with new expression, meaning, or message; it asks, in other words, whether and to what extent the new work is 'transformative.' [Citation.] Although such transformative use is not absolutely necessary for a finding of fair use, [citation] the goal of copyright, to promote science and the arts, is generally furthered by the creation of transformative works." [Citation.]

This inquiry into whether a work is "transformative" appears to us to be necessarily at the heart of any judicial attempt to square the right of publicity with the First Amendment....When artistic expression takes the form of a literal depiction or imitation of a celebrity for commercial gain, directly trespassing on the right of publicity without adding significant expression beyond that trespass, the state law interest in protecting the fruits of artistic labor outweighs the expressive interests of the imitative artist. [Citation.]

On the other hand, when a work contains significant transformative elements, it is not only especially worthy of First Amendment protection, but it is also less likely to interfere with the economic interest protected by the right of publicity. As has been observed, works of parody or other distortions of the celebrity figure are not, from the celebrity fan's viewpoint, good substitutes for conventional depictions of the celebrity and therefore do not generally threaten markets for celebrity memorabilia that the right of publicity is designed to protect....

[Cardtoons, L.C. v. Major League Baseball Players Ass'n, 95 F.3d 959 (10th Cir. 1996)], cited by Saderup, is consistent with this "transformative" test. There, the court held that the First Amendment protected a company that produced trading cards caricaturing and parodying well-known major league baseball players against a claim brought under the Oklahoma right of publicity statute. The court concluded that "[t]he cards provide social commentary on public figures, major league baseball players, who are involved in a significant commercial enterprise, major league baseball," and that "[t]he cards are no less protected because they provide humorous rather than serious commentary."....

We emphasize that the transformative elements or creative contributions that require First Amendment protection are not confined to parody and can take many forms, from factual reporting [citation] to fictionalized portrayal [citations], from heavy-handed lampooning [citation] to subtle social criticism [citation].

Another way of stating the inquiry is whether the celebrity likeness is one of the "raw materials" from which an original work is synthesized, or whether the depiction or imitation of the celebrity is the very sum and substance of the work in question. We ask, in other words, whether a product containing a celebrity's likeness is so transformed that it has become primarily the defendant's own expression rather than the celebrity's likeness....

We further emphasize that in determining whether the work is transformative, courts are not to be concerned with the quality of the artistic contribution—vulgar forms of expression fully qualify for First Amendment protection. [Citations.] On the other hand, a literal depiction of a celebrity, even if accomplished with great skill, may still be subject to a right of publicity challenge....[11]

Furthermore, in determining whether a work is sufficiently transformative, courts may find useful a subsidiary inquiry, particularly in close cases: does the marketability and economic value of the challenged work derive primarily from the fame of the celebrity depicted? If this question is answered in the negative, then there would generally be no actionable right of publicity....If the question is answered in the affirmative, however, it does not necessarily follow that the work is without First Amendment protection—it may still be a transformative work.

In sum, when an artist is faced with a right of publicity challenge to his or her work, he or she may raise as affirmative defense that the work is protected by the First Amendment inasmuch as it contains significant transformative elements or that the value of the work does not derive primarily from the celebrity's fame.

...[T]he trial court, in ruling against Saderup, stated that "the commercial enterprise conducted by [Saderup] involves the sale of lithographs and T-shirts which are not original single works of art, and which are not protected by the First Amendment; the enterprise conducted by [Saderup] was a commercial enterprise designed to generate profits solely from the use of the likeness of The Three Stooges which is the right of publicity...protected by section 990." Although not entirely clear, the trial court seemed to be holding that *reproductions* of celebrity images are categorically outside First

---

11. Saderup also cites ETW Corp. v. Jireh Publishing, Inc. (N.D. Ohio 2000) 99 F. Supp. 2d 829, 835-836, in which the court held that a painting consisting of a montage of likenesses of the well-known professional golfer Eldridge "Tiger" Woods, reproduced in 5,000 prints, was a work of art and therefore protected under the First Amendment. We disagree with the *ETW Corp.* court if its holding is taken to mean that any work of art, however much it trespasses on the right of publicity and however much it lacks additional creative elements, is categorically shielded from liability by the First Amendment. Whether the work in question in that case would be judged to be exempt from California's right of publicity, either under the First Amendment test articulated in this opinion or under the statutory exception for material of newsworthy value, is, of course, beyond the scope of this opinion.

Amendment protection. The Court of Appeal was more explicit in adopting this rationale....But this position has no basis in logic or authority. No one would claim that a published book, because it is one of many copies, receives less First Amendment protection than the original manuscript. It is true that the statute at issue here makes a distinction between a single and original work of fine art and a reproduction. (§ 990, subd. (n)(3).) Because the statute evidently aims at preventing the illicit merchandising of celebrity images, and because single original works of fine art are not forms of merchandising, the state has little if any interest in preventing the exhibition and sale of such works, and the First Amendment rights of the artist should therefore prevail. But the inverse — that a reproduction receives no First Amendment protection — is patently false: a reproduction of a celebrity image that...contains significant creative elements is entitled to as much First Amendment protection as an original work of art....

Rather, the inquiry is into whether Saderup's work is sufficiently transformative. Correctly anticipating this inquiry, he argues that all portraiture involves creative decisions, that therefore no portrait portrays a mere literal likeness, and that accordingly all portraiture, including reproductions, is protected by the First Amendment. We reject any such categorical position. Without denying that all portraiture involves the making of artistic choices, we find it equally undeniable, under the test formulated above, that when an artist's skill and talent is manifestly subordinated to the overall goal of creating a conventional portrait of a celebrity so as to commercially exploit his or her fame, then the artist's right of free expression is outweighed by the right of publicity. As is the case with fair use in the area of copyright law, an artist depicting a celebrity must contribute something more than a "'"merely trivial"'" variation, [but must create] something recognizably '"his own"'" [citation] in order to qualify for legal protection.

On the other hand, we do not hold that all reproductions of celebrity portraits are unprotected by the First Amendment. The silkscreens of Andy Warhol, for example, have as their subjects the images of such celebrities as Marilyn Monroe, Elizabeth Taylor, and Elvis Presley. Through distortion and the careful manipulation of context, Warhol was able to convey a message that went beyond the commercial exploitation of celebrity images and became a form of ironic social comment on the dehumanization of celebrity itself. [Citation.] Such expression may well be entitled to First Amendment protection....

Turning to Saderup's work, we can discern no significant transformative or creative contribution. His undeniable skill is manifestly subordinated to the overall goal of creating literal, conventional depictions of The Three Stooges so as to exploit their fame. Indeed, were we to decide that Saderup's depictions were protected by the First Amendment, we cannot perceive how the right of publicity would remain a viable right other than in cases of falsified celebrity endorsements.

Moreover, the marketability and economic value of Saderup's work derives primarily from the fame of the celebrities depicted....

Saderup argues that it would be incongruous and unjust to protect parodies and other distortions of celebrity figures but not wholesome, reverential portraits of such celebrities. The test we articulate today, however, does not express a value judgment or preference for one type of depiction over another. Rather, it reflects a recognition that the Legislature has granted to the heirs and assigns of celebrities the property right to exploit the celebrities' images, and that certain forms of expressive activity protected by the First Amendment fall outside the boundaries of that right. Stated another way, we are concerned not with whether conventional celebrity images should be produced but with who produces them and, more pertinently, who appropriates the value from their production. Thus, under section 990, if Saderup wishes to continue to depict The Three Stooges as he has done, he may do so only with the consent of the right of publicity holder.

....

The judgment of the Court of Appeal is affirmed.

GEORGE, C.J., KENNARD, J., BAXTER, J., WERDEGAR, J., CHIN, J., BROWN, J., concur.

Notes

1. *Constitutional Considerations. See* Town & Country Properties, Inc. v. Riggins, 457 S.E.2d 356 (Va. 1995) (statute prohibiting the use of a name for advertising purposes did not violate the constitutional commercial speech rights of real estate brokers who circulated a flyer advertising a house as having been previously owned by a famous professional football player).

2. *Altered Photographic Images and Actual Malice.* In Hoffman v. Capital Cities/ ABC, Inc., 255 F.3d 1180 (9th Cir. 2001), a still photograph of the actor Dustin Hoffman in women's clothing from the movie "Tootsie" was used to create a composite computer-generated image that depicted him wearing contemporary designer women's clothes. The altered image was published as part of an article on "Grand Illusions" that featured 16 modified stills from famous movies. The court held that the actor failed to state an action for appropriation. According to the court, the depiction was entitled to full constitutional protection because it was not pure commercial speech. Although the image appeared in a magazine advertising the designer's clothes, it was a "combination of fashion photography, humor, and visual and verbal editorial comment on classic films and famous actors." The use of the image did more than merely propose a commercial transaction. Because the speech in question was fully protected by the constitution, the plaintiff was required to show that the defendant acted with actual malice, namely that it intended to create a false impression in the mind of readers that when they saw the altered photograph they were seeing the actor's body. Because there were references in the accompanying article that made clear that digital techniques were used to substitute current fashions for clothes worn in the original stills, and the original stills were presented at the end of the article, it was not possible for the plaintiff to prove actual malice. The court noted that in many right-of-publicity cases the question of actual malice does not arise because the challenged use does no more than propose a commercial transaction and does not implicate the First Amendment's protection of expressions of editorial opinion.

Index